THE DIARIES OF SIR ALEXANDER CADOGAN, 1938–1945

Sir Alexander Cadogan, O.M.

The Diaries of Sir Alexander Cadogan OM 1938–1945

Edited by
DAVID DILKS

Professor of International History at the University of Leeds

faber and faber

This edition first published in 2010
by Faber and Faber Ltd
Bloomsbury House, 74–77 Great Russell Street
London WC1B 3DA

A CIP record for this book is available from the British Library

ISBN 978–0–571–26985–3

ACKNOWLEDGMENTS

My chief debt is to the late Sir Alexander Cadogan and his family, for allowing unrestricted access to papers, albums and diaries, for many helpful suggestions and for the patience with which they have awaited the completion of this book. Lady Theodosia Cadogan, in particular, has given me every possible assistance since the death of her husband.

For permission to see documents in privately held collections I am obliged to the Rt. Hon. Julian Amery, M.P., the Earl of Halifax, Mr and Mrs Stephen Lloyd, the British Library of Economics and Political Science, Cambridge University Library and the Library of Churchill College, Cambridge. Crown copyright documents are reproduced by permission of the Controller of H.M. Stationery Office. The Library of Congress has kindly allowed access to the papers of Mr Cordell Hull. For guidance in gleaning among the documents I am grateful to Lord Corvedale, Major Tom Ingram, the late Mr Donald McLachlan, Mr Kenneth Rose and Mr Gordon Waterfield.

Friends and colleagues have generously allowed me to draw upon their special knowledge. Amongst them I must mention especially Dr Sidney Aster, Dr Fay Carter, Miss Irene Cassidy, Mr Steve Endicott, Mr John Fox, the Hon. Margaret Lambert, Mr Fergus MacKenzie, Professor W. N. Medlicott, Dr Gottfried Niedhart, Mr Larry Pratt, Mr Michael Rooke, Mr Telford Taylor, Miss Jane Vieth and Mr Geoffrey Warner.

The many former collaborators of Sir Alec Cadogan who have responded to my questions will, I hope, forgive me if I do not mention them all by name. Some, however, have been able to help in a way which calls for more than general acknowledgment: M. Thanassis Aghnides, the Earl of Avon, Don Pablo Azcarate y Florez, Mr V. Cavendish-Bentinck, Lord Chandos, Sir Laurence Collier, Mr Jock Colville, Lord Gladwyn, Lord Gore-Booth, Mr Alger Hiss, Lord Inchyra, Maj.-Gen. Sir Ian Jacob, Mr Valentine Lawford, Sir John Martin, the Earl and Countess of Perth, the late Lord Reith, Sir Leslie Rowan,

Lord Salter, Lord Sherfield and the late Sir Llewellyn Woodward.

I am grateful to all those who have allowed me to reproduce extracts from private letters, and to those publishers and copyright holders for permission to reproduce material from published works. Full notes and a bibliography appear at the back of the book.

The responsibility for the interpolations and the selection of material is mine alone.

Typing and re-typing have been expertly undertaken by Mrs Christine Bassadone, Mrs Elizabeth Cashman, Mrs Joy Farquharson, Miss Joan Gartley, Miss Gil Pearson, Mrs Mollie Sidwell and Mrs Carol Wills.

I must record my gratitude for much encouragement to Mr Bruce Hunter, of David Higham Associates; to Mr J. F. Burrell and Mr Mark Farrer, of Farrer and Co.; and to Mr Kenneth Parker of the House of Cassell.

I would like to thank the directors and staff of the publishers, Cassell, and the printers, Clowes, for their part in the production of this book; it has been a happy co-operation throughout. Also Miss Hebe Jerrold, who has produced a first-class index, though having to work under much pressure.

Finally, I am deeply appreciative of my wife Jill's forbearance during the preparation of this book, and of her assistance in verifying the texts and notes.

DAVID DILKS

School of History,
The University of Leeds,
1 August 1971

CONTENTS

ILLUSTRATIONS

1884–1938
INTRODUCTION

Although the history of the Cadogans is traced as far back as the Marcher Lords of Wales and Prince Llewellyn, they came to prominence only in the eighteenth century, when the first Earl served under Marlborough at Blenheim, Ramillies, Oudenarde and Malplaquet, and the manor of Chelsea was acquired by marriage. Like others similarly placed the family provided a stream of younger sons serving in the Army and Royal Navy, in India, in the Church and in Parliament.

The fifth Earl and his wife, daughter of the Earl of Craven, had seven sons and two daughters. The eldest boy died in childhood and the second in middle age, so that the title eventually passed to the third son. Alexander, born in 1884, was the youngest child. His father, a keen supporter of Disraeli, held two Under-Secretaryships in the Ministry of 1874–80; and, being equally esteemed by Salisbury, joined the Cabinet as Lord Privy Seal in 1886. When Salisbury, after an interval of three years, returned to office again in 1895, he appointed Cadogan Viceroy of Ireland.

It was a methodical, orderly household, hierarchical to a degree not easy to realise at this distance of nearly a century. Not only did Earl Cadogan strictly discourage any disagreement with his own views, but the children must observe the respect due to age even among themselves. Explaining to a friend why, when nearing eighty, he still felt diffident about uttering to his brother what would look like a criticism, Sir Alec Cadogan recalled how often as a child he had heard the remark: 'Don't contradict your brother, he is older than you.' 'And so we never offered criticisms to each other, at least never from a younger to an older.'

That same elder brother, Edward, the one nearest to Alexander in age, observed with truth that while this conformity may have engendered the spirit of obedience and given the children a lesser conceit of themselves, it suppressed individual characteristics.[1] The unrelenting code of conventions within the family suffered no infringement. The fifth Earl, a creature of habit who could not abide the upsetting of his routine, had certain characteristics readily discernible in his youngest son—reserve, thoroughness, a high sense of duty, artistic tastes severely curbed lest they interfere with other claims upon his time, a loathing of personal publicity, love of the countryside. He had also more than a dilettante's interest in applied science, a hearty dislike of travel (it was a member of the Cadogan family who uttered the celebrated advice, 'Don't go abroad; it's a horrible place') and a positive passion for the Turf.

Alexander Cadogan, then, was brought up in a prestigious and wealthy family of high social standing. Besides the properties in London his father had Culford Hall, near Bury St Edmund's, with an estate of 11,000 acres, to which the entire family migrated in August. Each autumn a deer-forest would be rented in the Highlands. At Chelsea House and elsewhere, the Earl and Countess Cadogan entertained on the grand scale. Each morning in summer she would take a platoon from the Chelsea House stables for a ride in Hyde Park. In the afternoon, the barouche would convey her to the town houses of her friends and often to her mother's at 1 Great Cumberland Place, where all the family exchanged gossip in the manner immortalised by Galsworthy. Harold Macmillan, born nearby a few years after Alec Cadogan, remembered Chelsea House, standing at the corner of Cadogan Square, as

> . . . a kind of baronial castle, only outmatched in importance by Buckingham Palace. . . . On the steps outside there could generally be seen as we passed a splendid figure, with powdered hair or wig, blue coat, red velvet waistcoat, blue velvet kneebreeches, white or yellow stockings, and silver buckled shoes. This person, who commanded our deepest respect, we firmly believed to be Earl Cadogan himself, proudly surveying his tenants and his properties.[2]

For all the wealth of the household, the children were allowed no extravagances. They rose early, took breakfast in the nursery and then went to their mother, who would read from the Bible and make a commentary, enriched by a pronounced sense of humour. All the children seem to have been devoted to their parents. It being taken for granted that the boys would go to Eton, Alexander was placed in the house of A. C. Benson, an admirable teacher, minor poet and marvellous story-teller, masterful but not fussy, devoted to his house, sociable and warm-hearted, independent of mind. In his last year Alec Cadogan became President of the Eton Society, Editor of the *Eton College Chronicle* and Captain of the Oppidans. He loved the place deeply. At Balliol, where he read history from 1903–6, Cadogan worked moderately hard, played cricket for a light-hearted side known as 'The Erratics' against teams from villages to which the whole party was conveyed in a huge horse-drawn brake, and enjoyed the society of a coruscating and gay company. To his contemporary Lawrence Jones he seemed precociously wise and witty, 'with hair beautifully brushed, and the air even then of a Permanent Under-Secretary for Foreign Affairs, in neat tweeds, eschewing the grey flannel trousers of the rest of us'.[3] Called upon to adjudicate when a rash freshman removed the cap of a second-year undergraduate, who waxed very angry, Cadogan pronounced that the original request for the doffing of headgear should have been obeyed. 'Molotov may, on occasions, have contested a ruling by Alec Cadogan, but we others never did.'

Even Cadogan's escapades had a certain dignity and poise. He is credibly reported to have addressed a small crowd from the summit of a lamp-post in Trafalgar Square and to have thrown pennies down, after which he announced that since he had no more pennies he proposed to descend. On the last night of Henley he led to the Mayor's ball a decorous party of gate-crashers, who devoured 'in dripping flannels amongst his tailed and white-tied guests, the mayoral quails and trifles'. As a leading light of the Annandale Society, which practised the fine art of becoming 'buffy', a state well removed from drunkenness but bordering on gaiety, he caused huge waterfalls of crockery to crash down the staircases or even the steps of Balliol Hall. It was the custom before waterfalls to pay calls upon the studious. At the top of a tall staircase lived a gentleman of saintly character, much learning and spherical countenance. Alec Cadogan led the group which climbed up to worship Moonface, a ritual carried out on the knees with much incantation. No facetiousness marred the quality of adoration. Moonface, without a flicker of amusement, astonishment or even anger, peered at the visitors. He was killed, like most of Cadogan's Balliol contemporaries, in the Great War.

As the youngest son of a large family, Cadogan was modestly provided for. On leaving Balliol, to his slight disappointment, with a Second, he spent two years in preparation for the Diplomatic Service and passed first in 1908 in the competitive examination for three attachéships. The Foreign Office and the Diplomatic Service were then separate organisations, although temporary transfers could be arranged. After a short spell at the Office, in which his first duty was to make many copies of the manuscript letter, beginning 'My dear Brother and Cousin and Nephew', in which the Emperor Franz Joseph announced to Edward VII the annexation of Bosnia and Herzegovina, he was sent to the Embassy at Constantinople. There he spent two happy years learning the craft of diplomacy and playing upon the head of Chancery a series of ingenious practical jokes.[4]

* * *

In the summer of 1912, Alexander Cadogan married Lady Theodosia Acheson, daughter of the Earl and Countess of Gosford. The Cadogans had a son, Ambrose, and three daughters, Patricia, Cynthia and Gillian. Their married life was an idyllically happy one of complete devotion. On that subject it would be pointless to enlarge upon the tribute written by Sir Alexander and by his desire printed at the end of this book.

* * *

Alexander Cadogan's second posting abroad was to Vienna, where he found a congenial master in the newly-appointed Ambassador, Sir Maurice de Bunsen. High society there represented the most anachronistic survival of privilege in Europe. The highest nobility, the *erste gesellschaft*, were for the most part kindly, charming and cultured; 'they would not dispute' Cadogan recalled fifty years later, 'that in theory many excellent people might be found in the outer darkness, but they were not going to look for them . . .'. Niceties of manner and social custom had indeed been carried to the point of caricature. Profound shock was felt when Lady Theodosia innocently engaged so humble a conveyance as a one-horse cab to carry her to the palace of her relative Princess Festetics. When Alexander Cadogan attended a magnificent ball and enquired why most of the nobility had at a certain point moved to the landing at the top of the branching marble staircase, he was told that the Prime Minister would shortly arrive. Only after a little reflection did he realise that the real interest lay not in the fact that so distinguished a figure was expected but in another fact, to which no one present could recall a parallel: the entry of a mere Herr Baron into a palace in which no one below the rank of Graf had ever set foot.[5]

Cadogan soon won the confidence of his seniors. During the weekend of 27–28 June 1914, though still less than thirty years old, he was in charge of the Embassy. Vienna seemed tranquil. The aristocracy had migrated to Budapest for the social season. As the Cadogans were finishing their luncheon, a cypher officer telephoned from the Embassy to say that he had that moment received an alarming telegram. The consul at Sarajevo reported the murder of the Archduke Franz Ferdinand, heir to the throne of Austria-Hungary. Cadogan set off for the Embassy through the garden of the Belvedere Palace. Halfway down the wide path he saw a board which a couple ascending the path reached just as he did. The newly-posted notice announced the death of the Archduke. The husband read it out in tones of shock. He came to the fact that the murder had taken place at Sarajevo. 'Ah!' he said, 'happily that is very far away.'

* * *

During the First World War, Cadogan served in the Foreign Office and subsequently at the Peace Conference. The Permanent Under-Secretary, Sir Eyre Crowe, described him as 'the best man in the Office' when appointing him in 1923 as head of the League of Nations section. This was a small but influential part of the machinery. Its chief, with the aid of only two assistants, received and kept copies of papers on all subjects likely to come before the League, advised on the view which other governments were likely to take at Geneva and accompanied the British delegates at the Assembly, Council and more important committees. All this meant frequent and prolonged absences from home, for it was the high noontide of the League's authority and Sir Austen Chamberlain and his successors Mr Arthur Henderson and Sir John Simon attended frequently at Geneva. Cadogan made himself indispensable to them. He knew the business thoroughly, proffered advice with modesty and brevity and was often consulted by other delegations, and by the permanent Secretariat, who trusted him completely. When, in 1926, Sir Austen sent a formal letter to say that Cadogan had been appointed C.M.G., he added in manuscript:

> I take occasion to say again how admirably your League work is done. I know the difficult circumstances in which it has to be accomplished but you always managed somehow to provide me at the Council Table with all the information needed.[6]

Though he fought shy of enthusiasms and mistrusted fanatics—there being no lack of both in League circles—Cadogan was by no means a cynic. He came from experience to believe in the value and promise of Geneva, for most delegates went there with a genuine desire to do business and reach solutions. He dismissed the complaint that a Secretary of State, an amateur diplomat, must be worsted at Geneva, or that his other work would be unduly neglected. Those risks were outweighed by the value of acquaintance and discussion, whereby the statesmen were more likely to agree than by exchanging stiff notes, 'of which the first draft has probably been prepared by a subordinate anxious to score a point'.

Cadogan advised against the appointment of a permanent British representative, on grounds which are of particular interest when it is recalled that he held this post from 1946 at the United Nations. In that instance, geography and the meeting of the Security Council in continuous session left no option. At Geneva, however, the Council normally foregathered only once a quarter and the Secretary of State could get there in a day by train or an hour or two by air. Cadogan thought that a permanent representative could not be given sufficient latitude to make the best of Geneva's opportunities, in which event there would be a return to diplomacy by correspondence. Moreover, such representatives might well become a corps of professional debaters, carrying out their instructions to the letter and developing obstruction into a fine art. Some of the older hands at Geneva, indeed, could be relied upon to talk out almost any proposal, however harmless or even beneficial; whereas so long as the Secretary of State came regularly from London he could at least represent to the Cabinet at first hand the outlook, problems and idiosyncrasies of his foreign colleagues.

* * *

The subject of disarmament had preoccupied the League at intervals since 1919, when the drastic restrictions imposed upon Germany's forces had been declared the prelude to general reduction. In certain respects the problem had altered significantly since then. Britain had carried her unilateral disarmament, on land and in the air, to a point which nearly cost her independence in 1940. The principal naval powers had agreed at Washington in 1922 to limit their capital ship fleets. But the universal disarmament which the League was to promote had not been secured. Numerous commissions had brought forth innumerable papers and drafts; but no one had ventured to suggest precisely how many men, guns, tanks, aircraft each power should have.

In a memorandum written for Ministers in 1927, Cadogan had described all the obstacles to disarmament, which would prove impossible unless nations felt themselves secure. Regional arrangements were insufficient and attempts to organise something wider had thus far failed; and so, in the attempt to ensure early disarmament, the statesmen found themselves driven back to search for greater security. Disarmament, then, could not be imposed but would follow naturally from a genuine sense of security; which in turn would hardly follow, at least in the short run, simply from an agreement to disarm, depending as that must on good faith and confidence. Although this line of argument seemed to Sir Austen unduly negative,[7] its soundness can hardly be contested. All the same, Cadogan was in no doubt that an agreement would represent a solid British and Dominion interest; not because it would be popular but because it was on any but the strictest reading an obligation. He felt sure, moreover, that if the other powers did not disarm, Germany would rearm with impunity.

The Japanese attack on Shanghai provided an unhappy, even ludicrous, curtain-raiser to the Conference. Mr MacDonald was unwell and Sir John Simon could not leave London during the Far Eastern crisis. Mr J. H. Thomas, then Secretary for the Dominions, travelled out to represent Great Britain at the opening sessions. Cadogan, who had a very soft spot for Jim Thomas, went to meet the train and broke the news that they must attend a Service of Dedication, at which Archbishop Temple would preach. 'Oh 'ell', said Thomas, 'do I 'ave to go?' Cadogan insisted. Thomas was suddenly struck by a serious thought. 'Will Arthur be there?' This was Arthur Henderson, president of the Conference and Foreign Secretary in the Labour Government which had broken up amidst bitter recriminations some six months before. Thomas was one of the few Labour members who remained in the National Government, and had been viciously attacked for betraying the party. Cadogan had to say that Henderson probably would be present.

The two of them walked to the cathedral while Thomas reeled off anecdotes, the last of which had to be completed in the porch. Its theme, Cadogan recalled, 'was in no way suitable to our surroundings and I could only hope that it was not too widely understood'. They were placed in the front row, immediately beneath the pulpit, with two or three empty places beside Thomas. Just before the service began, none other than Mr Henderson appeared beside the steps leading to the pulpit. 'My God, there's Arthur,' exclaimed Thomas in considerable agitation. There was nothing to be done. Henderson and one or two others were ushered along into the front pew, so that the erstwhile colleagues were separated by one place only. 'I think I ought to shake 'im by the 'and,' said Thomas. Cadogan agreed. This was duly done, not without difficulty, behind the back of the stranger. A short conversation followed. 'It's all right,' Thomas whispered to Cadogan: 'I'm going round to 'ave tea with 'im this afternoon, and I'll 'ave it out with 'im.'

The service began. When the collecting-bags were passed to everyone save those in their row, Thomas beamed at Cadogan and remarked, 'Well, if you *'ave* put me in a front seat you've put me in a free one.' To his visible displeasure the Archbishop's pronouncement contained some strong criticism of the Versailles settlement. Thomas turned to Cadogan. ''oo wrote that bloody muck? Bob Cecil, I suppose.'

That evening the Secretary of State for the Dominions played bridge. Cadogan looked in just as the wife of a High Commissioner was laying her cards on the table and saying, 'I'm afraid, partner, it's not a very good hand.' Thomas leaned across the table, scanned the cards and said, 'Oh well, all me life's been one long bloody up'ill struggle.' No one batted an eyelid. Inferring that the guests were already acclimatised, Cadogan went back to his work.

After the inaugural sessions, Thomas was taken round to meet the principal delegates. He enjoyed the process; 'better than bull-fightin', as he put it. When M. Tardieu had explained at length the need for French security and Cadogan had translated, Thomas commented only 'Oh 'ell'.

'Qu'est-ce qu'il dit M. Thomas?'

Cadogan said that Mr Thomas had listened with great attention and interest and would report faithfully to his colleagues. Tardieu eyed the interpreter with thinly-veiled mistrust.[8]

Once the proceedings began in earnest, Cadogan spent more time in Geneva than at home, for the conference and its various committees worked more or less without interruption. The British delegation numbered between forty and fifty, representing eight or ten departments, with a host of secretaries, typists, clerks and cyphering staff. The principal representative of the War Office, General Temperley, has published a judgment which needs no gloss:

> For the first two or three days all was confusion, while those who were new to the job tried to sort themselves out and learn their various duties. Riding the whirlwind, magnificently capable and imperturbable, was Mr Alexander Cadogan. . . . He knew everything, was never in a hurry, never ruffled however irritating the caller might be, and he possessed an uncanny judgment of the right course to adopt in a given situation. He did not usually offer advice, but the man who consulted him and rejected it was undertaking a serious responsibility . . . a Secretary of State with him at his elbow had only himself to thank if he made mistakes. In the course of the Disarmament Conference his value became more apparent as difficulties increased.[9]

During 1932 the work of the conference dragged. Sir John Simon had only the faintest belief in the prospects of disarmament, allied with an unfeigned distaste for the atmosphere of Geneva. At the time, Cadogan, like Mr Anthony Eden, judged him more harshly than either thought fair in retrospect. The Service departments generally felt little enthusiasm, while the delegates at Geneva believed that the Foreign Office gave poor support and minimal guidance to its people at the conference. By the New

Year, 1933, very little progress could be recorded. Germany had withdrawn and had been lured back; Italy was playing off Germany and the West; the U.S.A. did nothing practical. On 2 February the Spanish delegate suggested that the General Commission might celebrate the conference's first anniversary by resolving itself into an hereditary Chamber.

Surprisingly enough, Cadogan still felt some optimism. The Under-Secretary at the Foreign Office, Anthony Eden, was in charge of the British delegation for long spells, although allowed little latitude by London. Cadogan found it most agreeable to work for someone so competent, straight and courageous. 'He seems to me to have a very good idea of what is right and what is wrong, and if he thinks a thing is right he goes all out for it, hard, and if he thinks a thing is wrong, ten million wild horses won't make him do it.'[10] For his part, Eden warmly admired Cadogan, who 'carried out his thankless task with a rare blend of intelligence, sensibility and patience'.[11] They combined, with assistance from the representatives of the other departments, to produce what became known as the 'MacDonald plan', presented by the Prime Minister at Geneva in March and daring to lay down figures of armaments for each country. For a time it seemed that this initiative might rescue the conference. That it was accepted by all as a basis for discussion testifies to the fairness of the plan. Within a few months, however, the fact had to be faced that with Hitler now in power, Germany was rearming and France less likely than ever to disarm.

After Cadogan had discouraged suggestions that he should become Secretary-General of the League or High Commissioner at Danzig, the Permanent Under-Secretary at the Foreign Office proposed the Legation at Peking. It was decided to hold this possibility open until the fate of the Disarmament Conference became clearer. By the late summer of 1933 Cadogan felt that there would be no point in delaying further. He accepted the Legation. This meant that High Trees, Chalfont St Peter, the Cadogans' well-loved home in the foothills of the Chilterns, had to be sold.

His last visit to the League coincided with the quarrels preceding Germany's second and final departure. 'I am getting alarmed', he confided to the diary which he had recently begun to keep, 'at the European situation; thank Heaven I shall be going 11,000 miles away.' Shortly after, just before the withdrawal ordered by Hitler, he recognised his desperate need for a change: 'Dull day—how I hate the Assembly and all its works, and how sick I am of this job—I scarcely realised it before'. Cadogan did not pretend to know the solution to Europe's problems. He recommended that if the French could possibly be persuaded, some limited German rearmament should be sanctioned. Realising that this sounded like rank heresy and weakness, he remarked characteristically: 'there's no weakness so reprehensible as the obstinacy which is afraid of being reproached for weakness!'[12] If the French refused, Britain should stand pat with them.

The Disarmament Conference droned on until June 1934 but was dead from April, when France, pointing to the steep rise in German spending on armaments, refused in effect to carry the discussions further.

* * *

The Cadogans sailed for China, with their three daughters, early in 1934. The official residence of the British Minister, the Legation at Peking, was a most beautiful house. Alas, by that time the troubles with Japan had caused the removal of the Government. Only a bare majority of the diplomatic corps still lived in Peking. Some had gone to Shanghai; the rest travelled about, with occasional visits to Nanking and Shanghai, searching, as Cadogan put it wryly, for the Government to which they were supposed to be accredited. This administration, commonly known as 'the Nanking Government', proved to be an inchoate body, dependent in all important matters upon the decisions of Chiang Kai-Shek, who in his turn insisted on remaining at Nanchang. He received Cadogan there graciously at the end of May, asking insistently, even after being told that China must not expect material or military help against Japan, whether England wished well to China? Cadogan tried to reassure him convincingly.

In order not to prejudice the eventual publication of Cadogan's diary and papers for his time in China, only the briefest account will be given here. Sir Miles Lampson, Cadogan's predecessor in China, had done much to foster close relations between the officials of the Legation and Consulates and the British commercial community. Sir Alexander followed the same course. He proved accessible and self-reliant. Soon after his arrival, two British naval officers were captured by pirates in the Yangtse. Asked whether he would telegraph to London to obtain permission to bombard the pirate vessels, Cadogan said 'Do it at once on my authority. I will send a telegram to the Foreign Office to say what is being done.' The officers were rescued within a day.

Chinese Ministers and officials, often hapless and helpless in the face of such outrages, showed themselves almost embarrassingly friendly to the British. As his acquaintance with them and the country deepened, Cadogan became confident that China would endure and that Chiang's Government deserved support, but thought the policy pursued by the Chinese, of refraining from direct negotiation with Tokyo, a doubtful one, for officials in the north might barter the country away. He saw no place for mediation by the League, favouring the tactic of a frank challenge to state grievances. As he put it to the Chinese Minister of Foreign Affairs, 'Give all you respectably can, and refuse courteously what you can't.' He would also have liked, but was overruled by the Foreign Office, a more systematic approach to the many niggling quarrels which arose between China and Britain over the interpretation of treaties; that is, to say that certain claims could not be admitted until the Chinese Government could do a deal on equal terms with others and make its writ run throughout China.[13]

In the autumn of 1934, when Cadogan went on a prolonged tour of

South China, the Japanese Foreign Office spokesman in Tokyo said that 'Great Britain is dancing as well as piping in China' and an officially-inspired newspaper proclaimed that the British Minister was plotting with the Chinese Finance Minister against Chiang and others who stood for co-operation with Japan. Cadogan, called upon for the first time to make numerous speeches about nothing in particular, told Eden how disconcerted he had been to find

> that constant practice brought a degree of facility—and futility—that reminded me of some of the more striking declarations on the policy of H.M.G. to which it has been our privilege to listen.[14]

At no time during his two years in China did Japan launch a full-dress military attack. Nonetheless, he felt sure that the volcano would erupt sooner or later:

> It is rather like the situation in Europe for the decade before the War. Everyone knew that it *must* come: no one could tell *when*: Germany would, we knew, choose her own time. Japan must explode in one way or another one of these days: no one knows when: it will be Japan who will pull the trigger.[15]

As for Britain's position, Cadogan felt much more doubt. Though he reported faithfully to the Office everything of note, the replies were scarcely beacons of illumination. In July 1935, his urging of a British loan to tide China over a severe financial crisis was twice refused. Only a few weeks before, the outgoing Foreign Secretary, Sir John Simon, had affirmed that Britain meant to maintain her position in China. Acknowledging that the decision about the loan might be correct—for Sir Frederick Leith-Ross, Chief Economic Adviser to the British Government, was shortly due to arrive in the Far East, a visit about which Cadogan had not been consulted and of which, to his anger, he learned from the Japanese—Sir Alexander yet had no doubt that something was sadly awry in British policy:

> with all their protestations that they mean to 'stay in China', they do *nothing*. And 'staying' will cost them something in money or effort or risk. The Chinese are becoming sick of us. And there is no use my 'keeping in touch' with them if I never can give them any encouragement at all.[16]

Sir Frederick Leith-Ross's visit, originating in Neville Chamberlain's conviction that Britain, facing a resurgent Germany, must try to make terms with Japan, failed to produce any basis of economic co-operation. The Far Eastern department of the Foreign Office, which had not been consulted until the decision to send Leith-Ross had been taken, never had any hopes that good would result. Within a few hours of his arrival in China it became plain that he knew practically nothing of the involved and subtle politics of the country. Nevertheless, he spoke freely to Chinese

Ministers and officials. More than once Cadogan had to remonstrate, particularly after Leith-Ross had suggested to the Chinese that they should recognise the Japanese puppet-state of Manchukuo, a step against which Cadogan had advised strongly. After a while Leith-Ross realised that he must tread more cautiously.

When Chiang asked in October whether there existed an 'understanding' between England and Japan, Sir Alec replied that there was not if 'understanding' meant any general agreement or treaty; but Britain hoped to remain on good terms with the Japanese, whose goodwill, or at least neutrality, was essential if others were to assist China's economic regeneration. 'What do you think of the future relations between Japan and China?' asked Chiang, following his habit of firing off questions at his interlocutor. Cadogan replied that although the subject was not easy for an outsider to follow, Japan seemed to have grievances, which he had never seen clearly formulated and which were made the occasion of vague demands. He felt that China had been wise to yield where resistance would be futile and where it could be done honourably. There had been no change in Britain's general Far Eastern policy since 1931, he added. Chiang in turn replied with a simple 'No' when Cadogan asked whether the Japanese were putting forth fresh demands.[17]

The plan evolved by Leith-Ross for an international loan to China, with the participation of Japan, was rejected by the Japanese Foreign Minister, Hirota. It would, he believed, serve the cause of 'certain Chinese groups' and increase China's difficulties. A week or two later, Cadogan sent a long review of the Far Eastern situation to the Foreign Office. Although it is a paper which does not readily lend itself to summary, its main features bear so markedly upon his later work that they must be set down here. Japan's policy, he wrote, had changed since the success of the aggression against Manchuria; she aimed to dominate the Far East and ultimately, perhaps, Asia; the Japanese military might at any moment become impatient of purely economic penetration and occupy Chinese territory, to which step China could offer little resistance in the military sense. It seemed that the Chinese Government had stiffened against Japan's intention to set up an 'autonomous' régime in the North and it would be a mistake for the British to identify themselves with Japanese policy. If this was a correct reading of it, and if the more irresponsible elements took control in Tokyo

> we should not be able to defend our position out here without a trial of strength, which we should wish to avoid at all costs and which only in the most exceptional circumstances could turn out in our favour.

But what was the element of bluff? Cadogan still recommended that the more outrageous actions should not be allowed to pass in silence, for each successful stroke encouraged the Japanese to go further and faster. If by this unheroic policy time could be gained, the situation might change. China and Japan might conceivably settle their differences; and if they did not:

> China has survived many invasions and assimilated many conquerors. I am no judge of the energy or of the endurance of the Japanese, but the power of stolid resistance of the mass of the Chinese people would seem to be illimitable.

As for Great Britain, her trade with China would not warrant the running of vital risks for its protection, nor, perhaps, would the loss of the very large British investment. But an abandonment of those interests, 'if it had the appearance of a retreat before the Japanese, might have the gravest repercussion on our position and prestige throughout the whole of Asia'. This view, which Cadogan had little cause to alter between 1935 and 1941, found general acceptance in the Foreign Office. Sir Robert Vansittart, sending the paper on to Eden, minuted simply:

> We shall get no consideration from the Japanese till we are stronger. It will then be less worthwhile to offend us. Japan certainly cares nothing about 'her moral position in the eyes of the world'. Whose morals anyway? Ours. Not hers.[18]

On 4 February 1936, Sir Alexander Cadogan received a private telegram from the newly appointed Secretary of State, Anthony Eden. It offered him the post of joint Deputy Under-Secretary, with seniority over the other official of the same rank, Sir Lancelot Oliphant. Rightly, Cadogan surmised that this post might carry the succession to Vansittart, the Permanent Under-Secretary. With intense regret at leaving China so unexpectedly and soon, but without hesitation, he accepted. Cadogan had two further interviews with Chiang Kai-Shek, for whose work and wide conception of patriotism he felt sincere admiration. Chiang said that China would make no more concessions to Japan. Russia was flirting with him, but he would not respond until the Communist question in China had been resolved.[19] Cadogan spoke of his desire to help China in his new post. The General and Madame Chiang Kai-Shek expressed their thanks and good wishes.

* * *

The position in Europe had, from a British and French point of view, altered greatly for the worse since Cadogan had recorded his alarm in the autumn of 1933, with open and flagrant rearmament by Germany, including the reintroduction of conscription; Italy's attack upon Abyssinia and triumphant defiance of the League; the dismissal of Sir Samuel Hoare after the abortive pact with Laval; cool relations between Britain and France; and Hitler's abrogation of the Locarno agreement in March 1936, when German troops re-entered the demilitarised zone in the Rhineland. To Cadogan this latter act, not opposed by the British and French, seemed a hinge upon which much must turn. If Germany was to be opposed, this was the moment; if not, mere condemnation would produce resentment without useful result. Asked by Eden to review the state of Europe,

Cadogan therefore proposed an avowed attempt to revise the Covenant, because it had not worked (as the Abyssinian episode had shown) and Germany could not be tied down to 'the vindictive clauses of a Peace Treaty which was really more in the nature of an armistice'. A revision of the Versailles settlement would be opposed by France and the successor states; but they would do well to face the fact that so long as they stood for the letter of the Treaty, Germany would cancel it chapter by chapter.[20] Vansittart thought this policy too heroic to be practical; Eden did not adopt it; Cadogan did not abandon it.

Having spent part of the summer at Montreux, where agreement was reached on a modification of the 1923 Straits Convention with Turkey, Cadogan again advised that Eden should challenge Germany to state her demands:

> I'm quite aware that one wants a long spoon in dealing with Germans, but by resolutely refusing to come to the table, even, we are letting them get all the soup. It can't be said that our 'policy' so far has been successful. In fact we haven't *got* a policy; we merely wait to see what will happen to us next.[21]

This was an uneasy time, with Cadogan's own position ill-defined and his impatience with the prevailing policy evident to anyone reading the minutes on Foreign Office papers. He thought Vansittart poor in exposition—'if he has any ideas or impressions, why can't he put them down straight on paper, instead of dancing literary hornpipes?'—and deficient in initiative: 'He pretends to be very slick and cute but I can't see that he does, or has any idea of doing, *anything*.' In that autumn Hitler recognised the Italian conquest of Abyssinia. He had probably, Sir Alec observed prematurely, made every sort of compact with Mussolini. 'Thus we "keep Germany guessing". It's an exciting game—for us!'[22]

Early in 1937, Eden told Cadogan that as he and the Prime Minister could not persuade Vansittart to take an Embassy, he would stay on for eighteen months anyway. Professing himself quite content, Cadogan explained the difficulties of knowing the limits of his authority in the Office and preached the importance of making contact with Germany. A day or two afterwards, Vansittart spoke to him about the redistribution of duties. Cadogan would take over all the work of Sir Robert Craigie, who was going to Tokyo, and more of a hand with that of Sir Orme Sargent. This was a step of importance, for it gave some precision to Cadogan's status as the senior Deputy Under-Secretary and allowed him some initiative in European questions.

When Sir Nevile Henderson was appointed to the Embassy in Berlin, ironically enough on Vansittart's recommendation, Cadogan approved his determination to make contact with the Germans; not because that policy would necessarily ensure peace, but because the ground must be tested in playing for the highest stakes. Moreover, to put the prospects at the worst, time must be bought:

> If everyone in Germany is mad, and if all are bent on our destruction, disaster *must* come. Therefore, the best we can do is to *put it off*. Therefore we *must* try and talk with some of them and encourage some of them. It's no use shutting our eyes and hiding our heads in the sand and doing nothing. If our rearmament is backward, we must have time. We must *do* something. It's no good, as Van does, forming no policy and merely saying 'Rearm'. He admits our rearmament goes slower than some people's. One more argument for doing whatever we can diplomatically. . . . I've endured nearly a year of 'loyalty' to the F.O., but there are other, and more important loyalties, and I think Van is rushing us to disaster. I must now lose no opportunity of being importunate and hammer away at them.[23]

Entries in the Diary, hurriedly written and assuming much, hardly do justice to either side of the argument. A document of May 1937, the record of Lord Lothian's interviews with Hitler and Goering, attracted a revealing minute from Cadogan and a commentary upon it by Vansittart. Sir Alexander argued from the premiss that Germany had suffered undoubted injustice from the Versailles Treaty and the manner of its application. German complaints, however, were vaguely expressed. The British were accused of encirclement and of thwarting German ambitions everywhere. Cadogan and Vansittart agreed in substance that Germany should be pressed for a more explicit statement. The former wrote:

> I'm not aware that we do—or indeed that we can—thwart all Germany's ambitions. It rather depends what these latter are, whether respectable or not. But that they will not, or cannot, tell us precisely.

At this point Vansittart noted in the margin that

> We are never told precisely just because the ambitions are not really respectable. If they were our difficulties would not be so great.

Cadogan then contested the view that if a premature attempt were made to remove German grievances, only an increase of her 'legitimate claims' would result. On the contrary:

> I believe that, so long as she is allowed to nurse her resentment to her bosom, her claims increase with her armaments—in fact, I should have thought that the history of the last few years proves that this is so. If we pressed her to explain herself, she would do one of two things: (1) She would refuse to do so, and thereby put herself in the wrong, and we should be none the worse off, or (2) she would have to formulate her claims. Surely she would be compelled to make these look as harmless as possible? She couldn't formulate the highest hopes of the wildest members of the Party. And if she had once been pinned down to a programme, wouldn't it be much harder for her later to raise the stake?

Nor did he see that Britain could or should prevent Germany from exercising economic domination over Central and Eastern Europe. He presumed that 'German hegemony' in Central Europe would not mean

> conquest in the ordinary sense of the word. In Czechoslovakia, Hungary, Yugoslavia, Roumania and Greece there are nearly 60,000,000 non-German inhabitants. It cannot surely be suggested that Germany could conquer and rule so many diverse elements. And if she could, I should have thought her hands would be full enough without any adventures against us.

Against this part of Cadogan's minute Vansittart observed that 'German hegemony' meant

> the conquest of Austria and Czechoslovakia, and the *re*conquest of Danzig and Memel; followed by the reduction of the other States to the condition of satellites—*military* satellites when required. This is a quite clear and comprehensible programme, but it is quite incompatible with our interests. We fought the last war largely to prevent this.

The last part of Cadogan's minute recognised its speculative nature but pressed for the examination of all alternatives

> seeing that our present line of policy does not, so far as I can see, point to any solution or appeasement. Our rearmament must, of course, go on at all speed. It is no solution in itself, and we ought to have an ultimate solution in view. And it will . . . be easier and better to make concessions from strength than from weakness.[24]

There is one other aspect of the situation in 1937 which is especially important as background to the Diaries. From July the Far Eastern crisis deepened as Japan attacked China. Cadogan attended the conference held at Brussels in the autumn. His conversations with the American representatives gave scant promise of any joint economic pressure or naval action. The First Sea Lord, Chatfield, told him on 20 November that there would not be much doing even if all the available capital ships were sent to the still unfinished base at Singapore. 'No good blustering unless we are sure we can carry out our threats,' Cadogan commented; and again a little later, when the omens looked still more unpropitious, '*We* shall come to no good, and I don't see how we're to defend our interests here, in the Mediterranean and the F[ar] E[ast]. Most depressing.' That was the central dilemma of British policy in the years covered by this volume, and one which it proved impossible to resolve until the United States entered the war.

* * *

Sir Alexander Cadogan's Diary was kept without a serious break from 1 January 1933 to the last year of his life. In the early stages entries often contained little but a record of engagements or movements. Within a year or two, however, it had become more than a diversion. Probably he intended it as an aid to memory and as the basis of a fuller record to be written at leisure. It was part of Cadogan's official duty to set down the gist of important conversations in Foreign Office papers. He never took copies for himself, and had neither time nor desire to repeat such material in his daily entries, which are often more useful in explaining the play of personality and the motives of policy than in recording its nature and development. Nevertheless, the Diary does contain occasional indications that its author, doubtless after a suitable lapse of time, would allow others to see it. 'I can't remember', records one entry in the summer of 1939, 'all of the details or the moment to moment worries. And perhaps that may make this diary more readable.' And again: 'I begin to wonder whether it is worth while setting out all these details of day-to-day worries, which melt, like the "neiges d'antan". But perhaps so.'

The Diary also provided a place for Cadogan to express himself without restraint, a comforting outlet in a life of excessive burden and business. As terse on paper as in speech, he enjoyed the luxury of saying in private what he could not utter elsewhere: 'I think he's got something pressing on his brain', 'a nasty mind but a nice wit', 'he has a soul above that sort of thing' and, simply, 'wish she'd go home', written respectively of a *Times* correspondent, Evelyn Waugh, a Private Secretary who failed to tell Cadogan that the Cabinet would be meeting at 10.30, and a tiresome female delegate at Geneva; while of a general angling for a wartime post in North Africa he wrote 'I told A[nthony Eden] "It is seldom that we get timely warning of impending disaster." . . .'

Only rarely is the Diary reflective. Cadogan was not given to prolonged self-examination on paper, which he would have thought a waste of time. Likewise any sustained attempt at literary elegance; a telegraphic style saved precious minutes and that was enough. For all his sensitivity to beauty in sound, colour and form, he hardly ever essayed the recapture of atmosphere or the evocative description. There are exceptions; for instance, his recollection of the scene when the British party joined their train at Murmansk in the winter of 1941. Normally, however, the language is matter-of-fact to the point of banality and Sir Llewellyn Woodward's reminder that the simplicity of Cadogan's official minutes may easily disguise his grasp applies with still greater force to his Diary and letters. Since they were not intended for publication, he made no effort to check for consistency of opinion or completeness of background, or to explain at length his assumptions. He disdained to sentimentalise or record petty scandal. And yet this document undeniably has a value which a more prim record would lack. No other permanent head of the Foreign Office in recent times appears to have kept a regular diary. No one else occupied a position in the British Government comparable with Cadogan's in the years 1938 to 1950. Others stood nearer to this or that Minister for shorter periods, but none—unless it be Sir Edward Bridges—stood so close to the centre of power for so long.

Until 1947, when he began to type, Cadogan made each entry in manuscript, usually after dinner or when he had finished the evening's boxes.

By the time he succeeded Vansittart, this had become a part of his routine. An ordinary entry would occupy half or two-thirds of a page in Cadogan's small script, written in three or five minutes. Occasionally, conscious that he might be recording something which would not easily be found elsewhere, he would write at greater length, even in times of the most dire pressure; for example, when the Cabinet rejected the Godesberg terms in September 1938, or when Mr Churchill became Prime Minister in 1940. Sometimes the Diary would be written up a day or two in arrears, a fact which its author would confess. Such indications have normally been included in this edition. Because the Diary was written in time of risk, strict precautions were taken for its security. In the first place, Cadogan, well-trained to his craft, was careful to include no information which would give the enemy a vital advantage. Completed volumes were placed in the Permanent Under-Secretary's safe at the Foreign Office, and an arrangement made for them all to be burnt, with other secret papers, should the Germans land. The Diary was never taken abroad during the war. For Cadogan's frequent absences we have to depend upon notes brought home for copying-up, or more usually on the letters written to Lady Theo. These letters, sent back in aeroplanes that might be shot down, are habitually vague about high politics. They do, however, convey the flavour of the main conferences and are freely cited in this book.

The fact that Cadogan kept a diary has long been known. An extract was quoted in Churchill's *The Second World War* some twenty years ago. Lord Birkenhead's *Halifax*, Colvin's *Vansittart in Office* and Thompson's *The Greatest Treason* print material from it. Sir Alexander supplied part of the diary to the Foreign Secretary, Lord Halifax, as a basis for the record which he compiled in 1939 of events leading to the outbreak of war. The original manuscript, however, was shown to one author only, Sir Llewellyn Woodward, when he was compiling the official history *British Foreign Policy in the Second World War*.

There is every reason to believe that Sir Alec Cadogan's Diary reflects faithfully his official advice, although the language and style are different. Most of his subordinates, no doubt, would have been astonished to learn what their chief, normally so fastidious and correct, was writing. The few who had penetrated the shell of reserve and divined that Cadogan's calm was the product not of nerveless placidity but rather of deliberate curbing of a lively temper, coupled with fine judgment and sense of proportion, would perhaps have been less surprised.

Like Sir Edward Bridges, Cadogan would give a visitor the impression that he had no business save that immediately in hand. Only the papers under reference would be visible on the desk, all others being locked away. Courteous without being effusive, well-dressed without being dandified, expressive but not extravagant in language, he conveyed the impression of a devoted public servant who had one ambition only, to get the public business through smoothly, pleasantly and quickly. Cadogan's observation upon his infant grandson—'he seems to have brought to a fine art the elimination of all unnecessary effort'—would serve very well as an epitome of his own administration. For most journalists he felt a kind of pity, and for many politicians an emotion bordering on contempt. 'Silly bladders! Self advertising, irresponsible nincompoops. How I *hate* Members of Parliament! They embody everything that my training has taught me to eschew—ambition, prejudice, dishonesty, self-seeking, light-hearted irresponsibility, black-hearted mendacity. Feeling better tonight', he added disarmingly, 'after dinner, and after above outburst!'

Away from the Office, Cadogan appeared completely relaxed and detached from its cares. If a golfing partner or a visitor began to talk of foreign affairs or politics, he would turn the conversation quickly. Though unclubbable, he was by no means unsociable. He enjoyed small dinners, but detested the babel and talk of cocktail-parties. 'The atmosphere was terrible: one lady fainted full-length on the floor and, seeing her lying there, I envied her and wished I had thought of the same thing myself.'

* * *

As Permanent Under-Secretary Cadogan valued promptitude, efficiency and good drafting. The problem of prolixity caused him anguish. He was heard to lament the abolition of the test in handwriting, and threatened to forbid dictation if the length of minutes were not curtailed. He could neither be deceived by scamped work nor browbeaten. For all his deprecatory remarks about his own physical courage, Cadogan faced the worst of the Blitz with complete composure and would often refuse to take shelter; like the French mathematician in the First World War who, having calculated that the chance of a direct hit would be small, announced that he would continue to sleep in his attic, 'protégé par la voûte impénétrable des probabilités'.

Cadogan had acute sensibilities. To those in some trouble, unless he judged it richly deserved, he would find a means of extending sympathy or help. He treated subordinates courteously, never indulged the habit of heaping blame upon them when situations turned sour, and knew how to convey reassurance. During the war, a leading light of the T.U.C., having consulted a comparatively junior official of the Foreign Office, used incautious words in a newspaper article. The official, apprehending Parliamentary questions, Soviet suspicion and American criticism, went to explain himself to the Permanent Under-Secretary. 'I remember vividly' he recalled long afterwards,

> how I walked up and down the carpet in Cadogan's room as I tried to extricate myself from this quandary. And just as vividly how, after a few minutes, and with a minimum of words, he absolved me, and sent me upstairs again feeling both contrite and innocent. He had a way of looking at one over the top of his spectacles, saying little or nothing, and yet inspiring one with something of his own innate calm and *sens*

de mesure—I don't want to say cynicism, because it wasn't that—and self-confidence.

In negotiation he was resourceful, straightforward and emollient, finding no use for excessive coyness or inflated claims. He had natural dignity and fine manners; was receptive, and a good listener even to those who bored or irritated him; mistrusted 'cleverness', by which he meant needless obscurity or a fondness for tortuous tactics; had a rare power of analysing situations in their broad features while grasping the details; and freely admitted his ignorance of finance and of the economic and social issues with which the Permanent Under-Secretary nowadays has to grapple endlessly. He did not believe that 'planning' of foreign policy could usefully be carried far, since the ingredients of future situations could not be predicted with sufficient accuracy. Although naturally concerned with the senior appointments, Cadogan had comparatively little interest in the formal machinery or procedures of the Office. If they worked, he was content; if they did not, something had to be devised. Believing that almost any machinery can be made to work if the personalities are not too abrasive, Cadogan submitted with an inward groan to the chore of reading long papers showing this or that theoretically perfect organisation, and with similar reluctance to the task of moving men around because two or three had decided that they could not collaborate. 'Why can't the blessed people pocket their whims and get on with each other?'

It would be easy but most misleading to conclude that the Diary somehow represents the 'real man'. It reflects a part of him—the dry wit, quick grip of essentials, intense practicality and lack of illusions—but distorts other features; for whereas a reader of the Diary might imagine Cadogan to have lived in a fever of irritability, most people who saw him at work day by day believed him to personify calm, moderation and common sense.

The official historian, with unique knowledge of the documents, paid tribute to Cadogan's

> remarkable powers of judgment and lucid expression. His minutes on paper after paper deal with almost every aspect of foreign affairs. They stood out at the time, and are likely to stand out in retrospect, as models of open-mindedness and sound conclusion. They bear no signs of haste or half-finished reasoning even when the writer gives a warning that he needs more time for reflection. They often have a certain irony, never any rancour or prejudice. Only their modesty is delusive; the reader of these short notes written (they are very rarely typed) in a firm quiet hand may not realise at once how great a mastery they show.[25]

Sir Alexander Cadogan cultivated no intimates and had no favourites. Although he would unburden himself with astonishing freedom in the company of a few trusted friends, even they would probably have described reserve as his most marked characteristic. These barriers were not aggressively erected or manned. It was simply that he valued his citadel's seclusion and would not allow his mental independence to be encroached upon. His old tutor A. C. Benson used to quote Aristophanes: 'Don't make your house in my mind' and Cadogan, when asked for advice, would often recall the words of Polonius while disclaiming any desire to share his fate: 'To thine own self be true.' He had in abundance the capacity to insulate himself from his surroundings and to shrug off, the more easily, perhaps, because of the Diary, the innumerable irritations and mishaps of a laborious life. So it came about that although devoid of vanity in the vulgar sense, he felt an inner conviction that his work was well done, and a deep satisfaction in it: 'I am no philosopher,' he wrote during the war,

> but it seems to me that deliberate search for happiness ends in disillusionment. (I am always so sorry for the 'pleasure-seekers' of whom we used to see pictures in some of our papers. I was always afraid they would never reach their destination.)
>
> My limited experience leads me to believe that happiness is nearly always a by-product—generally of 'blood, toil, sweat and tears'. It crops up in the most unlikely quarter and at the most unexpected times. And I don't believe that the present generation would disagree with that.[26]

The principal functions of the P.U.S. are to ensure the efficient administration of the Office, to be responsible to Parliament for the spending of the sums voted, to recommend promotions and dismissals, to receive Ambassadors and, most important of all, to advise the Foreign Secretary on issues of policy. In many questions the P.U.S., knowing the mind of his political chief, can give directions without further reference. He has to judge which papers—and they are not necessarily the obvious ones, for an ephemeral issue may have serious Parliamentary or party consequences—he will send up to the Secretary of State, whom he must guide by focusing, or contradicting, the views of officials lower in the hierarchy.

In those days the Permanent Under-Secretary and his small private office dealt with many administrative tasks. Thus it fell to Cadogan to decide at what hour the typists should leave the building in order to reach home before the Blitz began; to rule that the windows most frequently blown in by bomb-blast should be boarded up; to warn one distinguished Ambassador that his demands for meat-coupons seemed immoderate, and another that his Embassy's liberal use of high-powered cars was creating a poor impression in days of strict rationing of petrol; to hint to a courtier that the strictness with which the rules against divorce were then applied might be relaxed. 'He silly and sticky', Cadogan recorded. 'Said if those went, everything would go. It was laxity in these matters that accounted for all our recent troubles! I said I thought England did pretty well and the spirit of England was pretty good in Tudor times—Drake and all that—when Henry VIII's divorces were still hot news! He said that was quite different! Why? Ass.'

The entries in this published version of the Diary have been chosen to illustrate the range and nature of the duties shouldered by the P.U.S. thirty years ago, and to give some idea of his character, habits and recreations. The reader will soon realise that, for different reasons, work which occupied much of Cadogan's time he rarely described in detail; sometimes, as in the case of honours and appointments, because he thought the subject unworthy of further notice. In another area, the work of the organisations generically known as 'the Secret Service', the reason for omission is obvious. All the same, Cadogan desired that this edition of his Diary should be presented in a way which would show clearly the high importance which he attached to Intelligence. 'It is the missing dimension', he said, 'of most diplomatic history. I am sorry that so much has been published about it all, but now that milk is spilt you should use what you can.'

For the period covered by this volume, Cadogan kept no contemporary papers save the manuscript Diary and a very few personal letters. His private correspondence seems to have been destroyed, although that for the period 1950–68 has survived, and he removed no official or demi-official documents from the Foreign Office. In the last few years of his life he composed some short autobiographical chapters. Until his retirement from the B.B.C. in 1957, Sir Alexander had no opportunity to write memoirs. By then Mr Churchill's six volumes had appeared. Many documents from the pre-war archives of the Foreign Office had been published. Sir Llewellyn Woodward's official history was well advanced, and the first Alanbrooke volume about to come out. Cadogan thought he could add little of importance to the known record:

> It seemed to me that the chronicle had been fully compiled, and if there was any philosophising to be done, any lessons to be learnt, any morals to be pointed, any inferences to be drawn that might serve as a guide to likely future developments and the course that we should steer to meet them, that would call for skill and understanding that I do not possess.

The modesty was entirely sincere. For some years he maintained this attitude and the progress of his brother's memoirs did nothing to alter it. 'Look at Eddie's book', he would say gloomily, 'it only sold about six copies.' Family and friends persisted, however. To their urgings, Cadogan conceded, were added the prickings of a conscience warning against laziness, 'a complaint from which I have suffered all my life but which has not to my knowledge done me much actual harm'. Hence the draft chapters, covering subjects ranging from the Cadogans' time in the Vienna of Franz Joseph to the Disarmament Conference of 1932–4, Sir John Simon as Foreign Secretary, several of the wartime conferences and some of Sir Alexander's experiences at the U.N.

These chapters excited little interest with the Sunday newspaper or with the publisher to whom they were shown in 1966. There remained the possibility of publishing the Diary. Three new factors had entered into the argument since Cadogan had decided against this proposal ten years before: a thirty-year rule was shortly to apply to official papers, which meant that the full range of documents for the pre-war period would become available; a mass of new published material would make it possible to explain most of the references; and many of those mentioned in the Diary were now dead. Towards the end of 1967, he therefore decided to allow the publication of the Diary, though he still found difficulty in believing that it would be of interest. When a visitor quoted the saying that all the best English diaries have been written by bores, he exclaimed triumphantly 'There you are! I always said mine was no good.'

Not long before his death, the first typed versions—for the years 1938 and 1941—became available. Sir Alexander Cadogan had never before read them through. 'Even I', he said characteristically, 'became quite interested.' In discussions during these last months of his life he explained how he would like the book to be shaped and his wishes have been faithfully followed. In the first place, no material has been omitted simply in order to save his reputation as a prophet, or to shield his memory or family from criticism. Knowing that certain passages would produce that result, he insisted nevertheless that they be printed, even when clearly written in moments of frustration, exhaustion or anger.

The passages here reproduced represent rather less than half of the original. Most of the material left out describes the affairs of Cadogan's family circle, the weather, the company in which he lunched or dined, occasional weekends at the cottage near Northiam, his rather variable success as a golfer, the progress of the bulbs, plants and shrubs in St James's Park. In short, it is material which in bulk would be of no general interest. Nevertheless, examples have been retained in an attempt to convey the flavour of the original. Other parts have been omitted on different grounds: a few passages judged to be libellous; odd sentences which sharply criticise colleagues in the Foreign Office or the Diplomatic Service; occasional disobliging remarks which might give offence to those still living or to their immediate descendants; and some references to members of the Intelligence services or to activities which are still properly kept secret. It will be for others to judge, when the Diaries become available in their entirety, whether the balance has been fairly held. Sir Alexander accepted that the purpose of the interpolations and footnotes should be to make the text intelligible to an interested but not necessarily expert reader, and to show where further information may be found. He recognised that the character of the Diary would entail much explanation. As he wrote on a depressed day in the autumn of 1941, when he had persuaded himself that the diary must be dull:

> **I never have time or inclination to read it. I keep it scrappily and simply haven't the time to indicate what interviews are about, or to relate one thing to another.**

It has seemed best, even at the price of interrupting the flow of the text, to make frequent interpolations at the points to which they relate, rather than to place all the explanatory material at the beginning of each chapter. No attempt has been made to turn this into a history of British foreign policy or a biography.

Words italicised are those which Sir Alexander underlined in the original. Square brackets [ ] enclose interpolations by the editor, whereas material printed in parentheses ( ) appears in the same form in the manuscript. A few obvious slips have been corrected and for ease of reading some abbreviated words have been set out in full. Although Cadogan's holograph was rapid, clear and neat, with a revealing tendency to artistic flourish in the capitals, the Diary is not always legible with certainty. Where serious doubt exists about the transliteration it has been indicated by a question mark in square brackets. Omissions within the selected passages are indicated by ellipses. No alterations of language have been made.

THE DIARIES OF SIR ALEXANDER CADOGAN

1938–1945

I

January–August 1938
THE APPROACH TO MUNICH

On 1 January 1938, a long announcement from No. 10 Downing Street stated that the Foreign Secretary, in consultation with the Prime Minister, had reviewed the conditions which had placed increasing strain on the staff of the Foreign Office. They had concluded that relief could best be afforded

> by the creation of a new post in the Foreign Office, following the example of somewhat similar posts in other Departments. The Prime Minister has accordingly authorised the Foreign Secretary to appoint a Chief Diplomatic Adviser responsible directly to the Secretary of State.
>
> The functions of the new officer will be analogous to those fulfilled by the occupants of the similar posts attached to other Departments (Chief Industrial Adviser and the Chief Economic Adviser to the Government) and will include advising the Secretary of State upon all major questions of policy concerning foreign affairs remitted to him for that purpose, and representing the Foreign Office on any occasions, whether at home or abroad, on which the Secretary of State may wish to avail himself of his services.
>
> In order to give full effect to the purposes in view, it is necessary that the new post should be filled by a person of international reputation and authority, and accordingly Sir Robert Gilbert Vansittart . . . has been selected to be the first holder of the office.
>
> Consequently upon the above appointment, the Secretary of State for Foreign Affairs has appointed the Honourable Sir Alexander Montagu George Cadogan, K.C.M.G., C.B., Deputy Under-Secretary of State in the Foreign Office, to be Permanent Under-Secretary of State for Foreign Affairs.

The terms of the announcement, which Cadogan had not wholly approved, led to a good deal of comment. No such position had previously been known in the hierarchy of the Foreign Office, in which the work was organised in a pyramidal fashion, through the departments to Assistant Under-Secretaries, thence to the Deputy Under-Secretary, the Permanent Under-Secretary and, in matters of the highest importance, to the Secretary of State. It had proved difficult in 1935 to adapt this system so as to accommodate two Cabinet Ministers, Sir Samuel Hoare and Eden, in the Foreign Office. It proved far more difficult, indeed impossible, to modify the organisation of the Office in the sense of the communiqué.

Vansittart's post had been created not to meet a special need but because he represented, much more publicly than any other P.U.S., an attitude. His dismissal would immediately have engendered a suspicion that Britain's European policy was to be changed. He had refused an Embassy. Under the new dispensation, he kept the room normally used by the P.U.S., though he now had no Private Secretary or staff.

When Woermann, the German chargé d'affaires, asked a group of journalists for their opinion of the new appointments, six thought Vansittart had been promoted, six believed that he had been sidetracked, and six held opinions in between. Woermann telegraphed to Berlin:

> In view of Vansittart's personality, everything will of course depend entirely on what he makes of his position and what they let him make of it. A definite change of course in British foreign policy as a result of the changes in the Foreign Office is surely not to be expected at the present time, since Cadogan's views seem to coincide to a considerable extent with Eden's.

Assurances were later given in Parliament that Cadogan would be P.U.S. in the same sense as any of his predecessors. There was no intention of transforming the Chief Diplomatic Adviser into a species of Ambassador at large, or of conferring any special mission upon him. He would advise the Secretary of State upon major questions of policy, but would not be concerned with the day-to-day affairs of the Office. He and the P.U.S. would work on parallel lines.

As numerous entries in the Diary reveal only too well, Cadogan judged the whole system a mistake. Vansittart, who had not enough to do in the new post, was seconded to the Ministry of Economic Warfare in 1940, found himself a floating kidney there also, returned to the Foreign Office with fewer duties than ever and had his resignation gratefully accepted in the summer of 1941. The post of Chief Diplomatic Adviser was allowed to lapse and has never been revived.

Since it was not Cadogan's habit to read through old entries in the Diary, he had no opportunity to consider the balance or to correct impressions. The unfriendly references to Vansittart's position and views should not be read to mean that the two were on bad terms in private. They were not, although Cadogan in many respects represented the antithesis of his predecessor. Vansittart wrote long minutes in a style contorted, allusive and sometimes almost incomprehensible; harangued ministers and civil servants to the point where they judged him overwrought; was generally stronger in diagnosis than in prescription; lived rather grandly; and for all his warm-heartedness, charm, prevision and brilliance steadily lost ground. Cadogan, endlessly skilful in handling ministers, thought Vansittart a disastrously bad adviser in point of policy; seemed, with his matter-of-fact statements and short minutes, to personify calm and good sense; left no one in doubt that he was now in charge of the Office; and, though usually under-rated in the early stages of acquaintance, impressed and influenced a series of masters as diverse as could be: Eden, Halifax, Chamberlain, Churchill, Attlee and Bevin.

It would be misleading, and unjust, to suggest that Cadogan's disagreements with Vansittart derived simply from differences of method. For the first part of his tenure, Cadogan—holding a less black view of German intentions—was able to take a line which Ministers naturally found more palatable than Vansittart's incessant admonitions. Vansittart had his own sources of intelligence, outside the official machine, together with special skill in reading the signs. Cadogan acknowledged it, perhaps more handsomely than the facts warranted, in an entry of March 1939, just after the seizure of Prague: 'I must say it is turning out—at present—as Van predicted and as I never believed it would.' It was characteristic of him to supply this confession, without any attempt at self-exculpation, to Vansittart's biographer.

In the first half of 1938 Cadogan still had time for private reading and recreation. He then lived near Sloane Square and had no house in the country. At the weekends, however, Denham, twenty miles from London, lay readily accessible for golf. By the summer of 1939, when he bought a cottage near Northiam, in east Sussex, everything looked very different. A clear weekend had become a rarity, liable to interruption at any moment by messengers with red boxes and despatch-riders with pouches. An ordinary working day began at 9 a.m. and seldom ended before 11.30 p.m. or midnight. The Cadogans liked to entertain. So relentless had the pressure of business at the Office become, however, that they were less able than they would have wished to invite colleagues and friends to meals. Once the war began, the question settled itself. The Permanent Under-Secretary could not with decency escape many social commitments, some of which he enjoyed but more of which he did not. Here Lady Theo's skill in protecting her husband from unnecessary engagements and preserving a haven at home even in the war made, as he put it, always tolerable and sometimes agreeable a life which would otherwise have been impossible.

* * *

When Cadogan succeeded Vansittart, the essential problem of British foreign policy lay in the worldwide distribution of British interests. They were challenged by two powers of the first magnitude, Germany and Japan, at opposite ends of the earth; and athwart the lines of communication in the Mediterranean, exploiting and fomenting British difficulties in Palestine, stood Italy, a power with considerable nuisance value under a dictator of paranoiac tendencies. British and Commonwealth interests in the Middle East and Far East were scarcely inferior to those in Europe. Only in the most desperate circumstances, therefore, could relief be sought by conscious abandonment, and then with dire consequences. Had

Anglo-American co-operation been effective in the Far East, British policymakers might have been able so to manage their complicated affairs that the threats could be prevented from materialising simultaneously. In the absence of such co-operation, the British found themselves unable to concentrate sufficient force in the right place and at the right moment. That is in substance the theme of the first half of this book, the process reaching its apogee with the fall of Singapore and the loss of the two great ships sent there, inadequate because the exigencies of war in other theatres would not allow the despatch of a sufficient force.

The fear of damage to the capital ship fleet had influenced British policy in the Abyssinian crisis of 1935. Evident and growing perils in Europe and the Mediterranean equally disinclined the Cabinet in 1937 to place a large fleet at Singapore. Hence the strong pressure to remove Italy from the ranks of likely enemies. 'The intervention of Italy against us', the Chiefs of Staff advised in 1937, 'would at once impose conflicting demands on our fleet. Our policy must be governed by the principle that no anxieties or risks connected with our interests in the Mediterranean can be allowed to interfere with the despatch of a fleet to the Far East.'[1]

Rather less than two years later that doctrine had to be reversed. In the interval lay Eden's resignation, the Anschluss, the Anglo-Italian agreement and Munich. At the end of 1937, Japanese behaviour had become so outrageous that Chamberlain and Eden offered to risk the consequences of sending to the Far East eight or nine capital ships (leaving virtually nothing for home waters or the Mediterranean) if the United States government would do the same. President Roosevelt declined the suggestion, but did send Captain Ingersoll for secret staff talks in London. That development, notwithstanding the condition that the result would commit neither government, represented a kind of collaboration unknown between the two powers since the First World War; a fact without which Eden's attitude to Roosevelt's initiative of 11 January 1938 cannot be understood. Nor can Chamberlain's pressure for the Italian talks be understood if the Far East be left out of account. Noting in January that he hoped for an early start, he observed: 'It will be as well, for the Japs are growing more and more insolent and brutal.' And again in the same month: 'We are a very rich and vulnerable Empire, and there are plenty of poor adventurers not very far away who look on us with hungry eyes.'[2]

This is not to say for a moment that Eden was less aware than the Prime Minister of the dangers. To reduce the complicated differences between the two men to a sentence is perhaps unfair to both; yet it would not be too far wide of the mark to say that the Foreign Secretary, while agreeing that talks should be tried, sought stiffer terms than Chamberlain, had little confidence in the outcome whatever the terms, and wished to spend more on arms despite the financial risk.

As the Diary shows, Cadogan believed that the policy pursued in 1938 was in substance the right one, even though he might have preferred this or that phase to be differently handled or timed. Had he disagreed strongly, he would still have executed the chosen policy loyally: 'It is the duty of any Government Servant', he once wrote, 'at all times to offer his advice and express his opinion to the Minister whom he serves. . . .'

> You may think that an Ambassador, or for that matter any Civil Servant, can be placed in a very difficult position if he disagrees with the policy of the Government. To that I would reply that he was not 'hired' (as an American would say) to formulate policy: his duty is to supply his chief not only with all the relative facts that may help the latter in coming to his decision but also his own recommendations as to what should be done. But if he fails to convince, I think he has no real grievance: it will not be his job to present the matter to Parliament and take all responsibility for it. And I think his conscience should be clear: if he has honestly and fearlessly expressed all doubts about the proposed policy and has still failed to convince, he has at least done his duty and should not be too cocksure about his opinion against all other. He must remember, after all, that it is the Minister, and ultimately the Prime Minister, who will have to take the blame if the policy proves wrong, and the Civil Servant will be shielded. The obverse of that is, of course, that the Ministers will take the credit if all goes well! This may seem rather odd in theory, but I think it works pretty well in practice. Of course I have known one or two cases of Civil Servants resigning owing to their disagreeing with official policy. I never thought resignation justified. It always seemed to me a rather selfish indulgence of an unduly morbid conscience. What would happen if everyone arrogated to themselves the same right, and how could the business of Government be carried on?[3]

1938

Saturday, 1 January

Not a bad sort of day. Appointments out in Press this morning, and some puzzlement is evinced. Van[sittart]'s new post and Van himself, played up for all they are worth. 11 Capt. Ingersoll*, U.S. naval liaison officer, who arrived yesterday, came to see A. [Eden†] and me. Seems nice and his instructions seem to be helpful, but even he seems not clear on the *objective*. So after he'd gone, drafted a telegram to Washington to try and draw Americans and urge a naval demonstration *now*.

Sunday, 2 January

After tea went round to see A. about various things. He rather

* Capt. R. E. Ingersoll, director, War Plans Division, U.S. Navy; later C.-in-C. U.S. Atlantic Fleet.

† Anthony Eden. See List of Principal Characters (Appendix B, p. 831). Lists of abbreviations and codenames used in the Diaries are also printed in the Appendixes.

dismayed that Press had written up Van's post and duties too much, and thought P.M. would be annoyed. I said I didn't care so long as I had the substance and really conducted the work and had the responsibility and was not simply to 'polish up the handle of the great front door'. This he again assured me was so. But I pointed out that the question of 'duality' raised by [The] 'Observer' was bound to be in people's minds and would lead to Questions. (I knew it would, and had hinted that to him before.) He had had long letter from Maggie,* enclosing copy of Ivy's.† He said 'I'd thought of not answering her: I'll send her a picture postcard from the South of France'!

Tuesday, 4 January

N. Henderson‡ lunched. He had been rather puzzled by new appointments but I think understands.

Wednesday, 5 January

Went over to No. 10 at 11.30 for an hour's talk with Horace Wilson.§ I like him and our talk was useful and I think he wants to help. He said if Questions asked in House it must be made clear that mine is the responsibility and that I have the last word in 'advice'. . . . 5 Corbin¶ snooping about Anglo-Italian conversations. Reassured him. Said nothing would happen before A. met Delbos|| at Geneva.

Thursday, 6 January

Went to see Chatfield** at 11 and showed him draft telegram to Washington, designed to draw them. He didn't like it much and re-wrote some of it. But he wants to *follow* U.S. too much, but realises I don't like this. . . . 4.45 went to see P.M. Talked to him about Anglo-U.S. co-operation, 'recognition' of Abyssinia, Royal visit to France, &c. He is very pleasant, easy and sensible. Is going to write to A. about Anglo-Italian conversations and will show me draft. I

* Mrs Ronald Greville.

† Lady Chamberlain, widow of Sir Austen.

‡ Sir Nevile Henderson, British Ambassador in Berlin, 1937–9. See List of Principal Characters.

§ Sir H. J. Wilson, Chief Industrial Adviser, close confidant of Chamberlain. See List of Principal Characters.

¶ M. André Charles Corbin, French Ambassador in London, 1933–40. See List of Principal Characters.

|| M. Yvon Delbos, French Foreign Minister, 1936–8.

** Admiral Sir Ernle Chatfield, First Sea Lord, 1933–8; Minister for Co-ordination of Defence, 1939–40.

will draft him a telegram to Washington. Put to him point that Americans might be shocked by recognition, but he isn't worried. . . .

Got telegram from Van agreeing to my taking over at once Gladwyn Jebb*—who seems excellent.

Friday, 7 January

P.M. sent for me about 3.45. On Italian conversations (de jure recognition [of the conquest of Abyssinia]) warned him against opening up with Musso[lini] with a personal letter, and then leaving the difficulties—and possibly the break—to A. He quite saw the force of this, and will guard against it. On the F[ar] E[ast], had to show him Press report of fresh outrage in Shanghai. Asked if I should be content with simple apology and suggested time had come to tell the Americans we must do *something* (e.g. announce naval preparations) and ask whether they will take 'parallel' action. He agreed, and I sent off telegram. Also got his approval for A. to make a general declaration at the Council about our 'League policy'. Useful conversation, and he was very easy and sensible. With him about ¾ hour.

[The Foreign Office had received news of an assault by the Japanese on two British police officers in Shanghai. Captain Ingersoll's talks, lasting from 3–13 January, covered an exchange of codes; liaison; and Intelligence. It became clear that American forces could not be put into a state of full readiness until the President had declared a state of emergency, although some ships could sail at once. London now asked whether Roosevelt was likely to make this declaration. British preparations were as far advanced as they could be short of mobilisation. If the Admiralty had to announce further steps because of the incidents at Shanghai, would the President move in parallel? Sir Ronald Lindsay† was told that the response to such steps would be an announcement that the U.S. Pacific Fleet was being prepared for action, followed by another to the effect that the Pacific manœuvres would be advanced to early February.

Here the British Government found themselves in the familiar dilemma, for such moves would not commit the U.S. to war with Japan even if the British should be so embroiled. Moreover the despatch of the British Fleet to the Far East would take away the strongest card at a moment when the Italian talks were thought to be imminent. Chamberlain decided against it.[4]

Ingersoll's talks resulted in an agreed record but no commitments. His absence from Washington became known to the press. The publicity, which Roosevelt had hoped to avoid by sending him to London, embarrassed the

* Of the F.O., as Private Secretary. See List of Principal Characters.

† British Ambassador in Washington, 1930–9.

U.S. Government and probably retarded Anglo-American collaboration in naval matters.]

Monday, 10 January

Went to see Horace Wilson at 12 to explain to him that certain anti-Italian propaganda, about which he had asked me, had been done by News Department on A.'s instructions. Rather awkward, as I suppose P.M. objects to this, or is put up by H. W[ilson] to do so. H.W.'s interference in our affairs wants watching, but it will be just as well to keep in with him and look after him. . . . I warned H. Wilson of the danger of press gossip that Van has 'direct access to the P.M.'. This will be taken to mean that P.M., with Van, is running a rival foreign policy. This won't do and must be scotched. I'm all for Van having his boost but if it develops in any dangerous direction, I'll blow it to bits. Saw P.M. about 4 p.m. He quite easy and calm. Suggested we must wait for Roosevelt's reply before defining our position. Gave him draft declaration for Geneva which he examined, and made some slight alterations.

Tuesday, 11 January

12.30 went to see Chatfield. We have a telegram from Washington that Americans, *if* we declare our preparedness, will (1) 'Scrape their bottoms' (i.e. dock their battleships) and (2) advance date of manoeuvres. Chatfield obviously uneasy. And I agree that if we're going to be in negotiation with Musso[lini] in 2 or 3 weeks it *isn't* a good time to send our fleet away. So in the afternoon I wrote a minute to P.M. pointing out difficulties and submitting telegrams to Washington and Tokyo. To latter, rather menacing, but leaving questions open: and to former, appreciation of what they offer, telling them what we're doing in Tokyo and saying we may have to call on them shortly. . . .

Letter from A. about Far East. He has hoped that we will do what we are doing, so I think that's all right.

[On the subject of the projected negotiations with Italy, Cadogan believed that there would be little use in worrying unduly about *de jure* recognition of Italy's position in Abyssinia, since it seemed likely that members of the League would present the Duce with a series of such triumphs. 'The longer we leave it, the more will be the defections from the League front on this question, the more isolated we shall become, and the more foolish we shall look.' Moreover, he thought that the Italians had now made a definite advance; if no satisfactory basis for talks could be found, Mussolini would be confirmed in his suspicion of British intentions:

> The practical result is likely to be an accentuation of his nuisance value towards us in all its forms (propaganda, press campaign, subversive activities in Egypt and in the Arab world), the strengthening of the Berlin-Rome axis (possibly to the extent of a military alliance between Italy and Germany), an increase of tension in the Mediterranean, and joy in the German and Japanese camps.

Should these possibilities be realised they would provoke at least a demand for preventive measures, which in their turn would mean increased expenditure in Egypt and the Mediterranean theatre and a diversion of resources from home defence. Instead of thinking of a neutral Italy, as Sir Thomas Inskip, the Minister for Co-ordination of Defence was still doing, the British Government would have to revise all their war plans on the assumption of a hostile Italy. Nor could the issue be bounded by the Mediterranean:

> the situation created by such a hostile Italy in friendly relations with Japan and astride our Mediterranean communications will inevitably react on our freedom of action in the Far East.

Cadogan did not claim that successful talks with Italy would suddenly convert her into an ally, but he did hope that it would restore her to neutrality. And would not the practical effect of failure to recognise be

> to solidify the Berlin-Rome axis and increase the manifestations of its material strength and its capacity to front and insult us with impunity . . .? Moreover, is not Germany going to ask us a higher price for her friendship so long as we have a frankly hostile Italy on our flank rather than a mere neutral Italy?

Transmitting all this to Eden on 12 January, Cadogan added significantly that

> from the discussions I have had with the Prime Minister I am convinced that he is extremely anxious to reach an agreement if that be at all possible, with Mussolini, and that he attaches great importance to it.[5]

During the evening of 11 January, Sumner Welles, the Under-Secretary at the State Department, held a secret conversation with Sir Ronald Lindsay on behalf of the President. Roosevelt felt that the influence of the democratic states had been declining, and the worldwide situation deteriorating. He wished to take an initiative, designed to work parallel with the effort which the British were making with the Central European powers and to reinforce it. He proposed to urge upon the entire diplomatic corps, on 22 January, that their governments should agree on the fundamental principles to be observed in the relations of states: reduction of armaments, recognised laws of war, equal access to raw materials. If the response were favourable, the United States Government would ask a small number of governments to join them in forming tentative proposals. The speech which Roosevelt proposed to deliver recognised that agreement on these principles might not of itself establish peace, and stated explicitly that the U.S. Government could not abandon their 'traditional policy of freedom from political involvement'. The President would proceed only if assured by 17 January of the British Government's wholehearted support.

On the morning of 13 January there arrived two messages from Lindsay, recommending an immediate endorsement of this attempt to range American opinion behind the objectives of the democratic governments. To withold approval would annul all the progress made in the past two years in Anglo-American relations. 'I therefore urge respectfully but very earnestly that His Majesty's Government give their reply to this invaluable initiative with a very quick and cordial acceptance.' At Chamberlain's request, Cadogan discussed this development at once with Sir Horace Wilson; 'and he agreed' Cadogan recorded that day, 'that, desirable as it was not to appear in any way to discourage the President, it really seemed that he was taking and holding over our heads rather a hasty decision without full light on the situation here'.[6]]

Wednesday, 12 January

About 5.15 telegrams began to roll in from Washington—personal messages from Roosevelt to P.M. R. has wild ideas about formulating a world settlement! But must know by *Monday* whether we agree he should go ahead. Sent telegrams down to P.M. with a hurried minute. This is not the way to transact such business!

Thursday, 13 January

Went over in the morning to discuss Washington telegrams with Horace Wilson. He very anti-Roosevelt. I quite see all the difficulties, but it *is* important not to break with R. . . . Drafted telegram to Washington and sent it over to Horace W. Difficulty is that Lindsay now telegraphs pressing that we accept 'cordially and immediately'. Says R. *might* accept suggestions, but *not* in regard to timetable! So drafted a telegram appreciating R.'s initiative but saying that he probably doesn't appreciate what we are doing for agreement with Italy and Germany. Told him, and asked whether in view of this he wouldn't hold his hand (I wanted to add that, if he *wouldn't*, we'd go with him). P.M. arrived about 6 and I went to see him and Horace W. at no. 11. He hates R.'s idea, but I tried to point out that we mustn't snub him. But he wouldn't have my addition. Got off telegram containing message to R. (about 8), and a further telegram to Lindsay explaining our fears and objections.

Sent copies of telegrams to A. by aeroplane leaving early tomorrow.

[With the telegrams went a letter of explanation. The Prime Minister had viewed this initiative with 'the gravest concern' for reasons now explained to Washington; principally that it could cut across efforts to negotiate on more immediate issues with the dictators, who might take advantage of the President's proposals both to prevaricate and to inflate their demands. The President was asked to consider whether it would not be better to delay a little. Chamberlain, wishing to know the President's reaction before the following Monday, the date by which a definite British answer had been requested, asked Cadogan to explain to Eden that for this reason there had been no time to consult him.[7]]

Friday, 14 January

French Government have fallen, and Council may be postponed, so went over and suggested to P.M. that we should get A. back. He agreed—thank goodness—but I think rather reluctantly, and we got on telephone to A., who will be home by lunch tomorrow. Couldn't tell him why! (He is lunching with Winston [Churchill*] and Ll.G[eorge]† today—I warned P.M.!‡) Lunched with Herschel Johnson§ and Ingersoll at White's. Latter satisfied with his conversations and goes back on Tuesday. . . . Van came in just before lunch. I told him about Roosevelt. He of course rather anti-. But he went safely down to Denham.

Saturday, 15 January

Hear bag missed A. at Marseilles and that no aeroplanes are flying this morning (frightful gale). He coming by 10 a.m. train from Paris. So decided to go down to Folkestone with Oliver [Harvey]¶ to meet him. . . . Boat late, so walked with O. along the front for nearly an hour. Boat eventually came in, stern first, and crashed into pier! Had to go out again. V. bad crossing, but A. and Harold [Caccia]|| looked all right. A. read Washington telegrams. Thinks we have snubbed President too much. But this I don't believe. He wants to let President go ahead and doesn't believe a bit in P.M.'s initiatives regarding Italy and Germany. I think he exaggerates as much one way as P.M. does on other!

Back home about 7. A. and Bobbety** came to dinner and we had

* Winston S. Churchill. See List of Principal Characters.

† David Lloyd George. Prime Minister, 1916–22.

‡ At Eden's request.

§ First Secretary and Counsellor, U.S. Embassy, 1934–41; Minister to Sweden 1941–6.

¶ Private Secretary to the Sec. of State, 1936–9. See List of Principal Characters.

|| Asst. Private Secretary to Eden.

** Lord Cranborne, later Marquess of Salisbury, Parliamentary Under-Sec. of State for Foreign Affairs, 1935–8. See List of Principal Characters.

some talk after. . . . Telegram came in from Washington showing that President is giving us a little more time—but grudgingly, apparently. I got through to Washington (in about 5 minutes or less) and A. talked to Lindsay who fears President is disappointed. So we drafted a telegram to him designed to keep President sweet. They went about 12.30.

Sunday, 16 January

Went round to A. at 10.30 and found Oliver [Harvey] and Rex L[eeper].* Talked till nearly 12 (but don't think we advanced matters much) when A. went off to Chequers. . . .

A. rang up soon after 6 to say he had had 'fairly' satisfactory day with P.M.

Monday, 17 January

Have had no time for this Diary for some days, so my memory may be at fault.

Horace Wilson came in the morning to say P.M. rather horrified at A.'s attitude: thought A., before he went abroad, accepted idea of negotiations with Italy on basis of de jure recognition: now finds he is opposed and thinks he has 'run out'. Told H.W. he'd better go along and talk to A. himself. I advise A. according to my lights: it is difficult for me to try to adjust differences between them which are brought to my notice in this way. He went. A. sent for me after and told me about it. Is quite frank that there *is* a difference of view, or attitude, between him and P.M. Somehow—I forget how—later I told A. I had sent H.W. to him.

[On that day Eden wrote to the Prime Minister:

> I really do not feel that this initiative of the President need necessarily injure the attempts which we are making to improve relations with Germany, nor even have any repercussions on the conversations which I know you are so anxious to start with Italy. . . . I truly believe that with the world as it is now, it is almost impossible to overestimate the effect which an indication of United States interest in European affairs may be calculated to produce. I know that you fear that the dictators would resent the tone of his communication and that there would be, in consequence, a blast and counterblast between democracies and dictatorships. I do not myself think this would be the result, though I agree that neither of the dictators would like Roosevelt's initiative; they would probably, however, be constrained to conceal their dislike and might even become more negotiable. . . .

* R. W. A. Leeper, Head of the F.O. News Dept. See List of Principal Characters.

Simultaneously, Cordell Hull spoke vehemently to Lindsay of the sanctity of international law. *De jure* recognition of Italy's seizure of Abyssinia would be 'capitalised by desperado nations'; 'the repercussions in the Pacific area might be very serious in many ways'.[8]]

Tuesday, 18 January

All these days busy discussing with A. this question of Roosevelt's initiative. Whatever else may be decided, *we must not turn him down.*

Wednesday, 19 January

A. got back from F.P.C.* about 7.45. He had a rough passage and no one supported him, except perhaps, Malcolm M[acDonald].† P.M. produced draft of a very bad telegram. Dined hurriedly at home and went round to A. Oliver, Bobbety, and Jim Thomas‡ there. Malcolm joined us. We decided we *must let Roosevelt go ahead*, and I undertook to redraft P.M.'s telegram.

Thursday, 20 January

Got on to redraft of P.M.'s telegram and took it to A. He didn't like it, but I *must* try to get in some of the P.M.'s stuff. (Last night I suggested calling Van into conference, but he wouldn't! That's all I can do). . . . Message from A. about 5.15 asking me to come. . . . Find things went better. (A. had had interview with P.M., whom he shook, in morning). Agreed to let Roosevelt go ahead. That's the main point. Helped to draft telegrams for submission to F.P.C. tomorrow morning. *May* be great triumph. (I think Van was against, but he was hardly consulted).

Horace Wilson called about 6.45. Don't know what he's at or whether he's straight. Told him quite frankly what I had advised and why. 'What sticks out is American cooperation'. We *can't* throw that away.

Friday, 21 January

Meeting of F.P.C. in morning. Not very satisfactory, and apparently they don't like the telegrams to Washington and Malcolm [MacDonald] and Oliver S[tanley]§ commissioned to modify draft. . . . A. came back from F.P.C. with draft telegrams which *I*

* Foreign Policy Committee—or as Chamberlain used to call it on account of the prickly character of the discussions, the Fretful Porpentine Committee.

† Sec. of State for the Dominions, 1935–8, 1938–9, and for the Colonies, 1938–40. See List of Principal Characters.

‡ J. P. L. Thomas, Parliamentary Private Secretary to Eden, 1937–8; Financial Secretary to the Admiralty, 1943–5.

§ President of the Board of Trade, 1937–40. See List of Principal Characters.

think are all right. We got them off. I think he has won a great victory. Van wasn't consulted at all. I have tried throughout to keep A. from resigning impulsively because (I haven't told him this) either he wouldn't be able to make his case to the country, or would have to advertise fact that H.M.G. had repudiated American cooperation, which would be *fatal*. Pointed this out to J. Thomas. I'm afraid A. may think I haven't always given him strong enough support but I have been trying to prevent a break between him and P.M. for above reasons. However, both Jim Thomas and Rex Leeper volunteered to me tonight that A. was thankful for our support. Pray God it turns out all right.

I had had to draft a circular about treatment of papers in F.O. I thought it was only decent to let Van see it. He tried to insert a provision whereby I should send any papers of 'major importance' *through* him to S. of S. He knows that this is *not* A.'s intention, and he knows I know it. I said I wouldn't stand for this. Only condition on which I had taken on this sticky job was that I should deal direct with S. of S., and I won't keep it on any other. I stated this with unnecessary vehemence and A., loyal as he is, more than endorsed me and Van collapsed. I think V. is off his mental balance.

Saturday, 22 January

A., on reflection, is more pleased with yesterday than he had been. I told him I always was. Discussed with him the Dept.'s paper on German negotiations, which he approved. I sent off copy to P.M. and another with an explanatory letter to Horace Wilson. Talked to R. Leeper about how our Press should treat today's conciliatory speech by Hirota.* I said 'meet good manners with good manners' but don't go further.

[The paper on the proposed German negotiations summarised departmental opinions on the Western pact, disarmament, Germany's return to the League, Austria, Czechoslovakia and colonies. Prospects of progress under most headings looked rather doubtful. The 'reshuffle of central Africa' to which the diary for 24 January refers was intended to meet German demands for colonial restitution. Territories in a broad belt stretching across Africa would be subjected to internationally-agreed rules. Germany would be given a territory, not under mandate but to be administered according to these rules. The Foreign Office understood that no discussion should take place about colonies before other aspects of the general settlement has been broached, and that no recognition of Germany's right to colonies would be given in advance.[9]]

* Japanese Foreign Minister, 1937–8, who had spoken in the Diet of the traditional friendship between Britain and Japan and appealed for mutual understanding.

Sunday, 23 January

Telegrams from Lindsay, showing our messages are well received by Sumner Welles at least. He is 'confident' President will be pleased with them.

Monday, 24 January

A. asked me to lunch with him, and again P.M. wanted me to attend meeting of F.P.C. at 2.30. So did that. We talked shop at lunch (we were alone). I said what was important was that if—without any further clear lead from America—we had to open up to Delbos on *de jure*, we should at least be quite frank with Americans and tell them what we were doing. A. agreed heartily.

2.30 meeting of F.P.C. (Horace Wilson there!) P.M. explained his idea of a re-shuffle of central Africa. Quite good, as *presentation*, but it won't satisfy Germans. However, A., quite rightly, didn't criticise. Only made point—accepted by P.M.—that if we make colonial concession it is *only* as part of *general* settlement.

Had to draft telegram after to N. Henderson asking for his views. Got it done before 6 when there was a meeting of the Cabinet. . . . A. showed [it] to P.M., who liked it. Said I was to check it with minutes of the meeting, tomorrow.

Tuesday, 25 January

A. left for Geneva. Bobbety and Jim Thomas still here. There are leaks in the press about Roosevelt, since yesterday's Cabinet! . . . Polished off telegram to Berlin about Colonies, and got it approved by P.M. Van wrote angrily to say that he hadn't seen the F.O. paper for P.M. about points on which we want concessions from Germany. Should have been sent through him. I replied I couldn't do that—my instructions were to send straight to A. If I took it on myself to settle what to send to him *first*, I would be taking it on myself to decide on which points S. of S. wants to consult Chief Diplomatic Adviser, and I can't do that and refuse to do it. He agreed as to that, and I went and saw him and said I would keep him informed verbally of what was going on. I won't do more than that in absence of S. of S.

Wednesday, 26 January

Billy Gore* at 4. He hadn't got much to say—explained concessions we might make in Nigeria and Gold Coast and expressed

* W. Ormsby Gore, Sec. of State for the Colonies, 1936–8.

hope that we should tie up colonial concession with general settlement. Told him I thought P.M. made this clear. Van has seen minutes of F.P.C. meeting of Monday, at which I and the Chief Industrial Adviser attended! I said he must discuss this with A. He complained of H. Wilson. I said there he was—like the sun or the wind or the rain. We can't stop it and we'd better nobble him. But I expect Van will make trouble.

Thursday, 27 January

Tomii* came at 4.45—to sound me as to Hirota's speech. I said it was a very good, one, but I felt bound to remind him that we were at the mercy of 'incidents', of which there were several outstanding!

Horace Wilson came about 5.30 for a chat. I didn't get very much out of it. He's been playing about with Yoshida†, and I told him what I'd said to Tomii. He said P.M. wanted Nevile H[enderson] back next week and suggested N. should tell von N[eurath]‡ why he was coming. I said I'd telegraph that if he gave me the word, and when he rang up later I arranged a telegram with Sargent.§

Friday, 28 January

'D[aily] T[elegraph]' has a 'leak' this morning about Ingersoll and Anglo-U.S. naval plans. Talked to Rex L[eeper] about this. He must play 'village idiot'.... Horace Wilson and Parkinson¶ (C[olonial] O[ffice]) about preparing a paper for F.P.C. on colonial cessions to Germany. A bit hard on *us*, but I must make it go! Talked to Sargent about it, and he deputed Baxter|| as our representative in F.O.–C.O. discussions.

[Chamberlain telegraphed on 28 January that it was very difficult to proceed with Germany, Italy or Japan until Roosevelt's intentions were more clearly known. The rather delphic answer indicated that the President was content for Britain to begin negotiations with the European dictators, provided that *de jure* recognition were given only as part of a general settlement. A few days later came news that the President had decided to postpone the announcement of his plan for a short while.]

* Counsellor at the Japanese Embassy, 1936–8.

† Japanese Ambassador, 1936–8.

‡ German Foreign Minister.

§ Then Asst. Under-Sec., F.O.; later Deputy Under-Sec.; Cadogan's successor as P.U.S., 1946–9. See List of Principal Characters.

¶ Sir C. Parkinson, P.U.S., Colonial Office, 1937–40.

|| C. W. Baxter of the F.O.

Sunday, 30 January

6 I went to see A. just back from Geneva. He seemed to be in quite good form and cheerful.

Nevile Henderson dined, and we had quite a useful talk. I think he's very good.

[As the Diary for the spring of 1939 indicates, Cadogan modified this opinion later. He had known Henderson from Eton days and thought him sanguine, a prey to moods, and impressionable; liked him well in private life; and came only with reluctance to the conclusion that Henderson's apparently incurable indiscretion should compel his removal from Berlin. By 1938 Henderson had cancer, for which an operation was performed in the winter after Münich.]

Monday, 31 January

4 Baxter came to see me with first draft of his and C.O. paper, which seems to me excellent.

5 A., Van, N.H[enderson] and I went over to see P.M. Halifax was there, and H. Wilson. Long talk—till 6.45. Gave them Baxter's paper. Its indication of the difficulties and complexities of a 're-shuffle' brought P.M. to idea that we had better 'do the big thing' and give back Tanganyika, subject perhaps to frontier adjustments. Believe this is right. (Van must have squirmed!) ... A. rang up at 11.15 about torpedoing of 'Endymion'. Told him I couldn't do anything about it!

[Attacks on merchant shipping in the Western Mediterranean were resumed in late January. S.S. *Endymion* was sunk by an unidentified submarine. On 4 February another British ship was bombed and sunk. The anti-submarine patrols agreed on at the Nyon Conference in the previous September were resumed.]

Tuesday, 1 February

Meeting with A. and George Mounsey* and a lot of Admiralty representatives about 'Endymion'. Agreed what was to be said in Parliament, and that we should consider getting Nyon Powers to agree that all submerged submarines should be sunk in the patrol area.... 'C'† came round in afternoon with interesting information. Frank's‡ advertised visit to London is 'off'. Berlin say they can't give reason. When pressed—as arrangements have already been

* Sir G. A. Mounsey, Asst. Under-Sec., F.O., 1929–40. See List of Principal Characters.

† Admiral Sinclair, head of the Secret Intelligence Service.

‡ Dr Otto Frank, German Minister without Portfolio, was expected for a private visit to London on 4 February.

made here—all they will say is 'Mussolini'. Does this mean that lunatic is going off the deep end in the Mediterranean? I have taken precautions. Press story is that there's trouble in Germany—Reichswehr (Blomberg) versus Party (Himmler)—and that it is over Musso's scheme for intensification of campaign in Spain. Maybe. Told A. about it and told him to tell P.M. . . . (Have kept Van informed of secret information: he has written his usual minute—as result of yesterday's discussion—about his King Charles' head: Austria. This is ridiculous, but it'll only do him harm. I must try and think out where we stand, and what is a sane line to take.)

Wednesday, 2 February

Nothing more definite from Germany. 'C' called and told me of precautions he had taken—and warnings he had given! . . . 5.30 Nevile H[enderson] came for a talk. Told him of some of the secret news I have lately received. Meeting at 6 in Van's room with Horace Wilson (who had proposed it to me) Parkinson, Nevile H., Eastwood and Baxter. Went through their further paper on the 'new regime' in Central Africa.

Friday, 4 February

Awful day. Bobbety has brought back from Geneva a memo. setting out all the arguments *against* de jure recognition. They are none of them new, and it is an ex parte statement, with none of the arguments on the other side. But it impresses A. Horace W. rings me up that P.M. wants A. to fix a meeting with Grandi* for Tuesday to begin conversations. A. now digs his toes in. This is all wrong—he has agreed in principle to talks with Musso, and nothing has happened to change situation fundamentally. Spend a lot of my time arguing with him and Bobbety. Have to tell H.W. it's no use. A. is silly on this question—he doesn't like the medicine, and makes no bones about it; but then he seems to agree to take it, and uses every excuse—clutches at it—to run out. This makes very bad impression.

Saturday, 5 February

German crisis out in papers. Looks like victory in first round for the Party.

[Field-Marshal von Blomberg, War Minister, had been dismissed on 27 January; General von Fritsch, the Commander-in-Chief, was dis-

* Count Dino Grandi, Italian Ambassador, 1932–9.

missed on a trumped-up charge of homosexuality; Field-Marshal von Manstein was removed as deputy chief of the General Staff and became Commander of the 18th Division; von Brauchitsch became C.-in-C., and Hitler his own War Minister. Ribbentrop replaced von Neurath as Foreign Minister.]

Monday, 7 February

Lots of commentaries have come in on the instruction to Nevile H., and I am trying to edit them. John Simon* weighs in with pages —all on the wrong line.

Tuesday, 8 February

Edited instructions to N[evile] H[enderson], after consultation with Van. And drafted letter from A. to J.S[imon] explaining why we couldn't adopt his suggestions. A. more hopeful of Italian conversations since his interview with Grandi on Sat.† Thinks he can get something on propaganda and Spain and so slide easily into 'conversations'. Maybe. . . . 5 conference with Van, Sargent, and Strang‡ about paper on what we ask of Germany. Think we're all agreed. I have finished redraft of instructions to N.H. and drafts of what we say to French. Think we should instruct N.H.—contrary to his recommendation—to make communication to Hitler before latter's speech on February 20.

[On 8 February, Eden put his view to the Prime Minister:

> As I see it, the position is now this. Mussolini is in an extremely uncomfortable position. He has commitments in Abyssinia and Spain, neither of which is turning out well. He now sees a government in power in Berlin, which, it is quite true, is comparatively enthusiastic for the Rome-Berlin axis, but which is also apparently determined to pursue a more active foreign policy in Europe, with Austria as the first item on the list of intended victims. In such a position we have nothing to gain by showing ourselves over-eager. If Mussolini is really anxious to reach a settlement with us, then the opportunity we are affording him of liquidating his commitments in Spain gives him an excellent chance of proving his sincerity. He will now, moreover, have heard from Grandi how ready we are to take up this question without delay.

Chamberlain replied that he quite appreciated the strength of Britain's position, to be exploited in the bargaining.[10]]

* Sir J. Simon, Foreign Secretary, 1931–5; Home Secretary, 1935–7; Chancellor of the Exchequer, 1937–40; Lord Chancellor, 1940–5. See List of Principal Characters.

† When Eden had reminded Grandi of his pledge to the House of Commons that conversations would not begin until Italy's hostile propaganda abated.

‡ William Strang, head of Central Dept., 1937–9; Asst. Under-Sec. 1939–43. See List of Principal Characters.

Thursday, 10 February

Telegram from Roosevelt saying he is putting off his plan 'for days, not for weeks', until German situation clears. Apparently Hull thinks we are 'lukewarm' about the plan. Drafted telegram to Lindsay to assure them that we are *not*. A. sent it over to P.M., who probably won't agree. Dealt with Yoshida's ridiculous approach to A. It's really no good dealing with him on a 'personal basis'—he represents nothing. Japs are determined to eliminate us. Let us be polite, but not fooled. H. Wilson came at 4.45 to explain that he had not been responsible for 'Daily Mail' article on Wednesday about Anglo-Italian conversations, and for a general talk. . . .

Told H.W. what I thought about Yoshida (whom he's put up to make this démarche).

Rumours of German frontiers being closed, but can get no news.

[Cadogan received evidence that the article might have been inspired by Sir Joseph Ball, director of the Conservative Research Department, who is also said to have acted as an intermediary between No. 10 and the Italian Embassy. In 1967 Sir Alexander recorded that he knew nothing of any such conversations and that to the best of his belief he had never met Ball.[11]]

Friday, 11 February

A. went over to P.M. about telegram to Washington. Latter didn't like it, but A. managed to retain just enough, and I redrafted it and it went off. Also telegram to Nevile H. asking for his views on whether we shouldn't approach Hitler before Feb. 20. No definite news from Germany yet. . . .

Monday, 14 February

Don't know what this Austro-German meeting at Berchtesgaden means, and we have no news. But if it means a reaffirmation of [the agreement of] July 1936 I think we ought to take some account of it in our approach to Germany—i.e. not say to Hitler 'If we give you Colonies, you must do something about Austria and Czechoslovakia.' He will say 'I have done it about Austria.' We ought to note that he has done something which we hope is satisfactory—and hope he can do as much for Cz[echoslovakia]. But A. too rushed with questions to pay any attention and Sargent of course violently opposed to 'dropping' Austria. As I can trust Nevile H. to handle the situation all right (he *hates* the idea of mentioning Austria) I am not bothering. But the thing wants watching. 5 Coudenhove-

Kalergi* came.... Convinced that Hitler is going to move his legions into Austria tomorrow. Then why sign something with Austria yesterday?

A. has had talk with P.M. and I hope things are better—*he* thinks they are, which is the great thing. The P.M. himself put the notice in yesterday's 'Sunday Times' denying rumours of differences between himself and A.† A. has arranged there should be contact between Rex L. and Horace W. which I think excellent.

Tuesday, 15 February

Was summoned early to F.O. as there was a flap about Austria. Personally, I almost wish Germany would swallow Austria and get it over. She is probably going to do so anyhow—anyhow we can't stop her. What's all this fuss about? Meeting with A., Sargent, and others. Van there. He wanted to put in an instruction to Nevile H. to tell Hitler that we wanted to know what was going on about Austria, as our instructions 'dealt with Austria'. I got this watered down to 'include Austria'. And the P.M., I am glad to say, watered it down further. *What* is the good of brandishing Austria under Hitler's nose when we can't do *anything* about it? . . . Still no authentic news from Austria. Schuschnigg‡ has evidently had to give a great deal, but not quite clear whether he has given the police. As I say, I shouldn't mind if Austria *were* gleichgeschaltet.

[Although the official communiqué was couched in soothing terms, Schuschnigg had been forced to concede the legalisation of activities by the Nazis within Austria, and the appointment of the Nazi Seyss-Inquart to the key post of Minister of the Interior, which carried control of the police.]

Wednesday, 16 February

Hitler has evidently bullied Schuschnigg into a pretty bad 'agreement'. We have told N. Henderson, in any communication he makes to German Government, to say that we can't estimate effect of this yet, but that we have doubts about it and think it may detract from Austrian independence. French want to make a joint protest in Berlin. What folly! We are riding them off. Van, as far as I can make out, wants to *talk* big, but then—? He's an idiot with an idée fixe—a very simple one. He's all facade and nothing else.

* Count Richard N. Coudenhove-Kalergi, founder of the Pan-European Union, 1923, and of the European Parliamentary Union, 1947.

† The Prime Minister wrote to his sister: 'I saw Anthony on Friday morning and we were in complete agreement, more complete perhaps than we have sometimes been in the past'.

‡ Kurt von Schuschnigg, Chancellor of Austria, 1934–8.

Nothing constructive: with all his big *talk* he's got no idea at all. And *that* is what we are suffering from!

[Eden told the Cabinet on that day that he did not seek any decision from them, or desire 'to put himself in the position of suggesting a resistance which he could not, in fact, furnish'.

At the same meeting, the Cabinet considered a review by Sir Thomas Inskip of British spending on defence. He, having concluded that it lay beyond Britain's power 'to make proper provision in peace for the defence of the Empire against three major Powers', naturally pressed for action to reduce the number of potential enemies. The Chancellor, Sir John Simon, accepted with reluctance estimates of £1,650m. to be spent on arms by the end of 1941. Eden was authorised to tell the French, as the result of an earlier decision about the rôle of the Army, that the most Britain could send to the Continent, 'in certain circumstances', would be two Regular divisions and one mobile division.]

Thursday, 17 February

Long discussion (with too many people, but *not* Van) in S. of S.'s room about reply to private notice question about Austria. Only news we have is from Franckenstein* and we propose to quote him. . . . After lunch A. made me give my views to P.M. about Grandi's desire for an interview with him (P.M.). I said I knew G[randi] was getting instructions from Rome which won't arrive till this evening or tomorrow morning. We don't know what they'll be. If he sees P.M. it will be advertised that 'conversations' have been begun. Is this desirable? Won't Berlin think we are clumsily taking advantage of Austrian situation to break Berlin-Rome axis? Hadn't A. better sound out G. first? But P.M. wanted to see G. Wants to ask him about Austria. I don't mind that, if that is given out. We know G. has been lying low. A. wanted to see him yesterday, but he lay low—because he doesn't know what to say about Austria.

Now all this is very distressing. We have always known that Germany could swallow Austria. It's no good shouting about it (as Van wants) if we can't stop it (as Van admits we can't). I say go ahead with conversations. Musso may be playing with us. But can't we play too? Why should we now again turn our backs and do nothing: just that 'policy' has brought us all our troubles. Unfortunately, Jim Thomas comes in this evening with report of a 'unanimous' meeting of Conservative F[oreign] P[olicy] Committee†

* G. Franckenstein, Austrian Minister in London, 1920–38.

† This was the Foreign Affairs Committee, attended by supporters of the National Government. It took no votes, nor did it put resolutions to the Cabinet. Until Eden's resignation, Churchill attended regularly. Eden had several times addressed the Committee. See H. Nicolson, *Diplomacy*, p. 161; Eden, *Facing The Dictators*, p. 571.

who are breathing fire. But what do they want to *do*? Drafted telegram to Lindsay pouring cold water on his suggestion that President should be dissuaded from a 'Conference' and urged to take a hand in our 'conversations'. Fatal. (1) President never proposed 'conference' and (2) it would be most embarrassing to *us* if he were associated in our conversations. Let him plump out his plan as *his own.*

[Cadogan recorded long afterwards that he had found his task at this luncheon 'rather embarrassing as I didn't hold these ideas quite so passionately as Anthony did. I hope I did it loyally, but was probably not very convincing.'

On 16 February the Foreign Office learned of the President's intention to launch his plan later in the month, whatever Hitler might say on 20 February. Lindsay suggested that the President might instead be invited to indicate 'his willingness to assist through the diplomatic channel'. Cadogan minuted:

> This in practice would appear to mean an irresponsible interference in our negotiations. This seems to me to present considerable dangers to us—we are much more susceptible to U.S. influence than are Germany or Italy. The two latter countries can afford to ignore the President without worsening their situation: we cannot. . . .
>
> There are other considerations. Sir R. Lindsay makes some play of the fact that a 'Conference' is undesirable. But we have been twice assured that the President does not contemplate a Conference. . . . I have always thought that what was in the President's mind was to collect some Europeans, pick their brains and then produce his *own* plan.
>
> Further, I should have thought—though on this point Sir R. Lindsay must be the better judge—that Sir R. Lindsay's proposal would be full of 'involvements' for the President. I always thought that what the latter had in mind was a clear clarion call from his mountain top, addressed to the wicked European countries. I shouldn't have thought he wanted to get mixed up in our discussions. I should have thought that would arouse much more criticism in America than the President's original plan.
>
> Lastly, I don't think we *want* to have too much of a hand in shaping the President's action. It is to be *his* plan—an American plan. Let him bear as much as possible of the responsibility for it.

Eden telegraphed at once to Washington in this sense.[12]]

Friday, 18 February

Didn't see A. before his interview with P.M. and Grandi at 11.30. He got back about 1. Grandi had merely conveyed message from

Ciano* in general terms expressing desire of Italian Government for conversations. As regards Spain, said he thought his Government would accept British plan† subject to certain (? unspecified) conditions. Could say nothing about Austria. Pressed that announcement should be made *today* that conversations have opened. Told to come back in afternoon for answer. After G[randi] had gone, P.M. and A. had a set-to. P.M. very violent—said this was last chance of getting to terms with Italy (that jackass Ivy [the widow of Sir Austen Chamberlain] had been telegraphing to him [from Rome]): A. said that this was not now the moment to do it. In view of Hitler's performance in Austria, and before we know what he is going to say in his speech on Sunday, this is *not* the moment to crawl to Italy, of all countries. They evidently had a good row, and no result. I lunched with A., Bobbety, Thomas, Oliver [Harvey] at F.O. A. determined to hold out and will tell P.M. he can't share with him responsibility for announcement. Cabinet must be consulted. A. went over to P.M. at 2.30 (Grandi due at 3) and Bobbety and I went out for a walk. A. went back about 3.45. P.M. had agreed to a Cabinet tomorrow afternoon and told Grandi he would get his answer on Monday. All right so far, but I'm afraid there's a real rift, and they'll never work together. A. went off to his constituency‡ about 5. Round about 6 Rex Leeper brought me text given out by Italian Embassy, welcoming 'British approach'. This quite contrary to what had been agreed. Got Van and Horace W. to see me. Italian communiqué contains nothing *untrue*, we can only say it's 'unauthorised'. But I'm afraid the mischief is done. Can see no way out, unless P.M. would agree to give out that Italian communiqué was unauthorised, that *their* request was that we should announce conversations, but that this has to be considered. But I'm afraid that won't go. Will see A. when he gets back tomorrow morning.

Sun came into my room for first time about 4.45.

[The Italian communiqué, given to the press as 'semi-official' by the First Secretary of the Embassy, welcomed the 'new approach' of the British Government. It stated that the Italian Government thought the talks should embrace every subject, including *de jure* recognition, and that H.M.G. agreed. Warm satisfaction was felt that the British had now waived the Spanish question and that of the Bari Radio Broadcasts, which had been used as a pretext for the failure to start conversations.[13]]

* Count Galeazzo Ciano, Italian Foreign Minister, 1936–43. See List of Principal Characters.

† For withdrawal of 'volunteers' fighting in the Civil War.

‡ Eden represented the Warwick and Leamington constituency, 1923–57.

Saturday, 19 February

A. arrived back from his constituency about 12. Went to see him. And lunched with him, and the same party again, in the F.O. He quite decided not to 'crawl to Rome' and I agreed. . . . A. back [from Cabinet] about 6.45. Most of Cabinet against him—his only sure supporters S. Morrison* (not entirely reliable) and M. MacD. Between them have about 1½d! So it went against him: he notified his resignation and Cabinet adjourned till tomorrow at 3. At end of meeting, apparently, Halifax suggested compromise: announce negotiations, but at same time say that we shan't *give* de jure recognition till we're satisfied that Italian action in Spain is coming to an end. I told A. he should accept this. Or rather, he shouldn't refuse it, because that would put him in a false position. I don't think Italians will accept. But he can't refuse. Oliver [Harvey] is tiresome on this question, but I think I got him to be reasonable. About 7, Halifax and O. Stanley came to see him—presumably to put this compromise. Don't know what happened, and left at 7.45. A. dining with Malcolm. *If* he is offered this—I don't think he will be, because P.M. will say it is courting a refusal—he ought to accept. But they (he and P.M.) will never pull together, and we shall have further rows. Jim Thomas says if he accepts he ought to have a show-down with P.M. about conduct of foreign policy. I agree, but told J.T. I couldn't advise on that: that's a political question. Personally, as I told him, I entirely agree. But on the facts of the dispute, he ought to accept. I think he may.

Sunday, 20 February

Beginning of an awful week-end. Foul weather, to start with—dark and cold. A. asked me to come at 12.30. Walked with T. across Park. Found A. and Oliver [Harvey]. Malcolm M. had apparently rung up, after seeing P.M., to say latter would accept A.'s resignation. P.M. rang up soon after I got there, asking A. to come and see him, and he went at 12.45. Lunched at home and was at Office by 2.30. A. said it was settled he would resign. Thought Cabinet would last only a few minutes. Cabinet at 3 and A. departed, saying goodbye. Cabinet sat on. About 5, heard they had resolved into a Committee and there was talk of a compromise. This surprised me, as I understood A. and P.M. this morning had frankly and friendly acknowledged to each other that they couldn't work together. About 6.30 A. came back and Malcolm M. came in. Malcolm urged him not to resign, and I finally did too—urged him to accept compromise

* W. S. Morrison, Minister of Agriculture, 1936–9.

of *announcing* conversations but announcing at the same time that they would not begin till Italy had done something about the withdrawal from Spain. But I wasn't very helpful, as I had to point out that Italy couldn't accept this. And if she refused, his dear colleagues would always reproach him with having made conversations impossible. A. was adamant and he, being what he is, was right. He went off at 7.30 to hand in his resignation. It was accepted, and Cabinet met at 10. Meanwhile I got a wild S.O.S. from Phipps* in Paris and drafted a soothing reply which P.M. accepted and was telephoned back to Phipps by 10. . . .† An awful day, with all one's feelings lacerated and one's judgement torn in two.

[Lord Cranborne and J. P. L. Thomas resigned with Eden. Chamberlain concluded that the Foreign Secretary did not want talks with Germany and Italy and was therefore right to go:

> When I talked to him he always appeared to agree, but the moment we seemed really to be getting to close quarters there was always some reason why it was necessary to draw back. At last I made up my mind that it *was* 'now or never' and that I must make my stand, whatever the result, or give up my policy.

The Prime Minister thought that the penalties of a failure to open conversations promptly would be too severe. Mussolini would consider the talks cancelled and act accordingly:

> Italian public opinion would be raised to a white heat against us. There might indeed be some overt act of hostility, and in any case the dictatorships would be driven closer together, the last shred of Austrian independence would be lost, the Balkan countries would feel compelled to turn towards their powerful neighbours, Czechoslovakia would be swallowed, France would either have to submit to German domination or fight, in which case we should almost certainly be drawn in. I could not face the responsibility for allowing such a series of catastrophes.[14]

Chamberlain had indeed told the Cabinet on 19 February that he could not accept a decision in the contrary sense. With his catalogue of risks Eden would not have disagreed; but, as he said in his speech of resignation:

> in international affairs can anyone define where outlook and methods end and principles begin? . . . Of late the conviction has steadily grown upon me that there has been too keen a desire on our part to make terms with others, rather than that others should make terms with us. . . . I do not believe that we can make progress in Euro-

* Sir Eric Phipps, Ambassador at Paris, 1937–9. See List of Principal Characters.

† For similar message to U.S. Government see p. 56.

> pean appeasement, more particularly in the light of the events of the past few days, . . . if we allow the impression to gain currency abroad that we yield to constant pressure.[15]

Reflecting on these events after the war, Cadogan recalled that Chamberlain seemed to share the belief of Sir Horace Wilson that the conduct of foreign relations resembles the handling of trade disputes, 'whereas the composing of differences between employers and employed is different in kind from the elimination of national rivalries and antagonisms'.

Eden's tenure of the Foreign Office under Chamberlain, Sir Alec recalled, had been an uneasy time. Despite the intention of both to work loyally together, differences of view and temperament began to accumulate and intensify until:

> although I urged Anthony not to resign when he did, I had been forced to the conclusion that the partnership could not continue much longer. This tended to create in Chamberlain a certain feeling of isolation. Horace Wilson had been for long in many ways his right-hand man, in whom he had complete confidence, and he was not unnaturally inclined to turn to him for advice and suggestions.
>
> Horace Wilson had become an institution . . . and I came to the conclusion that we must make the best of him—for which I was doubtless criticised by members of my own Service. If I had tried to fight against him, I should only have been removed.

Cadogan never regretted the attempt at co-operation. Although various remarks in the diary for 1938 indicate an initial mistrust,* he came to feel that he had won Sir Horace's confidence. They remained on friendly terms to the end of Cadogan's life. He endorsed wholeheartedly Halifax's judgment:

> So far from feeling that Horace Wilson made things difficult between Prime Minister and Foreign Secretary, I always found him extremely helpful, when the pressure of work was heavy, in ensuring that I was fully acquainted with the thought of the Prime Minister and vice versa, and that neither was drifting into any misunderstanding of the other's mind.

As for the Prime Minister, Cadogan thought him right to keep 'a fairly tight hold' on foreign policy in such circumstances, though he had prejudices not easily eradicated: 'an almost instinctive contempt for the Americans and what amounted to a hatred of the Russians. (We can all be impatient with the former at times, and we have all come to loathe the latter.)' But it is right to note that on other occasions Cadogan used less vehement language to describe Chamberlain's attitude in both connexions. 'Another possible drawback was that he was, in a sense, a man of

* Sir Horace Wilson, shown passages from the Diary, has commented that he was by no means so influential at 10 Downing Street as they would indicate.

one-track mind. If, after much reflexion no doubt, he decided on a certain move or line of policy, nothing would deflect him.']

These judgments were elicited by a series of questions. Reading them through, Cadogan observed that their critical tenor was misleading and did not represent his feelings about Chamberlain: 'Like all other human beings he made his mistakes and had his failings, but on balance I had great admiration for him and, without any reserve, great affection.'[16]

Eden, Cadogan once remarked, had been unlucky in his chiefs. 'Baldwin could not be induced to take any interest in foreign affairs: Chamberlain took too much, and Winston was a rather too oppressive thundercloud overhead!' With his new Secretary of State, Halifax, the P.U.S. had long been on friendly terms. Halifax collaborated more smoothly with Chamberlain than Eden ever could have done. As Cadogan later put it, both were

> tormented day and night by their search for some peaceful settlement and I could not say that they were wrong in that, provided of course that they did not overstep certain bounds. But I don't think I am exaggerating when I say that Hitler was too quick for them and they never had the time to formulate any coherent course of action. . . .
>
> I am sure that Halifax, like Chamberlain, when he came into the F.O., strongly believed it to be his duty to make every effort to avert a war which we were almost certain to lose (short, of course, of overstepping the limits of what was honourable).[17]

Thus ended the second phase of Cadogan's partnership with Eden. They had been at one over Roosevelt's initiative, but on the merits of the Italian negotiation, as in most other questions of foreign policy, Cadogan agreed in substance with Chamberlain. He found Halifax easier to serve from day to day, but less expert and enterprising, than his predecessor. The lapidary and unexpected phrase 'all one's feelings lacerated' testifies to Cadogan's regret. He wrote to Eden:

> I do hope you are feeling . . . relieved and happy. Because you have reached, I am sure, the only conclusion *you* could reach.
>
> You have had the most awful time any man could have. I think you had to take a decision on one of the most difficult questions with which any man could have been faced. It was a problem far beyond my powers (and my distress at your leaving is increased by the reflection that I haven't been able to help you) but I am convinced that you have done right because you have remained true to *yourself*. And you need never be ashamed of that. Nor, I think, will you regret it.
>
> Personally, your going is a frightful wrench for me; as I hope you know what it meant to me to work for you. I owe you more than I can repay. You know that everyone in the Office who worked with you was devoted to you, but no one was as much as myself in your debt.

I've got to serve another master now, but I hope that, to make up for lack of official contacts, we may increase our unofficial ones.

And I look forward to the time when we may work together again.

In the meanwhile, take a little rest after your ordeal and come back fresh to take a part which may be only a little less important than that which you filled in office.

Chamberlain announced that conversations with Italy would begin. Any agreement must cover a settlement of the Spanish question. The Italian Government's acceptance of the British formula for the withdrawal of volunteers and the grant of belligerent rights had been notified just before Eden's resignation. He, however, had insisted that Italy must make a substantial withdrawal before official talks were opened.]

Monday, 21 February

Foul day again. Went to see Halifax about 11. He in 'temporary charge'. Tells me he hasn't been offered the post. I told him of dangers if he accepted. These were present to his mind and he may not accept. Talked to him about policy. Brave words butter no parsnips. Austria is gone: no good teasing (?) Hitler. He of course agreed. Promised to get him a draft reply to French for Cabinet tomorrow. . . . Dined at home. Everything is very hateful. A. came in to F.O. this morning to say goodbye. Horrible business. I think that, on the facts, an ordinary man ought to have stayed. A., being what he is, was right to go.

Tuesday, 22 February

Have been too busy, day and night, to keep this diary till today (27th) so my account must be sketchy. Things fairly quiet. Vote of Censure debate in House of Commons. I had to see Halifax in morning and had a talk with him. He doesn't yet know whether he will accept. Busy with him on draft reply to French memo about Austria, which must come before Cabinet tomorrow.

[On 18 February Corbin had presented a memorandum stating that because the independence of Austria constituted one of the major interests of European peace, the British and French Governments could not 'tolerate any *coup de main* or act of war likely to bring into question the *status quo* of Central Europe' and should tell Hitler so. The British reply remarked that words without deeds would be useless and might encourage Schuschnigg to rely on a military support 'unlikely to be forthcoming'. Nor could Britain accept what would amount to an automatic commitment to war. The British Government suggested the encouragement of Danubian unity, the use of influence at Berlin to modify the German attitude and the introduction of the Austrian question into the talks with Italy.]

Wednesday, 23 February

Lunched with Nancy A[stor]* to meet Lothian† and Garvin.‡ Latter talks as he writes—very emphatic bilge. Cabinet approved lines of reply to French. Halifax went off to P.M. about 7 to decide his appointment.

[On 21 February the United States Government were assured that Eden's resignation meant no change in the

> ultimate aims and purposes of British foreign policy. Crisis was brought to a head by differences of method and emphasis: in other words it was on tactics and not on strategy that the Prime Minister and Foreign Secretary disagreed. . . .
>
> There was above all no truth whatever in the press rumours to the effect that Great Britain now contemplated the negotiation of an agreement with the dictators at any cost. On the contrary, no agreement of any kind would be entered into with any dictator country unless it was entirely apparent that it was consonant with the principles which had hitherto guided British foreign policy and would result in general appeasement and hence in the preservation of peace.[18]

A few days later Lindsay was told that the President was keeping his plan in abeyance for the moment. Roosevelt thought the British procedure entirely right, and the prospects favourable. Thereupon Cadogan drafted a further telegram for Washington, explaining the purposes of the conversations with Italy and Germany and indicating that the desire to gain time was playing its part: 'Both these negotiations will doubtless be attended with many difficulties but if these regional agreements can be secured, it may be hoped that danger may be averted at least for a period.'

For a lasting improvement, it would be necessary to seek 'some scheme of general co-operation in Europe, both political and economic,' in which search the help of the United States Government would be of the greatest value.[19] Such ambitions, however, were soon rendered obviously unreal by events in Europe. On 12 March Sumner Welles told Lindsay that a chance to present the President's plan was unlikely to recur.]

Friday, 25 February

11.30 I saw Ishii.§ He had nothing to say, and quite clear that, contrary to what Yoshida has said to A.—and to Horace W.—Japan does *not* want our mediation.

* Viscountess Astor, M.P.

† Marquess of Lothian, Ambassador at Washington, 1939–40.

‡ J. L. Garvin, Editor of *The Observer*, 1908–42.

§ Viscount K. Ishii, formerly Japanese Minister of Foreign affairs, who was paying a private visit to London.

Tuesday, 1 March

P.M. has agreed Van can't go to Rome to help Eric [Perth]* (my argument 'Hoare-Laval' settled that, I think). H. now says they may send him over to Paris to comfort the French. Let him go! It amuses me, these silly attempts to keep him occupied. I never see him nowadays. He is annoying H. by firing minutes at him. It's not for me to save him from cutting his own throat. Got H.'s notes in order, approved draft statement for P.M. on L[eague] of N[ations], and outline of what we are to say to French about Italian conversations. H. has agreed to see Negus† tomorrow. (And he must receive Martin‡ with other Heads of Missions!) He agreed we should telegraph frankly to Rome, explaining.

Thursday, 3 March

Took opportunity this afternoon to see Horace W. about telegram to Roosevelt (which P.M. passed). He rather oyster-like. Don't quite trust him. Don't know what is plotted against F.O. Shall keep my weapon bright.

[Henderson had no more hopes than Cadogan of being able to help Austria, and generally expected little from his interview with the Führer. There at least his expectations proved well-founded. Hitler paid scant attention to the proposal about a new colonial régime in Africa, or to the mild warnings about Central Europe. He inveighed vigorously against the intrigues of the press, the meddlings of bishops and the iniquities of bolshevism. Though known as 'one of the warmest friends of England', he had been ill-rewarded for his friendship.

Germany would allow no one to interfere in the settlement of her relationship with 'countries of the same nationality' or countries 'with large German populations'. If England continued to oppose efforts to reach a just settlement, 'the moment would come when it would be necessary to fight'. 'The Austrian people must themselves be asked for their opinion'; and the Germans in Czechoslovakia 'must be guaranteed the autonomy in cultural and other matters to which they were entitled. . . . The present situation was in any case impossible in the long run, and would lead to an explosion.' England, he added, need fear no trouble from Germany. 'Some people' would 'make a bloody mistake' if they thought his statements on Central Europe pure rhetoric. If 'internal explosions' took place in Austria or Czechoslovakia, Germany would act 'like lightning'.[20]

* The Earl of Perth, formerly Sir Eric Drummond, Ambassador at Rome, 1933–9. See List of Principal Characters.

† The Emperor Haile Selassie of Ethiopia, in exile since 1936.

‡ Dr Martin, Ethiopian representative in London before the Italian attack; since Britain had not recognised the conquest, he remained in nominal office.

Hitler, Henderson judged, was prepared to risk a general war if others resisted his pretension to safeguard the interests of Germans living outside the Fatherland's borders. Vansittart minuted that this proposition contained a great deal of bluff, and if Germany interfered beyond a certain point in Czechoslovakia France might come to the latter's assistance. That would mean a European war with Britain involved:

> I submit therefore very earnestly that *we are incurring an enormous responsibility* in not speaking to Hitler a great deal more firmly and explicitly than we have yet done in this matter. At present he is being allowed to rave and threaten without check; and if he is not checked by being brought up against the hard reality described above and brought up quickly, he may carry himself and everyone else into disaster.[21]]

Friday, 4 March

Received, shortly before lunch, advance copy of N[evile] H[enderson]'s telegram about his interview with Hitler. It was *completely* negative. Had a word about it with Halifax. We must consider whether to try and administer oxygen to the conversations to keep them alive, or whether to announce what we have done in all good faith to show the friends of Germany what sort of response the latter has made, and so unite *this* country, showing them that we have done our best and that it is not *our* fault. That would save something from the wreck but it is rather a counsel of despair. H. went off to Yorkshire at 3.30 and I had a quiet afternoon and evening of spade-work.

Monday, 7 March

Lovely summer day again. Not much work in morning—had cleared off arrears. Talk with H., Van, Sargent, Butler* and Strang about what to say to Rib[bentrop].† All agreed on the right line—'half-way' as H. put it, 'between sorrow and anger'.

Tuesday, 8 March

Called on H. at 10. (Summer day again.) Discussed how to take Rib[bentrop], and I think we're agreed on the right line. Trouble is that either (a) Rib will be impossible or (b) he will in any case not report to Berlin what is said.... Went to see Horace W. about

* R. A. Butler, M.P., appointed Parliamentary Under-Sec. for Foreign Affairs when Lord Cranborne resigned. See List of Principal Characters.

† Joachim von Ribbentrop, German Ambassador in London, 1936–8. See List of Principal Characters. He was about to relinquish the German Embassy in London, on his appointment as Foreign Minister, and the intention was to make use of his first interview with Halifax to follow up Henderson's negative conversation with Hitler.

various things. *He* says Conwell-Evans* has it that Goering† has urged Rib to be forthcoming here, and he (C[onwell]-E[vans]) is meeting Rib in Brussels and travelling with him to London.

I have urged to say to Rib 'You Germans make vague complaints and utter general threats: it is this vagueness and generality that makes for apprehension and unrest. What is the matter? What do you want? Perhaps we might help you.' This is the advice I always gave the Chinese concerning Japan (and which they never took). Van against it, but H. says he 'doesn't disagree'. He saw P.M. tonight about the line he would take and said P.M. approved, but I don't know how strongly he put this point.

Wednesday, 9 March

Have been busy (March 12) day and night and haven't written this diary, which must be sketchy.

[In a speech at Innsbruck on 9 March, Schuschnigg announced that the Austrians would be invited on 13 March to say by plebiscite whether they wished for a 'free, German, independent, Socialist, Christian and undivided Austria'. Seyss-Inquart opposed the plebiscite.]

Thursday, 10 March

Rib came at 11. Had private talk first with H. and then Woermann and I called in about 11.45. Lasted till 1.15. Rib quite hopeless and wooden and useless. H. read him a lecture—or sermon—not too frightfully well, I didn't think.

[Halifax reported that no Anglo-German agreement could be one-sided. The British had no desire to obstruct peaceful agreement reached by peaceful means. Still less did they want a war in Europe, but

> the experience of all history went to show that the pressure of facts was sometimes more powerful than the wills of men: and if once war should start in Central Europe, it was quite impossible to say where it might not end, or who might not become involved.

Ribbentrop stigmatised Schuschnigg's proposed plebiscite as a fraud and a swindle. He asked Halifax to use British influence for its cancellation.[22]]

* Philip Conwell-Evans, who had many contacts among prominent Germans and had accompanied Lothian and Lloyd George on visits to Hitler; Hon. Sec. of Anglo-German Fellowship; became a close friend of Vansittart and from 1938 an opponent of appeasement.

† Field-Marshal Hermann Goering. See List of Principal Characters.

Friday, 11 March

News coming in all the morning that Germany is moving against Austria on account of latter's projected plebiscite. Lunched at No. 11 with P.M. Sat between [Sir Thomas] Inskip* and Mrs. Winston [Churchill]. Rib and Woermann there. I gave P.M. various telegrams and other news, and he decided to give Rib a talking to after, in his study, with H. and me. Both P.M. and H spoke quite well, but Rib quite impervious.† Germans are simply going ahead in Austria. During afternoon we had more news of their infamy. 5.15 H. went to tea with Rib and gave him more serious talking to. After that we drafted protest to German Government, sent it off, (8 p.m.) and repeated it to Paris. I gave it to Corbin who called 8.15. Got home to dinner about 8.40. Back at F.O. 9.30 and there till 11.40 drafting telegrams. H. very calm and sensible. Van has been like a cat on hot bricks, but H. doesn't care. I had it out with Van. I said 'it's easy to be brave in speech: will you fight?' He said 'No'. I said 'Then, what's it all about. To me it seems a most cowardly thing to do to urge a small man to fight a big if you won't help the former.' However, Van didn't come in to the picture and no one consulted him. It would have been criminal to encourage Schuschnigg to resist when we couldn't help him. At the end of the day, H. and I agreed our consciences were clear!

[Among the telegrams which reached Cadogan at the celebrated luncheon of 11 March 1938 were two of particular importance. One, from Berlin, stated that the German Ministry of War knew nothing of any troop movements. The idea of an approaching march towards the Austrian frontier was 'ridiculous'. Any troop movements could probably be ascribed to 'spring training'. The other, from Vienna, reported the presentation by Seyss-Inquart and another Minister of an ultimatum to Schuschnigg. The latter agreed under threat of civil war and invasion to cancel the plebiscite. Thereupon his resignation was demanded. Schuschnigg asked for the British Government's advice.

These facts were read out to Ribbentrop by Chamberlain, who spoke of the 'extreme gravity of the situation they disclosed'. Ribbentrop said that if the information were correct, this might be the best way of achieving a 'peaceful solution'.

During the afternoon Halifax telegraphed to Vienna that he could not advise Schuschnigg to take any action which might expose Austria to dangers against which Britain could not guarantee protection. Before he

* Minister for the Co-ordination of Defence, 1936–9.

† Cadogan confirmed in 1948 that the account of this lunch given in Churchill's *The Gathering Storm* is correct. He had some reason to believe, afterwards, that Ribbentrop was genuinely in ignorance of what was happening in Austria.

left the Foreign Office to see Ribbentrop, Halifax learned that Schuschnigg's answer was being demanded on pain of immediate invasion. At the German Embassy news arrived that Seyss-Inquart had just succeeded Schuschnigg; whereupon Halifax told the Reich Foreign Minister that:

> What we were witnessing was an exhibition of naked force, and the public opinion of Europe would inevitably ask when the facts were known what there was to prevent the German Government from seeking to apply in similar fashion naked force to the solution of their problems in Czechoslovakia or to any other in which they thought it might be useful. The conclusion must be that the German leaders were people who 'had no use for negotiation, but relied solely on the strong hand'.[23]

When he came home that evening, Cadogan lamented that since Ribbentrop was so stupid it mattered very little what anyone said to him. Chamberlain told his sister much the same thing, drawing some morals from the débâcle:

> it is perfectly evident, surely, now that force is the only argument Germany understands, and that collective security cannot offer any prospect of preventing such events, until it can show a visible force of overwhelming strength, backed by determination to use it. And if that is so, is it not obvious that such force and determination are most effectively mobilised by alliances, which don't require meetings at Geneva, and resolutions by dozens of small nations who have no responsibilities? Heaven knows, I don't want to get back to alliances but if Germany continues to behave as she has done lately, she may drive us to it. . . . For the moment we must abandon conversations with Germany, we must show our determination not to be bullied by announcing some increase or acceleration in rearmament, and we must quietly and steadily pursue our conversations with Italy. If we can avoid another violent coup in Czechoslovakia, which ought to be feasible, it may be possible for Europe to settle down again, and some day for us to start peace talks again with the Germans.[24]

The urgent questions now were whether the German Government were possessed by a lust for conquest; whether the German minority in Czechoslovakia would be used by Hitler as a pretext for another coup; and, if so, whether that prospect should evoke a British threat of war. Cadogan's curt judgment of 16 March, 'We *must* not precipitate a conflict now—we shall be smashed', shows how heavily the military outlook weighed with him, not the least because the threat to British and Imperial interests posed by Japan became daily more palpable.]

Saturday, 12 March

F.O. at 10. Cabinet at 10.30. H. told me they 'entirely approved all we had done'. Back at F.O. at 2.30. Was with H. for an hour or so drafting telegrams as a result of Cabinet. We can't *do* much, but must consider if there is anything we can plan for the future. Walked in Park 4.20–5.5. Then back and showed H. some telegrams. He saw Corbin, Masaryk* and A. Sinclair† from 5.30 to 7. After that I fixed up the last telegrams with him.

All this is disjointed and unintelligible. It is the result of Van's policy. We are helpless as regards Austria—that is finished. We *may* be helpless as regards Czechoslovakia, etc. *That* is what I want to get considered. Must we have a death-struggle with Germany again? Or can we stand aside? Former does no one any good. Will latter be fatal? I'm inclined to think not. But I shall have to fight Van, Sargent and all the forces of evil. God give me courage. So far we've not done wrong.

From the point of weather, this week has been lovely—sun all the time. Today began a bit overcast and was rather cold. Primulas in flower in the park, and a magnolia. One daffodil in flower in the open.

Monday, 14 March

Cabinet sat at 11. I was sent for about 11.30 and H. came out and gave directions for redrafting of part of the statement to be made in both Houses. H. Wilson, Van, and I got on to it. Had talk with H. and P.M. after Cabinet. Then with H. worked a bit on speech for P.M.—there was to be *Debate* in the Commons. Got to St. James' Club rather late for lunch with H[erschel] Johnson and Kennedy.‡ Latter very nice—frank and, I should think, friendly. Had to go down to House, where I attended Debate till about 7.30. Then went to P.M.'s room, where I found H. We had short discussion: they rather on the line of Winston's 'Grand Alliance'. I don't know about that. Went round to H. after dinner. Pointed out difficulties of dressing it up, for consumption here, as a 'League' affair, but thought it might be done.

[Cadogan told the German chargé d'affaires that British reaction to the use of force had been very strong; although the door was not closed to negotiations it would probably take a long time to get over the shock.[25]]

Tuesday, 15 March

Told Sargent about my discussions yesterday evening. He more in

* Jan Masaryk, Czechoslovak Minister in London, 1925–38.

† Sir Archibald Sinclair, Leader of the Parliamentary Liberal Party; Sec. of State for Air, 1940–5.

‡ Joseph P. Kennedy, U.S. Ambassador in London, 1937–41. See list of Principal Characters.

favour of simply backing French-Czech alliance. That certainly has merit of speed and simplicity. More talk with H. about this. . . .

Dined at the Palace—about 40 people. . . . Sent for by King. He rather fussed about Austria but sensible. Gloomy about French Government—against going to the League. . . . Didn't get away till 11.45. Mountains of telegrams to read on return.

France offensive apparently succeeding.

Wednesday, 16 March

Dined at home and tackled memo. on the situation and what we are to do about it. Sargent has painted his usual black picture, Strang has a more business-like paper on Czechoslovakia and what to do about it, Jebb proposes throwing Spain and Czecho[slovakia] to the winds and guaranteeing the Brenner. Latter doesn't make sense to me. I toned down Sargent's picture and came down against a guarantee to Cz[echoslovakia]. I shall be called 'cowardly' but after days and nights of thinking, I have come to the conclusion that is the least bad. We *must* not precipitate a conflict now—we shall be smashed. It *may* not be better later, but anything may happen (I recognise the Micawber strain). Go hard ahead with Italy—and she *may* eventually come in on Jebb's scheme. Rearm, above *all* in the Air. That is the policy of the line of least resistance, which the Cabinet will probably take. But I am convinced it is the lesser evil. Strang in his heart approves. Sargent against and I suppose Van will be wild. But can the Government weather the next few months on a policy of apparent inactivity? There are all sorts of intrigues afoot (Winston, S. B[aldwin] &c.) God knows: it's an awful situation, and God help us all.

Friday, 18 March

Discussion of the paper for F.P.C. with H., Van, Sargent, Malkin* and Butler. Van of course tried to cook it: he'll only do harm to his own case by over-statement. . . . H. got back about 6.30. F.P.C. unanimous that Czechoslovakia is not worth the bones of a single British Grenadier. And they're quite right too!

Dined at the Pilgrims' Dinner to Kennedy. . . . Was rung up by Warsaw in the middle of speeches. Kennard† says Poles will certainly march tomorrow unless Lithuanians accept *whole* ultimatum and stop boggling over trivial points. Expect Lithuanians in the wrong. Came

* Sir Will Malkin, Legal Adviser to F.O., 1929–45.

† Sir Howard Kennard, Ambassador in Warsaw, 1934–39.

back and wrote telegrams on menu-backs which H. approved, urging Kovno to give in and asking Paris to give similar advice.*

Saturday, 19 March

Talk with Rex Leeper (who agrees with me on the Czecho business, as do H., Butler, Jebb and most others, I think)....

Lithuanians have given in, so *that*'s over—for the moment! Italians are intensifying their bombardment of Barcelona, so sent telegram to Eric [Perth] to warn them that if that becomes known atmosphere will become impossible here for conversations.

Monday, 21 March

It's an awful life—working day and night . . . and the greater part of my days wasted in interminable drafting Committees, with boxes piling up in my room. In the morning went through with H. communication to French and draft statement to Parliament. . . . Thank goodness Cabinet are firm on doing nothing about Cz[echoslovakia]. Meeting of F.P.C. in afternoon.

A report of the Chiefs of Staff, who had been instructed by Chamberlain to consider the military consequences of a British decision to concert with potential allies against a German attack on Czechoslovakia, or to assure France of British support should she be compelled to honour her obligation to Czechoslovakia, concluded that Britain could send to the Continent a force of two divisions, 'seriously deficient of modern equipment', but at the price of preventing substantial reinforcement of her forces in the Mediterranean in the early stages. Of the 27 available fighter squadrons, 20 had only obsolete or obsolescent machines. No 3·7″ or 4·5″ anti-aircraft guns were available for home defence; there were no air-raid shelters. Save for a bridgehead at Bratislava, Czechoslovakia had no effective fortifications on her Austrian frontier, and the munitions centres at Pilsen and Prague would almost certainly fall to Germany at an early stage of the war.

On land, 'neither Great Britain nor France could render any direct assistance to Czechoslovakia, and the only method of rendering even indirect assistance would be by staging offensive operations against Germany'. The Chiefs of Staff thought the French unlikely to mount an effective attack on Germany. Should Italy and Japan elect to fight in a general war, the British Empire

> would be threatened simultaneously in Western Europe, in the Mediterranean and the Far East, by an immense aggregate of armed strength, and would be faced with the gravest danger.

* The ultimatum, sent after a frontier incident, demanded the establishment of diplomatic relations within 48 hours.

The British Fleet, seriously reduced in strength by the fact that 3 of our 15 Capital ships are now undergoing reconstruction, would have to be redisposed so as to maintain sufficient force to meet the German Fleet in home waters, while a Battle Fleet would be sent to the Far East, where we should stand on the defensive.

We could not, in these circumstances, maintain a sufficient fleet in the Mediterranean, and the Italians would therefore enjoy undisputed control of the Eastern Mediterranean. Our position in Egypt, Palestine and the Middle East would become critical.

A definite military alliance between Germany, Italy and Japan, the Chiefs of Staff concluded, 'would find us in the present year at a stage of rearmament when we are not yet ready for war'.[26]

Chamberlain's conclusions endorsed, and were doubtless to some extent influenced by, Cadogan's. Both were considering the usefulness of a guarantee intended to protect Czechoslovakia rather than to serve notice that an attack on her would provide the occasion of a European war. Neither thought the issue sufficiently clear, or British rearmament sufficiently advanced, to warrant so fateful a step. The Prime Minister recorded that weekend the blackness of the outlook:

> with Franco winning in Spain by the aid of German guns and Italian planes, with a French government in which one cannot have the slightest confidence and which I suspect to be in closish touch with our Opposition, with the Russians stealthily and cunningly pulling all the strings behind the scenes to get us involved in war with Germany (our Secret Service doesn't spend all its time looking out of the window), and finally with a Germany flushed with triumph, and all too conscious of her power. . . . As a matter of fact, the plan of the 'Grand Alliance', as Winston calls it, had occurred to me long before he mentioned it. . . . I talked about it to Halifax, and we submitted it to the Chiefs of the Staff and the F.O. experts. It is a very attractive idea; indeed, there is almost everything to be said for it until you come to examine its practicability. From that moment its attraction vanishes. You have only to look at the map to see that nothing that France or we could do could possibly save Czechoslovakia from being overrun by the Germans, if they wanted to do it. The Austrian frontier is practically open; the great Skoda munition works are within easy bombing distance of the German aerodromes, the railways all pass through German territory, Russia is 100 miles away. Therefore we could not help Czechoslovakia—she would simply be a pretext for going to war with Germany. That we could not think of unless we had a reasonable prospect of being able to beat her to her knees in a reasonable time, and of that I see no sign. I have therefore abandoned any idea of giving guarantees to Czechoslovakia, or the French in connection with her obligations to that country.[27]

In his Parliamentary statement of 24 March, therefore, Chamberlain enumerated the British obligations which might lead to the use of force: the defence of the British Isles or of any part of the Commonwealth; of France or Belgium against unprovoked aggression; of Portugal, Iraq and Egypt; and the more general instance of assisting victims of aggression under the terms of the Covenant. 'The case might, for example, include Czechoslovakia', though the obligation would not be automatic. The Government had decided against that on the grounds that it would deprive them of control over a vital question of foreign policy

> in relation to an area where their vital interests are not concerned in the same degree as they are in the case of France and Belgium. . . .
>
> But while plainly stating this decision I would add this. Where peace and war are concerned, legal obligations are not alone involved, and, if war broke out, it would be unlikely to be confirmed to those who have assumed such obligations. It would be quite impossible to say where it would end and what Governments might become involved. The inexorable pressure of facts might well prove more powerful than formal pronouncements, and in that event it would be well within the bounds of probability that other countries, besides those which were parties to the original dispute, would almost immediately become involved. This is especially true in the case of two countries like Great Britain and France, with long associations of friendship, with interests closely interwoven, devoted to the same ideals of democratic liberty, and determined to uphold them.[28]

This statement of the British position held good for six months.]

Thursday, 24 March

A frightful day and more wasted time. All morning with H. or P.M. jigging about the statement to Parliament. . . . Tried to do some work after, but had to go to H[ouse] of C[ommons] at 4.30. Rotten Debate. In interval went out to talk to John Simon about his winding up speech. But he was in one of his sour apple moods. We went back into House to hear Winston, and then I fled—can't stand John again. Home about 8. Dined at home, and must now sit down to neglected work. Every day this week about 6 hours of my day have been *wasted*. This is Democracy; but I suppose if we had a Nazi system I should have been compulsorily attending demonstrations.

Saturday, 26 March

Got to Cliveden about 5.30. Huge party—ordinary sort of crowd, plus the P.M. and Mrs. C[hamberlain]. . . . Sat between Lady Ravensdale and Mrs Fitzroy at dinner. Musical chairs after—won by P.M.!

Saturday, 2 April

Van has been away all this week, but it doesn't make much difference if he's here. He sends in minutes to the S[ecretary] of S[tate] snarling at some of Nevile H.'s telegrams which H. hands gloomily to me. I keep them for 2 or 3 days, then take them back to H. and say 'I'm very stupid: I can't remember what you told me to do about this'. He looks unutterably sad, and says 'I think perhaps we might burn it now!'

Tuesday, 5 April

Masaryk came at 11.30 to tell me what his people are doing (little enough, I suspect). Meeting in H.'s room at 12 to decide paper on Czechoslovakia for Cabinet. Van being silly, but rather crushed by H. . . . Had talk with H. These invaluable: he is very human. Sargent has been gassing outside Office, and of course it has got straight to P.M. (who is going to write about it). Told H. what I had wanted to do—and done—to stop this kind of thing.

Thursday, 7 April

Corbin at 5.30 on whom I urged that [League] Council should take least possible notice of German communication concerning Austria.

[On a Foreign Office paper of a few days before, pointing out that Germany's action in Austria violated the Covenant, Cadogan minuted that in view of the certain result of the plebiscite arranged for 10 April, it would be embarrassing to raise the issue: 'It is all very disturbing and humiliating, but if we have made up our mind to accept the fait accompli (as in Abyssinia) it seems to me that we don't improve matters by accepting it with a bad grace.' Halifax agreed.[29]]

Saturday, 9 April

Van is being tiresome—developing the technique of writing minutes on every paper he can lay his hands on and thus trying to become a super Permanent U[nder] S[ecretary]. Afraid the time has come for a remonstrance, which I shall make to H. on Monday. It's a great bore—why *will* Van be such an ass, and put me in the tiresome case of talking about one's 'position', like a housemaid? But there it is, and I must do it.

Monday, 11 April

Had to dine at H[ouse] of C[ommons] with American Committee in mufti. . . . Speeches by P.M. (rather flat-footed), American

Ambassador and Winston (ex tempore and not good). Home early—dropped here by American Ambassador, very full of his Windsor week-end—lyrical about Their Majesties and the Children!

Tuesday, 12 April

Cold at first, but the brilliant sun continued and warmed up. Azaleas coming out. 11.45 H[alifax] summoned meeting of Van, Plymouth,* Butler, Sargent, Strang and myself on Czechoslovakia. H. was psychoanalysing Van, and does it extremely well—and amusingly. Van shifted his ground a good deal. I think H. likes doing this—as I gathered from a talk to him afterwards! . . .

Had a talk to H. about 7. Talked about Eric D[rummond, Lord Perth], whom he wants to prolong for 6 months (this quite right, I think), Suez Canal Directors, and Van; H. would evidently like to get rid of latter, but I warned him how difficult it would be, and I don't know that it is necessary yet.

[The negotiations for an agreement with Italy, conducted in Rome, ended in mid-April. On the Italian side the new engagements amounted to little more than a reaffirmation of those already made and, in most instances, broken. Hostile propaganda was to be eschewed; Italian forces in Libya would be reduced; Britain would take steps leading to *de jure* recognition of the conquest of Abyssinia; Italy agreed to the British formula for the withdrawal of 'volunteers' from the Spanish Civil War and undertook to bring back all troops and material at its end. The entry into force of this agreement would await a settlement of the Spanish question. Italy disclaimed any desire to alter the status quo in the Mediterranean. At the time, it seemed probable that Franco would triumph within a few weeks. He did not. The agreement therefore remained in abeyance during the summer; Mussolini manifested an increasing irritation while the controlled Italian press glorified the contribution of Fascist forces to the successes of the Nationalists.

From 15 April Cadogan went on a week's leave to a house lent by Lady Astor at Sandwich. There he played a good deal of golf, caught a mild cold, did little work and reflected on the impending crisis in Europe.

Lord Halifax noted that he wished to be careful of backing proposals from Prague or from Berlin. 'In the former case', Cadogan commented on 20 April

> we should be taking an implied commitment to Benes,† and if his proposals were brushed aside by Hitler, we should be in a still more graceless position if we didn't support him. (I know that the meeting in your room the other day rather came to the conclusion that we *should*

* Earl of Plymouth, Parliamentary Under-Secretary for Foreign Affairs, 1936–9.

† Eduard Beneš, President of Czechoslovakia, 1935–8. See List of Principal Characters.

endorse a 'reasonable' Czech proposal. But I'm not quite sure that I agree, and I pointed out at the time that that might imply a commitment).

In the latter case—proposals from Berlin—these are likely to be pretty drastic, such as we should have some difficulty in pressing on poor Benes.

Consequently I agree that for the moment I don't think we should go further than impress Benes in general terms with the need for making a considerable effort. I don't even see why we should express an opinion on the 'reasonableness' of any proposals he may communicate to us. After all, I think we are agreed that it is not the 'reasonableness' of his plan that matters, but its settlement value, and on the latter we can hardly express an opinion.

Later, we *might* find an opportunity of putting in a word in Berlin in favour of Benes' proposals, or of telling Berlin that we have been giving advice in Prague and that, in our opinion (if it *is* our opinion), the Czechs have made a considerable effort.

But I am rather doubtful about the desirability of saying anything in Berlin at present.

If anything were to be said, I, in my obstinacy, would still think it should be on the line of trying to draw them as to what they *want* (without any guarantee that we shall help them to get it). I know that when you tried this on Ribbentrop, he merely said 'Oh! That is a long story'. But we should not grudge the time to listen to it. The Germans really have not the right to complain in general terms of the treatment of fellow-Germans in other countries—still less to utter vague threats of forcible action if their wrongs are not remedied, without being bothered to define their grievances or suggest where a remedy may be found. I have always believed that that is the line we ought to have taken long ago with Germany, and I'm not convinced it is even yet too late.

I have always been told that that would be putting the initiative in the hands of the Germans, but I believe that not to be the case—I believe it to be almost the reverse of the truth, because if one *could* pin them down to certain demands, they would have, as it seems to me, *less* freedom of action. At present they formulate no demands, waiting simply until they are ready and strong enough, at an opportune moment, to take what they think they can get. It seems to me that the initiative is always with them: we never know what they are going to demand, or take, next week.

Of course, we might expose ourselves to a snub—they might simply answer that this is no business of ours. But it might not be too easy for them to do that if we put the question in the right way. And if they do, they at once put themselves in the wrong, for what that may be worth.

They do the same if they pitch their demands too high. And there is no reason to suppose they will pitch their demands any higher simply because we ask them what they are. My experience is that German demands, like mushrooms, grow in the dark. They are always higher next week (naturally, because Germany has by then grown stronger), and if they *could* be got to define their wishes this week, ambitious though they might be, they will fall short of what they will be next.

Then there is one chance in 100 that the Germans might wish to show a sweet reasonableness, and you *might* get them to put their name to something reasonable, to which they might be held—for a time, at least.

However, I have said all this before, and never convinced anyone yet! So I shouldn't spoil your holiday with it.[30]

On 22 April Cadogan sent Henderson a revealing letter:

Thank Goodness, Austria's out of the way. I can't help thinking that we were very badly informed about feeling in that country. I've no doubt there's a section of the population hiding in cellars, and a number of those waving Swastika flags now may come to rue the day later, but we should evidently have been very wrong to try to prevent the Anschluss against the wishes of . . . a very considerable proportion of the population. After all, it wasn't our business: we had no particular feelings for the Austrians: we only forbade the Anschluss to spite Germany.

Cadogan had come to the conclusion that Britain could do nothing effective against the Reich's absorption of German minorities, or even against a German attempt to take a stranglehold on little countries:

We'd better put our defences in order (that goes much too slow at present) and try for a modification of the balance of Power—make friends where we can and secure our position at least in the Mediterranean, if that is possible.

What I wonder is, is it even now not too late to treat the Germans as human beings? Perhaps they wouldn't respond to such treatment. What I have always had in mind these last two years (and urged) is that we should ask them whether they won't let us try our hand at helping to remedy the grievances which they make so much of but which they don't make very clear.

No one knew precisely what Germany wanted or what she would do. Probably that was part of Germany's game:

but there is no reason why we should play it by putting our head in the sand and waiting for the next kick in the pants. (That is the policy which I always hear described as 'keeping Germany guessing', but it always seems to me that most of the guessing is done by us.)

Isn't it possible to psychoanalyse the Germans, try and draw them out? I'm told probably not: they would refuse to disclose their aims. That may be so, but if, with a professed desire to help them, we begged them to tell us what, in their view, was wrong, and how they would wish to see it put right, and if they refused, I still don't see that we should have done much harm.

Cadogan did not believe that this procedure would put the initiative into Germany's hands, or inflate her demands:

> If we could ever have got Germany to formulate what she wanted we could have held her to that for a bit.
>
> However, I appear to be the only person who thinks along these lines. No one seems to agree with me, so I must be wrong.[31]]

Monday, 25 April

My room has been repainted: beautiful new sandy carpet laid: precious blue leather chairs, new fire-irons &c.—and smell of paint. But quite good effect and with a picture and curtains (promised) will do quite well. Not too much work. . . . Discussion with H., Van, Sargent, Malkin, Strang about forthcoming conversations with French Ministers. H. continues to 'psychoanalyse' Van very well—and ties him in knots. This morning H. read me letter from Van, reciting conditions on which he had accepted his appointment—(1) that he should be in the same position as other 'Principal Advisers' (there is no analogy)—(2) that he should have 'direct access to P.M.' (H. and I agree this is moonshine) but he must make a 3rd point—that if foreign Ministers come here, he must take part in conversations! H. asked me what I thought! I said if he accepted the idea of a Chief Diplomatic Adviser (whatever that might mean), I didn't quite see how he could exclude him from such conversations! Though I left him in no doubt that I thought the C[hief] D[iplomatic] A[dviser] absurd.

L. O[liphant]* talked to me about Van this evening. He thinks he (V.) is mad.

Dined at home and worked. Wrote minute for S. of S. stressing that parrot-cry of 'Rearmament' is mere confession of failure of foreign policy. We *must* reach a modus vivendi with Germany.

Tuesday, 26 April

3 further meeting about Czechoslovakia. H. won on points.

Thursday, 28 April

First meeting with French at 10.30. Till 1, when we lunched at No. 10 . . . . Resumed after till about 5. . . . We got through non-contentious stuff, such as Anglo-Italian Agreement, procedure at Geneva, Spain and—less non-contentious—Staff conversations. Think it went fairly well. I impressed on H. that French come over

* Sir Lancelot Oliphant, Deputy Under-Sec., F.O., 1936–9. See List of Principal Characters.

here for 2 reasons—(1) to boost themselves (2) to tighten our leading string. We must look out for (2).

I had to give dinner (of 16) for most of Delegation at Carlton. Good dinner, and went so well that I couldn't get away till 11.30. Sat between Léger* and Cambon.† Sargent told me after that French *very upset* at our reluctance to embark on naval conversations. Don't believe this myself. They are simply trying it on us and hoping to have a 'grievance value'. Certainly Léger, who chatted to me for hours, never gave a hint that the French were displeased in any way.

[The meetings of 29 April began with a long statement by Halifax on the Czechoslovak question, the military aspect of which Britain regarded 'with considerable disquiet'. The Government could not go beyond the Prime Minister's pronouncement of 24 March. Nor, after the purges, could Russia be counted upon for any substantial contribution to the defence of Czechoslovakia. The result of the British examination of the military and political issues:

> was that, if the German Government decided to take hostile steps against the Czechoslovak State, it would be impossible, in our present military situation, to prevent those steps from achieving immediate success.

The view of M. Daladier, the French Prime Minister,‡ printed in full in the published British documents, was that Konrad Henlein, the leader of the Sudeten Germans, intended the destruction of Czechoslovakia. If France were to press the Czechs to further concessions, he thought there should be a rider; if they were not accepted, Britain and France would prevent the dismemberment of the country:

> We were confronted by German policy readily translated into action, designed to tear up treaties and destroy the equilibrium of Europe. In his view, the ambitions of Napoleon were far inferior to the present aims of the German Reich. . . . If . . . we were once again to capitulate when faced by another threat, we should then have prepared the way for the very thing we wished to avoid.

Daladier refused to agree that Britain and France were powerless to act in support of Czechoslovakia, though conceding that the Czech fortifications could now be turned because of the Anschluss. Chamberlain took up this point. Czechoslovakia was surrounded by German territory on three sides. He could not believe that Czechoslovakia could be saved, or that Britain and France were sufficiently powerful to make victory certain;

* Alexis St. L. Léger, Sec.-Gen. at Quai d'Orsai, 1933–40.

† Roger Cambon, Minister at French Embassy in London, 1924–40.

‡ See List of Principal Characters.

though 'he thought that a time would come when a gamble on the issue of peace or war might be contemplated with less anxiety than at present'.

Moreover, Chamberlain 'doubted very much whether Hitler really desired to destroy the Czechoslovak State or rather a Czechoslovak State', though that decision might admittedly be taken later.[32]

Cadogan would have been the first to place his own phrase 'awful rubbish', which he applied to Daladier's remarks about German hegemony, among those 'foolish and hasty reflections' which he admitted his Diary to contain.]

Friday, 29 April

Colder than ever but bright. At F.O. before 10, to talk to H. Van there—like a cat on hot bricks—said French were devastated by yesterday and almost thinking of 'making their own terms with Germany'. (What *does* that mean, even in an insane world?) I don't at all mind giving them something on naval conversations: we are committed to them in principle anyway. If it pleases them, let us say we are ready for them.

Meeting at 10.30—Czechoslovakia the whole time. Impassioned appeals by Daladier—putting the whole of Van's case about Germany 'hegemony'. Very beautiful, but awful rubbish. H. and P.M. put the answer pretty well, but we broke off for lunch with everyone looking rather blue.

Lunch at F.O. . . . We (British Delegation) had talk after. I found—rather to my surprise—that H[alifax] and P.M. were on my line, of asking Germans what it is they *want*. This is what I have been pressing for years. I merely nodded my head. Van—of all people!—seemed to concur!!! If things go my way, I'm quite content to sit and watch.

Went down to meeting 2.45 and H. put our point, using the phrase which I had written him. . . . 'German demands, like mushrooms, *grow in the dark*'. French seized on this and agreed. H. said to me 'You have won your point by a phrase'. Agreed we should both urge Benes to do his utmost, and that *we* should ask Berlin what they want! That produced agreement. P.M. intimated that we should be easier on naval conversations, and all ended in smiles.

H. received Kordt* at 5 and Crolla† (I was present) at 5.30. To latter he gave fairly full account of conversations. This is a good move—what I wanted: a 'follow-up' of our agreement with Italy. . . .

Just before H. left, at 6.45, I got the evidence that the French yesterday evening were delighted! H. said 'Show that to Van'! I said

* Theodor Kordt, Counsellor at the German Embassy, 1938–9.

† Guido Crolla, Counsellor at the Italian Embassy, 1936–9.

'He's already got it.' Of course he's a French agent, and the French know it and play upon his nerves. They don't try that on me.

Monday, 2 May

Corbin 5.15. . .—to my surprise—said his Government hoped we should get on without delay with our representation in Berlin. Submitted to H. draft instructions to Prague and Berlin and discussed them.

Tuesday, 3 May

5.15 went to H[ouse] of L[ords] to discuss with H. telegrams to Berlin and Prague to give effect to our conversations with French. Van had put in comments—mostly verbal and silly. H. thought nothing of them, but I got him to meet some of them so as to defeat Van's point—he wanted to come back on decision to *ask* Germans what they *want* (see April 29). That went all right, and we went to see P.M. who agreed generally, and made some useful suggestions as to form. I redrafted bits, and got H's approval and took telegrams back to F.O. about 7.45, and had them sent off. (Sargent is on leave, so I have all this on my hands, but not a bad thing.)

Thursday, 5 May

Franckenstein at 5.15. Rib[bentrop] has asked him to propagand for German Kultur in this country! He will wisely refuse. Hopes to stay here on his own. Many friends . . . are helping him. Tony Rothschild* came about German offers to buy Witkowice works. This significant. If they are prepared to pay $ or £ for it, it don't look as if they are going to march in and take it. Talked to Strang about it: must see Hankey,† as Admiralty have placed large order. . . .

Friday, 6 May

Talked to H. about his speech to [League] Council on Anglo-Italian agreement, which I didn't like at all. We changed draft a good deal. Heywood of Allied Newspapers called with a lot of information about men and material going over French frontier into Spain. I told him why I shouldn't like to see it published, and he said he thought Kemsley‡ would agree. Lunched at home. . . .

* A. G. Rothschild, partner in N. M. Rothschild and Sons.

† Sir Maurice Hankey, Secretary to the Cabinet and to the Committee of Imperial Defence, 1916–38. See List of Principal Characters.

‡ James Gomer Berry, first Baron Kemsley, chairman, Kemsley Newspapers, 1937–59, and Editor-in-Chief, *Sunday Times*, for the same period.

Masaryk at 5, to whom I told what instructions we had sent to Prague. He tried to show he thought we were doing the dirty on them. I said I could quite sympathise with this view, but how in Hell were we to help them? He had no answer to that. I said I knew I was talking like a schoolmaster—or a governess—but it didn't seem to me to be nonsense anyway. He said, if we made representations in Berlin, he hoped we shouldn't ask Germans what they wanted. I asked why not? He—à la Van—said because they would make impossible demands. I replied that I thought they would refuse to answer, so he needn't worry. But if they *did*, what they would demand now would be as nothing to what they would take some months hence. Let him look back for a moment at the course of events during the past 5 years, and the development of German aspirations. He didn't go on arguing, and I didn't tell him whether we should or shouldn't put the question to the Germans.

Van has been sniping at the S. of S. stupidly again, but the latter has dealt with him.

Saw Hankey about Tony R[othschild]'s story (see yesterday). He not very disturbed.

Saturday, 7 May

Had talk with Rex Leeper, who's still hypnotised by A. and very anti-Chamberlain. I think he's wrong in his views and inferences. Thinks C[hamberlain] is 'splitting the country'. I don't believe it a bit. That's what the old ass S[tanley] B[aldwin] says. Though *he* ought to be an expert—he's split the country before now.

Monday, 9 May

Corbin came to pump me about N. Henderson's interview with Woermann. Told him the minimum. Tony Rothschild came in. Gave him to see we didn't like idea of German control of Witkowice. New Court [headquarters of Rothschild and Sons] not inclined to it either, but he will let me hear further what his cousins think.

Wednesday, 11 May

Talked to H. in Geneva on telephone. He fussed about Nevile H's retort to our reproach to him for exceeding his instructions. I said that we had replied quite kindly but N.H. really *does* want a gentle jab in the mouth occasionally.

[Henderson had mentioned to Woermann that Britain was urging in Prague a 'comprehensive settlement such as, speaking quite confidentially, a state of nationalities rather than a national state would imply'.

Halifax thereupon told the Ambassador not to give interpretations of 'comprehensive settlement', partly because Germany might make public use of them. To this mild rebuke Henderson retorted that the force of his representations would be 'greatly diminished' if he were denied 'a certain latitude in expression of personal opinion'. The Foreign Office replied that the operation was a delicate one; the language used in Prague must be different from that used in Berlin. 'To take only one example; while we are emphasising in Prague the weakness of the military situation, we hope to make the German Government think long before doing anything likely to break the peace.'

Halifax reminded Sir Nevile in a private letter that

> whatever you and I may think about the ultimate lengths to which Benes may have to go or about the difficulty of really protecting Czechoslovakia if the Germans let themselves go in forcible measures, you should not in any conversation, official or private, let the impression be created that we and others should certainly sit by in all circumstances.[33]]

Thursday, 12 May

At last a hot summer day. Office has quieted down marvellously. Went over to see Horace W. about message I had had from P.M. as to suggestion he had received that he should talk to Hohenlohe*, who might influence Henlein. (I had found out that the 'suggestion' came from Van.) Horace showed me letter from Van to P.M., in which former said he had been approached by Henlein, who wanted to come over here, that he had spoken to H., who approved (H. said nothing to me about it) and that he had therefore answered encouraging. I said I didn't see any positive *harm*, and if Henlein had been encouraged it might be bad now to put him off. Lunched at home. P.M. sent for me—wanted to bring Nevile H. home before he saw Rib[bentrop].† Rang up N.H. and found he saw Rib last night. Told P.M. who agreed to do nothing.

Friday, 13 May

Press now have it that Henlein is here. Talked to Rab Butler about it, and he saw Van and told him not to press Henlein too hard. We now have report from Nevile H. of his talk with Rib[bentrop]. Latter says Henlein's points should be a 'basis for discussion'. (This better than I expected.) So I don't want Van to tell Henlein to come off his 8 points altogether: that will go straight back to Berlin, who

* Prince Max von Hohenlohe-Langenburg.

† Now German Foreign Minister.

will think we are double-crossing them. . . . Corbin at 4.15. Told him about Nevile H's interview and impressed on him that French *must* press Czechs, and that delay is dangerous. Dined at home. Saw first brood on the lake [in St James's Park].

[Vansittart told Henlein that 'he was now going too far and indeed some of his demands exceeded the bounds of the possible'. When Henlein replied that he had always been the apostle of conciliation, Vansittart 'hastened to assure him that I knew this to be true'. He pressed Henlein not to complicate the issue of the grievances of the German minority by introducing extraneous questions of foreign policy, and found him in general

> far more reasonable and amenable than I had dared to hope. . . . I would say that this visit opens up distinct possibilities, but no more than possibilities, and the odds are still that pressure will be put on Herr Henlein from Berlin to drive him out of any feasible agreement.

Henlein offered Churchill his word of honour that he had never received orders or even recommendations from Berlin.[34]

Saturday, 14 May

Calm morning, interrupted by appearance in my room of an anaemic-looking . . . man, who declared himself to be the Mexican Ch[argé] d'Aff[aires]. He had charming manners and expressed his deep regret that, on the first occasion when he had the honour of meeting me, he had to deliver such a message. He then handed me note saying he had been instructed to close the Legation and depart! I said I was very sorry too: I supposed we should have to do the same. He nearly wept and said how much he hoped our 2 Govts. would reach agreement. I said it didn't seem that his Govt. had chosen a terribly good way to go about it. I didn't know what else to say, and we parted with mutual expressions of highest esteem!

Monday, 16 May

Had talk with H. about Geneva and Henlein. He had, apparently, vaguely approved idea of Henlein visit. . . . 4 o'clock talk with H., Van and L. O[liphant] about the Henlein conversations. Think they may have done good, and we telegraphed them to Newton* for his talk tomorrow with Benes.

Tuesday, 17 May

Had talk with H. about his speech and other matters. Then consultation on Spain with him, Plymouth, Butler and Mounsey. 12.30

* B. C. Newton, Minister at Prague, 1937–9.

Corbin came and, as result of consultation, slipped it into him about material crossing French frontier [to Spain]. I said only chance was armistice, and if only French and Italians could get together, it might be arranged. But not much chance of this.

Thursday, 19 May

Corbin came again to make lame excuses about material going over French frontier. I spoke to him like a Dutch uncle. He can't expect Italy to give him same assurances as they have given us while they 'intervene' as much as Musso does.

Friday, 20 May

Had talk with H. about Embassies. He suggested Van for Washington and insisting on his going there. I said why I thought this was difficult.

H. saw Masaryk and pressed him about settlement with Henlein. . . .

Telegrams from Cz[echoslovakia] about German troop movements, but I am not unduly alarmed, and N.H. has got assurances from German Govt., for what *they* are worth. But everyone rather jumpy.

[As Halifax pointed out to a German visitor later in the summer, these denials might have carried great weight had not similar denials at the time of the Anschluss proved false. The telegram sent to Berlin on 21 May asked Henderson to remind Ribbentrop of British pressure upon Czechoslovakia to meet the just grievances of the Sudeten Germans. If Germany should nevertheless attack Czechoslovakia, France would be compelled to fight. 'In such circumstances His Majesty's Government could not guarantee that they would not be forced by circumstances to become involved also.'

That morning, Henderson telegraphed he had found Ribbentrop in 'a highly excitable and pugnacious frame of mind'. The Foreign Minister produced telegrams about the killing of two Sudeten farmers by a Czech major at Eger and to casualties 'amounting to nearly 100' of the previous day. Germany, he stated, would not wait much longer; and if provocation continued her 75 millions would act as one man. 'I regard position as extremely critical', Henderson commented.

That evening, when Henderson delivered the warning, Ribbentrop was 'clearly perturbed'. If war came, he avowed, it would be one of aggression, provoked by France. Germany would fight again as in 1914. In the early hours of 22 May Halifax replied:

> If resort is had to forcible measures, it is quite impossible for me or for him [Ribbentrop] to foretell results that may follow, and I would beg

him not to count upon this country being able to stand aside if from any precipitate action there should start European conflagration.

On the afternoon of 22 May Halifax once again reminded the French that Britain was not bound to them save in the event of unprovoked German aggression upon France.[35]]

Saturday, 21 May

News bad. H. arrived back from Oxford at 10.45. Had long talk with him. Decided we must *not* go to war!

Sent telegram to Berlin authorising warning to German Govt.—for what that may be worth. . . . 5.30 Jebb rang up to say there was 'very grave news' so dashed round to F.O. But not so bad—N. Henderson had found Rib in offensive mood, and there is more evidence of German troop movements. However, rang up H. and told him to come back. . . . H. turned up about 9.30. Took him to F.O.; where we reviewed news and drafted telegrams to Prague and Berlin. H. rang up P.M. who will be here for lunch tomorrow. Van rang up to butt in, and H. asked him to come tomorrow. Got away about 11.

Sunday, 22 May

F.O. at 10.30. Further talk with H. John Simon came about 11.45—and Van. J.S. takes our view strongly. We can't go to war. Drafted telegram to Paris warning them not to count too much on us. Heard that women and children of Embassy leaving tonight in special coach. Got H.'s authority to stop this folly. H. saw Dirksen* and had a good talk with him. Late lunch again. Back at F.O. 2.30. H. saw Corbin. I made first draft of statement to Parliament tomorrow. Cabinet at 5. . . . H. got back about 6.30. Cabinet quite sensible,—and anti-Czech! Drafted telegrams and got back about 8—dined at home. What a week-end! But H. is very calm and firmly on the right line. So, I gather, are Cabinet.

Monday, 23 May

Pretty quiet. Advised H. not to send for German Ambassador today. If the Germans *are* going to be moderate, they won't want it to look as if that was due to our pressure. So if he's got nothing particular to say, leave him alone—send for him perhaps tomorrow. H. is admirably calm and balanced and sensible.

Tuesday, 24 May

Long talk with H. in morning. Work slack and these talks about business and prospects very useful. He does *think*, and think *calmly*.

* Herbert von Dirksen, newly arrived from Tokyo as German Ambassador.

A great blessing. . . . Caught H. before he went to H[ouse] of L[ords]. We decided to send Strang to Berlin and Prague—an excellent move. . . .

Madriaga* called—with a veritable extravaganza of a plan for putting an end to the war in Spain. I have recorded it, but with all my misgivings. We've got somehow to persuade both sides that it's no use going on *fighting*. They must *stop* where they are. Then everything will solve itself. But it's not so easy as all that.

H. wants to sever French-Czech and Czech-Soviet connections. He's quite right, but I tell him this can only be done by some form of 'neutralisation'. We'll examine it.

Walked home and dined there, thank God.

Irises becoming lovely in the Park.

Wednesday, 25 May

Things continue fairly quiet in central Europe. We have to sit down under abuse from the German Government and Press. Nothing to be done. They are foul and blatant and stupid, and let's leave it at that and get on with it.

[Henderson wrote gloomily to the Foreign Secretary about Ribbentrop:

> He seeks popularity by quick results and his one idea is to win his spurs and to be regarded as a great man. If Hitler jumps a foot he jumps a yard, and I am appalled at the possibility of the fate of Europe being influenced by such a German Minister for Foreign Affairs in a situation like today.

The Embassy in Berlin advised afterwards that 'the necessary progressive psychological preparations' for military action against Czechoslovakia had been made in the Nazi press. There was little doubt that a 'bloodbath' in Czechoslovakia would have moved Hitler to act, although the German Army was not ready for a European war. The British Military Attaché, visiting the areas where preparations against Czechoslovakia would be visible, saw nothing to suggest that a move in force had been contemplated, though 'certain precautionary steps' had probably been taken.

The Prime Minister, however, felt sure that the Germans, having made all preparations for a coup, decided after the warnings that the risks were too great and were accordingly venting their spite on the British. 'But the incident shows how utterly untrustworthy and dishonest the German government is. . . . One thing is very clear to us, though we can say

* Don Salvador de Madariaga, Spanish Ambassador to France, 1932–4; delegate to the League of Nations, 1931–6.

nothing about it. The Anschluss and the Anglo-Italian agreement together have given the Rome-Berlin axis a nasty jar.[36]]

Sunday, 29 May

Went round to H. at 7 to discuss telegrams. Nothing much in, but situation appears quiet. He is thinking of butting in with a statement of what we think is right.

We may have to do that, but I should be in no hurry to do it. As I said to P.M., let us 'back no bills'. Also, as I told him, I want to keep a statement up our sleeve for dealing with the situation *after* we have got over this crisis (if we do). We *must* clear the air; we can't let Germany go on keeping the initiative, and we must call her into the open, as I urged upon A. on May 13, 1936!

Tuesday, 31 May

H. Wilson came to see me about Van's memo. on propaganda, which he had addressed to P.M. I said if P.M. didn't like that, he must refer Van back to S. of S. Talked about Spain, about which P.M. is (rightly) fussed.

Strang got back today from Prague and Berlin. Had long session with him, H. and Sargent 6–7.30. Decided to use big stick on Benes and sent off telegram to Paris and Prague.

[In Prague, Strang was told by Newton that the root problem was not the presence of the Sudeten Germans but the fact of a Slav state thrust into the heart of Germany and having treaties of mutual assistance with France and Russia. Germany was using the question to strengthen her military and political position. He favoured, and thought the Czechoslovak Government would welcome, the appointment of a British observer to tour the Sudeten country. The Czechs realised that something drastic must be done, and had been deeply impressed by Henderson's démarche in Berlin, whereby the British were thought to have committed themselves to intervene if there were a European war. The military attaché was not convinced that the Germans had intended any military action, although there had been troop movements. Newton, however, believed that the Germans had been deterred by British warning and the prompt military response of the Czechs.

In Berlin, Henderson judged that because Hitler's resentment was directed particularly against Britain, it was all the more necessary to make a renewed effort in Prague. Like Newton, he favoured the despatch of an investigator or commission; but he did not believe that Beneš intended a comprehensive settlement. A solution must involve self-administration for the Sudeten Germans and an adjustment of Czechoslovakia's foreign relations. The first measure, however, would lead eventually to incorporation in Germany. Should negotiations between Prague and Henlein break down, it might be right for the British and German Governments to discuss a settlement directly. Sir Nevile felt convinced that Hitler wanted a peaceful outcome.[37]]

Wednesday, 1 June

Strong S.W. gale and cold.

Nothing very much to record. Czechoslovakia remains outwardly quiet, but Henlein and Hodza* don't seem to get to grips.

Friday, 3 June

H. went off to Yorkshire at 1, after putting to Corbin my scheme for securing armistice in Spain, i.e. get promise from French that they will shut their frontier during armistice: then go with that promise to Rome and ask them to press Franco. It won't work, but no harm trying!

Wednesday, 8 June

Meeting at 3 with H., Van, Sargent, Strang, W. Malkin on possible schemes for 'neutralisation' of Czechoslovakia. Van opposed violently, but H. overrode him quietly and decided to put the matter to Paris.

Thursday, 9 June

Discussed with Sargent, H. Smith, Ingram and Roberts† questions related to Anglo-Italian agreement, i.e. what is a 'settlement in Spain', and how to get it. French have not taken badly my suggestion for armistice. (Though Van has!)

Wednesday, 15 June

Picked up H. at 10. He gave me a lot of gossip. P.M. wants to put Van into Reith's‡ place! They put themselves to an enormous amount of trouble to find Van a niche any other than the one he occupies! Horace W. has proposed Leithers§ for Washington. I said *NO*... if it has to go outside the Service, must go to important

* Milan Hodza, Prime Minister of Czechoslovakia.

† Respectively Charles Howard Smith, later Minister to Denmark and to Iceland; Maurice Ingram, head of the F.O.'s Southern Dept., 1937–9; and Frank K. Roberts of the Central Dept., later British Ambassador in Moscow and Bonn.

‡ Sir J. Reith, Dir.-Gen., B.B.C., since 1927; Chairman, Imperial Airways, 1938–9, B.O.A.C., 1939–40.

§ Sir F. Leith-Ross, Chief Economic Adviser to the Government 1932–46; Director-Gen., Ministry of Economic Warfare, 1939–42.

personage—not to someone from another Dept. I think that'll be all right. . . . Had to go to musical party at German Embassy. Atmosphere like the inside of a cow. Got away soon after 12.

Thursday, 16 June

Encouraging telegrams from Paris about Spain. They agree—with conditions—but I think we can go ahead in Rome. F.P.C. at 4. H. got through Czecho telegram but he has misunderstood my Spanish Armistice proposal, and has let them put in as a condition, 'substantial withdrawal'. This throws it all back in to that blasted N[on] I[ntervention] C[ommittee]. I explained, and I think he understood and felt guilty. Must write him something to show P.M. tomorrow. Walked home—V. hot. Dined at home.

Friday, 17 June

Gave H. a note showing why and how F.P.C. had missed the point of my armistice proposal. He quite saw it, and took me over to see P.M. I *think* he saw it (but wouldn't admit it—? fear of Simon and Malcolm M[acDonald]). But we got the telegram toned down perhaps sufficiently. H. saw Grandi after lunch, and I hope he may have made the matter clearer to him. Got off telegram to Paris about 'neutrality' of Czecho and to Rome about Armistice. Had to do this on my own as H. left at 3.45.

[The telegram to Paris suggested—on the ground that the root of 'the German–Czechoslovak difficulty' lay in the undertakings of France and Russia towards Czechoslovakia—that they might be remodelled. Czechoslovakia would be relieved of her obligations to France and Russia, whose commitments to her would remain intact. Germany would promise not to invade Czechoslovakia; and the latter's territory would not be used for aggressive purposes against Germany. The French did not respond.[38]]

Wednesday, 22 June

Our approach on armistice has been turned down by Ciano. Never mind—let that simmer: we may find Musso has something to suggest.

Thursday, 23 June

The House blew up about bombing of ships and I had to go down there about 7. But I refused to stay for debate and walked home. . . .

We shall have no peace, and shall make no progress, till this blasted Spain is 'settled'. Old Ivor [Lord] Plymouth and his N[on] I[ntervention] C[ommittee] are 'Old Man River' and will never settle anything. We *must* make a frontal attack on the thing—though my first has certainly failed!

Friday, 24 June

4.45 Corbin to ask about international commission on bombing. Barcelona getting anxious about this, and if we can set it up it may stop them bombing Geneva! Azcarate* at 5 also to ask about commission, and he hinted, verbally, that reprisals would be taken against Germany and Italy. Grandi at 6 with message from Ciano, who has heard of preparations in Barcelona and Valencia to bomb Italian towns. Italy would retaliate! I carefully avoided showing I knew anything about it, and read him a lecture.

Saturday, 25 June

'Times' reproduces my interview with Azcarate (only representing it as being with H.). This idiotic. A[zcarate] must have given it, but 'Times' ought really to consult us first. Talked to Rex Leeper, and sent explanation to H. 12.30 Grandi rang up! I said it was true A. told me that his Government were subject to great pressure to take reprisals on foreign instigators!

Monday, 27 June

Flood of work, and all the Departments very slow and inconvenient. Really, sometimes I do think we want to get a move on in the F.O.

Tuesday, 28 June

11.30 meeting at No. 10: P.M., Simon, H., L[eith] R[oss], Hopkins,† H. Wilson, Brenan‡ and myself. Inconclusive, but it cleared the ground—are we to come in on China's side with finance? (*Currency* credit a mere camouflage.) Got as far as we could by deciding to draft paper for Cabinet.

Friday, 1 July

Winston came to get material for an article on Austria. I got Sargent to help, but we couldn't tell him much (don't know). I tried to give him some phrases about Joy (through Strength) rides and labour camps.

* Pablo Azcarate y Florez, Spanish Ambassador representing the Republican Government.

† R. V. Hopkins, Second Secretary, Treasury, 1932–42.

‡ J. F. Brenan, served in China, 1905–37; adviser on Chinese affairs, 1938–43.

[The Italians had been told that until the Spanish question was settled, the Anglo-Italian agreement could not enter into force. Mere acceptance of the British plan for the withdrawal of 'volunteers' would not do. Settlement must at least mean that the Spanish issue had ceased to be a source of international friction. An armistice, followed by a substantial Italian withdrawal, would be preferred by the British Government. This suggestion was rejected out of hand by Mussolini, as were the alternatives. Ciano told Perth that the Duce no longer considered himself bound to conform to the agreement.[39]]

Monday, 4 July

Frightful telegram in from Rome about Musso's reaction to our suggestions. He evidently won't play at all. Discussed it with H. and decided we must be polite but firm. Awful day during which nearly my whole time was wasted.

Tuesday, 5 July

H. presided N[on] I[ntervention] C[ommittee] at 4 and got the blessed 'British Plan'* through at last. Discussed notes for Cabinet with him and drafted telegram to Burgos about their note re bombing. *Still* 15 boxes waiting for me. Put contents in large box for my home and then that bloody fool Jebb goes and sends me the *wrong* box. He's very clever, but *no* Private Sec.

Wednesday, 6 July

6 meeting with H. about reply to Musso. Van there and wants to 'stiffen it up'. I said important not to let Musso think we were 'excited'.

Friday, 8 July

More work on reply to Musso, now finally fixed up. H. talked to me about feelers from Hitler about a Goering visit, and about a speech he is contemplating. Asked me to think about them. But I have *no time to think*—that's just it. Also discussed help for China. N. Henderson came for a long talk in afternoon. Rather pessimistic but on no solid grounds.

[The British reply, given to Ciano on 12 July, stated that the 'volunteers' must actually be withdrawn. Ciano commented to the German Ambassador in Rome that matters had thus reached an impasse. Italy would 'wait and see how things developed. Each of the two parties was now free

* For the proportionate withdrawal of volunteers from each side in Spain, as a preliminary to the grant of belligerent rights. Franco refused; the plan was therefore stillborn.

to play the game as it saw fit. . . . On the question of supplying Franco with men and material, Mussolini was making full use of his regained freedom of movement.'[40]]

Monday, 11 July

Busy day—mostly on China and Spanish bombing. After tortured reflection, I'm convinced we should *not* help China—risk is too great. All very well for Brenan and Nigel R[onald]* to press it, but they aren't in daily contact with the awful European situation. Gave H. my notes for reply to the Hitler feelers.† . . . Awful rush, and towards end of [Parliamentary] Session all questions which Cabinet have shelved begin to converge. Long talk on things in general with Horace W.

Tuesday, 12 July

More talk with H. about China—picked him up at 10. He saw P.M. last night and—as I warned him—found P.M. against it. I suggested compromise of sounding Japs first. I think this would be all right—he doesn't like it.

Thursday, 14 July

Ascertained from H. that Cabinet yesterday turned down China loan. I shall have to tell Quo!‡ . . .

Gauleiter Forster called at 4, with Prof. Noe.§ Had 50 minutes of them. The Gauleiter a frank young gangster—rather nice. He talked quite openly: so, I hope, did I. He said what had we to do with Czecho? I said 'Peace'—amongst other things. I quite liked him, and I don't think he found me quite hopeless either.

Quo at 5. Painful interview, but he's a gentleman.

[Cadogan told Forster, who was known to be close to Hitler, that declarations by 'responsible people' in Germany about her discontents, coupled with her intensive rearmament, 'naturally produced a feeling of uneasiness and insecurity'.

Asked whether the English people still believed in self-determination, Cadogan said that they did; though that did not mean that a plebiscite could usefully be held in all circumstances. If people in Germany considered that there should be a plebiscite in the Sudeten area, that view

* First Sec., F.O., since 1930; Counsellor, 1939; Assistant Under-Sec., 1942–7; Ambassador to Portugal, 1947–54.

† This refers to the preliminary discussions on the visit of Captain Wiedemann. The initiative came from the German side; the British learned that Hitler wished to entrust him with a special mission of exploration.

‡ Quo Tai-chi, Chinese Ambassador, 1935–41.

§ Herr Forster was Gauleiter of Danzig and Professor Noe a Director of the International Shipbuilding and Engineering Co. of Danzig.

would contradict the attitude taken up when Schuschnigg announced the Austrian plebiscite. Forster said that Hitler had never done anything without obtaining an expression of the general will, and all his acts had been overwhelmingly confirmed by the vote of the people. On this Cadogan observed that 'the more normal technique was for action to follow rather than to precede a plebiscite'.

Forster several times expressed Hitler's desire for peace, assurances which Cadogan accepted.[41]]

Saturday, 16 July

Runciman* came at 12 and Sargent, Strang and I talked to him for an hour. He finally accepted mission as 'Mediator' in Czechoslovakia, provided both sides accept him. (I think this is a necessary condition.)

Sunday, 17 July

[After lunch] at Cliveden, T., Nancy [Astor], Lothian, two Nichols and I went to Royal Berkshire course. I played Nancy a single, giving her a half. My game (and particularly drive) simply faded out and she beat me 5 and 3. She then took P. Nichols' Rolls Royce and drove me home in it—a most hair-raising performance, 60 miles an hour and she shrieking with laughter. 'There's a corner coming—I'll slow down for that.' 'I hope so, indeed' was all I could say.

I was due with H. at 9.20. Went on with him to P.M. Had longish talk with him and H.W. as to how to take Wiedemann tomorrow.

[Wiedemann was known to be a friend of Hitler, and, like others, was received by Halifax and Cadogan because he might provide a means of by-passing Ribbentrop. A month before, Wiedemann had told a friend, who passed it on to Halifax, that *Mein Kampf* was not to be taken as gospel; and that Hitler wanted only a peaceable solution of the Sudeten problem within the Czechoslovak state. At this interview of 18 July, the Captain vowed that Hitler's attitude to England 'had always been one of admiration and friendship', though he felt that some of his advances had been rebuffed.[42]]

Monday, 18 July

Called at H's at 9.50. Wiedemann turned up at 10. 2 hours' talk, I had to interpret from the German, which was tiring. He authorised to suggest a Goering visit. We said delighted, in principle, but of course it would be better if Czech question cleared up first. He gave

* Lord Runciman, President of the Board of Trade, 1931–7.

most binding assurances that, *barring major incidents*, Germany determined not to resort to force. He said he was Hitler's adjutant (when H[itler] was a 'despatch-bearer') during war. Had to confess he never suspected his possibilities: thought him just a brave, reliable soldier.

Last night we had a *batch* of telegrams from Prague that all look bad, and we spent part of today in devising telegram to Newton warning that we may have to come out with our 'mediator' idea.

Tuesday, 19 July

'Daily Herald' announces Wiedemann conversation. Lunched with Layton* at 'News Chronicle'. Had to deny knowledge of Wiedemann.† . . . Dirksen came and I gave him message from an 'observer' in Czechoslovakia showing they had found no trace of military movements.

Wednesday, 20 July

4.40 Dirksen. I told him *we* weren't responsible for leak about Wiedemann. 6.30 went to see P.M. and drafted with him reply to question in Parliament tomorrow about W. Also got from him lines of what we are to say to Dominions.

[The Prime Minister stated that Wiedemann had had an 'informal conversation' with Halifax. He had not come to discuss any particular question; but the talk enabled him, owing to his contact with 'authoritative circles' in Germany, to renew the assurances already given by the German Government of their desire to achieve a peaceful settlement of outstanding questions.]

Friday, 22 July

H. Wilson came round to tell me Dirksen was going to see P.M. We concerted what he should say. Pole at 11.30 to try and find out what Forster had said to me about Danzig. I said we hadn't breathed the word! 1 p.m. went to try out Ford car. . . . H. Wilson sent me record of P.M.'s talk with Dirksen. Quite harmless,[43] but R. Leeper tells me Press are inventing all sorts of things. Forgot to go and drink cocktail with Anthony. Think I shall buy Ford. But time short before holiday, and I am rushed! Heard about 6 p.m. that King and Queen left Calais at 5.30. *That*'s a relief!‡

* Walter (later Lord) Layton, Editor of *The Economist* 1922–38; Chairman of *The News Chronicle*, 1930–50.

† Who had been recognised by a journalist on his arrival in England.

‡ They had made a State Visit to Paris.

Saturday, 23 July

Press (blast them!) are inventing all sorts of lies about the Dirksen interview. H. Wilson came round and we drafted a statement.

Sunday, 24 July

Had to go round in morning to pacify H. who is in a bad temper, and seems to expect us to produce all his speeches for him. If only he'd told us so, I could have done something about it. I should *hate* having my speeches written for me. Also there was a telegram from Prague showing Benes accepts Runciman idea.

Monday, 25 July

Kordt at 4 to complain of our communiqué about Dirksen interview.... Things get worse as time goes on. Shall I *ever* get away? Seems unlikely—there is so much to be done and I have *no* time of my own.

Tuesday, 26 July

Spent an hour with H. on his blasted speech. Got text of P.M.'s speech for today. Went over to see him and got him to cut out some bits about 'recognising Germany's restraint(!)' &c.... Runciman came and asked for Gwatkin.* I think [the request] rather objectionable but S. of S. wants to agree—will consult P.M.... Maurice Hankey talked to me ... about Van. I said I quite agreed, but what was to be *done*?!

Wednesday, 27 July

Picked up H. at 9.55. Had message from him after Cabinet to say they agreed about Gwatkin. Passed it on to Runciman.

Thursday, 28 July

McGowan† came at 12. Wants to sell 100,000,000 cartridges to Chinese but not good enough security. Wanted Government to help. We discussed means of juggling it up with some of his Government contracts, but came to the conclusion it couldn't be worked!

Forgot to say Ford car delivered at 10. I drove it on Embankment. It seems very nice. Then drove it to F.O. Bless its career!

Talked to H. about secret stuff concerning German preparations. I don't *think* I'm very much impressed by it on the whole.

Friday, 29 July

Had meeting at 12 with H., Van and Co., to clear up Czech

* F. Ashton Gwatkin, Counsellor, F.O.; Asst. Under-Sec. and Chief Clerk, 1940–7.
† Lord McGowan, head of Imperial Chemicals.

questions. Decided text of letter from H. to Rib. . . . 2.45 long talk with H. about Washington. Tried—and I think succeeded—in washing out Grigg.* H. asked me to see G. Dawson† about it this evening. H's choices are 1 Lothian, 2 Lytton‡, 3 Chatfield, 4 Grigg. G.D.'s are 1 Lothian, 2 Tweedsmuir§, 3 A. E[den] (but he admits latter is impossible!).

[As in 1937, the Cadogans had arranged to take their holiday in France. On 31 July they motored to Dover. 'The Hotel marked with a number of stars in A.A. book, but even they don't represent my language.' At Le Touquet Cadogan fared indifferently at the casino and on the links. 'Must give up golf' he noted despondently, not for the first time. He was not receiving Foreign Office papers and had to depend on the press for news of the Czechoslovak crisis, the rumours of impending German mobilisation and the efforts of Runciman's mission to find common ground, if such existed, between the claims of the Sudeten Germans and the authority of the Czechoslovak Government. On 24 August Gladwyn Jebb advised Sir Alec's immediate return to the Foreign Office. This Cadogan offered by telephone the next morning. He heard nothing further until the evening of 26 August, when Jebb again recommended return. Cadogan, irritated, replied that he must know definitely whether or not he was required.

Meanwhile, German military preparations and Czech countermoves formed an incongruous background for Runciman's efforts at mediation. Vansittart pressed for a clear warning to Germany by mid-August at latest. He received from some of his contacts among German officers and moderates the plea that Hitler be made to understand that the attitude taken up in the previous May had not been a pure bluff. Neither Halifax nor Chamberlain wished, however, to support so publicly a policy which might well lead to war; and Vansittart himself agreed that Czechoslovakia could not survive in its existing form.[44] The Chancellor, Sir John Simon, made a balancing speech:

> in the modern world there is no limit to the reactions of war. This very case of Czechoslovakia may be so critical for the future of Europe that it would be impossible to assume a limit to the disturbance that a conflict might involve, and everyone in every country who considers the consequences has to bear that in mind.']

* Sir Edward Grigg, Governor of Kenya Colony, 1925–31, M.P. 1922–5, 1933–45; several minor ministerial posts, 1939–42.

† Geoffrey Dawson, Editor of *The Times*, 1912–19, 1923–41.

‡ Earl of Lytton, Governor of Bengal, 1922–7; chairman of League of Nations Commission of Inquiry in Manchuria, 1932.

§ John Buchan, first Lord Tweedsmuir, Gov.-Gen. of Canada, 1935–40.

Monday, 29 August *Le Touquet*

J. S[imon]'s speech seems to me all right, and to have been received fairly well, except, of course in Berlin. I expect it was probably necessary, but we mustn't dare Hitler to be humiliated too much.

Tuesday, 30 August *Le Touquet*

'Daily Mail' this morning full of Van and all the conferences he attended, with a photo of his grinning mug. How *does* he manage to advertise himself so blatantly? Evidently a crisis going on, and I ought to have been back. Well, I gave them a chance to recall me. But I can't stay on here now after this week.

Played after tea with T. on Old Course. Very well too. . . . Total 78 (67 nett). Best score I think I have ever done here. *Why*?!

II

September 1938–March 1939
MUNICH AND PRAGUE

On 30 August 1938, most members of the Cabinet attended a long and disquieting discussion. Halifax reported measures which amounted to a partial German mobilisation. One view, he said, and for which there was much evidence, was that Hitler was bent upon force; others thought that while he had still not made up his mind, he 'was determined to have everything ready, using a mixture of bluff and force'. Many moderate Germans were pressing the British Government to go beyond the Prime Minister's statement of 24 March 'and had said that, if we did so, there would be no attempt to coerce Czechoslovakia and the Hitler régime would crack. For his part he received these messages with some reserve.' Chamberlain too had come to the conclusion that the risk of a bluff could not be run. No state should make threats unless ready and able to execute them. 'War in present conditions was not a prospect which the Defence Ministers would view with great confidence. . . . The policy of an immediate declaration or threat might well result in disunity in this country and in the Empire.' Britain, Ministers decided, should try to 'keep Germany guessing' as to her 'ultimate attitude'.

> Is it not positively horrible [wrote the Prime Minister] to think that the fate of hundreds of millions depends on one man, and he is half mad? I keep racking my brains to try and devise some means of averting a catastrophe, if it should seem to be upon us. I thought of one so unconventional and daring that it rather took Halifax's breath away. But since Henderson thought it might save the situation at the 11th hour, I haven't abandoned it, though I hope all the time that it won't be necessary to try it.[1]

This was the project of a meeting with Hitler, which had been discussed only between Chamberlain, Halifax, Henderson and Wilson. How soon Cadogan learned of it is not clear; probably from Halifax on 4 September. The disagreements between the Permanent Under-Secretary and the Chief Diplomatic Adviser continued during this crisis. For instance, Vansittart protested that Britain should not assist Germany to drive Russia out of Europe by enforcing the abandonment of her alliance with Czechoslovakia, or by deciding Czechoslovakia's fate at a Four Power conference:

> If we lend ourselves to the beginning of this process, the future is fairly obvious—in two stages. In the first Russia will be evicted and retire into sulky isolation. In the second she will be penetrated by Germany, and Bismarck's traditional policy of close Russo-German relations will follow. The consequences to Europe are too obvious to need enlargement here.[2]

Against those risks had to be set the more immediate hazards of a threat to Germany. Like Chamberlain and Halifax, Cadogan did not believe at the time, or after reading the memoirs and documents published in the following thirty years, that Czechoslovakia could have been preserved by a 'firm stand'. Admittedly Cadogan minuted in the middle of September 'It is worth bearing in mind that the German extremists may be bluffing a good deal more than we know.'[3] As the evidence of German armed strength, Hitler's determination, French defeatism, and British weakness in arms accumulated, however, he concluded that the risks could be run only in the last resort. Searching his memory in 1951, Cadogan recalled that 'of our top military, naval and air people whom I questioned on the subject, I don't think I found one who did not think that "appeasement" was right.'[4]

As a number of terse entries in the diary indicate, the relative weakness of Britain weighed heavily with Cadogan. Of Britain's fifteen capital ships, only ten were fully operational. The R.A.F. had scarcely any of the new 8-gun metal monoplanes in squadron service. The Army could bring no more than token assistance to France. As for substantial allies, Cadogan could feel little confidence in France, whose inadequacies became only too apparent under successive probings in September 1938. He accepted the prevailing expert opinion that the Red Army, in the immediate aftermath of the purges, could not provide a formidable offensive force. 'Pray God', he minuted gloomily on 21 September, 'we shall never have to depend on the Soviet, or Poland or—the U.S.'[5]

That is not to say that the military considerations were the only, or even the principal, consideration in Cadogan's mind. Like the Prime Minister he judged the issue, and Hitler's intentions, insufficiently clear to warrant a war which might be quickly lost and which could be won only at frightful cost. The skeletal Intelligence services had produced no definite evidence of a deliberate intention to swallow Czechoslovakia.[6]

As it was, the Prime Minister returned from Munich with mixed emotions; hoping, as he put it to Halifax, for the best while preparing for the worst. Cadogan's diary shows that he thought the policy pursued in 1938 the least undesirable option. It need hardly be added that while recognising the force of arguments in the contrary sense he refused always to join the more extreme and simplistic condemnations of Chamberlain.

1938

Friday, 2 September

We got away about 10.45. Wonder if I shall ever see Le Touquet again . . . L. O.[liphant] dined. He fairly calm and told me a certain amount about origins and progress of crisis. Cabinet settled nothing but authorised N.H. to tell Germans of his impressions.

Saturday, 3 September

Jebb came in morning. . . . He left stack of telegrams and papers, which I started reading. There's certainly enough in the Secret Reports to make one's hair stand on end. But I never quite swallow all these things, and I am presented with a *selection.* It's obviously touch and go—but not gone yet. . . . Runciman has done very well and is very canny.

Sunday, 4 September

Continued my most gloomy reading. . . . To F.O. H. turned up at 5. Had talk with him: he in good form—calm and quietly hopeful. Conference with H., H.J.W., Van., Sargent and Mallet*. Not much to be done for moment. It will be late tonight before we get Gwatkin's report of what Henlein has brought back from Berchtesgaden, and all turns on that. A short preliminary message is not unhopeful.

After my reading of all the papers, I gave some support to the idea of a *private* warning to Hitler that we should have to come in to protect France. I believe this advisable—Hitler has probably been persuaded that our March and May statements are bluff, and that's dangerous. Stayed on and said more on these lines to H. and H.J.W.

Monday, 5 September

Don't remember exactly all detail of these awful days, but I know we had numerous meetings, discussing advisability of giving Hitler another serious, and private, warning. In intervals got through what work I could. H. dined here, and we had a talk.

Tuesday, 6 September

In much the same state, till the evening, when H. Wilson came round to say he had been called on by Herr X (I shall probably never be able to fill in this name—the man's life is at stake, and I can't jeopardise it by putting the name on paper. I have disclosed it to *no one*, and shall not do so) who 'put conscience before loyalty'

* Ivo Mallet, F.O.; Asst. Private Sec. to the S. of S., 1938–41.

and said Hitler had taken his decision to 'march in' on 19th or 20th. We told H.W. to get P.M. down as soon as might be. Luckily, I had already persuaded H. not to go to Geneva on Friday.

[The unnamed visitor was Theodor Kordt, then chargé d'affaires at the German Embassy, whose brother Erich worked in Ribbentrop's private office and who had seen Sir Horace Wilson at No. 10 after being admitted through the garden gate.]

Wednesday, 7 September

H. saw Herr X this morning, and latter repeated his story. Wants us to broadcast to German nation. I said that fatal—and the suggestion almost makes me suspect Herr X. I had to waste 1½ hours in afternoon with King Boris.* Very pleasant and intelligent, but a waste of time at this juncture. Though I *did* give him the warning that if Hitler thinks we shall in *no* circumstances come in, he is labouring under a tragic illusion. He *might* pass this on through the Queen and Musso, but I don't think so. Lord and Lady H. dined. After dinner we had news from Bonnet† that negotiations in Prague suspended, and urging that we utter warning. Thinking troops might be moving, we drafted message from P.M. to Hitler. But we got H.W. round. He had broadcast which sounded better. We rang up B.B.C. and found that situation was being more or less held, so confined ourselves to asking Runciman whether there was anything we could do. H.J.W. stayed till 12.30.

Thursday, 8 September

Went at 11 with H. to meeting at No. 10 with P.M., J.S., Horace W. P.M. doesn't think warning message much good. Thinks he should go himself. I agree. H. thought better to send for Van. He against—Canossa. We argued with him and I think demolished him. Adjourned 1.30—I to produce possible draft of warning message, P.M. to produce draft saying he is coming . . .

I fixed up draft with Van. Meeting at 5. P.M. now against telling H[itler] he is coming and he produced no draft. He didn't like ours either. He seems to want simply to wait till after Nüremberg and then spring himself on Germany. I think we want to do what we can to prevent Hitler committing himself irretrievably at Nüremberg. Van. with me on this. He wants warning. I agree with P.M. that

* King Boris III of Bulgaria. He brought a message of friendship from Mussolini, amounting to a request that the Anglo-Italian agreement be implemented soon.

† Georges Bonnet, French Foreign Minister, 1938–9. See List of Principal Characters.

not much use. I still want P.M. to intimate his visit. Van suggested as alternative to summon British Press and endorse latest Cz[echoslovak] suggestions. I don't really like this. Adjourned 6.30. J.S. drafted telegram to Prague indicating what P.M. might say to Press and inviting Runciman's endorsement. H. took it to P.M. who approved. I'm not sure this is right. Depends on German Press tomorrow. Don't want to start a screaming match with Hitler. Corbin called 7.15, but I could only tell him no decision taken.

Friday, 9 September

Very difficult (writing Sunday) to sort out these awful days. Both Prague and Berlin reacted strongly against statement to Press. We sat most of the day in our usual huddle and drafted message of warning to Rib[bentrop] (so as not to take words out of P.M.'s mouth if he has to see Hitler) and telegraphed it to Berlin in time to send on by night train to Nüremberg. . . . I went round at 10.30 to Downing Street to see H.J.W.

[The warning, sent on 9 September, said that if France went to war in fulfilment of her obligation to Czechoslovakia

> it seems to His Majesty's Government inevitable that the sequence of events must result in a general conflict from which Great Britain could not stand aside.[7]]

Saturday, 10 September

Nevile H. rang me up at 8.30 to say he was sending reply by air, but couldn't get further than Cologne. I got an aeroplane off the ground here at 9.30 to pick up Messenger at Cologne. Message received about 4, and we met on it. N.H. violently against a warning and Ministers decided to hold their hand. I think right. Van. furious. We announce some naval moves (which impress German Naval Attaché). H.J.W. came here after dinner and we discussed draft for P.M. in event of 'Plan Z'.* This is an awful life.

Sunday, 11 September

After breakfast re-wrote H.J.W.'s draft for 'Plan Z'. Got car and drove to F.O. about 10.45. Discussed my redraft with H. before the huddle at 12. Huddle jiggered draft about. . . . Back at F.O. 2.30 to re-write draft again. All sorts of bothers and questions. Huddle again at 5.30. Re-draft approved—with further alterations. Decided *not* to take further naval steps. This right: though it gave Van

* That is, should Chamberlain decide to visit Hitler.

epilepsy. Yesterday, on N.H.'s recommendation we refrained from further warning owing to possible *irritant* effect. We announced naval moves (this rather contradictory). These have had great effect. To increase them would add to irritation (if irritation there is) and difference between what we have done and what more we might do is *not* sufficient to outweigh possible added irritant.

Monday, 12 September

These days (and nights) have been so awful that I have been unable to write Diary. (Pity—because they are just the interesting days). I think—I am writing on Thursday—that most of Monday was taken up with our meetings with Ministers. . . . I had to be back at No. 10 by 9.30. Picked up papers at F.O. on way and arrived punctual. We had text of Hitler's speech, which pulls no triggers. We adjourned, to sleep on it.

[Hitler's speech consisted of violent abuse of Beneš mingled with vague threats:

> I am in no way willing that here in the heart of Germany a second Palestine should be permitted to arise. The poor Arabs are defenceless and deserted. The Germans in Czechoslovakia are neither defenceless nor are they deserted, and people should take notice of that fact.

On the following morning the British Government learned from the Secret Service that all German missions had been told of the intention to invade Czechoslovakia on 25 September.[8]

Riots broke out in the Sudetenland, where martial law was proclaimed in the most turbulent zones. Shortly, Henlein fled to South Germany.]

Tuesday, 13 September

Meeting with Ministers in morning. Pretty inconclusive, but am glad to see they realise they can't sit back and do nothing after the speech. (I feared they might be tempted to do this). 3 p.m. further meeting with Service Ministers (and T. Inskip and Chiefs of Staff added). Waste of time. P.M. (quite rightly) won't mobilise [the Fleet] yet but ready to take precautionary measures. So I should have thought it quite easy to take all our decisions in about 5 minutes, but there were hours of talk. Duff Cooper* made a 'fighting speech', which fell rather flat. Got rid of the war-boys about 7.30. By then, telegrams had come in from Paris showing that Bonnet was completely deflated. Daladier demanded to speak on telephone to P.M. That hopeless. I said he must give a message, through Phipps. When it

* First Lord of the Admiralty, 1937–8. See List of Principal Characters.

came through, it was not quite so limp as Bonnet, but had *very* little backbone. That was not till 11. Meanwhile, Bonnet's messages showed that he at least was panicking, and the situation slipping. P.M. decided on Plan Z. We drafted a telegram—or rather P.M. really did, deciding on a quite simple form. Got it off to N.H. and rang him up about it.

[On 13 September Sir Eric Phipps found Bonnet 'very upset' and saying that peace must be preserved at any price; 'il ne faudrait pas que les Anglais nous poussent à la guerre.' The Ambassador attributed this collapse to a realisation of the imminent danger, Litvinov's* evasions at Geneva and Colonel Charles Lindbergh's hair-raising report of the overwhelming superiority of the German Air Force. An interview later the same day with Daladier proved hardly more reassuring.[9]]

Wednesday, 14 September

Cabinet—to be told what has been done! During it, saw H.J.W. and arranged for him to get P.M. to see King Boris. Lunched at home. N.H. came through from Berlin about 3.30—Hitler 'entirely at the disposal' of P.M. They want agreed communique. Rest of afternoon spent running between No. 10 and my telephone, fixing up with N.H. Finally fixed at 7, and agreed to issue at 9. Rushed home to 8.15 dinner and got back to F.O. 8.45 to inform Corbin. ½ hour talk with him. Then home—rather done in. But it's *right*.

Autumn crocuses just coming up! Shall I see them again, and what will they portend?

Thursday, 15 September

Got up at 6. Breakfast 7 and picked up H. and Lady H. in car 7.30. Got to Heston about 8.15. P.M. arrived 8.25. . . . Good send-off and take-off for P.M. Kordt there. . . . Picked H. up at 10.10 to walk to F.O. (All these days I spend about 15 hours out of the 24 with him. He is grand: always calm and wise and friendly.) . . .

5 meeting of H., J.S., Sam H[oare]†, Bridges‡ and self to discuss possibilities of plebiscite, &c. Van. deliberately excluded. Silly creatures—why don't they sack him?

Friday, 16 September

Had a good sleep, and luckily a pause today. Walked with H. to

* Maxin Litvinov, Russian Foreign Minister, 1930–9.
† Sir S. Hoare, Home Secretary, 1937–9. See List of Principal Characters.
‡ Edward (later Sir Edward) Bridges, Secretary to the Cabinet, 1938–46.

office. P.M. arriving this afternoon, so no need for further Simon-Hoare huddle. Met Sam H[oare] at the door, who told me of complaints that [W.N.]Ewer, V. Bartlett and V. Gordon-Lennox* are the darlings of the News Department. Believe this to be true: I'm afraid I'm becoming sick of R. Leeper. Saw him at 11 and gave him strong hint. 11.30 meeting with H. and Eric D[rummond] about Anglo-Italian relations. Not too conclusive. But wait for direct official approach from Musso. . . .

Grandi at 3.15, wanting to get in touch again!

P.M. landed at 5.30. I went over to No. 10 at 6 and he arrived 6.20. 6.30 meeting of Ministers. P.M. gave us his impressions. Thinks he has held Hitler for the moment. Quite clear that nothing but 'self-determination' will work. How are we to get it—or give it? I know Halifax will, by hook or crook. So will P.M. J.S. trying to evolve a semblance of Quid pro Quo. I think we'd better not try. Make the gesture to Hitler—we've never made one before—and trust to the result. Broke up without definite decision at 8. P.M. I think tired—though looks to me well. . . . I to see H.J.W. at 9.45. Spoke on above lines.

[Leeper was shortly afterwards put in charge of Propaganda, and taken away from the task of dealing constantly with the newspaper correspondents. 'Since Anthony's departure (and before) I have had constant complaints from No. 10 of the handling of the Press by our News Dept.,' Cadogan informed Halifax. 'Blame has been particularly attached to Leeper, not, I am bound to confess, without some reason. But he has been in a difficult position: I think he has tried to do his best: if he has failed, I attribute it to no base motives.'[10]]

Saturday, 17 September

Picked up H. at 9.40 and walked to F.O. Cabinet at 11—lasted till 1.40. Understand it didn't go too badly. Adjourned till 3. Got leave from H. and P.M. to see Corbin and tell him something—not too much! Also sent for Kennedy and had talk with him. (He's been got at by someone—I should judge Van!). . . Cabinet at 3. Sent for Grandi and gave him a little mild dope. Hungarian called to demand equal treatment for *all* minorities. Pointed out to him difficulty of issuing any declaration in favour of this principle. . . . Talked to H. and Gwatkin 6–6.30. Set a Committee to work on possibilities of a Plebiscite (as it appears Cabinet have decided on 'orderly transfer'). S. of S. had to go to No. 10 to deal with T[rades'] U[nion] C[ongress]

* Of *The Daily Herald, The News Chronicle* and *The Daily Telegraph* respectively.

and U.S. Ambassador. Back at 8 and I drove him to his dinner. No rush work tonight. I may try to work off some non-urgent papers. Daladier and Bonnet coming over tomorrow, so shall have a heavy day. H. again asked me (before Gwatkin) whether Van should be asked. I said really that wasn't my business: I left that to him and P.M., but I *had* to tell of my suspicions of Van's intrigues with Léger, Winston, &c., of which I am convinced. He told me later he had discussed it with P.M. and they agreed Van should attend, but H. to give him severe warning before meeting! Why not *sack* him?!

All the daughters at dinner.

[Describing his first meeting with Hitler, Chamberlain told his colleagues that it was impossible not to be impressed with the power of the man. 'He was extremely determined. He had thought out what he wanted, and he would not brook opposition beyond a certain point.' 'I had established', Chamberlain wrote to his sister, 'a certain confidence, which was my aim, and on my side, in spite of the hardness and ruthlessness I thought I saw in his face, I got the impression that here was a man who could be relied upon when he had given his word. . . .'

Hitler had told Chamberlain—falsely—that three hundred Sudeten Germans had been killed; the matter must be settled at once. 'I am determined to settle it: I do not care whether there is a world war or not.' In response to Chamberlain's remark 'there are many people who think . . . that you wish to dismember Czechoslovakia', Hitler said that he sought racial unity and 'did not want a lot of Czechs'.[11]]

Sunday, 18 September

Wednesday night, and I haven't written this Diary since Saturday last. Sunday an awful day. Daladier and Bonnet and their circus arrived by air and we met at 11.* Sat till 1.15. P.M. described his talk with Hitler. We had to listen to Daladier, with voice trembling with carefully modulated emotion, talking of French honour and obligations. But we brought him back to earth before lunch adjournment. He suggested question was how to (a) avoid war, (b) maintain *independence* (*not* integrity!) of Cz[echoslovakia]. . . . Meeting again 3.15–5, getting down to brass tacks. Reports on French Air Force coming in—too frightful. They have 21 machines (not in squadrons) equal to modern German machines! Adjourned for tea and our party started drafting message to Benes. Pretty stiff—telling him to surrender! P.M. decided that we must offer guarantee. Dominions don't even know of suggestion! Gave draft to French about 7.30 and adjourned for dinner.

* For the official record of these talks see B.D., Ser. III, Vol. 2, No. 298.

. . . French met us about 10.15 and we sat till 12.15. Agreed on communication to Benes, but Daladier must consult his Cabinet. Telegraphed text to Newton with message to hold his hand till we let him go by telephone. What a day!

[When Daladier said that France could hardly urge Czechoslovakia to give up part of her territory unless she were to receive an international guarantee of the rest, Chamberlain replied that this would be a serious commitment for Britain: 'she had no army which could march to Czechoslovakia, and it was a long way to send an air force.' Daladier explained that if he could believe Hitler's profession to want nothing beyond the Sudetenland, he would not press for a guarantee; but 'he was convinced in his heart that Germany was aiming at something far greater. . . . A British guarantee for Czechoslovakia would therefore help France in the sense that it would help to stop the German march to the East.' On those terms British Ministers accepted to join in an international guarantee of Czechoslovakia against unprovoked aggression, to replace the French and Russian treaties.[12]]

Monday, 19 September

Corbin telephoned 12.20 French Cabinet agreed. Telephoned on to Prague and informed Cabinet.

5 talk with H[alifax], Van[sittart], Malkin, Strang about procedure and proposals P.M. should put to Hitler.

6.15 had to go to Palace, where had nearly an hour with King. Latter very well informed and intelligent. I'm awfully sorry for him. He feels it acutely, sitting there in a room in the Palace unable to *do* anything. . . .

Came in on interview between H. and Winston. Latter seemed to be tamed somewhat, and I gather H. told him good deal of the truth about the French. Hoped for quiet evening, but after dinner found a rather rattled telegram from N.H. and a draft telegram by Gwatkin that puzzled me. So off to H. after dinner. We drafted reply to N.H. and I suppressed Gwatkin's draft. Home about 12. Rather dead.

Tuesday 20 September

An awful day. Don't remember what happened in morning. Lunched at home. Meeting of Ministers at 3. *I* thought waste of time: trying to think up details of settlement procedure. Hitler won't talk of details, and unless he accepts broad settlement, we needn't bother about them. J.S. in his element: I half asleep. I told H. last night of the King's condition, and he, I'm glad to say, went to see him this morning. In the evening reports began coming in of unfavourable

Czech reply. . . . Had to go to F.O. 10.15. Bad telegram from Prague. H. and I took it over to P.M. and H.J.W. and drafted reply driving the screw home on poor Czechs. Home 12.30.

Wednesday, 21 September

As I left house to pick up H., had telegram saying Benes had capitulated. Further discussion as to how P.M. should conduct conversation. He seems agreed he can't go further than he has gone, and he can't champion Poles and Hungarians. This is *essential*. I hope he'll stick [to] it. Lunched at home. Cabinet at 3. Joe Kennedy at 3.30 and I did what I could. Of course Press campaign is developing now here and in U.S. against 'Betrayal of Cz[echoslovakia]'. That inevitable, and must be faced. *How* much courage is needed to be a coward! . . . Discovered Van last night ordered fleet to Alexandria! However, I spoke to him and to Backhouse,* and in my judgment, seems to be the best thing to do, so, P.M. having left it to my discretion, was content to leave it. Poor H. taken up with T.U.C. till after 8 when I came away.

How I realise these scrappy notes give no idea of what I feel. We must go on being cowards up to our limit, but *not beyond*. I have tried to impress this. But what of the future?

Thursday and Friday, 22 and 23 September

Writing Sunday, I can't sort out in detail events of these days. They were mostly occupied in meetings of Ministers (to whom Malcolm MacDonald and Inskip have been added). News from Godesberg only very scrappy and unintelligible. What became plain, by Friday evening, was that Thursday's meeting [of the Prime Minister] with Hitler was 'very unsatisfactory'. P.M. therefore decided to write him a letter Friday morning making clear our attitude. Friday afternoon Hitler replied—also very unsatisfactory. Thereupon P.M. sent further letter 'asking for a memo.'. That was all I could get on the telephone from Horace W. In explanation, he could only say that they had had to ask for a memo. because hitherto 'It had been all words'. So I suppose Hitler is being asked to define exactly what he *does* want. That may be a good move, but it's rather late.

All these days have been awful—from 9.30 till about midnight—practically no break and one's mind gripped the whole time with this one awful obsession. We have been, at intervals, discussing war preparations (which is not cheering). And I have to hold Corbin

* Sir Roger Backhouse, First Sea Lord, 1938–9.

and Joe Kennedy at arm's length. The latter makes little secret of what he thinks of us!

News from France shows more and more the badness of their military (air) position and their growing disinclination to fight. So the Dictators will have it *all* their own way!

Saturday, 24 September

Hitler's memo. now in. It's awful. A week ago when we moved (or were pushed) from 'autonomy' to cession, many of us found great difficulty in the idea of ceding people to Nazi Germany. We salved our consciences (at least I did) by stipulating it must be an 'orderly' cession—i.e. under international supervision, with safeguards for exchange of populations, compensation, &c. Now Hitler says he must march into the whole area *at once* (to keep order!) and the safeguards—and plebiscites! can be held *after*! This is throwing away every last safeguard that we had. P.M. is transmitting this 'proposal' to Prague. Thank God he hasn't yet recommended it for acceptance. He returned by lunch time. I dropped H. at the Palace at 10. He then went to meet P.M. and lunched with him, so I hardly saw H. in the morning. . . .

Meeting of 'Inner Cabinet' at 3.30 and P.M. made his report to us. I was completely horrified—he was quite calmly for total surrender. More horrified still to find that Hitler has evidently hypnotised him to a point. Still more horrified to find P.M. has hypnotised H. who capitulates totally. P.M. took nearly an hour to make his report, and there was practically no discussion. J.S.—seeing which way the cat was jumping—said that after all it was a question of 'modalities', whether the Germans went in now or later! Ye Gods! And during Thursday and Friday J.S. was as bellicose as the Duke of Plaza Toro. At times he almost went berserk. I gave H. a note of what *I* thought, but it had no effect. P.M. left at 5.10 to rest. I told J.S. and Sam Hoare what I thought: I think the latter shares my view, but he's a puny creature. Cabinet at 5.30 and H. got back at 8 completely and quite happily défaitiste-pacifist. He seemed to think the Cabinet were all right. I *wonder!* They don't yet understand and they haven't seen the map. (They're going round after dinner to have it explained to them by Horace [Wilson]!) Pray God there will be a revolt. Back to F.O. after dinner. H. got back from No. 10 talk with Labour about 10.30. Drove him home and gave him a bit of my mind, but didn't shake him. I've never before known him make up his mind so quickly and firmly on anything. I wish he hadn't chosen *this* occasion! I *know* there is a shattering telegram from

Phipps about position in France: I *know* we and they are in no condition to fight: but I'd rather be beat than dishonoured. How can we look any foreigner in the face after this? How can we hold Egypt, India and the rest?

Above all, *if* we have to capitulate, let's be honest. Let's say we're caught napping: that we can't fight now, but that we remain true to all our principles, put ourselves straight into war conditions and *rearm. Don't*—above all—let us pretend we think Hitler's plan is a *good* one! I've never had such a shattering day, or been so depressed and dispirited. I can only hope for a revolt in the Cabinet and Parliament.

What *will* be written on the remaining pages of this Diary?

[Chamberlain told the inner ring of ministers that he thought he had 'established some degree of personal influence over Herr Hitler' who would not, he felt satisfied, go back on his word. Later in the day the Prime Minister said in full Cabinet that he believed Hitler

> extremely anxious to secure the friendship of Great Britain . . . it would be a great tragedy if we lost an opportunity of reaching an understanding with Germany. He thought he had now established an influence over Herr Hitler and that the latter trusted him and was willing to work with him.

Phipps telegraphed:

> Unless German aggression were so brutal, bloody and prolonged (through gallantry of Czech resistance) as to infuriate French public opinion to the extent of making it lose its reason, war now would be most unpopular in France.
>
> I think therefore that His Majesty's Government should realise extreme danger of even appearing to encourage small, but noisy and corrupt, war group here.
>
> All that is best in France is against war, *almost* at any price (hence the really deep and pathetic gratitude shown to our Prime Minister). Unless we are sure of considerable initial successes we shall find all that is best in France, as well as all that is worst, turn against us and accuse us of egging French on to fight what must have seemed from the outset a losing battle.
>
> To embark upon what will presumably be the biggest conflict in history with our ally, who will fight, if fight she must, without eyes (Air Force) and without real heart must surely give us furiously to think.
>
> It may be asked why I have not reported sooner in the above sense. The answer is that up to the last hour the French had hypnotised themselves into believing that peace depended upon Great Britain, and not upon Herr Hitler. They were convinced, that is to say, that if Great

Britain spoke with sufficient firmness Herr Hitler would collapse. Only now do they realise that Herr Hitler may well be meaning to take on both our countries.

Cadogan's prompt reply asked whether Phipps meant to include in the 'war group' those who felt that France must execute her obligations to Czechoslovakia. The Ambassador answered that he had meant the Communists paid by Moscow, who had been 'working for war for months'.[13]]

Sunday, 25 September

Cabinet in morning, so I didn't go to F.O. till 11.30. Nothing doing. . . . Cabinet again at 3. . . . Monteiro* came in to say Franco had offered neutrality in European War. Even crumbs of good news are good! Cabinet up about 6. H. sent for me. He said 'Alec, I'm very angry with you. You gave me a sleepless night. I woke at 1 and never got to sleep again. But I came to the conclusion you were right, and at the Cabinet, when P.M. asked me to lead off, I plumped for refusal of Hitler's terms.' He *is* a frank and brave man. I apologised. He asked me whether I *knew* I was giving him an awful night. I said 'Yes' but had slept very well myself. Seems Cabinet anyhow wouldn't allow P.M. to make any further concessions (and I'm sure country wouldn't). We now have to look forward to frightful ordeal, but we face it with clean hands. I'm *relieved.* French arrived for discussion at 9 p.m. We agreed that we can't accept Hitler's proposals. J.S. was turned on in his best manner, to cross-examine French as to what they would *do*. Awful. But French kept their tempers and they agreed to send for Gamelin. Cabinet about 11.30. Short meeting with French again. Home about 1.30. Record of 3 Cabinets in one day!

[At the Cabinet these notes were exchanged between the Prime Minister and the Foreign Secretary:

Your complete change of view since I saw you last night is a horrible blow to me, but of course you must form your opinions for yourself.

It remains however to see what the French say.

If they say they will go in, thereby dragging us in, I do not think I could accept responsibility for the decision.

But I don't want to anticipate what has not yet arisen.

N.C.

I feel a brute—but I lay awake most of the night, tormenting myself and did not feel I could reach any other conclusion at this moment, on the point of coercing Cz[echoslovakia].

E.

* Armindo Monteiro, formerly Portuguese Foreign Minister, now Ambassador in London.

Night conclusions are seldom taken in the right perspective.

N.C.

Cadogan hesitated before allowing Halifax's biographer to use this story, fearing that it might detract from the credit due to Halifax: 'But after all it does show that it *was* Edward who had the courage to make the decision. It was quite easy for me to do the little that I did. And any understanding reader would of course realise that.'[14]]

Monday, 26 September

Meeting with French at 10, put off to 10.30. Began with private talk P.M., Daladier, Corbin (then Gamelin*). Told French of our new—and further—undertaking to be with them at once if they are 'engaged in active hostilities' as result of German invasion of Cz-[echoslovakia]. Full meeting with French about 11. Told them of P.M.'s last message to Hitler being sent by H. Wilson. Told them it hinted at no further concessions but merely appealed for negotiation as against violence. Concocted with French message of warning to Warsaw about Teschen.† French left.

[On that afternoon the Foreign Office put out a communiqué:

> The German claim to the transfer of the Sudeten areas has already been conceded by the French, British and Czechoslovak Governments, but if in spite of all the efforts made by the British Prime Minister a German attack is made upon Czechoslovakia the immediate result must be that France will be bound to come to her assistance, and Great Britain and Russia will certainly stand by France.

At 4.10 p.m. on 16 September Chamberlain sent a message by telephone to Wilson in Berlin:

> Since you left, French have definitely stated their intention of supporting Czechoslovakia by offensive measures if latter is attacked. This would bring us in: and it should be made plain to Chancellor that this is inevitable alternative to a peaceful solution.

Hitler told Sir Horace Wilson that the Czechs must fall in by 2 p.m. on 28 September. 'Come what might, by negotiation or by force, Sudeten German territory would be in German military occupation on 1 October.[15]]

Tuesday, 27 September

Students of history may be puzzled by recent events. (a) (see yesterday) Gamelin seems to have put heart in to P.M., so we

* Gen. Maurice Gamelin, Chief of the French General Staff. See List of Principal Characters.

† Taken from Czechoslovakia by Poland after the Munich settlement.

declared 'solidarity with France' in event of her being engaged in 'active hostilities'. Cross-examination of Gamelin showed that 'active hostilities' probably meant a squib offensive (to bring us in) and then retirement on Maginot Line to wait (6 months) for our 'Kitchener armies'! This didn't suit at all, so John S. took up his pen and drafted telegram to Paris emphasising that we must 'fully concert' beforehand any offensive action!

Frightful afternoon—the worst I have spent. Was sent for to No. 10 about 3. Small meeting of Ministers, frightened out of their wits by Gamelin's conversation, by a telegram from Phipps about French feeling, and by Malcolm M[acdonald] (and Bruce*) on subject of Dominions. P.M. came in and out. Unfortunately Mason Macfarlane (M[ilitary] A[ttaché] in Berlin†) also here, and he painted gloomy picture of Czech morale. What does he know about it? Also meeting with Chiefs of Staff who were called in. Not very reassuring. But P.M. authorised Backhouse to mobilise Fleet. But all this produced a glacial period in Ministerial feet. But I got H's authority to send off telegrams proposing my 'timetable'. P.M. due to broadcast at 8. We were turned out of Cabinet room at 7.30 by electricians rigging microphone. P.M., Horace, H. and I adjourned to Horace's room. Horace had drafted telegram of complete capitulation—telling Czechs to accept Hitler memo. H. played up against it, and I spoke my mind. Poor P.M. (quite exhausted) said 'I'm wobbling about all over the place' and went in to broadcast. Back at F.O. after dinner as usual—I never get away before midnight.

[In his broadcast, presumably made with scant preparation, Chamberlain spoke of receiving countless letters of anxiety at the thought of war, of relief when the writers thought the dangers past:

> If I felt my responsibility heavy before, to read such letters has made it seem almost overwhelming. How horrible, fantastic, incredible it is that we should be digging trenches and trying on gas-masks here because of a quarrel in a far-away country between people of whom we know nothing. It seems still more impossible that a quarrel which has already been settled in principle should be the subject of war. . . .
>
> However much we may sympathise with a small nation confronted by a big powerful neighbour, we cannot in all circumstances undertake to involve the whole British Empire in war simply on her account. If we have to fight it must be on larger issues than that. I am myself a man of peace to the depths of my soul. Armed conflict between nations is a nightmare to me; but if I were convinced that any nation had made up

* Stanley Bruce, Australian High Commissioner, 1933–45.

† Col. (later Lieut.-Gen. Sir) F. N. Mason-Macfarlane.

> its mind to dominate the world by fear of its force, I should feel that it must be resisted. Under such a domination life for people who believe in liberty would not be worth living; but war is a fearful thing, and we must be very clear, before we embark on it, that it is really the great issues that are at stake, and that the call to risk everything in their defence, when all the consequences are weighed, is irresistible.[16]

The Chiefs of Staff at that afternoon's meeting no doubt took the line which they expressed formally a few days later. They had to reckon with the possibilities of Italian belligerency or glowering neutrality, and of Japanese hostility. Germany would be superior on land and in the air and even while attacking Czechoslovakia could man the western fortifications sufficiently to make a French land offensive costly and probably ineffective:

> It is our opinion that no pressure that Great Britain and France can bring to bear, either by sea, on land, or in the air, could prevent Germany from overrunning Bohemia and from inflicting a decisive defeat on Czechoslovakia. The restoration of Czechoslovakia's lost integrity could only be achieved by the defeat of Germany and as the outcome of a prolonged struggle, which from the outset must assume the character of an unlimited war.

The intervention of Italy or Japan, or of both, would create a situation which the Chiefs of Staff had earlier described:

> War against Japan, Germany and Italy simultaneously in 1938 is a commitment which neither the present nor the projected strength of our defence forces is designed to meet, even if we were in alliance with France and Russia, and which would, therefore, place a dangerous strain on the resources of the Empire. . . .[17]

At the end of the discussion, Chamberlain asked Sir Roger Backhouse whether he was satisfied that all necessary measures had been taken. Backhouse said that they had, though he would like to take further steps. Was the Prime Minister prepared to mobilise? Chamberlain hesitated for a few moments, then looked at Backhouse and nodded. Backhouse gathered up his papers and rushed off to the Admiralty. After the meeting, while Cadogan was still working on some papers in the Cabinet room, Sir Horace Wilson looked in. 'Do you realise' he asked, 'that we have not told Duff the Fleet is to be mobilised?' Cadogan confessed that he had not thought of this, though the First Lord had probably heard of it by then from Backhouse.[18]

Meanwhile, Sir H. Wilson had seen Hitler on the previous evening, but found him so impatient in temper and exalted in mood (Sir Horace's report speaks of 'insane interruptions') that he did not deliver the message until the morning of 27 September; whereupon Hitler said that 'What it boiled down to was that if France elected to attack Germany, Great Britain was under an obligation to attack Germany also. He could only take note of this communication.'

Wilson repeated the message slowly. Hitler thereupon repeated his interpretation. He would 'smash Czechoslovakia' if his memorandum were not accepted. He had prepared for all emergencies. Not for nothing had he spent 4½ billion marks on fortifications in the West.[19]

Nevertheless, at 10.30 p.m. on the same evening, 27 September, Chamberlain received from Hitler a letter indicating that German troops would not move beyond the territory which Czechoslovakia had already agreed to cede, that the plebiscite would be carried out by free vote and that Germany would join an international guarantee of Czechoslovakia. Thereupon Chamberlain, telegraphing to Hitler 'I feel certain that you can get all essentials without war and without delay', offered to visit Germany for the third time; Mussolini was asked to press for a peaceful settlement.

The news that the Fleet had been mobilised was not made known until late that night, well after Hitler's letter had been received, and cannot therefore have been the cause of his partial change of front. More probably the message delivered by Wilson, and the previous afternoon's communiqué, had given him pause.]

Wednesday, 28 September

4 a.m. this morning Roosevelt and another broadcast proposing Conference. 11.30 P.M. sent telephone messages to Hitler and Musso saying he ready to go to Germany again. About 2.30, while I was listening to T. Inskip holding forth to H. on insufficiency of our defences, telegram brought in from Rome saying Musso had got 24 hour postponement of German mobilisation (due 2 p.m. today). H. went off to House to hear P.M. 3.30 N. Henderson rang me to say Hitler invited P.M., Musso (accepted) and Daladier to Munich tomorrow. Dictated message and ran with it to House. Fished H. out of Peers' Gallery and we went along to behind Speaker's Chair and sent it in to P.M., who was still speaking. He used it as peroration —with tremendous effect and House adjourned—Thank God!

[This account disposes of the tale that the receipt by Chamberlain of the invitation to Munich had been stage-managed.

On this day Cordell Hull* told Sir Ronald Lindsay that should war break out the U.S. Government would not try to supplant British trade. 'The Ambassador', says Hull's record, 'seemed very much moved by this statement and expressed his deep satisfaction.'[20]]

* U.S. Secretary of State. See List of Principal Characters.

Thursday, 29 September

T[heo], G* and I picked up H. at 7.30. Drove down to Heston, and saw P.M. off. Drizzly morning, but a good show. Easy day—the calm in the middle of the typhoon! Joe Kennedy called for a chat. He says he'll tell P.M. I'm the man for Washington!... Quiet dinner and home—first time for *days*. Not much news from Munich, except that conversations 'very friendly', being renewed at 10 tonight. Poor P.M. must be half dead!

[The Munich agreement, signed by the four powers in the early hours of 30 September, undertook that the Czech evacuation of Sudeten German territory would begin on 1 October and end by the 10th; conditions governing this evacuation would be settled by an international commission, which would also determine in which territories plebiscites were to be held. There would be a right of option, available for six months, into and out of the transferred territories.

In a separate declaration, Hitler and Chamberlain recognised this agreement, and the naval treaty of 1935 as

> symbolic of the desire of our two peoples never to go to war with one another again.
>
> We are resolved that the method of consultation shall be the method adopted to deal with any other questions that may concern our two countries, and we are determined to continue our efforts to remove possible sources of difference and thus to contribute to assure the peace of Europe.

Friday, 30 September

'Times' this morning publishes the Munich Agreement. Looks to me quite good—not too unlike our 'Timetable'. Walked as usual to F.O. with H. Telegram from Munich confirming 'Times' text. Munich came through on telephone and gave us details of the 'Zones', which are *far* better than I expected. Home to Lunch. Maisky† came at 3.30, disgruntled and complaining. I explained the 'Zones' to him, which took some of the wind out of his sails. 4.40 took H. in my car, picked up Lady H. at 44, Eaton Square and started off for Heston [Aerodrome]. Awful crowd on the road, but luckily H. had brought his police pass. At one time, on Great West Road, I got on the wrong side of it and drove hard into a blinding rain storm. About ¼ mile short of Heston, heard the roar of a plane, couldn't believe it was the P.M.'s: it was then only about 5.30, but

* The Cadogans' daughter Gillian.

† Ivan Maisky, Russian Ambassador in London, 1932–43. See List of Principal Characters.

sprinted on the chance. Crashed through crowd at gates, brandishing the police pass, and constables opened up the crowd and let us right on to the concrete where we arrived as the pilot switched off and the P.M. stepped out. He shook hands first with Clarendon,* who brought summons from the King, then with H. and me. He broadcast a speech and got away fairly quickly. Rain began again as he finished. I got him to take H. in his car. He drove straight to Palace, history of which is as follows. In Eaton Square this morning I met Arthur Grenfell (whom I don't know), who congratulated me and said he had just left a note on H. suggesting King should go to Heston. I expressed doubt. Talked to H. and Lady H. about it and said I thought better P.M. should go straight to Palace. J.S. came into F.O. about 11. He had audience fixed with King for 12 and we suggested he should put this to H.M.

Took over an hour driving Lady H. back—awful crowd. Got to F.O. about 7.15. . . . Terrific demonstration in Downing Street. P.M. made speech from window. Last speech I heard from there—perhaps last speech made there—was Ll[oyd] G[eorge] on Armistice Day! Dined at home. Rumours of German violation of frontier—denied before coffee.

[This was the occasion when Chamberlain spoke of 'peace with honour' and 'peace in our time'.]

Saturday, 1 October

Corbin fussing about Polish ultimatum to Czecho[slovakia demanding Teschen]. Went over with H. to see P.M. with a draft message from himself to that brute Beck.† (P.M. looks v. well and cheerful). Then to a meeting with J.S., Strang, Horace Wilson and, later Gort,‡ to discuss arrangements for plebiscites, &c. . . . Nothing going badly wrong at present. Czechs and Germans don't want *troops*, but British Legion. This will be difficult. . . . Winston, G. Lloyd§ and others are intriguing with Masaryk and Maisky. But I don't feel suitably frightened. Duff Cooper resigned. Good riddance of bad rubbish.

[On 26 September, Hitler had told Sir Horace Wilson that telephone calls between Jan Masaryk and London and Beneš in Prague had been

* Earl of Clarendon, Lord Chamberlain, 1938–52.
† Col. Josef Beck, Polish Foreign Minister, 1932–9.
‡ Gen. Lord Gort, C.I.G.S., 1937–9.
§ First Lord Lloyd, Chairman, British Council, 1937–40; Colonial Secretary, 1940–1.

intercepted by the Germans. Later that evening, Goering read to Henderson extracts from these supposed intercepts, in which Masaryk was alleged to have said that he was working to overthrow Chamberlain's Government. This accusation came to the notice of Masaryk, who described it (28 September) as 'absolutely and utterly untrue'. The Germans supplied copies of the intercepts. Whether they were forged, or half-forged, is now impossible to determine. Doubtless Cadogan had his own sources of information. It is said that when Masaryk rang him up to protest against this rumour, Cadogan replied 'From one friend to another, Jan, be careful.'[21]]

Sunday, 2 October

Talked to Gwatkin and Strang, and we went on to meeting with J.S. and C.I.G.S. Joined by H. Discussed German-Czech demand for British Legion instead of troops, and agreed to telegraph arguments in favour of latter. Then discussed financial aid to Czecho-[slovakia]. Lunched at home. 2–3 wrote peroration for H. tomorrow.

Monday, 3 October

Debate today in both Houses. Finished off H's speech. Lunched at home. Went to H[ouse] of C[ommons] at 2.45 and sat through Duff (not very convincing), P.M. (quite good) and Attlee (not bad).* Then Sam Hoare, who had got to reply, hawked me out and he, Malkin, Strang and I worked up various points for him. Slipped home to a hurried dinner at 8. Back at 9, for further talk with Sam H[oare]. Went into House about 9.30 for Dalton's† speech. Extremely good and telling. Of course it's always easier to criticise, but it seems to be Government are getting rather knocked about in this Debate. Sam H., who seems to have a bad cold coming on, was too bad for words. Went home—at 11—depressed.

Tuesday, 4 October

Went over to Horace W. at 11.30. Long talk with him about prospects. Mustn't let this drop. I've seen so many failures by letting initiatives cool off. But of course everyone—including P.M.—is exhausted! Pray God I may have strength and guidance to suggest something. Talked to him about Press Department. R. Leeper must, I fear, go. Down to H[ouse] of L[ords] in afternoon to talk to H. Had good talk with George Mounsey about Van. G.M. had written

* C. R. Attlee, Leader of the Parliamentary Labour Party since 1935. See List of Principal Characters.

† Dr Hugh Dalton, Parliamentary Under-Sec., F.O., 1929–31. See List of Principal Characters.

me a rather cryptic paper, meant to voice discontent in F.O. about Van. Horace W. had told me this morning that this question would be finally tackled on P.M.'s return. I hope it will be! Down to House again at 7 to see Inskip about his speech, and was caught also by H. Jan Masaryk called about a particular point concerning the frontier. I said a word to him about my feelings, which I hope he appreciated.

[Mounsey's letter referred to a statement by Harold Nicolson to the effect that the Government had been guided by the advice of Horace Wilson, which was never inconvenient, rather than by that of Vansittart, which was always right but which the Government found inconvenient.

'If there is truth in the statement,' wrote Mounsey, who was evidently not alone in believing that Vansittart had been chattering too freely,

> the traditional discretion and reserve of members of this office should at least have safeguarded us from its public announcement in this fashion. The first duty of the F.O. is no doubt to advise the Government. Its second, but equally important, duty is to carry out the Govt.'s policy, whether it likes it or not. If it is true that in this case the F.O. conveyed its advice in such a way and with such effect that the Govt. could not trust it to carry out their policy but had to seek this service elsewhere, the inevitable result must be the immense weakening of the position of the F.O. among other Govt. Departments here and great loss of prestige with foreign countries. . . .
>
> To those of us here, and there are others beside myself, who feel convinced that the policy of the Govt. is the right one, it is very disquieting to read such a statement of the case; it is still more deplorable to feel that the reputation so long enjoyed by the F.O. for loyalty, self-discipline, and efficiency should be placed at the mercy of the self-advertising publicity campaign of a mischief-minded M.P.

Ciano told Perth on the evening of 3 October that Italy had decided to withdraw 10,000 men or more from Spain. He asked that the Anglo-Italian agreement should be put into effect at once. If not it would 'lose its interest for Italy'. Decisions, he said, had to be taken at the Fascist Grand Council, 6–9 October. Perth telegraphed: 'I feel that we have come to the parting of the ways'. Halifax replied on the evening of 5 October that he and the Prime Minister favoured early action but could not act so quickly. Parliament was about to adjourn and could not debate the issue until November, when there would still be considerable difficulties. It would help greatly if Italy could reduce her air forces in Spain.

The Cabinet decided on 26 October to bring the agreement into force without this latter assurance. France had already, on 4 October, recognised the Italian conquest of Ethiopia.[22]]

Wednesday, 5 October

A hourouche before lunch, when it appeared International

Commission had got into deadlock over percentage and census. We have to give way (because it was given away at Munich). Van in a splutter, and got H. to agree to tell N.H. to stick up for something we can't get. And of course we didn't. Went with H. to see P.M. about telegram to Rome on Anglo-Italian agreement. We can't be blackmailed in a hurry by Musso. P.M. can't tackle it till Parliament meets again in November. . . .

Went down to House to see H. and fix up final terms of telegram to Rome. (He had been canvassing it round the 'Dissidents'—Oliver [Stanley], W. Elliot* and Co.). Got it off.

Thursday, 6 October

Ronnie Campbell† arrived from Belgrade with strange story showing that Italians have access to all our documents here. Luckily there is a clue and I put it into the Admiral's [Sinclair's] hands, and we have laid plans! . . . Roumanian at 4.15, fussed—as well he may be—at Hungarians threatening to claim line which joins Czechoslovakia (Skoda works!) with Roumania. Asked him whether his Government were doing anything about it—after all, they ought, with fellow-members of Little Entente—to keep Hungary in order. But he shrugged his shoulders. Corbin at 5 to ask about our conversations with Ciano. Told him some, but as little as might be. Also told him about P.M.'s talk with Hitler. Dined at home—quieter. Parliament adjourned, thank God! H. said P.M. was very good. Stanhope yesterday in H[ouse] of L[ords] revealed that the 'Munich Timetable' was ours—mine!

Friday, 7 October

Italians have taken our reply about Anglo-Italian agreement pretty well, but it is clear our telegram was ambiguous, and they have taken the more favourable reading. Sent paper to H. asking whether we should leave them under this illusion or correct it. Home about 7.45—quite comfortable—and dined there. Thank God for a slight pause!

Sunday, 9 October

Read a bit and then tried my hand at a skeleton draft of a paper on future policy. But it's very difficult, as I don't know what it's to *be*. I only know the one we have followed is *wrong*.

* Walter Elliot, Secretary of State for Scotland, 1936–8; Minister of Health, 1938–40.

† R. H. Campbell, Minister at Belgrade, 1935–9. Not to be confused with R. I. Campbell.

Monday, 10 October

Corbin came at 4 to pump me more about Rome conversations. Was pretty frank with him, and asked him awkward questions about French recognition of Abyssinia. Talk with H. and Plymouth about Spain—interrupted by J.S. Feel now rather slack and relaxed—the result of the easing of the strain.

Tuesday, 11 October

Nasty telegram from Berlin tonight, showing that that viper Rib[bentrop] will probably ask for plebiscite *outside* the German occupied areas. He may offer compensatory plebiscites *inside*, but what are they worth? It would be a case of 'heads I win, tails you lose'.

Wednesday, 12 October

Heard from Berlin decision regarding plebiscite put off. But I fear it will come up and prove a snag.

Thursday, 13 October

After lunch got H. to approve telegram to N.H. stiffening him against plebiscites. (Luckily heard later—about 7—that plebiscites are decided against). . . . H. called me in this morning to consultation with Tom Inskip, and we demobilised the Fleet, Heaven help us!

Friday, 14 October

Eric Phipps looked in. He not very enlightening. . . . Message from Musso proposing conference early next week at Venice or Brioni on Hungarian-Czech affair. This necessitated messages to P.M., Berlin, Paris, Prague. Dictated drafts and got them approved. . . . After dinner, hear from G. Jebb that [Guido] Crolla says 'Hungarian request for Conference withdrawn' (the Hungarians never made it!) and therefore his démarche superseded.

Rang up P.M. in north of Scotland and told him. Rang up H. Bob Cecil* rang me about rumoured Czech intention to send back into Germany tomorrow 100 Sudeten German refugees. Rang up Strang and then F.O. and sent telegram to Prague instructing Newton to stop this if he possibly could. Rather a disturbed evening! And at 11.45 Walter Layton rang me up again about German refugees in Czechoslovakia, and I had to send a further telegram. Hope it may help them!

* Viscount Cecil of Chelwood.

[In mid-October, Cadogan attempted his first review of the crisis. He began from the premise, no doubt based upon constant reading of Intelligence reports, estimates by the Service attachés and reviews by the Chiefs of Staff, that Britain and France stood in a condition of 'dangerous inferiority to Germany in military strength'. Since that fact made it difficult to have a foreign policy, the Western Powers must increase their strength relative to that of Germany:

> There are many hard facts to be faced, and one is that in present conditions we alone cannot hope to equal Germany's military effort. (It seems doubtful whether we and France by our combined efforts could do more than attain something like equality with Germany.)
>
> It is not a question of this country being unwilling to make the sacrifices required; it is not a question of the difference between a totalitarian and a democratic State. The point is that Germany is far more nearly self-sufficient than these islands can ever hope to be and, with her closed economy, can concentrate the greater part of her industry on the production of engines of war. We have to import the greater part of our food, and consequently to maintain the value of the £ on the foreign exchanges. It is vital to us, therefore, to maintain our ordinary export trade. . . .
>
> But if we cannot compete with Germany in potentially aggressive armaments, we can and must at least put our defences in order. This again is a matter for experts, but it would seem to the layman that the essentials are the Fleet, the Air Arm and A.A. Defences. There is a great deal to be done, particularly as regards the last two, before our diplomacy can become effective again.
>
> And as regards defence, there is another point. We have inherited responsibilities all over the world, which have become more onerous with the rise to power of other nations such as Japan. In the Far East, we have British interests in China to defend. They are considerable, and are concentrated mainly in the hands of a not very numerous body of British individuals and concerns. It might not be intrinsically vital to protect them, though it might be important from the point of view of our prestige in Asia generally. What involves us vitally in the Far East is the necessity of protecting Australia and New Zealand against possible attack by Japan. These Dominions make some contribution towards their own defence, but it is very much to be hoped that, with the growth of population and of wealth they may find it possible to take a rather larger share, and to that extent leave us with a freer hand to deal with menace nearer home. . . .
>
> If we now make a great effort to put our defences in order, Herr Hitler will probably simulate indignation. He will say that all our talk of better Anglo-German relations resolves itself into a race in armaments. He is in fact already doing so, through his press. The retort is easy, viz. that our defenceless state left us practically helpless in the

recent crisis. That would be an unpleasant confession to make, but I do not believe it would necessarily be dangerous to make it. The Germans must know the details of our weakness, as well as we know most of the details of their strength. The people who are ignorant are the people of this country, and it would probably require enlightenment to spur them to the great effort that is needed of them. . . .

Rearmament is a vitally necessary first step. It is an essential insurance, but it is not a policy.

What can we have in mind as a reasonable and hopeful line of policy for such time as we may be strong enough to carry it out?

What follows is based on the assumption that there will be no sensational change in Europe, that Germany will continue on her present course, that there will be no collapse in Italy, that Russia will continue as aloof and unhelpful as she is now. (I should like to assume that conditions in France will not deteriorate, but that she will pull herself together and put her house in order.)

In the first place, we must, so long as these conditions last, give up any idea of policing Europe such as has come down to us from Versailles and the Covenant of the League. We simply cannot protect our own interests all over the world and at the same time claim a preponderant voice in the ordering of affairs in continental Europe.

For some time to come, we must be on the defensive. That involves the maintenance of the closest relations with France, dictated by the necessity of denying the channel ports to Germany. If we have need of France's friendship and support, she equally has need of ours, and there is no reason why France (a very uncertain guide) should dictate the foreign policy of the partnership. She has led us down the wrong path before now but perhaps, with the loss of her dominant military position on the continent, she may be expected to be more amenable.

The Iberian Peninsula is of great importance both to France and ourselves, and our object should be to strengthen our ties with Portugal, and to do our best to contrive that an independent and not unfriendly Spain should emerge out of the present welter.

The Mediterranean area is a direct interest of ours, being the highway to our eastern possessions and Dominions, and we should do everything we can to maintain the best relations with, and give such assistance as may be possible to, Turkey and Greece. It follows, of course that we should spare no reasonable effort to resume our former friendly relations with Italy. Of this there may be some prospect with rearmament in this country (and in France) and with the growth of the German menace which must cause misgivings to Signor Mussolini.

That is not to say that we are to abdicate from such positions as we have been able to create for ourselves in eastern and south-eastern Europe. . . . But any deliberate, uneconomic, 'encirclement' of Germany appears to me to be a mistake, and probably a costly one. When States like Turkey (and it may be Greece, Roumania and Yugoslavia) wish to be saved from being sucked into the German orbit, and when they can offer sound business, it would seem important to take advantage of the offer, and make every effort to turn it to good account.

German economic preponderance in certain countries of central and eastern Europe is bound to develop, provided the German economic and financial structure can stand the strain. It will be a fact to be reckoned with, like the rise of Japan, and it is very doubtful whether, with all our other commitments, we shall be strong enough to withstand it.

As an ignorant layman, I wonder whether we should try to withstand it.

I confess I am not expert in economics and am ready to admit that I may misunderstand the problem.

Which appears to me to be this: Germany has established an exchange control, which means that the mark hides behind a Maginot line. If the market were to be thrown open, the mark would undergo a serious devaluation. It is kept up by purely artificial means—by refusing to allow it to go upon the market for what it will fetch. Inside Germany it has a value. The German munitions worker is given a piece of paper which enables him to obtain goods of the baker, who in turn can pay his rent, and his internal commitments with it. That piece of paper would buy very little abroad. Germany has to import certain materials for her munitions manufacture, and she does this by taking from exporters (such as they are) such foreign exchange as they earn, and compensating them with the bits of paper that the baker accepts. With that foreign exchange she buys tropical and other products which do not exist in Germany, and for which she cannot find adequate substitutes.

With her neighbours, who produce what she wants, and who want some of the things she produces, she has elaborated clearing up or barter systems. She takes food and raw materials from Hungary, Yugoslavia and Roumania, for which she pays in goods (generally, now, munitions). These countries are bound to fall in with this plan, because Germany is their natural market for their food or raw materials, and they cannot find a better market elsewhere, and they can only get payment in kind from Germany.

This system, if developed, will enlarge the German economic sphere and develop and complete her 'autarky'. Some prophets of evil see the German system spreading and ousting us from the markets of the world. But is that development to be apprehended? It is understandable that, for instance, Roumania may be caught in her grip by the necessity of finding a market for her wheat (? and her oil). Germany's oil consumption may be almost unlimited. But her wheat consumption cannot be. She could not consume, in addition to the wheat of south-eastern Europe, the wheat of the Argentine and other parts of the world, and it is difficult to see why or how these countries whose products cannot be taken by Germany should be caught in the toils of German 'autarky'.

She cannot eat her way into markets whose produce she cannot assimilate.

Germany as an 'autarkic' Power looks pretty formidable—almost as formidable as the British Empire might be. But is there not a limit to 'autarky' and must not Germany re-enter the field of foreign trade and exchange if she is to progress beyond certain more or less narrow limits? Is it a bad thing that Germany should be a powerful economic unit? Of course if our traders and exporters cannot compete with their German rivals, the outlook is bad. But we may have faith that they can, and on that assumption will not an economically powerful Germany increase the general volume of trade, out of which we may expect to get certain pickings, at least? But how to switch Germany over from her closed-economy, autarkic system to a system of free exchange and trade? That is a problem of experts, far beyond my ken.

The moral seems to be:—

(1) The League system, and 'collective security', are, if not dead, in a state of suspended animation:

(2) Far from ordering the affairs of Europe, we, and the French, are on the defensive:

(3) Let us make those defences good:

(4) We must try to maintain our influence in Western Europe and the Mediterranean:

(5) We must cut our losses in central and eastern Europe—let Germany, if she can, find there her 'lebensraum', and establish herself, if she can, as a powerful economic unit. I don't know that that necessarily worsens our commercial and economic outlook. I have never heard that Mr. Gordon Selfridge ruined Harrods. (Oddly enough, small shops flourish under the shadow of both of them.) I know that it is said that 'Mitteleuropa' will turn and rend us. But many things may happen before that.

We must, of course, keep such markets as we can, and we cannot forego the right to take advantage of any openings. But I believe that any deliberate, uneconomic 'encirclement' of Germany will be futile and ruinous.

(6) We must do everything possible to foster our trade with other parts of the world and with the Empire. We must do what we can to facilitate commercial exchange with the United States. Unfortunately, the Americans are the spiritual heirs of the Dutch, and open their mouths rather wide. The Trade Agreement with America would be worth considerable material concessions. Not only in the economic field, but politically in the Far East. The Americans may be backward in giving any promise of material assistance, and still more backward in implementing it, but the shadow of possible trouble with America has undoubtedly restrained Japan in recent times from doing as much damage as she would like to do to our interests in the Far East.

All this is rather negative-defensive.

Can we take any initiative? Can we make the Germans guess, and so reverse the process, under which we have suffered for years, of the Germans 'keeping us guessing'?

Hitler has got all that he said he wanted. That is quite different from Hitler saying that he has got all he wants, and that again would not mean that Hitler does not want a number of things that he does not happen yet to have mentioned. It is quite impossible to challenge Hitler to say what he *does* want? Is it too late—I suppose it is, because now we are relatively too weak—to admit that Versailles was a temporary, and very bad, expedient, and suggest a conference which should review the Peace settlement and put it right? I suggested that 2½ years ago, but it was considered too difficult, as it would reopen the questions, not only of the Treaty of Versailles, but also of the Treaties of St. Germain and the Trianon. The Treaty of St. Germain has now disappeared, lock, stock and barrel, and the Treaty of Trianon is being torn to bits by Poles and Hungarians.

I know it will be said that any such conference will be useless and probably dangerous: that Germany would put forward impossible demands. She probably would—probably five times what she would have put forward a year ago and a fifth of what she might demand next year. But would there not, even now, be an advantage in getting her to state her terms and obtaining some sort of (even temporary) fixation of them, rather than allow German aims to grow and grow with military strength? However, it is probably too late for that now, and we should look to our defences, to retain what we may and in the hope that all Hitler's grandiose plans may not work out quite so easily as he expects.[23]

This view seems to have coincided with that of Halifax. He told Ambassador Kennedy, for instance, that Hitler could proceed in Central Europe while England would seek her future in the Mediterranean, with the Dominions and in friendship with the U.S. This same conception of abandoning the European heartland in favour of holding the rimland appears more explicitly in a long letter from Halifax to Sir Eric Phipps of 1 November.[24]

In respect of the Far East, Cadogan minuted separately:

The fact is that we are faced, at the other side of the world, with a situation not unlike the one that confronts us here (though the structure of Japan is probably not so solid as that of Nazi Germany). And the problem, fundamentally, is the same: are we to fight Japan now, and prevent her possible accession of strength, or wait for a possible war later?

Can we, and should we try to, confine and restrain even the economic expansion of Japanese millions? If Japan had adopted different methods in China, we might have seen a real Sino-Japanese cooperation that might have absorbed Japan's energies at least for a considerable time and diverted them from regions where they would prove a more direct menace to ourselves.

It is as difficult to find the answer to the Far Eastern problem as it is to the European one.[25]]

Saturday, 15 October

More fuss about refugees. Not too much work. Gave H. my reflections on future policy, and some stuff on rearmament for his Edinburgh speech. Told him I was going to take afternoon off—he coming back to work, but that's all right for him if he's had a day's hunting with the Heythrop. Lunched here and T. and I motored to Denham. Lovely calm day—a bit of sun and mild. Played 18 holes.

Monday, 17 October

Hungarian at 12.15, with a map, to show me what his beastly Govt. are claiming of Czechs. Not so bad as I thought—I suppose Berlin are putting the brake on! George Lloyd at 6.30 about Roumania. Says we *must at once* buy 600,000 tons of Roumanian wheat. But we don't want the damned stuff—and the question is are we going to declare economic war on Germany? (No one can pretend that it is a commercial proposition.)

Tuesday, 18 October

Picked up H. as usual in morning. Fine and warm. Told him about my misgivings about Roumanian wheat &c. We must settle first in principle what we want to do. . . . Talk with H. and Maurice I[ngram] about Anglo-Italian situation. Then concocted with H. what he should say to Cabinet tomorrow. Polished off work and home to quiet dinner. Afraid invitations are beginning to come in, and I shall be subjected to that awful corvée of over-long meals making conversation to people (at the top of my voice) whom I don't want to meet.

Wednesday, 19 October

Walked to F.O. without H. Lovely morning but rather windy. Cabinet all morning. Drove with H. to lunch at 88 Eaton Square. He had had talk with P.M. but can't make out that he'd got much of a line from him. He won't 'broaden basis' of Cabinet, and indeed I don't know how he could. He is apparently thinking of a Ministry of National Defence—a very good thing.

Thursday, 20 October

11 Nevile H., who said he was exhausted—as he should be—but

didn't look so. He rather annoyed that we hadn't expressed our thanks to him and Embassy! I know—but no thanks have been handed round to anyone so far as *I* know! He told me privately (and I quite approved!) that he had put Goering up to objecting to our guarantee of Czecho[slovakia].

Monday, 24 October

Committee on Palestine at 3.—P.M., J.S., Malcolm M., Zetland,* Sam Hoare and Walter Elliot. Decided partition was dead and best procedure to call Arabs and Jews into conference in London? Jan[uary].

Tuesday, 25 October

Long chat with H. about future policy, &c. He told me Hailsham† resigns [as Lord President], and Runciman‡ comes in. Stanhope to Admiralty. [Earl]De La Warr takes his place§: Herbert Samuel‖ to be asked to come in. Malcolm M[acDonald] to retain Dominions¶ as well as Colonies for the present.

Monday, 31 October

As usual, after a short holiday, a pretty awful day trying to catch up. Had a talk with H. this morning about future policy. Gather P.M. wants to 'follow up Munich', but I don't know that his ideas are more definite than that. But of course it means that we have to produce yet another 'paper'. Spoke to poor W. Strang about it tonight. . . . Jebb says gossip is that P.M. is angry with me for swinging H. against Godesberg terms and wants to send me abroad! I'll go nowhere except to Washington! I'll resign rather than anything else—and they'll have to accept my resignation. But I don't believe the story.

Wednesday, 2 November

Still overwhelmed with arrears of work. Dined at home and got through some of it. Long and frank talk with H.J.W. this morning. I shd. *say* this discounts story of Oct. 31.

[By the Vienna Award of 2 November, Hungary gained territory at the

* Marquess of Zetland, Secretary of State for India, 1935–40.
† 1st Viscount Hailsham.
‡ 1st Viscount Runciman.
§ As President of the Board of Education.
‖ 1st Viscount Samuel.
¶ The Dominions Secretary, Lord Stanley, had just died.

expense of Czechoslovakia. As both powers had requested the arbitration of Germany and Italy, rather than Britain and France, Cadogan thought it futile to protest.]

Monday, 7 November

I am still trying to write—in intervals of interruption—a paper on policy. But everyone has weighed in with bright, or dark ideas and I am getting more and more muddled. Only thing to do is to go ahead on my line of a frank challenge to Germany to state her grievances. I *know* that there are arguments against this, but I feel it's right and I can think of nothing better. Nor can I see that anyone has suggested anything better. The only alternatives are (a) fight Germany (b) continue to do nothing. The former, I suspect, would lead to disaster, the latter has proved to lead nowhere else.

[In this paper, Cadogan again assessed the results of Munich. On the debit side Hitler was said to have brought off a bluff:

> This is not entirely true. It is not, in poker parlance, a bluff to bid high on four aces, which he held in his hand. What he did for the first time on a large scale was to resort to power-politics. For this he had the strength in his hand and we have to recognise that that, after five years of Nazi rule, is the situation. In any case his success in getting all and more than he was entitled to, without shedding a drop of German blood, may have reinforced his position in Germany.

On the other hand, Cadogan went on, war had been avoided 'at the moment when we were least prepared for it' and the German people realised how nearly Hitler had led them into an unnecessary war, a fact which might have 'shaken their belief in his leadership'. Some might count it a further advantage

> that we have learnt that we cannot any longer aspire to police Europe as we did in the post-Versailles-Covenant era, or join in crusades where our direct interests are not threatened.
>
> We are back in the old lawless Europe and have got to look out for ourselves. It is not always profitable to look too much at the mistakes of the past, but surely our great mistake has been to act too long on the belief that the Versailles settlement could be maintained. And yet, if that really was our policy, we ought to have reacted against the occupation of the Rhineland, when we could have done so effectively. We did not and the policy is now out of date.

In the rest of his paper Cadogan reverted to a familiar theme; Germany should be challenged to state her grievances. Her only remaining avowed aim was the retrocession of colonial territory, for which it would not be easy to find a *quid pro quo:*

> It is to be feared that Germany now will find some pretext for refusing consultation because she may think that she is strong enough to obtain by force what she requires.
>
> Even so, from the point of tactics alone, it seems right that we should propose . . . an examination of the difficulties, fears and suspicions that seem likely to make Europe shortly uninhabitable. There is then the hope that if we can show ourselves to the German Government (and through broadcasting to the German people) to be reasonable, Herr Hitler will not succeed in inducing his people to follow him into his wilder adventures.

Cadogan hoped that a four-power meeting might be summoned soon, even if there were not time for proper preparation. A meeting without concrete result might

> leave us in no worse a case than we are at present, awaiting the next German blow. Germany's great advantage has always been that she has chosen her own time, the initiative has been left to her. If we broach questions for which she is not ready we may at least dislocate her time-table and embarrass her. . . . If the German Government is, in effect, unwilling to embark on any useful negotiation, is there much harm in that being made apparent?

The purpose of a conference would be remedy of grievances, exchange of assurances and, in the end, a reduction of armaments; and the first step would be consultation with France.[26]]

Wednesday, 9 November

Finally finished off, and gave to H., paper on policy. Upshot is—my old King Charles' Head—ask Germans what they want: make them good offer (broadcast it to German people). That'll disincline German population from following Hitler into wilder adventures. . . . Left F.O. with H. at 5.15, dressed in uniform and got to Guildhall [for the Lord Mayor's Banquet] 6.20. Tiresome reception. P.M. had great ovation. . . . P.M. spoke for 45 mins. Moderate speech, v. well delivered. Crept away . . . soon after. Met H. in cloakroom. I said 'How the devil did you get here?' He, looking very sad, 'I got permission from a Shewiff'!

Friday, 11 November, Armistice Day

On Wednesday evening I saw poor Nevile H. who has what he told me frankly was a malignant growth under his tongue. He was being operated today. And then later they've got to do something to his neck. Sounds bad. I *am* sorry. . . . Packed H. off before lunch in rather a bad temper and with a *mass* of papers—some of them designed to elicit a decision as to our future policy, on which we *must* have some idea before we go to Paris. He asked me how to get rid of Van. I said that was hardly my job, but I'd think!

Sunday, 13 November

Dined at home and went and had good talk to H. after. Stoked him up about secret reports we have had all tending to show Hitler, Rib[bentrop] and Co., are 'exaltés'.

Monday, 14 November

5–6 talked to H. about his brief for Foreign Policy Committee on future of Anglo-German (and European) relations. Went with him at 5.50 to meeting in P.M.'s room of F.P.C. Quite a useful discussion. P.M. agrees only line of advance (beyond rearmament) is through Musso. But we can't tell for sure yet what prospect that holds out. Stayed behind with P.M. and H. to discuss prospects of Paris visit.

[Halifax gave the Committee a résumé of secret reports to the effect that the German Government, and especially Hitler, were becoming increasingly hostile to Britain; and that they intended the disintegration of the British Empire and if possible the domination of the world. In Germany, said the Foreign Secretary:

> Munich might be said to have had two diametrically opposite results. In the first place, the German people as a whole realised with horror that Hitler's policy had brought them to the verge of war and were profoundly grateful to the Prime Minister, both for having avoided war and for having assisted them to achieve what a number of them regarded as their legitimate aspirations. In the second place, this reaction in German public opinion had infuriated some of the highest Nazi leaders, not excluding Herr Hitler, and had resulted in a desire to re-establish Nazi prestige by depicting Great Britain as the enemy of the German people.

Chamberlain pointed out that these reports were by no means so precise as many received in the summer. 'There was no suggestion that Herr Hitler contemplated any immediate aggressive action.' The Prime Minister drew the moral that the Italian end of the Axis must be tackled.[27]]

Thursday, 17 November

Dinner to King of Roumania at F.O. . . . Had talk afterwards with [King] Carol, who was of course insistent on need for economic help *now*.

Tuesday, 22 November

Went to call on King George of Greece and had an hour with him.

He said the expected things and made the expected appeals for help, and I threw small douches of cold water.

Wednesday, 23 November *Paris*

Caught Golden Arrow at 11 with Chamberlain and Halifaxes. Also Strang, O. Harvey and Cleverly.* Awful crossing—gust of 100 m.p.h. at some points in England. But didn't feel uncomfortable. Spent some time on deck with H. Arrived Paris about 5.50—a bit late. Drove to Embassy. Large crowds and quite good reception (though the 'Times' says we were hooted!)

Thursday, 24 November *Paris*

Called to see H. about 9.30. Quai d'Orsay at 10. Talks went on till 12.30—and quite well. I think we and French see eye to eye, but the French give me the appearance of drifting. Daladier evidently drinks, and it has rotted him. A pity—he's a good man. Lunch at Elysée. . . . Talks again 2.45–6.30. Had some trouble about guarantee to Czecho[slovakia], but slid out of it. French renew the Delbos guarantee. We can say so, and they say they will.

[During these talks, Daladier remarked that German fortifications on France's north-eastern frontier were being constantly improved and extended. He looked for the closest collaboration with Britain in all matters of defence. When Chamberlain said that 'the present attitude of Germany had brought before His Majesty's Government the possibility of a quarrel between Great Britain and Germany rather than between France and Germany' Daladier at once offered a reaffirmation of France's will to support Britain in such circumstances. A long and unsatisfactory discussion took place about the guarantee offered to Czechoslovakia at Munich. Daladier's and Chamberlain's views differed markedly, the former saying that France had offered to guarantee the new frontier (which had turned out worse than that shown on the Godesberg map) in order to make Czech acceptance easier; while Chamberlain retorted that he had never conceived of a guarantee under which Britain might have to act alone. Both recognised that since the new Czechoslovakia was already within Germany's orbit the guarantee would not in practice operate.[28]

Towards the end of November, the Foreign Office heard that on 9 November Hitler had declared 'conditions were all against an Anglo-German understanding. If foreign powers would not meet German demands, then Germany would take for herself what she could not get by negotiation.' Ribbentrop was reported as saying at about the same date that if no agreement could be reached with England, Hitler was

* O. S. Cleverly, Principal Private Secretary to P.M., 1936–9.

'determined not to shrink from war in order to destroy her. Germany demands an unrestrained hand in the East, and will suffer no English interference in this sphere. . . . The colonial question is of secondary importance.'[29]

On 28 November an officer of the Intelligence service brought Cadogan material which seemed to show that someone at 10 Downing Street was in contact with Ribbentrop through Fritz Hesse, press adviser to the German Embassy in London. Cadogan decided that he must speak to Halifax. 'Don't want to,' says the diary, 'as he's getting rather fed up, and I don't want to give him reason for resigning. But we must stop this sort of thing.' Sir Alexander, guessing that Halifax would tackle Chamberlain, felt that if the Prime Minister had not inspired the approach he should know of it; if he had, he should know the twist which Hesse had given it (for example, saying to Ribbentrop that it proved Britain would give Germany everything she asked for in 1939).

Halifax spoke to Chamberlain on the evening of 29 November. 'He aghast (H. thinks genuinely)' Cadogan recorded that night, 'and wants to follow it up, but H., on my prompting, said I *must* have 24 hours' notice before he does (to save our source).' The diary, although it contains several further references to this episode, does not round it off. A member of the Prime Minister's staff was eventually warned by Sir Horace Wilson against indiscreet talk. Cadogan noted that 'this will put a brake on them all.']

Friday, 2 December

Corbin came and told me of representations his Government are making in Rome about this vulgar and impudent (organised) outburst in Italian Chamber about Tunis, Corsica and Nice. I sent account down to P.M. . . . Suggesting we should, as Corbin asked, also give the ice-creamers a crack on the head. Dined with Swedes for Crown Prince. . . . Had talk with C[rown] P[rince] who was disturbed (as I am) to find P.M. confident that Nazi regime is crumbling. Most dangerous: must counteract it: have already spoken to H.

Saturday, 3 December

P.M. approves representation to Italy, so got that off and told Corbin.

Tuesday, 6 December

12.30 went to see P.M. He told me [H. von] Dirksen has been sounding Runciman as to an agreement on *something*—? gas. I said that was rather ridiculous. We've signed innumerable gas protocols. We might say that was interesting but we must go further. P.M.

agreed. Got him to agree that, pending more about Schacht's* visit (of which he has heard nothing more) Gwatkin should be told to go easy about his talk with Goering.†

Thursday, 8 December

P.M. at House at 6.30. He wanted to talk to me about Greece. Rob Hudson‡ (who's an eel) had been talking to him about 'lack of co-ordination'. What's his job but to produce co-ordination? Had half an hour's talk on all sorts of subjects.

Saturday, December 10

Things still delightfully quiet, and I have worked off all arrears. Just before lunch, Gwatkin had a message from Goerdeler§ outlining plan of a (army) revolution in Germany, to take place before the end of the month. G[oerdeler] wants a 'message' from us. He had already sent us a 'programme', which we couldn't subscribe to—too much like 'Mein Kampf'—and that rather put me off him. But he *may* want something merely to show his fellow conspirators that we shan't fall upon a divided Germany, and would want to work with any decent regime that might come out of the mess. I drafted hurriedly the kind of message (very non-committal) that we might send him, and sent it up to H. I don't believe much in this, but if there *is* anything in it, it's the biggest thing of centuries.

T. and I motored to Eton. . . . What a delightful place Eton is. I feel to draw fresh inspiration from it whenever I go.

[Goerdeler's proposal was essentially this: Britain and France should suggest to Germany a negotiation for the settlement of outstanding issues, on the condition that the policy of violence, internal and external, should cease. If this note were rejected, Britain and France would break off diplomatic relations with Germany, in which event Dr Goerdeler undertook that appropriate action would begin in Germany to produce an administration prepared to talk on these terms.

Vansittart described Goerdeler as 'a stalking horse for Germany's *military* expansion'; a not unfair observation, as Cadogan's commentary on the programme indicates:

> We are asked to 'liquidate' the [Danzig] Corridor; to give Germany a block of colonial territory, to be administered 'according to the

* Hjalmar Schacht, President of the Reichsbank, 1923–30, 1933–8.

† A project suggested by Goering's friend Prince Max von Hohenlohe.

‡ R. S. Hudson, Secretary, Dept. of Overseas Trade, 1937–40; Minister of Agriculture and Fisheries, 1940–5.

§ Dr Karl Goerdeler, Mayor of Leipzig and a leader of German opposition to Hitler.

principles of International Law'; to give Germany an interest-free loan of £400 to £500 million.

In return we get a promise that Germany will return to a free exchange system; an assurance that Germany 'aims' at no hegemony in S.E. Europe; a German guarantee of the status quo in the Mediterranean; a German promise to co-operate in the Far East. . . . We are expected to deliver the goods and Germany gives us I.O.U.s.

I really don't think we can have anything to do with this.[30]]

Sunday, 11 December

I sent for 'C' to consult him about the G[oerdeler] story (see yesterday). He very sceptical. I think I am too, but don't like to ignore it altogether. . . . I went at 7 to see P.M. He would have none of it: and I think he's right. These people must do their own job.

Monday, 12 December

P.M. sent for me in morning and showed me parts of his speech to F[oreign] P[olicy] A[ssociation] on Tuesday. We toned down the passage about Rome visit. Instead of 'We are going to Rome', 'We have planned to go to Rome' &c. But he didn't give me the rest of it. Told me to write to Eric D[rummond, Lord Perth] to warn Italians that we may not bring off visit if they go on behaving like this. . . . Drafted letter and showed it to P.M. at the House in afternoon. He approved. . . . About 7 p.m. I asked for and got on loan, a copy of P.M.'s speech. Very feeble and bad.

[Cadogan's letter to Rome indicated that unless Italian manners towards Britain and France mended somewhat the visit would have to be cancelled. Demonstrations like the one recently organised, or at least allowed (when Ciano's speech in the Chamber had been interrupted by cries of 'Tunis, Jibuti, Corsica'), coming but a fortnight after the implementation of the Anglo-Italian agreement, cast some doubt on the professed intention not to disturb the *status quo* in Mediterranean countries.

Lord Perth answered that he was still most anxious for the visit to take place. The agitation against France was dying down; cancellation would be regarded by Mussolini as a personal insult, 'a thing that he never forgets or forgives' and would play into the hands of extreme supporters of the Axis.[31]]

Tuesday, 13 December

Tackled H. early about P.M.'s speech. He rang up No. 10, but they said it was already distributed! Rather bad. . . . Speech went fairly well, but it got applause in the wrong places (as I had predicted) and I don't think P.M. did himself much good. I think he's missed an opportunity.

Wednesday, 14 December

Talk with H. and Dirksen about submarines and Anglo-German relations in general. P.M. wants his Monday speech written by F.O.! . . . Life is an awful rush, and I can't keep this Diary properly —wish I could.

Thursday, 15 December

R. L[indsay] said frankly that the Lothian appointment [as Ambassador in Washington] *might* be undesirable from the 'Cliveden Set' point of view, but he didn't want to press it.

Ivone K[irkpatrick]* turned up from Berlin. He has been told by his friend K— that Hitler will bomb London in March! . . . I then saw H. and told him the K. story. He saw P.M. at 7, and latter summoned a meeting of the Ministers concerned for 10 a.m. to-morrow. Glad he takes it seriously. . . . Schacht saw P.M. today and told him straight there was no 'appeasement' with Hitler.†

Kirkpatrick had been told by a retired German official close to General Beck (who had recently resigned as Chief of the German General Staff) of preparations for a sudden air attack on London. These plans were supposed to be completed in three weeks, and the informant wanted the British to take some precautions. The Cabinet decided to bring the A.A. regiment from Lichfield and place the guns where they could be seen from the German Embassy.[32] It is possible that this official may have got wind of the plan drawn up by Keitel, on Hitler's instructions, for a full-scale onslaught on Britain and France by Germany and Italy.[33]

The gist of the Intelligence provided by mid-December from secret sources was summarised thus by Gladwyn Jebb:

'(a) Germany is controlled by one man, Herr Hitler, whose will is supreme, and who is a blend of fanatic, madman and clear-visioned realist.

(b) His ambition and self-confidence are unbounded, and he regards Germany's supremacy in Europe as a step to world supremacy. He has been peculiarly susceptible, since Munich, to extremist influence.

(c) At present he is devoting special attention to the eastward drive, to securing control of the exploitable riches of South, and possibly more of, Russia.

* First Sec., British Embassy in Berlin, 1933–38. See List of Principal Characters.

† Dr Schacht was dismissed as President of the Reichsbank on 20 Dec. 1938.

(d) He also intends to subject Eastern and South-Eastern Europe to Germany's political and economic hegemony, to vassaldom, if not worse. Polish and Roumanian integrity are threatened.
(e) He means to secure the return, sooner or later, of Germany's former Colonial possessions, or a satisfactory overseas equivalent; but that does not seem at present to be the primary objective.
(f) He is devoting close attention to the Middle East; he intends to extend his influence to South America, and to make the Japanese give him special privileges in China.
(g) Britain, meanwhile, is Enemy No. 1 of Herr Hitler and the Nazi Party. He is embittered and exasperated over the British. His extremist advisers, who are particularly anti-British, feed him on tales of British 'decadence'.
(h) The eastward drive—the Ukraine in particular—is the order of the day. But Herr Hitler is *incalculable*, even to his intimates. He is capable of throwing the machine he has created, regardless of settled policy, and on his own initiative, in *any* direction at short notice. He can personally precipitate a conflagration, whatever the consequences to his régime may be.'[34]

Monday, 19 December

Saw final version of P.M.'s speech. Quite good. He took most of Leeper's stuff and a sentence or 2 of mine. . . . *Perishing* cold. H. tells me Van wants to resign!

Wednesday, 21 December

Talk to H. in evening about our policy regarding Italy and Rome visit. He has had talk with Van and advised him to put off decision as to his future, though agreeing that he is a 'fifth wheel' in F.O. Hope he won't be deterred from going! But P.M. rather disturbed at the idea of his going into Parliament!

Thursday, 22 December

3 secret meetings of C[ommittee of] I[mperial] D[efence] on Kirk[patrick]'s news. We got thro' a certain amount, and it seems we *are* going ahead, but I sometimes wish we were a Totalitarian State.

[This meeting decided to accelerate air raid precautions, the provision of anti-aircraft defences and preparations for civil defence. All departments were to ensure that their war plans were brought to a state of readiness within three months, i.e. before the end of March 1939.[35]]

Saturday, 31 December

So ends the year. It has been a strenuous and anxious one, but thanks be to God we are all alive and well. What the coming year will bring, I hardly dare to conjecture. It will be big with fate in any case. It seems to me that, unless there is revolution in Germany, we must flounder into war. And the former hope is slender indeed. I can only pray God to help me to do what little I can in my sphere, and to bless us all and bring us all safely through.

[Musing upon the events of this winter with the benefit of twenty-five years' hindsight, Sir Alexander found it hard to delimit the frontier between hope and belief, or to pinpoint the moment when the latter had to be abandoned. Chamberlain, he guessed, had taken longer to see the light than Halifax:

> But I cannot be sure. Hitler's open atrocities against the Jews in the autumn of 1938 certainly deeply impressed Chamberlain. . . . And of course Halifax was no less shocked. Many people who did not know Chamberlain personally had the impression that he was a gullible and obstinate old man. During all that ghastly time I saw almost as much of him as I did of Halifax and I will say, from my observation of him, that nothing could be further from the truth. He was haunted day and night by the prospect that he saw clearly enough, he gave everything of his strength to try to avert it. Many people thought he was a cynic. Cynicism was a virtue with which he was perhaps not sufficiently equipped, or he would not have been taken in by Hitler's rather transparent 'piece of paper'. On the other hand he had quite a streak of the sentimental and emotional in him, which betrayed him into uttering those unguarded words to the crowd in Downing Street after his return from Germany.

Cadogan's view of Germany, and of Russia, was a practical one. It remained so in 1941 and 1945. The idea occasionally pressed upon him by younger colleagues, that Britain's foreign policy should be based upon 'the fight against evil' or some other ideological motive, he consistently rejected as unreal and absurdly luxurious for a country of limited means and worldwide vulnerability. It follows that he did not during the war feel any qualms of conscience about alliance with Russia. In February, 1939 he brought decisively to a close an argument being pursued in a Foreign Office paper:

> I personally—with all humility—think it otiose to discuss whether Fascism or Communism is the more dangerous to us. It is quite plain that, *at the moment*, the former is the more dangerous, because it is the more efficient, and makes more and better guns and aeroplanes. Some people forget the years, say 1920–26, when the only danger was 'Bolshevism.'
>
> That has now faded, mainly because the General Strike showed

people, who couldn't see pikestaffs, that conditions in the U.K. were slightly different from those in Russia.

I don't say that the Bogey of Fascism will fade and finish so quickly or dramatically. But he *may*.

I abominate both Communism (as practised in Russia) and Fascism or Nazism. I don't like oysters or oatmeal biscuits, but it has never occurred to me that it would be profitable to devote any of my time to discussing which of them I dislike more. (As a matter of fact, neither of them disagrees with me: perhaps it would be fairer to say that I have lost no time in meditating upon the comparative disadvantages of measles and mumps.)

If the S. of S., in the months to come, has a little more leisure, it might interest him to read these essays, but I think it would be unfair to ask him to do it now.

Let them lie for a bit, and bring up on June 1. (What sort of a world shall we be in then?)]

1939

Monday, 2 January

G.C.M.G.*announced this morning [in the New Year's Honours], so am beginning to get flood of telegrams and letters, which adds to one's work. . . . Eddie has got K.B.E.—a tardy recognition of his devoted work†—and Edith Hillingdon‡ is a Dame! So the family have done well, and when they retire they can set up a co-operative ironmongery store.

Tuesday, 3 January

Dame A. Livingstone§ at 5, who wants to bring a deputation on Spain to H. on Saturday afternoon. Poured a douche of icy water on her (and subsequently got H's refusal by telephone). Also got H. to authorise me to write to Governor of Bank¶ (who is off to Germany tomorrow), referring to fact that he had never said a word to H. about his trip and warning him to engage in no serious negotiations!

Wednesday, 4 January

Found a livid Governor of the Bank [i.e. Norman] on my doorstep. But calmed him down. He said everything arranged with P.M.

* Knight Grand Cross of the Order of St Michael and St George.

† Cadogan's elder brother Edward, M.P. 1922–3, 1924–35, 1940–5; honoured by being made a Knight Commander of the Order of the British Empire for his services to boys' clubs in the East End of London.

‡ Cadogan's niece, daughter of his eldest brother.

§ Dame Adelaide Livingstone, a stalwart of the League of Nations Union.

¶ Montagu C. Norman, Gov. of the Bank of England, 1920–44.

and Chancellor. I said that might be so, but my S. of S. knew nothing; hence his concern at press reports. If he (Governor) had taken offence at any phrase in my letter, he must know it was my drafting—not H's. He calmed down a bit. But it seems to me that it is a stunt of No. 10 (he said he had discussed it with Horace W.) As he left, I said 'Well, I hope you will let us know of any results'. He said 'There won't be any results!' I said 'Tant mieux'. . . . Drove H. home and he dined here. He has talked to A. [Eden] about rejoining Government, but A. still rather sticky. H. wants a good re-shuffle, but says Hore-Belisha* has nobbled Gort—and Creedy.† So suppose he will stay!

Friday, 6 January

Corbin came at 4 and I gave him line we shall take in Rome. This will leak, but I can't help it: we *must* reassure French and he was evidently greatly relieved.

[Shortly before the Prime Minister and Halifax left for Rome, Lord Perth reviewed the international position of Italy. Mussolini remained sole master of Italian policy, he wrote; Italian and German aims in South-east Europe conflicted; a section of the Fascist party believed the democracies to be 'on the run'; Mussolini, however, did not desire a general war, and sincerely sought good relations with Britain; and 'Italy's policy will continue as before to be based upon what will seem to us to be blatant and undisguised self-interest, and nothing will impress her except a conviction of real strength in others.'

Cadogan commented:

> The moral of this despatch seems to me to be that we must show Mussolini, in as friendly and polite a manner as possible, that the Democracies are *not* 'on the run', and that they will not make unjustifiable concessions simply because the Italians shout loudly enough for them. Unless we can establish that, we shall get nowhere.
>
> . . . we must not leave out of account . . . that Italy has grabbed the whole of Ethiopia. To develop that country properly will take Italy, at the very least, 20 years. So that, during those years, it is ridiculous for Italy to clamour for parts of the former Roman Empire which she covets. It may be that Italy resents having had to conquer Ethiopia instead of being presented with chunks of Africa by France. But after all, we had something to resent in the Ethiopian performance, too. And she cannot use her conquest, which we have eventually with some difficulty condoned, as an argument for us, or the French, now giving her more.

* L. Hore-Belisha, Secretary of State for War, 1937–40, against whose continuation in office several junior Ministers had recently protested to the Prime Minister.

† Sir H. Creedy, P.U.S., War Office, 1924–39.

Cadogan noted on another paper at the same time:

> It is of course galling for them [the Fascists] that we retain control of the approaches to the Mediterranean. But I don't see that they have any better claim to Gibraltar than we have. And as regards the eastern approach, which involves the tutelage of Egypt, I am quite convinced that we are more fitted to exercise that than they are.
>
> Finally, even we can lay some claim to prestige, and we cannot be expected to make territorial, or other, concessions on demand.
>
> If Italy wishes to develop her Empire in peace, she must understand that depends on loyal co-operation with us: she will then have all the security that she wants, and if such co-operation is proved over a period, we might then consider whether any of her grievances are legitimate.
>
> But if we were *now* to make further concessions to Italy, there would be no finality and no security.

These minutes were taken by the Prime Minister to Rome.[36]]

Tuesday, 10 January *En route London to Rome*

T. and G. came to see me off at Station—mainly, I think, for the fun of promised communist demonstration, which hardly materialised. P.M. and Halifax turned up just before 11. Calm crossing. Lunched on train with P.M., H. and Dunglass.* Paris 5.45. Drove to Quai d'Orsay. Talk with Daladier, Bonnet, P.M., H., Phipps and Léger. Desultory—no proper secretariat or interpreter, and we just sat in chairs. P.M. and H. tried to talk French. That sort of talk always rather ineffective. Caught 7.30 train at Gare de Lyon. Worked at P.M.'s speech and a few other things after dinner with H.

[The principal point of the conversation at the Quai d'Orsay was the French Ministers' insistence that they would and could cede not an inch to Italy. Chamberlain asked whether the sudden change of Italian attitude towards France was connected with the project which Hitler was said to be nurturing for the Ukraine. Bonnet answered that this might well be so: the object being to keep France occupied in the Mediterranean while Germany moved in the East.]

Wednesday, 11 January *Rome*

Slept fairly, but not too, well. Up and had breakfast just before Genoa, where we arrived at 10. Some sun, and reasonably mild. P.M. reviewed guard of honour. Great enthusiasm—and obviously spontaneous. And that was the same all the way along. Noel Charles†

* Later Earl of Home and Sir Alec Douglas-Home; Parliamentary Private Sec. to Chamberlain, 1937–40; Foreign Sec., 1960–3; P.M., 1963–4; Foreign Sec., 1970–.

† (Later Sir) N. Charles. Minister at Embassy in Rome; later British High Commissioner in Italy.

and Nosworthy* joined us at Genoa. Arrived Rome 4.20. Met by Musso, Ciano and many dignitaries. Great show of guard of honour &c. British colony all penned together and very enthusiastic. . . . Drove, with Anfuso† and O. Harvey to Villa Madama—which is really beautiful—even at this time of year. Great crowds on the way and enthusiastic clapping and saluting. After tea, went to write our names at the Quirinal. Then to Palazzo Venezia, where the 'Big Four' had a talk of 1½ hrs. while we all kicked our heels in Sala del Consiglio. I talked to Grandi most of the time. Then back to Villa, where P.M. and H. gave us account of their conversation. Which seems to have been friendly enough, but not very productive. Banquet at Palazzo Venezia at 9. . . . Saw a number of old Italian friends—including Imperiali‡, who hardly looks older than he did 15 years ago! Musso and Ciano took us round the Museum after. Home about 12.15. P.M. has rather a cold, but doesn't seem bad.

[The British party were accommodated grandly in the only completed wing of the residence designed by Rafael for the Popes on the slopes of Monte Mario; more grandly than conveniently, for, believing every room to be wired, they could converse only in the most guarded terms.

Mussolini spoke at this first meeting of Italy's need for peace, attachment to the Axis and determination to stand loyally by the Anglo-Italian agreement. He denied any intention to make demands on Spain after the civil war had ended. At the second meeting, on 12 January, Chamberlain spoke of Germany's attitude, 'giving rise to a great deal of anxiety and doubt, not only in his mind but all over Europe . . . a general suspicion that Herr Hitler had it in mind to make some further move in the near future which would be likely to upset a great part of Europe. . . . Some people though it would be in the direction of the Ukraine; others that, although that might be the ultimate aim, it would be preceded by a sudden attack in the west. Here Signor Mussolini shook his head emphatically. . . .' Mussolini said he was convinced of the defensive purpose of Germany's admitted rearmament. To this Chamberlain replied that 'German military forces were now so strong as to make it impossible for any Power or combination of Powers to attack her successfully. She could not want further armaments for defensive purposes; what then did she want them for?'[37]

'Effective contact' recorded Ciano on the first day, 'has not been made. How far apart we are from these people! It is another world. We were talking about it after dinner with the Duce, gathered together in a corner of the room. "These men are not made of the same stuff" he was saying, "as the Francis Drakes and the other magnificent adventurers who

* Commercial Counsellor at the Embassy in Rome.

† Filippo Anfuso, head of Ciano's private office.

‡ Formerly Italian Ambassador in London; and representative at the League, 1921–3.

created the empire. These, after all, are the tired sons of a long line of rich men, and they will lose their empire."' Nor did Ciano fail to observe the deep unease of the British Ministers about Germany. 'They would be ready for any sacrifice if they could see the future clearly' he concluded understandably but wrongly, judging that in league with Germany and Japan, Italy could get whatever she wanted. 'The British do not want to fight.'[38] Cadogan's Diary shows his awareness of this mood.]

Thursday, 12 January

I had a talk with P.M. Suggested to him we must before he goes, get Musso on subject of Hitler and latter's intentions. We must take away from here some assurance that Musso will try to restrain Hitler, and leave behind us here the idea that, if Hitler is *not* restrained, there'll be a blow-up. P.M. I think quite ready for this but must of course choose his moment. 10.50 to Pantheon to lay wreath, and ditto at Tomb of Unknown Warrior. Great reception. 11.30 Quirinal. P.M. and H. received in audience, while we waited. King* then came in and we were presented. Then lunch. I between Musso (who had King on his other side) and Bastianini.† Musso very pleasant, and we talked nearly the whole time. I reminded him of a former meeting (1924) and he told me of his visit to London in 1922. I flattered him, and drew him, about Rome. He told me of what he had done and was doing and of the reclaiming of the marshes, Ostia, &c. We talked about Americans (arising out of Lima Conference). He affected to take not much account of them. He admitted there wasn't such a thing as an Aryan race—only an Aryan language. Said only 20% [?] of Germans were fair haired. Rest were Dinarios, Alpinos, &c.‡ Talked about F[ar] E[ast]. Told him he's like C[hiang] K[ai] S[hek]§ who wasn't a bit communist. No communism in China.¶ He said he had sympathy with Chinese, and had helped them with an Air Mission, &c. (Didn't say he'd since withdrawn it!)

After lunch walked around Palace and I had another talk with Musso. He lectured me on Etruscan and early Roman history (but I don't know how much he knows about it). Talked to me also about their youth training, beginning at the age of 6, and ending at 55! I said there was quite a bit of that that we might copy in England. We talked French the whole time.

* King Victor Emmanuel III.

† Guiseppe Bastianini, Italian Under-Sec. for Foreign Affairs, 1936–9; Ambassador in London, 1939–40.

‡ The text is rather illegible at this point, and the ethnology equally doubtful.

§ Chiang Kai-Shek. See List of Principal Characters.

¶ There seems to be no explanation elsewhere in the Diary of this extraordinary and cryptic remark.

Drove back with P.M., whose cold rather more troublesome today.

In afternoon we all went to display in Foro Mussolini. Had to stand in a rostrum with Musso, Starace,* &c., for 1½ hrs. Good show, but rather too long. P.M. and H. went on for further talks at Palazzo Venezia. I went to tea at Embassy. Dined at Embassy. . . . Then on to the Opera. Sat in box with Edda Ciano,† Ela‡ and Grandi. Falstaff dull, but 'Boutique Fantasque' very well given. On to supper at Excelsior with Ciano. To give him time to get there, we drove round Rome for about ½ an hour. Coliseum and other buildings floodlit. But it was raining, and out of a modern low-roofed car one can't see much. Supper began about 12.

['I thought' says Halifax's diary, 'there was no reason that the entertainment should ever end, but it eventually did about 1.30 a.m. and we got back to bed about 2 a.m. The Italian habit of life is very different from mine.'

After dinner on 13 January Chamberlain remarked to the Duce that despite assurances which the latter had given he still felt unhappy about Hitler's intentions. The Prime Minister said, in the words of his record:

> that the German press had on more than one occasion been somewhat contemptuous about the fighting qualities of the democracies, indicating that in no circumstances would they be prepared to come to the test of war. Such an attitude betrayed a grave misapprehension; democracies would fight under certain circumstances and had been ready to fight last September, and it would be a terrible tragedy if aggressive action were taken under a misapprehension as to what lengths the democracies might be prepared to go to.

Both Chamberlain and Halifax found Mussolini quiet and reasonable in the talks, even though he made it plain that there would be no discussion of Franco-Italian difficulties until the Spanish war was over. On the other hand, he did not attempt to endorse the claims on French territory made a little earlier during the 'entirely spontaneous' demonstration in the Chamber.[39]]

Saturday, 14 January

P.M. tells me he spoke last night to Musso as I had advised him—warning against the danger of contemptuous propaganda in the German Press (this is a nice way of putting it) and saying that that way danger lies. If he spoke properly, our visit has not been in vain.

* Sec.-Gen. of the Fascist Party, 1931–9.
† Wife of the Foreign Minister and daughter of Mussolini.
‡ Lady Perth.

Down to Embassy for P.M. to receive Staff. Then up to the Villa for Italian press. Left Villa at 11.35 for station. Tremendous show—Musso very beaming. Left at 12.5. Review of guard and great show at Turin at 9 p.m. Found Air Officer commanding was an old friend of Geneva (Disarmament) days!

Tuesday, 17 January

In view of all the secret reports, spent whole morning writing a warning against an 'attack in the West', i.e.—principally—Holland. Lunched with Maisky. He trying hard to pump me on Rome visit, and not disdaining to put the most leading questions.

H. got back about 4. Gave him my notes on Rome visit and on 'attack in the West' and went off to P.M. at 4.30.

[Between mid-December and the British party's return from Rome, further disquieting evidence had been received from secret sources: Ribbentrop was reported to be convinced that England could be successfully blackmailed, Hitler that Germany's declining strength in relation to that of the West argued for an early stroke. It seemed certain that at least some members of the Führer's entourage were seriously considering an attack on Britain and France. 'At any rate' said Jebb's summary, 'all our sources are at one in declaring that he is barely sane, consumed by an insensate hatred of this country, and capable both of ordering an immediate aerial attack on any European country and of having his command instantly obeyed.'

Cadogan's paper, 'Possibility of a German Attack on the West', admitted that his intentions could not be divined:

> We cannot know whether Hitler will decide to go East, remaining on the defensive in the West, or whether he will deal with the West first, so as to gain a free hand in eastern Europe. It would seem more logical (and more in accordance with *Mein Kampf*) that he should first acquire control over the resources of eastern and south-eastern Europe, and then, thus reinforced, turn against the West. It seems most unlikely, and contrary to all tradition, that he would deliberately engage himself on both fronts simultaneously, although we have reports to this effect.

If Germany moved west, Britain would be the chief object of attack, and the general design to deprive her of French help either by air bombardment or by invasion of Holland.

> It has always been held that the independence of the Low Countries is a vital interest to this country, and in these days of air and submarine warfare this seems to be more than ever true, and I should have thought that we should be bound immediately to do all that lay in our power to prevent or hinder it.

> . . . Once in command of Holland and the Dutch coast, Germany would aspire to dictate terms to us, under threat, regarding the colonies, and she might at the same time bribe Poland and perhaps other countries with promises of colonial loot. (And she might make a present to Japan of the Dutch East Indies.)

Halifax, in his covering note, made reservations about some of the sources and about Hitler's unpredictability. Nevertheless, the theme running through all the reports—that Hitler would soon attempt a *coup*, with the danger-period beginning towards the end of February—could not be missed. That *coup* might take the form of an attack on the West before the British and French rearmament deprived him of Germany's advantage.[40]]

Thursday, 19 January

Passed papers for circulation to Foreign Policy Committee on German peril. . . . L[eith] R[oss] came at 3.15. That dirty dog Warren F[isher]* is trying to put him into D[ominions] O[ffice] in place of Harding. Complete waste of talent and knowledge. Promised to do what I could to spike this, but he will let me know when he wants me to move. 6 H.J.W. came over. Began about Van, who thinks he shouldn't go in present critical state. Well, I agree. Said Van had seen P.M., who found him in most nervous state (!). From that he went on to my paper on 'attacks in the west' (see Jan. 17). I don't *think* he was trying to throw cold water on it. I said I had risked being thought nervous, but personally I wouldn't take responsibility of ignoring all these reports. Anyhow, it won't do us any harm to brace ourselves to meet a shock in 6 weeks' time—we shall be all the better for it. He evidently strongly in favour of taking U.S. into our confidence. That all to the good. P.M. has to speak at Birmingham Saturday week. I urged he should now come out firm and confident. H.J.W. said he would make suggestions on that line.

Monday, 23 January

Foreign Policy Committee at 3. They didn't pooh-pooh our paper, and were quite prepared to face risk of German attack. P.M., H., Sam Hoare and O. Stanley all said we must come in if Holland attacked. Agreed to take U.S. into our confidence. Fixed up with P.M. after draft of statement to Parliament on Rome visit. Got it off in Bag to Rome for Ciano's approval. Then discussed Bonnet's draft of speech to be made tomorrow containing very awkward passages.

* Sir Warren Fisher, Permanent Sec, to the Treasury and Head of the Civil Service, 1919–39.

Got back to F.O. about 6 and gave instructions for draft to Washington and statement for H. to make to Cabinet. Saw Margerie* about Bonnet's speech. This is going to be *very* difficult.

Tuesday, 24 January

Corbin came at 11.30 and I talked to him about Bonnet's speech. Got him to suggest a formula that may make it possible, but it's difficult. If *we* want French to give us an all-round guarantee, they naturally expect the same in return. But the circumstances aren't the same. Didn't press him too hard, and God knows what Bonnet will say, but it won't do much harm. . . .

7.15 Herschel Johnson, to whom I gave our telegram to Washington (approved by P.M.). He hadn't much comment. He said 'It makes me feel quite sick'. 4.30 H. had meeting of prospective signatories of manifesto. Don't know what they agreed. All my spare moments consulting H. about telegram to Washington and his statement for Cabinet tomorrow. An awful day.

[The telegram to Washington is noteworthy not only because it indicates the difficulties of assessing secret Intelligence but also because it disposes of the legend of a bemused administration awakened from roseate dreams only by the events of March. The text, as approved by Chamberlain, was sent in Halifax's name:

> I have received a large number of reports from various reliable sources which throw a most disquieting light on Hitler's mood and intentions. According to these reports Hitler is bitterly resentful at the Munich Agreement which baulked him of a localised war against Czechoslovakia and demonstrated the will to peace of the German masses in opposition to the warmongering of the Nazi Party. He feels personally humiliated by this demonstration. He regards Great Britain as primarily responsible for this humiliation and his rage is therefore directed principally against this country which he holds to be the chief obstacle now to the fulfilment of his further ambitions.
>
> As early as November there were indications which gradually became more definite that Hitler was planning a further foreign adventure for the spring of 1939. At first it appeared—and this was confirmed by persons in Hitler's entourage—that he was thinking of expansion in the east and in December the prospect of establishing an independent Ukraine under German vassalage was freely spoken of in Germany.
>
> Since then reports indicate that Hitler, encouraged by Ribbentrop, Himmler and others, is considering an attack on the Western powers as a preliminary to subsequent action in the east. Some of these reports

* Roland de Margerie, First Sec., French Embassy, 1933–9; later Private Sec. to the Minister for Foreign Affairs.

emanate from highly placed Germans of undoubted sincerity who are anxious to prevent this crime; others come from foreigners, hitherto Germans, who are in close touch with leading German personalities. They have received some confirmation in the reassurance which Hitler appears to have given to Monsieur Beck concerning his plans in the east, as well as in the support which Germany has recently given to Italy's claims against France.

There is as yet no reason to suppose that Hitler has made up his mind on any particular plan. Our reports show that he may:

(i) Push Italy to advance her claims by force and use his obligations to Italy as a pretext for embarking on war. This course would have the advantage of ensuring the participation of Italy from the outset.

(ii) Begin by launching an attack on Holland. The President will have noticed the recent deterioration of German-Dutch relations and the critical tone adopted towards Holland by the German press. Once in command of Holland and the Dutch coast, Germany would aspire to dictate terms to us and paralyse France. She might at the same time bribe Poland and perhaps other countries with promises of colonial loot; in that event the Dutch East Indies might be allocated to Japan.

(iii) Put forward impossible colonial demands in his speech of January 30th in the form of an ultimatum. This seems the least likely hypothesis.

(iv) Make a sudden air attack without pretext on England and follow up this initial surprise by land and sea operations against the western powers. We have received definite information from a highly placed German that preparations for such a coup are now being made. He has, however, no information to show that Hitler has yet made up his mind to execute this plan.

In the last few days we have received reliable information to the effect that the German Government are pressing for the conversion of the Anti-Comintern Pact into a pact pledging the signatories to give each other military assistance against unprovoked attack by a third power, that the Italian Government have agreed, and that the Japanese Government are now considering the matter. Our information is that the German Government wish this pact to be concluded in time for it to be announced by Herr Hitler in the speech he is expected to make on January 30.

All the reports are agreed in forecasting that the danger period will begin towards the end of February. This is borne out by independent reports to the effect that orders have been issued for mobilisation about the middle of February. We have already received news of preliminary mobilisation measures, and the formation of a reserve regiment composed of time-expired conscripts has been recently established in

Bavaria. Moreover the economic and financial crisis with which Germany is now faced might well compel Hitler to take some action, and the choice before him is either to slow down his rearmament and to abandon his policy of expansion, or else launch into some foreign adventure in the hope that it will both distract attention from domestic difficulties and supply him with the material resources which the country urgently requires and can no longer buy abroad. There can be little doubt that a man of Hitler's temperament may be tempted to choose the second alternative. Another motive for his doing so might be that he was not sure of the loyalty of his army, and might feel that the surest way for a dictator to deal with a doubtful army was to give it occupation.

It may seem fanciful and even fantastic to attribute such designs to Hitler and it is as yet impossible to speak of them with certainty. His Majesty's Government have no wish to be alarmist, but today, as in July, August and September of last year, it is remarkable that there is one general tendency running through all the reports, and it is impossible to ignore them, particularly in view of the character and proved reliability of the informants. Moreover, Hitler's mental condition, his insensate rage against Great Britain and his megalomania, which are alarming the moderates around him, are entirely consistent with the execution of a desperate coup against the Western powers. The removal of moderates such as Schacht and Wiedemann is symptomatic. It has been suggested in some quarters that the German people would not follow Hitler on such a course and that a revolt would ensue. We have examined this aspect, but the authorities on Germany whom we have consulted including anti-Nazi Germans of sound judgment are agreed that Hitler's orders would be carried out and that no revolt can be anticipated at all events during the initial stages of a war.

His Majesty's Government have carefully considered the situation in the light of these reports and have decided to accelerate as far as possible the preparation of their defensive and counter-offensive measures. In the meantime they are employing such methods as are available to them for bringing home to the German people the wantonness and folly of embarking on aggressive adventures. They will lay such public emphasis as they can on the point, in the hope of deterring Herr Hitler from committing himself to something irrevocable in the speech which he is expected to make on January 30th.

Finally, in the event of Germany picking a quarrel with Holland, His Majesty's Government are considering the desirability as a matter of tactics and precaution of being ready at once with a proposal to both Governments for the selection by neutral governments of a board of three arbitrators. Such a proposal might not prove effective, but if arbitration were rejected or over-ridden by Germany, the issue would be clear and His Majesty's Government would have *locus standi* for appropriate action.

In the next few days His Majesty's Government will be considering carefully what further steps they might take to avert or to meet a situation such as they have cause to apprehend, and I will of course keep the President informed of any decision taken.

In view of the relations of confidence which exist between our two Governments and the degree to which we have exchanged information hitherto, His Majesty's Government feel bound to state frankly their apprehensions as to the future and to indicate what measures they feel able to take. It would, of course, be a great help to them if the President had any further suggestions to make.

It is impossible as yet for the Prime Minister to decide whether he will himself utter any public warning to Germany before Hitler makes his speech on January 30th. The Prime Minister is due to speak at Birmingham on January 28th and, if possible, I would let the President know beforehand what line the Prime Minister would propose to take. If the President were disposed to take an occasion for any public announcement, it might be more valuable if he were to do so before January 30th.[41]]

Wednesday, 25 January

Gather from H. that Cabinet was all right. But no decision on Holland, though I understand that is left to F.P.C. tomorrow. Meeting on Spain (how often have I written these words in last 2 years?) at 5. 'Times' want to go off at half-cock tomorrow with article on German menace. Agreed with H. to hold them in: it won't help if P.M. is going to speak out on Sat.

Thursday, 26 January

Went over to see Horace Wilson, who had shown signs of scrapping with our News Department. Think I put a stopper on that. . . . 3 Foreign Policy Committee. Quite a good meeting: agreed to fight for Holland, and on various precautionary measures (including re-conversion of 'Repulse' to a battleship!). I had heard this morning that P.M. in his speech on Sat. will talk about 'peace and conciliation'. So I urged the reverse on Horace this morning, and he seems to have passed it on.

[M. Bonnet said that in case of war in which the two countries were involved all the forces of Britain would be at the disposal of France just as all the forces of France would be at the disposal of Britain. Four days later Hitler announced that if Italy went to war Germany would be with her.]

Friday, 27 January

Azcarate at 12.30—very miserable but talking big about further resistance in Catalonia, and of course trying to make our blood freeze about Italian designs in Spain.... Herschel Johnson called to ask if we had any more to tell him—particularly in regard to P.M.'s speech. Had to say nothing. (P.M. left at 3 and no one knows what he will say. I couldn't get much out of Horace, who is probably trying to keep on 'peace and conciliation' line.) Fixed up with H. what, exactly, we should say to French, Belgians and Americans as result of yesterday's discussion.

Saturday, 28 January

Awful hourouche this morning. 'Times' have been very stupid about the 'Manifesto', emphasising that it was in the German broadcast before the Press. Idiots! Or worse. And Randolph Churchill rang up Kenneth Clark* to say he had heard the thing was arranged in F.O. and could K.C. confirm. K.C. rang up Rex L[eeper]. Had to stop this getting into [the *Evening Standard*'s] 'Londoner's Diary'. Tried to get Sam Hoare at Cromer, but he out shooting. Then Kingsley Wood,† but he away. Finally got S. of S. (who is in London) to ring up Beaverbrook. Which he did—with success. B. will suppress R.C.'s poisonous scoop.

H. saw Corbin and Cartier‡, and I saw Herschel Johnson, to tell them as much as we could of Thursday's F.P.C. decision.... Listened to P.M. at Birmingham. Quite good enough, I think.

[The manifesto took the form of an appeal by a group of British notables (Lord Willingdon, Lord Derby, Lord Dawson, H. A. L. Fisher, Montagu Norman, John Masefield the Poet Laureate, and others) to the leaders and people of Germany to join in a 'supreme effort to lay the spectre of war and enmity between nations'.]

Monday, 30 January

Don't remember that much of interest occurred. We were all waiting for Hitler's speech tonight. Much too much attention paid to these periodical performances and we are too much 'agog'.... Met H. there [F.O.] and we glanced at such reports of the speech as had come in. Nothing much in it—so the *situation is not changed.* Went over to P.M. at 10. I *hope* he isn't too relieved at the speech and won't now think that everything is for the best in the best of all possible worlds. I don't *think* so.

* Sir Kenneth Clark, Director of the National Gallery, 1938–45. A signatory of the 'Manifesto'.

† S. of S. for Air, 1938–40.

‡ Baron de Cartier de Marchienne, Belgian Ambassador, 1927–46.

Tuesday, 31 January

Wrote a bit for the P.M. to say in the House about Hitler's references to economics, and took it over to H.J.W. But—as usual—he didn't use it. I'm *afraid* there is a surge of optimism—'Hitler Boom in City', which is undignified as well as silly. And that ass Geoffrey Dawson says 'the P.M. is right'. However, I don't think the P.M. is quite such an ass as G.D. thinks. Nevile H. called in afternoon. Filled him up with a good deal about our strength—he wants a bit of stiffening.

[Towards the end of January the Foreign Office learned from Litvinov that a German trade delegation would soon arrive in Moscow. A member of the German Embassy said privately that there would probably be a large German credit, Germany buying raw materials and supplying machinery and, perhaps, arms. 'There is as yet no indication of any impending political or military contacts' the British Ambassador advised. On 1 February, Corbin pointed out to Sir Alexander that Hitler's speech had contained, exceptionally, no attack on the Soviets. On this and other signs Cadogan minuted:

> If we may believe that the Germans have found that their project for acquiring a dominating position in the Ukraine was not so realisable as they had thought, it may well be that they have turned their minds to obtaining a form of economic co-operation with, if not domination of, the Soviet with a view to benefiting from the almost unlimited sources of raw materials which that might put at their disposal. The transformation of the anti-Comintern Pact into a simple pact of mutual assistance against unprovoked aggression by any third party might be designed by the Germans to convince the Soviet Government that they are no longer their chief enemy and that German policy is not directed entirely against the Soviet and all its works. It seems to me that we shall have to watch very carefully the development of any tendency towards a *rapprochement* between Germany and the Soviet.[42]]

Friday, 3 February

Walked to F.O. with H. Meeting with him, Van, O. Sargent, Malkin, Strang about possible violations of Holland's integrity. Van of course wants a 'warning' to Germany about Holland. I'm not at all sure (may be what Germany wants). But it might be done in general terms.

Saturday, 4 February

Not much of a rush. Maurice Ingram stopped me as I was going out—some hitch that the Admiralty were making about surrender of Minorca. But I settled him on the stairs. Lunched at home, and we went down in the car to Sevenoaks [where the Cadogans were looking for a cottage]. But beastly city-dwellers' villas.

Sunday, 5 February

Seems that Catalonia, at least—if not all Republican Spain—has collapsed. Went round to F.O. and looked at telegrams: rang up S. of S. and got his approval of instructions to urge (in guarded terms) surrender on conditions. . . . F.O. rang me up. Corbin had been fussing again, but had caught G. Mounsey. Rang latter up. French have lost their nerve, and fear Italian advance on Pyrenees frontier! G. M[ounsey] had sent telegram to Burgos asking Franco to use only Spanish troops!

Monday, 6 February

Picked up H. and walked to F.O. Discussed answer to P[arliamentary] Q[uestion] about Anglo-French solidarity in case of attack on France (by Italy)—arising out of Bonnet's speech. H. sent for Van. To my surprise, H. suggested a very strong draft, really promising help in all circumstances. To my greater surprise he later put it across P.M. Very satisfactory (and it eventually 'went' v. well in the House). . . . Went to help H. draft telegram to Washington saying what Cabinet *had* decided last Wednesday. This still v. doubtful, so we sent draft over to P.M.

[Chamberlain stated in Parliament:

> It is impossible to examine in detail all the hypothetical cases which may arise, but I feel bound to make plain that the solidarity of interest by which France and this country are united, is such that any threat to the vital interests of France from whatever quarter it came must evoke the immediate co-operation of this country.

The telegram to Washington confirmed that a German invasion of Holland would compel Britain to declare war, and an attempt to dominate Holland by force or the threat of force would be regarded as a menace to British security. This message was sent after the Belgian Government had refused to believe that Germany was contemplating a seizure of Holland; and in any event, said her Foreign Minister, Belgium was convinced that her only chance was to remain strictly neutral.[43]]

Tuesday, 7 February

P.M.'s statement yesterday has gone very well. It *may* be a turning point. P.M. approved our telegram to Washington and it went off, so I sent for Herschel Johnson and gave it to him. . . . H. kept sending complaints that he hadn't enough work. So I kept on sending back messages that that would give him time to *think!*

Thursday, 9 February

Maisky at 6 to complain that Arcos [Russian trade organization] building had been raided by police. Tried to persuade him it *hadn't*, but his story differed so from mine that I promised to get further and more detailed report. . . .

A lot going on, but difficult to enter everything in this Diary. I am sick of it by the time the day is over! This is a critical time. There's a curious lull in Germany. Either there's an internal tug-of-war, or they're preparing some awful devilment or—they're feeling devilish uncomfortable. I hope, and think, that P.M.'s statement of February 6 *may* have been psychologically just very well timed!

Friday, 10 February

11 Promotions Board lasting all morning—discussing how to get rid of Duds. Rather useful—we made a 'Black List', with several suggestions for procedure. If H. plays, he will be a greater purger than Stalin!

Saturday, 11 February

After tea Jebb rings me up . . . has heard Musso is going tomorrow to demand demilitarisation of Corsica, ditto of Bizerta and condomium in Tunis. Well, if so, the answer is a triple NO. I don't believe it myself. Anyhow it won't keep me awake. I can't believe that Italy will do more than bluff. But of course that's dangerous.

Sunday, 12 February

Back about 6.15. Dined at home. Ought to write speeches for H. But I *won't*. Sometimes I *must* have a let-up and be lazy, and think of other things (I've been dreaming of a cottage). And besides, that's *his* job.

Monday, 13 February

Picked up H. as usual. Further discussion at 11 with him and the pundits on recognition. Glad to say he has moved in directions of immediate, unconditional recognition. He went to see P.M. at 12.15, and I gather that latter agrees. I rang up Eric Phipps (with H's authority) to tell him so. . . . Less work—actually for 10 minutes or so—for the first time for over 12 months—I had nothing to do!

5 Azcarate came to explain that he might tomorrow ask us to put Negrin's* 3 points to Burgos as being a *proposal* of the Spanish Government. This is awkward from various points of view. Corbin about 6.30 to give us to understand that his Government are moving in the same direction as ours, but will do nothing final (he thinks) tomorrow. L. Kennedy† on recognition. He seems quite sound and will write accordingly, I hope.

Tuesday, 14 February

3.15 Herschel Johnson whom I put wise about Spain—recognition of Franco. . . . 7.15 talk with H. and Mounsey about telegram to Burgos, trying to get Franco to talk on Negrin's 3 points.

[Negrin offered an end to the war if Franco would give assurances on three points: the withdrawal of all foreign volunteers, abstention from reprisals, and the freedom of Spaniards to choose their government.]

Wednesday, 15 February

Cabinet in morning, so nothing much doing. Have been so busy last 2 days that I have left this diary and can't remember what happened. Cabinet seem to have agreed in principle to recognition of Franco, but want, if possible, to get some assurances (about reprisals) first. Don't mind this, so long as it doesn't delay recognition.

Thursday, 16 February

Found Azcarate had been round to carry the thing a stage further —practically offering surrender on terms. Drafted telegram to Burgos with H. and G. Mounsey. (Pray Heaven, with any luck, 'Spain' will be over soon.)

Friday, 17 February

Nothing much—have a good deal of trouble about moving people out of the Office, owing to 'War Room' being constructed in our basement. . . . Maisky at 4. Gave him our police reports. Observed they tallied with his account and asked him to accept our explanation (for which I vouched). He—stupidly—pretended to be still suspicious. I worked him on to the ground of demanding that police should always apply to him for permission to enter (on grounds that

* Juan Negrin Lopez, Spanish Prime Minister, 1937–March 1939.

† A. L. Kennedy of *The Times*. Diplomatic correspondent, B.B.C. European division, 1942–5.

Arcos building has diplomatic immunities). He said he would like me to put this demand forward. I said that I supposed the same would apply to the London Fire Brigade! This flummoxed him, and he asked me to do nothing until he had consulted his Government! I should have thought he was too clever a man to let me score like that!

Sunday, 19 February

Rob Hudson called in the evening about Press leakages concerning his trip.* (Rather think he is responsible for them!)

Tuesday, 21 February

Called on H. at 10.... He agrees with what I wrote him yesterday—that we can't go on like this about Spain. On *Thursday* last, Spanish Government asked us to make representation on their behalf. We agreed, and showed Azcarate draft of a telegram to Burgos. We are *still* without an answer. That only proves that there *is no Government* on the anti-Franco side. I had urged that we should say that, unless there is an answer by noon tomorrow, our hands are free and we can (and will) take our own decisions. H. had met Azcarate last night dining with Maisky and had put this to him.

1 p.m. P.M. sent for me (H. wasn't available). He was fussed about Spain. Told him what H. had done. He said he was very glad.... He said he'd got to speak in Sunderland tomorrow. Had thought of using 'Come the 3 corners of the world in arms, and we shall shock them!' Said someone had suggested to him that that might be too obviously aimed against anti-Comintern Pact (? H.J.W.)! I said not a bit. And the magic number 'three' had been broken by the inclusion of Hungary, making up to 4! Hope he will use it.†

... Told H. of my conversation with P.M. and he got latter's approval for a telegram to Paris saying we wanted to recognise not later than Friday!

Wednesday, 22 February

Czech Ch[argé] d'A[ffaires] at 3.15. His Government will give declaration of neutrality but want our guarantee.

French have now replied they will recognise on Monday. We're clinching that. Cabinet this morning agreed to Chinese exchange equalisation fund guarantee. 2 good moves.

[The Cabinet agreed to set up an exchange stabilisation fund in order to hold up the sterling value of the Chinese dollar. This would be a banking

* To Germany in March with Oliver Stanley for trade talks.

† He did.

operation rather than a direct loan, and therefore less provocative to Japan.]

Thursday, 23 February

Lull in work continues. But Joe Kennedy came round in the morning and filled an hour. After his resumption of contact with the U.S., I can hardly understand a word he says. It's a different language.

[Kennedy had been in London less than nine months when he told the astonished Halifax that he did not care for the post of Ambassador. He felt better in America, where he was 'as independent as a hog on ice'.]

Friday, 24 February

Found Hudson was going to have a broadcast message to German people put out on German broadcast! Stopped it. Quiet talk with H. for ¼ hour before lunch. He thinks we've done enough in way of 'firm' speeches. Told him we certainly haven't done too much. If he likes to ease up and talk about weather and crops, I shouldn't mind for a bit, but we should have to watch and see how things go. . . . Comparative lull—2 nights this week I've had no box at home after dinner. But this doesn't necessarily mean a healthier atmosphere in Europe! Nevile H. is completely bewitched by his German friends. Van, on the contrary, out-Cassandras Cassandra in a kind of spirit of pantomime. Must talk to H. about it. He ought either to rebuke Van or recall N.H. I don't know which is the sillier of the 2, or which destroys his own case the more effectively. Van, I think. What a prize ass he is! I have *not* pushed to get rid of him so far, but I think now I ought to.

[Henderson, who had returned to Berlin on 13 February after four months' absence, reported to Cadogan his first impression: 'the Germans are not contemplating any immediate wild adventure and that their compass is pointing towards peace.' Simultaneously Chamberlain had become more optimistic about the prospects. 'He feels' wrote Joseph Kennedy after a long talk on 17 February,

> that America's action [rearmament and a warning speech by Roosevelt to the Senate Military Affairs Committee] psychologically and Britain's tremendous amounts for defence have had a very definite effect on Germany and may do the trick.
>
> . . . It is very difficult to reconcile his two points of view: his hope that appeasement will still be worked out and his fear that Hitler has in his hands, and is quite likely to use them, the means of causing a world war. He definitely does not think Mussolini will cause it.[44]

When the Prime Minister wrote in an even more hopeful sense to Henderson, Halifax immediately added a damping commentary:

I am afraid the business of getting the bridge built between Paris and Rome is likely to be more difficult than the P.M. appears to feel. . . .

I do not myself feel there is any hope of making any sense of colonial discussions, as I think I said to you before you left England, unless and until your German friends can really show more than smooth words as evidence of friendly hearts.

Two days later Henderson reported that Hitler had lately become 'very alive' to German popular feeling against war, and was 'determined democratically to respect it'. Treated rightly, Sir Nevile believed, Hitler would become 'gradually more pacific'.[45]

Very different predictions had been reaching the Foreign Office. Upon one of them Cadogan commented:

I have the profoundest suspicions of Hitler's intentions: I believe they are strictly dishonourable, and I believe what he would like best, if he could do it, would be to smash the British Empire. When it comes to prophesying what his next move will be, I find myself in the same difficulty as the writer of the memo. We neither of us know. The writer admits that Hitler's plans change from week to week: but that does not deter him from telling us as an absolute fact that Hitler is going to engulf Czechoslovakia in May. It was only a few weeks ago that the writer was going about London assuring people that Hitler was 'coming West'. The one theory may be as correct as the other, or neither or both. The writer remarks that he was 'spoken to frankly, under the eyes of the uniformed Nazis', which he finds surprising. But I think it can be accounted for: moreover he is just the sort of personality that the Nazis would choose for conveying any message, threat or hint that they wished to convey. This may be the explanation: but we must bear it in mind.

As regards the reliability of the active facts (such as they are) that he gives us, I think it will be found that his information regarding the railways does not tally very closely with the very detailed information given us by the Industrial Intelligence Section. . . .

The only one thing certain in a very uncertain world is that we must be prepared as best we can for anything. (I believe we have already done some good by our accelerated preparations and by showing determination.) We must take every precaution we can to strengthen ourselves in the Mediterranean and in the West, and even to guard against possible trouble simultaneously in the Far East: and we must not allow ourselves to be distracted too much by the week's story.[46]]

Litvinov told Seeds in February that the Russian Government and public opinion saw no sign that Britain and France would do anything but continue to capitulate. Russia would therefore 'keep aloof', all the more readily since her interests were not directly threatened. 'Herr Hitler and Signor Mussolini', said Litvinov, 'are as frightened of war as you are but they now know from experience that you will never fight.' The Embassy in

Moscow surmised that in the event of a European war, the Russian attitude would probably be one of 'nervous neutrality', designed to avoid antagonising Germany. A little later, in early March, the military and air attachés advised that Russia would not be capable of a telling offensive against the Reich, though Colonel Firebrace predicted that the Red Army would put up a formidable resistance against an invader.[47]

Meanwhile, the Foreign Office had been considering possible points of co-operation with Russia. The Far East had been suggested; but there the familiar difficulties prevented Britain from offering anything effective:

> We cannot, at present, provide China with arms and munitions. It seems that the Americans are unlikely to join in economic action against Japan (which, without U.S. co-operation, would be worse than useless). As regards active operations against Japan, I think these are ruled out, owing to the situation in Europe. If Germany, Italy and Japan attack us simultaneously, we should have to do what we can, but we should probably be rather on the defensive in the Far East. This is one of the problems which is being examined with a view to the Staff conversations with the French. It *may* be that, as a result of those conversations, we should be able to indicate to the Russians our prognosis of events in such a case, and endeavour to find out what, if any, contribution could be expected from them. But I shouldn't have much expectation of any useful or dependable result.[48]

By the end of February, the time when the danger period foreshadowed earlier should have begun, the tenor of the Intelligence reaching the Foreign Office about Germany had become much more reassuring. Nevertheless, the German army was working at high pressure and the Foreign Secretary telegraphed to Washington that

> While recent secret information suggests that any plan for mobilisation early in March may have been postponed, reports have recently reached us pointing to the possibility of a military occupation of Czechoslovakia.
>
> Hitler is clearly preparing for every possible eventuality. Rumours of one or other of these plans are continually reaching us and cannot be lightly discounted. On the other hand, there is no evidence at present that any of them has been irrevocably adopted by Hitler and the date fixed for its being put into force.
>
> . . . Our general impression is that there has been an abnormal amount of military activity in Italy of late but that it is at least premature to deduce that Signor Mussolini has decided to resort to war in the immediate future . . . there are reports from sources that cannot be ignored that instead of risking a major war by pressing her demands on France, Italy might seek cheap glory in the annexation of Albania.[49]

Monday, 27 February

A fuss this morning about the P.M.'s statement on recognition [of Franco's Government] this afternoon. But the fuss was made by the Nit-Wit-in-Chief (Cleverly), and I think the P.M. had what he wanted.

3. Discussion with H., Van, Sargent, Malkin and Uncle Tom Cobley about Franco-Italian relations—in particular the 'concentration-race' in N. Africa. We agreed on lines of a draft telegram to Paris offering to intervene in Rome and urging them to do nothing silly without consulting us.

[Chamberlain announced that Britain would recognise the régime of General Franco as the Government of Spain and had noted with satisfaction his stated intention to maintain the traditional independence of Spain.]

Tuesday, 28 February

While dressing—about 9—message to say H. laid up with 'flu.... Saw P.M. (with Rab Butler). Gave him analysis of the scramble in Parliament yesterday, and suggesting a way out. He seemed quite pleased. He agreed we can't give *any*—even 'de facto'—recognition to Barcelona side.... Wrote some stuff for P.M. for debate on Spain.

Went at 6 to House to see P.M. He had 'got away with it'. Showed him telegram I had sent to Paris based on our discussion of yesterday. He approved heartily.

Thursday, 2 March

Called on H. and found him sitting up in his dressing gown. Talked about that booby Lothian who came back from U.S. very satisfied that he had 'put it across' America and was 'swinging' American opinion. But we have a copy of a letter from Roosevelt, showing he *fairly* put his foot in it. H. had been only amused, but I said we must really reconsider his appointment. So he has referred to P.M....

Corbin came—mainly to hint to me that his Government rather disturbed about our representation on subject of reinforcement in N. Africa.

Friday, 3 March

Met P.M. in Park. He agrees about Lothian, and we're telegraphing to R. Lindsay.

[At the weekend Cadogan caught influenza, and was away from the Office for a few days. Lindsay advised strongly in favour of Lord Lothian's appointment.]

Friday, 10 March

All the Press carries a ridiculous 'rainbow story' (as [W. N.] Ewer called it). Much too optimistic. Traced it to interview given by P.M. yesterday evening to Lobby correspondents. He really shouldn't do this—or at least he should consult H[alifax] before. He talked of Disarmament, which is a dangerous thing to do, and of Franco-Italian relations. I had happened to be with Horace W. yesterday evening (he wanted to talk to me about Leithers) about the time the P.M. was doing it, and he gave me no *inkling* of what was afoot. H. quite nettled, and wrote a rather reproachful letter to P.M.

Corbin came about 6—about staff conversations, still trying to voice suspicions of our démarche in Paris on the subject of troop concentrations—and of course put me through the mill about the P.M.'s statement.

[Halifax reminded the Prime Minister of the difficulties in synchronising relations with the press between No. 10 and the Office. He pointed out that publicity for hopes of early progress in disarmament—'which, however desirable, I cannot regard as probable'—would not do good in Germany at that moment; and asked that in future Chamberlain should consult him in advance of such talks to journalists. The Prime Minister confessed his error but did not repent of the substance of his talk.[50]]

Saturday, 11 March

Walked to F.O. with H. Press full of Slovak crisis. I said (a) it *appeared* to be settled—for the moment—(b) for God's sake don't let's do anything about it. . . . Kell* came to raise my hair with tales of Germany going into Czechoslovakia in next 48 hours. Maybe. Told H. but let him go off to Oxford. Warned P.M. . . . Jebb rang up after [dinner] to say S.I.S. have some hair-raising tales of Czecho[slovakia] for the 14th. It can wait.

[On 9 March, Henderson again told Cadogan that he entirely disbelieved 'wild stories of attacks in various directions'. Sir Alexander replied on 13 March:

> At the end of your letter you express the wish that we could rearm a little more quietly, as you say that the noise we make about it leads Germans to believe that we want after all to attack them. I suppose Germans *can* hold such a fantastic belief, if instructed therein by Goebbels. But with all the vaunting of their own strength, I can't imagine they can believe we could attack them successfully.
>
> What seems to me to be a far greater danger is that they might believe they could attack and smash us (and France), because then they might be led into having a try at it. For that reason, I had always hoped

*Maj.- Gen. Sir Vernon Kell, head of M.I.5 until 1940.

that, when the time came (and thank heaven it has very nearly come), we should advertise our strength as much as possible. Surely you have often yourself said that that is the only argument that the Germans understand?

On the same day, Halifax recorded 'a negative improvement in the situation, in that rumours and scares have died down, and it is not plain that the German Government are planning mischief in any particular quarter. (I hope they may not be taking, even as I write, an unhealthy interest in the Slovak situation!)'[51]]

Monday, 13 March

H. off to Sunderland, for his speech, at 12.30. Slovak situation still v. obscure. We have S.I.S. news that the Germans are prepared to walk in. I showed this to P.M. this evening, observing that the one question we couldn't answer was whether the Germans *would* put their plan into operation. Anyhow, he's disillusioned with Hitler! Van in a neurotic state. Says we must stop Oliver S[tanley] going to Berlin. I told P.M. that, *if* there is an 'Einmarsch' in the next 2 days, we should certainly have to consider the question. He agreed. ... George Lloyd at 5 about Greece.* He spoke for an hour to O.S. and me. On the whole, his report encouraging. Apparently the King† and Metaxas‡ have the situation fairly well in hand, and their medicine—if it does not prove an emetic—may do the Greeks good. Saw Ogilvie-Forbes§ this morning before his return to Berlin. I think he's sensible and capable.

Tuesday, 14 March

H. back from Sunderland. Told him of my talk with P.M. He inclined to agree that, in case of German 'direct action' O[liver] S[tanley] shouldn't go to Berlin. All sorts of reports of what Germany is going to do—'march in' tonight, &c. Probably true. Talk with H., Van, O. S[tanley], Malkin, Sargent. Nothing to be done to stop Germany. But O.S. shouldn't go. Van wants to withdraw Nevile. I against—it's futile. But of course Van doesn't like N. in Berlin. ... Corbin at 3.15 to pump me. French are thinking—he says—of an 'enquiry' of Berlin. I said there was nothing we could do to *stop* it. Question is one of saving our face. This can be done with least loss of prestige *after* the event, by registering disgust. Rob Hudson at 4.30 with all sorts of arguments (of course) in favour of O.S. and his going to Berlin. When he'd gone, and before—2 minutes later—H. went

* Which he had visited as chairman of the British Council.

† King George II of the Hellenes.

‡ Gen. Ioannis Metaxas, Greek Prime Minister and Foreign Minister, 1936–41.

§ Sir G. Ogilvie-Forbes, Counsellor at the Embassy in Berlin, 1937–9.

to see P.M., I warned H. to accept Hudson's arguments with a grain of salt. . . . H. rang me up from House with instructions to draft telegrams to Berlin and Paris. The former quite useless—and P.M. realises it, but wants to be 'on the record'. Latter explaining our position about guarantee. 7.15 H. got back and I and O.S. tried to persuade him that Rob H[udson] must be taken with a grain of salt. O. Stanley came about 7.30 and confirmed that R. Hudson had 'exaggerated'.

Wednesday, 15 March

Rung up at 6.30 by Resident Clerk, who has been bothered by Miss Layton about refugees in Prague. She wants the Legation to take them all in. Folly! German troops going in at 6.30 this morning. Walked to office with H. We must have statement in both Houses this afternoon. Cabinet, during which I got to work on statement. Went over with it to No. 10 at 12.30, and discussed it with Horace, H. and P.M. till 2, when they went off to lunch. I had a sandwich and glass of cider in the Cabinet Room and got statement in order. H. made it at 3. P.M. had to make speech, as there was a debate. Said he would base himself on statement, and did so, but added that he would go on with his 'policy' (? 'appeasement'). Fatal!

Thursday, 16 March

Picked up H. on way to office. Awful amount of work. Corbin at 12.45 to say his Government wanted us to join in a 'protest'. Czech Chargé [d'affaires] to say German Embassy demanded delivery of his Legation. I said anyhow he and his staff could stay here. Awful day—like last Sept[ember]. . . . Talk with H. about his speech on Monday. Don't know *where* we are. We ought perhaps to take a stand (whatever that may mean) but after P.M.'s speech, can we? He speaking again at Birmingham tomorrow night. Think he's been binged up to be a bit firmer. Dined at home and must now tackle *mountains* of work. Begin to doubt whether I can carry this job, and whether I am the right man for it.

[Halifax told the German Ambassador on 15 March:

I could well understand Herr Hitler's taste for bloodless victories, but one of these days he would find himself up against something that would not be bloodless. . . . The conclusion which everybody in this country and far outside it would draw must be that [the German Government] had no great desire to establish good relations with this country, that they were prepared to disregard world opinion and were seeking to establish a position in which they could by force dominate Europe and if possible the world.[52]]

III

March–August 1939

FLOUNDERING INTO WAR

The German occupation of Prague, and the Italian occupation of Albania three weeks later, gave the signal for a new policy of British and French guarantees in Eastern and South-eastern Europe. The first few weeks covered by this chapter were a time of intense strain, uncertainty and anxiety for Cadogan, however calm his demeanour. Thereafter, when the guarantees had been given, shortly followed by the decision to enforce conscription in peacetime, he felt less harassed. Though the pressure of business and the worry of decision remained severe, the uncertainty of 1938 had largely gone.

As Chapter II showed, the British Government had been surprised not by the nature but by the timing of Hitler's latest stroke. Vansittart complained sadly of Henderson's failure to foresee the event and of the official optimism disseminated on its eve. 'But nothing seems any good; it seems as if nobody will listen to or believe me. I shall never know why.'[1] This understandable lament does not entirely meet the point. The British Government heard every kind of rumour, some accurate, more not. What was lacking was a machinery for the collation and assessment of Intelligence. As Cadogan put it, recalling the events of mid-March 1939:

> For weeks or even months beforehand it was not difficult to guess what Hitler's next move might be: in fact it had of course been common talk for some time . . . we were daily inundated by all sorts of reports. It just happened that these were correct; we had no means of evaluating their reliability at the time of their receipt. (Nor was there much that we could do about it!)[2]

Equally, Winston Churchill was not correct in saying that Ministers had no inkling of Mussolini's seizure of Albania, though justified in adding that at any rate they had no conviction of what was coming. In this same month, just after a British guarantee to Poland had been given in order to warn Germany off an attack wrongly supposed to be imminent, there was established a Situation Report Centre, with a representative of the F.O. and the three Service Directors of Intelligence, to bring together the material received from abroad and issue a report each day 'in order that any emergency measures which may have to be taken should be based only on the most reliable and carefully co-ordinated information'.[3]

The two principal features of the six months described by this chapter are the negotiations at Moscow and the attempt to persuade Hitler that an attack on Poland would provoke more than a token effort by Britain and France. The talks at Moscow could scarcely have succeeded once Hitler had shown himself willing to pay a price which the British and French, whether or no they had made pledges to Poland, could not match. The fact that Germany paid a good price indicates either a conviction that the British and French were going to take their Polish guarantee seriously or a determination to snuff out those whom Hitler had described in 1937 as Germany's hate-inspired antagonists. The risk that he might seek to fulfil this purpose by agreement with Stalin, who even before Prague had announced that Russia would not be drawn 'into conflicts by war-mongers who are accustomed to get the others to pull the chestnuts out of the fire for them', was by no means ignored by British policy makers. On the contrary, it was a subject of frequent comment in the Foreign Office and at meetings of the Cabinet. Here also the Intelligence services, though reporting many rumours, did not provide hard and timely information about the Nazi–Soviet negotiations.

The outward form of other developments looked, perhaps, worse than the reality from a British point of view. Franco had triumphed in Spain, but soon indicated that the Duke of Wellington had not erred in saying that there is no country in which foreigners may interfere with so little profit. The British gave him to understand that until Spain dissociated herself from the Axis there would be no loans or money.

Admittedly Germany and Italy signed the Pact of Steel, but only after Japan had declined to join a three-power military alliance, and even then Mussolini stipulated that Italy should not be expected to fight until 1942 or 1943. The Japanese refusal can hardly have failed to impel Germany towards the Nazi–Soviet Pact. From Tokyo the Russians, on the other hand, were admirably informed by their spy, Richard Sorge, who reported that Germany had been trying to commit Japan against Britain. Stalin may well have reasoned, therefore, that he had the less incentive to make terms with the West. Moreover, Germany was obtaining secret information from London about the Anglo-French negotiations in Moscow, a leakage of which Cadogan did not become aware until 1940; and until September 1939 Russia had an agent in the Communications Department of the Foreign Office. This is not to say that the negotiations in Moscow would otherwise have ended differently. Hitler could, in effect, offer Stalin the Baltic States and half of Poland. Britain and France could not.[4]

On the afternoon of 17 March 1939 M. Virgil Tilea, the Roumanian Minister (1938–40), told Halifax that his Government had been presented by Germany by what seemed to them 'something very much like an ultimatum'. Could the British say what they would do if Roumania were a victim of German aggression? The situation might be saved if a 'solid block' of Poland, Roumania, Greece, Turkey and Yugoslavia could be created, with British and French support. At a later interview Tilea informed Cadogan that his Government had refused the German proposals but had received others, of which he had not particulars.[5]

That evening Chamberlain spoke at Birmingham. Having refused to repent of Munich, he asked whether the occupation of Prague denoted the end of an old adventure or the beginning of a new?

[Is this, in fact, a step in the direction of an attempt to dominate the world by force? . . . no greater mistake could be made to suppose that, because it believes war to be a senseless and cruel thing, this nation has so lost its fibre that it will not take part to the utmost of its power in resisting such a challenge if it ever were made.]

1939

Friday, 17 March

All these days have been beastly (I am writing on Monday 20th). Climatically, dark, cold and N.E. wind—most depressing. Politically, awful. Really worse than last Sept. . . . In afternoon, got copy of P.M.'s Birmingham speech. Not too bad.

Tilea came to see me and S. of S. in the evening, with story of German 'ultimatum' to Roumania. On that, S. of S., O.S. and I drafted telegram to threatened States, referring to this threat to Roumania, and asking them, more or less, what they will do about it.

Saturday, 18 March

Having repeated to Bucharest our telegram to the 'threatened States', R. Hoare* asks us to hold it up, and subsequently we got from him démenti of it from Roumanian M.F.A. I sent for Tilea and confronted him with this. He could only say he *knew* it to be true, but he could not tell me he had it direct from his Government. We got P.M. back from Birmingham and there was a Cabinet at 5. They, as far as I can make out, were bellicose, but it was left for a meeting of P.M., J.S., H., Oliver [Stanley] tomorrow to draft final telegram of instructions.

[If a report by the Yugoslav Minister, intercepted by the Germans, is to be believed, Tilea told him that in order to safeguard Roumania's security he had 'made the utmost possible use of his instructions'.[6]

At the Cabinet Chamberlain proposed that Britain approach Russia, Poland, Yugoslavia, Turkey, Greece and Roumania. On the reported threat to Roumania, the Chiefs of Staff said through Admiral Chatfield that German access to her oilfields would do much to nullify a British blockade. Political control, sure to follow, would be still more serious, since Germany could then move straight to the Mediterranean, relying on Bulgarian friendship. However, little could be done to help Roumania directly.]

* Sir Reginald Hoare, British Minister in Bucharest, 1935–41.

Sunday, 19 March

Meeting at 11.30. P.M., H., J.S., O. S[tanley], Horace W. and myself. By then replies came in from various capitals where, in spite of R. H[oare]'s hold-up our Representatives had taken action. All of them, in reply to our question 'What will you do', said 'What will *you*?'

P.M. said he had foreseen this, and to meet it, and stop it, had idea that we should put before France, Poland and Soviet a text of a declaration of 'non-intéressement'. This seemed a good idea, and we drafted it. Met again at 4.30 and got draft into shape.

Nevile H[enderson], recalled from Berlin, dined and *would* talk till 11.30. I got to bed at 1.

Monday, 20 March

Picked up H. at 9.45. Cabinet at 10.30. Saw H. at 12.45, but he absorbed in his speech. Told me Cabinet had approved draft telegram to certain amendments: I was to get it into shape and get P.M.'s approval. This I did, by about 5. 5.45 Corbin came and I gave him formula. He expressed horror—and there is *some* force in his objection. We propose to publish a Declaration that, *in the event of a further outrage*, we will consult. Point: c'est tout. So I warned H. and P.M., both down at the House; held up telegram and went to see them, with Horace W., at 7.15. They touch[ed] it up* and I sent it off.

These are awful days. The crisis is worse, really, than last Sept., but the public don't know it. It's more critical and more imminent, and more acute. And I'm afraid we have reached the cross-roads. I always said that, as long as Hitler could pretend he was incorporating Germans in the Reich, we could pretend that he had a case. If he proceeded to gobble up other nationalities, that would be the time to call 'Halt!'. That time has come, and I must stick to my principle, because on the whole, I think it right. I don't believe that he can gobble all Europe, or at least I don't believe that, if he does, it will do him much good. But we must have a moral position, and we shall lose it if we don't *do* something now. P.M.'s speech was all right on sentiments, but the country—and other countries—are asking 'What are you going to *do*?'. If we say plainly, we risk goading Hitler into attacking us. But that is a risk that must be taken. This country has taken risks before. But of course we are *not* ready (nor ever shall be).

* The amended version said that the British, French, Russian and Polish Governments would immediately consult together about joint resistance to action threatening the independence of any European state.

P.M. has sent a letter to Musso. I have struggled against his drafts which all looked much too much like asking for another Munich, which would be fatal. *I* wanted to send him a warning that he can't bully France. P.M.'s final draft has a hint of this, so it's not too bad, but I don't quite like it. Life is Hell. Dined at home.

[The Foreign Office had heard on 17 March that Mussolini might emulate Hitler by presenting an ultimatum to France or occupying Albania. It was thought that a warning of Anglo-French refusal to consider claims presented in such a manner might deter him. The letter which Chamberlain sent contained nothing so explicit, though it did say that if the German performance in Czechoslovakia heralded 'attempts at control of other States', war would be inevitable.

There was, of course, the possibility of 'buying' Italy; but that, Cadogan thought, would be a harder task than it looked:

> Doubtless Italy's historic policy has always been to sell herself to the highest bidder. But by breaking with the Axis, Mussolini would be confirming the pretty complete failure of his policy, and Dictators don't like doing that. He would want a big price—which would have to be paid principally by France. And there is the danger—a very great one—that any approach to Italy now might give him the impression that, after all, the Democracies *are* frightened. Mussolini may not want to go to war, but he may be encouraged to bluff up to a point at which retreat is impossible for him, and then the spark is put to the powder. But we shall be on the watch for any possible weakening of the Italian Govt. and must do our best to turn it to account in the best possible way.[7]]

Tuesday, 21 March

It's impossible to keep this Diary up. I work day and night and have no time for it (I am writing on Saturday 25th). The French visit has made this week a nightmare. Superimposed upon a crisis, it has rendered everything impossible. I don't remember the exact sequence of events. I know that, in the upshot, France agrees to our new declaration, and Moscow also (provided French and Poles sign) but this has only gradually emerged during the last few days.

Wednesday, 22 March

Meeting between P.M., H., Bonnet, Corbin, Bressy*, Strang and self at 5. Clear by now that Poles won't play on Declaration. We agreed that, when they had refused, we and French should offer to guarantee a Polish-Roumanian mutual Guarantee Pact.

* Pierre Bressy, Bonnet's Private Secretary.

[Halifax said that the British Government thought it was now a question of checking German aggression, whether in Western or Eastern Europe. Bonnet emphasised that to get Poland in was essential, for Russian aid would otherwise be ineffective. The strongest pressure, even to the point of threats, should be put upon Poland. Halifax agreed that 'very plain language' might be needed. It transpired, under Chamberlain's questioning that France had produced 100 aircraft during the last month, instead of the 400 predicted by Daladier in the previous November. Britain's production had risen from 250 per month at the time of Munich to 600. Admitting the seriousness of France's weakness in the air, Bonnet asked Halifax in private to think of the position on land. Here, said he, was France, with some 40 millions, facing Germany and Italy with about 120 millions. If the French people could not look for substantial British help until, say, eighteen months of a war had elapsed, the consequences might be 'profound and irretrievable'. Acknowledging all the difficulties, traditional, industrial and practical, Bonnet begged for the introduction of conscription in Great Britain.[8]]

Friday, 24 March

Had to be at No. 10 at 9.45—P.M. talking to Labour. He explained quite frankly that *we* weren't cold-shouldering Russia—it was the misgivings of Poland and others.*

Saturday, 25 March

There are neither week-ends, nor nights nor days. Corbin came to pump me—I told him as little as possible. . . . 12 meeting with H., Van, Sargent, Malkin, Strang to discuss what to do next. Lunched at home and resumed at 3. Quite useful.

Sunday, 26 March

Got first impressions of Musso's speech—pretty offensive. Revised Strang's draft embodying results of our yesterday's discussion, and drafted short statement for P.M. for tomorrow—refusing to give information as to course of negotiations. . . .

Whole situation looks as murky as it can be, and all the little States are weakening and showing funk—even Turkey. I must say it is turning out—at present—as Van predicted and as I never believed it would. If we want to stem the German expansion, I believe we must try to build a dam *now*. Of course, as to whether, if Germany really does gobble S.E. Europe, she will *really* be stronger to attack us, I still have some doubts. But Mason MacFarlane thinks she will, and

* For a statement of Chamberlain's 'profound distrust' of Russia see Feiling, *Life of Neville Chamberlain*, p. 403.

he ought to know more about it than I. If we are set on this course, we must set about it quickly and firmly. It *might* act as a deterrent to avert war, though I confess I think the chances of that are rather slight. But on the whole, it is probably the right thing to do.

Pieris Japonica at Queen Anne's Gate showing pink bud. Most daffodils are out. There was a red rhododendron in flower in Richmond Park.

I picked up H. at 9.20 and we went on to No. 10. R.A.B. there. We discussed approach to Polish and Roumanian Governments—involving our guarantee. P.M. approved in principle.

Monday, 27 March

Foul day again and drizzling. Fairly easy morning. Lunched at home. In afternoon busy on draft telegrams giving effect to our decisions of last night. 5 p.m. Foreign Policy Committee on drafts. To my surprise, no strong objections—even from J[ohn] S[imon]—to our guarantee of Poland and Roumania. Back to F.O. at 7.30 and got telegram off.

Tuesday, 28 March

W. T[yrrell]* and Anthony [Eden] conspiring [at a lunch at the Cadogans' flat]. A.E. says basis of Government must be 'broadened'. W.T. suggests S.B.† should be taken in as a stool-pigeon to lure the Labourites. This seems to me rather over-elaborate!

But we *must* do *something* about our military strength. I talked to H. about it this morning. There are, I know, frightful difficulties, but it is the test by which other countries (including Germany) will judge us. Wrote him something, which he sent to P.M. He told me tonight that P.M. has authorised doubling of territorials (I don't of course, mean to say that I had any hand in this!!). That will be something: but I fear not enough.

Wednesday, 29 March

Cabinet in morning, to which H. exposed our policy in regard to Poland and Roumania. They seemed to take it all right. But we haven't yet had a reply from French saying that they agree.... In evening Ian Colvin ('News Chronicle') came and saw H. and me and Rex L[eeper] and gave hair-raising details of imminent German thrust against Poland. A nice young man—rather precious. I was

* Lord Tyrrell, one of Cadogan's predecessors as P.U.S., 1925–8; Ambassador in Paris, 1928–34.

† Stanley (then Lord) Baldwin.

not entirely convinced. I am getting used to these stories. But H. seemed impressed, and we took him over to P.M. about 6, when he told his story. French have now agreed, and we have told Warsaw and Bucharest to go ahead. H., who stayed behind with P.M., came over later and said latter agreed to idea of an *immediate* declaration of support of Poland, to counter a quick putsch by Hitler.

. . . I at F.O. at 10.15 to meet H. and R.A.B. Drafting Declaration for immediate use (and telegrams to Paris and Warsaw) till 1 a.m.

[Ian Colvin's account seems to indicate that in the later stages of the second meeting Cadogan half-suggested that Chamberlain should be succeeded by Halifax. Shown this record in 1964, Sir Alexander had no recollection of the conclave in the Prime Minister's room, though he remembered well the meeting between Colvin, Halifax and himself in the F.O. He could only conclude that this remark had been made in jest. 'I don't think I can possibly in all seriousness have invited the company to consider doing a Delcassé!'[9] As Cadogan's diary shows (see, for example, the entries for 22, 26 and 27 March) Mr Colvin's information was not the origin of the guarantee to Poland, though the announcement was precipitated as a result of these talks on 29 March.]

Thursday, 30 March

To No. 10 at 2.30. Cabinet had played about with our Declaration and P.M., H. and I tried to put it in shape for F.P.C. at 4. Saw [A.] L. Kennedy [of *The Times*] and gave him the low-down—hope I can trust him. Florescu* at 5—nothing much to say—trying to pump me. Sent telegrams to Paris and Warsaw, asking if we could make interim declaration of support of *Poland* tomorrow. . . . Lots of work, and I'm exhausted. Can't give a coherent view of what is happening. The great question is shall we *now*—and how—challenge Hitler and try to stop the rot? I *think* we must (if Poles agree: Van says in any case—I think he's wrong). But it's a *frightful* gamble. Mowing begun in Parks.

[Chamberlain put the dilemma thus:

> If we take no action, there is a risk that we shall find that Poland has been over-run. On the other hand, if we utter a warning such as is now proposed, we shall be committed if Germany persists in aggression.

The Chiefs of Staff thought that although Poland would probably be conquered in a campaign of two or three months it would be preferable,

* Of the Roumanian Legation, deputising for Tilea.

if Britain did have to fight Germany, to do it in alliance with Poland. Ministers agreed with the announcement which Chamberlain would make the next day.

The Intelligence available to the British Government at that stage, correctly as we now know, did not indicate an immediate German *coup* against Poland.[10] Chamberlain said as much in the House on March 31. However,

> certain consultations are now proceeding with other Governments. In order to make perfectly clear the position of His Majesty's Government before those consultations are concluded, I now have to inform the House that during that period in the event of any action which clearly threatened Polish independence, and which the Polish Government accordingly considered it vital to resist with their national forces, His Majesty's Government would feel themselves bound at once to lend the Polish Government all support in their power. They have given the Polish Government an assurance to this effect.

The reasons for which Britain had embarked on the new policy were summarised by Cadogan in May:

> The principal object of our guarantee to Poland was to deter Germany from any further acts of aggression, and by obtaining a reciprocal guarantee from Poland to ensure that, if war must ensue, Germany would have to fight on two fronts. We have been told that this is essential. Germany is unable at the moment to embark on a war on two fronts. If she were free to expand eastward and to obtain control of the resources of Central and Eastern Europe, she might then be strong enough to turn upon the Western countries with overwhelming strength.
>
> Our object was, therefore, beginning with our guarantee of Polish independence, to build up a peace front to the East and South-east of Germany consisting of Roumania, Poland, Turkey and Greece. Of this combination Poland was the key, and Poland's position would be precarious in the face of a hostile or perhaps even of a neutral Soviet Union. Our only practicable lines of communication with Poland in case of war would lie through Russian territory.
>
> We therefore wished to be assured of at least the benevolent neutrality of the Soviet Union, and better still of the probability of assistance being afforded by that country to Poland and Roumania in case of attack.[11]

Towards the end of his life, Cadogan read through his Diary for the first three months of 1939 and confessed that it left

> the impression of a number of amateurs fumbling about with insoluble problems. It is necessary to try to recall the situation of those times. Our own military capabilities were deplorably inadequate. We

were being swept along on a rapid series of surprises sprung upon us by Hitler with a speed that took one's breath away. He was pursuing his tactic of 'one by one'. And it was that in the end that drove Chamberlain to take a sudden and surprising decision to guarantee Poland. Of course our guarantee could give no possible protection to Poland in any imminent attack upon her. But it set up a signpost for himself. He was committed, and in the event of a German attack on Poland he would be spared the agonising doubts and indecisions. You might say that this was cruel to Poland. I wouldn't agree with that, because our military situation must have been known to them and they should have been quite aware of the imminence of the peril that threatened them. You might say that it was cynical. On a short view, perhaps it was. But it *did* bring us into the war. . . . And in the end we, with our Allies, won it. Though of course the poor Poles cannot be expected to appreciate the result for them.[12]

Neither at the time nor in retrospect did Cadogan believe that the guarantee had effectively given the control of British policy to Poland or stultified the later negotiations at Moscow, though it carried many obvious drawbacks—commitment to an unstable position, provision of excellent material for German propaganda, and a straining of the Dominions' loyalty.]

Friday, 31 March

F.P.C. meeting at 9.45. P.M. said he must show text of declaration to Cabinet, so it was called for 12. Meanwhile O. Stanley said the City wanted steadying, so agreed that P.M. should answer question at 11 saying we have no confirmation of the rumours and announcing that he would make a statement before House rises. F.P.C. approved revised draft of Declaration. Horace and I afterwards drafted telegram to Musso. I got back to F.O. about 11.30 and got H. to approve draft to Musso[lini]. Went to H[ouse] of C[ommons] about 11.45. Waited on Cabinet in P.S.'s room. They finished 12.45—didn't alter draft. H. and I went back to F.O.—he to see Maisky, and I to see Joe K[ennedy]. Latter very tiresome: I gave him declaration and he said it would be regarded in America as a 'subterfuge'. I retorted rather hotly, and he promised to do his best with his beastly newsmen. . . . Back at F.O. at 2.45 and, as there wasn't anything frightful or urgent, went out and walked round lake in the Park. Saw scyllas in bloom. I was feeling pretty awful by now, but sight of flowers and mowing machines and domestic couples of ducks restored my balance. Aras* at 5—to give me 'explications' which very considerably fogged his ramblings of yesterday. H. went home at 5. Polished off a lot of

* Tewfik Rüstü Aras, Turkish Ambassador, 1939–42.

work—disturbed by Layton about his wretched correspondents in Berlin. *Nobody* has *any* mercy on me. By the way, in the Park this afternoon I met Raczynski*, coming back from the House, seemingly pleased. The die is now cast and Hitler may bomb us. But I think we've done right.

. . . Pretty tired. The strain is more than one knows at the time.

Saturday, 1 April

A tiresome symposium with H. at 11 to make notes for P.M.'s speech on Monday. These things always rather futile, and I very draggled and tired.

Hitler's speech gives the impression that he was rather embarrassed to know what to say. Jebb rang up to say H. wanted meeting tomorrow at 12. I protested violently: it just cuts the heart out of the day, and I've had *no* week-end for 3 weeks. Even in times of crisis, H. goes off to Yorkshire on a Friday afternoon. When he's in London, he's at a loose end and doesn't know what to do with himself, so ruins everyone else's day. Fixed it for 6 instead.

Sunday, 2 April

Went round to H. Tinkered with his statement for tomorrow, and P.M.'s speech, and a few odds and ends. There's nothing in Musso's reply to P.M., and there's a testy telegram from Litvinov.

All daffodils out, and most primroses. Country beginning to look very nice. The earth's a good place, if only Hitler weren't on it!

Dined at home. Rang up H.J.W. after dinner, and gave him some comments on our notes for P.M.'s speech.

Monday, 3 April

Went to House . . . at 3.45. Greenwood† and P.M. both fairly dignified—and dull. 5.30 meeting with H., Van, Sargent, Malkin, Strang and Makins‡ on how to take Beck. 7 went to House with H. to P.M.'s room to discuss with him, J.S., H.J.W., R.A.B. and Ivone what J.S. should say in winding up. Latter had a fairly good draft, and we didn't help much. Stayed afterwards with P.M. and H., discussing N. Henderson's return. I don't see much harm, if it's done quickly and naturally. Told P.M. I had advised Brocket§ not to go

* Count Edward Raczynski, Polish Ambassador, 1934–45. See List of Principal Characters.

† Arthur Greenwood, Deputy-Leader of the Labour Party.

‡ Roger Makins of the Central Dept.; later Lord Sherfield.

§ Second Lord Brocket, Chairman of the Anglo-German Fellowship.

to Germany to junket with Hitler on his birthday and had advised B[rocket] to advise Kordt not to issue invitations to others.

Tuesday, 4 April

I am writing on Friday, having been on the Bridge since Tuesday and no time to do anything. My memory is therefore rather at fault. Meeting at 11. H., myself, Strang, with Beck, Potocki* and Raczynski. Quite fairly satisfactory. Beck is ready to give us reciprocal guarantee in case of attack on *us*, but it remains to be seen whether he will move in case of attack on Holland, Belgium, Switzerland, &c. . . . 5 meeting in P.M.'s room—P.M., H., Strang, and I and the Poles. Beck quite good on his guarantee to us, but very sticky about guarantee to Roumania—says he must talk to them first.

Dinner for Beck at F.O. . . . After dinner Kemsley produced text of Jim Stanhope's† speech on 'Ark Royal'! Why do we keep exhibits like Jim in the Cabinet!! Kemsley undertook to try to suppress it. Peake‡ kept it out of B.B.C. and tried to suppress agencies. I was told off to hunt Joe Kennedy to stop it in America. But with little success! Bed about 1.

[On 3 April the Foreign Office had received a report (from an informant connected with the German War Ministry) to the effect that the Luftwaffe might make a lightning attack on the British fleet. The Cabinet thereupon authorised Lord Stanhope to say that some of the Fleet's anti-aircraft defences were manned. Of *Ark Royal* he announced: 'Shortly before I left the Admiralty it became necessary to give orders to man the anti-aircraft guns of the Fleet so as to be ready for anything that might happen.'

Embarrassed explanations had to be made in Parliament. The story, it appears, had been 'planted' by Admiral Canaris§; another, to the effect that German submarines were patrolling in the Channel and Thames Estuary, was successfully planted on Vansittart by a different German agent.[13]]

Wednesday, 5 April

Dinner at Polish Embassy. . . . After dinner H., I, Strang, and Poles (Van was left out!) agreed statement for P.M. tomorrow.

* Count Joseph Potocki of the Polish Ministry of Foreign Affairs.

† Earl Stanhope, First Lord of the Admiralty, 1938–9; Leader of the House of Lords, 1938–40.

‡ Charles Peake of the News Dept., F.O.; British representative with the French National Liberation Council, 1942–4; Political Liaison officer with the Supreme Allied Command, 1943–5.

§ Admiral Wilhelm Canaris, head of the Abwehr (German Military Intelligence) 1935–44; executed by the Gestapo, April 1945.

Thursday, 6 April

Went with H. at 10.0 to see P.M. and show him draft statement, which he approved. Sat on talking about Nevile H. They agreed he ought to be changed. Came back and told Raczynski that statement all right. Saw Nevile H., who had been given hint of his move by H. Was just in time to stop a bad answer to a private notice question on Albania.

Poles spent 3 hours in my room in afternoon drafting 'Heads of Agreement' with me, Strang, and W. Malkin. Dined at home, picked up H. and landed at F.O. at 9.30 for meeting with Poles. Agreed 'Heads of Agreement'.

Good Friday, 7 April

H. went off about 11.15 to Church (3-hour service!). Then news came in about Italy's ramp in Albania. I was ready packed for Stanmore, but told T. at lunch that I probably couldn't go. Raczynski came and initialled 'Heads of Agreement'. Lunched at home at 1 and saw Beck off at Victoria. . . . Aras 3.45 and Simopoulos* at 4.15. About 4.45 saw H. who had been brought back to F.O. and decided not to go to Yorkshire. Discussed Albania with him. Decided we can't *do* anything to stop it. I take line that this proves Musso a gangster as Czecho[slovakia] proved Hitler, and we must set up a barrier with Greece and Turkey. Admiralty fussing about their ships in Italian ports. Told them to hang on till tomorrow. H. summoning service Ministers and Chatfield for tomorrow 11.30.

Saturday, 8 April

Went with H. at 11.30 to a meeting of a scratch crew at No. 10. J.S. (in chair), H., Sam Hoare, Hore-Belisha, Kingsley Wood, Jim Stanhope, Ernest Brown†, Buck de la Warr, Chatfield. Decided nothing to be done about Albania but, in principle, Albania is like Czecho[slovakia]—proof of Musso's, as of Hitler's, evil intentions, and we must put a full stop, which in this case means agreement with Greece and Turkey parallel to our Polish agreement. Decided to ask P.M. to return (he is doing so tonight) and to recommend summoning of Parliament (for which Attlee &c. are asking) probably on Thursday. . . .

Crolla has a message from Musso[lini], which he is trying to deliver to H. If he can't get him, he will bring it to me. Heard later he had got him.

* C. J. Simopoulos, Greek Minister, 1935–42.
† Minister of Labour, 1935–40.

Easter Sunday, 9 April

After breakfast, F.O. sent round a telegram from Athens saying Greek Government had news from a reliable source that Musso was going to occupy Corfu between April 10 and 12. Well, that's the kind of rumour one gets every 5 minutes these days, and God alone knows whether it's true. If Musso does it, we go to war, that's all. . . . Picked up H. at F.O. and we went to see P.M. at No. 10. Crolla, whom I met, had been with H. again, giving him renewed assurances that Musso won't attack Corfu. But what are they worth? H. gave him good warning, and we are telling Greeks we have done so, and asking Musso to repeat his assurances to Athens. P.M. quite calm and sound: seems to agree we must tie up Greece and Turkey. . . . After lunch motored to F.O. and walked in Park, meeting H. and Dorothy [Lady Halifax]. 2.45 we approved telegrams to Rome and Paris. 3 went with H. to meeting of Chiefs of Staff and Chatfield. Decided to concentrate Mediterranean Fleet (who are now strung out over Villefranche and other ports) somewhere S[outh] of Malta. I came home for tea and T. and I went to Park and walked for an hour and a half. On return, found Crolla had seen H. again and renewed assurances about Greece, and said that Musso agreed to repeat assurances to Athens. 7.30 Barrington Ward* to see me. I told him to soft-pedal. We shall have quite enough abuse of 'Ice-creamers'. Difficulty is to steer between provocation and impression of impotence. If you are too bellicose, you provoke Dictators into doing something irrevocable. If you are too passive, you encourage them to think they can do anything.

What an Easter! Dined at home.

Monday, 10 April

Saw H. before Cabinet. Tilea and Cretzianu† called 11.30, to put me through one of their catechisms (which I resent profoundly). What they want is a provisional, unilateral guarantee. Didn't encourage them to think they'd get it. . . . H. appeared at 1.20 after a 'fair' Cabinet. Hurled one sentence at me about a guarantee for Greece and told me to make notes for F.P.C. meeting this afternoon at 4 (what about?). . . . Wrote, with M. Ingram's help, notes for H. Went with him at 4 to F.P.C. He hadn't had time to read my notes, so when called on to open the proceedings, he started reading them. J.S. looked down his nose. Awful rambling discussion, but general sense was we must do something about Greece and Turkey. After,

* R.M. Barrington-Ward, Assistant Editor of *The Times*, 1927–41; Editor, 1941–8.

† Of the Roumanian Legation.

with P.M. and Chatfield, discussed fleet movements. Seems fleet will have to go to Malta—which seems a bit of a risk. Came back and, with H. and M. Ingram, made first skeleton draft of declaration for P.M. and telegrams to Turkey.

On return from dinner found message from Corbin and Herschel Johnson to ring them. Corbin said Reuter had issued 'communiqué' denying that we are going to guarantee Greece. After hunting round all London on telephone, find this is a mis-statement. Barrington Ward rang up about 10.45 to say rumours of Cabinet dissensions. Put him wise. Think Corbin's story is merely designed to scare us into haste. He in league—so Peake, whom I got at last on telephone, tells me—with 'D[aily] T[elegraph]' who will have attack on Government tomorrow for 'indecision'. (Seems they are running H. against P.M.—Silly.) Anyhow, the Reuter story is a mare's nest. H. Johnson (whom I had seen this afternoon) wanted to know if H. really made formal request for despatch of U.S. fleet to Pacific. I said he had made it half jokingly. They'd better discuss it tomorrow.

[The developments in South-east Europe upset the agreed British naval strategy, which counted on a friendly or neutral Italy allowing the passage through the Mediterranean of capital ships to Singapore. Indeed, a sub-committee of the Committee of Imperial Defence had suggested before Prague that if war broke out in Europe Britain should take the offensive in the Mediterranean and hope that Japan would stay out of the war in the early stages. Immediately after the Czechoslovak crisis, and in order to assuage Australian anxieties, Halifax asked whether the U.S. Fleet could not be moved back to the Pacific. Roosevelt agreed in part and the transfer was announced on 15 April.]

Tuesday, 11 April

H. set me to work to draft ideas for P.M.'s statement on his speech. 12 went with him to see P.M., who had drafted a different form of declaration—much too weak (I suppose Horace has been at him again!) only talking about an 'unfriendly act'. Drove H. back here to lunch, and on the way we read telegrams, including some from Angora [Ankara], showing Turks have lost their nerve and want some ginger. . . . F.P.C. at 3, when it was agreed to go further than 'unfriendly act' and to give definite guarantee to Greece and ask for Turkey's support. Desultory and rambling discussion of telegrams to Angora and Paris. Got back about 4.30 and re-wrote them and submitted them to H., who finally approved. This—as in the Polish case—is an interim measure to guarantee Greece, who is in the front line. We shall then have to try and get Turkey into a more comprehensive arrangement, but that is a matter of time. Strang, Maurice I[ngram] and I started draft on those lines.

Wednesday, 12 April

Can't remember exact sequence of events (am writing on Friday). Submitted in morning re-draft of longer telegram to Angora, which H. approved. Don't think much else happened the rest of the day, except that, in the evening, Corbin came round with a text of a declaration his Government are going to make tomorrow, backing us, but *also* guaranteeing *Roumania!* Got H. to join in talk and we tried to get Corbin to dissuade them. He didn't think he could do it. H. went over to see P.M. about 7.30 and latter strongly against.... H. turned up at 9.30 and we drafted telegram to Paris protesting, which I telephoned to F.O. Then he rang up Corbin and used the same arguments. But it won't be much good, I think. H. left about 11, and I so tired that I could do nothing more. Life is a complete nightmare: shall we ever wake up?

Thursday, 13 April

Found George Lloyd on my doorstep urging that we should give Roumania guarantee! I said as if I hadn't been up all night about it, and turned him out. Tilea then rang up with the same request... and I snubbed him. Cabinet at 11. Corbin called and gave me reasoned exposé of Daladier's views on Roumania. And they were unanswerable. Sent record over to H. at Cabinet. Cabinet finished 12.15 and I was sent for. They had agreed to Roumanian guarantee! Drafted telegrams in Cabinet Room with P.M. and H. Lunched at home. Back 2.15 to help H. with his speech. Did some work and had to go at 6.30 to House to coach J.S. for his winding up speech. He pretty awful, as usual.

Friday, 14 April

Slight panic after last few days' activities. Discussion with H., L. O[liphant], Maurice I[ngram] and Strang about new approach to Russia. Decided on.... H. left for Yorkshire at 3.15. P.M. gone to Chequers! I hate these lulls—they are always ominous. But at least I had one and feel played out. Tilea and Corbin called. Home earlier —7.45—very tired.

[Russia was asked to make a public declaration that in the event of a resisted attack upon one of her European neighbours she would give armed assistance if desired. Cadogan noted a few days later that this proposal was made 'in order to placate our left wing in England, rather than to obtain any solid military advantage'.[14]]

Saturday, 15 April

H. rang up about 11 to say he had a letter from Hamilton, Rector of St. Paul's, Knightsbridge, who had invented a proposal that Hitler should summon a Conference on his birthday, and has given this to the Duke of Buccleuch (who flew to Germany this morning) and Brocket, who is going this afternoon! Ye Gods and little fishes! *Is* the world upside down? However, H. had given the Rector a mild cold douche and asked me to continue the good work. I sent for the Rector at 11.30, and gave him plainly to understand we didn't think anything of this idea, and above all those 2 . . . must make it perfectly clear that they have no *sort* of official approval of any kind.

Fortunately, later in the morning, H. Johnson brought round the text of a message Roosevelt sent last night to Hit[ler] and Muss calling on them for assurance of non-aggression against certain countries and proposing a conference himself. So he's beaten the Rector (who has just rung me up again!) by a short head.

Corbin at 12. French jumpy about Tangier and are sending 2 cruisers: want us to do the same. Really. I'm not Lord High Admiral, and as we are concentrating fleet in Mediterranean, we mustn't interfere with *that.* Subject to that, and French convenience, I don't mind if we send a ship.

Bill Bentinck* at 1.15 to say Egyptian army is being sent to war stations. Really, I'm not G.O.C. Egypt. I don't want to stop them going there but told him to tell Miles Lampson† to ask *why!*

Rex L[eeper] rang me up about 11 to say that Poliakoff‡ hears Hitler is going to reject Roosevelt 100%. Probably!

Monday, 17 April

I lunched with L[eith]-R[oss]. Discussed his trip to Roumania, &c., and decided to try and stymie that awful Rob Hudson sticking himself in. . . . Talks in afternoon with H. about a number of things —mainly Turkish situation. He fresh from a long week-end, ready to raise lots of questions. I rather fagged.

* V. F. W. Cavendish-Bentinck of the F.O.; Chairman, Joint Intelligence Committee, 1939–45; Ambassador in Warsaw, 1945–7.

† Sir Miles Lampson, later Lord Killearn; British High Commissioner in Egypt, 1933–6; Ambassador in Cairo, 1936–46.

‡ Vladimir Poliakoff, journalist of Russian extraction.

Tuesday, 18 April

Don't remember exactly what happened, but I know I had an awful rush. Had to try to write some of H's speech for tomorrow. He's the devil when he has a speech in the offing.

[The Russians suggested that Britain, France and Russia should make an agreement for mutual assistance; offer all help to states lying between the Baltic and Black Seas and bordering on Russia; discuss promptly the means of giving such help; sign conventions on the military and political aspects simultaneously; and agree not to conclude a separate peace.

Cadogan's minute, hurriedly drafted, accepted the prevailing opinion that Russian military assistance would be of doubtful value outside her own frontiers:

> We have to balance the advantage of a paper commitment by Russia to join in a war on one side against the disadvantage of associating ourselves openly with Russia. The advantage is, to say the least, problematical. . . . If we are attacked by Germany, Poland under our mutual guarantee will come to our assistance, i.e. make war on Germany. If the Soviet are bound to do the same, how can they fulfil that obligation without sending troops through or aircraft over Polish territory? That is exactly what frightens the Poles.[15]]

Wednesday, 19 April

Read to H. my appreciation of the Moscow telegram putting the mischievous Soviet proposals. He approved. . . . 5.30 F.P.C. to settle reply to Turkey. M. Ingram gave good explanation of the case, and they approved draft without much difficulty. They then discussed (in a preliminary way) Soviet proposals. I gave them my views and there was general approval, though S. Hoare—and Oliver S.—are still hankering after the Soviet.

Got back about 7 and approved finally telegram to Angora. Sent telegram to Paris urging them not to reply to Soviet before consulting us, and asking them exactly what proposals *they* had made to Soviet.

[On 19 April Daladier begged the British Government, through Phipps, to introduce conscription; it could only be a gesture, but he thought it would be a vital one for friends and foes alike. Phipps hoped that the Cabinet would give 'immediate and most serious consideration' to this plea, at a 'moment when the imponderables count more than mere material considerations. . . . German propaganda is terribly busy in France just now, and only by the adoption of this measure can it be countered.'[16]]

Thursday, 20 April

Lovely spring day. Hitler's birthday!! I had arranged that H.M.

should not wish him 'happy returns' (as we don't want any of them!) but only 'congratulations' on his 50th birthday—blast him! Picked up H. at 9.45. Told him about F.P.C. yesterday evening. Pole at 10.40. Corbin at 11.45. I hinted to Pole that they mustn't be intransigent about Danzig now that we have guaranteed them. H. got back at 1 from C.I.D. P.M. has agreed to Conscription! Hopes to announce it on Tuesday and we want to have N.H. back in Berlin on Monday.... H. busy in afternoon, but got back about 6.30. Got him to approve telegrams to Paris and Rome trying to get the 2 parties together—I think that is a great chance. Also telegram to Paris about sending back Ambassador. Authorised E. P[hipps] in last resort to tell Daladier about conscription. May be necessary to do this in any case, to get him to get a move on with Italians.

Friday, 21 April

E. Phipps argued for ½ an hour, trying to persuade Daladier and Bonnet to send Coulondre* back to Berlin. They wouldn't: so he had to tell them about conscription. They burst into tears and flung their arms round his neck and agreed to *anything* we liked! But I suppose they'll leak!

Saturday, 22 April

(Much worried in morning by Admiralty who are *all* half-wits and keep on referring to me about movements of Mediterranean Fleet, with different suggestions from each Department). Finally Cunningham† (D.C.N.S.)—King Half-wit, rang me up and I got angry. So ordered the Fleet to concentrate at Alexandria between May 2 and 15. Lunched at home. T. and I went to Kew. Very beautiful, but rather between seasons. Daffodils and some blossom rather over. Azaleas and magnolias not out. Met Ullswaters. He 84, she, I think, 85. They had one bathchair between them!

Monday, 24 April

Gafencu‡ 11. He very nice—forthright, good looking, sincere (as I should judge) and a good talker. He was apparently reassured by (1) Beck and (2) Hitler!!

Tuesday, 25 April

Walked with H. in morning. Meeting of F.P.C. at 11 about reply

* Robert Coulondre, French Ambassador in Moscow, and in Berlin, 1938–9; Dir.-Gen. of the Cabinet of the President of the Council, 1939–40; Ambassador at Berne, 1940.

† Admiral Sir Andrew B. Cunningham, Deputy Chief of the Naval Staff, 1938–9; C.-in-C. Mediterranean, 1939–42; First Sea Lord, 1943–6.

‡ Grigore Gafencu, Roumanian Foreign Minister, 1938–40.

to Soviet. Didn't last long—all agreed to turn them down. . . . I found Hore-Belisha showing H. draft of P.M.'s statement for tomorrow on conscription. There were one or 2 howlers we corrected, and, as H[ore]-B[elisha] had to go to No. 10 for a meeting, he gave me a lift there, and I charged him to put our amendments (which, as a matter of fact, went through). I to F.O. to approve telegrams to Berlin and Rome instructing [Noel] Charles and N.H. to inform their beastly Governments of what we are doing, and why.

Wednesday, 26 April

H. got back from Cabinet about 11.30. Things all right *there*, but he has to go and help P.M., with T.U.C. at 12! . . . Quiet afternoon, only slightly disturbed by Corbin. Got *quite* clear of papers (marvellous to relate) as I *hope* to go away tomorrow morning.

Drove home with H., who had also seen Corbin, from whom he learned nothing doing between France and Italy.

Thursday, 27 April

Am taking an 'Easter', having been done out of all semblance of one this year. T. and I started about 11 in the car. Arrived Cooden (68 m.) at 1.20. Walked up to Club House to try to find a game. Failed, but played round by myself after tea. Out in 41—playing fairly well, especially with wooden clubs. But had some accidents on the way home—47! Still, I'm playing much better than I was at Le Touquet at end of Aug.! Nice and peaceful, and I swept *all* foreign affairs out of my mind. Country looking beautiful. Fresh green, daffodils nearly over. Lilac coming out.

Monday, 1 May

May Day! *Very* cold, quite dark and *torrents* of rain. I can't think why L. O[liphant] dragged me back. Cabinet in morning: hardly saw H. till 6 p.m. and no work to do! L.O. himself didn't show up! If it had been a fine day, I should have killed him. . . . 6 talk with H., R.A.B., Strang and Ivone [Kirkpatrick] about Hitler's speech. Decided to draft a reply which is *right*. We have always left the field too open to Hitler. He can be answered—and should be.

Tuesday, 2 May

Got Kirkpatrick's draft reply to Hitler before lunch and tinkered with it a bit. . . . Back at 2.30 to show reply to Hitler to H. He made some suggestions, which I worked on and sent down to him at

H[ouse] of L[ords] before 5. Liberian Minister at 5—wants a guarantee for Liberia!

Saw H. at 7.20. P.M. wanted further alterations to reply to Hitler. Also fussed about last Sat's BBC remark that Poland 'alone' is judge of when our guarantee applied. H. wants telegram to Warsaw to correct this point. But this rather delicate.

Wednesday, 3 May

Put finishing touches to telegram to Warsaw (which Van says is 'admirable'!!). About 4 o'clock got to work with H. on reply to Hitler. We got another draft into shape. 5.15 Corbin, who asked what we were doing about Russia. I said waiting for a reply from his Government! Went to see H.J.W. about a telephone intercept, which looks as if No. 10 were talking 'appeasement' again. He put up all sorts of denials, to which I don't pay much attention. But it's a good thing to show we have our eye on them.

[The 'delicate' telegram to Warsaw stated that the British Government stood by their guarantee; 'and their determination to implement it is as strong as their confidence that Poland would not lightly reject an equitable settlement because she felt that she would have . . . [their] support in any war that might ensue from such rejection.' The Polish Government, however, must take Britain fully into their confidence and should, if they wished to establish that their independence was 'clearly' threatened, consult before taking irrevocable action.[17]]

Thursday, 4 May

I had to go to the Palace at 11.30 to present Afghan and Nepalese ministers and had 2 talks, before and after, with the King. He was very bad with the Ministers—quite stiff and speechless. He told me after that if people were as shy and frightened as that, the only thing was to dismiss them! I agreed. But the charge of shyness lies elsewhere!

Friday, 5 May

F.P.C. meeting 3 till 5 on reply to Russia and Pope's proposal!*

H. told me after that Kordt has intimated that Hitler wants to negotiate, and hopes we'll give him a reasoned and helpful reply—soon—about Naval Treaty. Don't quite trust Kordt. Pope's proposal

* Pope Pius XII proposed to send a 'paternal message' to Britain, France, Germany, Italy and Poland, inviting them to discuss in conference questions threatening to bring about a war.

sprung on H. yesterday by Godfrey*. We had a meeting on it, and that ass Van says we must include Russia! How *could* we?!!

5–7.30 working up telegrams to Moscow; Bridges came to help and we were joined by H. about 7.

Tuesday, 9 May

Had a fairly quiet day and talk with H. about draft reply to Hitler, which P.M. wants remodelled. Worked on this. And on telegrams to Poland, trying to restrain Beck from going off the deep end at once if Danzig declares for the Reich. Suggesting to him that he might begin by 'quarantining' Danzig.

[On 10 May Henderson remarked, in one of his numerous letters to Cadogan, that the Germans believed that Hitler would do as he had invariably done before and 'get away with it without war'. Against this Cadogan noted 'I am afraid Hitler may think the same'. Nor, added Henderson, did the Germans believe that the British and French would 'let loose a world war for Danzig'.[18]]

Thursday, 11 May

O.S. and I settled with H. telegram to Vatican about Pope's proposal (which is now suspended—Hit[ler] and Muss say 'There is no threat to peace!').

Friday, 12 May

Announcement of Turkish Pact in House this afternoon. Was bipartite, as the French and Turks are still scrapping over Hatay† and we couldn't get the French into a Tripartite.

[Cadogan minuted:

The Soviet Govt. have now rejected our proposals and reverted to their own, specifically including Finland among the States to be guaranteed.

(Which, incidentally, is an enlightening comment on the Soviet proposals—the Finns simply won't *have* any guarantee from the Soviet.)

This question of the inclusion of Finland will now have to be taken up with the Soviet in connexion with the whole question of Anglo-Soviet relations in face of aggression, and therefore it wd. not seem necessary for the S. of S. to raise it separately with M. Maisky.[19]]

Tuesday, 16 May

F.P.C. on Russia at 6, till 8.5. Chiefs of Staff have now swung

* William Godfrey, Apostolic Delegate to Great Britain, 1938–53; later Archbishop of Liverpool and of Westminster.

† The former Sanjak of Alexandretta, transferred to Turkey soon afterwards.

round to 'whole-hog' alliance with Soviet.* P.M. annoyed. Oliver S[tanley] in favour. I must confess that our formula is so like—or can be represented as being so like—an alliance, that we'd better go the whole hog if we're to ensure that Russia doesn't go in with Germany.

Wednesday, 17 May

F.P.C. decided last night to let Van—who had lunched with Maisky—try him out informally on our new formula. Coached him and he saw Maisky at 12.30. Not much success. . . . In afternoon, H., Van, W. Malkin, Strang and I cooked up new formula, which H. got approved by P.M. at 6. Van was told to go ahead on it with Maisky, who promised to telegraph it to Moscow.

Thursday, 18 May

About 5 had talk with H., Van, W. Malkin and Strang about Russia. Devised possible formulae to satisfy Russians if—as seems certain—they refuse our proposals. It means an alliance, but I am coming round to think that that must be our choice.

[The Soviet Government stated that the British proposals placed Russia in a position of inequality

> inasmuch as they do not contemplate an obligation by Great Britain and France to guarantee the U.S.S.R. in the event of a direct attack on the latter by aggressors, whereas Great Britain and France, as well as Poland, enjoy such a guarantee as a result of the reciprocity which exists between them.

It was true that Britain had not offered Russia a guarantee in the event of a direct attack upon her. Nor, however, had Britain asked Russia for a guarantee in the event of an attack on the British Isles. The real ground of the Russians' objection, Cadogan judged, lay in their feeling that whereas Britain, France and Poland had all made reciprocal arrangements for mutual assistance, Russia had no such treaty save the Franco-Soviet pact, and accordingly stood to get nothing from the declaration asked for:

> The Soviet Government also seem to fear that the mere fact of their making the proposed declaration might provoke a direct attack upon the Soviet Union by Germany, and that in the absence of a direct guarantee from Great Britain and France to Latvia, Estonia and Finland, such an attack might be aimed at the Soviet Union through those countries.
>
> There is also the possibility, in the Soviet view (such are their suspicions), that Germany might attack the Soviet Union through Poland or

* They had previously believed, admittedly in judging on different terms of reference, that the advantages of alliance with Russia would not offset the naval disadvantage of Spanish hostility. They feared throughout a German-Russian alignment.

Roumania with the connivance of, or at least without provoking the resistance of, those countries. Seeing that our guarantee to those countries depends on their offering resistance, we might not be involved, and the Soviet Union would be left alone to deal with a German aggression.

If the Soviet Government really entertain this fear, it is evident that we shall have to undertake some commitment to allay it.

Cadogan's paper then set out the consequences of an alliance. On the debit side, it might impel Hitler to further aggression and consolidate his régime, or offend in varying degrees Italy, Spain, Japan, the Vatican, Portugal, Finland and Yugoslavia. The material assistance to be expected from Russia would not be very great. On the other hand, a pact might provide the only means of averting war. 'Germany is impressed only by a show of strength, and Italian policy has always been to reinsure with the stronger side.' There were signs that the guarantees must be made more effective. Should the eastern front, built up on Poland, collapse, Germany would be freed from the fear of a two-front war. Moreover, Germany and Russia might combine:

> It is noticeable that during the past few months anti-Soviet propaganda in Germany has been almost completely damped down: we know that certain members of the German General Staff are in favour of an understanding with the Soviet Union, and we have some evidence that they have lately again been advocating it.[20]]

Friday, 19 May

Maisky conveyed to Van this morning that his Government reject our proposals and stick to theirs. Blackmail, of course, but there it is. . . . F.P.C. at 2.30. They were informed of Russian refusal and, as I expected, they could do no more than take note of fact that we are coming up against choice between Soviet alliance (or pact of mutual assistance) and breakdown—with all consequences. *My* opinion (much against my will) is hardening in favour of former. P.M. hates it. O. Stanley, S. Hoare, M. MacD[onald], Chatfield, I think Inskip, Burgin* in favour of it. To them I think I should add H. P.M., S. Morrison and (?) J. Simon against. All agreed it must be a Cabinet decision. Also agreed that, as our bull point against Russian proposals was Polish and Roumanian dislike of association with Russia, and as rumour casts some doubts on this, we *must* consult those countries at once.

Back to F.O. about 4.30. Drafted message for Van to give to Maisky (purely holding). Drafted telegrams to Poland and Roumania putting problem before them and designed to elicit their views.

* Dr Leslie Burgin, recently appointed Minister of Supply.

Saturday, 20 May

I dictated paper for Cabinet on Russia. Rather delicate, weighing up the pros and cons. In his present mood, P.M. says he will resign rather than sign alliance with Soviet. So have to go warily. I am, on balance, in favour of it. So, I think, is H.

Sunday, 21 May

Van rang up from Denham to say Wohltat says Schnurre* is going to Moscow tomorrow. He in a flap; I drafted telegram to H. (at Geneva) suggesting he might at least show Maisky we know this (if we do!). . . . Corrected my dictation of last night. Copy has gone to H. and another to R.A.B. and I sent copy to H.J.W. who has since rung me up expressing approval. P.M. doesn't get back till 11.

Monday, 22 May

Went over about 12 to see P.M. about Cabinet paper. He had approved it, and only made certain verbal alterations. Long talk to H.J.W. after. Asked him to jog P.M.'s memory about O[rme] S[argent]'s appointment as Deputy [Under Secretary of State] (shall have some trouble here, I expect) and about Nevile H.'s successor. P.M. wanted to approach Scandinavians and get them to offer mediation in Danzig question. Probably silly, and shall have to try to prove it so.

Tuesday, 23 May

5 went over to H[ouse] of C[ommons] to see P.M., who approved telegram to Warsaw about Scandinavian mediation. He then talked to me about a 'League umbrella' for our Russian arrangement, and I promised to draft something for him, which I did, sending copy to meet H. in Paris tomorrow morning and to Sam Hoare.

[Chamberlain had now come, very reluctantly, to accept that it might be necessary to sign a triple pact. He hoped that it would contain some reference to the Covenant of the League of Nations, which might later be modified, so that Britain would not be tied up for all time with the Soviet Government. Cadogan thereupon submitted a draft. 'I do not pretend to think that anything on the above lines will help very much, but the Prime Minister attaches some importance to it both as regards a section of opinion in this country and in the Dominions,' he told Halifax. 'I do not think it

* Schnurre was special commissioner for economic affairs in the German Foreign Ministry and had been due to visit Moscow for some time. The Russians denied that he was coming.

would matter very much one way or the other in Germany: it will not be popular in Italy, where there are bitter memories of League sanctions, nor in Japan, where there is apprehension of sanctions to come.'[21]

The Japanese, as their Foreign Minister often announced, were working for the creation of an economic bloc which would be largely self-supporting or at least invulnerable to economic strangulation. Even if she absorbed China, Japan would still lack essential materials, especially mineral oils and iron ore, which could most nearly be found in Borneo and Malaya.

Sir R. Craigie, the British Ambassador in Tokyo, was told by the Japanese Vice-Minister for Foreign Affairs of his Government's anxiety about the Moscow negotiations. Though Craigie was careful to avoid the use of arguments in that connexion to deter the Japanese from joining the German-Italian military alliance, he reported that the two subjects were inseparably linked in Japanese minds. Cadogan replied that he had been anxious to keep these issues distinct, in order to avoid giving the impression that a bargain might be struck. For the moment the extreme elements in Japan seemed to have been defeated; any indication of gratitude or gratification might strengthen them and would in any event leave Britain in a weaker position:

> Our attitude should rather be to show ourselves generally indifferent as to whether or not Japan joins the Axis alliance, and when they try to make our flesh creep, to counter this by doing the same as you in fact did [pointing out that from a European point of view an arrangement with Russia might suit Germany better than one with Japan, and that Anglo-Russian talks were not therefore necessarily injurious to Japan]. . . .
>
> If they raise the subject, we should emphasise that it is difficult to see what advantage they hope to get from an alliance with the Axis Powers. Probably the extremists argue that an alliance with Germany and Italy would immobilise us in the Far East, but can it reasonably be argued that it would be in Italy's power to contain the British fleet in the Mediterranean or possible for Germany easily to overcome the physical and geographical difficulties in the way of affording Japan any material assistance in a conflict with Russia? It is no doubt these and similar considerations which have enabled the moderate elements to put up so prolonged and successful a resistance.

Cadogan thought that the extreme party's lack of success had led them to institute a drive against British interests in China, in order to scare Britain away from an arrangement, even one limited expressly to Europe, with Russia.[22]]

Wednesday, 24 May

H. landed 9.45 and we drove to F.O. Had a talk with him: told him P.M. apparently resigned to idea of Soviet alliance, but depressed. Suggested line on which he might cheer him up and he went over to No. 10 at 10.50. Cabinet till about 1. They agreed to Russian alliance and H. and I drafted statement for P.M. in House.

Friday, 26 May

Corbin rang me up to say French Government accepted formula, so we told Seeds* to go ahead.

[To Seeds' astonishment, Molotov,† the Russian Foreign Minister, said that Britain and France wanted to continue conversations indefinitely but were not interested in concrete results; while the reference to the Covenant would only drag in all the cumbrous machinery of Geneva.

Sir Percy Loraine's first impressions as Ambassador in Rome had not been hopeful. By deciding to convert the Axis into a military alliance Mussolini had openly cast the lot of his country with that of Germany, justifying this as a defensive measure against the threat of encirclement by rich and jealous democracies.[23]

At their first encounter, Mussolini asked Loraine whether in view of the Anglo-Turkish declaration, the impending treaty with Russia and the general policy of encirclement, the Anglo-Italian treaty had any value. Encirclement of Germany would be treated as being directed against Italy too. Why, he demanded to know, was Britain dishing out guarantees to countries which had not asked for them and certainly did not require them? Sir Percy argued back: 'Unless my language has given him pause' he telegraphed, 'which I cannot reasonably hope, I fear the die is cast and that the only argument is the visibility of overwhelming physical strength.' According to Ciano's record, Mussolini's countenance during this interview 'became absolutely impenetrable; it looked like the face of an Oriental god sculptured in stone'.[24]]

Monday, 29 May

Telegrams received last evening show that the Russians have been most tiresome and contemptuous of our proposals, and P. Loraine had a *bad* interview with Musso. Rang up L. O[liphant] before lunch. He read me reply to Moscow, approved by H., which I approved, subject to some modifications.

Wednesday, 31 May

Rang up L. O[liphant]. He very alarmist about Russia. So rang up C. Peake. He told me to listen to Wireless [for a report of a speech by

* Sir William Seeds, Ambassador in Moscow, 1939–40.

† Vaycheslav Mikailovich Molotov, Russian Foreign Minister, 1939–49. See List of Principal Characters.

Molotov]. Which I did. Not so bad. Rang him up again after, and he agreed it was no catastrophe. I think L.O. jumps at everything to show that his Bols[hevik] friends are as black as he paints them.

Thursday, 1 June

'C' came to see me about Roumanian oilfields. Said regular scheme wd. have to be worked out. Of course—je ne demande pas mieux—told him to get on with it.

Tulips being taken up.

Friday, 2 June

4.15 Dirksen about restrictions on Germans coming here, and low-flying over German fleet!

Saturday, 3 June

T. and I left in car about 2.30 for Eton. . . . Saw Dorothy H[alifax]. But *very* few people I ever saw before. 30 years ago I shd. have known everyone but now, nobody. Where are my contemporaries? They weren't *all* killed. But I suppose their boys have all left Eton.

Sunday, 4 June

I ought to work, but life has been so beastly for a year that when I get a peaceful week-end I become completely lazy. One *must* be, sometimes!

Monday, 5 June

5 Foreign Policy Committee on answer to Soviet. Agreed more or less on lines it should take. Discussions as to whether W. Malkin should go out. This frightfully inconvenient, and it was difficult to discuss in Committee. H. saw P.M. after, and they incline to getting Seeds home.

Tuesday, 6 June

H. fussing about his speeches—which give more trouble than anything else in the year. They get added to, and re-written, so that they become like a patchwork quilt, and a very thick and heavy and uncomfortable one.

Wednesday, 7 June

2 degrees hotter—84 in shade. Picked up H. Life still clouded and disturbed by his damned speeches. . . . Seeds ill, so we can't call him home. Got in touch with Strang, whom we shall have to send out. . . .

Am trying to get H. to persuade P.M. to approve O. S[argent] as Deputy. Think I have succeeded, but it is difficult. *Hundreds* of other appointments held up till this is settled.

Went over to H.W. in morning to draft statement for P.M. on Russia, which went fairly well.

[Chamberlain said that general agreement on the main objects had apparently been reached. Britain and France had made it clear that they were ready to give Russia, 'immediately and without reserve . . . full military support in the event of any act of aggression against her involving her in hostilities with a European Power'. There remained one or two difficulties, especially the position of states which did not want a guarantee and upon which it would be manifestly impossible to impose one.]

Thursday, 8 June

Corbin called and said no good slapping text down in front of Russians—must argue with them. I quite agree. Dined F.O. (King's Birthday). Sat between Corbin and Maisky. Talked a lot and tried to talk to him on Corbin's line—showing him quite frankly the difficulties and saying we must find, together, a way over or round them.

Friday, 9 June

11 Foreign Policy Committee. They agreed on Corbin's line.

Monday, 12 June

Saw Strang before his departure for Moscow. H. had approved draft memorandum, so sent for Corbin and gave him a copy. . . . H. and Phipps saw P.M. at 11 and discussed letter to Daladier. Decided—rightly—that it must await our Soviet agreement, &c.

Dined with R. Tree to meet Hamilton Fyshe [Fish] Armstrong*—one of these earnest, never-let-up Americans. . . . An *awful* evening. Sat in dining-room till 11, then stood in ante-room till 12, then went up to drawing room where I stood, talking to the Armstrong, or he talking to me, till 1. They do get their *teeth* into it, these Americans, and can't allow themselves any relaxation. Why not talk of wild flowers, or fornication, or any human subject?

Tuesday, 13 June

Walked with H. to F.O. and talked Tientsin (which is ugly). Sent for Howe,† and he convinced us, more or less, that it was all

* Editor of the American journal *Foreign Affairs*.

† R. G. Howe; served in Peking 1934–7, and in F.O. 1937–40; Asst. Under-Sec., F.O., 1945; Gov.-Gen. of the Sudan, 1947–55.

right. Later news shows Japs are not planning anything so very menacing after all. . . .

4 meeting on Danzig to hear Makins' report of his talk with Burckhardt. Upshot, do nothing now.

Wednesday, 14 June

12.30 Hungarian came to deliver note about 'unbearable' situation of Hungarian minority in Roumania and talking of 'important territorial problems' between Hungary and R[oumania]. I said at once that I must make most express reserves about this; we didn't recognise a 'territorial problem'. And I said he must substantiate allegations about treatment of minority. . . . 3 meeting with H., Malkin, O.S. and Ivone about French draft for Russian agreement. Referred to P.M.

[The Japanese had been increasing their pressure on European interests in China. Four Chinese, alleged by the Japanese to be terrorists who had plotted the murder of an official, took shelter in the concession at Tientsin and were protected by the British authorities from arrest by the Japanese, who thereupon instituted a blockade. The Consul-General's advice, supported by Craigie, had been to hand the men over. This the Far Eastern Department had declined to do, although the legal position was by no means secure and the physical one still less so.]

Thursday, 15 June

H. fussed—as well he may be—about Tientsin. I think we've bungled this. I blame myself—and I am of course responsible—for not taking more interest in it. Had to spend half the day holding H's hand. Corbin at 12.30. Gave him redraft of Russian agreement. Tilea at 1. . . . H[alifax] sent for me at 4 and kept me till 5.15. We got H. Johnson round (as Joe [Kennedy] was at Ascot) to consult him as to advisability of asking U.S.G[overnment] to warn Japs that they were going a bit far. . . . H.J. called again at 7.30, after consulting Joe, to agree that we might send our telegram to Washington, and we added a paragraph. I rang up H. about 7.45, and he agreed. Meanwhile everyone *poured* papers upon me, and, after dining at home, must get to work. What a life, and what a prospect!

Those damned dahlias being put in again.

Friday, 16 June

Talk with H. and Howe about Tientsin. H. still very fussed. As I have said, I think this thing has been mishandled. But I believe Japs were out for a show-down anyhow, and we have got to meet it.

H. had a talk with P.M., and Chatfield, and they seem to be discussing despatch of capital ships! Fixed up with P.M. now about Sargent, and S. of S. has told him. So that's something. Lunched at home. Approved a 'Reuter message' about Tientsin brought me by C. Peake. H.J.W. rang up about 7.30 very fussed about it—he thought it too strong—it had just appeared on tape as 'Government statement'. Confess I had no idea it was of that nature, but on re-reading it don't think it'll do any harm. S. of S. bowled off to Yorkshire at 4. Bruce* came in about 6—fussed about what he was to tell his Government.

[Australia and New Zealand had been assured on a number of occasions since 1937 that a battle fleet would be sent to Singapore in the event of serious trouble with Japan, regardless of the European situation. On 20 March 1939 the Australians were told that this undertaking no longer held good, a painful fact which the Tientsin crisis confirmed. In mid-June, only eleven of Britain's capital ships were instantly available: six were needed for Home waters and the Atlantic, three for the Mediterranean. Hence the remark in Cadogan's diary entry for 19 June. In a report of 24 June, the Chiefs of Staff said that in September (when the battleships *Revenge* and *Renown* would be available) seven ships could be sent to Singapore if the Mediterranean were denuded. The Committee of Imperial Defence decided on 26 June that no lesser number could be sent in any event, and that these seven ships could not be spared. Therefore Britain must negotiate with Japan, at the risk of further damage to her Far Eastern interests; for the naval co-operation of the U.S.A., the one factor which might have redressed the balance, would plainly not be forthcoming.[25]]

Sunday, 18 June

Tientsin looks ugly. Went round to H. at 9.50. Howe turned up at 10 and we discussed Tientsin—rather gloomy—and Soviet negotiations, which aren't going *too* badly.

Monday, 19 June

11.30 F.P.C. Very glum and sticky meeting. Chatfield produced report by Chiefs of Staff, showing we can send *2* ships to F[ar] E[ast]! C[hatfield] himself thought the picture painted unduly black. Of course the Committee settled nothing. After it, with H., passed draft statement for P.M. to make in House—and I hear it went fairly well. . . .

* Australian High Commissioner.

5.30 saw Shigemitsu* with H. S[higemitsu] very sticky and tiresome and Japanese. I told him Jap authorities had said they had evidence, but they wouldn't produce it to us because they feared it might come into hands of Chinese police. Couldn't he ask them to produce it to us? He havered. I said, couldn't he ask them whether they *had* such evidence? He still havered. However, H. and I put this to Craigie in a telegram. H.J.W. came to see me, and I told him what we were doing, and he rang up later to say P.M. approved.

Tuesday, 20 June

I've had a frightful week (am writing on 25th) and can't remember the details. It has all been overshadowed by the Tientsin mess and the intolerable—and suspicious—mulishness of the Russians in our negotiations. I can't remember all of the details or the moment to moment worries. And perhaps that may make this Diary more readable. As regards Tientsin, we have bungled the thing sadly. F[ar] E[ast] Department and Mounsey have been working in their little groove and *never* referred a paper to me. That puts me in the awkward position that I can't explain, or shift the blame. I saw copies of the telegrams, which I read hurriedly (I read hundreds a day) and I did *not* ask what it was all about. I ought to have. And the P.M. is very annoyed, and there will be a drive against F.O.

The Russians are impossible. We give them all they want, with both hands, and they merely slap them. Molotov is an ignorant and suspicious peasant.

[From Moscow, Strang acknowledged that Molotov stood nearer to the final source of authority than Litvinov ever did; but he knew no foreign language, very little at first hand of the outside world, and not much more about the subject-matter of foreign relations or the technique of negotiation:

> The result is that, although of course Molotov has very clear ideas about the essential objects of Soviet policy in these negotiations, there is little give and take in the discussions and he seems to be quite impervious to argument. . . .
>
> As you will see from the Ambassador's reports, Molotov's technique is stubbornly and woodenly to repeat his own point of view and to ask innumerable questions of his interlocutors. . . .

Cadogan minuted at the end of the month, on the question of a Russian guarantee of the Netherlands and Switzerland:

> . . . we must dig our toes in. If that leads to a breakdown, I doubt

* Mamoru Shigemitsu, Japanese Ambassador, 1938–41.

whether we should really be worse off, as Soviet insistence on this point would mean that they did not intend to have an agreement anyway.[26]]

Monday, 26 June

Picked up H. in morning. He very tiresome about his beastly speeches. I lost my temper. Altogether a bad day—masses of distracting work on a variety of complicated and quite insoluble problems. . . . F.P.C. 6–7.45. Roughed out draft telegram to Moscow with H. . . . I completed telegram to Moscow and did masses of other work. Very tired, stale and dispirited.

Tuesday, 27 June

Japs have agreed to negotiation in Tientsin, so that looks a *little* better.

Wednesday, 28 June

(Am writing on July 3, so remember nothing. Life has been impossible lately.) Generally speaking, Tientsin has died down, as Japs have agreed to negotiate in Tokyo and barrier incidents *seem* to decrease. As regards Soviet, we are going to the furthest limit without any very sure hope—on my part—that the dirty sweeps will respond.

Thursday, 29 June

All these days are awful. There is no issue anywhere; I am too overwhelmed with work to think. I *must* get away. And on top of it all I have all the moves to consider—and Horace W. to manœuvre against. . . .

Dined at Chatham House for speech from H. that had been the bane of our lives for days. At last moment Van said we must put teeth into it. That quite right I think. So I sat down and wrote 2 pages—a moving paraphrase of 'We don't want to fight, but by Jingo if we do' &c. Went quite well.

[Halifax said:

British policy rests on twin foundations of purpose. One is determination to resist force. The other is our recognition of the world's desire to get on with the constructive work of building peace. If we could once be satisfied that the intentions of others were the same as our own and that we all really wanted peaceful solutions, then . . . we could discuss the problems that are today causing the world anxiety. . . .

But this is not the position which we face today. The threat of military force is holding the world to ransom, and our immediate task is—and here I end as I began—to resist aggression.]

Monday, 3 July

Most of morning spent drafting statement on Danzig to be made in House. Interrupted—of course—on a dozen other questions. Gave it to Kennard to vet. Meeting about 5 on Russia (Soviet are still being incredibly tiresome) and Danzig. 5.45 H. went off to see P.M. about both questions. He in a bad temper. I've done my best and reply by getting equally angry. Worked after dinner again. This is not life at all.

Tuesday, 4 July

4 discussion with H., O.S., I.K., W. M[alkin] on Soviet. Latter are being simply mulish. F.P.C. at 5. Decided on a sort of ultimatum to Soviet. Came back about 6.30 and drafted telegram to Moscow with O.S., and W. M[alkin].

Wednesday, 5 July

P.M. approved our draft to Moscow and we showed it to French, but they want several modifications.

Thursday, 6 July

Came down to breakfast and found Trish [Patricia] and C[ynthia]. Trish said 'I'm engaged to Gerry Coke!' I confess I was so surprised that I probably didn't come up to the situation.

Saturday, 8 July

Not too much to do in morning. Gave parting instructions to O.S. and L.O. Russian negotiation still in progress.

Wednesday, 12 July — *High Corner*

Arrived High Corner* about 1. . . . Had tea there—our first meal. After tea I mowed a bit. Then our first dinner—not too bad. So here we are settled in, and resolved to spend the night here. It seems awfully nice and quiet, and cosy. Hope it will prove a success, and God bless us here.

Sunday, 16 July — *High Corner*

Fine day, but windy. Went to Robertsbridge to pick up G[illian] at 1. Lovely road with beautiful views. Walked round to look at views in afternoon. T. and G. cooked dinner. . . . Frightful things

* The Cadogans' newly acquired cottage near Northiam in Sussex.

happened. T., melting lard, produced clouds of acrid fumes that darkened the countryside. The sole, when put in the pan, exploded with a noise like a Brock's benefit. But eventually something more or less eatable was produced. And sausages and bacon.

[On the day of the Cadogans' departure, Sir Percy Loraine had another stiff argument with Mussolini. The Duce started from the premiss of Germany's taking Danzig; he said he was determined to stand by Italy's obligations to Germany; and although there were hints of co-operation between the great powers

> The whole totalitarian outlook on things is getting wider and wider apart from our own; I feel practically as if the common language formally used for the discussion of international affairs had been destroyed. There seems to be no junction between our lines of thought; it was as if, yesterday morning, I was talking about cricket and Mussolini was talking about chess.[27]

Sir Nevile Henderson had already told Cadogan of his conviction that Hitler had 'no immediate intention' of staging a military *coup* or enforcing a 'constitutional change' at Danzig. The Ambassador disbelieved in Russia's good intentions:

> I feel intuitively that the Germans are getting at Stalin. Goering said to me the other day, 'Germany and Russia will not always be enemies'; *absit omen*, but if Poland does not talk a little less about her bravery and think a little more about the realities of her geographical position, we may yet live to see a fourth Partition.[28]

Chamberlain, by no means surprised at the slow progress in Moscow, announced that a *coup* in Danzig would raise issues affecting Polish independence and reaffirmed British determination to uphold it. Cadogan's Diary makes little mention of politics in the last three weeks of July, and no reference to the public row which followed talks between Sir Horace Wilson, Robert Hudson and Goering's official Wohltat, in which a large British loan was said to have been offered if Germany mended her ways. Towards the end of the month, Craigie and the Japanese Foreign Minister found a formula which damped down, for the moment, the Tientsin crisis. On 26 July the U.S. Government denounced their commercial treaty with Japan.

As it appeared in London, Russia was asking not only for protection against 'indirect aggression' through Finland and the Baltic States but also for a licence to interfere in their internal affairs and go to war if that led to trouble. This could only drive them into the arms of Germany. By contrast, even the British guarantee to Poland did not cover the contingency of an indirect attack through, say, Lithuania. Molotov said on 24 July that he foresaw no insuperable difficulty on this point. Since Britain and France had now agreed that the military and political agreements should enter into force together, military talks should begin in Moscow at once. Strang had no doubt that 'if we want an agreement with them we shall have to pay their price or something very near it'.[29]]

Monday, 31 July *High Corner*

Nothing to record these days. Lovely lazy life, with occasional jobs, both inside and out. E.g. last night after dinner I cleaned all the silver!

Tuesday, 1 August *High Corner*

G. Jebb arrived at 12.15. Walked him round the views, and he gave me the news. Tho' there isn't much. Mainly Kemsley's talk with Hitler, which seems to me as harmless, and as useless, as most such.

Thursday, 3 August

Torrential rain (a very good day to go to London). Arrived F.O. 11.40. Saw H. at 12. He seems fairly well, but doesn't anticipate a real holiday. I told him he *must* have one. We shall see. He told me about Kemsley's interview with Hitler. Latter said we should both put down on paper what we want. K[emsley] didn't follow this up, but has been made to write to Dietrich* to ask if H[itler] will put down his desiderata. H. fussed about Far East. He thinks we can go a long way on police, neutrality of Concessions, &c. When we get on to currency and silver, we shall have to stall, and in the end we cannot give way. Russia—military talks will now hold the stage. Lunched at Club with Ivone. Talked with R.A.B. at 2.30. He as inscrutable as ever.

Monday, 7 August *High Corner*

Calm bright sunset—a good omen, I hope. So ends a charming holiday—that I had dreamed of but never hoped to realise. I am as fit for work (outdoor) as ever I was, and enjoy it as much. The view at sunset was so peaceful and lovely: I hope it bodes that we may spend some days here in peace. Back to London tomorrow. Thank God for my holiday, and give me strength to face and deal with what may come. T's courage and resourcefulness have made this holiday possible. I shall dream in London of High Corner—now to be called 'Thatched Cottage'.

Wednesday, 9 August

H. arrived about 12. Discussion with him, Van, Strang, Malkin

* Dr Otto Dietrich, head of German Press Bureau, 1934–45.

and Ivone K. of further possible formulae for 'indirect aggression'. Later, discussion with Mounsey and N. Ronald of Far East, which is heading for almost inevitable deadlock.

Thursday, 10 August

11 further talk on Far East. Department and G. Mounsey rather anti-Craigie, and think S. of S. is 'appeasing' too much. Explained to G.M. after that I don't think S. of S. is under any illusion as to ultimate success of concessions to Japs, but we *must* avoid definite break with Japan during these 2 months.

H. left in afternoon for Yorkshire. About 6, got telegram from Danzig that Hitler has invited Burckhardt* to Berchtesgaden. Should he tell Beck? I thought so, and I rang up H. at 8 and got him to agree to telegram advising Burckhardt to tell Beck. Burck[hardt] also wanted to know if there was anything we wanted him to say. Gave him the 'firm' background for his guidance, but not as message.

Friday, 11 August

Better day (climatically). Woken at 7.30 with scare telegrams from Angora reporting Roumanian fear that Germany was going to invade *them*. Spoke to H. on telephone at 10.15. Told him I thought this bosh and that I proposed to say we had heard gossip but had no *facts* in corroboration. Roumanian C[hargé] d'A[ffaires] called 11.45 to repeat the same thing, and I tried to reassure him (after consulting Admiral [Sinclair]) as above.

12. Raczynski came to read me acrimonious exchange of notes between P[olish] G[overnment] and German Government, former saying that any action by latter against Polish contractual rights and interests would be regarded as an 'act of aggression'. P[olish] G[overnment] ask us and French to make 'preventive démarche' in Berlin. I tried to tone R[aczynski] down and later telephoned the story to H. with a draft reply to effect that, in view of Burckhardt visit, we do *not* think this is the moment for a 'preventive démarche'. H. agreed, and I sent off telegram. It's difficult to conduct affairs of this kind with H. in Yorkshire and P.M. in Scotland! I hope their trust in me is not misplaced. . . . At end of dinner I got Most Immediate telegram from Craigie sent me by Ashley Clarke.† (N. Ronald seems also to have broken down—Howe has already collapsed!). I devised a (bad) answer to it, and then got down to other work. A hell of a week. What would the old bureaucrats of 20 years ago have thought of it!

* League of Nations High Commissioner at Danzig.

† Of F.O.; later Chief Clerk and Ambassador in Rome 1953–62.

[Strang advised that it might, after all, be worthwhile to attempt a further approach to Molotov. The Prime Minister agreed that a fresh effort should be made to find a formula which would 'not appear to give Russia a right, covered by our guarantee, to interfere in the internal affairs of other States'.[30]]

Saturday, 12 August

Talked to H. at 10.15. Kept him calm. French agree we should *not* go in for 'preventive démarche'. Agreed telegram to Angora about agreement. . . . Hitler has decreed 'Spannung'* for the 15th, which means the opening of the 'battle of nerves'. Hope mine will be all right!

Sunday, 13 August

Ridsdale† rang me up about D[aily] T[elegraph] having got hold of story of Burckhardt's visit to Berchtesgaden. Asked him to try and damp it down. Read innumerable telegrams.

Monday, 14 August

Saw Makins on his return from Bâle where he had seen Burckhardt. Really nothing definite resulted from interview. But Hitler apparently undecided, rather distracted, rather aged. We shall see.

Tuesday, 15 August

All the various crises still with us. Discussion with H. of F[ar] E[ast]. He agrees to taking a firm line about economic questions. I can't see what else we can do. If we give way, we lose China, America and Europe. And the Japs won't go *to war* about silver. And we shall have to stand a bit more squeezing for the next few months.

. . . The 'Times' had a report (which they wouldn't publish) about German-Italian proposal to Vatican for 4-Power Conference. This would be very awkward, and I explained to H. best way I could think of parrying it.

Wednesday, 16 August

All sorts of worries about how much to tell everyone about Burckhardt interview, and about military talks with Russians. . . . X‡

* Beginning of the 'period of alert'.

† W. Ridsdale, F.O. News Dept.; Head of Dept., 1941–53.

‡ An official of the Intelligence services.

called at 10.45 with a scare report from the Hague: but it only confirms, I think, what we already expected, and I am not unduly disturbed.

[The British and French military missions had arrived in Moscow on 11 August, the British having been told to go very slowly until the political accord was settled. This instruction Halifax rescinded on 15 August. Admiral Drax, leader of the British delegation, reported after five days of meetings that they had found not a point upon which agreement could be reached:

> They make it plain that in their opinion we came here as suppliants asking them to give us a Treaty of assistance. In consequence, any unpleasant jobs must be done by us. They demand that if the Soviet armies are to help the Allies, Britain and France must obtain the approval of Poland and Roumania for Soviet armies to move through their territory in the desired directions. . . . They have once or twice threatened that the continuation of our discussions would be useless if an early reply is not received.'[31]

The talks broke down on this point.]

Thursday, 17 August

A great deal of my time taken up talking on telephone to H. and collecting stuff for his and P.M.'s pouches. This rather complicates matters, having S. of S. in Yorkshire and P.M. in north of Scotland.

Friday, 18 August

Received salmon from P.M., so hope he is having good sport. . . . 'C' has news from v. good source that Chief of Railways saw Hitler on Wed[nesday] night and said he could arrange transport for Party Rally or for mobilisation, but not both at once! Unconfirmed report says H[itler] chooses Rally.

Dined at home. At end of dinner Van rang up in high state of excitement to say he had been telephoning to S. of S. who must come back at once. P.M. should also. S. of S. had told him to speak to me. I asked him to come round, and gave him cold supper. I have never seen a man nearer nervous collapse. *His* source has told him H[itler] has chosen war, to begin between 25th and 28th. I have my suspicions of his source. Still, one can't ignore it. Spoke to H. who will be here noon tomorrow. Agreed *not* to send for P.M., yet. Eventually calmed Van down a bit and packed him off about 11. This is the beginning of the 'War of Nerves'. And I have seen the first casualty!

Saturday, 19 August

Wrote out my proposals for an approach to Musso. S. of S. at 12 and he, Van and I had a talk. Agreed in principle (1) send telegram to Rome for Musso (2) draft letter from P.M. to Hitler (3) *not* to bring back P.M. (he is due early Monday morning).... Had draft telegram ready at 4 for H., Van, Strang, Makins. Long sitting, till 7.30. Approved and despatched telegram to Rome. Also letter to meet P.M. on the way, explaining situation, what we had done, and enclosing draft letter to Hitler.... Took steps to recall Newall*, Pound†, Bridges, &c., *all* of whom are on holiday.

[The letter which was sent that night to Chamberlain, in Halifax's name but drafted by Cadogan, summarises the situation so clearly that it is printed here at length:

When I was in London earlier in the week, Van gave me a good deal of information which came from a reliable source which he disclosed to me, and which I can disclose to you when I see you, in regard to what had recently been passing between Berlin and Rome. The upshot of this was to the effect that shortly before the meeting of Ciano and Ribbentrop at Salzburg, Mussolini had weighed in with a memorandum to Herr Hitler in the sense of saying that Italy was of course 100 per cent with Germany, but that there was a series of admirable reasons why Germany should take no precipitate action.

The effect of this was said to have been so to irritate Herr Hitler that the Salzburg meeting was immediately arranged. At this Ciano began by maintaining the Italian position, but subsequently, having been whisked off to Berchtesgaden, somewhat wilted under Herr Hitler's pressure. This pressure was exerted on the line of giving assurances that any action in regard to Danzig or Poland would be so conducted as to ensure its local character, that other Powers would not in fact join in, and that accordingly Italy had nothing to fear. Nor, in fact, did Herr Hitler demand anything of her than that she should remain in a friendly posture of neutrality, thereby protecting Hitler's left flank.

Van told me last night that he had had further information from his sources to the effect that, Italian anxieties having been thus allayed, it was pretty well decided in Berlin to take action against Poland any day after the 25th of this month. The actual dates given were between the 25th and the 28th.

We heard through another Secret Service source two days ago that the railway authorities in Germany had conveyed to Herr Hitler that

* Air-Chief Marshal Sir C. L. N. Newall, Chief of the Air Staff, 1937–40; Gov.-Gen. of New Zealand, 1941–6.

† Admiral Sir Dudley Pound, First Sea Lord, 1939–43.

they could not conduct both the transport for the Nuremberg Rally and for mobilisation simultaneously; and accordingly Herr Hitler must take his choice between them. The first information was to the effect that he had chosen the Nuremberg Rally, but I understand that both the Admiral and Van's sources are now disposed to be of one mind in the sense of thinking that the Nuremberg Rally will be, in comparison with previous gatherings, symbolic—the railways being absorbed by troop transport and the meeting being only for those who can get there on foot or by car.

We have in the course of the last six months had so many dates given to us that one is naturally sceptical about any repetition of them, and I do not suppose that we should exclude from our minds the possibility that all this may have its place in the general nerve storm which we have been told was designed to rage during these weeks. On the other hand, the information seemed to me too circumstantial to ignore, and the actual dates given were, so it is alleged, given to the Italian Government, which obviously increases their significance. The general appreciation involved also coincides with the picture that you will have seen painted in Henderson's telegrams, in the attitude of the Italian Ambassador at Berlin, and is pretty faithfully reflected in the last report that Loraine gives of his conversation with Ciano. And if the appreciation is in fact a true one, it is also a black one, and there is no time to lose.

Apart from what I have set down above, there are indications that Herr Hitler still believes that we do not mean to fight, or that, alternatively, he can crush Poland before we can come in. It might be asked whether, if he has not been convinced by our declarations up to date, he will be any more convinced by a further declaration now. None the less I do not think that we should be justified in sparing any effort to bring the truth home to him, and with that in mind I would suggest that we should find means of conveying to him a clear message on behalf of H.M.G., defining our position, possibly by one or other of the methods suggested by Henderson. It is for consideration whether this should best be done through the agency of someone like [General] Ironside*, who might speak verbally to Hitler, or by means of a letter to Herr Hitler from yourself. Henderson's advice on this point has been, as I see it, inconsistent. On the one hand he deprecates anything that would echo May 21st, 1938, and in the same breath recommends Ironside, which I would have thought would certainly have that effect. But it is fair to add that the sources with which Van has been in touch have been hitherto in favour of the Ironside method; and as you know Herr Hitler has himself from time to time dropped a hint that he would like an Englishman to go.

We have telegraphed to Henderson this afternoon to ask him his considered judgment on these alternatives, but unless he adduces very

* Later Field-Marshal Sir Edmund Ironside, Governor of Gibraltar, 1938–9; Insp.-Gen. of Overseas Forces, 1939; C.I.G.S., Sept., 1939–May 1940.

strong reasons against it, my own judgment is pretty clear that I should favour the approach being made by means of a personal letter from yourself on behalf of H.M.G. to Herr Hitler. I should suppose that this would produce whatever effect it would produce in the way of clarifying the situation without the counter disadvantage of publicity and alleged intimidation.

It seemed to me important, while we were considering action at Berlin, that we should if possible make some effort in Rome, with the object of encouraging Mussolini not to abandon his restraining efforts. I am accordingly sending tonight a telegram to Loraine, of which I enclose a copy. I hope you will not disapprove. If Mussolini wants to play at all, this perhaps gives him some encouragement.

I am not telling either the Poles or the French at present of our approach to Rome.[32]]

Monday, 21 August

Picked up H. early. Went with him to see P.M. at 11.30. Discussed letter to Hitler, and all phases of the crisis. Frightful day, but don't (Wed) remember all details. Further session at No. 10 in afternoon. Home for hurried dinner. H. came round after and we drafted some telegrams.

[Admiral Sinclair had received a suggestion that Goering would come to London if he could have a discussion with Chamberlain. It was decided on 21 August to agree, and secret arrangements were made for 23 August. Nothing further was heard until the Thursday, 24 August, when a message came to the effect that Hitler did not think the visit would prove immediately useful.[33]]

Tuesday, 22 August

Session with P.M., H., and H.W. again in morning. P.M. (or H.W.) had produced re-draft of letter to Hitler. H. started making some niggling criticisms. I said I had a much more fundamental one to make—I didn't like the passage about 'here are my proposals:—(1) (2) (3)' &c. P.M. agreed. News this morning of Soviet-German Pact.* But I'm glad to say P.M. quite firm about its not altering things.... Van was called in (first time) for part of this morning at No. 10. Cabinet at 3. Called over there soon after 6 to give effect to their decisions. Letter to Hitler agreed and despatched. Awful rush. Home 8.30. Lothian dined. I interrupted by telephone calls. Finally sent for about 10 by H. He had Van, in state of excitement, with a

* A telegram from the U.S. Government, who were excellently informed of the German-Russian talks, sent on 17 August, was not received in the Central Dept. of the F.O. until 22 August. It bore no priority marking.

draft telegram of pure 'appeasement' to Rome. I said 'You've changed your stance.' He said that was a thing he never did (he's 'always right'!) H. decided to hold it up till we get Loraine's account of his talk with Ciano tomorrow. Home at 12, exhausted.

Wednesday, 23 August

The kind of lull that comes in the middle of a typhoon. Loraine's telegram interesting and hopeful.* Glad we didn't send Van's message. All German military preparations going forward. But that doesn't surprise me—'War of Nerves' anyhow. H. at one point said to me 'Do you think this means war?' I said 'Yes: I think it does, but I believe it doesn't'. That is my mental (or spiritual) state. Surprised to find Admiral felt the same way this morning.

Home 8.15 and dined there. These crises are really too tiresome. We can't go on living like this in Europe. There's no point in it.

Recalled everyone from leave and sent diplomats back to their posts.

Musso is nibbling and P. L[oraine] says he 'is confident' he won't fight.

Thursday, 24 August

A black day (meteorologically too—cooler). Terms of German-Soviet Pact out. I told H. only thing to do was to say to Musso: 'We can't urge Poles to agree to Danzig's incorporation in Reich. *If* Hitler will agree (a) that Polish rights must be safeguarded and (b) that settlement must be internationally guaranteed, that would give us a basis on which we might approach Poles.' P.M. agreed, and we got off a telegram before lunch—almost Totalitarian!

Otherwise everything as black as black. Parliament met, with statements in both Houses. Lunched at home. This is the calm spot in the middle of the typhoon, and I really hadn't much work. There's really nothing to do. We've got to wait and hope. In one way, it's not so bad as last year. Then, there was the awful question *ought* we to fight or ought we not? Now there's no question that in certain circumstances we *must*. It just depends whether these circumstances—out of our control—arise.

[Chamberlain assured Hitler that the Nazi-Soviet pact, whatever its nature, would not affect Britain's

> obligation to Poland which His Majesty's Government have stated in public repeatedly and plainly and which they are determined to

* Ciano had told him that Italy wanted peace and that Mussolini was disposed to use his influence with Hitler in that direction.

fulfil. . . . If the case should arise, they are resolved, and prepared, to employ without delay all the forces at their command. . . . It would be a dangerous illusion to think that if war once starts, it will come to an early end, even if a success on any one of the several fronts . . . should have been secured.

Chamberlain then expressed once again the conviction that war between Britain and Germany 'would be the greatest calamity that could occur'. If a calmer atmosphere could be secured, Germany and Poland might negotiate about their differences, preferably on the understanding that a settlement must be guaranteed by other powers.[34]

Although the risk of a German-Russian agreement had been freely mentioned in the deliberations of the Cabinet and Chiefs of Staff, it appears that the Intelligence services did not provide any clear pointer to its imminence or nature. The German desire for closer relations with Russia was known, though alleged to be completely at variance with Hitler's views. The Foreign Office had no evidence of a corresponding desire on the Soviet side. Indeed, such information as reached the Foreign Office from Russian sources seemed to show a Nazi-Soviet pact unlikely. The Northern Department had therefore judged the more serious danger to be a Russian retreat into isolation.[35]]

Friday, 25 August

Can't remember exactly events of this day (I've been doing about 16 hours a day work). But in course of morning we heard Hitler had sent for N.H. at 1.30. Don't know what this means. I think I spent most of morning at No. 10. Afternoon, N.H. rang me up* to say Hitler had made him a communication and had suggested he should fly back to London. Should he agree? I said yes. Went and told P.M. and H. We received later Hitler's 'proposals'. They aren't proposals at all. He says 'Polish Question must be settled *first*: then I will make an offer to England'. Discussed this after dinner at No. 10. Agreed we must get preliminary draft before N.H. returns. Got back to F.O. about 11.30 and H. started dictating a draft reply, before a large audience. And a v. bad reply. I couldn't interrupt him. But towards the end made some notes of my own and when he had finished, said I had made an 'essay in brutality', read him out what I had written. Everyone very tired. Back at 1.a.m.

[The Anglo-Polish Treaty was signed on this afternoon. Hitler's message consisted of a series of assertions and threats. Polish provocations had become intolerable; Germany would abolish 'these Macedonian conditions on her eastern frontier'; the 'problem' of Danzig and the Corridor must be solved; a war between England and Germany would be

* This call was intercepted by the Germans; D. Irving (ed.), *Breach of Security*, p. 96.

longer and bloodier than that of 1914. After the 'solution' of the German-Polish problem, however, the Führer would make a large offer. He would 'pledge himself' for the continued existence of the British Empire, and place the power of the Reich at its disposal, if his limited colonial demands were fulfilled in due course and his obligations to Italy left untouched. He regarded Germany's western frontiers as final.[36]]

Saturday, 26 August

Got to F.O. early and elaborated my draft with which Departments agree. Went over to No. 10. H. wouldn't put up my draft, but I gave copy to H. Wilson. They jiggering about with words. N.H. arrived about 1. Nothing essential to add to Hitler's message. Met again 1.30. H.J.W. and R.A.B. sent off to produce draft (*what* a party). I sat in garden with P.M. (while H. went to see Raczynski) and tried to put ginger in to him. He, I think, quite receptive. Draft produced about 4—*quite* awful. I corrected worst errors, and let it go at that. Cabinet won't have it. Let them fight their own battle. Cabinet at 6 till 8.30. Rushed home for dinner and back at once. Found, as I thought, that Cabinet wouldn't have draft and we got it more or less into shape. Home at 1 again.

Sunday, 27 August

Heard Dahlerus*—'mystery man'—arriving about 1. Jigged about with draft at No. 10 in morning. Dahlerus at 2.15. He, P.M., H. and I. He didn't add much to what we know. Cabinet at 2.30 for 3, but we didn't finish with D[ahlerus] till 3.40. Then I took him over to F.O. and he remained in my room, telephoning at intervals to Goering, till about 5.30. Meanwhile I had to interview Corbin in waiting-room and deny that I knew anything of 'mystery man'. I tried to pump the stuff into Dahlerus. Meanwhile 'C' has information of dissensions in German General Staff and produced a spy whom he wants me to send back with N.H. Arranged that. Cabinet did nothing—remitted draft to J.S., H.J.W. and me.

[The line which Chamberlain, Halifax and Cadogan took with Dahlerus in numerous talks amounted to this: Britain did not want war if it could be honourably avoided, intended to fulfil her commitment to Poland and therefore looked to Germany to negotiate sincerely with Poland. At the meeting on 27 August, Chamberlain told him that the Poles would fight rather than surrender the Corridor. The maximum they could give up would be Danzig, subject to special Polish rights. Lord Halifax understood from Dahlerus that the Germans now appreciated British

* Birger Dahlerus, Swedish businessman and friend of Goering.

determination to go to war if they invaded Poland. Cadogan said 'This gangster attitude will have to cease.'[37]

Halifax was continuing to keep contact with Ciano, whom he assured that the precautionary measures in the Mediterranean did not portend war.]

Monday, 28 August

Last night H. and N.H. rigged up some instructions to N.H. for guidance in his talk with Hitler. At N.H.'s suggestion, they included offer of Non-Aggression Pact with Germany! I managed to kill this with P.M. and H. Masses of messages from Dahlerus, who saw Goering again last night. But they don't amount to much unless one can infer from them that Hitler has cold feet. 'C' getting news of trouble with reservists in Germany. Cabinet at 12 for final jigging about of draft. I went over while they were sitting and went in after. Drafted telegram to Warsaw asking Poles to say they agree to direct negotiation. Got affirmative answer at 4 just as N.H. was leaving. . . . Text finally approved after lunch and telegraphed to Berlin. Quiet evening. Worked off arrears. Inspected War Rooms. Dined at home.

[The British reply noted that Hitler had made no proposals about the nature or mode of a settlement of Germany's differences with Poland, to which the British Government had obligations that they intended to honour:

> They could not, for any advantage offered to Great Britain, acquiesce in a settlement which put in jeopardy the independence of a State to whom they have given their guarantee . . . the next step should be the initiation of direct discussions between the German and Polish Governments on a basis which would include the principles stated above, namely, the safeguarding of Poland's essential interests and the securing of the settlement by an international guarantee.
>
> They have already received a definite assurance from the Polish Government that they are prepared to enter into discussions on this basis. . . . The results of a decision to use force have been clearly set out in the Prime Minister's letter to the Chancellor of the 22nd August.[38]

Hitler announced calmly, when Henderson handed over this message, that Germany must have Danzig, the whole Polish Corridor and 'rectifications' in Silesia. Sir Nevile observed that the Chancellor must choose between moderation (and understanding with England) and war. Hitler spoke of the Poles' unreasonableness and threatened to annihilate them.

He declared that he was not bluffing, to which Henderson retorted that Britain was not bluffing either. Hitler replied that he fully realised it.[39]]

Tuesday, 29 August

Walked to F.O. with H. and Dorothy. Sat in Park and joined by P.M. and [Mrs] Annie [Chamberlain]. I had had message from Dahlerus, which I was able to give them, that he thinks things satisfactory, and hopes 'nothing foolish' will be done on either side to upset things. Nothing much in the morning.* Further messages from Dahlerus who seems to think things are going well. . . . About 5 X† got back in N.H.'s 'plane from Berlin. He had some interesting—and not unhopeful—items of news. 6 H. and I went over and sat in garden of No. 10 with P.M. About 7.15 heard N.H. was seeing Hitler. Summary of reply expected about 9. . . . Got summary about 10 and went round to H. with it. We went over to No. 10. It looks pretty bad, and between us we knocked up a fairly hot draft by 12.30. Then H. and I and Kirk[patrick] went to F.O. to look at text now coming in. This was really quite different, and quite better. Sketched outline of different reply. Finished 2.30 a.m. and left it to Kirk to put in shape. Home 2.45 a.m.

[Henderson's first telegram described the interview as stormy. Hitler said that while he wanted British friendship more than anything in the world he could not sacrifice Germany's vital interests; for Britain to make a bargain over such a matter would be unendurable. He repeated that direct negotiations with Poland, though accepted by Germany, would be bound to fail. That, Henderson replied, would depend on the Chancellor's attitude. If he attempted to impose his will on Poland by force, Britain would fight. Hitler's written reply rehearsed Polish transgressions and 'barbaric actions of maltreatment which cry to Heaven'; stated that Germany wanted the return of Danzig and the Corridor and warned that 'in the disorganised state of affairs obtaining in Poland' incidents impossible for Germany to tolerate might occur. Nonetheless, Germany was willing to negotiate directly with Poland and had no intention of contesting Polish independence; she would therefore accept the offer of British good offices in securing the arrival in Berlin of a Polish plenipotentiary, who must arrive on 30 August.[40]]

Wednesday, 30 August

Kirk called here 9.20 with his draft. I looked at it and we went to H. On to F.O. where we had further discussion, and H. and I to No. 10 at 10.30. Dahlerus arrived about 10.45 and told us of his talk with Goering in the early hours. *Says* Hitler *may* offer plebiscite on certain conditions. This throws a new light (and there are still

* Cadogan told Corbin that he did not see how Hitler, having announced his aims categorically, could beat a retreat without discrediting himself.

† An official of the Intelligence service.

rumours of trouble in Germany). I took D[ahlerus] back at 11.30 when Cabinet met. Saw Corbin and gave him text of Hitler note and outline of what I know of our reply.

H. back about 1. I got D. to ring up Goering and put various questions to him. He seeems hopeful of Hitler (1) offering plebiscite (2) not putting proposals in form of 'Diktat'. But (3) a Pole *must* come from Poland to get terms 'with full powers to sign'. Told him this unreasonable.* Lunched at F.O. with H. putting finishing touches to reply and telegram to Warsaw. Went over to P.M. for approval. H. went to bed at 5. Then trouble began. Corbin came down with an objection from his Government to a passage in our Note to Hitler. And Van blew up. By desperate efforts managed to compose the differences and get P.M.'s approval. Home about 8—mad with fatigue. Things must now take their course. D. left Heston about 6. I can't help thinking Germans are in an awful fix. In fact it's obvious, even if one discredits rumours of disturbances. God help us: I don't *think* we've given away anything essential *yet!*

[At midnight, Henderson saw Ribbentrop, who read out 'at top speed' a long list of German demands and then asserted that it was too late for negotiation anyway since the Polish emissary had not arrived. He refused to give the Ambassador a copy. Henderson immediately afterwards pressed the Polish Ambassador to ask for an interview with Ribbentrop. Both Poland and Germany had mobilised. 'The Poles', Henderson wrote to Cadogan, 'must put themselves in the right by making a gesture of some kind, or else we must all fight. Possibly the second would be the best but the responsibility is too great for me to encourage the idea.' On the evening of 31 August the Poles agreed that their Ambassador should visit the German Foreign Office to determine the basis of negotiation but not to receive the German proposals, which might be accompanied by some form of ultimatum. Colonel Beck said that he would not go to Berlin, 'as he had no intention of being treated like President Hacha†'.[41]]

Thursday, 31 August

Pretty hectic day. Picked up H. Ciano rang him up, trying to put wind up. Wanted us to urge Poles to abandon Danzig and discuss other questions! Consulted P.M. Gave Ciano flat refusal. While we were over at No. 10 C[iano] rang up again and said Musso wanted to propose Conference for revision of Versailles, but wanted to know

* Halifax reinforced this, saying that Dahlerus must make it absolutely plain in Berlin 'that we were prepared to do our best in negotiation only if it really was negotiation and not dictation on the Czecho-Slovak model.'

† The President of Czechoslovakia, who had been compelled to sign away his country's independence under the threat of the immediate bombing of Prague.

(before putting it to Hitler!) whether we and French agreed. We got Corbin round to No. 10 and he rang up Paris, who will give us a reply later. . . . Daladier's reaction to Conference proposal very hostile. P.M.'s first reaction was that we must have demobilisation first. French don't like even this. . . .

About 8 more telegrams in from Warsaw—Beck's reaction to our reply to Germans and his reply to our proposals. Agreed on telegram to Warsaw. Got home about 8.45 and tried to eat dinner, interrupted by F.O., Joe Kennedy (twice) and Corbin.

Heard later Germans had broadcast their offer to Poles, which *looks* very good. They add the lie that Poles have known of this for 2 days and not answered, which can be taken as rejection! Told Peake to kill this lie (11.30). Much more happened during the day. Can't give full or connected account—too tired. But it *does* seem to me Hitler is hesitant and trying all sorts of dodges, including last-minute bluff. We have got to stand firm.

IV

September 1939–June 1940

THE TWILIGHT WAR AND THE COLLAPSE OF FRANCE

The War Cabinet quickly decided, on military advice, that since time would work in favour of the Allies their strategy should be adapted to a long war; to build up resources, train the armies, impose the utmost economic pressure. 'The fate of Poland', Roosevelt was told on 14 September, 'will depend on the ultimate outcome of the war; i.e. on our ability to defeat Germany, and not on our ability to relieve pressure on Poland at the outset.'

Military commanders had been given instructions that only military objectives, defined in the narrowest sense, should be bombarded. The Germans were doing likewise. So long as this continued no really serious damage could be done to Germany or Britain from the air. The War Cabinet thought that attack involving loss of civilian life in Germany would not materially help Poland, and were subject to strong pressure from France to do nothing which would provoke retaliation and thereby hinder the concentration of troops. As for Britain:

> every week is of value to us in increasing our reserves in aircraft, anti-aircraft guns, etc., and generally improving the security of the base from which our offensive operations will ultimately be launched.
>
> A delay in the inception of the air war is all to the advantage of the defence of this country and of our sea-borne trade. . . .
>
> On balance . . . it was considered that the early initiation of intensive air action would not materially improve our chances of winning a short war, while the possession of an Air Striking Force relatively intact and with increased reserves will go far to ensure that the Germans for their part cannot win it . . . on purely military grounds it was concluded that we should therefore adhere for the present to our existing policy.[1]

The Chiefs of Staff continued to represent that bombing of industrial centres must diminish British aircraft production, and the French that their factories were still in process of being moved out of the most vulnerable zones.

* * *

Early in September, Cadogan received a telegram from Washington, which seemed 'to give us a line on the "leaks" of the last few years. Fear someone in the office is compromised.' Because he was habitually cautious in his reference to all such questions, the Diary does not show how long Cadogan had known of this particular breach of security. Nor does it indicate what steps had been taken to counteract it. An entry of 21 September, however, calls the revelations of the Intelligence authorities' enquiry 'awful'. It soon transpired that a member of the Communications Department, handling the cypher traffic, had been spying for Russia. He was arrested on 27 September, tried promptly and sentenced to ten years' imprisonment. Cadogan reluctantly decided that the whole Department, apparently recruited by haphazard methods, must be reorganised; this involved the movement of some staff, and the dismissal of others. Halifax generously offered to explain to them. Hence the grateful entries of 30 October and 1 December.

* * *

The conclusion of the Nazi-Soviet pact provided Hitler with yet another triumph over the British and French, whose military missions had to creep ignominiously away from Moscow while Ribbentrop and Stalin toasted the downfall of the British Empire. It freed Germany to strike east or west. On land and in the air she was stronger than Britain and France; at sea far weaker, though the fleets of Britain and France were not much greater than those of Germany, Italy and Japan combined. But Germany and Italy had an advantage in that they could concentrate their navies to defend their interests while Britain had to disperse her navy fully to defend hers; and Japan had virtual immunity from naval and air attack within home waters.

All the same, Hitler had paid a price in the longer run for Russia's political neutrality and economic goodwill. Russia rapidly moved into the Baltic States and Finland; she might be expected to oppose Germany in the Balkans, especially in Roumania. Plainly, the signature by the leader of the Crusade of an agreement with the anti-Christ, left other parties to the original pact in an exposed posture: the Japanese Government, which had been virtually at war with Russia on the Mongolian frontier, fell. Mussolini, no more consulted than the Japanese, was confirmed in his intention to remain neutral. By a calculated indiscretion, Ciano exclaimed to Loraine on 31 August, 'Can't you understand that we shall never start a war against you and the French?'[2] General Franco, whose hostility might have rendered the Straits of Gibraltar impassable, declared Spanish neutrality and continued throughout the war to show scant gratitude to Hitler and Mussolini.

The Russians had less difficulty than others in accommodating themselves to the change of sides. True, Stalin did say in the last stages of the negotiation that to insert a phrase about friendly relations would be going rather far, considering that for six years the Nazis had poured 'pails of manure' over Russia. However, he drank privately to the health of the

German nation's beloved Führer. And on 31 August Molotov described the pact to the Supreme Soviet, justly, as 'a turning-point in the history of Europe, yes and not only of Europe.

'Only yesterday, German Fascists were conducting a foreign policy hostile to us. Yes, only yesterday we were enemies in the field of foreign relations. Today, however, the situation has changed and we have ceased to be enemies.' And referring to Stalin's speech of 10 March, he remarked pithily: 'It is now evident that in Germany they understood these statements of comrade Stalin correctly on the whole and drew practical conclusions from this. [*Laughter*]'

Like others who had never believed much in Russia's good faith or offensive capacity, Cadogan refused to regard the Nazi-Soviet pact as a major disaster. He recognised, of course, that it left Poland still more vulnerable and might make nonsense of the guarantee to Roumania, the operation of which was not conditional upon a German attack. Should Russia invade Roumania, there was practically nothing the West could do with Turkey neutral, and precious little if she were not. 'The action of Soviet Russia has changed, or may have changed, the whole situation so profoundly that our obligations can fairly be considered to have been modified', Cadogan remarked. 'I am aware that this is pure Hitlerian doctrine, but in this case it seems forced upon us by circumstances over which we have no control.'[3]

In some respects, the advent of war simplified the issues for those who had to conduct foreign policy. There was no longer the need to consider from day to day how the balance should be held in respect of Germany. It was now simple to say that unless the wrong done to Poland were righted, there could be no peace. The arguments for keeping Italy and Japan neutral had certainly not been weakened, however; which meant that concessions had often to be made when the War Cabinet and Foreign Office would have preferred a very different stance. Ciano told Loraine in September that the British line was by far the best one. Each evidence of British goodwill helped him with Mussolini.[4] The new Japanese Government promptly offered the British the 'friendly advice' that they should withdraw their troops and warships from those parts of China under Japanese control. About the Far Eastern situation there was little to be done, in the absence of an effective American policy. However, in his dealings with the Japanese, Sir Robert Craigie showed himself fertile in expedients and skilful in procrastination; and the Japanese evinced no keenness to press matters to extremes.

The desire to keep Italy out of the war, partly dictated by a wholesome respect for German power, partly by a desire to hold the Mediterranean open for Middle Eastern and Imperial reasons, restricted further the range of military policy available to the Supreme War Council, which had been set up by the British and French Governments. Before long the proposals for action in South-eastern Europe were being mooted; whereupon Cadogan pointed out:

I don't see myself how any such action could be contemplated with a hostile Italy, and therefore it seems to me necessary to explain to the French how essential it is to keep Italy neutral while we are consolidating the front in Turkey and Greece, and to try eventually to secure Italy on our side to enable us to initiate, eventually, any action in that region.[5]

Nine months later, Mussolini resolved some of these difficulties, to the relief of many. 'Am rather glad,' wrote Cadogan on 10 June 1940. 'Now we can say what we think of these purulent dogs.' Though hindsight would suggest that the Allies could only have profited by fighting Italy during the twilight war, the Chiefs of Staff consistently advised otherwise. Moreover, it is worth remembering that Mussolini's decision to enter the war was taken only after the collapse of France, an event which overturned the basis upon which every British Government of recent years had made its strategic assumptions. Chamberlain, Halifax and Cadogan, all of whom had been so powerfully influenced in 1938 by the evidence of French feebleness, were perhaps a little less surprised than Churchill by the cataclysm of May 1940.

* * *

For the moment, the main tasks of British foreign policy were to manage the naval blockade as effectively as possible, without doing serious harm to relations with the U.S.A.; to concert as closely as might be with the French, a task often so difficult as to justify the celebrated remark about the near-impossibility of winning a war by means of a coalition; to attract the approval and full-blooded support of the Dominions, in men, money and munitions; to avert, or at least to stave off the reckoning, with Japan and Italy; to get all possible help from the U.S.A.; to induce some European powers, especially Belgium and the Scandinavian states, to depart from the strict interpretations of neutrality.

* * *

Chamberlain and Halifax found themselves in considerable difficulties on 1 and 2 September 1939. The French insisted that they must gain time for evacuation. The British Government had no official knowledge of the German terms until the night of 31 August and could not mention their private information without compromising Dahlerus and Goering. At least Hitler had made it fairly plain by the timing of the invasion of Poland that he did not seriously expect the terms to be considered; and had thereby relieved Halifax and Cadogan of the anxiety they had long felt lest, by producing specious terms which the Poles would reject, Hitler should persuade many in Europe, the U.S.A. and even in Britain that the British Government had precipitated a general war by giving Colonel Beck a blank cheque.

One day after the war, when Cadogan had become the first British permanent representative at the United Nations, his Soviet colleague made some sneering aspersions upon Chamberlain, his Government and the United Kingdom itself. Cadogan, who had penetrated Chamberlain's reserve and had found that a rewarding process, replied that Britain was the first power to declare war on Germany in 1939, and the only power to fight, with the Empire and Commonwealth, through every day of two world wars against Germany and of the war against Japan:

> No one seemed to pay much attention—least of all the Soviet delegate, who sat back expressionless in his seat taking no further notice, secure in his reflection that, having said his piece dictated from Moscow he could count on a further tenure of his office. . . . My remarks were never challenged. Perhaps I was thought to be unworthy of notice.
>
> But it may be a good thing sometimes, as one is swept along in the ceaseless rush from one crisis to the next, to make a little reckoning similar to the foregoing. Anyhow it gives me satisfaction, and a little courage, and a little hope.[6]]

1939

Friday, 1 September

Days and nights have been so awful that I can't remember the sequence. It was this morning, I think, that I was woken up by the telephone at 7 to say that Danzig had declared its incorporation in the Reich, and, later, that Germans had crossed the Polish frontier. I think (I am writing Sept. 3) that I spent most of the day at No. 10. H. and H.J.W. and I lunched there. By the evening, we had instructed N.H. to present (which he did at 9.30 p.m.) a warning (not an ultimatum) to the German Government, calling on them to withdraw (no time-limit).

[Dahlerus rang Cadogan up from Berlin shortly after noon, having seen Goering and Hitler. The Führer had said that he would like to discuss matters with the British and Dahlerus wished to come to London. Cadogan said he could see no hope on either score, a message which he repeated, with the Prime Minister's sanction, an hour later:

> Nothing to be done on lines indicated: matter has been taken out of our hands.
>
> Any idea of [British] mediation while German troops are invading Poland is quite out of the question.
>
> The only way in which a world war can be stopped is (1) that hostilities be suspended and (2) German troops should be immediately withdrawn from Polish territory.[7]]

Saturday, 2 September

Walked with H. and D. [Lady Halifax] through Buck[ingham] Palace gardens.* Purple autumn crocuses out. No answer from Germans. We are simply waiting. . . . I found message summoning me to No. 10 (3.15). Went over (and stayed there till 1 a.m.). Trouble is the French. We can't simply wait longer for a German reply. But the French don't want to present ultimatum till noon tomorrow, with 48 hrs.' notice. Found Ciano had been ringing up with proposal for 5 Power Conference. And I think Bonnet has probably committed himself to it too far—trying to wriggle out. P.M. committed to making statement this evening to Parliament. Cabinet in afternoon, who wanted ultimatum to expire at midnight tonight. But we couldn't budge the French. Awful evening, ringing up Bonnet and Daladier. Told Ciano we couldn't look at Conference unless G[erman] troops withdrawn. He said useless to press that on Germans. Finally Daladier agreed a statement for P.M. to make at 7.30 —no time limit—merely saying we were consulting French as to procedure. This infuriated the House. I came home to dinner, but in the middle was told I must go to No. 10 '*At once: at once*'. Went round in car. Found P.M., Annie and H. and H.J.W. having dinner, and finished my dinner there. P.M. told me about the House and the trouble with his own colleagues. We got Corbin and telephoned to Daladier, and then to Bonnet. But couldn't move them. Finally agreed *we* must act at 9 a.m. with time-limit till 11 (my suggestion). Cabinet at about midnight. (I was present at this as at the afternoon one.) Everything tied up and I drafted the necessary telegrams. Home 1.30 a.m.—usual time. Awful thunderstorm. Dead beat.

[Halifax' record says:

> the general feeling [in the House] . . . was that the French were trying to run out of their engagement to Poland and were taking us with them. For this . . . there had never been the least ground. The sole reason for the French delay was General Gamelin's desire to secure further time for completing mobilisation. . . . I could not acquit some members of the Cabinet of having fed the flames of suspicion.

Churchill now joined the Government as First Lord of the Admiralty, and Eden as Secretary of State for the Dominions.]

Sunday, 3 September

Drove in car to F.O. about 9.30. No news. Dahlerus rang up 10.50 to say German reply on its way. Only hope was to ask Goering to

* The King had given Halifax a key.

fly over. I said 'Rats'. I went over with H. at 11 to P.M. 11.10 still no news. P.M. due to broadcast at 11.15. 11.12 definite message from Berlin that no reply received so P.M. let fly at 11.15. Very good. 11.30 J.S. rushed in to complain that W[ar] O[ffice] had not received 'Let go' message. But he was cut short by first Air Raid Warning and we dispersed to our shelters. All clear after about 20 minutes and H. went off to House. Newall called about 12 to ask when he could start operations from France. Says warning was due to approach of 2 machines to Beachy Head. (Subsequently rumoured they were French.) . . . Very hot and sunny. No work—only working off arrears. In a sense, there is relief; doubts resolved.

Monday, 4 September

Air Raid warning about 3 a.m. Woken up and went down to basement. Damned nuisance. All clear after about ½ an hour.

Walked to F.O. Still very muggy. Peirse (Air Ministry) rang me up to say Dutch in a flap about aircraft flying over their territory last night. They apparently complain that our leaflet-dropping bombers crossed their territory. Peirse says quite untrue. (But leaflets fell on Dutch territory.) I asked him about Air Raid warning. He said he thought H[ome] O[ffice] had loosed it off, due to these rumours of aircraft over Holland. I said anyhow why in Hell did they want to wake London over that. He said they were enquiring into it. . . . Raczynski—no news. Corbin ditto.

Managed to prevent Rob Hudson being made Minister of Economic Warfare. Fixed this with H. and Horace. They are appointing Cross,* whom I don't know. . . . Trying to arrange to get N. Henderson and staff safely out. Dutch being helpful.

Left office about 7.20—drove H. back. Just before leaving had telephone report from Hague that German bombing squadron crossing Dutch territory for England. But they have never (10.45) turned up! So I suppose this is one of the stories to which we shall have to get used in the next few weeks, or months, or years.

Tuesday, 5 September

No news. H. got back before lunch. Our airmen *say* they bombed ships in Wilhelmshaven last night. But how did they know they were there? The night before they said they hadn't crossed Holland, but the evidence produced to me this evening by Dutch Minister seems to me to prove that they *did*. If they didn't know they were over Holland, how can they say (in bad weather) that they were over an

* R. H. Cross, Minister of Economic Warfare, 1939–40; of Shipping, 1940–1.

individual ship? Moreover they've bombed Esbjerg!! Lunched at home. Ordered shelter. . . . Took H. away about 7.50. He says Gort had satisfactory conversation with Gamelin yesterday. Meanwhile Poles seem to have cracked: Hitler will conquer Poland and then make peace offer, and . . . [the French] will want to accept! Well, in war, we have to go through these awful times.

Wednesday, 6 September

Woken by Raid at 6.45. Nothing happened, but 'All Clear' didn't go for about 2 hrs. It's a damned nuisance, these things. . . .

Very depressed. We shall fight to the last, and may win—but I confess I don't see how! Italy is merely waiting to see which side wins. Poland is sunk, and it will *look* to Italy as if Germany was winning. And I don't see what we can do. However, the only thing to do is not to be despondent in these early stages. We have a long row to hoe! I have no definite work, and feel I ought to be active somehow, and that probably contributes to my depression.

Thursday, 7 September

Picked up H. and Dorothy. Drove to Park and walked through it. He promises to take up at Cabinet question of publicity, of which poor Charles Peake is worried to death. . . . Feel better today—perhaps because busier or perhaps because news not quite so bad. Reports of Musso's illness followed by telegram from Loraine showing that King [Victor Emmanuel] may have taken over army, with Prince [Umberto] of Piedmont and Graziani.*. . . Plan of Germans is now quite evident—conquer Poland and then ask what we are fighting about. (Answer quite easy!) But until then, they probably won't attack us, or at least confine their attack to military objectives.

Friday, 8 September

Picked up H. at 9.30. Rehearsed with him his daily statement for Cabinet. *Lovely* day and *blazing* hot. 'C' came over about his revolution in Czecho[slovakia], Austria, Poland, Bavaria, &c. There is something in this, but it may misfire. All sorts of bothers about Staff and reorganising Communications Department. O.S. comes in and makes a suggestion. No sooner do I try to do something than L.O. comes in with a different one. Then O.S. changes his mind. L.O. (who has nothing to do) has second thoughts. This evening I lost my temper and said I would only see them together and what we agreed

* Marshal Rodolfo Graziani, formerly Viceroy in Ethiopia; Commander of Italian forces in North Africa, 1940–2.

on I'd bloody well do. They drive me mad. Ogilvie-Forbes came in morning and N.H. at 3.30. They haven't really much to say. They were well treated or not ill-treated. N.H. rather excitable and silly. . . . Johnson (Herschel) at 4. U.S. reacting strongly against Japanese 'advice' to evacuate concessions. But will they stand by us? This necessitated re-drafting telegram to Paris which H., R.A.B. and I had agreed on. Paravicini* more hopeful about German morale, but with no good reason. Newall rang me up to tell me we are sending (with the French) 'planes to Poland. But how? German advance in P[oland] pausing, but they are beginning to transfer troops to the west. French fiddling about with Siegfried line. But what can they do? Busier, but depressed.

Saturday, 9 September

6 Buck House to see the King. Called in about 6.10 and stayed till 6.50. He rather depressed—and a little défaitiste—result, I think, of a talk with Joe K[ennedy] who sees everything from the angle of his own investments. Back to No. 10 at 7 to see H.J.W. who showed me Press announcement of a '3-year war'. Asked how I thought that would go down. I didn't see any harm, provided it was put to the Press properly. Telegraphed it to Paris, with appropriate explanation.† H.W. rang up P.M. (at Chequers) who approved. H. left at 3.15 for Yorkshire. S. Hoare, Belisha and Hankey holding the fort!

Sunday, 10 September

Drove to F.O. at 10. Pole came at 11.15 with urgent appeal for effective action on Western Front. I sent it over to the Rump Cabinet at 11.30.

. . . we motored to Denham. Lunched there. T. and I strolled over the course. Clouded over. Very depressing. I suppose all the amusements of life must now be in abeyance, and will they ever be revived?

Monday, 11 September

'C' says leaflets doing no good. He has failed to get Air Ministry to support his revolution in Cz[echoslovakia]. And they are quite right: I read today a v. good paper (approved by War Cabinet this evening) by Chiefs of Staff against dispersal of our air effort. . . . Saw Raczynski with H., who told him we couldn't say more about our

* C. R. Paravicini, Swiss Minister in London.

† This statement, to the effect that the Government were preparing for a war of at least three years, was issued because the War Cabinet wanted to kill rumours that their action would be influenced by events in Poland.

war plans than our '3-year War' and referred him to experts on subject of air activity. War Cabinet again at 6. P.M. decided to fly to France tomorrow for meeting with Daladier. Sent for me to tell me to draft communiqué of meeting! which I did. Dined at home. Worked till 11.15. Cooler this evening. Feel less depressed. Due to fact that I know French are going to make big push against Siegfried line: also perhaps to pause of German armies in Poland.

Tuesday, 12 September

Generally, outlook not so black. Germans are definitely held in Poland for the moment and are 15 miles from Warsaw. Ironside says they are *not* broken (but in a pretty bad way!). It has begun to rain in Poland (drizzle here). May it *pour*! Ironside also thinks French push may have some success. So feel better.

[The meeting of Chamberlain and Daladier passed off well enough. Chamberlain described British plans for mobilising industry and obtaining supplies from the U.S.A. Neither side wished to give the impression of forming a Balkan *bloc* against Italy. Daladier said he was pleased by Spain's attitude. The Sous-Préfet invited Chamberlain to come and fish in the Somme 'as soon as circumstances permit'.]

Wednesday, 13 September

Raczynski called in evening, trying to find out what happened between P.M. and Daladier yesterday. Fortunately couldn't tell him, as didn't know. Debate in Lords on bombing and unfortunately at 1 p.m. I got tape announcement that Germans were going to bomb even 'hamlets' in Poland, owing to activity of 'francs-tireurs'. . . . We can't commit ourselves to reprisals at this moment.

Drove home with H. who had just been seeing High Commissioners. They have got the wind up about our Air Force. But I can't quite make out why. I think they are the most undependable busybodies. Bruce is bad: I suppose they haven't really enough work to do.

Thursday, 14 September

Germans held for the moment in Poland but, unless there is good heavy rain, there will be a further and more disastrous 'pincers' movement. Fact is no small semi-industrial country can stand up for 10 days against one of the 'Big Five' (or Four or Three?) . . . O.S.—old croaker—going about saying we had decided to do nothing till March 1940. G.J. had already told me H. Hopkinson* was saying

* Of F.O., then serving in the War Cabinet Secretariat.

the same. I asked H. this evening if this was so, and he assured me that the date for the French push against the Siegfried line holds good. If it comes off, shall wash their heads. Still nothing happening and we must possess our souls in patience. Much talk of Germany turning next on Roumania. God grant that she may be so foolish. Of course she can overrun the country, but the dispersal of effort, if we can give her a whack on the Western Front, will be a Godsend.

Friday, 15 September

Poland has been crumpled up. I suppose we must lose the war for 4 years before we win a decisive battle. Spent most of afternoon in conference with H. on Balkan and Turkish situation (all very glum) and Belgium. Outlook pretty black. Gather from H. that P.M. impressed with power of the air in Poland and wants to 'gain time'. But what are Germans doing meanwhile?

Sunday, 17 September

G.J. rang up at lunch time . . . at news of Russian invasion of Poland. Said Tilea *must* see me this evening. What can *I* do for him? However, said I'd be back at 7 and T[ilea] could call 7.30. Awful drive up to London—took 2 hours 25 minutes. Everyone in the world using their car for last time before rationing, and all wanting to be back before dark.

. . . Tilea came at 7.30. I, of course, could do nothing for him. Dined at home and worked—*stacks* of telegrams.

Monday, 18 September

Fearful day: callers to waste my time, and masses of papers. Everything gloomy—loss of 'Courageous'.* French attack postponed for a week. We don't know what Russians are at—we don't want to go to war with them—nor what effect it will have on Turks. . . . H. Johnson came about Far East. Americans evidently won't take any 'commitment' but will nevertheless blame us if we clear out. Cambon came about communication to Russia. War Cabinet want to issue communiqué about Russian performance. Late in evening showed him text of latter and draft of communication to Russia. After dinner . . . message from Cambon, deprecating our draft communication to Russia as being 'dangerous' and submitting one that seemed to me to be much more so. Anyhow they don't object to our communiqué.

* Aircraft-carrier, sunk by a U-boat in the Bristol Channel.

[The British Government, said the communiqué, had learned with horror and indignation of Russia's invasion of Poland. Their obligations to Poland would not be altered by it, and they remained confident that Poland would be restored at the end of the war.]

Wednesday, 20 September

Talks with R.A.B. and H. about Far East. I urged no withdrawal, and can't suggest anything about silver that Japs would accept. H. said that was unhelpful. I agree. But one can endure these things slowly in the F[ar] E[ast]. . . . Corbin rang up to say Daladier wanted another meeting with P.M. on Friday. Went to see P.M. after dinner. He agreed, but wanted D[aladier] to come to him, if possible, and wanted to know agenda.

Friday, 22 September

Picked up H. at 9.30 and we arrived at No. 10 at 9.40. Hush-hush party consisting of P.M., H., Chatfield, self, Ismay and Bridges. Left Victoria by special at 10. Arrived at Hove 11. Drove to Town Hall. No-one knew what was happening. Town Clerk had been warned to accommodate meeting of 'Government officials'. Wandered about passages of an awful Victorian building, hung with Victorian pictures of dead Aldermen. A functionary asked H. if he was a 'Government official'. He said 'Yes'. We had been decanted at the back door and had to walk round to the front entrance. Some people recognised P.M. and I heard 'Chamberlain! Cor Blimey!' Corbin joined us, and we had a long wait for the French, till 12.15. Meanwhile the Town Clerk recognised us and sent for the Mayor, who arrived breathless—the local butcher, I presume, but quite nice. 12.15 Daladier, Gamelin, Darlan,* Dautry,† Jean Monnet,‡ a General and young Chambrun arrived.

We discussed first a Salonica or Stambul expedition. P.M. threw gentle showers of cold water on it, and the French didn't seem entirely convinced by their own argument. It's moonshine to me. *Only*, if one could do it *quickly* and *effectively* enough, it would throw Hitler out of his stride. But I don't think we can.

1.40 lunch at Prince's Hotel. I sat between Dautry and Chambrun. Former, after a bad air crossing and one glance at the menu, asked for a 'canapé' and a 'tasse de thé'. So I had a gap next to me.

* Admiral François Darlan, C.-in-C., French Navy, 1933–40; Vice-President of the Council, Vichy Government, 1941–2.

† Raoul Dautry, Minister of Munitions, 1936–40.

‡ French economist; Chairman, Franco-British Economic Co-ordination Commitee, 1939–40; Commissioner for Armaments, Supplies and Reconstruction, French Council of National Liberation, Algiers, 1943–4.

Not too bad a lunch and we resumed about 3. Talk about munitions production and reinforcement of the air and A.A. in France. Our special left at 4 (Jean Monnet came with us) and we got back at 5.

Saturday, 23 September

H. asked me about our 'War Aims'. I told him I saw awful difficulties. We can no longer say 'evacuate Poland' without going to war with Russia, which we don't want to do! I suppose the cry is 'Abolish Hitlerism'. What if Hitler hands over to Goering?! Meanwhile what of the course of operations? What if Germany now sits tight? Gamelin doesn't look to me like flinging himself on the Siegfried line. What do we do? Build up our armaments feverishly? What for? Can we last out the course? 'Time is on our side.' Is it? What are the Germans doing meanwhile? Must try and think this out. . . .

Maisky at 6 with H. M[aisky] very embarrassed: of course he knows *nothing!*

Monday, 25 September

General Carton de Wiart* called, just back from Poland. V. interesting. Says the German of 1939 is not the German of 1914. On equal terms, he scarcely held his own with the Pole. But of course he had an overwhelming might of material. And Poles had not prepared *any* defensive positions. On the last day, 2 German mechanised Divisions had run ahead of their petrol, were stranded, and could have been wiped out by an Air Force.

Tuesday, 26 September

11.15 Corbin rang up to say Polish Ambassador in Paris had notified French Government last night of new Pres[ident]. French Cabinet this morning had decided to refuse to recognise! Let H. know—he was seeing Raczynski. This came as complete bombshell to R. . . .

Raczynski came in evening—very distracted. Couldn't comfort him much.

Wednesday, 27 September

Saw Maisky with H. at 5. He gave evasive and silly answers to questions we put to him on 23rd.† Quite useless talking to him—he knows nothing and is told nothing by his Government.

* Lt.-Gen. Adrian Carton de Wiart, V.C.; retired 1924; head of British Military Mission to Poland, August 1939; commander, Central Norwegian Expeditionary Force, 1940; Prime Minister's military representative with Chiang Kai-Shek, 1943–6.

† Halifax had asked, *inter alia*, whether Russia wished to discuss a general war trade agreement.

I am *very* uneasy at the meeting of Rib[bentrop], Molotov, and Sarajoglu* in Moscow. It's a sinister party, and I don't know what it means.

[The Führer observed to Dahlerus on 26 September that the British had always interpreted his restraint and patience as weakness, but that they should not let themselves be deceived. He would soon wage the war toward the West, in such a way as to stun the British. This hardly seemed promising material for a negotiation. He must have 'a free hand in regard to Poland', but would guarantee 'the status quo of the rest of Europe', including the Low Countries and France. The mood of German troops in the West, however, 'was one of extraordinary eagerness for combat'. Dahlerus set off for England once more.[8]]

Thursday, 28 September

6.30 heard Dahlerus had arrived. Went home soon after with H., dined at home, fixed up D[ahlerus] to come round and see me at 10. He stayed talking till 12.15. He really hadn't much to say. He's like a wasp at a picnic—one can't beat him off. He's brought very little from Berlin. He spent most of Tues[day] with Goering and Hitler, but their 'terms' are as to be expected: give us a free hand in Central and E. Europe and we will guarantee the British Empire.

Friday, 29 September

Ronnie Campbell† arrived. Prince [Paul] has told him a story that makes it seem that Goering (? possibly) *might* bump Hitler off if he can be assured we shall not dictate another Versailles. 3 p.m. meeting of P.M., H., self, and Dahlerus. He told us his story but it didn't get us much further. P.M. spoke on same lines as I had spoken last night—No assurances, no promises, no signatures of present regime are worth *anything*. Germany must do some *deed* as evidence of good faith.... Dahlerus dined with me and T. at Carlton [Hotel].

Sunday, 1 October

Listened at 9 to B.B.C. I shall bend all my efforts to getting Ogilvie—if possible—anyhow *someone*—sacked.‡ It consisted of German communiqués claiming 10 British machines shot down, and Hess' speech. Why the *Hell* should we broadcast Hess' ridiculous propaganda muck?

* Sükrü Sarajoglu, Turkish Minister for Foreign Affairs, 1938–42; Prime Minister, 1942–46.

† R. I. Campbell, Minister at Paris, 1938–9; at Belgrade, 1939–41; in Washington, 1941–5. Not to be confused with R. H. Campbell.

‡ Sir Frederick W. Ogilvie, Dir.-Gen., B.B.C., 1938–42.

Monday, 2 October

Wrote a bit for P.M.'s statement tomorrow on situation produced by German-Soviet agreement.*

Friday, 6 October

R.A.B. about administrative questions. I can't stand these. I am suddenly told that a Department in the Ministry of Obfuscation has to be reorganised: it must come back 'under control' of the Ministry of Circumlocution. But there is a great difficulty, as the Head of the Department—Col. Shufflebottom—ought not to be there, and I ought to substitute Mr Piffkins. (Other people tell me this is a ramp, and that the real man is Nuffkins.) I don't know S. or P. (or even N.). I can't grasp what they are supposed to be doing. I have no data to go upon: how the *Hell* can I decide? But I was at it all day—and work accumulating.

Saturday, 7 October

Called to War Cabinet 12.30 for discussion on reply to Hitler.† I had talked to H. about this: the line, according to me, is to say frankly (and P.M. hesitates to say this) that *we won't make peace with Hitler*. Get rid of Hitler: that is my *war* aim—not peace aim. Do that first: then you will win the war. Remove him, and there will be such disunity in Germany that they *can't* win. The French will object to this, and some members of the Cabinet. But it's right. And it *should* work, *if* we couple it with an assurance that we don't want to *dictate* a peace. Not a v. useful discussion. . . . Back to F.O. to draft reply to Hitler and work off a *mass* of arrears. 8 p.m. sent down first draft of reply to P.M. and H.

[Cadogan wrote at this time:

'War Aims' or 'Peace Aims' are loose terms.
They connote:

(1) what forced us reluctantly to take up arms;
(2) what our immediate object may be in righting wrongs;
(3) what we may conceive and aim at as a better order in Europe and the world.

As regards (1), the events of the past 2 years are a sufficient answer. We may be criticised for not having taken up arms earlier. We cannot

* They had announced that (a) Poland was now partitioned between Germany and Russia and (b) all responsibility for the continuation of the war rested on the Western Powers.

† Who had addressed the Reichstag on 6 October.

be reproached for resolving—and announcing our resolve—not to condone a further outrage such as that which was committed against the Czechs last March.

That is the negative side of our 'War Aims'—to deny to Germany the ever-increasing encroachment on the rights and liberties of others. To have allowed another outrage to pass unchecked would have been to hand over Europe to terror and oppression.

As regards (2) we can only assert that our object is to deliver non-German populations from domination and terrorism. And on that we are resolved.

To ask us to define, here and now, the conditions in which we shall give them back their freedom is unreasonable.

Much will depend on the state of Europe after the war, and they themselves could not now say what guarantees they would require for their defence and for their development.

Unless we know the duration of this war and its intensity, we can form no estimate of the state of Europe when the victory is won: what the groupings of Powers will be: how far the resources of all will have to be exhausted.

For that reason it is really impossible to frame any definite proposals under (3).

We all know instinctively what we want—that every man and woman in Europe should have a chance of leading a decent and orderly life and developing his or her ability to the fullest for their own advantage and for the common good.

But in what happened to be favourable circumstances, we failed to achieve this. We must try again, sobered by the knowledge of the great difficulties. But we should be over-ambitious if we planned our edifice now, without knowing what materials we shall have wherewith to build.[9]]

Sunday, 8 October

Corbin called this morning; very fussed about our procedure of saying we are going to 'examine' Hitler's speech, and reply on Wed. The French are very difficult. If we reply at once, they reproach us for not consulting them. If we take some days to consult them, they say this will 'produce a bad effect'. I argued with him, but of course to no purpose. I could only say that we were already committed—as we are—to 'examining' and had already announced a reply on Wed. We can't now simply ignore Hitler's speech. He also trotted out the silly French arguments against attacking *Hitler*. I said I quite saw these but, as an *immediate war* aim, I thought it would be invaluable to get rid of Hitler. The French say that it's not only Hitler, but the German nation—'Il faut en finir'. Yes: but how? The French are a logical race: oughn't they to stop and ask themselves *how* to 'en finir'? They didn't know how at Versailles. Reported to H. and sent copy to P.M. H. had his redraft ready about 6. It's much longer—as Sam Hoare wanted—but I don't know that it's the better for that. Winston came over after Cabinet—about 6. He thinks it too long. He told us German ships were out in N. Sea this afternoon. . . .

Corbin rang up again at 8.30, bleating about the press reactions to our announcement of a reply on Wednesday. I don't know what he means, and I can't make out that he does either.

Monday, 9 October

P.M. has produced new draft reply to Hitler. Spent 3–4 p.m. trying . . . to graft on to it essential passages of H's draft. Meeting at 4 P.M., H., Winston, H.J.W. and self, on draft. Quite useful—got it into shape, more or less. Adjourned 6–7 for Horace to have it retyped. Then met and approved it. Quite good, I think.

Wednesday, 11 October

Dahlerus rang up from the Hague. I think he has nothing, and this confirmed by telegram just received. If we insist on change of regime in Germany, nothing doing. Then nothing *is* doing, and we must look forward to air raids tomorrow night.

Thursday, 12 October

Smuts* wants to change reply to Hitler and H., Makins and I worked on possible draft for giving effect to his wishes. But they won't do. . . . P.M. made his statement, which went well. Dahlerus rang up but I wouldn't talk to him. Says he wants 'guidance' on P.M.'s statement. It's clear enough, and what D. has been able to send us is useless.

[Hitler had argued simply that since Britain and France had failed to save Poland they might as well make peace. The only question at issue on the British side was whether to enter into such an exchange. It was thought best to pin upon Hitler the responsibility for the expected holocaust. Chamberlain replied appropriately on 12 October, offering no hope of a negotiation but saying that it was not British policy to exclude from her proper place in Europe a Germany able to dwell in friendship with others:

> The peace which we are determined to secure, however, must be a real and settled peace, not an uneasy truce interrupted by constant alarms and repeated threats. What stands in the way of such a peace? It is the German Government, and the German Government alone.[10]

* Jan Christian Smuts, Prime Minister of South Africa, 1919–24, Sep. 1939–48.

Various unofficial approaches in the next few months, in most of which Halifax and Cadogan had little belief, were answered in this sense.

Chamberlain's speech was immediately condemned by the German Foreign Office as 'an outrageous insult to Germany', a calculated rejection of the hand of peace held out by the Führer. There could now, Ribbentrop said on 14 November, be only a war of annihilation between England and Germany.[11]]

Friday, 13 October

Telegram this morning from Dahlerus who was rung up at the Hague by Goering at 9 last night to say Germans would not answer P.M.'s statement, which was a declaration of war!

[Cadogan minuted that Dahlerus might be rather stupid and was on his own admission ignorant of international affairs. But because he had direct access to Hitler and Goering he was not to be ignored, and he had done no harm.[12]]

Saturday, 14 October

Heard news of sinking of 'Royal Oak',* which is most inopportune to say the least.

Sunday, 15 October

Stacks of telegrams. One from Dahlerus, which is to me significant; he says 'atmosphere more hopeful' in Berlin: has had 2 hours' talk with Goering, and he speaks of new proposals. This, after G[oering]'s first reaction to P.M.'s speech (see Oct. 13) means either that the Germans think they still can bluff us out or that they really are in a tight corner. And I don't absolutely exclude the latter. . . . H. also inclined to be hopeful. . . . This rain *should* hamper a German offensive in the West!

Monday, 16 October

About 6 p.m. news of air attack on Rosyth which seems to have failed, and news of German offensive in West, but nothing about this in 9 p.m. B.B.C. broadcast.

Tuesday, 17 October

More messages from Dahlerus, who is annoyed at me not welcoming him here. But if he has any 'proposals', he has only got to give them to Nevile Bland.† Admiral [Sinclair] has a story from his 2

* Battleship. Sunk at anchor in Scapa Flow by a U-boat.

† Sir G. N. M. Bland, Minister to the Netherlands, 1938–42, Ambassador, 1942–8.

German Generals that they will be in Holland today! (It's always 'tomorrow'.) Meanwhile they seem to convey that Hitler has 'bad news' from Italy: is in an excitable state: has given orders which Goering refuses to carry out: and that latter has been dismissed! We shall see! . . . German attack in west renewed, but no appreciable results, apparently.

Thursday, 19 October

Dahlerus still bothering, but I drafted a quietus, which was approved, with alterations.

[The telegram reminded Dahlerus that he had no commission to approach the Germans on Britain's behalf. She could not consider any proposals which did not right the wrongs done to other nations and provide guarantees of reparation and protection against aggression. These objectives might require large internal changes in Germany. If he therefore felt it impossible to proceed, the British Government could only accept the position.[13]]

Friday, 20 October

Went to Ministry of Information at 3.30 to see Findlater Stewart* and attempt to strangle their 'Intelligence' Section, which seems desirous of building up a Foreign Service and a Secret Service. Won't have this. . . . I think we were agreed to strangle it.

Saturday, 21 October

H.J.W. rang up to say F. Stewart in a frightful stew about letter from H. to Macmillan† asking to take back Foreign Publicity Department. This is the last shred of the Ministry of Information! Perth (and C. Peake) had been pressing for this. I spoke to H. about 3 weeks ago about it, but I couldn't press it hard, as I hadn't got all the arguments. Recommended him to see Perth. As a result, he and P[erth] walked to F.O. one morning recently, and a draft to Macm[illan] appeared. I don't know who drafted it; I saw it and approved—and approve. But it appears fairly to have put the cat amongst the pigeons! Warned H. after the Cabinet. He said: 'Oh that's all right: this morning P.M. told me he was thinking of winding up the Ministry and asked whether I'd mind taking back the F[oreign] P[ublicity] D[epartment]. I said that, far from minding, I'd just proposed that to Macm[illan]!' So I did no more about it.

* Sir S. F. Stewart, P.U.S., India Office, 1930–42; temporary Dir.-Gen. of Ministry of Information, Sept.–Nov. 1939.

† Lord Macmillan, Minister of Information, 1939–40.

Sunday, 22 October

G. J[ebb] rang up twice saying there was a frightful stink about Ministry of Information. There'll be more, before *I*'ve done with it.

Monday, 23 October

H.J.W. did *not* turn up to see H. about Ministry of Information—as threatened—at 10.30. So I suppose he has found that P.M. *is* in favour of winding it up! I told H. all about the shamozzle, but was glad to find him unmoved. . . . 'C' has got report on interview with his German General friends. I think they are Hitler agents.

I *don't* know what Hitler is going to do about the war. No one is waging it at present. (And I'm damned if I know how *we* are going to do it.) The only hope of a decisive result is a collapse in Germany, and I am being driven to the conclusion, by a study of millions of reports, that we can't look for that *yet*. What is the answer?

[The gist of Admiral Sinclair's exchanges with the 'Generals' was this. They were allegedly suggesting that they might capture Hitler, after which a military junta would take over and make peace. The British intermediaries, Major H. R. Stevens and Captain S. Payne Best, who ran a network of Intelligence-gathering activities from The Hague, were told that nothing should be given to the Germans in writing. Wireless messages passed to and fro in the next fortnight.]

Tuesday, 24 October

'C''s Germans have put 2 questions and I discussed with H. answer to give them, and subsequently drafted it. . . . Showed H. my draft reply to Germans, which he approved. We went over to P.M. with it at 6.30. He approved generally, with verbal alterations. Discussed war aims with him, and evolved some sort of line. Dined at home. Masses of work, till midnight. Must cut it down somehow.

Wednesday, 25 October

3.30 talk with R. Leeper, and later with H., about War Aims. Not v. conclusive. Benes at 5, till 6.15. He obviously trying to get our recognition of his 'Provisional Government'—which he has failed to get in Paris. Corbin about Mooney (American) who has seen Goering and got the usual stuff.

Dined with Tilea. Aras, Momtchiloff, Simopoulos and Soubbotitch.* What a party! Sat talking Balkans till 11, when I tore myself away. They were plotting a Neutral Balkan Bloc, and I encouraged

* The last three the Bulgarian, Greek and Yugoslav Ministers respectively.

them where and how I could. I left them drafting telegrams to their Governments. I only gave Tilea the advice that they should call a meeting on *economic* grounds.

['The usual stuff' consisted of a prolonged statement by Goering to the effect that Germany would be prepared to allow the reconstitution of Poland and Czechoslovakia, in some undefined form, under the economic and military protection of Germany. Responsible statesmen from Britain, France and Germany should meet on neutral territory.[14]]

Thursday, 26 October

A lot of work, which carried me on, with interval for dinner, till 11.30. That is my earliest hour nowadays. I must cut it down somehow.

Saturday, 28 October

10.45 talked with H. and Van about messages which V[ansittart] has received from K and Max Hohenlohe.[15] Decided on answer to give—much on lines of that given to D[ahlerus] and the Generals.

The diary does not reveal the identity of 'K', and the papers do not appear to have been released in the Public Record Office. It is possible the 'K' connotes Admiral Canaris, head of the Abwehr (German Military Intelligence), whose name is spelt with a 'K' in the entry for 20 December. On the other hand, Cadogan recorded on 26 June 1953 a visit from none other than Dahlerus: 'He says—and he gave me some evidence—that Canaris turned against Hitler long before we knew he did.'

This 'K' may have been the man who had given Kirkpatrick secret warnings in the previous December.

Sunday, 29 October

Read Aldous Huxley. Good for the soul—not Aldous Huxley, but the relaxation of reading and getting one's mind off the daily track. We are, after all, although bureaucrats, human beings. And no human being can go on for ever chained to a wheel: it's bad for him and he becomes rotten. Must relax, cynically, if you like.

Monday, 30 October

Walked alone to F.O. Caught by air raid warning in Lower Grosvenor Place. So took taxi to F.O. Went up to my room to collect papers and while there 'All Clear' sounded. Another of these 'electrical defects'. It's an outrage!

H. grateful for my diary. Discussed Communications Dept. worry.

He will consult P.M. and wd. like high legal opinion—e.g. Lord Chancellor. Fortified by that, he wd. be prepared to see the doomed members. This is much the best, but I hadn't liked to suggest to him such a horrible duty.

... P.M., during week-end, had studied messages from Max Hohenlohe and K., and our draft reply. After lunch H. showed me P.M.'s reactions and I drafted on them.... Fixed up draft reply to Hohenlohe with H.

Tuesday, 31 October

Put replies to Hohenlohe and K. in final form and gave them to Van.... Fresh message from our German Generals in Holland. Doesn't get us *much* further, but must keep them on hook. Devised outline of reply with H. Then Menzies* came over with further message, which doesn't alter situation much. Went over with H. to see P.M. at 6.45. There for about an hour, drafting reply, which we shall have to look at again in the morning. There's *something* going on in Germany. That's about all one can say. 'Change of Guard' in Rome. All to the good.

[Cadogan told Signor Bastianini, the Italian Ambassador, that two things were indispensable: the restoration of a Polish state and a positive collective guarantee that Germany would not resume tomorrow what she was unable to accomplish today. Chamberlain had deliberately not closed the door to the Germans; but these guarantees could plainly not be supplied by someone who offered a German peace and at the same time threatened a war of annihilation. Bastianini remarked upon Cadogan's misgivings about Russia's easy conquests and the benefits which she might derive from a long war, or from a postwar period when the rest of Europe would be exhausted.[16]]

Wednesday, 1 November

Cabinet were told of our contact with Generals and didn't like it. Told H. that first impact was bound to be unfavourable and rouse suspicion. He mustn't listen too much to Winston on the subject of 'beating Germany'. We must try every means of helping G[ermany] to beat herself....

Had to redraft (for the nth time) reply to Generals. P.M. frightened by the Cabinet!

Thursday, 2 November

Cabinet did nothing about reply to Generals—as Winston away till

* Col., later Maj.-Gen., Sir Stewart Menzies, who succeeded Admiral Sinclair as head of S.I.S.

Sunday night! This may be all right. R. sends telegram tonight from Lucerne 'Hermann proposes meeting Scheveningen'. That *may* mean what it says, or it may mean invasion of Holland!

Friday, 3 November

More messages from Generals, who want an answer, and seem to expect 'negotiations'. This is awkward, as Winston's suspicions aroused, he is away till Sun. night and no one dares answer without his approval. Went over with H. to P.M. and agreed on reply merely saying we hoped to give answer Mon. or Tues. Further complication in that they have concealed earlier exchanges of messages from Cabinet, and I don't know how long we shall be able to keep this up.

Word through Christie* that the 'Hermann' message *was* a warning about Holland. But S.I.S. think nothing of the source.

Monday, 6 November

H. sent car for me at 9.30. He had to go on to see Winston (about Generals).... H. returned about 10.30 having nobbled Winston.... Saw H. afterwards [i.e. after lunch]; he gave me text to reply to Generals, which I sent off. They are expected in Holland again tomorrow morning.

Tuesday, 7 November

About 7.15 news of Leopold-Wilhelmina offensive† and of our talks with Generals yesterday—said to be 'satisfactory'.

Wednesday, 8 November

11.30 Palace to introduce Ecuadorean, whom I had primed to be chatty and who played up. Had some talk with the King: told him how I thought we should advise he reply to Leopold and Wilhelmina. After Ecuadorean left, the King commented on his chattiness. I said 'Yes: I thought he'd do that to Y.M.: he did it to me yesterday!'... 3.15 Corbin about Belgian enquiry as to what France would do if Germany invaded Holland (which she looks like doing).... 5.30 went with S. of S. to P.M. with draft reply to Leopold and Co., and message from Generals. Approved general lines of former, which has

* Who had been deputed to listen to Hohenlohe's proposals.

† King Leopold III of Belgium and Queen Wilhelmina of the Netherlands made an appeal for peace to the German, French and British Heads of State.

to be recast. As regards latter, agreed to tell Cabinet minimum to-morrow.

Thursday, 9 November

Saw Menzies. General did *not* come into Holland yesterday, but expected today! 'Nothing immediate contemplated'. Does this refer to coup or to invasion? Hitler missed by a bomb yesterday! P.M. laid up with gout, and Cabinet did not consider draft reply to Leopold-Wilhelmina. Dutch Minister anticipates invasion this week-end, but gives me no reasons. He may be right. . . .

All the leaf has come off with a bang in the last 4 days. They started pulling up those beastly dahlias this afternoon. The head gardener, who was there, assured me they were going to put in tulips, as they had got them in any case. Called to F.O. at 11.30. There had been Cabinet after dinner to discuss C.I.G.S. and C.A.S. conversations in France today. Drafted telegram at midnight, with H., to Brussels, insisting on conversations.

[The German propaganda apparatus, attributing the bomb explosion at Munich to the Secret Service's 'time-honoured British method of assassination', denounced British brutality and lack of scruple. Among other leading characters alleged to have been despatched by the same method were listed Nicholas II, the Archduke Franz Ferdinand, Jean Jaurès, T. E. Lawrence, King Alexander of Yugoslavia and Louis Barthou. The bomb had in fact been planted by a German.

On 11 November, Ribbentrop ordered that Dahlerus' attempt at mediation must cease, since the British had clearly indicated their rejection of the German position.[17]

Meanwhile, Major Stevens and Captain Best had fallen into a trap. As Cadogan had surmised on 24 October, the 'Generals' were agents of Hitler. When the two British officers arrived at the meeting-place, Venlo, they were seized and whisked off to prison in Germany, and the Dutch officer who accompanied them was shot dead. According to Professor Trevor-Roper, this kidnapping brought 'disastrous consequences to their rickety organisation'.[18]]

Friday, 10 November

Our men, who met, or were to have met, Gen[eral] yesterday, bumped off on Dutch-German frontier. Discussed matter with H. and Menzies. . . . Numerous reports of imminent invasion of Holland. . . . Cabinet approved draft reply to Leopold and Wilhelmina. Gave it to Corbin. . . . Van in evening with results of his contacts with Hohenlohe, which I think is nothing, and K., who appears to be working with the Generals. Discussed it with H. and decided to give a cold douche to Hohenlohe, who seems to be working with Goering + Hitler. Generals and K.—it seems—are working with Goering-Hitler. But I don't know that we shall keep any contacts with these now.

Reports seem to show that Germany will invade Holland tomorrow or the 15th.

Sunday, 12 November

Had fully thought Germans would be in Holland by now, but they're not.* Wonder whether it does mean that there are divided counsels and that the Generals are exercising some restraining influence? . . . G.J. came round to ask what we were to do with the Press about the brawl in Holland. Decide to issue 'D' notice.

Monday, 13 November

Talk with H. and Sargent about latter's idea of taking over anti-Comintern Pact, and thereby roping in Italy, Japan and Spain. Attractive, but there are difficulties. Will talk to Loraine about it—it may afford an opening for talking privately to the Italians and getting together with them. . . . Van has had more from Christie about his communications with Hohenlohe. Don't think they'll do much good, but might be followed up to gain time. . . . Holland has recovered her nerve, according to Dutch Minister, who accuses us of panic!!

Wednesday, 15 November

The Generals are still alive—and apparently unaware of the frontier incident. 12.30 Kennedy (Times). Tried to ensure he wouldn't put his foot in it on war aims. . . .

Friday, 17 November

Meeting of Supreme Council at No. 10 at 11.15. Daladier, Gamelin, Darlan and Vuillemin,† and P.M., H., Chatfield. V. interesting discussion as to whether in event of invasion of Holland and/or Belgium, we should bomb the Ruhr. That was our proposal, and French argued against, and I think they were right.

Saturday, 18 November

War Cabinet at 11.45. Roger Keyes‡ made a havering report of his

* Sunday 12 November was in fact the date fixed by Hitler for the German offensive in the West (Nuremberg Docs. C-62). Bad weather brought about a postponement.

† Gen. Joseph Vuillemin, C.-in-C. French Air Force 1938–40.

‡ Adm. Sir R. Keyes, liaison officer with the King of the Belgians; Director, Combined Operations Command, 1940–1.

talks in Royal Circles in Brussels. Winston urged we should not change our Ambassador at this moment! I said I would discuss it with S. of S. I'm not going to be drawn into *this* argument in Cabinet. Reply from Generals—fairly meaningless—which I submitted to P.M. before lunch. He sketched outline of reply, which needn't be discussed before H. gets back.

Sunday, 19 November

Spoke to H. on telephone this morning. He enjoyed his outing with the hounds yesterday, and wasn't stiff as a result. I had nothing to tell Cabinet, so didn't go. Tiresome letter from Winston about successor to Admiral.* (At Cabinet yesterday he also raised question of prolonging [Sir R.H.] Clive in Brussels. Must fight against both of these. He ought to have enough of his own to do without butting into other people's business.)

Monday, 20 November

Had to prepare for War Cabinet, who are suddenly discussing Enemy Exports and Far East. . . . War Cabinet at 11.30 to 1.30. Didn't have much to say—rather a waste of time. Winston fussed about magnetic mines.† Decided in principle to stop enemy exports. . . . Promotions Board 3 till 4.15 with everyone at their most leisured and tiresome. 4.30 meeting with Winston, Chatfield and Dominions about defence of Singapore and Australia. . . . I was only asked one question—about Siam, about which I know *nothing*, but said something.

Tuesday, 21 November

P.M. annoyed about draft which I sent him last night for his statement about enemy exports, as it wasn't explicit enough. I could only say that I must have misunderstood. As a matter of fact, draft prepared by W. Malkin and Attorney Gen. and approved by Cross, who were all present at yesterday's Cabinet, and apparently got the same impression that I did! . . . H. returned about 3.15. Had a good deal to discuss with him. He went off to see P.M. at 6. On his return, I found he had gathered P.M. was annoyed with me about this morning's draft. But really not my fault! . . . G.J. came in—about 11—to say Germans had given out a statement about Munich bomb

* Sinclair had died in office.

† About a dozen merchant ships had been sunk at the entrances to British harbours, although they had been swept for mines. On 23 Nov. two magnetic mines were recovered intact from the mud-flats near Shoeburyness, and a remedy was soon found.

outrage, connecting it with Venlo incident. Rang up C. Peake: told him to point out to Press that the story didn't hang together. Bed after midnight—exhausted.

Wednesday, 22 November

Collected C. Peake, Menzies and others to draft statement for Press in reply to German stuff about bomb outrage. Got a very good one. But Cabinet preferred to say nothing. Perhaps they're right. . . . About 7 got radio from Berlin showing that Gestapo have taken over (if they did not always have!) our communications with the 'Generals'. So that's over.

Dined at home and made very little impression on the *stacks* of muck that everyone throws at me. Depressed.

Thursday, 23 November

Corbin at 12. Gave him latest Dahlerus news and such explanations as I could give him of Venlo incident.

[Dahlerus had visited Berlin a few days before, finding Goering allegedly anxious for peace and still desirous of a meeting with the British and French on neutral ground.[19]]

Friday, 24 November

Cartier at 11.30, to protest against our seizure of enemy exports. I rather snapped at him—with good reason. . . . H. told me [pocket battleship] 'Deutschland' out and Winston had given instructions to pursue her into Norwegian territorial waters, according to doctrine of 'hot pursuit'. May be all right! . . . 5.15 Chatfield and M. Hankey to discuss Danube scheme with H., O.S. and me. A difficult problem! Hankey rather Winstonian: Chatfield and H. rather wistfully correct. I rather inclining to press the button! . . . Navy has lost touch with 'Deutschland' so similar orders have been given to Air Force. *And* discovered that orders were not in line with doctrine of 'hot pursuit' but gave free hand. Rather odd. But in that case, no worse to act with air arm than with navy. . . . Horace rang up to explain that probably Cabinet didn't know what they were doing. P.M. doesn't seem to mind. I rang up H. and found that he *had*, really, known what he was doing. So I don't see why I should bother. Told Horace, who agreed. Then Resident Clerk rang up to tell me that orders to Air Force hadn't gone off—should they? I said yes!

Saturday, 25 November

Met H. at Palace gate. Told him about my telephone calls last night about the 'Deutschland'. Funny people these politicians are! H. v. distressed at idea of blowing some rock into the Danube, but appears to have agreed that we should go into Norwegian waters and hammer the 'Deutschland' to bits! Fact is, they didn't know what they were talking about, and hadn't thought about it. He seemed—or looked—rather reproachful when I said I had loosed the R.A.F. last night. But it was only logical! However, I'm getting in hot water all around, as I had to assume, yesterday evening, sole responsibility for ordering preparations on the Danube, which was quite right, but they are probably unnecessary. Now I have authorised an outrage by our Air Force. If I hadn't, and if the 'Deutschland' had got through, I should have been hanged on Tower Hill. Luckily everyone has lost touch with the 'Deutschland': no one seems to know where she was nor where she was going, so I hope we shall have a quiet day.

Sunday, 26 November

We seem to have heard nothing more of the 'Deutschland' up to this morning. In some ways I am rather relieved! Cabinet discussed revised instructions yesterday morning.

Monday, 27 November

Talk with H., R.A.B. and [R.G.] Howe about Far East. Authorised telegram to Craigie telling him to go ahead and try to get settlement of Tientsin question on lines (quite orthodox) which he indicates. Though why he should think there is any chance of success, I simply can't think. Talked to H. about Lothian's meaningless letter [from Washington] and agreed to draft one to him trying to elicit what he means. I think he's a phrase-monger. Tiresome letter from Menzies, with whom I sympathise. Am trying to binge up H. to get decision [on Sinclair's successor] tomorrow. M[enzies] is in difficult position, and it's silly of everyone to go on funking Winston.

Tuesday, 28 November

6.30 meeting at No. 10 with P.M., H., Winston, Kingsley and Hore-B[elisha] about 'C''s successor. H. played his hand well and won the trick. Winston told us of announcement by Berlin of sinking of cruiser 'London' class, which may be 'Dorsetshire', 'Norfolk' or poor old 'Suffolk'.* No news from C-in-C, so fear she may have been sunk without trace.

* This report proved false.

Wednesday, 29 November

Menzies this morning said that he had from the v. *best* source, report that Germans had abandoned any idea of offensive. Tonight, report that telephone communication between Holland and Germany cut off! I believe all the stuff we get is put out by the Germans and put out to puzzle us! After all, that's what *we* do!

Friday, 1 December

H. interviewed Communications Dept. He did it very well. Most painful, but it went off better than I expected.

Monday, 4 December

Talked to H. about this ridiculous summons of League Council and Assembly on Finnish question.* Inevitable, but insane. We must send R.A.B. there!

Tuesday, 5 December

Find H. has dictated record of events August 18–September 3 based on this diary. It is hailed as a wonderful connected account, and it is suggested Woodward† should be got in to complete and perfect it for posterity!

Wednesday, 6 December

Meeting at 11.45 under R.A.B.'s presidency, about forthcoming League meetings. Very woolly, but I got some decisions out of them. R.A.B. said he was chiefly 'concerned to keep our moral position intact'. Before he's finished, he'll be much more concerned to keep his mental position intact. H. gave me lift back at lunch-time. Told him of our deliberations. He very frightened of 'going to war with Russia'. I don't want to do that, but we must 'keep our moral position intact'....

Letter from Perth who has had a talk with Bastianini. Italians will of course take the line that, if we are fighting 'aggression', we must show a bold front to the Russians. Otherwise they will doubt our bona fides. Talked to H. about this: it reinforces what I say: that if expulsion of Russia is proposed, we must vote for it.‡ Corbin 6.15. I think we've agreed on the line at Geneva. Talk to H. about Dahlerus

* Russia had invaded Finland on 30 November.

† E. L. (later Sir Llewellyn) Woodward, diplomatic historian.

‡ Cadogan minuted: 'we may have to go a long way in reprobating what Russia has done in condemning her aggression and even, as in the case of China, of affording such assistance to Finland as we can, while making it plain that our primary effort must necessarily be directed against Germany—the real originator of all these disturbances.'[20]

and Villard.* He hankering after 'peace' again. But I explained why it's no use ingeminating 'peace'. . . .

9.30 box . . . containing things that would require a week's study, about M[iddle] E[ast] campaign, for Cabinet tomorrow. Sent these on to H. saying I hadn't and couldn't read them, and this wasn't the way to do business. Lots of work after, including accounts of telephone conversations which the French want to include in their publication. As far as I can see, they'll do them more harm than us.

Thursday, 7 December

Got off telegram to Rome promising to buy £20,000,000 of goods in next year. This as a bait before Fascist Grand Council meeting on the 9th. . . . 3.30 Colban† about Norwegian shipping questions. Ticked him off about sticky attitude of his Government in regard to Blockade. . . . Talk with R.A.B. before latter's departure for Geneva.‡ He deplored this Geneva meeting 'But', as he said 'it gives me an opportunity'!!

[Tilea told Halifax that it was necessary to decide whether the British and French guarantees to Roumania would operate against Russian, as well as German, aggression. He thought that with a little British encouragement Turkey would offer Roumania a mutual defence pact against Russian aggression. Halifax pointed out the numerous difficulties, including those of transport and the uncertain Italian attitude.[21]]

Friday, 8 December

Hear Dahlerus is arriving this afternoon! Corbin at 12 about Roumanian guarantee. He had been already told of H's talk with Tilea yesterday. Tilea is trying to rush us again, and French are inclined to fall for it. Told Corbin I couldn't say much more until we had seen Numan.§. . . Meeting at 3.30—H., Numan, O.S., Bowker,¶ self and an interpreter. We put Numan through a catechism, upshot of which is that they would throw Roumania (Bessarabia) to the wolves, but that their frontier is on the Bulgarian frontier. *And* they are doubtful whether Russia is ready for the 'grand jeu'. I think this is probably a sane, though perhaps somewhat cynical view. H. broke off at 5, but we had Numan on our hands—on economic and financial questions—for another hour.

* O. G. Villard, an American journalist who had recently visited Germany and reported on the state of German morale. File C 19120/G, F.O. 371/23013.

† Erik Colban, Norwegian Minister in London, 1934–42, Ambassador 1942–6.

‡ Where Russia was expelled from the League of Nations.

§ Numan Menemencioglu, Sec.-Gen., Turkish Ministry of Foreign Affairs, 1937–42.

¶ R. J. Bowker, F.O.; later Ambassador at Rangoon, Ankara and Vienna.

[Numan added that the Russians were unlikely to go beyond Bessarabia unless they intended to seize the Dardanelles and therefore go to war with Great Britain.]

Sunday, 10 December

Tiresome business about a Jap ship [*Sanyo Maru*] with German goods. I had said she must come in . . . but, as a sop to the Japs (of whom we're frightened) said she wouldn't be kept long. Reported this to War Cabinet at 5. Winston took the silly line that this was making a hole in our Blockade. But 10 mins. before he had been painting the danger of the Japs seizing some of our shipping! If M.E.W. had had their way, they'd have let her through. It was I, last night, who stopped her on my own! W. S. C[hurchill] very downhearted. Had been down at Chatham talking to Drax,* who is not very stimulating. T. Phillips† told me not to be depressed. J.S. took me along for ½ hour talk after. He fussed—from Home political point of view, of course—about Soviet situation.

Tuesday, 12 December

X at 5 till 5.45: most painful interview. If people are sacked, for no reason given, doesn't that show them that they are simply 'impossible'? But they all come and ask me 'Why?' Inviting the answer 'Because you are such a nincompoop'. But that is the answer I can't give! Dined at home and worked. I have N. H[enderson]'s book‡ on my shoulders now. I got it yesterday, and he wants an opinion by Thursday. He damned well won't get it. Do people think I lead a life of leisure?

Wednesday, 13 December

In afternoon saw Duke of Wurtemburg, 'Père Odo'§—who told me a long and enthusiastic story about a Halder–Beck plan to get rid of Hitler, Goering, Rib[bentrop], &c. They of course want us to give guarantee that we shall keep the ring. I said we'd already gone as far in this direction as it was safe to go. He very nice but I should think rather credulous. . . . We went to see the Marx Brothers in 'At the Circus'—I don't see why I shouldn't relax sometimes and damn the work. Quite amusing. Groucho Marx quite good—he talks about his

* Admiral the Hon. Sir R.A.R.P-E-E-Drax, head of British Military Mission, Moscow, 1939; C.-in-C. the Nore, 1939–41.

† Rear-Admiral Sir Tom Phillips, V.C.N.S., 1939–41.

‡ *Failure of a Mission.*

§ The Duke Carl-Alexander of Württemberg, a cousin of Queen Mary, had become a monk and was known as Dom Odo.

'Aūnt—I would have said Ănt, only I'm showing off before the monkeys'!

Thursday, 14 December

H. picked me up at 9.20. He had seen X* last night, who has a scheme for Goering to bump off Hitler and form a Government! My Père Odo insists G[oering] himself must be bumped off! Let them get on with it, and I will then render my judgement!† News of 'Graf Spee' battle. Quite good.‡ Lot of trouble about this blasted 'Sanyo Maru'. Wish I had never mentioned the 'secret' naval goods, which excite everyone. It's simply, as we see from the manifest, goods for Jap navy.

Friday, 15 December

Had to go to Palace at 12 to introduce new Venezuelan. It went fairly well; I told the V. beforehand that he must talk, and I told the King he must help the V. out with his English. So they both talked at once! Had sit-down talk and a cigarette after with H.M. He talked of the 'Graf Spee' battle and his trip to France. Said he'd never felt so cold in his life. He indulged in some rather disparaging reflections on Hore-Belisha, but I couldn't quite make out why.

Tuesday, 19 December

Meeting of Supreme Council at Quai d'Orsay at 9. Long discussion on Balkan Front and we headed the French off the worst pitfalls. Also discussed help to Finland, acceleration of despatch of troops to France, purchases in America, Fécamp broadcasting station, &c. Quite a good meeting.§... Arrived Le Bourget 1.40. Found a state of 'alerte' (German 'planes near Rouen). So had to wait. Got off at 2.10. I with Ironside again. (Yesterday he—like the King—inveighed against Hore-Belisha!). Fine till the Channel: then we met cloud. Went over it, but over England had to come down through it. As it was getting late, it got darker and darker as we descended. Bumped a good deal, and saw nothing till we were on the chimney pots at Hendon. Unpleasant. Landed at 4.

* A Swiss citizen, not the 'X' of 12 December.

† The British Minister to the Vatican made a somewhat similar reply when told by the Pope in January of opposition to Hitler on the part of certain German generals.

‡ The German pocket-battleship *Admiral Graf Spee* was forced to take refuge in Montevideo by the spirited action of the British cruisers *Exeter*, *Ajax*, and *Achilles*. She was scuttled on 17 December.

§ The French agreed to make no separate peace. They wished to do more than eliminate Hitler at the end of the war, urging that the Allies should retain strategic command of the Rhine.

Wednesday, 20 December

Menzies came over with a story . . . of Kanaris' [Canaris] man having said—after handing out the usual stuff—that Germany was 'finished'. Promised to send us written report of conversation. . . . Menzies now sends written report, which doesn't seem to me to contain anything on the lines he had indicated.

Thursday, 21 December

Nothing very interesting: just a day of swimming against the tide, which is overwhelming me. And kind friends will send Xmas cards! Do they really suppose that I have a moment in which to acknowledge them?

Friday, 22 December

I attended Cabinet at 11 for discussion of question of our intervention in Scandinavia. Agreed to make representations, as suggested by French, to Norway and Sweden, but decided we might go further and 'switch the war into Scandinavia', i.e. offer to assist in protecting the Swedish iron-mines—which would mean 'protecting' them also against Germany, i.e. put a stranglehold on supplies to Germany. This might be a vital point in conduct of the war, but it may be difficult to do without being a bit high-handed. Discussion finished at 12.30 and I set to work to draft sketch of how we are to proceed. First thing is a telegram to Paris.

Saturday, 23 December

Finn came with a long story about the Dane whom H. saw last Sunday and who appears to be misrepresenting him utterly in Berlin! Spoke to H. on telephone later about this and was able to authorise the Finn to give the Dane the lie. Finn also said French in Helsinki, and in Paris . . . had said that Supreme Council decided to send French and British troops to Finland!

Anthony [Eden], Chatfield and M. Hankey came to see me about the Scandinavian business. They entirely approve our telegram, but don't want to go too fast. (I agree that there are obvious snags.)

Maisky came! to protest against arrest of Doschenko.*. . . Corbin came 4.30 and I flung in his teeth the French indiscretions about Finland (above). He looked pained.

* A. A. Doschenko, of the Soviet Trade Delegation. After enquiry at the Home Office, Cadogan told Maisky that Doschenko had 'unfortunately been indulging in activities which do not commend themselves to H.M.G.' Because the evidence could not be disclosed in court, Doschenko was deported. File N. 7763/G, F.O. 371/23702.

Sunday, 24 December

French reply came in agreeing about Norway and Sweden. . . . Cleared off work after tea. Suppose I must now tackle private correspondence!

Monday, 25 December

Talked to H. on telephone about draft to Scandinavian Governments. He thought mine went a bit too far, but says he'll come up tomorrow to discuss it, for Wednesday's Cabinet. I also talked to H. about the approach to Musso re Balkans: let's go easy on that till we know whether we are going to do anything, and whether we are going for Scandinavia. We can't do *both!*

Tuesday, 26 December

Back at F.O. at 2.30. H. had arrived. Had a peaceful talk with him—no rush of papers so, for once, one has time to think and discuss. My theme was: *don't* talk to Scandinavians about iron-ore, or to Musso about Balkans, until you know what you *can* do, and *want* to do, in either sphere. Why bother them unnecessarily? H. agreed. We sent for Hollis from Cabinet Offices, who told us that Chiefs of Staff had reached same conclusion. It's obviously right. I'm awfully tempted by the Scandinavian scheme, but we must (a) know that we can reasonably hope to do it effectively and (b) give it a reasonable appearance of decency. H. going to dine with Winston.

Wednesday, 27 December

Attended War Cabinet 11.30–1.30. P.M. said he hadn't anticipated we should really open up to Scandinavians about our plans, but that, in making the written communication urging them to support Finland (and hinting that we should help) we should say, incidentally, that we can't stand this flow of iron-ore to G[ermany] through territorial waters, which G[ermany] violates with her submarines. This is mixing vinegar with oil. It could be done, but I am puzzled how to link up the 2 subjects, and I was glad when the Cabinet agreed to make the written communication first, and then in a few days—early next week—to talk about iron-ore. H. raised question of approach to Italy. But meanwhile François-Poncet* has gone ahead and done it! Without any violent reaction.† Agreed to consult Percy L[oraine] as to whether it should be left at that. After

* André François-Poncet, French Ambassador at Rome, 1938–40; Member National Council, 1941; arrested by Gestapo, 1943; liberated, 1945.

† Ciano told him that if Bessarabia were invaded by Russia, Italy would intervene. He did not rule out action in the Balkans on the side of the Allies.

Cabinet, told O.S. to tell French H. would make written communication to Scandinavian Ministers this evening—which he did.

Thursday, 28 December

Dahlerus at 11* (till 12.15). He now rather more concerned about *Sweden* and consequently more robust! Talked a lot about Finland and not much about Germany. I think he has got our view on the latter, and I pumped more into him. He lunched here.

Friday, 29 December

Rang up H. but had little to say to him. Told him of our decision yesterday evening to grant [economic] alleviations to Italians. Tilea at 11—for nearly an hour. Burden was that Roumania was convinced there would be a German and/or Russian drive against her in the Spring and she must have material assistance. He gave me particulars of German plans for improving transport of oil to Germany. Maisky at 12 to protest further about Doschenko. He complained of his being in prison. I said 'That's nothing: you've been in prison. All my friends have been in prison. Benes many times, and a certain Delegate of the I[rish] F[ree] S[tate], with whom I made friends, had been in no less than 6 English prisons, and was none the worse for it'! . . . Got abreast of my work and home by 8. Street lamps in Whitehall alight. But shrouded to reduce their brilliance to that of about 2½ glow-worm power.

1940

Monday, 1 January

Misty and cold. Walked to F.O. Fairly quiet morning. Report by Chiefs-of-Staff, which shows that Scandinavian operation would be advisable *provided* (a) a stoppage of ore supplies would really deal a fatal blow, and (b) we have full co-operation of Norway and Sweden. Latter probably, as far as I can see, impossible. . . .

H. arrived rather late, about 3.15. I shook him on Scandinavia and made him read C[hief]s of S[taff] report.

. . . Talk with H., O.S. and Collier. H. is shaken and went to see P.M. at 5.30. Back about 6.30. P.M. seem to feel same way as we do. But they've got to fight Winston tomorrow morning! H. told me Hore-Belisha must be got out of W.O.† and will be offered Ministry

* He had insisted on coming, despite discouraging messages from Halifax.

† Chamberlain seems to have reached this decision because of the bad relations between Hore-Belisha and Lord Gort, commanding the British Expeditionary Force in France.

of Information. This blinding—and exquisitely funny. I hadn't time to get my breath, but on thinking it over, came to the conclusion that Jew control of our propaganda would be major disaster.

Tuesday, 2 January

Talked to H., O.S. and Collier. Told them I didn't, on the whole, mind 'doing Narvik' now.* It seems to me that it is a thing that can stand on its own feet. *But*, don't let them think that that will *help* to the 'larger operation'.†

Told H. I thought P.M. ought to have consulted him about appointment of Horeb to Ministry of Information. H. said 'He did'. So I supposed it was settled. No use merely criticising after the event.

Wednesday, 3 January

11.30 H.J.W. came about Hore-Belisha's appointment. Told him what I knew and that I understood it was settled so hadn't criticised it to H. But if question was still open, and since he asked my opinion, I thought it catastrophic.

. . . 6.30 Corbin again—gave him aide-mémoire which we propose to give to Norwegian and Swedes.

Thursday, 4 January

Told H. P.M. had much better make one bite of the cherry and get rid of H-B altogether! He will get the worst of both worlds if he merely shifts him. H. said he saw this, and would put it to P.M.

. . . H. tells me that P.M. has sacked H[ore]-B[elisha] from W.O. but offered him B[oard] of T[rade]. This just misses the point. P.M. had an awful interview and had much better just gone the little bit further and said he had no post to offer him. He would thereby have gained credit in some quarters and not lost much anywhere. Oliver [Stanley] to W.O., J. Reith to Ministry of Information. One can only spend the night in prayer imploring the Almighty that H-B. may refuse B[oard] of T[rade]. But H-B will take no account of Jehovah in this.

Friday, 5 January

Corbin came to see H. at 4.30 about communication to Norway

* That is, using sea power to interfere with the iron-ore passing from the ice-free Norwegian port of Narvik to Germany. The plan involved the laying of a minefield in Norwegian territorial waters, in order to force the ore-ships out to sea, where they could be attacked or captured.

† That is, to aid Finland against Russia and place troops on the Gällivare ore-fields in Sweden.

and Sweden. French agree, but want changes in form, about which I see no difficulty. H. tells me Hore-Belisha will only accept Board of Trade provided, (1) it is boosted as a sort of post of 'Minister in charge of Economic Policy' (J.S. says 'Will the Treasury come under him?') and (2) he remains in War Cabinet. P.M. won't agree to either.

While I was in my bath Corbin rang me up and after I had finished, I rang him back. He had just heard the news from the Agencies, who have it. He was fussed because Genthier due here on Sunday to discuss with O. Stanley who now goes to W.O. According to him, Sir A. Duncan to Board of Trade. Never heard of him. J. Reith at Ministry of Information. If this means H[ore]-B[elisha] has definitely gone, I'm sure it's a good move!

Saturday, 6 January

Hore-B[elisha] has fairly collared the Press, the worse organs of which smell a plot by the 'Generals'. . . . Not much doing, but Corbin insisted on coming after 1 o'c to question me about Hore-B. I don't think he had any illusions, but I assured him there was no *political* reason whatever for the resignation. . . . Cottage nice and warm. Read a bit of Ted Carr's book,* which is good.

Monday, 8 January

Found H. had had painful interview with Colban on Sat. But I hadn't expected much else! Prytz† had not taken it so badly. . . . Corbin at 4 to ask how our representations to Norway and Sweden had gone. Told him all I knew, but said that Colban was then with S. of S., and I would let him know later what transpired. Alec H[ardinge]‡ rang up because Colban is to see King tomorrow to convey message from [King] Haakon.§ Promised to send him all material in good time. Fact is, this Narvik business is silly—as I knew it would be. I continue to think we *can* do it—if Winston insists—but (a) it won't be very effective in itself, and (b) it *must* prejudice the 'larger scheme'. H. saw P.M. about it and finds latter is of same view more or less. We must now persuade Winston—if we can—that we must climb down as gracefully as we can. H. says P.M. was very worried, over the weekend, about the Horeb 'pother'. And he puts the blame on H. Says H.-B. would have accepted Ministry of Information (which I doubt) and, if he had thought he couldn't offer him that, he wouldn't have set the whole thing in motion by sounding

* *The Twenty Years' Crisis*. E. H. Carr, then Director of the Foreign Division of the Ministry of Information.

† Bjorn Prytz, Swedish Minister in London, 1938–47.

‡ Private Sec. to King George VI, 1936–43.

§ King Haakon VII of Norway.

Oliver [Stanley]. So if H. had produced earlier his objection to putting H.-B. at Ministry of Information, he'd have done nothing, and left him where he was! Surely this is a bit weak: if H.-B. ought to go from W.O., he ought to go! However, P.M. seems happier now —why, I don't know. Meanwhile, most unscrupulous campaign continues in Press. It's *very* bad luck that there's *no* war—or other news to swamp it. Parliament will flare it up again next week, but after that I hope it'll be forgotten!

Tuesday, 9 January

3.13 D.N.I.* He, personally, rather apprehensive of results of German reprisals on Norway. 3.30 meeting with H, Van, R.A.B., Collier†... [and others] on Narvik and Scandinavia. Interesting and useful but no very concrete results except that we ought to say to Norwegians—and Swedes—'Well, if you are so anxious we shouldn't interfere with Narvik traffic, what will *you* do about it?' Might ask Norway to stop *all* exports of ore to belligerents, and Sweden to reduce production or export. But I confess I don't see why they *should*.

Wednesday, 10 January

Advised H. about Narvik as above.... 7 talked to H. about Scandinavia. Cabinet this morning settled nothing, as Andrew Duncan‡ said we couldn't proceed on lines H. and I wanted because, he said, we had only one week's supply of ore ourselves! Really!! Someone might have thought of this before. Wallenberg§ has arrived here and S. of S. will see him tomorrow. Though why, because Swedes are frightened of our infringement of Norwegian neutrality, they should be brave enough *themselves* to be unneutral to Germany, I simply can't imagine. This so-called Scandinavian 'plan' is not a plan: it's a hang-over. We were all intoxicated by vision of Soviet threatening northern Scandinavia. That might have given us a chance. But that vision has been dispelled. And yet those funny old boys in the Cabinet still seem to think, in some hazy way, that there is some opening for us to do what we want. There is *not*—at present. H. asked me to postpone my week's leave, which I had hoped to take next week. (I've had one Sat. off since August 8th).

* Adm. John Godfrey, D.N.I. 1939–42.

† Laurence Collier, Counsellor at F.O.; Minister to Norway, 1941; Ambassador to the Norwegian Government, 1942–50.

‡ Sir A. R. Duncan, President of the Board of Trade, 1940, 1941; Minister of Supply, 1940–1, 1942–5.

§ Marcus Wallenberg. Swedish banker and financier, delegate to trade negotiations with Great Britain, 1939–43.

Lady Theodosia Cadogan

Cadogan on his way to the House of Commons, 28 September 1938, with Hitler's invitation to Chamberlain to attend the Conference at Munich

Rome, 11 January 1939. Cadogan, Halifax, Chamberlain and Lord Perth

Thursday, 11 January

Talked to H. about Scandinavia. Told him on the whole it was simply a hang-over. We have now made our threat about Narvik. I'm not convinced that it would be worth while to carry it out. How can we get out without loss of face? Only thing I can suggest is that we should call on Norway at least not to help Germans with pilots.

. . . 6.30 further talk with H. about Scandinavia before he went to see P.M. at 7. He now convinced that W.S.C. on wrong tack. He had had interview with Wallenberg at 3 and had got—of course—nothing out of him. Heard later P.M. shares his view. Fear this will produce something like a Cabinet split. They will discuss it again tomorrow.

Friday, 12 January

Had final talk to H. about Narvik and Scandinavia. Told him I was against Narvik. Prepare for 'larger operation' and hope for opportunity for it—which doesn't exist now. Discussed with him absurd idea of sending out Sam Hoare. . . . Saw H. Cabinet turn down Narvik—while keeping it as a threat, or lever to get what they can out of Norway and Sweden. But *what*? They seem to have parted on the note that Sam Hoare should go out! I told him this ridiculous. What would he think if Goering or Himmler went to Brussels or the Hague? He said it was trying to have every suggestion negatived. I said it was my duty to negative stupid ones. He left for Yorkshire at 4.15.

Saturday, 13 January

Didn't go to Cabinet. [Sir Edward] Bridges came over after about story, which I had since received, of German plane which crashed in Belgium on 10th with 2 Staff officers and complete plan of German invasion of Low Countries. Very odd. But one can't ignore these things and all precautions taken.* Had long talk to Collier about this ridiculous idea of sending Sam Hoare to Sweden.

Sunday, 14 January

Woken by F.O. at 3.45 a.m. Telegram from Brussels that Belgians expect invasion of Belgium, Holland and Luxembourg at dawn today. Having ascertained that this conveyed to all proper quarters, went to sleep again. V. cold and rather foggy. Walked to F.O. getting there about 10.30. Sent off telegram to Brussels saying that in these circumstances they *must* agree to Staff conversations. Rang up H. and put

* It was genuine; but the British naturally asked whether it was a plant, intended to provoke the Belgians into asking for assistance, and thus to provide a pretext.

him wise; he approves. Cabinet 12.30—Chatfield,* Service Ministers, C.I.G.S. [Ironside] and Pound. Winston told us of his talk with Keyes on telephone this morning. King had laid down certain conditions—wants certain assurances about no separate peace, restitution &c. He (W.S.C.) had rung up P.M. (Chequers) who was furious at Belgians laying down conditions and they had concocted a pretty damping reply. But as W.S.C. unfolded his tale it became clear that, on these conditions, Leopold would invite us in *at once*. I don't think he or P.M. had quite tumbled to importance of this. Oliver spotted it and I supported him strongly. Decided we must talk to P.M. again. Chatfield got him on telephone at 1.30. He still recalcitrant, but agreed to cancel first message and to have another Cabinet later. Cabinet rose at 2 and I had to go to see Corbin and tell him all about it at 2.20. Lunch 2.45! Went to see H.J.W. and Bridges about 4.45. P.M. back at 5.30 and sent for me. Still annoyed. I agreed thing might be a fake but couldn't be ignored and Leopold's offer could not be turned down.

Cabinet at 6. Drafted a better reply to Leopold—giving him 80%. Cabinet rose 7.45. Rather foggy. Couldn't get taxi until 8.20. Saw Corbin at 8.30 and gave him text of our reply. He doubtful. Dinner about 8.50. Went round to H. about 9.50 and gave him the news: took him on to see P.M. Home about 11.15.

Monday, 15 January

Still no attack! V. cold. Walked to F.O. No reply from Brussels yet. Lunched with H. at Dorchester. Sam H. there. Tried to talk them out of this ridiculous and nefaste idea of sending Sam to Scandinavia. Didn't succeed too well. Cabinet at 3 (I didn't attend). 3.30 Aras as unintelligible as usual. Telegram from Paris showing Gamelin has told Belgians they must invite us in by 8 p.m. or he'll send his men back to billets!

Dined at home. Worked until 10.30: then went to pick up H. and to F.O. Leopold's reply coming in: he wriggles out. (Probably old Keyes has got it all wrong†). Rang up Paris. Ronnie C.‡ says nothing happened by 8 p.m. so I suppose that's all over! Home about 12. As Bridges said—just like a peace-time week-end!

Tuesday, 16 January

A rush getting H's telegrams ready and drafting a telegram from the King to Haakon proposing Sam's visit. Told H—for the *last*

* Now Minister for Co-ordination of Defence.

† He had.

‡ R. H. Campbell. Now Ambassador in Paris.

time—that this was a *bad* plan. Only thing to do is to form our 'expeditionary force' gradually in *Finland*, and then we shall have it on the spot when we want it.

. . . Fairly quiet day. Thank God there was opposition in the Cabinet to Sam visit.

. . . I conclude that all this scare is *quite probably* a German fake. *But*, as I told H. before the Cabinet this morning—in case they felt they had been fooled—they must act *exactly* the same next time. If it was a fake, it was done, either to get us into Belgium first, which would give Hitler a propaganda point with his own people, or with the idea of 'crying wolf' in the hope that we shall ignore the real information when it comes along. If therefore they are too sceptical in future, they will be playing the German game.

Wednesday, 17 January

12.30 meeting with Ted Carr, Waterfield,* and Leeper about British Council. I said only solution was to lock Reith and G. Lloyd in a room together. And I'm glad to say they agreed.

6.30 meeting with P.M., H., W.S.C., Chatfield, Hankey, and Menzies, about sabotage in Sweden. Quite satisfactory and hopeful.

Cabinet this morning turned down idea of Sam's visit to Sweden. Thank God! Gather the fur flew!

[Some members of the Cabinet favoured the despatch of British troops to help Finland, an action which might be so developed as to place them in control of the Swedish orefield. The Chiefs of Staff, however, advised against any attempt at capture in the teeth of Norwegian and Swedish opposition. Chamberlain supported them, remarking that such a policy would have disastrous effects not only in the Dominions but also in the U.S.A.; and to retain American support was vital for financial and other reasons.]

Thursday, 18 January

Corbin . . . keeps hinting that we want a Supreme Council on Scandinavia, and indeed I think so. We can't do *both* and Balkans, and we must choose between the 2—or have a strategic reserve for either. And the War Cabinet must first make up *their* mind.

Friday, 19 January

I *had* meant to begin my 'holiday' today, but no point in going to the cottage with the ground like iron and 6 ins. (as I understand) of

* A. P. Waterfield, Deputy Secretary at the Ministry of Information.

snow, and the pipes all frozen up. Fine morning, but temp. at 10 a.m. still only 32°. A nice quiet day. . . .

Had a talk with Menzies. He rather convinced of overwhelming German attack in West, from Jan. 25th onward, but he's rather mercurial, and *rather* hasty and superficial (like myself!).

Saturday, 20 January

Dutch Minister to protest against one of our 'operational sweeps' having netted 2 Dutch ships. I must say I don't quite know what these 'sweeps' are supposed to be doing. . . .

O. Sargent dined, and we went to 'Black Velvet'. Vic Oliver quite good. I think the modern Revue is quite a good sort of entertainment —a million times better than most films.

Monday, 22 January

Pointed out to H. that the ridiculous paper given him on Fri.—'as from' the German Govt.—by X (from Y) was absolute bilge. Both X and Y are (a) 'Pacifists' and (b) Half-wits. If the Germans want to say anything to us, they won't use this drain for their communication. Also, why was the paper Roneo'd? (I shd. very much like to know this!) . . .

Had talk with Ronnie [H.] Campbell who is over here on 'private affairs'. He thinks all these rumours leading up to a last peace offensive. I agree with him. Talk with H. Seymour,† Clifford Norton‡ and W. Strange about League Work—particularly 'Bruce Report'.§ How tiresome everyone is, and how particularly tiresome the League is. Dine at home. No box!

More snow this afternoon. Shall we *ever* take refuge in the cottage?

Tuesday, 23 January

Talked to H. about trouble over removing Germans from Jap Ships—which looks ugly. (Far Eastern Dept. are very unlucky: they never refer things to me and always get into trouble). . . . 3.30 Honours Meeting with H.J.W. Awful scrap with Darlan, who refuses G.B.E. (Because Gamelin has G.C.B. and Georges§ G.B.E.). Agreed to offer him G.C.M.G.

Wednesday, 24 January

Not quite so cold, but still freezing. Everything still going wrong,

* Sir Horace Seymour, Asst. Under-Sec. of State, F.O., 1940–2.

† Returned from Warsaw to F.O., 1939; Minister at Berne, 1942; Ambassador in Athens, 1946–51.

‡ On the economic and social work of the League.

§ General A. Georges, French C-in-C.

even in small details, and everyone in a bad temper. Not feeling too well, either, these last days. . . . 4.15 had a talk with H. about possible peace terms. He in pacifist mood these days. So am I, in that I should like to make peace before war starts. *But* you can't make peace with Hitler except on terms he would and could never accept. May be a good thing to put these terms, *if* you can formulate them. What worries me, as I told him, is that all this lavish news of an attack in the West *may* herald a peace offensive in which we *may* find Roosevelt and the Pope associated. If so, we can't simply turn it down: we *must* put up some alternative. What? We left each other completely puzzled.

Thursday, 25 January

H. saw Shigemitsu about 'Asama Maru'* and tried to patch up an agreement. It is really tiresome that at critical moments we always get let down in the Far East. But tempers have cooled a bit. Went to see H. J. Wilson about N.H. who wants to retire on a medical certificate. That probably the best solution.

Friday, 26 January

Urgent message from L. O[liphant]† this morning which seems to show that that silly old Roger Keyes either misunderstood or misrepresented (or both) King Leopold. Why use these ridiculous unofficial busybody 'emissaries'? They don't know the background, so they don't understand and they can't report correctly, because they're not trained to it. He seems not to have taken L. O[liphant] into his confidence, so I must draft a message to L.O. explaining the whole silly muddle! P.M. wants draft of a speech for next week correcting (but not letting down too hard) W.S.C. Did my best. . . . 5 until 6.45 meeting with H., Van, O. S[argent], I. K[irkpatrick] and Collier on Scandinavia and 'Peace Offensive'. No conclusions that are not useless. Report (belated) . . . that our secret documents were communicated in July and Aug . . . to the German Government! I can trust *no-one*. Must go into the whole thing.‡

Saturday, 27 January

Menzies at 4. Peace offensive—as I thought—developing. German

* The blockading British forces had removed 21 Germans from this Japanese ship. Some were later returned and the Japanese agreed in February, with undue difficulty, to a compromise.

† Now Ambassador in Brussels.

‡ The diary does not show the result.

Minister at the Hague wants to meet N. Bland. Authorised this. Message from a good contact throwing out hints of the usual peace terms but, apparently, rather subordinating them to elimination of Hitler. Full report coming by Bag. We shall see.

Sunday, 28 January

[F.O.] H. there. Talked to him about Paris telegrams about Supreme Council meeting. French say Finnish question urgent and want to meet Feb. 1 or 2. But *that* won't help Finland: it's no use politicians meeting until technical advisers ready.

Monday, 29 January

French have agreed to postpone Supreme Council meeting until after meeting of Chiefs-of-Staff on Wednesday.

Tuesday, 30 January

Hitler's day! Not too much of a rush, though God knows, what with 'Asama Maru' and American complaints of our Blockade (*and* Italian) we have enough on hand.

... Dined at home and listened to summary of Hitler's speech. Quite harmless muck—no 'peace offer' thank God!

Wednesday, 31 January

Agreed with H. that P.M. need say nothing about Hitler's speech.

... 4. went to see Horace W. and he promised to help me to have disposal of all the money I want for security measures.

Friday, 2 February

About lunch-time telegram from Roosevelt about his awful, half-baked, idea of sending Sumner Welles (!) over here with a flourish of trumpets to collect data on which Roosevelt is to proclaim basis of peace!

... 5.15 Menzies with text of the new 'peace offer'. 7 P.M. and H. about Paris meeting (decided to take Winston!) and Roosevelt.

Saturday, 3 February

Finished draft reply to Roosevelt. Went over to P.M. with H. about 5.30. Got finished about 7.45. Got telegram off, cleared up some things and home, where dined.

[This long telegram set out fully and clearly the difficulties of talking usefully about peace while the Nazis remained in power. Other despatches were answered in the same sense:

. . . the President has no doubt observed that no announcement by any leading Allied statesman would justify the belief in Germany that Allied Governments intend upon victory to partition Germany. If German people do believe this it is because the German Government by means of their propaganda are forcing this belief upon them in the hope that by this means they may counteract any craving for peace among the German people and may be better able to reconcile them to further hardships and sacrifices.

As to the inevitability of a tremendous offensive in the spring this too has for some time been put about by German propaganda as part of the war of nerves on which they are engaged. It must be realised that this war of nerves is directed not only against the belligerents but also against the neutrals. By keeping the neutrals on tenterhooks, especially those neutrals in close proximity to Germany, the German Government hope to create among them the general fear lest a continuance of the war will eventually involve them in hostilities either directly or indirectly. We do not therefore feel that this kind of propaganda is necessarily conclusive as to peace being more difficult of attainment later. . . .

I am gratified to note that the President is convinced of necessity that any peace settlement must include 'guarantees that there would be no renewal of aggression during any of our life-times.' That is really the kernel of the difficulty and it is clear that the President appreciates the fact. It might not be so difficult to devise a settlement that apparently righted the wrongs done in recent months: whole difficulty is to find some means of assuring Europe that this *could* not be followed sooner or later by a renewed attack on the rights and liberties of the weaker European States.

We cannot imagine how such an assurance could be attained so long as Germany remains organised on the present lines and is under the direction of her present rulers. To demand as the condition of a peace that the present German regime shall be overthrown or changed may have one or other of two effects. It might encourage the German people to throw off Hitler's regime or it might unite them behind Hitler from fear that the Allies and America are trying to disrupt Germany so as to destroy her. The former alternative is rendered rather remote by the fact of the complete grip which Hitler, the party and the party machine seem to have on a population that is traditionally and remarkably amenable to discipline. The latter alternative is to be feared because it is the obvious line for Hitler's propaganda machine to take and because we should have to anticipate that they would use it skilfully and to the full.

But to be quite frank there would be the utmost difficulty in persuading people of this country and I believe of France that *any* settlement is worth signing with Hitler or present regime.

We have hitherto felt best method of handling this difficulty is to state the conditions which while not such as to invite rejection by considerable elements in Germany, are such as Hitler would find it impossible to accept. I infer that this is not far from the President's thought. . . .

The announcement of mission of Mr. Welles will of course produce a sensational impression throughout the world more particularly if it makes public full purpose of this initiative.

It may be that the President feels he cannot obtain data that he requires from his regular representatives in various capitals. But such a sensational intervention will raise hopes in some quarters and give rise to discussion—much of it ill-informed—in nearly all and if the President after weighing all considerations that I feel bound to submit to him feels full disclosure would best contribute to the ends he has in view, it would seem of great importance that he should give clear indication in announcement of his own conviction that first essential purpose to be achieved is durability of any settlement arrived at.

I must frankly admit to a good deal of anxiety lest the effect of this move however carefully presented should be to cause embarrassment to the democracies from which Germany, still unconvinced of the failure of policy of force, will reap advantage.

There is no doubt greater unity in France and England than there is in Germany but there are always elements in the community which do not share general opinion, and what I fear is that public announcement of the President's initiative will at once bring these elements into open and vocal prominence in countries where 'freedom of information' already exists. Since German public and press will remain dragooned and controlled there will ensue a false appearance of unity in Germany which will contrast very unfortunately with an apparent disunity in democratic countries. Period of waiting while Mr. Welles collects his information will be a critical one, and I am concerned at the thought that it may be used by German Ministry of Propaganda to emphasise divisions in ranks of their opponents, and thus alter the situation to our disadvantage.

I am most anxious to avoid giving the President the impression that I do not fully appreciate the impulse which has inspired him to courageous proposal. On the contrary you may assure him that I will certainly cooperate to the best of my ability. But I earnestly hope that he will consider very seriously possible effects of a public announcement of purpose of Mr. Welles' mission before this becomes absolutely necessary.[22]]

Sunday, 4 February *Paris*

Raining, but still cold. Went to Charing Cross to catch special leaving at 10. Enormous party—P.M., H., Winston, Oliver and Kingsley [Wood]. Winston in a strange spurious naval costume, clasping the 'Lord High Admiral's Flag!' P.M., rather tentatively, showed his colleagues our Washington telegrams. Winston—after a 2nd sherry—read them through and, with tears in his eyes, said 'I'm *proud* to follow you!' So *that* was alright. Embarked on destroyer—'Basilisk'—about 11.45. Lovely day at sea—sunny and much milder. Passed a floating mine. Machine-gunner tried it, but made the most awful practice. Then a few shots from a sub-calibre gun and we holed and sank it—without explosion. Got into Boulogne about 1.45 and special to Paris. [At dinner] sat between Léger and Darlan (latter very nice). In bed at 12.

Monday, 5 February *Paris*

At Embassy at 9.30. Found H. in his bedroom. Winston had been holding forth in his dressing-gown for nearly 2 hours! Meeting at Ministry of War at 10. Rode French off their silly Petsamo scheme, and got them to accept our idea. Agreed Chiefs of Staff should meet after lunch.

... Meeting with French about 6.15. Everything agreed and merry as a marriage bell.

[The French and British agreed that Finnish resistance must be assisted, but equally that it must be done with Norwegian and Swedish consent. The plan for seizure of Petsamo might mean war with Russia; whereas the British proposed the preparation of a force which would go to Finland's aid across Northern Scandinavia and of another which would defend Norway and Sweden if a German threat against the south materialised.]

Tuesday, 6 February

Train stopped at 5 a.m. and of course I woke—and couldn't sleep again. Embarked on 'Boadicea' at 9.15. C.I.G.S. carrying dirty little blue paper parcel. I admired his luggage, which he confessed was a kilo of butter!

Foggy and consequently calm. Clearer in mid-channel. Found another mine. Hit it first shot and it blew up. Our escort 'Beagle' dropped depth charges for our amusement. The 'Lord High Admiral's flag' gave rise to an incident: in the mist, as we approached Dover, another destroyer signalled 'Why the Red Ensign?'!!

Wednesday, 7 February

Reply from Lothian reporting his talk with President who, I think, is shaken by our arguments.

... 6. went with H. to P.M. and got Washington telegrams approved.

[Sumner Welles should make it clear to Hitler and Mussolini, Lothian suggested, that the U.S.A. would not allow a *blitzkrieg* or a successful aerial and submarine blockade against Britain and France. President Roosevelt answered, in effect, that although he would not dispute the rightness of some such step, it was politically unpractical. Not a quarter of Congress would support it. It was an election year. If he raised the issue, it would produce a violent campaign of an extreme isolationist character. Only events would compel the American public to face realities.[23]]

Friday, 9 February

Drafted telegram to Washington in reply to Roosevelt, but by the time I'd done it, his 'splash' was coming out on the tape. His announcement of Welles' trip not too bad, but that croaker Cordell Hull also announced talks with neutrals about a 'peace settlement', which 'might be extended to belligerents'. Saw C. Peake with H. and gave him the line of comment for Press and B.B.C.

Saturday, 10 February

Produced redraft of telegram to Washington, but advised against sending anything, now that Roosevelt has splashed all his stuff. Our press quite good, and don't feature it. P.M. agreed to send nothing.

[Early in February Loraine asked the Italians to sell some arms and ammunition. Mussolini refused, because he did not wish to reduce Italy's stocks and intended to fulfil Italy's commitments to Germany. When Loraine was told this on 8 February, he said that the decision destroyed the basis of the economic negotiations, and that Britain would stop the shipment of coal from Germany to Italy.[24]]

Sunday, 11 February

Corbin at 12.15 to ask about the Sumner Welles stunt. He not too gloomy about it. Told him of Musso's ban on arms sales to us, which disturbed him.

Tuesday, 13 February *Thatched Cottage*

Grey, and snowing lightly. Cold still rather bad. Impossible to do anything in the garden with snow and frost. But spent a nice lazy day, taking some exercise and fresh air, thinking not at all of the war and reading various books.

Tuesday, 20 February

Several boxes from F.O. Mostly tiresome questions about relations between Ministry of Information and F.O. in realm of propaganda. The kind of question I *hate*: one can form no judgment of it: everyone is making his own propaganda! Dined at home and worked. I was going to write 'a pleasant holiday', but it wasn't, as the weather was so utterly foul. But it was a welcome rest. I was lazy and did more or less what I liked when I wanted to—which is very unlike my normal routine. . . . Fortunately, we kept well during our stay in the cottage and I hope we have benefited by it. It was an oasis.

Wednesday, 21 February

Had talk with H. who hadn't much to tell me that I didn't know (except communication from Pope to which I don't pay much more attention than I do to all these stories).*

. . . Papers coming in in floods—a bloody life. Dined at home and worked myself silly.

[The French pressed for immediate occupation of the principal Norwegian ports, in order to give Sweden greater security. They pointed out that Norway, by protecting in her territorial waters armed German ships carrying British prisoners, had infringed neutrality herself. When Finland appealed, Sweden might go to her aid, or allow the allies to do so; if not, they would still dominate Germany from the north, be placed to stop the shipment of Swedish minerals by sea and able to bomb the Gällivare mines.[25]]

Friday, 23 February

About 6.30 P.M. sent me over his Birmingham speech. I suggested two alterations. About 7.15 H. back from Cabinet. They had reacted strongly against Maisky's suggestions of last night to R.A.B. about peace terms for Finland. I am v. glad. R.A.B. very disgusted—I am sure he saw here another chance of 'appeasement'. Apparently Cabinet still undecided about minefield in Norwegian waters. Of course it is really only a Winston stunt, and ill-conceived. Tho' I shouldn't mind doing it. Phillips (Admiralty) and Attorney-Gen.† came over to touch up draft. But I think it will never be used.

Saturday, 24 February

Summoned to Cabinet at 11.30. Sam, Winston and Oliver and Anthony. They asked what had become of the draft statement about Norwegian waters. I knew S. of S. didn't want this party to play about with it and that it must await the Cabinet on Monday. (I had been told to go slow with its circulation). So I could only express

* Pope Pius XII had told the British Minister to the Vatican earlier in the month that part of the German Army was ready to act, even at the risk of civil war, if the union of Germany and Austria were respected. On 17 February Halifax replied that Britain must act with France, and see a 'definite programme authoritatively vouched for', including reparation to Germany's neighbours, guarantees of security and freedom of choice for Austria.

† Sir Donald Somervell, K.C.

surprise that they hadn't got it, look as daft as I could and promise they should have it as soon as possible. They agreed to adjourn and meet again if there was any point in the draft they wanted to raise. I went back and arranged they shouldn't get it much before lunch-time.

Drafted reply to Finns about President's suggestion for our intervention in Moscow. This involves telling them that Maisky had put to us terms which we did not see fit to pass on.*

. . . Reported to H. on the Cabinet. Got him to approve and circulate reply to Finns and also to French suggestion that we should immediately seize Norwegian ports! Heard Hitler was speaking at 7 this evening. Left with H. at 6.30. T., G. and I dined 7.30 and went to Little Review. Quite amusing. Joyce Grenfell v. good. . . . Kirkpatrick had promised to let me know if Hitler said anything, but no word from him, so I suppose he said nothing.

Tuesday, 27 February

Corbin came to see me about 6.45, disturbed by his talk with H. this morning, from which he inferred we were weakening on Scandinavia. Did my best to reassure him! I said H. may have dwelt on the difficulties. But it was no use pretending the difficulties did not exist, because they *did*, and they were rather formidable. I took the war into his country by asking *how* the French proposed to get over these. He had no idea. Had to wait at F.O. until about 8.10 to see a draft telegram from Winston to Roosevelt. (I deprecate this procedure). It contained what I thought a quite poisonous sentence, which I cut out and went home to dinner. After dinner, telegram from Rome saying U.S. Ambassador had heard Finns asking for German mediation. Don't believe this. We must ask Finns. But that raises the point—should we tell them not to do anything without consulting us. Rather tricky, so went round at 10.30 to see P.M., who approved a telegram saying that, in view of point reached in our discussion with Finns, they should *inform* us before committing themselves.

Wednesday, 28 February

Cabinet took no decision and I had to tell Corbin so. 5 Lonsdale Bryans, with his ridiculous stale story of a German opposition ready to overthrow Hitler, if we will guarantee we will not 'take advantage'.

* British policy was to damage Russian interests without fighting her; by supporting the Finns to prolong the war and thereby prevent Russia from helping Germany and from plotting mischief in the Balkans.[26]

Let him talk, and then broke it to him that this was about the 100th time I had heard this story.[27] He lacks charm to an extent that is positively astonishing. I couldn't get him out of my room. . . . That half-wit Tavistock* is bringing out a pamphlet. I advised H. to let it come out. A bit of rope.

Thursday, 29 February

11.45 Corbin called with report of Finnish Minister's démarche to Daladier last night, and telegram from French Minister in Helsingfors showing that Tanner† was completely defeatist after his visit to Stockholm. So it's not quite clear what the Finn attitude *is*. Sent over to Cabinet record of my talk with Corbin. . . . Saw H. after and got from him rather vague account of Cabinet meeting. Got Bridges to come over and drafted, with him, a telegram to Helsingfors to try and elucidate where, exactly, we were. . . . Corbin came at 6.30 with further news from Paris. French Government convinced Finnish decision will turn on *number* of men we can promise and *date* when they will arrive. Gave H. record of this at 7.30. . . . These days are awful. T. and G. went to film. I remained to grapple with *mountains* of work.

Friday, 1 March

Cabinet decided to approach Norwegians and Swedes in accordance with plan. . . . 4.30 gave H. revised draft, but Finn coming to see him. Was present. Finns ask (1) 50,000 men in Finland in March (impossible), (2) 100 bombers at once (3) promise that our force be employed *anywhere* in Finland and (4) assurance that we shall act in spite of Sweden. Looks as if they want a get out. Got Cabinet (minus P.M.) together at 6. Heard same demands (with 30 instead of 100 bombers) made in Paris and that Daladier has gaily accepted (though he knows it's impossible!). How like the French! Cabinet thought it better not to refuse demands seriatim, but show that we're prepared to all that's materially possible *as a first step* and that more will follow. H.J.W. and I left Cabinet and made a draft, which S. of S. and J.S. approved. Got it off. I rang up Corbin and explained (without recrimination). Then H. and I saw Gripenberg.‡ As regards Swedish attitude, he fortunately put his question in the form 'If Swedes tomorrow say No, what will you do?' I said 'We shall go ahead with all our preparations'. This rather successful.

* Succeeded later in 1940 to Dukedom of Bedford as 12th Duke. The pamphlet, *The Fate of a Peace Effort*, published letters exchanged between himself and Halifax.

† V. Tanner, Finnish Minister of Foreign Affairs, 1939–40.

‡ G. A. Gripenberg, Finnish Minister in London, 1933–41.

Saturday, 2 March

Cabinet 10.30. I didn't attend. Corbin sent me round a note showing again what Finns demand. Cabinet decided that it simply wasn't *fair* to promise Finns what we couldn't perform (thro' no fault of our own). So I rang up Corbin and explained that we can't do more. As regards Finn demand for immediate delivery of 100 bombers, this simply can't be done. At least, of course it could be done, but they'd be no damned use if they got there. They require 3,000 men and *tons* of equipment to enable them to operate. We have bombers on the way or earmarked for despatch, and I told Corbin we were accelerating these and that we didn't like to promise what couldn't be performed! . . . Corbin rang up again to say his Government couldn't understand doubt and hesitation in Helsingfors. I said *I* could. They'd been promised one thing by the French and another by us. *We* had kept to what could be done! He rather tamed.

Sunday, 3 March

Corbin at 12.45. I had some digs at him. He said Finns appeared to be in some doubt. I said not surprising, seeing what different things they were promised in London and Paris. But I said I thought Finns themselves would know that the French promise of 50,000 men in Finland in March was just simply materially impossible. He agreed that it was a 'mistake'. . . . Gripenberg rang up asking to see me. So I had to be at F.O. at 3. Object of his visit was to plead for more bombers immediately. I could only say I would pass it on. I told him what we were doing and reminded him of the limits of material possibility.

Monday, 4 March

Found H. pretty defeatist about Scandinavia. I said (1) we must know whether Finns are going to appeal to us: Vereker* thinks they will settle that question tomorrow. Let us take our fences in order. If they won't appeal, that settles everything and we do nothing. If they do, we must keep up pressure on Swedes and probably threaten publication. H. went to see P.M. at 11.15. Back at F.O. at 2.45. Cabinet had decided to do nothing until we know whether Finns *are* going to appeal. That probably right. G. Lloyd at 6.30 about his blasted British Council. Corbin at 6.45. He said he thought we ought to make joint démarche in Helsinki to show identity of views. I said I thought that a very good plan, seeing the great divergence that had been made apparent, in the matter of figures, between Paris and

* G. G. M. Vereker, Minister at Helsinki, 1940–1.

London. I thought that had already been cleared up but I would suggest further instructions. H. was with P.M., so sent him over account of my talk with Corbin with a draft telegram to Vereker. Approved.

Tuesday, 5 March

O.S. just back from sick leave very aggressive and says even if we can't—or aren't asked to—help Finland, we should go into the orefield. But he, and Collier, have always emphasised that our great weapon with the Scandinavians is the opprobrium latter will incur from stopping us *helping Finland*. They will incur no opprobrium for defending their own orefield; in fact, they will have the world behind them!

. . . Dined at home and worked. B——y fools at F.O. hadn't sent my box and I had to ring for it. Shall raise ten thousand hells tomorrow.

Wednesday, 6 March

Lunched with Archbishop [Lang, of Canterbury]. Only Masseys* and a Chaplain . . . there. Rather embarrassed after, when Archbishop asked me, in front of Massey (who knows) what we proposed to do to help Finns! He very bellicose. Awful gloomy Victorian gothic house, with a frozen garden and lawn, now used by a balloon—the 'Arch-Blimp'.

Aras at 3.30 who *may* be useful in suggesting a triangular deal with Italy—Turks taking armaments and Italians buying our coal with proceeds. . . . 6.30 Lonsdale Bryans, whom I liquidated in as friendly a manner as I can do. . . . Telegram coming in from Helsinki which seems to show Finns are throwing up the sponge. Secretly, I shall be glad. I believe ours is a hare-brained scheme which hasn't been thought out properly by anyone, and I am shocked at the levity and stupidity of our Gen. Staff.

Thursday, 7 March

Corbin came at 12.30 with message showing that Finns are entering into pourparlers with Soviet, thought doubtful whether there can be any basis of discussion. (This later confirmed by telegram from Vereker.) . . . Saw H. when I got back and he gave me lines of telegram to Helsingfors putting matters squarely before Finns and pressing for an answer. (1) Will they appeal for troops? (2) Would they sooner rely on material? (3) Do they intend to negotiate? As

* Vincent Massey, Canadian High Commissioner in London, 1935–46.

usual in a crisis, I have to deal quickly with S. of S. and P.M., and am then subjected, ex post facto, to sniping fire of criticism from O. Sargent and Collier, and my time is taken up. . . . 5.30 went with H. to discuss with P.M., Ismay* and Newall. Main question—shall we send 50 bombers? I against. Decision deferred—in view of H's talk with Gripenberg—until tomorrow. Found 13 boxes in my room.

Friday, 8 March

Have never had so much work. Constant procession of Office Keepers through my room, carrying 4, 5 and 6 boxes each. Don't know what's happened. . . . Drafted telegram to Helsingfors in accordance with Cabinet decision, saying that *if* they appeal for Allied military help, we will send 50 bombers. 3.30 Corbin came and showed me telegrams showing that Finn Delegation has gone to Moscow! . . . Bastianini came to see H. who put before him basis for agreement. Gather it went well.

[The War Cabinet had agreed that ships carrying German coal might proceed, with the exception of those still in Belgian and Dutch ports, to Italy.]

Saturday, 9 March

Ralph S[tevenson]† rang up to give me message from Rome which looks as if we'd settled the coal question. A smack in the eye for Rib[bentrop] on his arrival in Rome, when I expect he hoped to rope the Italians into the war. There may be something in 'appeasement' yet!!

Sunday, 10 March

We drove to Heston to meet Sumner Welles. He arrived about 12. Crowds of photographers and cinematographers took us as we shook hands. One of them cried 'Sir Alexănder, do that again.' So I did it again! . . . H. just going over to P.M. with Pound about 'Marine operation'. French agree but want no warning. We agree, I'm glad to say. H. had seen Corbin and had message from Gripenberg, as a result of which we sent message to Oslo and Stockholm asking what will happen when our expeditionary force appears off their ports! We *may* get through yet. French appear determined to.

* Gen. Sir H. L. ('Pug') Ismay, Sec. to the Committee of Imperial Defence, 1938–40; Chief of Staff to Minister of Defence and Deputy Sec. (Military) to War Cabinet, 1940–6.

† R. C. S. Stevenson, Principal Private Sec. to S. of S., 1939–41.

Monday, 11 March

Directly I had packed H. off to Cabinet, Corbin appeared, to make a grand remonstrance about our backwardness in Scandinavia. I retorted—saying that it might be picturesque and romantic . . . to promise the Finns 200,000 men, but it wasn't playing the game. However, I supposed it didn't matter much, as the Finns themselves must know that it was a fairy story. A minute after he had started, H. rang me up from No. 10 to say we must have a statement for the House this afternoon, promising help 'with all our available forces'. Corbin stayed until 12.15. Dashed off the statement with R.A.B. in 10 mins. Gripenberg waiting to see me. He was merely renewing appeal for bombers immediately. Sent over both records to No. 10. . . . Found Cabinet had agreed on Statement, which P.M. made, and on immediate despatch of 8 bombers. 42 to follow. Telegrams from Helsingfors, one saying that Govt wanted us to approach Scandinavians. In view of Corbin's complaints of our 'discouragement' of Finn Gt, gave instructions to telegraph accordingly. Dined at Dorchester with H.—Sumner Welles, Crew,* Snell,† Pound, A.E[den], Oliver S[tanley], Herschel Johnson. General talk after—quite interesting, but S[umner] W[elles] clam-like.[28] Got back and found Corbin on the telephone saying we ought *not* to approach Scandinavians—this some sinister move of Tanner? I said maybe, but we couldn't, in view of his talk with me this morning, turn down any Finn request. How tiresome the French are.

[In his conversation with Sumner Welles, Chamberlain said it was impossible to deal with the German régime, which had destroyed confidence. Welles asked whether this opinion would still hold if Poland and Czechoslovakia could be restored and provision made for a disarmament which made for security? Yes, Chamberlain replied, because Hitler 'personified a system with which the British Government had learned from bitter experience it was impossible to make terms. . . . We could not be satisfied with any settlement from which it did not clearly emerge that Hitler's policy had been a failure.'

Welles was deeply impressed by Mr Churchill, a fact which it was proposed to pass on to the latter. Cadogan, however, minuted that he 'felt some delicacy about asking the Sec. of S. (or the P.M.) to authorise our telling Mr Churchill that he made a unique impression on Mr Welles. I take comfort from the fact that Mr Churchill will already have that conviction, so nothing is lost.'[29]

* Marquess of Crewe, Viceroy of Ireland 1892–5; numerous ministerial offices 1905–16; Ambassador at Paris, 1922–8; leader of Independent Liberals in House of Lords, 1936–44.

† Lord Snell, Deputy Leader of the House of Lords 1940–44; formerly a Labour M.P., 1922–31.

The mission had no result. President Roosevelt spoke to Lothian about the definition of Allied war aims, which should not include the disintegration of Germany. He talked also of disarmament and abolition of offensive weapons; but the whole issue became academic upon the German invasion of Norway.]

Tuesday, 12 March

Found letter from Corbin reinforcing what he said last night. Agreed with H. to try to telephone to Stockholm and Oslo to suspend. But too late. Doesn't matter. . . . Rumours of peace settlement, but vague. Meanwhile that hysterical Daladier has *fairly* spilled the beans to the Chamber. Don't know where we are. French insist on postponing 'marine operation for 2 months'! I think we must face up to French. This is 1920–24 over again—they take the bit between their teeth. We should jab them in the mouth.

[Finland made terms, which included the cession to Russia of the Karelian Isthmus, in Moscow on this day. The Cabinet had agreed on 12 March to reactivate the plans for military landings at Narvik and Trondheim, with later descents upon Stavanger and Bergen. Whether Norwegian and Swedish permission would have been obtained remains doubtful. Had Finnish resistance lasted longer, the Allies might have proceeded regardless; as it was, the agreement signed at Moscow meant that these plans were again abandoned. Most of the force earmarked was sent instead to France. Unhappily, the Royal Navy's codes and ciphers were deplorably insecure. The German Intelligence services read almost everything of importance to do with the Norwegian operations and were able to judge the dispositions of the Home Fleet. The postponement of the planned operation against Norway was known at once from the interception of signals ordering the dispersal of the submarine force lying off the Skagerrak.[30]]

Wednesday, 13 March

So the Finns have capitulated. I don't blame them, as we could only (honestly) offer them 13,000 men by second half of April. And I don't blame us, as we couldn't (honestly) promise more. A black day, but there it is. Passed draft of statement for P.M., which I hear later, from R.A.B., that he didn't like. Gripenberg came round, but he had no news. . . . 2.50 telegram for Helsingfors confirming 'peace'. Rang up Chatfield, who said he was holding everything here but that stuff in transit was already in Finn control. Sent for Gripenberg and asked if he could stop it. He rather disconcerted—said Finn G[overnmen]t had bought it. So didn't press him. Told Chatfield, and he agreed. He asked what he was to do with the 'expedition'? Some store ships had sailed. I said they must be recalled and 'standstill' for the rest. He agreed and said he would see P.M. . . . 5.30 H. and Van about Lonsdale Bryans, who is still trying to be busy. Settled to put kybosh on him. (*I* shall have to do it tomorrow!) . . . Gloomy interview with Corbin. Beastly day and very depressed. But I'm secretly relieved. Our plan was amateurish and half-hatched by a half-baked staff.

[Cadogan's relief is not difficult to understand. Either the force would have failed at once, thus enhancing the Russian triumph, or it would become a liability, entailing naval losses and reinforcements on land which Britain could not provide.]

Thursday, 14 March

Awful article by Ll. G[eorge] for America. . . . Showed it to H., who showed it to P.M., who thought it best to let it go, and stage an attack on the old fool in the House when it's out. Talk with H. and Chatfield about Scandinavian Expeditionary Force. Decided to disperse it and tell French. Better face facts.

Friday, 15 March

Letter from [Clifford] Norton, declining Ministry of Information* post. Very tiresome. . . . Thought of all other possibilities and lit on I. K[irkpatrick]. Obviously the man for the post, but I never thought Department would spare him. But they say he already has to spend half his time doing the Ministry's work for them.

Saturday, 16 March

Cabinet 10.30. Everyone very gloomy—particularly, of course Winston. I suppose we *have* suffered a reverse over Finland, but we've been through tunnels before, and one sometimes comes out on the sunny side of the hill. Corbin at 12.30 to complain of his talk with H. yesterday. I think latter *was* a bit mandarinesque. It's rather silly to talk of encouraging a Scandinavian bloc *now*. Only a display of strength will have any effect on neutrals. At Cabinet Chatfield talked about 'strong diplomatic action in Sweden'. As I told Anthony afterwards, diplomacy is rather hamstrung by being deprived of the necessary apparatus—military strength. *Words* don't do anything.

Monday, 18 March

Hitler and Musso[lini] met this morning on the Brenner, but we

* Mr Butler described one of its officials as resembling 'a nonconformist accountant in a disorderly house which was extending credit'.

have no indication, so far, of what it all means. Ciano *was* not to have gone, but did, and before leaving said 'Crisis has been overcome.' But one doesn't know what these double-crossing monkeys mean. Everything very black for the moment.

[They reached no formal agreement. Mussolini averred that Italy still intended to move with Germany but must choose the moment, since Italy's resources could not stand a long war.]

Tuesday, 19 March

Talk with H. and O.S. about our attitude to Scandinavians. No use offering to back their 'bloc'. Must warn them that certain actions of theirs would affect our 'vital interests'. In fact the big stick. But is ours thick enough?

. . . R. Campbell looked in. Says Daladier determined to resign! Corbin at 6.45 urging us to stop Narvik shipments. In view of that and R. C[ampbell]'s news, didn't break it to him that H.M.G. turned down Narvik. Told H. after, who agrees, and will raise matter at Cabinet again. Walter Monckton* about Ministry of Information appointments. *Hope* that's getting straightened out. W. Strang about Belgian approach to us about assistance to Holland and Belgium.

[M. Paul-Henri Spaak, the Belgian Prime Minister, had asked what Britain and France would do if the Germans attacked the Netherlands but not Belgium.]

Good Friday, 22 March

H. arrived at F.O. before 11. He had been worried all night by W.S.C. who wants to take [Dr Hjalmar] Schacht off 'Conti di Savoia' at Gib. We had decided yesterday that game hardly worth the candle. H. went to meeting with Winston and P.M. Rang me up soon to tell me to find out what American reactions would be. I got hold of Herschel J[ohnson] and *his* reactions weren't good! Went over and joined them at No. 10 and told them. But they decided to take him off—not intern him, but send back to Italy. I want to hear first whether we have found him, before telling Americans and Italians.

[Reynaud now proposed, in preparation for the Supreme War Council's impending session, that the Allies should control shipping in Norwegian territorial waters and occupy vantage points on the coast; sever German communications from the Caucasian oilfields, even at the cost of a rupture

* Sir W. T. Monckton, Dir.-Gen. of the Press and Censorship Bureau, 1939–40; Deputy Dir.-Gen., Ministry of Information, 1940, Director, 1940–1.

with Russia; and study the possibility of sending submarines into the Black Sea.

The War Cabinet were not prepared to occupy strategic points in Norway, and the Black Sea proposals ignored Turkish neutrality; but they did favour the mining of the Rhine and action against the Narvik ore traffic.[31]]

Wednesday, 27 March

Cabinet at 11, which I attended. Ranged over all questions to be discussed with the French tomorrow. Quite useful: stiffer line with neutrals, and 'Narvik' *soon.* Caucasus doubtful: cross-examine French on their ridiculous 'Black Sea' idea (if it can be dignified by that name) and discourage Balkan adventure. But, insist on fluvial mines and offer Franco-British Declaration. . . . Heston, where we met Reynaud,* Campinchi, Laurent-Eynac†, Léger and others. Bitterly cold N. wind. Back at F.O. at 7. C. Peake tells me French Press (Havas, therefore official) have put out that 'Allies' 'have decided' to police neutral waters! These French!! Sent him round to Dorchester to tell H., who, with P.M., is seeing Reynaud tonight at French Embassy.

Thursday, 28 March

Supreme War Council at 10. Sat between H. and Kingsley [Wood]. V. long statement (too long) by P.M. But we got moving. Lunch at Carlton. . . . Drove back with Winston who was v. gracious and insisted on taking me in his car. Tried to efface some of his suspicions of me. Met again 3. Finished 4.15. Quite good meeting. Results: note, on our lines to Scandinavians April 1 or 2. Start laying 'fluvial mines' April 4. Lay mines in Norwegian territorial waters April 5. Lay fluvial mines from the air April 15th. 'Study' Baku. Anglo-French declaration on solidarity.

[The Supreme War Council realised that this policy might provoke a German reaction in Scandinavia and thus, in turn, allow an Allied landing in Norway.]

Friday, 29 March

H. gave me timetable of fluvial and Narvik mines. Had meeting . . . to work it out and to plan necessary drafts. Corbin at 6.30. Asked

* Paul Reynaud, Minister of Finance, 1938–40; President of the Council, succeeding Daladier, 1940. See List of Principal Characters.

† Ministers of Marine and Air respectively.

him to get his G[overnmen]t to make, on Monday, similar communications to Swedish and Norwegian Ministries. Stacks of work. Heard Ministry of Information were announcing Ted Carr's resignation and *Ivone's appointment.* Rang up Reith and said I couldn't have this. I knew nothing about it. Neither his Ministry nor I.K. himself had said a *word* to me. He agreed.

Saturday, 30 March

No Cabinet, so H. had nothing to do but waste our time with one of his dreadful drafting meetings. The longer they last, the more niggling, and ineffective, they become. Hitler doesn't do this! We were drafting the various communications to Scandinavians, declarations about fluvial mines and 'Narvik' mines &c. Didn't get away till after 1.30.... Back at F.O. 5.30. Joined H. and Winston in discussion of next week's programme. Further drafting Committee till after 7. Worked till 7.45. Drove H. home. He beginning to demur at my getting away on Monday, but I must get away *some* time and *no* time is a *good* time. Rang up Reith about I.K. Said he could have him as far as I was concerned, but he must fix up terms with I.K.

Sunday, 31 March

Telegram from Paris—as I expected—saying that French have gone back on fluvial mines.*... Talk with H. and Winston. Found they were prepared to go on with Narvik. I said we ought to barter Narvik against fluvial mines and gave them heads of argument, and put them on paper. They went to see P.M. at 6.45 (who was seeing Corbin at 7.15). Gather he accepted my arguments. We *must* press the French on this. It's the *only* chance of ever getting our mines. Worked till 7.30. H. tells me Chatfield is to be shed: has been offered N.Z., but refused.

Monday, 1 April

Having worked all over the weekend, nothing very much to do, or no undue pressure. Glad to find P.M. was absolutely firm with Corbin last night. Said 'No mines, no Narvik.' This is the only line. The French seem to say that it was *Daladier*† who objected. I don't believe this, and it's a dirty trick. About 12 Corbin rang up to say his Government agreed with the text of the communication to be made today to Swede and Norwegian. But, he said, the P.M. had promised him 'a further communication on that matter'. I said (having just

* The French requested, for fear of reprisals, three months' delay.

† Now Minister for War, but estranged from Reynaud.

been rung up by H.) that I could give him the 'further communication', which was that we weren't going to say anything today to the Scandinavians, and hoped Reynaud wouldn't, either. Corbin said 'Yes: and was there no *constructive* suggestion?' I said 'No.' They must chew on it. We really must try to bring them to heel. They talk about 'vigorous prosecution of the war', which means that *we* should do it, provided we remove the war as far as possible from France!

Tuesday, 2 April

Corbin 12.30. Ostensibly to ask for P.M.'s statement for this afternoon, but really to sound me as to our attitude. I kept a stiff upper lip. He finally asked me outright whether we were expecting his Government to go back on their refusal to allow fluvial mines. I said we were certainly hesitating to indulge in 'Narvik' alone and we were hoping the French would reconsider their attitude. He had evidently been instructed to convey to me the impression that they won't. We shall see. Inactivity will be more embarrassing for Reynaud than for us. Oliveira* came for the nth time to say goodbye! I actually cleared up all work and said goodbye to H., hoping to be off tomorrow until Sunday. As regards the French, I said keep them on tenterhooks for several days. 'Narvik' can wait, and we *must* try to get fluvial mines. He agreed. No box—only telegrams. And I do hope we may get off tomorrow, that we may have fine weather and that I may blow my cold away. It is still there—of the lingering kind. Some tulip buds.

Wednesday, 3 April *Thatched Cottage*

Primroses are coming out, but not full out yet. Our fruit trees are just beginning to bud. Very late, but so much the better. The herbaceous plants seem all alive-oh, and have made some growth. Meadows greening up nicely and copses purpling.

Friday, 5 April *Thatched Cottage*

Pouch shows Daladier is the obstacle (? for political reasons) to R.M.O.† Winston has gone over, but I doubt if he can over-persuade him. We seem to be committed to 'Narvik' on April 8. If we do that, goodbye to R.M.O.

My cold came to nothing much. I cough a bit and snivel. But I hope I've dug the worst of it into the kitchen garden.

* Dr R. R. de Oliveira, Brazilian Ambassador, 1925–40.

† The mining of the Rhine.

Sunday, 7 April *Thatched Cottage*

French absolutely refuse R.M.O. We lay 'Narvik' mines tomorrow morning, *if* the S. gale subsides. This I think silly—unless it induces Hitler to do something sillier. *Masses* of stuff to read. A very pleasant holiday, which I enjoyed and which, I hope, did me good.

A row of peas and a row of broad beans coming up.

Monday, 8 April

Back to the treadmill again. Everyone—even H.—making allusions to my 'holiday'. Considering I've had only a fortnight since last Aug[ust] Bank Holiday and very few Sundays! H. himself has perhaps had less. 'Narvik' mines laid this morning. . . . Boheman† at 12. He not reproachful—only commiserating! Says we have done the silliest thing in history—in our own interests. And I think he is right, but I had to argue with him.

. . . Reports of German ships out in the North Sea, but I don't think we've done anything but lose a destroyer—'Glow-worm'.

[The Germans had broken British signals revealing the plans to mine the entrance to Narvik and put in a small force. They practised a successful deception, moving what seemed to be empty ore-ships up to Narvik. The Admiralty misinterpreted the German naval movements, failing to realise that they heralded landings in Norway; the First Cruiser Squadron accordingly left Rosyth without the troops held ready to assault Norwegian ports in the event of German landings.]

Tuesday, 9 April

Rung up at 8 to say Germans attacking Oslo. At F.O. at 9.10. Cabinet met 8.30. I joined them about 10. Fixed up communiqué with H., H.J.W. and Reith showing German attack put in motion before we laid a mine and assuring Norway of full support. Cabinet again at 12. No news from the Fleet—'wireless silence'—rather ominous. Germans seem to have got in to Narvik! How?! . . . Meeting at No. 10 with Reynaud and Daladier at 4.15. Told them of our dispositions. Agreed to summon Belgium to invite us in. (French say Brussels have impression that attack is coming in next 3 or 4 days.) Denmark has been wiped out. We sent such reassuring message as we could to Norway. Got Corbin's concurrence in draft to Brussels at 8.15. . . . If the German adventure in Norway is an operation in itself, I like to think that it is suicidal (that's what I told Herschel Johnson). But I think it is a prelude to, and a distraction from, an attack in the west. We shall see.

† Erik Boheman, Sec.-Gen., Swedish Foreign Office, 1938–45; headed Swedish delegation for war trade agreements with Britain, 1939–45.

Wednesday, 10 April

Masses of telegrams. Situation rather obscure. Went to Cabinet at 11. Things don't look v. good. Strong German force in *Narvik*, and we lost 2 destroyers. As in the case of Jutland, Admiralty put this straight out, saying we had 'withdrawn'. Later learned we sank 2 German destroyers, a supply ship and a munitions ship and 5 or 6 merchantmen, and shot the place up. Even Germans admit they've lost 2 cruisers. On the whole think we didn't have a bad day. Lunch at Dorchester, where H. spoke—very well. . . . Boheman at 3. He marooned here and consequently very bellicose. But he may be of some use to us. Got H. to see P.M. about Admiralty communiqué and persuade latter to talk to Winston. Corbin complained of it bitterly!

Thursday, 11 April

Rung up last night 12.45 a.m. to say French were sending Coulondre and General Mittelhauser* to Sweden on a mission of 'encouragement'. They would be here for meeting at No. 10 at 8.30. Got up at 7 and when starting off at 8.15 told meeting postponed till 9.30. Meeting of P.M., H., Winston, Oliver, Sam Hoare, Chiefs of Staff. French as above and Corbin. Agreed on instructions to Mission. As soon as I got minutes—about 12.45—drafted instructions. Lunch at 1.45 (C. here). Back at 2.30. Got H. to approve instructions—also Corbin. Got them to Air Ministry by 3.30. French had left for Scotland at 2. Our people (Admiral [Sir Edward] Evans and [Maj.-] General [E. O.] Lewin) joining them later. C's of Staff got cold feet about one paragraph. Sent amendment to Lewin, who not up yet from Aldershot. 5 went to P.M. to report. He approved. . . . Back to F.O. Evans stopped by storm in mid-England. Lewin has got through. Drafted telegram to Stockholm to serve either purpose—whether Mission arrive or whether they don't. News of northern war not too bad. We've knocked them about pretty hard. Had several talks with Boheman, who, I *think*, is straight with us.

Friday, 12 April

Had discussion with H., Strang and Makins about Chiefs of Staff paper regarding going into Belgium without B. consent and without waiting for German attack. Attended Cabinet 11.30. Not v. much news—nor much to be expected till we land at Narvik. Both Swedes (Boheman & Co) and Norwegians urge that Narvik won't cut much ice. We must have Germans out of Trondhjem. Got back about 12.30

* Previously Chief of Staff of the Czech Army.

and saw Colban. He agreed to Norwegian broadcast to hearten his people and encourage guerilla tactics. . . . 4 Cabinet again on Belgian question. Decided to tell Belgians that if Holland attacked* and they (B's) do nothing, we will nevertheless go in. H. doesn't like this. But I think it's right. Drafted telegram to Paris—as we must get French concurrence first. And I don't think we shall! . . . G.J. has filled up my box with a mass of undigested stuff—like a rag-bag.

Saturday, 13 April

Went to Cabinet. P.M., J.S., Sam H[oare] and H. impressed by message showing that Narvik alone is no good and we *must* attack Trondhjem (easier to do it *now* than in a few days when it will be reinforced). Winston against—and made interminable speeches. But we got something out of him. Pray heaven it may not be too late. I drafted telegram to Sweden and Norway designed to encourage them, and we got it off after lunch. Winston reluctantly sent telegram to Paris asking for power to divert Chasseurs Alpins from Narvik to elsewhere. (French have since shown they're as keen on this as we are!) Drafted telegram from King to Haakon. Got it approved by P.M. and H.M. and sent off. To be in Press tomorrow. Masses of work. Cartier [de Marchienne] came at 6.30. Rather embarrassing interview. Sent account to H. Cartier clamouring for answer, which he won't get until tomorrow. Stalled him off. Awful day.

Sunday, 14 April

A bad weekend. Though very good news of Narvik this morning. I hope we have liquidated N[arvik] and—still more—purged Winston and the Cabinet of the Narvik obsession. Let's now leave that alone, and get on with Trondhjem, which is the only thing that matters in Scandinavian eyes. Cabinet at 11.30 at which it was decided to land a token force today. (Later heard this was postponed, and got H. to ring up Winston and urge him to get on with it. He *said* he would.) This morning before Cabinet gave H. draft letter to Cartier, which he niggled about. It was only a time-saving reply, and I told him so. And sure enough, during Cabinet, message from Cartier that it didn't answer his questions. H. promised to see him later in afternoon, and after Cabinet, discussed with P.M. what he should say. . . . At 5 H. called me in to help with Cartier. H. went to P.M. at 5.30 and left me with C[artier] to draft a new letter. He got back about 6.20 and didn't quite like draft, but agreed alteration with C.

*** On this day the British military attaché at The Hague was told, in effect, that there could be no military collaboration with Holland.**

[The attempt to hold Trondheim turned on the Norwegians' ability to cut railways (which they failed, and in some instances, refused, to do) and on neutralisation of the German air effort. The possibilities on the latter score were much over-estimated by the British Staffs. The whole Norwegian operation was undertaken without proper consultation between the Admiralty, the other Service departments and the Intelligence staffs; and was characterised by a lack of information about the topography and of machinery to focus and accommodate the differing needs of the three Services.]

Monday, 15 April

Cabinet at 11. Not much news. A good air day. But the party ashore at Namsos report adversely on facilities.... Lot of telephoning after [dinner], while I was trying to work, about the Hambro Norwegian broadcast ... which I had put out at 6.30. Seems to be rather too optimistic and Press are bombarding with questions, but after consulting Winston and Oliver [Stanley] told Broad* to say we had 'no comment' on this Norwegian Govt. message.†

Tuesday, 16 April

Cabinet at 11.30. Not very much news. We had a good air day yesterday—in particular at Stavanger. Short Cabinet, as P.M. was going to preside meeting of Milit. Coordination Committee. Heard later they had taken some quite sensible decisions. May go bald-headed for Trondhjem.... Percy L[oraine] at 3. Suggested he ought to go back. He doesn't think so, and he may be right. H. agreed later.

Wednesday, 17 April

Admiral Evans called and I commissioned him to go to Norway. Cabinet till 12.30. Evans called again and I had chat with him. He says Lewin is not such a fool as I'd think.

Thursday, 18 April

Cabinet 11.30. (always have to go, now). Scandinavia seems in good shape. We have landed altogether 7,000 men, slightly ahead of schedule, without losing one. 'Suffolk' got home—rather badly damaged, but no disaster. Quite a good air day. 12.45 came back to see Corbin. French v. pessimistic about Italy. I can't help thinking

* Philip Broad, a First Secretary of the F.O.

† Presumably by C. J. Hambro, President of the Norwegian Storting, who had arrived in Stockholm on 10 April. It was to the effect that British and French help was now assuming 'great proportions', evidenced by the recapture of Narvik. All Norwegian authorities were to give the Western Allies every assistance.

that, *at present*, it is largely a smoke-screen and a success in Scandinavia would make a great difference. . . . Drafted telegram to Paris urging reconsideration of decision not to tell Belgians that we come in, whatever happens, if Holland violated.

Friday, 19 April

Cabinet 11.30. Not v. much news. 'Suffolk' beached at Scapa. Corbin 12.45. Told me Reynaud was sending a letter to P.M. about Scan[dinavian] campaign. French evidently nervous that we haven't got our heart in it. Want to make it seat of major operations (so as to remove the war from France!). But doubt if that's physically possible.

Saturday, 20 April

Cabinet 10.30. All Trondhjem plans upset. 'Frontal attack' given up, and we can't expect anything for a month! This was recommendation of C's of Staff, approved by P.M. and Winston. But it seems to me awful! . . . Dined at home and spent most of the time after writing a paper urging 'frontal attack' on Trondhjem. I am sure the risk is great, but is it so great as waiting for a month?! And what *will* the French say?!

Sunday, 21 April

Sent H. my note about Trondhjem, but I don't suppose he can do anything about it now. D.N.I. tells me Namsos plastered with bombs and burning! . . . Cabinet at 5. Scandinavian situation certainly doesn't look too good!

Monday, 22 April *Paris*

A long Cabinet till 1.30. Namsos situation bad, and a long discussion as to what Kingsley Wood should say to the Press. He a chicken-hearted little mutton-head. . . . Left with H. for Hendon at 4.30. Off the ground about 5.10. Took 1 hr. 35 mins for the trip to Paris. Sam H[oare] and Newall with us. Lovely day and comfortable trip. Drove to Embassy and had a talk with P.M.

Tuesday, 23 April *Paris*

Lovely day again. It was 75° yesterday and chestnuts in bloom. Air-raid last night. At 12.10 a.m. heard a 'plane overhead and thereafter gunfire. Meeting at Quai at 9.30. V. satisfactory. Agreed to go into Belgium on invasion of Holland and to bomb marshalling yards and refineries at once!* Pole and Norwegian attended at the end.

* That is to bomb the Ruhr immediately upon any aggression in the West. This policy the French had long opposed, fearing retaliation.

Wednesday, 24 April

Was late for Cabinet, as thought it was 11.30 but it met at 11. So missed some of the reports. Gather that things still go badly—our Namsos force falling back, after heavy mauling, on N[arvik]. Winston made an oration about the possibility of coming back to 'frontal attack'—almost on lines of my minute!

Thursday, 25 April

H. had met Ismay, who had given him most gloomy account of Norway—that we must get out. Cabinet 11.30, but the gloom was not as bad as all that, though we're abviously in a bad fix. P.M. says of Winston 'he's grand—when things are going right'! Certainly he is rather mercurial, and chops and changes. Decided to reinforce Eastern Mediterranean. Good thing to do. Italy has piped down for the moment, but if things are going to go badly in Norway, we shall want a big stick handy.

Friday, 26 April

A pretty awful day. Cabinet in morning, at which it was decided we must clear out of central Norway. Pretty awful! Benes at 4—for an hour and a quarter!—on necessity for setting up and recognising Cz Government. Corbin at 5.15. French have heard of our decision as to impossibility of holding on—and are incensed. But *they* don't convoy at sea, and *they* don't have to—or can't—grapple with *air* attack, which is the whole problem. Told me Gamelin coming over and wants to see P.M. and Winston. Meeting arranged for 9.30, with preliminary meeting at 9 of P.M., H., Service Ministers, C's of S. and self. Gulped some dinner at 8 and H. picked me up at 8.40. We explained frankly to Gamelin, Corbin and Mittelhauser, and they hadn't got much to say. Reynaud coming over tomorrow.

Saturday, 27 April

Cabinet at 10.30. Lasted all morning. V. gloomy. We must get out, but it's an awful débacle. But there it is, and must be faced. P.M. got H. and me to lunch with him. Meeting with Reynaud and Daladier and the whole outfit at 2.30. They agreed in principle we can't hold on, but want to 'save face'. We had a meeting after with Massy* and Staff which showed that we'd better not try.

By 6.30 went back to F.O. to find a whole day's accumulation of work. Told O.S. what had happened. He in one of his frozen, pessimistic, useless, 'I told you so' moods. Think I shall have to fix [? fire] him.

* Lt.-Gen. H. R. S. Massy, C.-in-C. forces operating in Central Norway.

[The British Ministers explained to Reynaud that the Royal Navy could not afford the continuing strain of the Norwegian operations and that German superiority in the air was producing a devastating effect which aircraft based in the U.K. had not the range to challenge. Chamberlain also emphasised the imminent danger of war with Italy. The Supreme War Council agreed to give up the idea of taking Trondheim but accepted Gamelin's suggestion that the force at Namsos should be withdrawn gradually to the north, in order to hold up the German advance on Narvik. However, this decision was later reversed and immediate evacuation agreed upon.[32]]

Sunday, 28 April

Much happens these days which I can't remember, or haven't the time to record. A damp dark morning . . . Cabinet 10.30. Lots of talk—not much done. Massy brought in at the end. Strong as ever on need for immediate evacuation. So there it is: it's going to be awful, and there was a deal of discussion about what to do with the Press and Parliament. H. and I saw Corbin at 12.45. He fears his people will think we are going ahead too fast in evacuating *at once*. But we explained difficulties and dangers—we've got to face up to it sooner or later, and the sooner the better if that involves less risk and loss. . . . Saw Colban, who was extremely embarrassing, asking me what truth there was in rumours of our calling off our attempt to recapture Trondhjem. I could only evade question by saying 'we would do our damnedest'. Worked until 8. Got King's approval of message to Haakon. Authorised R.A.F., if necessary, to impress Norwegian work on aerodrome at Narvik. Dined at home and worked. Everything as black as black. But my only reaction to that is to go on doing my work as well and as hard as I can. Not much use, but still.

Monday, 29 April

Cabinet 11.30. There had been a telegram early from Reynaud asking for reconsideration of evacuation plans. Can't consider holding on till it's too late, but glad to hear from Ironside at Cabinet that we have adopted Gamelin's plan of a delaying retreat northward from Namsos. . . . Colban at 3.30. Very awkward: his Government have heard of our order to retire, and enter violent protest (endorsed by [Maj.-Gen. B.] Paget, our Commander on the Dombaas front!). Told him I didn't know military dispositions, but that I did know Paget hotly engaged. And enlarged on difficulties. Reported to H. and told him he really ought to see Colban—which he did later. . . . 6. Corbin. Joined by H. Corbin was beginning to bleat about our going back on S[upreme] W[ar] C[ouncil] resolutions, when I cut him short with this morning's decision regarding Namsos.

Tuesday, 30 April

Discussion with H., R.A.B., and O.S. about Italy and Yugoslavia. R.A.B. of course, 'appeasing'. I still think we should answer at once with declaration of war. (We must however agree first with French and *Turks*). Cabinet at 11.30. Long talk about Scandinavia. We have removed [King] Haakon and Govt. Otherwise, situation remains same. Then, an inconclusive discussion about Italy. Gen. sense *against* declaration of war. But H. agrees to put the whole case as soon as possible before French. . . . Corbin at 7.30—had evidently had news from Paris casting doubt on Norwegian resistance (which doesn't seem to matter 2d one way or the other, so far as I can see, except as regards tankers). Told him Haakon was going to Tromso, so that looks all right. H. had frank conversation with Colban about offensive and childish message from that wind-bag Hambro, who is sitting pretty in Stockholm. . . . We've got some nasty days in front of us. But it seems that Roosevelt has sent a *very good* message to Musso[lini]. News of our diversion of shipping out tonight and we had to put out a statement. I authorised one at 7.45 which, I hope, is not entirely on the wrong lines.

This morning, at Cabinet, we were discussing evacuation from Gib. of 'old men, women and children'. P.M., with a hawk-like look, said 'How do they define old men?'

Wednesday, 1 May

Cabinet 11.30. Not v. much news. Rather heavy losses of bombers. Evacuation of Andalsnes begun successfully last night. Barrage of stories being laid down on us by Germans—attack on Belgium, attack on Holland, attack on Maginot Line, attack on Hungary, invasion of England, &c.!

. . . 7.30 Corbin with an appeal from Reynaud, on his bed of 'flu, to hang on to Namsos. Even Corbin realised that this was a 'useless démarche'. But I sent it on to H. and P.M. French offer us more troops and material, but I explained, for the nth time, that the whole difficulty was *getting* them there and *keeping* them there. And the French (though I never say this) have done absolutely *nil* towards this. It is *our* ships and *our* aircraft that are shot down.

Thursday, 2 May

Cabinet 11.30. Not much news. Discussion as to P.M.'s statement for this afternoon. Sent telegram to the Hague asking Dutch to prepare to blow up aerodromes on islands and mainland. (They won't dare.) Also telegraphed to Paris to explain that Gen. Audet* himself has advised against leaving rearguard near Namsos. P.M.'s statement seems to have gone fairly well. . . . H. rather gloomy and wants talk on general prospects. To my mind, *whole* thing turns on *air production*, which seems to be awful. Probably Kingsley's [Wood's] fault. He has the air, now, of a dog that's stolen the ham off the sideboard.

Friday, 3 May

Admiral Evans came in about 10.30. He had left Stockholm 10.30 last night! He had many stories but no very clear impression. Cabinet 11.30. We have embarked successfully from Namsos, but convoy will be bombed all day. French destroyer (the only one) sunk. Later heard [destroyer] 'Afridi' also sunk. Foreign Press not too bad. . . . Corbin at 5 to ask that we should not announce withdrawal from Namsos. I said that we might wish to defer it for some hours, for various reasons, but it must be faced. No good being ostriches when the Germans were trumpeting it round the world.

Saturday, 4 May

Drafted telegram to Hambro giving assurance that we should hang on to Northern Norway. . . . To F.O. at 5.30. Found 20 boxes! Talked to I.K., which is always cheering. Got through as much as I could. Home 8. Dined and worked. Planning conquest of Iceland for next week. Shall probably be too late! Saw several broods of ducklings.

Sunday, 5 May

Lots of work and Dormer† came for about ¾ hr. He seems quite well. He arrived . . . [with Norwegian emissaries] this morning. I gather they're *all* a bit disgruntled—small blame to them, poor darlings. But we're not going to sit quiet too long under their rather offensive reproaches. Considering their complete inefficiency—and treachery—they oughtn't to get off without retort. As for the Swedes—I drafted a telegram to Stockholm saying what I thought of *them*. Which did me a lot of good. I leave it to Mallet‡ whether to use it or not.

. . . Koht§ has been broadcasting and we couldn't stop him—even if we wanted to. But I don't understand Norwegian. Sent masses of papers to H., who gets back for dinner. He'll be furious. But I had

* Commanding a brigade of Chasseurs Alpins.
† Sir C. F. J. Dormer, Minister at Oslo, 1934–40.
‡ Victor Mallet, Minister at Stockholm, 1940–5.
§ Halvdan Koht, Norwegian Foreign Minister, 1935–40.

Cadogan and Halifax in St. James's Park, August 1939

Churchill, Harry Hopkins and Cadogan aboard H.M.S. *Prince of Wales*, August 1941

Quebec, 18 August 1943. Front row: Eden, Roosevelt, Countess of Athlone, Churchill. Back row: Earl of Athlone, Mackenzie King, Cadogan, Brendan Bracken

20 boxes between lunch and dinner yesterday, and many today. Put up to him plan for Iceland, amongst other things, which he must get Cabinet to decide tomorrow.

Monday, 6 May

Saw Howard-Smith* and gave him his instructions—to land Marines first, and then go ashore. He leaves tonight for Clyde—sails tomorrow morning. Long Cabinet and a very bad and gloomy one. Cork† reports all military against a frontal attack. Doesn't give his own opinion, which would seem to be different. Telegraphed to ask him. Cabinet now wobbling about Narvik—which won't *do*. They approved Iceland.

Tuesday, 7 May

Rather better Cabinet. Cork seems to want to go ahead, and decided to let him. Discussion about bombing. On all considerations, I think we ought *not* to begin. No decision reached. . . . Talked to H. about 'Smaller War Cabinet'. P.M. seems to have got away with the Debate, more or less. Dutch have made up their minds Germany will invade them tomorrow morning. Must go to bed early!

Wednesday, 8 May

Cabinet 11.30. Cork definitely recommends attack and Cabinet gave authority. Yesterday's debate went badly, but I don't think it's fatal. In my view, N. C[hamberlain] the best P.M. in sight. The *only* alternative is H. and that would be the end of him. Nett result: we lose an admirable S. of S. Talked to C. Peake on these lines. Corbin at 5.15, from the House. He less gloomy than yesterday. Dined at home and worked. What a life! P.M. seemed well and quite cheerful this morning, but I gather debate will weaken Govt. But *what* are we going to put in its place? Winston useless. Then? Attlee? Sinclair? Sam Hoare!

Thursday, 9 May

Govt. pressed to a Division last night and majority dropped to 81. So this is serious! Lovely day—tulips almost at their best and everything smiling, except human affairs. Walked to F.O. H. went off to see P.M. about 10.15. Back by about 11. He very gloomy—thinks P.M. will go and fears he (H.) may be asked to take over. Cabinet at

* C. Howard-Smith, Minister at Copenhagen, 1939–40; at Reykjavik 1940–2.

† Admiral of the Fleet the Earl of Cork and Orrery, commanding all forces in the Narvik area.

weaken Govt. But what are we going to put in its place? Winston useless. Then? Attlee? Sinclair? Sam Hoare!

Thurs. May 9. Govt. pressed to a Division last night & majority dropped to 81. So this is serious! Lovely day — things almost at their best and everything smiling, except human affairs. Walked to F.O. H. went off to see P.M. about 10.15. Back by about 11. He says Prime-Minister P.M. inclined for & fears he (H) may be asked to take over. Cabinet at H. of C. at 11.45. But we had to wait about, as that blasted H. of C. was sitting & wrangling & intriguing. C.I.G.S. explained, with a map, Narvik operations & I had a talk with Pound. About 12.15 P.M. appeared, looking v. tired and "offended". Cabinet sat till 1.35, in an air of gloom. Lunched here — Dormers, Adele, Bentinck, G. H. went over to No 10 at 4.30 to meet P.M. & Winston. This is his account:— P.M. said main thing was national unity: Labour must come in to the Govt. If they wouldn't come in under his leadership, he was quite ready to resign. Agreed to talk to Labour leaders & Attlee & Greenwood came. Then were asked (a) will you come in under present

Two pages from Sir Alexander Cadogan's Diary, 8 and 9 May 1940

leadership, (b) under any other? They must consult Party. Answer to (a) almost certainly "No", to (b) probably "yes". So after they had gone, P.M., Winston & I discussed possibilities. P.M. said I was the man mentioned as the most acceptable. I said it would be hopeless position: If I was not in charge of the war (operations) and if I didn't lead in the House, I should be a cypher. I thought Winston was a better choice. Winston did not demur. Was very kind & polite but showed that he thought this the right solution. Chief Whip & others think feeling in the House has been veering towards him. If N.C. remains – as he is ready to do – his advice & judgement would steady Winston.

I said I personally welcomed this, as it kept H. with us. (I think he is not the stuff of which a P.M. is made in such a crisis. We should have a good S.of S. & get a doubtful P.M. But I'm not at all sure of W.S.C.) However, there it is – waiting on Labour decision. It would not be – or might not be – a bad solution. But how beastly the H. of C. is! With what delight they jump on a good man when he is down! I gather that this morning there was rather a "morning after" feeling in the House. But too late! The trade of politics is indeed a

H. of C. at 11.45. But we had to wait about, as that blasted H. of C. was sitting and wrangling and intriguing. C.I.G.S. explained, with a map, Narvik operations and I had a talk with Pound. About 12.15 P.M. appeared looking v. tired and 'effarouché'. Cabinet sat until 1.35 in an air of gloom. . . . H. went over to No. 10 at 4.30 to meet P.M. and Winston. This is his account:—

'P.M. said main thing was national unity: Labour must come in to the Govt. If they wouldn't come in under his leadership, he was quite ready to resign. Agreed to talk to Labour leaders and Attlee and Greenwood came. Then were asked (a) will you come in under present leadership, (b) under any other? They must consult Party. Answer to (a) almost certainly 'No', to (b) probably 'yes'. So after they had gone, P.M., Winston and I discussed possibilities. P.M. said I was the man mentioned as the most acceptable. I said it would be hopeless position. If I was not in charge of the war (operations) and if I didn't lead in the House, I should be a cypher. I thought Winston was a better choice. Winston did *not* demur. Was very kind and polite but showed that he thought this right solution. Chief Whip and others think feeling in the House has been veering towards him. If N. C[hamberlain] remains—as he is ready to do—his advice and judgment would steady Winston.'

I said I personally welcomed this, as it kept H. with us. (I think he is not the stuff of which a P.M. is made in such a crisis. We shd. lose a good S. of S. and get a doubtful P.M. But I'm not at *all* sure of W.S.C.) However, there it is—waiting on Labour decision. It would not be—or might not be—a *bad* solution. But how beastly the H. of C. is! With what delight they jump on a good man when he is down! I gather that this morning there was rather a 'morning after' feeling in the House. But too late! The trade of politics is indeed a dirty one. I don't think they'll get a better P.M. than Neville. But all their beastly little envies and jealousies and susceptibilities have to be 'appeased'. If only it means the disappearance of Sam Hoare, all this will not have been in vain!

Friday, 10 May

Woken up 5.40 a.m. with news of invasion of Holland and Belgium. Made sure that everyone was warned. Dutch Minister going to see H., who rang me up soon after 6. Got up about 6.30. Breakfasted 7.30 and was at F.O. 7.50. Cabinet at 8. Not much news and not much to settle. Germans have relieved us of a number of embarrassing questions by invading *both* countries. Cabinet over about 9. Went for ½ hr. walk at 9.20. Met Rab and Mrs B. They very indignant about

Parliamentary proceedings. As well they may be! Back 9.50 and H. went out. Rung up by Kirk[patrick], who wanted to put out on B.B.C. at 10.30 what I thought a thoroughly bad statement (he seemed rather excited). Gave him a better version. Cabinet again at 11.30. Discussed bombing of Ruhr. No decision. . . . Joined H. who had Kleffens and Welter* with him. They had had a bad journey! Cabinet 4.30. Decided to see how land attack developed—Ruhr put off tomorrow night. R.M.O. to start 9 this evening. Labour refuse to serve under Neville, who resigns. Winston to form Government. . . . Confused news, which seems to show Germans not having it *all* their own way—except at Rotterdam. But it is difficult to know what to believe. All chance of holiday gone, of course!

Saturday, 11 May

Thank God, H. continues at F.O. Other Cabinet changes (since given out by B.B.C. at 9 p.m.) none too good. I'm afraid Winston will build up a 'Garden City' at No. 10, of the most awful people—including Brendan Bracken!†. . . News very confused, but it seems that German parachutists are a *real* danger and a new problem. Our armies could get into position by noon tomorrow, but have no news of their progress. Most critical days. And here we are Cabinet-making!

[Cadogan wrote at once to Chamberlain

> to say how deeply I have sympathised with you in all your difficulties, and how glad I am to think that the country, by your generous decision, will still benefit by your services.
>
> During these troubled years, I have been privileged to watch your conduct of affairs from close quarters, and there is no one of your numberless followers and admirers who would pay you a more wholehearted tribute than I should.
>
> And I shall remember to the end of my days the many personal kindnesses you showed me.

Chamberlain replied that he had been greatly touched by Cadogan's letter:

> Your cool head and strong common sense have been of great value to us in these difficult years; there can have been few more difficult in all the history of the Foreign Office.
>
> If we get safely through our present dangers you will be wanted more than ever. I hope I may be there to give such help as I can.[33]]

* E. N. van Kleffens, Netherlands Minister for Foreign Affairs, 1939–46, and C. Welter, Netherlands Minister for the Colonies.

† Brendan Bracken, M.P., became Parliamentary Private Sec. to Churchill. See List of Principal Characters.

Sunday, 12 May

Not very much news—very confused. Parachute attacks in Belgium and Holland producing great confusion. But main thing is our and French troops seem to be getting on to their positions without much loss. Very critical days. H. came in about 12.30. . . . S. Hoare now to go to Madrid! I suppose they want him safely out of the country! . . . B.B.C. gave out more Cabinet appointments—including J.S. as Lord Chancellor.

Before I forget it must give table-plan of Cabinet since April 8:

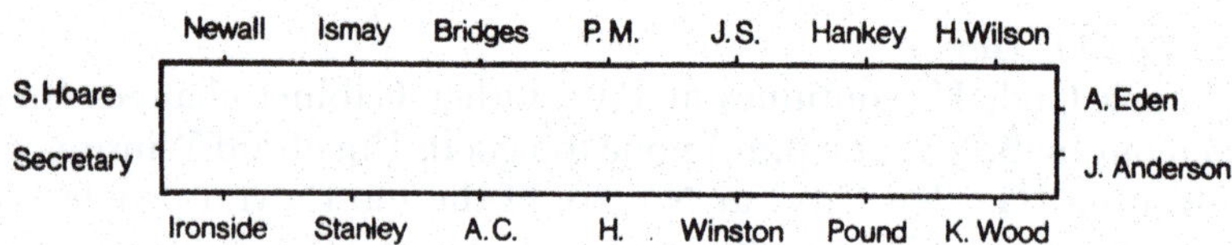

Monday, 13 May

Masses of telegrams. Things look pretty black. Holland cracking and Belgium not too good. H. yesterday offered Madrid to S. Hoare who refused—will take nothing short of India! Lunched at home. Nothing but bad news all day. Cabinet at 6.30.

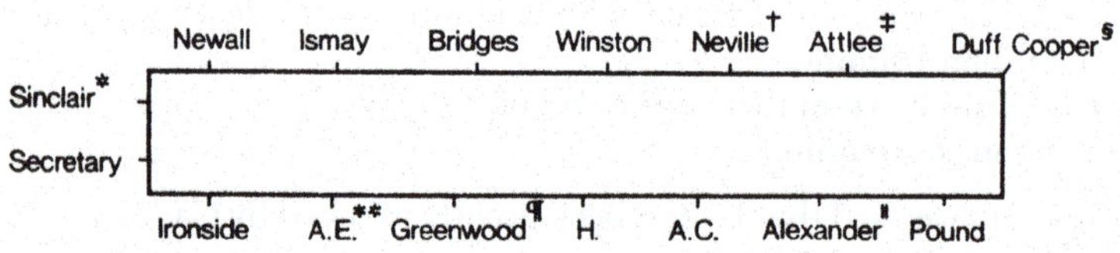

* Sir Archibald Sinclair, Secretary of State for Air.
† Lord President of the Council.
‡ Lord Privy Seal.
§ Minister of Information.
‖ A. V. Alexander, First Lord of the Admiralty.
¶ Minister without Portfolio.
** Anthony Eden, Secretary of State for War.

Plus ça change! And do Greenwood, Attlee, Sinclair and Alexander strengthen the party so? Awful discussion about bombing the Ruhr. Decided (I think rightly) to put it off for 4 days. Home 8.45. Dined at home. Lot of work. Cartier about 11 to protest against British troops going through Brussels, contrary to 'agreement'. Said I was unaware of any agreement. Anyhow the essential was to get, by the best way, on to the best defensive line to protect his beastly country. But rang up C.I.G.S's A.D.C. 'pour acquit de conscience'.

Tuesday, 14 May

Lovely morning—warm sun. Rung up about 8.30 by Makins who said French were in a flap about an appeal from Queen Wilhelmina, which looked as if Dutch might capitulate. Put him on to Alec Hardinge and Dutch Minister—*we* had heard nothing of it. Cabinet 11.30. Situation still very obscure. C.I.G.S. thinks big attack coming in West. Winston still doubtful. Saw Kleffens with H. before Cabinet. K. in good heart—a nice fellow, and *he* doesn't look like capitulating.

. . . Cabinet at 7.—on Reynaud's message to Winston, showing that Germans have broken through at Sedan, and imploring air aid, which we can't give, in great measure. Very gloomy and unpleasant meeting—worst I have ever attended in that beastly room. Cabinet rose 8.10. Found Corbin wanted to see me. Made rendezvous here for 8.25. He wanted to know what decisions had been taken. Told him from memory but advised his A[ir] A[ttaché] should go to Air Ministry. Things never looked blacker. But they've looked that before.

Wednesday, 15 May

An awful day. Cabinet at 11. Our R.A.F. did their damnedest—and very effectively too—in the battle yesterday. Resulting v. heavy losses. Don't know where this will end. News still v. bad. Georges says the hole in the line has been 'plugged', but I gather counter-attack can't be mounted owing to other German thrusts. . . . Cabinet this morning decided to start bombing Ruhr. Now the 'Total War' begins! 5.30 talk with H., Dalton, Drogheda,* Van, O.S., Nichols,† &c., about trying to hold off Muss[olini]. Smaller meeting later to decide what to do if Italy attacks Yugoslavia tomorrow. Corbin at 7.

* 10th Earl of Drogheda, Joint Director, M.E.W., 1940–2; Dir.-Gen., 1942–5.
† P. B. B. Nichols, Foreign Office.

V. gloomy. Pressed request for more fighters in France, which we can't spare from A.D.G.B.* Especially if we are beginning on the Ruhr.

[Churchill telegraphed to Roosevelt:

> I trust you realise, Mr President, that the voice and force of the United States may count for nothing if they are withheld too long. You may have a completely subjugated, Nazified Europe established with astonishing swiftness, and the weight may be more than we can bear. All I ask now is that you should proclaim non-belligerency, which would mean that you would help us with everything short of actually engaging armed forces. Immediate needs are, first of all, the loan of forty or fifty of your older destroyers to bridge the gap between what we have now and the large new construction we put in hand at the beginning of the war. . . . We want several hundred of the latest types of aircraft . . . anti-aircraft equipment and ammunition . . . to purchase still in the U.S.A. . . . I am looking to you to keep the Japanese quiet in the Pacific, using Singapore in any way convenient.

The President made a prompt reply, probably as helpful as it could be at the time. On the two vital points, however, he could offer nothing very comforting. The loan of destroyers would require the sanction of Congress, which he was reluctant to seek at that moment. As for Japan, the U.S. Fleet would remain at Pearl Harbor for the time being.[34]]

Thursday, 16 May

The blackest days I have ever lived through. But there are doubtless worse to come. I am writing on 17th and can't remember details. Cabinet in morning at which we received blacker and blacker news from France. Finally Dill explained plans for withdrawal in Belgium. This infuriated Winston, who said we couldn't agree to that, which could jeopardise our whole army. Sprang up and said he would go to France—it was ridiculous to think that France could be conquered by 120 tanks (but it may be!). He said he would leave after lunch, and asked N.C. to 'mind the shop!'. . . Awful afternoon. Much of my time wasted. 6 meeting of Committee presided by N.C. about what to do in Mediterranean if Italy comes into war. Not much! Dined at home. Cabinet announced for 10. Went there and met H. and John Anderson.† Cabinet put off till 10.30, then 11. Waiting for telegram from W.S.C. in Paris to be decyphered. Talked with H. and J. Anderson about plans for home defence. Cabinet, under N.C., assembled at 11. Winston's message showed situation

* Air Defence of Great Britain.

† Home Secretary. See List of Principal Characters.

desperate and endorsed appeal by French for all the Fighters we can give them. Agreed by midnight, to send 6 squadrons.* I give full marks to Newall, who is *admirable*—I retract all that I may ever have said and thought to his discredit. Home 12.30 and did some work.

[In Paris Churchill had found the situation incomparably worse than he had imagined. On a map at the Quai d'Orsai, showing the fronts, there had appeared 'a small but sinister bulge' in the region of Sedan. 'Où est la masse de manœuvre?' Churchill asked. General Gamelin shook his head. 'Aucune,' he said.

For once the Prime Minister was struck speechless. Evidently the abandonment of Paris was being prepared, for clouds of smoke were rising from the garden and he could see venerable officials heaping archives by the barrow-load on the flames. Gamelin begged for more fighters, to attack the German tanks. 'Mon général,' Churchill replied, 'on ne peut pas arretêr les chars avec des avions de chasse. Il faut des canons—Poof! Mais si vous voulez nettoyer le ciel, je demanderai de mon cabinet.']

Friday, 17 May

Cabinet at 10. W.S.C. gave account of his trip. French evidently cracking, and situation awful. Nothing much to be done and no decision to be taken. Kennedy turned up at 11. W.S.C. saw him and got from him President's reply to his appeal. I'm quite convinced that Pres[ident] will do all he can, but he can't go ahead of his public. And even then, what can they do to affect *this* battle? . . . All kinds of worries: these days are dreadful and my knees are beginning to go! Gather French haven't fought at all—simply shattered by air-tank attack. Troops and guns hardly used. Our Staffs living in the days of the Zulu war. H. went to a meeting of a Ministerial Committee to consider how we proceed when France has capitulated and we are left alone. Just as well to prepare for that.

Never did I think one could endure such a nightmare. . . . Very tired. But how these Chiefs of Staff (and the P.M.) endure—*never* getting any rest—I can't think. They're wonderful—at least I think Pound and Newall are. Ironside I think so stupid as to be impervious to anything.

Saturday, 18 May

Situation less awful, but still very grave. Whatever happens, R.A.F. have covered themselves with imperishable glory. Cabinet 11.30. Beaverbrook† came, about aircraft production. I got a bad

* In addition to the 4 squadrons which the Cabinet had agreed earlier in the day to despatch.

† Minister of Aircraft Production, 1940–1. See List of Principal Characters.

impression—that he was trying to rush things into the shop window. Anyhow his proposals met with strong opposition from Newall, in whom I am beginning to have complete confidence. It's amazing what our Air Force have done. . . . Cabinet 5.30 about what we do if France collapses and—most of the time—what we do anyhow now about aliens. Which I found dull. News still obscure and grave—though not so grave as I had expected. Morale of French troops may be improving. Germans have thrown *everything* in, and if we can slash them, we may do something. Weygand* recalled.

Sunday, 19 May

Cabinet at 10. News pretty bad—Germans now driving N.W. to cut through to Channel ports between us and French. French army not fighting. French Cabinet changes—Pétain brought in [as Vice-President of the Council]—for prestige. Gamelin (thank heaven) sacked. . . . Went down to Kew. It's a lovely spring with sparkling air and wonderful blossom and the whole world looking like paradise—and Hell let loose. Back 4.45. Cabinet summoned at 4.30. Anyhow missed that bus, and had a cup of tea and got to F.O. 5.30. Sam at 6. Says Bracken had come to him with urgent message from W.S.C. that he must go to Spain *at once*. This quite contrary to what H. told me. I said if that was P.M.'s wish it must be done, and kept him on the hooks talking. About 6.45 H. returned from Cabinet and I went to see him. He said he had discussed matter at Cabinet and W.S.C. had told him to go slow for some days! So I put Sam into his room. They soon sent for me. Eventually H. said he would see W.S.C. We kicked Sam out and went over to Admiralty House. W.S.C. said he had sent *no* message to Sam, and rang for Bracken, who denied that *he* had. Dirty little dog has got the wind up and wants to get out of this country! However, they all want to be disembarrassed of him and agreed to send him out. This hard on Peterson† and difficult to arrange, but as long as I see the last of Sam, I don't care *what* happens. . . . News very bad—French won't fight. Can Weygand rally them? B.E.F. threatened with extinction. Cabinet instructed Gort to try to fight his way southwards along the coast.

* General Weygand. Recalled from the Levant to replace Gamelin as Commander-in-Chief. In June appointed Minister of National Defence in Marshal Pétain's Government.

† Sir Maurice Peterson, Ambassador at Madrid, 1939–40. It had already been decided in April, before there was any question of Hoare's appointment, that he should be replaced. Peterson, not knowing this, made no attempt to conceal a bitter conviction of ill-treatment.

Dined at home—late. Listened to Winston's broadcast. We must fight on, whatever happens. I should count it a privilege to be dead if Hitler rules England. I had not thought I should have to live through such awful days.

Monday, 20 May

Another glorious day. Only man is vile. Walked with H. and D[orothy, Lady Halifax] through Palace garden. H. wanted to talk about S. Hoare. I said there was one bright spot—there were lots of Germans and Italians in Madrid and therefore a good chance of S.H. being murdered. H. looked pained, but D. agreed heartily. Peterson came in about 11 and said Spaniards would certainly refuse—from fear—a 'Special Mission'. Cabinet 11.30. Pretty grim. Germans still driving on. See no hope of any counter-stroke.... S.H. and Lady Maud fussing around. I passed them on to poor Makins. Walking down the passage, to make conversation, I said 'It must be difficult for you, so suddenly, to adapt yourself to living in a new country.' She said 'It may be easier than to adapt oneself to living in an old country in new conditions'!!! That's it! The rats leaving the ship. The quicker we get them out of the country the better. But I'd sooner send them to a penal settlement. He'll be the Quisling of England when Germany conquers us and I am dead.

... Reports of French counter-attack, but doubt them, and all is confusion. Weygand *may* rally France. Léger gone.

Tuesday, 21 May

Cabinet at 11.30. Unfortunately W.S.C. began by saying situation more hopeful. Which resulted in a most awful tale of woe being unfolded. French Command are in complete confusion and helpless. C.I.G.S. who got back this morning, gave us an account. He (C.I.G.S.) had been blown out of bed by a bomb in Calais last night, but of course *that* hadn't affected him. He had found Billotte* completely foutu. Eventually he *shook* him, and he said B. seemed a little better after. He had then caught Weygand who was up in the North, and had denounced B. to him. There are masses of troops there, trained and with good material, but the command paralysed. *If* Weygand can get a grip, we may yet do something. Meanwhile German tanks galloping through Arras, Amiens, Abbeville, and all our stores gone! *What* a situation!... That little blighter S. Hoare at 5. He determined to fly out of this country as soon as he can get a plane. H.

* Gen. Billotte, commanding the First Group of Armies; killed in a car accident later this day.

asked me why he was in such a hurry. I said 'Because he's frightened.' H: 'You don't *really* think that?' I: 'I certainly do, he's the first rat to leave the ship.' And what the Hell can he do anyway in Spain? Brute.

... A miracle may save us: otherwise we're done. Reynaud told the truth to the Senate this afternoon. He made a generous reference to the R.A.F.—certainly merited.

Wednesday, 22 May

Cabinet 10.30. Winston had left at dawn for France. Neville in charge. Not much news—mainly because there is no co-ordination and no communications. What there is, is black as black. We put the Guards into Boulogne all right. ... Cabinet 7.30. Winston back. Pleased with his talks with Reynaud and Weygand. As regards latter, says he 'looks too young to be entrusted with so important a command'. W[eygand] *has* a plan. Counter-offensive should start tomorrow. But will the French fight? The command seems to have collapsed. C.I.G.S. says troops all right. But Dill* says they have never fought anywhere, and Ismay seems inclined to agree. Our fellows will probably fight—as it is their only chance of getting out! What an appalling situation. Cabinet this morning discussed legislation for this afternoon giving Government full powers over property and persons. This ought to have been done 12 months ago. ... I asked Newall this evening if he'd had a good day. He said his reports weren't all in yet —but so far we had bagged 7. 'The sort of stuff one gives away to the beaters—no good birds—Heinkels!'

Thursday, 23 May

Cabinet 11.30. News awful. Tanks galloping all round Etaples, Montreuil, Boulogne, Calais, Poperinghe, (!) &c. B.E.F. cut off from supplies. Weygand says he is putting in a counter-attack. But no signs of it, and without communications, I don't see how anything can be shaped [?] ... The public don't grasp the situation at all. Sam's agrément received—thank heaven. So we can get him out of the country in a few days. Good riddance of v. bad rubbish. He wasted a lot of my time. Corbin for exchange of news. I don't think he's more gloomy, really, than usual. Cabinet at 7, which I didn't attend. Don't know what they did. This morning we decided in principle to get out of Narvik and I hope to goodness we can do it successfully—

* Gen. Sir J. Dill, V.C.I.G.S.; succeeded Ironside as C.I.G.S. on 27 May. See List of Principal Characters.

wish we have never gone in. Maule Ramsay and Mosley* arrested! Quite right. But there are 1,000's of others who ought to be. . . . *If* Weygand can stage good counter-attack on flank attack in next 24 hrs, we *may* avert complete disaster. But that is all the time he has.

Friday, 24 May

Cabinet 11.30—pretty gloomy. Tanks galloping all over N.E. France. No news of counter-offensive. Dill sent over to Gort. Dunkirk still more or less open and we *may* get supplies and ammunition in to the B.E.F., but not likely! R.A.F. did as well as usual. . . . Van approached . . . with suggestion we should offer to discuss Mediterranean with Italy. I'm all for it—if it will stave off war with Italy for a few days. Ministry of Information had better news this evening—that gap between the armies had been reduced to 10 miles. But I don't know where they got it from, and no good news is true news.

[On 24 May the War Cabinet authorised Halifax to say that if Italy remained neutral, Britain would take account of 'reasonable' Italian claims at the peace conference, at which Italy would appear on an equal footing with the belligerents. Halifax was authorised on the next day to take immediate account of Italian claims, on the same conditions. This offer was put by Halifax to the Italian Ambassador on 25 May.[35]]

Saturday, 25 May

Cabinet 11.30. Just as gloomy as usual. Gort seems—inexplicably, rather—to have withdrawn 40 kms! But everything is complete confusion: no communications and no one knows what's going on, except that everything's as black as black. Boulogne taken, Calais heavily besieged. Dunkirk more or less open, and that's the only exit, for our B.E.F., if they can ever be extricated. Meanwhile they have little food and practically no munitions. If *only* that Great French Army could give them a smack on the flank, we should have defeated Hitler. They *may* be preparing something, but there is no sign of it, and I haven't heard of a Frenchman fighting anywhere. And every day that passes lessens our chances. . . . G. Lloyd at 3.30 with H. He agreed to try and overhaul S.I.S., which wants it *badly!* H. saw Bastianini at 5 and seemed to think his interview wasn't unsatisfactory. . . . G.J. came in with a conversation which seemed to show that H's conversation had raté completely. Sent him round to see H. G.J[ebb] rings me up 11.15 to say he has seen H. and

* Capt. A. H. M. Ramsay, M.P. 1931–45; interned 1940–44; and Sir O. Mosley, formerly a Labour Minister, now leader of the Fascist party in Britain.

subsequently Paresci.* Will give me report tomorrow morning. Stacks of work. What a bloody life!

[Paresci told Jebb that Lord Halifax's conversation with the Ambassador had left a bad impression by offering no concrete proposals. Immediate satisfaction of Italy's claims was called for. To this Jebb retorted that short of total defeat in war Britain would not hand over Gibraltar and Suez.]

Sunday, 26 May

Cabinet at 9. Reynaud coming over here for lunch. Plain that French are in very bad way. Letter from Spears† showing they are talking about capitulating. They say they have 50 Divisions against 150 and insufficient material. Bastianini came to see H. and me at 12. Nothing to be got out of him. He's an ass—and a timid one at that.... Cabinet at 2. W.S.C. gave us account of his conversation with Reynaud at lunch. R[eynaud] doesn't *say* that France will capitulate, but all his conversation goes to show that he sees no alternative. H. went over to talk to Reynaud at Admiralty. I went back to F.O. Summoned to Admiralty at 5. Found W.S.C., H., Neville, Greenwood and Attlee. Discussed situation. W.S.C. seemed to think we might almost be better off if France *did* pull out and we could concentrate on defence here. Not sure he's right. He against final appeal, which Reynaud wanted, to Muss.‡ He may be right there. Settled nothing much. W.S.C. too rambling and romantic and sentimental and temperamental. Old Neville still the best of the lot. I suggested *immediate* withdrawal of best troops and Bofors guns from Narvik. But this wasn't smiled on. Back at F.O. 6.30. H. saw Maisky. Soviet accept Cripps.§... Home 7.30. Walked in Chelsea with T. Told her more frankly what the situation is. She very brave and sensible. Dined at home and worked. It is a strain—daily and hourly looking the ugliest facts in the eye. A non-stop nightmare. God grant that I can go on without losing faith or nerve. But where to?

Monday, 27 May

Writing this on May 28th, I have rather forgotten sequence of events. Cabinet at 11.30—as gloomy as ever. See very little light anywhere.... Cabinet again at 4.30, which decided to dissuade Reynaud from making his panicky appeal to Italy.... Cabinet again at 10 until about 12. Position of B.E.F. quite awful, and I see no hope

* G. Paresci, press attaché at the Italian Embassy.

† Maj.-Gen. Sir Edward Spears. Churchill's personal representative with French Prime Minister.

‡ Reynaud wished to use Mussolini as an intermediary to obtain terms from Hitler.

§ As Ambassador in Moscow. See List of Principal Characters.

for more than a tiny fraction of them now that Belgium has capitulated. I urged 'no recrimination'. Only ray of light is our Air Force, which is marvellous. After the afternoon Cabinet H. asked W.S.C. to come out into the garden with him. H. said to me 'I can't work with Winston any longer.' I said 'Nonsense: his rhodomontades probably bore you as much as they do me, but don't do anything silly under the stress of that.' H. came to have tea in my room after. Said he *had* spoken to W., who of course had been v. affectionate! I said I hoped he really wouldn't give way to an annoyance to which we were all subject and that, before he did anything, he would consult Neville. He said that of course he would and that, as I knew, he wasn't one to take hasty decisions.

[Mussolini sent a hostile reply to an approach by Roosevelt. Cadogan noted on this document:

> of course Mussolini is not going to, and, in fact, dare not make any separate agreement with the Allies, even if he wanted to. He is simply wondering how much of the general 'share-out' he will be allowed by his 'Ally' to take, and whether he will ultimately get more, or less, by spilling Italian blood for it. We can't tell which way he will jump, but I hope we shan't delude ourselves into thinking that we shall do ourselves any good by making any more 'offers' or 'approaches'.[36]]

Tuesday, 28 May

Cabinet 11.30. Dill brought in unnamed British liaison officer, who left Belgium yesterday and paid tribute to their fighting and to the King. Silly old Roger Keyes also came, but he's stupid, sentimental and quite inarticulate. Prospects of B.E.F. look blacker than ever. Awful days! . . . Morton* at about 5.30, who hears from Monnet that Reynaud should be displaced by Weygand. Think this is possibly right. We ought to have direct contact with Weygand: we only get his views through Reynaud (and de Margerie†. . .). I agreed he should talk to W.S.C. and gave him copy of my letter to R. Campbell expressing my doubts. 6 sent for to H. of C. Discussion with W.S.C., H., Attlee, Greenwood, Sinclair and N.C. of reply to French about appeal to U.S. and approach to Italy. Neither are any use and product of panic. Corbin came and I told him about our decision. He, *personally*, agrees.

[On 28 May Ciano let Loraine see that Italy would soon enter the war. Afterwards, Halifax wondered whether it might not have been possible to

* Major Desmond Morton, Personal Assistant to Churchill.
† Now Private Sec. to Reynaud, Minister for Foreign Affairs.

bribe Mussolini; 'but I do not think we could ever have offered him enough to tempt him, and Loraine always disliked the idea of offering anything to Ciano. He never felt able to hand him £50,000 on the golf links.'[37]]

Wednesday, 29 May

Walked to F.O.—only sane moments I have. Everyone—principally G.J.—wanted me to see 100 people and read 1,000 long papers before 10.30. Can't be done and I reacted. Cabinet 11.30. News unpleasant. We have got off 40,000 men and taking them, at present, at rate of 2,000 an hr. But the end will be awful. A horrible discussion of what instructions to send to Gort. W.S.C. rather theatrically bulldoggish. Opposed by N.C. and H. and yielded to a reasonable extent. Fear relations will become rather strained. That is Winston's fault—theatricality. Discussion of what to do with ice-cream-vendors. Drown the brutes is what I should like to do. . . . Discussed evacuation of Narvik (which has been taken—at last!) with H., Sargent, Collier and Ismay. Very nasty. . . . H. rang me up about telegrams from Paris and Rome, but we agreed to consider tomorrow.

Thursday, 30 May

Corbin called with draft appeal to U.S. Silly! Cabinet 12.30. W.S.C. produced much better instructions to Gort, ordering him to come away before the end and giving some latitude about final capitulation. Squadron of Defiants* shot down 35 Germans with *no loss*! Marvellous! . . . Cabinet 5.30 till 8. We have got off 102,000 men—wonderful performance. Everything v. black, but there are signs of strain on the Germans too. . . . P.M. off to Paris tomorrow morning. French look like running out and putting blame on us. And he must hearten them and keep them in the fight or we must cut out and fight alone—and cut a good figure too, I hope. V. tired, but how these others—Chiefs-of-Staff, &c. stand up to it, I can't think.

Friday, 31 May

P.M. in Paris. Cabinet at 11.30. By noon, we had taken off 164,000 men—a miracle! Lunched at home. Went with Theo to choose rugs. Just as well to give away Treasury notes, which will be worth nothing, for goods of value! Discussion with O.S. and Collier about Narvik. Colban coming to see H. Luckily he had not spotted our defection! But telegrams from Dormer show that we must take Norwegians into

* Bolton-Paul Defiant; 2-seat fighter.

our confidence. So had a hurriedly scratched-up meeting of Cabinet at 5 and approved telegrams to Cork. . . . Corbin about 6.30—completely défaitiste—said French line couldn't hold and all their industry would be lost. French people must ask 'What can we hope?' I said 'Nothing' if they capitulated. But they *are* in a fix—quite helpless and no stomach for the fight. *I* think we'd be better without them. If we keep them in the fight, we've got to give them air protection and drain away our defences and so fall between two stools. Better say 'All right: if you can't stick it, get out or give in: We go on alone.' And *that* would bring in U.S. Well: we shall see what Winston brings back: it was questions like these that he was going to discuss frankly.

[Sir Ronald Campbell reported to the Foreign Office that Churchill had handled the French magnificently. At the end of the Supreme War Council's meeting he spoke of the implacable will of the British people to fight on to the bitter end and to go down rather than succumb to bondage. Reynaud responded in similar vein; 'but one felt that it came rather from his head than his heart'.[38]]

Saturday, 1 June

Cabinet 11.30. Evacuation marvellous. We have got off 224,000, including about 34,000 'Allies'. But a fearful strain on R.A.F. and Fleet—particularly in destroyers. Decided can't go on after tonight. W.S.C. and Attlee returned from France. They had had—superficially—satisfactory talks with French. But unless we pour in troops south of the Somme and give our whole Air Force, I foresee they'll do *nothing*. Gort came in at 1.20. Cabinet rose and greeted him and P.M. said 3 or 4 sentences very well. Gort then gave us a story of events for ¾ hr. French—with exception of Laurencie's* party—evidently worse than useless! Dreadful! I should like to be quit of them. Cabinet rose 2.15.

Sunday, 2 June

Cabinet 6.30. French howling for assistance on the Somme. Perhaps we should give them a token, but it's so much down the drain. It won't do any good—It won't prevent the French reviling us. I'd really sooner cut loose and concentrate on defence of these islands—come the 4 quarters of the world in arms! We should really be better off! Decision postponed for report of Chiefs of Staff. Labour members, Neville, H., and, I think, A. Sinclair, think with me. Sentimental Winston rather doubtful.

* Gen. B. L. de F. de La Laurencie, commanding two French divisions in the area of Dunkirk.

Monday, 3 June

Cabinet 11.30. Dowding* there and exposed the extent of the strain on R.A.F. fighters. Discussion as to reply to be sent to French appeal for help on Somme. Glad to say it was decided *not* to fall between two stools and not to send our fighter protection over to France. That would be fatal. . . . H. fiddling about with my draft message from King to Lebrun.† Left him to it.

Tuesday, 4 June

Cabinet 11.30. Discussed reply to French appeal. W.S.C. trying hard to send out fighters to help them. But they're *no use*. If I could see any sign of the French fighting I should take a risk. But they don't. And they ignored our 24 hour warning of raid on Paris yesterday, and the pilots were all at lunch! 40 machines on the ground, and 4 got off! But I'm afraid W.S.C. will have his way. A lecture by Ironside‡ on plans against invasion. He seems to be doing something.

Wednesday, 5 June

Cabinet put off until 12.30. German attack developing on Somme. Reynaud howling for all our fighters. W.S.C. had meeting with Air Staff, Dowding and Beaverbrook, but I don't know what passed. I do *hope* we're not uncovering ourselves to help a helpless France. Cabinet decided to stop Italian cargoes. Dalton v. offensive and got everyone's back up.

. . . King of Norway sent tiresome message. Preparing to do a 'Leopold'. Drafted reply urging him not to be an ass—or a traitor. Got it approved by W.S.C. and Neville.

. . . Corbin to plead for fighters and for 'setting Balkans alight'. A number of tiresome questions and everyone, including myself, rather short of temper.

Thursday, 6 June

Van has been made a Privy Councillor! What on earth for? he has now, by well-earned dismissal, achieved a G.C.B. and a P.C.!! Found H. this morning sealing up a lettter to Van—congratulating him, I suppose! H. *is* a queer fish.

A harassing morning—everybody wanting everything at once.

* Air Chief Marshal H. C. T. Dowding, A.O.C.-in-C. Fighter Command, 1936–40.

† Albert Lebrun, President of France, 1932–40.

‡ Now C.-in-C. Home Forces.

Cabinet 12.30. Attack on Somme seems to have been more or less held yesterday. But pretty weakly. Reynaud still howling for an Air Force, but, as far as I can gather, Winston hasn't quite given it yet. I'd like to see the French put up a much better show before I'd risk all to help them.

Friday, 7 June

Battle sways. Our Division (our only one!) has been badly knocked about—over a wide front.* French seem to be holding a bit better. Still howling for fighters. We had 144 in action for them yesterday, and should have more today, so they've no great cause for complaint. . . . About 7.30 Alexander came over about the 'Umbria'—the Italian ship with 5,000 tons of bombs which has got through the Canal. Agreed that she might be brought into Port Sudan for 'export control' and that we should try to bribe the Master to sink her before she gets to Massawah!

Saturday, 8 June

Cabinet at 10. French holding fairly well, but tricky situation on W. of line—where we are—in Havre-Rouen area. Cabinet discussed eternal question of denying supplies of oil to Germany and got not much further. I talked about it to Dalton after. He the 'new broom', talking of 'vigorous action'. Due to ignorance, and half to egotism. Back about 12 and H. went off to Yorkshire. . . .

Back after lunch to tackle masses of work. Asked 1st Sea Lord what had happened at Narvik. Seems we evacuated all right and got King and Government, &c., on board. . . . I am in conference with Ronnie C[ampbell] as to how to salve wreckage if France collapses. A depressing topic!

[Assessments of Germany's new economic position were drawn up in June and July. It appeared that despite stocks of oil and petrol captured in France, absence of an assured source of supply still constituted a weakness; and German plans for the invasion of the U.K. might even be diverted by attacks on oil supplies. The Cabinet agreed to practise this policy of bombing, or harming by sabotage, refineries, petrol dumps and communications.[39]]

Sunday, 9 June

Battle in France continues: German thrust to Rouen and Havre, but nothing catastrophic yet. . . . Cabinet 7. Looks as if 'Glorious'

* The 51st Highland Division, the 52nd Lowland Division, and the remnants of 1st Armoured Division were in France.

[aircraft-carrier] and at least one destroyer sunk. Otherwise Narvik party seem well set on way home. In France great pressure all along front, but nothing broken yet. General de Gaulle* came over to see P.M., who found him in good heart. Better telegram from Reynaud.

[General de Gaulle, then Under-Secretary for National Defence, brought an expression of the French Government's 'will to continue the struggle even, if need be, in the Empire': de Gaulle thought the Prime Minister unconvinced, for he refused further assistance in the air. He did undertake, however, to send to Normandy a Canadian division and to leave the 51st Highland Division in France.[40]]

Monday, 10 June

Pitch dark—and remained so all day. Walked round Park. F.O. at 10. H. back. Cabinet at 12.30. French more or less holding, but in reply to a question whether they will continue to do so, Dill blithely says 'No'. What fun! W.S.C. said he was going over to France after lunch, but subsequently cancelled it—largely, I suspect, because French Government are packing up and leaving [Paris] today.†...

6. Musso declared war. Am rather glad. Now we can say what we think of these purulent dogs. Fairly busy. Told Phillips (Admiralty) he could *forthwith* do what he liked. Corbin came in gloomy mood for chat. Old text—that we should put everything we have into the battle in France. I'm not at *all* sure.... Duff did a gorgeous broadcast at 9‡—saying *all* that he has been boiling to say for 2 years. Hope we can give the Italians an early and hard knock.

[When Ciano announced to the French Ambassador that Italy had declared war, François-Poncet replied 'The Germans are hard masters. You, too, will learn this.' Loraine, whom Ciano summoned next, did not bat an eyelid. He merely wrote down the formula, confirmed that it should be immediately effective, and withdrew.[41] He is supposed to have said from the doorway, 'I have the honour to remind Your Excellency that England is not in the habit of losing her wars.']

Tuesday, 11 June

Cabinet 12.30. Not much news as French G.Q.G. and Goverment have moved. But French seem to be holding pretty well. W.S.C. off to France again this afternoon.... Bastianini at 4 to protest against cutting off communications between Embassy and Consulates, and

* General Charles de Gaulle. See List of Principal Characters.

† For Briare, near Orléans.

‡ Duff Cooper, now Minister of Information, reviewed the Italians' martial record in unflattering terms.

against arrests of last night. I said I'd enquire about former (and got it put right). As regards latter, I said lessons of last few weeks had been taken to heart and we were not going to take any chances. He waxed indignant—said he would give me his word of honour that no Italian would engage in 5th Column activities; that if he had known of anyone doing so, he would have come round and told me at once. I said I would accept that, but would suggest that many things might be done without H.E.'s knowledge. He said that our action had come as a 'disagreeable surprise'. I said we had all had some disagreeable surprises in the last day or two. We parted courteously. . . . Dined at home. We should be bombing northern Italy now!

Wednesday, 12 June

Cabinet 11.30. Pretty gloomy. Haining* thinks Paris may not be entered for 24 hours. P.M. and A.E. still away but on their way back. Awful nightmare. . . . 3.15 Corbin to get news—he's completely cut off and I had not much to give him. . . . Cabinet 5.30 which I did not attend. Saw H. after, who said Winston had brought back news that French were evidently cracking. Well, if they must, let them crack and let us concentrate on our own defence and the defeat of Germany, instead of dribbling away to France all that we have that is good—and losing it. But what a look-out! God give us courage. Bombing attack on N. Italy last night a flop—owing to bad weather and French opposition!

Thursday, 13 June

H. rang up at 9 to say P.M. sent for by Reynaud and going over to France—wants H. and me to go with him. Got to F.O. 9.50 and told H. starting from Dorchester at 10. G.J. motored me there and we got to Hendon at 10.30. W.S.C. got up late and didn't turn up till 11. Flew in Flamingo with H. and Capt. Berkeley.† P.M., Beaverbrook and Ismay in other machine. Out to Weymouth, where saw a mined tanker being towed to the beach. Over Channel Islands and to Tours. Thunderstorm and rain as we arrived on pock-marked bombed aerodrome. No one expected us and I got hold of French A.F. officer who was very helpful and supplied cars to take us to Préfecture. Complete chaos. But managed to impress who we were. Préfet at last arrived and got Reynaud on telephone. Arranged to meet 3.45 and went off to lunch at a hotel. V. good lunch and W.S.C. in v. good

* Lt.-Gen. Sir Robert Haining, V.C.I.G.S.; Intendant-General, Middle East, 1941.
† Who acted as interpreter.

form. . . . Baudouin* arrived—a wet blanket. Préfecture at 3.45. R. [H.] Campbell turned up. Only Reynaud there for French. He said French army bust and asked us to release him from no-separate-peace-agreement.† He said he had been heartened by Roosevelt's message allowing publication of his appeal. So we said make another—last appeal, and meanwhile we won't answer your question. Spears and R.H.C. told me he hadn't been in this mood at noon. But old Pétain completely défaitiste—also Weygand: it's not *his* war. Reynaud improved later, but he's v. mercurial. Off the ground soon after 6. Landed Hendon about 8.30. Dined at home. Cabinet 10.45 till 1.15. Good message from Roosevelt which crossed Reynaud's last appeal. We sent appreciative message to Roosevelt, another to Reynaud saying he'd got all he wanted, and a message of solidarity from France to England. Home about 1.30. V. tired. Had about 5 hours in 'plane which *should* be restful—but rattling.

Dahlias being put in!

[During the meeting at Tours, Churchill had begged the French to fight on, in North Africa if need be. He launched into a magniloquent expression of faith, comradeship and resolution: 'We shall listen to no peace proposals emanating from Hitler. . . . The war will continue, and can but end in our destruction or our victory.'[42]

That evening he drafted the message which the Cabinet sent to France on 14 June:

> In this solemn hour for the British and French nations we renew to the French Republic our pledge and resolve to continue the struggle at all costs in France, in this island, upon the oceans, and in the air, wherever it may lead us, using all our resources to the utmost limit, and sharing together the burden of repairing the ravages of war.
>
> We shall never turn from the conflict until France stands safe and erect in all her grandeur, until the wronged and enslaved States and peoples have been liberated and until civilisation is free from the nightmare of Nazism. That this day will dawn we are more sure than ever. It may dawn sooner than we now have the right to expect.

For Fighter Command this last phase had the most serious implications. In their anxiety to sustain the French, Ministers had pressed Dowding until he became desperate. In ten days the Command had lost

* Paul Baudouin of the French Foreign Office; Foreign Minister, June–Oct. 1940.

† That is, the agreement reached by the Supreme War Council on 28 March that neither Britain nor France would negotiate or conclude an armistice or peace except by mutual agreement.

250 Hurricanes, which were coming forward at the rate of only two per day. When Britain's reserve had been drained away, would Hitler turn upon her and win the war? 'I don't mind telling you', Dowding said to Halifax with deep emotion, 'that when I heard of the French collapse I went on my knees and thanked God.'[43]]

Friday, 14 June

Germans entering Paris. Everything as black as black. Even Turks running out. . . . Censor at 7.30 said message intercepted to effect that Pétain has formed a Government. If true, that means capitulation and all lost.

Saturday, 15 June

Cabinet at 10. French army seems to have disintegrated. After, Neville brought up proposal—which he didn't think much of (nor I) —for fusion of British and French Governments—I had meanwhile drafted telegram to Bordeaux, suggesting French Government should come here. That is the most practical step. Draft approved. I broke away at lunchtime—I've had 10 weeks non-stop and it's too much, almost, even for me! . . . Went out in a deluge of rain and picked peas and dug potatoes for our dinner, which was excellent. Did some writing after, but won't look at work! Everything *awful*, but 'Come the three corners of the world and we will shock them'. We'll all fight like cats—or die rather than submit to Hitler. U.S. look pretty useless. Well, we must die without them.

V

June 1940–May 1941
A YEAR ALONE

Seven generations earlier, the first Earl Cadogan had been the principal Staff Officer and Director of Intelligence in ten campaigns to Mr Churchill's most illustrious ancestor. 'Nothing', wrote Churchill in his *Marlborough*, 'disturbed his fidelity to his chief or the mutual comprehension between them.'[1] On the eve of a battle in Flanders, Marlborough reconnoitred the positions. He threw down his glove, and then told Cadogan harshly to pick it up, which, to the general's amazement, he did at once. That night, when Marlborough said that he wished the main battery set up at the place where he dropped the glove, Cadogan was able to reply 'It is there now', for he had realised by intuition the purpose of the supposed insult. Seeing Alec Cadogan and Winston Churchill together, as they listened to the agonising tale at Tours on Thursday, 13 June 1940, Sir Edward Spears was reminded of that story:

> Now here were the descendants of the two great leaders, brought together as their forebears had been by virtue of the services their Houses have rendered, generation after generation, to the country. Later, recalling this scene, I thought how fortunate England has been to be served through the centuries by such men, and by others imbued with the same transcendent loyalty, though bearing lesser names. At that moment it was only the old story of the Flanders battlefield that flashed in my mind, a vivid picture, as I watched the two men in that small room at Tours.[2]

Cadogan's dismay at Churchill's accession to the Premiership, however oddly it may read now, was widely shared in Whitehall. It did not last long with many, and certainly not with Sir Alec, who quickly came to place Churchill in a class apart from any other statesmen he ever served. An entry from his diary in March 1940, already quoted in the previous chapter, refers to Churchill's suspicions of him. Probably they did not amount to very much. Cadogan was identified to some degree with the policies of 1938 and 1939; and the Prime Minister generally cared little for diplomats, whom he thought inclined to give themselves airs for no particular cause and in some instances to owe their positions to the operation of Buggins' turn, or for the F.O. as an institution, which he thought slow-moving, apt to search for smart paper solutions and to hedge its bets. 'If you want a line of policy from a F.O. memorandum' he would say, 'you must send either the paragraphs with even numbers or those with odd numbers. Every alternate paragraph begins "On the other hand...."' To his private secretaries he would often abuse the Foreign Office. One of them, Jock Colville, remarked that he had been equally hard on the Treasury. Which did he dislike the more? 'The War Office' said Churchill.[3]

It was therefore of particular importance that the influence of so masterful and imperious a Prime Minister, deeply interested in foreign affairs, should be moderated and balanced. 'Always stand up to him' said Halifax. 'He hates doormats. If you begin to give way he will simply wipe his feet upon you.'[4] Happily for the Foreign Office and for the Allied war effort, neither Halifax nor Eden nor Cadogan was in the least inclined to grovel to the Prime Minister. In the result, the Foreign Office preserved a much stronger position during the Second World War than under Lloyd George in the First. The fear that Churchill would recreate something analogous to his 'Garden Suburb', (Cadogan's entry for 11 May 1940), soon proved illusory. Eden, in particular, had a special relationship of confidentiality and affection with Churchill, despite an age-gap of twenty-three years. As Churchill records, they thought alike on many issues, even without consultation; and being by nature tough and tenacious, the Foreign Secretary was very often able to get his own way in the long run. As for the Permanent Under-Secretary, Churchill soon exempted him from his strictures upon the Office at large. They had moved in the same social milieu all their lives; Alec Cadogan was entirely fearless, straightforward and loyal; he could not be bullied, he clearly knew his business and he had neither reason nor desire to curry favour. 'What a privilege it has been', he recorded on the night of Churchill's death, 'to have served him during his grandest period, and to have won, as I dare to think that I did, some regard and even affection from him.'

Reflecting upon his relations with Churchill, Cadogan took down his copy of the Alanbrooke diaries and said: 'Here is a passage which struck a chord with me. After a row Winston declared that Brookie hated him and must be sacked. Pug Ismay, as usual, went along to make the peace; and Brooke replied "I don't hate him, I love him; but when the day comes that I tell him he is right when I believe him to be wrong, it will be time for him to get rid of me." That was my motto too, both with Winston and with Anthony.'

* * *

As soon as it was clear that France would capitulate within a few days, the Russian Government sent an ultimatum to Lithuania, and then to Latvia and Estonia. Invasion followed. Bogus elections were set up. Shortly afterwards Russia formally annexed these states. The Soviet Government sent its warmest congratulations on the 'splendid success' of the German armies in France before presenting, on 26 June, an ultimatum to Roumania. Bessarabia and Northern Bukovina were taken on the next day.

Cadogan was cultivating the garden of his cottage while Ministers and their advisers agreed in London to propose a Franco-British union, providing for common citizenship, a single War Cabinet, unified command of all armed forces and joint organs of foreign, defence and financial policy. This document, telegraphed to France on 16 June, came too late to save Reynaud and would probably have made little difference anyway. Cadogan was not alone in feeling much relief that it never became operative.

Very soon, General de Gaulle was left as the standard-bearer of free France. At this stage he was for the British a mysterious figure. 'I can't tell you anything about de Gaulle' said Cadogan to Foreign Office colleagues after their first meeting at 10 Downing Street, 'except that he's got a head like a pineapple and hips like a woman.' Soon he knew a good deal more than that, for the relationship between the U.S.A., Britain and the Free French occupied more time at high level and over a longer period than any other issue of foreign policy in the war except, perhaps, that of Poland. There stood de Gaulle, self-identified with the historic greatness of France and pledged to its revival, owing everything to Britain and disliking the fact; and Churchill, sometimes lost in admiration of his resolution and aggressive spirit, more often irritated at his bad manners and tiresomeness, or furious because de Gaulle kept playing into the hands of his American opponents and sowing discord between Prime Minister and President. 'I know that there can be, and indeed are, Frenchmen who do not like the British', he once said to a sulky de Gaulle. 'They have a perfect right to their opinion; mais ce ne sont pas les Français que je recherche.'[5] For his part de Gaulle felt among those with whom he dealt in Britain, whether Ministers, military leaders, businessmen, officials, journalists or whatever, an enviable loyalty and assurance, a community of aims. To resist the British machine

> when it set itself in motion to achieve something, was a severe test. Without having experienced it oneself, it is impossible to imagine what a concentration of effort, what a variety of procedures, what insistence, by turns gracious, pressing and threatening, the English were capable of deploying in order to obtain satisfaction.[6]

* * *

On the night of 15 June, heart-warming messages reached 10 Downing Street from Australia and New Zealand. Both offered their unconditional support. 'If H.M. Government in the United Kingdom decide to fight on,' said the telegram from Wellington, 'we pledge this Dominion to remain with them to the end, and we are confident this policy is unchangeable in the Dominion . . . whatever the decision . . . in these most difficult circumstances, it will be understood, accepted and supported by us to the end.' Mr Churchill replied at 3.30 a.m.: 'I am deeply touched by your message, which is only in keeping with all that the Mother Country has ever received in peace or war from New Zealand.'[7]

And later in the day he sent a telegram to his fellow Prime Ministers in the four Dominions:

> I do not regard the situation as having passed beyond our strength. It is by no means certain that the French will not fight on in Africa and at sea, but, whatever they do, Hitler will have to break us in this Island or lose the war. . . . We shall let you know at every stage how you can help, being assured that you will do all in human power, as we for our part, are entirely resolved to do.

1940

Sunday, 16 June

G.J. rang up—as he always does—to say awful things were happening which he couldn't tell me on the telephone. Just to 'warn' me. Fat lot of good *that* does! 4.45 Mallet rang up. Could I come up at once*: I should be wanted to leave 'on a sea trip tonight'. So packed and had hurried tea and started 5.20. Car behaved splendidly and we got home 7.5. G.J. and H. arrived. Orders are to leave with Winston, Attlee, A.E. and Chiefs of Staff from Waterloo 9.40. Embark in 'Galatea' midnight for Concarneau, or some point on coast of Brittany, to meet Reynaud. Packed and dined. But at 8.50 F.O. rang up to say trip off. 9.30 rang up to say trip on again. (I had kept my bag ready packed!). Jumped into taxi and got to Waterloo at 9.55. Found special waiting, but P.M. had just gone back again to No. 10. So came home. Cabinet offices warn me to be at a moment's notice. Life rather like that of a fireman. (Only with no hope of putting out the fire!). Got into bed and at about 11.45 Cabinet Offices rang up to say Reynaud resigned and Pétain formed a Government. There might be a Cabinet meeting—would I stand by. I said I would 'lie by', in bed—turned out the light and went to sleep!

Monday, 17 June

Pétain Government formed and P. broadcast at 12.30 ordering France to cease fighting. Cabinet 11. Pretty gloomy. No news of French fleet. Darlan assures us it will never be surrendered (and P. later confirmed this to Ronnie C. But I don't know!). Sent off telegram of reproach and urging again that fleet must be kept out of German clutches. . . . Drogheda came in with suggestion that all

* From the cottage.

ships for France be diverted. Went over to P.M. and H. and got their approval and told Pound. No news from France. Tape says Hitler and Musso meeting to decide on terms. What a nightmare! It will almost be a relief when we are left alone to fight the Devil, and win or die. Dined at home. About 11 p.m. summoned by P.M. Found him storming at Corbin—who was singing in chorus. P.M. had a scorching message to Pétain and Weygand. I tried to tone it down a bit, but failed. So sent it off. Showed him a snorter which I had drafted, but he wouldn't read, but he said 'send it off at once. minutes count'. So off it went. Home about 1.

[Churchill's message expressed his profound conviction that Pétain and Weygand would not deliver the French Fleet to Germany. 'Such an act would scarify their names for a thousand years before history.']

Tuesday, 18 June

Cabinet 12.30. Winston not there—writing his speech. No reply from Germans: French situation still uncertain. Can't get them absolutely tied up about their fleet. . . . Morton came over with a scheme of Monnet's for a declaration of help to France if she continued resistance overseas. Corbin came later, with obviously the same idea. It's not a bad one. He is sending Monick* today or tomorrow to Bordeaux and wants M. to take such a message. Got S. of S's blessing in principle and sent for Morton to get P.M.'s approval. Dined at home. P.M. sent for me at 10.30 (hope this won't become a habit). H. told me he had approved Monnet idea and that the 2 M's were going tomorrow and G. Lloyd with them. I think this all right, though idea of G.L. going was raised by H. at Cabinet this morning and didn't create a furore. P.M. incensed with Belgians. Calmed him down a bit and told him what I'd already done. Beaverbrook came in. Left P.M. orating to him and home about 12. 2.30 a.m. Newall rang me up to know whether he should make special arrangements to fly Bonavista† to Bordeaux. Never heard of him. Went to sleep again.

Wednesday, 19 June

Told H. about the Bonavista worry, the de Gaulle broadcast, &c. Told him this can't go on. No. 10 Hall is like behind the scenes at the circus and every crank in the world is getting hold of P.M. and getting half-baked decisions. I won't go on unless this is stopped. H. talked to

* E. G. M. Monick, financial attaché at Washington, 1930–4; London, 1934–40.

† Col. Bonavista, French Military Mission in London, who was sent out to persuade 'technicians, soldiers and pilots' to join de Gaulle in London.

P.M. who apparently agreed. Anyhow result is that Spears humbly sends me draft of another broadcast by de Gaulle. I said it must cease and rang up Duff, who agreed. Air raid last night over eastern England—singularly and suspiciously ineffective. . . . P.M. sent for me at 10.30 to discuss Swedish destroyers. Beaverbrook, Pound and Phillips. Home 11.45.

Thursday, 20 June

Cabinet 12. Another air raid last night—did a bit more damage, but not much. Long discussion of Eire. Neville made proposals that looked like coercion of N. Ireland. W.S.C. opposed in passionate speech. . . . 3.15 Spears and de Gaulle. Explained to latter why I thought he should keep quiet* until situation clears. He accepted that and said that, if he was convinced that Weygand was organising resistance overseas, he would be first to offer his services. Meeting at 5. about Russia. Don't believe she is doing more than assure her own *defence*. 6.30 Corbin . . . He pressing request that we should drop food for troops in Alsace. But this, of course, really silly and only have propaganda value. However, I rang up Newall about it. . . . No circus at No. 10 tonight—thank God! French envoys have been to Tours to get German terms. French Government to Perpignan prepared, apparently, to go to N. Africa.

Friday, 21 June

Corbin came in afternoon, and S. of S.—cowardly—laid on me task of telling him (1) we *won't* feed his troops in Alsace from the air (2) we won't let the French gold go from Halifax to Martinique and (3) we maintain most of our restrictions on French shipping. Corbin says this will create v. bad impression. And so it may—but nothing like so bad as that which greater events will inevitably create. Corbin went after to see P.M. and sent me a very snotty note. But I can't help it. Lots of work and tiresome interruptions. 8.30 [R. H.] Cross rang me up—evidently pressure is being brought on him to release French ships, on ground that it will 'make all the difference' to the French 'decision' (? on the armistice terms). Of course it won't. Told him so.

Saturday, 22 June

Don't remember what happened (writing on 23). I have had a most scarifying 48 hrs. Cabinet in morning. . . . To F.O. at 5.10. Every sort of fuss and bother. Dined hurriedly 8.30. Cabinet 9.30.

* That is, not broadcast for the moment.

Proposed to send Phillips and G. Lloyd to Africa. Cabinet adjourned about 12.30. Home 12.45. Bridges rang up to say I was to draft 'instructions' for G.L. who is now not starting till tomorrow. (Weather in any case hopeless). But what do they want him to be instructed to do?! Went to bed at 1. Everyone all over the place and W.S.C. endorses any wild idea.

Sunday, 23 June

At F.O. 9.40. Could not draft 'instructions' to G. L[loyd]. Could only put down *questions* as to what our policy *is*. Winston hadn't thought of that! Cabinet (at 10) came to conclusion idea of sending G.L. half-baked. After Cabinet—about 12.15—P.M., Neville, H. and I saw de Gaulle and agreed on declaration he should broadcast tonight, with corresponding declaration by H.M.G., about formation of 'National Committee'. He is to go away and consult and report later. . . . Masses of worries which H. wanted to discuss in his slow way. Spears and de Gaulle arrived about 7, when H. had gone to the King. After a tussle got de G. to alter his declaration, taking out names—in particular *his*. H. back at 8 and got him to agree declarations by 8.30. Made all arrangements for broadcasting with C. Peake. Monnet called, to urge de G. idea all wrong! Back about 9. Began dinner. 9.15 Van rang up from his country retreat to say he had Corbin and Léger with him and de G. must change his broadcast! He had rung up H. (dining with O. Stanley) who agreed, and said P.M. must be consulted. I said how the Hell could this be done before 10? Tried to ring up H. but couldn't get through, so got in taxi and caught him. I said we couldn't change our minds every 5 mins. There were only 2 alternatives:—Deny B.B.C. to de Gaulle, or let it rip. He favoured latter, and I got him to ring Van and tell him so. Came home to dine and stacks of work, only a part of which could I tackle. I've never been so nearly driven *mad*.

[General de Gaulle said that the French National Committee would account to the legal French Government, when one existed, or to the representatives of the French people when conditions allowed them to assemble. The British Government announced that it would deal with the Committee, so long as it represented all French elements resolved to fight Nazism, on all matters concerned with the prosecution of the war.]

Monday, 24 June

An awful day—which I can't well remember. 3 Cabinets—at 10, 6 and 10.30. Most of the time discussing the awful problem of the French fleet. And we didn't get much further. . . . I dictated a draft communication to the French about the Fleet. This discussed by Cabinet, who jigged it about, but didn't decide to do anything with it. Adjourned 1.15 a.m. and air raid warning sounded. Went over with H. to F.O. War Room, where we remained until 4.15! Very boring.

Tuesday, 25 June

A bit tired. 9 a.m. Alec H[ardinge] rang me up—said King wanted to see me at 10. Presented myself, and found H.M. fussed by reports that that wicked old King of Sweden* is intriguing with Hitler to depose Haakon and put in the grandson with a Regency. Haakon—and Olaf†—came in. I promised to draft a message from H.M. to Gustav. Which, on return, I did—or gave instructions to O. Sargent to do it. Dull Cabinet, who wouldn't face up to communication to French about Fleet (but Winston used most of it in his statement to Commons). Quiet afternoon, thank Heaven!

[Churchill said that the new French Government had been informed that the indispensable condition for their release from the obligation to make no separate peace had not been met. He had read Article 8 of the armistice (whereby the French fleet would be demobilised under German or Italian control in specified ports) with grief and amazement. The British Government would not now state their policy; but 'neither patience nor resolution will be lacking in any measures they may think it right to take for the safety of the Empire'.]

Wednesday, 26 June

Having washed my hands of de Gaulle—Van having butted in and I having handed de Gaulle over to him—I now find that Van is getting into difficulties with him and wants me to take him back again. Not on your life! I told Van he must now see it through. So like him to want to shuffle it off directly it begins to get difficult! And he is boxing the compass—one day for de G. and the next against. I'll have nothing more to do with it.

R. Campbell dined and we had a long talk. He left about 10.45, when I had to get down to work. Had a lovely 8 hour sleep last night—v. tired after the night before. These air-raid warnings are almost worth it if they make one so tired. Autumn crocuses cut down today.

Thursday, 27 June

Drove back to F.O. with H. He had been told by P.M. that he

* King Gustav V of Sweden.

† Prince Olav of Norway, later King Olav V.

must have a flat in F.O., so wanted to inspect rooms 'at once'. Everybody wants everything done 'at once'. But owing to limitations of time and space, impossible to do more than one thing at a time.

Friday, 28 June

A regular bear-garden. Everyone wanting everything at once. Dalton ringing up hourly to try to get a large finger in the Sabotage pie. I wrote a minute on it last night, which S. of S. must see first. I also wrote him (S. of S.) a broadcast for Sunday. I am now told it's not wanted. Cabinet at 12. Nothing of much interest. . . . War Cabinet at 5.30 to which I didn't go. In future I go only on Mondays and Thursdays. Sorry not to watch it from day to day, but it *does* take up an awful lot of time and make life almost impossible. They seem to have discussed an Anglo-French landing at Casablanca—which is one of the few good ideas of recent times.

De Gaulle came to see H. this afternoon and I was present. I am still not impressed. But his main point was sound: 'I ought to get on to French territory (N. Africa). If I go there now, I am arrested and "supprimé". Let me raise a "troupe" here and then I will land.' Maybe something in it. Anyhow he is the only hope—I see no other.

Saturday, 29 June

Cabinet at 10. W.S.C. at Chequers, so we got through by about 11.15. . . . T. and I drove to Park and sat and read. Quite peaceful. Then walked a bit in the middle of the Park, but it is parched and seared with guns and trenches—beastly. . . . Meinertzhagen* came round to talk to H. and me about blocking the Park Door. He is very gloomy on easy possibility of German descent upon London. I am not terribly impressed: I think it must be more difficult than he makes out. Report from A.E. of a tour in Sussex and Kent, which certainly makes it seem that the Germans can take a penny steamer to the coast and stroll up to London!

. . . Certainly everything is as gloomy as can be. Probability is that Hitler will attempt invasion in next fortnight. As far as I can see, we are, after years of leisurely preparation, completely unprepared. We have simply got to die at our posts—a far better fate than capitulating to Hitler as these damned Frogs have done. But uncomfortable.

Monday, 1 July

This is the zero hour for Hitler's invasion of England—the actual date favoured by the tipsters being about 8 July. Lovely day. Walked

* Col. Richard Meinertzhagen, W.O. 1939–40; Home Guard, 1940–5.

to F.O. Cabinet 11.30. Not v. interesting. Have sunk 3 more Italian submarines, which is good. They surrender before they are really hurt!

3.30 meeting with H., Hankey, G. Lloyd, Dalton, D.M.I. and 'C' about Sabotage, &c. Quite useful, and I hope we'll get it on a proper footing, with both drive and control. Hungarian at 6. He sounded me on peace negotiation rumours. I assured him, both personally and officially, that there was no sort of foundation at all.

[In Madrid, Sir S. Hoare found Germans everywhere, the influence of the Embassy minimal and its machinery hopeless, and enemy influence in command of the press. The Foreign Minister, Colonel Beigbeder, spoke to him of the great but platonic sympathy between Spaniards and Italians:

> Look round and tell me whether you see any signs of Spain going to war. If we had wished to go to war we should have been making preparations since last September. . . . You will find quantities of evidence that we are lacking in all the essentials for carrying on a campaign.[8]]

Tuesday, 2 July

H. fractious. Very frightened by a howl from Sam [Hoare] about our admitting Negrin* here. I said I was responsible (I first obtained assent to his admission last Nov.). He was fractious about that. I said 'all right: turn him out.' But that, if you please, would annoy Attlee, of whom he's almost equally frightened. What cattle these politicians are! And what moral cowards. Very annoyed with him: and he's becoming slow and tired and havery. . . . H. fussing about his bloody Flat in F.O. which he wants *at once*. Hell: and it's a *frightful* inconvenience and can't be done at once. . . . The Pope is making tentative half-baked suggestions for agreement. Silly old H. evidently hankering after them.

Wednesday, 3 July

Should have been one of my days off from the Cabinet, but I was summoned about 12.30. I don't know why—except that H. shoved under my nose a pencil note 'Note to French'. Cabinet were discussing something quite different—control of spiders, or something—but I got to work on a draft note to French explaining why we were blowing their fleet out of the water. 1.30 heard Cambon was still waiting to see me. Went back and saw him. He delivered a formal protest against seizure of French ships in British ports. Argued that it

* Formerly Prime Minister of Republican Spain.

was silly, as it would ensure that other French ships in French ports would now obey Bordeaux. Couldn't tell him that we had taken measures to see that they did not. Was present (5.15) at similar meeting between H. and Corbin, on the same unreal basis, and with the same limitations on us. Got to work drafting reply to Cambon's protest. Heard, about 8.15, that battle at Oran had broken out. . . . H. picked me up 9.25 and we went to see Winston. He approved note to French. Lot of talk. Got note in final shape and signed by H. at midnight. G.J. and I dropped it at French Embassy.

[The French fleet was mainly disposed at (a) Portsmouth, (b) Alexandria, (c) Oran and Mers-el-Kebir, where lay the two modern battle-cruisers, *Dunkerque* and *Strasbourg*, two battleships, cruisers and smaller vessels. On 3 July, Operation 'Catapult' was implemented: the seizure or destruction of all accessible French ships. Vice-Admiral Sir James Somerville gave the French at Oran an ultimatum; 'Surrender, scuttle your ships or be sunk.' Only *Strasbourg* escaped, to Toulon. The French Admiral Godefoy's ships at Alexandria were immobilised. Most of the French vessels at Portsmouth were taken without fighting.]

Thursday, 4 July

Result of naval operations yesterday not too good, but Winston was able to make good enough showing in House and had a good reception. H. had to make statement in Lords, with which I helped him. Discussion of Jap demands with H[orace] Seymour and Ashley C[larke]. I am convinced we must stand out against closing of Burma Road, even at risk of war. If we give way, Americans will give us up, with hopeless results, not only in Pacific but also on this side.

[On 19 June Craigie had reported from Tokyo, not unexpectedly, a stiffening of Japanese demands. The Director of Military Intelligence had said that the Japanese felt they would 'earn the obloquy of their descendants' if they failed to avail themselves of the opportunities now open. In more concrete terms, Britain must close the Burma Road, the frontier at Hong Kong and the military establishment at Shanghai.[9] On 28 June Cordell Hull told Lothian that the U.S. could do nothing effective. It would be better to retreat, while refusing irrevocable concessions. How the two parts of this policy were to be reconciled he did not vouchsafe. The political effect of closing the Burma Road might well be more serious than the material, and Chiang might feel obliged to make terms with Japan.[10]

This business was argued at several Cabinets. Broadly speaking, the Chiefs of Staff were throughout in favour of yielding; so were Churchill, Chamberlain and Lloyd, on the time-honoured grounds that Britain could not afford to fight Japan as well as Germany and Italy. That argument was, of course, much reinforced now that the French fleet could not hold the Mediterranean. Halifax and Cadogan judged that Germany was trying to embroil Britain with Japan and that it would simply play her game to give way.[11]]

Friday, 5 July

Further discussion with H. about Burma Road. Feel stronger than ever that we should not give way. Quite apart from Chinese feelings, if we do, the Americans—or a large section of opinion—will say 'the English are beat anyway'. And we don't want that. Cabinet at 12 and Winston took the wrong turning, dwelling on all the inconvenience of war with Japan. Well, we all see that, even if we *do* believe that Japan will declare war (which I still beg leave to doubt). But if they *do*, what shall we lose, and how shall we weigh that against what we may gain? However, none of these feeble Labour champions of China spoke up, except, to some extent, Alexander. Support from Amery* and Duff [Cooper], but that's hardly good enough. No decision—told to explore some half-way house. Don't mind doing that, but it's hopeless to do as Winston suggested—try to put the U.S. on the spot. They simply won't stand there.

. . . Discussion with H., H. Seymour and Ashley Clarke of new draft to Tokyo. Eventually approved—not too bad—H. had further talk with P.M. on the subject. . . . Winston had a triumph in the House yesterday on French fleet. What funny people we are! Of course it was right and vital, but I should have thought there might have been a more regretful tinge in it. It was very necessary, but it was *not* pleasant! Like having a tooth out.

Saturday, 6 July

Cabinet at 10. Rather a rush to pack H. off with the right stuff. He got back about 12 and we settled final form of telegrams to Tokyo about Burma Road. Glad to say we *don't* surrender, but temporise. And later, telegram came in from Washington, showing that was exactly what Hull asked of us.

[Craigie was told to explore the possibilities of a negotiated settlement. Halifax again suggested to the War Cabinet that Japan would not risk total war if her demands were refused, though she would probably blockade Hong Kong. Craigie, admitting that further demands would follow, nevertheless favoured acquiescence. The Japanese Foreign Minister refused to compromise.]

* L. S. Amery, Secretary of State for India and Burma, 1940–5.

Monday, 8 July

Poor Corbin at 10.30 about French breaking off relations.... Nothing much doing. We are still awaiting—and I hope preparing for—invasion. The lull betokens awful happenings! Dined at home and worked.

Tuesday, 9 July

Telegrams coming in from Craigie, and they are no worse than I expected. I still believe there's a good element of bluff in their attitude.... We seem to have damaged the 'Richelieu', but I can't make out how much. An engagement with the Italian fleet, but they ran.... On way back from lunch met Miss X—employed at No. 10 since Lloyd George's days. Asked her about present turbulent conditions of work. She described Winston's late meetings as the 'Midnight Follies!'

Wednesday, 10 July

Nothing much of interest. Work has slackened off. I hope this is not merely an ominous lull, but really means that with the disappearance of so many countries we wretched diplomats don't have to make such a tale of strawless bricks.... 3.15 meeting on Far East. Cabinet, led by Winston, evidently bent on surrender. That is easier, but I think it's wrong.... Not much work. Only a stream of telegrams about Turkey and the Balkans, which I can *not* understand. These esoteric speculations as to the backstairs intrigues of that deplorable part of the world are quite beyond my comprehension, and I'm afraid I ignore them.

Thursday, 11 July

6. meeting with H., N.C. and Attlee about Sabotage, &c. P.M. (put up to it by Morton) is against Dalton taking over and wants to lump the whole thing under Swinton.* This sloppy: we want to get someone to take a grip on Sabotage, &c. and pull it into shape. *I* think Dalton the best man. And the meeting agreed to recommend this. With Van as his Chief of Staff! Mightn't be bad, *if* Van will get down to a job of work, which I doubt. Otherwise M. Peterson would be best.

Not much work—it really has eased off. Will Hitler invade? I, personally, doubt it, but would never say so. Every day he gives us is a gain. Convoy came in on July 9 with 250,000 rifles (with ammunition) and over 300 75's.

[Until the Special Operations Executive was established, 'irregular

* Viscount Swinton, Air Minister, 1935–8.

projects' had been initiated by the Director of Military Intelligence, or by his naval counterpart the D.N.I., or by S.I.S., which executed them. The Minister of Economic Warfare accepted with relish the task of co-ordinating this ungentlemanly warfare. 'Set Europe ablaze' said Churchill. This was easier to command than to achieve. Indeed, if Dalton's diaries and papers are to be taken at face value, he sometimes came nearer to setting Whitehall ablaze. The purpose of S.O.E. was to exploit every means of making the enemy uncomfortable: strikes, propaganda, terrorism, riots, boycott and bribery. This programme, Dalton told Halifax rather gratuitously, could not be executed by ordinary departmental machinery.[12] Cadogan gave up Gladwyn Jebb to the new organisation, Henry Hopkinson replacing him as Private Secretary. Rex Leeper took charge of 'black propaganda'. This arrangement was probably the best that could be made at the time. The clandestine activities of S.O.E., sometimes needing the support of the armed services and usually carrying political implications, were bound to produce frictions with other departments.[13] Cadogan did much to reduce them. He had not Halifax's moral objections to many of the strokes which S.O.E. wished to bring off. ('You'll never make a gangster', said George Lloyd with feeling to the Foreign Secretary.) Though he did not believe that the activities of S.O.E., even if wildly successful, could have a decisive effect, Cadogan tried by frequent consultation with Jebb, and by intervention within the Office, to ensure that S.O.E. was not blocked at every turn. 'Whenever I try to destroy anything anywhere', lamented Dalton, 'I am caught in some diplomatic trip wire'[14]; to which Cadogan might justly have retorted that S.O.E. nevertheless achieved a good deal and would have made many more mistakes but for the Foreign Office's restraint.]

Friday, 12 July

Quo* at 5.45. Difficult interview. He came for 'enlightenment' on various points arising out of his talk with H. yesterday, when latter broke it to him that we were ratting over Burma Road.

Saturday, 13 July

Cabinet at 10. Stymied Dalton from declaring all French goods 'enemy exports'. (He was doubtless trying to rush this through in H's absence!). . . Discussed Far East with R.A.B. and others. Craigie has given away 110%. I was always against it. We've been bluffed. But it was Winston who resolutely refused to call it. Simopoulos† at 6 to protest against our sending a tanker into Cretan ports, which has resulted in Ice-creamers bombing Greek ships. Really! I asked him what representations his Government were making in Rome!

* Quo Tai-chi, Chinese Ambassador.

† Greek Minister in London.

Sunday, 14 July

Winston rang up in rather a flap about Far East. Feared that, by boggling over trifles, we might lose agreement. Told him I didn't think so, as agreement gave Japanese *all* they wanted. There were a few 'trifles' that we *must* boggle over. Japanese are showing up in their true colours which used, proverbially and practically, to be worn by the Dutch . . . Winston sent me script of his broadcast for tonight. All right, except in one point of detail, which I corrected. . . .

Winston at Cabinet told us of his inspection of the coastal area and was optimistic. Some discussion of tea ration, and a discussion of this topic, between Winston and A. Greenwood, can be *quite* dispassionate!

Monday, 15 July

H. back and he havered for a bit about F[ar] E[ast]. His havering is becoming an ingrained—and very disastrous—habit.

[Hull, forewarned by Lothian that the Burma Road might be closed, expressed 'much regret and disappointment . . . , not only on account of the blow that would result to China in the general contest with Japan, but on account of the interest this Government, engaged as it is in international commerce, has in seeing all arteries and channels of trade kept open.' This offered nothing; and Britain agreed to close the road until 18 October, that is for the rainy season only.

A new Japanese Government took office in July. Its Foreign Minister, Matsuoka, declared with candour to Craigie that Japan was 'determined, and in fact compelled by circumstances, to set up a new order in the Far East'. Since Great Britain was resisting, it was difficult to see how a 'fundamental clash of interests and purpose could be avoided'.[15]]

Tuesday, 16 July

Gloomy conferences with H., R.A.B. and the F[ar] E[ast] Department about our far eastern surrender to Japan (insisted on by Winston). Trying to dress up public statement, but, as I said, it's like trying to walk an invisible tightrope in a dark room.

Wednesday, 17 July

More tiresome conferences on F.E.—making bricks not only without straw but also without clay. Corbin lunched alone with us and we took a tender farewell (he's off tonight). Further havering conference on F.E. at 6.

Friday, 19 July *Thatched Cottage*

After tea, T. and I walked across the fields to Ewhurst. A long walk—certainly 4 miles, up and down hill. No sign of war here. We were never stopped on the way: one or 2 road blocks: no soldiers.

Saturday, 20 July *Thatched Cottage*

Walked around in Rye—as charming and as peaceful as ever. Then on to Winchilsea, and a bit of a walk there. A lovely clear sky, and I've never seen such a picture of peace!

Sunday, 21 July

A very enjoyable week-end and a very welcome rest. The cottage looking very pretty and friendly. We had a good time there. Hope we may go again.

Monday, 22 July

There's a *vast* accumulation, including stacks of undigested material for H's speech in Lords on Wednesday, which will be the bane of my life. H. completely preoccupied by his broadcast tonight, which was *not* v. effective. He showed it to Joe Kennedy, who said 'The God stuff's all right: the rest isn't tough enough!'

Tuesday, 23 July

Dictated stuff for H's speech on Far East. . . . Séance with H. on his bloody speech. . . . Germans take H's sermon of last night as a challenge and gnash their teeth and threaten destruction of British Empire. Well, let them try.

Wednesday, 24 July

H. fussing about his speech for this afternoon and wanting me to do six things at once, immediately. Then proceeded to waste ¾ hr of my time by making me sit by while he very slowly dictated 'headings' from a mass of material I had given him. . . . Got back to tackle neglected work and, with H. stuck in House of Lords, got through it. Very wetting and persistent rain all afternoon. Was able to get back home with most of my work done. Must tackle Bills!

Thursday, 25 July

Various worries—principal being (as I expected) wild protest from Sam H. against Dalton making announcement this *afternoon* of rationing of Spain and Portugal. Dalton has schoolboy ideas of doing things *now*. A most elementary pitfall. Spoke to H. and then rang up Dalton, who came round. Got him to agree to postpone his announcement till Tuesday. Cabinet 11.30—but there was nothing in which

I was interested. They began on India and P.M. put Leo Amery on the spot,* which was rather embarrassing, so I came away! Gave H. a minute for P.M. explaining why it's no use his trying to get Weygand's collusion in setting up a Government in N. Africa. . . . I, having nothing to do for the first time for months, started writing minute on necessity for concentrating our propaganda on *Hitler* and *Hitlerism*. (Van and the French—good advisers!—had ridden us off this.) H. called me in and I found Van. H. had a letter from Nevile H[enderson] pretty well on my line, and I said I was already writing something.

[The French had urged, according to Cadogan's note, that since all Germans were equally wicked, Allied propaganda should be directed not against Hitler, or even against Nazism, but against Germany. Cadogan wrote:

> I don't accept the thesis that all Germans are equally wicked, but even assuming it to be true, I maintain—and have always maintained—that it was not very clever to put that in the forefront of our propaganda.
>
> Even if it is a true reflection, it is not a helpful one, because it leads nowhere. It can only point to the necessity for massacring or—on a longer view—sterilising all Germans. And I don't think that is really practical politics.
>
> At the present moment, Hitler is presumably on the crest of the wave. Any attacks that we make on him will not (on the French assumption) appreciably strengthen his position.
>
> But there are elements working against Hitler. There is a rather impressive volume of evidence to show that, in spite of military triumphs, there is no great enthusiasm for the war in Germany. There is a certain lassitude in Germany and if, after all their efforts, the Germans are asked to embark in small boats to land on mined beaches in this country, or to run the gauntlet of our fighters in troop-carrying 'planes, it may be that that will not redound to Hitler's popularity.
>
> It seems to me that what we want to get into the minds of the Germans is that we do not desire that even they shd. be denied the right to live in peace, and even comparative plenty, and that it is only Hitler and his system that stands between them and the exercise of that right. . . .
>
> If Hitler produces a specious plan for a 'New Europe' (and if we have been able to produce no better one), probably our best line of attack wd. be as suggested in a recent telegram to Washington—viz. that this all looks very nice but is of course in reality simply designed to subserve

* Churchill insisted upon seeing private telegrams which had passed between the Viceroy and Amery (some of which reflected freely upon himself) and half-accused Amery of misleading the Cabinet.

Hitler's end of domination. The economic paradise which he depicts is really only a German playground: the other States of Europe are to supply him with food and raw materials for the manufacture of his munitions (which is Hitler's 'cure' for unemployment) for the domination of the rest of the world and for the denial of freedom to all other peoples. . . .

The removal of Hitler, if that could by one means or another be brought about, must have a profound effect. It is difficult to believe that Goering, his successor designate, or any other of the German leaders could maintain German unity in the way that he does. When people sometimes speak to me of the marvellous efficiency of the Dictatorships, I always remind them that they may be rather deficient in stability and continuity, and offer to review the position with them again 6 months after the death or disappearance of either Hitler or Mussolini.

I submit therefore that our propaganda should concentrate against Hitler and the Nazi system. They may not be so all-powerful as they look, and dissension in Germany would be worth a number of Army Corps.[16]]

Friday, 26 July

Funny pause. I should judge Hitler doesn't like the look of invasion and is trying to tempt us to parley. (We have had various feelers in different quarters*). But if that fails, I think he will attack. And I think that will fail too. And if it does, the whole face of Europe will be changed. French making difficulties about our representation at Vichy.

Saturday, 27 July

Menzies for a chat. He has news that invasion *will* come. Hope so. Back at 7.45. Dined at home. Raczynski† came round about 9.30 with news of impending Russian occupation of large part of German-occupied Poland. Looks like German-Russian collusion and as if G. had bought off Russian interference in her Balkan plans.

Monday, 29 July

Cabinet at 11.30 in Central War Room. Quite a good air battle over Dover. These Jap savages have arrested 11 Britishers. One has committed suicide. We can't stand this. . . . Talked to Horace S[eymour] and Far Eastern pundits about arrests. H. will ask Cabinet tomorrow for authority to 'pick up' a number of Japanese in India,

* On 19 July, in the Reichstag, Hitler had appealed 'once more to reason and common sense in Great Britain . . . I can see no reason why this war need go on'. Diplomatic approaches were then made through Sweden, the Vatican and the U.S.A.

† The Polish Ambassador.

Malaya and here. We really *must* stand against them now. Surely even Winston will realise that we can't 'appease', any further.

Tuesday, 30 July

Arranging for arrest of suitable Japanese as reprisal for their performance.... Can't make out what the Germans are doing. Various good indications that they *are* going to attack us. But why haven't they done so? And what are they doing with these costly and half-hearted air-raids? 25 shot down yesterday at Dover against 2 of ours. Must be something very deep.*

Glad to hear from Bridges that old Neville C. is going on all right—they won't have to do another operation, and hope to have him right in 2 or 3 weeks. I devoutly hope this is so.

[Earlier in July, Lothian had wired that it would be extremely difficult to obtain destroyers from the United States unless the Americans were assured that the British fleet would cross the Atlantic if Britain were overrun. On the last day of the month Churchill sent his formal request to the President; fifty or sixty old destroyers for use at once in the Western Approaches against U-boats. Thereupon Lothian suggested that these vessels might be exchanged for long leases of British bases in the West Indies and Bermuda.]

Wednesday, 31 July

Quo at 11 with message from Chiang Kai-Shek to P.M. Quite courteous and dignified. Hideous day, with ghastly hammering going on the whole time overhead—work on H's flat.... O.S. back from leave. Told me I.K. might be leaving Ministry of Information. I.K. came in 5 mins later! To say his job was fading out. But I don't know how we can accommodate all these people!...

What are we to expect? At the risk of being proved wrong to-morrow morning (which I don't mind) I do *not* think Hitler is going to be fool enough to attempt an invasion. He has concentrated our attention on these islands, and he will then, with his filthy Italian friends, thrust at Gibraltar and Egypt (though I'm bound to say our 'intelligence' gives nothing to corroborate this theory. But then they're awfully bad). Anyhow, that's what I would do if I were Hitler, damn him.

Thursday, 1 August

Cabinet 11.30. Agreed to take reprisals on Japs. And to withdraw

* The figures of aircraft noted as shot down on both sides in these months in the Diary are of course subject to post-war 'correction'.

Shanghai garrison—subject to Craigie. . . . Had talk with H. about Cripps'* telegram complaining that Molotov won't receive him. Decided to tell him he must stay in Moscow, nevertheless. And damned good for him! About 7 went over to see P.M. to get his authority to meet fresh appeal for rescue from Daladier & Co. He harangued me on world situation and suggested he should send personal message to Konoye.† I sent minute to H. rather endorsing this.

Friday, 2 August *Thatched Cottage*

Fine sunny day, northerly breeze. Left with T. for Cottage just before 11. Went round by Benenden and, in absence of all sign-posts, lost our way. . . . Hay has been cut, and they were making it. Sat in north garden after lunch. Walked a bit past Dixter. Scythed amongst the birch and fruit trees before dinner.

Sunday, 4 August *Thatched Cottage*

Church full of soldiers, which made it more cheerful. Lazy after-noon—v. hot. After tea motored to Camber. No one stopped us—no sentries—no notices. But the moment we got on the sands we were arrested! A very nice junior officer arrived and released us. Back home, and went on scything. The lull in the war continues and one day's newspaper (or Broadcast) is exactly like another's.

[When he at last consented to receive Cripps, Molotov left him in no doubt that Russia would not jeopardise her good relations with Germany, which had brought political, economic and strategic benefits. Within that limitation, Russia thought that it might be possible to get on to better terms with Britain. It would help matters if no questions like that of the Baltic States' gold (which the British had refused to hand over to Russia) were allowed to arise.[17]]

Friday, 9 August

Meeting at 10.45 with H. and Wavell‡ and experts. W. *not* very impressive. Stacks of work to catch up and many interruptions. No great news, except 60 German aircraft shot down yesterday in Channel. (They were active over *our* heads, but I didn't know until after that any of them were German!) . . . Meeting with H. on Baltic States shipping, gold &c. Everyone strikes me as stale and

* Sir Stafford Cripps had succeeded Seeds as Ambassador in Moscow.

† Prince Fuminaro Konoye, Japanese Prime Minister, July 1940–Oct. 1941.

‡ Gen. Sir A. P. Wavell, C.-in-C. Middle East, 1939–41; C.-in-C. India, June 1941; C.-in-C., S.W. Pacific, Dec. 1941–June 1943; Viceroy of India, 1943–7.

tired (myself included!) G. Lloyd at 4. He's becoming a bore—as supplementary Foreign Secretary.

Saturday, 10 August

'C' came in for a talk. He says his 'best source' 'expects nothing this month': German police given leave up to end of Aug.

Sunday, 11 August

H. rang up at 12.30 to discuss draft telegram to Cripps. I hate doing work this way on the telephone, and he was rather vague and havering, but I hope I have put the draft telegram in shape for Cabinet on Tuesday.

Monday, 12 August

Cabinet 12.30. Good air battle yesterday—62 brought down: lost 25. Another going on this morning over Portsmouth.

Tuesday, 13 August

H. back. Went with him to Cabinet at 12. Settled instructions to Cripps. Air battle raging again today. Yesterday's results marvellous. . . . 5.30 Bridges, about manning of F.O. at night. Explained to him I am always 'on the bridge' till midnight. No use wasting other people's time.

[The War Cabinet doubted the value of a major concession to Russia at this stage. Evidence of Britain's determination to defend her interests might be as useful as one-sided concession. Cripps was told that *de jure* recognition of Russia's control of the Baltic States would be refused, not least because of the precedent which would be created in respect of German and Japanese conquests. Russia's control might be recognised *de facto*, but the gold would in no circumstances be handed over until British losses there had been compensated. There ensued an inconclusive argument by telegram. On 20 August Sir Stafford was instructed that for the time being he need attempt no negotiations with the Russians. It was becoming clear that a partial British release of the Baltic assets might have wide repercussions, practical and psychological, in the U.S.A. In September, Halifax informed Maisky that there could be a deal on Baltic questions only if the Soviets renounced their claim to the gold, Britain abandoning the claim to compensation. Trade talks had meanwhile come to nothing.

Cadogan's view of Russian motives is indicated plainly enough by the Diary entry for 17 August.[18]]

Wednesday, 14 August

5.30 went with R.A.B. to see Bevin* about his complaints of the

* Ernest Bevin, Minister of Labour, 1940–5; Foreign Secretary, 1945–51.

'citadel' nature of H.M. Foreign Service. As I expected, he was v. reasonable when we talked to him. I *think*—in spite of rather woolly talk—that he has practical ideas. He has to go to hospital to have his tonsils out and promises, in his bed, to write us a paper. This sounds practical.

Roosevelt has really, I think, weighed in with destroyers. Cabinet meeting about it at 6.30 which I did not attend. We *must* give a very easy quid for the quo, and I understand Winston now agrees.

Air action yesterday marvellous. We shot down 75 for sure: 21 'probables' and 29 'damaged'. We lost 13 machines, but saved all pilots except 3! Amazing! Unfortunately, they got 8 Blenheims on the ground . . . and we seem to have lost 11 out of 12 Blenheims on a patrol.

Thursday, 15 August

This was the day Hitler was to be in London. Can't find him. . . . Air-raid warning at 7.20 but luckily lasted only 10 minutes. . . . B.B.C. announced we had shot down *88* today, and lost 19, pilots of 5 of which had been saved. Marvellous!

Friday, 16 August

Discussion with H. and others of Italy's outrages against Greece. Can't do much. . . . Total bag today 161—against 27 (but many pilots saved).

Saturday, 17 August

Meeting with H. on Russia. Cripps argues that we must give everything—recognition, gold, ships and trust to the Russians loving us. This is simply silly. Agreed to tell him to sit tight. We will see what we can do here with Maisky. Exactly nil, I should say. However H. proposes to begin by asking Maisky and Madame to dine*—and threatens to ask me too! Extraordinary how we go on kidding ourselves. Russian policy will change exactly when and if they think it will suit them. And if they *do* think that, it won't matter whether we've kicked Maisky in the stomach. Contrariwise, we could give Maisky the Garter and it wouldn't make a penn'orth of difference. However, I see no reason to object. . . . Theo and I left at 2.30 by car for Eton. Walked in the Playing Fields. Fell in with Vice-Provost (Marten) who invited us to tea. . . . Very pleasant. We strolled round

* When Maisky gave a luncheon, a sumptuous affair in a conservatory overlooking Kensington Gardens, Robert Boothby, M.P., exclaimed: 'What a relief, in these days of rationing, to share the simple life of the proletariat.'[19]

again after. *What* a delightful place. We saw one 'student' on a bicycle with (a) a rifle, (b) a pair of cricket pads, and (c) a steel helmet. *How* that would puzzle Hitler, who, by the way, has ceased his air attacks today. Has he had enough?

Monday, 19 August

Numbers of German planes brought down yesterday now about 140—to our 22, I think. And only about 16 pilots lost. Today, Germans quiet in the air and 'C' tells me there is a meeting of German Air Staff summoned in Berlin. It wouldn't surprise me! Talked with H. about a number of things and gave him my snippets for his speech tomorrow. Cabinet at 12. Nothing v. much. Beaverbrook seems undisturbed by destruction of machines on the ground,* which he says he's replaced. It was stupidity—or disobedience—leaving 2 hangars stuffed with aircraft. They ought to be dispersed.

Wednesday, 21 August

We must wait and see what Hitler will do. Can he redouble his air attacks on these islands? Can he break them off? My belief is that, if he finds invasion is 'off', he will have a winter campaign in N. Africa, and send a couple of thousand planes to help the ice-creamers and then where shall we (or M[iles] Lampson) be? The Americans have come clean with their destroyers, I think—which is something to the good. W.S.C.'s speech yesterday was clever, and successful.

Thursday, 22 August

Cabinet at 11.30. Approved Winston's message to Pres. about destroyers, &c.... Air-raid warning about 3.30. I never heard sirens. T. woke me up. I refused to move until I heard guns. She came in later to say she had heard them. By time I got down 'all clear' sounded, and I went back to bed.

Friday, 23 August

About 5 telegram from Lothian to say Americans don't like P.M.'s procedure and must stick to their exchange of letters idea.† Lothian rang me up to emphasise that this was the only possible course. Went over about 6.30 with D. Scott and Dean‡ to see P.M. He rather

* 46 aircraft had been destroyed at Brize Norton on 16 Aug.

† That is that the two transactions should come together. The destroyers could be transferred only if there were a consideration which could be certified as adding to the U.S.A.'s security.

‡ D. J. M. D. Scott, Asst. Under-Sec. of State, F.O., 1938–44; P. H. Dean, Asst. Legal Adviser, F.O., 1939–45.

incensed and won't have exchange of letters. Says he doesn't mind if we don't get destroyers. Won't expose himself to a wrangle with Americans, having made us definite gift, haggling over the extent of ours. Dare say he is right. Sent provisional telegram to Lothian, and P.M. will dictate his message in car on way down to Chequers.

Saturday, 24 August

Received P.M.'s draft message to Pres.—very good. But he rang me up to say he had had a message . . . which changed aspect of things. . . . But I don't think it means anything, and I rang up P.M. again to say I thought he'd better send his message all the same. (I had sent it down for H. by despatch rider, for his approval). P.M. said I must anyhow get 1st Ld. and 1st Sea Ld's approval first. . . . Lothian came through, fussing for P.M.'s message. I said there was a hitch and explained to him broadly. He not disconcerted. Told Chequers of my conversation. They seem to think P.M. won't send message tonight anyhow.

Sunday, 25 August

Telegram from Lothian urging P.M. to send reply. It had been telephoned to Chequers and P.M. agreed message might go off. Got Herschel Johnson round and gave it him, telegraphing it to Lothian.

Monday, 26 August

There was an A[ir] R[aid] W[arning] last night 10.30–11.20. Then we went to bed. And another one 12.30 for about ½ hr., but I remained in bed and slept well. Fine morning. H. back from his Chatham-Dover visit. He hadn't seen much of a battle, but was impressed by his tour of defences. Cabinet at 12.30. Not much of interest. Weather was bad over Berlin, so a lot of our bombers brought back their bombs. But others dropped them. We sent over 81 machines. . . . All clear (which didn't wake me) not until 3.30. Certain amount of damage done, I gather—mostly in Coventry-Birmingham area, but nothing vital.

[On the morning of 27 August, Churchill formally offered 99-year leases for naval and air bases in Newfoundland, Bermuda, the Bahamas, several West Indian Islands and British Guiana, He accepted the drafts of letters which Lothian had prepared, and amended after conference with Roosevelt and Hull.]

Wednesday, 28 August

Had to see Swiss [Minister] in afternoon about our violation of

Swiss air: had meeting in morning with H., A. Sinclair and an Air Marshal. Plain that we can't avoid Switzerland but better not to tell them that frankly at this stage. So I stalled. The A.M. was encouraging in talk we had with him about various aspects of air war. . . .

No Cabinet today—Winston gone down to Dover to dispute the supremacy of the Straits. . . . A.R.W. went on till 4 a.m. Bomb dropped near here at 1 a.m. and servants said 'something' had fallen in garden. Inspected with Wardens, but found nothing. 'All clear' woke me up for a moment.

Thursday, 29 August

Discussed with H. and David S[cott] Lothian's telegrams about destroyers. . . . Cabinet at 12. Winston agreed to give way to Americans on procedure.

He had been to Dover and Ramsgate yesterday. Beaverbrook rather fussed—or affected to be—about our aircraft losses and damage to factories. Winston thinks German scheme is to hammer Kent promontory flat and then attempt invasion.

Saturday, 31 August *Thatched Cottage*

After tea walked with T. up to Dixter. A raid came over—17 bombers accompanied by fighters. 10 mins. later, I had hardly said I shd. like to see about 10 coming back, when all 17 reappeared. Perhaps we got some of their fighters. After dinner 9 o'clock news said 46 enemies down to 21 of ours, but 10 of our pilots saved. But it's beginning to be a toll of our machines!

Monday, 2 September

Cabinet at 12. V.C.A.S. and P.M. seem quite happy about the air. . . . Dined at home. A.R.W. 10.30 till—?

Wednesday, 4 September

Talk with the King about de Gaulle—who didn't impress him much—and partridges, which appear to be good. Also about coming winter—assuming we survive it—and how to amuse troops and maintain morale. We can think of that a fortnight hence.

V. good news of air battle, 41–5. A.R.W. about 9.10—still going on, so far as I know. There's a Cabinet at 9.30 on A.R.W.'s, I'm glad to say, and I believe idea is to do away (I hope so) with this awful wailing, lamenting defeatist noise, and also to cut out warnings to a large extent. Hope they'll take drastic decisions.

Friday, 6 September

A.R.W. at 8.45 but I shall take no more count of these, as they are daily and constant, and interfere less and less with our routine. Lovely and blazing hot day. Pretty busy, but with nothing v. interesting. Lot of air battles, in which we seem to be doing well. I suppose Hitler thinks he can wear our fighters down, but, according to figures of J[oint] I[ntelligence] C[ommittee] his fighter figure is already reduced *below* ours. (This I can hardly believe.)

Saturday, 7 September

Big air battle over London, of which we could see something. All clear about 6.30, and I went to F.O. and collected work. A.R.W. again at 8.30 and machines droning overhead. Gunfire. About 11.15 4 or 5 terrific explosions. (There was a big fire started in the Docks area by the 5 o'clock raid). Went up to bed, but the battle got a bit hot and about 12.15, I think, T. and I went down to the basement. She insisted on my taking a camp bed, and settled herself in arm-chairs. Not too comfortable, but cool, and an awful noise at intervals. Bombs on Pont Street, Victoria Street and Westminster. Frightful blaze still going on in docks. All clear at 4.45 and we went up to bed. A good explosion from a delayed bomb ¼ hr. later. But slept.

Sunday, 8 September

Yesterday afternoon very good—we got 99, losing 21 or so. They are coming over now in succession, but I hope that has nuisance value, mainly. T. is marvellous—her nerves are much better than mine, I know that! Slept(?) in basement. Air-raid went on until 5.45. I got a bit of sleep, but woken up by noisy patch at 3.45.

Monday, 9 September

Cabinet 12.30. Everyone—even Anderson and Beaver—quite cheerful. Went over to basement with H., Grey and Jones. Sent round circular saying people must try to get home by Black-out.

Tuesday, 10 September

Long talk with H., and later Strang, about further 'peace' offer through a certain [Dr Ludwig] Weissauer in Switzerland. It's just the same as the others, and put out with the same motives. H. saw this.* . . . About 4 went over with H. to see P.M. about 'peace' offer and reply to be sent. He took the line I expected, which doesn't differ

* The proposals were received on 9 September. Cadogan's reply on 11 September was regarded by Weissauer as a refusal.

from H's. It's a question not of *what* to reply, but *how* to reply. We left him to think it over. Back with H. to P.M. at 7.30. He was in bed in flowered Chinese dressing-gown, puffing large cigar. He read us his draft reply which is all right.

Thursday, 12 September

Went to see N.C. before Cabinet. He very thin and rather frail, but seems fairly well and alert. Cabinet 12.30. We had a marvellous air battle late yesterday afternoon. Brought down 89. Lost 28 but many pilots saved. Lovely barrage last night. London guns more than doubled. One third of raiders turned back. Little damage.

[Early in September, an economic agreement was made with Spain, after spirited haggling and in despite of strong German pressure. Hoare, lamenting the rigidity of Dalton's attitude at the Ministry of Economic Warfare, thought that there was still a chance of keeping Spain out of the hands of Germany and even of 'bringing her into our own orbit'. 'It is a physical effort for Dalton to keep his hands off any ship on which he can lay them', Halifax wrote, 'but he has not really, I think, behaved too badly over the particular concessions for which at your insistence I have pressed him.' Dalton gave way with a groan. 'He [Hoare] wants to keep them sweet; I want to keep them short.'[20]

Spain had still made no move to enter the war. With the increasingly obvious failure of the German air attack upon the British Isles, the Allied position at Madrid slowly improved. The naval attaché, Captain Hillgarth, worked with considerable success to minimise spying and sabotage at Gibraltar and mischief-making in the port. On 13 September Cadogan wrote to Hoare:

> We are given details of the arrangements which Hitler has made to invade these islands, and I have no doubt that he has made them. Whether or not he will decide to put them to the test, is another question. . . . I should have thought he would be rash to try unless he has obtained air superiority, which he most emphatically has *not*. He has troubled London a good deal lately with night bombing (which has not given him any military advantage). Everyone complained of the fine weather and clear skies that enabled him to come over at night, but our gun barrage profited equally from these conditions and cramped his style. Now we have wet and overcast weather, of which he takes advantage to come over unseen and dive on Buckingham Palace, and other military objectives. I have no doubt we shall find the answer to that. . . .
>
> I have not hitherto been able to write to you at length; may I take this opportunity of expressing all our admiration and gratitude for the good work you have been doing in Spain?[21]]

Friday, 13 September

Went to see N.C. before Cabinet, which took place at 11 in War Room. Rather gloomy—mostly about damage (considerable) caused by raids. During it, we had news of attack on Buckingham Palace, and Cabinet sent message of sympathy and congratulation.... After dinner, about 10 or 10.30, numbers of incendiary bombs fell all round, and on, these premises. Firemen said there was a bomb on our roof and we must get out.... Bomb was really on roof next door and was quickly put out. But houses down the street burning badly. We all went back and to bed about midnight. Got quite a good sleep.

Monday, 16 September

Cabinet in War Room at 12. Not quite so gloomy. Wonderful day in the air yesterday—185 to 25 (11 pilots safe). Also damage reports not so alarming.

The French ships have forestalled us in Dakar, and so 'Menace' is off! I cannot truly say I am sorry!

Lunch at home. A.R.W. at 2.10 but couldn't wait for it to end, and drove to F.O. getting there at 3. An underground meeting with Heads of various Depts. to discuss methods of carrying on work under these conditions. We *must* take over I[ndia] O[ffice]!

Tuesday, 17 September

Long talk to Catroux (with Morton), just arrived. He is more impressive than de Gaulle, and seems very nice. Dined at 8 as Cabinet at 9 in War Room. Drove myself there through the barrage. Messages show people on spot want to go on with 'Menace'. I warned against possible result of another Oran. But everyone in favour. Drove home about 10.30—rather quieter. But v. noisy later, and got to sleep late.

[The original proposal had been for de Gaulle's forces to take Duala. Then there seemed a good prospect of securing the bigger prize of Dakar. Various delays followed: Vichy no doubt heard of the plan; the naval forces at Dakar were reinforced. The estimates supplied to the Cabinet about the local position appear to have been unduly optimistic. It was necessary to choose whether to go on, with the certainty that the operation would become a major one, or to abandon the enterprise. The Cabinet had indeed decided, on learning that the Vichy ships had reached Dakar, to call off the operation, for they had no desire to quarrel further with Vichy. They had then reversed the decision under pressure from de Gaulle and the commanders of the task force.

From this unhappy episode Halifax drew the conclusion that fruit in the French colonial empire must not be picked until self-evidently ripe.[22]]

Wednesday, 18 September

Cabinet decided to go on with 'Menace'. Air battle took place while we were sitting. Haven't heard result yet. . . . Usual Blitzkrieg. Some heavy crumps about 11.20, but quieter later and I got some sleep. White autumn crocuses full out.

Thursday, 19 September

Damage last night severe to houses and fairly heavy in casualties, but public services said to have got off comparatively lightly. Beaverbrook told me 2 of his factories got it. Railways said to have improved. Poor Lady G[osford]* bombed out of her flat and took refuge in Claridge's.

Friday, 20 September

Oil bomb on F.O. 2nd Floor last night. Not so very much damage. Cabinet at 12 in War Room. Mostly about 'Menace'. French ships from Dakar headed off from going to Duala, but two of them got back into Dakar.

Saturday, 21 September

Saw Retinger† and told him P.M. anxious about Sikorski's‡ safety, and he should find other quarters.

Sunday, 22 September

P.M. furious because, in sacking X on his instructions, I put some kind words into the telegram about his past services. After all, the man had given the whole of his life, and we are sacking him on hearsay evidence. Winston is very babyish in some ways. . . . Herschel Johnson at 1 about a telegram from Washington that Pres. had news that invasion will take place at 3 p.m. this afternoon. It doesn't say whether it's dep. Calais at 3 or arr. Dover! As I told him, dates and hours are always meaningless. The thing must turn on the weather.

Monday, 23 September

Cabinet at 5. Rather gloomy. 'Menace' going none too well and [cruiser] 'Cumberland' hit. Beaverbrook gloomy about production (but I discovered he was doing this on purpose). Lost 9 machines for 10 this morning. Invasion expected tonight.

* Lady T. Cadogan's mother.
† Sikorski's confidant.
‡ See List of Principal Characters.

Saturday, 28 September *Thatched Cottage*

We went to see bomb-hole—a bomb wasted: as far as you could get from human habitation, and didn't even obstruct the lane.

Sunday, 6 October

A welcome holiday. I didn't enjoy it as much as some, although the family were there. The weather was moderate, nothing to do in the garden, a sort of feeling one oughtn't to be away from London and a grim winter impending. Not that I'm glad to be back!

[The Germans announced on 27 September that they, Italy and Japan had signed a pact; it was clearly directed against the U.S.A. Meanwhile Japan had secured from Vichy the right to pass troops through Indo-China and to use air bases in Tonkin. It was plain that the condition upon which the Burma Road had been closed—that special efforts be made to produce a lasting peace in the Far East—would not be met. Craigie had now concluded that reopening the Burma Road would not lead to a Japanese declaration of war.

The Vichy administration had asked several times that without overt raising of the blockade some food-ships should be allowed to reach French ports. The Cabinet replied, through Madrid, that while they were ready for a discussion about trade between French colonies and the unoccupied portion of metropolitan France, they would not relax the blockade unless assured that Vichy would act independently in respect of French territory overseas.]

Monday, 7 October

Long talk with O.S. Nothing dreadful has happened—except Japanese Pact! But decided to announce tomorrow that we will reopen Burma Road. Talked to H. Asked him if W.S.C. was going to blame Dakar on F.O. or S.I.S. If so, very unfair, as he took the decision on his own and never consulted or informed either. I was only told of the original decision *after* it had been taken. . . . Cabinet (considerably enlarged) at 5. Discussion mainly on Blockade of French Africa. I drafted a telegram with Dalton and got it approved by H. Winston then began holding forth about disgraceful articles in 'Mirror' and 'Sunday Pictorial'. He got the Attorney Gen. in but I gather latter said no case for prosecution.

Wednesday, 9 October

Talk with H. and Collier about Soviet and U.S. in relation to Japan-Axis Pact. Also with P. Nichols. We had discussed with him yesterday reports of German plan for invasion of Egypt via Syria.

Rather far-fetched, but not impossible. Saw Gwatkin about Office arrangements. We have got what we want out of I[ndia] O[ffice], which is the beginning of the solution.

Thursday, 10 October

Pretty noisy last night. St Paul's Cathedral damaged. Showery morning. Drove to F.O. Had talk with H. about Cripps' telegram from Moscow proposing fresh approach to Soviet. Might be a good way of drawing Molotov. . . . Home about 7.10 and just got my bath before the Blitzkrieg. Didn't go to Cabinet today as there was nothing special, and it was held in P.M.'s room at the House, which H. says is already uncomfortably crowded.

Friday, 11 October

I walked to F.O. Had to make a detour through Downing Street as Parade blocked by un-exploded bombs. Cabinet off. . . . H. had gone to see P.M. at 2.30 about blockade of French W. Africa and stoppage of munitions to Dakar. I'd go slow on former (P.M. agreed to that being discussed on Monday) but see no reason why we shouldn't do latter, if Admiralty can do it. Pound fussed about this, and kept ringing me up, even unto dinner-time. Compromise reached by sending message to Vichy through Madrid that we'd much sooner they recalled munitions ship rather than that we should have to stop her. Home about 7. Just got my bath (or three-quarters of it) before Hitler intervened. Poor Horace Seymour bombed out of his flat last night. But he hasn't changed! (and literally—because he had to wear the suit he slept in!).

[On this evening, Neville Chamberlain's resignation was announced. Cadogan, distressed at the news that the cancer was incurable, allowed himself unusual freedom in his letter of regret:

> I am not going to write about the events of the last two and more years—I can't presume to usurp the function of the 'historian', though I do anticipate his judgment. But I do want to say how happy I was to serve you and to enjoy, as I dare to believe, your friendship. I shall always treasure that as a very happy memory, and I shall be very proud of it. I have tried to serve several Ministers and even—at further remove—several Prime Ministers; and I did what I could for a perfectly dizzying succession of Delegates at Geneva! But I have never learnt so much as I did from you, nor felt my loyalty so completely engaged. Nor have I met such sympathy.

Chamberlain replied shortly before his death:

> It has been a great pleasure to me to work with you in what has been the most important part of my duties. I hoped our association might have lasted longer, but I have to accept what cannot be avoided. Therefore it is a real satisfaction to me to be able to look back on so many associations with loyal and devoted friends; among whom [he added in manuscript] I am proud to count yourself.[23]]

Saturday, 12 October

Everything lately points to German drive through Balkans against Egypt, coupled—possibly, though this more doubtful—with attack on Gibraltar, with or without invasion of England. (Last I have lately thought *very* doubtful,* but it's still there, and if our attention relaxed, Hitler would seize on a favourable opportunity to try it). Our anti-night bombing devices don't seem to be coming to much yet!

[Cripps thought that the Russians did not want Germany to win the war. If Britain were to exploit that fact she must make some attractive offer for the long term. Russians feared that after victory the Allies would form an anti-Russian alliance, and therefore be more dangerous than a victorious but war-weakened Germany. He suggested that if the Russians would behave as friendlily to the British as to the Germans, and be at least 'benevolently neutral' to Turkey and Persia should they be attacked, Britain should promise (a) to consult with Russia about the post war settlement; (b) to enter no anti-Russian alliance; (c) to recognise until the end of the war Russia's *de facto* sovereignty over the territories she had taken in 1939–40; (d) to supply commodities useful for self-defence against the Axis; (e) to guarantee Russia against attack from Turkey or Iran. The arrangement would be secret, and would include a trade agreement. If the Russians refused, they would be told that Britain would not undertake (a), (b) or (c).

Although neither the War Cabinet nor the Foreign Office had much hope of this approach, Cripps was told to proceed, bearing in mind that *de jure* recognition of Russia's conquests could not be granted. Molotov refused even to see Cripps, who had to present the draft eventually to Vyshinsky.† The Russians did not bother with it. According to a report reaching the Foreign Office in December, Maisky had said that Russia was content to see the two sides exhaust themselves. He was in the daily habit not of setting down the losses against each other but of adding them together in one column.[24]]

* The J.I.C. reported in the same sense in this month; Maj.-Gen. Sir K. Strong, *Men of Intelligence*, p. 118.

† Andrei Vyshinsky, formerly Russian State Prosecutor; Vice-Commissar for Foreign Affairs, 1940–9.

Monday, 14 October

Meeting with H., R.A.B. and O.S. about Cripps' proposals for trying to swing the Russians more to our side. I'm all for trying it myself, though I have little hope.

Tuesday, 15 October

Diary has become rather difficult, as it was very noisy last night and T. decided today to evacuate to the Carlton Hotel! Cabinet at 5 to decide on reply to Cripps, authorising him to go ahead, subject to certain cautions. . . . Slept in Grill Room. Always loathe Hotels, and in these circumstances grisly. Slept not at all.

Friday, 18 October

Awful rush to get ready for Cabinet at 11.30. They approved draft to Madrid* and took decision on blockade of W. Africa—to pick up a few ships when possible without serious clash.

Monday, 21 October

In present circs. of our squalid existence in a hotel, I can't keep up this diary. I don't remember what happened this day. There was a Cabinet at No. 10 at 5—P.M. away and nothing v. interesting. We dined with the H's at the Dorchester to meet Philip Lothian. The Dorchester is the worst spot on earth to live in. We dined on the 6th Floor, to an accompaniment of 4·5" guns, which knock the glasses off the table, tear your eyebrows out and snap your braces. Poor Dorothy evidently completely rattled, but H's deafness, I suppose, stands him in good stead.

Friday, 25 October

Woken up at 6 by a telegram from S. Hoare. His French colleague says Laval† is pressing for complete co-operation with Germany; message from King or P.M. to Pétain might avert this. P.M. and H. had already been woken and presumably have the matter in hand, so why wake me? Went back to bed again. Fine but cold.

Found P.M. had drafted message, and also one to Weygand and one to Roosevelt. Last all right: the one to W. I was doubtful about: we have already covered that ground and it's no good going on nagging. H. and I played about with the draft from the King and

* About relations with Vichy.

† Pierre Laval, formerly Prime Minister and Foreign Minister of France; became Vice-President of the Council in June, and became Foreign Minister again on 28 October; dismissed 13 December.

went over to see P.M. about it. He approved in final form and I got the King's assent and got it off about 12.30.

Monday, 28 October

The dirty ice-creamers attacked Greece at 6 a.m. Luckily I wasn't woken. Arranged messages from P.M., King &c., to King of Greece and Metaxas. Greek Minister called but had no fresh news.... 5 Cabinet—discussing what we could do to help Greece—not v. much! Agreed to intensify bombing of Italy—and Rome.

[The Italian ultimatum demanded the occupation of 'strategic bases' in Greece. When the President of the Council asked which they were, the Italian Minister could not answer. General Metaxas said that he regarded this as a declaration of war.[25] He applied at once to Britain for help at sea and in the air, but did not ask for troops. The Cabinet regarded themselves as bound, both by self-interest and by the guarantee to Greece, to send this assistance.]

Wednesday, 30 October

Frightful rush, as H. called me in about 10.30 and kept me for nearly an hour and then wanted, at once, all his telegrams and a note on Negrin—on which papers could not be produced. So I was in a very bad temper.... Worked in F.O. and Hotel till 8 and again after dinner. In *foul* conditions. How I *loathe* Hotels. And in the middle H. rings up and I have to sit in an airless sentry-box for ½ hour. I can't go on like this.

Thursday, 31 October

Talk with the pundits—including Van!—about Iraq.* Van wanting to be 'tough'. What a child he is—and suffers from childish complaints like vapours and irritations. Nothing rational about him at all—just silly uninformed impulse. Tried again to binge up H. about attacking Italy, before he went to see P.M. at 12.30. No one takes any interest—they have a Narvik-Dakar complex and they can't see that there is a *great* opportunity and a *great* prize to be won, worth any risk. Whereas all the Dakar and Libreville† schemes will only do us harm, even if they did succeed. Toned down a telegram (v. discouraging) from P.M. to Palairet‡ and told P. Nichols to tone up Air Ministry. (I gather latter are quite forthcoming). Tinkered with telegram to S. Hoare for Vichy calling for a showdown. Can't go on like this. They announce agreement with Germany. They say

* Where Rashid Ali, a politician favourable to the Axis, had displaced Gen. Nuri-es-Said earlier in the year.

† Taken by the Free French forces on 13 November.

‡ Sir Michael Palairet, British Minister, later Ambassador, to Greece, 1939–43.

it doesn't cover certain points. Then they must tell us what it does cover. . . . Have arranged to take a 2nd Floor suite, which might make life seemingly human again.

Friday, 1 November

Cabinet at 12. Glad to say we put 5 tons of bombs on Naples last night and are going to concentrate on Italy—even at expense of Germany. It's the *only* thing to do. Frightful discussion about Negrin. Any Spanish topic makes the politicians go all hay-wire and Attlee, otherwise a dormouse, becomes like a rabid rabbit. Why? . . . Feel slightly better—or less ill. But the cold is unbelievable—and the cough!

Monday, 4 November

Cabinet at 5. Thank Heaven, we *are* doing all we d——d well can, in the air, for Greece.* Got back to F.O. soon after 6 and sent off telegram to Palairet telling him what we hoped to do. He may tell King and Metaxas, but they *must* be discreet about it as we are skinning ourselves to the bone in Egypt—until beginning of next month.

Tuesday, 5 November

Talk with H., Strang, R. Campbell and Mack† about our general attitude and future policy toward Vichy. I hope we may play down de Gaulle, who I think is a loser, and there are signs that P.M.'s faith in Spears may be waning!

Wednesday, 6 November

Simopoulos in afternoon to say his Government don't want to attend Allied meeting here. This very suspect, and I told him he'd better advise them to think again.

Thursday, 7 November

Home 6.45 and worked before and after dinner. Masses of it these days—this is the 3rd week O.S. has been away with his phlebitis. He shd. be back on Monday.

Friday, 8 November

A ridiculous telegram from Brazzaville, showing that that ass de

* Four squadrons—one of Gladiators, three of Blenheims—were initially sent; rather to the dismay of Eden, who was in the Middle East and concerting with the Cs.-in-C. there plans of which the Cabinet did not then know.

† W. H. B. Mack, head of French Dept., F.O., 1940–2; British Civil Liaison Officer to Allied C.-in-C., N. Africa, 1942–3.

Gaulle is contemplating 'summoning Weygand to declare himself'. Just exactly what de Gaulle should not do at this moment. Drafted a reply to that effect and sent it to P.M. (whose faith in de Gaulle—and Spears—is, at last, I think, shaken).

Saturday, 9 November

P.M. has approved reply to Brazzaville, also message telling de G. to come back here.

Monday, 11 November

12.30 Simopoulos, with scraps of information and a Greek army bulletin which even he seemed to think rather optimistic! . . . 3.30 P. Lothian, who has produced very good message from P.M. for President putting all our cards on the table (which I think is right).* . . . 5 Cabinet. Good day (and weekend) in the air. Naval news not so bad—22 out of 36 of the Halifax convoy (attacked by [pocket-battleship] von Scheer) have already turned up. Amusing passage between P.M., Sinclair, Beaverbrook and Duff about Sinclair's interview to 'Daily Express' declaring Hitler a 'military objective'.

[On this day the Fleet Air Arm inflicted much damage on the Italian Navy in Taranto harbour. Half the Italian battle fleet was disabled.]

Tuesday, 12 November

Cabinet at 5. Anthony gave an account of his trip [to the Middle East]. Very interesting and, on the whole, encouraging. Cabinet decided to send air reinforcements to Egypt, to replace those sent to Greece, in teeth of strong (and rather overdone!) opposition by Beaverbrook. Didn't get back, in Blitzkrieg (fine and bright moon) until about 7.30.

Wednesday, 13 November

Sloane Square station was blown up last night. I always said that, as they took 2½ years to rebuild it, it was sure to be bombed directly it was completed. I never saw such a mess. The new station one huge crater, and, at the bottom, a train crushed under an avalanche of concrete blocks and steel girders. They think about 30 people killed. We had only one window broken. . . . V. tiresome meeting at 3.30 with Gladwyn about finance of S.O.E. Didn't understand anything about it, but settled something.

* This message, pointing out that Britain could no longer pay for the munitions she was ordering in the U.S.A., was sent in an amplified form a fortnight later, and led to the President's decision to propose Lend-Lease. Its gist is sufficiently indicated by Lothian's cheerful remark on returning to the U.S.A : 'Well, boys, Britain's broke; it's your money we want.'

Thursday, 14 November

Neville C's funeral service at 12. Coldest thing I've ever known. All the windows blown out of Henry VII's Chapel [Westminster Abbey], and no heating. The cloisters felt warm by comparison. Rather too long a service. . . . Margot Asquith pushed into the family procession!* . . . 3.15 Simopoulos to say he will represent his Government as an *observer* at Allied meeting. Told him why I deplored this.

Tuesday, 19 November

Gave instructions for telegram to Madrid about relations with Vichy—offering to open economic conversations in Madrid—and got a telegram drafted to Washington to urge necessity of economic help to Spain—on conditions: but the Americans are being tiresome and making two difficult conditions, i.e. *public* declaration of non-belligerency.

Wednesday, 20 November

Got H's approval to draft telegram to Madrid inviting Vichy to economic talks and giving certain assurances as to status quo meanwhile. P.M.'s approval will have to be obtained.

Thursday, 21 November

Quiet night. Further attack on Birmingham foiled by our tampering with [German directional] beam. Drove down to (new) House with H. to discuss matters with him. He had to be there at 11 for Opening of Parliament. As I drove away, saw King driving up in a car. O Tempora! O mores! . . . Cabinet at 3. Main thing was they approved our seizure of the Brazilian ships carrying enemy goods. . . . Greeks really are whacking the ice-creamers, but of course it can't last and I suppose the Germans will snuff them out. Our fighters seem to have cleaned the sky of the Wops.

Saturday, 23 November

Sent in a minute to H. urging 100% effort *at once* against Italy in view of Greek success. Latter may be short-lived. He sent minute down to P.M. at Chequers. . . . Came back at 5.30 or so to Lansdowne House, to which we have transferred. Rooms are cheap and seem very nice. There must be a snag somewhere—service I suspect and, obviously, band at dinner.

* Widow of the Prime Minister, the Earl of Oxford and Asquith. She had for some time made a habit of taking part in such processions, at weddings and funerals alike.

Sunday, 24 November

Telegrams from Belgrade asking for a communication encouraging them to think we shall help them to resist. Sent these to P.M. with draft (acquiescent) reply. . . . P.M. wanted to put off consideration until Cabinet tomorrow, but H. got on telephone to him and we got off the right telegram.

Monday, 25 November

V. quiet night—the Germans are concentrating, I'm afraid, on the industrial towns and ports. . . . Cabinet at 5. Nothing very interesting. I got H., on Sat., to write to P.M. again on necessity of hitting *Italy* for all we're worth in the next few days. A strange report from Stockholm that units of Italian fleet may wish to desert to us! Don't believe it.

[Halifax recorded of this day's proceedings:

A Cabinet at 5 went on until 7.15 and might easily have stopped at 6.15. Then a meeting of the Defence Committee at 9.30 which I was invited to attend and at which Winston turned up in a grey romper suit. It was all I could do to keep my face straight on first entry. He talked from 9.30 till 12, round and round and across. It is quite shattering to me the love to talk some people have.[26]]

Thursday, 28 November

3.30 I attended longish talk between H. and de Gaulle. Latter made a better impression. Less pompous, and talked rather well, firmly but with restraint. We drew him on Weygand, but he would have none of him—nor of Noguès.* He thinks there is nothing to be done with Vichy. We can only make them small concessions—that will only defer their 'grandes décisions', and meanwhile playing with Vichy may offend the mass of the French people. He says Darlan is the root of evil, and determined to produce a clash with us. He himself is sending troops to Egypt to fight Italians (all to the good) and plans an operation in Djibouti (which I don't mind).

Gladwyn came in about a brewing row between his people and Minry. of Information about broadcasts. I said that, so long as this battle didn't divert everyone's attention from the war, I didn't care a damn what happened.

Friday, 29 November

12.45 Bobbety† about that ass Van's ridiculous (and vulgar)

* C. A. A. P. Noguès, Resident-General and C.-in-C. Morocco, 1936–42.

† Lord Cranborne.

broadcast. Dominion High Commissioners—especially Bruce—are upset about it; and particularly because Van threatens more! Told H. who promised to talk to the ass.*

Saturday, 30 November

Americans have agreed to be reasonable about Spain. After all it concerns *us* more immediately than them.

Monday, 2 December

Discussion with H., R.A.B., Sargent and Nichols about Turkey and the Balkan situation. We have probably done all we can and Hugessen† is (rightly, I think) against pressing the Turks too much to pronounce what they will do in every hypothesis. . . . Cabinet at 5. Gloomy news about shipping.‡ U-boats got right into an unprotected convoy. Agree terms of P.M.'s letter to Pres. Discussion—as usual heated—about Jew illegal immigrants into Palestine.

Wednesday, 4 December

Had a talk with H. about his war aims paper. Difficulty that I see is that to proclaim 'democracy' and 'liberty' enables the enemy to say that we stand for the 'Front Populaire' and the 'Red' Government in Spain. And millions of people in Europe (I would not exclude myself) think that these things are awful. Even to talk about reinstating all these small countries is rather absurd. The last 20 years has shown that they *can't* stand by themselves and must *not* be taken too seriously—equal vote at Geneva, &c. Some form of Federation must be evolved. But *there* one runs up against difficulties!

H. spoke (much too mildly, I'm sure) to Van about his vulgar and ridiculous broadcast. The 'Daily Herald' are attacking it. It may do a deal of harm.

Monday, 9 December

Very heavy attack on London last night. B.B.C., House of Commons, and railways hit. 85 killed so far and about 500 seriously injured. Raid lasted from 5.30 to about 6 a.m. I got to sleep about 1 and didn't wake up again. . . . Cabinet 5. Attack on Italians at Sidi Barrani opened at dawn, and seems to have opened well, at least. Beaverbrook very pleased at his adaptation of the Merlin 3 engine.

* Vansittart was making a series of broadcasts to America about Germany. They were not notably moderate in expression.

† Sir Hughe Knatchbull-Hugessen, Ambassador at Ankara, 1939–44.

‡ In October, 442,000 tons of British, Allied and neutral shipping were lost; in November, 376,000 tons; and in the seven months beginning 1 May 1940, 3,239,190 tons.

(Also says we produced more aircraft in November than in October, and more this week than last—86 bombers instead of 68.) He also says he presided over a hopeful meeting about countering the night bomber.

Tuesday, 10 December

[Telegram] to Cairo—as result of P.M.'s telephone call to H.—asking whether military situation (which looks very good) did not afford opportunity of pushing Egypt into war. Didn't get away until after 7.30 with a box *full* of work. Dined in Restaurant. Barbarous. Worked.

Thursday, 12 December

Curious how difficult I find it to remember all that happened. What we have been doing is anyhow unimportant. What *is* important is our sweeping victory over the Wops.* P.M. says tonight about 25,000 prisoners. I have sent minute to the interested Depts. to point out that we must make the most of this *at once*. . . . News of Lothian's† death. A great blow. Who will succeed him? P.M.'s list is Van, Pound, Rob Hudson‡ and someone else (I can't remember). All catastrophic. My list is Gerald Campbell§ (but he has offended our Dictator) and Anthony [Eden].

Friday, 13 December

P.M. is sounding Ll.G about Washington, and Ll.G. is 'interested'! R. Lindsay¶ is thought of. Talk with H., Strang, Roberts and R.A.B. about Spanish and Portuguese Islands. I'm sure we shouldn't initiate anything. So, I think, is H. And I believe even P.M. comes to that view. . . . Before he left H. asked me to think over what our terms would be *if* Italians crawl to us. I had already thought of this and told him roughly. *First*, we must have the *fleet*.

[Lord Halifax had been wondering whether it would be worthwhile to offer a bribe to Laval, and had concluded that the process would be both unprofitable and unpleasant. The unpleasantness, Cadogan remarked, would be immaterial:

* The victory at Sidi Barrani of Lt.-Gen. Sir R. O'Connor's Western Desert Force.

† Lord Lothian had been subject to spells of drowsiness for some time. A Christian Scientist, he refused medical treatment.

‡ Now Minister of Agriculture.

§ Sir Gerald Campbell, High Commissioner in Canada since 1938; Minister at Washington from Jan. 1941.

¶ Formerly Ambassador there, 1930–9.

The difficulty is that Laval's attitude is dictated by his belief that Germany will win.

It would therefore require a very large sum to persuade him to throw over his German friends. That would probably mean permanent exile from France and certainly from French political life.

Then I should certainly give Laval very little before he had delivered the goods and I am not quite sure what goods we should expect him to deliver.

Even if we got Laval on our side, we should have handicapped ourselves with an incubus. So long as he stayed there, though, once the Germans are out of France, the French people will see to it that Laval goes too. There is not enough market value in him.

Mr Churchill added on 15 December: 'He is no longer worth buying.'[27]]

Saturday, 14 December

H. called at F.O. at 10. He had been worried all night by P.M. about Spain. True the Spaniards have behaved v. badly about Tangier, and we sent them a snorter last night.* But I do *not* think it means they are in with the Germans,† and I do *not* think that, on that assumption, we should jump into the islands. Strang, Roberts and I had a talk with H. and primed him before he left at 10.50 to lunch with P.M.

. . . Laval dégommé and replaced by Flandin!‡ This *can't* be a change for the *worse*. 26,000 [Italian] prisoners in N. Africa! Had talk this evening with 'C' who thinks German plan is to do a 'Norway' on W. coast of Peninsula. This I think much more likely than attack on islands. On the other hand, Germany may seize Italy!

Sunday, 15 December

I found P.M. had sent telegram last night to Washington telling them to sound President informally about appointment of Ll.G. as Ambassador! I ascertained that H. (who met P.M. at lunch yesterday) had agreed to this, but they had both forgotten to approach the King!

Monday, 16 December

H. came in . . . to say Ll.G. had refused on health grounds. He made me drive with him to H. of L. to discuss. I said my next

* The Spaniards had recently occupied the International Zone, incorporating it into Spanish Morocco, and had dismissed British subjects from the administration.

† The Joint Intelligence Committee, under Cavendish-Bentinck, reported in this month that Franco would not co-operate with the Germans, and that they would not try to force their way into Spain.

‡ As Foreign Minister in Pétain's administration.

preferences were (1) R. Lindsay (2) Chatfield + G. Campbell. Heard later Winston inclining to Oliver Lyttelton.* Don't know him. Does he know America? Cabinet at 5. They approved our line on Tangier, but wanted S.H. to use some 'rough talk'. Home about 6.45. Worked before and after dinner. Drafted the 'rough talk' and wrote a minute to H. about Lie's broadcast—which is on the right lines—recognition on the part of small European nations that they must be British Dominions.

[Mr Trygve Lie, acting Foreign Minister of Norway, had advocated a closer alliance with the Atlantic countries, the British Empire and the U.S.A., during and after the war.]

Tuesday, 17 December

H. now suggests the combination Willingdon†–Campbell for Washington. Not bad. Don't know what P.M. will think. Gave H. my draft of 'rough talk' to Spain. He took most of it.

[On that afternoon, Beaverbrook told Halifax that he ought to take the Embassy at Washington himself. 'Whether his feeling was due to genuine conviction about Washington or to a desire to get me out of the F.O., I am not quite sure' wrote the latter.[28]]

Wednesday, 18 December

Absolutely quiet night. What is up?! There *was* some fog, but that is not enough to account for it. H. has had a letter from P.M. asking him to go to Washington. He doesn't want to, and I suggested how he should put his doubts to Winston. He and I went over to see Winston at 11.40—about Portuguese suggestion for Staff talks. I then left them to discuss Washington. . . . P.M. pressed him on Washington and would appoint Anthony in his place. H. left at 7 to see A. . . . A. *says* he won't take F.O. He may have to! H. asks me to think of other candidates. There are very few. Mine would be Malcolm M[acDonald] but I gather P.M. regards him as rat-poison on account of his connexion with Eire ports.‡ ? Alexander. But that means an awkward shuffle of the Cabinet. ? G. Lloyd. Might be awful: might be good. Rather a gloomy prospect altogether.

* President of the Board of Trade, 1940–1; Minister of State Resident in the Middle East, 1941–2.

† Formerly Viceroy of India.

‡ MacDonald, as Dominions Secretary, had negotiated the treaty of 1938 with Eire, whereby Britain had renounced the use of Berehaven and Lough Swilly. Churchill had strongly opposed the agreement.

Thursday, 19 December

H. went to see Winston again about Washington. Looks as though Winston beginning to press him.

[Churchill assured Halifax of his close accord, political and personal and of his admiration of the Foreign Secretary's work. At their interview Halifax said that everything seemed to him to weigh against the proposal. On 20 December, however, he received a second letter from the Prime Minister, putting the proposal more definitely: 'you are, I am sure, the one person best qualified for this paramount duty'.[29]]

Friday, 20 December

H. showed me a letter from Winston v. definitely pressing him about Washington. Saying it was *the* important spot: that he could have Gerald Campbell, so as to free him to come back here occasionally: he could resume his seat in War Cabinet whenever he did come back.

Picked up H. at 11.45 to go to Lothian Memorial Service in Westminster Abbey. Dorothy there, furious at Winston's letter. Declared she would see P.M. herself. . . . H.—and Dorothy!—went off after to No. 10. Saw them on their return. They had found it useless. Dorothy recognised this—had realised P.M.'s object really was to get rid of H. I said that had been my own conclusion. (When H. had said to me this morning that it was *not* a plot to get rid of him, I didn't contradict him as, if in the end he stayed, it would have done no good to have injected poison into their relations). It's true, I'm afraid—and Winston is making a grave mistake—at this end.

[The Prime Minister told Lady Halifax that Washington would give her husband the opportunity to do a piece of work reflecting much personal credit. He had been conscious of certain currents of opposition to Halifax's tenure of the Foreign Office. The Foreign Secretary's diary observes that for anyone not to consider the personal advantages would seem unintelligible to Churchill: 'nothing could have been kinder than he was, but he and Dorothy were certainly talking a different language and she said she felt . . . an abyss between his thought and hers'.

Halifax concluded that he had no choice, and in the event, he found the Washington Embassy a heartbreaking task during the early stages and a rewarding and refreshing one later. At the official lunch of farewell, in early January 1941, Halifax recalled the words of a railway official in India whom he had thanked for the excellent arrangements: 'It has always been a very great pleasure to see you off.' 'No doubt many of you here today are animated by feelings no less kindly than those of that station-master.'

In 1946, at the moment of his own departure from the Foreign Office, Cadogan wrote to Halifax: 'I so much enjoyed working for you that I look back, even to those hideous years, with a pleasant memory. I think I should have gone mad with anyone else.'[30]]

Sunday, 22 December *Thatched Cottage*

Walked past Dixter on Ewhurst path down to the bottom. Then right to the railway, where I found an old gentleman, a sort of plate-layer, eyeing doubtfully a football in the ditch by the side of the permanent way. He asked me—did I think this suspicious? I said everything was suspicious nowadays. The ball was plainly visible: it couldn't have been lost. It was spherical—blown up—so it wasn't thrown away. He said—how did it get there? I said 2 boys had been throwing it about in a compartment of the train, and it had gone through the window. He said that it would then have [been] *on* the track, till I reminded him that inflated footballs bounced. However, I didn't want to touch it any more than he did. I wanted neither a football nor an early grave, so I told him to 'report' it. This filled him with importance and we walked along the line for ¾ mile in pleasant, banal and rather unintelligible converse. . . . Quite a pleasant weekend. I have had 13 out of 52 this year!

Monday, 23 December

H's appointment in press, and Anthony to succeed him. . . . Had talk with H. who is resigned (both senses) and rather resentful. . . . Cabinet at 12. Saw A. before we went in, and greeted him on his return. At a point in the proceedings, P.M. made little speech voicing Cabinet's gratitude to H. for assuming this most important task. I looked up and saw the Beaver opposite me, hugging himself, beaming and almost winking. I didn't know what to do: I don't want to be privy to any of the Beaver's schemes (if it *was* his scheme). So I tried to look cordially shocked. I left Cabinet before the end to go and put in writing the amendments F.O. recommend in his broadcast to the Italian people (6 p.m. this evening). . . . P.M. sent for me about 3. I thought to be sacked! But he wanted to protest against all our amendments to his broadcast. I persuaded him to take one, but had to let him discard the others. He then kept me for a chat. Explained that there was growing criticism of H. which led to attacks on 'F.O.'!

Tuesday, 24 December

About 11.45 went to see H. Wilson and [R. V.] Hopkins about our financial difficulties in U.S.—and about Dutch and Belgian gold, which we must try to snaffle. We *can* snaffle the Belgian, but I don't want to be harder on them than the Dutch. 12.30 Machtig*—about Gerald Campbell. Arranged with him a preliminary sounding, but then heard P.M. was raising difficulties (I don't know what—what a bore he is!) and I had to hang everything up. Told A. about the Belgian gold and he agreed and I wrote to H.J.W. . . . We're not bombing tonight or tomorrow. Wonder whether the Germans will fall into the trap! No alert so far (9.30). If they bomb and we don't, we can score on it. Anyhow I'm glad we don't.

Wednesday, 25 December

Swiss complain that we violated their air last night—when we hadn't a machine over Europe! This seems to prove that the Germans do it, and I hope we can make capital out of that. There was no air activity on either side last night: Thank Goodness we decided not to bomb. We should have looked fools, talking what Joe K[ennedy] would call all that 'God stuff', if we had bombed and the Germans had not.

Friday, 27 December

A. arrived soon after 10. Went to Cabinet with him at 12. Not much news, except that Americans are being *very* tiresome about financial matters. Maybe Pres. wants to be able to show Congress that he has got all he can out of us.

Sunday, 29 December

Home for tea soon after 5, after talking to A. at Frensham about our trying to torpedo a ship going in to Porto Delgado. I think, and Admiralty agree, that we had much better make a clean breast of it to Salazar† and apologise, as he must know about it (Portuguese have one of our unexploded torpedoes). A. agreed.

Monday, 30 December

Very heavy attack last night—mostly incendiary on the City. Could see a tremendous glow when I went to bed. Dirty dogs. . . . Cabinet at 12. Decided to advertise attack on City—quite rightly. This may help us enormously in America at a most critical moment. Thank God—for all their cunning and industry and efficiency—the Germans are fools. Lunched at home. Awful accumulation of work. H. came in in afternoon. Have had very nice note from him. . . . A. now living in F.O. Don't know whether that will turn out a good thing or a bad.

* Sir Eric G. Machtig, P.U.S., Dominions Office, 1940–8.

† Dr Antonio de Oliveira Salazar, Prime Minister of Portugal, 1932–68.

[Eden occupied high office for the whole of the war. For five years he was a member of the Defence Committee, for four and a half Foreign Secretary and a member of the War Cabinet, and for the better part of three Leader of the House of Commons. He travelled once to Ankara, twice to Washington and Quebec, thrice to Athens and Moscow and four times to Cairo, in addition to attending the conferences at Teheran, Yalta, San Francisco and Potsdam. 'As Permanent Under-Secretary and therefore my principal official adviser', he wrote, 'Cadogan was at all times wise and thorough. These qualities, and his exceptional experience, enabled him to take much of the burden off me.'[31]

It would be pointless to pretend that their relations were invariably untroubled. But a diary kept in telegraphic style by a much-harassed official does not always contain considered views. Argument and ephemeral troubles are apt to receive a disproportionate attention. For every recorded disagreement, there were doubtless many agreements mentioned briefly or not at all. It is well to remember that according to the published evidence and to the testimony of those who saw them together, Cadogan and Eden had high respect for each other. Sir Alec did not re-read the whole of his Diary for the war years. When, however, he saw again his entries for the first half of 1941, he said:

> I see that I sometimes wrote rather sharply about Anthony. I don't think any Secretary of State I served excelled him in finesse, or as a negotiator, or in knowledge of foreign affairs. When something had to be done, Anthony would long to do it. That quality was perhaps carried to a fault; but it was on the whole a good fault for a Foreign Secretary. No one worked harder. And then to take on the Leadership of the House! How he endured those awful gaseous Members I shall never know.]

Tuesday, 31 December

A. in rather a flap. When he was at W.O. he seemed admirable, but I fear that here he is getting as jumpy as ever. Talk with him, David S[cott] and Whitehead* about P.M.'s proposed message of appeal to Pres., which we approved, and message about destroyers and their shortcomings, which we disapproved. Or at least we said it should be in a different form, denying story that we couldn't man them and explaining their defects, details of which would be given to N[aval] A[ttaché]. . . .

I generally write a little homily on New Year's Eve. I haven't much to say tonight—except that worse things have happened during this year than we could have expected. But one thing is much better than anyone could have hoped—and that is the British spirit. I am amazed at the courage of my fellow-countryman. I am rather a

* T. W. Whitehead, adviser on American affairs, F.O., 1940–3.

physical coward, and I can't say how I admire the courage I see all round me. T, in the first place, is marvellous. I couldn't have thought she could stand the kind of thing she's been through. But she is far braver than I am, and more practical and more helpful. Such a spirit can*not* be beaten. Everything—on paper—is against us, but we shall live. I don't frankly, see how we are going to win, but I am convinced that we shall not lose. And if you hang on—like a bull-dog—it's funny what things do happen. The enemy is a very good facade. But if it cracks, it will crack suddenly and cataclysmically. . . . God bless us and bring us through the awful year that is coming to us. I hope I may not fail.

1941

Wednesday, 1 January

Got further evidence against Muselier.* . . . Talked to A. [Eden] about Muselier. P.M. of course wants to hang him at once. I pointed out possible effect on de G. movement and suggested we must consult de G. first, who is away in the country. A. agreed. Home about 7.

H. H[opkinson†] rang up to say Morton instructed by P.M. to proceed at once against Muselier and Co. I said P.M. ought to talk to A. first. A. rang up later. P.M. still insists. I said all right provided he realises what is at stake. Awful lot of work and some correspondence. A few have congratulated me on the K.C.B. already. Hope many more won't do so!

Thursday, 2 January

12.30 A. and I saw de G. and broke to him news about Muselier and Co. I had a talk to him after about Indo-China. de G. affects to be sceptical about Muselier.

[The documents appeared to prove that Muselier, secretly in touch in Vichy, had attempted to transmit to Darlan the plan to attack Dakar and that he was plotting to hand over the *Surcouf*, a French submarine.[32]]

Friday, 3 January

de G. came to see me and A. at 10.45. He made an impassioned, but quite undocumented, defence of M. Of course he doesn't want a scandal! We promised to hasten impartial investigation. . . . I tried

* Vice-Admiral E. Muselier, Commanding Free French naval forces, 1940–2.
† Private Sec. to Cadogan.

to get the Muselier story straight. There isn't a case—yet. . . . It was that baby Dictator Winston who ordered immediate (and premature) action. . . . de G. has worked himself up into being a passionate advocate of M. Found A. had slipped away to the country. Got away about 6.50 with lots of work.

Saturday, 4 January

Alexander rang me up this morning to say that M[uselier]'s lot should be alleviated. I agreed: I wanted to hand him over to Admiralty. But when Alexander realised that P.M. had had a hand in the affair, he went all wankly and said we should be very careful! I said I was quite prepared to take responsibility of making M. more comfortable. But I discovered later that Alexander had rung up P.M. and asked whether Admiralty could take over M. and P.M. had said 'No'! How frightened of the P.M. all these people are. (So am I, because he's impulsive and undependable.) So when Admiral Dickens* came to see me later I said I could do no more. M. had been moved from Pentonville to Brixton, which is better, and I rang up A. Maxwell† and told him to do the best that Brixton allowed.

Monday, 6 January

5.30 discussion with A., O.S., R.A.B., Collier and Maclean‡ about Russia. Glad to find A. not 'ideological' and quite alive to uselessness of expecting anything from these cynical, blood-stained murderers. P.M. has now authorised removal of M. to Greenwich (where Byng was kept, before being shot!). Home soon after 7. Masses of work.

Tuesday, 7 January

I had talk with A. about rumours of German move into Balkans, which looks imminent. The Greeks are in a flap. I believe there's more to be done, now, in Albania than in Libya. A. has put this to P.M. who, I think, agrees.

Wednesday, 8 January

A. told me to telegraph to Palairet that we are prepared to send Wavell at once to Greece. This is a good move. Got away about 7, after talk to R.A.B. about Bevin's paper—long promised—which

* Admiral Sir G. C. Dickens, principal naval liaison officer with Allied navies.

† P.U.S., Home Office, 1938–48.

‡ Fitzroy H. Maclean, then in F.O.; later resigned and led British military mission to Yugoslav partisans, 1943–5.

doesn't amount to much in practice. Thing to do is to treat it very gingerly and politely.

Thursday, 9 January

X* has now confessed that the Muselier documents are forged! So we are releasing everyone and P.M. apologised to de G. at 5 this afternoon! I gather he did it fairly well, though he said to A. before 'When I'm in the wrong' (I didn't know he ever admitted he *was*) 'I'm always very angry'!

Friday, 10 January

A. brought Hopkins† along to introduce. Seems simple and nice. Fixed up tel. to Turks telling them we are helping Greece and trying to get them in or at least assurances of their coming in. (Defence Committee last night decided on quite adequate assistance to Greece.)... 3.30 Brazilian, to whom I grovelled about Muselier 'affaire'. P.M. yesterday apologised to de G. But won't have anything to do with Muselier! *We* have got to apologise to him!!

[On this day Harry Hopkins spent three hours with the Prime Minister, whom he assured that

> The President is determined that we shall win the war together. Make no mistake about it. He has sent me here to tell you that at all costs and by all means he will carry you through, no matter what happens to him—there is nothing that he will not do so far as he has human power.

A few days later, after seeing off Lord Halifax at Scapa, Churchill and Hopkins dined in Glasgow with Tom Johnston, Secretary of State for Scotland. Churchill wept when Hopkins said:

> I suppose you wish to know what I am going to say to President Roosevelt on my return. Well, I'm going to quote you one verse from that Book of Books in the truth of which Mr Johnston's mother and my own Scottish mother were brought up: 'Whither thou goest I will go; and where thou lodgest, I will lodge; thy people shall be my people, and thy God my God.'

And then, very quietly, 'Even to the end'.

At this stage, the Lend-Lease Bill still had to pass Congress. Information from Bangkok suggested that Thailand and Japan were planning, probably for April, simultaneous movements by the former into Laos and

* A member of the F.O. staff.

† Harry Hopkins, U.S. Secretary of Commerce, 1938–40; special adviser and assistant to Roosevelt, 1940–5; christened by Churchill 'Lord Root-of-the-Matter'.

Cambodia and by the latter into Southern Indo-China and Saigon. Such an advance would bring Japan to the borders of Burma, leaving Malaya and the Dutch East Indies the more dangerously exposed. Butler gave the Thai Minister a warning on 8 January.[33] At the end of the month the Thai Prime Minister said that Japanese warships would patrol off Indo-China and Thailand so long as Japan continued to act as 'mediator' in the dispute between Thailand and Indo-China; whereupon a further warning was given against an alliance with Japan or economic concessions damaging to Britain. This elicited a satisfactory answer.]

Sunday, 12 January

Spoke to A. on telephone and sent him down a draft telegram to Angora, urging that Turks must resist an *occupation* of Bulgaria. German game is, I think, plain. They are concentrating a large, aggressive, force in Roumania. Everyone says they can't embark *now* on a Balkan campaign. But what they will do is to occupy Bulgaria as they have done Roumania. Then threaten Greece into making peace or—pounce on her. We *must* try to get the Turks to help forestall this.

Tuesday, 14 January

Not too much to do, and A. fairly calm. Wrote him a minute about S.O. [Special Operations] activities, which don't seem to me much good. They can produce nothing but the old schemes, . . . which are all problematical, and they want a completely free hand. Not much further news from Balkans. German plan is evidently to infiltrate into Bulgaria. We can't get the Jugs to say they will resist this—nor even, yet, the Turks. Though both will resist an attack.

[Informed of British plans for placing extra air and mechanised forces in Greece, Prince Paul said that the effect would merely be to bring the Germans into the Balkans. They would triumph there. The British proposal he judged 'rash and mistaken'. Yugoslavia, he stated, would resist the passage of German troops; but a later message indicated that this resolution might not hold good if the British set up a front at Salonika. Churchill minuted before the Cabinet on 14 January:

> The evidence in our possession of the German movements seems overwhelming. In the face of it Prince Paul's attitude looks like that of an unfortunate man in a cage with a tiger, hoping not to provoke him while steadily dinner-time approaches.[34]

From January the Luftwaffe began to operate seriously in the Mediterranean, with the result that Allied shipping had to face attacks more effective than those previously mounted by the Italians.]

Wednesday, 15 January

Devised telegram to Belgrade conveying message to Prince Regent, who has lost his head and his nerve.

Thursday, 16 January

Freezing more than 8°. Cabinet 11.45. We got down officially 2 raiders over London last night. (Later I heard probably 5.) There was an alert about 11.30—rather noisy—and one again in the small hours. But I slept well. Wavell has seen Metaxas who (probably prompted by Prince P.) refuses all aid in men. Even refuses guns, if accompanied by crews! Lunched at Flat. Defence Committee at 6 to consider Wavell's telegram. I sent O.S. off with A. They got back about 7.15. Agreed, of course, that we can't force assistance down Metaxas' throat. C's of S. drafting telegram repeating our arguments. I think these Balkan States are probably wrong. But they are all terrified. And it *may* be that the Germans are hoping to lure a small British force into the Balkans, to destroy it.

Friday, 17 January

Freezing 11°. Fairly quiet night. A frightful day in which everyone lays hand on every box they can find, crams into it all the worst and most complicated Files, and throws them at my head. So I effected nothing, beyond trying (without success) to keep my chin above water. Really nothing of importance—as so often happens when one is busiest.

Saturday, 18 January

Telegrams this morning from Tangier showing Weygand has decided to re-enter the war,[35] but can't do it till he gets material—and how can we supply that to him? Asked Chiefs of Staff to study question. Reports coming in of German-Italian designs on Tunisia. Warned Vichy and Weygand of this. (A. away. Spoke to him on an inaudible telephone.) A. says Winston has rung him up and deprecated attack on *one* Dodecanese Island. So do I. But we *do* want the *lot*. Otherwise we're cut off from Turkey. Told C's of S. that A. shared Winston's view.

Monday, 20 January

Milder. Incredible slush and filth. Drove to F.O. Not an awful lot doing. P.M. wants attack on Sardinia studied! C's of S. produce a paper, urging, much more sensibly, capture of *Dodecanese* and hankering after (much more difficult) capture of Sicily. Lunched at home. Bought some shirts (my laundry having been bombed!). Dupuy* at 3.45. Tried to ease him off: he wants to be a negotiator. I want him to be a postman. Cabinet at 5. Shipping losses rather bad again. Tobruk to be attacked tomorrow. As Greeks refuse our assistance (from funk) we'd better go on in N. Africa. Cabinet listened 6.10–6.30 to Pres. R[oosevelt]'s inaugural speech, which came through very clear.

Tuesday, 21 January

Stacks of telegrams from Angora. I suppose the Turks *are* all right, but they're not very convincing in the rôle.

Thursday, 23 January

Meeting 11.30 with G.J. and Nelson† about Roumania. Seeing that turmoil has begun there, decided to jump in at once, even though our arrangements not complete. A. agreed and got P.M.'s concurrence.

Monday, 27 January

3.15 meeting with G.J., C.D., Phil Nichols and others. Agreed to go ahead with trying to 'keep the pot boiling' in Roumania, though I fear this may be difficult.

Tuesday, 28 January

Talk with A. about his idea of him, or me, or someone else, doing a tour of the Middle and Near East. Don't think I should help much, though quite prepared to go if asked. Would be a blessed relief from the tide of boxes that overwhelm me twice or thrice daily. But I am rather too much of the same calibre as Hugessen and Co. and I don't quite see what I should contribute. On the other hand, a big gun—A. or a Minister—will merely scare them [the Governments] out of their wits. . . . 3.30 Bulgar. V. nice little man, but what he says doesn't go. He wants to know whether we can offer Bulgaria air assistance. I want to know whether they'll ask for it!

Home about 7.30, with a full box.

Thought I had a cold coming on. But I'm not sure: it may be talking too much yesterday, and smoking too much and too generous libations of Kümmel. We'll see tomorrow morning!

* Pierre Dupuy, Canadian chargé d'affaires at Vichy. He had recently talked with Marshal Pétain and Admiral Darlan.

† Sir F. Nelson of S.O.E.

Wednesday, 29 January

It was the Kümmel!

. . . C[lifford] Norton talked to me about . . . help for Turkey and I later impressed on A. necessity for avoiding appearance that we are deserting Greece and falling back on a backward Turkish defence line.

[General Metaxas died on 29 January. M. Koryzis became Prime Minister and General Papagos C.-in-C.]

Thursday, 30 January

Quiet night. Still dark and cold (34°). Walked to F.O. Shipping losses still ominous. A heavy day. . . . Talk to A. about last night's discussion. It was agreed to offer Turkey 10 squadrons.* This quite good.

Friday, 31 January

Saw final draft of P.M.'s message to Ismet.† But hear that Chiefs of Staff are looking at it again. Maybe that's because there's a wire in from Wavell saying Benghazi will take a month at least. More or less settled that A. is to go out. Managed to keep abreast of work by shirking A.'s meeting on French propaganda.

Monday, 3 February

Cold 30°—light snow falling. Walked to F.O. Found that O.S., in my absence, had simply passed on every box to me with the label marked 'On return'. This is really a bit thick, and I was snowed under! . . . Grappling with *tons* of boxes. I must reorganise the F.O. It is getting out of hand. I had a rubbish heap thrown at me by F[ar] E[ast] Department, which I rejected. Bennett‡ came down and explained matter to me. I said that I couldn't be expected to waste my time grubbing in these garbage heaps. Cabinet at 5. Nothing very exciting. . . . Home about 7.45. *Masses* of work. Warning just gone (11.10 p.m.). Turkish M.F.A. has answered our offer of air help in just the same sort of timorous, sticky terms employed by the Greeks. I fear my suspicions of Turkey are confirmed. They have given us *no* concrete proof that they have any backbone at all. A depressing day.

Wednesday, 5 February

11.30 meeting on Far East, with A., Horace [Seymour], and Bennett. Looks pretty black. And later in day there were Jap telephone talks that look very ominous.

* Britain was already committed to help Turkey if she was attacked and to supply munitions meanwhile.

† Gen. Ismet Inönü, President of Turkey, 1938–50.

‡ J. Sterndale Bennett, head of the Far Eastern Dept., 1940–2, 1944–6.

Thursday, 6 February

Cabinet 12.15. Complete Italian rout in N. Africa,* and Wavell expects to be at Benghazi 'in a day or 2'. Discussion of undertaking to Dutch about E. Indies. Admiralty tiresome† and it had to be adjourned for discussion between the two Departments. . . . Some more very bad-looking Jap telephone conversations, from which it appears they have decided to attack us. A. was seeing Hopkins and I went in and guardedly gave them the news. We then went over to see P.M., about 6.50. Found he had been 'Cabinet-making'—consequent on poor G. Lloyd's death. A. sympathised at this extra burden, but P.M. said he liked it—as he evidently did. Showed us the list, and asked what we thought of Bernard Norfolk.‡ I thought it very good. A. asked how he had thought of it. W.S.C. said he had been through a list of Dukes—Buccleuch, Westminster, Bedford, Manchester—we didn't stop to hear the rest! Instructed H. to pass on to U.S. government our information about the machinations of these beastly little monkeys. Home about 7.30.

Friday, 7 February

A. saw Shigemitsu and told me after he was afraid he might have gone too far, as S. seemed surprised and shocked. I assured him it was all right: a little of that medicine was good for them. . . . 3.20 meeting with A. and Chiefs of Staff on F[ar] E[ast]—particularly in regard to our position vis-à-vis Dutch in E. Indies. We wanted to give Dutch a sort of guarantee, but Staffs against it—particularly Admiralty. Didn't reach any agreement. Benghazi fell today!

[Eden asked Shigemitsu outright whether Japan intended to attack British territory. Britain would not concede Japanese claims to domination in the Far East and would defend herself vigorously. He felt sure that the Ambassador would have left the Japanese government in no doubt about the unity and spirit of the Empire? 'We were absolutely convinced that . . . we could not fail to secure final victory.' Shigemitsu asked whether he should transmit all this to Tokyo. Eden said that he should.[36]]

Saturday, 8 February

Preliminary reply from the Turks, not too discouraging. They even

* This advance cleared the Italians from Cyrenaica. 130,000 Italian prisoners, and a mass of equipment, had been taken.

† Admiral Phillips spoke of British inferiority to Japan at sea. Ten months later he went down with his flagship, *Prince of Wales*, after an attack by Japanese aircraft. The Secretary for India, Mr Amery, who had also a very poor opinion of Pound, wrote after this meeting: 'The Admiralty is rotten at the top.'

‡ Joint Parliamentary Secretary, Ministry of Agriculture, 1941–5.

seem to contemplate A. visiting Angora. Lunched with A. at Savoy. H. Hopkins, H. Johnson, R.A.B. and O. Sargent. We impressed on H.H. the danger, not only in F.E., but also to our Cape Route, of any Jap adventure in the region of Malaya. And we asked him to follow up Donovan's* good work in the Balkans. Didn't get away till nearly 3.30. Went back to F.O. with A. and helped him to dictate minute to P.M.

Monday, 10 February

Dined at home and attended Defence Committee 9.30 till 12.30. Settled A. and Dill should go out. Decided to stop at Benghazi and run over to Balkans. Dill inclined to say our first obligation is to Turkey. P.M., rightly, I think, said he wouldn't accept that. Greece was fighting and Turkey was doing nothing but evade rather plain obligations. We ought to do all we can to help Greece. That may encourage Turkey. Abandonment of Greece would confirm Turkey in what I believe to be their quite equivocal attitude. We'll give them what's left over.

[On 11 February, the C.I.G.S. telegraphed to Wavell:

> General feeling is that assistance to Greece and/or Turkey must come first apart from strain on Navy and R.A.F. which advance to Tripoli would involve.]

Tuesday, 11 February

I and R.A.B. to carry on, calling in Bobbety if wanted. Don't think I shall do this often!

Wednesday, 12 February

5.30 talk with R.A.B. about work. We shall work together all right. 7 P.M. sent for me to discuss various things, including method of work. He evidently does *not* want Bobbety associated with it!

Friday, 14 February

P.M. has gone to look at 1st Armoured Div., so I wasn't harried, but a lot of work. Bulgarian Minister at 12, whom I lectured and told he must fight the Germans! I believe he's of that opinion himself, but it's a grim prospect for his country. . . . 3.15 Dutch Minister, who wants combined Anglo-Dutch-U.S. warning to Japs. Pointed out U.S. [constitutional] difficulty and told him what we had already done. Promised to see if there was more we could do.

* Col. William Donovan, head of O.S.S. (Office of Strategic Services), had recently toured the Balkans on Roosevelt's behalf and had expressed his confidence in British victory.

Saturday, 15 February

Showed R.A.B. some telephone conversations which seem to show Japs are climbing down. If this is really so, how valuable this form of eavesdropping has been!

[Churchill's account remarks that he 'became conscious' of a stir in Japanese circles. 'They were evidently in a high state of excitement, and they chattered to one another with much indiscretion. In these days we kept our eyes and ears open.' It seemed that war might be imminent; alternatively, the activity might be a cover for Japanese depredations in Thailand and Indo-China. 'I ought to let you know' the Prime Minister telegraphed to Roosevelt, 'that the weight of the Japanese Navy, if thrown against us, would confront us with situations beyond the scope of our naval resources'. The Japanese could take what they wanted in the Dutch East Indies, raid the coasts of Australasia, plunder the trade routes and communications across the Indian and Pacific Oceans. Quite apart from grievous economic effects, the threat of a major invasion of Australia and New Zealand, which had already sent their best troops to the Middle East, would enforce the withdrawal of the Fleet from the Eastern Mediterranean, with disastrous consequences for the North African campaign and the Turkish attitude.

Very soon after this, it was learned that Matsuoka, the Japanese Foreign Minister, would visit Berlin, Rome and Moscow. Shigemitsu assured Churchill that Japan had no intention of attacking Britain or the United States, a statement which Hull disbelieved. At a second interview, on 4 March, the Ambassador again emphasised Japan's desire not to fight Great Britain.[37]]

Monday, 17 February

12.30. Soubbotitch.* Told him I was disappointed with his Govt. for their backwardness in Yugoslav-Turkish talks. Only hope for Balkans lay in their getting together. . . . 3.30 Iraqi Ch. d'A. who said he hoped we were now satisfied by the change of Govt. Wd. we give them $750,000? I said we welcomed the new Govt. and were waiting to see what they wd. do. First thing we wanted them to do was to kick out Italians. When they'd done that, we might consider doing things to help them. . . . R.A.B. brought me message from Matsuoka, conveyed to him by Shigemitsu. All very nice, but meaningless. But there may be some significance in fact that he thinks it necessary to send such a message!

Tuesday, 18 February

Various telegrams which make one feel that unless we can make really good show in Balkans, we'd better clean up Africa and get the victorious 'Army of the Nile' alongside Weygand in Tunisia. Put

* Dr. Subotić, Yugoslav Minister in London.

O. S[argent], Strang and H. Seymour on to it and will consider sending minute to P.M.

[The Prime Minister took charge of the Foreign Office in Eden's absence. Cadogan was soon receiving characteristic minutes from him. These are some examples from February and March:

'We have received nothing but ill-treatment from Vichy. It would have been better to have had [as Pétain's successor] Laval, from our point of view, than Darlan, who is a dangerous, bitter, ambitious man, without the odium which attaches to Laval . . . an end should be put to the cold-shouldering of General de Gaulle and the Free French movement, who are the only people who have done anything for us, and to whom we have made very solemn engagements.'

'The zeal and efficiency of a diplomatic representative is measured by the quality and not by the quantity of the information he supplies. He is expected to do a good deal of filtering for himself, and not simply to pour out upon us over these congested wires all the contradictory gossip which he hears.'

'All this goes to show that we should continue to give increasing support to General de Gaulle. . . . I am sure Darlan is an ambitious crook. His exposure and Weygand's weakness will both, as they become apparent, inure to the credit of de Gaulle.'

'I am in principle in favour of constitutional monarchies as a barrier against dictatorships, and for many other reasons. . . . The main policy of the Foreign Office should . . . be to view with a benevolent eye natural movements among the populations of different countries towards monarchies. Certainly we should not hinder them, if we cannot help.'

'Monsieur Stoyadinovitch should be treated with formal courtesy, but kept under constant surveillance. The Governor [of Mauritius] should be informed that he is a bad man. . . . Food and comfort should be appropriate to the scale of a colonel.'[38]]

Wednesday, 19 February

Eventually—about 12.15—got the Department's and O.S.'s lucubrations about Tripoli, Balkans, German infiltration into N. Africa. Stacks of minutes and drafts, of course—quite indigestible. Dictated, in 10 mins., minute for P.M. setting out arguments, with bias in favour of abandoning our friends and going on with Tripoli.* A shot in the dark—as I don't know what is entailed—but felt bound to put it up. Squared Van and enlisted R.A.B. and sent it over. It will probably produce explosion! . . .

Dalton sent for me at 5.30 on excuse of discussing N. Africa. Really he wanted my opinion on whether to protest to P.M. about indiscretion of Brendan B[racken] who is attacking him. I said he

* Where General Erwin Rommel had just arrived to command the German troops.

wouldn't effect anything definite in that quarter, though I should like to see P.M. warn B.B. about his indiscretions again, if that would have even a temporary effect. These irresponsible unscrupulous amateurs are Fifth Column!

[Earlier that afternoon Dalton had seen Vansittart, who said that he had not been consulted about Eden's visit to the Middle East, against which he would have advised. He thought Eden would get nothing from the Turks. Vansittart added that his position in the Foreign Office became more and more impossible.

Immediately afterwards Cadogan arrived. 'So I get the personal contrast at its most vivid,' Dalton wrote. 'No doubt there is much to be said for C. Steady, common-sensible, unruffled. . . .' Cadogan too expressed his doubts about Middle Eastern affairs, on the lines of his minute to the Prime Minister. He feared that the Greeks might have to make a separate peace, but that even that would be better than having Greece devastated to the last acre or putting in British troops and seeing them trapped. He felt sure that the Germans had been trying to entice a British force into Greece, and did not believe the Turks or Yugoslavs would move. If they would, to put British troops into Greece would be a different matter.[39]]

Thursday, 20 February

P.M. rang up about 11.30 and gave me instructions for an angry note to Shigemitsu. Cabinet 12. P.M. announced A.'s trip and gave a little review of the questions he will have to settle, leaving room—I was glad to see—for the possibility of Tripolitania. I got an answer from him to my minute which was quite moderate and not discouraging. I'm sure all these things are in his mind, but I felt bound to point them out.

The Cabinet's instructions were that Eden was to represent H.M.G.

> in all matters diplomatic and military. . . . His principal object will be the sending of speedy succour to Greece. For this purpose he will initiate any action he may think necessary with the Commander-in-Chief of the Middle East, with the Egyptian Government and with the Governments of Greece, Yugoslavia and Turkey.

This directive was endorsed by the Cs.-in-C. Middle East. Wavell had already sent forces to Greece, and neither he nor the Air Officer Commanding, Air Chief Marshal Sir Arthur Longmore, believed that an advance to Tripoli would offer a feasible alternative at that time. The Greeks had from the start determined that they would resist the Germans, if necessary alone.

Saturday, 22 February

Fine morning but cold N.W. wind. 33°. Walked to F.O. Surprisingly enough, P.M. has swallowed message to Prince Paul, with unimportant alteration of one word! Telegrams beginning to come in from A. of his discussions with Wavell. Seems we could spare about 3 divisions and one armoured which *might* hold 'a line' in Greece. This might be a gamble worth trying. . . . P.M. sent me his re-draft of aide-mémoire he proposes to give to Shigemitsu on Monday. I made some suggestions, and returned it. Also sent him draft telegram to Washington summarising all the Jap talks that gave their game away. . . . [A. V.] Alexander, who rang me up about something else, says we've contacted a pocket battleship in the Indian Ocean. If we could do that in, *that* would impress the 'Dwarf slaves'.

Sunday, 23 February

Telegrams in from A. who seems to have plumped for helping Greece (he's in Athens now). That is certainly respectable, but we must eventually be beaten there. Telegram from Belgrade suggesting message from King to Prince Paul. Had it telephoned to P.M. and suggested he should advise King to send it. He agreed. But, tonight, King jibs—says it's too peremptory.

Monday, 24 February

P.M. arrived just before 12, when he was due to see Jap, and Turk immediately after. He sent for me to ask what to say. I gave him the dope. . . . Had a talk with R.A.B., who is exercised as to the figure he will cut at his first attendance at the Cabinet this evening. He needn't bother! . . . Read Chiefs of Staff report endorsing proposals for a Balkan expedition to help Greece. On all moral and sentimental (and consequently American) grounds, one is driven to the grim conclusion. But it *must*, in the end, be a failure. However, perhaps better to have failed in a decent project than never to have tried at all. A. has rather jumped us into this. But it is impressive that *Wavell*, and Dill endorse him. Cabinet at 5. Menzies* there. He evidently doubtful, but the general sense was to go ahead with it. It's a nasty decision, but I *think*, on balance, I agree with it. P.M. evidently made up his mind.

P.M. seems to have seen the Greek this afternoon, and I got a message during Cabinet that an agency was putting out that Greek had said his country didn't want help until invaded. This of course a lie, but I suggested to P.M. that it might be useful to us to let it go, to camouflage our plans! He agreed.

Wednesday, 26 February

Had a meeting at 3.30 with R.A.B., Menzies, Bruce and Shedden†

* R. G. Menzies, Prime Minister of Australia, 1939–41.
† Sir F. Shedden, Secretary to Australian War Cabinet, 1939–46.

—mainly about Far East. What irresponsible rubbish these Antipodeans talk!*

Thursday, 27 February

Cabinet at 5.30. P.M. very gloomy on shipping situation, which is murky enough (and an argument against this Balkan expedition). I raised question of revision of Italo-Yugoslav frontier and Cabinet agreed to give A. some latitude.

[The Turkish military situation proved to be a most disappointing one. Marshal Chakmak and his officers explained that they would not declare war when Germany attacked Greece—which should have been a Turkish obligation—because, lacking modern weapons, they would be a liability. Eden was successful in persuading the Turks to allow the diversion to Greece of supplies intended for, or *en route* to, Turkey. This was indispensable, for there were no other stocks available. Rather surprisingly—for the point could hardly have been passed *à outrance*, and the Turks knew perfectly well that they were at risk—they agreed.

Eden's telegram summarised the discussions thus:

> Turkey undertakes in any event to enter the war at some stage. She will of course do so immediately she is attacked. But if she is given time by Germans to re-equip herself she will take advantage of it, and will then make war at a moment favourable to the common cause, when her weight can be used with real effect.[40]]

Friday, 28 February

Telegram from A. at Angora, which puzzles me. It is couched in jaunty and self-satisfied terms, talking of the 'frankness' and 'friendliness' and 'realism' of the Turks. The 'reality' is that they won't do a damned thing. Has he had his head turned by crowds of hand-clapping Turks? And what is he now to say to the Yugoslavs and Greeks? The former will now of course curl up, and we shall be alone with the Greeks to share their inevitable disaster. The Turks at least in their recent declaration talk about their 'zone of security'. To A. they appear to have said quite flatly that they will only fight if attacked (which of course they won't be—yet). But he seems quite happy. What's bitten him?

[Churchill replied:

> Obvious German move is to overrun Bulgaria, further to intimidate Turkey by threat of air attacks, force Greece out of the war, and then

* Of this passage Sir Robert Menzies wrote: 'My colleagues and I went to the Foreign Office to discuss the problems of the Far East. The results were hopelessly disappointing. Cadogan's attitude was one of remoteness and almost indifference. I said with some bitterness of spirit: "Well, the only conclusion I can reach is that you have no policy in relation to these matters at all." '

turn on Yugoslavia, compelling her to obey; after which Turkey can be attacked or not, at their hostile convenience.

Your main appeal should now be made to Yugoslavia. . . . I should like you so to handle matters in Greece that if upon final consideration of all the factors . . . you feel that there is not even a reasonable hope, you should still retain power to liberate Greeks from any bargain and at the same time liberate ourselves.[41]]

Saturday, 1 March

Glad to find P.M. has sent a sobering telegram to our temperamental Secretary of State, saying 'You appear to have got nothing out of the Turks'. And that is true: he is going on a lemon-gathering expedition, and he has only got that ninny Dill, with him. (Wavell is in Cairo). I rang up No. 10 to make sure Wavell was being kept informed. This stunt trip is a most disastrous one. And A. seems quite gay about it. The only explanation I can conceive . . . is that A. expected the Turks to react strongly against our giving all our help to the *Greeks*. And of course the Turks *didn't*. They—quite rightly, don't expect to be attacked—yet. But that doesn't help the Greeks—or *us*. What the hell is A. going to say to Greeks and Yugoslavs? It's a diplomatic and strategic blunder of the first order. And what will Menzies say? (We shall have an interesting Cabinet on Monday!) Talked to O.S. and R.A.B., who share my amazement at A.'s Angora telegram. . . . B.B.C. tonight announce signature of Axis Pact by Bulgaria and entry of German troops. A real answer to A.'s silly antics.

Monday, 3 March

I sent message to P.M. asking what I was to do at Cabinet about the Balkans. Cabinet haven't seen the telegrams and will be sure to ask. He authorised me to read A.'s raspberry from Ankara. Which I did, and left them all looking rather blue-nosed. (Menzies had already seen it). Everyone's reaction is the same—how *can* one account for the jaunty tone of a recital of *complete* failure? Germans have swarmed over Bulgaria, and there we are. I confess everything looks to me as black as black. Shipping situation very bad, and I don't see where we are to turn. I'm sure a forlorn hope in Balkans will only do us harm—in France and Spain. I *wish* we could have gone on into Tripoli and joined up with Weygand. Probably now too late (if *ever* it was possible) as Germans seem to have landed. Complete silence from A. since his raspberry telegram!

Tuesday, 4 March

P.M. sent for me at 1 to talk about relief for unoccupied France, which is on Cabinet agenda for this evening. I *thought* I got him to see that we should probably have to give way.

... Cabinet 5.30. No further news from A., so could take no decisions. P.M. opened up on relief for France in entirely wrong sense. R.A.B. didn't realise what had happened and I had to chip in with contrary view. Completely confused discussion, ending in instruction to me to reconcile everything in draft telegram to Washington!

Wednesday, 5 March

Cabinet at 5.30 on A.'s telegrams from Athens. He has really run rather ahead of his instructions* and *agreed* to things which Greeks will take as commitments and on which they may make decisions as to their policy in a critical moment. He may have had to do it to prevent an immediate collapse. But really I think his head is turned a little.

[Eden telegraphed that he had found in Athens 'a changed and disturbing situation and the atmosphere quite different from that of our last visit'. The retirement from Thrace and Macedonia to the Aliakhmon line, which the British had thought to be agreed on 22 February, had not even begun. Papagos wished to 'dribble our forces piecemeal up to the Macedonian frontier'. This the British refused. They thought it equally disastrous to withdraw the offer of British military support; and therefore finally accepted three Greek divisions, little more than half the force earlier expected, for the Aliakhmon line. Meanwhile Prince Paul had promised Hitler that Yugoslavia would join the Axis.

The troops available for despatch to Greece were mainly Australians and New Zealanders. Both Governments acquiesced, though Menzies protested at the signature of this agreement without Australia's prior consent.[42] It was thought that Japan might attack Australasia at any time.]

Thursday, 6 March

A. has evidently committed us up to the hilt. Telegram this morning gives text of agreement signed with Greeks. ... Cabinet at 6. Awkward discussion†. P.M. evidently thinks we can't go back on A. and Dill, and I don't think we can—though I would if I could see any better alternative! K. Wood, Alexander and J. Anderson evidently

* Eden's instructions empowered him 'to formulate with the Greek Government the best arrangements possible in the circumstances. ... In an emergency he must act as he thinks best.'

† 'When this [the agreement] was revealed to them, it gave rise to mixed emotions in some of the members—annoyance that they should have been rushed in this way, secret satisfaction that if the thing went really wrong there was a good scapegoat handy!' Cadogan to Halifax, 18 March 1941.

out for A.'s blood. Finally decided to defer decision till we get A.'s answer to telegram which P.M. sent him last night. Meanwhile Palairet telegraphs saying we can't now let Greeks down, and A.'s answer will be the same.

Friday, 7 March

Cabinet at 12, which practically decided to go ahead in Balkans. On a nice balance, I think this is right.

[Churchill assured Eden immediately that by this decision the Cabinet had taken upon itself 'the fullest responsibility'. The fact that Cadogan's views on the Balkans situation shifted several times in a matter of weeks (c.f. the entries of 16 January, 10, 19, 22, 24, February, and 6, 7 March) testifies to the complexity of the issues.]

Saturday, 8 March

Had just got into bed, and trying to go to sleep when, at 12.30, Winston rang me up from Chequers about some telegrams from Belgrade which I hadn't seen. Nothing for it but to get up, dress and go to F.O. and ring him from there. Found messages from Prince P[aul] showing he was sending an officer to Athens to find out what help he could expect. This *may* be a good sign. So rang up Winston and told him I'd send a telegram to Athens urging that the utmost encouragement should be given. (Have since been ticked off by A. for doing anything from here except through him!) So I needn't have been to all that trouble! But just as well to do it, as Winston talked about the F.O. being 'shut down'. Must see about this.

. . . Wonder whether Yugoslavia really will do anything! What a chance to give the bloody ice-creamers the final kick in the pants!

Monday, 10 March

Cabinet met in the Dollis Hill War Room.* I left with R.A.B. at 11.30 and we arrived on time. Arrangements impressively good. P.M. not there—has slight bronchitis. I in a difficulty, as I didn't know this, and didn't know how much he'd want me to tell them. Gave them a hazy general impression (there isn't much definite news, as a matter of fact). Menzies then held forth for 40 mins. on Australian war effort. Very impressive, but no one but an Australian would have done it! However, he didn't do it badly.

Wednesday, 12 March

P.M. sent for me about his telegram to Roosevelt about supplies to France and N. Africa. It's not a good message—rather woolly—

* In the north-western suburbs of London.

not up to his form. After changing some detail, I suggested a change of shape. But he wouldn't have it!

Friday, 14 March

No decisive news. Jugs. still hesitant. Turks tightly enclosed in their shell. I really have more hopes of the former than of the latter. Look at the latter's form: they have so far carefully evaded every obligation they ever took! But I haven't *much* hope of the former. . . . 4.15 Maisky, to introduce his new Counsellor. I rather like Maisky, although—or perhaps because—he's such a crook. P.M. instructing A. to stay in Middle East. I believe that's right! We can carry on here, I hope.

Sunday, 16 March *Thatched Cottage*

Heard a bomb or 2 last night, but can find out nothing about them. Misty morning and cold. Went out about 11 and dug in kitchen garden. About 11.30 sky cleared and thereafter it was a cloudless summer day—quite a hot sun. Dug again after lunch till 3.15. Then picked up T. and we wandered down the meadows and picked primroses. I actually sat in sun for a bit. Really heavenly at last to get a glimpse of spring. But Hitler will make it hell. Picked some crocuses—as an experiment—and the first 2 doz. daffodils. Left 5.30. Home 6.50. Not too much work and no real news. A satisfactory day, and I feel a different man for the digging and the sun.

Monday, 17 March

3.30 talk with O.S. and P. Nichols about B.B.C. But as I. K[irkpatrick] has been run over by a motor-car, can't do much about it yet. Meanwhile P.M. storming about idiocies of B.B.C.—which *are* idiocies. The place *must* be properly controlled. . . . 5 Cabinet. 3 submarines destroyed and we have got Berbera. But the shipping losses continue! P.M. hopes to do something with Americans, to get them to help.

[On 18 March Cadogan wrote a short survey for Halifax:

R.A.B. and I constitute a happy little Duumvirate here under the all-seeing eye of the Most High. . . .

The Shipping position really causes the most worry here at the moment, and a Balkan campaign, conducted via the Cape, will be an added strain.

Night raids have begun again, but have so far generally been rather scattered. They seem to have been curiously ineffective against vital points, and you will have noticed that our night fighters have started what the P.M. calls 'clawing them down'.

I am glad to say I think we have come through the winter without any illusions, and I don't think any time has been wasted and our effort has been maintained at a high pitch. We must expect a terrific opening, soon, of the Campaign of 1941, but I don't think we are ill prepared. The sober calculation of our experts is that, at the present rate of wastage, Germany, by the end of this year, will only have increased her operational strength of aircraft by 400, which means that, given our lead in quality, we shall have an Air Force at least equal to her. . . .

I attended today the Pilgrims' lunch to Winant.* The P.M. gave a very good performance, and Winant made what I expect was a very good speech. But his delivery and manner was hurried, so that it was impossible to appreciate it fully, though he *does* get across the idea that he is sincere and in almost all respects the antithesis of Joe Kennedy. In private conversation he is completely inaudible.

Walking back from lunch at the Savoy, I found the P.M. and Seal getting out of a car to inspect the work on the 'fortress' which is being built on the old Whitehall Gardens site, and tacked myself on to them. The work being done is impressive, but not so much so as Winston's progress round the works, with his cigar, up and down ladders, puddling through half-set concrete, talking to workmen about their private affairs, putting to any sufficient audience the question 'Are we downhearted' and really enjoying himself thoroughly. And no doubt giving a good deal of pleasure. . . .

On the whole—till the storm breaks—life goes on here much as you knew it. There are no more discomforts. I suppose rationing has been tightened up, but the only result of which I am conscious is a slight reduction in the kitchen books. Though that is not much consolation when one reflects that Kingsley Wood will get all one's savings—and more.

To come back to where I began—the Balkans. I am pretty confident that we are doing the right thing in doing the most for Greece. We can hardly expect a material success, though it is hoped that both Dill and Wavell—neither of them uncautious—endorsed the policy unreservedly. But even if it is—immediately—a failure, I don't believe it is wrong.[43]]

Thursday, 20 March

Balkan news better. Turks really forthcoming after A.'s talk with them in Cyprus.† And they may encourage Yugoslavs. Only the 'Atlantic' looks bad. At end of Cabinet, P.M. said 'I'm not afraid of the air, I'm not afraid of invasion, I'm less afraid of the Balkans—but —I am anxious about the Atlantic'. . . . P.M. ringing up all after-

* J. G. Winant, U.S. Ambassador, 1941–6.

† This hope proved rather illusory. Sarajoglu's colleagues in Ankara thought that he had been too forthcoming.

noon about distribution of 'Eden' telegrams and so forth. But he seems in quite a good mood. Caught up arrears and came home 7.30 without much in my box.

Friday, 21 March

Everything fairly quiet, and I wasn't overwhelmed with papers, and P.M. quiescent. Yugoslavs seem to have sold their souls to the Devil. *All* these Balkan peoples are trash. Poor dears—I know their difficulties. They've got no arms, and no money and no industry. But then they shouldn't have behaved as Great Powers at Geneva—in spite of everything that Philip [Noel] Baker might say.

Saturday, 22 March

Had hoped to get to cottage. But there were telegrams from Belgrade suggesting message from King to Prince Paul. And the P.M. with a crashing telegram to Tsvetkovitch.* P.M. was on the telephone all the morning from Chequers. And he had the idea of carrying out [Operations] 'Shrapnel' and 'Brisk'. Meeting of Chiefs of Staff on latter arranged for 6 p.m. So my week-end went west. . . . Meeting with C's of S. at 6. Rather inconclusive. We set out the arguments but the recommendation rather depends on the *value* to *us* of the islands, if we get them. Study will be made of this, and report to P.M. tomorrow.

Sunday, 23 March

Quiet day in F.O. No signs of life from Winston. Balkans still a large question mark. Yugo[slavia] dithering and Turks drawing back into their shell.

Monday, 24 March

All the news from the Balkans is bad: the Yugoslavs are collapsing and the Turks are running out. The former are hard to blame, but the latter are the villains. So far, they've done *nothing* but evade *every* obligation. They now *refuse* to inform Yugoslavia of their declaration† to A. in Cyprus (see March 20). . . . Cabinet at 5. After we met, I got Transocean message that Jugs are off tonight to sign Pact. Told Cabinet. A. is doing all that is possible, and that is unavailing. Can only ask G.J. to blow up the Jug train! But he probably can't do that. Home 7.30.

* Dr Cvetković; Yugoslav Prime Minister since 1939.

† Turkey had agreed to propose to Yugoslavia an exchange of views in the event of a German attack on Greece.

Tuesday, 25 March

Jugs are signing—silly, feeble mugs. . . . P.M. sent for me at 3.15. He showed me telegram from Roosevelt agreeing to [aircraft-carrier] 'Illustrious' being repaired in U.S. Then he spoke to me about 'Son of a bitch', which I took to be Tsvetkovitch, but found he meant Stoyadinovitch.*

Wednesday, 26 March

P.M. sent for me about 3 to show me telegram he wanted to send to Belgrade. Upshot was that R. C[ampbell] was not to break with the Government. This quite right, provided he at the same time does not relax efforts to put another Government in their place! P.M. agreed and added a sentence I drafted.

[The telegram read:

> Do not let any gap grow up between you and Prince Paul or Ministers. Continue to pester, nag and bite. Demand audiences. Don't take NO for an answer. Cling on to them, pointing out Germans are already taking the subjugation of the country for granted. This is no time for reproaches or dignified farewells. Meanwhile, at the same time, do not neglect any alternative to which we may have to resort if we find present Government have gone beyond recall. Greatly admire all you have done so far. Keep it up by every means that occur to you.

Yugoslavia had the best army and air force in the Balkans. Eden had already authorised Campbell to secure a change of government by any means available, including coup d'état.[44] The British had indeed been giving money to one of the Serb parties, which had left the Government when the majority determined to capitulate to Germany. On the night of 26 March, the Prime Minister was arrested, the Regency abolished, King Peter II proclaimed, and Prince Paul dethroned. General Simović, to whom Colonel Donovan had spoken confidently of the Allies' prospects on his visit, became Prime Minister. Although there were Croat ministers in his Government, he lacked the support of Dr Matchek, leader of the Croat Peasant Party. For this and other reasons the new Government moved cautiously.[45]]

Thursday, 27 March

Good news on arriving at F.O., of coup d'état in Belgrade. Went to see P.M. at 11.40. He due to make speech at 12. Gave him his phrase 'Yugoslav nation has found its soul', which was featured by evening papers. We sent off telegrams to the President (U.S.), Belgrade and Angora. And he advised A. (hung up by weather at Malta) to return to Cairo. . . . Somewhat puzzling and rather discouraging news from Belgrade. Government seem to have put out

* Dr Milan Stoyadinović, Yugoslav Prime Minister, 1935–9.

a statement that their foreign policy isn't changed! Cabinet at 5. P.M. very elated. I threw a little cold douche, but pointed out that independent, and previous, reports on Simovich (from Athens and Angora) were good. Duff said H. Nicolson* had lunched with Soubbotitch, who was depressed. I said of course he was—he had missed the bus—hadn't resigned in time! P.M. said King ought to send a message 'before we went to bed'. . . . Back to F.O. 7.45 and dictated message from King and arranged for it to be submitted to P.M. Back for dinner about 8.10. (It looks as if Yugs *may* attack Italians at midnight! Prince P[aul] asking to come here! We can't allow that, but we'll get him out somewhere.)

Friday, 28 March

About 6 P.M. sent for me and gave me, to read, draft of a long telegram to A. on strategy. Gist was—what do we want of Turkey? Turkey won't be drawn into an offensive, and perhaps shouldn't be. We ought to say to her 'After events in Belgrade, Germany may be shy of attacking Yugoslavia, may pretend she never meant to attack Greece, and may turn her whole assault on *you*! Hadn't we, Greeks, Turks, Yugs better say if one is attacked all will defend: a strong defensive. Meanwhile, you Turks, don't get crumpled up in Thrace. Strategic retirement as a precaution. Then Hitler, with his 30 Divisions, may sheer off our 70. He may attack Soviet.' Told P.M. of our news of German armoured Divisions being rushed back to Cracow [Poland]. This rather in line with his ideas. But German order given *before* Yugo coup d'état. Yugo going canny. But I hope they're all right. Home about 7.30. P.M. will broadcast on Sunday night and says he may want to consult me. R.A.B. and O.S. going away, so my week-end done in!

[The Joint Intelligence Committee had suggested that an assault upon Russia would be Hitler's next objective.

> I noticed reports from Poland [wrote its chairman, Cavendish-Bentinck] that the Germans were increasing the length of the runways of the airfields in Poland and reinforcing these runways. It occurred to me that this was not being done for the benefit of Lufthansa! A little later we received reports that the Germans were beginning to subsidise again Bolshevik organisations in the Caucasus. These two pointers led me to suggest to my colleagues on the J.I.C. that the J.I.S. (its advisory sub-committee) should be directed to prepare a report on the possibility of a German attack on the Soviet Union.

* Harold Nicolson, Parl. Sec., Ministry of Information, 1940–1; M.P., 1935–45.

The report was prepared and was based on all sorts of information additional to the two items mentioned above. . . . If I remember right, it took a little time to convince the Chiefs of Staff that the Germans intended to go for the Russians.[46]]

Sunday, 30 March

[Cruiser] 'Sheffield', while stopping a French convoy, has been fired on by French coastal guns. Returned fire, to some effect, but is being bombed and this is unpleasant. Lunched at Flat and then went back to F.O. Found Admiralty had informed P.M., who didn't seem too excited. We must wait for more facts before we can put out statement. . . . News of naval battle [at Cape Matapan] v. good—3 Italian 8″ cruisers and 2 destroyers sunk, also probably a 6″ cruiser. What news for Matsuoka, who is arriving in Rome!

Home about 6.45. P.M. rang me up from Chequers to say French now bombing Gib[raltar]. Drafted telegram for him to send to Vichy through Washington warning them that if this goes on we bomb Vichy, and pursue them everywhere! He approved it. Also on his instructions drafted telegram to Wavell to warn Italians that if they scuttle ships in Massawah we won't feed an Italian in Africa.

Monday, 31 March

Had to go to meeting of Defence Committee at 9.45. About Djibouti. P.M. presided, and we rambled post-prandially. Home about 11.30.

[On this day Rommel launched his first attack against the weakened British force in North Africa.]

Wednesday, 2 April

A flap, because Admiralty have news that 'Dunkerque' going from Oran to Toulon—presumably for repairs. P.M. sent for me about 11.30 and found him and 1st Lord [Alexander] and 1st Sea Lord [Pound]. He told me to draft message from him to President. Got back to Office and found Zaleski* waiting for a talk. But I got message drafted and took it to P.M. at 1.15. He read it through and said 'Awfully good' and passed it.

Thursday, 3 April

Home reasonably early, but rung up by Hollis at 10.10 to summon me for meeting of Defence Committee at 10.30. P.M. had reply from President indicating—rather vaguely—that he would 'understand' an attack on 'Dunkerque'. I argued against it—which no one else dared! I agreed that it wouldn't bring French into *war* but might

* Polish Minister for Foreign Affairs, 1926–32, 1939–41.

mean transfer of Fleet. I asked how long repairs would take. 3–6 months, said Pound. I asked which was the better chance—2 torpedoes tomorrow or 3 months' bombing in Toulon. But A. Sinclair wouldn't help. Only one who helped—feebly—was Attlee. Alexander—though Pound and Phillips *hate* it—agreed, as usual, with P.M. So P.M. gave the order. But I hope U.S. representations *may* prevent it, and we have 2 big ships going through those waters tomorrow, which are more likely to.

Also discussed Italian civilians in E. Africa, and the appalling situation at Benghazi. Very gloomy. Finished about 12. I had to walk a long way before getting a taxi.

Friday, 4 April

P.M. sent for me about 7. Sat with him till 7.50 while he dictated—very slowly—some quite useful telegrams. He *was* going to Chequers. At 7.10, said 'make dinner at 9'. At 7.20 'I'll dine here and go down after'. At 7.30 'Put me through to Mrs Churchill: we can't go down tonight.'! Hope he won't have a meeting at midnight. Got away just before 8. P.M. told me he'd heard nothing of 'Dunkerque' and thought it 10 to 1 against her moving. Told him I hoped he'd win his bet. As regards Libya, he said 'No news, good news'. I hope we shan't get any.

Saturday, 5 April

Had a message from President that Vichy said 'Dunkerque' would not move for 10 days anyhow. This satisfactory. Sure news that Germany will invade Yugoslavia tomorrow morning. All the right people informed, but I don't know what we can do. Telegram from A. to say he's going back to Cairo today and leaving there for England tomorrow.

Sunday, 6 April

Rung up at 7.45 with news (fully expected) that Germany has declared war on Yugoslavia and Greece. This should put an end to all the dither in Belgrade.* No news at all. Soubbotitch called at 12.45 but *he* had no news. Asked for a 'message' and I gave him what I could, though I can't make pronouncements on behalf of the British Government.

. . . Rung up after dinner by No. 10. P.M. wants O'Malley pulled out at once.† In regard to my record of talk with Soubbotitch, said we should send official message if I thought it necessary. Got No. 10

* Simović had refused to allow a visit by Eden. Dill, who did go to Belgrade, failed to make an agreement. Fruitless staff talks were held on 3 April.

† From Budapest; Sir O. O'Malley was British Minister there.

to telephone him draft. Also received draft telegram from P.M. to President about 'Dunkerque', proposing to announce in H[ouse] of C[ommons] that he will sink her if necessary. I see no objection in principle—I always thought we ought to give some warning—but suggested amendments from security point of view. Alexander rang up about this draft. Evidently doesn't like it, but daren't say so to P.M. I suggested line he should take, but he said he would consult Pound. Best thing he can do.

Monday, 7 April

4.30 Hungarian, on whom I declared war. He not surprised but, I think, sad. Not much news from Balkans. Germans took a knock from the Greeks in Rupel pass (that is official). But they are apparently penetrating into Yugoslavia, and I haven't heard of a Jug firing a shot yet. . . .*

Cabinet at 5. V. gloomy. Bad air attack on Piraeus last night. At least 6 ships and valuable cargoes lost. Menzies evidently worried and rather critical. Jugs (according to 'C') seem to be very uncooperative. Shipping losses v. bad. We *may* stand at Tobruk, but v. doubtful. Altogether gloomy. Went over to see P.M. at 7.30 about military liaison with Jugs. He had other things on his mind, but was going to see Chiefs of S. . . . We ought to get a good liaison with Jugs at once. No use waiting for that farceur [General] Carton de Wiart to go out tomorrow.

Thursday, 10 April

Cabinet rather gloomy. 2,000 prisoners and 3 of our Generals taken in Libya. . . . Left F.O. 3.30 for Paddington to meet A., who arrived punctual. Drove with him to F.O. Gather he thought Libyan disaster due to muddle by our high military command, which I can *quite* well believe. He then went to see P.M. W. Monckton came about things I knew nothing about. (I suppose outsiders think I read and study each one of the 1200 or so communications that are received daily in the Office!) However I was sympathetic. 7 had a talk with A. in his flat. P.M. had been rather tiresome to him—saying he had never wished to help Greece! I said that must be his mood: no one could have supported A. more stoutly and consistently in his absence than P.M. had done.

[The Japanese Foreign Minister, Matsuoka, passed through Moscow, where he saw Stalin and Molotov, and thence to Berlin, where the Foreign

* Many of their aircraft were destroyed on the ground, despite Dill's urgings to disperse them; and the tactics of the Yugoslav army appear to have been ill-co-ordinated. All the same, Hitler had to postpone his attack on Russia in order to mount these Balkan operations; which in turn may have cost him the Russian campaign.

Minister assured him that Germany was in the 'final phase of her battle against England'. 'Should Russia some day take a stand that could be interpreted as a threat to Germany the Führer would crush Russia. . . . Germany had to be protected in the rear for her final battle against England. . . . It was now only a question of time until England would admit having lost the war.' Ribbentrop then pressed for an early Japanese assault upon Singapore. Matsuoka's responses were guarded.

Churchill thought it opportune to send Matsuoka a few pointed reminders. For examples:

> Did Japan's accession to the Triple Pact make it more likely or less likely that the United States would come into the present war? . . . Is Italy a strength or a burden to Germany? Is the Italian Fleet as good at sea as on paper? Is it as good on paper as it used to be? . . . Is it true that the production of steel in the United States during 1941 will be 75 million tons, and in Great Britain about 12½, making a total of nearly 90 million tons? If Germany should happen to be defeated, as she was last time, would not the 7 million tons steel production of Japan be inadequate for a single-handed war?

This document, transmitted to Moscow for delivery to Matsuoka there, was intercepted by the Germans and shown to Hitler. Still less pleasing to him must have been the news that Japan and Russia had signed a neutrality pact on 13 April. Stalin and Molotov made a tremendous fuss of Matsuoka, who shortly assured Churchill that Japanese policy was determined only after a very careful balancing of all the facts; and 'once determined, I need hardly tell your Excellency that it will be carried out with resolution but with [the] utmost circumspection, taking in every detail of changing circumstances'.

On return to Tokyo, Matsuoka told the German Ambassador that if Germany and Russia went to war, Japan could not remain neutral.[47] Nevertheless, the pact signed with Russia provided an open encouragement to Japan's southward expansion. Simultaneously the British heard that Japan had now concentrated between twelve and fifteen divisions for the purpose of attacking Malaya directly or through Thailand. The Thai Government had repeatedly refused to give an undertaking not to join in any aggression directed against Great Britain, though they said they would resist military encroachment by Japan. In addition to strategic significance, Thailand had rubber and oil.[48]]

Tuesday, 15 April

Telegram about 6 to say that Yugoslavs have capitulated! Sent it in to A., who was seeing Greek Minister. A. went over to P.M. after. Saw him when he got back and found him quite cheerful, and he said P.M. was the same. Greeks have withdrawn their left wing to keep touch with us. N. Africa not too bad.

Wednesday, 16 April

No confirmation of Yugoslav capitulation, but their effective resistance evidently at an end. Meanwhile it seems—from our most reliable source—that Germans yesterday broke through on our right down the [Greek] coast—which was considered by our G[eneral] S[taff] nitwits to be impossible! It *may* not be true, but I think it is. Libya (or should I say Egypt) a little better, but the outlook is glum indeed. When, in a few days, the Germans have rolled up the Balkans, they will cross over and turn us out of Egypt.

Thursday, 17 April

Awful Blitz last night (450 machines). Couldn't sleep till all clear at 4.30. Fine morning and warm. Walked by devious way to F.O. Area Piccadilly, St James' Street, Pall Mall, Lower Regent Street pretty well devastated. Cabinet 11.30. Admiralty hit. From his place at Cabinet table, Winston observed this gave him a better view of Nelson Column. Quite true. Papagos has asked us to evacuate and we agree to try. No one knows what happened. N. Africa looks a bit better. Winston says it's all right, referring to tenuity of enemy forces. But then how the hell did they get there? I'm not satisfied. Nor is Margesson.*

Friday, 18 April

Can't make out what's going on in Greece. Germans seem *not* to have broken through and we are retiring. This afternoon Wavell seems to have ordered [General H. M.] Wilson to stand on Thermopylae, though I thought idea was to evacuate. 3.30 talk with A. about Soviet. He has the usual itch to *do something*. Nothing doing—yet. Promised to draft a telegram to Cripps. . . . (A. yesterday accepted Van's resignation, though I understand they are going to cover him with ridicule by giving him a Peerage! Good God!!) Tried to grapple with arrears of work (*I* must have a Dukedom).

[In response to Halifax's enquiry, Cadogan gave this account of Vansittart's retirement:

> It was not till towards the end of Anthony's 2 months' absence in the East that I realised that I had seen very little activity on the part of the Chief Diplomatic Adviser. I asked Henry Hopkinson whether he had been sending him papers as usual. He said that no, as a matter of fact, he had not. So Van had seen nothing whatever for about 6 weeks. Though this had rankled, Van said not a word to me and, the matter having gone so far, I observed a masterly inactivity.

* Capt. D. Margesson, who had succeeded Eden at the War Office in Dec. 1940.

On Anthony's return, Van sent him a fiery letter, claiming that all pledges made to him had always been broken, but that he had never expected anything different, &c. &c. He announced that he wished to retire on reaching the age of 60. . . .

Anthony sent for him, made him take back the letter, and accepted the resignation. All very friendly and pleasant, I understand, and you will now have the advantage of Van's guidance in Their Lordships' House.[49]

Vansittart said to Dalton that he felt himself to have 'warmth of feeling and of temperament, which cannot live side by side with the cold fish—A.C. and R.A.B. who, with Halifax, once made a terrible cold trio'.[50]]

Monday, 21 April

Nothing much doing till Cabinet—a rather gloomy one—at 5. We had been expecting to have to decide whether to evacuate from Greece or not, but a telegram came in about 4 showing that Greeks are asking us to. Fleet should have bombarded Tripoli at dawn this morning, but so far, no news. Perhaps they have to observe wireless silence. N. Atlantic sinkings not so bad, but these things always go in waves. Must say outlook is pretty black, though I don't think I had expected much different. What to do? Only thing—if it is possible—is to take *great* risks in cutting Sicily-Tripoli communication and then mopping up Wops and Huns in N. Africa. If we could do *that*, situation would change radically. But I don't know what the possibilities are.

[The Greeks said 'We are sorry we haven't been able to do more. Thank you very much for all your help. And now please go as soon as you feel you should in order to save as many as you can of your own troops.' Koryzis, the Greek Prime Minister, had committed suicide on 18 April.]

Tuesday, 22 April

Had a talk with A. about general outlook, which is murky. We must get out of Greece as soon and as best we can. The real battle of the war is coming in N. Africa. The Navy seem unable to stop convoys from Italy to Tripoli, and we are going to take a—perhaps vital—knock in Egypt. I have been rubbing this in, and I *think* we are doing all we can. Bombardment of Tripoli yesterday morning was a flop. It's a race against time, with most of the odds against us. Iraq* has gone well—Cornwallis† seems excellent. But Turks are

* Rashid Ali, in German pay, had seized power in Baghdad on 3 Apr. Although he said he would abide by the Anglo-Iraqui treaty, troops were promptly sent from India and held in readiness at Basra.

† Sir Kinahan Cornwallis. Just arrived in Baghdad as Ambassador (1941–5); formerly Adviser to Iraqui Ministry of the Interior, 1921–35.

putrid: N. Africa and Spain and Vichy! *gone*, unless we can have a success in Libya. And I don't see it.

Thursday, 24 April

Cabinet at 12. Not v. much news, except that Winston told Cabinet of Roosevelt's decision to police the Western half of Atlantic. Which is *very* good. No sinkings. Also good. News from Greece bad, but we seem to have won a respite in Libya—or Egypt.

Friday, 25 April

A. saw Shigemitsu, who gave him Matsuoka's reply to P.M. which was complete rubbish, invoking Hakko-Ichiu,* which appears to be a state of complete peace, comparable to that of the country graveyard.

Monday, 28 April

3. Meeting with A., Van(!), O.S., Strang and H. Seymour—on what to *do*! We are in that awful period when everything is going wrong and those in authority feel they have got to *do* something. In a quiet moment I got A. alone and said 'Please don't do anything for the sake of *doing* something! Don't throw in small packets here and there to get chewed up. I know it's disappointing and humiliating to look forward to another year of the defensive, but *don't* squander the little you've got.' He professed to agree. I begged him to believe that diplomacy could only be prepared in our munition factories. But will o' the wisps have a fatal attraction for him and Winston.

Cabinet at 5, till 7.30. Hopelessly rambling. Winston tired, I think. Bevin made some more than usually fatuous remarks, which annoyed the P.M., who immersed himself in papers and let the Cabinet rip for half hr. Hopeless waste of time! . . . Defence Cttee. at 9.30—till 12.30. More diffuse and useless than ever. 5½ hours of my day wasted. V. tired.

Tuesday, 29 April

Evacuation going fairly well. That's all that we're really good at! And we anticipate that 5,000 German air-borne troops are going to wipe us out of Crete! Our soldiers are the most pathetic amateurs, pitted against professionals. Dill is the most unimpressive—if charming—personality I have ever come across. Almost I am persuaded to believe in Ironside! Dined in Flat and worked hard. Tired, depressed and defeatist!

* In loose translation, 'all the world one family'.

Wednesday, 30 April

These dirty Iraquis are attacking us at Habbaniya.* We have authorised bombing. Talk with A., H. Seymour and Strang about Syria,† (the great danger) Iraq and N. Africa. . . . Met P.M. who said 'So you've got another war on your hands tonight!' News awful. Bad sinkings again in Atlantic. Libya-Egypt seems to be going badly —at least according to Germans—and Plymouth wiped off the map.

Thursday, 1 May

Cabinet 12. Nothing much, and no more frightful news than we had yesterday. We then resolved ourselves into Defence Committee and Menzies, quite rightly, made a stink about the telegram sent at 4 a.m., as result of last night's 'Midnight Follies', heartily endorsing American suggestion that they should send their Pacific fleet into the Atlantic. Anything more insane! We were able to telegraph to Washington to suspend action. But Winston very obstinate that this was the right thing to do. He who was convinced Japan was coming into the war last year [and] insisted on closing the Burma Road (a capital mistake), is now determined that *nothing* will make them come in. And he suffers from the delusion that any cold water thrown on any hare-brained U.S. suggestion will stop the U.S. coming into the war! Even the American naval authorities were themselves against this insane proposal.

Friday, 2 May

3.30 Defence Committee, about Djibouti, Crete and Iraq. All news murky. Our (still) total inadequacy in material renders us powerless everywhere. And our Staff are a handful of charming amateurs, pitted against the best professionals in the world.

Saturday, 3 May

Wind still N.E. (43°). Beastly day. Walked [to F.O.]. First of all a flap because P.M. had sent us a copy of the President's message of last night of which he (W.S.C.), who is tired and depressed, had taken a jaundiced view. He sent with it an unsuitable draft reply. I discussed with D. Scott and Whitehead and we spoke to A. about it. Attlee called, and took our view. Iraq situation pretty bad. Are we really going to be beaten by Iraquis?! Authorised A[ir] O[fficer] C[ommanding] to say that if Habbaniya encroached upon, we shall

* The principal R.A.F. base, the defenders of which gave the Iraquis an ultimatum before counter-attacking on 2 May.

† Where Vichy gave facilities to the Axis.

bomb Bagdad. . . . Meeting with A., Attlee and C's of S. about 4.30, about Crete and Iraq. Doubts about being able to hold former. Turks have offered mediation in regard to latter. Drafted a v. cagey reply, with which A. left at 6 for Chequers, together with redraft of reply to Pres. Home about 7.15, with lots of work. A lovely night and a warning went about 10.30, so we shall be Blitzed!

Sunday, 4 May

After days of awful gloom, things look—oddly—rather better. Re-shuffle of Government in Spain better, our 16 successes in the air last night better, and there is secret news to show that Germans are not comfortable in Libya. Only Iraq looks bad.

Monday, 5 May

Cabinet at 5. Plymouth attacks have been bad. Concentrations on areas like this are serious. *What will win the war*, as I have said before, is the *defeat of the night bomber*. Lip-service is paid to this principle, and some progress has been made, but I don't think the P.M. realises its supreme importance.

Came home, at 8, with a bagful of work. Which I have scamped. There is too much.

Friday, 9 May

Meeting at 4 on Spain, with A. He is always jumping about the room, itching to 'do something'. He has to be humoured, but the best one can do is to restrain him. About 6 saw him about Djibouti, where he and P.M. (latter's fault) have got at 6's and 7's. Meeting on Persia—to see what we can '*do*'. I've told him 100 times—make more *tanks*!! Discussion about the future régime in Abyssinia. A tiring and harassing and unsatisfactory day. I'm afraid I don't suit A. in his present phase. I'm a crusted bureaucrat—he wants a Philip [Noel] Baker. Well, well, I shouldn't be sorry to leave. My back is almost broken after three years. Youth must have its fling and —I am afraid—you never can prove it's silly except by giving it its most expensive head. I'd rather not be there then.

Sunday, 11 May

5.30 Addis rang me up [at the cottage] with this story: a German pilot landed near Glasgow, asked for the Duke of Hamilton.* Latter so impressed that he is flying to London and wants to see me at No. 10 tonight. Said I shouldn't be in London before 8. Fixed

* M.P., 1930–40; served in R.A.F., 1939–45.

meeting for 9.15. Half hour later, heard P.M. was sending to meet His Grace at airfield and wd. bring him to Chequers—so I needn't be tr-r-r-oubled!

. . . London awfully knocked about last night. And I fear Westminster Hall and Abbey got it. Also Parliament, tho' I don't care about that. I wish it had got most of the Members.

False alert about 9.50, but I suppose we shall get it again tonight.

T. is marvellous—completely unconcerned and fearless. Only wants to bomb Berlin. I'm sure she wd. pilot a bomber there if she could.

Monday, 12 May

(Writing night of 13th). In all the years I have kept this beastly diary I have never been so hard pressed. Mainly due to Hess, who has taken up *all* my time and I am 48 hours in arrear with work. Talk with A. and Duke of Hamilton, who says it is Hess!* Sent for 'C' and consulted him about sending I. K[irkpatrick]† up to 'vet' the airman. He agreed. Got I.K. about 1.15 and gave him his instructions. 3.15 meeting with A. and I.K. Duke came at 4. Packed them off in plane at 5.30 from Hendon. Cabinet 6. 'Tiger' [convoy to Malta] got in all right with loss of one ship. . . . 9 o'clock wireless repeated German announcement about Hess. A. rang up. Met him at F.O. at 10.45. Had got text of German announcement. . . . We went to see P.M. in C[abinet] W[ar] R[oom]. He already had text of an announcement, which included remark that H. had come here 'in the name of humanity'. This won't do—looks like a peace offer, and we may want to run the line that he has quarrelled with Hitler.

[The German official notice stated that Party Member Hess had seemingly lived

> in a state of hallucination, as a result of which he felt he would bring about an understanding between England and Germany. . . . The National Socialist Party regrets that this idealist fell a victim to his hallucination. This however will have no effect on the continuance of the war which has been forced on Germany.

'In my opinion', Ciano confided to his diary, 'it is a very serious matter: the first real victory for the English.' Ribbentrop arrived unexpectedly in Rome but his explanations were hardly believed; and Mussolini said privately that he was glad of the Hess affair, which would

* Rudolph Hess, deputy Führer, 1933–41.

† Who had known Hess before the war.

'bring down German stock, even with the Italians'. At dinner, so Ciano unkindly noted, Ribbentrop 'repeated his slogans with that monotony that made Goering dub him "Germany's No. 1 parrot"'.[51]

Hess, in talks with Kirkpatrick, spoke at length about Germany's bad treatment by England in the past, her unity, her certain victory. All the same, the Führer would leave the British Empire alone if Germany might have a free hand in Europe. Though she had admittedly certain demands to make of Russia, Germany did not intend to attack. Hitler, Hess declared, had known nothing of his intention.

The British put it about that Hess's flight betokened a growing split in Germany over the policy of collaboration with Russia. If Hitler continued with it, he would insist on benefits in the short term, since the policy would have to be abandoned in the end. Russia would by then have made vital concessions, and having lost potential allies, would be left to face the Germans.[52]

Since March the Foreign Office had been receiving numerous warnings of a German attack upon Russia. Hitler was reported to have told Prince Paul that he intended to invade on 30 June. At Cripps's suggestion, the Yugoslav Minister in Moscow spoke of this to Stalin and Molotov. Cripps delivered a separate warning from Churchill. Other rumours in the same sense began to circulate freely in Moscow during April. Stalin seems to have taken little notice.]

Tuesday, 13 May

Frightful day—mostly on Hess—constant interruption. Talked 10.50 to I.K. and dictated his account of his interview. Undoubtedly it is Hess. But can't see why he's come here unless he's mad. Doctors say he isn't. Took account to P.M. at 12. He told me to settle how H. was to be kept. He wants him to be a 'State Prisoner'. Consulted Malkin. Tried to get through to I.K. who must evidently stay there for a bit. Lunched late in Flat and left early after. Tried to grapple with work, but what with interruptions and having to go round to give Dominion High Commissioners the low-down on Hess, didn't have much time. Horace S[eymour] looming in and out of my room about Iraq—like ghost. S. of S. like a cat on hot bricks—or John Simon. Got away at 8, with no work done. Everyone is butting in on Hess—John Anderson, G.J., 'C', Geoffrey Shakespeare,* M.I.5. Hell! Brought back a *Pantechnicon* of work, of which I broke the back tonight. Quite exhausted.

Wednesday, 14 May

Hess is the bane of my life and all my time is wasted. . . . 6 went over to No. 10. P.M., A., 'C', and Duff [Cooper]. P.M. decided he

* Parl. Under-Sec., Dominions Office, 1940–2.

must make statement in Parliament tomorrow about Hess. A. left and we had to wait while P.M. dictated. *How* slow he is. What he dictated was all wrong—explaining what Hess had said (peace proposals) corresponding exactly to what Germans put out this afternoon. I said that, on that, Hitler would heave sigh of relief. *And the German people.* They would say 'Then it *is* true what our dear Führer has told us. Our beloved Rudolf has gone to make peace.' They *may* think him rather silly, but they won't think him a traitor, which is what *I* want them to *fear.* However P.M. and that ass Duff brushed me aside (8.30). Home 8.50. Dined and worked. Rang up A., who had been summoned to meeting at 12.30 a.m. on this. (He was in bed.) Think he took my point of view, but said he wouldn't go to meeting but would see P.M. in morning.

He rang me up about 12.30 to say P.M. had got on to him in a raging temper (had been dining with the Beaver[brook],* who apparently took our view). Wanted A. to attend meeting, but A. said 'I didn't sleep v. well this afternoon'! Finally, in a temper, P.M. said he would make no statement tomorrow. Je ne demande pas mieux!

Thursday, 15 May

Cabinet at 12. P.M. in v. good form—has got over his tantrum and admits our view correct. This confirmed by conversations of German P[risoners of] W[ar], who are simply distracted. Mood of German public will be the same. . . . P.M. rang up to ask whether I had report of I. K[irkpatrick]'s talk with Hess today. Said I could only instruct him at lunch to go over, and that took 1½ hours. He furious—said why did he sit comfortably at Turnhouse 1½ hours away from H. I said I didn't think he was at all comfortable there—he had to be near his plane, but I would tell him to stay at the Hospital. I.K. came through about 5, but had got nothing much fresh.

Saturday, 17 May

V. little news from Middle East, which is the critical theatre. Hess arrived all right in London this morning—tho' all the Press knew it! Lunched at Flat. T. and I went to Kew. White double cherries marvellous. But pink blossom killed by frost. Crab good. Azaleas not out and magnolias over. Back just before 5 and I went to F.O. Ridsdale fussed because Duff has raised ban on reports of what Hess is said to have said. Rang up A., who agreed ban must be maintained. Got P.M.'s authority. Masses of work. A. rang up about

* Appointed Minister of State, 1 May; Minister of Supply, 29 June.

7.45. He had been speaking to P.M., who enquired whether it wd. be all right to raise ban with warning that all speculation was unauthorised. I said this wd. be all right.

Monday, 19 May

P.M. still hankering after his stupid statement about Hess. Insisted on reading it with great gusto to the Cabinet. Fortunately (with the possible exception of A. Sinclair) they were *unanimous* against it, and I think he has dropped the idea. Afterwards stayed behind with A. to discuss a telegram to Washington about attitude to be adopted now to Vichy. I.K. came in to report. P.M. agreed we ought to draw Hess by pretending to negotiate, and he came out with my idea of J. Simon for the part.

Friday, 23 May

Cretan news not too bad, but the Navy are suffering and finding it difficult to carry on. These Germans *are* marvellously efficient. Nothing like it has ever been seen. I caught Defence Cttee. as they were breaking up at 1 with a problem of whether to bomb a German raider slinking along N. Spanish coast making for Bordeaux, within S[panish] territorial waters. Thank Heaven, Winston decided it wasn't worth the risk.

Saturday, 24 May *Thatched Cottage*

Went to see H. Wilson at 11.30 about getting our [F.O.] young men back from peeling potatoes in the army. . . . News of sinking of 'Hood'.* . . . Later, news there had been a battle with [battleship] 'Bismarck'. Admiralty 'think' we have sunk 'Bismarck'. Later still, forces still in contact, which looks bad. . . . reached cottage about 5. Leaden skies, gale and drizzle. This *always* happens. After tea went round garden. *Nothing* has grown at all for 4 weeks—this due to constant N. wind, frost, no rain and no sun. Devastating! Only thing flowering is chieranthus. Walked the usual round to Primrose Wood, in waterproof suit. Beastly! Gale still raging. *What* a country! Why do the Germans want to conquer it? If only they knew!

Monday, 26 May

Cabinet at 5. Poor Winston very gloomy—due of course to 'Hood' and Crete. In latter place things look black. Only ⅓rd of our Medi-

* Britain's largest and fastest capital ship; sunk in the Denmark Straits in the early morning of 24 May. Only three of her company survived. The *Prince of Wales* was severely damaged also.

terranean Fleet undamaged, and once Germans start reinforcing by sea, we're done. Message came in that our carrier aircraft had been airborne from 3 till 5 without contacting 'Bismarck'.

A tiresome and most acrimonious discussion about publication of figures of recent sinking of convoy. Cabinet (including A., against my advice) in favour. Winston furious, and Cabinet climbed down to him. Then a discussion on conscription in Ulster. Cabinet again against Winston (rightly). He made passionate appeal: to back down now, in face of clamour, would show that the mainspring of resolution was broken &c., &c. That is all very well. But what he does is to jump to decisions—ill-considered—and then say that it shows weakness to recede. It shows stupidity to jump to them. A very gloomy and unpleasant Cabinet. Max was on edge and very pugnacious (on the surface). Bevin was almost the only supporter of the P.M. on Ulster. But he made a most timid and rambling statement. I wrote to A. 'Bevin's spiritual home is Delphi.' Poor Winston will recover all right if we get a bit of good news. Tonight he was almost throwing his hand in. But there is a bit of the histrionic art in *that*.

Tuesday, 27 May

Cabinet at 10.30. 'Bismarck' seems to have been crippled during the night and should be sunk this morning.* Winston agreed to chuck conscription in N. Ireland. . . . Awful news from Crete. We are scuppered there, and I'm afraid the moral and material effects will be serious. Certainly the Germans are past-masters in the art of war—and *great* warriors. If we beat them, we shall have worked a miracle.

Wednesday, 28 May

Cretan news terrible—it's another disaster. Private telegrams from Miles Lampson to A. about lack of air support in Crete and saying this has bad effect on morale everywhere—including Anzacs. Went with him to see A. Sinclair and Portal. They've done all they can. The difficulty is rather geography than supply.

Thursday, 29 May

Cabinet at 12. Horrible decision to take—whether to go on with evacuation from Crete, with all the damage to the Fleet, or to abandon our men. Decided to go on—for the present.

Friday, 30 May

5.15. talk with A. about Turkey and Russia. He keeps on feeling

* She was sunk at 10.40 a.m. Churchill telegraphed to Roosevelt: 'The effect upon the Japanese will be highly beneficial. I expect they are doing all their sums again.'

that there's something to be *done*—diplomatically—and there is an underlying reproach that we can't think of things. Fact is that with our military weakness and the sensational ineptitude of our commanders, diplomacy is completely hamstrung. For instance—Russia. You can't do anything nowadays with any country unless you can (a) threaten (b) bribe it. Russia has (a) no fear of us *whatever* and (b) we have *nothing* to offer her. Then you can juggle with words and jiggle with drafts as much as you like, and you'll get nowhere.

Saturday, 31 May

4 meeting with A. and Chiefs of Staff, mainly about Armistice terms for Iraq. Rashid Ali (*and* Gabbrielli!*) have collapsed and fled to Iran. Chiefs of Staff have come to conclusion that Germany is *prepared* to attack Russia. I agree, but *I* believe that Russia will give way and sign on the dotted line. I wish she wouldn't, as I should love to see Germany expending her strength there. But they're not such fools (as *our* General Staff). But we must consider how we can use threat or fact of bombing to Baku.

* Italian Minister in Iraq.

VI

June–December 1941
THE WORLDWIDE WAR

At the beginning of June 1941, neither side had any prospect of an early victory. The British and Commonwealth forces, although turned out of Greece and Crete with much loss, still held Egypt and the Suez Canal. The Axis ruled most of Europe, but not Spain or Portugal. Hitler was clearly massing a great army in the east, either for the invasion of the Soviet Union or for the enforcement of harsh economic terms. With the collapse of the rebellion in Iraq, Germany and Italy lost the immediate prospect of establishing a threat to the flank of the British position in Egypt and Palestine. Turkey's attitude therefore became more significant than ever. She continued to supply chrome and other materials to Germany, against which the British felt unable to protest unduly. In this situation British diplomacy could do comparatively little until reinforced by the accession of allies and the prestige of success. In sum, the war had from a British point of view reached an intermediate stage. The phase of acute and immediate danger to the British Isles had passed, although the war in the Atlantic threatened their economic, and therefore political and military, survival; the honourable but hazardous attempt to establish a bridgehead in the Balkans had collapsed; the Russians seemed hardly aware of their impending fate and deaf to warnings; while the Americans, though adopting a sterner line towards Japan, felt unable to demonstrate plainly that effective economic sanctions and preparedness to fight must go together.

To land an expeditionary force in Europe was beyond British capacity in 1941 or 1942, however stridently the Russians might call for it. There was little the British could do, then, in the short run, to mitigate the German attack on Russia, save to wage war in the Middle East; to send supplies, largely from the U.S.A., through Persia or by means of the murderous convoys to Archangel; and to co-operate in subversion. This the Soviets suddenly agreed to do in August. Negotiations of the utmost secrecy began with the GPU, the Russian secret police, in Moscow. Only Stalin, Molotov and Beria knew, and the two Russian representatives did their own typing.[1]

Dalton and his staff at the Ministry of Economic Warfare must in any event have occupied a delicate position in relation to the Foreign Office, exacerbated in this instance by the Minister's manners and mental habits. A good deal of Cadogan's time between July and November 1941 was evidently spent in composing differences about the demarcation of duties between the Ministry of Information, the B.B.C. and the S.O.E. in respect of political warfare. Dalton believed that Eden suspected him of interfering unduly in foreign policy. Eden denied it. Dalton, partially reassured, complained that Cadogan had written him 'a most gawky letter'.[2] For a while the issue was smoothed over.

At the end of July, and again in September, Dalton opposed papers put to the Cabinet by Eden on questions of blockade. In respect of propaganda to enemy and occupied countries, a new organisation came into being. It was christened the Political Warfare Executive and was responsible to the Foreign Secretary, the Minister of Information and the Minister for Economic Warfare jointly; or, should they disagree, to the Prime Minister. Shortly afterwards, Dalton protested to his party leader, Attlee, at the failure of the Foreign Office to consult the M.E.W. adequately and of its efforts to 'drill holes in the blockade. I have constantly to fight against appeasement, by way of blockade concessions in the occupied territories. . . If the Foreign Office had had their way, the blockade by now would be leaking like a sieve, and the hour of victory would have been postponed by months, if not by years.' He also felt alarmed at the attitude of the Political Warfare Executive. 'I am now conscious of being faced by a combination of two Conservative Ministers and three principal officials, all of whom are anxious to reduce my influence over the new P.W.E. to a minimum.' Dalton concluded that unless Labour Ministers were better treated each must consider his position.[3]

Again the immediate crisis died down, to revive briefly in November. Dalton wrote a sharp letter to which Eden took exception and upon which he was reported to have minuted: 'This looks like a lecture by the Doctor on how to run my job.' However, Cadogan and Dalton's lieutenant, Gladwyn Jebb, had an amiable talk. Eden told Dalton that Jebb had the confidence of the Foreign Office and sent back what Dalton's diary describes as a 'most reasonable and friendly letter'.

Such episodes, which loom large in Dalton's papers, find only brief mention in those of Cadogan, who probably judged that the Foreign Office, with a political head so close to Churchill, could always uphold its position in any serious conflict; and the last thing he wanted was for the Office to be saddled with any more responsibilities. The repercussions of clandestine activities occupied, he felt, enough of his time already. 'Latter part of morning' he recorded on 19 October, 'taken up with X's exploit. Why *will* our odd Service Depts. employ degenerate lunatics?'

1941

Sunday, 1 June

A General Clark has gone and signed a rather feeble armistice with the Iraqis. Don't know who he is, or on what authority he did it. Sent a telegram to Cornwallis (got A.'s approval on telephone) pointing out that he must somehow get a good deal more. . . . Back at F.O. 6.40. Found A. had been fussing on telephone and wanted 2 messages sent to Iraq. He had 'gone out for a drive' so couldn't get him. Home 8.10. A. rang up 8.45 and I got his approval of messages. He rang up again 9.15 very excited, to protest against Storrs'* broadcast about Iraq on the 9 o'clock news. It wasn't v. good, but I couldn't see that it was so very bad. I'm afraid I snapped at him. . . . I just turned him on to Kirk. If he is so sensitive to all the winds that blow, he'd better sit in London—and get another Permanent Under Secretary.

Monday, 2 June

A. arrived soon after 11 and we and R.A.B. and C. Warner† discussed what he should say to Maisky. Germans are evidently ready to attack Russia. And they will do so if they don't get what they want. I think they *will* get what they want. I hope they won't, because that would give us time, and it must be *some* effort for them. Lunched at home. Cabinet at 5. Bevin critical (quite rightly) about Crete. Short discussion of Arab policy and of Cyprus. We then got through our paper about reform of Diplomatic Service. Only the Chancellor against—and he not from conviction. A. saw Maisky at 7. Seems to have been quite a useful interview. Bevin made the one 'mot' I have ever heard him make. Cabinet ended on discussion of proportionate pensions for unsuitable diplomats. They were then breaking up, when Attlee said he must just mention a decision taken with the Minister of Agriculture for elimination of unremunerative cows. Bevin asked 'Do they get proportionate pensions?' Dined at home. Lot of work. A. still a bit jumpy but better.

Tuesday, 3 June

Talked with N. Bland about his abortive appointment to Rio. He annoyed, because it had leaked out—which makes him look a fool. A. approved it and got King's approval before weather-cocking for no good reason. I think there is growing resentment about Crete (fostered by the B.B.C.), and I don't mind, if it is to produce changes in our War Museum. *That* is the service that wants purging—not ours. They think in terms of Crècy and Agincourt and are the most feeble-minded set of blind mice imaginable. A. shows some disposition to come up tomorrow to discuss Syria, and I shall certainly encourage this and put the wind up him. Because we are heading for just the same disaster there!

* Sir Ronald Storrs, then in the Ministry of Information.

† Of the Northern Dept.

Wednesday, 4 June

11.30 hastily summoned meeting with P.M. and C's of S, nominally to discuss Syria.* Actually, there was only desultory conversation about anything that came into the P.M.'s head—in that order. Meeting on Syria fixed for 6 (later put off till 10). We adjourned 12.45. . . . 4.45 meeting with A. and C's of S. on Syria. I said I should like it postponed—I think it's a bad gamble. But I don't think he's convinced. My chief argument is why—a week before your effort in N. Africa—do you blunder into a war with Vichy. *Stacks* of work had now accumulated. . . . Dined at home and grappled with my mountain of papers. Defence Committee at 10, but A. didn't insist on my attending, so I left him to it.

Thursday, 5 June

Defence Committee last night decided to go on with Syria. P.M. takes the cynical view that he has to face a debate on Crete on Tuesday. So we'd better begin the Syrian venture on Saturday and take the two together!

Monday, 9 June

Cabinet at 5. Can't make out what's happening in Syria. [General] Wilson's technique—directly an operation begins—is to dry up completely and give *no* news at all. P.M. very angry at this, as he has to make statement to House tomorrow. He said 'it's damned bad manners'. He discussed course of debate tomorrow. He said: 'People criticise this Government, but its great strength—and I dare say it in this company—is that there's no alternative! I *don't* think it's a bad Government. Come to think of it, it's a very good one. I have *complete* confidence in it. In fact there never has been a government to which I have felt such sincere and whole-hearted loyalty!'

N. Henderson dined. I.K. came in at 10 to report on [Lord] Simon's interview with Hess. Nothing useful transpired. H. recited all the rubbish that he's treated us to for the past month.

Tuesday, 10 June

. . . Maisky came to A. with a cryptic, incomplete and wholly useless answer to his approach.

* Gen. Catroux, representing the Free French in the Middle East, had suggested that a coup be staged against the Vichy régime in Syria, accompanied by a declaration promising independence for Syria and the Lebanon. After the German invasion of the Balkans and use of Syrian airfields, the War Cabinet agreed.

[The Russian Ambassador said that no negotiations, economic or political, were in progress between the Russian and German Governments. Russia regarded her relations with Germany as being regulated by the Nazi–Soviet pact of 1939 and felt no anxiety about Hitler's military intentions. Three days later, by which time Eden and Cadogan had given still more specific warnings, Tass put out an official communiqué, dismissing rumours of war as an 'obvious absurdity'.

After conversations with Hess, Lord Simon thought him probably deranged. With the aid of copious notes, Hess explained why he had come and how Germany had been unjustly treated. Unless she made terms, Britain would be doomed, though the Führer would regret it. If they could agree, Europe would be Germany's acre; Britain would keep her Empire. Hess gave half a hint of the forthcoming attack on Russia. Simon left convinced that the flight to England had been Hess's own scheme.[4]

The Anglo-French force had gone into Syria on 8 June. An armistice was signed 5 weeks later.]

Wednesday, 11 June

J.S. came about 11 and recounted to me his interview. Very interesting. He has very definitely formed the impression that H. is telling the truth—strange though it be. He says (1) H. is of a very second-rate intellectual ability (a conclusion I had reached from the conversations) and (2) in his present mental and nervous state he would be quite incapable of acting a part. So there is nothing to be done along these lines, and when they have been followed to their end we must decide how best to exploit H.—mendaciously. . . . A shemozzle at 7.45, as Duff had spilled the beans about German-Russian situation, and given out a lot of stuff about Stalin 'giving way' which would completely queer our pitch with the Russians if there was a chance of our playing with them. He had not even said a word to A. I left A. at 8.5 telephoning wildly to Ridsdale (who apparently can't do anything about it) and trying to telephone to P.M. (who was dining with the King!)

Friday, 13 June

A dull and tiresome day, plodding thro' papers. (Rather unlike this day last year—our flight to Tours!). . . Wrote a short minute on night-bomber. A defeat of the night bomber is not, as the Cabinet seem to think, a *defensive* action, but (if done in time) the only *offensive* that *might* produce an *early* victory. I'm sure they're not pressing on with it hard enough. Anyone who asks for this is regarded as a craven who has got the wind up from a Blitz. 'London can take it,' and all that nonsense.

Saturday, 14 June

Just like a week-day—worked till nearly 8 (lunching at home) and then had to talk to A. on telephone to fix up a message to the Turks (and do a lot of other work). Turks are evidently going to sign up with Germany. I always knew they were dirty dogs. We are sending them a last—and pretty stiff—message. But it won't do much good.

Sunday, 15 June

'C' came in about Hess, who's going off his head. I don't much care what happens to *him*. *We* can use him. There's a meeting tomorrow between Winston and Simon about him, at which I hope to be present and to get decisions on how to treat and how to exploit him—alive, mad or dead. *No* news from Libya—not even on 9 o'clock news. We were supposed to bring off our great coup today.

Monday, 16 June

Rung up by 'C' at 8.30 to say Hess has thrown himself over the banisters and broken his thigh! Told A. in the brief moment I saw him—he has a frightful day of engagements. . . . Maisky at 3, and I gave him a number of particulars of German concentration on Russian frontier. Cabinet at 5. Fairly good news of fighting in Libya—which is pretty tough. Discussion about publication of shipping losses, which continue to be *very* serious. Afterwards J.S. gave Cabinet an account of his interview with H[ess]. Rode P.M. off his idea of announcing the broken thigh—which would be simply silly. He agreed that, in regard to H. 'Mum's the word'. That's what I wanted and I will now get on with my propaganda. A. kept me till 8.10 discussing whether there were any further last-minute representations we could make to these . . . Turks.

Tuesday, 17 June

Meeting at 11.30 to discuss what we do about propaganda in case of German-Soviet conflict. O.S., O. Harvey, R. Leeper, [Clifford] Norton and others. Quite useful. . . . Col. Rees (nerve specialist) to see me about H[ess]. Latter is definitely paranoid, and we have got another—and a rather awkward—lunatic on our hands for the duration. Rees says this persecution mania must have developed, in some form, *before* his departure from Germany. . . . These . . . Turks have gone and initialled.

Wednesday, 18 June

V. hot and sunny. V. gloomy. Our great offensive in Libya has ended in a bloody nose—for us. Most depressing. The Germans are magnificent fighters and their Staff are veritable Masters of Warfare. Wavells and suchlike are no good against them.* It is like putting me up to play Bobby Jones over 36 holes. We shall learn, but it will be a long and bloody business, and we shall have to go through endless suffering and disappointment. Had a talk with A. and S. Cripps, which veered on to propaganda. I said the *machine* could work in other hands than Duff's. I suggested a standing item in Cabinet agenda should be 'Information'. But I doubt if they'll do it. And Winston won't desert Duff. . . . Turks are definitely signing tonight—damn them—and we've given guidance to the Press, so far as we can. F.O. will be blamed of course!

Sunday, 22 June

F.O. rang up at 9 to say Hitler has attacked Russia. A. seeing Maisky. *I* can't do anything about it. We can only hit Germany as hard as possible. We shot down 28 German planes for 6 yesterday, and I've just heard we got 27 for 1 today. . . . Winston broadcast at 9. But he's overdoing the mud-slinging.

[Jock Colville,† remembering the Prime Minister's part in promoting armed intervention against the Soviets in 1918–19, asked whether he would not be awkwardly placed when Hitler invaded Russia. Not at all, Churchill replied; 'if Hitler invaded Hell, I would at least make a favourable reference to the Devil in the House of Commons.' He took a more sanguine view than most experts of Russia's prospects. His speech, deliberately withheld from Eden and Cadogan lest it be toned down,[5] promised that

> Any man or state who fights against Nazism will have our aid. Any man or state who marches with Hitler is our foe. . . . It follows therefore that we shall give whatever help we can to Russia and the Russian people.

Litvinov, then Russian Ambassador in Washington, told Halifax that when he first heard of the German assault, he felt sure Britain had done a deal through Hess. He was proportionately relieved by Churchill's speech.[6]

The first German advance was made along a wide front by some 160 divisions. In the first month a deep penetration was made. By the end of

* On 21 June Wavell was relieved of his command and appointed C.-in-C. India in place of General Sir Claude Auchinleck, who assumed the appointment of C.-in-C., Middle East, in early July.

† Asst. Private Sec. to the P.M.

July Hitler was disputing with his military advisers whether a thrust should be made for Moscow, or whether to continue the advance on a broad front, especially against Leningrad and the Crimea. The latter course was chosen.]

Monday, 23 June

A. saw Maisky, who accepted our offer of help, such as it is. . . . Cabinet at 5. Fraser* there. Long argument—without any result—about Ministry of Information. Lasted till 7.45, when we got text of an impossible broadcast Sikorski wants to let off at 10.30. Tried to put it into shape, and left A. to grapple with S.

Friday, 27 June

H. Wilson came to see me about O. Lyttelton's appointment, and to say that Henry H[opkinson] had been recommended as his assistant! This really is the limit, but, as a patriot, I must agree to the best man going, to prevent the thing being a flop. But it's the devil. I shall take Loxley [as Private Secretary].

Saturday, 28 June

Our secret news shows that Germans are not having it *all* their own way in Russia.

Sunday, 29 June

Russians still seem to be inflicting some damage on Germans. The surprise Russian big tank seems to be a success. But we can't hope for too much.

Monday, 30 June

Cabinet at 5. Dill v. gloomy about Russian prospects—which is the only hopeful sign. We seem to have no plan for harrying Germans in West. Spoke to A. about this, who also worried. 'Daylight sweeps' no use, as the Germans ignore them! And we lose masses of bombers at night. No plans for raids. Nothing doing! The effect throughout the world will be frightful. And they expect 'diplomacy' to effect something!

Tuesday, 1 July

Walked, and met A. He had spent from 11 p.m. till 2 a.m. with P.M. But I gather nothing much emerges. We are not prepared to take advantage of this Heaven-sent (and short) opportunity of the

* Peter Fraser, Prime Minister of New Zealand, 1940–9.

Germans being heavily engaged in Russia. We shall look awful fools! But there it is.

Wednesday, 2 July

Russians still being hammered, but they haven't absolutely gone up in smoke yet. Syria is awful.

Friday, 4 July

Maisky came to see A. about what Russia will do in regard to recognising Poles, Czechs and Yugs. A. sent for Sikorski and I joined them. We told S. of Russian proposals, which he didn't like in their entirety, and A. saw Maisky again later.

Saturday, 5 July

About 11 Retinger* rang up on behalf of Sikorski to say latter would receive Maisky at his (S's) headquarters at Rubens Hotel between 3 and 6 p.m. I thought this rather odd, but rang up Maisky and told him. He demurred to calling on S. Wanted to meet on 'neutral territory'. Suggested they should meet in my room. He wasn't enthusiastic, but eventually got him—and S.—to agree. . . . They met courteously and shook hands and we sat down to talk. Zaleski also there (which wouldn't help matters). However, Sikorski v. good. Firm but courteous. Only real difficulty question of release of Polish *political* prisoners in Russia. But M. agreed to submit this to his Govt. I didn't take much part, but perhaps my presence may have averted a row! . . . At end, Sikorski said to Maisky 'Your troops are fighting'. And later: 'You hate the Germans as much as we: you ought never to have made agreement with them in 1939, and we should have been fighting side by side all this time.' M. took it very well, laughed and said 'All that is past history.'

[Sikorski said that he could accept no departure from the frontiers of August 1939, and were he to recognise even implicitly a surrender of Poland to Russia, it would, as Cadogan's record puts it delicately, 'make it difficult, if not impossible, to create enthusiasm among the Polish soldiers who are at present in Soviet gaols or concentration camps, or deported under distressing conditions'.

Russia, said Maisky, favoured the formation of 'an independent Polish national state . . . the régime to be established was the exclusive concern of the Poles. . . .'

* Temporary chargé d'affaires in Moscow, 1941.

At a renewed meeting on 11 July, Maisky said that Russia would now denounce the agreements with Germany of 1939 in respect of Poland, resume diplomatic relations with her, and allow the creation of an independent Polish Army on Soviet soil. 'What would happen', Sikorski asked, 'if the Polish and Soviet armies marched victoriously into Polish territory? Who would govern this territory. Poles or Russians? He would be satisfied if Monsieur Maisky said that the Poles would govern it.'

Maisky said that 'at the moment this question was perhaps a little academic'.

Cadogan pressed him for early signature of a Polish-Russian agreement, excluding frontiers.[7]]

Wednesday, 9 July

10.30 A. and R.A.B. and I received the Russian Mission. Golikof seemed quite a live little man. The rest all looked like private detectives. They naturally press that we should *do* something. And we're *not* going to do anything—much. This is pretty hopeless. . . . Cabinet 6.30 to discuss Stalin's request for an agreement.* I had talked with A. and O.S. and R.A.B. about this. I am in favour of giving them all they want—no haggling. Winston wants to do the same and to send a personal message to Stalin. A. against that. . . . Winston insisted, and the sheep baa'ed in chorus. So he sends his message, but we don't have a Treaty or 'agreement' but an 'Agreed declaration'. Rather afraid this is one of our famous half measures.

Monday, 14 July

Russians hanging on, but Germans have crossed [Dnieper] river and can now debouch into open country. (1) Have Russians got a strategic reserve (2) can German transport keep the pace going? About 7 we got Japanese intercepts showing the monkeys have decided to seize bases in Indo-China—by the 20th.† Went back to F.O. after dinner and consulted with F.E. Department. Made rough draft telegram to Washington. But struck me later the best thing we can do is to use publicity—publicise Jap intentions and publicise the assurances they have lately given us.

Tuesday, 15 July

Discussed action about Japan again with F.E. Department. Meeting at No. 10 at 12.15. P.M., A., 'C' and Pound. P.M. approved our

* Under two heads: (a) mutual help, (b) no separate peace.

† Sumner Welles had shown Halifax on 10 July 'a lot of fairly definite stuff suggesting that the Japs had made up their minds to have a go'.

proposed action—publicity, and consultation with U.S. as to what we do if and when Jap move becomes patent.

Wednesday, 16 July

At the party this afternoon, Winston came up to talk to T. He said: 'I see a lot of Sir Alexander now—I suppose I ought almost to call him Alec.' I said: 'I've never dared to call you, to your face, what I've called you, behind your back, now for more than 40 years!'

[After this reception, at Buckingham Palace, Churchill told Cadogan of the plan he was considering; a visit to Roosevelt in August. If it materialised he hoped Cadogan would accompany him.

In mid-July, Prince Konoye formed his third Cabinet and excluded Matsuoka, the former Foreign Minister, who was certainly favourable to the Axis, possibly mad, and (in the judgment of Hull, daily reading the most secret Japanese code) 'as crooked as a basket of fishhooks'. The Vichy Government allowed Japan to place troops and occupy bases in Southern Indo-China, including Saigon. The Russians had every reason to believe, if they credited the excellent Intelligence supplied by Sorge's ring in Tokyo, that Japan would not move against them.]

Monday, 21 July

Cabinet at 5. Lasted till nearly 8. [Harry] Hopkins there again. This is rather absurd, and we had to get rid of him before the end on the excuse that we were going to discuss home affairs, and then discussed—America and the Far East! P.M. digs his toes in against any assurance to the Dutch. He's frightened of nothing but Japan. Long and tiresome discussion. A. fought him and found, of course, no support. Brendan there for first time. This didn't stop Duff sleeping. 9.45 Defence Committee. An appalling ramble. Decided to do 'Puma' in August. I then put up A. to ask how far the objective [the Canary Islands] was from the mainland. None of C's of S. could answer! (Ye Heavens! After Namsos and Crete!) Alexander said 500 miles (I had said 120). Pound measured it roughly on a Mercator's projection of the world hanging up on the wall. Said he made it about 150! This is really shattering. Meeting lasted till 12.30.

Wednesday, 23 July

About 6, Maisky and Golikov and Kharlomov* called on A. and I was there. They subjected us to a cross-examination as to what we were going to do in the North. M's attitude, as usual, very suspicious.

* Rear-Adm. N. Kharlomov, later Russian naval attaché in London, 1942–4, and head of Russian military mission in London, 1944–6.

We got Hollis,* and then Pound over to help us. They didn't go till 7.15.

Thursday, 24 July

These stupid Dominions of course get cold feet, and don't want to freeze Japanese assets without an assurance of support from U.S. They *must* know that they can't *get* this. D[ominions] O[ffice] wanted to send a telegram agreeing that we should seek it. I watered it down, and we caught A. at 8 p.m. and he, luckily, killed it.

[On 25 July President Roosevelt, having asked Japan to withdraw from Indo-China, froze all Japanese assets in the U.S.A. This policy cut Japan off from the supply of materials indispensable to her war economy. Britain simultaneously took similar action. The Dutch, with natural apprehension for the fate of the Netherlands East Indies, did likewise on 27 July, severing one of Japan's principal sources of oil. Eden told the Netherlands Government than an attack on the East Indies would lead the British 'to do the utmost in their power, though H.M.G. must remain the sole judge of what action or military measures were practicable'. Much would depend on the Americans' attitude. By early August, Thai resistance to increasing Japanese demands had hardened.]

Sunday, 27 July

Quiet morning, except that there was a telegram from Cripps, showing that *he* has been negotiating at the other end a Polish-Soviet agreement—and has got rather more than we got out of Maisky! A. agreed I should get hold of Maisky . . . and get him to check up on this before we say anything to the Poles. . . . W. S[trang] and I saw Maisky who had heard—or affected to have heard—nothing from Moscow. . . . No box, and none last night—first time for *months*.

Tuesday, 29 July

Talked to A., who told me of P.M.'s plans and said he thought I ought to go with him. I should be only too glad. . . . About 7 A. got back from P.M., who agrees to my going. Home just before 8 and broke it to T., who took it v. well. Poor dear—it's dull for her.

Wednesday, 30 July

Saw A. and Strang about Polish-Russian business. Both sides are crooks, but it looks as if we may get a signature this afternoon.

* Maj.-Gen. L. C. Hollis, senior Asst. Sec. to office of War Cabinet, 1939–46.

[The agreement annulled the Nazi-Soviet pact in respect of Poland and embodied promises of mutual aid and support in the war against Germany. Frontiers were not mentioned. Sikorski had to overcome much opposition among his exiled compatriots before signing this document.

Towards the end of July, R. A. Butler left the Foreign Office to become Minister of Education. Since he was occasionally the target of barbed comment in the diary, it is well to record a part of Cadogan's valedictory letter:

> I write you a line . . . to say how greatly our satisfaction at your promotion was dimmed by regret at losing you from here.
>
> You have always shown the greatest patience in face of your own difficulties and you have helped us out of many of ours and we shall miss you badly. But I reserve to myself, as I told you, the right to appeal to you occasionally on ticklish matters.[8]]

Sunday, 3 August

Special left [Marylebone] at 12.30. Down the old familiar line through Rickmansworth. Arrived Wendover just before 1.30. Picked up P.M. (in his grey-blue 'rompers'), Dill and Pound. Freeman* already on board. Also the 'Prof'.† Lunched with P.M., Pound and Dill. P.M. warmed up and was in quite good form. Reckoned that for past 48 years he had averaged a ½ bott. of champagne a day. Got the 'Prof' to work out this in figures—and in tons, which was impressive. When translated into volume, he was v. disappointed to find it wouldn't half fill the dining saloon. V. good lunch—tomato soup, sirloin of beef (in unlimited quantities and quite excellent), raspberry and currant tart.

[Cadogan spent the first part of this journey, through Wembley, Harrow and Moor Park, looking out for landmarks and scenes affectionately remembered from his daily journeys between Rickmansworth and London. Much of this Chiltern country was then still unspoilt and peaceful; but the expansion of London since 1933 had been rapid, and he was shocked to see how the sprawl of new buildings smothered the country. At lunch Churchill made a remark in that sense, to which Cadogan replied that if one wished to look at the brighter side these houses should be viewed as the encampment of the anti-Bolshevist horde.[9]]

Monday, 4 August *H.M.S. Prince of Wales*

About 10 drove to the harbour [Thurso] and taken in launch to destroyer 'Oribi'. Stayed on the bridge. Flat calm but misty and dull.

* Air Chief Marshal Sir W. R. Freeman, V.C.A.S. 1940–2.

† Lord Cherwell (Professor Lindemann), Churchill's scientific adviser from 1940; Paymaster-General 1942–5, and 1951–3.

Interesting going in to Scapa through the booms. (Took something over an hour, I suppose). Went on board 'Prince of Wales' and saw our cabins, and found Harry Hopkins* on board. . . . Took a long time circling slowly out of the harbour. . . . Three destroyers in escort. Weather cleared, and there was a bit of sun.

Tuesday, 5 August *H.M.S. Prince of Wales*

After lunch P.M. asked H. H[opkins] to play backgammon. H.H. 'Yes, but I play well.' P.M. 'That's all right: I play low.'. . . We do ourselves well on board—we took on a cargo of grouse in Scotland, and we have some very nice beef. Masses of butter and sugar. After dinner quite a fairly amusing film 'Mr. X', of spies in Russia. We had to apologise to H.H. for any fancied reflection on his new friends.

Wednesday, 6 August *H.M.S. Prince of Wales*

Fair morning but dull. Calm night. Up at 7.30 and breakfast at 8.30. Walked a bit with Dill and went upon Bridge. Did some work, then on deck again to see the destroyers from Iceland join up. They were 3 mins. ahead of time, and found us in mid-Atlantic, in a patch of fog!

After lunch, drafted something for P.M. about F[ar] E[ast].

H.H. produced a tub of admirable caviare, given him by Joe Stalin. That, with a good young grouse, made a very good dinner. As the P.M. said, it was very good to have such caviare, even though it meant fighting with the Russians to get it. When H.H. refused a second brandy P.M. said 'I hope that, as we approach the U.S., you are not going to become more temperate.' Film after dinner, 'The Devil and Miss Jones'. Bad.

Thursday, 7 August *H.M.S. Prince of Wales*

Bad Film after dinner 'The High Sierras'. Awful bunk. But the P.M. loves them and they keep him quiet. After, he played H.H. at backgammon. I couldn't see that H.H. was as good as all that. I crept off about 12.30, leaving them at it. P.M. demanding that we should get in tomorrow evening (which we could quite easily do). 1st Sea Lord equally (but silently) determined that we *shan't*!

Friday, 8 August *H.M.S. Prince of Wales*

Film 'Lady Hamilton' after dinner. Quite good. P.M., seeing it for 5th time, moved to tears. At the close he said 'Gentlemen, I

* Harry Hopkins was on his way home from Moscow.

thought this Film would interest you, showing great events similar to those in which you have been taking part.' Left him and H.H. playing backgammon. H.H. ended up a winner of seven guineas.

Saturday, 9 August *H.M.S. Prince of Wales*

Up at 7 and breakfast about 8. Then found that, by U.S. ships' time, it was only 6.30! A long day. We had to put out to sea to kill time, and eventually came in through lines of U.S. destroyers and dropped anchor by the 'Augusta', with the 'Arkansas' lying beyond. Usual long period of waiting. Then our party went over to 'Augusta' and we were presented to the President. That over, P.M. and he retired for a tête-à-tête lunch, and we had a very unsatisfactory, dry, déjeuner à la fourchette in the Ward Room. Then Sumner Welles took me to the 'Arkansas' where he sat down at a table, with a pile of papers in front of him, like a judge, and went drily through a number of matters, mainly Far East, and 'commitments'. Back on board about 3.30. P.M. already there and in bed. He got up about tea-time and told me of his talk with President. Main thing is application of Plan IV on August 20.* Started off about 6.45 for dinner with President in 'Augusta'. Flashlight groups before dinner, with Fala, the President's dog, in the middle. President sat at head of table with P.M. on his right and me on his left—General Marshall† on my other side. We had quite a lot of talk, and he certainly has great, and natural, charm. He made a short speech or talk after dinner, sitting down. P.M. followed, with more elaborate statement —not his best. C's of S. were then called on without notice and all three acquitted themselves, I thought, extremely well.

[Lord Halifax had asked Cadogan to get on to good terms with Welles; 'he has been playing the game very well lately, and is all out to help.' Welles wished to know whether the British Government had entered into any secret commitments. Cadogan assured him that they had not, save that the Senussi had been told that they would be freed from Italian rule and the Yugoslavs that the issue of Istria might well be considered at the end of the war.

Sumner Welles said that the Japanese now realised, because of the economic measures, that the period of the U.S.A.'s 'extreme patience' was over. If Japan continued to seek the military domination of 'the entire Pacific area', war was inevitable; and he had said as much to the Japanese Minister in Washington. Welles favoured the postponement of a showdown

* By which the United States Navy 'took over' the America-Iceland stretch of the Atlantic.

† U.S. Chief of Staff, 1939–45.

to a moment more propitious. The President did not wish Britain to make even an occupation of Thailand a *casus belli*. Sir Alec said that he entirely agreed, and thought the Prime Minister would probably do so. However, he added, Mr Churchill had recently seemed to believe that Japan would take on all comers. Only with reluctance had he authorised the promise to the Netherlands Government of limited assistance if Japan attacked the Dutch East Indies.[10]

At dinner, Roosevelt conversed charmingly about his country estate at Hyde Park, where he hoped to grow Christmas trees for the market. Afterwards the party talked about immediate business. The President indicated that he would consider 'parallel' declarations by the U.S.A., the British and the Dutch, designed to restrain Japan, and a joint Anglo-American declaration of principles.

The next morning, while Cadogan was breakfasting in the Admiral's cabin, he heard a great commotion. It came from Mr Churchill, storming round the deck. He wanted immediately drafts of the 'parallel' and 'joint' declarations, and indicated in broad outline the character of the latter. Sir Alexander wrote out suggestions, had them typed and gave them to the Prime Minister, who expressed general approval.[11]]

Sunday, 10 August *H.M.S. Prince of Wales*

Drafted scheme of 'parallel' declarations by U.S., selves and Dutch, designed to restrain Japanese from further devilry and to provide mutual aid. Also, President last night said he might be prepared to make a joint general Declaration of principles, so started rough draft of that. P.M. approved both, with alterations.

11 combined Church service on quarter deck attended by President and his party and 250 U.S. seamen and marines, who were mingled in with our men. Very impressive. 3 good hymns—'Onward Christian Soldiers', 'O God, our help in Ages Past' and 'Eternal Father'.

Sat about on deck. Talked to S.W. Gave him some dope about Hess, which I think interested him. Lunch President in Ward Room. I sat between Gen. Marshall and Harriman. Short speeches again by Pres. and P.M. Former awfully good—just like his fireside chats. Very hot by now and sun brilliant. Pres. left soon after lunch. I changed and went ashore on a shingly bay with P.M. (in his Rompers!), Harriman, 'Prof', Martin and 'Tommy'.* We clambered over rocks. P.M. like a schoolboy and insisted on rolling boulders down a cliff. . . .

We gave a dinner on board, to Admirals and Generals and Sumner Welles. Sat and talked to S.W. after, and he stayed after others had

* Respectively J. Martin, Churchill's Principal Private Sec. since 1941; Cmdr. C. R. Thompson, Personal Assistant to the Minister of Defence (i.e. Churchill), 1940–5.

gone. He improves on acquaintance, but it is a pity that he swallowed a ramrod in his youth. But I suppose that can happen in any family with sporting tastes.

Monday, 11 August *H.M.S. Prince of Wales*

Went over with P.M. to 'Augusta' at 11, and had long discussion with President and S.W. on Atlantic islands, Far East and joint declaration. It all went very well. We didn't of course get 100% of what we wanted on F[ar] E[ast], but we must remember that it must be read in conjunction with the Joint Declaration, which will give the Japanese a jar. Back to lunch and spent a pretty busy day drafting telegrams to London. . . . Bed about 1. While I was in bed reading, Hollis brought me telegram from London showing that they agree in general. Pretty quick work! Quite a satisfactory day and I dropped quickly asleep.

[Cadogan reported to Eden that the meeting should produce a great moral effect, though there would be no immediate or striking results. The President had agreed that Plan IV should come into effect on 20 August. This would be of the utmost assistance from the naval point of view In respect of Thailand, Sumner Welles had so far 'been rather sticky', saying that 'the time for warnings is past'. There Cadogan took issue with him:

> he wants to gain time by a continuation of these negotiations which have been going on (as we know) for some time now. That *might* gain time, but if we are to allow the Americans to proceed on that line we must at least insist that the time isn't gained at China's or anyone else's expense, and that meanwhile the economic measures are kept up and screwed up. On this last point Welles has given me satisfactory assurances.
>
> I have hobnobbed with him a lot and have tried to get through his reserve. I believe him to be sound at heart and Edward [Halifax] assures me this is so. . . .
>
> P.M. and President appear to hit it off very well, and whatever factual results we bring back, there will be a great many 'imponderables'.[12]]

Tuesday, 12 August *H.M.S. Prince of Wales*

Beaverbrook arrived. And locked the bathroom door. But I outflanked him through his sitting room and bedroom. Went over to 'Augusta' with H.H. about 11.30 and fixed up with S.W. drafts of Joint Declaration, announcement of meeting and joint telegram to Stalin. Then another meeting with Pres., at which the Beaver was also present. Went without a hitch. Lasted till after 1, when I had lunch in Ward Room. Got final texts checked with S.W. and went to take my leave of President, and so back to ship, where I worked hard on telegrams to London. Sailed at 5. Grey drizzly weather but an impressive night as we sailed down the lines with 2 U.S. destroyers astern. They are coming with us to Iceland. Clocks on 2 hours, so we dined at 9. Film (the world's worst) began not much before 11, so I didn't get to bed before 1 or after.

[The Joint Declaration, or Atlantic Charter as it was henceforth known, read as follows:

> The President of the United States of America and the Prime Minister, Mr Churchill, representing His Majesty's Government in the United Kingdom, being met together, deem it right to make known certain common principles in the national policies of their respective countries on which they base their hopes for a better future for the world.
>
> First, their countries seek no aggrandisement, territorial or other.
>
> Second, they desire to see no territorial changes that do not accord with the freely expressed wishes of the people concerned.
>
> Third, they respect the right of all peoples to choose the form of government under which they will live; and they wish to see Sovereign rights and self-government restored to those who have been forcibly deprived of them.
>
> Fourth, they will endeavour, with due respect for their existing obligations, to further the enjoyment by all States, great or small, victor or vanquished, of access, on equal terms, to the trade and to the raw materials of the world which are needed for their economic prosperity.
>
> Fifth, they desire to bring about the fullest collaboration between all nations in the economic field, with the object of securing for all improved labour standards, economic advancement, and social security.
>
> Sixth, after the final destruction of the Nazi tyranny, they hope to see established a peace which will afford to all nations the means of dwelling in safety within their own boundaries, and which will afford assurance that all the men in all the lands may live out their lives in freedom from fear and want.
>
> Seventh, such a peace should enable all men to traverse the high seas and oceans without hindrance.
>
> Eighth, they believe that all the nations of the world, for realistic as well as spiritual reasons, must come to the abandonment of the use of force. Since no future peace can be maintained if land, sea or air armaments continue to be employed by nations which threaten, or may threaten, aggression outside of their frontiers, they believe, pending the establishment of a wider and more permanent system of general security, that the disarmament of such nations is essential. They will likewise

aid and encourage all other practicable measures which will lighten for peace-loving peoples the crushing burden of armaments.'

This document was endorsed, with varying degrees of enthusiasm, by the Governments of Belgium, Czechoslovakia, Free France, Greece, Luxemburg, the Netherlands, Norway, Poland, Russia, Yugoslavia. At the time, and afterwards, Cadogan thought the sixth article the most significant.

When, in the late afternoon of 12 August, Cadogan took the draft telegrams for approval, he found the Prime Minister standing in the Admiral's cabin reading a document:

> As I came in he lowered the paper in his hand, took off his spectacles and said 'Thank God I brought you with me.' The simplicity of the seven word tribute and his manner of saying it were proof of its sincerity, and I was deeply moved and puffed up with a great pride.[13]

The British had suggested 'parallel' communications by the U.S.A., Britain and the Netherlands to the effect that further Japanese encroachment in the South-west Pacific would bring forth counter-measures, even if they should lead to war. Roosevelt was asked whether he would seek from Congress an undertaking to help any third power attacked by Japan as a consequence of these declarations. The President declined to go so far. He did give the Japanese a warning, but not in the terms agreed with Churchill, who announced on 24 August that if the U.S.A. were involved in war with Japan, Britain would fight at her side. Lord Halifax said at this time that he asked himself every night whether he could have done more to bring the U.S.A. into the war? Certainly the task of dealing with an administration so ill co-ordinated proved a frustrating one, which Halifax compared with 'a disorderly day's rabbit shooting'. 'Nothing comes out where you expect and you are much discouraged. And then, suddenly, something emerges quite unexpectedly at the far end of the field.'[14]

Churchill told his Ministers that he now felt convinced Roosevelt would do all he could to help in war and consolidate the peace. Soon the new convoy system would operate, whereby so long as one American merchant ship was escorted by one warship, any number of British merchantmen could join in. The zones in which enemy ships would be shot up were to be extended.

He did not think the Japanese would go to war with Britain. The Americans had given serious warnings and were gaining time by a 'rather humbugging' negotiation about the conditions upon which the neutrality of Indo-China and Thailand could be guaranteed. It was hoped to spin out this process for perhaps three months, by which time Britain would be able, or so he then thought, to put a very strong fleet into the Far East without denuding the Mediterranean.

As for the Atlantic Charter, the Prime Minister had pointed out to the

President that whereas in 1917 the Allies had spoken of a war to end war, with all committed to disarmament at its close, and of making Germany pay, they now proposed, while disarming Germany, to make no promises and no attempt to ruin her. Rather she should be 'fat but impotent'.[15]]

Wednesday, 13 August *H.M.S. Prince of Wales*

After tea started work on Cabinet paper giving account of our stewardship. P.M. has got one of his untidy colds coming on. Film after dinner. One Donald Duck, and thereafter appalling slapstick by Laurel and Hardy [*Saps at Sea*]. P.M. hated it, and thought I'd chosen it (as I had—I hate the dramas that he likes).

[Mr Churchill went at once to his cabin, pausing only to remark 'a gay but inconsequent entertainment'.]

Saturday, 16 August *H.M.S. Prince of Wales*

Yesterday evening, about 8, we sighted a convoy of 72 ships, in good formation. We went right thro' the middle of them (they doing only about 7 knots), turned back again thro' another part of the line and then up through them again. It was a remarkable sight. The forest of funnels looked almost like a town. The evening was fine and it was a beautiful and inspiring sight (though it is disturbing to see what a target they offer, and how little protection they have). They were in 13 columns of 6, and keeping v. good formation. Good luck to them.

Monday, 18 August

[On train back to London] long lunch. Winston did himself well, finishing up with a Benedictine. 10 min. later he called for a brandy. The attendant reminded him he had had Benedictine. He said: 'I know: I want some brandy to clean it up.' (Next morning I found him eating cutlets and bacon for breakfast!)

Monday, 25 August

We went into Persia this morning.* Things seem to be going 'according to plan'.... Cabinet at 5. Lasted till nearly 8. Very rambling, but not unuseful, as there was a long discussion (H. was there) of the recession in America. The Beaver, back from the U.S., thumping the table and saying P.M. must do something 'dramatic'. I think it *is* true that the President lags behind a bit, and the American public want a jolt and are ready for a jolt. I wonder whether a statement by the P.M. would help—to effect that we are all right and can

* Russian forces moved in simultaneously. The purposes were to suppress German influence, capture the oilfields and secure a route to the Caspian.

defend ourselves, but that to get a (quick) victory and to impose the 8-point Declaration on the world, America must come in. Till she comes in, we shall not get the American war effort (as in this country) keyed up.

Thursday, 28 August

Cabinet at 11.30. H. Morrison* violently opposed the Beaver's proposal for relaxation of black-out on roads. P.M.—rightly, I think—said that we ought to take advantage of this lull to intensify work in factories and ports and on the roads. I left them before they reached any conclusion. . . . 3.30 Moghaddam.† What a man! He described to me, with dramatic gestures, how he had always been devoted to England and had worked for the closest relations, and how his people—and the Shah—had for centuries pinned their faith to Great Britain. And I *know* he's bitterly anti-English and would work against us in any way he could!

Monday, 1 September

Lunched with Tony R[othschild] at New Court [the Rothschild Bank buildings]. Hadn't seen the City since the fire. Queen Victoria St. an extraordinary sight. It has disappeared and is quite open. Curious effect, rather like being behind the scenes at Buffalo Bill's show. . . . Cabinet at 5. Wasn't heckled on anything that mattered. Had to put up 2 papers—on milk for children in Vichy France and unoccupied countries, and naturalisation of Frenchmen. Didn't win on either—but didn't lose: Cabinet merely prevaricated.

Tuesday, 2 September

Hot and sunny. An awful day. P.M. rang up at 10.10, raging about Germans and German Legation in Persia. Was able to show him we had already done everything. Max Beaverbrook rang up to say P.M. wanted him to see Hess! Would I tell S. of S.? Did so later, and on his instructions got Max to undertake to keep us fully informed. H[erschel] Johnson‡ about Mexico. P.M. sent for me about 12 to show me his letter to de Gaulle. I got his approval for telegram to Persia and one to Moscow about Baltic fleet. Lunched at home. 3.30 [Habsburg] Archdukes Robert and Felix! Gave them cold comfort. Everyone fussing at once and H. H. hopping in and out. . . . H. Seymour about a mass of tiresome questions and I had to

* Herbert Morrison, Home Secretary, 1940–5.

† Mohammed Ali Moghaddam, Persian Ambassador, 1940–1.

‡ U.S. chargé d'affaires.

ring up Hollis to say I wouldn't do what Chiefs of Staff wanted. Brendan rang up about that egregious Moore-Brabazon's gaffe, and I had to send a telegram to Cripps about it. Amery sent for me to complain he wasn't informed about Persia and F[ar] E[ast]. What a day! Home 8.5. Dined and did a lot of work.

Wednesday, 3 September

6 meeting at No. 10 of Defence Committee on Persia. Quite plain now that P.M. is planning grandiose warfare in Persia. Well, A. might stop him if he was here, but as he chooses to be on holiday, I can't keep up a 3-cornered wrangle between Frensham [where Eden had a house], No. 10 and F.O. Got some of his phrases inserted in to the telegram to Tehran. But he won't like it. But would he be able to ride P.M. off his Persian campaign?

7.30 took draft telegrams (revised) to Tehran to P.M. Found him sitting (in rompers) in garden with Max. Joined them for 20 minutes or so. P.M. approved drafts. (I last sat there with poor old Neville [Chamberlain]—when was it? Sept. '38 or '39.)

Thursday, 4 September

Maisky at 5. Gave him latest dope. He wanted to see P.M., with A., tonight or tomorrow morning. Fixed him up for tonight at 10 and got A. to come up. . . . Sent for Geoffrey Dawson, who turned up just before 7.30, to rate him about 'Times' treatment of Persian question.

[Maisky talked to Churchill and Eden in grim terms of Russia's burdens and plight. This might, he said, prove a turning-point. If Russia were defeated, how could Britain win? The Prime Minister, sensing 'an underlying air of menace in his appeal', reminded Maisky that but four months earlier the British had not known whether Russia would fight against them on Germany's side. 'Whatever happens and whatever you do, you of all people have no right to make reproaches to us.'

By now, Russia had lost more than half the Ukraine. Leningrad had been encircled but not taken. Hitler then turned the weight of the German effort to an onslaught upon Moscow, while the southern armies pressed on to the lower Don. By mid-October the Germans appeared to be on the point of capturing Moscow.]

Friday, 5 September

Poor A. had to stay here all night. He rang me up at 11.45 p.m. to tell me about the Maisky interview. Stalin message pretty black. demands a 'diversion' and/or pretty considerable material help. . . .

Cabinet 12.30. Cabinet confirmed we can't do diversion, and discussed material help, of which we can offer something substantial. . . . A. went off to C's. of S. meeting to revise P.M.'s draft reply to Stalin. Cabinet thought this morning it was a bit too negative. (Personally I think Stalin's message lays it on a bit thick. Our evidence does not show imminent Russian break.) Saw A. after his return. He says Beaver is pressing for him to go out at once to Moscow. I think this a mistake. He went over to P.M. again about 6 and wasn't back at 7.40 when I left. I've got a lot of foul things on my hands. . . . I *hope* to get away tomorrow and leave all this mess. I am completely muddled and exhausted. I must reform Office work on my return. They must *not* fling 30 lb. files at me. It will be much more work for them, but they *must* (1) set out the case shortly and (2) put down *exactly* what they propose. Was just getting to sleep at 12.10 a.m., when Winston rang up to say Cripps was coming home and must be stopped. I told him to dictate a telegram and send it to the Resident Clerk. About 12.30 he rang up again to say that *he* ought not to send the telegram—it ought to come from the S. of S. I said that was all right, rang up Resident Clerk and dictated telegram.

Saturday, 6 September

A. in a flap on the telephone from Frensham. It's hopeless conducting business like this. A. sees no papers, he is dragged up to London for 24 hours, dines with P.M. They both happen to see an intercept which makes it look as if we might get Germans out of Afghanistan. So they get on the hop, and I get messages to say that it must be done *at once*. But there are considerations of which they are blissfully ignorant, poor children. Had to go round to I.O. Amery away. Could only find Sir L. Wakely*—a typical Civil Servant. Tried to stick some pins in his backside—it was already 1.10—and contrived with Lawford† to leave the baby in other arms than mine.

[The Cadogans went for a fortnight's leave to their cottage. A messenger arrived every few days with a box of papers. 'Not very much news' says the Diary for 9 September, 'but a telegram from Cripps showing that, in spite of all outward appearances, Stalin is feeling very dicky.' Most of the time was pleasantly passed in walking, gardening and reading.]

Sunday, 14 September *Thatched Cottage*

After lunch continued grubbing and digging. After tea, scythed some grass for T. to get her bulbs in. . . . At end of dinner, T.

* Dep. Under-Sec., India Office, 1934–41.

† Nicholas Lawford, Asst. Private Sec. to Eden.

produced a Welsh Rarebit of a strength and savagery almost unknown. What will be the result?

Monday, 15 September *Thatched Cottage*

About 3, T. and I motored to Hastings. Climbed thro' barbed wire on to the Front, walked along it, and sat for a bit on the only half-acre of beach left open to the 'public'. Such a seaside town a most depressing sight nowadays. Blind windows and peeling paint and only one or two asthmatic residents sitting in the shelters.

Saturday, 20 September *Thatched Cottage*

This is our last night here. A very pleasant and unexpectedly long holiday. News, from the Russian front, has been pretty bad throughout. Perhaps we are in a better state than I should, last spring, have expected. But everything is pretty murky, and how exactly we are going to *win* this war, I shd. like someone to explain. While it lasts it's completely bloody.

Sunday, 21 September

A winter and dark nights to look forward to. The Russian news is bad—Kiev is gone and the Germans are driving straight to the Caucasus, and I see no hint of an end to the war.

Wednesday, 24 September

Cabinet at 6. . . . A. gave an account of his attempt to reconcile de Gaulle and Muselier. Hardly had he done so when Morton sent in a report of an interview between the two at which de G. insulted M. Only thing to do to get them together and ''ave it out', as Jim Thomas would say. Got Morton to summon them for 7.30 and told I. Mallet to put them in separate rooms! Left A. to it at 7.50.

[A. V. Alexander, First Lord of the Admiralty, had the task of providing a link between General de Gaulle and the Admiral. Eventually Muselier consented to join the National Committee, provided that he might have 'une conversation à fond' about its purpose. 'Ce n'est pas un comité, c'est une comédie' said he. All the negotiations were carried on in separate rooms. Eventually de Gaulle concluded that the matter could now be arranged. 'Ce n'est rien, tout cela. Ce ne sont que les troubles de l'émigration.'[16]]

Thursday, 25 September

Meeting with A. about Turkish Chrome. Turks are most awful brigands. We daren't threaten them—we can't bribe them. 1st Lord rang me up later to tell me most he cd. offer in the way of destroyers, but I fear it's not good enough.

[The British and Russians had assured Turkey on 10 August that they intended scrupulously to observe the independence of Turkey, would give every possible help if Turkey were attacked by a European power, and had no claims on the Straits.]

Friday, 26 September

Polished off some things with A. at 4—he wanting to go down and establish himself in his new country house.* A further de Gaulle worry, just as he was starting. X. has intrigued with Y. to protest to P.M. about the new Conseil! What the Hell has it got to do with Y.? whose only business—though he uses a W.O. 60 h.p. car for the purpose—is to arrange Punch and Judy shows for Free French children! A. wrote a snorty minute in reply, I'm glad to say. Settled . . . about fire-watching [at F.O.]. I shall have to do it. V. tiresome, but that is the only way I can bring compulsion to bear on our 'high-ups', who haven't shown up too well in this business.

Monday, 29 September

This diary *must* be dull. I never have time or inclination to read it. I keep it scrappily and simply haven't the time to indicate what interviews are about, or to relate one thing to another. It can only be an *aid* to memory and if I am ever spared any leisure in a possible world, I may be able to build something of these strawless bricks. But I doubt it! Generally, life here is almost like peace-time—no air raids. But dull and depressed. Little social life, and one's whole mind is spoiled and dominated by this bloody war. One feels almost unpatriotic in allowing one's mind to dwell on anything rational (not 'rations'!) or pleasant.

Tuesday, 30 September

Didn't see A. till 7.30. Seems matters in House went well, and Winston's speech† a success. A. had spoken to him frankly last night about the Beaver's various performances, and he had taken it well.

Monday, 6 October

Walked with Eddie [Cadogan] to Queen Anne's Gate. White autumn crocuses, at their best, look quite lovely, and contrast so

* Binderton, in west Sussex.

† About Russia, Persia, the Battle of the Atlantic and Allied shipping losses.

well with the bedizened trollops of dahlias. P.M. seemed depressed but cheered up a bit. German drive (long known to us) against Moscow beginning. The Bols[heviks] are in for a thin time—and so are we all, probably.

Wednesday, 8 October

A. worried about increasing pinpricks between us and Russians in Persia. He saw Maisky this evening—without getting much out of him. . . .

Russian situation evidently very bad in centre and south. I fear we are nearing end of campaign though, let us hope, not a complete collapse.

Thursday, 9 October

Cabinet 12.15. Russian situation bad, but perhaps not quite *so* bad as I had thought. Max B[eaverbrook] returned, but didn't appear at Cabinet. P.M. went out to see him. M.B. apparently confident—but then of course he left Russia 5 days ago.

[The initial reception of Beaverbrook's party in Moscow had been frigid. Eventually a protocol was signed, specifying the supplies which the U.S.A. and Britain would make available in the next nine months. These consisted mainly of tanks, aircraft, guns and ammunition. No promise was made about their transportation, though both powers undertook to help. The few military conversations uncovered no common ground, for the Russians would not or could not understand why the immediate establishment of a Second Front was not feasible.]

Monday, 13 October

Cabinet meeting. . . . Agreed Russian situation pretty 'grim'. Max gave light-hearted account of his Moscow mission which, as I know from my sources, was a complete newspaper stunt. He *is* a scamp! After Cabinet settled telegram to Mexico about resumption of relations.

Wednesday, 15 October

Defence Committee at 10. Glad to say we killed operation 'Ajax'. It *might* succeed in itself but then, as Joe Kennedy would have said, 'Where the Hell do we go from here?' We examined, more favourably, better prospects in Mediterranean area. Home 12.15.

Thursday, 16 October

Frightful day. 10.30 talk with A. about (1) Far East (2) Abyssinia, before Cabinet at 12.15. Cabinet lasted till 1.40. Boxes meanwhile piling up. On Abyssinia P.M. took wise line that we must not saddle ourselves with a Protectorate—and all the responsibility that implies. Perhaps the Emperor can't govern well, but we can't keep everyone on apron-strings. 'The grant of self-government implies the grant of mis-government. I mean, otherwise there wouldn't be any fun in it at all'!

[Japan was now reported to have some 28,000 troops in Indo-China. Admiral Nomura, Japanese Ambassador in Washington, told Halifax on 16 October that he

> did not anticipate any sudden change of policy. The Emperor has been in favour of peace, and even if a general were made Prime Minister, it was unlikely that the Emperor's wishes would be disregarded. . . . Everybody in the Japanese Cabinet wanted understanding with the United States, and the only difference was as to the price that should be paid for it.[17]]

Friday, 17 October

Mild. Various talks with A. about Far East (Konoye's resignation looks bad*) and other things. . . . 3.15 till 5 Defence Committee. They decided on Mediterranean operation. Not *quite* so much work, and caught up arrears a bit. Maisky had a telegram today from Molotov, still in Moscow, and defence of city being prepared.

Monday, 20 October

10 Defence Committee. Alexander† there. . . . Beaver had circulated a paper . . . which was simply a 'Daily Express' Leader. 'We must help Russia'. *He* knows, as well as anyone, why we can't. He's playing some game. I couldn't make out what it was, but gradually it dawned on me that it was this: by waving his arms frantically and barking that he 'disagreed fundamentally' with the Government, he put a certain amount of wind up Winston. Then he switched over to 2 particular controversies he has had with W.O. and A.M. about supplies to Russia, and got Winston—in order to avoid worse difficulties—to back him over those! What a monkey. Home 12.45 a.m.

Tuesday, 21 October

3.45 meeting of P.W.E. Dogfight between Dalton and Brendan. Inconclusive. . . . Frightful ramble at Defence Committee. We talked

* He was succeeded by Gen. Hideki Tojo.

† Lt.-Gen. H. T. Alexander, Then G.O.C.-in-C., Southern Command.

about everything on earth till 11, when we started on the Agenda—and left it at 11.5. Finished soon after 12.30 a.m. I'm rather tired!

Wednesday, 22 October

Rather a *good* report on Russia, from a good source.

Thursday, 23 October

Moghaddam came to say good-bye (thank heaven).

Friday, 24 October

11.50 A. sent for me: he had Maisky with him, whining because we hadn't declared war on Finland, Hungary and Roumania. Quite silly.

Sunday, 26 October *Thatched Cottage*

Not a bad day, but coldish N. wind and one or two very light showers. Out earlyish. Carted barrow-loads of soil and ashes to put on roots of young trees. Pruned (very bold!) the young fruit trees. After lunch gathered vegetables, mulched fruit trees and planted 2 new clematis. . . . Russia doesn't look too bad. Resistance still going on, but Cripps, of course, asking for a 'second front'. The obvious. If *only* we could have struck, even in Libya, by now. But there is a delay—how long exactly, I don't know.

Monday, 27 October

Defence Committee at 10. Old Pound heavily and convincingly killed [Operation] 'Whipcord' and we buried it and put up a little headstone. Poor Winston very depressed. Got away by midnight.

Tuesday, 4 November

Defence Committee at 10—till 1 a.m! . . . Far East. Examined redraft of P.M.'s telegram to Roosevelt. I suggested appeal to R. to warn against Japanese attack on Yunnan. P.M. agreed.

Wednesday, 5 November

Cabinet at 12.15. . . . P.M. produced his redraft of telegram to Roosevelt, but he had left out the guts—proposal for a fresh warning. So I scribbled a para[graph] for insertion and he accepted it.

[General Chiang Kai-Shek appealed for help in the defence of Yunnan, upon which China's ability to protect the land approaches to Burma and Singapore largely depended. Churchill's telegram finally read:

What we need now is a deterrent of the most general and formidable character. The Japanese have as yet taken no final decision, and the Emperor appears to be exercising restraint. When we talked about this at Placentia you spoke of gaining time, and this policy has been brilliantly successful so far. But our joint embargo is steadily forcing the Japanese to decisions for peace or war.

It now looks as if they would go into Yunnan, cutting the Burma Road, with disastrous consequences for Chiang Kai-shek. The collapse of his resistance would not only be a world tragedy in itself, but it would leave the Japanese with large forces to attack north or south.

The Chinese have appealed to us, as I believe they have to you, to warn the Japanese against an attack in Yunnan. I hope you might think fit to remind them that such an attack, aimed at China from a region in which we have never recognised that the Japanese have any right to maintain forces, would be in open disregard of the clearly indicated attitude of the United States Government. We should of course be ready to make a similar communication.

No independent action by ourselves will deter Japan, because we are so much tied up elsewhere. But of course we will stand with you and do our utmost to back you in whatever course you choose. I think myself that Japan is more likely to drift into war than to plunge in.

The President replied that while he would do what he could to sustain China another formal warning to Japan might inflame rather than deter.[18] On 10 November Churchill announced that if the U.S.A. became involved in war with Japan, 'the British declaration will follow within the hour'.]

Thursday, 6 November

I returned to F.O. after dinner—my first night of sleeping in as fire-watcher. 9–10 crawled over the roof with Bill Bentinck and the professional fireman. But didn't learn much. Worked after and then went to bed in my room. Was quite comfortable, with a nice fire flickering.

Saturday, 8 November

News tonight of loss of 37 bombers! This is awful! Due to 'weather'. For 20 years I have been complaining of the complete inability of the Air Ministry to learn *anything* about the weather. This is proof, at least, that I was right, but that is small consolation.

[Stalin had sent an indignant telegram about a leakage of information concerning the British declaration of war on Finland, Hungary and Roumania. He added that he did not wish to see Generals Wavell and Paget unless they were coming to discuss plans for the post-war period and for a mutual treaty on military aid.

On 19 October, Stalin had issued his most famous Order of the Day, enjoining resistance to the last. The German armies were held just outside Moscow. Hitler gave instructions on 13 November for one last effort to take the city. This attack, launched in early December, broke down completely in the extreme cold. Nor had Leningrad fallen.]

Tuesday, 11 November

Soon after 1 A. sent for me to tell me about Stalin's reply to P.M.'s message about Finland. It is thoroughly *bad*—cantankerous and offensive. I don't know what it means. 3 G.J., whom I warned that a campaign was hotting up against S.O.[E].... Cabinet at 5. Our catastrophic losses in the air over the week-end due to hopeless ignorance about weather conditions and rather too much enthusiasm on part of Peirse.* P.M. angry, and said his instructions had been ignored. *Bombing does NOT affect German morale:* let's get that into our heads and not waste our bombers on these raids. Long discussion on Ethiopia, during which I—like Pound—went actually to sleep, I think. We were then turned out and War Cabinet left alone to deal with something—? Russia. Hope they're not being silly.

Wednesday, 12 November

12 saw A., who told me about last night's discussion of Stalin's message. He is to be fairly stiff with Maisky. Lunched with Poles.... Raczynski complained after about Russian treatment of Poles, and I passed this on to A. before he saw Maisky this evening.... De Gaulle—who was baulked of an interview with A.—came to see me. Main point was Djibouti, and I elicited from him that his idea was that, whatever the conditions of a surrender, Free France must administer the territory. So it appears that neither P.M. nor A. really came to an understanding with him on this point, and this must be cleared up....

Defence Committee at 10—till 12.45.... Stalin's prickly message. Decided to ignore it.

Friday, 14 November

3 talk with A., O.S. and Warner about Stalin. Maisky has hinted to A. that he realises Stalin's message was unfortunate. Agreed to leave him alone for moment. But A. would have to go out to Moscow —after Libya has developed—and Cripps should stay there till then.... Authorised Admiralty to intercept French ships in China seas carrying rubber from Indo-China for France–Germany. Think this is all right, but must inform A. tomorrow.

* C.-in-C., Bomber Command, 1940–2.

Saturday, 15 November

Maisky 10.15. Talked to him about Yugoslav revolt and he promised to ask Moscow to stop Communist fighting Mihailovitch.* . . . Kamimura† at 3.30. But it is as useless talking to him as to any other Japanese.

Sunday, 16 November

These week-ends are awful. Ministers get time to 'think', which I think they do on country walks, in the course of which they lash themselves into a frenzy—about nothing much. Then, on returning home, they seize the telephone receiver like a drunkard seizes the bottle, and the whole place flares up. *That* shows you what would happen if we had a Cabinet of 'non-Departmental' Ministers. And the P.M. sits somewhere in the country, like a spider in the middle of his web, and tickles them all up. I don't believe it produces much beyond frayed nerves and tempers.

Monday, 17 November

Special Cabinet about Stalin, which I didn't attend. They approved draft telegram which I wrote for S. of S. yesterday morning. . . . Cabinet at 5. No great news. P.M. told them in confidence that our offensive in Libya was due tonight. Long discussion of India and question of internment under 18B and control of Press. Waste of time for me, for whom work was piling up. Home at 8 with a *stack* of papers.

[The telegram, sent on 21 November, assured Stalin that the Prime Minister wished to work with him. Soon Eden would visit Russia to discuss the war and post-war prospects. 'The fact that Russia is a Communist State and that Britain and the U.S.A. are not, and do not intend to be, is not any obstacle to our making a good plan for our mutual safety and rightful interests.'

It promised that if the Finns did not within the fortnight cease their operations against Russia, Britain would declare war on them.[19]]

Tuesday, 18 November

11 talk with A. about Finland. Agreed we might try idea of sort of ultimatum to Finland on original Soviet offer (if Russians will agree). That would be more respectable than declaring war on them out of the blue—for no particular reason.

* Gen. Draža Mihailovitch, leader of the Cetnik guerrillas in Yugoslavia.

† S. Kamimura, Counsellor, Japanese Embassy, 1941–2.

Wednesday, 26 November

Found all sorts of things waiting for me. Principal among them draft for Cabinet on Russia—our 'Volga Charter'. O. Harvey had already told me P.M. had agreed to my going with A. to Russia—probably Sunday week. This draft v. bad and I started re-writing it. . . . 5 caught A. with latter and he approved.

Thursday, 27 November

Cabinet at 5 on Russia. P.M. in a hopeless mood, opposing violently the paper we had circulated—without having read a *word* of it. So there is nothing to be done but redraft it somewhat and add a draft of the kind of thing we hope to sign—to show what our objectives (and our limitations) are.

After dinner (at home) tried my hand at this drafting. But after a bit one gets bored with a subject and can't get on with it. I can sometimes sit down and write straight out something that makes some sort of sense—like the Atlantic Charter. But once one gets niggling about and altering phrases, I lose sight of the whole thing, and get lost.

Friday, 28 November

Maisky came in afternoon with message from his Government about what they could do to transport us from Archangel to Moscow. *Admiralty* says we can't get to Archangel. M. says this is nonsense! Got A. to approve a draft Anglo-Russian declaration (not mine—and not a good one—as thin as restaurant coffee) and circulated it to Cabinet. A. tells me Max has told him P.M. is still in an anti-Russian defeatist frame of mind.

[On 24 November, Hull told the British Ambassador and others that the U.S. Government wished to try for a temporary agreement with Japan, 'primarily because the heads of our Army and Navy often emphasise to me that time is the all-important question for them, and that it is necessary to be more fully prepared to deal effectively with the situation in the Pacific area in case of an outbreak by Japan'. This tactic was abandoned, however. Instead, Hull presented to the Japanese envoys on 26 November a note demanding, *inter alia,* withdrawal of all Japanese forces from China and Indo-China and of support to any government in China other than that of Chiang.

Five days later, and undoubtedly basing himself on Intelligence derived from the intercepted Japanese messages, Hull said that

> the diplomatic part of our relations with Japan was virtually over. . . . it would be a serious mistake for our country and other countries

interested in the Pacific situation to make plans of resistance without including the possibility that Japan may move suddenly and with every possible element of surprise and spread out over considerable areas and capture certain positions and posts before the peaceful countries interested in the Pacific would have time to confer. . . .

Hull complained to the British Ambassador about the manner in which his efforts to postpone the row had been blown out of the water by people who did not understand how delicate was the balance, indicating that he was resentful of Roosevelt's receptivity to advice from those outside the State Department.[20] On the next day, the Americans had the decypher of a telegram from Tokyo asking the Japanese Ambassador in Berlin to tell Hitler and Ribbentrop secretly:

. . . that there is extreme danger that war may suddenly break out between Anglo-Saxon nations and Japan through some clash of arms, and add that the time of the breaking out of this war may come quicker than anyone dreams.

Admiral Phillips had just arrived in Far Eastern waters with the battleships *Prince of Wales* and *Repulse* but without the aircraft-carrier *Indomitable*, which had been damaged in running aground in the Caribbean.]

Monday, 1 December

Cabinet at 6. P.M. against taking any forestalling action in Thailand. Think he is right. Japs are evidently in a fix, and announce that they want to continue conversations in Washington. P.M. also decided *not*, at present, to publish documents on origin of war. I think he is right again. A. wants to publish them, but I think this is 'ideological'. Why rake up controversy now? Have them ready by all means. Does A. realise that *he* is responsible for the great and tragic 'appeasement'—not reacting to German occupation of the Rhineland in 1936? How lucky he is—no one has ever mentioned *that*! and *that* was the turning point.

Wednesday, 3 December

Meeting with A. at 11.45 about F[ar] E[ast]. Things look critical, but American attitude seems firm and sound. Agreed draft to Washington. . . . Defence Committee at 5.30 about F.E. and Russia. . . . Didn't reach any final decision about our trip to Moscow, but P.M. seemed to accept idea of sending a telegram to Stalin warning him we don't come with Divisions in our pocket. This is essential, before we go. Though Max urges that we go out blind and put it across Stalin. I'm sure this is wrong.

Thursday, 4 December

Cabinet at 6. We had had very good telegram from Roosevelt

about Far East, which removed many of P.M.'s doubts, and he said we could not guarantee Dutch. Discussed Russian trip. Appears now that we shall not even have material to offer to Russians—in place of Divisions. A.—rightly—made a stink about this, but agreed to go. P.M. again stamped on A. Sinclair for suggesting postponement. Dined at home. Back to F.O. by 9.45 to draft telegrams. Went over to see P.M. at 11, and eventually got drafts passed. Home about 12.30—rather tired.

Friday, 5 December

5.30 went to see P.M. who gave me instructions about declarations of war this midnight on Finland, Hungary, and Roumania. I shall have to ring him at midnight. He off to Chequers. A. left for Binderton this afternoon. Dined at home, worked and prepared packing. But an awful night, as Finn reply came in about 11.30 and a telegram from Washington (a good one) with messages from President about Far East. Spent about 1½ hours telephoning to A., P.M. and F.O. Finally fixed up decision to declare war on Finland, H[ungary] and R[oumania], and got P.M.'s approval to reply to President. Bed about 1. Very tired.

Saturday, 6 December

Found report of reconnaissance of Japanese armada moving west, south of Cambodia point. Rang up A. Broke into meeting of C[hiefs] of S[taff], who didn't seem to know quite where they were. Informed Winant. Later saw Dutch and told them what had been planned about a warning, and asked them to get ready. But all may be now in melting-pot if the monkeys are going for Kra Isthmus. Later heard that they had gone into west coast of Indo-China. This gives us more time. We may yet get a joint warning. P.M. has approved message to Thai P.M. Dined at home and packed—so far, 10.30 p.m., quiet. I thought A. might postpone trip, but he says not. This Diary will (if we start tomorrow) be continued on scraps of paper.

(*31 December*) I have assembled the scraps of paper, and endeavour to formulate the result as follows:

Sunday, 7 December

During dinner we were told (gossip from a porter on a platform) that Japan had attacked the U.S., and, later, we had a message to say that we couldn't embark at Thurso, owing to weather, and must be prepared to embark at 8.30 at Invergordon.

[Japanese aircraft, based upon carriers standing some 275 miles off, succeeded in a space of two hours in wrecking a large part of the U.S. Pacific Fleet in Pearl Harbor. Seven of its eight battleships were sunk or damaged. The U.S.A. now had two battleships operational in the Pacific, Japan ten. For the time being, then, Britain and the U.S.A. had naval command only of the Atlantic. The Japanese promptly attacked Hong Kong, Malaya, the Philippines, Borneo, Thailand and the Dutch East Indies.

On 12 December Churchill transferred Burma to Wavell's India command. It had rice and some oil, provided the only means of sending supplies to Chiang in South-west China and was essential to the protection of Eastern India, where many of the munitions factories lay. In the autumn of 1941, India had possessed not a solitary aircraft capable of fighting the Germans or Japanese on level terms; not a single modern tank; and less than three dozen anti-aircraft guns. Touring in late October and early November, Wavell had been horrified by the lack of organisation at Rangoon and by the 'completely unwarlike' atmosphere at Singapore. He had then thought it unlikely that the Japanese would attack Malaya.[21]

The Intelligence organisation in the Far East was lamentably thin, and the effectiveness of the Japanese air power much under-rated.]

Monday, 8 December *H.M.S. Kent*

Breakfasted about 7.45. A. joined us, but only drank a ½ bottle of soda-water—had had a very bad night, being sick and feeling like nothing on earth. . . . Apparently P.M. wants to be rung up. I told him A. was ill and he got round a naval surgeon, who found a temperature and diagnosed gastric 'flu. A. rang up P.M., who said he was off to America! A. horrified, but didn't succeed in dissuading him. He then rang up Attlee and Winant, who both agreed it should be discouraged. Attlee said he would oppose it at Cabinet at 12. (Will he?!) . . . [about 5 p.m.] I rang up P.M. He said his plans were all made, so evidently Cabinet had not (of course) stood up to him. I said A. was distressed at idea of their both being away together. He said 'That's all right: that'll work very well: I shall have Anthony where I want him!' Does this mean that we shall have to stay indefinitely in Moscow, to conduct 3-cornered conversations? Returned to tea in 'Kent' and we sailed about 6. A fairly full muster for dinner, but sea became lively after, and many went thoughtfully to bed.

Tuesday, 9 December *H.M.S. Kent*

Sun at noon only about 5° above horizon. Passed a floating mine.

I asked Capt. to shoot it but first he said it was too close to ship and then he said it was too far off to hit. Read and slept most of the day. A. still has temperature. Our party very much thinned out by mal de mer.

Wednesday, 10 December *H.M.S. Kent*

The vibration and motion in the stern of the ship are uncomfortable. We do about 24 knots. And then, on top of all, telegram in afternoon reporting loss of 'Prince of Wales' and 'Repulse'. Very depressing. Crossed Arctic Circle about 8 p.m.

Friday, 12 December *H.M.S. Kent*

We ran into fairly thick fog this morning, but nevertheless hit off pilot boat and picked up pilot and several Russian naval officers. I went up on Bridge—rather crowded with Russians. Curious scene. There was no daylight: the pilot boat ahead of us had a search-light astern which she trained on us, while we trained ours on her. Our own light lit up the bridge and the foc'sle. Wisps of fog kept intervening and blotting out everything, and a great deal of hooting, not very well co-ordinated, told us whether we were ramming the pilot boat, or where she was when we had lost her. Eventually anchored about 3. . . .

After we had anchored, 3 Russians came aboard—2 from the Commissariat for F[oreign] A[ffairs], of whom one seemed respectable and spoke intelligible French. The other, whom I called 'Frog-face', was alleged to speak English, but it must have been some local dialect unknown to me. The third was in military uniform and frankly spoke only German, so I avoided him—for purely linguistic reasons. A. up again by teatime and dined in his cabin. Maisky went ashore to discuss plans and came back in favour of train which, he says, will take only 60 hours. That, if correct, is much the best plan. If we go by air, we shall have to divide the trip in two, and stop off at Archangel. This likely to be beastly, and moreover one is liable to be held up anywhere for a week. (Nye* has the story of a secret rule in the Air Ministry to the effect that, if an officer simply *must* be at a given spot by a given time, he must travel by *train*!) Russell, of our Embassy,† came on board and seems energetic and efficient. Speaks fluent Russian. *He* says we shall take 5 days by train. Anyhow it's best in A.'s state of health.

* Gen. Sir A. Nye, V.C.I.G.S., 1941–6.

† J. W. Russell, then 3rd Secretary.

Saturday, 13 December *En route Murmansk to Moscow*

Quiet night in the ship. After Breakfast packed and went on deck. Pretty dark. Wandered on to Bridge and exchanged reflections with Quartermaster, who was not enthusiastic. He said, quite wisely, 'I shan't be coming 'ere for my 'oneymoon!' About noon we suffered from an influx of Russians—the former ones and some new ones. They all wanted lunch, of course, and got it. Left for the shore about 2, and landed at a jetty where guard of honour was drawn up. Oddly enough, it was a scene of eerie beauty. Snow-covered setting, dimly lit by a lemon-coloured glow on the southern horizon. In the foreground a very new Union Jack and a blood-red Red Flag illuminated by searchlight—a spot of brilliant colour on the pastel background—the kit of the guard showing faint mauve tints against the snow. Got into cars to drive about 15 miles to Murmansk. 'Frogface' got in with me. As we were starting, an unknown lady swathed in fur, got in and sat on the strapontin. She said 'I komm with you'. Which was obvious but not very explicit. However, she turned out to be quite pleasant, and, unlike 'Frogface', had a certain command of current English. After about half an hour we stopped on the top of a hill and looked down on Murmansk. It was a lovely sight. The glow on the horizon, on the far side of the town, was still just sufficient to light the snow on the ignoble roofs and it looked really fairy-like. Then drove down into the town and the station, where we found the train waiting. Accommodation not too good. I have to double up with O. Harvey in a cramped and antediluvian sleeping compartment. There is a lavatory, where water (cold) runs hopefully for 2 seconds and then relapses into a thick and completely black fluid. We have our own dining saloon where A., Maisky, O. Harvey and myself are to regale ourselves.

Sunday, 14 December *En route Murmansk to Moscow*

Dawn came at 10.35, when the sun—oddly enough, very suddenly—came over the horizon. We are running through snow-covered forest, and the effect is beautiful. A clear blue sky and the fir trees covered with rime and snow. The sun, for the few hours it is with us, is never more than a degree or two above the horizon, so that it is always sunrise (or sunset—the two run into each other) and there is a pink-mauve glow all day. The topmost branches of the highest trees just catch the sun and look like branches of coral. Breakfast was late. The attendant has no use for clocks. Some time in the morning we got out and walked somewhere. There were 45° of frost, but it was still, and didn't feel cold. Our train drags at its tail two open trucks, in which there are A.A. guns and crews. They do watches of two hours! They had icicles hanging from their eye-lids, but seemed quite cheerful! Good food on the train. And good vodka. But much disappointed by compressed caviar, which has no taste.

Monday, 15 December *Moscow*

Misty early, but then lovely again. Got to Vologda 11.30, where we walked. 54° of frost! . . . at 5, we stopped . . . and Cripps came aboard. . . . A. joined us for dinner. We arrived Moscow about 12.30. It was snowing as we stepped out on platform under a battery of searchlights. A group, headed by Molotov, advanced upon us. We went to meet them. Cinemas whirred, but I couldn't get into the front rank, what with Cripps and Molotov and Commissars and interpreters and Ogpu men. A. inspected large guard of honour and shook hands with engine-driver. However, it was probably the right thing to do. Drove through a *complete* black-out with Admiral Miles to National Hotel. Unpacked and got into bed 1.45. Hotel old-fashioned—like 'Beau Rivage'* only almost more so. Sitting-room with grand piano. Bathroom with a tap that squirts water impartially into the basin and on to the operator.

[The prospects for these talks in Moscow did not look unpromising. Stalin had recently stated in public that Russia sought the liberation of her own peoples, not the subjugation of others; the Germans had not taken Moscow; the entry of the U.S.A. into the war should strengthen Eden's hand. Hull telegraphed from Washington, though it was unnecessary, a warning against the conclusion of any secret agreements with Russia.

At the first meeting, Stalin said that he wanted not a declaration, 'algebra' as he termed that, but an agreement, 'practical arithmetic'; to cover wartime collaboration and post-war reconstruction. Poland would receive East Prussia. Germany would be split up into three or four states. Russia's western frontier in Finland and the Baltic would revert to that of June 1941; Russia would want the Curzon Line as her boundary with Poland (giving Russia less than she had under the Nazi–Soviet pact, but much more than she had under the Treaty of Riga of 1921); Russia would also require Petsamo from Finland, and substantial territories from Roumania. Britain might, if she wished, have bases in Norway and Denmark. Russia did not want to 'bolshevise' Europe. Stalin accepted that Britain could not yet open a Second Front in Europe; nor could he in the Far East. He said that he thought it must come to war with Japan and apparently looked for a contest in the spring.

* The hotel used for many years by the British delegation at Geneva.

Eden explained that he could not negotiate an agreement about the frontiers.[22]]

Tuesday, 16 December *Moscow*

Slept fairly well. Grey and snowing lightly (as it was last night). Had a talk with A. and helped him with his notes for talk with Stalin. Latter anxious for a tête-à-tête, but A. has persuaded him that Cripps also should attend. Cripps gave us his draft of an agreement, which contained certain good points. I married it to our draft (to the sound of gunfire). As I finished, warning sounded, about 1 p.m., and we were hounded out of the hotel to a neighbouring Tube Station. There we descended into the *depths* by escalator, and were shown into a magnificent marble hall, out of which opened cubicles with beds, telephones &c. All clear at 1.30. (I think the thing was a fake, just to show us what would happen if necessary.) Lunched in Hotel. Food very good. Afterwards drove out to the point on road from which Napoleon surveyed Moscow. But too misty and snowy to see much. Walked great part of way back. Drove round Kremlin and past Embassy. A. went off to see Stalin at 7. Back about 11. Seems to have been quite satisfactory, though S. indicated his ideas of future frontiers, which would raise a lot of questions.

Wednesday, 17 December *Moscow*

Still dull. Maisky came round at 11 with translations of the texts of the two draft treaties which S. gave A. last night. Nothing much wrong with them,* and by lunch he and I and A. had provisionally agreed texts. After lunch in hotel went for walk in town. Not very attractive. New wide streets (as in Nanking) but rather a squalid huddle of modern buildings. Went into fur shops and Mostorg. In latter, a whole counter of Father Christmases and Xmas tree decorations being sold! F.C. has to be called 'Grandfather Frost'! Rather noticeable that *books* (cheap editions) seem to attract many buyers. . . . At Kremlin at midnight. Stalin, Molotov, A., Cripps and self. We met in a gaunt modern office. Photos of Lenin, Marx, Stalin. Nothing much else. A long sort of refectory table, at one end of which we sat

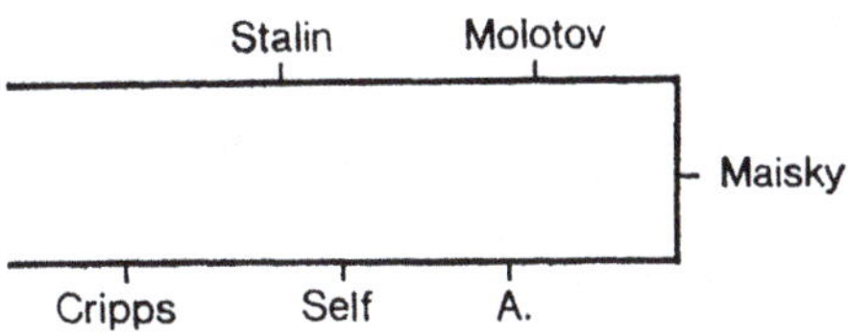

* The agreement about frontiers would, according to Stalin's proposal, have been contained in a separate and secret protocol.

Stalin said our work (on drafts) was interesting, but what really interested him was Russia's future frontiers. He wants us, here and now, to recognise Russia's 1941 frontiers, i.e. including bit of Finland, Baltic States and Bessarabia. We told him we couldn't do this (and he had given no warning of this requirement to us). Argued, inconclusively, till 3 a.m. and then left without anything settled.

Difficult to say whether S. is impressive. There he is—a greater Dictator than any Czar (and more successful than most). But if one didn't know that, I don't know that one would pick him out of a crowd. With his little twinkly eyes and his stiff hair brushed back he is rather like a porcupine. Very restrained and quiet. Probably a sense of humour. I thought at first he was simply bluffing. But I was wrong.

Thursday, 18 December *Moscow*

To Kremlin at 7. We both had suggestions for 'formulae' for bridging our gap, but they were mutually unacceptable, and we were both quite frank in recognising that there *was* a gap that probably couldn't be so bridged. Back about 8.30 and went early to bed.

[The Foreign Secretary explained once again that Britain could not simply accept Russia's demands there and then. Stalin appeared unimpressed. He merely said: 'It is a pity.'

Surmising that microphones would be installed in every room, Eden arranged during the drive back to the hotel with Cripps and Cadogan that the listeners should now be treated to a chorus of complaint. This tactic the three of them adopted with a will.[23]]

Friday, 19 December *Moscow*

A. left for front at 8 a.m. . . . Cripps went to see Molotov at 5, but got little change. A. back about 7. He had taken opportunity to have long and frank talk with Maisky, who was not entirely pessimistic.

Saturday, 20 December *Moscow*

Pretty clear Russians won't sign treaties if we don't recognise their 1941 frontiers. Snack at 6 and went to Kremlin at 7. Recognising failure, we had brought short draft of usual colourless communiqué. On arrival, found Russians had a much better one, which we at once accepted. Everything finished by 8.30, when Stalin invited us—and *whole* Delegation—to dine at 10. Rang up Delegation to give them glad tidings. Most of them had already dined! Went back to Hotel and returned to Kremlin at 10. Received in different part of premises. Walked first through what looked like series of modern booking-halls, then through largest conference room I have ever seen, into a rather gaudy suite which included (where we dined) Catherine the Great's Throne Room. But decoration I should guess at early 19th century. I sat next to Stalin, with Dunlop (as interpreter) on my left. Toasts began at once, and were first drunk in what Stalin called 'Russian whisky'—Vodka treated with burnt pepper and chilis. S. told us he never went to bed before 4, but didn't get up before 11.30. Had some words before dinner with Timoshenko.* He was rather tight. (He drank pretty consistently for the next 7 hours, so that I marvelled that he was sober at 5 a.m.). Dinner ended about 1 and we adjourned to a private cinema theatre. Quite a good film of the Russian forces, which came to an end about 3. Stalin said then he would show us another film of 'our Japanese friends'—a rotten film which lasted till 4.45. Everyone drinking the whole time—champagne mostly. Voroshilov,† who was sitting next to Stalin, very uproarious at first. He later became ominously quiet. An A.D.C. came to try and pull him away, and got him half way to his feet, from which position he relapsed on to Stalin's lap. Latter got up and took a turn round the room. Voroshilov's symptoms became graver later, and he was carried away at 4. a.m.‡ We left at 5. It was by now Stalin's sixty-second birthday.

Timoshenko very blatantly confident about German loss of morale. Stalin also confident, but in a quiet way.

[Stalin's frontier demands had not abated. Indeed, they varied little during the war. What is remarkable is that even at this stage, after six months of desperate crisis and with the German armies at the gates of Moscow, the Russians should have formulated their policy so precisely and pressed it so confidently. The communiqué stated that the two parties had agreed about the conduct of the war, the need for the utter defeat of Germany

> and the adoption thereafter of measures to render completely impossible any repetition of German aggression in future. Exchange of views on questions relating to post-war organisation of peace and security provided much important and useful material which will facilitate a future elaboration of concrete proposals on this subject.
>
> Both parties are convinced that the Moscow conversations constitute

* Marshal S. K. Timoshenko, People's Commissar of Defence, 1940–1; in command Western (Central) Front, July–Nov., 1941; then commanded on South-western and Southern Fronts, 1941–2, Western Front, 1943, Ukraine, 1944.

† Marshal K. E. Voroshilov, member of Politburo 1926–52, of State Defence Committee 1941–5, and numerous other bodies; later President.

‡ When Stalin asked 'Do your generals ever get drunk?' Eden replied 'They don't often get the chance.'

a new important forward step towards closer collaboration between the U.S.S.R. and Great Britain.

Significantly, Cadogan said to the U.S. chargé d'affaires in Moscow that it might be best for the British and American Governments to concert their attitude towards post-war problems and then to present their joint view to Russia.[24] Sikorski told Stalin that he could not agree to the Curzon Line, or to the surrender of Vilna; he did not wish Russia to have the whole of Lithuania; and Poland, although she wanted East Prussia, did not desire a frontier as far west as the Oder.[25]

Churchill, who had reacted strongly against Stalin's demands, reached Washington just as the British party left Moscow. On the whole, the Prime Minister succeeded better than anyone had dared hope. Despite a minor brush with Cordell Hull when de Gaulle's forces took the islands of St. Pierre and Miquelon (whereupon the State Department issued a statement talking of 'so-called free French ships' and Hull lectured Halifax *in extenso*), general agreement was reached on a unified command in the South-west Pacific, to devolve upon the luckless Wavell. That unique instrument the Combined Chiefs of Staff Committee was established in Washington, with British representatives permanently stationed there. Vast plans were set in train for increased production of warlike stores. Most important of all, the Americans showed no disposition to concentrate everything on the Pacific theatre. The Prime Minister lived in the White House, just across the corridor from the President, who would 'blow in' as he pleased. 'He is the only Head of State', said Churchill, 'whom I have ever received in the nude.'[26]

Monday, 22 December *En route Moscow to Murmansk*

Kremlin at 5, to say good-bye. Back to Hotel and then station. Train left 6.30.

Thursday, 25 December *H.M.S. Kent*

We were up to time last night, but it was broken to us this morning that we were 3 hours late—no one knows why. Arrived at Murmansk 12.15 instead of 9.12. Pretty dark. Got into a car to drive the 15 miles to Vianga. An enormous Russian naval officer sat on strapontin in front of me, so that I could see nothing ahead, and as a snow-blizzard came on, the side windows became obscured. So that I might have been a pill in a box. And—although travelling slow—we skidded and swerved and bumped alarmingly. The most unpleasant drive, lasting best part of an hour, that I have ever had. After reviewing guard, we got on board 'Kent', followed by a crowd of Russian vultures, who had scented food. There were so many that we all, except A., were crowded out of Admiral's quarters and had no turkey. I got a snack in the Ward Room—a plate of wet ham and a glass of water. What a

Christmas dinner! Some delay occurred over getting luggage aboard, and as it was getting rapidly dark, Captain began fussing. Eventually, luggage arrived, and we made to get under weigh. I took great pleasure in herding Russian officials and Trade Unionists (*13* of them we are taking back with us) out of the way of sailors doing their jobs. *Some* revenge for being done out of my lunch. Got off about 4.30 and soon got into rough water, and *all* the Russians disappeared, and were no more seen! I confess I didn't enjoy dinner myself. 24 knots in a rough sea isn't much fun in the after part of the ship.

Sunday, 28 December *H.M.S. Kent*

Church (a scratch one) at 10.45. Somewhat interrupted by pom-pom practice during the hymn.

Monday, 29 December

Having made very good time—were generally doing 24 knots and during one hectic, rattling night 28—we were ahead of time and arrived in the Clyde this morning. A lovely sunrise as we were passing Ailsa Craig. Arran looked beautiful. Quite warm. Anchored off Gourock about 2. Got special off at 3. Before leaving ship Maisky—to his delight—inspected guard of honour of Marines! Lunched on board before leaving. Train comfortable and got us to London at 12.45 a.m.

Wednesday, 31 December

Anglo-Australian-Dutch landing in Portugese Timor has produced a crisis—Salazar (who must be rather an ass) maintaining a tiresome sanctimonious attitude.

So ends 1941—what a year again! But it does look as if we may be at the turn. Disasters in Far East cloud the nearer scene, but on a long view all that matters is defeat of Germany, and that, with her failure in Russia and in Libya, and with entry of U.S. into the war, now seems to be coming into sight.

T. and the family all well, thank God! T. has slaved to look after me, and I owe her everything.

VII

January–September 1942
REVERSES

Although the Japanese attack on Pearl Harbor, and the most fortunate and unusual loyalty of Hitler in declaring war on the United States, gave everyone a new confidence in the outcome, there were few encouraging signs for the immediate future. The Prime Minister had said boldly, for at the time he could do none other, 'give us the tools and we will finish the job'. All the same, and excepting an internal convulsion in Germany, that was a task beyond the British Commonwealth's strength. Few could believe by the end of 1941 that an economic blockade, however rigorous, or strategic bombing, however vigorous, would win the war. The makers of British policy, then, felt conflicting emotions: on the one hand, intense relief that the manpower, money and manufactures of the United States would henceforth be freely available; as a counterweight, consciousness that the American forces, even before Pearl Harbor, were inadequate, that the Pacific Dominions and colonial territories were dangerously exposed, that the British hold on the Middle East must remain tenuous until Rommel could be routed. In Washington, Mr Churchill had secured a prize of the first order in the undertaking that the European theatre would take priority. Otherwise he brought home what Eden succinctly described as 'lots of jam for tomorrow, but not much today'.

Small wonder, with the Japanese taking the Dutch East Indies, Singapore, the Andamans, much of Burma; with the dreadful losses of shipping in the Atlantic and Russian convoys; with a groundswell of press and Parliamentary dissatisfaction; with the Germans almost in Moscow and on the borders of Egypt, that the Prime Minister should now feel the weight of the war press upon him even more suffocatingly than in the summer of 1940. Cadogan always said that he had found the first nine months of 1942 the hardest time of his life; not from exhaustion or an excess of work, but on account of the sense of impotence bred by successive military setbacks and consequent diplomatic weakness.

There were, of course, elements of strength in the Allied position which were not immediately apparent in this grim winter. First among them, paradoxically, stood Hitler's continued control of German policy. Had he not gone to war with Russia and the United States it is hard to see how the Axis could have been defeated. For those reasons Cadogan felt glad, in retrospect, that a wartime meeting decided, purely on account of practical difficulties, not to attempt Hitler's murder. Second, a close co-operation between the British and Americans had been developing for twelve months in the vital fields of Intelligence, espionage and subversion. The British read all the *Abwehr* hand-cyphers from 1940, and the machine-cyphers from 1942. The Americans gave the British in 1941 the means of unravelling the most secret Japanese codes. Spanish diplomatic messages between Madrid and Washington were consistently read from 1942, Vichy diplomatic codes from 1942, and Italian naval traffic from 1941. No doubt numerous other codes and cyphers had been broken.

Unhappily, the dictators seem to have been as well informed of the Allies' proceedings as the Allies of theirs. Count Ciano continued to receive intercepts of some British diplomatic telegrams. The codes used by Mr Robert Murphy* in the Mediterranean, broken by the Germans, gave away American contacts with General Weygand and probably caused his dismissal by the Vichy Government. If the Americans were greatly aided in the crucial battle of Midway Island by decyphering the Japanese signals, the cryptanalysts of the Axis scored a much more significant success in reading the cypher mainly used for Atlantic convoys between February 1942 and June 1943. They studied carefully, for example, the Admiralty's daily signal about the supposed whereabouts of the U-boats. Moreover, the Germans were monitoring some of the telegraphic exchanges between Ankara and London, and between London and Moscow. British methods, reflected Goebbels, were extraordinarily careless:

> [I can only hope that this is not the case with our own secret communications as well; for if the British knew in detail about us everything that we know about them it could have very grave consequences.[1]]

1942

Thursday, 1 January

Pole at 5, and tried to pump me about Stalin's attitude to Balkan States. All our private conversations have evidently leaked, and it was *not* too easy to stall him.

Friday, 2 January

Defence Committee at 3. Mostly about Falkland Islands. If *necessary*, we must call Americans in. But we *must* bar Argentines.

Saturday, 3 January

Simopoulos and Milanovitch† at 11 to communicate Greek-Yugoslav treaty of 'Union'. Very good.

* R.D. Murphy, President Roosevelt's personal representative, with the rank of Minister, in French North Africa.

† Greek Minister and Yugoslav chargé d'affaires respectively.

Sunday, 4 January

Dutch are furious at decisions being taken in Washington without being given a chance of expressing their opinion. They are quite right! . . . I got van Kleffens* on telephone and gave him ridiculous message (very tactfully) from P.M. telling him to cancel his departure for Washington tomorrow. He—in a huff—had already decided not to go.

Monday, 5 January

Cabinet at 5. Not very much news. Latest tank battle in Libya seems to have been pretty hot—we lost 60! A. had argument with Dalton about supplies for Greece.

Tuesday, 6 January

Simopoulos at 5. He had heard (how?) that Dodecanese were 'discussed' in Moscow. Reassured him. Then a sudden rush of work but got thro' most of it before dining at home.

Friday, 9 January

Talk with A. 1.15. He said House in very bad mood. Thought a reshuffle would be difficult to resist.

Saturday, 10 January *Thatched Cottage*

Hens not laying yet! Walked down into valley towards Ewhurst—to get shelter; then left and up thro' fields. T. came out into garden for 10 mins. before lunch. In afternoon did the same sort of round, only rather longer, in reverse direction. 2 primroses out in garden. Daffodils showing an inch or so—and an iris in bud! Otherwise no signs of life. . . . Winter jasmine in full flower.

[Cadogan spent a week's leave of miserable weather at Thatched Cottage. In his absence a minor crisis in the Yugoslav emigré Government resulted in the deposition of Simović, who had led the abortive coup in Belgrade nine months before. The Graeco-Yugoslav treaty was signed in the Secretary of State's room on 15 January, beneath the gaze of Pitt. In mid-week a messenger brought Cadogan a box with many papers but little news, which he summarised thus: 'Malaya sticky, Libya slow and Russia hopeful.']

Monday, 19 January

Cabinet at 6. Not v. interesting and interminable, rambling talk. P.M. seems prepared for the worst in Malaya but not hopeless yet.

* Netherlands Minister for Foreign Affairs.

Otherwise optimistic. Long argument started by Earle Page* about the 3 agreements initialled by P.M. in U.S. E.P. can never state a point (I don't know whether he ever grasps it). P.M. finally lost his temper—which was a good thing. I left the Cabinet still sitting at 8.45. New cook—who will be disgusted by these hours!

[Mr Churchill recorded that the attitude of the Australian Government (Mr J. L. Curtin, the Australian Prime Minister, had just stated that an evacuation of Singapore would be regarded as 'an inexcusable betrayal'), press criticisms, carping by Parliamentarians, the atmosphere of the lobbies, all gave him 'the sense of an embarrassed, unhappy, baffled public opinion, albeit superficial, swelling and mounting about me on every side'.

Aware of his strong position, and adamant that he would surrender none of his responsibilities, he determined to demand a vote of confidence. In an oration of nearly two hours, coolly received, he defended himself vigorously, even truculently, on 27 January. The speech certainly had the merit of laying bare the truth about the Allies' vulnerability in the Far East, and their inability simultaneously to meet three major enemies in theatres ranging from the Atlantic, the Channel, the North Sea, Central Europe, the Mediterranean, North Africa and the Middle East to the Indian Ocean, Burma, Malaya, the Pacific and Australasia:

> In two and a half years of fighting we have only just managed to keep our heads above water. . . . It looks as if we were in for a very bad time; but provided we all stand together, and provided we throw in the last spasm of our strength, it also looks, more than it ever did before, as if we were going to win. . . .
>
> While facing Germany and Italy here and in the Nile Valley we have never had any power to provide effectively for the defence of the Far East. . . . There never has been a moment, there never could have been a moment, when Great Britain or the British Empire, single-handed, could fight Germany and Italy, could wage the Battle of Britain, the Battle of the Atlantic and the Battle of the Middle East, and at the same time stand thoroughly prepared in Burma, the Malay Peninsula, and generally in the Far East, against the impact of a vast military Empire like Japan. . . .

The debate lasted three days, concluding with another speech by Churchill on 29 January. The vote of confidence was accorded by 464 to 1.]

Tuesday, 27 January

Michiels† at 4, to complain of P.M.'s speech, which, he said, had

* The special Australian envoy to the War Cabinet continued to attend meetings when Australian affairs were discussed.

† Jonkheer E. Michiels van Verduynen, Dutch Ambassador, 1939–52.

given away the whole of their case on co-ordination. Saw A. about it when he got back from House and we agreed to see Michiels tomorrow morning (tho' I don't think we can comfort him). Gather P.M. did not make very great impression—too long. Summary on B.B.C. tonight sounded quite good.

Wednesday, 28 January

Wellington Koo* at 3.30 about P.M.'s speech. Everyone dissatisfied with that!

Thursday, 29 January

Law told me debate had gone all right. Good vote. But news is bad all round (except in Russia) and Germans claim Benghazi. Our army is no good!

Friday, 30 January

Discussed with A. paper by C.I.G.S.,† who wants to take nearly all that we send to Russia and to distribute it in packets all over Middle and Far East, India, Australia and New Zealand! We probably must submit, and we shall have to tell Stalin that it is because he can't do anything to relieve Japanese pressure on us. But I wonder whether it is not possible to avoid so great a *dispersal* of effort—just what the enemy want us to do.

Saturday, 31 January

No papers, so listened to news at 1. We've retreated into Singapore island. That *must* surely be indefensible against the air. Coming on top of our loss of Benghazi, most depressing. I'm afraid our soldiers seem very incapable.

Sunday, 1 February

Good dinner at home and not too much to read. The news was not so much worse as it usually is nowadays.

Monday, 2 February

Cabinet at 5. After last week's debate P.M. hectors more brutally a more subservient Cabinet. He flew at Amery. Latter said 'Is that the view of the Cabinet?' P.M. said 'Yes'. No one else said anything. Cabinet seem to expect Singapore to hold out for a bit. Don't see how it can. Long wrangle about 'consideration' for Lease-

* Chinese Ambassador, 1941–6.

† Gen. Sir Alan Brooke had recently succeeded Dill.

Lend. A. put up a fight to meet the State Department. Confess I am a heretic on this point. I think their article 7 about Imperial Preference* is rather impertinent blackmail. But H[alifax], D. Scott, [Nevile] Butler† and others think passionately the other way. P.M. carried the day against A. . . . Russian news alone good. (Even C.I.G.S. is prepared to admit they've done *something!*).

[On 2 February the Government of Husein Sirry Pasha resigned in Cairo, after the intervention of King Farouk. Sir Miles Lampson quickly presented an ultimatum to the King, demanding the installation of a government with popular support, which in practice meant a government of the Wafd, and threatening force if the demand were not met. The King gave way.]

Tuesday, 3 February

Fresh snowfall—and awful slush. Drove to F.O. Talk with A. and M. Peterson‡ about Egyptian crisis. Decided we can't have an apparent Palace Victory and we may have to kick Farouk out. . . . Little news. Russia seems to be going on all right. Lull before storm at Singapore. I tried to reassure Wellington Koo.

Wednesday, 4 February

Egyptian situation moving rapidly to a crisis. Expect we shall have to kick out the King. . . . I warned A. that I have fear Japs may contain us (4 Divisions of us!) in Singapore island, already rendered useless, and turn against Burma, cutting Burma Road. This ought to be their game! . . . We still seem to be rushing backwards in Libya. Russian front seems all right.

[The Prime Minister and Cabinet, committed to the eventual independence of India, had received much evidence of revived antagonisms between its communities, and especially between Moslems and Hindus. By a proclamation of 1940, the Moslems had been promised that they would not be coerced; the Indian war effort was vital in the Eastern theatres, and never more so than now, with the Japanese overwhelming Burma. Churchill hoped that the different communities might elect their best men to serve in a Constituent Assembly, with the promise of Dominion status, and the right to secede from the Empire, after the war. It appears that at one moment he intended to visit India himself in order to press some such solution; but the fall of Singapore killed that plan. President Roosevelt had

* Which in effect required its eventual abandonment.

† Nevile M. Butler, head of American Dept., F.O.; later Asst. Under-Sec. of State, F.O., 1944–7; and Ambassador to Brazil and to Netherlands.

‡ Now Under-Sec. of State, F.O.

got it into his head that the expedients adopted during the American War of Independence might somehow be applied to India. 'States which have no overseas colonies or possessions', wrote Churchill, 'are capable of rising to moods of great elevation and detachment about the affairs of those who have.'

Japanese troops took Rangoon on 8 March. Immediately afterwards, Sir Stafford Cripps went out on the War Cabinet's behalf to consult Indian leaders. Despite his efforts, Congress rejected all proposals which would retain 'even a partial measure of British control in India'.]

Thursday, 5 February

Cabinet 5.30. Item 1 was India: item 2 Russia (Stalin's [territorial] demands). I went over at 5.30 and with great delicacy sat in the Hall. I had taken a lot of work with me. P.M. came in rather late and saw me there. After a few minutes sent Bridges out with a message that he thought it rather rude to keep people in the Hall (he often keeps the Lord Chancellor there!) and would I come in; so I joined the party. Lively discussion on India, which doesn't concern me, but distracted me from my work! At the end, P.M. floored everyone by announcing *his* remedy, which is brilliantly imaginative and bold and was generally welcomed! (I think he brought me in to witness his performance!). Thereafter a short discussion on Russia, in which P.M. showed himself mulish. (Of course he's right, really.) Max [Beaverbrook] supported A. strongly, but not very effectively.

Friday, 6 February

A harassing day. V. cold. So many interruptions that I didn't finish reading my morning distribution of telegrams until 5 p.m.! . . . Cabinet at 12. Came to a decision about 'consideration' for Lease-Lend, but don't believe Americans will accept it. Then a tiresome discussion of Stalin's demands. Traversed all the old ground and got no further. Agreed to put up draft to Washington. Got away 1.45.

Monday, 9 February

Michiels at 12 about co-ordination. Luckily Australians have now agreed to Far East Council* in London and P.M. has fixed a meeting for tomorrow and invited Dutch. M. wanted to know whether he should come with his P.M. I said he should. . . . Cabinet at 5. First about Russia. Cabinet accepted my draft (though P.M. didn't like it). Then a general meeting. *Very* gloomy. Japs have

* The function of this body, which became known as the Pacific War Council, was to focus the views of the Dominions, the Dutch, the Chinese and the British. There was a parallel body in Washington. The Council did not meet in London after Aug. 1943.

penetrated 5 miles into Singapore island. Our generals are no use, and do our men fight? We always seem to have 'Indian Brigades' or Colonials in front line. As P.M. says, what will happen if Germans get a footing here? I tremble to think. Our army is the mockery of the world. Then about 130,000 tons of shipping sunk in a week! Poor Winston v. desperate. (And A. tells me he's fussing about his health.)

Tuesday, 10 February

News all round frightful. Singapore is going to be a bloody disaster and sinkings—especially of tankers—are climbing up to a murderous figure.

[In January, the shipping losses (British, Allied and neutral) totalled 419,907 tons; in February, at which point the Germans penetrated the codes more thoroughly, the figure rose to 679,532 tons; and in March to the staggering total of 834,164 tons. The loss of shipping in this one year aggregated nearly 8,000,000 tons.]

Wednesday, 11 February

4 Bridges about delimitation of O. Lyttelton's functions. (I never can grasp these questions—nor their terminology). P.M. has postponed his plan for the moment (see Feb. 5). Singapore situation renders it impossible: he must remain here to take the bump.

[That day, Wavell telegraphed from Singapore: 'Morale of some troops is not good, and none is as high as I should like to see.']

Thursday, 12 February

The blackest day, yet, of the war. Singapore evidently only a drawn-out agony. Burma threatened. Meanwhile we are bullying Chiang Kai-Shek in India about his seeing Gandhi. So China will go out of the war when Burma collapses. Meanwhile, 'Scharnhorst', 'Gneisenau' and 'Prinz Eugen' cockily steamed out of Brest this morning and up the *Channel* in broad daylight, and so far I have been unable to hear that we have been able to knock any paint off them. We are nothing but failure and inefficiency everywhere and the Japs are murdering our men and raping our women in Hong Kong. . . . I am running out of whisky and can get no more drink of any kind. But if things go on as they're going, that won't matter.

Friday, 13 February

German battle-cruisers eluded us and must be home by now. Another blow. Poor Winston must be in a state.

Sunday, 15 February

Winston broadcast at 9. Announced fall of Singapore. His broadcast not very good—rather apologetic and I *think* Parliament will take it as an attempt to appeal over their heads to the country—to avoid parliamentary criticism.

Monday, 16 February

Talked about P.M.'s broadcast to A., who took same view as I did. He was going to lunch with P.M. 12 Dutchman about these infernal liaison arrangements. Gave him satisfaction. Cabinet at 5. P.M. truculent and angry—and havering. I should have thought that he, with his 40 years' experience of the House, would know it's no use getting prickly about stupid criticism. All news as bad as it can be. . . . Defence Committee 10–12.15. Glad to say general consensus of opinion was that it's no good frittering away inadequate forces on the forward line, and better to concentrate on Burma-Ceylon-Australia! But can we persuade Dutch of the rightness of giving up Dutch East Indies?

Tuesday, 17 February

P.M. rather prickly in the House today and Ridsdale told me it didn't go down very well. He *will not* give up Ministry of Defence.

['The trouble about this suggestion', as Lord Beaverbrook pithily remarked, 'is that either the new Minister of Defence will disagree with the Prime Minister on strategy and will get the sack, or agree with the Prime Minister, in which case his appointment will be superfluous.'

Churchill's absence in Washington, at a time when vital decisions must be taken about the Far East, had provoked much questioning about the nature of the British war machine. Not everyone was wholly reassured by Attlee's presence at the helm. This phase coincided, as Mr R. A. Butler recorded in his inimitable style, with the expression of

> a curious inverted conscience on the part of the Private Members of the Conservative Party. They saw things going very badly for the country and their own interest (as they have expressed it to me). They began to search their conscience as to whether they had told the truth to Chamberlain. They came to the conclusion that they hadn't, and that they must therefore tell the truth to Churchill. There was nobody to give them good advice about Politics.

The Prime Minister soon realised, despite the vote of 29 January, that Parliamentary discontent had by no means evaporated. On 4 February he bowed to the demand for a Ministry of Production, to which Lord Beaverbrook was appointed. Meanwhile, Sir Stafford Cripps had returned from the Embassy in Moscow with the highest reputation. He refused the

Ministry of Supply in late January. After the fall of Singapore, the Prime Minister knew that he must make further changes. According to Lord Beaverbrook's contemporary account, Attlee said that he did not want Cripps, who had been expelled from the Labour Party, to lead the House. 'Having excommunicated Cripps in the peace, he is not going to make him assistant Pope in the war.'[2] Beaverbrook himself, meanwhile appeared to live on the edge of a nervous and physical collapse. He resigned the office which he had held only a couple of weeks. Attlee's objections having been overcome, Cripps began a brief and embarrassed tenure as Leader of the House.]

Wednesday, 18 February

Gave lunch at Claridges. . . . A. there and gave me a lift back. Discussed with him plans for Cabinet changes. Main thing is that P.M. should accept in principle *smaller* War Cabinet. A. would see him at 5 and press this. . . . Further talk with A. at 7.30. P.M. accepts smaller Cabinet and has two alternative schemes (dropping Kingsley [Wood], Greenwood, bringing O. Lyttelton back and bringing in Cripps. Max stands down a bit—he's conscious that he is unpopular!).

Thursday, 19 February

A. had long session last night with P.M. till after 2 a.m. Result, at present, is that he stays at F.O. Cripps to lead the House. War Cabinet—P.M., Attlee, A., Cripps, Anderson, Bevin and O. Lyttelton, who will do Production (Max travelling). Kingsley remains Chancellor *outside* War Cabinet. Greenwood dropped. Glad A. stays with us. Alternative scheme would have been Bobbety [Lord Cranborne] nominally Sec. of S., with Attlee over him—a bad arrangement.

Michiels at 12. Wanted us to press Stalin to move against Japs. Told him not much chance, but agreed we ought perhaps to try. Flap with A. about the not surprising Dutch annoyance at Washington having, without saying a word, altered conclusions of Tuesday's Pacific Council. Wellington Koo at 4.30 to pump me about the Council's doings. I really think we must have a better liaison with Chinese.

Friday, 20 February

G.J. at 5 with draft 'Charter'. (But I hear from A. that P.M. is going to take S.O.E. away from Dalton—and divide it between us and Chiefs-of-Staff! Help!). . . Home usual time and dined. Not too much work. Hankey Bannister have played up and have sent me 3 each of Claret, Port and Whisky!

Saturday, 21 February

Still dull and beastly cold (29°). Trying to snow as I walked to F.O. Nothing of great interest. Lunched at home. Read for a bit after, and then T. and I walked to Leicester Galleries. On the way looked at the new Rembrandt in National Gallery. Very striking. Went on to see Epstein's lump of alabaster Jacob and the Angel. Two unpleasant apes in questionable posture. Quite beastly. So obviously disconcerting that the asses who gape at it think there must be something in it. But there isn't. I don't know whether alabaster has any war uses. If so, this is a frightful waste.

[In the early months of 1942, the difficulties of finding a working arrangement with the S.O.E. caused Cadogan much trouble. Sometimes the erratic proceedings of S.O.E. agents led to immediate political difficulties, with the consequences of which the Foreign Office had to cope; more seriously for the long term, the development of S.O.E.'s activities might produce, and in some instances did produce, conflicting foreign policies. The responsible Minister, Dr Dalton, took exception to 'a most graceless, clodhopping' memorandum by Cadogan of early February. A few days later he was told by Eden that had he been Secretary of State in 1940, he would have kept these activities under the control of the Foreign Office. In the ministerial reshuffle Dalton was moved to the Board of Trade, S.O.E. remaining under the new Minister of Economic Warfare, Viscount Wolmer.* Dalton tried, unsuccessfully, to arrange that Political Warfare at large should be handled by Cripps, since it was essentially a task requiring 'a Left Wing mind'.[3]

For the moment, Gladwyn Jebb remained at M.E.W. Cadogan appreciated the delicacy of his position, and tried to help. Frequent meetings of officials, which the P.U.S. attended with an inward groan, were supposed to ensure harmony between S.O.E., the Foreign Office and the Political Warfare Executive. 'These S.O.E. people' Cadogan noted gloomily in March, 'have a jargon, which lays down a dense smoke-screen.' The diary for April refers to 'interminable S.O.E. worries'; for June to fortnightly gatherings to consider S.O.E.'s plans; and for July to troubles between S.O.E. and P.W.E.]

Monday, 23 February

Had meeting with O.S., O. Harvey and Strang about future of S.O.E. . . . G.J. came over at 3 to join our S.O.E. party. He said Wolmer had been told by P.M. to carry on. But this, I should think, is hopeless. We discussed alternatives and I finally put to S. of S. appoint O. Stanley (or Swinton) to be directing Head (Permanent U.S., as it were) responsible (a) to him, and (b) to Chiefs-of-Staff.

* Later Earl of Selborne; Minister of Economic Warfare, 1942–5.

He agreed, and I drafted him minute to P.M. (Omitting names).... New Cabinet at 6. Looks very much like the old! Grigg replaces Margesson, Cripps replaces Greenwood. Moyne disappears. And Kingsley had crept in again!* *How?!*

Outlook uniformly gloomy. For months we shall suffer disaster. Week's sinkings worst ever!

My work is decreased in volume and importance: I'm stale as stale, and should like to find a fresh field.

[Stalin now issued an Order of the Day distinguishing between the German people and 'the Hitler clique'. It was regarded by some, though not by Cadogan, as a warning that unless a favourable response were soon made to his frontier demands, Stalin's enthusiasm for his British and American allies might wane.]

Tuesday, 24 February

Meeting with A. and others at 5 about Stalin's frontier demand. Americans are sticky about it—quite rightly. How funny A. is! Because it fits in with his trip, he is quite prepared to throw to the winds all principles (Atlantic Charter) which he has not drafted. This amoral, realpolitik line was never his. We shall make a mistake if we press the Americans to depart from principles, and a howler if we do it without them. But P.M. can be trusted to see to that! 5.30 Winant came to see A., who was going to enlist his help.

Wednesday, 25 February

P.M. stands by his decision to give S.O.E. to Wolmer. I dare say it will work, but he's not very inspiring.... A. told me of this morning's Cabinet discussion of Stalin's demands and wanted me to help him in drafting memo for Winant, to be submitted to another Cabinet at 7. Main point is to try to get U.S. to agree to *tripartite* discussion here in London.

Friday, 27 February

Same weather at first, but turned brighter—$32\frac{1}{2}°$. $35°$ after lunch. No work. I'm very bored. Dined and lunched at home.

Saturday, 28 February

Found P.M. had sent a rather silly telegram to Stalin. Cancelled

* Sir P. J. Grigg, formerly Permanent Under-Sec. at the War Office, now became Secretary for War in place of Capt. Margesson; Sir S. Cripps became Lord Privy Seal and Leader of the House; Lord Cranborne replaced Lord Moyne as Colonial Secretary and Leader of the House of Lords; Sir Kingsley Wood remained Chancellor of the Exchequer but left the War Cabinet, though he continued to attend when Treasury business was discussed.

it (or held it up) and rang up A. He agreed and I sent him down some modifications and additions.

Sunday, 1 March

P.M. against asking anything of Stalin in Far East, but agrees to discuss the draft tomorrow.

Monday, 2 March

Meeting with A. and others about message to Stalin. Everybody (O.S. and Ashley Clarke) have had a go at this, and urge that the only thing to do is to send out a 'High Military Officer'. I point out that we offered to send Wavell last Autumn and Stalin demurred, and we took V.C.I.G.S. with us to Moscow—with no result. They seem to have forgotten this. A. accepts idea of revised draft of message to Stalin (with some quite useful additions by Ashley Clarke) and will speak to him about it. A. spoke to me of the general situation. He feels—as I do—that for the last fortnight there has been no direction of the war. War Cabinet doesn't function—there hasn't been a meeting of Defence Committee. There's no hand on the wheel. (Probably due to P.M.'s health). Brendan and Cripps urge that A. should be Deputy Defence Minister. This was my idea also. Hope he can keep the F.O.—and I can run it. . . .

Cabinet 5.30—over soon after 7. Nothing much. News from everywhere—except Russia—bad. There's something wrong with *us*, I fear.

Tuesday, 3 March

10.45 meeting with A. and others about this wretched message to Stalin. P.M. evidently reacted strongly last night against our alterations. I still say that it's worse than nothing to send the P.M.'s original draft painting a black picture with a hint of blacker to come. But A. evidently thinks he can't over-persuade P.M. . . . Department produced yet two more drafts of P.M. message as result of our meeting this morning. I can do no more—I am confused by drafts: there are now at least five. If the P.M. accepts *any* it will be the one nearest to his original. Heard later from Ismay that A. had approved *both* the new drafts! I don't know what that means, as they were quite different! Fact is P.M. is in a sour mood—ill, I think—and frightens anyone—including A. I quite sympathise with them!

[The claims which Stalin had coolly put to Eden in December, at a moment when the Germans were at the gates of Moscow, raised the gravest issues. As the Prime Minister had immediately pointed out from Washington:

> Stalin's demands about Finland, Baltic States and Roumania are directly contrary to the . . . Atlantic Charter, to which Stalin has subscribed. There can be no question whatever of our making such an agreement, secret or public, direct or implicit, without prior agreement with the United States. The time has not yet come to settle frontier questions, which can only be resolved at the Peace Conference when we have won the war.

This view corresponds closely with that which Cadogan upheld for the next five months. His Secretary of State, however, favoured a more accommodating line, and on grounds to which Cadogan's diary entries do not do full justice. At the end of January, Eden pointed out to the Cabinet that if Germany were defeated and France remained weak for a time, there would exist no counterpoint to Russia in continental Europe. Russia would naturally be tempted to trade upon her immense prestige in such circumstances by working for the establishment of Communist governments in most European countries. If Hitler were defeated, it seemed certain that Russian forces would stand much farther westward than in 1941 and that the Soviets would not accept in victory frontiers shallower than those across which they had been attacked in 1941.

As matters turned out, the line which Cadogan favoured triumphed in the treaty of May 1942, but only for the moment. A change of policy on the Russians' part might diminish the force of Eden's argument; the weakness of Cadogan's (see the diary for 3 May) is that it depended on the proposition 'frontiers can easily be agreed on later'. They could not. While the kind of treaty signed in 1942, therefore, avoided many difficulties with the Americans and the Poles, it merely postponed what Churchill later called the brute issues until a time when the Russians were better placed to enforce their claims. When that time came, Eden opposed Russia's demands more vigorously than Churchill.

Under stress of the Far Eastern disasters and the stalemate in the Western Desert, the Prime Minister had now modified his attitude towards Russia's frontier claims, always excepting the Russo-Polish border. He even feared that if a flat negative were returned, Russia might be tempted to a separate peace with the Nazis: 'The increasing gravity of the war', he telegraphed to Roosevelt on 7 March, 'has led me to feel that the principles of the Atlantic Charter ought not to be construed so as to deny Russia the frontiers she occupied when Germany attacked her. . . . I hope . . . that you will be able to give us a free hand to sign the Treaty which Stalin desires as soon as possible.'

Without awaiting the American response, the Prime Minister injudiciously told Stalin that he had telegraphed in this sense. Cadogan confessed himself puzzled about the Russians' motives. If they won, they could seize the Baltic States and the British would certainly not go to war on that score. Were they looking for a grievance? If so, surely the demands would be more extensive?[4]]

Wednesday, 4 March

Had a talk with A. about general situation, running of the war, &c. Poor old P.M. in a sour mood and a bad way. I don't think he's well and I fear he's played out. Told A. I was becoming a 'second-fronter' and gave him certain arguments which he agreed ought to be considered. Had another talk with him later about message to Stalin and got him to send a minute to P.M. saying (1) he'd sooner send nothing than a mere recital of gloomy facts, and (2) he would prefer bluntly to invite Stalin to consider the Far East as part of the whole war.

Thursday, 5 March

3.30 talk with A. and others about Russia—urgency of not letting them slip. . . . Trouble in Cabinet. Winston having agreed in War Cabinet to Indian plan, puts it to other Ministers with a strong bias *against*, and finds them unanimously of that way of thinking! Talk—only talk—of resignations from War Cabinet—who met again at 6. Poor old Winston, feeling deeply the present situation and the attacks on him, is losing his grip, I fear. The outlook is pretty bloody.

Friday, 6 March

Discussion with A. about Russia. P.M. is now going to send a message to Stalin simply renewing pledges about quotas. This is all right. And we are pressing for an early view from Roosevelt about Stalin's frontier claims. A. told me after that P.M. is thinking of going to Russia, and I shd. have to go with him. Crisis in India seems to be still acute. P.M. will probably have to give way. (Otherwise I think Cripps' resignation at stake.) Awful lot of work. Dined at home. Never felt anything like the cold.

Saturday, 7 March

A. at 10 at F.O. Talked to him about de Gaulle-Muselier worry* (which got me telephoning at midnight last night). P.M. sending a good telegram to Stalin about maintaining quotas—nothing else for the moment. We *are* going to study possibility of a 'second front' in West! No decision yet about India. Cabinet at 10.30 about it. Maisky at 11.30. His Government hear Rib, Ciano and Japanese

* De Gaulle had now dismissed Admiral Muselier as Commissioner of the Navy and the Merchant Navy in the French National Committee.

Ambassador in Berlin are congregated in Sofia and expecting Sarajoglu. Much as I distrust Turks, I hardly believe this, but telegraphed to Angora.

Sunday, 8 March

Telegram from Angora conveying categorical denial of Rib-Ciano-Sarajoglu story. Passed it on to Maisky.

Monday, 9 March

Cabinet 5.30. O. Lyttelton there. We have just saved an immediate disaster in Burma (where [General] Alexander has arrived) but everything else looks pretty black. But I'm glad to see Cabinet rise in their wrath against the disreputable Press, and appoint a Cttee. to report on the further powers they should take for dealing with them.

Tuesday, 10 March

The de Gaulle worry continues. I think Admiralty have been egging Muselier on, and I had to ring up First Lord. . . . De Gaulle consented to come and see A. at 4. Gather interview was stormy.

Monday, 16 March

Cabinet 5.30. Not much news, except of fearful sinkings—nearly all on American coast. Americans *do* certainly seem to be terrifyingly inefficient. And we have lent them about 40 naval vessels! Air-raid warning this morning. Portal* said they were 'calibrating their beams' so they are probably planning resumption of raids on this country. Hope we give them a warm reception. P.M. had a decent message from Stalin today. . . .

Before the Cabinet, First Lord and Admiral Dickens came to see A. and me about the de Gaulle worry. Of course the Admiralty support Muselier and want to thrust him back on de G. We explained this was probably impossible—de Gaulle wd. go, and we couldn't contemplate that yet. De G. had asked to see Dickens and we agreed he should go. D. said it wouldn't do much good (I agree): 'The General will only make a face like a female lama surprised bathing'!

Winston has had a small operation.

Thursday, 19 March

No news—except of continued sinkings at a rate we can't stand.

* Air Chief Marshal Sir C. F. A. Portal, Chief of the Air Staff, 1940–5.

All the fault of the inefficient Americans, and I'm glad P.M. has sent a message to the President about it.

Friday, 20 March

Talked to A. about interception of [Vichy] French reinforcements for Madagascar. In view of our plans, I think this necessary.

Saturday, 21 March

Not much doing. We are in a period of awful—and perhaps disastrous—stagnation. I *hope* we are planning aggressive action (I believe so), but I haven't been to Defence Committee lately and am not in the Inner Councils (I am all for their being kept secret!) so don't know. I am personally convinced, in spite of all the obvious risks, and chances of disaster, that we must *do* something active in the next four months. I have said so to A. (it is easy to say!) and he assures me that opinion in the highest circles inclines in the same direction. . . . Haven't seen a glimpse of sun *all this week*.

Sunday, 22 March

Awful feeling still persists, of a *lull*—no-one doing anything, but losing time. Telegram from Wavell this evening asking whether, in the event of losing N. Burma, our forces should try to struggle back into India, or go with the Chinese. And suggesting that the latter might have a good 'political effect'. That depends! If they can be supplied with ammunition and are fit to *do* something, the effect might be good. But if they do nothing but eat Chinese rice, I should say it isn't a good idea. But we must get more information on these points—there isn't enough to go on.

Monday, 23 March

Cabinet at 6. Lot of time taken up by Winston explaining his correspondence with Curtin and Casey.* Sinkings continue as bad as ever. We seem to have had quite a good naval action putting a convoy into Malta. Maisky has told A. of Soviet reaction to U.S. communication about Stalin's demands. It amounts to 'Thank you very much for this information' and a renewal of the demand to us! Just what I feared. A. will want to go ahead. I shall have to resist.

Tuesday, 24 March

Meeting with A. and others about Russia. I had to go into opposi-

* Rt. Hon. R. G. Casey, Australian Minister in Washington, had just been appointed Minister of State Resident in the Middle East and a member of the War Cabinet.

tion. I'm sure it's wrong, in view of President's attitude, to give Stalin all he asks. A. evidently annoyed, but I can't help that. . . . 4. Kulski,* whom I had to rate for Polish intrigue against our policy vis-à-vis Soviet and for their raising contentious issues with the Russians at this moment. . . . Old Nintchich† wasted hours of my time this morning describing his plan for visiting Moscow. Fat lot of good he'll do there.

Dined at home and received Sargent's drafts to Washington and Moscow about Stalin's demands. Re-wrote them rather heavily and sent them on to A.

[Roosevelt, who was transacting the business of the State Department with Sumner Welles while Hull took ten weeks' 'rest', had replied robustly that he felt sure the U.S.S.R. would not 'quit the war'. The Allies should not agree on frontiers till the war's end; and the Russian demands conflicted with the Atlantic Charter. However, the Cabinet decided, largely on military grounds, to concede the Russian demand that until the frontier questions had been settled, there could be no discussion of others. Since Britain was a European power, to whom post-war collaboration with the Soviets was essential, she would negotiate a treaty recognising Russia's demand for her frontiers, other than that with Poland, of 1940. The President received these tidings with a marked lack of keenness. He let Lord Halifax know that he would be compelled to say publicly that he had known of British intention. He expected this attitude to be taken as a sign of disapproval.[5]]

Wednesday, 25 March

Met A. in morning. He evidently determined to give in to Stalin. Cabinet at 12 to settle matter. P.M. has now been brought round, so I have no doubt Cabinet will agree. I fear they will be wrong. But I have put my views, both orally and in writing, as clearly as I can, and *I* may be wrong. I hope so, for if it turns out as I expect, we shall be in a mess.

Went off at 1 with G.J. to lunch at his Baker Street H.Q. [of S.O.E.]. Not frightfully impressed there. Went on after to Welwyn [in Hertfordshire], where we had quite a good show of explosives, &c. But that is operational stuff—not S.O. And it is the S.O.'s political follies and misjudgments that give us all the trouble. Went on to Hertford where we saw some good parachute dropping and more explosives. All quite good. . . . A lovely spring day in the country, but everything dead—only crocuses showing.

* Counsellor at the Polish Embassy.

† Dr M. Ninčić, Yugoslav Minister of Foreign Affairs.

Thursday, 26 March

Met A. Cabinet decided in his favour and approved of telegraphing Washington first (they *would*: a good half-way decision). I expect they'll get an out-size raspberry from Roosevelt. I've done all I can and if they get into a real mess, will do my best to help them out.

Sunday, 29 March *Thatched Cottage*

Wind dropped last night and it was a God-given day today—sun the whole time. Like summer, and swarms of bees busy on the crocuses—which are *lovely!* One old bumble bee—I suppose tight—collapsed in the cup of a purple crocus and I left him sleeping there. Hoed in the morning, and a bit after lunch. T[heo] and I then walked down the fields and round up by Dixter. Masses of lambs, and many twins.

Tuesday, 31 March

Message from A. that I should ask the Turk to lunch on Thursday. I told Oliver I wouldn't. In the first place I saw him yesterday: in the second it's too short notice and I can't scratch up a party: in the third I don't want to meet him too much these days—they are suspicious of us, and rightly in view of A.'s policy about Russia. . . .

A. in very tiresome mood in the country. Scribbles unhelpful instructions on every paper. Good deal of work. Dixon has produced a paper which will give A. a headache—on reaction in Turkey to our Russian policy.

[Lord Beaverbrook, seeking a cure for his asthma in America, had been talking to the President and reporting to Lord Halifax, who regarded his visitor's performance with a mixture of awe, amusement and detachment. 'What are the relations between Bevin and Attlee?' asked the Ambassador in one of their gossips. 'Oh, very good indeed', responded Beaverbrook. 'Like two high and distant mountain peaks, and both with snow on them.'

The nature of Beaverbrook's consultations remained, to the Foreign Office at least, more or less a mystery. The Prime Minister told Stalin that Beaverbrook would 'help smooth out the treaty question with the President'. Cadogan, who mistrusted Beaverbrook, probably felt that nothing could be done about this ill-defined mandate, and that the American attitude to Stalin's claims would not alter. Beaverbrook telegraphed once or twice to Churchill from the Embassy, and sent to Eden a message ending '*Nil desperandum*; which you will be able to translate because you were at Eton.'[6] Some of Beaverbrook's less official messages also came to Cadogan's notice. He had at this stage no idea that Beaverbrook desired to prise Halifax out of the Washington Embassy.]

Good Friday, 3 April

Another extraordinary telegram from the Beaver, meaning nothing. But it talks of a 'plan'—apparently in connexion with the Stalin demands. *We've* had no 'plan'. On the other hand the President has been telegraphing to the P.M. about a 'plan'—apparently political-military. Are the two connected? Impossible to say. After consulting O.S. I dictated a telegram to Washington trying to find out what the Devil the situation *was*. Left him to read Beaver's telegram to A. and my draft (as I couldn't get A. on telephone before lunch). . . . Yesterday heard 'Richelieu' and 'Jean Bart'* and other units going from Dakar to Toulon. Found this morning that at 2 a.m. Admiralty had sent orders to stop them. Ascertained that this was with P.M.'s approval. Warned A., who didn't object. Later, Admiralty got cold feet and asked did A. realise implication of possible war with Vichy? I said of course he did, but it was not for Foreign Secretary to weigh up military advantages and disadvantages of such an eventuality. Don't know what they'll do. Have they the *force* to stop these ships?

Easter Sunday, 5 April

Good news of raid on Ceylon—27 Japanese planes down and about the same number damaged. The dirty little monkeys can't afford this!

Tuesday, 6 April

Cabinet 5.30. Japanese fleet (⅔rds of it) seem to have come into Indian Ocean, ignoring Americans, who remain in San Francisco, and we seem to have lost [cruisers] Dorsetshire and (?) Cumberland.† Outlook pretty gloomy all round. Sinkings not quite so bad, but this only because U-boats are out of torpedoes! Selborne dining with P.M., so I hastily prepared note from A. to P.M.

Wednesday, 8 April

P.M. seems to have more or less kept his (and our) end up with Selborne last night. . . . Not very much work. News everywhere as depressing as usual. Can't see any daylight. And meanwhile I sit here doing less and less—impotent. Wish I could find another job!

* Seven months later, during the Allied landings in North Africa, the battleship *Jean Bart* was gutted by fire at Casablanca. The battleship *Richelieu*, at Dakar, joined the Allied fleets after the conquest of North Africa, in the spring of 1943.

† In fact the *Cornwall*; both ships were sunk.

Thursday, 9 April

3.15 went to see C.I.G.S. about various things.... Found him rather impatient with our attitude of giving *everything* Russians ask and getting *nothing* in return. Of course the Russians are fighting—but for themselves and not for us—but I do sympathize with him rather. 5.30 meeting with A. and many others about the form of our Treaties with Russia. A., determined to go ahead, gallops gaily over the ground, which will give way under him, one of these days. We're selling the Poles down the river, and everyone will suspect we're going to do the same to them, and we're annoying and disgusting Roosevelt. And to what purpose?

Saturday, 11 April

Went to see Selborne at 10. He determined to shed G.J. (which I regret). Discussed plans for liaison.... Maisky at 12.45 about the Japanese in Teheran. Told him we might have to send troops in.

Sunday, 12 April

Saw Maisky and Orbay* and tried to get them to get their respective Governments to damp down the hate about the Angora bomb explosion.

[A month before, an unsuccessful attempt had been made to blow up the German Ambassador in Ankara, Herr von Papen. The Turks began an enquiry, but did not press it unduly when clear evidence of Russian inspiration emerged. Aware of the dangers of too much talk about assassination, the German Government made no great fuss.]

Monday, 13 April

Cabinet 5.30. H. Hopkins, Marshall and Casey there, so there was rather a crowd. Sinkings are quite disastrous. If we are going to lose the war, that is how.

Tuesday, 14 April

An awful day, for the odd reason—that I had no work to do! Bored stiff. Had to have recourse to 'Times' crossword puzzle.... Not much news. We're going to have trouble in America over our Russian agreement. But I warned A. of *that!*

Thursday, 16 April

No work to do—which will drive me mad. Don't know what's

* Huseyin Rauf Orbay, Turkish Ambassador, 1942–4.

really going on—and refrain from asking. Lunched with de Gaulle. Sat between him and one of his military officers. He's not very inspiring. That old half-wit Roger Keyes there—abusing Alexander like a pick-pocket, which I don't think is *quite* the correct thing to do before foreigners, but I couldn't make a scene. However, I will report him. Some lunatics are harmless, but others ought to be put under restraint. . . . 5.30 meeting with A. and others about a treaty with China. Managed to persuade him that this wasn't a good moment for us to take initiative. Agreed to consult Americans—so as to stop them cutting in ahead of us.

Friday, 17 April *Thatched Cottage*

I haven't had enough to do lately—wasting my time—better employed hoeing onions. Left soon after 3 and arrived at cottage soon after 5. It clouded over half-way. All the daffodils out, but the kitchen-garden hasn't made much progress—this perishing E. wind I suppose. After tea we went round garden and then I walked down fields and turned right into the wood. I've never seen such masses of wild flowers—primroses, violets, anemones—carpets of them—and celandines. Also other whose names I don't know—I know very few—and I found an orchis. Up by Dixter. Black-out now not till 9.30. Heard a cuckoo!

Saturday, 18 April *Thatched Cottage*

At the ponds we found a small boy fishing. He had a jam-jar with some 2 inch gudgeon in them. We said 'What are you going to do with them?' He said, 'Give them to the cat.' A satisfying answer.

Monday, 20 April

Unpleasant half-hour with G.J. who had just been sacked by Selborne. Very sorry for him, and think it's a mistake. . . . Cabinet at 5.30. Nothing much. Sinkings are still terrific. Pound has gone to U.S. to try to do something about it. Found my room full of boxes on return and had to lug home two portmanteaux full. Worked 8.45 until nearly 11, and didn't finish then. I complained last week of not enough work, but I don't want too much!

Tuesday, 21 April

Turk at 11 about the Angora bomb. Gave him the usual good advice, though it's plain to me that the Russians are more to blame. Long talk with Bruce Lockhart* about changes at S.O.E. Advised

* Sir R. Bruce Lockhart, Dep. Under-Sec., F.O., and Dir.-Gen., Political Warfare Exec., 1941–5.

him to get on with G.J. on his tri-partite agreement. Lunched at home. 3.30 Stephenson (of D[ominions] O[ffice]) about participation of Dominions in our Treaty with Soviet. They don't relish it, mostly! . . . 5 Raczynski with a reply to our note of April 17th. Had to argue with him mildly, though I agree with all that is said therein! (Hear Russians are sending people here by air. What does this mean?!)

Wednesday, 22 April

Told A. I must know rather more about our military plans. It isn't that I want to know out of idle curiosity—and indeed I'd rather *not* know too much detail—but I must have some guidance, without which I can't advise in a number of matters of policy affecting, e.g., Anglo-Russian relations. He told me all I wanted to know and I didn't encourage him to tell me more!

12.15 Promotions Board, to discuss changes at S.O.E. and to find a place for G.J. They were not very helpful and this is a twin problem! Now that G.J. is going, I think O.S. and others, who have always girded at him, begin to realise that the last state will be *much* worse than the first. Unless it gets so bad that we have to crash S.O.E. altogether. Had further long talk to B. Lockhart, but he explains with reason, that there isn't place in any of *his* show for G.J.

G.J. came for long talk about 6.30. I tried to draw him as to how new system would work, but confess I don't see how.

Thursday, 23 April

Meeting 11.30 to discuss certain documents which suggest Hitler *may* 'switch' to attack through Syria &c. There are *no* positive indications, but it is a *possibility.* Undertook to write a note for A. about it. Message from Joe about our visitor from Moscow [Molotov] who may, I suppose, be expected any minute. Looks as if he'll give us a rough passage over the Treaty (which, I hear, on the other hand, is beginning to cause a stink amongst M.P.s—egged on by Victor Cazalet!*). . . . Saw A. when he came back from Secret Session. P.M. appears to have had a good innings of 1½ hours. Discussed Moscow telegram with him. Difficult to know what to make of it. Told him of my hope to mix up all three wrangles—Treaty, Strategy and Supplies—in one tri-partite Conference. But I read Joe as objecting to this—at present.

[The Japanese Navy had now become so menacing in Eastern waters that the War Cabinet determined to seize Madagascar, largely in order to

* Capt. V.A. Cazalet, M.P., Political Liaison Officer to Gen. Sikorski, 1940–3.

secure the harbour of Diego Suarez. Although the Prime Minister's first instinct had been to let Free French forces take the island, as de Gaulle had more than once proposed, it was decided to make this a purely British expedition. The ships left Durban on 28 April; the first troops landed on 5 May; by 7 May the resistance had ceased.]

Friday, 24 April

Meeting with P.M. and Chiefs-of-Staff (and Mountbatten) at 11. About Madagascar. As usual, Cs. of S. get cold feet when an operation is ready. This time they plead that Laval's accession to power [as Prime Minister] has changed situation. I told A. it had *not*, in essentials, and the meeting decided *not* to interfere with the operation—there is another week in which we can do so! But it is silly planning these things and then calling them off. Let's risk *something*.

Saturday, 2 May

Talked to Raczynski about [Polish] President's projected broadcast for tomorrow about Lwow and Vilna. It's silly to rub this sore spot, but I can't help feeling some sympathy with them. He promised to see if anything could be done, but of course they have internal stresses and strains. . . . T. and I drove to Kew. Sunny, but cold there and the blossom (most of it not quite out) hasn't been improved by the icy blast. Met Cripps there. . . . Good deal of work. Am getting down to my last drop of alcohol!

Sunday, 3 May

Maisky has given Soviet reply to our draft Treaties. Pretty bad: they cut out all we had put in to save the Polish case and American susceptibilities. It's curious that A., of all people, should have hopes of 'appeasement'!! Much better say to the Russians 'We can't discuss post-war frontiers: we want to work with you, now and later: let's have a mutual guarantee. Frontiers can easily be agreed on later. If you like, we will try to get U.S. collaboration—so far as their Constitution allows them to go. If not, we offer you all *we* have. But don't ask us *now*, at the cost of all our principles, to agree to a situation which *we* can't influence!' I believe, still, it would be better not to crawl to the Russians over the dead bodies of *all* our principles.

Monday, 4 May

4.30 meeting with A. and others about Soviet. Glad to find he realises we can at least go no further, and no use haggling. 5.30 Cabinet. Not much news. . . . Short discussion after about Russia.

All members of Cabinet sound (except perhaps Cripps, who didn't know what he was talking about, as he hadn't seen the drafts of the Treaties).

Tuesday, 5 May

Madagascar was launched this morning, but don't know how it is going. Roosevelt has played up well. . . . Meeting in A.'s room at 10 p.m. on Russia. Glad to find he is determined at least not to throw the Poles down the drain and faces the possibility of a failure of the negotiation. I urged again that we should try to switch the discussion on to some alternative form of Treaty—mutual guarantee, or something. No use haggling—as all through the summer of 1939—on the present drafts. Agreed Department should try to draft something.

Wednesday, 6 May

5. Dejean* with a note of protest at Free French not having been taken into our confidence about Madagascar. Pointed out undesirability of Frenchmen shedding French blood: we had settled to do without F.F. participation, and it might have been embarrassing to the General to tell him so. As to future, pressed that the General should come and see S.-of-S. (which he has hitherto declined to do!).

Thursday, 7 May

Diego Suarez has surrendered. Cabinet at 12 about Russia. Everyone (except Cripps, who was late) was—quite rightly—against A. giving watered down terms to the Russians. This would be *fatal*. Just what we shouldn't do. P.M. evidently hopes the Treaty is off the map. 'We must remember that this is a *bad* thing. We oughtn't to do it, and I shan't be sorry if we don't.' Agreed P.M. should include in his Sunday broadcast a warning about gas. Auk [General Auchinleck] says he can't attack! But I don't think P.M. will stand this. . . . P.M. sent for me about 6. Found him sitting in garden with [General Sir A.] Nye. Pound had suggested to him idea of putting Muselier in Madagascar. Told him complete breach between M. and de G[aulle] was imminent, but told him I'd try and hold former. Saw [C.] Peake† about this. P.M. wanted A. to ring him up (A. in Edinburgh for a speech). I arranged for A. to ring me first. . . . A. rang after dinner and he agrees we should try to get de G[aulle] to swallow the Muselier arrangement.

* Diplomatic Counsellor, French National Committee.

† British representative with French National Committee since February.

[No sooner had Cadogan reached the cottage on 9 May than he learned that Molotov might arrive in Scotland on Monday morning, and that he must be met by the Permanent Under-Secretary.]

Sunday, 10 May

Comfortable flight, though about ½ way we got above cloud—very pretty, but cold. Landed at Tealing (Dundee) at 6.2. . . . Then to the station, where we found the special, with Maisky and Co. . . . Bed earlyish. Quite comfortable. My cold a bore, but not bad yet.

Monday, 11 May

Got up at 3.45. Very cold. Started for aerodrome in the dark at 4.30. Hung about till nearly six, with no news, so returned crestfallen, and damned cold, to the train and breakfast. Ordered the train into Edinburgh—Dundee is too beastly. . . . Back to the train at 7. We dined there and left about 11 for Dundee. I went to bed and slept.

[On the following morning, 12 May, the whole party again rose at 3.45 and left at 4.30, in the dark, for the airfield. By 6 a.m. it was plain that nothing would happen, since Molotov's plane could not be allowed to cross the North Sea in daylight. All returned, cold and crestfallen, to Dundee station. Again the train was ordered to Edinburgh.

The usual round of visits—the Castle, the Royal Mile, Holyrood House—was therefore made for the benefit of the Russians. At Holyrood, to Cadogan's mild surprise, they evinced much interest. They seemed to have been specially coached in the proceedings of the 'Imperialist' court of the sixteenth century, and to find a particular fascination in every detail of the room where Rizzio was murdered. Thereafter the train returned to Dundee, where Cadogan learned that Molotov would again be delayed. There was nothing for it but to arrange another outing.

Maisky pressed to be taken, with all his following, to Balmoral. Cadogan, wondering whether the Russians' briefing had induced a confusion between Mary Queen of Scots and Queen Victoria, did not dare enquire 'for fear that I might be led into a dissertation on the many notable differences between the two Queens, which would have to be wide-ranging, and possibly embarrassing'.

The best that could be arranged at short notice was a drive past the Castle. 'The Russians' recorded another member of the British party,

> were endlessly tricky and boring. They had a miniature Soviet in a closed compartment each time we suggested an outing, and emerged with insulting and impossible requests. When we took them for drives, they ostentatiously went to sleep whenever we came near to the entrance-gates of an attractive country-house. But they gave themselves

away, a bit, by all suddenly waking up when we passed Balmoral. There was an absurd picnic. . . . While Maisky told the usual Soviet humorous stories, a rather young-looking Soviet admiral (who was rumoured to have reached his high rank by stuffing his senior officers into the stoke-hole) kept running off after grouse, in the hope of catching them in his uniform cap.

When on the next day there was still no sign of Molotov, Cadogan rang up the Foreign Office to announce that unless definite news were received, he proposed to leave. After a journey of twelve and a half hours, the special train reached London on the evening of 14 May.

Cadogan returned to work the following morning. 'Met A. in Park' he noted. 'He tells me P.M. wants to replace H[alifax] by the Beaver! Ye Gods!!' It seems clear that neither Eden nor Cadogan, and still less Halifax, had any notion that the Washington Embassy had been suggested to Beaverbrook, and accepted, in the previous September; or that on 12 May, while Cadogan was awaiting Molotov in Scotland, Churchill again offered the post to Beaverbrook. Moreover, President Roosevelt agreed. It is not known why this arrangement was not acted upon.[7]

Adopting Cadogan's proposal, Eden now submitted to his colleagues the draft of a treaty providing Russia with a post-war alliance against German aggression, but omitting any recognition of new claims:

> With the disappearance from the Treaty of any mention of frontiers it would no longer be necessary for us to safeguard the Polish position and to reassure our other Allies in Eastern Europe by the insertion of special stipulations about the confederation of these States and about collaborating in the post-war settlement with the other United Nations.
>
> If Mr Molotov, on arrival, proves unwilling to meet us on the above two points, it will, I believe, be of little use to embark upon prolonged discussion of alternative formulae for getting over the difficulty. On the other hand, it would be highly undesirable from both the Russian standpoint and our own that his visit should end without the signature of a Treaty, which is widely expected both here and abroad.

Dr Goebbels, who had been studying the intercepts, knew of Stalin's demands and about the divergent attitudes of Britain and the U.S.A. He wrote in his diary:

> In their predicament they [the British] are ready to grant the Russians everything they ask for. Above all they would permit them to swallow up all the small border states without further ado, quite apart from Germany which the British would just love to see destroyed and decimated. The United States are offering major resistance to this.[8]]

Monday, 18 May

5.30 Cabinet until 8.10. But not much news. Discussed Russian convoys and decided we must send the present one, but put the situation to Stalin. This is right. Sinkings still awful, but people seem to mind less.

Tuesday, 19 May

Meeting with A. and others about Russia. Discussed possibility of another diversion—i.e. an agreement that on cessation of hostilities and for transition period 'pre-war' frontiers must be observed (to prevent claim-jumping). There may be something in this.

Wednesday, 20 May

Left F.O. at 6.30 with A. for Brookmans Park* to meet Molotov. His train (my old special) due at 7.22. We arrived 7.15 and I recognised it steaming in. We raced on to the platform (through the rain which had begun to fall) and boarded train almost immediately after it had drawn in. Short talk to M., who seemed at the top of his form and most chatty. Cinemas and microphones in the saloon. Russian party drove off to Chequers.† A [Daily] 'Mirror' man there. How the devil do they get these things?!

Thursday, 21 May

Russians arrived at No. 10 at 11.30. M. said he had come to discuss (1) Treaties (2) Second Front, and was going on to Washington. P.M. presided and Attlee was there. We really only had a general discussion. As regards (2), P.M. said this involved technical questions and suggested Russian General should get in touch with C.I.G.S. M. said he wanted to discuss it 'on the political plane!' (Blackmail!) Adjourned 1.45. . . . Further meeting presided by S. of S. at 3.30. Russians as wooden as ever. We discussed Treaties. Their attitude is: 'We have made large concession in agreeing to leave Polish frontier for later settlement. What concession do you make?' They ignore that we have *made* the great concession about the Baltic States! No conclusion. We agreed to try a draft exchange of notes, but it will be no use. Adjourned before 5.30. I then dictated records of the meetings.

Friday, 22 May

10.20 meeting with A. and others about Russia. Don't think A. has got many illusions left (and he appears to have been stiffened by Cabinet yesterday) in spite of that ass Oliver H[arvey]. 11 meeting

* A station some 18 miles from London.

† Where the three principal members of the Russian party each had, in addition to the usual guards, a female Cerberus to keep constant watch on the bedrooms. A pistol was laid out with Molotov's despatch-box every night.

with Russians at No. 10 on Second Front, presided by P.M. Only a general discussion, which followed expected lines*.... Lunch at No. 10. Sat between A. Sinclair and Martin. Excellent lunch and many toasts, from which I have scarcely recovered.

Meeting at 4. (Arrears meanwhile piling up). Wearisome further discussion of Treaty and little progress. Broke up about 6.30. A. and P.M. went down to Chequers. I dictated record and grappled with 25 boxes, both before and after dinner.

Saturday, 23 May

Meeting at 3 in F.O. Put our alternative (mutual assistance) Treaty to Russians who examined it, but of course said they couldn't pronounce on it and that it would have to await M's return to Moscow. M. then asked to have further discussion of the existing drafts. So we went wearily through them again. M. produced what he described as 'concessions' but could make no suggestion on the crux—the Polish frontier. So we faced a deadlock again and suggested M. should go on to America and return *here* to conclude discussions. He curiously anxious to finish here *now* and offered to stay some extra days. He *may* have asked for fresh instructions. We agreed, of course, and Russians returned to Chequers with understanding that they could call a meeting for tomorrow if they liked. Must keep A. firm on Polish question. I *think* he'll be all right. But he is subject to temptation and that ass Harvey's advice†. However, he went away to the country. I stuck here.

Sunday, 24 May Whit Sunday

Russians have told A. they have fresh instructions on Polish frontier question. A. rang up to say he had asked Maisky to put proposal in writing, but M. wanted a meeting today, which A., of course, wanted to avoid. He asked me to ring up M. at Chequers, which I did. But, of course, M. very cagey and pressed for a meeting. So I had to fix one at 4.... A. arrived 3.45. He had wisely come to the conclusion he should press our alternative mutual assistance treaty on the Russians. Russians arrived at 4. Unfortunately, they had come a long way on the Polish frontier question, and it will be difficult to break on that! They still won't look at our alternative Treaty, so we went through the drafts of the others and agreed to

* 'Molotov', Cadogan wrote, 'had all the grace and conciliation of a totem pole.'

† The tone of these references to Harvey derives from Cadogan's irritation at discovering that the former, who had always opposed vehemently any appeasement of Germany and Italy, should now be anxious to make unrequited gestures to Russia.

put the points to the Cabinet tomorrow. They *are* extraordinary people to deal with—they wear their suspicions on their sleeve! A. now longing to get out of his promise about frontiers. (Winant has been twisting his tail.) But it's a bit late for that now!

[During this meeting, Cadogan pointed out to Maisky that the mutual guarantee now offered went some way beyond anything Britain had offered to France.]

Monday, 25 May

Hear that last night Maisky rang up A. to say that they might consider our alternative Treaty. Seems Winant twisted *their* tails last night. They asked for a meeting at 3 today. . . . F.O. at 2.45 and saw A., just arrived. Russians at 3. Molotov said that he hadn't final instructions yet, but thought he could discuss our new Treaty. Which we did. No great difficulties that we can't get over. Russians left about 4. Cabinet at 6.30. Winston and all delighted at idea that we may be free of our old difficulties, and welcomed idea of new Treaty.

Tuesday, 26 May

Russians last night agreed our Treaty. Much of the morning taken up by the Russians trying to slip in various amendments. But none of them were vicious. Cabinet at 1, when Russian Treaty was explained to them. Winston relieved and delighted, and bouquets were heaped on A! . . . 6. Signature of Treaty, under searchlight and cinemas. Russians left about 7 and we had Cabinet. . . . A very satisfactory ending to a long and tiresome and embarrassing exchange. Everyone pleased. The Americans particularly, I think. Winant was at the lunch, and Harriman, and the latter came up and spoke to me enthusiastically after. I think the visit has done the Russians good.

[In 1963, looking through the diary and reflecting on the lessons of this negotiation, Cadogan remarked on the Russians' freedom to make such complete changes of policy overnight. The negotiator must still judge, of course, whether the other side was adamant or was bluffing. 'I only mean to emphasise that in dealing with the Russians it is useful to bear in mind that they can, if they find it convenient, make right-about turns without exposing themselves to any embarrassment. . . .'[9]]

Thursday, 28 May

Rommel has begun his attack on Libya, but it's difficult to make out what, if anything, has happened. Congratulations from everywhere to A. on his Russian treaty!

Saturday, 30 May

Not much news of Libya battle, but it doesn't seem to have gone *wrong yet!!* 50 aircraft operated against this country last night, of which only half crossed the coast, and we shot down 7. That's very good. Kharkov battle seems to be stabilised.

Sunday, 31 May

Heard on wireless about our 1,000-plane raid on Germany. Grand! Can't make out what's happening in Libya battle, but nothing seems to have gone irretrievably wrong *yet*. The convoy seems to have got through to Russia with loss of 7 out of 35. No naval losses reported.

Monday, 1 June

6. Cabinet. Libya battle seems to have quite good possibilities. Portal couldn't add much to what is already published about the great raid. Sinkings bad. . . . We're planning to send another large bombing force over the Ruhr tonight. . . . As P.M. said, 'We've had worse weekends.'

Thursday, 4 June

Meeting at 5 with R. Law, O. S[argent], W. Strang and Gwatkin about reconstitution of Economic Section, or development of General Dept. into something of the sort. Agreed in principle.

Tuesday, 9 June

Greeted Molotov and drove with him and Maisky to Chequers. Discussed plans on the way. Very good breakfast on arrival—kedgeree and a whole York ham. Rang up A. and fixed plans. . . . Meeting at No. 10 with Russians at 12. Talk mostly on 2nd Front and supplies. Finished at 2. Lunched in A.'s flat. Russians, Max [Beaverbrook], Leathers* and R. Law there. Sat between Leathers (whom I like) and Sobolev.† Meeting with Russians after, in A.'s room, about publicity, communiqué, &c., and a number of minor questions. V. friendly and easy. Finished about 5.30. Had to dictate record of this morning's talk and tackle a mass of work, which followed me home.

* Lord Leathers, Minister of War Transport, 1941–5.
† A. A. Sobolev, Counsellor of Russian Embassy.

[Cadogan had to leave Chequers that morning in a rush. During the afternoon, a messenger brought into his room an official despatch-box, marked 'From Chequers. Most Urgent.' It contained nothing but the P.U.S.'s slippers. 'I think', he said, 'that the world would be a better place if these red boxes were invariably used for such purposes.']

Wednesday, 10 June

Rather cold and beastly. Glad to see they are putting tall antirrhinums in the border by Guards Memorial, instead of those horrible dahlias. Tried to catch up on my arrears of work (without much success). 11.15 discussion with A. and a large party... about publicity and presentation of the Treaty, &c. 1.15 left with A. for Soviet Embassy. He inveighed against House of Lords. I said that—apart from a few recent creations—I thought them, on the whole, a damned sight better than the H. of C. Molotov and Co., Sikorski, Raczynski and Retinger at lunch. Sat between Maisky and Retinger. Fixed up communiqué and plans with Maisky after. Back at F.O. 4.40. Got through as much of the mountain of work as I could, and then went, at 7, to No. 10 for a farewell to the Russians. Broached a bottle of champagne of which I drank only a compulsory sip in a toast. Russians left just before 8. I said goodbye—A. has got to see them off at Cheddington (in Buckinghamshire) at midnight! (Maisky made no bones about indicating to me that that was expected!). What savages! P.M. in quite good form—and his rompers!

[The Foreign Office continued to receive occasional feelers for peace, put forward by groups or individuals allegedly hostile to Hitler. Often there was reason to suspect that the offers were 'plants' concocted by the German Intelligence services to embroil the British in a negotiation which could at a suitable moment be blazoned before the world as an example of perfidy and disunity in the alliance. In the circumstances of 1942, with their armies controlling most of Europe, few Germans were likely to make proposals which could provide even a basis for discussion. No doubt it was also from a desire not to give the Russians any further ground of complaint that Eden confined himself to the following public statement:

> The longer the German people continue to support and to tolerate the régime which is leading them to destruction the heavier grows their own direct responsibility for the damage that they are doing to the world.
>
> Therefore, if any section of the German people really want to see a return to a German State which is based on respect for law and for the rights of the individual, they must understand that no one will believe them until they have taken active steps to rid themselves of their present régime.

Urged by Bishop Bell of Chichester, who had heard about an opposition focused on Beck and Goerdeler, Eden still refused to make a move, a policy with which Cadogan warmly agreed. The Secretary of State laid it down that he must not even appear to enter into such negotiations; and he must be able to say so to the Americans and Russians.[10]]

Sunday, 14 June *Thatched Cottage*

I weeded and hoed the long border and continued bedding out. After lunch gave the delphiniums in North garden some liquid manure and did more bedding out. Altogether planted about 300 antirrhinums and nemesia and 2 doz. stocks. Picked pinks. . . . We seem to be being completely worsted and outwitted, as usual, by Rommel. I suppose he's a very good general, but I am quite convinced that our own (including C.I.G.S.) are blockheads, who cannot learn anything.

Monday, 15 June

5.30 Cabinet—very gloomy. Libya bad, sinkings awful (tho' P.M. doesn't seem to think so). Malta convoys badly mauled. No good news from anywhere. Bad weather prevented us from bombing on any scale.

Thursday, 18 June

Had many discussions with various people about the new 'Economic Department'. Found a little draft circular on my table this morning which, in a parenthesis, seemed to throw all future foreign policy into the new Department. (Now I know why G.J. is so pleased with his new appointment!). This won't do, and, after all my consultations, think I see a way out.

Friday, 19 June

Libya is evidently a complete disaster—we are out-generalled everywhere. P.M.'s arrival in Washington announced this morning.

Sunday, 21 June

I to F.O. to learn that Tobruk had fallen. It held out for 8 months last time, and for about as many hours this. I wonder what is most wrong with our army. Without any knowledge, I should say the Generals. *Most* depressing.

Monday, 22 June

Cabinet at 5.30. They hadn't really any more news. Approved

drafts of statements for House about Libya and Malta convoys. Sinkings are still more frightful. Sevastopol seems to be going. Altogether pretty gloomy. A good telegram from P.M. to Auchinleck (and a gentlemanly one!).

[In June, British, Allied and neutral shipping losses totalled 834,000 tons, a figure equalled in 1942 only by the losses in March.]

Tuesday, 23 June

No particular news: Rommel seems to be massing for attack on our frontier positions tomorrow—or earlier. Our poor diplomacy has of course been dealt a fearful blow, in Turkey, Spain, Portugal and elsewhere.

Thursday, 25 June

We are now retiring out of chunks of Egypt. We have suffered one of the most decisive defeats ever inflicted.

[That defeat had derived in part from the excellence of the Intelligence reaching Rommel. Because American supplies were vital in the Middle Eastern theatre, and on the obvious general grounds, the U.S. military attaché in Cairo was supplied with most secret material about Allied plans and movements. Unhappily, his signals were so insecure that the decodes were reaching Rommel as swiftly as they reached General Marshall in Washington. Not until the attaché's recall in July was this damaging leakage stopped.[11] By then Auchinleck had taken personal command in the desert; the supply lines of the Axis armies were severely extended; the Allies enjoyed air superiority, exercised with notable flexibility and skill. Rommel's headlong progress towards the Nile was over. At the end of June, when there seemed to be no stopping him, Mussolini had arrived at Derna in preparation for the ceremonial entry into Cairo, thoughtfully bringing his own white charger. After a fortnight's residence in North Africa, he returned to Rome.]

Monday, 29 June

3.15 saw A., who said P.M. was in good form, though I don't know why. Rout of our 8th army in Egypt seems to be as complete as any in history. . . . 5.30 Cabinet. Winston at Chequers, so Attlee presided—like a soured and argumentative mouse. The news looks pretty sticky to me. Only sinkings not so bad. Long wrangle about instructions to Leith Ross on Post-War relief. (When *is* Post-War?). Cabinet sat till 8.10. Home 8.20. Dined there and tried to grapple with mass of work.

[The Prime Minister had gone to Washington to persuade Roosevelt that the Allied invasion of mainland Europe was not a practical operation in 1942, whatever the Americans might have said to Molotov. On the morning of 21 June, a message was brought to Roosevelt. He handed it across the table to Churchill: 'Tobruk has surrendered, with 25,000 men taken prisoners.' Churchill was deeply shocked. 'What can we do to help?' asked the President. 'Give us as many Sherman tanks as you can spare, and ship them to the Middle East as quickly as possible.' The Americans sent more than three hundred.

Returning to London at the end of June, Churchill found that a by-election had gone very badly for the Government. On 1 and 2 July the Commons debated the motion 'That this House, while paying tribute to the heroism and endurance of the Armed Forces of the Crown in circumstances of exceptional difficulty, has no confidence in the central direction of the war.'

The motion was lost by 475 to 25, 'les vingt-cinq canailles', as Churchill described them picturesquely, 'qui ont voté contre moi'.[12]]

Wednesday, 1 July

7. Went to see A., who had retired upstairs, about the Russian offer of 3 Polish Divisions. We must get Polish consent and I couldn't get hold of Raczynski this evening. Will see him tomorrow morning. A. said debate had been rather deplorable. But I gathered it hadn't done much harm to (1) the country, (2) the Gov., but only to Parliament. Well, I don't mind about that. Discovered that M.I. estimate of German casualties in Russia is 6½ million gross; 4¼ million now away from front and 3¾ will never go back. This seems to me unduly high.

Thursday, 2 July

Yesterday's debate a deplorable spectacle. Talk with A. about Egypt (arrangements for evacuation, &c.)... P.M. apparently in a high state of dudgeon this morning, but A. tried to calm him. He spoke at 3.30 and I later discovered he did extremely well.

Friday, 3 July

12. Cabinet. News from Egypt better (though one hardly dares say so). Discussed evacuation from Egypt and telegram to Russia about 2nd Front.

Sunday, 5 July

After the debate on Thursday, P.M. told A. he was going to Cairo! He had a plane ready, and had consulted Attlee and Bevin who had, of course, agreed—or rather had not ventured to disagree! A. had to argue for two hours to convince him of the absurdity of this. Finally Winston said 'I see what you mean—you think I would be like a fat old bluebottle on a cowpat!'

Monday, 6 July

10.30 Edward [Halifax] came for about an hour. He looks very well and we discussed all sorts of things. (Except his possible replacement!)... 5.30 Cabinet. Egypt seems better. The Russian convoy situation bad. I don't know *how* we can keep this up. Russian front not too good.... P.M. furious about Generals ordering surrender—and he's quite right. Says we ought to make it clear that any General ordering surrender will, after the war, be tried for his life and have to justify himself. The Gen. in Tobruk ordered surrender, it seems, to 'save bloodshed'. But how much blood did he let by doing so? Unfortunately, he's a S. African, so *we* can't do anything about him.

Tuesday, 7 July

Warned A. of P.M.'s idea of stopping *preparations* for 2nd Front and telling Russians frankly. We *can't* do this. It will have bad effect. Besides, we must be *prepared* in *case* there is a break, when we should want to slip on to the Continent without delay. Also warned him of what Portal told me of possibliity of our flying over S. Sweden, if necessary. He agreed.

Wednesday, 8 July

Had a talk with A. 'Second Front' in Europe this year definitely off. President wants to do 'Gymnast'.* *I* think that simply a dispersal of effort, but if it will keep Russians going, may be worthwhile. Wrote a paper for A. tonight suggesting how it might be presented to Russians. But I'm not sure! Very gloomy outlook and Cabinet yesterday seems to have been very depressing. Chiefs of Staff have no ideas and oppose everything. P.M. said 'We'd better put an advertisement in the papers, asking for ideas'!

Thursday, 9 July

Gave A. a paper I wrote last night on how to put change of plans to the Russians. He thought it ingenious. He took me off to Cabinet at 12. Subject—Post-War Relief. P.M. arrived in high dudgeon, and enjoyed himself enormously. He devoted himself to attacking Cabinet

* Projected landings in French North Africa.

decision, taken last Monday week in his absence—to tell Americans that, as part of general plan for relief, we should be prepared to keep on 'a system of rationing after the war'. His line was: 'Are we to tell the British soldier, returning from the war, that he is to tighten his belt and starve, in order that Roumanians may batten on the fat of the land. I've never heard of such a thing.' In vain, A., Cripps, Attlee, Bevin and Co., told him that nor had they—that that was an outrageous proposition, but didn't happen to be the one that they had subscribed to. That didn't matter: Winston began again 'Are we, who alone saved the world during a whole year, to go short while Americans eat what they will, free of all restriction?' &c. &c. No arguing with that. Kingsley was on velvet. He and P.M. the only ones against the rest of the Cabinet and Kingsley felt quite safe with such support. He kept interjecting comment—and got roundly smacked on the head. He insinuated that the B. of T. had quickly sent off their instructions after the snap division in the Cabinet. Dalton, quick as lightning, said 'the B. of T. work quite quickly when not obstructed by the Treasury.' Great fun. And Winston enjoyed it more than anyone (except me).

Monday, 13 July

Lunched with A. in his flat. J.F. Dulles* there [at F.O.]. I had expected to meet Allen D[ulles].† So it was a shock. J.F.D. the woolliest type of useless pontificating American. Said to be 'close to' Welles. Heaven help us! . . . Cabinet 5.30. Outstanding news was sinkings for the week—364,000 tons. This, of course, if continued, leads us straight to early disaster. Russian perhaps not so bad as might have been. But I have no great confidence in Egyptian situation. We have no initiative. Only about 8 ships of the Russian convoy got thro'. This is not good enough. Defence Committee are discussing tonight and I hope they'll decide to discontinue.

Wednesday, 15 July

11 talked to A. about various things, including our operational plans. *We* have made up our minds against 2nd Front this year. This, I am afraid, is right—sad though it might be. We want Americans to do 'Gymnast', President would probably be willing. But Marshall against. I fear his idea is that, if [Operation] 'Sledgehammer'‡ is off, America must turn her attention to the Pacific. This is all rather

* American lawyer; later adviser to U.S. Sec. of State at meetings of the Council of Foreign Ministers, 1945–9; Sec. of State, 1952–9.

† Head of the U.S. Office of Strategic Services in Europe, 1942–5.

‡ Plan for an assault on Cherbourg or Brest in 1942.

disquieting. Marshall and H. Hopkins flying over tonight. We have decided, I am glad to say, to sail *no* more northern convoys to Russia. It really isn't good enough. Nearly 500 tanks at the bottom of the sea as a result of last attempt. (Only 4 ships out of 33 safe at present.) That does the Russians no good. P.M. consulting President about this, and how to put it to Russians.

[Eventually eleven merchant ships in this convoy, PQ17, staggered on to Archangel; the other twenty-three were sunk.]

Saturday, 18 July

Saw Maisky at 12.30 and let him read copy of P.M.'s telegram to Stalin about Russian convoy. He had been prepared for it, so didn't take it too badly. Gave me Soviet reply about 'northern operation', which was to the effect that Soviet army are too busy. That rather exonerates us!

Wednesday, 22 July

Asked A. about Hopkins-Marshall conversations. He confesses he doesn't know much about them. Defence Cttee. hardly meets nowadays, and of course Cabinet aren't brought in. Apparently we hope to educate Americans to realisation that 2nd Front in Europe is impossible this year. P.M. wildly keen about 'Gymnast'. I *believe* Pres. favours this, but it seems H. H[opkins] and Marshall don't. So it looks like our doing *nothing*. Which will be rather fatal to the Russian situation.

[Matters were settled by 25 July. The Americans agreed that in view of British opposition there was no point in continuing to press for 'Sledgehammer'. All attention was therefore to be concentrated on 'Gymnast', shortly rechristened 'Torch'.]

Friday, 24 July

A. . . . showed me Stalin's reply to P.M. about convoys and 2nd Front. Pretty stuffy. Cabinet to discuss it at 5 and he wants me there. . . . 5. Cabinet. Very interesting. Decided no reply to Stalin for present, but meeting early next week with Maisky, [Rear-Adm.] Kharlamov* and Pound to explain naval difficulties. Then long discussion about war plans—'2nd Front'—'Round Up'† and 'Gymnast'. U.S. and British Staffs agreed on a paper—and so am I, provided it means what I think it should mean. We must try to make

* Now Russian naval attaché.

† Plan for the liberation of France in 1943.

this clear. Agreed paper now to be remitted to President and War Cabinet.

Saturday, 25 July

Raczynski came in morning, very fussed about arrest of Polish agents in Russia. I promised to consult A. and see what we could do about it. . . . Message that A. agrees we ought to try and help Poles. Rang up Raczynski and told him I'd let him know more tomorrow.

Sunday, 26 July

Russian news looks bad. In Egypt the Auk, after his good old 1916 battle of artillery barrage and infantry attack(!), seems to have been brought to a standstill! I wish de Gaulle were C.I.G.S.

Monday, 27 July

Mass of work—as always, if I am occupied for 3 or 4 hours at meetings, the whole office fire at me colossal files defaced with interminable minutes.

Wednesday, 29 July

Left F.O. at 10.45 and picked up Maisky and his A[ir] A[ttaché] at 11. Reached Bomber Command about 12. Long discussion with [the C.-in-C.] Arthur Harris, who told Maisky of his possibilities, limitations and plans. M.—as was to be expected—critical and insistent. *Would* keep on pressing, e.g. that we should bomb Frankfurt-a[m]-M[ain] as it was an important industrial centre. Useless to assure him that F-a-M is in its (proper) place on our list, and that we have compiled positive encyclopaedias on the relative importance of all possible targets! . . . A. tells me his visit (to U.S.A.) now probably postponed to late in Aug., and he doesn't think he'll take me. Don't know which I should prefer.

Thursday, 30 July

Lovely day. Met A. in Park, who said P.M. off to Egypt—had had a Cabinet about it at 1 a.m. Asked me to bring H. (who was coming to see me at 10.30) to talk to him about it. This we did, and I brought a telegram to me from Archie Kerr* urging meeting between P.M. and Stalin. A. went off to see P.M. Heard he was fixed on the trip, and I shall have to go with him. . . . Martin tells me P.M.'s doctor, Attlee and Anderson trying to dissuade him from going! Heard later he insisted on doing so, but probably Saturday

* Sir A. Clark Kerr, Ambassador in Moscow, 1942–6.

night—not tomorrow night! . . . Bore not knowing one's plans. Don't know yet for sure, as P.M. has still to be tested tomorrow morning for 'high flying'.

Friday, 31 July

Went to Cabinet War Room at 11 to pick up P.M. and we started for Farnborough about 11.30. P.M. and Mrs. C[hurchill] in one car and I and [Sir] Charles Wilson* in another. Our blood pressures were satisfactory, and we were put in the 'Chamber'. Taken up to 15,000 ft. and kept there ¼ hour (with a little oxygen). Felt no effects at all. Nor, apparently, did P.M. We then came down and I, as usual, became very deaf, and slight pain in head. P.M. complained of pain, but we discovered that was due to clumsy adjustment of his oxygen mask, which was pressing. Clemmie peeked at him through port-hole. Blood-pressures good after. . . . Arranged now we start tomorrow night.

[The entries for 3 to 20 August are taken from Cadogan's letters to Lady Theodosia; the interpolations draw upon published accounts and upon a record which Cadogan composed in retirement.]

Monday, 3 August *A.C. to T.C.* *Cairo*

We got off all right on Sat./Sun. night from a West Country airfield. I don't give you the name—not out of any consideration for secrecy—but because I'm not sure of it myself.

The P.M., his doctor, Private Secretary, A.D.C., Valet and Detective got off the ground about 12.30 a.m. We followed about an hour later. Clemmie and Jack Churchill† came down to see them off, and they were going to spend the night in the special and get back to London early in the morning.

We flew in two 'Liberator' (American) bombers. They are beautiful 4-engined machines, but of course *not* very comfortable. I slept in what is known as the Bomb Bay, which I shared with (Ld.) Hardinge (whom I didn't know before). He seems to be bottle-washer‡ to the A[djutant]-Gen[eral], Adam. The latter, with Alan Brooke and Bobbety§, left 24 hours before us for Malta. Brooke and Adam came on here this morning.

To return to our plane, they had done the best they could with it, having made little shelves on which there was a mattress with bedclothes and pillow, but you can't stand up without cracking your

* The Prime Minister's doctor; later Lord Moran.

† The Prime Minister's younger brother.

‡ Officially Military Assistant.

§ Lord Cranborne was now Colonial Secretary.

head against some steel projection on the ceiling, nor sit up in bed without ditto. However, it wasn't too uncomfortable, and I think I slept for about 4 hours.

We landed at Gib at 8.30 (7 hours' flight). A lovely morning, and one gets a wonderful view of the Rock and the whole lay-out, and Algeciras, from the air.

We went straight to Government House where P.M. had already arrived. . . .

P.M. lay on his bed in his underwear and held forth to us. He seemed none the worse for the journey. We didn't have to go very high—not over 12,000 ft. . . .

It was a lovely day at Gib—very hot sun but a nice breeze. After lunch a soldier, Sir Colin Jardine,* (whom I'd never heard of) took me round the defences. They are rather wonderful—the whole Rock has been honeycombed with passages, workshops, ration stores &c.

The Governor is Mason MacFarlane—Military Attaché in Berlin before the war, and lately head of our [Military] Mission to Russia. I had, of course, seen him in Moscow and knew him before that.

We got off the ground at 6 p.m.—*very* hot until we got high up—started up the Mediterranean, then cut across the African coast and went inland, keeping south of the trouble and making for the Nile, then down to Cairo, where we landed at 8 a.m.—14 hours for, I think, about 2,200 miles—good going. Both our planes started together, as we had to have an escort until dusk, and we eventually beat the P.M. by nearly an hour.

I was surprised to find that at that hour, although the sun was hot, there was quite a nice breeze.

Miles [Lampson] and everyone drawn up to meet us. I chatted with him for about 20 mins. and then jumped at his suggestion that I should go on to the Embassy, which I did, driving for about ½ an hour—past the Pyramids. (I got about 6 hours unbroken sleep in the plane: I had to be woken just as we were arriving!)

Jacqueline† met me at the door—expecting, I suppose, the P.M.—and we had a chat while I drank coffee and ate fresh figs. She wanted all sorts of tips as to how to treat the P.M. I did my best for her!

Small lunch party here—I sat next to Tedder,‡ the Air Marshal, whom I had met in London.

* Maj.-Gen. Sir C. A. Jardine, Deputy Fortress Commander, Gibraltar, 1942–3.

† Lady Lampson.

‡ Air Chief Marshal Sir A. W. Tedder, A.O.C.-in-C., Mediterranean; later Deputy Supreme Commander, S.H.A.E.F.

Smuts arrived in the middle. I'd never met him before. He's certainly impressive and very good company—one of the few men whom I think the P.M. really respects, and to whom he will listen. . . .

About 5.30 Auchinleck blew in, and had a long conference with the P.M. and C.I.G.S. I joined them at the end to discuss minor matters when they had finished their consultation on the graver issues! Auchinleck looks very much thinner than when I saw him in London, but very hard and fit. He had to go back to the battle before dinner.

Tuesday, 4 August *A.C. to T.C.* *Cairo*

I suppose you hardly remember this house [the Embassy]. It's a good one, and quite liveable, but there are only two air-conditioned rooms (given up to the P.M.) and not enough bathrooms.

Miles has stored away his most treasured Chinese possessions, but there are still masses lying about. He himself seems very well.

Wednesday, 5 August *A.C. to T.C.* *Cairo*

I think I had reached lunch-time yesterday in my record of our doings. Nothing much interesting in the afternoon. I spent most of the time sitting in the shade in the garden, while the P.M. held a meeting of Auchinleck, Smuts, Wavell* and other military, naval and air big-wigs. He must have enjoyed himself immensely. Photographs were taken in the garden, but I'm afraid I'm only on the outer fringe of the group, which will probably be cut off, before publication. Quiet dinner here—except for rather loud monologues by Winston. We got to bed about 1.30 as he was due to start for the Front at 5 a.m. this morning! He's due back in a few minutes (5 p.m.), but I suppose he will be quite fresh. Before lunch I called on Cannellopoulos, the Greek 'Minister of State'—a chatterbox.

[Eden had asked Cadogan to arrange an interview between Cannellopoulos and the Prime Minister. Each time he was approached by his Private Secretary, Leslie Rowan, however, Churchill merely said 'Can't—ellopoulos'. Rowan eventually suggested that Sir Alec himself should tackle Churchill, which he did from the foot of the staircase at the Embassy in Cairo. Churchill listened as he climbed the stairs, put on a very serious face and then, retreating nimbly up the last few steps, said 'Can't—ellopoulos' and vanished down the corridor. Summoned to the bathroom a little later, Cadogan found the Prime Minister wallowing about like a porpoise, and throwing his sponge up and down to the chant of 'Canellopoulos! Can'tellopoulos! Canellopoulos. . . .' In the end he saw him.[13]]

* Now C.-in-C. India.

Friday, 7 August *A.C. to T.C.* *Cairo*

[On 6 August] P.M. . . . went to the Palace at 11 p.m. for a secret audience of the King. He got back soon after midnight, and held forth to Miles and me till 2.30! Poor Sir Charles Wilson, who considers himself responsible for the resistance which the P.M.'s constitution puts up against the various strains imposed upon it, is becoming distracted!

I think we shall leave here Sun. or Mon. and be back here again towards the end of next week. When, exactly, we shall get home I really can't say. Winston paints his future plans with broad sweeps of the brush, but it's a different picture each time.

He wanted to send me off to Beirut yesterday for a day, to grapple with Spears.* But I managed to scotch that!

[Churchill had by now lost confidence in Auchinleck, and had been unfavourably impressed by stories of poor morale, undue numbers of officers behind the lines ('the gabardene swine') and inadequate staff work at the headquarters of the C.-in-C. Middle East. Like almost everyone else, Cadogan included, Churchill failed to appreciate the decisive nature of the First Battle of Alamein, just fought under Auchinleck's leadership, which marked the beginning of Rommel's defeat. Rommel himself was under no illusions.]

Saturday, 8 August *A.C. to T.C.* *Cairo*

[Yesterday] I spent a peaceful afternoon, as I usually do, sitting most of the time in the garden and conducting my interviews there. It certainly is a very pleasant place, if one can take it at one's leisure, as I can, having nothing to do with the purely military and operational work on which the P.M. is busy. . . .

After tea, an Indian Prince arrived to call on the P.M.—a tall, inscrutable, impassive figure, beautifully dressed, with an immaculate turban and a great panache of gauze flowing from the top of it. The P.M. appeared in his rompers and what he calls his 10-gallon hat—a sort of Mexican affair. . . . The Indian registered practically no surprise at all, but I don't know what he was thinking.

After that, the Army photographers and cinema operators were admitted to the garden to photograph Winston and Smuts playing with baby Victor [Lampson]! What England will think when the Film is released, I really cannot imagine. (I don't appear in the Film: I was standing behind the operators making suitable noises to attract Victor's attention).

* Now head of the British Mission to Syria and Lebanon.

Before dinner I had a long walk round and round the garden with Smuts, who's a dear old boy. (He left in the small hours this morning.)

Dinner was rather a frost. We assembled as usual at 9 but the P.M. didn't put in an appearance until 9.30, looking like a thunderstorm. Poor man, he had just heard that the key General [Gott], who was to be given the main appointment in the scheme of changes he had been arranging here,* had been shot down while flying back from the Front to Cairo. It really is bad luck. So poor Winston sat speechless and desperate during dinner and had hardly recovered before the small hours. The American General Maxwell,† who sat next to him, and who didn't know what had happened, must have thought he was a frightful flop. I explained to him afterwards. It was delightful in the garden—quite a cool breeze. Winston kept me and Miles up until 2.30 discussing everything on earth. He was due to start off on a visit to a unit at 5.30 a.m.! But he put it off, and finally didn't go until 8.30.

Today I had another peaceful morning receiving in the garden, sitting under a flame-flowered tree, viewing the Pyramids in the distance and watching the hoopoes pecking on the lawn.

I had to go to a lunch which Casey gave for de Gaulle (who arrived yesterday). Luckily I didn't sit next to that General, but between Catroux‡ and de Benoist (Suez Canal) who are both very agreeable.

Friday, 14 August *A.C. to T.C.* *Moscow*

Days in Cairo seemed much alike—too hot to do anything much in the day time. I don't remember that anything of note happened during most of the 10th. In the afternoon the Lampsons took me out to their country house on the edge of the Fayoum Oasis—a mud construction of many little courtyards. Not bad: better than Paomachang§. Camped next door was a 'Long Range Desert Group' patrol, with 2 officers who came to tea. These patrols are self-contained units which operate behind the enemy's lines, staying there sometimes 2 or 3 weeks. After tea the officers rushed us all over the desert in one of their little American Scout cars, which can go anywhere and do anything at 30 miles an hour. . . .[14]

We left for the aerodrome soon after midnight but for one reason or another didn't get off the ground till 2.30, arriving at Tehran at

* Gen. Sir H. R. Alexander to be C.-in-C. Middle East, with Lt.-Gen. W. H. E. Gott as G.O.C. Eighth Army. With Gott's death, Gen. Sir B. C. Montgomery was appointed to command Eighth Army.

† Maj.-Gen. R. L. Maxwell, commanding U.S. forces, Middle East.

‡ Gen. Georges Catroux, C.-in-C. Free French Forces, Levant, 1941–3.

§ Near Peking.

8.30. I slept a bit, but the Liberators are *not* built for comfort. My travelling companions this time were Wavell, Alan Brooke, Tedder (Air Officer Commanding in Egypt) and Jacob* of the War Cabinet Offices.

We had meant to go straight on to Moscow, but we were too late, so resigned ourselves to staying in Tehran for 24 hours.

The Legation is certainly very nice, with a lovely garden, in which I sat most of the morning. The P.M. went off to lunch with the Shah, and the rest of us lunched in the Legation.

Saturday, 15 August *A.C. to T.C.* *Moscow*

We got up at 4 a.m. and left the house at 5 and the aerodrome at 5.30. After our machine had been going half-an-hour, the pilot said something was wrong with one of the propellers and he thought it best to turn back, but we should have to circle over the aerodrome for 2 or 3 hours to get rid of some of the petrol—we were too heavy laden to land. So there we circled. When we eventually came down we went back to the Legation while they diagnosed the machine's complaint. The verdict soon came that we should have to stay the night, while a plane was sent to get the necessary spare part from Bagdad.

We got news that we were offered a Russian machine to take us on to Moscow next morning. A very good and comfortable passenger machine of American make [Douglas DC3]. Armchairs, a Persian carpet on the floor, radio-gramophone and all comforts. The pilot was to be the famous Russian pilot who flew over the Pole some years ago [Colonel Gratchov].

[The Colonel's reputation as a pilot of exuberant habits was promptly confirmed. He flew the aircraft at a belt of tall trees, and then banked so steeply that even the imperturbable Tedder, sitting in front of Cadogan, felt moved to turn round and murmur 'When *we* were very young. . . .' This was the bumpiest flight of Cadogan's experience; as the Dakota rushed low along the western shore of the Caspian Sea, 'the faces of some of my companions were beginning to assume unnatural and unbecoming hues.'

The pilot stopped to refuel at Baku before passing over vast reed-beds in the Volga delta and flushing, to the delight of the C.I.G.S.s, egrets, herons and duck. The virtual absence of defences between the Caucasus and the Caspian delighted him less. From Kuibyshev, where the whole party had to consume refreshments intended for the P.M. on the previous day, the last leg to Moscow took three hours. Repeating his

* Lt.-Col. (later Lt.-Gen. Sir) Ian Jacob, Asst. Sec. (Military) to the War Cabinet.

earlier performance, Colonel Gratchov scattered the large group of dignitaries on the airfield, just missed the buildings, circled triumphantly and landed at 7.20 p.m., after a journey of fourteen hours.

Brooke, Cadogan, Tedder and the others were bidden to dine with the Prime Minister at his dacha just outside Moscow. Before dinner Churchill told Sir Alexander of his first meeting with Stalin, on the previous evening. He had explained, with copious illustration, exactly why the Second Front could not be opened in Western Europe in 1942. Having disputed the reasoning, Stalin conceded that the decision lay outside his control. He heard with apparent approval the Prime Minister's account of the bombing of Germany and the plans for 'Torch', the landings in North Africa which the British and Americans planned for the autumn. Stalin even said jovially that he hoped no details of this highly secret affair would appear in the Russian press! In short, Churchill thought the meeting a good one; that he had cast off the millstone of the Americans' half-promise of a Second Front in 1942. According to Tedder, Churchill talked at table of Stalin as a peasant whom he could handle. Tedder, convinced that there were microphones everywhere, was horrified. 'Méfiez-vous', he scribbled on a menu-card, passing it along to the Prime Minister. 'He gave me a glare which I shall never forget, but I am afraid it was too late.'

Incredibly, the C.I.G.S. too did not realise until visited by the Polish General Anders on 14 August that all the rooms had ears. When it was pointed out to the Prime Minister that since there would almost certainly be a microphone in the wall of each room in the Kremlin, he must be very careful, he said 'we will soon deal with that. The Russians, I have been told, are not human beings at all. They are lower in the scale of nature than the orang-outang. Now then, let them take that down and translate it into Russian.'

The second meeting with Stalin took place after 11 p.m. that night, 13 August, in a sparsely-furnished chamber at the Kremlin. As in Beaverbrook's mission of the previous autumn, and Eden's of the winter, Stalin's line now hardened. He made gratuitously insulting remarks about the British Army's cowardice. Eventually the Prime Minister had had enough. He cracked his hand on the table, wound himself up almost audibly, and burst into a torrent of oratory. 'I have come round Europe in the midst of my troubles—yes, Mr Stalin, I have my troubles as well as you—hoping to meet the hand of comradeship; and I am bitterly disappointed. I have not met that hand.'

Tedder said that for about five minutes Churchill spoke 'in the most lucid, dramatic, forceful way I have ever heard anybody speak'. Both interpreters had failed to take a note. Only Cadogan had scribbled down the Prime Minister's words. He began to read them out but Stalin held up his hand. 'I do not understand the words, but by God I like your spirit.' The meeting ended at 2 a.m.

On the way back, Cadogan asked the Prime Minister: 'Shall I tell

Stalin in confidence that you are hesitating whether to accept his invitation to dinner tomorrow after what has happened?'

'No: that is going too far, I think.']

Saturday, 15 August (cont.)

I was with the P.M. by 11 next morning. The country-house, or 'Dacha' is quite well run, with a biggish garden, and in the garden the most colossal and luxurious dug-out you ever saw—the walls covered with coloured marbles or wood panelling: I don't know how many rooms, an electric lift, refrigerators and complete kitchen, offices &c. Very ridiculous and really rather vulgar!

In the garden are also clumps of raspberries dotted about the lawn, and beds of strawberries (besides flowers). The raspberries are excellent. Disposed as they are, they can't be netted, but I suppose there are no birds.

[After lunch, Cadogan gave Molotov a sharp reply to Stalin's memorandum of the previous day, adding that the Prime Minister felt puzzled and disheartened.

The usual Kremlin banquet began in Catherine the Great's State rooms at 9 p.m., by which time Stalin seemed to have modified his view. The meal consisted of nineteen courses, interspersed with innumerable toasts. Soon Stalin proposed the Prime Minister's health. Churchill replied shortly. Thereafter Molotov had to make the running. He uttered laudatory speeches about all the eminent Russians present, detailing their contributions to the winning of the war. Each had then to make suitable acknowledgement and to propose a toast to another of the company. After some hours, Cadogan felt that this self-perpetuating process was beginning to lose its pristine freshness. Moreover, he had noticed the Prime Minister's obvious boredom. When his health was proposed, therefore, Cadogan determined to break up the party. He simply said: 'Mr Molotov, I am deeply honoured by your kind words. May I now suggest a toast? Gentlemen, I give you death and damnation to the Germans.' The party drank up enthusiastically.

Driving home with the Prime Minister, Cadogan was amazed at the violence and depth of his resentment and could only surmise that Stalin's leg-pulling, passed through the mangle of an interpreter, had perhaps sounded unduly heavy or even deliberately hostile. 'Anyhow,' said Cadogan to Sir Charles Wilson, 'he was like a bull in the ring maddened by the pricks of the picadors. He declared that he really did not know what he was supposed to be doing here. He would return to London without seeing Stalin again.'

At the dacha, Churchill, Cadogan and Rowan sat at a long table and wrangled over the communiqué. The Prime Minister said that the Russian draft would be calamitous. Cadogan disagreed. Churchill pressed his point. Cadogan stormed back at him. 'I had never', records Wilson, an eye-witness, 'seen anyone talk to the P.M. like this.' At last Churchill said: 'Well, you have been in the Foreign Office all this time. Do as you think. But I want it recorded that I thought it would be disastrous.'

Authorised again to take his own line, Cadogan said he could not do that if the Prime Minister thought it would be disastrous. There was a silence. Churchill rose to go to bed. Cadogan got up, said 'Good night' and left for his hotel. It was now 3 a.m.

By 10.30 the next morning, when Cadogan returned to the dacha, Churchill had repented. The Ambassador, Clark Kerr, dissuaded him from acting upon his first wish, to leave Moscow forthwith. While Brooke, Tedder and Wavell tried with indifferent success to make their Russian colleagues understand the rudiments of cross-Channel operations, Cadogan was telephoning hourly to the Kremlin, only to be told 'Mr Stalin is out walking.' It was not until 6 p.m. that Stalin agreed to see Churchill alone at 7. Imagining that this would be a short encounter, the Prime Minister asked Sir Alexander to look after General Anders, summoned to dine at 8.30.

For the first hour in the Kremlin, Stalin made no response to the approaches of Churchill, who said he was leaving at dawn. The Russian then suggested drinks at his house. He uncorked a large number of bottles. When his red-headed daughter Svetlana came in and kissed him, Stalin glanced at Churchill to see how he reacted. 'I confess', said the latter, in recounting all this to the Cabinet, 'that I acquired a quite definite physical impression.' Thereupon Stalin wondered whether they might not invite Molotov, who was fussed about the communiqué. 'There is one thing you can say in defence of Molotov; he can drink.'

The three, with their two interpreters, then sampled a series of dishes; vegetables, pig, chicken, beef, fish. Much chaff and banter were exchanged. By now it was well after midnight. At the dacha, Cadogan was still doing his best to entertain General Anders when a message called him to the Kremlin. There he found the company in great good humour, still sitting at the groaning board, and surrounded by a large number of bottles. Cadogan, having already eaten one dinner, politely declined an invitation to share a sucking-pig. Stalin fell upon it with zest.

The great men had reached the stage of bandying reminiscences. After some talk about the collectivisation of the farms, Churchill asked, 'What happened to the . . . ?' 'Kulaks?' prompted Cadogan in a whisper. Stalin replied with a straight face that some of them had been given an acre or two in Siberia, but had proved 'very unpopular with the rest of the people'. Within a few minutes the troublesome communiqué had been agreed:

> A number of decisions were reached covering the field of the war against Hitlerite Germany and her associates in Europe. This just war of liberation both Governments are determined to carry on with all their

power and energy until the complete destruction of Hitlerism and any similar tyranny has been achieved. The discussions, which were carried on in an atmosphere of cordiality and complete sincerity, provided an opportunity of reaffirming the existence of the close friendship and understanding between the Soviet Union, Great Britain and the United States of America, in entire accordance with the Allied relationships existing between them.

There was just time to take leave of Stalin and Molotov, drive to the hotel, gulp down a cup of coffee and leave for the aerodrome. Notwithstanding torrents of rain, guards of honour paraded and national anthems were played. The aircraft took off at 5.30 a.m.

Churchill now felt quite sure that the Russians would fight on to victory. Indeed, Stalin had spoken of his forthcoming counterstroke. Like Clark Kerr, Cadogan was convinced that the two men had made genuine contact. It had scarcely been possible, when bearing nothing but bad tidings, for the British to press the claims of Poland; but at least they had not met what Cadogan expected, a hint from Stalin that if the Western Allies could not do more, he did not know how much longer Russia could stand the strain. On the contrary, 'he repeatedly said that he himself was astonished at the spirit and determination of his people. He didn't know them; he had never dreamt that they could show such unity or resolution.'[15]

For most of the ten hours' flight Cadogan slept. Wavell, whose brains, character and economy of language he esteemed, was meanwhile composing a 'Ballad of the Second Front.' He gave the original to Cadogan as they landed:

> Prince of the Kremlin, here's a fond farewell;
> I've had to deal with many worse than you.
> You took it, though you hated it like hell;
> *No Second Front in 1942.*

The party reached Tehran at 3.20 p.m. on 15 August.]

Monday, 17 August *A.C. to T.C.* *Cairo*

The P.M. had set his heart on my seeing the Shah—I can't think why—so an audience had to be fixed and I just had time to have tea, unpack and have a bath and dash off to the Palace to be presented at 6. He's a nice and intelligent young man, but he mumbles so (though he speaks good French) that I only heard about 50% of what he said. (Flying always makes me deaf for an hour or two.). . .

Today I spent a lazy day with nothing much to do. The P.M. *talks* of spending a week here, but I hope to push him off earlier.

Tuesday, 18 August *A.C. to T.C.* *Cairo*

We got to bed quite early last night—about 12—so I had a good rest.

This morning it was overcast, but about the same temperature. With the Nile rising, it is getting damper, which makes the heat rather more oppressive. The days average about 95° and the minimum at night seems to be always 72°. But I gather it might be much worse, and there is generally a pleasant little breeze when we sit out after dinner.

Wednesday, 19 August *A.C. to T.C.* *Cairo*

This morning poor Auchinleck came to say goodbye. He has refused the new appointment that was devised for him,* so I suppose he disappears altogether. I am very sorry for him: I expect he is a good chap, but one way or another I think he can't have been up to the job.

Thursday, 20 August *A.C. to T.C.* *Cairo*

I have now discovered that there is no chance of a plane before tomorrow night (Friday) and as the P.M. is probably leaving on Sat. or Sun., I think I shall wait and go with him—possibly in less discomfort.

He went off yesterday afternoon to the Front again for 24 hours, and is due back this afternoon. I expect he will be very excited. . . .

I see the English Press have been pretty good on the P.M.'s tour. The fact of his having visited Joe damps down a good deal of criticism that might have been levelled at him.

I'm looking forward to getting home: I'm rather bored here now, as I have no particular business here and there's not much to do—it's too hot for sight-seeing.

Friday, 21 August *A.C. to T.C.* *Cairo*

The P.M. got back about 6 p.m. yesterday, and then had a conference from 7 to 9. He was in terrific form and had enjoyed himself like a schoolboy, having bathed twice. He held forth the whole of dinner, ragging everyone. Sir Charles Wilson, his 'Personal Physician', is one of his principal butts. To Winston's delight, poor C.W. fell ill of the usual local tummy complaint, and Winston now goes about saying to everyone 'Sir Charles has been a terrible anxiety to us the whole time, but I hope we'll get him through!' Last night

* A command in Iraq and Persia. He became C.-in-C., India, in 1943, on Wavell's elevation to the Viceroyalty.

at dinner Winston held forth to the whole table on medicine, psychology &c. (all Sir Charles' subjects) and worked himself up to a terrific disquisition. I suspect (and I inferred from Sir Charles' expression) that it was pretty good nonsense. And I think Winston must have had an inkling of that too, as he ended up 'My God! I do have to work hard to teach that chap his job!'

Sunday, 23 August *A.C. to T.C.* *Gibraltar*

Spears arrived in the middle of lunch. P.M. spoke to him after and then turned him on to me, and I had to listen to *his* side of the case for an hour or more. . . . Got off the ground 7.30. Not a very comfortable night. I occupied one of the better places *outside* the Bomb Bay, but they took us up to 15,000 ft and it got very cold, and lack of oxygen made breathing rather difficult. They eventually fixed us with oxygen masks, but rather too late. Arrived Gib about 9.30.

Monday, 24 August

Off the ground 1.50. Ran into bad weather in home waters, but nosed our way in over Milford Haven and landed with the last light at Lyneham [Wiltshire], about 8.50. . . . Special got off quickly and we had a much needed dinner. P.M. in cracking form.

[Cadogan, to his surprise and relief, found no great arrears of work awaiting him in London. After reporting to Eden and acquainting himself with the latest phases of the planning for 'Torch', he went for a week's leave to the cottage.]

Sunday, 6 September

Russians seem to be holding, temporarily, at Stalingrad and enemy seems to have failed in Egypt. Nice holiday. But not too sorry to be back. I haven't really done much honest work these last five weeks.

Monday, 7 September

Cabinet 5.30. Not much news. Anti-submarine campaign doing well. During last week Germans have made comparatively little progress in Russia at great cost.

Agreement is now reached with U.S. on plans for 'Torch'* but I fear it won't happen before November.

Tuesday, 8 September

Had a hard time with Warner and Ward† trying to sort out a

* At the end of August the U.S. Chiefs of Staff had suggested a more modest scope for 'Torch' than was acceptable to the British. Churchill had to intervene with the President.

† C. F. A. Warner and J. G. Ward of F.O.; later Ambassadors in Brussels and Rome respectively.

frightfully muddled file about co-ordination of Chemical Warfare. It has been complicated by no-one, no Government, daring to call a spade a spade, and we haven't faced up to the question whether, in view of P.M.'s declaration, if Stalin says he is retaliating against a German gas attack, we *automatically* throw gas on Germany. Same difficulty in regard to Roosevelt's declaration concerning Pacific. Must try to get this faced and straightened out.

Wednesday, 9 September

Grappled with some sticky Files—the worst about co-ordination of Gas Warfare. An *awful* mess by our Department, complicated by ineffably silly and irrelevant papers by [Sir Edward] Bridges. Don't know how I shall get it straight.

Thursday, 10 September

Tried to sort out the awful tangle caused by our promise to retaliate with gas if Germans use it against Russians. . . . Winston enjoying himself enormously, reviewing Home Guard on Horse Guards' Parade, with Marines' Band.

Monday, 14 September

Cabinet at 5.30. . . . P.Q. convoy [to Russia] has lost 12 ships (out of 40) and that is all we know. They are in danger zone for 4 more days! Damage done to them by torpedo-bombers 450 miles from their base! Outward Atlantic convoy also cut up. And attempted landing at Tobruk a complete fiasco. This not surprising—seeing it was arranged by Harwood.* On other hand our bombing has been good. We have dropped as much, this fortnight, as in whole of August—average 1,800 tons a week! In last two raids on Düsseldorf and Bremen we dropped 700 and 750 tons. Equal to 3½ Coventrys! Stalingrad hard pressed, but still there. Will probably shortly go. P.M. has confidence in continued Russian resistance. Maisky is intriguing everywhere with the ignorant and disgruntled, stirring up a 'Second Front' campaign. Although he knows the truth.

[Maisky, having long enjoyed a most unusual latitude in his relations with M.P.s and the press, had just granted an interview to American correspondents, criticising British failure to keep the Russians informed, open the Second Front, match America's offensive spirit and so forth. Eden gave him a warning on 18 September. Less than a month later. Eden had to reproach Maisky severely for talking to two journalists about 'Torch', the plans for which had been confided to him in the strictest

* Admiral Sir H. Harwood, C.-in-C., Mediterranean, 1942.

secrecy. Knowledge of this indiscretion had come from 'sources which we must regard as absolutely trustworthy'. Eden brushed aside Maisky's denial.[16]]

Tuesday, 15 September

Talk with A. at 6.15 about Casey's proposal to establish branch at Bagdad, and we dictated minute to P.M. protesting. A. complained of P.M.'s galumphing about and meddling with everything. C.I.G.S. has been this afternoon to say that P. J. Grigg* realised P.M. was trying to push him out!

Saturday, 19 September

A. rang me up. He's been having trouble with P.M., who wants to make peace with Vichy French in Madagascar. Why, I don't know—except that he says 'Annet's† quite a good chap: Clemmie met him in a train somewhere once.' That doesn't seem good enough.

Monday, 21 September

Talk with S. Hoare at 3 about 'Torch'. He is going to have a very unpleasant time, and I think ignorant C's. of S. minimize the difficulties and danger. . . . Cabinet 5.30. Not much news. 27 ships out of 40 of Russian convoy got in. Germans claim to have sunk 38! P.M. not v. well, I think.

Tuesday, 22 September

Slept at F.O. [for fire-watching]. My section had a silly sort of drill with hoses, from which we learned nothing.

Thursday, 24 September

10.45 meeting with A. and Strang about 'Torch'. Gave A. my views (reinforced by S. Hoare) that Joint Planners skimmed rather lightly over the difficulties we are going to have in Spain for the fortnight before operation comes off. Wrote him a minute to P.M. on the subject.

Sunday, 27 September

No news. But *my* indications are all rather hopeful: German campaign in Russia has *not* been a success and internal situation in Germany isn't very rose-coloured. But then, we shall probably have some *frightful* reverse tomorrow.

* S. of S. for War since Feb. 1942.

† Armand Annet, Gov.-Gen. Madagascar, 1941–3.

[The French had become convinced that Sir Edward Spears, British Minister to Syria and the Lebanon, was deliberately undermining the French position there. The French, despite the known wishes of the British, had not announced elections or the transfer of a good deal of administration to the local authorities. Arriving on the scene in early August, General de Gaulle was soon talking about forcing the British out of French territory in the Levant should they fail to meet his terms, and arguing that the Allied command in the Levant should be in French hands.

On 30 September, Churchill and Eden pressed on de Gaulle the importance of early elections, and refused the transfer of the command. The latter averred that he could not accept 'British demands for a preponderant position'. He complained of the behaviour of British representatives in the Levant. The great difficulty, retorted Churchill, lay in working with the General. Wherever he went there was trouble. He had shown no desire to assist the British, and had proved the greatest obstacle to their effective collaboration with the Americans.

Neither the British nor de Gaulle, however, sought a breach. In October, relations improved a little, though the problems in the Levant remained unresolved.[17]]

Monday, 28 September

3 meeting with A. about 'Torch' and Madagascar. I said that *if* de G. gives us guarantees about Syria we must honour our (implied) promise about Madagascar and let him in *at once*.

Cabinet 5.30. American bombing effort here is a flop—for the old reason that they won't *learn*, and won't profit by our *experience*. It really is rather tragic. And we have to handle them so gingerly. Dined at home and worked—on a few enormous files with *acres* of confused minutes. I really must protest about this.

Tuesday, 29 September

No news. Except a long telegram from A. Clark Kerr reporting a rather disturbing conversation with Wendell Wilkie* which shows that Anglo-American relations—personal, national rather than political—must be carefully nurtured.

Wednesday, 30 September

A. and P.M. had a pitched battle with de Gaulle—quite indecisive, I understand from Desmond Morton. On their instructions I put a stop on all outward telegrams from de Gaulle!

* Defeated Republican candidate in the U.S. Presidential election, 1940.

Friday, 2 October

A. has had a hard time with P.M. Cripps wants to leave Government—or at any rate War Cabinet—as he is 'not satisfied with the conduct of the war'. P.M. wants to jump at this and kick him out. But it seems C. might accept a useful job abroad—or at home, and there is idea of making him M[inister of] A[ircraft] P[roduction]. Don't know if he'll accept. Anyhow, A. will become Leader of the House but will retain, nominally, F.O. That will devolve a bit more on me, but Law would become sort of 'Acting S. of S.'. I have to have this arrangement worked out at short notice, but agreed to do nothing for the moment—for secrecy's sake. There was a Balfour–Curzon precedent during Peace Conference, but don't know whether that can be invoked.

Saturday, 3 October

Stacks of paper and *acres* of minutes, about which I am now really going to make a protest. I shall demand only *one* minute—from Head of Department—and that will give them so much extra work that they will protest. And that will make them keep their Departments in order! It's intolerable and the limit has now been reached. Worked till after 11.

Monday, 5 October

Saw A. who told me that he had managed, during week-end, to arrange that Cripps should suspend his resignation until after 'Torch'. I am glad—as it would have had a most disturbing effect. How unprincipled these politicians are. When it suits their political book, they put their 'conscience' before the national interest.

'The P.M. appeared in his rompers and what he calls his 10-gallon hat—a sort of Mexican affair. . . .'

The illustration drawn by Sir Alexandra Cadogan in his letter of 8 August 1942 to Lady Theodosia. See page 468.

VIII

October 1942–September 1943

THE DEFEAT OF ITALY

Mr Churchill said after the war that September and October of 1942 were for him the most anxious time of all. The shipping situation remained desperate; no one could tell whether Russia would hold out; Alexander and Montgomery were still preparing their onslaught against Rommel; the landing in North Africa must be hazardous; the Japanese controlled the Indian and Pacific Oceans, and much of South Asia. Though the Government won a handsome vote of confidence in July, the Leader of the House, Sir Stafford Cripps, reached the conclusion by the end of August that the machinery for the central direction of the war had serious faults. He proposed a War Planning Directorate separate from the Staffs responsible for action; or, as the Prime Minister termed it, 'a disembodied Brains Trust to browse about among our secrets and add to the already immense volume of committees and reports'. On 2 September Cripps sent in his resignation, which as we have seen he was persuaded to suspend until 'Torch' was launched. He told Eden on 2 October of his conviction that 'we should all get on much better without W.' It is clear that Sir Stafford also felt Pound to be unequal to the post of First Sea Lord. In the previous February the C.I.G.S. had confided to his diary that with Pound it was impossible for the Chiefs of Staff to function as they should. Brooke replaced him as Chairman in the following month. Devoted to Pound, Cadogan can hardly have failed to notice his growing drowsiness at meetings but makes no mention of it in the diary.

Evidently Cripps' resignation could not remain long in abeyance. Just as Smuts was leaving for South Africa, on 19 November, he spoke to Eden about the impending Cabinet changes. 'I said', Eden recorded that night, 'that I didn't want to lead the House. He said that he feared I must. W. had spoken to him of his utter confidence in me and it was necessary to spare W. every possible burden. No one else could take this on.'

Thus it was settled. Cripps' tenure of the Leadership had in any event been an unhappy one. Eden, by contrast, did the job outstandingly well. It obliged him, as he points out, to be 'almost continuously at hand in the House of Commons during the day'. In those times the House met in the mornings and afternoons. The War Cabinet or Defence Committee frequently sat into the early hours, after which the Prime Minister, refreshed by his post-luncheon sleep, liked to talk. Somehow the multifarious business of the Foreign Office, entailing much travel abroad, had to be fitted in as well.

'This meant', Eden observes, 'a ruthless burning of the candle at both ends for the best part of three years, for which excess there is always a price to be paid.'[1]

It also meant that Cadogan saw less of Eden than he wished, and explains his sharp remarks about the difficulties of access to him. Had Eden been less knowledgeable and quick on the point, or Cadogan less experienced and dependable, the system could hardly have been proposed, let alone practised. That it worked is a tribute to them both.

1942

Tuesday, 6 October

No heating in F.O. till Nov. 1., so we shall freeze. Winant last night gave A. a communication from his Government proposing we should tell the Chinese on the *9th* that we abrogate the 'Unequal Treaties' and submitting the text of an agreement to this end. I wish they'd give us a *little* more notice! However, I think it's all right. A. got Cabinet this morning to approve in principle. But Americans propose to tell the Chinese of these glad tidings *confidentially*. This of course quite silly: (a) it would lose its point, and (b) the Chinese wouldn't keep it 'confidential'. So, at 10.45, we instructed Department to draft two sentences of a declaration announcing our intention. By *1* o'clock the Department produced a bad draft. Why are Departments so *frightfully* slow? What *could* they have been doing all the morning? . . .*

4.30 A. called me in to his conference with Winant. Latter, quite rightly, wants to take this opportunity of a *joint* U.S.–British declaration, so the Department's jejune draft won't do. I drafted letter to Winant agreeing in principle, making certain reserves and proposing publicity with a new joint draft. Gave it to Ashley [Clarke], who hadn't been through it with his fine toothcomb till 6.10, when I sent it to A. at Cabinet, and got it back soon after approved. He will give it to Winant at 8. Really our Departments rather overdo the caution and meticulous. It may be a fault on the right side, but it's sometimes a blunder on the wrong! Hit and miss is sometimes better then holding one's fire.

Friday, 9 October

Cabinet at 7, which I had to attend as A was away, about 'manacling' prisoners [of war, as a riposte to German reprisals against Allied prisoners]. Cabinet have made fools of themselves, as they didn't

* The three countries signed Treaties on 11 Jan. 1943 which abolished extraterritorial rights and other concessions of Britain and the United States in China.

come clean about the 'tying up' order and they didn't consult the Dominions. P.M. away so everyone could ramble, and they did, till 8. The Attlee rang up P.M. to give him their 'conclusions' and get his consent, which wasn't got until 8.15.

Monday, 12 October

Cabinet 10.30 (p.m.) to discuss 'shackling' of prisoners. P.M. just back from Edinburgh in a silly fighting mood. On A.'s instructions I timidly put up suggestion for appeal to Protecting Power. To my surprise, it went, and we drafted statement for P.M. in House to-morrow.

[This statement contradicted the one which the Prime Minister had just made in Edinburgh, for in effect it offered a truce, in respect of the shackling of prisoners, to the Germans. As Churchill used to say, 'I have often had to eat my words, and I confess that I have always found it a wholesome diet.']

Tuesday, 13 October

Had to mug up question of coloured U.S. troops for Cabinet at 12. Wild discussion there. Everyone spoke at once while P.M. read papers (a formality he had omitted). Discussion was on a low level, e.g. Bobbety tried to impress Cabinet with *his* (Colonial) difficulties. Said black official at C.O. had always lunched at a certain restaurant which now, because it was patronised by U.S. Officers, kept him out. P.M. said 'That's all right: if he takes a banjo with him they'll think he's one of the band'! I with difficulty slipped my piece in. No one took any notice, but the eventual solution was quite sensible.

Wednesday, 14 October

Winant 4.30 about extraterritoriality. I gave him our reply to read, and he scrutinized it so carefully and so slowly that it was 5.15 before he finished. I had to go to Cabinet at 5.30 so sent him up to A. and told Ashley to stand by. Smuts at Cabinet. He is a wonderful old boy —fresh as new paint. P.M. welcomed him effusively and he replied. Then we started on usual business. In connexion with C.I.G.S.'s report, P.M. asked Smuts to say something about prospects in Egypt. He gave us a long, lucid, balanced exposition—quite admirably. The upshot was optimistic—I hope not unduly so.

Thursday, 15 October

A. told me result of his interview with Maisky. Latter denies all indiscretions and stoutly denies that he is being moved to Stockholm.

(On Monday Brendan [Bracken] told me that X had told him that M. had told him (X) that he was going! What *is* one to believe? The Russians are doing a lot of lying, but I can't think *why*.)

Friday, 16 October

A's doctor says he mustn't see people, or talk. (He's going to Chequers tonight for a party with Smuts, which will go on till 3 a.m.!) He had been going to see the Turk and dress him down about chrome.* So asked me to do it. Turk couldn't come till 3, so we shall have to make late start. . . . Turk was quite punctual. Dealt with him.

Monday, 19 October

12.30 talk with A. and others about the de Gaulle hitch (he has sacked Dejean for agreeing with us about Syria). . . . 5.30 Cabinet. A. not there, as he was off to Bomber Command for the night. P.M. asked me what I thought about France! Not easy to improvise on that subject! John Anderson was holding forth about something, and Smuts said to me 'Is that Andrew Duncan?'! . . . Smuts confined to me that a weekend at Chequers was 'like a tornado'!

Tuesday, 20 October

Americans have rejected most of our amendments to China Treaty and are going to present draft to Chinese tomorrow or next day! Really, their behaviour is most cavalier! . . . 4 talk with A. and a large party about our amendments to China Treaty. Think most of our amendments are rather exaggerated. Beckett† an excitable stickler. Washed most of them out. 5 long discussion of reply to P.Q.‡ for tomorrow about mischievous and impertinent Soviet suggestion that Hess should be tried at once! As Hess was in jug here while Russians were German accomplices, Russians ought logically to be put in the dock with him! Succeeded in retaining in draft reply a nasty cut at the Russians.

[On 14 October, the Russian Government demanded the trial of all war criminals already in Allied hands. *Pravda*, on 19 October, stated that the British, in taking the view that Hess should not stand trial until the end of the war, was ignoring his crimes and providing a refuge for gangsters. Eden complained vigorously to Maisky on the 20th and said in Parliament

* Which Turkey was supplying to Germany.

† Sir W. E. Beckett, 2nd Legal Adviser, F.O., 1929–45.

‡ A Question in the House of Commons.

that British proposals for the establishment of a United Nations Commission for the investigation of war crimes had been accepted by all governments except that of Russia. Hess would be treated like any other war prisoner, and would not be brought to trial now.

On Eden's instructions, Clark Kerr tried to discover from Stalin and Molotov on 5 November the root of Russian suspicions. Stalin began to study the *Pravda* article during this interview, but 'dropped it like a hot potato'. He said he wanted the British and Russian Governments to agree. Hess did not merit 'all this trouble'. Stalin had genuinely feared, the Ambassador surmised, that Britain intended to send Hess back to Germany.[2]]

Wednesday, 21 October

Had to attend Pacific War Council at 6. Review by P.M. (they hadn't met since May!) but no business done.

Thursday, 22 October

6.30 talk with A. and others about the China Treaties. Americans really have bounced us over this, and behaved v. badly. A. had stormy talk with Maisky this morning about Hess. I gave him beforehand my explanation of inexplicable Russian attitude. Apparently Maisky admitted it was 'partly' correct.

Saturday, 24 October

Chen* at 11, whom I told of American presentation of draft Treaty in Chungking today. Told him we should be presenting a similar one in a day or two.

Sunday, 25 October

News from Egypt seems all right, but no signs of decisive blow—suppose one can't expect that.†

Monday, 26 October

Cabinet 5.30. Telegrams from Alexander, who seems satisfied. Nothing seems to have gone frightfully wrong yet. Nearly 1,500 prisoners. Some discussion as to what to do about Soviet propaganda re Hess, and I shall have to produce a review of the whole Hess episode! Russians are beastly. Maisky was at lunch today and rushed up to A. on arrival, without a word about Egypt or anything else, and said something 'very serious' had happened. Two ships (American) had been ordered from Iceland to discharge here. A. rightly said that Americans gave instructions to their own ships.‡

* Dr Chen Wei-cheng of the Chinese Embassy.

† The Second Battle of Alamein opened on 23 October.

‡ The P.Q. convoys assembled in Iceland before sailing to Russia.

Tuesday, 27 October

Fine but cold. Ban on Central Heating lifted yesterday, so I sent message to Gwatkin asking for a little warmth. Pipes became scarcely tepid by about 7.30 p.m. . . . 5. Alba,* to whom I gave a retort to the ridiculous remark in the paper which he gave me the other day, to the effect that the Spanish Government thought there was no fundamental difference between the 2 belligerents. We shall broadcast (not literally) this exchange to U.S. and Soviet and perhaps others.

Wednesday, 28 October

Talk with A. and others at 12.30 about Russia. Decided to give Russians a pretty hard crack about their Hess performance. A. persuaded P.M. about representations to Russia, but gave me draft to shorten—Departments are *fearfully* diffuse. . . . No great news from Egypt. We were told not to expect it. But, with our superiority, I confess I had expected a *little* more. R.A.F. have established supremacy, but I *do* want to see our *Army* do something good.

Thursday, 29 October

'C' showed me a lot of what looks like good news of Egypt. 7.10 called to Cabinet, who were discussing remonstrance to Stalin about Hess propaganda. We practically got our draft through. It was left to me to put it in shape. . . . Must give up weekend with A. away and P.M. in London in a state of over-excitement.

Friday, 30 October

Maisky at 3.30 to enquire about our negotiations with Swedes. As he was leaving I asked if he was going to be in London this weekend. He said 'No' and, smiling, 'because I shall have to be here *next* weekend.'† I said I hoped it would prove to be an edifying one, and he, still smiling, said 'I hope so.' Very odd in view of his recent attitude. . . . Much warmer, so they've put the heating on full.

Sunday, 1 November

Egypt seems all right, but I don't like the look of the German reinforcement programme. It's difficult for them: but they are wonders at doing marvels. I wonder whether we pressed on hard enough!

* 17th Duke of Alba, Spanish Ambassador, 1939–45.

† That is, the time laid down for the Allied invasion of North Africa, 'Torch'.

Monday, 2 November

Meeting with A. and others about his idea of visiting U.S. (which he ought to do). But letters and telegrams from Halifax don't encourage it in the near future. This largely because latter seems to think P.M. will be going soon. But I don't think he will: his doctors have definitely said that he oughtn't to do any more of this flying! Cabinet 5.30. No very definite news. Alexander seems confident and a pretty big battle seems to have been joined. Sinkings for Oct. 570,000 tons. Pretty bad, and the U-boats have got into another convoy. Poor Edward [Halifax]'s second son Peter killed in Egypt. Killed so far reported about 1,700. We have taken about 1,300 German prisoners and 1,900 Italians. I *hope* it's going to be all right, but I begin to have nasty doubts. We never seem to have any *surprises* for the Germans—or feints. . . . The gallant French generals, when hearing how near the [North African] operation was, have cold feet and ask for 3 weeks' delay. I *hope* this has been refused.

[In mid-October, the British Government received secret messages from Admiral Darlan, Commander-in-Chief of the French Forces, and General Giraud, who had escaped in a spectacular fashion from prison in Germany and was living in Southern France, then unoccupied. Each asked for the supreme command of the rumoured American expedition to North Africa; each claimed that he could rally the French troops there. As Admiral Darlan had given away British naval secrets to the Germans, helped Rashid Ali's rebellion in Iraq, tried to arrange for French merchantmen to bear supplies to Rommel and generally identified himself in every way with the policy of collaboration, there was no desire in London to make any kind of terms with him. Giraud, however, was contacted and, in early November, brought to Gibraltar by submarine and aeroplane. He imagined still that the command of the expedition would be his, and talked also of landings in Southern France. For forty-eight hours General Dwight D. Eisenhower, who had been appointed Allied Commander-in-Chief, North Africa, had to argue doughtily.

As matters turned out, all these arrangements came to nothing, for the moment anyhow. When Giraud arrived in Algiers he found that no French commander would recognise his authority; for by chance Admiral Darlan happened to have come to North Africa to see his son in hospital. He had seniority, and carried something of the mystique of Marshal Pétain. Under American pressure, Darlan ordered a cease-fire and 'in the name of the Marshal' assumed authority in French North Africa. Thereby the Allies took without further opposition Morocco, Algeria and most of Tunisia.

Experience at Dakar and in Syria had indicated that the Allies would do better in North Africa if there were no Fighting French contingent in the expeditionary force. On the insistence of Roosevelt, Churchill did not break the news to de Gaulle until the first landings had taken place.]

Tuesday, 3 November

'C' had news, which he 'phoned me this morning, which certainly seems to show Rommel is in a fix. I am *inclined* to think that R. cries 'wolf' to get more help sent him. But this certainly looks good. . . . Meeting with A., who appears to have had difficult Cabinet this morning about 'Atlantic Co-operation'. P.M. of course excited about Egyptian news, and his excitement took the not unexpected form of 'Damn Europe: we'll be strong enough to go our own way.' Discussion seems to have been complicated by introduction of '4-Power' paper, though that was not yet officially before the Cabinet.

[The '4-Power paper' is a brief description of proposals for the post-war world which the Foreign Office were examining. Its gist was that the highest political power would reside in a Council of the U.S., Russia, Britain and China, with regional organisations in Europe, the Far East and the Middle East. On this the Prime Minister minuted:

> It sounds very simple to pick out these four big Powers. We cannot however tell what sort of a Russia and what kind of Russian demands we shall have to face. . . . I cannot regard the Chungking Government as representing a great world-power. Certainly there would be a faggot-vote on the side of the United States in any attempt to liquidate the British overseas Empire.
>
> I must admit that my thoughts rest primarily in Europe. . . . It would be a measureless disaster if Russian barbarianism overlaid the culture and independence of the ancient States of Europe. Hard as it is to say now, I trust that the European family may act unitedly as one under a Council of Europe.

The War Cabinet, on 27 November, generally accepted the principle of Four-Power co-operation, with China as one of the Four, and decided not to make proposals at that time about the World Council or regional arrangements.[3]]

Wednesday, 4 November

'C' at 4. Good news from Egypt, and an excellent telegram from Alexander. Official announcements still—rightly—very cautious. Giraud coming out tonight—if our arrangements work. Saw A. about telegram to Moscow re Hess. He agreed we'd better 'come clean' about [Lord] Simon having seen Hess. Also disposed to agree to flight over Spain, if necessary, of 20 Hudsons tomorrow night. They are required in Gib. to deal with U-boat concentration.

Thursday, 5 November

Saw A. at 10.30 about flight over Spain. He had mentioned it last night to P.M. and Portal—who didn't know much about it. I said I thought it had been vital, but of course if it wasn't, it was the last thing we wanted to do. A. will fix this. . . . 'C' heard the Giraud affair had been rather muddled (by (a) Americans, and (b) Admiralty) but it really is hoped to get him out tonight. . . . Victory [at Alamein] really seems to have been a smashing one. What an effect this may have all round! 'May God prosper' (as Stalin said) 'Torch'! P.M. v. over-excited. Night before last he sent for 'C' at 11 p.m. About 11.15 he said 'You look v. tired; you'd better go to bed'. 'C' admitted he was, and would. At 2.15 a.m. P.M. rang him up to ask a quite unnecessary question—and then apologised!

Friday, 6 November

Talk with A. about telegrams from S. Hoare concerning representations made to him by Spanish Government who are at last evidently getting worried about 'Torch'. Agreed draft reply for submission to meeting with P.M. and Chiefs of Staff at 12.30. At this meeting (U.S. General Bedell Smith* also there), P.M. v. excited—giving orders for the church bells to be rung on Sunday. In vain we pointed out that the bells were probably rusted up and the ringers all in the Army. That didn't matter. Agreed telegram. Some discussion of the President's silly decision that de Gaulle should be told nothing beforehand. The U.S. General evidently did not agree, but the President's telegram was rather a testy message and can't be ignored, so there it is. Our convoys are through the Straits—Pound produced a chart with the positions marked. . . . I *hope* our part in 'Torch' is now all tidied up. Egyptian news very good—I hope bell-ringing will be justified: I think so.

[A good deal evidently depended on the attitude of the Spaniards. Even in February Hoare had been able to report that despite weighty German propaganda, the disasters in the Far East, and the failure of the Libyan offensive, Spanish feeling was more anti-German than ever before. For some time the Germans had operated detection-posts near the Straits of Gibraltar. When it came to the notice of the British Intelligence services that they were preparing to instal radar and infra-red apparatus on Spanish territory, just west of the Bay of Gibraltar, Hoare waited at once on General Franco, whom he delicately reminded that petrol, for the supply of which Spain depended on the goodwill of the Allies, must have been used in the construction of these buildings. Soon afterwards Admiral Canaris, head of the Abwehr, who had close connexions with Spain and prided himself on his special influence there, was told to remove these

* Chief of Staff, Allied Forces, North African and Italian campaigns, 1942–4.

agents and dismantle the station. When Sir R. Campbell made similar protests at Lisbon against the performances of Axis agents, the Portuguese Minister said with a straight face that it would be so much better if warring powers would eschew espionage and concentrate entirely on counter-espionage!

As the appointed date for 'Torch' drew near, General Jordana, the Spanish Foreign Minister, made no great trouble about the accumulation of forces. A completely successful deception plan was practised upon the Germans and Italians, who expected a renewed assault upon Dakar and concentrated some forty submarines accordingly in the vicinity of the Azores. The convoys of troops entered the Straits of Gibraltar undetected on the night of 5 November.

When the landings took place, on the coasts of Morocco and Algeria, Hoare had satisfactory interviews with Franco and Jordana. The feeling was growing, he told Churchill, that Franco would resist any German demands for passage through Spain. 'I have . . . never ceased dinning it into the heads of official and unofficial Spaniards that, first, we are now overwhelmingly strong and secondly, we have no sinister intentions against Spain.'[4]]

Saturday, 7 November

Lunched in F.O. with A., who has had a slight relapse of his cold. [The Viceroyalty of] India has apparently been suggested to him—Bobbety to replace him. He seems toying with idea. I tried to dissuade him. After lunch went over with him to Admiralty War Room to see charts of 'Torch' development. All good and up to time. One transport torpedoed, but floating all right and will soon be in tow. . . . 5.30 to Soviet Embassy, where there were 10,000 people. But as about 9,900 came from Whitechapel, Hoxton and Limehouse, I didn't know many of them, and fled. . . . About 7 got the code message to say 'Torch' is on, at 1 a.m. Giraud got to Gib. yesterday.

Sunday, 8 November

Not much news yet. P.M. hears that [Admiral] Darlan* is under 'protective arrest' in N. Africa, but I don't know where he got this from. . . . Apparently we got ashore near Algiers and near Oran, although there was some 'trouble' in the latter port. Situation at Casablanca unclear. French naval units seem to have gone out to fight us. . . . Giraud is all right, and has broadcast. De Gaulle lunched with P.M. A. there. De G., surprisingly, took the right line: Free French must not split—he will serve under Giraud. . . . Not much news on broadcast. De G. has given a good talk. Hitler has made a

* Now Vice-President of the Council, Vichy Government.

speech—ridiculous, containing only wild threats of air reprisal on Britain. Egypt seems to be going well. Can't make out yet whether Germans mean to stand at Tobruk. But what with, anyhow? Hope things are all right—think so.

Monday, 9 November

Smuts at Cabinet was, rightly, very insistent on importance of Tunis, without which rest of Africa is not much use. And I can't make out that we're yet doing anything very effective about it.

Tuesday, 10 November

Hear that Darlan has signed armistice covering all N. Africa. Papers say we are in Oran. Fighting, apparently, still round Casablanca. Talk with A., who agrees to help de Gaulle to get in touch with Giraud. Think we should now help de G. all we can—seeing he has played up well.

Wednesday, 11 November

A. with a temperature, in bed. Cripps asked me to see him. Obviously wanted to take A's place in the House tomorrow and to make a speech on international affairs that would, as he put it, 'go round the world'. With advice from A., took steps to contrive to scotch this! . . . Germans are occupying rest of France—and Corsica. I don't think we mind either much. Africa looks better. Armistice signed covering all N. Africa, including Tunisia. Germans have got some air into T. but I hope we're now pressing on from Algiers. If we don't get Tunisia, we haven't got much. So next day or two will be critical. Casablanca seems all right now. Fog bad this evening, and Loxley* and I had to navigate our way home on foot with torches. Dined at home. No work—this is a condition that is becoming pleasantly frequent. P.M. seems to have made a good speech in the House. v[on] Thoma, hearing three Italian Generals were to put in with them, begged that this should not be so, or that, if it must, barbed wire should be put up between him and them. Meanwhile, the three Italian Generals, hearing that they might be put in with v. Thoma, begged that they should be spared this!

Thursday, 12 November

A. still in bed. Went to see him with draft telegram to Mack† warning of danger of playing in too much with Darlan. If Darlan

* Peter Loxley, now Cadogan's Principal Private Sec.

† W. H. B. Mack, now British Civil Liaison Officer to Allied C.-in-C. (Eisenhower), N. Africa.

would give us fleet and Tunisia, I should be very grateful—and then throw him down a deep well. . . . Read Chiefs of Staff paper on future strategy and wrote something rather critical of it for A. As I said, it is rather a view from a War Office window than a view of Allied Strategy. They are very mouse-like people.

Friday, 13 November

8th Army have turned German retreat into a rout, I think. Tobruk taken today. N. Africa hopelessly obscure. Americans are playing with Darlan, Noguès,* Giraud and Juin†! What a party! Telegraphed to Mack to try and find out what *is* going on. On military side, things seem to go all right, but I shan't be happy until we get to Tunis and Bizerta. . . .

After dinner Strang rang me up to say that Pleven‡ had told him that *Vichy* had put out, through Darlan and Noguès, announcement that Darlan had taken over in N. Africa and ending with 'Vive la Maréchal! Vive la France!' Apparently alleged that this has American endorsement! I told S. to tell A., and to say that this leaves me completely bewildered. Where are we? And what is going on? We have *no* news from Mack. De Gaulle can *never* work with that crowd.

Saturday, 14 November

An awful tangle in N. Africa. Eisenhower and Cunningham§ have made agreement with Darlan, Giraud, Noguès, Juin. *What* a party! A. and P.M. still seem to take this lightly. P.M. has telegraphed to Eisenhower 'Anything for the battle. Politics will have to be sorted out later.' That's all right, but will they be? Talk with A. and others about 'getting Italy out of the war'. This, as much as 'getting Turkey into the War' (P.M.'s pet scheme), a complete chimaera. So we told A., who left for Chequers at 12. . . . Rang up A., and gave him such news as we had. He agreed we might telegraph to Mack asking for a *little* more news. Also read him statement that de G. wants to put out. He said de G. mustn't. I said I and Charles Peake would do our best. . . . C.P. at 4.45. Coached him for his talk with de Gaulle at 5.15. Masses of work. C.P. at 7. to report. The Americans

* C. A. A. P. Noguès, French Res.-Gen. in Morocco.

† Gen. A. P. Juin, C.-in-C. French forces in N. Africa since Nov. 1941; C.-in-C. French forces in the Tunisian Campaign, 1942–3.

‡ René Pleven, member of the French National Committee.

§ Naval C.-in-C. for 'Torch'.

and naval officers in Algiers are letting us in for a *pot* of trouble. We shall do no good till we've killed Darlan.*

Had to walk home in fog (physical and spiritual).

Sunday, 15 November

Long telegram in from Eisenhower explaining why it is necessary to make a compact with the Devil—Darlan. Well, it may have been, but this is going to present us with awful problems, and is dirty. . . . Spoke to A. at Chequers on telephone and made him read Eisenhower's telegram. He was *rather* horrified—not sufficiently. He rang me up later to give me text of a telegram P.M. was sending to President—rather on lines of his telegram to Eisenhower of yesterday. A. tells me he and P.M. are thinking of sending me out—partly to sort out this tangle—which is inextricable—and partly to be at their elbow to restrain them [from] doing stupid things in regard to broadcasts to Italy &c. I don't think I can do anything on the first, and as regards the second, would that mean by being stuck in Algiers or Gib. indefinitely? I'm not convinced of the utility of this and must discuss it with A. tomorrow. . . . Charles Peake at 4.15. Gave him his marching orders for his interview with de G. Latter must hold his temper until he has seen A. or P.M. tomorrow. He got back from Gen. de G. about 7.30—to Travellers' [Club], where I picked him up. Told A. and got his authority to put a stop on de G., in case latter, spurred on by Pleven, breaks out tonight. . . . I wish these crises wouldn't always happen when the P.M. is in Bucks and the S. of S. motoring from Bucks to Sussex. It's *not* the way to do business.

Monday, 16 November

A. didn't arrive till about 12.30. Saw him at once and impressed on him—if that were necessary—all the disadvantages and dangers of a pact with Darlan. He went off before 1 for an interview, with P.M., with de G. I went over to No. 10 with him at 12.50, and left before de G. was shown in. . . . Back 2.45 and saw A. He said interview had gone off fairly well. De G. said he could have no part nor lot in this. P.M. said that was right and that de G. was in an easier position than most of us. Discussed with A. suggestion that I should go out. I said I was ready to go anywhere, and do anything, but should rather like to know, before starting, what I was supposed to do. I can't get them out of the present tangle which, for military reasons, they *accept, temporarily*. If I am to *stay* at Eisenhower's elbow, that raises other questions, which he must decide. If anything, I thought *he*

* This is not, of course, to be read literally; see the entry for 30 Dec.

ought to go to *Washington*. . . . Another talk with A. before Cabinet at 6. Drafted message from P.M. to President cautioning that any agreement with Darlan must be only *temporary*. At Cabinet, P.M. reviewed situation. No-one very excited. Smuts thought that Eisenhower, in the circumstances, had done right. P.M. would not consider A.'s draft. No doubt they will discuss that later tonight. Nothing further about *my* movements! Got away 7.45. Dined at home. There's a Defence Committee tonight, and I may know more tomorrow morning. It's a bore not knowing to what part of the globe one may be catapulted next day. What would Crowe* have thought of it?!

[Churchill telegraphed the President about the depth of feeling stirred in Britain by the arrangement with Darlan, who had 'an odious record'. It should be 'a temporary expedient, justifiable solely by the stress of battle'. On 17 November Roosevelt put out a public statement confirming this view and approving the sentiment that no permanent agreement should be made with Darlan.]

Tuesday, 17 November

X† (but I don't know that he's reliable) says Americans have been playing with Darlan all the time. I wouldn't put it past them. But if it could be proved, I would have a God Almighty show-down with them. . . . Libya still goes well, cleaning up the rout. Tunisia is rather a question-mark. But my inside information seems to show that the Axis are not too comfortable there, *yet*; if only we can get on quick enough, in sufficient force.

Wednesday, 18 November

Having messages from all my sleuths that I am going out to Gib—went and saw A. and asked him what it was all about. Bedell Smith has been very busy suggesting to P.M. that I should go. Pretends Eisenhower wants it. A. said P.M. was rather doubtful about it. A. rang up Winant (who advised telling Washington) and B. Smith, who confirmed that Eisenhower wanted conference in Gib on Saturday. A. went off to Cabinet at 12, and I got a message from him saying P.M. *did* favour my going. Telegram drafted to President. This means my leaving tomorrow night and coming back, if conditions favourable, on Sunday. Had some talk with Strang about the line to take.

* Sir Eyre Crowe, P.U.S., F.O., 1920–5.

† A French source, not the 'X' referred to earlier. It is not clear what Cadogan meant by 'all the time'. Most accounts date American contacts with Darlan from about 8 Nov., when he had already been in Algiers three days.

Thursday, 19 November

Heard . . . that Bedell Smith now has doubts about my going out with him and had put them to P.M. who seemed to share them. Told A., and observed that I am not going out if P.M. has any doubts about it. I may be a mug, but I'm not such a fool as that. Later, copy of telegram from President arrived. He also seems doubtful. That put the lid on it. Went with A. to see P.M. at 12.30. P.M. asked me if I wanted to go. I said that wasn't the question: did *he* want me to go? He said he thought it might be 'premature'. I said in that case I must obviously wait, and we sent off a telegram to President saying I *wasn't* going. Rang up T. and cancelled all arrangements. (I had always smelt a doubt about this, and had made no arrangements myself!) . . . Rather glad I'm not in the train! There really is nothing much for me to do with *Eisenhower*. He would produce all his (perfectly good) military reasons. President has now announced that the arrangement with Darlan is only provisional and local. It remains to settle with *him how* it is to be ended, and then to give instructions to Eisenhower.

Friday, 20 November

Saw A. at 10. He wanted to talk to me about proposed Government changes and appointments. Looks as if he'd stay, but will have to take on Leadership of House, so that there will have to be an Assistant or Deputy S. of S. Understand a 'Protocol' is coming from Eisenhower for our approval. He urges to be authorised to sign at once. . . . Have now got the famous 'Protocol'. The business part is all right, but the preamble amounts to recognising and confirming Darlan as High Commissioner. A. left this morning, so had to ring him up at once. Then began the usual week-end business of discussing with him papers he hadn't seen, and drafts thereon. P.M. (at Chequers!) has seen Protocol and wants to agree it at once! Apparently v. impatient and angry. I don't believe Roosevelt *can* sign it in its present form, in view of his declaration of Nov. 17. Later read A. draft telegram to Washington and discussed it with him. Had it telephoned to Chequers. He and P.M. must fight it out on long-distance line. But I suppose I shall be woken up all night! What a way to do business!

Saturday, 21 November

Luckily a quiet night, and thank goodness a Cabinet fixed for this morning at 12.15. We really can't settle these things on the long-distance telephone. Saw A. at 11.30 on his arrival and primed him.

At Cabinet P.M. read telegram from Joe announcing his offensive. He *says* enemy line breached on a 22 km. front. Then we got down to the argument about N. Africa. P.M.'s line was 'You can't pull this man (Eisenhower) about while he's fighting a battle,' and he of course summoned C.I.G.S. in his support. But that's all agreed. Point is that Pres., as appears from his message this morning, has the same misgivings as we have about the Protocol, and we only want to help him with suggestions as to *how* to get out of it. P.M. battled most unfairly, and in the end we could only get him to agree to message to Pres., saying we share his views, particularly that agreement should not be in the form of Protocol or diplomatic document. Fact is Darlan has bluffed and diddled U.S. and U.K. P.M. ended with a tirade against de G. 'He has been battening on us and is capable of turning round and fighting with the Axis against us'. That is just untrue. Tiresome he may be, but sound on essentials. Find this was all due to de G's lunch at No. 10. Clemmie had asked him whether French fleet would come over. He at once answered 'Certainly not'. She (innocent soul) took this to mean de G. thought it *oughtn't* to. What he really meant was 'That blighter Darlan will never give it to you'.... Back at F.O. 3.30. A. off to the country again! Had approved draft broadcast by de G. for this evening. P.M. sent for me at 4.15 and said broadcast was disgraceful and must be stopped. I argued uselessly. Commissioned C. Peake to put stopper on the Gen.—which he did. P.M. reshuffling his Cabinet, which makes him excitable. Cripps to leave War Cabinet and take Aircraft Production. A. to lead House. Law* for India! Who is to help with F[oreign] A[ffairs]?! *Masses* of work. Dined at home and worked.

Sunday, 22 November

Addis† rang up about 7 to say there was a message from Darlan, sent through Allied H.Q., to all French diplomats abroad, announcing that he has taken (with the muzzled Marshal [Pétain's] consent) military and *administrative* control of the French *Empire*!! He *is* a Card! Told Addis to sit on the message and draft one to Washington, for the President, observing that this seems in conflict with the latter's statement that any arrangement with Darlan was purely *local*. Rang up A., who agreed. Darlan has made *rings* round Eisenhower and old mother Cunningham! What a man! Cabinet changes announced tonight—Cripps M[inister of] A[ircraft]

* Richard K. Law, Parl. Under-Sec. of State, F.O., 1941–3. See List of Principal Characters.

† J. M. Addis, 3rd Sec., F.O., 1938; with Allied Force H.Q., Mediterranean, 1942–4.

P[roduction], [Herbert] Morrison to take his place in War Cabinet, Bobbety Privy Seal, Oliver Stanley* C[olonial] O[ffice]! Nothing about F.O., or Law.

[Darlan's message showed that he interpreted Roosevelt's 'temporary' to mean 'until the liberation of France is complete', and that he regarded himself as holding his authority from Marshal Pétain.]

Monday, 23 November

Cabinet 5.30. No definite news from Tunisia. Our pursuit of Rommel must pause for a bit. Russian counter-offensive round Stalingrad seems good. On all fronts, we have shot down a vast number of Axis planes in the last week. (C.-in-C. Bomber Command is bored because 'Italian towns don't burn as well as German—too much marble and stuff'!). P.M. had just received a telegram saying Eisenhower had signed a 'Protocol', modified. He apologised to A. A. said 'I don't blench'. P.M. said 'I don't blush'. . . . Darlan has 'brought over' Dakar. But where to?!

Tuesday, 24 November

Met A. in Park and asked what we were to do about F.O. work now that he was leading the House. He said we could go on as before. But we can't! He leaves London lunch-time Fri.: gets back lunch-time Mon., and will now have to spend Tues., Wed. and Thurs. in the House. Quite impossible! Darlan situation where it was. He is now 'Emperor of the French'. Washington say we can let Darlan's message (Nov. 22) go forth through ordinary commercial channels! I dare say it's all right. . . . Met Nancy Astor. . . . She said we must lunch with her some time. Asked where we were living: had we a cook? I said 'Yes'. She said 'Oh well then, I'd better lunch with you!'

Wednesday, 25 November

Saw A. for a moment about 6.30—this arrangement under which he leads the House can't last for very long.

[Darlan's appeals that the French Fleet should cross to North Africa had been ignored. The Germans planned to seize the vessels, but were thwarted. On 27 November, 73 ships were scuttled by French officers in Toulon.]

* He had been out of office since he left the War Office on the fall of Chamberlain's Government.

Sunday, 29 November

Winston broadcasting at 9. Quite good—sober jubilation—no rash promises. News still seems good—Russians must, I think, be doing well. There may be a battle at Agheila, but we already know something about that from our 'best source'. I am only rather puzzled about Tunisia: hope it's all right.

Monday, 30 November

Cabinet 5.30. Not v. much news. Sinkings not *quite* so bad. . . .

Some discussion of future plans. P.M. had an outburst which seemed to show that he had come round to offensive in the West next year. I asked A. what it meant, but he said he was 'bewildered'. Russian news continues good.

Saturday, 5 December

Every sort of flap about Eisenhower's 'negotiations with Boisson'.* These generally take the form of the Vichy French telling the Americans what they want, and the Americans giving it to them with both hands regardless of our interests or feelings. A. of course in the uttermost region of Sussex, and the P.M. *might* be reached (somewhere in the N. of England) by field telephone about 12.45 p.m. *What* a way to do business! If the Foreign Sec. must consult the P.M. on day-to-day, or minute-to-minute, business, they really ought to stay together.

Monday, 7 December

A. arrived about 12 and I saw him about the silly P.M. broadcast to Hong Kong and Malaya. I don't think he'd read what I'd wrote him, but told me he approved and would I settle it. That's the way business is done nowadays. . . . Cabinet 5. Not much news, except that Tunisia goes v. badly. Sinkings less bad. A snap decision at the end to unshackle prisoners. Everyone talking at once, whispering and passing notes. I was told to take the necessary action. Not easy, but drafted a telegram to Berne, which I showed A. after. He took it to P.M.

Tuesday, 8 December

Swiss appeal about shackling has now come in. They ask us not to reply before 12th—to avoid appearance of collusion. This is silly. . . . Picked up A. in his flat and to Savoy for dinner 8.15. De Gaulle, Catroux and Strang. V. pleasant and quite interesting, but not v.

* Pierre Boisson. Gov.-Gen., French West Africa.

helpful. De G.'s one remedy is 'Get rid of Darlan'. My answer is 'Yes; but how?' No answer.

Monday, 14 December

Cabinet 5.30. Not much of interest. Tunisia not going well, so P.M. on his usual (and to me well-founded) complaint that, out of about 110,000 men there, there are only about 10,000 fighting men. It does seem rather hopeless. Sinkings not quite so bad.

Wednesday, 16 December

Had to go over to House to see A. about this ridiculous declaration Roosevelt has put in the mouth of Darlan—without ever consulting us. We agreed to try to get some changes, but on return found it was already on the Tape! We *must* try to get some Supreme Allied Council. I put that up to A. yesterday. I don't know how it can be done, but there's no other cure. At present our policy is not being directed by State Department, but *by Gen. Marshall*!*

Thursday, 17 December

Thank Heaven that rotten Parliament have adjourned, so we may be able to get down to some work. Americans butting in in Djibouti and bogging our negotiations. This, with their performances in N. Africa, China and probably Italy, shows that we must, as I have proposed, devise some sort of *political* liaison. Will talk to A. about that tomorrow. Good news from Libya: we seem to have cut into Rommel's force.

Friday, 18 December

Cardinal and Apostolic Delegate, have message from Italian Government that Musso, High Command and Military Staff will leave Rome if we won't bomb it! This great fun! We know Germans are trying to stop it. If they succeed, they will have the responsibility and we can make oceans of bad blood! Devised telegram to Washington, as proposal has been put to Americans and we must stop them doing anything foolish.

Monday, 21 December

Americans are being obstructive and silly about Rome evacuation. Cabinet agreed to send them a sensible telegram.

* U.S. Chief of Staff.

Tuesday, 22 December

It took two Office Keepers to carry in my boxes! Home at 8 and worked hard after dinner. My appeal for brevity useless and during Christmas I shall forge a thunderbolt. People are becoming worse and worse.

Wednesday, 23 December

3. talk with A., Law and O. Harvey on trips. Evidently A. not wanted on P.M.'s possible trip. Law inclined to advise him to gate-crash. I advised *against*, but I think he ought to do a trip on his own as soon as may be.

Friday, 25 December *Thatched Cottage*

Very good lunch—soup, chicken and plum pudding—with brandy butter made of my best '78! Then I felt I must get some exercise. Walked along Hastings road till turning to Robertsbridge, then doubled back left to Beckley and so home. At 3 o'clock, as I passed a cottage, I heard the King's voice and stopped to listen. Heard almost every word of his broadcast. . . . News today of Darlan's assassination. If order is maintained in N. Africa, this may be a blessing.

Saturday, 26 December *Thatched Cottage*

After the news this evening an awful American . . . did a broadcast about Darlan. Seemed to be devoted to trying to prove America had not backed the wrong horse (which they did), without any regard to Allied interests. I *must* keep my temper with Americans, but it's going to be a hard job!

Sunday, 27 December

Seems that Giraud will succeed Darlan. De Gaulle affects to regret Darlan's demise, as he says that latter was making him (de G.) numberless converts!

[At Eisenhower's instance, Giraud now became High Commissioner for French North and West Africa, and Commander-in-Chief, Civil and Military.]

Monday, 28 December

3. discussion of Chinese demand for termination of lease of New Territories. Decided to recommend to stand pat and do no more than admit that discussion may take place after the war. We are on perfectly firm ground. Cabinet 5.30. P.M. gloomy—on account of

Tunis. There, we are going through our usual teething trouble of incompetent command and organisation, and it looks v. bad. Cabinet heartily endorsed decision to stand pat on New Territories, and P.M. gave impassioned speech (which cheered him up) on those people who got up each morning asking themselves how much more of the Empire they could give away. Americans object to H[arold] Macmillan's appointment,* but P.M. has sent pretty sharp riposte. N. Africa seems quite quiet, and Frenchmen getting together—which shows how wrong Americans were in saying that only Darlan could rally N. Africa. Americans becoming impossible at all points, and are lecturing us now on Persia, about which they know nothing. I urge that we should put our foot down *now*—it will only be more difficult and more dangerous later.

Wednesday, 30 December

5.30 went to see Pound to arrange telegram to Cunningham authorising him to deny charges that Secret Service was in any way connected with Darlan murder.

Thursday, 31 December

We're certainly in a very different position from what we were a year ago. There's a light at the end of the tunnel, but I can't see an exit yet. Thank God, T. and the family well. T. remains a solid rock, and looks after me and sustains me. God bless us all in 1943.

1943

Friday, 1 January

Nothing much doing. A silly, ill-informed and ill-natured article on the Foreign Service in the 'Times'. . . . A. rang up about it, and said he would talk to J. Astor.† . . . Hear Astor has said he has told Casey‡ (in charge of 'Times') to send Philip Graves to see me about the continuation of article in tomorrow's issue. . . . No sign of P. Graves so, about 7, rang up Casey. He (whom I don't know) seems to be quite silly (or dishonest). Anyhow Graves wasn't instructed to come here. In that case, I said, could 2nd article be held up. He promised to ring me later, which eventually he did do—at 7.45—to say he had arranged postponement.

* As Minister Resident at Allied H.Q., N.W. Africa.
† J. J. Astor, Chief Proprietor of *The Times*, 1922–66.
‡ W. F. Casey, Deputy Editor of *The Times*, 1941–8.

[This article alleged that the organisation of the Office still bore the imprint of the nineteenth century, with the result that newer aspects—particularly those of economics, finance and propaganda—were neglected. Relations between the F.O. and P.W.E. and the foreign services of the B.B.C. represented awkward compromises, while the Ministry of Information and M.E.W. stood formally independent of the F.O., leaving it in control only of the antiquated machinery of diplomacy.

The sequel, published on 4 January, pointed to an absence of planning in foreign policy, neglected in the organisation of the Foreign Office. But the change in Britain's status required a departure from the empirical approach of trying to ensure that no single state was stronger than Britain, the diplomacy of the 'two-power standard'. The F.O., too enmeshed in its own traditions, could not provide this organ for planning, which should embrace all the appropriate departments, be analogous to a Ministry of Defence co-ordinating the Services, and relieve the Foreign Secretary of many departmental and administrative functions.]

Saturday, 2 January

Saw Ridsdale about the 'Times' worry. He agreed with me that we'd better do no more about it now. I got A. to accept this. But how badly the 'Times' office is run . . . an article about our Service, cutting across the proposals which A. has on the stocks, and it's not even *shown* to the Diplomatic Correspondent, [Iverach] McDonald, who is horrified. . . . About 6 Pleven turned up with a statement de Gaulle wants to publish. A stupid move. He is in negotiation with Giraud and he has got impatient and wants to blurt it all out to the Press. I asked whether de Gaulle despaired of negotiations. Pleven said No. I said I asked because this was the sort of statement that might be put out by someone who had. I begged him to urge the General at least to postpone it: his last message to Giraud was only sent yesterday morning. Rang up A., who endorsed this and I passed on his message. But the reply came that the General had reflected long and was determined to publish in tomorrow's morning press. Told A., who was annoyed, but there it is. I wouldn't muzzle de G. now and (inevitably) let the Press know we were muzzling him. But A. said P.M. ought to know. . . .

Pleasant New Year's greetings from wine-merchant, who cut my allowance by more than 50%! However, I've supported no hardship in this war yet! Dined at home—suppose I shall be kept up all night by this de G. affair, tho' I hope A. and P.M. will fight it out between them on the telephone.

[General de Gaulle's statement ascribed the confusion in North Africa to the lack of Fighting France's official representation there, which hampered Allied military operations and then enfeebled resistance in metropolitan France. He proposed the enlargement of the provisional central authority.]

Sunday, 3 January

De G. won, and got his statement in the Press. By that, he's probably done for himself. Got off to A. a draft of a frank telegram to Washington trying to dispel their baleful suspicions about our relations with de G. But nothing will cure them.

Monday, 4 January

3 meeting with A. about shackling of prisoners.* Not v. conclusive, but I think he agrees not to back down entirely before the Germans. He told me, after, that P.M. might send for me to his foreign rendezvous if Free French question arises. When P.M. gets back, A. will go to America and will want me to come with him, (I've already travelled 27,000 miles during this war!). Cabinet 5.30. No great news. We're stuck in Tunisia, and bombing effort has died out, and we have *not* built up our bomber force! Only Russian news good.

Monday, 11 January

Cabinet at 12, as P.M. off later in the day [to the Casablanca Conference]. P.M. more hopeful about N. Africa, though I don't quite see why. Decided to have destructive bombing on the principal French U-boat bases—subject to previous general warning.

[Arrests had been made at the end of December, supposedly in connexion with the murder of Darlan and a plot against Mr Robert Murphy, by Giraud and his deputy. More arrests, made on 12 January, were freely ascribed in the press to the influence of elements hostile to de Gaulle.]

Wednesday, 13 January

12 talk with A. about arrests in N. Africa. He wanting to tell Macmillan that it's all an anti-de Gaulle ramp. Maybe: but I said go easy: I won't guarantee that de Gaullists aren't in the plot, and if Americans can show, or think, that we're trying to shield potential murderers, the Washington-London situation will become much more acute.

Saturday, 16 January

It looks as if we *may* be attacking Rommel. (But fear he's getting

* A British statement of 4 January said that all shackled prisoners in British hands would be unshackled.

away). Raczynski at 12.30 about fresh German drive against Poles in Warsaw. 1,000 new arrests in last 2 days. . . . Was rung up after [dinner] about message from P.M. directing A. to see de Gaulle tomorrow and to pack him off to meeting in Africa with Giraud. Spoke to A. about it. See one difficulty, which we tried to get over by message which I had sent to P.M. Now trying to fix de G. for 12 tomorrow.

Sunday, 17 January

A. arrived about 11.30. Strang and I talked to him about the P.M.'s proposal. De G. arrived at 12 and A. and I saw him. He is a species of mule: he refuses to go, and nothing A. or I could say would move him. He said he would meet Giraud next at Fort Lamy, but he would not meet him in an 'Aréopage Allié'!* We said surely he had sufficient confidence in himself (this nettled him) to hold his own and plead his own good case. What did he expect of any private meeting with Giraud if he turned this down? He said quite bluntly that the solution was for an enlarged National Committee to take over in N. Africa. Giraud could be added to their number and be appointed commander of the forces! Most he would do was promise to reflect, and see us again in the afternoon. He turned up at 5, with Pleven, with a message for the P.M., refusing. We used all our arguments again and expressed our conviction that the results would be most unfortunate. But he wouldn't budge, so we had no alternative but to inform P.M.[5] This, I should think, is the end of the Free French movement. Roosevelt will say to P.M. 'Look at your friend: this is how he behaves.' And Winston will have to agree with him—and shed de G. A *great* pity. But in point of fact, would de G., being what he is, *ever* collaborate with *anyone*?

. . . 145 machines dropped 380 tons of bombs on Berlin last night! They want to give an encore tonight, but I don't know how the weather is.

Monday, 18 January

Hitler evidently annoyed at bombardment of Berlin, as he struck at London with weak forces last night. About 30 machines between 8.30 and 9.30 and 30 more round about 5 a.m. Very noisy barrage. We got 12 down—not too bad. We raided Berlin with the same sort of force as the night before (150 or so) but I fear we lost 22.

Cabinet 11.30 about de G. situation—which they agreed we must leave to stew. . . . 9 p.m. radio announces relief of Leningrad and

* Areopagus, the hill at Athens where the highest judicial court sat.

various other Russian successes. To me it seems that Germans are probably shortening their whole lines.

[Churchill's answer to de Gaulle was despatched from Casablanca on 18 January. In it he pointed out that the invitation to attend the Casablanca Conference came from the President as well as from himself, and that refusal would mean the failure of the Prime Minister's efforts to bridge the gap between de Gaulle and the U.S. Government. 'If he rejects the chance now offered' Churchill telegraphed to Eden, 'I shall feel that his removal from the headship of the Free French Movement is essential to the further support of this movement by H.M.G. . . . For his own sake you ought to knock him about pretty hard.']

Tuesday, 19 January

Received P.M.'s reply to de Gaulle. Pretty hot, but not more than circumstances justify. . . . A. had asked de G. to see him at 3. But de G. 'busy'. . . . 5 Cabinet, to modify P.M.'s message to de G. Soon after 6 Pleven came round to see Strang to say that de Gaulle anticipated P.M.'s message would be sharp, and he couldn't trust himself not to burst out with remarks that he would afterwards regret! What a baby! So we sent him the reply by the hand of Peake, reminding him that time was short and that A. was at his disposal. But it's no use—if he *did* go out there, he'd simply fall foul of everybody.

Wednesday, 20 January

Telegram from P.M. saying he wants to go to Cairo, and then meet Turks. Drafted bits of a reply to him explaining why Turks impossible. Had appointment with A. at the House. Went there and waited. Some tomfools in the House made a scene about a matter of *no* importance, so A. was clamped to the bench. I kicked my heels until 12.45 and then came away. This is really *intolerable*, and making a farce of Parliamentary Government. . . . Saw A. just before 3 and showed him draft. . . . De G. came to see A. and me at 5. He now agrees to go! But if his 'plane can't get off tonight, he will have missed the bus! Cabinet 5.30 to discuss P.M.'s telegram and decide on lines of reply. Everyone against his going to Cairo—but we shall see! Back about 6.15 and drafted message, which I got A. to approve. *Masses* of work had accumulated. Dined at home. A. rang me up to say strings of telegrams in from P.M.—one of which may necessitate Cabinet tonight!

Friday, 22 January

De G. got off last night! Telegram from P.M. agreeing, apparently

—and reluctantly—not to go to Cairo. Drafted reply clinching it. Also, with Strang, drafted a telegram giving estimate of de Gaulle's probable reaction to proposals.

[When de Gaulle at last arrived at Casablanca on 22 January, Churchill spoke sternly to him. The General was unmoved. 'His country has given up fighting,' cried Churchill afterwards, half-angry, half-admiring. 'He himself is a refugee, and if we turn him down he's finished. Well, just look at him! Look at him! He might be Stalin, with 200 divisions behind his words. I was pretty rough with him. I made it quite plain that if he could not be more helpful we were done with him.'

Asked how de Gaulle had taken this, Churchill had to admit 'he hardly seemed interested. My advances and my threats met with no response. England's grievous offence in de Gaulle's eyes' he said after reflection, 'is that she has helped France. He cannot bear to think that she needed help. He will not relax his vigilance in guarding her honour for a single instant.'[6]

Surprisingly, the President's meeting with de Gaulle passed off well. Roosevelt felt attracted by 'the spiritual look in his eyes'. The long-awaited encounter with Giraud proved less satisfactory. For the moment the proposal that the Committee in London and the Imperial Council in Algiers should be fused under their joint leadership could not be realised. By accident, or more probably by Harry Hopkins' skilful stage-management, the two generals were brought together before numerous cameras. They shook hands, with no excess of cordiality.

When Oliver Lyttelton visited the U.S.A. in the previous summer, Roosevelt had given him oral messages for Churchill about plans for the post-war world. The President said that he would be satisfied with nothing but the complete surrender of Germany. Thereupon the Allied armies would apparently march into Germany to smash up weapons heavier than machine guns. An international inspecting force would try to prevent Germany from rearming. Infraction would be punished by 'quarantine' and if necessary, and after warning, by bombing. The Russians, Americans and British would maintain an international force. Others—for instance, France and Poland—would contribute to this force but would not be allowed to recreate armies.[7]

It is clear that the British Government did not expect such questions to be discussed at Casablanca, for neither Eden nor Cadogan was asked to accompany Churchill. On 20 January, however, he asked whether the War Cabinet would think it well to include in the communique

> a declaration of the firm intention of the United States and the British Empire to continue the war relentlessly until we have brought about the 'unconditional surrender' of Germany and Japan. The omission of Italy would be to encourage a break-up there.

This question was considered on that day by the War Cabinet, who replied that Italy too should be included. The Diary does not indicate any consultation with Cadogan; but he would certainly have seen the minutes promptly, and makes no mention of any protest. 'Unconditional surrender' was not, after all, mentioned in the communique. At the Press Conference on 24 January, however, the President said that the allies would enforce it on all their enemies. Churchill thereupon supported him.

Roosevelt probably wished to avoid a conditional surrender of the kind which had had such numerous embarrassments and recriminations after 1919, to heighten the conviction that the allies and their enemies dwelt upon different moral planes, to reassure Stalin, and to satisfy the demand for an explicit statement of war aims.

As Cadogan's diary for 12 August 1943 indicates, he disliked the demand for unconditional surrender. It contains no evidence, however, that he believed that policy to have prolonged the war significantly. After all, there was no lack of other grist for Dr Goebbels' mill. Systematic bombing of German cities, enjoined by a directive at Casablanca, is an example. Any more detailed statement of Allied conditions, as Churchill pointed out to the Cabinet a year later, would hardly be likely to reassure the German people. Both he and Roosevelt denied publicly any intention to enslave them.]

Monday, 25 January

Met by O.S. and O. Harvey who told me of telegrams showing that P.M. is determined on his jaunt. So I suppose I shall have to join him. Cabinet at 12—they capitulated, of course, and agreed to P.M.'s plans.

Tuesday, 26 January

It has been agreed that I should start in afternoon, and then that it might be 1 p.m. Went to F.O. at usual time and was then told, at 11.5, that I must be ready there with my luggage at 12. Said I couldn't be—but was! . . . Arrived Plymouth 2.30 . . . Ascertained that we couldn't start tonight, as our Catalina was still at Stranraer—weatherbound. They might have told us this before we left Hendon! Walked in town to survey damage, which is not quite so impressive as I had expected.

Thursday, 28 January *Malta*

Off ground in a Hudson at 4.30 [a.m.]. Shut up in dark, so I couldn't read, and didn't manage to sleep. When dawn came, we were over a thick cloud-layer. Near Gib, this cleared off, and it was lovely. We landed just before noon and drove to Government House. . . . Malta, arriving about 9. Perfect landing—in fact, in the dark, I didn't realise we had touched down. Met by Station Commander, [Group Captain] Le May, and taken to a dilapidated hut, where we had the usual meal of pink sausage, a soggy bit of toast and some tinned beans. To drink, a battered enamel teapot yielded a fluid alleged to be tea, all ready mixed with reputed milk and sugar. But I must say Le May gave us a whisky and soda after in his hut. We were then given another hut with 2 beds and dirty sheets. The pillow was so black that I dressed it in my shirt. Lay down and got to sleep perhaps before midnight.

Friday, 29 January *Cairo*

Soon after dawn we passed Benghazi, and later came down at El Adem. Very cold, but there was a mobile canteen where we got a cup of hot chocolate. Landed about 12.15 and got to Embassy before 1. Went up to do a superficial wash. P.M. burst into my room, which he paced up and down, expatiating on the prospects of his visit to Turkey and explaining how he was going to handle the Turks. I grunted assent through face towels.

[It was agreed that since Ankara was too unsafe, the British party should rendezvous with the Turks at Adana, near the border with Syria.]

Saturday, 30 January *Adana*

Left Embassy 8.30 and off ground 9.30. I travelled in P.M.'s plane, which has been made very comfortable, with a saloon with armchairs and windows. Crossed Canal and hit off Gaza. Then up the coast. Fine at first, but then we ran into bad weather with heavy thunderstorms. Saw several water-spouts and a few flashes of lightning. Followed coast up to Tripoli, then straight across to Adana, where the weather was better. Landed about 12.30 and met by Sarajoglu* and Numan [Menemencioglu]. They took us to a special train at the edge of the aerodrome, in which we lunched while we trundled slowly out over the flat, flooded country for about ¾ hour, (probably not more than 6 miles or so). There, on a siding, we found the President's special, and were hitched on to it. We went along and were presented, and then left P.M. and President [Inönü] alone together for about half an hour. (When I asked P.M. later what had happened, he said 'Nothing'!). They then joined a full meeting in a big saloon and P.M. took hours doing a slight translation into French of his opening statement. This, in English, was an excellent document, but what it sounded like to the Turks in P.M.'s French, I have no idea! However, he gave the English text to Inönü, who

* Now Prime Minister.

pretends to read English. We then adjourned to a smaller meeting—Inönü, Sarajoglu and Numan and P.M., Snatch* and I. Quite a useful talk, which P.M. conducted v. well. Turks, I think, very relieved to find that we aren't pressing them to do anything definite. Frightened, of course, of Russia, about which we gave them such reassurance as we could. Large and convivial dinner in President's coach, at which I sat between Numan and [Lieutenant-Colonel A. C.] Arnold (our M[ilitary] A[ttaché]). Went off quite well. P.M. held forth to us for a bit afterwards in our saloon, but we got to bed soon after midnight. He's right not to press the Turks.

Sunday, 31 January *Nicosia*

Up fairly early. Found a most suspicious member of the Lepidoptera family on my sheet, which I slew. Consultation with Sir Charles Wilson confirmed me in my opinion that it was a bed bug. Quite a good breakfast. The waiter offered me 'Bekanek'. I have forgotten my Turkish and tried to recall what this might be, until I realised that it was bacon and eggs—and not bad either. P.M., in bed, sent for me. Either last night, or this morning, he had dictated a paper which he entitled 'pensées matinales', about the future of the world, which he proposes to give to Inönü. I didn't see anything much wrong with it, though we altered a few details. He was awfully proud of it. Meeting (à 6) about 11, which went off very well.

[Long afterwards, Cadogan recorded that he 'never saw men so resolutely disinclined to be drawn into a war. They were very friendly and pleasant, and I am sure their sympathies were genuinely with us, but when the conversation began to veer towards anything like practical action on their part it seemed that they found more than usual difficulty in hearing what was said.'

The Turks had already shown themselves co-operative in allowing the British to build up stores on Turkish soil. One of the principal merits of their belligerency would have been the vulnerability of the Roumanian oilfields, upon which the Axis relied heavily, to bombing from Turkish airfields. This advantage, however, would have worked more obviously to the Allies' benefit than to the Turks'; and it became plain during this conference that President Inönü and his colleagues looked upon Russia as the principal threat. Perhaps Mr Churchill, in his heart of hearts, did not disagree. Like Eden, Cadogan had expected no other attitude from the Turks. Saracoglu was evidently not convinced by the Prime Minister's evocation of the international organisation which was to restrain aggressors, or by his assertion that he had never known the Soviet Union to

* Sir Hughe Knatchbull-Hugessen, Ambassador in Turkey.

break an engagement. Turkey, said Saracoglu, was looking for something more 'real'. All the defeated countries would become Bolshevik and Slav if Germany were beaten.

The 'Pensées matinales' claimed that the new world organisation would embody the spirit, but lack the weaknesses, of the League. Admittedly, no one could be sure that the victors would not quarrel among themselves, though they would make intense efforts to prolong their honourable association. 'Great Britain will certainly do her utmost to organise coalition resistance to any act of aggression committed by any Power. . . .'

The military men agreed on increased supplies of modern weapons to Turkey. This was the only practical result of the Adana conference. Turkish Ministers argued throughout 1943 that their country was not yet ready to enter the war, in which towns would suffer destruction at the hands of the Luftwaffe. Turkey's determination to cling to her neutral position and keep her forces intact against Russia was well known to the Germans from the intercepts.[8]]

Sunday, 31 January (*cont.*)

Lunch about 12.30, during which our train, very slowly, got under way. Plan was that P.M. in his 'plane, in which I had a seat, should go to Cyprus, leaving at 1.30: the other plane to Cairo direct. During lunch, P.M. said he had a lot to do in Cairo (he hasn't) and would cut out Cyprus. On arrival at aerodrome we made our farewells and boarded plane. Pilot got aboard and P.M. told him we were going to Cairo. Pilot said that was the first he had heard of it: he thought we were bound for Cyprus. Before he could start up engines, P.M. changed again and said we would go to Cyprus. We then started moving, and were brought up with a sudden lurch—offside wheel had left the runway and sunk about 2ft. in the mud. Turkish soldiers were harnessed to the wheel with a piece of string—which broke. (After all, a Liberator weighs about 20 tons). The afternoon was now getting on, and there wasn't going to be too much light to land in Cairo (the other Liberator was hemmed in by our stranded machine). So P.M. and his party were transferred to the other Liberator and I was assigned to the Lodestar. Just as P.M.'s plane was ready to take off, his own Liberator was freed, a digging party having dug out a runway and the lorry, plus the Liberator's own engines, having coaxed it up on to the tarmac. But P.M. went on and I followed in Lodestar, leaving P.M.'s plane to bring on the rest of the party next morning. We got off about 4 and hit N.E. end of Cyprus about 4.45. I'd no idea it was so big an island (160 miles long) and we flew on and on down the S.E. coast, finally turning inland and landing at

Nicosia about 5.30. Met by A.D.C. and drove to Government House. Tea on arrival and then Winston put me on to draft telegrams, which I did for a bit in an *icy* office. After a bit, couldn't bear it any longer and went into drawing-room, where there were 2 open fires and only the Governor (Sir Charles Woolley) and Tommy [Thompson], and installed myself by the blaze and finished my work. . . . Discussed telegrams with Winston in his bedroom and got to bed fairly early.

Tuesday, 2 February *Cairo*

Went, about 6, to American Embassy to see film of troops entering Tripoli &c. V. good. Dined at Embassy. . . . Sat between Winston and Randolph. The latter a dreadful young man. He has been an incubus on our party ever since Casablanca. . . . *Very* silly of Winston to take him about. Father and son snapped at each other across me, which was disconcerting. However, we got Winston on to the Omdurman campaign, on which he held forth, at the dinner-table, till 11.30. Lampsons then returned, and in the confusion, I slipped off to bed about midnight.

Thursday, 4 February *Castel Benito*

Breakfast (good) at airport at 3 a.m. Off the ground at 4.15, arriving at Castel Benito about 9. . . . We spent part of the morning driving round . . . trying to catch up with Winston's procession and parade. Failed, but saw a good deal of the place. Then had to track down lunch at Montgomery's H.Q. Landed up there about 1 and found a picnic lunch going on. Every sort of good thing to eat (I had had nothing since 3 a.m.). P.M. introduced me to Montgomery and we sat together. . . . Drove off, about ½ hour, to a parade ground where P.M. reviewed N.Z. Division. Men looking frightfully fit and extraordinarily smart after 1,600 miles of fighting. Then to the Port, where we made a tour of inspection in a naval vessel. First 2 big ships had been got in this morning. I went to Alexander's camp, where I was allotted a van with a camp bed and a small bucket of cold water. I dined in his mess, which consists of a van with flaps on either side, ante-room under one flap and dining room under the other. All these vans dispersed, and tucked away in bushes (a sort of white brown) and camouflaged with branches. Quite a pleasant spot. After dinner there was a raid on Tripoli (about 10 miles away) and we watched the barrage, which afforded quite a good display.

Friday, 5 February *Algiers*

Off the ground about 4: arrived Algiers about 9. C.I.G.S. and I were taken to Eisenhower's house, where we had an excellent bath, shave and breakfast. Lovely day, and we pottered between Eisenhower's and Cunningham's houses—both in the same garden—meeting and talking with various people—[Robert] Murphy, Macmillan &c. Lunch with Eisenhower. P.M. there, and a largish party including Giraud, Noguès, Boisson, Peyrouton.* I sat next to Giraud, whom I found charming, and very ready to tell me the story of his escape from Germany. In the afternoon I had séance with Macmillan and R. Makins,† trying to clear up the mess caused by Murphy's having obtained Roosevelt's signature to documents purporting to confirm Casablanca agreement (which Winston hadn't seen!). This took some time: we got Murphy to agree an amended version, then put it across P.M., who subsequently saw Murphy. Also agreed next stages of Godefroy‡ drama with P.M.

[Although they never became effective, these documents are of considerable interest, revealing as they do not only the reasons for General de Gaulle's mistrust but also the amateurish way in which President Roosevelt did business. The first paper, dealing with the re-equipment of French forces in North Africa, stated *inter alia* that Roosevelt and Churchill agreed that General Giraud be given all facilities for bringing about the union under one authority of all Frenchmen fighting against Germany. The other paper recognised Giraud as possessing 'the right and duty of preserving all French interests' until the French people were able 'to designate their regular government'. Macmillan could only surmise that the President, pressed for time when approving these documents, had failed to realise their significance. Eden, in London, asked the Prime Minister by telegram whether he had seen these papers and been consulted about them, since they purported to carry his approval? Churchill answered 'No'. He settled with Murphy a revised text, which caused a prolonged delay in Washington. The note which Macmillan and Murphy jointly gave to Giraud on 28 May said simply that every facility would be given to him and to the French National Committee under de Gaulle to bring about the union under one authority of all Frenchmen fighting against Germany.[9]]

Saturday, 6 February *Gibraltar*

Luxurious bath in Eisenhower's enormous bathroom. Breakfast

* B-M. Peyrouton, previously Res.-Gen. of France in Tunisia and Morocco; Gov.-Gen. of Algeria, 1943-50.

† Who after serving with the Minister Resident in West Africa had come to join Macmillan's staff.

‡ Adm. Godefroy commanded the French naval squadron at Alexandria, immobilised since 1940; he refused to recognise Darlan's authority or to allow the ships to be used by the Allies.

with C.I.G.S. Eisenhower joined us. Strolled round the demesne with Macmillan, chatting about things in general, rather apprehensive of the numerous sentries with Tommy-guns behind each bush. . . . Landed Gib 5.15. . . . About 10.45 we drove up to the top of the Rock. Then, at a given signal, *all* the searchlights went on, *all* the guns fired (tracer) and *all* the rockets went off. Most impressive spectacle! And if I were an Axis airman, I should keep well away.

Sunday, 7 February

Landed at Lyneham [Wiltshire] about 10. P.M., who had taken off from Algiers, about half an hour behind us. Greeted by Portal, who said he hoped we'd had a good trip. Both C.I.G.S. and I said yes, but that it was *damned* uncomfortable. I won't be dragged around the world again in these conditions, which are filthy. I don't think P.M. has ever looked into our 'plane, or realises how beastly it is. Told C.I.G.S. never to cease chasing Portal on Chiefs of Staff Committee. Sure he'll play up. . . . At 5. T. woke me, saying there was a message from Lawford that there was a Cabinet at 5.30, and I needn't go to it. Got up and rang up Lawford, who said Cabinet was about India, so I fussed no more. Subsequently discovered that Winston—contrary to what he had said—attended it, and gave account of his trip. So I ought to have been there! A. sent for me at 7.30! Rather hard, without a car, but I caught a taxi and ordered a car to bring me home. Had talk with A., who doesn't seem fussed. I had just read a ridiculous minute . . . setting up howls about. P.M. having thrown the '4-Power Plan'* down the drain. Rubbish, and A. doesn't feel this. It always happens when one goes abroad, that the little quill-drivers in their cells pass a fine tooth comb through everything and wail that we have 'sold the pass'. Do them a lot of good to go abroad—and stay there.

Monday, 8 February

Cabinet at 5.30. P.M. not there, but he, fortunately, sent a message to say that he agreed with our new line on shackling. It involves his eating his words of Oct. last, so I expected trouble. Perhaps he didn't realise this!

Tuesday, 9 February

Archie Kerr at 11 to report on his interview with P.M. last night. Latter decided to communicate 'Morning Thoughts' tel quel to Russians, with suitable explanations. This I think right. A. spoke last

* See p. 488.

night to P.M. about visit to Washington. Latter favours it. . . . 6.30 talk with A. about Washington agenda. He alarmed that we haven't got everything à point. I told him much better so—let's talk at random and exchange ideas: that will get much better results at both ends. . . . I shirked Fire-Watching—or rather P. L[oxley] announced that I wasn't going to do it. A good P.S!

Monday, 15 February

We—or rather Americans—seem to have taken a knock in Tunisia. Russian news marvellous. Nearly 500 machines on Cologne last night and nearly 250 on Milan.

Tuesday, 16 February

10.30 meeting with A. and others about bringing Turks and Russians together. (I don't quite know how it's to be done! Or what subject can be broached in particular—the whole trouble is that the Turks simply fear and distrust the Russians!). . . . 12.30 meeting with O.S. and Bruce Lockhart about treatment of Italian 'feelers'. I feel we must soon abandon the quite mulish and ostrich-like attitude of O.S. and Department.

[The Foreign Office received approaches from Italy in December 1942, and told the Americans and Russians. It was not then thought likely that the Fascist regime could be overturned until Italy's military position was worse. Whether Count Ciano was responsible for these overtures is doubtful. It is certain, however, that by the end of that year he had become the mainspring of a group anxious to explore the channels of a negotiated peace between the Axis and Russia, or even between Italy and the West. The Duce felt differently. He seems to have received from Hitler a deciphered American telegram showing up the activities of the anti-German group. This probably did no more than confirm an intention already formed. At all events, Ciano was deposed as Foreign Minister on 5 February, being replaced by Mussolini himself with Bastianini as Under-Secretary. Grandi, the latter's predecessor as Ambassador in London, was dismissed from the Ministry of Justice.[10]]

Friday, 19 February

P.M. still has temperature of 101 so our trip, fixed for Monday, is put off. P.M. had planned to take Leadership of the House, as well as F.O.,—and winning the war! I see some damn fool has given Winston a lion—which I suppose will travel in future in my 'Liberator'!

[During the weekend Cadogan was taken ill. He had therefore to remain in England when the Secretary of State left for Washington in March.]

Friday, 5 March

Nothing to record of these boring days of illness. Had a temp-[erature] for about a week. But didn't feel bad. Only for 2 days no appetite and not much sleep. Then began to pick up. But Dr [McCall] says I *must* go slow—3 days in bed after temp normal, and must go away for a fortnight. A great bore! On Friday 26th a telegram from Winston fussing about my health.* Sent reassuring reply and told McCall to ring up Charles Wilson and give full report. Winston has had slight pneumonia, but seems to be making very good recovery.

Friday, 19 March *Thatched Cottage*

Read after lunch (Livingstone's 'Education for a World Adrift', which I find v. good. Mainly because it leads up to my only 2 poor ideas—service to the State, and service to one's neighbour). Then I walked down fields and right through 'wild-flower garden' and up through the copse again.

Sunday, 21 March

Broadcast by Winston at 9. Very good—mostly on post-war prospects, which he has hitherto eschewed. No actual news, though Winston gave us a hint that Montgomery is moving. So ends a v. good holiday. It took me a week or so to recover from McCall's most efficient drugs. But for this last week I have been fit and now feel very well.

Monday, 22 March

Mack at 3, to elicit circumstances of de Gaulle's latest antic in appointing a Governor of French Guiana. . . . 5.30 Cabinet. P.M. greeted me with enquiries about my health. *He* looks and seems very well. 8th Army have launched attack in force, and things look well so far as they go. N. Tunisia not so good, and Burma pretty rotten. Our troops (like the 8th Army) have to learn by *experience*, before they become the world's best soldiers. Russia looks like slowing up.

Tuesday, 23 March

Last night I sent a minute urging that we make clean breast of it to Stalin—i.e. that we can't send more northern convoys until August or September. I'm sure this is best. He seems inclined to agree, and directed me to attend meeting this morning of Chiefs of Staff, who

* To Lady Theo: 'We are both very sorry to hear of your husband's illness . . . all sympathy . . . great care. . . . Be quite sure he is fit before he resumes work.'

were drafting alternative messages. In afternoon agreed drafts with Ismay: these to be sent to A. with instructions (and arguments) to press for the clean breast.

Wednesday, 24 March

Went with R. Law to see P.M. (in bed) at 10.15. Explained to him de Gaulle's antics in Guiana and got his approval of a telegram to Macmillan asking whether these are likely to compromise success(?) of de G.-Giraud meeting.

[On 16 January, the Soviets announced that all Polish inhabitants of that part of Poland occupied by Russia would lose their nationality and become Russian citizens. Polish welfare organisations there were disbanded. These measures caused distress among Polish troops serving with the Allies, many of whose families were affected; a fruitless series of protests; and an equally fruitless appeal from Sikorski to Churchill. Cadogan is stated to have surmised, in a talk with the U.S. chargé d'affaires, that this action might have been partly a retaliation by the Russians against what they thought a 'chauvinistic' attitude recently shown by Sikorski. The Ambassador in Moscow, Clark Kerr, on leave in London in February, said that he would not rule out a separate peace by Russia if the West appeared to be doing little to help. Molotov's warmest response to the Ambassador's jokes consisted of removing his very thick glasses, wiping them and putting them on again. M. Tadeusz Romer, the Polish Foreign Minister, had been trying to smooth out some of the frictions between the two governments.[11]]

Saturday, 27 March

12.30 Raczynski, with a wail about failure of Romer's negotiations in Moscow. His Government want us to intervene. I said I couldn't decide this, but would put it to P.M.

Sunday, 28 March

396 bombers over Berlin last night dropped about 1,000 tons of bombs! . . . I had to leave for F.O. about 6, as Chiefs of Staff were again deliberating on their recommendations regarding Portuguese Islands. I waited till 7.45 but their report didn't come, so came home to dinner and received it after. I have no comments to make, as theirs is a purely military weighing-up of considerations and doesn't affect our view of the *political* elements, already telegraphed to Washington. But I durst not refrain from pointing out that they seemed to have left out a chunk! No German bombers yet, but they will probably come.

Monday, 29 March

Lunch at Claridges . . . for Spellman.* S. very nice. Told me he had to broadcast to America from N. Africa. He had no material with him except Bible and Atlantic Charter. I said they were both good documents. Latter was a little vague and might yet cause us some embarrassment but, I supposed, no more than the Bible would cause him. He didn't mind!

Tuesday, 30 March

P.M. rang up just as I had broached my poached egg. About a telegram from A. [in Washington] on American post-war notions which annoyed him. (I hadn't seen it). Also said he would see de Gaulle at 6 this evening. I asked had he received request for an interview. He said no, and I said I had questioned him the other day only on whether, in principle he *would* see de G. if asked. Said I'd find out what had happened. After many enquiries, found that de G. had *not* requested an interview, but that the egregious X† had told Massigli‡ that P.M. would see the General. Sent minute to P.M. explaining the circumstances,—which I am glad to say elicited rebuke to X. P.M. won't make any appointment until requested. . . . Massigli at 4. He gave me little news except that Catroux advised postponement of de G's departure until he (C.) could report more fully on his conversations. . . . 7.15 Maisky, to whom I gave a copy of P.M.'s message to Joe about convoys. He took it, perhaps, less badly than I expected. Dictated report to P.M. and left F.O. about 7.40. T. had thrown a huge sherry party—terrific rabble—but I missed them all.

[This telegram of 30 March told Stalin that the sailing of the March convoy must be postponed, on account of the presence at Narvik of a strong German battle-fleet; and that convoys could not be resumed on the northern route at least until September. Stalin's short reply of 2 April referred to 'this unexpected action as a catastrophic diminution of supplies', which must affect the Soviet troops' position. Churchill acknowledged the force of this. Stalin sent a friendly reply on 12 April.[12]]

Friday, 2 April

Went to see P.M. (in bed) at 10, about de G. He asked why I 'changed with every gust that blew'. (In view of telegrams showing that Catroux was double-crossing de G., I thought latter should go

* Cardinal Spellman, Archbishop of New York, 1939–67.

† Not the 'X' referred to on p. 494.

‡ René Massigli, Commissioner for Foreign Affairs, French Committee of National Liberation, 1943–4; Ambassador in London, 1944–55.

out.) I said it was the situation that changed—not I. He accepted this. Agreed to see de G. at 12 and wanted me there. This destroys our week-end. Interview passed off well. But of course I don't know how long effect will last! de G. won't start before Tuesday and will see A. (due back tomorrow) first. . . . P.M. sent for me 3.30 to show me Joe's reply about convoys. Might have been worse. P.M. delighted with it. He may be right. Told me other things that Maisky had said to him, of which I made record. Back to him at 5.45 to show up my work. He held forth on every conceivable topic until 6.45.

Saturday, 3 April

Pretty busy at F.O. in morning, but no particularly bad worry—except telegrams from Algiers about Giraud-de G. situation. Looks to me as if Catroux is double-crossing de G. De G. evidently thinks so too! I sent a minute down to Chequers saying that on balance of unpleasant alternatives, I thought de Gaulle should go out on Tuesday.

Sunday, 4 April

Telegram from Eisenhower deprecating de G. coming out at present. P.M. agrees. I told Mack to convey message through Massigli. A. got off yesterday. . . . Started for Hendon about 1.30. When I got there, heard he wouldn't arrive until 2.30. He finally didn't till 2.45. . . . He looked rather tired (and unshaven!). P.M. wanted him to go to Chequers. I said he'd better get it over, but make the condition at once that he goes to bed by midnight. He agreed, and drove off to F.O. . . . A. v. pleased with himself, as I think he has a right to be.

[General de Gaulle thereupon published a communique implying that he had been prevented by Eisenhower from leaving for North Africa to conclude a French union. This episode caused violent feelings at Allied H.Q. in Algiers. Catroux decided that he had better go to London after all, which he did on 8 April. The terms he bore from Giraud were still not acceptable to de Gaulle.

In Washington, Eden's talks had ranged over many subjects. 'If American ideas and British ideas differ,' Cadogan had said to the U.S. chargé d'affaires, 'we are quite prepared to re-examine the lines along which we have been thinking, but it is important for us to learn without delay what progress you have made and what sort of approach you are taking.'

The Americans felt that the British had not exercised all possible control or influence over de Gaulle and his advisers. If it were not British policy to support some of de Gaulle's pretensions, the visit to Washington would provide Eden with a good opportunity to say so. According to the

American record, Cadogan said there was 'no desire on the British side to back General de Gaulle for any position of primacy'; that he and Strang had thought during the Syrian episode of the previous summer that it might be possible to 'drop de Gaulle entirely' with 'Torch', but that unfortunately the feeling stirred up over the matter of Darlan had so strengthened him in Britain that this was not feasible.

Eden took Strang with him to Washington. Strang, absurdly, was suspected of being behind press articles hostile to Darlan and the Americans' pact with him. Hull told Strang that no one who knew anything of American policy could imagine it to be based upon anything but the highest moral considerations; he also complained of the British press and the criticisms of the Free French, and in general showed himself unsympathetic to de Gaulle. Eden replied that nothing the Prime Minister, or he, or anyone else, could say would engender British admiration for Vichy. Nevertheless, Eden thought there was a sufficient general agreement and no point in trying to settle details prematurely.

It was twelve months since Roosevelt had stood out against Russia's frontier demands, feeling, as Halifax noted after one of their talks, 'quite confident that if he could see Stalin he could settle it in five minutes.' On the merits of the issue, the President had now changed his view. If Poland got East Prussia and, perhaps, some concessions in Silesia, he thought she would gain by accepting the Curzon Line. He no longer objected to Russian claims on Finland or the Baltic States.

As for the ordering of the world after the war, Roosevelt suggested a General Assembly of all the nations, to meet once a year and blow off steam; an Advisory Council with the Four Powers plus six or eight others representing regions; and a Committee to take the vital decisions and wield executive powers. China, he insisted, must be one of the four, partly because in a serious conflict of policy with Russia she would line up with the U.S.A. Churchill was not anxious to treat China as an equal of the other three, as he had minuted to Cadogan on 22 March; while Eden left his American hosts in no doubt that Britain did not wish to see China supreme in the Far East. China was in a chaotic state and would, he thought, probably undergo a revolution. He surmised that Roosevelt was using America's interest in the Pacific as a means of leading her people to shoulder international responsibilities.

After reading through these and other papers about the security of the post-war world, Cadogan set down views which his later experiences at Dumbarton Oaks and San Francisco, and at the United Nations, confirmed in a painful manner. If the Great Powers could maintain their harmonious relations, he wrote on 13 April 1942, and agree to use force when needed, German and Japanese aggression would be contained and it would not be difficult to build 'ancillary organs which might have their uses'. If these conditions did not prevail, the ancillary organs would be 'card castles'. There was therefore no purpose in discussing for the moment the details of their organisation. The first step would be to sound the

American and Russian Governments about the rôle of each after the war. If agreement could be reached, an effective policing of Europe, in collaboration with other powers, might be achieved. The grim feature was the dependence of everything on agreement between the three powers and on their resolve to use force if need be. Such agreement should be earnestly sought before planners began to design 'all the outbuildings of the future Palace of Peace'.[13]]

Wednesday, 7 April

Lunch at Spanish Embassy—for Winston. Marvellous lunch. Sat between Monteiro and Villaverde. Towards end of lunch Winston did his tricks and held the attention of the table. After, he slipped it in to Alba about closing of frontier against refugees and escaped prisoners. He gave me a lift back.

Thursday, 8 April

Tunisian battle seems to be going all right. But I think Rommel's armour has slipped away, and the Italians this time, without waiting too long, have commandeered some lorries and got away without waiting for the trouble. Small blame to them!

Sunday, 11 April

T. picked about 1,000,000 daffodils, which we with great difficulty got into the car. How G. found a place, I don't know. I thought we should be taken for a funeral and that people would raise their hats to us.... 500 machines on Frankfurt last night. I think they all came over the cottage. Quite a pleasant week-end. But the cottage is for long, hot, summer days and a hammock.

Thursday, 15 April

Winston had had telegram from Roosevelt about administrative set-up in 'Husky'.* A. and I examined it and went over at 10.45 to see Winston in bed. He had already drafted a reply, which we approved. A cataract of boxes today, all containing 100-page memos, with an acre and a half of minutes. 1.30 lunched with Winston at No. 10 and Sikorski and Raczynski. P.M. told them we were ready to try our hand at intervention on their behalf in Moscow, but warned them also against provocation.

[On 13 April Germany announced the discovery in the Katyn Forest of evidence that the Russians had murdered, mainly by shooting in the back of the neck, some 10,000 Polish officers. At the luncheon on 15 April,

* The Allied invasion of Sicily.

Churchill said 'Alas, the German revelations are probably true. The Bolsheviks can be very cruel.' On the next day, learning of an imminent Polish appeal to the International Red Cross for an investigation, Eden and Cadogan asked for the insertion of a sentence condemning German propaganda methods and leaving the Russians a loophole. Raczynski did secure the inclusion of a qualifying phrase, and the issue of a statement about German crimes in Poland.

The Prime Minister had also told Sikorski that Poland must be strong and independent, and that her eastern frontier must be revised, with compensation in the west. How the first part of this policy was to be secured he did not say. *Pravda* started referring to 'Hitler's Polish allies' and Stalin telegraphed explicitly about the collusion between Hitler and Sikorski's Government, provoking thereby a retort from Churchill:

> His position is one of great difficulty. Far from being pro-German or in league with them, he is in danger of being overthrown by the Poles who consider that he has not stood up sufficiently for his people against the Soviets. If he should go, we should only get somebody worse.[14]]

Monday, 19 April

Cabinet 5.30. We seem to have been rather promiscuous in our bombing, and to have made some boss-shots—particularly at Stuttgart! Sinkings much better. Battle in Tunisia being staged, and will break out soon. Long argument about church bells. P.M. determined to have them rung again—quite rightly. [Sir J.] Anderson* brought up all the bureaucratic objections in his best governess manner. And many of the Cabinet against P.M. But he bulldozed them into submission, I'm glad to say.

Tuesday, 20 April

7 A. to talk about Palestine and other things. (He told me idea of his going to India [as Viceroy] is now off. I thought it would be. It was Amery's† idea and obviously P.M. wouldn't let him go. Candidate is now Gwilym Lloyd George.‡ Rather insignificant!).

Good Friday, 23 April *Thatched Cottage*

Sorted out and started cleaning my carpentry tools. (I wonder when I shall be able to use them again!). About 5.30 a lovely evening, and I continued my weeding. Short showers, and after dinner, about 8.45, it turned to heavy rain again. This will do a lot of good—but I wish it wouldn't come *just* in the Easter holiday.

* Now Lord President of the Council.

† L. S. Amery, Secretary of State for India and Burma.

‡ Then Minister of Fuel and Power.

Archbishop [Temple] of Canterbury is now bleating on the wireless. I should say an almost model bad broadcast.

Saturday, 24 April *Thatched Cottage*

Messenger arrived after lunch with a special box containing the Anderson Committee's draft report on the structure of Government after the war, on which A. wanted comments. In spite of its first sight attraction, I don't think 'supervising Ministers' will work. We must have Cabinet Committees, and I gave A. my views on the alternatives suggested. Also wrote him the homily which I have been revolving— 'Beveridgism is not enough'.

[Cadogan's homily is revealing of the man, and is almost the only surviving paper by him on a subject other than foreign policy or international organisation. It sprang from the discussions about the reform of national insurance, and many other measures of material betterment promised for the peace; discussions in which, as it seemed to Cadogan, the emphasis had so far been misplaced:

> Comfort and well-being are to be ardently desired, and sought; but, as we have learnt to our sorrow, they *alone* cannot be relied on to bring happiness to the individual, security for the State or real progress in the world. Nor do we necessarily attain to them if we make them the *one* object of our search. . . .
>
> Modern war is a very unpleasant business: it has none of the glamour of the days of chivalry (except perhaps for the fighter pilots). But we may hope that that is compensated in some degree by the 'totality' of modern war conditions, where the whole population is united, in various spheres of action, in doing . . . a job which they know is worthwhile. . . . Much as the Englishman loathes war, and much as he has had to suffer from it, I wonder whether the average individual is not more at peace within himself than he was before this war broke out, and whether he will not dwell with more satisfaction on the part that he has played in these hard times than he will on the occasional relaxations and diversions which, if he was lucky, peace afforded him.
>
> Can we carry any of this co-operative effort forward into the 'Peace'? We must, if we are not to repeat the errors of 1919–39.
>
> To take one case, if we are to 'police' Europe, compulsory military service will have to be continued in some form. It is not very complimentary to our people to assume that they only want 'benefits' and are not ready to assume obligations. If it could be put to them in the right way, surely there would be a response? If we have to keep up a considerable military force, surely conscription is the fairest, most democratic and cheapest way of doing so?
>
> How can we prolong and turn to good account all the co-operative

> and gallant effort that has been put into the Home Guard, Fire Services, &c.? I can't answer the question; I should only like to be sure that it is put, and considered... it does seem to me that the emphasis is too much on material well-being. It is a reproach to us that this should be so—it derives from the fact that there has been too much inequality in this country. That is being rapidly corrected now by war taxation.
>
> Those who have been denied the ordinary comforts and decencies of life, to an extent which I find it hard to imagine, naturally attach to these a primary importance. Their lot must be bettered, and until it is so, perhaps we can't expect them to realise that that is the ultimate aim and that that will not necessarily bring them happiness. But even amongst those so placed, I should be surprised to find that there were many who would not be ready—even glad—to assume obligations together with their benefits. I suspect that they would be proud to do so....
>
> It is idle to deny that religion no longer plays the part it did. Perhaps one day we shall have a new Revelation, but we can't sit and wait for it. But we can perhaps prepare for it. Keep ourselves keen and avoid a moral atrophy, by setting ourselves to some form of common endeavour, some kind of sacrifice—our duty to our neighbour, to the State, to the world.
>
> All this has been said before, and is being said, doubtless much better. There's nothing new in it. But old things want burnishing. It is a hard doctrine to preach, but I believe there are more men and women ready for it than we know of.

As Cadogan composed this letter, Eden was telling Sikorski that the Russians were about to break off relations with Poland; but Stalin had said he would refrain if the Poles withdrew their application to the Red Cross and blamed Germany for Katyn. Sikorski refused.[15]]

Monday, 26 April

Soviet rupture with the Poles, which I learnt from my box on Saturday, announced tonight. This heavy Russian plunge is, I think, indicative of a bad conscience. It's a bad move, anyhow, and Goebbels must be happy.

Tuesday, 27 April

Had talk with O.S., W.S. and [Frank K.] Roberts about the Polish-Soviet row. Clearly we must try to plaster it over, but it won't be easy, and Russians probably will make it a condition that their frontier be settled and that has probably been their intention all along. Talk on same subject with A. Decided he should ask P.M. to send fairly stiff message to Stalin .... 5.30 A. called me in to a talk with Raczynski, who had brought draft Polish statement on the row.

A. went off to see P.M. I criticised statement on general ground that, while we are trying to bring about a reconciliation, statements won't help, and on several particular passages. R. went to No. 10 at 5.45, when Sikorski was due. Cabinet, called for 6.15, had to wait a bit. P.M. gave Cabinet homily on the trouble, but I don't know what he has decided to do about approaching Stalin. Agreed to muzzle B.B.C. and damp down Press.

Wednesday, 28 April

Had to be at F.O. by 10 to discuss with A. a draft Polish declaration which P.M. had written last night. Quite good. Sikorski and Raczynski came at 12 and we put it to them, and they took it fairly well. We mucked it about a bit, without any essential change. . . . Back at No. 10 at 3 to get P.M.'s approval of final form of declaration. Poles then came and accepted it. Afterwards P.M. dictated a telegram to Stalin and A. and I went over at 4 to look at it. It was a little hard on the Poles and a little soft on the Russians, but we got it modified a bit. . . . Department produced a rather bad draft of instructions to A. C. Kerr for use with Molotov. A. sent for me at 7.30 about it and I tried my hand at putting it right. Got away about 8, A. dining with P.M. and will discuss with him the revised telegram to A.C.K., so I (10.45 p.m.) am momentarily expecting to be summoned! A filthy day. Masses of papers to clear up after dinner this evening, and I'm running out of drink! Damn!

Thursday, 29 April

Talk with A. at 10.20 about Soviet-Polish worry. Didn't decide much, except that it would be a good thing for him to see Maisky. M. has been left out in the cold and is consequently disseminating poison in press and other unsavoury quarters. A. saw him at 12 and gave it to him pretty straight. But I don't suppose it'll do much good. . . . 1. meeting of Defence Committee to which A. and I went, hoping to get Cabinet Members to approve policy in Soviet-Polish worry. But we came into a discussion of Far Eastern strategy with Wavell, Peirse and Somerville.* I left at about 1.30 (when it was settled to have a Cabinet in the afternoon for our purpose.) . . . Cabinet approved what we had done. P.M. then announced his intention of leaving for Washington on Sunday night. No one liked it—no one, except Brendan [Bracken], dared oppose. P.M. blithely rode down all opposition.

* Respectively C.-in-C., India; A.O.C.-in-C., India, 1942–3, and Allied A.O.C.-in-C., S.E. Asia Command, 1943–4; C.-in-C., Eastern Fleet, 1942–4.

Friday, 30 April

Found a telegram from A. C. Kerr suggesting alterations in P.M.'s message to Stalin. This delay a bore. Some of A.C.K.'s suggestions good, and I, with O.S. and W.S. drafted amendments. Took O.S. round with me to P.M. at 11.30. He in bed smoking a cigar. He approved our amendments and we got them off. Raczynski at 12. I put to him a draft statement in which Polish Government would withdraw their appeal to Red Cross.* I know how difficult it is for them, but I urged him to do it in *their own* interest, as their own friends here criticise them for the appeal. He promised to submit it to his Government. . . . 4.30 had to go over to No. 10 to get P.M. to withdraw an amendment he had made in his message to Sikorski on Polish Day (Sunday). Had to wait about 20 mins. He agreed at once. Then started haranguing me on Egypt. Meanwhile Department sent me copy of today's 'Soviet War News', with a disgraceful article about Polish Government. P.M. sent for Maisky. Kept me hanging around until M. arrived. Then we kicked Maisky all round the room, and it went v. well. P.M. told me of his (barren) interview this morning with de G., who was doing his celebrated mule act. (I have got to make a record of this—without much material!). Didn't get away until 6.15. Raczynski came back with only partial agreement of his Government. Think it will just do. Rang up A. and gave him account of today's doings. All this takes time! And there were a score of boxes waiting for me, which I got home by 8 p.m. Dined and worked till 11. Finally fixed up with Raczynski on telephone text of the statement, which will be put out by P.A.J. [the Free Polish News Agency]—not Polish Govt. I got A.'s concurrence (doubtful) and rang up News Department to get them to give the thing a fair wind. Rather tired!

[The Prime Minister's telegram drew Stalin's attention to Goebbels' suggestion that Moscow intended to set up a Polish Government on Russian territory. No such government could be recognised by Britain.

Soviet War News had alleged that the Polish Government in Britain did not represent the Polish people. In the interview of 30 April, Churchill told Maisky in terms that the 'emigré character' of Sikorski's Government was 'not unconnected with a double occupation of Poland'. Maisky pointedly referred to Poland as a country of 20 millions next door to one of 200 millions. Churchill retorted hotly; and less than a week later, when Maisky told Eden that the British were 'too tolerant of Polish feelings', he was

* The Prime Minister had told Sikorski that the British Government had a right to be consulted beforehand. It would in any case be useless to arraign the Russians in matters of honour; they would only be provoked to further brutality.

reminded that it was on account of Poland that Britain had gone to war. Stalin pressed for a reconstruction of the Polish Government, and said that the Poles were trying to play off one ally against the other. They thought themselves clever tacticians; but 'God has given them no brains'.[16]]

Saturday, 1 May

A tiresome telegram from Moscow, still protesting against the line we are taking with the Russians. I *suppose* A. C. K[err] will have presented P.M.'s message, anyway. I hope so. Drafted a telegram telling him this, but otherwise agreeing that he could go slow with Molotov—depending on Joe's reaction to P.M.'s message. Got A.'s concurrence on telephone.... A. rang up to say P.M. now wanted to take out stiff paragraph at the beginning of his message, which we put in yesterday, and was doubtful about approaching Soviet concerning Poles in Russia. I said this was all wrong. The stiff paragraph was a trump, and we must raise the Poles-in-Russia question—more especially as Pres. R[oosevelt] has done so. A. said P.M. would think that was all right, provided *we*, in our representations to Molotov, backed him over Poles. I said that was all right, and in our instructions. It was true that we gave A.C.K., in our telegram this morning, latitude to begin tentatively, but of course we should maintain the Poles in our programme. We must see first what happens at the Stalin interview. That will almost certainly broach the question. Anyhow we must follow it up and, if necessary, send A. C. Kerr another telegram impressing this on him. On A.'s instruction, sent message to P.M. to this effect.

Sunday, 2 May

Polish Pres. is recording a broadcast for tomorrow containing tiresome remarks about Lwow, &c. (see last year! [page 449]) I thought we could let it go. But W.S. tells me S. of S. has to be consulted. I left him to do that, as I understand A. is in a cat-on-hot-bricks mood, and I choose not to deal with him on the telephone.... We went to St. Paul's for the Polish Service. Not v. impressive, though the Polish choir was good. I knew there had been awful internal rows about this in the Polish Government. (What exactly, the trouble was, I never could make out.) However, none of the Cabinet came to blows in the Cathedral.

Monday, 3 May

Had talk with A. on his arrival. Question of his going to India is coming to a head again. I think it's folly, but there appears to be no one else.... Cabinet 5.30. No v. good news. Weather has been against bombing, and the Americans have achieved *nothing* for the last fortnight. Sinkings for the week worse again, but the total for April was good. In Tunisia no great progress can be reported, but our information shows that Axis are in a bad way. Germans planning thrust on Kursk, but there are some formidable Russian armies there. We're rather in the doldrums at the moment, but doubtless things will liven up.

Tuesday, 4 May

A. tells me he may *not* go to India—maybe O. Lyttelton. My morning's work rather curtailed by Frank O. Salisbury who wanted an hour's sitting of me for presentation picture of the signature of our Russian treaty last year. He produced a lightning sketch in chalks which was probably very like me, but I look very thin and hungry and pessimistic. . . . 6. Raczynski. Had to tell him we *can't* take on active charge of Polish interests in Russia. I'm awfully sorry, but I'm *sure* that could only lead to disaster. Dined at home and worked. P.M. off [to Washington] tomorrow, with a party of 150! Including the Beaver!

Thursday, 6 May

W.S. told me of his 1.30 a.m. worry with Retinger about Sikorski's immediate reaction to Stalin's statement to the press.* Why *will* everyone (Poles and de Gaulle) *rush* into publicity at half-cock? They are quite incapable of conducting their own affairs and should really consult us *first*. Rang up Raczynski and found he had been double-crossed by Retinger, who had told him Sikorski had 'consulted the S. of S.' However, S.'s statement is not too bad. Later, heard Polish National Council were getting under way and proposing to put out a '5-point statement'. Rang up Raczynski again, and found it wasn't as bad as all that. He will meet Council this afternoon and try to muzzle them, but he has a tough job. . . . A. wanted to see me at 3.30 at House of Commons. Went down there. He excited about Archie C.K's telegram to me (which he hadn't seen) about ammunition for discussion of frontiers with Stalin. I told him it was no good giving him advance copy of telegram, (on which he would only scrawl 'A.C.—Please speak') and he'd better wait to see it when Department had expressed their opinion and put up draft reply. He accepted this—*and* the draft reply. . . . Raczynski came to me after his meeting with National Council. He has done as well as one could

* To the effect that Russia desired a strong, independent Poland in close alliance, if the Polish people wished, with Russia against Germany.

expect. I reported to A., who *may* want to make further representations to Sikorski. 6. Maisky came to A. with Joe's [Stalin's] reply to P.M. Not too bad. Discussed with A. how to proceed, and decided to summon Sikorski and Raczynski for tomorrow morning on this and National Council worry.

Friday, 7 May

10.30 had a talk with A. who had got the jumps about our telegram to A.C.K. regarding a possible discussion of frontiers. He had passed it yesterday, and hadn't read it properly and raises all sorts of objections now he sees it in print. Sikorski and Raczynski called at 11 and we told them something of Joe's message. Didn't make much progress, but asked for their collaboration in controlling Polish Press here. Meanwhile Vyshinsky* has put out a savage and disgraceful attack on Poles. They left about 12 and I drafted telegram to Moscow to clear up the instructions to A.C.K. . . . 1. Cabinet on Egypt—to consider C.-in-C's observations on use of force. These can be ignored and M[iles] L[ampson] can be told to go ahead, as and when necessary, with knowledge that he has, ultimately, force behind him. . . . A. approved my telegram to A.C.K.

Saturday, 8 May *Thatched Cottage*

Woken up at 4 a.m. by the wind, which had then developed into a howling, raging gale. This bore along with it banks of leaden clouds and successive downpours. Tried to go out about 10, but couldn't stand against it. I am well acquainted with the Outer Hebrides, but never have I known such a gale. It is ripping and cutting the fruit trees, uprooting the irises, shearing trusses off the poor old pear-tree and strewing the place with wreckage. Remained in shelter of the cottage, which somehow seems to stand. I suppose it has borne this for 4 centuries! And the pear tree, perhaps, for as long! Made one or two attempts to go out in afternoon, driven back every time by the blustering, blundering, damaging gale. . . . Marvellous news—we have both Bizerta and Tunis. Wonder whether enemy can give us much trouble in Cape Bon Peninsula. I hope not, as we seem to have unchallenged air superiority. What a long way from Norway to here!!!

Monday, 10 May

A. got back to F.O. about 11.40 and I went to see him about a number of telegrams which have now come in from P.M. [in

* Vice-Commissar for Foreign Affairs.

Washington]. The most important is a message he wants to send to Stalin about Polish-Soviet difficulty. This seems to be on wrong lines and I drafted amendments. Also a telegram from A. to P.M. explaining them. . . . After Cabinet discussion of telegrams to P.M. suggesting modifications of his message to Stalin. It amuses me to see how, in his absence, *every* member of the Cabinet makes, simultaneously, sweeping suggestions. If he were here, every rabbit would crouch dumb.

[The main purpose of Churchill's visit to Washington, his third in eighteen months, was to persuade the Americans that an assault on Italy should follow the capture of Sicily, which had been agreed upon at Casablanca. He hoped by knocking Italy out to gain Turkey as a belligerent, and thereby the use of her bases to bomb Ploesti and sweep the Aegean; to cause 'a chill of loneliness over the German people'; to secure the Italian fleet and enable British naval strength to be diverted to the Bay of Bengal and the Pacific; to take the weight off the Russian front by forcing Germany to expend many divisions in the Balkans. Although it was at once agreed that a major cross-Channel operation would not be feasible in 1943, Churchill could not secure a decision at that stage to launch an invasion of Italy.

Each day Roosevelt complained bitterly, or perhaps contemptuously, of de Gaulle's 'well-nigh intolerable' attitude, and 'Messianic complex'. The Prime Minister asked his colleagues to consider whether de Gaulle should not now be eliminated as a political force? On 23 May Eden and Attlee replied, with ample reasons, 'No'. Churchill said sorrowfully of de Gaulle, 'I brought him up from a pup, but never got him properly trained to the house.' He agreed to await the outcome of the talks between de Gaulle and Giraud, and urged the Americans not to carry this issue to the point of a quarrel with Britain.

The other principal political issue in these talks—apart from some inconclusive discussion about the post-war world, in which Churchill pressed the importance of regional arrangements for security—was that of the Azores, Portuguese territory. If bases there could be used, they could provide air protection to the Atlantic convoys, fuel for the ships and staging-posts for aircraft. The Prime Minister wished to ask Portugal for these facilities, and to intimate that if not freely granted they would be taken anyway. A diplomatic approach was preferred by the War Cabinet. Churchill again agreed to postpone the decision.[17]]

Tuesday, 11 May

At Salisbury's Hampstead house for another sitting at 9.30. Lasted an hour. The picture awful. Justifies Kenneth Clark's remark about Salisbury's 'ghastly efficiency'. I look as if I were just going to bark.*

* The only people pleased with the picture were the Russians, whose taste it suited exactly. Stalin's interpreter, Pavlev, admired it warmly. 'It is so "like".'

. . . Talk with A. at 5 about Azores. P.M. has got on to this again with great vigour. Agreed we might *ask* Salazar for facilities but must *not* seize them. Defence Committee 6.15, which confirmed above.

Wednesday, 12 May

6 talk with A., O.S., Strang and Jebb about future organisation of the world. Quite useful, as they agreed to begin on the basis of trying to agree with Americans and Russians what we put into the various armistices and what our respective functions, and their scope, will be. On that we may build something practical. Intercepted message from [General] v[on] Arnim* 'We have fired our last cartridge. We are closing down for ever.' This is a really wonderful performance. It will be very interesting to see, in the next few days, what will be the repercussions. I *don't* believe in Italian collapse, though J[oint] I[ntelligence] C[ommittee] still maintain Germany won't help Italy, and in that case latter's outlook is indeed black! *What* changes since last July!

Saturday, 15 July

Papers about Administration of Huskyland have become an absolute *jungle*. I think the excellent Bob Dixon†. . . knows too much about his subject. He has made it quite incomprehensible to others. Yesterday we had drafts ready to go to Washington. I rang up A. in the country saying I would send them off without showing them to him, as they followed minutes he had approved. He agreed. They were then taken to W[ar] O[ffice] who said P. J. Grigg wouldn't agree them. He had gone—as is the custom of S's. of S.—to the country. I said they must send them down to him as he must discuss them with A. *I* won't discuss them with P.J. One might as well argue with a stone wall. He is a 'strong man' which means that he hasn't the intelligence, or the courage, to see anyone else's point of view. This morning he sends the papers back, saying he maintains his view and couldn't talk to A., as he wasn't on a scrambler! Well, you can't do business like that. So the telegrams haven't gone and I wash my hands of it. . . . Massigli at 5. Spoke quite straight to him, saying everyone saw that de G. insisted on Algiers as meeting place so that discussion could take place under pressure of demonstrations. He didn't demur—much. I agreed to consider suggesting a compromise

* Who had succeeded Rommel in North Africa.

† Pierson J. Dixon; served in F.O. 1940–3; on staff of Minister Resident at Allied Force H.Q., Mediterranean, 1943; Principal Private Sec. to Eden and then to Bevin, 1943–7.

to Algiers. Authorised Mack to do this. . . . went to 'It's foolish but it's fun' (6.30). Nervo and Knox—wholesome knockabout (best form of wit) salted with a good deal of vulgarity. Not a bad show. Left before the end.

Sunday, 16 May

A., I'm glad to say, agreed to send off telegrams to Washington about Administration of Huskyland . . . .

Monday, 17 May

A. didn't arrive (with a cold!) until lunch-time. Really, it's impossible to work like this. He marks every paper 'A.C.—please speak' and then one has no opportunity of speaking to him! . . . 4.30 saw A. for a few moments about a number of things. 5.30 Cabinet. V. good Lancaster attack on German dams!* Sinkings much better. 15 U-boats sunk this month so far. (We want to keep up that rate). Discussion on Thanksgiving Service on Wednesday. Morrison had sent out written invitations to Lords and Commons, giving date and time, so it's the talk of the town! Decided to postpone from noon to 6 p.m.

Wednesday, 19 May

Few German fighter-bombers have been making these nights in London rather noisy—we have 2 or 3 alerts, and an amount of gunfire, which interferes with sleep—a bore. And we don't shoot down quite enough of them. It's going to be a nuisance, but I suppose we shall find a cure. . . . 5.20 T. picked me up for St. Paul's Thanksgiving Service. We had good seats, next to the aisle. (But it was damned cold.) A dignified service, and luckily Hitler didn't bomb King, Lords, Commons and everything else. What a target!

Thursday, 20 May

Going out to lunch, on Horse Guards Parade, I saw a mounted Policeman coming through the archway, followed by a crowd of about 200, mostly women. Waited to see what it was, and found Montgomery, in battle-dress and black beret, walking with another officer behind the Policeman. Joined and congratulated him, but the cinematographers became so thick on the ground that after a bit I told him I couldn't stand it any longer, and left him! The Provost Marshal ought to ask him why he's improperly dressed. He *is* a good advertiser! And so was I, pushing up to him, I suppose!

* In the Ruhr. Dortmund and Kassel were flooded as a result.

Friday, 21 May

Cabinet at 12, about propaganda to Italy and Administration of Husky. Attlee read out ridiculous telegram from P.M. demanding immediate (and surprise) occupation of Azores. Agreed to meet on this at 5. . . . Got F. Roberts about 3.45. Saw A. with him at 4. Drafted reply to P.M. and had it copied in time for 5 o'clock Cabinet. Rambling discussion. Everyone (except Morrison) against P.M.—which they wouldn't have been if he'd been here! They discarded my draft which argued the case in some detail, and sent merely a message saying 'Why such a hurry? Let's wait till you get back.' This no use, because (a) Winston will say there *is* a hurry, and (b) when he gets back, he'll swing them to his view! Attlee also told Cabinet of telegrams that are coming in from Winston about de G. Former (under American pressure) wants to execute latter.* But is this the moment, when de Gaulle and Giraud *may* be getting together?

Sunday, 23 May

A. wanted to see me 8.30 before Cabinet at 9. Dined soon after 7.30 and kept the appointment. All the trouble about P.M.'s messages about de Gaulle. We had draft replies (prepared by W. S[trang] and Mack—very good ones). Cabinet jigged them about a bit and I had to stay after to put them straight with [Sir Edward] Bridges.

Monday, 24 May

Reply from P.M. about Azores, which makes it plain that it's *his* plan, which he wants to force on Pres., with *our* help. I'm sure *our* draft (see May 21st) ought to have been sent. Prepared a new version, incorporating most of our original arguments, and gave it to A. before lunch. . . . Cabinet at 3 about Azores draft. Cabinet—like any such large collection of arrogant and ignorant men—a hopeless body for drafting. I undertook to produce new draft, which I was able to submit to A. by 5.15. . . . Ordinary Cabinet 5.30. Sinkings *much* better, and we have destroyed 26 U-boats this month so far! 2,040 tons dropped on Dortmund last night! At the end, Cabinet agreed—with some difficulty—my latest draft about Azores.

Saturday, 29 May

Nothing much doing, and no news—this interval between now and 'Husky' will be bleak and dull. Bombing goes on, but it palls. . . . Telegram from P.M. summoning A. to Algiers. Rang him up: he

* Not, of course, literally.

quite ready to go: it will probably only be for 3 or 4 days, i.e. they will be back end of next week. We can carry on somehow.

Sunday, 30 May

P.M. wants to make Wavell Governor-General of Australia and replace him by the Auk. But Attlee protests!

[The Prime Minister flew direct from Washington to the Mediterranean. Consultations with Eisenhower and the Mediterranean commanders at Casablanca showed a preference on the part of the British for an early attack on the mainland of Italy. General Marshall refused to commit himself. Meanwhile, devoted mediation by Catroux had helped to bring de Gaulle and Giraud together. On 29 May Churchill asked that Eden should come to Algiers:

> He is much better fitted than I am to be best man at the Giraud-de Gaulle wedding. He ought to be conscious of the atmosphere and in touch with the actors in what may easily be a serious drama.

In fact, Eden had no occasion to intervene in the French negotiations. On 1 June a difference arose between de Gaulle and Giraud about the dismissal of Noguès, Peyrouton and Boisson. Giraud favoured a delay; but on 2 June the press announced that Peyrouton had asked de Gaulle to convert him into a soldier and that de Gaulle was placing him at the disposal of the French C.-in-C., Levant. Agreement was announced on 3 June for a new Committee of National Liberation, to exercise power over the territory and forces hitherto controlled either by Giraud as C.-in-C. or by de Gaulle's Committee, and under the co-presidency of the two. The new organisation pledged itself to re-establish the laws of the Republic and to surrender power to a provisional Government as soon as the liberation of metropolitan France allowed. Within a few days, de Gaulle resigned over the matter of control of French forces. The Americans, however, were determined that Giraud should retain effective command of the Army. Other issues, not in themselves significant, inflamed the President's dislike of de Gaulle, and apprehension about his motives and plans, to a point where this question became a major factor in relations between Churchill and Roosevelt on the one hand, and Churchill and the Foreign Office on the other. Before leaving for North Africa, de Gaulle had said to the Foreign Secretary, 'Je conserverai le meilleur souvenir du peuple britannique'. Eden understood that this genial memory did not include the British Government.

Nevertheless, de Gaulle owed his political survival largely to the British. On 17 June Roosevelt strongly suggested to the Prime Minister that the time had now come to break with de Gaulle. Even Churchill did not try to defend the terms of the President's message; Eden, as usual, had the task of trying to persuade the Prime Minister to reason with

Roosevelt. 'We shall be hard put to it', says Eden's diary for 18 June, 'to keep in step with Americans, or rather pull them into step with us, over the French business, and not commit some folly which will give de Gaulle a martyr's crown or control of the French army or both.'

This particular difficulty was eventually resolved, after the refusals, counter-refusals, resignations and other *hauteurs* inseparable from French politics of the period, by the constitution of a committee, upon which the General sat, responsible for the armed forces' training and organisation. Neither the British nor the Americans had yet decided on the degree of recognition which they would accord to the Committee.]

Monday, 31 May

Alba at 4 to protest against cartoons of Franco. I reacted fairly strongly and went at him about arrests of Jews in Tangier. Winant at 5. Very inaudible, but discovered that he meant to imply that Roosevelt is incensed at the idea of 'armistice' with Italians. I said that if it would smell sweeter under any other name, we'd be quite ready to call it 'Conditions of Surrender'. Discovered after that there must have been some misunderstanding, as the draft emanated from Eisenhower and was called 'Terms of Surrender'. So shall have to see him again. . . . Cabinet 5.30. 31 submarines sunk during May and our sinkings less than for a *long* time. I submitted to Cabinet our plan for dealing with Yugoslav Government crisis,* and they approved generally, though Cripps had some silly remarks to make. (A great chance for the Cabinet, in A.'s absence, to become—all of them—Foreign Secretaries, which they *love*!) Also consulted them about putting screw on Switzerland about transit of war material. Cripps rightly pointed out that Press reports this afternoon showed Germans and Swiss apparently coming to loggerheads, so agreed this could wait for day or 2. Couldn't get away from dinner till 10.15, so had to read late. (How I hate these social occasions—they bore and tire me.)

Tuesday, 1 June

Saw Winant about 'Armistice', and other matters. Amongst latter, drew him about his interview with Monteiro,† at which latter complains of having been 'threatened'. But it appears this was about Wolfram—not islands.

Thursday, 3 June

P.M. wanted to go on to Moscow. A. dissuaded him and offered

* Factious disputes within the Cabinet, mainly between Serbs and Croats. A Government under Dr Trifunović failed to satisfy Croat members.

† Portuguese Ambassador.

to go instead, but I gather this is all 'off'. I let on to Attlee, thinking he'd know—but he *didn't*!

Friday, 4 June

Alba at 12, very exuberant with what he called a 'very nice' message about Tangier. It contained nothing tangible, but was polite so I said that we appreciated the friendly intention, but hoped there would soon be a satisfactory solution. He looked rather crestfallen, so I thanked him for the Spanish destroyer search for possible survivors of shot-down Lisbon plane.

Saturday, 5 June

Went to F.O. and saw A., whom I found well and in good form. He seems to think everything going all right.

Monday, 7 June

5.30 Cabinet. No news these days. Weather has made bombing impossible. Sinkings *much* better, U-boat destruction admirable. Alexander, with the aid of a map, gave us a lecture on Tunisian campaign and made some general, and optimistic, remarks about future prospects. He did it awfully well. . . . Defence Committee 10.30 about Azores. I helped to argue against P.M. and in favour of 'diplomatic approach'. No very firm decision, except to get R. C[ampbell] back. After, talked to A. about India. P.M. still trying to make him go. This silly.

[The Secretary for India, L. S. Amery, had had Eden in mind for the Viceroyalty since the summer of 1940. Eden himself felt the lure of the post, and the Prime Minister half-inclined to the proposal. However, the King weighed in strongly against Eden's departure. 'From the point of view of the general conduct of the war he is, I know, very much in your confidence', he wrote to Churchill. 'He is, so to speak, your Second-in-Command in many respects, and, while I appreciate your readiness to let him go, I cannot help feeling that you might well find the loss of his assistance and support too great an addition to the heavy burden you already have to bear.'

This was written on 28 April. Five weeks later the issue had still not been resolved. On the one side, Churchill claimed that only Eden's appointment as Viceroy could redeem the situation; on the other, Eden reflected that inter-allied relations were now of the first importance. Moreover, he was not readily replaceable either as Leader of the House or as Foreign Secretary. Cadogan made no secret of his relief that Eden had decided to stay.[18]]

Wednesday, 9 June

Met A., and he took me round the Park. P.M. still pressing India on him. He, I think, determined to resist. . . . A. told me this evening that P.M. now agrees to appointment of Wavell to India—Auk to succeed him. This probably good.

Thursday, 10 June

Telegrams from Lisbon show that we might approach Salazar* about the islands with some success.

Saturday, 12 June *Thatched Cottage*

Rather gray in the morning, but it developed into a lovely day, with a cool S.W. breeze. In morning, lifted daffodils by the Barn and in the N. border, prepared ground and bedded out antirrhinums, mixed nemesia. After lunch, went on with the work, including stocks. Masses of peas and excellent broad beans, just at their best. Sat in hammock for ½hr. before tea—that was my only rest. . . . Rather stiff after a day's stooping—but I hope that won't do me any harm. . . . Pantelleria surrendered yesterday. More than 2,000 tons of bombs on Düsseldorf and Munster last night. I'm glad of this—it brings to an end a 12 days' complete lull in bombing, which is bad for the enemy; it is wrong that they should form false ideas. Our new lupins are marvellous. *All* the damned hens stopped laying with a click 4 days ago. I've cursed them, and given them cabbage.

Tuesday, 15 June

Cabinet at 5. Pres. [Roosevelt] and Smuts have given the all-clear about the Azores and we have telegraphed to R. H. C[ampbell] to go ahead. . . . Deadlock seems to persist between de G. and Giraud. P.M. becoming again temperamentally anti-de G. But de G. is no fool and when he behaves as he does, we must suspect he has some reason for so doing. I believe he has satisfied himself he has a strong following in N. Africa—as well as in France. In which case, if we break with him, there will be complete confusion.

Wednesday, 16 June

10.30 talk with A. about 'Lifebelt'.† He agrees to see Monteiro at the same time that R. H. C[ampbell] sees Salazar. Discussed details of procedure, and various other subjects—Joe's rather tart reply to P.M.'s message outlining operational plans, &c. . . . 4.30 discussion

* Portugese Prime Minister and at this time also Minister of Foreign Affairs and of War.

† Possible operations against the Azores.

with A. and a party about Armistices and post-war plans. 5.30 Cabinet on former. A most frightful discussion in a much too large party, including Evatt,* Selborne, Leathers &c. P.M. in recalcitrant mood, but we eventually got authority to open up with Americans and Russians about Armistice terms or 'Terms of Surrender'. Then had a similarly futile discussion about Austria, though not quite so bad.

Friday, 18 June

Roosevelt has lost his patience (and his head) about de Gaulle, and is asking for the latter's head on a charger. P.M. of course disposed to agree with him. But of course it's most unwise. I don't know what case there was against St. John the Baptist, but public opinion was less formed—and less formidable in those days. (I'm slipping into Van's style.) *We* shall be hard put to it to make a case against de G. Talked to A. on the telephone. He has tempered the P.M. somewhat, and we can't do more. . . . Good deal of work—amongst other things an extremely well done despatch by [Sir O.] O'Malley† making the case against the Russians for the Katyn murders, and drawing the inference that it was terrible to be on friendly terms with a Government that can do such things. I pointed out that, years before Katyn, the Soviet Government made a habit of butchering their own citizens by the 10,000's, and if we could fling ourselves into their arms in 1941, I don't know that Katyn makes our position more delicate. The blood of Russians cries as loud to Heaven as that of Poles. But it's very nasty. How can Poles *ever* live amicably alongside Russians, and how can *we* discuss with Russians execution of German 'war criminals', when we have condoned this?

Saturday, 19 June

R. Campbell broached 'Lifebelt' to Salazar yesterday. Got, of course, no definite answer, but the interview not too bad. A. at the same time, saw Monteiro, who took it well and will be helpful.

[Dr Salazar quickly agreed in principle, subject to talks about the conditions; but refused the suggestion of a visit by Eden.]

Sunday, 20 June

Lawford rang up to say A. wants to go to Lisbon to negotiate. He really wants to go there to gather a chaplet of flowers! I said he

* Dr H. V. Evatt, Australian Minister of External Affairs, 1941–9; Australian representative in the U.K. War Cabinet, 1942, 1943.

† Ambassador to the Polish Govt. in exile, 1942–5.

shouldn't go until it was clear we should get what we wanted, and even then I didn't see why he *should*, and Salazar would probably be embarrassed. It appears he had broached this to P.M., who of course approved excitedly. The idea of anyone travelling anywhere always fires him! . . . Went to listen to band in Green Park and read G. J[ebb]'s 'Late Night Final' edition of the 'Four Power Plan'. Don't find much wrong with it, but constant repetition makes it boring.

Monday, 21 June

Talk with A. and others at 12 about Lifebelt and de Gaulle. He was seeing Monteiro at 12.30—and seems to have had quite a satisfactory conversation. M. seems to favour idea of his going to Lisbon. . . . Cabinet 5.30. . . . Long discussion about de Gaulle situation. I agree that, if you ask me whether we can safely put French army in hands of de G., I answer a thousand times no. If that means that he then resigns from the Committee, that is altogether deplorable, but it can't be helped and we must make the best of it—by blackening de G's face as much as possible. V. unfortunate, but there it is.

Thursday, 24 June

10.45 talk with A. about a P.Q. concerning a British soldier, who seems, quite rightly, to have thrown an American financier through rather a high window. Pretty busy.

Friday, 25 June *Thatched Cottage*

Not many flowers, though the lupins are still doing manfully. Peas and beans in abundance. Raspberries coming ripe. Hens laying again!

Saturday, 26 June *Thatched Cottage*

Maisky rang me up yesterday afternoon to say he had a message from Joe. It sounds pretty formidable, as it quotes from earlier P.M. messages!

[This exchange of telegrams with Stalin had been proceeding for six months. He had been dissatisfied, naturally enough, by the Casablanca decisions, which held out no certainty of a re-entry into Northern France. By the end of May, Stalin knew that the operation had been put off until 1944. He sent a sharp protest to the President, whereupon Churchill commented that he could not allow a useless massacre of British troops in order to remove Russian suspicions. 'I am getting rather tired of these repeated scoldings considering that they have never been actuated by anything but cold-blooded self-interest and total disdain of our lives and fortunes.' He again explained the physical impossibility of a landing in 1943. Stalin's retort complained angrily of lack of consultation. Molotov had earlier in the year given assurances that no approaches from Nazi Germany to Russia would be entertained. The Foreign Office advised Eden, who agreed, that Russia was not contemplating a change of policy. Churchill had had his doubts.[19]]

Monday, 28 June

I read sharp exchange of telegrams between Joe and P.M. on second front. Maisky trying to see A. P.M. advised not having anything to do with him. But this silly and I told A. so. He said he would see M. (Told me later Maisky is recalled to Moscow—and Bogomolov*—for consultation. I don't like this.) . . . Cabinet 5.30. Not much news, but Battle of Atlantic goes well. We dropped 7,000 tons of bombs on Germany last week. P.M. trundled out Syrian question as prelude to violent attack on de Gaulle. Attlee (!) reacted quite well! P.M. makes it an Anglo-American issue, and says 'I won't break with Roosevelt'. Nobody wants him to, but he might reason with the man, or at least not out-Roosevelt him. However, it was useful, as we got P.M. into a corner where he admitted he would like to recognise the Committee of Liberation—but not, of course, ahead of America.

Tuesday, 29 June

Saw W.S. about our policy regarding assurances to Spain in connexion with Lifebelt. I don't want to give any more, or renewed assurances. They shouldn't require renewing, and this is not an occasion for doing so. Lots of work had accumulated. P.M., following an American lead blindly, is getting himself into awful mess over French in Algeria. He plunges ahead without knowing the *facts*.

Thursday, 1 July

Drafted minute from A. to P.M. suggesting an A.-Winant-Maisky body, en permanence here, for discussion of political questions.† Am sure it is right, but don't know whether P.M. will agree.

Friday, 2 July

5.30 talked to A. about various things, principal of which a

* A. Y. Bogomolov, Russian Ambassador to Allied Governments in London, 1941–3.

† This is the germ of the European Advisory Commission, established by the Foreign Ministers' meeting at Moscow in October, but with restricted functions.

ridiculous telegram from Roosevelt, who wants to pour armies into Peninsula, to protect Portugal, at expense of *all* our other operations. Glad to say Defence Committee are killing this. I'm sure I know what it is—the old American fear that the 'boys' will get bottled up in the Mediterranean!

Monday, 5 July

Rung up by A. while in my bath to say that Sikorski and party (including Victor Cazalet) were killed last night taking off from Gib[raltar]. Verified from Resident Clerk that Poles had been informed. This is a great blow: there's *no-one* to take his place. . . . 5. talk with A. and others about Benes'* desire to sign treaty with Soviet. We can't *stop* it. Russians now say we have *no* self-denying ordinance, and they seem prepared to sign. Decided thing to do was to appeal once more to Russians not to do so. If they insist, we must at least urge that treaty must not be directed in any way against Poland and, if possible, should provide for Polish accession. Cabinet at 6. Best week ever of sinkings. U-boats certainly sunk: May 36. June 13. July—so far 1. War Cabinet after discussed President's proposed message to Italians on 'D-day'. Agreed to urge that message should not be sent out till we see how operation goes, and that we should suggest a few amendments showing that *we* have *some* part in 'Husky'. Got draft for P.M.'s statement in House tomorrow about Sikorski.

[The Prime Minister used this draft without significant change. Sikorski's death, it need hardly be said, provided too good an opportunity for Goebbels' propaganda machine to miss, especially after the accusations and counter-accusations between Poland and Russia about Katyn. Accordingly the Germans, as in the instance of Darlan's murder six months before, stated as a fact that the British had once again organised the removal of an inconvenience. Cadogan's papers contain no sign that he, or anyone else in a position of importance in the British Government, paid attention to the charge. Not until a short while before his death did it gain any serious currency. Cadogan, who had been throughout the war in such intimate contact not only with turbulent Polish politics but also with the Intelligence services, dismissed the whole story with contempt:

> I see that a Herr Hochhuth says Winston arranged the murder of Sikorski. Of course it is absurd. We didn't even try to murder Hitler, let alone Sikorski. Winston was personally devoted to him; he stood above those wrangling Polish politicians; he was no more anti-Russian than most of them, and a good deal less than some. We all needed him. If I were dead, someone would be saying that I murdered him.

* Now President of the exiled Czech Government in London.

The cause of the crash at Gibraltar remains mysterious. What is certain is that there had been earlier attempts to sabotage aircraft used by Sikorski. A well-constructed bomb with a time-fuse was found while his plane was over the Atlantic in the previous year.[20]]

Tuesday, 6 July

10.30 talk with A. and others about Polish affairs. Mikolajczyk* to be P.M. That's possibly all right. Difficulty arises over C.-in-C. who is *not* to be in the Cabinet. (That all to the good.) Not v. much work and v. little news. This period of waiting (now drawing to a close) has been trying. Papers this morning report German assaults on Russians. All to the good, but I doubt whether it's a very serious affair. Another talk at 5.30 with A., who had to see Polish Pres[ident] at 6 about C.-in-C. Choice lies between Sosnkowski and Anders.† Former avowedly anti-Soviet. But I doubt whether latter much better, really, from that point of view. Depends on what Russians think. We have consulted A.C.K., but don't know when we shall get his views. A. will ask Pres. for a little more time. Am inclined to think that Sosnkowski is the straightforward choice, and Anders rather too much an unknown quantity. (He didn't impress me.) Azores discussion opened (apparently favourably) in Lisbon yesterday.

Wednesday, 7 July

A.C.K. telegraphs he knows nothing of Sosnkowski but definitely thinks Anders a persona *non* grata with Russians. This rather confirms my idea. A. had a not unsatisfactory talk with [Polish] Pres. last night. Pres. wants Sosnkowski as C.-in-C. and wants to make appointment without waiting, and before formation of Government. There are objections (obvious) to this and A. charged W. Strang to talk to Raczynski about it. Without much effect. Lunched with A. Massigli and Strang there. Massigli fairly hopeful and helpful. I had a talk with him after. Tried to interpret to him P.M.'s emotionalism in regard to France. . . . German attack in Russia *seems* fairly serious. I wish these next 3 days would pass quickly.

Thursday, 8 July

Defence Committee 10.30. About Azores: but that point was

* Stanislaw Mikolajczyk, Deputy Prime Minister, 1941–3; Prime Minister of exiled Polish Govt., 1943–4; Deputy Prime Minister, 1945–7.

† Kazimierz Sosnkowski, Minister of War 1920–3, 1924; Inspector of Polish Army, 1927–39; Minister of State, 1939–41. Wladyslaw Anders, then commanding Polish forces in Russia.

settled in 3½ minutes. Rest of the time, till midnight, taken up with rambling gossip. But Pound showed us diagram of where our 'Husky' convoys are and will be at different hours. Most exciting.

[At this meeting the Prime Minister insisted that nothing would induce him to recognise the French Committee of National Liberation. He inveighed against de Gaulle, whereupon the Foreign Secretary retorted that the Americans had mishandled the French issue from the start. Their treatment of the General would make him a national hero. When Cadogan supported his chief, the Prime Minister said he had been 'frequently wrong'. 'A turbulent and rather ludicrous interlude', remarks Eden's diary.

In a paper of 13 July, Eden set down the reasons for the belief that the U.S.A. did not want a strong French administration built up in Algiers. The argument for a strong France was based on the premise that 'Our main problem after the war will be to contain Germany.' The same argument applied, however, if the potential enemy was Russia. Churchill even imagined that he and Eden might have to part on this issue. This mood passed, however. After the President admitted on 22 July that he was moving to a 'limited acceptance' (not 'recognition') of the Committee, the issue was postponed for discussion at Quebec, where Eden was able to point out that the purpose of recognising the Committee would be to build up its collective authority, that Britain had to live twenty miles from France and that refusal would merely strengthen de Gaulle. Cordell Hull thereupon accused the British of financing de Gaulle; the implication being that since the British were in turn dependent upon the U.S.A., American money had long been paying for attacks upon herself.[21]]

Friday, 9 July

Poles are getting into a knot. Saw A. and Raczynski about it. Pres. has appointed Sosnkowski C.-in-C. On those terms Mikolajczyk won't form a Government. It would be bad to announce S., who resigned on signature of treaty with Soviet in 1941, if a Government can't be formed. Urged appointment be kept secret until after Sikorski's funeral (next Thursday). R. seems to agree. He says really the fundamental difficulty is that opposing forces are manœuvring for position after the war. What a people! And Sikorski not yet in his grave! . . . 'Tonight's the night'. It is very exciting—and anxious. We are trying something that's never been tried before. If it succeeds, it will have tremendous effect. If it fails, it will be a rather bloody nose for us. Well, we've taken them before. It's a terrific operation.

[The initial assault for 'Husky' involved nearly 3,000 ships and landing-craft, carrying 160,000 men from many ports of embarkation.]

Saturday, 10 July *Thatched Cottage*

Heard on 10 o'clock news that we'd landed in Sicily. No more. But it's something to have got troops ashore. The whole thing is such an experiment that there might well have been an initial and disastrous failure.... 'Agency messages' dwell on the difficulty of the operation—which is ominous—but it's not wrong!... Rang up [R.] Cecil* after tea. He hadn't got much extra details, but it seems that British, Canadian and even American troops are ashore. Only 3 ships sunk (carrying vehicles). Casualties not heavy. Enemy not boasting. But he says everyone seems fairly satisfied. Sat and read Somerset Maugham. Hot bath and dinner. 9 o'clock news provided no more details.

Borders are quite good, but a bit thin. Some v. good orange daisies and cherry phlox. Beastly night tonight. Still raining—and blowing.

Sunday, 11 July

News continues good. All the same, feeling depressed. Perhaps the weather, perhaps sense of futility while great things are happening. Box didn't contain too much work.

Monday, 12 July

Cabinet at 6. Sinkings are rather spoiling the record, with 2 ships of 36,000 tons to be added to the list. Sicily seems all right, but there are hard times ahead. We have 160,000 men and 600 tanks ashore, and we've got Syracuse. Germans apparently being held in Russia. Then P.M. gave us a lecture on 'Basic English', which has caught his fancy. Wants to push it; said he would broadcast, if necessary. Someone asked 'In Basic English?'!

[The Prime Minister had suddenly taken it into his head that a widespread use of Basic English 'would be a gain to us far more durable and fruitful than the annexation of great provinces'. He contemplated daily teaching of Basic English by the B.B.C. A Cabinet committee under Amery was duly appointed to investigate and report. Towards the end of September, the Prime Minister was 'shocked' to discover that urgent pressure of business had prevented the Ministers from holding even a preliminary meeting. Cadogan alone, it seems, had given the matter due attention; for he composed on the official stationery of the Foreign Office a lengthy document entitled

BAR-JI ENGLISH
PRELIMINARY REPORT OF THE LORD PRESIDENT'S COMMITTEE.

Much thought [said the bogus report] was being devoted to the

* Asst. Private Sec. to Cadogan.

debasement of English to a point where it could serve as a medium of communication between Anglo-Saxons and other races (o.r.). For this purpose—of Keeping the Foreigner in his Place—was required a limited range of forceful and easily memorised admonitions.

Considerable research has convinced us that this purpose would best be served by the standardisation and widest possible adoption (by Anglo-Saxons) of the colloquialisms employed by the barge-workers of this country. . . .

Unlike the Chinese language, which has five 'tones', Bar-Ji English has only one tone—authoritative-minatory—easily acquired by the Anglo-Saxon. Many cases have been reported to us of Anglo-Saxon functionaries of no great linguistic attainment or education, such as Embassy butlers in Turkey, China and other countries, who, with a comparatively elementary equipment of Bar-Ji English, can reduce the o.r. of those countries to a condition of docility bordering on panic.

Prolonged experimentation with what may be called the raw material of Bar-Ji English shows that the number of nouns can be reduced to 1163 and the adjectives to 1. A considerable number of verbs would have to be retained (together with their participles) but the Mixed Sub-Committee, which has not yet completed its study of this particular subject, says, in an Interim Report, that 'the less said about some of these verbs, the better.' With this we entirely agree. . . .

The average Englishman will find little difficulty in segregating from his vocabulary the particular expressions required, which will have been compulsorily memorised by the o.r. of the country he intends to visit.

These will meet all ordinary requirements. For instance, when the French porters come on board at Calais, all he will have to say is 'Nah then, yah bloody nigger, drop that!' The French porter will infer from this that the visiting Anglo-Saxon is minded to make his own arrangements for the transport of his baggage from boat to train, at a rate of remuneration which he deems to be just. This would be very difficult to convey in any of the current European languages and would involve a serious waste of time. . . .

It is perhaps unnecessary to counter the objection that it would be unsuitable for o.r. to reply in Bar-Ji English, when addressed. The answer is, of course, that no reply is needed or, indeed, expected. We feel confident that a little further study will result in producing a suitable medium for the dissemination, and enforcement, of Anglo-Saxon culture throughout both hemispheres.]

Wednesday, 14 July

Talk with A. and W. S[trang] about our attitude to Algiers. A. has been wrestling for a week with P.M. who, I think realises he's made rather an ass of himself in these matters. . . . 5. meeting with

A., Massigli, Viénot,* M. Peterson, Casey, Spears &c., about Syria. Hope it may have been useful. M.P., for all his violent and bloody-minded talk, doesn't show up much at these meetings. Spears, as a matter of fact, not too bad. Casey gives me goose-flesh. Massigli smothered everything—in the good old manner—with beautifully worded French talk and an appearance of omniscience.

Friday, 16 July

Howard,† and later O.S., about the (very vague) S.O.E. reports of Italians wanting to surrender in Balkans and Samos. But who are they to surrender to?! Papers marked by P.M. to Chiefs of Staff and F.O. 'Action this day', so had to devise a letter to [Major-General L. C.] Hollis‡ giving our rather unhelpful views.

Monday, 19 July

Cabinet 6. (until 8). Sicilian news good. 20 U-boats sunk this month so far. Sinkings not so good—but not bad. P.M. objects to foreign pronunciation of foreign names: calls it Pentellărea, and ridicules Pantelleíra: asks if we are to talk about Afreéca and Parée! C.I.G.S. played up nobly by calling Porto Empedocle Porto Empedoakle. P.M. didn't bat an eyelid. A rambling discussion, in course of which P.M. said we should have to consider, after the war, segregating 3 or 4 million German males for some years, to arrive at a balance of population with France. A. Sinclair hit the nail on the head by pointing out that you could only arrive certainly at this result by shooting millions of German *women*.

Wednesday, 21 July

3. meeting of the Attlee Committee on administration of Italy. Short and amateurish and thereby all the more effective. It has wiped out *acres* of minutes by E[conomic] and R[econstruction] Department.

Friday, 23 July

Talk with A. at 11.15 about plans. P.M. has fixed (or is fixing) Quebec meeting. A. will go too, and wants to take me. P.M. rather wants him to go to Moscow. But what could he say? Alternative is to go there after Quebec. But will that be pleasant interview? Joe has

* Pierre Viénot, diplomatic representative in London of French Committee of National Liberation, 1943–4.

† Douglas F. Howard, then serving in F.O.; later Ambassador at Montevideo and Minister at the Holy See.

‡ Senior Asst. Sec., office of War Cabinet.

ignored Roosevelt's invitation and has never replied to P.M.'s message on opening of Sicilian campaign. If he can sulk, I suppose we can too, and I am rather in favour of leaving him alone. If we tell him of Quebec, he may send someone there, whose arguments will reinforce the Americans, who are as keen as Joe on a cross-Channel spring operation. Failing that, the Americans want to waste strength in the Pacific. Very awkward. I think I should take the risk of leaving Joe out and, if he protests, remonstrate with him for his bad manners.

[In the late afternoon of 24 July the Fascist Grand Council met. Count Grandi, formerly Italian Ambassador in London, moved a motion hostile to Mussolini's continued conduct of the war. In the early hours of 25 July it was passed by 19 votes to 7. That afternoon Mussolini was dismissed by the King and put under protective arrest. Marshal Badoglio formed a Government at once. The Fascist Party organisation, and all the imposing facade erected around the Duce in more than twenty years of power, collapsed. Badoglio announced that Italy would continue the struggle at Germany's side.]

Monday, 26 July

Papers have Mussolini's resignation! ... 2.45 saw O.S. and Howard about Grol's* request for an interview with me. Grol at 3.30. Found to my surprise that he would favour the *majority* of the Government going to Cairo with King P[eter]. Only disturbed at idea of splitting Government and starting next Monday! I said I quite agreed: *I* thought majority of Government ought to go, but I wouldn't dictate the date. 5. discussed with Dixon and after, for 2 minutes, with A. the Italian situation. Cabinet 5.30. Winston not too excited. He will telegraph to Pres. but does not mind our getting on with a telegram to Halifax instructing latter to try and get agreement of U.S.G. as to what we are to *do* if faced with offer of surrender. (Hitherto we have written *acres* of minutes with no result.) P.M. outlined plans for trips. This was in War Cabinet. When the rag tag and bobtail came in, A. and I left to clear up a lot of work. ... These are stirring times. P.M. is keeping his head, but Washington are going off the rails with excited abuse of Badoglio and the King. It's too early for that.

[Churchill telegraphed that night to Roosevelt:

> I don't think myself that we should be too particular in dealing with any non-Fascist Government, even if it is not all we should like. Now Mussolini is gone I would deal with any non-Fascist Italian which can deliver the goods.]

* Dr Milan Grol, Yugoslav leader, later Vice-Premier.

Tuesday, 27 July

Sobolev at 5.30 with Russian reply about War Crimes Commission. They are evidently obstructing. They agree to Dominions taking part if Ukraine, Byelo-Russia, Latvia, Estonia, Lithuania and Karelo-Finland are also separately represented. Indicated that this must make indefinite further delay. Seems to me Russians are trying to saboter [sic] Commission for fear of Katyn being brought before it! Dinner at Dorchester 7.15 with Inter-Allied Friendship. Such things can only end in inter-allied murder. [Prince] Olav of Norway spoke for *one hour and 20 minutes*, and said *nothing—twice*. Then Romer, the Pole (next to me) was called on and produced innumerable typewritten sheets. Then the President of the Belgian Senate (the only one who could make a speech). Then Arthur Evans, M.P., (whom I knew nothing about) brayed with the voice of a donkey. Nor was that the only point of resemblance. All in a temperature hovering round 100° and a complete lack of oxygen. Why must such things be? Then Cassin* was put up to talk. . . . So I took leave of the Chairman, Wickham Steed,† who had made some of his interventions in French quite unnecessarily, and fled. Luckily found a taxi and was home at 10.45, and able to get thro' some work. But is there no Society, or Board, or Committee, or Proctor, or Interventor who can forbid this kind of thing, set the place on fire at a suitable moment and crucify the Chairman? We are overburdened with regulations, but the long-suffering public have no protection at all against the worst evils that are inflicted on them. We boast of liberty of speech, but if that means that one man can mumble away for 1 hr. 20 mins, while 150 people sit morally and mentally enchained, I do not call that one of the 'Four Freedoms'!

Wednesday, 28 July

Various talks in afternoon, mainly concerned with trying to sort out the tangle in our Italian armistice terms produced by about 6 bodies of excellent bureaucrats writing square miles of minutes. Yugoslavs giving trouble again: Government running out on Cairo trip and King P. much too feeble to call them to heel. . . . Defence Committee at 10.30. Discussed armistice terms and Ike's mad idea of broadcasting a bowdlerised version. P.M. got Pres. on the telephone and squashed latter idea. But Ike authorised to put out a

* René Cassin, Commissioner for Justice and Public Education on French Committee of National Liberation, 1941–3.

† Former Editor of *The Times*.

proclamation. P.M. mainly preoccupied about our prisoners. Sent short threatening telegram to King of Italy.

[In the House on 27 July, Churchill had given a cool welcome to the Badoglio régime. The telephone call made by the Prime Minister after the Defence Committee was intercepted by the Germans. It is recorded thus:

CHURCHILL: We do not want proposals for an armistice to be made before we have been definitely approached.
ROOSEVELT: That is right.
CHURCHILL: We can also wait quietly for one or two days.
ROOSEVELT: That is right.

They agreed to contact the King of Italy. The exchange is quoted in the War Diary of the German High Command with the comment, 'This is complete proof that secret negotiations between the Americans and Italy are under way.'

Almost unbelievable confusion characterised the Italian armistice talks. The Americans had a plan for a surrender in two stages: first, the immediate signature of a document containing only military terms and second, the dictation of political and economic terms to a civil administration. In the British view this procedure would carry a serious risk, that of making the Italians feel cheated when the victors imposed stringent conditions after disarmament. Eisenhower's broadcast would have concerned the military terms only.[22]]

Friday, 30 July

V. hot again. A. up until 3 this morning. P.M. suddenly called a Cabinet for nothing—except his state of over-excitement—and they sent off messages which seem to have cut across all that we have done in the last 36 hours. . . . 12.30 Allied meeting and lunch with A. Allies evidently disturbed by Eisenhower's proclamation, and all in rather suspicious mood. Spoke to Viénot after. He wants (1) French participation in armistice (I should think so!), and (2) a statement to make it clear that Amgot* is not the model for *liberated* countries. . . . No news—but I didn't expect it. Italian 'Government' can't know where they are. Think we are entering on Catania battle.

Saturday, 31 July

11.30 Romer, about their contacts with Hungarians. Had to turn him out in the middle, as A. rang up, in an awful flap, about a telegram from Pres. suggesting, apparently, *new* armistice terms (Ye Gods!). Got rid of Romer, got hold of President's telegram and

* Allied Military Government of Occupied Territories.

discussed it with O.S., Dixon, Jebb and Fitzmaurice.* They abounded, of course, in minute criticism, but that is not the point. Finally fixed up with A. on telephone a minute to P.M. pointing out that President's proposals revert to 2-stage arrangement (being purely military terms). As such they are not too bad and if an emergency arises we may have to use them as such. But meanwhile *do* ask the Americans to look again at our *complete* armistice (they have had it for weeks). If we have time to agree on that, surely it's better to present it in the first instance? This went on until 1.40.... Rushed through some work and had a flap with A. (who, however, is fairly calm) about this question of whether or no we should ask Joe to the Conference. We *must*. He agreed, and I dictated a minute from him to P.M. in that sense.

Sunday, 1 August

Contrary to expectation, everything calm. P.M. has telegraphed, more or less as I wanted, to Pres. about armistice terms. But I gather he won't contemplate Russian participation in forthcoming meeting. Meanwhile Ike has blown off again with a (so far as I know, unauthorised) proclamation to the Italians, saying that unless they make peace, we start the Blitz again. This is the way *not* to do it. I think his Mr Crossman† ... has taken charge.

[By the last week in July, the discussions with Portugal about the Azores had still not reached a conclusion. The Ambassador in Lisbon insisted that the Portuguese were showing goodwill, but a renewed proposal for a visit by Eden would be regarded by Salazar as an attempt to rush him. Eventually an agreement was signed in mid-August, to become effective in October.]

Monday, 2 August

Cabinet at 6. Sinkings of U-boats wonderful, 91 in 92 days—for certain. June sinkings 380,000 tons. Attack in Sicily started last night, and not too badly, apparently.... Defence Committee at 10.30 p.m. Tiresome discussion about S.O.E. activities in France and Balkans. But some agreement seemed to be reached. Then we rambled all over the place, and finally lit on second item on agenda, Azores. On this, P.M. was simply tiresome and mulish, insisting on date September 15th, and getting v. excitable at times, and silly. Subsequently A. got

* G. G. Fitzmaurice, 3rd Legal Adviser, F.O., 1929; seconded as legal adviser to M.E.W., 1939–43.

† R. H. S. Crossman, Deputy Director, Psychological Warfare, Allied Forces H.Q., 1943.

him to agree to something reasonable. Then a discussion of American decision to cancel bombing of Rome tomorrow, and Marshall was called on telephone. Luckily I got away at 1.15 a.m. Rather tired, but more bored and discouraged.

Wednesday, 4 August

5.30 Viénot, with formal request from Committee of Liberation to be associated in Italian Armistice. I was as kind as I could be, but had to give him rather a douche. By the way, Cabinet at 1, which decided to urge U.S. Government *not* to make Rome an open city. *Volleys* of red boxes, with all sorts of complications.

Thursday, 5 August

5. talk with A. and Winant about the Italian wail put out through Lisbon. Nothing to do about it. . . . I got him to drop it. Discussion about Yugoslav crisis. Agreed it was no use forcing the King out to Cairo if his Government wouldn't go with him. (And they won't.) So that's that. And I'm not sorry. I think it was always rather a silly idea.

[On 10 August King Peter dismissed the quarrelsome Cabinet and appointed a government of officials under Dr. Pourić, formerly Yugoslav Minister in France. In October, the King and Cabinet moved to Cairo, accompanied by R. S. Stevenson, the new British Ambassador to the Yugoslav Government.]

Friday, 6 August

Various more or less direct approaches from Badoglio through Lisbon, Barcelona and Tangier—which I discussed with Dixon. The one through Tangier . . . definitely invites 'negotiation'. We can't negotiate, but I don't think we ought to ignore it. Why not put our 'surrender terms' through it? Put this to A. later, and he very frightened. Said we must demand 'unconditional surrender'. I said if there were any virtue in these words, we could use them. Had a draft telegram to P.M. telephoned to him, which later he approved. . . . 3.30 Turk. He kept on invoking the Alliance and saying what good allies they had been. I kept on insinuating that they'd been awfully good neutrals. 5 Sobolev, whom I informed about Italian approaches.

Tuesday, 10 August *Thatched Cottage*

Messenger arrived after lunch. Nothing much to read and little of interest. Italians still nibbling at us through Tangier, but I think

Badoglio is falling more into German grips. Roumanians also nibbling, but I don't care what happens to them.

Wednesday, 11 August

I am very fit. Thank God for my Holiday. I just needed it, and have profited by it. Find—as I expected—that A. is very cagey about saying a *word* to the Italians, who are contacting us from all round. It's the old complex—the old ideology—that *terrifies* him and makes him see ghosts. How silly! I'd start talking to them at once. I haven't got such lack of faith in our diplomacy that I daren't open up with friend or foe. This was the grand fault of our policy 1933–38—see my poor Diary *passim*. But I think Winston and F.D.R. are too big to be frightened by this turnip. I must have some plain speaking with A. this week.

Thursday, 12 August

Went up to see A. Found him jumpy and bad-tempered, so left him. *Stacks* of boxes—all containing long-term plans in millions of words. So sent them back saying I was not to be bothered with these things now. . . . 3.15 W. Tyrrell for a gossip. (He evidently sees the foolishness of 'unconditional surrender', and I'm afraid I let him see that I agree!) . . . 5.30 Romer to plead for Anglo-U.S. declaration about German deportations from Poland, and to warn against any discussion of Polish frontiers! I went so far as to tell him I thought that subject would inevitably be brought up—by the Russians! . . . A. rang up after [dinner] about the Americans' (rather rude) gate-crashing on Azores.

[Churchill suggested using the term 'honourable capitulation' in the Italian negotiations. Since the Allied demand for 'unconditional surrender' had already been stated in public, however, Eden felt that it must be sustained. Signor Berio* was answered accordingly on 14 August, and also reminded that Roosevelt and Churchill had already said that the Allies wished to see Italy occupy a respected place in the new Europe. On the next day, just before Eden and Cadogan left for Quebec, an intermediary said on Badoglio's behalf that Italy would accept 'unconditional surrender' if allowed to join the Allies in fighting Germany. Churchill and Roosevelt, at Quebec, decided to follow this up.[23]]

Friday, 13 August

Our Clipper weatherbound at Lisbon, so we can't start before Sunday. . . . 11. talk with Macmillan who, I think, is sensible. He

* Of the Italian Foreign Office.

off this afternoon. . . . Salazar's answer now in: he had said October 15th, we October 1st, he now October 8th. Silly. Rang up A. and recommended accepting October 8th. Agreed to draft telegram on that line, which he subsequently approved by telephone this evening.

Saturday, 14 August

A. has approved our reply to the Italian approach through Berio (Tangier). Won't lead to much, I think!

Sunday, 15 August

A. decided—wisely, I think, to wait for the Clipper tomorrow, rather than take a bomber tonight. So here I am for another 24 hrs. . . . Telegram has been received from Lisbon to show that Italians wanted to surrender—on condition they could fight on our side. We collected Nye, Hollis and O.S. and we drafted a somewhat discouraging paper pointing out all the obvious snags and the doubtfulness of the advantages. Had this telephoned to A. and to Attlee, who apparently agreed. In bed by about 2 a.m.

[Cadogan flew to Quebec with Eden and Brendan Bracken on 17 August. He kept a diary during this trip, but the entries printed for 20 August, 7 and 8 September are taken from letters to Lady Theo.]

Wednesday, 18 August *Quebec*

Awake and got up early. A low layer of thin cloud below us, and another high above. Promise of sunrise in between. This gradually broadened out until the floor below and the roof above us were a mass of pink and gold with, in the west, most unbelievable blues and greens.

Went and sat with pilot. Soon after 10.30 he pointed to a patch in the cloud below and said 'There's land. You've crossed the Atlantic!' . . .

Met by naval launch with N. Robertson* and M. MacD[onald]† on board, taken ashore and chucked into a mob of pressmen and then whisked in a car and up to the Citadel, where, on the terrace, we found Pres., P.M. and Athlones.‡ Got photographed with them. A. and I had a talk with P.M. He, as I expected, had nibbled at the Italian bait, and was determined to try and swallow it. Pres. and Chiefs of Staff with him, so there it is. Anyhow he has safeguarded it

* Norman A. Robertson, Canadian Under-Sec. for External Affairs, 1941–6, 1958–64.
† British High Commissioner in Ottawa (1941–6). See List of Principal Characters.
‡ The Earl of Athlone was then Gov.-Gen. of Canada.

by saying no *negotiation* and no *commitment*. (He has agreed to Marshall being Supreme Allied Commander in the West.)

Friday, 20 August *A.C. to T.C.* *Quebec*

I've been pretty busy as, with enormous Delegations here, there is a good deal going on, and it's not easy to conduct affairs some 3,000 miles from home, with the P.M. in a huddle with the President in one building and the Foreign Secretary and myself in another, a quarter of a mile apart. We shall end up in a glorious muddle!

The P.M. went off fishing all today, with the President. Cordell Hull arrived about lunch time, and Anthony and I had a long session with him this afternoon. A dreadful old man—vaguer and wordier than Norman Davis,* and rather pig-headed, but quite a nice old thing, I dare say. We didn't make much headway with him, and certainly didn't persuade him to recognise the French Committee.

It's not an amusing Conference, as the P.M. lives in one world and we, about 500 of us, live in another. Anthony goes round to some meals with the President and P.M., but I've seen very little of the Bigwigs. . . .

I shall get very fat. I believe there *is* a rationing system. One waiter told me one mustn't have more than three lumps of sugar in a cup of tea. Very good food in unlimited quantities.

Saturday, 21 August *Quebec*

V. busy again. Hull at 1. (till 2). We at last got some agreement on Italian surrender terms. Agreed to differ about French recognition, and discussed some minor topics.

Sunday, 22 August *Quebec*

Had long sitting with Americans. Hull has given us U.S. 4-Power draft [about post-war security] which looks good. Main difficulty remains this beastly question of recognition of French Committee, on which Hull too tiresome. We jig drafts about all day and all night. . . .

Meeting at Citadel at 5.30—P.M., Pres., A., Hull, Dunn,† Atherton,‡ H. H[opkins] and self. We had prepared the ground and had quite a useful discussion—on the terrace, which was v. pleasant. Lasted till nearly 8. Pres. said to me 'Cadogan, I want to ask you a

* Head of U.S. delegation to London naval talks, 1935–6, and to 9-Power conference at Brussels, 1937; an old friend of Cadogan.

† James C. Dunn, adviser on political relations, State Dept., 1937–44.

‡ Ray Atherton, chief of the division of European Affairs, State Dept., 1940–3.

riddle—where is the original of the Atlantic Charter?' I said 'That's an easy one, Mr President; it doesn't exist!' Hull made a typical intervention. He said Norwegian Minister in Washington had approached him with the request that, if the Germans evacuated Norway, the latter might be allowed to send a token force with troops of occupation. This was duly weighed and approved, and then Hull croaked 'I don't know but what I oughtn't to check up on that. It may have been Palestine'. Everyone looked pained.

Dined in Hotel with G.J. and had a lot of 'Washing up' to do. It's hard work being P.U.S., Chancery and everything else combined.

[Hull, at this resumed talk of 22 August, said to Eden, who continued to press him hard about recognition of de Gaulle, 'I never knew you were such a politician'; he allowed it to be inferred that he, Hull, was by contrast a 'statesman'. Eden asked whether the Secretary of State had not heard Lloyd George's definition of a statesman: 'a politician with whom one happens to agree'? Even Hull was amused; but on the main question, he would not budge. 'You see *buggies* everywhere', he said with emphasis. This turned out to mean 'bogies'. After the next day's equally futile encounter, Cadogan described Hull to one of the British delegation as being 'as vindictive as an old woman about whom someone had been spreading scandal'.

These days, tiring as they were, provide an excellent example of Cadogan's capacity to concentrate wholly on the business in hand until he could make no further progress, at which point he would cease to worry. On 22 August it was decided, after a frustrating morning of abortive attempts to make mental contact with Hull and telephonic contact with Sargent in London, to take a picnic to the country. Eden, Cadogan and Lawford found a delightful place at the edge of a wood, where they ate a 5-course meal with plates and napkins, knives and forks. Cadogan, dressed in clothes he might equally well have worn in Whitehall, complained mildly of the pears' softness and the peaches' tastelessness but obviously enjoyed himself.]

Monday, 23 August *Quebec*

3 Long session again with Hull, which dragged on till dinner. . . . Went with A. to Citadel after. Talk with President, Winston, Hull, Dunn, Ath., H.H. Brendan there part of time. P.M. in very good form, but that resulted in our being kept up till 1.30. At one time he was pacing about haranguing us, H.H. said suddenly 'Now I'll tell you, Mr P.M., what's going to happen'. The P.M. halted and looked inquiring. 'Your pants is coming down' said Harry.

(This afternoon P.M. had some iced water. He took a sip and said

'This water tastes very funny'. 'Of course it does' said H. 'it's got no whisky in it. Fancy you a judge of water!')

Tuesday, 24 August *Quebec*

Hull at 10.15. We have agreed to differ about recognition, and use different formulas. But it's been an exhausting business. Went up to Citadel with A. at 11.30 and found W.S.C. stark naked drying himself. Got his final approval and came back here. From then till tea-time . . . was busy 'washing-up'. This now practically complete. . . .

Dined with G.J. and N. L[awford]. Sat and talked to Pound after, who then took me to see a film of 'artificial harbours'. (Not very convincing to a purely lay mind.) As I came out (about 10.30) saw G.J. running up and down the hall with a scared look. He pounced on me and said A. (who had dined in bed) had been summoned to the Citadel and had left 10 minutes ago. I was to follow. Jumped into a car and penetrated to the dining-room in the Citadel. Found Pres. and P.M. had been alarmed at a seemingly rude message from Stalin. But read properly it really wasn't so bad. A. and I calmed them down and got away about midnight.

[This message from Stalin protested against the handling of the Italian surrender negotiations:

> To date it has been like this . . . the U.S.A. and Britain reach agreement between themselves, while the U.S.S.R. is informed of the agreement. . . . I must say that this situation cannot be tolerated any longer.

He wanted a three-power commission to handle questions of negotiation with powers detaching themselves from the Axis. For different reasons, Churchill and Roosevelt did not favour this proposal, which was dropped when the Russians accepted the British suggestion of a European Advisory Commission in October.

There was nothing for it but to use different formulae about the French Committee. The British statement of 26 August recognised the Committee as 'administering those French overseas territories which acknowledge its authority, and as having assumed the functions of the former French National Committee in respect of territories in the Levant'; noted sympathetically the Committee's wish to be regarded as the body qualified to ensure the administration of all French interests, a request to which the British Government would give effect 'as far as possible'.]

Wednesday, 25 August *Lake Jacques Cartier*

About 5.30 got away in car with A., N. L[awford] and Charlesworth for Lake Jacques Cartier. Pretty drive, but I find the pine forests rather monotonous after a bit. Arrived at the Camp on the lake at 7.30. Pretty cold (2,500 feet up) and nice to have a roaring log fire in our cabin. A. and I in one cabin and the 2 others in another. We fed in the central cabin. Quite good food—grilled trout. But we had forgotten the Whisky, and there was nothing to drink. I *hate* tea or coffee with meals. Early to bed.

Friday, 27 August *La Cabane*

A. and I started for La Cabane at 5.30. V. bad road, but better scenery than on ours. 2 or 3 miles short of La Cabane, met two cars with Detective and Martin. They said P.M. was 'shooting the rapids' in a canoe, and they had come to pick him up! I don't know how they were going to do it, as there was an impenetrable thicket between the river and the road.

We drove on, and found Tommy and Moran, and had a gossip. M. rather worried about P.M.'s health. P.M. and family arrived soon after 8. He had a drink, and then insisted on a bath, while A. talked to him. So we didn't get dinner till 9, which looked bad, as A. and I had to get back to Quebec—we weren't asked to stay the night!

Very good dinner and, to my surprise, we got away at 10.30. Portal and Brooke also came, in another car. They had arrived just in time for dinner, from the Lac des Neiges. In 2 days Portal had caught 104 trout, and Brooke 93—averaging 1½ pounds, the biggest 3¾ pounds!

Sunday, 29 August *La Cabane*

Moran and I went out fishing about 9 a.m. But it was too bright and sunny and we were sent (I think) to the wrong places! I caught 2, but not good ones. Got back for lunch. W.S.C. in terrific form, singing Dan Leno's songs and other favourites of the Halls of forty years ago, together with the latest Noel Coward. I went thro' his broadcast and got one or two things altered. He luckily then went to sleep. I sat on the duckboard and read till tea. After that we fished. I went to Portal's Bay and caught eight, all in about ¼ hr. Biggest three pounds. V. good evening. Back about 8. More singing at dinner.

Monday, 30 August *La Cabane*

P.M. dictating more of his broadcast. About 1.30 he went off to have a bath. Ismay arrived and we eventually got lunch soon after 2. After lunch went thro' new bits of broadcast with P.M. and concocted some more. I think it's finished now! . . .

P.M. got in just after 8 and by the time he'd had a drink and a bath it was 9 o'clock. We had meant to start back for La Cabane at 10.30, but P.M. started a monologue which went on till 11.30, so we reached the Cabane at 2 a.m. I crawled off to bed at 2.30. Rowan and Ismay (with whom I was sharing a room) had to sit up with P.M. till 3.45! But Ismay didn't wake me coming to bed.

Tuesday, 31 August *En route Quebec to Washington*

P.M. arranged to start at 9.30, but by 8.30 he was bustling about and shouting for a start at 9. He's surprised to have a cold. But of *course* he has a cold. Lovely sunny and fresh morning. We drove (at P.M.'s bidding) at a terrific speed and got to Quebec about 10.20.

I had a bath and attended to various things. Then to Citadel where P.M. had invited Canadian Cabinet to listen to his broadcast, and lunch after. Sat between Mack. King* and Minister of Justice (St. Laurent). 3: attended meeting of Canadian Cabinet which lasted till 4.30. Then a chat with N. Robertson and back to Hotel to pack. Left them 6.15 for Wolfe's Cove station, from where special started at 7. Most luxurious—air conditioned, saloon in back coach, wide beds, porcelain baths and good food.

[At Quebec agreement was reached on the full terms of the Italian surrender. Eisenhower, however, did not wish to use them at this moment; the landings in Italy were scheduled for 3 September, and he looked for the earliest possible acceptance of the military terms. On that day, therefore, the 'short terms' were signed on Badoglio's behalf, in strict secrecy, near Syracuse. The 8th Army had just crossed the Straits of Messina to the toe of Italy. Then ensued a further confused period. The Allies had hoped to take the airfields round Rome with the Italian Government's connivance. On 8 September it was discovered that the Germans had forestalled the intention. Badoglio appealed to Eisenhower to call off the announcement of the armistice; but he, because the Allied troops were already on their way to the hazardous landing at Salerno, refused. The news was broadcast on that evening. German forces took Rome; Badoglio and the Ministers left for Brindisi; the Italian fleet, after serious losses from German attack during the journey, reached Valetta harbour on 11 September. On the following day, Mussolini was rescued from captivity by a daring airborne operation mounted by Hitler's orders, and carried off to a meeting with him at Munich. Eventually the fallen leader established a puppet government in the north. Italy now had no effective indigenous administration: the Allies, fighting their way up the peninsula, ruled the territory they took; the Germans ruled the rest.]

* W. L. Mackenzie King, Prime Minister of Canada, 1921–30, 1935–48; S. of S. for External Affairs, 1935–46.

Wednesday, 1 September *Washington*

Dinner with R. C[ampbell]* and sat in garden after till 10.30 when I was summoned by telephone to White House. Found P.M. there, very excited about Italian armistice negotiations. We discussed telegrams and he then took me down to Map Room in Basement, where we found Pres. Ismay came with us, and General Marshall joined us about 12. Discussion went on until 1.30. Agreed to authorise Eisenhower to send air-borne Division 'at appropriate moment' to Rome area. Seems that, on that Italians will sign. Home before 2.

Thursday, 2 September *Washington*

3 to S[tate] D[epartment] to see Breckinridge Long† (who is spoken of as possible successor to Welles.‡ Rather a dry stick of a man (Lincoln through the wrong end of a telescope) and, I am told, difficult. However, he wasn't so bad talking generalities. . . . Summoned to White House at 10.30. Went round there and found P.M. not available. He was still not available at 11.30. I told Martin I would wait till 12 and then go home. I don't know what sort of message he gave to P.M., but latter turned up at 11.58, with apologies which I received in silence. It's really too much. What he wanted was to give me instructions about drafting two messages to Stalin about the Mediterranean Commission and the 3 Power meeting.

Friday, 3 September *Washington*

To White House to try to see P.M. But he was engaged, so left drafts for him. . . . Good dinner, after which (at 10) called on Hornbeck§ and sat gossiping with him till 12. Then home and to bed —no summons to White House, thank Heavens. But I don't know what Winston's doing. Hungarian affairs have also blown up, and I must see him about them. All our plans are changed again. Winston will, I think, settle down in U.S.!

Saturday, 4 September *Washington*

Went round to White House. Found Winston in bed. Pres. had drafted message to Stalin which was pretty muddled, as he hadn't seized the difference between proposal for Mediterranean Commission and 3 Power Conference. We tried to straighten this out, and discussed other matters. 1.30 Press lunch for P.M., who did awfully well in reply to questions . . . Summoned by P.M. to White House.

* That is, R. I. Campbell.
† Asst. Sec., State Department, 1940–4.
‡ Sumner Welles, Under Sec. of State, 1937–43.
§ Stanley K. Hornbeck, U.S. State Dept.

Got there soon after 5. P.M. still tinkering with draft to Stalin. I passed between him and Pres., and agreement was finally reached.

Plans all changed. Avalanche* put forward to 8th–9th, so P.M. can't launch himself on to the sea over that date, and has elected to return here after his Boston trip. Think he is right. As he shouldn't fly, he couldn't get to the *other* side in time. I got his leave to send a telegram to A. asking whether I may stay with him over the critical date.

[This Cadogan was keen to do, for he confessed himself quite charmed by Washington: the old houses, the tree-shaded streets, the parklike surroundings of the more modern buildings and the magnificence of the Mellon gallery.

> I can't begin to describe it [he wrote to Lady Theo on 4 September]: it's one of the most lovely buildings I have ever seen. Seldom more than half a dozen pictures in any one room, hung to the best effect on the most beautiful panelling—unbelievable Rembrandts, Van Dycks, Italian primitives, Goyas, el Grecos. . . .
>
> I hadn't been through 3 rooms when I received a telephone summons from the P.M. to go to the White House. And I was there till 8, running between the P.M. in bed and the President in his study. The P.M.'s sleeping arrangements have now become quite promiscuous. He talks with the President till 2 a.m. and consequently spends a large part of the day hurling himself violently in and out of bed, bathing at unsuitable moments and rushing up and down corridors in his dressing-gown.]

Monday, 6 September *Boston*

We hung about in large Hall for some time, being marshalled, and then processed into the Theatre. Ceremony quite well done. Winston's speech very good. He went flat out on Governor Dewey's† appeal for an alliance but it was done quite cleverly and discreetly. (I had had various brushes with him while he was in bed on the train—he had wanted to leave China out of the Great 4 in a most pointed and wounding way. He changed it, with much blasphemy.)

Tuesday, 7 September *A.C. to T.C.* *Washington*

We started back at 3, going through some lovely country, and got back here at 8 a.m. this morning.

Winston enjoyed himself hugely, making V-signs from the train window at all the engine drivers on the line and at all the passers-by. He quite unnecessarily rushes out on to the rear platform of the car,

* The Salerno landings.

† Thomas E. Dewey, Governor of New York, 1942–54; Republican candidate for Presidency, 1944, 1948.

in a flowered silk dressing-gown, to attract and chat with anyone he can find on the platform at stopping-places. Makes Clemmie and Mary* do the same—only they are conventionally dressed!

Wednesday, 8 September *A.C. to T.C.* *Washington*

Here I still am—you will have seen from the news why the P.M. stayed, so as to be in close touch with the President over these few critical days. . . .

The P.M., oddly enough, is fairly calm, or was, when I saw him last this afternoon.

I haven't really had much to do today, and have bought some olive oil, marmalade and anchovies! I don't know what else to get. I can't get a ham—it is on 'Points'—as are a surprising number of things. Which is very good for the Americans, but rather a bore for us!

Thursday, 9 September

Saw Joe's reply about Commission and 3-Power meeting. He insists Moscow for latter (and Tehran for the later 'Big Boys' meeting). So I shall have a jolly autumn. Planned provisionally to return by bomber, leaving here Sunday. P.M. won't sail till later. But plans may change. . . . Winston showed me his reply to Joe. Fear he accepts Moscow, but there it is. . . .

Dined at home and read, while R. C[ampbell] worked. (It is quite pleasant to see someone else doing this!)

Sunday, 12 September

Harriman† came to see me at 10.15, on his way to Hull about agenda for the 3-power meeting. Hope he gets something out of the old lady! He promised to see me later in the day.

Monday, 13 September

Harriman rang me up yesterday afternoon. He hadn't much to say: he and Dunn were going to try to put 'something in writing' before the old lady this morning. The o.l. might then see me this afternoon or tomorrow morning. But I doubt whether anything will come of it. Pres. returns tomorrow morning. I wish I could see *him*. P.M. said to me 'the Pres. will take a lot from you'. Anyhow, one *might* get something *definite*. Harry Hopkins might help, but I don't know where he is or how he is. Harriman may have good intentions but I think he is rather ineffective.

* Mary Churchill, the Prime Minister's daughter.

† W. Averell Harriman, U.S. Ambassador in Moscow, 1943–6. See List of Principal Characters.

IX

September 1943–May 1944
THE BEGINNING OF THE END

This chapter covers the period separating the landings in Italy on 3 September 1943 from the launching of 'Overlord', the most ambitious operation of its kind ever undertaken, on 6 June 1944. In the realm of diplomacy, Anglo-American relations remained cordial. The conversations which Stettinius* held in London during the spring of 1944 showed that the two governments were thinking similarly about the plans for a better ordering of international relations in the post-war world. All the same, American doubt of British intentions in the military field had grown. When, in November 1943, Lord Halifax asked point-blank whether there was not a good deal of suspicion of Britain's intention to undertake 'Overlord' wholeheartedly, Stimson† admitted it. He had said as much to Churchill, who replied, 'Well, we have given our word and we will do it.' Halifax remonstrated that it was not unreasonable to keep freedom of decision until one saw how matters looked nearer the time. That, Stimson conceded, was elementary; but if the thought were half-hearted, the preparations would never be properly made. 'It is like the old steamboat on the Mississippi which worked its whistles and its paddles from the same engines. The funnel for the whistle was so big that when the whistle went it stopped the paddles.'[1]

The Prime Minister and the British Chiefs of Staff therefore found themselves deprived of some freedom of manœuvre in the Mediterranean and in the conferences at Cairo and Tehran, for Stalin was aware of Anglo-American differences, small as they were when measured against the scale of agreement, and none knew better than he how to extract the utmost purchase from them. For the moment, despite these signs of strain within the alliance, the task of defeating Germany remained so immediate and burdensome that it provided a sufficient incentive to unity. For all his disbelief in the virtues of 'unconditional surrender', Cadogan's Diary contains nothing to indicate that he thought Germany would be defeated by other than military means. By this stage, Anglo-American collaboration in all matters of covert propaganda, espionage and other clandestine operations had become continuous and intimate. The British saw the results of the contact established by Allen Dulles in Berne, whereby

* Edward R. Stettinius, Jr., Under Sec. of State in the State Dept., 1943–4; Sec. of State, 1944–5. See List of Principal Characters.

† Henry Stimson, U.S. Secretary for War.

thousands of the most secret German documents were passed over. Admiral Canaris and his staff were rightly suspected by the British of disloyalty. Although too cautious to record it, Cadogan is almost certain to have known, from his regular gossips with 'C', Menzies, of the feelers put out by Canaris through his agents in Spain and Portugal. Menzies was apparently not interested. Probably he felt as Cadogan did about another approach, allegedly inspired by von Papen, the German Ambassador in Ankara, of December 1943; that leaving aside all the other political difficulties, the terms of a deal, even one which entailed the overthrow of the Nazi Government, were unlikely to be tolerable until the military balance had tilted much more heavily against the Axis. von Papen's approach, for example, suggested that Germany should maintain the Anschluss and 'rent' Danzig and the Corridor from Poland.[2]

The invasion of Italy safely launched, Cadogan left the Prime Minister and flew home.

1943

Saturday, 18 September *Thatched Cottage*

Went round estate. Not much doing. Quite a few apples gathered. Autumn crocuses rather over. Later walked down fields and up by Little Dixter. Picked 2 small mushrooms! Masses of blackberries. . . . Already feel refreshed.

Thursday, 23 September

Saw A., who told me P.M.'s idea of Cabinet reconstruction. Oliver L[yttelton]* to be Chancellor. Anderson to take Production. Attlee to be Lord President. Brendan [Bracken] to have W.O.(!) Dick Law Information. Bobbety Dominions. Beaver Lord P.S. and Leader in House of Lords. Dick Law a bad appointment. I suggested he should take Jowitt's† place (who is to be A[ttorney] G[eneral], Simon being displaced by [Sir Donald] Somervell), and Camrose‡ should have Information. A. put this to P.M. this evening, who seemed to take to it.

Saturday, 25 September

Part of Government changes announced today. (The other day Winston said to A. 'Except for you and me, this is the worst Government England ever had!')

[The Chancellor of the Exchequer, Sir Kinglsey Wood, died suddenly on 21 September. Sir John Anderson replaced him at the Treasury, Mr Attlee

* Minister of Production, 1942–5.

† Sir W. A. Jowitt, Minister without Portfolio.

‡ W. E. Berry, 1st Lord Camrose; Chairman, *Daily Telegraph* and Amalgamated Press Ltd.

became Lord President in his stead, and Lord Cranborne succeeded Attlee at the Dominions Office. Lord Beaverbrook returned to the Government, but not to the War Cabinet, as Lord Privy Seal. Richard Law, later Lord Coleraine, became Minister of State.]

Sunday, 16 September

T. and I drove to St. Paul's for the 'Battle of Britain' Service at 10. Fortunately not too cold. Service quite good but uninspiring. Archbishop [Temple] *read* a dull sermon. Perhaps just as well he did so, as he avoided putting his foot in it. . . . Lunched with T. at Ritz. Then to Sloane Gdns.* to rescue some clothes and tinned food. Suppose it is the last time I shall set foot there. Very sad—it was nice while it lasted. How forlorn and abandoned a disused house looks—and reproachful.

Monday, 27 September

As often happens, when I have worked over a weekend, there is a shortage on Monday. So I was bored. (I grumble when there's too much to do, and the same when I am idle, but the *spasmodic* flow of work *is* rather tiresome and disconcerting.)

Tuesday, 28 September

Cabinet at 5.30. Nothing v. interesting there. P.M. rather snappy with poor Syfret†. . . . (A. tells me poor dear old Pound has a tumour on the brain.)

Thursday, 30 September

Found a S. American file with 3½ acres of useless minutes by under-employed bureaucrats. Sent it back to D. Scott‡ with disobliging remarks. They're intolerable. . . . 6. Talk with A. and others about our eternal problem of Russian frontiers. Couldn't help much! . . . An awful day—more papers than I have ever received. Everyone knows too much of his subject and has become awfully muddle-headed (Amgot, etc.). A large and sharp axe required. Had to decide *not* to go to the cottage tomorrow. This bores T., and upsets her plans, but a rush 'getaway' with masses of stuff waiting, is too exhausting and chancy. I'd sooner polish off, and rest here. Tomorrow, there will probably be nothing. Still no answer from Joe about [the Foreign Ministers] Conference, though offensive and silly message about agenda.

* Where the Cadogans had formerly had a house.

† Admiral Sir E. N. Syfret, Vice-Chief of Naval Staff, 1943–5; C.-in-C. Home Fleet, 1945–8.

‡ Asst. Under-Sec. of State, F.O.

Saturday, 2 October

Joe insists on Moscow for the Conference! About 11.30 p.m. A. rang up in a flap to say P.M. had heard Sforza* was arriving at Prestwick tomorrow morning. Could we send someone to meet him, arrange accommodation, &c? Of course we can't send someone to meet him, even if he *does* arrive, which is unlikely. Anyhow, I don't see why we should make a fuss of Sforza, who's a dud.

Sunday, 3 October

No news of S[forza]. But in view of flap, and a good deal of work, decided I couldn't go down to Denham. . . . Good deal of work till 6.30. Still no news of S., so did no more about it.

Monday, 4 October

Moyne† at 11, about Palestine, Greater Syria, Arab Federation and Ethiopia. These are among the many subjects of which I am ignorant. I listened gravely and arranged an interview for him with M. Peterson, which seemed to damp his spirits, as it would mine. . . . Cabinet put off till 7 and lasted until 8.20. P.M. leads a very disorderly life. Sinkings for September only 106,000 tons—nearly the best month. Good progress in Italy. Alexander‡ has rather outrun his transport and may have to pause a bit. Cunningham there, in place of poor old Pound, who, I fear, is finished. I *am* sorry.§

Tuesday, 5 October

1.15 lunch at Claridges with Poles—Mikolajczyk, Raczynski, Romer, A. and O'Malley. Poles very intransigent and we got nowhere. . . . Cabinet 5.30 on our paper about Germany, for guidance at Moscow meeting. Perfectly *hopeless*. P.M. didn't want to discuss the question at all (being too difficult) so took semi-humorous-critical line. Others, who spoke, wandered all over the place. A. lost his temper—quite rightly—and said if he couldn't get *any* guidance he'd rather not go to Moscow and anyone else who liked could go. This pulled things back on to a rather more practical basis for 5 minutes, but then it wandered off again. I never witnessed such deplorable proceedings. P.M. can be a very good leader in war time.

* Count Carlo Sforza, Italian Minister of Foreign Affairs, 1920–1; leader of Free Italians, 1942; joined Badoglio Government, April 1944.

† Lord Moyne; Deputy Minister of State, Cairo, 1942–4; Minister Resident, Cairo, 1944.

‡ Gen. Alexander was now C.-in-C. Allied Armies in Italy.

§ Adm. Cunningham now replaced Pound as First Sea Lord.

Tehran, November 1943. Cadogan, Eden, Ismay, Clark-Kerr

Yalta, 9 February 1945. Front row: Churchill, Roosevelt, Stalin.
Back row: Lord Leathers, Eden, Stettinius, Cadogan, Molotov, Harriman

The picnic in Virginia, 10 September 1944. A page from one of the Cadogan albums

But he *can* be the worst chairman of a Cabinet imaginable. Smuts there—and Edward H[alifax] (who was shocked).

Wednesday, 6 October

3.30 Gousev.* Quite stupid and inarticulate. Can only make up for his shortcomings by saying 'How are you?' in a voice of thunder.

Thursday, 7 October

3. A. had meeting with Allied Ministers about prospects of Moscow Conference. They didn't seem very disturbed and asked very few questions.... Stacks of paper work. Everyone makes the most elaborate plans, and counter-plans (on paper) how to run different parts of the world. It all turns out in practice, of course, quite different. I lose interest.... P.M. has ordered his plane to be ready to take him to Tunis tonight! He is excited about Cos, and wants to lead an expedition into Rhodes!! I think A. and others have dissuaded him.

[Cos, Leros and Samos, the Italian-held islands in the Dodecanese, had been occupied by the Allies after the Italian surrender. Cos was retaken by German forces on 4 October. Churchill, distressed at what seemed to him American indifference to the Ægean operations, wanted Marshall to join him at Eisenhower's headquarters. Roosevelt refused.]

Saturday, 9 October *Thatched Cottage*

Returning across fields, saw T., Mrs Tree and Burchett busy in the field, so inferred the 12 pullets had arrived. So they had—looking very well. But their food not. They look indignant. Had laid one egg on the way! Premature confinement owing to shock, no doubt.... Wandered out for a bit and then read—Harold Laski's book.† What warped and puny minds these ideologists have! And when they get down to the core of the matter, and try to analyse it, they take refuge in mumbo jumbo which of course hasn't any sense, and can't even be read as English. I'd like to put them in power and give them responsibility—not for more than 10 minutes, but that might be sufficient to prove, even to their stunted intelligences, their futility, prejudice and chicanery. But I suppose not: they wouldn't face the truth: they are more frightened of that than [they] are even [of] their 'Fascist' bogeys (which include poor old Neville Chamberlain who,

* Feodor Tarasovich Gousev, now Russian Ambassador, replacing Maisky; he had previously been a butcher, then a functionary of the OGPU and later Soviet Minister in Ottawa.

† *Reflections on the Revolution of our Time.*

Laski tells us, modelled his policy purely on the lines of fear for his own 'privileges'! Ye Gods! What roaring insanity! No—wicked mendacity, and conscious, sinful, unrepentant mendacity. Laski is an ass, but not a fool, and he *knows* that what he writes is cowardly libel. And damned nonsense, too).

Monday, 11 October

P.M. commanded me to lunch to meet Sforza. Clemmie and R. Law there. P.M. gave S. a good schooling! These parties mean that *I* have to draft a minute of the conversation—none too easy!

Tuesday, 12 October

11. Nils Bohr.* What a man! He talked, quite inaudibly, for ¾ hr. —about what, I haven't the least idea. For some time past I have feared I am going deaf, but I was relieved to hear from O.S. that he listened to N.B. on Saturday for 1½ hrs. without hearing a single word. It's a growing, lazy habit to mutter away a jumble of ill-arranged thoughts. 11.45 Raczynski about poisonous attacks by the 'Week' and other gutter rags. P.M. made statement about Azores, which he must have enjoyed.

[The Prime Minister was able to announce at last that in virtue of the Alliance of 1373 and later agreements, Portugal had granted 'certain facilities' in the Azores, without prejudice to Portugese sovereignty, for the protection of merchant shipping in the Atlantic. Britain would furnish supplies to the Portuguese armed forces. Sir Samuel Hoare ascribed the absence of a hostile reaction in Spain to General Franco's change of attitude and to a general conviction there that Germany was now too weak to retaliate.[3]]

Wednesday, 13 October

Italy duly declared war on Germany at 4 and our tripartite statement about 'co-belligerency' put out by B.B.C. at 9.

[Badoglio had wished to postpone a declaration of war until the Italian Government had returned to Rome. The Allies insisted that Italy should act promptly, and announced that when the Germans had been driven out the Italians would have the right to choose their own form of government.]

Thursday, 14 October

P.M. rang up at 9.30. Mostly about Duff [Cooper]. Said Duff seemed to think he had had a 'firm offer' of Algiers, but that that

* Dr Nils Bohr, Danish atom scientist.

wasn't so at all. Had been rather shocked, when Duff dined with him 2 nights ago, to find him a vehement 'de Gaullist'! I was to show Duff all the necessary papers to prove some of de Gaulle's delinquencies! . . . Bucknell* at 5 with a note saying State Department think Brazil and China should be added to Mediterranean Commission! Told him why *I* thought *not*. Home to dinner. Then received Joe's answer about convoys. It's outrageous, but I don't like—for that reason—to pass it on tonight to P.M. without moderating comment, so am holding it, to deal with tomorrow morning.

[While the British agreement with Portugal about the Azores was being negotiated, it had become clear that the Americans also wanted considerable facilities there. Indeed by early September the U.S. Chiefs of Staff were asking for an American occupation, with a force of 10,000 men. As usual, Churchill was more willing than Eden or Cadogan to support American wishes. However, he accepted Eden's view that Britain should do her best to get for the Americans what she had got for herself. If they wanted more, they must make the running themselves.

The U.S. Government's effort failed. Dr Salazar said that he would strain Portuguese neutrality to the point of allowing the Americans the same facilities as the British. When the Americans proposed to send an operational squadron, Salazar said that Portugal would resist by force. Several months of wearisome talks produced a solution whereby the Americans wore British insignia, with their own alongside in a less conspicuous form.[4]

On 21 September Molotov had 'insisted' that the northern convoys be resumed. Churchill told Stalin in a message that the Allies would do their best to sail four convoys of thirty-five ships each, between November and February 1944; 'this is no contract or bargain, but rather a declaration of our solemn and earnest resolve.' Stalin's reply of 13 October took strong exception to this phraseology. The convoys, he stated explicitly, were an obligation, and the Prime Minister's message 'a kind of threat addressed to the U.S.S.R.'. There followed some paragraphs about facilities for British personnel servicing the convoys in Russia.[5]

Eden was by now on his way to Moscow. Churchill left the handling of the matter to him, but determined not to accept the message. On the afternoon of 18 October, therefore, he had an amiable conversation with M. Gousev, said that the Foreign Secretary would deal with the question of convoys in Moscow, handed back the offending message in an envelope and ushered the Ambassador to the door. He even used the correct phrase '*nul et non avenu*', found in handbooks on diplomacy.]

Friday, 15 October

P.M. has developed unpleasant habit of ringing up at 9.30 to ask

* Howard Bucknell, Jr. In State Department, 1940–3; thereafter Minister at U.S. Embassy in London.

if I have seen various things that have come in during the night and which are sitting in his office. Of course I haven't. Went round and saw him in bed at 10.30 and gave him Joe's answer. I warned him, before he read it, that he'd lose his temper, so the result wasn't so bad. He snorted as he read it and, at the end, said 'I'll stop convoys.' But I suggested another reply, and he calmed down. . . . Agreed his telegram to Pres. accepting latter's idea, based on alleged information from Lisbon, that he could approach Portuguese direct on Azores. It saves *us* trouble.

Monday, 18 October

P.M. rang up about 11 to say he proposed to see Gousev this afternoon at 3 and return him Stalin's message about convoys—which he would not answer. I told him I thought this quite right. We shall help, rather than hinder, A. by refusing to allow Stalin to wipe his boots on us. 3 meeting with [Stanley K.] Hornbeck and our pundits. No great points of difference that I could see. I was called away to the telephone in the middle—P.M. to tell me about his interview with Gousev. He seems to have done it v. well, having quite a friendly conversation and then gradually edging G. out of the room with Stalin's answer in his hand! I'm glad that's done. We must, on occasions, treat Stalin rough, and he's well in the wrong on this occasion. Poor A. is to settle the matter in Moscow (he arrives there this evening). About 5. P.M. sent round his draft reply to a P[arliamentary] Q[uestion] tomorrow about the 5 Senators. Not a good one. Discussed it with R. Law, D. Scott and N. Butler.* Caught P.M. just before Cabinet at 5.30 (he was just out of bed). But no time to explain our ideas, so merely warned him we had suggestions, and expressed hope he wouldn't open discussion in Cabinet. He asked me to put my suggestions in writing, which I did during Cabinet and passed them across to him and he read them. About 7 Cabinet got on to Home questions, so I left. No work, and I was preparing to go home at 7.30 when I was summoned again to a smaller meeting at No. 10 about the Senators. Finally, P.M. agreed to a course which is quite in line with our thought. We should have preferred him to make a detailed reply to the Senators on the lines of his original draft. But he was definitely against this, and Smuts even more so, but he accepted our amended draft of his reply to P.Q., which was our 2nd line of defence and is, I think, all right. He then informed the meeting of what he had done about Stalin's message on convoys.

* Head of American Dept., F.O.

They, of course, approved. I think—as I have said—that it's all right. It's a strong measure to return a communication, but this, after all, was not an official note—only an item in an exchange of personal messages, and was damned offensive.

[Five U.S. Senators visiting war-fronts had made charges of unfair action or bad faith against the British. Churchill had proposed to rebut the charges *seriatim*, but decided instead merely to announce that a full statement of the facts had been drawn up and would be published if necessary.[6]]

Tuesday, 19 October

Cabinet at 6 about U.N.R.R.A.* Quite futile. P.M. did his usual bit—only rather longer than usual—about not condemning the British worker to equal rations with the Chinese. That, of course, not the point. Dick Law brought them more or less to the point and everyone, being tired of the subject, agreed our instructions to the Delegation, not knowing what they were. Stayed on after Cabinet (which also decided to rebuild House of Commons), to do P.Q.'s with Dick L. and P.M. Home 7.45, and dined there. About 9 received for P.M. tiresome telegram from Lisbon showing President is going to ask *much* too much, and tactlessly, of the Portuguese. Sat down and studied File and drafted message from P.M. to President. 'Staff meeting' in W[ar] C[abinet] R[oom] at 10.30. P.M., C's of S., Lyttelton, Leathers, Smuts and self. Gave P.M. my draft to President. He approved it, and that settled that, without rambling discussion. Then decided on bombing Sofia—and how. Then had discussion about 'Overlord' v. Mediterranean. Quite interesting, and rather useful. P.M. says there must be another Staff meeting somewhere before the 'Big Boys' meet, and after we see result of Foreign Secretaries' meeting.

[The Prime Minister wished to give extra strength to some of the Mediterranean operations, at the expense of preparations for 'Overlord'. The Chiefs of Staff had already recorded their unease that the rigidity of the Quebec decisions was hampering the exploitation of success in the Mediterranean.]

Wednesday, 20 October

Telegram from A. to show that his meeting yesterday (on 2nd front) wasn't too bad.

Friday, 22 October

Summoned, with Dick Law, to P.M.'s bedside at 10.30. He, in a

* United Nations Relief and Rehabilitation Administration.

padded and flowered dressing gown—and cigar—held forth on everything, including Harold's tactics before, and at, the Battle of Hastings. This sounds irrelevant, but it didn't seem so at the time. Our real object was to discuss draft telegram to [Harold] Macmillan about 'broadening the basis' of the Italian Government. Undertook to do re-draft. 1.30 lunch at Spanish Embassy. . . . P.M. . . warmed up after his third glass of brandy. Abused Primo [de Riviera] for having closed Casinos in Spain—he having once won £600 in 24 hrs. at San Sebastian. . . .

Air raid about 7.15—we've been having a lot of them lately at night. 3–10 machines, but a bore and gunfire wakes one up. Provided we don't get another late, I find this a much better hour. P.M. went down to Chequers. I've sent some minutes after him, so shall be rung up all night. Moscow talks go pretty well.

Monday, 25 October

Moscow goes almost suspiciously well. My task is complicated by the P.M. suggesting—or *sending*—spasmodic replies to A.'s telegrams which really require some modification. 'De minimis non curat Dux', but he'll gradually get into an awful mess if he doesn't avoid some of the smaller and more tiresome little traps. However, he's fairly patient. . . . 3. Viénot. I broke to him the idea of removing the Political Military Commission to London *without* a regular French Member. He didn't take it at *all* nicely. . . . Defence Committee tonight on German 'rocket'. Didn't feel I should barge in. I am apprehensive—they have evidently got *something*—but sceptical.

Tuesday, 26 October

6. talked to Mallet about Staff prospects. We are suffering from not having taken in 'temporaries' early enough. *Now* we haven't accommodation for them! Rather a nasty 'survey' from Alexander about future of Italian campaign. Germans *may* mass to defeat us there in detail. In which case, all this 'Overlord' folly must be thrown 'Overboard'. Defence Cttee. last night discussed the German 'rocket'. They evidently take it rather seriously. O.S. on a scheme for bringing Turkey in. I said that in present circumstances, it looks as if we can spare *nothing* from the Italian campaign, so not much hope. But agreed it could go to Planners.

Wednesday, 27 October

6. Cabinet on Moscow talks (which continue to go well, and I think we've tied up all the loose ends) but mainly on the 'Overlord'

v 'Italy' issue. Whole Cabinet—and Smuts particularly—very definite that we *can't* be tied, in changing circumstances, to the Quebec decisions. Must have a Staff meeting again in first half of November. Winston will fight for 'nourishing the battle' in Italy and, if necessary, resign on it. Most useful discussion. Then discussed Russian demand for Italian ships.* Agreed we can't give A. carte blanche. Then, I'm glad to say, decided to approach U.S., Dominions, India and Dutch on publicity campaign about Jap atrocities.

Thursday, 28 October

11.15 Michiels, about the form of 'consultation' with Small Powers for ordering the affairs of Europe. His Government would find it 'inacceptable' to have foregone decisions put before them. But I can't see why that's worse than being outvoted by 3 or 4 to 1. These little Powers are inclined to get on the high horse—and it gives them a lot of satisfaction to do so—but in the end it's the Great Powers that carry the burden. After all, the contribution that Holland has made to the winning of the war is in the order of ·0001 %. Some others are almost a minus quantity. . . . Lunched at Mansion House for 'Frogface' [Gousev]. Sat between Solvert and Fefer (who had just enough English to convey to me he was a Russian poet, and to ask who was our favourite English poet. I don't know: fortunately the Lord Mayor proposed the toast of the King before I could reply. . . . 5.30 talk with O.S. about A.'s refusal to meet Numan [Menemencioglu] in Cairo on his way home. Explained in a telegram to A. how it might be quite useful, and followed it up with another showing how our minds are working about pushing Turkey into the war.

Friday, 29 October

Went to see P.M. (in bed) at 10.30. Made pretext that I wanted to know his decision about appointment of N. Charles as High Commissioner in Italy. He said it could wait until A's return. I really wanted to know whether I could have a weekend. Asked if he would mind O.S. being in charge tomorrow—I wanted to go away this afternoon—would be back on Sunday. He agreed, apparently readily. Told me he plans to leave on Nov. 10.

[The Moscow Conference of Foreign Ministers, which brought Eden, Hull and Molotov together, was perhaps the most useful and businesslike Allied meeting of the whole war. Molotov and his military colleagues asked every conceivable question about 'Overlord' and appeared at last to be

* That is, for a part of the surrendered Italian fleet.

satisfied that the British and Americans seriously intended to put all their strength into it. Eden settled the vexatious issue of the convoys. He agreed with Molotov's suggestion that a Russian mission to Marshal Tito's* Partisans should operate in contact with the British mission.

The main achievements of the Conference lay in the establishment of organs for Allied co-operation: an Advisory Council for Italy on which the Russians had a seat; the Allied Control Commission for Italy; and, much the most important, the European Advisory Commission, to make plans for the armistice and its enforcement and to meet in London. Eden would have liked a wider function, namely, that the Commission should consider European political problems as they arose, before and after the armistice. For this proposition there was much to be said. It would have provided a machinery for constant consultation, on a basis of equality, for which spasmodic conferences at high level could provide no substitute. However, neither Molotov nor Hull would agree.

The three Governments promised to hold informal discussions about the World Organisation, and recognised 'the necessity of establishing at the earliest practicable date a general international organisation, based on the principle of the sovereign equality of all peace-loving states, and open to membership by all such states, large and small, for the maintenance of international peace and security.'

There was virtually no talk about Poland. Early in October, Eden and Cadogan had had a fruitless talk with Mikolajczyk. The Poles insisted that their eastern territories should not be surrendered and refused to agree to an official discussion of the frontier question by the Foreign Ministers. Hull would not make a move of any kind. Molotov gave a bleak response to Eden's attempts to raise the issue informally, though he did his best to prevent the supply of British and American arms to the Polish Underground Army, which, in close touch with London, clearly presented one of the principal obstacles to Russian control of the country. As Cadogan pointed out afterwards to Count Raczynski, the Poles themselves, by refusing to allow discussion of territorial concessions, had left Eden with no cards to play.[7]]

Monday, 1 November

A. has postponed his departure—owing to weather—till tomorrow morning. Agreed now that he should see Numan in Cairo. Moscow has gone very well and if he can get something out of the Turks we can drape him in garlands. P.M. has agreed to meet Pres. in Cairo Nov. 20—for staff talks. No agreement yet for a meeting with Joe, who won't come further than Tehran. . . . 5.30 Cabinet. Less than 100,000 tons sunk (we budgeted for 550,000) and at least 23 U-boats

* Marshal Josip Broz Tito, President of Yugoslav National Liberation Committee and leader of Partisan forces; Prime Minister of Yugoslavia, 1945–53; President from 1953.

destroyed during Oct. Progress in Italy slow. Russians have cut off Crimea. P.M. will give House in secret session tomorrow some warnings about the German rocket. [Lord] Cherwell lays 5 to 1 against it. So do I. But they're preparing *something*, there's no doubt.

Wednesday, 3 November

P.M. sent for me at 5 to show me a fiery telegram to A. about Turks. (A. left Moscow this morning: should be in Cairo tomorrow morning, when he will meet Numan.) P.M. had put in that if Turks don't do what we want 'our interest in Turkey lapses'. I changed this into 'We cannot plead Turkey's case with the Soviet.' Also he had said that Turks must come in and that we should not be bound by our 'Hardihood' undertakings. I don't know what these are, nor how far they have been disclosed to Turks, so I got him to substitute that, if Turks came in 'we should be in the battle by their side, and our assistance would be limited only by our ability to provide it'(!) ... P.M. in good form and under the influence of (suppressed) excitement.... P.M. seems to plan to start for Cairo on 10th or 11th. Don't know whether I shall go with him. Rather gather A. angling *not* to go. He's had *his* show—and a very good one—and may not relish another tiring tour as second fiddle!

Thursday, 4 November

Aghnides* in morning to question me about Mediterranean and European Commissions. Also to protest against their not having been told of signature of 'Long Terms'.† (*What* a muddle that was!)

Friday, 5 November

Got intelligence of Germans sending vessels—or going to—through the Straits both ways. Asked A. to tell Turks to stop it!

Saturday, 6 November

A. has had his first interview with Numan and received a raspberry.

Sunday, 7 November

A. still finding Turks completely sticky. But Americans agree to delay removal of landing craft from Mediterranean.

[Eden's bargaining position was not a strong one, for the operations in the Ægean had just failed. Stalin pressed hard at Moscow for Turkish

* Thanassis Aghnides, Greek Ambassador in London, 1942–7.

† The 'Short Terms' was in effect the simple document of the Italian surrender; the 'Long Terms' was the full-scale document of surrender. See Maj.-Gen. Sir K. Strong, *Intelligence at the Top*, pp. 104–23.

belligerency. Eden asked him why? Eventually Molotov, having shown that the prospect of British submarines in the Black Sea was not a welcome one, agreed that the first step should be a request for air bases.

Eden talked with Numan at Cairo between 5 and 8 November. The Turks evidently feared the Russians deeply. Eden asked in the name of Britain for air bases, and in the name of the three Allies for Turkish entry into the war, though not for offensive operations, by the end of the year. Numan would do no more than put these requests to his colleagues. Both were refused on 15 November.[8]]

Monday, 8 November

Cabinet at 6 (till 8.10). Lot of chat—P.M. filling out time, I think, so as to guillotine our Suez Canal paper at 7.55. He succeeded. But, of course, it is *not* really urgent and can wait.

Tuesday, 9 November

P.M. rang up just before 8 to ask for draft of a message to C[hiang] K[ai]-S[hek] inviting him to Cairo. I should have thought he could have done this better himself!

Wednesday, 10 November

Had talk with A. at 4, but short—he off to bed, as he expects P.M. to keep him up till 3 a.m. and he has a speech to make in House tomorrow. . . . Cabinet about 7 on War Criminals. Smuts destroyed P.M.'s rather mild paper, and latter agreed to revise it.

[The limited independence of Syria and the Lebanon had been announced by the Free French, and recognised by the British, some two years earlier. After strong British pressure, elections were held in the summer of 1943. In both countries Nationalist governments were returned. The Lebanese administration proposed to rid itself of the Free French. This was in October. Simultaneously, preparations for the meeting of a provisional Consultative Assembly at Algiers were maturing. Giraud, whose influence had declined, resigned from the French Committee on 8 November leaving de Gaulle sole President. The Committee's stated purpose was to bring in representatives of the political parties and the Resistance. Giraud remained Commander-in-Chief.

The most acute phase of the Levant crisis coincided with these changes. The French arrested several Lebanese Ministers, including the President, and dissolved the Assembly. French troops fired on a demonstration in Beirut. Riots took place elsewhere, and neighbouring states gave the Lebanon assurances of support. Churchill, far from content with the changes in the French Committee, seized the chance to bring matters to a head with de Gaulle. The British Government demanded reinstatement of the Lebanese Government and the recall of M. Helleu, General Catroux's deputy; otherwise British troops would assume responsibility for law and order. The French Committee gave way, against de Gaulle's wishes. But for tactful and expert handling at Algiers, this episode would have done a quite disproportionate amount of damage. As it was, it left its mark on British relations with de Gaulle, and reinforced powerfully the French conviction that Sir Edward Spears was dedicated to the destruction of France's place in the Levant. Churchill would not, however, agree to his replacement.[9]]

Friday, 12 November

Talk with A. and M. Peterson about French folly in Lebanon. They have overstepped all limits. . . . Cabinets on Lebanon at 3.30. All agreed on firmness with French. P.M. (who left at noon) had left draft telegram to Pres. practically proposing that this was the best opportunity for finally ridding ourselves of 'that turbulent Knight' de G. We, and all the Cabinet, opposed this and found ourselves opposed by—the Lord Cherwell!! Bridges tells me P.M. directed that in his absence Lord Cherwell should attend Cabinet meetings. An unwise decision, as Lord Cherwell's main achievement is to unite against him any body of men with whom he comes in contact. So he's not a good advocate!

Saturday, 13 November

5. Frogface with message from Joe. He agrees to meeting in Tehran about 27th. Molotov will not go to Cairo on 22nd. (C.K.S. has agreed to be there!), but will come with him (Joe) to Tehran Forwarded it to P.M. Leros looks bad. Russians doing marvels. . . . Getting stale, and tired. Have had no holiday this year, and don't see when I shall get one. Anyhow, I don't think I want one at this time of year. But T. ought to have a rest.

Monday, 15 November

5.30 Cabinet. Not much news. Got them to agree a telegram to Casey indicating that if the French won't agree our demands we may have to take over.

Tuesday, 16 November

5.30 Cabinet—mainly about Greek policy. A. didn't get it all his own way, and I think that's right. I'm doubtful about a complete and sudden break with E.A.M.* and holding a pistol to the head of the King. . . . No news at Cabinet except *bad* news of Leros. Talk of,

* The Communist Greek 'National Liberation Front'.

and plans for, 'evacuation' brings back the bad old days of '40 and '41. But it's on a smaller scale of course. We now have Turkish reply—a web of words meaning nothing, but that the Turks funk coming into the war and look for every loop-hole.

Wednesday, 17 November

Lebanon hasn't flared up yet, but that doesn't mean that it won't if we leave it alone. Leros lost last night. First German success for more than a year. And our front in Italy bogged down. P.M. arrives at M[alta] tonight. 6. talk with A. about Poles, who, as I have long suspected, have at last hinted that they want to be *forced*. But we must have agreement with Americans first. . . . Told A. I wanted to go away tomorrow till Mon. Have had no leave this year (bar sick-leave in February).

Thursday, 18 November

12.45 talk with A. and others about Lebanon. He arranged Cabinet for 5 p.m. Explained to him—what he already knew—that I was going away! I have had no leave—O.S. has had masses and refuses to go abroad.* I have got to take on another strenuous trip next week—I must get home for a few days and have a bit of a rest. In this, my sixth, year of my present job I have had no real holiday, unless you count Washington.

Saturday, 20 November *Thatched Cottage*

Noisy bombardment woke me up last night. It began again at 7 and restarted at 8. Apparently attack on Rye and Hastings. Went on intermittently during the morning. There was a luncheon break and then it began again until tea. But the wireless says nothing about it. . . . Messenger arrived 3.45. No very great news. P.M. on way from Malta to Cairo—'not too well'. Don't know what that means. We start Tuesday night. . . . Catroux seems to have done nothing—though we have given him an extra 24 hours. Read official papers between tea and dinner. Battle of Hastings seems to have died down for the moment.

Sunday, 21 November

Box arrived 8.15. Containing lots of telegrams. Looks as if we shall muddle out of Lebanon crisis more or less all right.

* Sir Orme Sargent declined to attend any of the conferences, or indeed to go abroad for any purpose. He was supposed to suffer from claustrophobia in ships and aircraft.

Monday, 22 November

Found the Lebanon had kept people busy—even a Cabinet meeting yesterday afternoon. Catroux has given way on $\frac{3}{4}$ of our points and I think therefore our ultimatum for Wed. morning cannot be maintained, i.e. we should not march in automatically if the *last* of our demands not met. . . .

Message from A. that we shan't be able to fly tomorrow or next day, owing to weather, so start tonight! Cabinet 5.30 Greece and Lebanon. Cabinet gave A. free hand on former. Drafted telegram to P.M. giving our views on latter.

[Cadogan and Eden left Lyneham in a Liberator in the early hours of 23 November, reaching Cairo, via Gibraltar, the next day.]

Thursday, 25 November *Cairo*

10.30 A. and I started off to the Villa to pay respects to P.M. I went on . . . to see Harry H[opkins] at President's Villa. He produced a draft communiqué (which he had given the night before to Wang Chung Hui*), which I looked at. It is bad drafting but the substance looks all right. At noon a party collected in the garden for photography. Great crowd—all the Anglo-American notables and a few Chinese. Met the Chiangs and had a talk with her. She seems all right—very smartly dressed—white jacket with a beautiful spray of rubies on it; jade and pearl earrings. C.K.S. looks rather small and wizened but well. . . . I had discovered some serious flaws—and an omission—in the communiqué and gave A. a redraft to take off to his Thanksgiving dinner with the Pres.

[Cadogan told Halifax afterwards that the Americans had behaved 'rather badly' about the communique. He had to spend much of this afternoon discussing changes, punctuated by Dr Wang's 'I think I prefer the original text,' to which he could only reply 'I'm sure you do, Dr Wang. My point is that I definitely don't.'

The talks dealt largely with military questions. From the start, Generalissimo Chiang was present in Cairo and Chinese affairs took up a disproportionate amount of time; Roosevelt made Chiang a rash promise about an early operation across the Bay of Bengal, which Churchill eventually persuaded him to give up; the intimate conferences with the Americans for which the British had looked were much hampered; and the difficulties of dealing with the Americans were by no means confined to the communiqué. At lunch with Eden on 25 November Churchill confessed that poor progress was being made. Roosevelt was 'a charming country gentleman';

* Sec.-Gen., Chinese Supreme National Defence Council, 1941–7; Member, Praesidium, People's Political Council, 1943–8.

business methods were almost non-existent; and the Prime Minister must accordingly play the unwonted role of courtier, seizing opportunities as they arose.

These few days in Cairo revealed disquieting tendencies which were felt to the end of the war and beyond: an American assessment of Chiang's significance which bordered on the ludicrous, a growing suspicion of British intentions, a fundamental misunderstanding of Russia's. From Great Britain's point of view the timing of the conference could scarcely have been less fortunate, with her position in the Far East almost as bad as it could be, Cos and Leros just fallen, and the Italian campaign bogged down. The Prime Minister had to endure much with a good grace, including explanations from the President of other powers' higher morality. 'Winston, you have four hundred years of acquisitive instinct in your blood and you just don't understand how a country might not want to acquire land somewhere if they can get it. A new period has opened in the world's history and you will have to adjust yourself to it.'

It was only Russia's absolute refusal to compromise her neutrality with Japan, and therefore to attend a meeting with Chiang, which vitiated the President's insistence upon inviting to Cairo Molotov and a Russian military representative.[10]]

Friday, 26 November *Cairo*

Harriman turned up about 11.30. Didn't (of course) like my changes in the communiqué. So we didn't get much further. . . . I got to President's Villa at 3.30 (about communiqué) where we were joined at 4.15 by A. Just as he arrived, P.M. sent over a new and revised version of his own, which more or less got us over our difficulties, and we accepted it. Then went down and joined P.M. and President and the Chiangs, and sat and gossiped there for a bit. I exchanged courtesies with C.K.S. through Wang. C.K.S. very graceful and friendly. . . . P.M. and Sarah [Churchill] came to dinner. Small party—only about eight of us. P.M. talked to the whole table from 8.30 till 11.30. Then to me and A. and Miles [Lampson] from 11.30 till 1.35. Then expressed surprise at having a sore thoat!

Saturday, 27 November *Tehran*

Landed at Tehran at 1. (2.30 local time). . . . Found A. and Winant. P.M. has lost his voice entirely (of course) so the dinner of the three great ones was off, and they are all dining separately (P.M. in bed). Harry Hopkins came in for a talk. Dined at the Holmans'.* Archie Kerr running backwards and forwards between here and the

* A. Holman, Counsellor at the British Legation, Tehran.

Russians, trying to make plans. Back to Legation. Harriman came in. . . . He lectured A. and me on how to conduct international Conferences, and how they usually developed. I've forgotten a great deal more about that than he ever knew. True enough it is that this meeting looks like being all over the place, but that is ever the way with the Great Men. Bed by 12.

Sunday, 28 November *Tehran*

Russians now claim to have unearthed a plot, and think it safer for President to move into a house in their compound. This he has now done. Sat about all morning in the garden, doing very little work. P.M. appeared about 12.30. His voice isn't right yet. . . . At 4, P.M. and A. went off to the Soviet Embassy for a meeting of the Big Three. But as all the Staff went, and Harriman and A. C. K[err] didn't, I couldn't. . . . Don't know *what* this meeting will produce. P.M. and President *ought* to have got together, with their staffs, *before* meeting Russians. But that, through a series of mischances, has *not* happened. A. came in about 7.30. As I had anticipated, things had gone pretty badly. Without any previous Anglo-American consultation, President, in his amateurish way, had said a lot of indiscreet and awkward things. A. went off again to dine with Russians and for another talk after. President became 'indisposed' during dinner and disappeared.* Only record I have of what passed, after, between President and P.M., is quite scrappy and woolly and useless.

[Cadogan's language indicates a degree of scepticism about the plot. Although two Russian works have claimed that an attempt to assassinate the Big Three was thwarted only by the excellence of Soviet counter-intelligence, there is no evidence of any serious planning by the Germans.

It was Stalin who had insisted upon Tehran as the venue for the Conference, known to be unsuitable in almost every particular. The American Legation lay a mile from the British and Soviet buildings, which adjoined. The supposed plot, of which Molotov admitted he had heard no more than rumours, enabled him to press that the President should move into the compound of the Russian Embassy. Churchill urged this course strongly. He seems to have been the only one of the British party to take Stalin's solicitude at face value. All members of the staff in the villa were members of the N.K.V.D. 'I wonder', says Lord Ismay politely in his memoirs, 'if microphones had already been installed in anticipation!' There is little need to speculate on that score. It may be taken for granted that all the private conversations of the American delegation were monitored.[11]]

* This illness was described as 'an acute digestive attack'. It was thought at first that Roosevelt had been poisoned. *See* H. L'Etang, *The Pathology of Leadership*, p. 92.

Monday, 29 November *Tehran*

A. appeared about 10.30. He rather in despair about this hazy conference. Chiefs of Staff got together this morning, but I gathered from Brooke and Portal at lunch that no progress was made. . . . Back to Legation garden about 2.45. Winston appeared and chatted for a bit. He seems better. 3.30 to Russian compound for ceremony of handing over Stalingrad sword.* P.M. made a short speech and handed it to Stalin. Latter replied shortly, kissed the scabbard and handed it to [Marshal] Voroshilov—obliquely, so that the sword slipped out of the scabbard and the pommel hit V. on the toe. Otherwise it went off very well. Photographic orgy afterward, into which I did not push. Back for tea, did a little work. Winant, (who clings like ivy, and is a great bore) wasted some of my time—though I haven't got much else to do with it. A. back about 7.30. They don't seem to have made *any* progress on their operational talks—rather the reverse, as the President promises everything that Stalin wants in the way of an attack in the West, with the result that Winston, who has to be more honest, is becoming an object of suspicion to Stalin and much of the work of the Moscow Conference is being undone. Stalin looks to me to have put on a little weight. He does *not* look well in his Marshal's uniform, and rather uneasy, pulling down the flaps of his tunic and trying to arrange his feet and his trouser-ends. I am bored by this Conference—have little to do and am wasting my time. . . . We have decided to spend another day here—Wed. We certainly shan't get any results unless we do.

Tuesday, 30 November *Tehran*

Same lovely weather. Gather the Great ones had the usual woolly (and bibulous) evening last night. Nothing v. definite seems to have emerged. Joe seems to have pulled Winston's leg and latter to have risen to every fly. Nothing for me to do but hang about, so went . . . sight-seeing. . . . Bazaars quite good—as a sight. Nothing in them. A squalid town of bad taste. Back 12.45 to find a tiresome telegram from London about the Cairo communiqué. Had to go over to Soviet building to see Harry H. and to draft a reply for Winston. He already in at lunch with Joe, so I sent it in. . . . A. had given Molotov and Harry H. lunch at Legation to try to get down to political questions. They seem to have made a start, at least. We went to a curio shop after lunch, but full of rubbish. Sat about in garden, talked to A. about his lunch conversation. Told him we *must* send *some* news to London, who must be wondering what on earth (if anything) is

* A Sword of Honour presented on behalf of the British people.

going on. But he didn't seem to think that mattered. *I* can't draft a telegram as *I* certainly don't know what's going on. Usual Staff meeting 4.30. A. back soon after 6. They seem to be agreed. Did a bit of work. Dinner at Legation quite successful. Joe and the President and the principal members of their Staff attended. Cake with 69 candles. I had a few words with Joe before dinner. He admitted he had put on weight—thought that must be due to these, the first, few days' holiday he has had since the war began. He was in quite good mood. Winston began toasts during the soup, and they went on till nearly 12. President left soon after, and was followed by Joe. I got to bed before 1.

[After much chaffing, Churchill had drunk to the proletarian masses and Stalin to the Conservative Party. A waiter, absorbed in Stalin's speech, tipped a huge confection over interpreter Pavlov. Though covered from head to foot in ice cream, he continued his translation without the slightest pause. He was subsequently awarded the C.B.E.]

Wednesday, 1 December *Tehran*

Same lovely weather. Decided we must get off tomorrow morning, so all remaining discussion must be crammed into today. Winston had to chuck his lunch at Legation, as he must lunch with Joe and Pres. A. joined them there. Back about 4. They tackled the Polish question, and it would seem that Russians stand about where they did, though they would agree to Poland going as far west as the Oder. But I don't see that we've got anything very definite in exchange out of the Russians, e.g. on resumption of relations with Polish Government in London. It seems all a bit woolly.

About 7.45 had to go over to the President's villa to work on a draft communiqué. I had already drafted the usual kind of thing. Found a new draft on more (and better) journalistic lines. . . . P.M. came in about 11, having apparently finished up. He in very good form. I persuaded him not to take A. in his plane. He himself has always been strong against putting all our eggs in one basket. (But my real reason was that, if I could get A. in mine, we need only start at 8.30 instead of 6.15 a.m.!) Packed and got into bed as it struck 1. (We have summoned Inönü to Cairo.)

[Stalin had no need of secret Intelligence to show up the differences between the British and Americans. As Harry Hopkins put it on the way to Tehran, 'You will find us lining up with the Russians.' Roosevelt, although avoiding private talks with Churchill, had no such inhibitions with Stalin. Doubtless this policy derived from a desire to convince Stalin that the British and Americans would not present him with a series of *faits accomplis*.

Its effect was serious for the British. The C.I.G.S. said simply, 'This Conference is over when it has only just begun. Stalin has got the President in his pocket.' It was at Tehran, Churchill used to remark, that he realised for the first time what a small nation Britain was. 'There I sat with the great Russian bear on one side of me, with paws outstretched, and on the other side the great American buffalo, and between the two sat the poor little English donkey who was the only one . . . who knew the right way home.'

In private, Roosevelt spoke to Stalin about a three-tier organisation for the security of the post-war world: an assembly, an executive committee and the 'Four Policemen'. Stalin said, very much as Eden had done nine months before, that the Four would hardly be welcomed by the small nations of Europe, and that he did not believe China would be very powerful after the war. On the more immediate military issues, Stalin held the others to 'Overlord' in May or June, pressed the claims of a supporting operation in the South of France at the expense of the Italian campaign, and promised to fight against Japan when Germany collapsed. On the Polish frontier question, Russia insisted on a line so drawn as to include Lwow, Königsberg and the northern part of East Prussia. Stalin averred, and it was an argument for which Churchill and Eden felt much sympathy, that Russia must have security in the west. The Americans shied off the issue, on account of the election due in 1944; upon which Eden observed that if no solution could be found, Polish-Russian relations, with the Red Army crossing Poland, would in six months' time be infinitely worse and the election much nearer. Stalin did say that Poland could in compensation go as far west as the Oder. He did not indicate whether he meant by this formula that the new Polish frontier should run up to the Western Neisse.

He evidently enjoyed teasing Churchill. 'I can't understand you at all; in 1919 you were so keen to fight and now you don't seem to be at all? What happened? Is it advancing age? How many divisions do you have in contact with the enemy? What is happening to all those two million men you have in India?' And more in the same vein, taken in good part.[12]]

Saturday, 4 December *Cairo*

Started off about 10.45 to airport to meet Pres., Inönü and Numan, who arrived soon after 11.30. . . . 3.30 A. and I drove out to Ismay's villa, where we found him and Numan and P.M. and had a preliminary talk till 4.45. Stopped a minute or two at P.M.'s villa on way to President's, where we had a full-dress meeting. Anglo-U.S.–Turkish, lasting till nearly 7. Afterwards, Snatch [Knatchbull-Hugessen] said to me 'the Turks have come a long way'. I said 'Yes: but along a familiar road which I seem to have travelled before'. However, it's not too bad *if* they are handled fairly and decisively. . . . Dinner with Pres. Soviet Ambassador in Angora also present (he had funked attending our meeting as he had received no instructions!) Sat between Harry H. and the Soviet Counsellor. P.M. not too well, and cried off dinner. However, he appeared in his rompers just as I hoped we might be going home. Turks and others left soon after, and we got away about 12.15. Climbed into bed at 1.

Sunday, 5 December *Cairo*

Wrote short paper for A. on how Turks should be handled.... Meeting at President's Villa at 3, with Turks and Americans. Went fairly well until Numan intervened, when everything fell flat. Adjournment at 4 for photographers. Resumed for a bit until nearly 5, when it was decided that a Committee should take it on at 6. Drove home with A., changed, and back at 6, till 8.15. Quite hopeless, and quite clear to me that Numan (probably in German pay) is straining every nerve to twist and turn and prevaricate. It's really *no good* going on like this. We shall get nowhere unless we are pretty tough with the Turks and put them on the spot. Snatch and Helm* still keep on saying how well the Turks are coming along. I keep on saying so they are, but in the wrong direction. They used to say they would come in when the moon turned blue: now they say they will when it turns pink. I don't see much difference myself. I should think the Russians would consider we had been a bit soft with them.

Monday, 6 December *Cairo*

Old Smuts arrived. Meeting with Turks at President's Villa at 5. Very rambly. P.M. who had not, I think, understood the position, began to realise how the Turks were turning and twisting. Meeting broke up about 7 and I went back to Embassy and wrote out a little prescription for dealing with Turks (firmly). Dinner party at Embassy in honour of Turks (about 24 people). A. approved my prescription and told me to give it to P.M. Numan brought a draft communiqué, and we had the usual shamozzle after dinner trying to get it agreed. Got to bed before 2.

Tuesday, 7 December

Some small new changes in communiqué, and we spent the next hour and a half chasing Turks and Russians on the telephone trying to get them to agree. Couldn't get final confirmation much before 12.

[These three days of talks with the Turks produced little result. President Inönü pleaded his country's unpreparedness. He did agree to make air

* A. Knox Helm, Counsellor at the British Embassy, Ankara, 1942–6.

bases ready by February, when the Allies would ask permission to send in aircraft, and expressed Turkey's readiness 'in principle' to come into the war.

The Turkish Government said in January 1944 that they would fight as soon as successful operations in the West were under way. At the same interview, Numan told Knatchbull-Hugessen that the German Ambassador, von Papen, 'knew considerably more about what is going on than was good for him'. This was indeed an understatement, for the British Ambassador's valet, in the Germans' pay, was regularly handing over photographs of most secret papers, of interest not only for their contents but also because they helped the Germans to break some of the British diplomatic cyphers. The Germans knew promptly from this source of the scale of R.A.F. infiltration into Turkey; saw signals describing the state of relations between Russia, the U.S.A. and Britain; got the minutes of the Foreign Ministers' meeting in Moscow, and of the Cairo and Tehran Conferences. When the valet gave his contact at the German Embassy the reports showing the increased infiltration of British Service personnel into Turkey, von Papen had to decide on a balance of risks. He saw Numan and let him understand plainly that the Germans were well informed. This was the occasion of Numan's remark that Papen knew more than was good for him. Hugessen immediately wrote a telegram in that sense. The valet thereupon sold a photograph of it to the Germans.[13]

Cadogan had for some time known of the insecure Turkish cyphers, to reading which the Germans attached particular importance. In January 1944 he learned that von Papen had been securing papers from an agent in the British Embassy. Thereafter the leakage was soon stopped, although it was not until the capture of German documents in 1945 that the full story transpired. The information which the Germans derived from Cicero (as the valet was known to them) they put to little use, save that von Papen was the better placed to utter stern warnings to Numan. That situation suited the Turks well, for they could and did exploit it in their dealings with the Allies. Very naturally, they sought the advantages of belligerent status for the peacemaking, and the supply of arms, without the inconvenience of heavy involvement in the fighting.

In April 1944 the Turkish Government cut off the supply of chrome to Germany, and in August severed diplomatic relations. Turkey at last entered the war in the spring of 1945.

In October 1943, on his way out to the Moscow Conference, Eden had a meeting with King George of the Hellenes in Cairo. The Greek situation, seen from London, bore unpleasant similarities to that of Yugoslavia: the future of the monarchy in doubt, the resistance movements split, Britain supplying arms and money to rival factions, a strong Communist element struggling for post-war mastery, the Government in exile necessarily reflecting these tensions and uncertainties.

Early in October 1943, E.L.A.S. (the military wing of the Communist-dominated National Liberation Front), attacked the much smaller anti-Communist E.D.E.S. under Colonel Napoleon Zervas, despite an agreement of three months earlier. E.L.A.S. had so far received the larger share of British money and supplies, which had been used to suppress anti-Communist forces. S.O.E., with the support of the military authorities in the Middle East, had in effect been promoting a policy in Greece at variance with that of the War Cabinet, although in 1942 Eden did secure instructions that the British officers in Greece should, save in the most exceptional circumstances, support the groups favourable to the King and exiled Government.

On his return from Moscow, Eden proposed that British support should be withdrawn from E.L.A.S. (which he thought of little value as a weapon against the Germans) and a deliberate effort made to win the support of the non-Communist majority in Greece. Since the King was unpopular, the British must make it plain that they would not force his return; they must also try to safeguard his interests by asking him to nominate a Council of Regency while the Greeks decided the future of the monarchy.

On 3 December in Cairo again, Eden spoke to King George on these lines, to which the State Department had agreed. However, Roosevelt saw the King three days later and advised in the opposite sense. Apparently forgetting that he had been shown the British proposals in advance, Roosevelt complained that the British had not consulted him. He even took it upon himself to remonstrate with Churchill about Eden's alleged efforts to rob King George of his crown. After this episode, the King would not give the public pledges which the British plan required. A direct breach with E.L.A.S. was therefore hardly feasible, and a temporary truce between the factions was patched up in February.[14]]

Wednesday, 8 December *Cairo*

11. Talk with A. and Rex Leeper* about Greek situation. Roosevelt has sold the pass by giving the King advice diametrically opposed to ours—in the face of his own advisers! It really is too tiresome: he is less interested—and certainly less expert—in Europe than we are.

12.15 went with P.M., A. and Miles [Lampson] to the Palace for an audience. The King [Farouk] still in a wheeled chair as a result of his motor accident. He said that that, according to his religion, has been 'pre-ordained'. Later in the conversation, P.M. found that his hardest-worked trouser button had thrown its hand in. He apologised—saying it had doubtless been pre-ordained, but was none the less embarrassing.

Thursday, 9 December *Algiers*

Expected to arrive Gib. about 9 or 10, but the man who called me

* Ambassador to Greek Government in Cairo from March 1943; in Athens from Oct. 1944. See List of Principal Characters.

at 8 said we were coming down at Algiers to refuel. Very odd. Landed there about 9.30 with one engine conked out. Gathered it had been giving trouble all night. Told that they could tell us in about 2 hours whether and when it could be put right. Went to a café on the aerodrome and had weak coffee and cheese sandwiches.... About 6 left with A. and Winant for a farm about 25 miles inland, the H.Q. of his Battalion of the 60th. Dined there and watched boxing contest. All very hearty and tiring. Back about midnight. Found that Portal, not content with our 'Liberator', had also ordered the York to Tunis—two large planes for 3–4 people. Everyone got so indignant that I went to bed and slept for about 8 hours.

[Lord Halifax asked for the 'lowdown' on these conferences. Cadogan's reply indicates a degree of optimism which he soon ceased to feel:

> You will have seen such official accounts as there are. I can only add that the personal relationships were, I think, excellent, and that we are entitled to expect good concrete results from the convivial junketings and rambling talk. The latter is very useful: if Winston is stimulated (by various means) into airing his views on all topics under the sun, it gives Stalin some insight into his character. Roosevelt probably knows all about that already, but if he, in his turn, tells anecdotes about himself and his ancestry, that also gives Uncle Joe material which he is able to turn to good—and possibly quite beneficent—use.
>
> U.J. has a good sense of humour, and is very adept at pulling Winston's leg. He can get a rise out of Winston with great skill and certainty—and enjoys it. I believe that is all very much to the good. Winston, when properly started off, has very few reticences: U.J. is shrewd enough to spot that, and must, I think, have satisfied himself that he was reading an open book, that there was no concealment or duplicity and that he could have faith. And I believe that *has* done something to improve Anglo-Soviet relations.
>
> Then, in Cairo, Winston fell for Madame Chiang Kai-shek. He had, as you know, breathed fire and slaughter against her, which, on her Indian performance, was not surprising.* But it is a good thing that that should have been mitigated. Chiang Kai-shek himself made an impression on the Prime Minister and President. To me, who hadn't seen him for seven years or so, he looked, though fit, rather shrunken and small. But he was in very good form, very gracious and dignified....
>
> Being fresh to it, I am rather appalled at the haphazard, amateurish surroundings of the President. How *do* these people carry on? At Tehran I was invited to discuss a draft of the communiqué with Major Boettiger. Major Boettiger may be an excellent fellow—even an excellent son-in-law—but I don't know what qualifications he has for communi-

* She had sharply and publicly criticised British policy in India whilst on a visit.

qué-drafting. I found him sitting on an untidy camp bed in a rather squalid pavilion in the Russian compound. My dinner was waiting for me, so I gave him one or two hasty observations and extracted from him a promise that he wouldn't disturb me again that night unless he got into extreme difficulty. However, I suppose we can't talk if we trail Randolph [Churchill] around with us. Harry Hopkins seems the only practical and more or less effective member of the entourage; even his methods are a trifle unorthodox. But his language is refreshingly emphatic.]

Friday, 10 December *Gibraltar*

Beastly morning—torrents of rain and low cloud. Hectic telephone conversation between Algiers and Tunis, as a result of which we agreed Portal should come on to Gib. with his 2 giant planes. We meanwhile secured a 'Dakota' to take 13 of us to Gib. . . . Lunched at 12 with Massigli. . . . Catroux very agreeable. . . . Landed Gibraltar 5.30. . . . P[ortal] says he can only give us 4 places on his York. . . . Left soon after midnight for airfield. I put A., Leathers, Winant and Howard to bed, and settled myself conspicuously in a chair. About 1 a.m. Portal and his party boarded the plane. Portal said I must have a bunk. I said I was quite happy as I was. 1st Sea Lord said he'd take my trousers off. I said that would be very draughty, and retired quickly to bed. So we won the rubber 5–3, and Portal's secretary had to sit up.

Saturday, 11 December

Told we were going straight through to Northolt, but as we came over Lyneham pilot ordered to land. So we landed. . . . Arrived London about 1. T. there: she had been on the move, trying to meet me, since 6.30 a.m.!

Tuesday, 14 December

5.30 Raczynski. I told him he must get from A. direct what had passed about Polish-Soviet relations. He took this well, and told me what points he would put to A. . . . Angora telegrams . . . show (*not* to my surprise) that the Turks are running out completely.

Wednesday, 15 December

Meeting with Chiefs-of-Staff at 11.15 about reply to Turks. Decided on reasonable line of reply, making an advance in our offer, but implying that this would be the last and that anyhow it was conditional on our going ahead at once with preparatory work on airfields. . . . P.M. has got pneumonia again and Moran is rather fussed about his heart. Specialist being flown from Cairo. He [Churchill] is, so far as I know, at Carthage.

Thursday, 16 December

5. meeting with A. and others about Yugoslavia (Mihailovitćh). I get confused with all these muddled Balkan situations. They bore me. . . . Drafted brief for A.'s talk with Poles tomorrow. He's very chary of it, but I think he must be frank. News given out this evening of P.M.'s illness. Have had no direct news. Clemmie going out.

[Resistance in Yugoslavia centred broadly on two groups: the Cetniks, led by General Mihailović, and the Partisans, whose outstanding leader was Josip Broz, known as Tito. The Partisans were Communist, the Cetniks Royalist, in sympathy. They fought each other frequently. The British found themselves in several dilemmas. In the first place, they had their obligations to King Peter and his exiled Government. Their military authorities, and S.O.E., naturally favoured support of the guerrillas most active against the Axis, and these seemed to be the Partisans. Those with an eye to the political future of Yugoslavia could not take so simple a view, for the result might be to place the Communists in control when the enemy's forces were driven out. Efforts to reconcile the Cetniks and Partisans broke down. The Russian Government would have no truck with Mihailović, whom they accused of collusion with the Italians against Partisan groups.

In May 1943 Eden did his best to insist that Mihailović must, if he were to receive continued British support and supplies, resist the Axis and try to collaborate with the Partisans. Mihailović accepted, but did little in either direction. Some British supplies were by now going to the Partisans. In July 1943 Brigadier Fitzroy Maclean was appointed to lead a liaison mission with Tito. By October he was reporting that the Partisan movement counted for more than the British authorities had previously recognised, that it would collaborate with other resistance groups but not with the Cetniks, and that Mihailović could never unite Yugoslavia. If full British support were given to the Partisans, the most probable result would be a Communist state, in close relations with Russia. Churchill decided to run this risk, on the grounds that the Partisans were indisputably doing more damage to Germany. On 10 December, in Cairo, he told King Peter that the British had 'irrefutable' evidence of the Cetniks' collaboration with the enemy; in the near future, the British Government might suggest the dismissal of Mihailović from his post as Minister of War.

Tito had by then set up a 'Provisional Government', which purported to deprive the Royal Government in exile of all its rights and standing. Eden had returned to London from Cairo ahead of the Prime Minister, who fell seriously ill at Carthage and then convalesced at Marrakesh until 14 January. Brigadier Maclean and the Royalist Yugoslav Government were still at Cairo. A policy had therefore to be found by triangular exchanges of telegrams. The Foreign Secretary suggested that King Peter should proceed to Tito's headquarters and form a new Government there. The British Ambassador to the Yugoslav Government, R. C. S. Stevenson, and Brigadier Maclean, advised that this was not practical politics. The former telegraphed on 25 December.

> Our policy must be based on three new factors: The Partisans will be the rulers of Yugoslavia. They are of such value to us militarily that we must back them to the full, subordinating political considerations to military. It is extremely doubtful whether we can any longer regard the monarchy as a unifying element in Yugoslavia.

These assumptions were not accepted by the Southern Department of the Foreign Office or by Cadogan. Eden did not wish to place all the cards in Tito's hands by telling him at once that Mihailović's immediate dismissal would be called for, but preferred to use this as a possible bargaining counter if Tito were prepared to discuss a *modus vivendi* with King Peter. The Prime Minister entered into a direct correspondence with Tito, whom he told on 8 January that 'no further military support' would be given to any but the Partisans; the British Government would be glad if Mihailović were dismissed; and that he hoped Tito would 'understand' that Britain would 'in any case remain in official relations' with King Peter. Tito sent a general reply after a long delay, saying that he quite understood the Allies' engagements to King Peter and would try not to inconvenience them on that score, although the 'internal political situation' created in the struggle represented 'the irresistible desire of all patriots'.[15]]

Friday, 17 December

12.30 attended interview between A. and Raczynski, which went quite well. A. calmer and did it well. . . . P.M. seems to be making steady progress. Berlin bombed again last night. But, as soon as weather permits, we must get busy on the 'ski-sites'* across the Channel. This is *urgent*. We want Winston home to prod people.

[Eden at this interview told Raczynski that he had not been able to secure a renewal of diplomatic relations between Poland and Russia. He also described Russia's frontier demands and the proffered compensation, which he thought too much to be digestible.

On 20 and 22 December, in Cadogan's presence, Eden held similar talks with Mikolajczyk, Romer and Raczynski. As a result, the Poles gave an undertaking to co-ordinate with the Russians their military action in Poland. Privately, the Ambassador remarked to officials of the Foreign Office that Britain's policy was one of appeasement, of storing up trouble

* For the launching of the 'V' pilotless weapons.

by postponing a showdown. Mikolajczyk said that his people were expecting Poland to emerge with her eastern provinces intact and her western ones increased.[16]]

Saturday, 18 December

Odd telegram from Stockholm, showing that a Swede (unnamed) has just returned from Berlin, after conversation with Himmler,* with Hitler's authority, with proposals for a 'clandestine' meeting in Stockholm between 2 Germans and 2 British. Object said to be to 'clarify terms of surrender'. First, we must find out who this Swede is, and test his credentials. Then we must inform Russians and Americans and perhaps propose to them to listen to the Germans, and agree with them the terms in which we are to present 'unconditional surrender'. Personally, I think this, if there is anything in it, is designed (1) to split Allies (2) perhaps to stiffen German morale by showing crushing nature of our terms or (3) possible the old trick of trying to threaten us into a compromise peace by the bogey of their 'secret weapon'. But I don't think we are entitled to ignore it altogether. It is odd: Bormann† is alleged to have been present at X's interview with Himmler. (3) is perhaps unlikely, because the Germans would be more likely to do this *publicly*.

Sunday, 19 December

Telegram from R. Stevenson about Tito's 'Executive's' declaration, containing attack mainly directed against Mihailovitch, but incidentally, also it seems, against the King [Peter]. This is very tiresome. Only thing to do is to try to get Tito to acknowledge the King. This T. won't do so long as King employs Mihailovitch. But it's rather hard for King to throw over M. at T's dictation. Spoke to A. on telephone. Telegraphed to R. Stevenson instructing him at least to dissuade Yugoslav Government from putting out anything silly.

Then the Turks are frightened at the idea of the 3 C.'s-in-C. going to Angora. (I'm not surprised.) But the job can be as well done by somewhat junior officers, with the Ambassador's backing. I promised A. to attend C's. of S. meeting on this tomorrow morning. . . .

Got full text of the Tito declaration, which isn't as bad as it might have been. Leaves a loophole open for the King. Good deal of telephoning to A.

* Heinrich Himmler, leader of S.S.; Minister of Interior, 1943.

† Martin Bormann, confidant of Hitler; Leader of the Party Chancellery and Member of the Cabinet, 1941–5.

Monday, 20 December

Saw A. about Yugoslavia. He has come to the (right) conclusion that the only thing to do is to drop King Peter into Tito's H.Q. . . . 5.30 Cabinet. No great news. P.M. seems to be going on well. In spite of lovely weather here, there was cloud over N. France and we couldn't do much against 'Crossbow'* (which is becoming urgent, although Cherwell still affects to pooh-pooh it). Cabinet agreed about Yugoslavia and action to be taken on Stockholm telegram.

Wednesday, 22 December

11.45 Alba. Brought me a little list of Spanish grievances, which I exchanged, with gusto, for a list of British. 12.15 talk with A. about Greece and Yugoslavia. Slight symptoms in Greece of a desire to sink internal differences. As regards Yugoslavia, news from R. Stevenson seems to show that our cock won't fight. Tito comes out even stronger against the King. Is this Moscow? . . . I dined upstairs with A., Mikolajczyk, Romer, Raczynski, O.S. and O'Malley. V. good dinner and we talked after, trying to instil sense into the Polish mind but, my goodness, that's a difficult job!

Friday, 24 December *Thatched Cottage*

All afternoon our bombers, some of them 4-engined, were roaring home from the Pas de Calais. Hope they have knocked 'Crossbow'. Radio tonight says that 1,300 went! . . . Winter jasmine, of course, blooming. It's mad. Purple crocuses just showing tips: yellow coming up nicely, and just some signs of daffodils. Primroses in the pavement go on flowering regardless of everything.

Monday, 27 December *Thatched Cottage*

Quiet read—but annoyed by the stuff I read: Sacheverell Sitwell's 'Splendours and Miseries'. He might just as well have called it 'Colanders and toothbrushes'. It doesn't mean anything at all. I suppose he's experimenting in some surrealist style, but I wish he *wouldn't*.

Wednesday, 29 December *Thatched Cottage*

Fed chickens and in to tea, after which I pursued my course of light reading in front of a log fire—a good change from my usual life. 9 o'clock news gave account of engagement with Blockade Runner and enemy destroyers in the Bay [of Biscay]. 3 of latter sunk. This, on top of the sinking of the [battle-cruiser] 'Scharnhorst' is good.

* 'Crossbow' was the committee set up to devise countermeasures against the V-weapon attack. The name came to indicate the entire operation.

Germans have had a miserable Xmas—may they have a much worse New Year!

Friday, 31 December *Thatched Cottage*

It's been a wonderful year in many ways: a complete change in the war situation. Germany is beat—but when? That cowed herd of people can do nothing to help themselves, except fight like caged rats. And if they continue to do that, it will take us a long time to wipe them out. They *may* break at any moment, but I don't expect it. Meanwhile, I suppose we must, in the spring, embark on the most hazardous enterprise ever undertaken. If it goes wrong, it will set us back 2 years. I don't mean to be pessimistic, but it will be an awful gamble. But I don't exclude a German crack before we have to make this hazardous throw.

1944

Monday, 3 January

Cabinet 5.30. No great news. Our bombing of 'Crossbow' seems to have achieved something, but nothing very decisive. Berlin is getting basted. Dined at home. Masses of work.

Tuesday, 4 January

Russians are doing wonders—have crossed the '39 Polish frontier. But that presents us with some problems! Raczynski and O.S. were clamouring to see me today, but I simply hadn't the time! Our bombings of 'Crossbow' seem to have had some effect, but not an awful lot. It's difficult.

Wednesday, 5 January

12.15 O'Malley with text of Polish Declaration about Russians' crossing of Polish frontier. Not bad at all. Sent him back to Romer to try to get it even better. 1.15. A. in a flap, asking for it. Told him I'd approved it and given O.'M. his instructions. It contains almost *all* the amendments he wanted, and he was busy. He doesn't like it if one sends him too many papers, but is always ready to complain if *one* slips past him. . . . About 4, got O'M. with the Polish text, A. tamely admitted it was quite good. Struggled on with work, but my boxful of 'stinkers' still waiting.

[The declaration stated that

The Polish Government, as the only and legal steward and spokesman of the Polish nation, recognized by Poles at home and abroad as well as by Allied and free Governments, is conscious of the contribution of Poland to the war and is responsible for the fate of the nation. It affirms its indestructible right to independence. . . .

The Polish Government expects that the Soviet Union . . . will not fail to respect the rights and interests of the Polish Republic and of its citizens. . . .

Eden commented to Churchill, recuperating in Marrakesh, that efforts to secure a favourable press had not proved entirely successful. 'The truth is that in the present atmosphere of overwhelming Russian victories there is public impatience with the Poles. This may not be just, but it is the truth.' Two days later, Stalin wired that to judge from the declaration of 'the Polish emigrant Government' and other statements, there was evidently 'no foundation for reckoning on the possibility of bringing these circles to reason. These people are incorrigible.'

The published Russian reply of 11 January condemning the alleged inaccuracy of the Poles' statement of 5 January stated that the Soviets did not 'consider the 1939 frontier inalterable'; proposed that the frontier should run roughly along the Curzon Line, with compensation for Poland in the West; and attacked the credentials of the Poles in London.

The Polish Government in exile, detached from its people, has proved incapable of establishing friendly relations with the U.S.S.R. or of organizing an active struggle in Poland against the German invader. Moreover, its mistaken policy clearly plays into German hands. The interests of Poland and the U.S.S.R. demand the establishment of friendly relations between our countries and the joining of the two peoples in the struggle against the external enemy. . . .

Eden pressed the Poles hard to make a conciliatory reply. Their next statement, of 14 January repeated Poland's desire for an agreement with Russia on terms just and acceptable to both. Poland would discuss, the British and Americans participating, 'all outstanding questions'. This formula included frontiers and had been reached only after much heart-searching. The Foreign Secretary urged that Russia should not refuse, but again to no avail. A Russian retort of 17 January rejected negotiations because the Poles had not accepted the Curzon Line in advance. In the view of Soviet circles, stated Tass, the official Soviet News Agency, the Polish Government did not 'wish to establish good-neighbourly relations with the Soviet Union.' This reply, Eden told Gousev, came 'like a blow in the face'. Simultaneously, *Pravda* published reports of a supposed meeting between senior British officers and emissaries of Ribbentrop, or even Ribbentrop himself.[17]]

Thursday, 6 January

Telegram from P.M. suggesting Poles should be sent out to him [at Marrakesh] and that I should accompany them. Talked to A. about this, who approved and drafted reply. If Poles agree, we may start out this day week. Just kept abreast of a cataract of boxes. . . . O.S. away, O. H[arvey] ill—so that I get vast and undigested files from the Depts. I have snapped at them.

Friday, 7 January

Romer at 11. He and Mikolajczyk ready to go to P.M. I said they could start about next Thurs. and I would accompany them. Then had some talk on the general problem. He went so far as to hint that he, personally, was wondering whether an understanding could be reached with the Russians that the region between 1939 frontier and Curzon Line was 'litigieux', its fate to be settled at Peace Conference by U.S., U.K., Soviet and Polish agreement. He almost went so far as to say Polish Govt. might agree to an intimation to Soviet that they were 'prepared to contemplate' that whole or part of this region might be ceded to Soviet. This is a distinct move forward, but I don't know whether he can deliver the goods. Told A. and telegraphed to P.M. . . . Was gradually working off arrears, when several more 'stinkers' arrived—including Palestine and German Armistice terms! Russian news wonderful. Dined at home and swam upstream against arrears of Files.

Saturday, 8 January

Telegram from P.M. who says he *may* be coming home earlier than he thought, in which case Poles and I need not go out. Will let us know within 48 hrs.

Sunday, 9 January

Telegram from P.M. showing that he probably *is* contemplating coming home soon. But this crossed one from A. saying we were still in midwinter and he'd better be careful. So I shan't think of my plans yet. A. apparently in his usual week-end flat spin. So I avoided talking to him on the telephone. Fussed about the proposed handling of Turkey—i.e. going back to the old haggling. Of course this is silly. But I am now convinced (by Snatch's recent reports) (a) that it would or might be a disaster to get Turkey into the war now and (b) that the only importance she has is as 'cover' to deceive Germans. Therefore, we'd better go on haggling and sending stuff in though, in practice, it will be wasted. Think he took this view later in the day.

Monday, 10 January

P.M. clamouring for a decision about handing over Italian ships to Russia. C's of S. don't see eye to eye with P.M. (or with President, who shares Winston's view). Got Dept. to draft message from P.M. to Pres. which Rumbold* told me was in accordance with what C's of S. settled at their meeting this morning. A. approved it and I took it to Cabinet to show to [Admiral] Cunningham. He said it was not at all in accordance with C's of S. view. I asked him, with his colleagues, to produce redraft after Cabinet. I left Cabinet at 6.30 and at 6.40 Ismay rang me up to say C's of S. had met and Cunningham was sending over [Captain] Lambe at once to see me. Nothing had happened by 7.20 so I rang up Admiralty, who hadn't heard of Lambe since 11 a.m! But Cunningham was sending over someone at once to see me. About 7.30 a wet-eyed young civilian appeared, but he didn't seem to know much more than I did what the Admiral wanted. I said he must go back and get Admiral to approve a draft which must then be sent over direct to S. of S. at F.O. tonight, as a telegram must get off to P.M. Explained to A. and left at 8. I suppose I shall be rung up at midnight—and probably pulled out of bed. But I shall resist valiantly.

Not much news, except Russian, which is marvellous. Attacks on 'Crossbow' have been fairly good, but we are just not keeping abreast of them. Dined at home.

Tuesday, 11 January

Coldish—rained later. A wearisome and tiresome day. My cold developing slowly! I expected to be rung up late last night, but this didn't happen. (I begin to wonder whether it is worth while setting out all these details of day-to-day worries, which melt, like the 'neiges d'antan'. But perhaps so.) Instead A. rang me up at 9 in a pet. Said I'd let him down last night. Why hadn't I done as he told me, and gone to Chiefs of Staff meeting? I said (a) he *hadn't* told me, but that (b) on hearing, at 6.30 yesterday evening, that C's of S. were meeting, I offered to go over and join them but Ismay said it was over! Got to F.O. at 9.50. Couldn't get A. till 10.25. Told him I was going to C's of S. at 10.50 and asked for a line, which I suggested —and got. (He had calmed down, more or less.). . . Gave them idea of draft reply to P.M. which they approved. Guaranteed to let them have written text ½ hour. I had then to go on to Cabinet about Yugoslavia. Cabinet (except Sinclair) made no difficulty. Meanwhile P.M. has produced an alternative suggestion for meeting Joe about

* Anthony (later Sir Anthony) Rumbold, then serving in the F.O.

ships—i.e. 'lending' him [battleship] 'Malaya'. 12.40 helped A. to dictate a telegram to P.M. about Yugoslavia. 12.50 talk about how to take Poles this afternoon about Soviet declaration. . . . At 3.15 to join A. and Poles. Latter quite hopeless but have undertaken to do nothing supremely silly without consulting us further. . . . 5.15 talk with A., [A.V.] Alexander and Cunningham at which we—*at last*—fixed up reply to P.M. about Italian ships for Soviet. O'Malley brought draft declaration which we might urge on Poles. Good in its general line, but much too controversial for us to dare to give to Poles as a British draft. (They might well give away that we were authors.) O'M. wouldn't have this but A. agreed with me and O'M. will try another version on them tomorrow morning.

Wednesday, 12 January

O'Malley showed me forecast of what, after discussion with Romer, he thought Poles might put out. This all right, if they'll do it. . . . Poles weighed in with a typical Polish declaration. But they agree to wait to discuss it with us tomorrow before putting it out. I told A. we must talk straight to them. (They probably want it.)

Thursday, 13 January

Nothing much in morning (except work!) Wellington Koo* at 11.30. Lunch with A. in his flat for Gousev. There were old Lloyd G[eorge], Bevin, Bruce,† Bobbety, Camrose, Walter Layton, Alexander, Vincent Massey, J. Anderson. Towards end of lunch Ll[oyd] G. collared the talk. I suppose he's not strong enough to take part in Parliamentary Debates, so seized on this opportunity. His theme—we ought to have had a Second front in 1942. What was the difficulty? In 1918 he had demanded American troops, and had got 1,300,000 in a few months. Everyone regarded this whole performance as a joke (as it was) but in view of Gousev's presence, I thought the old man *must* be checked a bit. I reminded him that in 1918 he had all the French ports and railways open to him. Alexander chipped in with a few other obvious criticisms. Ll[oyd] G. waved them aside in the old, grand manner and continued on his course. For us, all this very amusing, but I wonder what Gousev thought of it. And what he will report to his Govt.! 5–7.30 session with A., O'Malley, Mikolajczyk, Romer and Raczynski. Gave them our version of draft declaration we should like them to make. They pretty mulish, but I think they're moving a bit. Read them P.M.'s message which

* Chinese Ambassador.

† Australian High Commissioner.

Cadogan and Bevin

The Cadogans' cottage at Yateley, Hampshire. Watercolour painted by Sir Alec after his retirement

At the United Nations, 25 October 1946

shook them. They're so *silly:* they seem to be bringing themselves to the point where they might hold out a hand to the Soviet, but they *cannot* resist putting some itching powder on it.

Friday, 14 January

Mikolajczyk and Romer . . . at 12. Their Cabinet had come a *little* way to meet us, but were still silly. Told them so, and sent them back with a draft of our own. We had meanwhile had a Cabinet at 11, which had been quite useful, and endorsed us . . . further interview with Poles. They finally had seen sense. We got Ridsdale in and gave him instructions to give it a fair wind with our Press (which he tells me he can do). Not surprising that after all this I had seventeen boxes waiting for me. A. saw Gousev at 4. He sticky, but then of course he daren't be anything else, poor mutt. . . . 6.30 Winant, whom I posted on the Soviet-Polish question. He promised to help. Made inroads in my papers. Home at 8, and dined there and more or less finished off my work. Wrote two fulminations to the Office about length and complexity of minutes, and shortcomings of Communications Dept. Cold really seems to have receded for the moment. . . . Shall probably have a jolly weekend.

Monday, 17 January

A. didn't arrive till 12.30. We then had discussion of Soviet flat-footed and bloody-minded reply to Polish declaration. I'm beginning to share Polish suspicions that Soviet intentions are wholly dishonourable. Don't see what we can do for the moment, except perhaps mobilise P.M. (who is due at 10 a.m. tomorrow). . . . 4 meeting with 'C' and others about leaks, apparently, in Angora. Von Papen appears to be well supplied with our secret documents. Cabinet 5.30. No great news. We seem to have knocked 'Crossbow' about a bit. Russian news continues very good. Soviet have allowed 'Pravda' to reproduce a story of a negotiation between Ribbentrop and British officials in a Pyrenean town, for a 'separate' peace. This is quite monstrous. We tell the Russians *everything* and play square with them. They are the most stinking creepy set of Jews I've ever come across. Got A. to agree to issue dementi here (as it's got about in the Press) and to demand a dementi of the Russians. They *are* swine!

Tuesday, 18 January

Winston arrived this morning and went straight to House, where he made a 'dramatic' entry. A. says he seems well but looks a bad colour (Press say 'pale'). But he complains of his legs and says he can't walk or even stand for v. long. That may be result of 'M. and B.' [drugs]. . . . 3.30 talk with A. and O.S. and others about Greece. Then about Polish-Soviet situation. Agreed we should move P.M. to telegraph to Joe on certain lines. [F.K.] Roberts undertook to produce draft. I saw A. after about Egypt and other things. About 7.15 I rang up Roberts about his draft. He had only just produced it. Depts. have no *idea* of 'First things first'. Got it, through O.S., about 7.45. Rang up A. to say it wouldn't be ready for dinner—I'd send it round after, if necessary. Dined at home. Redrafted message to Joe—or rather, wrote a new one, and did some other work.

Wednesday, 19 January

Mild, but dull. Nothing much in morning. 12.15 went to Palace to present new Venezuelan to the King. Unprofitable conversation about the weather and the climate. The King made some contributions overwhelmed by rhetoric on the part of the Venezuelan. But this was in—to me—quite unintelligible English, given in sonorous and minatory declamation. We did our best about it, but our interjections were feeble and to him, probably, inappropriate. It had never struck me before to what degree one is at a disadvantage if a foreigner takes one's own language and bludgeons one with unrecognisable sounds and most un-English mien and gestures. One ought to reply in polite Chinese, or meaningless gibberish. . . . . Meeting with A. at 3 about Poles. Conclusion—after some talk—seemed to be that one couldn't do better than my draft of last night, and A. is putting it to P.M.

Thursday, 20 January

12.15 went to No. 10 for a talk between P.M. and A. and the Poles. Nobody there when I arrived but P.M. shortly appeared at the garden door and I greeted him. He looks and seems well and vigorous. A. joined us and we admitted Mikolajczyk, Romer and Raczynski. P.M. gave it them hot and strong, poor dears, but that's right. M. said he would have to consult his Govt. this afternoon. When he gets their reply, P.M. will draft message to Joe.

Friday, 21 January

3. Raczynski, who stayed an hour and a half adjusting an agreed record of yesterday's conversation, and telling me what he could—not much—about his Govt's reactions.

[In the early hours of 22 January, Allied troops landed at Anzio and Nettuno, south of Rome, but nearly 100 miles north of the Allied lines.

The Germans reacted quickly and virtually sealed off the beach-head. At one time they seemed likely to cast the British and Americans back into the sea. Churchill later called this his worst moment of the war.]

Monday, 24 January

Our landing, at Anzio, on Saturday morning, *seems* successful. 12.45 talk with A. and others about Argentine, which seems to be taking a better turn. . . . 4.30 talk with A. and others about Turkey. Agreed on P.M.'s line of withdrawing [military] Mission and stopping further shipments and awaiting Turkish reactions. 5. Raczynski, who produced note of further amendments they want in the 'agreed' record, and a note asking silly questions. Cabinet at 6. P.M. in good form. *No* losses of ships due to enemy action last week. Russians doing well in North. We seem to have pounded 'Crossbow' pretty well. Fri. night's raid on London (which I forgot to mention, and was *frightfully* noisy) doesn't seem to have done much harm.

Tuesday, 25 January

Cabinet at 5.30. Poland, Agriculture, Japanese atrocities and Palestine! Went on till nearly 8. P.M. asked me to give him draft message to Stalin on quite good lines. This I did, with much other work, after dinner at home. Much of it is a re-hash of my earlier draft.

Wednesday, 26 January

Gave my draft of message from P.M. to Stalin to O.S. and Dept. to worry. They, of course, haven't the faintest inkling of what is wanted for this sort of draft, and boggle over every word. Carcano* at 11. He didn't seem to know much. I said it was good that the Argentine had taken the plunge: they must now strike out in the right direction. In that way we might arrive at restoration of relations of confidence. Tried to disabuse him of idea that we and U.S. had been at cross purposes. . . . A. had approved my draft and sent it to P.M. But in the meanwhile the silly old man had dictated one of his own (after asking me to give him one). Without any pride of authorship, I must say I think mine is better than his! But I can do no more than attempt to tinker with his. Raczynski at 6. Told him of P.M.'s intention of sending message to Stalin without waiting for Polish reply. He quite approved. But reminded me P.M. had promised to show it to Poles. They won't like P.M.'s draft! Agreed tinkerings with O.S. (who also hasn't got the hang of P.M. messages).

* Don M. A. Carcano, Argentinian Ambassador, 1942–6.

[In general, the British had been well content to follow the lead of the U.S.A. in South American issues. The Government of Argentina, however, had refused to break off relations with the Axis, and had made only token efforts to control the operations of the German and Japanese Intelligence services. In June 1943 President Castillo's dictatorship was overthrown by a military junta under President Ramirez, in which Colonel Juan Perón soon emerged as the principal figure. The new regime showed plainly enough that it intended to play off the Axis and the U.S.A. as long and as profitably as might be. Receiving evidence of the complicity of the Argentine Government and German agents in the overthrow of the Bolivian Government, Hull proposed that the U.S.A. with British support, should try to secure the downfall of Ramirez's Government. The British demurred. They did obtain, however, evidence of German subversive activities organised from Argentina. Fear of its disclosure may have assisted President Ramirez's announcement, on 26 January, that Argentina would break off diplomatic relations with Germany and Japan. Early in February the German military and air attachés and the Japanese naval attaché were arrested. Shortly afterwards, a further *coup* by officers under Colonel Perón displaced President Ramirez. The U.S. Government refused to recognise the new regime unless it met American conditions, which it declined to do. Under strong pressure from Hull, Eden told the British Ambassador in Buenos Aires to communicate with the Government of Argentina only on routine matters. British interests there were greater than those of the U.S.A. Moreover, two-fifths of the tiny British meat ration was imported from Argentina.]

Thursday, 27 January

Gave A. text of our tinkerings with P.M.'s draft to Stalin. Cabinet at 12.15 at H. of C. to consider draft. P.M. accepted our amendments. . . Back at F.O. at 2.30 to tackle mounts of papers, of which I had to send a lot in to A. (That's largely his fault—owing to his horrible habit of scribbling remarks and queries on advance copies of telegrams.) A. saw Beneŝ* at 5.45 and showed me after, at 6.15, two amendments B. proposed to P.M.'s message. Both, I think, good. . . . 7.45 went with A. to see P.M. about Beneŝ' amendments. He accepted them. I told them of 'Isvestia's' attack on Poles in connexion with Katyn and that Poles would probably react in their Press. He said they should be urged not to. So went back to F.O., soon after 8, and rang up Raczynski who appeared to agree, and promised to speak at once to Mikolajczyk. But I think I know latter has already committed himself.

[This message told Stalin of the discussions with the Poles, and disclosed that Churchill had pressed them to accept the Russian proposals in return

* He had recently been in Moscow.

for the 'fine compensations' offered. It also pointed out that the creation of a rival government in Poland, and disturbances there, would raise serious issues between the Allies.]

Friday, 28 January *Thatched Cottage*

Alba at 12. He only came really to bid a friendly goodbye, but I had to impress on him that we were fully behind the American suspension of oil shipments. However, he thinks as I do, and we parted on most friendly terms. He expects to leave for Madrid tomorrow morning. . . . T. and I started for cottage at 3.15. Arrived 5.5. Quite a lot of crocuses showing yellow. Winter jasmine in full bloom. Anemones blooming. Primroses still blooming in pavement. (All the early things are yellow—jaundiced, I suppose, by our climate.) Tulips just pushing through. I wonder whether they'll flower. Pullets all look most robust, but they don't lay an egg and one died suddenly earlier this week. . . . Not much news, except from northern Russian front. Another 1500 tons on Berlin last night, making a total of nearly 20,000 tons since Nov. 18!

Saturday, 29 January *Thatched Cottage*

Raid which interfered with 9 o'clock news. Russian news v. good. Another raid on Berlin last night (2nd night running). Absence of news from our Nettuno bridgehead [at Anzio]. When is this bloody war going to end? I'm tired of it, and getting rather stale altogether—getting myopic from constant close-up view of the grindstone.

Monday, 31 January

Ferguson at 3.30. Sent by [Lord] Kemsley with reference to my remarks . . . about Alexander Werth's* broadcasts of the 'Russian point of view'. Explained that I had no intention of imputing blame to Lord K. or 'Sunday Times'. I only thought—and still think—it a work of supererogation for B.B.C. to broadcast from London 'Russian point of view'. I see no likelihood of Moscow broadcasting 'British point of view'. I had taken it up with Brendan [Bracken]. Cabinet at 6. P.M. v. despondent about the Nettuno landing. Said this had now become an American operation, with no punch in it. We were clinging to a bridgehead and rendering it defensively fireproof. A bad prospect for this operation and a bad omen for greater ops. later. Heavy and successful work in the air. Significant that Germans announced raid on London with 600 machines. About 230 were put in the air, 100 crossed the coast, and 25 reached Greater

* *Sunday Times* correspondent and B.B.C. commentator, Moscow, 1941–6.

London. Germans obligingly added that their loss—25 machines—was a v. small percentage. We didn't know we'd shot down so many! Best month yet of sinkings. 8 U-boats destroyed—4 probables.

Wednesday, 2 February

5.15 meeting with A., O.S. and Ismay about Italian ships for Soviet. Joe had sent most offensive reply about our offer of [battleship] 'Royal Sovereign' and an American Cruiser, saying this was 'of no significance' without attendant 8 destroyers and 4 submarines. There are various alternatives. Least bad, I advised A., was to offer British and American over-age vessels, explaining that efficient ships are required for 'Overlord' in which Joe has evinced some interest. A. agreed and went over to see P.M. Don't know what happened. 5.30. meeting with O.S. and all the Pundits on 'Dismemberment of Germany' (what a waste of time!) and 'Unconditional Surrender'. On latter, agreed on lines of draft paper for the Cabinet. On former, must talk to A. tomorrow and try to get some sense. Quite useful.

Thursday, 3 February

4.30 talk with A. about 'elevation' of Missions. He objects to Cuba: I object to the lot, but don't care much. So we go ahead, except for Cuba. (And I expect P.M. will try to re-include Cuba so as to assure his supply of cigars.)* 6 talk with A. about Spain—he is still infected with his anti-Franco views. Also talked to him about 'Dismemberment of Germany' which means nothing and never did mean anything and is advocated by those who never stop to think what it does mean. Agreed to turn E[uropean] A[dvisory] C[omsion] loose on it first. Dined at home. V. good Russian news—Rovno and Lutsk and encirclement of ten German Divisions in Ukraine. 1,100 U.S. aircraft over Wilhelmshaven today.

Friday, 4 February

12 Palmella† to say Salazar can't come here, and to urge reticence about suspension of oil to Spain. I expressed regrets about former, and gave all assurances regarding latter. . . . 2.45 talk with A. and others about Stalin's reaction to our communication about Poles.

* Cf. Churchill to Eden, 5 Feb: 'I must say I think Cuba has as good a claim as some of the other places—la perla de las Antillas. Great offence will be given if all the others have it and this large, rich, beautiful island, the home of the cigar, is denied.'

† Duke of Palmella, Portuguese Ambassador, 1943–9.

Stalin's actual reply to P.M.'s message not yet received. We agreed to put up, over week-end, brief on which P.M. might talk to Poles. 3.15 Winant, about Censorship, and I managed, tactfully I hope, to urge him to close his own gaps.

Saturday, 5 February

P.M. is having a glorious week-end, grinding out masses of telegrams on foreign affairs which is not very convenient. He, from Chequers, sends up draft to F.O., for immediate despatch unless Foreign Sec. sees objection. F.S. 60 miles away at Binderton. No time to get Dept's observations. Also, he has arranged for Mikolajczyk to have lunch with him tomorrow. I wish he *wouldn't*. He swears he's not going to continue serious discussion, but only to 'prepare' M. Meanwhile Stalin's answer has come in—I haven't seen it yet. But P.M. will not be able to deny that he has received it, and, in the course of a good lunch, will inevitably [?] be drawn by M., and we shall never know what has passed. I have asked A. to try to get O'Malley included in party, and I think he is going to try. Then P.M. had drafted a message to Tito (which as a matter of fact I think is all right) and a number of telegrams on Italian ships for Russia (which is rather more a head-ache for the Admiralty). I left F.O. at 6 and left them to it—our migratory statesmen must settle things direct between them. But it's hopeless, during week-ends, to conduct affairs on this plan:-

.Chequers

.London

.Binderton

Walked home and dined there. Russian news v. good. 'Attacks repulsed' on our Nettuno Bridgehead. Don't like the latter, and think the Italian situation depressing and ominous for the future.

Sunday, 6 February

Hear A. has got to go to Chequers for lunch! Joe's answer now in. Not too bad—rather on the lines of his talk with A. C. K[err]. Nothing much to do but some quiet reading. . . . At F.O. 3.45. Not much doing and no news of Chequers party. Nettuno news bad. We have taken rather a knock, and seem to be hemmed in. I wish our Staff had studied in Germany. Home 6.30. Read. Dined at Ritz. Polished silver.

Monday, 7 February

Cabinet 5.30. The Nettuno Bridgehead definitely a disappointment: not yet a disaster. May it be a lesson from which we may learn. Sinkings good. Russian news marvellous. C.I.G.S. now says situation on E. front very like that on W. front in summer and autumn of 1918. (But there are other factors.) Good results on 'Crossbow'. Dined at home. Meeting with A. and others at 10 p.m. on Polish question. P.M. pressed the Poles pretty hard at lunch yesterday. He has now produced draft telegram to Joe informing him of this talk and saying that if Poles won't agree he (W.S.[C]) will pledge himself to Russians to support their case at Peace Conference. This, as it seems to me, is putting all the aces (including the Ace of Trumps) in Joe's hand. A. quite agreed, and dictated a minute to P.M. suggesting that the reply to Joe can wait a day or two, during which we can continue to work on Poles.

Thursday, 10 February

6.30 talk with A. and others about Bulgarian peace-feelers (and [Colonel W.] Donovan's* fantastic antics in connexion therewith) and Greece. . . . Went on to dine at Savoy with A. and Poles (Romer and Raczynski). Don't think they've come on at *all*, though O'M. who was there also, thought they had. He's rather like Snatch with his bloody Turks!

Friday, 11 February

Spent some time with O. Harvey and O'Malley drafting terms of a possible Polish-Soviet agreement. Sent it off to A. before lunch. Don't know when he will see it, as he's occupied in the House with a continuation of this contemptible 'debate' about 'certificating' M.P.s. It merely gives Aneurin Bevan the opportunity to sling about libellous charges, for which he would have to pay heavily, were it not for 'privilege'. He and his kidney are mere barnacles on the bottom of the 'ship of State'. In any decent country they'd be bumped off. To that extent am I 'Fascist'—and proud of it! . . . Saw A. in afternoon about our Polish-Soviet draft, which he sent on to P.M. Then dashed off to the country (A.—not I!) Kept busy till 7.30. Dined at home. Paid bills. Don't like the 'Bridgehead' news. Jumbo [Wilson]† or Alex[ander], or both, will get the sack.

* Chief of the U.S. O.S.S.

† General Sir H. M. Wilson, Supreme Allied Commander, Mediterranean, Jan.–Nov. 1944.

Saturday, 12 February

P.M. approved our draft Polish-Soviet agreement text. O'M. to try it on Poles. . . . 'Evening Standard' had headlines about Bridgehead situation being 'desperate'. I know of no reason for this, and don't believe it to be true. That crook Max [Beaverbrook] is—for reasons best known to himself—bedevilling everything. He is opposing the Health proposals, opposing our line on Article VII, going about telling Americans that Labour [Ministers] are going to walk out of the Cabinet. What is he up to? What does he want? Does he want to be P.M. at this moment? Or is he manipulating finance? Why the heck does the P.M. keep him? A. told me he doesn't see how any Cabinet that includes Max can possibly pull together. He *is* a monkey [?]. On the 9 o'c. news a confident statement by Alex and Jumbo which I suppose has been designed as a corrective.

Sunday, 13 February

Not much doing. O'Malley has been wrestling with Poles, and they go back and back.

Tuesday, 15 February

Saw A. at 10.30, who had had session with P.M. into the small hours. Latter seems to think that we needn't assume complete Polish–Soviet breakdown, and that we can try on the Poles an intermediate stage, wherein they accept Curzon line as a provisional, war-time, ad hoc dividing (administrative) line. This follows, more or less, a draft which he made some days ago. While we were talking, P.M. rang up and asked A. to send me round. . . . P.M. in bed, rather becolded and damp. We went through his original draft and altered it a bit, and I undertook to send him and A. a redraft, which I did at lunch time. Nothing else exciting. . . . 6.45 O'M. told me Mikolajczyk was handing in his resignation to the President. Told him to inform A. (at Cabinet). 7.15 A. and O'M. appeared in my room and we sent for Romer. Told him to hold his crisis and come and see P.M. tomorrow afternoon, when latter would have proposals in a slightly different form to put to them. He agreed. . . .

In a spare hour on a recent Sunday I measured my travels—since the war—on my globe. They work out at 57,000 miles!

A. complained last night to the P.M. that he can't do both F.O. and the House. P.M. made it plain that he's got to stick anyhow to the latter. P.M.'s remedy was to 'delegate more to the F.O.' (but that really doesn't make sense) or 'let Bobbety have a hand in it' (but that is even more hopeless). A possibility is to appoint B., but I rather hope not. I expect it will blow over. Pressure on A. is rather severe now, with Parliamentary difficulties, and Hall* ill.

Wednesday, 16 February

Black fog for ½ hr. after lunch. Gousev at 12.15. Rated him about 'Pravda' article.† He completely wooden. I nearly lost my temper. . . . 5.30 session with P.M., A., O'Malley, Mikolajczyk, Romer and Raczynski about the eternal Polish-Soviet question. Poles have moved a *bit* but not far enough. P.M. gave them his revised draft message to Stalin. They don't like it, but took it away to chew on. Didn't finish till 7.30. Dined at home and worked. We had 1025 bombers out last night—893 over Berlin. The fantastic German claims about their raids in London encourage me to think that we have smashed up 'Crossbow' and that they are trying to dress up these air raids as 'retaliation'.

P.M., in conversation with Poles, did say we couldn't tell whether this year's operations would go well or ill. He did add that in two or three years the Great Powers 'might get tired of the war'. I don't know what he meant, nor what effect this may have had on the Poles!

[In conversation with Clark Kerr on 2 February, Stalin had said that he wished the Polish Government to accept the Curzon Line. That Government must be 'reconstructed' before the Soviets could resume relations. But after the war the Poles would be free and independent; the Russians would not interfere with their choice of government. The written reply ran on similar lines, and insisted on the annexation of Königsberg. This claim Churchill divulged to the Poles for the first time at Chequers on 6 February. Mikolajczyk refused to accept it or the Curzon Line. The establishment by the Communist Party in Warsaw of a 'National Council of the Homeland', he felt sure, presaged a Russian intention to set up a rival Polish Government. At this further meeting of 16 February, the same ground was traversed. In essence the Poles would accept a line of demarcation (not a settled frontier) running east of Vilna and Lwow. Churchill and Eden once more said that Britain could not prevent the Russians from marching through Poland, and if no agreement were made, they might set up a puppet regime.

Mikolajczyk could not persuade his colleagues, but allowed the Prime Minister to tell Stalin that the British proposals were put forward with his acquiescence. Churchill stated that the Poles were willing to discuss the frontier, though they could not yet announce their willingness to cede territory. He hoped that they would soon be allowed to return to Poland

* George Hall, M.P., Parliamentary Under-Secretary of State, F.O., 1943–5.

† An article of 12 Feb., containing a bitter attack on the Polish Government in exile.

and establish a civil administration in certain districts. With the consent of their Underground leaders the Polish Government had ordered full collaboration with the advancing Soviet armies; and when diplomatic relations were resumed they would include in their administration only men determined to co-operate with Russia. Britain would support such a settlement at the peace conference and guarantee it thereafter. Rejection of this offer would have serious reactions on Russia's relations with the U.S. and Britain.[18]]

Thursday, 17 February

Talked to O'M. about his consultations with Poles. He has a new formula, which is ingenious; while reserving all Polish rights, it leaves it to Russians to say what bits of Poland they will allow Poles progressively to administer. (The answer is, probably, 'none', but Poles with their suicidal tendency might like this: quite likely Stalin would.)... 3 meeting with A. and O'M. Latter authorised to continue his conversations with Poles and try to marry his draft to P.M.'s and put it across them.

Friday, 18 February

11.30 meeting [on 'Overlord' security] wasted my time till 1.20, when they adjourned to 4—so my weekend had gone west.... 3.30 meeting with A., O.S., O'M. and Roberts about Poles. O'M. has produced an ingenious draft, which he thinks he can put across Poles. I pointed out it wanted re-arranging (it's a patchwork quilt) and indicated points in order. Roberts commissioned to re-write it. 4 o'c. committee went on till after 6. I didn't have much to do. They adjourned till 11 on Mon. I've handed over to O.S. as I plan to get away tomorrow morning and not get back before lunch on Monday. Found 13 boxes waiting for me. Looked at R.'s redraft, which seems all right, and briefed O.S. Home at 8. Dined at Restaurant (which is running out of whisky) and worked off papers. A pretty beastly day.

Monday, 21 February

Nearly all windows [at F.O.] gone.* I installed in O.S.'s room. Worked hard. 3.30 talk with A., O'M[alley] and Romer. Cabinet at 6. Said last night estimated at 25 machines over London, as against 30 on Fri. night. But they have made a good mess of Whitehall. Meanwhile, during the last 48 hrs. we and the Americans have so basted Germany that their defences are exhausted, and we only lost 10 last night, out of about 700. (We got down 5 of the Germans, and

* The Foreign Office had lost most of its windows and several doors, No. 10 all its windows and most of the tiles.

this ought to be improved.) Masses of F.O. problems, Spain, Italy, Americans and oil &c. Cabinet went on till 7.50. Home about 8 with *stacks* of work, and I don't know when I shall catch up again. Dined at home and worked. *Never* again shall I come up on a Monday morning. It's *hopeless*, and one never catches up. Don't know how A. does it. Suppose he doesn't. . . . P.M. speaking tomorrow. Just as I was sitting down to dinner, Millard* rang me up to read out P.M.'s draft of what he will say about Poles. All right, with one exception, about which I made suggestions.

Wednesday, 23 February

V. noisy night again last night, for an hour or so. About 100 planes over London, which is a considerable increase on recent ventures. But I don't think they can do much more. 10 shot down, which is not bad, but not good enough. Fairly quiet morning. A. busy at House with F[oreign] A[ffairs] debate. . . . Was getting down to work (of which not too much) when O.S. picked me up to take me off to that frightful 'Red Army Day' at Soviet Embassy. Ten thousand people packed like sardines. One long-haired man smoking a pipe. By the way, this morning, an American . . . came and talked to me for nearly an hour about his recent time in M[iddle] E[ast]. Quite interesting, but they *do* talk—these Americans. As he did the whole of the talking, I expect he will say he had a *vurry* interesting interview. Back at F.O. 6.30. Home to a lavish dinner. We today suddenly received supplies of haddock, kipper and chicken and ham!

Thursday, 24 February

Dined at home and washed up during another raid—not quite so noisy. No news except from Russians who have taken Rogachev and Dno. Raid lasted from 10 to 11. Hope we shan't be woken up again. Only got 5 last night out of 90 across the coast and 15 over London. Not enough. P.M. was having a meeting today, I think. It's extraordinary how officials and Service men want prodding the whole time. 11 night before last was not so bad. But we ought to be doing *much* better, and these raids will go on until we *do*.

Friday, 25 February

3 talk with Bridges about Chiefs of Staff sitting on papers sent them by P.H.P.† (on which they should *not* be the final authority).

* Guy Millard, Asst. Private Sec. to Eden, 1941–5.

† The Post-Hostilities Planning sub-committee of the Chiefs of Staff Committee.

[During the weekend Cadogan developed a feverish cold. He was away from the Foreign Office for a week.]

Monday, 6 March

3–3.40 meeting with A. and others about Polish question. Don't see what to do, but am determinedly opposed to an Anglo-Soviet agreement giving the latter what the Poles won't give. What *won't* be said about 'another Munich'! Besides it's useless, as well as being wrong. . . . 5.30 Cabinet. Max against continuing correspondence with Stalin about Poland. But he was in a minority of 1. P.M. undertook to revise his draft message.

[The proposals made, after so much effort, in Churchill's message of 21 February were curtly dismissed by Stalin on 3 March in a message which Eden called 'cavalier as well as dusty'. He went on:

> I don't like even to refer to the possibility that we should break with the Polish Government in London. I should prefer to ignore the issue but, if it has to be mentioned, should it not be on [the] basis 'of course we shall continue to recognise Polish Government in London'? . . .
>
> But over and above all this Soviet attitude on this business raises most disquieting thoughts. Is Soviet regime one which will ever co-operate with the West? . . .

Eden told the War Cabinet that matters could not be left thus. Britain had an obligation to the Poles and, having persuaded them to offer concessions, should protect them against Russian intransigence. Churchill's message to Stalin of 7 March therefore repeated that the British proposals would have given Russia a de facto occupation of the Curzon Line. The War Cabinet would be sorry indeed if Russia could have no relations with the Polish Government, which Britain would continue to recognise.[19]]

Thursday, 9 March

3.45 talk with A. and R. Campbell about Wolfram. Told him he must warn Salazar that, if he doesn't play up on Wolfram, he will be bracketed with Franco—or worse!

Friday, 10 March

12.30 Palmella, about Timor. That is sheer pantomime.* Gave him some urgent warnings about Wolfram. . . . A bloody rush of boxes, and I was kept hard at it, with various interruptions—notably by

* In December 1941, a small Dutch and Australian force landed in Portuguese Timor, before the Japanese assault of Feb. 1942. (See Diary entry for 31 Dec. 1941.) Dr Salazar regarded the Allied landing as a breach of Portugal's sovereignty and protested. Later he asked that Portuguese troops might participate in the recapture of the island from the Japanese.

Warner on Finnish terms. Russians are doing their best to get Finns out of war. Finns will be fools if they don't agree (though of course no one would trust Joe to stick to his terms). Dined at home with T. and G. and did as much work as I could. I am tired, and not very well and *stale*. I've done this job for over 6 years, and it's *wearing*.

[Portugal had made an arrangement with Germany in January 1942 to export up to 2,800 tons of wolfram in the year beginning 1 March 1942. The Allies, after prolonged haggling, secured a larger amount, and the War Cabinet were now trying to effect a complete embargo on supplies to Germany. When Campbell proposed this on 23 January, Dr Salazar hedged. He refused a complete embargo on 28 March, but gave way on 5 June.]

Saturday, 11 March

Saw Frogface [Gousev] at 5 and told him we agreed with Soviet reply to Finns. Put various questions to him, to which of course he hadn't the answer. Home 7.15. Dined there and worked. No great news—the war gets duller and duller.

[Further exchanges between Churchill and Tito had brought the British Government little comfort. The Marshal (as he now described himself) insisted that the Yugoslav Government in Cairo be dissolved and the National Council of Liberation recognised as the sole Government. The Council would not then refuse to co-operate with King Peter, although the future of the monarchy must be decided after the liberation. Churchill again tried unsuccessfully, in a message of 9 March, for a composition between Tito and the King, while Eden asked the King, who had returned from Cairo for his marriage to Princess Alexandra of Greece, to reform his administration.]

Monday, 13 March

12 discussion with Ralph Stevenson, O.S., Rose* and [Pierson] Dixon about the line to be taken with King Peter. It's all pretty hopeless. As a first step we must get him to re-form his Govt. Of course that won't do much. His only chance lies in co-operation with Tito. But we don't know yet whether Tito agrees! . . . 6.30 Cabinet. No great news, though sinking of submarines goes on merrily. Russian drive wonderful, though that doesn't make *F.O.* work any easier. (Russians have rushed in and arranged to appoint an Ambassador to Italy,† without a *word* to *us*. This is both meaningless and disgrace-

* M. E. Rose, then serving in F.O.; Minister at Bonn, 1960; Ambassador at Leopoldville, 1963.

† The Russians had simply accredited an Ambassador to the Badoglio Government; but the Allies were still technically at war with Italy, and Italian affairs were under the Allied Control Commission.

ful and I got A. to approve telegram to Moscow.) Quite regardless of the lateness of the hour, P.M. indulged his capacity for non-conduct of business. I got away at 8.15. Only result was that War Cabinet postponed decision on War Criminals and postponed—still more decisively—decision on 'Unconditional Surrender'. P.M. trying to arrange to spend weekend of 23 March with Pres. at Bermuda, to discuss a number of operational and political questions. Don't suppose A. can go with him, so I suppose I may have to. Shouldn't mind a sea-voyage—might do me good. Still have beastly bronchial cough, though better.

Friday, 17 March *Thatched Cottage*

Winter jasmine, with great discretion, has given up the effort of providing bloom. Walked round after tea with T. Chickens all laying like machine-guns.

Monday, 20 March

3.30 Viénot, whose pointed enquiries I did my best to parry. He says he senses that Pres. has lately 'battu en retraite' about the French Committee, but didn't know why. I said the Pucheu trial* might be one reason! 5.30 Gousev with texts of communications exchanged between Finn and Soviet govts. *Here*, the Soviet Govt. are being quite reasonable. I wish they would be as regards the Poles! 6 Cabinet. Nothing v. interesting. There had been a small meeting at 5.30 at which, I gathered from A., he had had a row with P.M. about France. But I didn't get details. P.M. looked flushed and was very woolly. Hope he's not unwell.

Tuesday, 21 March

10.30 talk with A. about Yugoslavia. He fears, rightly, that if we get King P. to dismiss his Govt., Soviet may recognise Tito. He dictated message to P.M. on this. Agreed Stevenson should catch Peter on his return from his honeymoon tomorrow, and sound him as to what he contemplates. Cabinet at 12.15 about Polish-Soviet question, and had to mug up the case beforehand. Agreed P.M. should send telegram to Stalin pointing out that the leaks of which he complains, come from Soviet Embassy! Agreed that we should draft statement acknowledging failure in negotiations, and imputing some

* Pierre Pucheu, formerly Vichy Minister of the Interior, was arrested in Dec. 1943 by the French Commitee for National Liberation. He was executed on 20 March. The Prime Minister had been much displeased by this and other arrests; the President pressed de Gaulle to postpone arrests and trials until after the liberation.

blame to Soviet. Cabinet then wandered. P.M. confessed he was tired, so stepped from one irrelevant topic to another....

Found 17 boxes awaiting me after lunch, and they came on in an incessant stream. Message at 6.30 from A. (at Cabinet) that he was sending over draft from P.M. to Stalin, and he would want to see me about it after Cabinet. He came over at 8.30! I gave him one or 2 amendments and got home just before 9, bearing a stack of foul files. P.M. this morning confessed he was tired—he's almost done in. A. can't bear his double burden any longer. Everyone's exhausted. I've carried my little job for over 6 years, and I wasn't on a bed of roses before *that*! However, I suppose we've got to plug along. Worked till nearly 11, then rather exhausted.

[The reader of tartly-worded entries about Churchill, Eden and others, should bear these last sentences in mind. Cadogan himself toiled long and despatched a huge volume of businesss, but he at least could normally reckon on finishing work by midnight. The Prime Minister, by contrast, had often hardly begun work at that hour. The C.I.G.S. recorded sadly: 'I'm afraid that he is losing ground rapidly. He seems quite incapable of concentrating for a few minutes on end.... He kept yawning and said he was feeling desperately tired.' Cadogan's diary entry for 19 April is written in a similar sense. As for Eden, his burdens were abundantly more than any one man could carry. Several discussions with Churchill in March failed to produce a workable division of labours. On the 16th the Prime Minister said to him, 'You will have to go on as you are for a few months longer.' Eden, however, was approaching the point of breakdown. His notes for 24 March record a troublesome Secret Session which kept him at the House nearly all day and played havoc with his work:

> Hate these endless crises first in Foreign Office, then in House. One or other would be bad enough.
>
> Some talk to Brendan Bracken when House rose. He is convinced that I should give up Foreign Office. I am so weary I hardly care so that [? long as] I am released from one.

And two days later, on Sunday at Binderton:

> Politically a most harassing day. Winston rang me up at least three times, during one of which he read me out the greater part of his speech though it was coming to me by despatch rider. Winant telephoned twice and Alec and the Office several times. I had heavy boxes and two speeches of my own to prepare. Very exhausting.

On the following evening, 27 March, the Prime Minister agreed that Eden's two posts must be divorced. It transpired, however, that he did not wish to work with any alternative Foreign Secretary.[20] It is not certain whether Churchill seriously thought of appointing Cadogan, on the model of P.J. Grigg's elevation from the post of P.U.S. to Secretary of State for War. The rumour was widely bruited abroad. One version had it that Cadogan was to be a species of puppet Foreign Secretary with Lord Beaverbrook twitching the threads behind. This prospect is not without its humour.]

Thursday, 23 March

10.30 discussed Polish tangle with A., giving him minute explaining it, and draft telegram to Moscow. He approved and told me to clear it with P.M. Saw P.M. (in bed) at 11.30, fixed it with him and was back at 11.45 and got telegram off. Not too much work, thank Heaven. Lunched at Club and got hair cut. Jock Colville at 3 to say P.M. when stepping into train at 1 (to visit Americans) wanted to hold up our telegram to Moscow for a day or 2. Sent further telegram to A.C.K[err] telling him to hold his hand, *unless* he was asked for an explanation by Stalin or Molotov. . . . P.M.'s trip definitely off, as Pres. must go away for a month's rest. He *may* come over here before 'Overlord'.

Friday, 24 March

Dined at home, and worked after on a damned speech that A. has to make to Nonconformists on Tuesday. I'm not good at this.

Saturday, 25 March

A violent reply from Joe. A complicated worry about Turkish chrome,* and a number of other stinking questions. Sent special messenger down to A. at 6 with a draft reply from P.M. to Stalin—so as to try to avert an unreflected outburst by former. . . . Germany evidently nervous about her Balkan flank. She has swallowed Hungary, and seems to be in the process of doing the same with Roumania. But these are extra commitments for her. Noisy raid last night about midnight, and I suppose that, with this moonless period and the interminable spell of fine weather, we can expect it nightly for 10 days or so. A great bore. Meanwhile our own offensive over Germany continues at full pressure. We are bogged down in Cassino and, indeed, in Italy. It looks to me like a Passchendaele, beloved of Generals.

[Stalin's letter of 23 March insisted on the Curzon Line, reminded Churchill that it had in effect been accepted at Tehran, and refused his

* The Allies had withdrawn their military missions from Turkey in February, and had suspended exports to her of cotton, wool and copper. In late April, after a threat of blockade, Turkey suspended the supply of chrome to Germany.

proposal that although Russia would occupy the territory up to the Line a final decision on the frontier should be postponed until the peace conference. Russia, said Stalin, was merely claiming restoration of her legal right to territory which 'even Curzon and the Supreme Council of the Allied Powers recognised in 1919 as being non-Polish'. Her dispute was not with Poland, but with the 'émigré' Government in London. The people of Russia would regard a statement which the Prime Minister proposed to make in the House as an undeserved insult. Stalin himself would regard it as an unfriendly act towards the Soviet Union. Attempts to discredit Russia did not, he added somewhat gratuitously, provide a good basis for Allied co-operation in the future.

The proposed statement to which Stalin objected so strongly said that Britain continued to recognise the Polish Government with which she had been in unbroken relations since 1939; that she now thought all questions of territorial change must await the peace conference, and that no forcible transfer of territory could be recognised.

Stalin's message perturbed Churchill deeply, as well it might. A few days later Eden minuted on a Foreign Office paper:

> I confess to growing apprehension that Russia has vast aims and that these may include the domination of Eastern Europe and even the Mediterranean and the 'communising' of much that remains.[21]]

Sunday, 26 March

A good many crises and worries. Telegrams from Roumania which don't amount to much. Everyone willing to be very brave if they can be assured of 'Anglo-American' assistance. But it's only Russia that can help. Winston's broadcast coming through. What he says on foreign affairs all right—except a bit about Turkey which we're asking him to take out. . . . Telegram from Moscow showing that Russians now, suddenly, agree to play with Roumanians. What unpredictable creatures they are!

Monday, 27 March

3 talk with A. about Polish-Soviet crisis. He approved generally my draft reply from P.M. to Stalin. . . . 4.45. Raczynski, about the situation as between Underground Movement and Soviet Army. Bad! Cabinet 5.30—which rambled on till 8.5. Decided to do nothing about Soviet-Polish crisis for a few days at least.

Wednesday, 29 March

12.45–1.10 talk with King of Greece at Claridges. He roamed rapidly and spasmodically over all Greek topics. Made it clear he was determined to refuse to sign 'constitutional act'. Told me, in confidence, that Tsouderos,* in a private letter, had advised refusal! . . . 6.30 talk with A. and others about Yugoslavia. Tito has handed us a lemon.† Diplomacy depends entirely on military performance and *all* our difficulties, with Russia, in Yugoslavia, Turkey and Spain, are due to our check (to put it at its lowest) at Cassino. Dined at home and worked. A. told me today it was practically certain he would have to give up F.O. Bobbety probably in his place. (Daily Worker' tips me, as a nominee of the 'Cliveden Set'. I've had no truck (or even contact) with an Astor for about 3 years!)

Thursday, 30 March

Not much doing. House wasting its time over this ridiculous defection and 'defeat' on Education Bill.‡ 5 Gousev to whom I handed out some rather tart memoranda on 3 questions. He quite wooden.

Friday, 31 March

We sent out 950 aircraft last night, mostly on Nuremburg. We lost 94! This is too much. It is curious that, after all the controversy, the Americans prove to be right. With their Fortresses, they wander over Germany by day, now, and have *much* fewer losses. *We* are a target for night fighters. I wonder what we'll do about it. We can't go on like this.

Monday, 3 April

Palmella at 12. I told him we were relying on his advocacy (he goes home tomorrow) of a complete embargo on Wolfram! 12.30 talk with A. and others about a week-end spate of minutes by P.M. on all subjects. . . . Cabinet 5.30. Nothing on agenda, but P.M. roamed over all topics till 8. Longest discussion on bombing targets in France. Agreed Defence Committee must look at it, and it must come back to Cabinet. All agreed we must do the best for Overlord, but considerable doubt as to whether railway targets, involving possibly

* E. Tsouderos, Greek Prime Minister in Exile, 1941–4.

† A decision of the Anti-Fascist Council that King Peter should not return to Yugoslavia after the war. Eden was trying to put King Peter of Yugoslavia 'on as good a wicket as possible internationally' and to raise him 'above the internal dissensions of his country', by suggesting a declaration that the people of Yugoslavia would be able to choose their government freely after the war, until which time internal quarrels should cease.[22] After much persuasion, the King at last agreed that M. Subasić, formerly Ban (Viceroy) of Croatia, should come to London. The Ban was appointed Prime Minister on 1 June 1944.

‡ On 28 March the Government had been defeated by one vote on an amendment to the Education Bill. Churchill announced that the amended clause would be deleted, the Committee Stage resumed and the issue regarded as one of confidence. On 30 March the voting was 425–23.

huge French loss of life, and about which experts are not unanimous, are the best.*

Tuesday, 4 April

Several of the more disreputable papers canvass my appointment as S. of S.—deprecating it. I most cordially agree with them! Jim Thomas† tells me it's been going all round the Lobbies, on the grounds that that is what P.M. wants—so that he should have complete control of F.A., I suppose! He *may* have toyed with the idea, but it's a bad one.

[The leaders of E.A.M. announced from Greece the establishment of a Political Committee of National Liberation, Communist-controlled. This event provoked a series of mutinies among Greek armed forces in the Middle East. Tsouderos, who had been unable to elicit from the King the appointment as Regent of Archbishop Damaskinos, offered his resignation on 6 April. The British Ambassador to the Greek Government telegraphed to the Foreign Office on April 7: 'What is happening here among the Greeks is nothing less than a revolution.'

He strongly urged that the King of Greece should not go out to Cairo. The King decided otherwise, with the support of Churchill, in charge of the Foreign Office during Eden's absence. 'This is an occasion' telegraphed the Prime Minister to the unfortunate Leeper, 'for you to show those qualities of imperturbability and command which are associated with the British Diplomatic Service.' He telegraphed again on April 9:

> Our relations are definitely established with the lawfully constituted Greek Government headed by the King, who is the ally of Britain and cannot be discarded to suit a momentary surge of appetite among ambitious émigré nonentities. Neither can Greece find constitutional expression in particular sets of guerrillas, in many cases indistinguishable from Banditti, who are masquerading as the saviours of their country while living on the local villagers.[23]

King George arrived in Cairo and proclaimed that a representative Government would be formed. M. Veniselos, formerly Minister of Marine, became Prime Minister. The mutinous units were meanwhile being surrounded and starved out. This process took a couple of weeks, during which Churchill described King Farouk, who was trying to intervene, as 'wallowing like a sow in the trough of luxury'. By 25 April the mutinies had collapsed without the loss of Greek life. M. Papandreou, leader of the Social Democratic Party, who had just been brought out of Greece, re-

* The estimates of French casualties proved much exaggerated, and the dislocation of the French railway system had reached such a pitch by D-Day that German reinforcements could not be brought quickly to Normandy.

† J.P.L. Thomas. Now Financial Secretary to the Admiralty.

placed Veniselos as Prime Minister, and eventually succeeded in forming a Government of all parties.

Wednesday, 5 April

Aghnides at 5 for a long wail about the Greek situation. . . . He says Tsouderos must go—none will serve under him. King's message (against A[ghnides]'s advice) refusing to accept Tsouderos' resignation produced resignation from all the other Ministers. He says King *must* go out to Cairo. His impression is that Veniselos, although a nonentity, is perhaps the best provisional solution.* I can't help thinking R. Leeper has botched all this. I think he's become *too* immersed in Greek politics and Tsouderos pulled the wool over his eyes. Anyhow, to my limited understanding, he has made the whole thing completely unintelligible.

Thursday, 6 April

Had a talk with A. He staying on for a month or 2 anyhow. Gather that any re-shuffle presents a difficulty in that Attlee demands more places for his party! A. going to take a fortnight from tonight completely off work.

[The Prime Minister, desperately keen not to lose Eden from the Foreign Office, asked him to rest for three weeks. 'You are my right arm; we must take care of you.']

Sunday, 9 April *Thatched Cottage*

T. and I motored to church. Parson more melodramatic than usual, but only 12 mins.

Monday, 10 April

Went to 'Something for the Boys' at the Coliseum. An American musical show, slick without being tuneful, well-drilled and quite uninteresting. There was one good tune. The rest was jazz, which all sounds alike to me—a pulsating noise, such as one hears when one has run upstairs too fast. . . . Shall have an awful fortnight with the P.M. in charge [of the F.O.], complicated by Stettinius, but hope to get through.

Wednesday, 12 April

11.30 [Ed. R.] Stettinius came. Dick Law also attended. S. very pleasant. Looks like a dignified and more monumental Charlie

* Shown this passage, and the entry for 15 December 1944 (p. 687), M. Aghnides has commented that he does not recall having put these points as emphatically as Sir Alec's Diary would suggest.

Chaplin. We had a general talk, mainly about European Commission, French Civil affairs and future World Organisation. . . . Summoned, with Dick Law, by P.M. for 3 p.m. (thus avoiding boring S.O.E. meeting at 3.30) . . . on President's 'directive' about French Committee and Hull's statement on same subject. He must have lunched well, as he ambled, or rambled, all round the subject most pleasantly and it was not till 5 that we approved, with some alterations, a telegram he proposed to send to Pres. 6.30 small meeting, P.M., Bevin, Lyttelton, 'C.', F. Stewart and Ismay, about 'Overlord Security'. Came down in favour of ban on foreign cyphers &c, to be submitted to War Cabinet tomorrow. P.M. kept me after to read to me letters he had just received from Randolph [Churchill]. Altogether he kept me away from my work for three hours today on matters which shouldn't have taken more than twenty mins. How does he get through his work? Between 11 p.m. and 3 a.m. I suppose. In view of this, lucky not to have too much work.

Thursday, 13 April

6.30 Cabinet, till 8.20. Cabinet approved cypher ban in connexion with Overlord security. I had to point out where and to what extent it was not watertight. Cabinet had no answer. P.M. said we must stop French wireless from Algiers. I pointed out we *couldn't very well.* He then muttered something about an appeal to de Gaulle, so I have now drafted him a message.

Friday, 14 April

10.30 Raczynski. 11 Gousev. 11.30 Alba. None of them had anything of great interest. Except that Gousev said Japanese had repeated their proposal of last Sept. to send a Mission through Moscow to 'Western Europe'. This an evident 'peace feeler', probably at German dictation. Russians have rightly turned it down. 12.30 meeting with N[igel] Ronald, O.S., O.H. and others about 'King-Planner'. Decided to recommend I. K[irkpatrick].* But this is not an easy one either, as we should have to abstract him from P.W.E. in teeth of Brendan's opposition. . . . Masses of work, in O.S.'s absence. His badly trained juniors send me in ill-digested stuff. 6.25 went to see P.M. to tell him about R. Stevenson's talk with King Peter. P.M. dictated telegram to Molotov telling him what we are doing. P.M. rather fractious—or depressed. Hadn't had his afternoon

* Ivone Kirkpatrick had been Controller of the European Services of the B.B.C., under the guidance of the Political Warfare Executive, since 1941; he became Deputy Commissioner for Germany in Aug. 1944.

sleep, I think. Planned to take it in car on the way down to Chequers this evening. . . . *Floods* of ridiculous files. Brought them home and tackled them after dinner there.

Saturday, 15 April

Dick Law was going to lunch at Chequers and I gave him a minute to P.M., and briefed him, about French Civil affairs. Have since heard P.M. seems to be coming round. . . . Quite an amount of work, but no fireworks from Chequers.

Sunday, 16 April

P.M. keeping quiet, but things are plainly coming to a head in Egypt and I must move him to do *something*. Had already yesterday sent him draft telegram to Cairo. Told Martin at Chequers to draw his attention to latest telegrams. . . . Minute from P.M. (written this morning) proposing to do nothing before consulting Cabinet on *Wednesday*. But that too late. However, he rang up before 6 with a draft message to King Farouk telling him to hold his hand while he consults Cabinet. This all right, but I had to get him to make some minor changes. . . .

My work more or less cleared off, but I had some papers of G.J.'s to read on future organisation of the world (as I suppose I shall have to be dealing with this in Washington next month).* As usual, the people who have been thinking on these things, have thought themselves into a complete fuddle and are carelessly prodigal of words. They become so prolix as to be unintelligible, but by the time they reach that stage I think they have no thought of their own. A *lot* of pruning will be required.

[The issue of 'unconditional surrender' continued to trouble the Foreign Office and Cabinet at intervals until the end of the war. Churchill, desiring not to fuse the Germans together 'in a solid desperate block for whom there is no hope', understood the slogan to mean that after surrender they would have no right to any particular form of treatment. The Chiefs of Staff agreed with Eden that the Germans should be encouraged, even in defeat, to have hope for the future, and Churchill told Parliament on 22 February 1944 that 'unconditional surrender' did not mean enslavement or destruction of the German people. 'If we are bound, we are bound by our own consciences to civilisation. We are not to be bound to the Germans as the result of a bargain struck.' The War Cabinet agreed that the principle should not necessarily be applied to satellite states of the Axis. When this was put to the Russians in March, they agreed to an

* This meeting was postponed until August.

announcement. The U.S. Government did not, though willing to consider individual instances.

General Eisenhower, now Supreme Commander for 'Overlord', suggested in mid-April the issue of a statement about the principles upon which defeated Germany would be treated. In Eden's absence, Churchill minuted to Cadogan on 19 April:

> I have pointed out to the Cabinet that the actual terms contemplated for Germany are not of a character to reassure them at all, if stated in detail. Both President Roosevelt and Marshal Stalin at Tehran wished to cut Germany into smaller pieces than I had in mind. Stalin spoke of very large executions of over 50,000 of the staffs and military experts. Whether he was joking or not could not be ascertained. The atmosphere was jovial, but also grim. He certainly said that he would require 4,000,000 German males to work for an indefinite period to rebuild Russia. We have promised the Poles that they shall have compensation both in East Prussia and, if they like, up to the line of the Oder. There are a lot of other terms implying the German ruin and indefinite prevention of their rising again as an armed Power. . . .
>
> On the other hand, they know that 'unconditional surrender' was interpreted in a very favourable manner in the case of the Italians, and we see now what the Roumanians are offered if they will come over.

He still thought that a statement should follow a military victory. General Marshall too had been looking for a definition, but told Dill* that they were up against an obstinate Dutchman who had brought the phrase out and didn't like to go back on it.[24]]

Monday, 17 April

11.15 Stettinius rang me up to say he had 2 messages from Washington about French civil affairs and wanted to send Doc. Matthews round with them. Latter turned up at 11.45. Upshot is Washington (Pres.) won't look at any verbal changes in the 'Directive'. A feather in P.M.'s cap. . . . At No. 10 at 3 but P.M. still lunching with Alexander and Ike. So went back to my room and was summoned at 3.20. P.M. had lunched well. Eventually I was able to put the 2 messages before him. He (1) inveighed against de G. and (2) said he wouldn't do anything today on these messages: they went 'too far'! I asked did he then want to fight de G's battle? This angered him. I oughtn't to have tried to reason with him in his state! So I left him, and charged Martin to bring him up to the scratch tonight. Cabinet at 6.30—nominally. Actually we didn't begin till 6.45. Maharaja of Cashmir [Kashmir] there. That involved a long welcome from P.M. Chiefs of Staff did their tricks, and P.M. then

* Field-Marshal Sir John Dill, now head of the British Joint Staff Mission. Washington.

reported on F[oreign] A[ffairs]. We didn't finish till 8.25. At the end, P.M. asked me what had been done about the cypher ban. I said I had sent out all circulars at 5 p.m. He asked when ban came into force. I said midnight tonight. He said 'Crikey!' I said no point in giving them longer notice. But I added I should like to stay in the Cabinet Room as I was frightened to go back to my office!

Tuesday, 18 April

11 talk with—or rather from—Bowman,* with R. Law, G.J., and Webster† and N. Butler. My God, these Americans *do* talk. I was told Bowman was pretty good—and so he may be. But by 12.50 we had got *nowhere*. So I then suggested an agenda for our next talk. He proposed Monday. This quite hopeless. Got him to agree to come tomorrow at 11 and talk to a definite agenda. . . . 6.35 went to see Brendan about getting Kirk for 'King-Planner'. He promised me answer tomorrow—but it won't be the right one.

Wednesday, 19 April

An awful day. P.M. sent for me at 10.15. Went over a number of questions he's been sitting on for last few days. I had another meeting with Bowman due at 11. But couldn't get away from P.M. till 11.20. Joined discussion till 11.40 when had to change into tail coat to go to Palace and present Mexican Ambassador. Back about 12.20. Discussion continued till 1. . . . Back at F.O. 2.45. Tried to start on my work. Summoned by P.M. at 3.30 for talk with Stettinius on world organisation. Had to leave at 4 to see Wellington Koo—incensed about cypher ban. Tried to calm him. 6 an awful meeting with O.S. and all the rest about 'Western Bloc'. O.S. being more O.S.ish than I've ever known him. Fortunately had to go at 6.30 to Cabinet. Egypt: P.M., I fear, is breaking down. He rambles without a pause, and we really got nowhere by 7.40. N. Chamberlain would have settled it in 6 minutes. P.M. undertook to draft telegram tonight. That may come out all right. But he wasted about 150 man-hours. Then paper on Turkey. Equally hopeless. And then Anglo-American differences on blockade questions. Rather more practical result reached on this. I really am fussed about the P.M. He is *not* the man he was 12 months ago, and I really don't know whether he can carry on. I left Cabinet at 8.30 to discuss further matters on

* Isaiah Bowman, Vice-Chairman, post-war Advisory Council. Dept. of State, 1943–4; special adviser to Secretary of State, 1943–5.

† C. K. Webster, served in F.O., 1943–6; member of British delegations to Dumbarton Oaks and San Francisco; later Professor of International History, London University.

which I am not concerned. Home 8.50 and dined there, and tackled till 11.30, a *stack* of muck. Noisy raid last night at 2 a.m. We shot down 13 out of 58. Not bad. Warning without gunfire for half an hour from 10.30 tonight. Now want to go to *sleep*!

Thursday, 20 April

Cabinet 6.45 approved P.M.'s telegram to Cairo about Egyptian crisis (which is all right). Gousev called just before Cabinet and gave me latest Finnish-Russia exchange, which I read to Cabinet. They agreed we had no comment to make on proposed Soviet reply. I got away from Cabinet about 7.30. . . . About 10 went to see P.M. He and Clemmie playing bezique. Luckily it soon came to an end and I got P.M. to approve (a) telegrams to Washington and Madrid going ahead on Hull's plan about Wolfram (b) formation of tribunal with F[indlater] Stewart as Chairman to administer [cypher] 'ban' (c) agrément for Ruegger.* And got home soon after 11.30. Not bad. Lots of paper work undone.

[In the latter part of 1943, General Franco made a number of helpful moves, including the imposition of a low limit on exports of Wolfram to Germany. Nevertheless, Spain remained a centre of German espionage and subversive activity, and still had a division fighting against Russia. In January 1944 the U.S. Government cut off oil supplies to Spain and allowed the fact to transpire publicly. Then the U.S. Ambassador was told to demand a complete ban on the export of wolfram to Germany. The British, anxious not to make the best case the enemy of the good, and equally anxious to ensure the expulsion from Spain and Tangier of enemy agents, obtained on 17 February an offer which met most of their desiderata. Churchill and Eden wished to close at once. 'Our difficulty', Eden noted, 'has been mainly one of securing effective co-ordination at the Washington end and in this respect I fear that our recent troubles over Spain are by no means unique.'

A second leakage in Washington caused a stern German protest and a prolonged delay. American hostility to any kind of face-saving arrangement derived from the imminence of the Presidential Election in the U.S.A. Hull said publicly that the time for giving way to neutrals had passed. He suggested on 17 April that the British should supply the oil to Spain, exports of wolfram being reduced to a minimal figure. In other words, the effect on Spain would be the same, but the British would carry the odium. Churchill agreed on 21 April. After two further changes of mind in Washington, Eden announced the settlement on 2 May.[25]]

Saturday, 22 April

9.15 P.M. rang up saying he wanted to see me at 10. Explained I

* As Swiss Minister.

had Committee but would slip away at 10.30. Which I did. Found him having breakfast in bed. At the moment he appeared to be eating a cold cutlet. Said he was tired after his speech yesterday. A tiresome telegram from Pres. urging we still press Spaniards for complete Wolfram embargo. Does the Pres. know nothing of Hull's suggestion (which we had decided to accept)? P.M. agreed we must stick to this and I undertook to submit draft message. Went back to Committee, which finished about 11.30. They had so much paper before them that they were stifled! Very satisfactory.

Sunday, 23 April

P.M. didn't ring up personally, but I got some snotty little notes from him. . . . Back at F.O. 4.30 but nothing doing. Left there about 6, having cleared everything, including even Honours recommendations for Wed. meeting.

Monday, 24 April

11 Bowman came for discussion with Webster and me. Went quite well. 12.30 discussion with A. and others about French 'civil affairs' and Yugoslavia. Both v. sticky! 1.15 lunch with O. Stanley and Bowman. Latter is very nice, but he *is* a gas-bag. 3 talk with A., Stettinius and Winant about various points left over, including French civil affairs and Wolfram. A. fairly frank about both. Work had meanwhile accumulated. Cabinet at 7. P.M. rambled as much as lately, and he hadn't finished at 8.20, when A. said he must go off for his dinner for Stettinius and I went with him.

Tuesday, 25 April

12.15 meeting with A., Stettinius, Winant and Gousev. Idea was to put G. wise as to what we had been doing. G. looked like a cow about to calve—surprised, suspicious and rather resentful. . . .3 went over to No. 10 where P.M. received Mikolajczyk and 3 Poles brought out of Poland. Gen. Tabor* gave us an account of the organisation of the Underground Army. 5.30 Raczynski about cypher and bag ban. . . . Bridges about how to get P.M. to apply his mind to papers on future World Organisation. Spoke to A. about this at 7.30. Dined at home, washed up and worked. Strenuous days, which I start by cooking breakfast! (Mrs X. has left, so we have no one. Think we must get rooms in a hotel.)

At this meeting with the Poles Churchill said once more that he stood for an independent Poland but could not guarantee the whole territory of

* Pseudonym of Gen. S. Tatar, Deputy Chief of the Polish General Staff in London.

1939. He favoured the Curzon Line with compensation in the west and a broad outlet to the sea. The Poles insisted that they should retain Lwow and Vilna, whose populations were Polish and anti-Russian, and that they should not be cut off from other East European States.[26]]

Friday, 28 April

10.30 Stettinius and his party called to say good-bye. S. very easy and friendly and understanding, though I don't know what he's like really.

[A few days later, in Washington, Halifax found Stettinius 'bursting with admiration' for Cadogan:

> He told me [Halifax wrote] that if he was suddenly made Chairman of a big Railway, . . . and was given his choice of eight men from England, he would certainly want you by reason of your complete honesty, sure gentlemanlike instinct and composure! You may get this sort of tribute every day, in which case you won't value it. In case you don't get it every day, I thought it might cheer you up.
>
> Stettinius has come back in very good heart.
>
> I have seen alternating reports lately that either you or the Beaver are to become Foreign Secretary. Of the two, and this you can also take as a further compliment, I should much prefer you!

On this paper Cadogan endorsed a single sentence: 'I hope Mr. S. will get the Big Railway, and remember me!']

Sunday, 30 April *Thatched Cottage*

A blazing summer day—all day. Was pretty lazy in the morning. How nice it is to command one's own time—and do nothing. Picked a lot of wallflower, gold and russet. Sat in chair in N. garden reading till lunch. Put up hammock seat. After lunch I sat similarly, T. in hammock. . . . About 3.45, roused myself and went on with my weeding of iris bed, till tea. After tea ditto, T. resting in hammock—which she richly deserves: I hope some days of this may do her good. The evening was such as one gets sometimes in July! How nice—but we do want rain. If only it would rain all night every night. Perhaps I've never stayed here exactly at this season before. It certainly is lovely, and I've fallen in love with the cottage. We've been here through frost and snow and May gales and autumn discomfort, but it's really heavenly now. The daffodils are over, except the very late white ones. And the narcissi are still out, and the spiraea arguta like little snowmen. And the wallflowers a warm cloth of gold and bronze. The old pear tree in full bloom, and the view, clear enough, softened by the sun haze. And no wind. It's quiet and kind. . . . I should like to see this place in 20 years' time—but probably shan't.

Air activity went on all day. The cuckoo cracking his throat against the roar of the bombers.

Ribes over—yellow alyssum at its best. Lilac coming out.

So lovely tonight that T. and I went out after dinner to gaze at the view—she to gather eggs.

Monday, 1 May *Thatched Cottage*

Another gorgeous summer day. Was fairly lazy in the morning, but finished weeding the irises, which are all on the point of bursting into bloom. After lunch I tried to sketch the N. side of the cottage. I haven't tried to wield a pencil for 20 years or more, and my old fingers (stiff with weeding) don't take to it kindly. But it's absorbing, and I may improve!

[As 'Overlord' approached, a settlement of the Allies' relationship to the French Committee became a matter of the highest importance and urgency. When France was liberated, how would government be carried on? To whom would officials owe allegiance? When would elections be held? To what degree would the Allies be responsible? How would civil war be prevented?

These were questions which Eden and Cadogan wished Britain and America to take up jointly with the French Committee in the autumn of 1943. Some progress was made in converting the State Department, none with the President, and little with the Prime Minister. Roosevelt issued a directive to Eisenhower in March 1944 allowing him to consult the Committee or authorise them to appoint civilian administrators, but not confining him to dealing with the Committee. On 9 April Hull made a broadcast which went beyond the terms of the directive.

General Koenig had been appointed by the Committee in February 1944 to command the armed forces of the French Resistance, and in April to liaise with Eisenhower for operations based on the United Kingdom. Eisenhower's deputy, General Bedell Smith, had a helpful talk with General Koenig in mid-April. Eden hoped that the Committee might now be invited to pursue matters with Eisenhower's headquarters through Koenig's mission. Once again, however, Roosevelt intervened. All arrangements with the Committee, he insisted, must be tentative until agreement had been reached on a 'civil affairs formula'; and no arrangement could preclude consultation with other groups in France. In the Foreign Office this document was described as wholly unacceptable, but the Prime Minister refused to quarrel with Roosevelt, about whose hostility to de Gaulle Hull spoke very strongly to Halifax. Churchill told Roosevelt that he wished to invite de Gaulle to London for talks with Eisenhower. To this the President assented, so long as Eisenhower did not become involved with the French Committee on a 'political level'.]

Thursday, 4 May *Thatched Cottage*

No news at all except of bombing. Seems to me—as I have said before—that 2 factors have proved our night-bombing wrong—(1) development of German night-fighters and (2) extension of the range of fighter escorts. We have heavier losses, and the Americans less. But I don't know whether we can switch now—probably not. German radio, I see, says we had loaded our invasion ships 2 days ago, but that they were being unloaded. I know we had prepared an 'exercise' for 2 May, but I suppose the gale stopped it.

Monday, 8 May

4.40 talk with A. about France. This has got into a mess again, as Pres. has now sent another 'directive' to Eisenhower, which practically repudiates Hull's statement. 5.10 Viénot with complaints of failure of Eisenhower-Koenig conversations to progress, and of our communications ban. Wants to send Paris* out to Algiers. . . . Recounted our interview to A. and drafted minute from him to P.M. putting up Viénot proposal. It won't go thro'. I see no solution. And meanwhile Algiers, cut off from here, are drifting further and further away. I have written a minute tonight to A., suggesting we must get away from 'directive' and C.C.A.C. and all the letters of the alphabet, and consider how we are to help France recover, *and work with her.*

Tuesday, 9 May

5.15 G.J. about World Organisation. I gather Dominion Premiers, as was to be expected, got nowhere this morning. Saw A. at 5.30 about my minute about France—see above. He says, rightly, that he has put all these points to P.M. already. He thinks only solution is for him, or someone else (? me!) to go out to Algiers to conduct the negotiation on 'civil affairs' there.

[An interdepartmental committee under Richard Law had for some time been thrashing out the British proposals for the post-war international security organisation. The purpose, as he expressed it, was to retain the better features of the Covenant of the League of Nations, but to make the

* J. E. P. Paris of the French diplomatic service; commissariat of Foreign Affairs, London, 1942; Counsellor to French mission with Allied Governments, London, 1944.

new machinery more effective. The Prime Minister attached importance to Regional Councils for Europe, the Americas, Asia and, perhaps, Africa. On 11 May a meeting of the Dominion Prime Ministers showed clearly that they shared Eden's reservations.

> Their principal motive [he records] was a reluctance to be included in regional councils limited geographically to their own part of the world, when their future could be as much effected by events in areas where they would not be represented. In other words, regional councils would make the effective working of the British Commonwealth more difficult.

Revised texts were produced, incorporating, with the Dominions' approval, the possibility of a regional organisation for Europe, in which the U.S.A., Russia and Britain would be represented. It was understood that this body would be subject to the authority of the World Organisation in the settlement of political disputes. Churchill minuted later in the month:

> We have no idea of three or four Great Powers ruling the world. . . . We should certainly not be prepared to submit to an economic, financial and monetary system laid down by, say, Russia or the United States with her faggot-vote China.
>
> The Supreme World Council or Executive is not to rule the nations. It is only to prevent them tearing each other in pieces.[27]]

Wednesday, 10 May

Talk with A. at 5.30 about France. Evolved with him draft telegram from P.M. to President which might enable Eisenhower and Koenig to get on with their talks. But neither P.M. nor Pres. will probably accept it.

Thursday, 11 May

Talk with A. at 10.30 about his talk with P.M. on France last night which lasted till 3.15 a.m. P.M. is sending message to Pres. suggesting that we get de G. and, if necessary, one or 2 of the Committee over here this month to negotiate agreement on 'civil affairs' *here*. That might be the best solution. . . . 'Overlord' probably put off for about a week. This is just tolerable, but if it is for longer, we shall be exposed to every kind of difficulty in many quarters.

Friday, 12 May

10.30 [Lord] Selborne about P.M.'s cancellation of orders allowing

French contingent to be sent to Far East. *Why* does P.M. want to drive France further and further away from us? Selborne is going to protest from his point of view. 11 I.K. about P.W.E. which is a *scandal.* 1,250 people in London, and 500 at Woburn, none of whom know what they are *supposed* to do. 11.30 G.J. and Webster about World Organisation, which is getting into a *frightful* tangle. If I could have 24 hours I could sort it out, but I haven't got *half* an hour. . . . 3.40 talk with A. about Yugoslavia. This is hopeless. We can only go on pressing the ridiculous little King to shed his beastly Govt. and get a new one. But *that* won't do much. 4.45 talk to A. about French communications—Eisenhower wants Koenig to be allowed to send cypher telegrams. Had to dictate minute for P.M. (who's on the train) to get his authority. No one else can give it. . . . Grappled with waves of paper. Home to dinner and worked till after 11. I really haven't got time—or strength—to give proper attention to the mass of stuff that's slung at me. Italian offensive opened last night.

Saturday, 13 May

12 Viénot. Luckily P.M. last night agreed to Koenig's telegram being despatched so I could tell him this. S. of S. had also hinted at 'other arrangements' for consultation and I could confirm this. His complaint was that *all* French Press Correspondents were to be prevented from going in with the 'débarquement'. This is folly, and I have said so. . . . Gousev at 4 to say Russians agree to make agreement with Norwegians on lines of our agreement with latter. . . . Got ridiculous mass of paper from G.J. (which I had been allowed to glance at last night) back from S. of S. who says he's 'had a word' with Bridges, and will I 'have a word' with B. and settle the thing. As I don't know what this magic 'word' is, as I haven't seen the minutes of Thurs. morning's meeting with Dominions, and as I haven't been given the time to study the matter, I have minuted it that I would be charmed to 'have a word' with anyone—the King if necessary—if only someone would explain to me what the HELL I am to say. Have summoned G.J. for tomorrow. Have added that, if this is the way work is to be done, I scratch from Washington and all other engagements, paying all the forfeits if necessary. How I *hope* to get to bed.

Sunday, 14 May

Saw G.J., and tried to sort out the muddle about World

organisation. But he couldn't help much. Rang up Bridges and can't say I got much help from him. At last, in the afternoon, managed to get hold of minutes of Thursday's meeting with Dominions. Now I see my way more or less. But harried about Portuguese wolfram and Spanish agreement and a number of other tiresome things. . . . Before leaving at 7 got on to the World Organisation business, which I *hope* to straighten out tonight. But although I gave orders my box was to be home before 8 or immediately after 9, I still (9.30) haven't got it, and have had to ring up Resident Clerk. I can *never* get these arrangements to work! . . . Our Italian offensive doesn't seem to have gone wrong yet, but it doesn't seem to have achieved anything striking. Finally got my box and straightened out World Organisation!

Monday, 15 May

12.30 saw A. Gave him my minute on World Organisation, which he accepted, and settled up with him question of Algiers' reply to Koenig, and 'King Planner'. On latter, I drafted him letter to Brendan, asking for I.K. at latest on September 1. . . . Dined at home and washed up. Have just heard de G. announces that F.N.C.L. is Provisional Gov. of France. That puts *everything* in the soup just as we were settling it and bringing the crazy President to reason!

Tuesday, 16 May

Italian battle seems to be going all right. Brooke says he is 'very pleased' but I don't know how good a judge he is.

Wednesday, 17 May

3.30 meeting with Dominion officials on World Organisation. Quite useful, I think. But all this is going to be very difficult. . . . News from Italy is, I think, good. God grant it may remain so. The Germans have *not* got many reserves there, unless they denude, dangerously, other fronts.

Thursday, 18 May

. . . meeting with P.M., A., C's of S. and Bedell Smith about French situation. Bedell S. evidently expects violent reaction from Pres. against 'French provisional Gov.'. So we don't get anywhere. P.M. says, as usual, 'Don't ask me to quarrel with Pres. over de G.' No one asks him to but we do wish he would *reason* with Pres. He won't. Cabinet 6.15 on Turkey. They agreed fairly easily to our stepping up economic pressure on Turks. . . .

Tried to sketch out first draft of P.M.'s speech on World Organisation (for F.O. debate next week) but didn't get v. far. Tired. Going to bed.

Friday, 19 May

Talk with A. and Bobbety about Fraser's* violent reaction to our re-draft of paper on World Organisation. This is all to the good—we may frighten the P.M. off his stupid line. Drafted minute sending it on to P.M. Wrote passage for P.M.'s speech on World Organisation.

Monday, 22 May

Cabinet 5.30 put off till 6 because nothing on agenda. But the shorter the agenda the longer the ramble and they hadn't finished when I left at 7.50. A. brought up Portuguese wolfram. P.M. had drafted a telegram to Salazar about the minimum compromise. Dept. (without consulting me) had plumped, v. surprisingly, for the American plan to invoke Alliance for pushing Portugal into war. This simply silly. Told A. I preferred P.M.'s message, and it was agreed. From Lisbon telegrams tonight it seems that that was right. Battle going well. Anzio should come into action v. soon now.

Wednesday, 24 May

A good madhouse in A.'s room at 10.30. A., and 16 other people, fluttering pages of P.M.'s draft speech (for this morning!) looking over each other's shoulders and all talking at once. Towards the end when asked my opinion, I said that if I could have a chance to read the damned thing I might express one. From the smell of it, I didn't see anything wrong (it's rather a good speech).

Thursday, 25 May

Rung up by L. O[liphant] who had had a terrible morning with the 'bloody Belgiums', who were mortally offended by a—I must say unhappily worded—passage in P.M.'s speech of yesterday. Did I pass it? I can't remember! Took L.O. back to F.O. and we drafted a passage for A. to insert in his winding-up effort this afternoon. Don't know whether he used it.

Tuesday, 30 May

5.30 Cabinet, as usual, put off till 6.30 as there was nothing on agenda. Usual result that we rambled incoherently till 8.45. I was

* Prime Minister of New Zealand.

mad with rage. Oh! for N. Chamberlain on these occasions! Italian news good. Shall we take advantage of it and destroy German armies where they are? Our generals—even Alexander—not so good at this. . . . Our charlady, who was to have come back today, will be away another week, which gives T. all the housework. I wish Winston could realise this. Of course *he* can stroll over to the Annexe at 9 or 10 and at a nod a dozen Marines spring to attention and produce dinner —*and* old Brandy. I wonder has he the least idea of the difficulties of life for the ordinary British subject?

Wednesday, 31 May

11.30 talk with Nigel R[onald], G.J., and Webster about minute to P.M. trying to clear up mess about Memoranda on Future World Organisation. Telegram from Halifax today showing that old Hull wants to get on with a meeting, even without waiting for exchange of papers. . . . Rumours of postponement of D-Day, but I can't get them verified.

X

June 1944–February 1945
FROM OVERLORD TO YALTA

The period of nine months covered by this chapter always seemed to Cadogan the political as well as the military turning-point of the war. Until July 1944, the British Empire had more men in contact with the enemy, the world over, than had the United States. Thereafter the balance tilted ever more rapidly in the other direction. With it went the balance of political weight within the coalition. Though the Combined Chiefs of Staff achieved what General Marshall rightly described as an unprecedented co-ordination of two great powers' military effort, they found no political counterpart. Had the European Advisory Commission enjoyed more than the most lukewarm American support, it might have helped to supply that deficiency. When Hull returned to Washington from Moscow, however, he had found his principal colleagues hostile to the establishment of the E.A.C. in London. Winant, the American representative, receiving very circumscribed instructions, pointed out that such an attitude must cause discouragement on the British side and indifference on the Russian. Eden had taken the same line.

The most important work of the Commission was to prepare terms of surrender for Germany and to propose zones of Allied occupation. Roosevelt did not like the suggestion that the north-western zone should be British and the south-western American. His view, however, does not seem to have percolated to the State Department. At the Quebec meeting in September 1944, he accepted the E.A.C.'s proposals which *inter alia*, placed the Russian zone's western boundary within about a hundred miles of the Rhine, and failed to provide explicitly for communication through the Russian zone between the Western zones and the Western sectors of Berlin. Churchill appears not to have understood in time what was going on in the Commission.

In the military field, the advance of the Red Army left the Poles and their sympathisers with little bargaining power. Germany's failure to push the Allied armies out of Normandy meant that the end could not be long delayed. Her troops could not be brought quickly to the place of landing on account of the skilful destruction of the French railway system; her aircraft, produced in ever greater numbers, could often not be flown for lack of fuel; and after June 1944, when the Americans captured a copy of the codebook, all the U-boat communications were broken, with the result that nearly three hundred were sunk in eleven months.

Cadogan's main work in this period concerned the Dumbarton Oaks and Yalta Conferences. At the former he dealt with a subject which he thoroughly understood, and was the principal British delegate. Before the latter, he had seen enough of Russia's attitude not to expect too much. He looked on Yalta much as he had looked on Munich. Both agreements entailed serious injury to the rights of states which could not defend themselves against large and predatory neighbours; both reflected the military and geographical facts; neither was a matter for pride or for fierce self-reproach, since it hardly lay in British power at the material time to do other; both looked better on signature than in the hard after-light.

1944

Thursday, 1 June

Had talk with A. at 11 about French affairs. Pres. is simply not normal on this subject. Polished off some work with A. and then went to Cabinet at 12—mainly about French affairs and de G. Very woolly—went on till 1.30. Situation complicated by Dufour case which may come on while de G. is here. P.M. said in that case he must either warn de G. or not invite him. Hopeless discussion as to how we could delay or quash proceedings. At 1.30 decided A., Attorney-Gen., Cripps and Anderson should meet in afternoon. Met at 3.15. . . . Decided to offer £1000. But we must also get French to release Dufour from French forces. This, if it doesn't settle, will probably delay case. . . . I was just getting down to a dozen boxes, when P.M. sent for me. . . . P.M. furious with Duff [Cooper]* for delaying transmission of his invitation to de G. He dictated telegram to Duff telling him to transmit it at once and giving such assurances as we can—not v. much in view of President's attitude. P.M.'s gestation very slow and didn't get away till 8. Dined at home and did a lot of work. Plans (so far as we can make them) remain unchanged. P.M. not so jumpy as I might have expected.

[It appears that Dufour was a British agent and a deserter from the French forces, who had been imprisoned by them and had escaped. In September 1943 he brought an action in the British courts against French officers, including de Gaulle, for maltreatment. The Foreign Office had told Viénot that the British Government could not interfere with the courts and, as de Gaulle did not enjoy diplomatic immunity, recommended a settlement out of court. de Gaulle regarded the whole affair as a deliberate attempt to discredit him, dismissed the officers who attempted a settlement, and ordered them not to appear. Cadogan's references show that the case was not a mere fabrication on the part of the British.[1]

* Now British representative with the French Committee of National Liberation.

General de Gaulle arrived early on June 4 and went to see the Prime Minister, ensconced near the south coast in a special train. This arrangement had numerous inconveniences. There was only one bath and one telephone. Churchill, records Eden, seemed to be perpetually in the one and Ismay forever on the other. The conversation at lunch, despite the Prime Minister's best efforts, did little to cement his relations with de Gaulle; for Roosevelt had refused to permit talks on political matters between the three countries and de Gaulle did not want to discuss the administration of liberated France with the British alone.]

Saturday, 3 June

Fine again, but strongish N.W. wind. De Gaulle dithering and trying to make conditions! Otherwise fairly quiet day but a lot of paper work. . . . I to F.O. at 4.30. De G. is now coming tonight, with a party of 141. Those damned Turks have gone and let German (disguised) warships through the Straits [the Dardanelles]. We shall have to have a row with them, but that will upset 'cover' as we were on the point of concluding an economic agreement with them! Salazar has agreed to wolfram embargo, but on all sorts of unacceptable conditions. T. and I dined at Ritz. I paid innumerable bills and wrote letters after. Thank goodness I've got that off my chest. But no money in the Bank!

Monday, 5 June

Grey, overcast and w. wind. But pundits say it is going to be *beautiful*, so the expedition is on! I hope they are not as infallibly incorrect in wartime as in peace. Gather talk with de Gaulle didn't go so badly yesterday. He agreed to broadcast,* providing some changes were made in Ike's statement. He was given to understand that this might be done. He refused to discuss civil affairs, in absence of Americans. This, from his point of view, quite sensible and not incorrect. That is where we have landed ourselves! Lunched at home. 4 o'c saw A. and Duff. Latter had a suggestion from Viénot for opening the way to discussion with de G. A. saw V. about 4.15. By 5, however, I learnt that SHAEF [Supreme Headquarters, Allied Expeditionary Force] had had to tell de G. (what they might have told him yesterday) that it was too late to make changes in Ike's statement.† So de G. refuses to broadcast! Only fair to SHAEF to say that yesterday they expected a longer postponement. Cabinet 6.30. We endured the usual passionate anti-de G. harangue from P.M. On this subject, we get away from politics and diplomacy and even common sense. It's a girls' school. Roosevelt, P.M. and—it must be

* Immediately after Eisenhower, on the morning of D-day.

† It transpired that 40,000,000 copies had already been printed.

admitted de G.—all behave like girls approaching the age of puberty. Nothing to be done. During Cabinet, news came that de G. has forbidden his liaison officers to embark. Well, that puts the lid on. We always start by putting ourselves in the wrong, and then de G. puts himself *more* in the wrong. He deserves to lose the rubber. A. said he would see Viénot and explain—rightly—that in these circumstances there was nothing more to be done. Winston says *he* will come out of it all right. But I don't think he will. Agreed to close with Salazar's best offer on wolfram. P.M. informed the Cabinet that the expedition has sailed. The weather, up till dark, looked worse and worse. God help us all. Anyhow Rome fell yesterday and is in our hands, more or less intact.

Tuesday, 6 June

Bright morning, but cold N.W. wind. News good so far. We are said to have three Divs. ashore and light casualties. Weather, of course, bad. 11 saw A., who had had an awful night with P.M. and Viénot till 3 a.m.* De G. now says he *will* broadcast, but V. too frightened to ask him for his script.† He was to record at 12.30. Got Duff round about 11.15 and told him he must see de G. and try to get his script and tell him not to be silly about his liaison officers. But Duff couldn't get an audience till afternoon, so it was agreed we should have to check de G. from the disc and stop it if it was too bad (it wasn't of course).... In middle of dinner listened to the King's broadcast and the news. Nothing much definite in the latter, tho' everyone seems satisfied. Home 10.30 and did a little work. Absence of definite news, and calm, rather an anti-climax.

Wednesday, 7 June

Same beastly—and unpropitious—weather, cold cloudy and this damned N. wind. Things seem to be going all right—but these are early days. Americans on beach E. of Vire got held up. Our ships are trying to help them. German Panzer Div. on E. end of our line. Can't tell yet how things will go. And of these critical 72 hours, I suppose about 40 have been occupied by all the High-Ups wrangling about purely imaginary and manufactured grievances against de Gaulle! A. kept up till 3 a.m. again, and on telephone to P.M. from 8.30 till

* Viénot had come at 1 a.m. to say that de Gaulle would not change his mind about the liaison officers, whereupon Churchill spoke violently against him. Later, Duff Cooper persuaded de Gaulle to let some of these officers go.

† The Foreign Office seems to have been misinformed. De Gaulle had said not that he refused to broadcast but that he would not do so immediately after Eisenhower, whose text ignored the F.C.N.L. entirely.

10 this morning. Saw him at 11.15 but at about 11.20 P.M. rang up again on the same subject, till 11.40. Cabinet this evening to discuss the matter, and we agreed outline of draft letter to de G. designed to open conversations with us, with or without Americans, on civil affairs. Pres. is so odd on this question that I think he must have made secret agreement with Pétain and/or Laval! Went off with Duff and O. Harvey to draft letter. . . . Cabinet at 6, but agenda was cancelled and it was announced that it was to be only War Cabinet + A. Sinclair. A. had told me to come, but I said I'd better keep out—he could send for me if he wanted me. I understand de G. the only topic, and there will be a lot of washing of dirty linen in private, and they won't want an onlooker! Wasn't sent for, and got through my work. Dined at home. Listened to news which is, I think, good enough for the moment.

[Meanwhile Eden was giving dinner to de Gaulle, whom he tried to persuade to begin conversations with the British. The Americans had already refused to take part. But it would be a time-wasting and humiliating business, the General objected, to reach agreement and then go along to them for approval. Eden recommended the policy of 'she stoops to conquer'.

Two days later de Gaulle relented to the extent of allowing Viénot to open discussions between officials and without American participation.[2]]

Thursday, 8 June

Wind still too much in N. Coldish, cloudy and rain in afternoon. News seems to be all right. Nothing yet at all decisive. But Alex in Italy seems to be planning to overrun the whole country. A dull day as far as I was concerned. . . . Saw A. about 5.30 about Sosnkowski* going to Italy. He had no great news. He had prevailed on P.M. in small hours this morning to let him send letter to Viénot proposing Anglo-French conversations with reference to U.S. He has impressed on V. that this is the last chance, so I hope de G. will be gracious!

Friday, 9 June

Not v. much to do. Had planned to go to cottage. But as A. has to go this afternoon to Bradford, and won't be back at Binderton till 7 or 8 p.m. tomorrow, and will consequently be out of touch, and as the de G. question is boiling and P.M. has crashed into Yugoslav policy, O.S. asked me if I wd. stay here, and I gathered A. wanted me to also. So rang up T. at 11.30 and said cottage was off. . . . P.M., who seems to have been baffled in his attempt to go to Beaches, is mucking

* Polish Supreme Commander.

up foreign affairs instead. He arranged to see King Peter and Ban* at 3 this afternoon to tell them to go out to Vis to get in contact with Tito. This contrary to F.O. advice, but I'm not sure he's wrong to take the gamble. But he behaved badly. A. had been kept up till 3 a.m. for three nights running, so went to bed last night and didn't go to see P.M. Latter sent for [R.S.] Stevenson, to whom he blackguarded F.O. conduct of foreign policy, which is improper and embarrassing. P.M., A. and King and Ban met at 3.30, and it was agreed all should leave tomorrow night—Peter stay in Malta and Ban go on to Vis to negotiate with Tito. I think this right. As regards de G. worry, A. sent letter to Viénot proposing Anglo-French negotiation. This afternoon V. brought back a not entirely unsatisfactory reply, which Duff was to take to P.M. V. was asked to press de G. in any case to get Commissioners [from Algiers] here at once. They could return with him if he goes back early next week. Haven't heard result of either démarche yet (11.10 p.m.). Tho' kept here for alarums, I had a dull and idle day, so started re-studying Memoranda on Future World Organisation. Shall probably have a movementé if not accidenté day tomorrow!

[In June, Tito had been forced to flee to Vis, an island off the Adriatic coast, where he was protected by British troops. His position was nevertheless a strong one, for he knew that the British did not wish to lose him entirely to the Russians, and that having enforced the dismissal of Mihailović, they could not break with the Partisans. At Vis, Tito was visited by Subasić. They agreed on 16 June that the Royal Government and the National Liberation Committee would collaborate. Tito said he did not intend to impose Communism on Yugoslavia after the war. This was disbelieved by most expert opinion in the Foreign Office. The Tito-Subasić agreement did not refer to a possible return of the King, whom Tito evinced no desire to meet. Both sides had already accepted that the form of government must be decided when the war was over.[3]]

Saturday, 10 June

Talk with O. Harvey, Mack and Dixon at 12.45 about the French worry. Saw the French party again and told them that on reflection, only thing to do was to go ahead discussing agreement with Viénot (de G. refuses to bring Commissioners here). This would be a *tactical* victory for de G. But why should that matter? If we don't do this, de G. will go back next week with nothing done, and we shall be back again in the old deadlock. They all agreed, but doubted whether I could put it across A.—and P.M. P.M. rang up about 4, v. angry

* The Viceroy, Dr Subasić.

about change of Govt. in Italy—as well he may be. This has been bungled, as P.M. puts it, 'by that old woman Mason Macfarlane'.*... Don't quite see what we do. Nothing unconstitutional has been done. Of course we can refuse to recognise Bonomi crowd, but that may be unwise. P.M. has diverted A. to Chequers this evening, and they will have to discuss it. I have sent material to A., who rang me up from Chequers at 7.30. Talked to him about France. I had sent him a message about 5 through Lawford in Bradford and got the answer that he agreed with me. Now that he has to tackle P.M. about it, he's weakening rather, and becoming, like the others, temperamental about de G.: 'Why can't de G. help *me* at all?' We haven't helped de G. much. However, we shall see. Stevenson today persuaded Peter and the Ban to leave for Malta and Vis tonight. He goes with them.

[Badoglio had resigned on 8 June, to be replaced by Signor Bonomi. His all-party Government was formed on the conditions that Prince Umberto should summon a Constituent Assembly at the end of the war and that the oath of allegiance should not commit ministers to support the dynasty. The Bonomi Government received Allied approval on 18 June.]

Sunday, 11 June

Rather milder, but rather beastly. Low cloud—practically no sun —but wind more in S. News from France all right. We have widened and apparently consolidated our bridgehead. We have got the Germans on the run in Italy. A. flying from Chequers to Binderton. Gather he failed with P.M. last night—they had a shouting match till 2 a.m. P.M. refuses negotiation with Viénot. Everything becomes madder and madder.... At F.O. about 4. Oliver H. had been talking to A. about France. A. wanted me to send for Viénot and press him to get de G. to get a Commissioner here—perhaps Mendès-France,† on plea of monetary question. V. came at 5.30 for an hour. He rehearsed the whole situation: Committee had decided to join only in tripartite conversations. That may have been silly, but at least de G. has now gone further and agreed to conversations between us and V. (preliminary). Are we now to refuse that? Some question of prestige or school-girl pride? Why can't we 'déblayer le terrain' with the Committee's diplomatic representative? V. said that if we could do that, and if things went well, Commissioner would be sent. But no, apparently, P.M. won't have it. There's just one chance in a

* Lt.-Gen. Sir F. N. Mason-Macfarlane, Chief Commissioner, Allied Control Commission, Italy, 1944.

† Pierre Mendès-France, Finance Minister in French Provisional Government.

million Pres. may reply to P.M. that Winant can join in discussion. That would clear everything up, but it won't happen.

P.M. going to the 'beaches'. I thought on Tues., but I now hear tomorrow.

At end of our conversation, V. asked whether P.M. was going. I said I didn't know: I had read in papers that he wanted to go with assault force, and doubtless would be impatient to get there. Why did he ask? (I knew full well). He said that, between us, it would create a v. difficult situation if P.M. went before de G. I could only shrug my shoulders. It was then 6.30 and I rang up A. He said P.M. leaves tonight. After discussion, we agreed better say nothing to P.M., as it could only have a bad effect—unless A. gets an opening. He won't!

Monday, 12 June

Nothing much doing. P.M. went over last night. . . . 5.15 talk with A. and others about France. He agreed to ask P.M. to authorise us to begin discussion, on official level, with Viénot. This would be a *start*—and it's the only step forward I can think of. . . . Cabinet at 6. P.M. away, so we got through quickly. Some particulars of 2nd front. We on the beaches, have landed over 200,000 men (Allied total 400,000) 1,200 tanks, 30,000 vehicles and 40,000 tons of stores. A marvellous performance. But stiff fighting expected within a week. Germans in Italy seem to be almost en déroute.

Tuesday, 13 June

Appears we had pilotless aircraft over last night (there were two alerts that woke me up). 4 identified overland: of which 2 in Greater London area—some damage in Bethnal Green: 4 fell in the sea (!) and 3 possibles. Not v. impressive. Hope some will return and fall in Germany! They didn't fly higher than 8,000 ft and only 250 mph. at most. A sitting target! . . .*

Some progress with de G. P.M. has been prevailed on to allow conversations with Viénot, and de G. to go to France tomorrow. But the Pres. is rushing to break *all* the plates tonight at 9.45 by saying that the French currency is backed by Eisenhower! On A's instructions got Chancellor to agree to try to persuade Winston to send a message dissuading Pres. Don't know if it went. Don't much care: if he makes the announcement I hope we shall dissociate ourselves from it (we weren't consulted). That will leave all the odium—and the guarantee of £400,000,000—on the cracked President!

* The speed of the V-1, which varied from bomb to bomb, was in fact in the region of 350–390 m.p.h.

Thursday, 15 June

News continues all night. Counter-attacks everywhere. But that is a good thing. Enemy frittering away reserves instead of collecting them for a big punch. Lunch at Mexican Embassy. . . . Speeches! Mexican Ambassador read a dull one. P.M.—after v. good lunch—replied—quite well, but he said (a) that [cypher] ban would be lifted in a few days and (b) that we should soon have a battle in Normandy a million a side. He'd better have said neither.

(By the way, at 8 p.m. last night . . . Mack rang me up to say de G. had done a bolt in Normandy. Last seen going W. towards Carenton and had booked a room in Bayeux. I said that if he became a nuisance he must be put under 'polite restraint' and that an officer must be detailed to ask him his intentions. But he's back this morning, thus confirming my feeling that it was rather a scare!)

V. little work. Italian news wonderful. A. was going this evening with King to France (which he's got no business to do). Tomorrow morning there's a debate in the House on France and a discussion in Cabinet on Oil. Dick Law was deputed to take the House and I was asked to take Cabinet. I know nothing about Oil and didn't feel like doing battle with Max, so protested. Anyhow, A. now staying. So hope I can get away for week-end.

[General de Gaulle returned very much cheered by his reception in Normandy, where he left a lieutenant who quietly took over the administration. De Gaulle then returned to Algiers, without meeting the Prime Minister again, and without the recognition of the F.C.N.L. as the Provisional Government of France. In Washington, the Secretary for War, H. L. Stimson, had concluded that America must recognise de Gaulle. He told Hull that Roosevelt too was beginning to realise the fact, but found Hull adamant: 'He hates de Gaulle with such fierce feeling that he rambles into almost incoherence whenever we talk about him. . . .'[4]]

Friday, 16 June

Pilotless aircraft made their first big attack last night, beginning about 11.30. Alert went on all night. As a matter of fact, I slept well. I gather about 130 over, up to 7 a.m. Good deal of damage, but not many casualties reported yet. All clear about 9.

Monday, 19 June

A. didn't arrive till after 3. His windows had been blown out! 4 attended his meeting with Allied representatives about the [cypher] Ban. He had meant to announce its removal tonight, but at 3 P.M. rang up to say that wasn't certain. So A. thanked them for their forbearance, said he had hoped to announce raising of ban, but owing to attack on London, that might be difficult. They took it well. Cabinet in War Room at 5.45. Some discussion of the new attack. Decided to call it officially 'Flying Bombs'. We seem to be getting the measure of it. Goebbels' wild propaganda is encouraging. It does, of course, no military damage, and the population take it very calmly. It's a nuisance—that's the proper description. Cabinet, after some discussion, decided to lift the Diplomatic Ban at midnight. So I had to leave, about 6.45, to get out the necessary circulars &c. and didn't hear Chiefs of Staffs report. But news seems good: we have, for the moment at least, cut the Cherbourg Peninsula, and the rout in Italy continues. Warnings on and off all day, but not much doing. A bomb in Tottenham Ct Rd this morning. But up to 6.30 they had only sent over 24 since daylight. Our fighters learning the technique, and plans for balloon and kite barrage. . . . Hear Rockets are almost ready to operate. Don't know much about their performance.*

Friday, 23 June

About 5.30 R. Law came to say Leathers† had received request from Gousev to provide special train to take 300 of his staff to Blackpool. A. (who had heard of this on leaving for country) wanted me to protest to Gousev. Latter came at 6.30 (in middle of 'immediate danger' warning). He said he only wanted 3 special *coaches.* I promised to consult Leathers, which I did after Gousev had left. L. said he couldn't provide 'special' coaches, but would see to it that accommodation would be stretched to provide for Russians. He agreed to inform Soviet Embassy. 7.30 Gousev rang me up to complain of completely 'negative' answer. So I rang up Ministry again and they agreed to hint to Soviet Embassy that in practice it *would* be all right. Funny how the Russians are the first to panic. They did the same in Feb. Leathers had agreed his course of action with [Herbert] Morrison,‡ so I thought there was no need for me to take it up with A. or P.M. . . . Warnings all day, but since 8 a.m. I've heard no bangs. Wonder whether it is reconnaissance planes trying to spot damage. They won't see very much! 24 hrs. ending 6 a.m. this morning, 104 Bombs crossed the coast. 60 got to London. We shot down 37 and the balloons got 7.

* Weight 12·65 tons; warhead approx. 1 ton; range 207 miles; max. speed 4,000 m.p.h.; flight time 4 mins.

† Minister of War Transport.

‡ Home Secretary, 1940–5.

Saturday, 24 June

Gousev raising Hell again. Leathers rang me up. I said I didn't want to question his ruling, but if he could give a hint to Soviet Embassy that in practice it would be all right, he might do so. He agreed. Later Gousev sent angry note to A., who, on telephone, says he will wash Gousev's head. . . . Good deal of work. P.M. rang me up about message to Pres. on French negotiations. I think I fixed up a text between him and A. . . . T. seems all right, but it will be a long process. It *is* bad luck!* We ought, I should judge, to have Cherbourg within 48 hours. Resistance in Italy stiffening, but I think that's what Alex wants. Russian offensive seems to have opened well.

Sunday, 25 June

A. flapping about the Argentine—he's got that ass Winant with him. Seems to be half persuaded to appease Hull by withdrawing Kelly.† I got him to wait a bit. A row with the Argentine means a fairly heavy cut in our meat ration. I told him I thought we had already asked about as much as we were entitled to of the inhabitants of these islands. Why should we do more for a purely ideological-election whim of old Hull—for it is nothing more. He agreed. Stopped on my way home at the band, but combination of a trombone solo by a sergeant, and A. L. Kennedy, was too depressing. So got home before 7.

[While Hull made no secret of his desire to overthrow Colonel Perón's Government, the British argued that denunciation and attempted dictation merely strengthened its position. In deference to the State Department, Kelly had been told to confine his contacts with the Argentine Government to matters of routine business. In June, the U.S.A. decided, without consultation, to withdraw their Ambassador. Churchill, as usual, felt more inclined than Eden to meet American wishes. The Foreign Secretary advised that Hull's position was an unreasonable one. Moreover, nearly half the British meat ration came from the Argentine, and there was a very large investment of British capital. Kelly was 'recalled for consultation' at the end of June, under pressure from Roosevelt.[5]]

Monday, 26 June

We have met some opposition in Italy. Cherbourg not yet quite taken,‡ and nothing definite on Normandy front. . . . 5 talk with A. about Argentine. He agreed to be fairly firm about Hull's folly, and dictated a good minute to P.M. Later a talk about set-up in Italy.

* Lady Theodosia had broken a bone in her foot.

† Sir D. Kelly, Ambassador at Buenos Aires, 1942–5.

‡ It fell on 27 June.

All these frightful minutes and papers and Committees of 6 months ago have of course resulted in a hide-bound situation of entirely the wrong shape. We shall have to shake it into some other shape, but I'm blessed if I know what. Must think over it [sic]. Bovenschen,*... v. annoyed because we have gone ahead with discussions with French without waiting for him. Serve him right.... We're in rather a nasty (temporary) pause. Russian offensive goes well—at least it seems to. Stalin comes out every 8 hrs with an 'Order of the Day'—whatever that may be.

Tuesday, 27 June

Not a bad night. Fine early, but became awful later—violent squalls in a S.W. gale, and heavy showers. We've had *one* fine day this June. Bad for unloading, bad for air cover in Normandy and bad for flying-bombs. Alerts on and off all day. 12.30 talk with A. about Argentine. At one moment this morning it was difficult to concentrate. The alarm bell outside my room went wrong, with the result of constant tintinnabulation: the sirens went: flying bombs roared overhead, and there was a thunderstorm!... 5 talk with A., Macmillan and others about Italian lay-out. And at 5.30 again about Argentine. We *must* differ from old Hull, but I don't know whether A. and P.M. will face it. We can stall for a bit.

6. Cabinet—at its worst—mostly about flying bombs. Morrison rather over-played his hand and annoyed P.M. Latter monologued for hours. We could have got thro' by 7, but sat till 8.55!

Wednesday, 28 June

Lunched at Chinese Embassy. Large party.... While we were gathering for lunch, two flying bombs passed over. All the guests edged away from the windows (quite rightly). I—a late arrival—remained near the door!

Thursday, 29 June

Lunched with A. at F.O. for Turks.... Interpreted after between Turk and Herbert Morrison. Talked to latter after about 'Democracy', on which we see, I think, eye to eye. (He is an instinctive, and rather uninstructed, totalitarian!)

Friday, 30 June

Our thrust in Normandy seems to have been held, which is disappointing. Russians doing well, and we seem to have got Germans on

* Sir F.C. Bovenschen, Joint P.U.S., War Office, 1942–5.

the run again in Italy. But I gather P.M. has had to give way to Americans and we shall skin poor Alex for 'Anvil'.* I'm not *sure* this is wrong, but it's rather heartbreaking. . . . Talk with A. at 3.30 about Spain. He's still got the bug—or perhaps he fears that many MP's still have. I'm glad to say he's remaining firm—as yet—on Argentine, refusing to be dragged at old Hull's heels. . . .

These are unpleasant times. I'm not at all sure of our offensive capabilities in France, and I don't know whether the flying bombs are going to become more of a nuisance. And what about the 'Rocket'? It can't affect the war, but may be a very considerable embarrassment. And T. laid up for at least another 3 or 4 weeks.

Saturday, 1 July

This morning telegram from Kelly rather ratting and urging his withdrawal. All the Latin Americans are withdrawing, and Pres. has sent appeal to P.M. A. annoyed and defeatist. Obviously nothing for it but to give in, while expressing doubts and dislikes. Drafted message from P.M. to Pres. Don't know whether it's accepted. But principle of withdrawal *is*. . . . We seem to be hung up in Normandy, but I don't think it's *bad*. If *only* we could have some clear fine days. It is said that our 'cover' plans were so good that we deceived even the 'Bon Dieu'. I hope that's the correct explanation—otherwise he's the worst strategist ever!

Sunday, 2 July

I was so tired last night that I slept from the moment I laid my head on the pillow. I was woken by a bump at 7 but went to sleep again 10 min later, till nearly 9. Last 24 hrs has not been good. We've done little against the Flying Bombs. There appears to be a check in Normandy. Our propagandists keep on bellowing that we 'retain the initiative'. But if we don't do anything with it, what then? Russia and Italy seem all right. Not much work. Lunched at home and 'All Clear' went soon after we had begun. And it has lasted till now—why, I can't think. It is ideal for F/B's. I suppose they're saving them up for tonight. . . . Have just heard on 9 o'clock news that poor old Norman Davis is dead. I *am* sorry. He was a capital old rascal and I was *very* fond of him, and looking forward to negotiating with him in Washington on future world organisation.

Monday, 3 July

V. noisy night from 4 a.m., or earlier, onwards, and I didn't sleep

* Landings in the South of France, renamed 'Dragoon'.

at all. This is becoming a bore, and with the perfectly b——y weather we've been having the last four days we can't do anything about it! I thought 'Crossbow' a joke, but it's going to give us a headache—no mistake.... 5.30 Cabinet, which lasted till 8.55. P.M. wasting time more than usual even. Don't like the look of Flying Bomb. It's doing almost as much as Blitz at its worst. And we're not getting the better of it. Certainly not with *this* weather. P.M., who had pooh-poohed it, was impressed by figures of tonnage dropped and damage done. Casualties not so bad. Otherwise news all right. Dined at home soon after 9. After what I had heard, I turned our passage into a dormitory. Better get away from flying glass at least.

Tuesday, 4 July

Alerts most of the day, but I heard very few crumps.... After I left Cabinet last night, P.M. kept members of Inner Ring and they finished at 9.45. All P.M. said was 'Oh! we've missed the 9 o'clock news'!

Wednesday, 5 July

Pres. has imperiously insisted on his Staff's demand for 'Anvil' (rather late) at expense of Alexander's campaign. P.M. had really no alternative but to submit, but I'm glad to say he sent a pretty hot telegram to Pres. today.

Thursday, 6 July

5 meeting with A. and others about Turkey (who are ready to break off relations—on terms—but pretend to want to come into the war. I don't know that we want them to!)

Friday, 7 July

11.30 went over to Cabinet, which was due to discuss future world organisation. Alexander was lecturing them on Italian campaign. I had to wait till 12.10. Then went in. Met Alex coming out and greeted and congratulated him. P.M. announced he had to lunch with a 'Royal Person' and would have to leave at 12.30, so he took various other items and then left us to 'the Peace of the World about which, in present circumstances, I am rather lukewarm'. This hopeless and v. naughty. In his absence, Cabinet easily approved reference to A.P.W. Committee* of A's paper inviting instructions to our Delegation. But if P.M. is going to evade the issue and snipe, we

* Armistice and Post-War Committee.

shall be v. uncomfortable in Washington. Cabinet approved going ahead with Turkish rupture of relations with Germany—but *not* on basis of Turkish proposed exchange of notes.

Saturday, 8 July

We opened an attack on Caen this morning, which is said to be 'going well', but one never knows what that means.* Russians have taken Baranovice, and we advance—slowly—in Italy. So nothing very sensational, but I think things go well with us—and v. badly with the Germans.

Monday, 10 July

Cabinet at 5.30 till 8.10.... Normandy looks fairly good, and Russia v. much so. F/B attack reduced, but we shall have a job (in this weather) to hold it down. Casualties not high, but housing problem—due to blast—serious. Morrison—as usual—v. pessimistic, but Willink† not so.... There *is* a rocket! But we don't know much about it. One has fallen in Sweden and we're trying to get hold of it. Cabinet this evening approved our urging Turks to break off relations, and to seize any opportunity of getting Americans to join with us in recognising French Committee as Provisional Govt.

Tuesday, 11 July

10.30 talk with A. and others about France. A. wanted to recognise the Provisional Govt. on July 14. But a message from the Pres., which is quite good in other respects, shows we can't do *that yet*.... 6. talk with A. about Polish-Russian situation. Poles want us to propose a visit to Moscow by Mikolajczyk. We agreed to pass this on—we must, I think.... We have made local—very local—gains in Caen area. Germans are putting up stiff resistance in Italy, but I understand that's what Alex wants them to do. Russians press on. If only we could get a week's fine weather, we might make some headway against the F/B's. But this b——y weather is ideal for them. 3 fine days since June 6! There never *has* been such meteorological bad luck.

Wednesday, 12 July

11 Bolivian Chargé d'Affaires, who said that Hull had consulted his Govt. on 'economic sanctions' against Argentine. I said we had heard nothing of this. Folly!... 5 Venezuelan to show me a telegram

* Caen was taken on 9 July.
† H. U. Willink, Minister of Health.

he had decided to send to his Govt. urging them to protest against Flying Bomb. I said very nice, but no use! Hope I didn't cold-douche him too much.

Saturday, 15 July

Lunched . . . at Turf [Club]—quite good. About 5 people there, and a general air of the family vault. . . . A few alerts, but few bombs. Don't know why. Weather ideal for them. Russian news good. We seem stuck. I *hope* we may break out one of these days, but I'm not sure. It will be serious if we don't do so within a week or 2. I remember that [Gen.] Nye has always said to me 'Monty is a very *cautious* General'. He must now have about 1,200,000 men, and material in proportion. The Germans, as I know, are hanging on by the skin of their teeth.

Monday, 17 July

Not much doing in morning. 4.45 talk with A. and others about Turkey. In view of Soviet (and U.S.) attitude, I think we must press them to *declare war*. But there are many considerations against. 5.30 Cabinet, which is becoming more and more rambling, disorderly and voluble. News not bad, but not v. good. What are we doing in Normandy—with 1,229,000 men and a *mass* of material (255,000 vehicles! Over a million tons of stores!) Maybe we have a plan. There is no inkling of it. Cabinet agreed we must go for Turks coming into war. I slipped away at 8.10! Cabinet having several other items to take. P.M. is evidently ageing, and the rambling talk is *frightful*. Whatever little the Cabinet settled would have been settled in 7 mins. under Neville Chamberlain. F/B's rather better, but no *cure* in sight. And they damage 11,000 houses a day! P.M. takes the light hearted bull-dog view of it until faced with figures like this, when he is (I hope) a little bit disconcerted. It's serious. Owing to delays (A's fault) we shan't be ready to start for Washington by sea next Monday, and must go by air, which I hate, on Sat. week. Dined at home and worked.

Tuesday, 18 July

12.45 talk with A. and others about Greek situation. His feet getting cold (owing to Left pressure) about supporting Papandreou* against E.A.M. But he agreed to do it. . . . Told Michiels† I thought Germans were more stretched than many people believe.

* Georgios Papandreou, Greek Prime Minister.
† Dutch Ambassador.

[Papandreou, leader of the Republican Socialist party, had formed a Government of National Unity on 8 June. At the end of that month negotiations with the Communist-dominated E.A.M. broke down, E.A.M. having refused to appoint ministers to the five places reserved for them by the Lebanon agreement. Eden announced on 27 July that the British Government were continuing to support Papandreou. E.A.M. came into the Government on 2 September.]

Wednesday, 19 July

We made a tank break-through E. of Caen yesterday, but I'm *afraid* it's held up. C. Peake,* who'd been at Portsmouth this afternoon, told me this evening that Bedell Smith and Americans are rather down in the mouth, and rather critical of Monty. . . . 5.30 talk with A. and others about Turkey. (O.S. went resolutely off on a week's leave—which is a bore, with O. Harvey away). Agreed that, unless C's of S. can offer some tangible assistance, we'd better stick to our plan of 2 bites to the cherry. Then a long discussion with R. Stevenson about Yugoslavia. A. feeling the draught in Parliament but I don't see what we can *do*. A. says the Ban [Dr Subasić] must get Serbs into his Govt. I agree. But that's what the poor man is trying his utmost to do. I don't see what *we* can do.

Thursday, 20 July

Defence Committee in Map Room at 12.15. Agreed to revert to our line of '2 bites at the cherry' with Turkey. Agreed to support Papandreou in his line. C.I.G.S., who was in Normandy yesterday, gave us a lecture, with map. Not very reassuring. We're rather stuck, and as far as I can make out we had meant this to be a real break-through. And it is *not*—yet. Everyone blathers about a German 'collapse'. I wish I could see a sign of it. P.M. off to Normandy. King [George VI] going to Italy tomorrow night. And proposes to see Umberto, to which I object. . . . 3 A.P.W. Committee. An *awful* meeting. . . . Eventually we got down to our question of Future World Organisation, when the meeting were so sunken in sloth and garrulity and muddleheadedness that they let it pass. Letter from Winant announcing that Hull is going to take part in discussions. I drafted telegram expressing surprise that we should suddenly be faced with a proposal for radical change of basis. . . . No alert since about lunch-time I think. I suppose they're saving up. I said to Portal this morning that I thought the wicket-keeping hadn't been

* Now Political Liaison officer with Supreme Allied Commander.

so good these last 24 hrs. But he said on the contrary, it was better but the bowling was stronger. They had launched 137 and we had destroyed 73.

Friday, 21 July

Papers full of attempt on Hitler's life.* Don't know what it means. Not v. much, I think. Possibly an excuse for a purge. Anyhow, it seems that he has stamped on any opposition. Talk with A. and others about it at 11.30. 'Others' rather unduly excited about it. I threw a few little cold douches. . . . 4.30 another meeting with A. about Germany, but we have *no* news. In spite of constant interruptions, I managed to keep abreast of a ghastly amount of verbose papers. . . . This weather is foul. I think we had planned our advance on American front in Normandy, introduced by another 7,000 ton bombardment. But there was thick cloud down to 600 ft., and heavy rain. Providence has no idea of strategy.

Saturday, 22 July

Slept well. But in last 24 hrs. Germans launched 204 F/Bs—record number. About the usual percentage got to London. *Filthy* weather—quite dark with low cloud—breakfasted by artificial light. 56°! Floods of paper. 11.30 talked to C. K. Webster. He starts on Mon. and as meeting is now put off till Aug. 12 he will be kicking his heels in Washington. I warned him against the dangers, to us and to himself, of getting involved in conversations. . . . 'C' came in, but he had no news—except the significant fact that the revolt seems to be headed by Witzleben, Hoeppner and Fromm,† and we haven't heard that any of these are jugged yet. . . . A number of alerts today, but no noises. I gather Monty . . . ought to have gone right through this week. The Americans—and Tedder‡—are furious with him. Tedder says that, awkward though it would be, he may have to 'go to the P.M. about it'. Monty puts out stuff about 'very light casualties' and does a lot of publicity stuff in his sweater and beret. I don't believe he's a general at all, but just a Film Star. Russian news all right, but we can't leave everything to *them*. We do well enough in Italy. I wish we could get Alex here.

* The abortive attempt on Hitler's life at his headquarters in East Prussia. Although hints of a plot had reached British officials in Portugal some time before, Cadogan seems to have been taken by surprise.

† Field-Marshal von Witzleben was to assume, according to the plan, command of the Armed Forces, and Gen. Hoeppner of the Reserve Army; Gen. Fromm had behaved equivocally, but had swiftly put himself on the right side after learning that the plot had miscarried.

‡ Now Deputy Supreme Allied Commander.

Sunday, 23 July

Col. X . . . at 11.30. about a possible contact with Gen. Reinhard, G.O.C. in Holland. Authorised giving him a wireless set, though I don't expect anything of it. But we shall have to consider telling Russians about it. . . . Telegram from Washington summarising U.S. paper on future world organisation. V. good—except that there is a good deal about 'territorial trusteeship'!

Monday, 24 July

6.0 Cabinet. P.M. not depressed by his visit to France. Attributes delay (possibly rightly) to weather, which is unprecedently frightful. Cabinet went on, in the present tradition, till 8.30. We rambled around every subject, with no result. Haven't been able to get at A. at all. We *must* discuss U.S. views on 'World Organisation', especially 'territorial trusteeship'.*

[In mid-July, Churchill telegraphed to the President in detail about the indispensability of Argentine supplies in maintaining the meat ration, and adding: 'You would not send your soldiers into battle on the British Service meat ration, which is far above what is given to workmen. Your people are eating per head more meat and poultry than before the war, while ours are most sharply cut.' Roosevelt made reassuring noises in reply, but sent a statement which Hull was about to issue. It lacked nothing in vehemence, and made it impossible, for the moment at least, to recognise the government of Argentina.

Even the negotiations for a new meat contract bred further arguments with the Americans. Hull spoke loftily of 'the petty commercial advantages of a long-term bargain with a fascist government'. The whole issue, indeed, had become almost an obsession with him. Lord Halifax, congratulating himself silently on being in Hull's presence for half an hour with no mention of the Argentines, enquired about the Secretary's health and found that he had unleashed a torrent. The Argentines, said Mr. Hull, had been partly to blame for his feeling run down. For the moment, and in view of the impending Presidential election, Churchill ruled that no long-term meat contract should be signed.[6]]

Tuesday, 25 July

12.45. Talk with A., Mikolajczyk and Romer. Tried to get him to agree to go to Moscow—on the chance. But he wouldn't. These Poles are blind fools and M. is weak. . . . 3.45 Discussion with A., Kelly and the Department about Argentine. Agreed to consult Washington Embassy about possibility of a show-down with old Hull. 7.15 meet-

* Cf. Churchill's remarks quoted on p. 432.

ing with P.M., A., and the Poles. P.M. kept us waiting till 7.50. Then rambled till 9.10. These hours are very trying! However Mikolajczyk did agree to take his courage in both hands and start for Moscow tomorrow night. This in spite of the Soviet having this afternoon announced their intention to negotiate with Polish National Council.* But even this may be checkmated by the stupid Poles having, last night, without consulting us, put out one of their recurrent and ridiculous 'declarations' stigmatising the Council as 'usurpers'. I like and respect M., but by Heaven what a mess they've made of their case!

Wednesday, 26 July

Dined here . . . and worked after. Afraid wrote angry strictures on a number of awful Files from O.S.'s depts. He allows them to spread themselves on paper and they compose symposia of unheard of length, leading nowhere. I sent them all back. O.S. has promised to come back Friday. I must say the Normandy news is a little disappointing. We now have 1½ million men there, equipped as never an army has been equipped before, and our advances if any, are measured in yards. I think I was right in rebuking the Dept. the other day for a minute in which they forecast the end of the war in mid-Aug. . . . I see *no* reason to think it won't go on for 3 years more.

Thursday, 27 July

Gale and low cloud held! Mild. Press v. gloomy about Normandy but found out later this had been put out by a junior American numbskull in SHAEF—probably anti-Monty. . . . Back at F.O. at 2.20 to mug up agenda for A.P.W. Committee, to which A. insisted on taking me at 3. There till after 4. Might just as well not have been. But P.J. G[rigg] was not so tight. Tried to grapple with flood of minutes. Have sent a snorter to O.S. saying I think his S[outhern] Dept. is completely addle-pated and incompetent. Verbosity is a terrible (lazy) disease. A. insisted on my coming to Cabinet at 6. Agenda F/B and exchange of prisoners in Pacific. I was only faintly interested in latter. We rambled till 8 on F/B and then cut out the rest of the agenda. However, I had taken a good deal of work there and got through it. But found *stacks* afterwards, which I brought home. . . . O.S. and O.H. must *not* again be away together. And I *must* reform office procedure. I have already told O.S. that I will only receive *one* minute from his Dept. I shall make this a general

* The 'Lublin Committee' which, Stalin telegraphed to Churchill, was the only force in Poland strong enough to set up an administration.

rule. Worked till 10.30. Rather tired—I've been on the stretch for 5 weeks, including weekends. T. took plaster off yesterday!

[The Russians now said they would send an aircraft to Tehran to fetch Mikolajczyk to Moscow. Both Eden and Cadogan had believed that they would find a pretext for postponement. Mikolajczyk, who had been encouraged in Washington to stand out against Russian demands, set off at once.]

Friday, 28 July

We seem to be stuck against heavy opposition in Normandy, but the Americans have done well on the west flank, getting, apparently, to Coutances. A fairly quiet day in F.O., after these last exhausting days. . . . T. can put her foot to the ground a bit, on crutches. . . . Raczynski at 12.30 about various points, all of which had already been turned down, but which I suppose he had to raise again, pour acquit de conscience.* A salvo of F/Bs at lunch time, and another one going on now (10 p.m.). Otherwise quiet. 6 saw Gousev and asked him to get denial from his Govt. of reports that Polish underground troops, after joining Red Army in recapture of a Polish town, are disarmed and arrested. He woodenly eventually agreed to communicate with Moscow. . . . Russians sweeping all before them.

Monday, 31 July

5.30 Cabinet. News good enough all round. Americans, and even we, have done well in Normandy. Russians sweeping on. And we're not doing too badly in Italy either. F/Bs seem to be kept down to the former scale, or even a trifle below it. Last week we dropped over 10,000 tons on Germany. They dropped 220 tons on London and 295 elsewhere. So that's not too bad. I don't know any more about the rocket. Got away from Cabinet at 7.15. They probably rambled for another 2 hours! Dined at home, and did a certain amount of work. Quiet day so far—few alerts. We may get a packet tonight, but it's clear and still and looks, at least, more settled. And that may help us—and the battle.

[By now advance units of the Red Army had moved to within a few miles of Warsaw. General Bor, leader of the Home Army in Warsaw, responded to a Russian broadcast and gave the signal for an uprising. On the afternoon of 1 August, 40,000 Poles turned upon their German conquerors. The Russians made no effort to help the revolt. Indeed, they

* For Cadogan's letter of 28 July, pointing out that Britain could not give effective air support to an uprising in Warsaw, see Raczynski, *In Allied London*, pp. 320–1.)

forbade British and American aircraft to land at Russian bases after dropping supplies. Warsaw lay otherwise outside the range of Western help.

Thus it came about that Mikolajczyk was colloguing with the Russians at the very moment when the only solid base of authority remaining to the London Poles was being destroyed. Stalin showed himself a little more forthcoming than usual in his talks with Mikolajczyk. The Lublin Committee, while willing that he should be Prime Minister, wanted 14 places out of 18 in the new Government.

During August and September the Germans killed or took nearly 200,000 Poles, one-fifth of the population of Warsaw; Stalin rejected, with no excess of cordiality, pleas that Russia should help; Roosevelt, with the election imminent, did not exert himself unduly; the War Cabinet in London fumed at their own impotence. Churchill, half-regretting afterwards that they had not threatened to cut off the northern convoys, wrote that 'terrible and even humbling submissions must at times be made to the general aim'.[7]]

Tuesday, 1 August

5. Raczynski, asking again for the impossible. Indications from Moscow are that Mikolajczyk *may* be able to do something there, so the quieter we keep here the better.

Wednesday, 2 August

5.45. Raczynski. They have heard that the Polish rising started yesterday at 5 p.m. No further news from Mikolajczyk.

Thursday, 3 August

I went to Cabinet at 7. in anticipation of (1) Ethiopia and (2) World Organisation coming up about then. Sat in waiting-room (doing some of my work). Joined by R. Hudson. At 8.10 we were told we shouldn't be wanted! So came home and dined. Luckily no accumulation of work. It's terrible that we have a P.M. who simply *can't conduct business*. It's all hot air! T. is able to walk a bit without crutches.

[There was now only one clear day left before Cadogan's departure for the Dumbarton Oaks Conference, in respect of which he had received no instructions.]

Friday, 4 August

11.30. Cabinet, which took our 'Future World Organisation'. P.M. cynically jocular—which bodes ill. Neither he—nor anyone else—would take it seriously, and at 11.55 he said 'There now: in 25 mins. we've settled the future of the World. Who can say that we aren't efficient?' Deplorable. I think I had a little of the sympathy of the Cabinet!

Saturday, 5 August

Dined early at 7.30. About 8.15 P. Loxley and [Tom] Bromley* came to pick me up, and we left for Euston about 8.30. Pretty good crowd at station but not so bad as I had expected. Comfortable sleeper. Only drawback no towels. 'Gentlemen', said the Attendant, 'use the bed cover'! Slept fairly well in spite of rather violent shaking—I expect the permanent way wants attention.

[Halifax and Cadogan learned just as they were boarding the *Queen Mary* that the Russians needed another week for preparation. This chance offered a welcome opportunity for consultation with the Americans.

After a restful voyage, they were met at New York by Stettinius and a military band on 12 August, and flew at once to Washington.]

Sunday, 13 August *Washington*

Breakfast on terrace at the shady end of the house [the Embassy] was agreeable—quite a nice little breeze. Press conference at 4. H. held forth for ½ hr or so and then put me up and I gave them 5 min. or so, and answered questions, which were not difficult. I think it went all right.

Monday, 14 August *Washington*

H. and I took the Delegation to present them to old Hull. He made a rambling speech about democracy and the future of the world. I replied suitably and simply, and shortly—as I didn't think it was up to me to indulge in stump oratory.

Hull afterwards kept H. and me and gave us a half hour sermon on Argentina. I should have thought H. might have reacted a bit more strongly, but he probably knows best. Then H. and I talked with Stettinius and called on Dean Acheson,† and got home for lunch.

[The purpose of the Dumbarton Oaks Conference was to give substance and precision to the various Allied statements of intention to set up an international organisation. Revival of the League of Nations could be ruled out, since the U.S.A. had never been a member and Russia had been expelled four years earlier for the attack on Finland.

Before the Conference opened, Cadogan found general agreement

* Cadogan's Principal and Asst. Private Secs. respectively.
† Asst. Secretary of State, 1941–5.

between the British and American delegations; the exception was the issue of a veto. The U.S. Government seemed to believe that Permanent Members of the Council should be able to use the veto in matters where their own interests were involved. To this Cadogan replied that there would be strong opposition in the Commonwealth to a method whereby Britain could veto action against herself but the Dominions could not.[8]

Halifax gave a number of small dinner-parties, at which Cadogan was able to talk privately with leading American politicians of both persuasions. Pains were taken by the U.S. Government to avoid the fiasco of 1919, when opinion about the League of Nations had split on party lines.

The Ambassador said that he wished to leave Washington in 1945, but Cadogan did not like to suggest himself as his successor.]

Wednesday, 16 August *Washington*

Delegation meeting 9.45. Dominions at 11. Berendsen,* New Zealander came to consult me beforehand. Said he was embarrassed, as his Govt. did *not* approve our line. (They have never told us this before). I told him he'd better tell us frankly—that's what our meetings were for. *We* couldn't settle such differences here across the table and he'd better get his Govt. to get in touch with London. So at the meeting he let off steam. I think . . . there may be simply a misunderstanding. However, I am sure he felt all the better for it. . . . We went to a showing at the O.W.I., of a film 'British Imperialism'. As the O.W.I. invited H., I suppose they thought they'd done a good job from our point of view. But it wasn't too good. Best point was that it only lasted 18 minutes.

Friday, 18 August *Washington*

11.15 started off with H. to the Pentagon to see Gen. Marshall. Had long and interesting talk with him. He quite optimistic, and showed us with maps, the situation up to date. (Advance elements only about 12 miles from Paris.)

[General Marshall said that since the Germans had not much more to put into the battle, Eisenhower would push on and take the risk of local setbacks. American Intelligence about Germany's lack of oil coincided with that of the experts in London.]

Sunday, 20 August *Washington*

Soon after 11.30 Stettinius picked me up and we walked down town for a bit discussing plans in a preliminary way. Then we got into his car and drove to National airport to meet the Russians, who arrived at 12.30. Same reception ceremony as on our arrival.

* C. A. Berendsen, New Zealand Minister in U.S.A., 1944–8, thereafter Ambassador.

Monday, 21 August *Washington*

Left with H. for Dumbarton Oaks at 10.15. Met by batteries of cameras. Meeting opened at 10.30 with speech read by Hull. Gromyko* followed, and then I. Went all right, I think. Rather hot, sitting under blazing searchlights with cameras going the whole time. Then adjourned to garden for about ½ hr. of more photography. I took Gromyko aside and talked to him about procedure, and a few other points. He's much better, personally, than Gousev, but obviously terrified of departing a hair's breadth from his instructions. . . .

Gladwyn called at 2.30 and we had a word about procedure and then went to a meeting of the 'Steering Committee' at 3 and settled various points of procedure. Gromyko was insistent on the Soviet idea of getting agreement of broad *principles* first, and filling in detail later: I can't object to this, and it was settled to take the Soviet paper as basis of our discussions. . . . Left at 8 for Conference Banquet at 8.15 at Carlton. Stett. swore to me more than once that there would be no speeches. But I'm not to be caught that way and, during my walk, I thought up 2 or 3 sentences for use in case of necessity. Luckily, for towards the end of dinner I found Gromyko, on my right, drafting a speech on the back of a menu. In the end, I had to get up and say something, and don't think I disgraced myself. My main point was appreciation of the arrangements for our welcome and of the delicacy with which our hosts had struck a nice balance between friendly meeting and military display, which might set the tone of our discussions here.

[Cadogan's speech pointed out that in the new organisation responsibility must be commensurate with power. The Great Powers' goodwill was essential to make the machine work, though they must not establish a dictatorship. The Conference should concentrate upon guiding principles and basic instructions, rather than detailed regulations. Peace—that is, the absence of war—would not be a sufficient ambition. Means must be found to turn the benefits of applied science into constructive channels, so that freedom from fear and freedom from want would march together. Halifax noted in his Diary that day that Cadogan's speech was much the best of the three.]

Tuesday, 22 August *Washington*

Dumbarton Oaks 10.30. Gromyko expounded the Soviet thesis. I—and the Americans sometimes—made critical comment. Stettinius asked me privately to continue in afternoon with statement of British

* Andrei Gromyko, Russian Ambassador in Washington, 1943–6; Russian representative on the Security Council, 1946–8.

case. This seemed to be waste of time but I realised that he wanted opportunity for presentation of American plan. So I agreed. 12.30–1 I prepared some notes for statement. Lunched in cafeteria and walked round garden. Meeting at 2.30, at which I continued our general principles—very shortly. U.S. Delegation followed with an exposition of their plan. Great waste of time, but, having got that over, we agreed to go into Sub-Committees tomorrow, to get down to the detail.

Wednesday, 23 August *Washington*

The Press are revolting against the State Department's repressive methods. More especially as Reston, of the N.Y. Times, comes out with details of all our 'plans'. There has been leakage somewhere, and of course all the other correspondents are furious at Reston's scoop. I think the only cure is to give them a bit more. But Stett. is frightened. The Organisation Cttee. covered a good deal of ground, but at the expense of leaving a lot of the more difficult questions for further consideration. We adjourned 12.15 to go to the White House for reception by President. Hull, Gromyko, H. and self pulled in first. President greeted me with his 'Hulloallec'. Then we presented our Delegations and stood in a circle round his desk while he gave us a little sermon. I thought he looked well: he's lost a lot of flesh, but looks hard and fit, though rather older. Went back to Dumbarton Oaks for lunch, and then had talks with my Delegation about how to take the afternoon discussion in Security Cttee. 2.45 meetings of Heads of Delegations about how to handle Press. Decided to explain why we couldn't give them results, or texts. 3.15 Security Cttee., which didn't go badly—much on the lines of the Organisation Committee of the morning.

Thursday, 24 August *Washington*

Dumbarton Oaks at 9.45 to meet about 15 representative Pressmen, with Stett. and Gromyko. Press presented a written protest against the restrictions placed on them, and we handed them a most discouraging reply. I hope this is all right, though I doubt it. It's quite true that we can't tell them what we agree on, but I should have thought we cd. have given them a good deal of harmless stuff that would please them. But in these matters I can't go an inch further than the Americans.

We didn't get to our Organisation Sub-Committee till about 10.45. Followed our usual procedure of running thro' papers and agreeing easy things, leaving all the difficult ones for further consideration. I raised our point about parties to a dispute not voting, and pointed out all the difficulties that this raised. I think the others listened, and will consider it, but of course we got no decision. . . . U.S. Govt. have arranged a week-end in New York for us, from tomorrow afternoon till Sunday. I had refused, as I was engaged to dine with Chinese tomorrow and with Grews* on Sat. But Stett. this morning said my refusal hadn't gone down awfully well, and muttered something about the Pres. taking an interest in the trip. So I said Grew must get me out of my difficulty with the Chinese, and postpone his own party. This he willingly and effectively did.

Friday, 25 August *Washington*

At Dumbarton Oaks at 11, where we had a meeting in Stett's room of myself and G.J., Gromyko and Soboleff [A. A. Sobolev] and Stett. with 2 others. We really got through quite a lot. Stett. had to leave for lunch 'down town' but the rest of us lunched under the trees and we really got through quite a bit more. Gromyko is personally very reasonable. Whether he will present our arguments to his Govt: whether, still more, they will pay any attention to him, remains to be seen.

[Harmony between the Great Powers was acknowledged on all sides to be vital. That agreement, however, left all the difficult questions unanswered once the delegates abandoned the plane of rhetoric and began to debate the machinery of a working organisation. For examples, what should be the rôle of regional groupings? Would powers feel any obligation to make serious sacrifices for remote parts of the world? What rôle should be allotted to the smaller powers, a question in which, because of the Commonwealth, the British view differed, at least in emphasis, from that of the U.S.A. and Russia? Most important of all, should a Permanent Member of the Council (to which it was decided to add France) have the right of veto in disputes to which it was a party?

The Russians, tenaciously guarding their neutrality in the Far East, refused absolutely to have anything to do with the fifth 'Great Power', China. A Formulation Committee, keeping no minutes, drafted almost all of what became the United Nations Charter. A Steering Committee worked on larger issues of policy.[9]]

Monday, 28 August *Washington*

11 at Dumbarton Oaks, for Steering Committee, where we had quite a useful discussion. Americans accept our point of view about

* J. C. Grew, Special Asst. to Secretary of State, 1942–4, Under-Secretary of State, 1944–5.

voting power on Council. . . . 5.30 Dominions meeting. Gave them full account of our doings. They didn't seem to have any objections.

Tuesday, 29 August *Washington*

10.30 Stett., Gromyko and I received large Press gathering at Dumbarton Oaks, to tell them that we weren't going to tell them anything. I let Stett. make the running—it's his job, and he did it reasonably well. A few questions were put but as, in reply to any serious ones, his stereotyped answer was 'That point is under discussion, so I can't say anything', they got tired of it. Finally one questioner said 'Is it true you went to a night-club in New York?' S. said 'No', and the question came back 'Why not?'! . . . 3 meeting of Steering Committee, where we made some progress. After, had tea with Stett. and Gromyko. Former had to leave us, and I sat on talking to G., who's a very nice and very sensible fellow.

Thursday, 31 August *Washington*

Got to Dumbarton Oaks just before 12, when we had meeting of the Steering Committee. Quite useful, and I think we're making progress—on non-controversial points. Lunched there, and worked after. 3 Sub-Committee on Security. Rather a silly farce, but we didn't disclose any points of difference.

Friday, 1 September *Washington*

Saw Stett., who told me various things—the most important being that the Administration are getting cold feet about the controversy over the power of the Pres. to commit the U.S. 'quota' of armed forces.* He thinks they will have to put in a reservation providing for 'constitutional processes'. This pretty serious, but it's for them to say what they can and what they cannot do. . . . I've done no Conference work today; we've devolved it all on our subordinates who do it much better than we do. So it's a very good plan. Home at midnight.

Monday, 4 September *Washington*

Dumbarton Oaks at 11, for Steering Committee, till 1. Quite hopeless, as the Russian can contribute nothing—merely says 'I have no new proposals to make'. I have telegraphed to London asking for authority to make *our* concessions: Ed. S[tettinius] is prepared to make his, and we can then say to Gromyko 'Where are

* The proposal was that states should maintain a 'quota' of forces instantly ready to move at the order of the Council.

yours?' Probably won't have any effect, but it's the only thing to do. Lunched with Ed. S. and Gromyko. Latter left early to see a Doctor and I told Ed. that he, as Chairman, should remonstrate with Gromyko for going back on all that Sobolev does on Formulation Committee. This is hopeless. Purely formal meeting of Organisation Sub-Committee at 3. Just to give a run to those members of the bloated U.S. Delegation who aren't on the Steering Committee. What a waste of time! But only for an hour. . . . Worked and had tea and a Dominions meeting at 5.30 till after 6.30. They're very tiresome—they want to have the best of both worlds and they mustn't be allowed to bully us too much. I'm beginning to react against them. That's the medicine they want, I think. . . . with Edward at 10.30 to call on Harry Hopkins, who wanted to talk to us about the future of Germany—and did so till 12. He wants to eliminate the Ruhr (as against [Jean] Monnet's scheme of internationalism). Attractive, but I don't know how practical it is.

Marvellous war news—we seem to be in, or at, Antwerp.

Tuesday, 5 September *Washington*

We had a telegram from F.O. yesterday afternoon saying that P.M. might come round to idea of international Air Force.* I told them that various things had been bringing me to this same idea—my talk last night with [Senator] Burton, and Mike [Lester] Pearson's (Canadian) reservation at yesterday's Dominions meeting about Canada being 'consulted' before her 'quota' was even used. Bless my soul—if we put in such provisions, the world will say 'Where are the 'teeth' you promised to put into the Covenant? We are back where we were before'. I believe the International Air (or any other) Force is technically unsound, but politically it may have merits. Anyhow, as there is a chance of our changing our minds on this subject, I told them I was going to warn Stettinius. We and the Americans have fought this thing together and we can't suddenly desert them on the field of battle. . . . With Stett. to Soviet Embassy, where we had quite pleasant lunch. Gave Stett. the warning after.† He didn't seem unduly disturbed. . . . Telegram from A. this afternoon telling me to get in touch with P.M. on Sept. 10 as he may want me at Quebec.

Wednesday, 6 September

I worked till 11.30, when I had a meeting with our men o' war

* The Russians had proposed such a force, to come under the direct control of the Security Council.

† Cf. F.R.U.S., 1944, I, p. 769.

about International Air Force. They maintain—quite rightly, I expect—their technical objections, but I explained, and they accepted, political arguments in favour. . . . Dumbarton Oaks again at 3. Telegram has now come through from F.O. giving us a little latitude, but not much. They are quite right. Talked to Ed. and we agreed it wasn't good enough to summon Committee at short notice. Fixed it for 10. a.m. tomorrow.

[By 29 August, the Americans had come round to the view that a party to a dispute, whether a Permanent Member or not, should not vote upon it; whereas the Russians insisted on unanimity of the Great Powers in all circumstances, so that a Permanent Member should have a veto in a dispute in which its interests were involved.

Eden telegraphed on 6 September that Britain could not accept the Russian view; and Cadogan remarked to Gromyko that even if Britain and America did support it, no other government would. There would therefore be no World Organisation. Gromyko stood pat. Cadogan, doubting whether he understood the arguments, suggested an intervention in Moscow. Roosevelt telegraphed to Stalin, who replied that the understanding reached at Tehran implied the unanimity of the four Great Powers. Russia had to be mindful of 'certain absurd prejudices' on the part of other powers, which frequently hampered 'an objective attitude' towards the Soviet Union. On 13 September, Gromyko told Cadogan that Russia's insistence on unanimity was 'final and unalterable'.[10]]

Thursday, 7 September *Washington*

Steering Committee at 10. Had telegram from F.O. showing that we could propose a (*very* slight) concession on International Air Force. Showed this to Ed, who didn't mind my proposing it at meeting. When I did so, he made some rambling remarks which appeared to show that he might go even further. I asked him after to give me his ideas in writing, but I haven't got them yet. I was able to put in a few concessions on other points but Gromyko put practically none. Ed., Gromyko and I lunched together and Ed. and I tried to hammer him on the main point—the Great Power Veto. But he was quite wooden on that. Best he could say was that we should 'leave the point open'. I explained to him again and again that this was an illusion and that, if one 'left it open' one simply wouldn't get a World Organisation. From some of the things he said, it became clear that he didn't understand the point himself, so *can't* have put the arguments properly to Moscow. So I came home and drafted telegram to London suggesting Archie Kerr should be instructed to put them to Molotov. . . . 4 meeting with Dominions, which lasted till 6. I kept my temper—a most remarkable achievement.

Friday, 8 September *Washington*

10.30 meeting of Steering Committee fixed, but Gromyko didn't turn up—I knew he was being grilled by the President on the crucial question of parties to a dispute voting. He arrived about 11, and he, Ed. and I had a private talk. He eventually gave in about economic and social questions, and expected that I should give in on question of simple or ⅔rds majority vote on Council.* I said I'd only do that if Soviet gave in on the vote of parties to a dispute. So that remains the only big question at issue. It's quite a simple question—'Do you want a World Organisation or do you not?' However, we're making *some* progress.

Saturday, 9 September *Washington*

10 large meeting of all Embassy and other British Missions' Staffs, a periodical affair at which everyone reports on his job. I reported in three sentences what we had done at Dumbarton Oaks. . . . Further meeting of Steering Committee at 10.15 [p.m.]. Got home 12.15. Got through a certain amount, but the Russians are slow and sticky and rather stupid.

Sunday, 10 September *Washington*

An astonishing day. Lovely sunny weather with cool air. Started off at 10 in a car with Ed. S., Edward, H. H. Kung,† and Wellington Koo. Joined 15 other enormous limousines at Arlington Bridge and thence proceeded with police motor bicycle escort and sirens to drive through Virginia. Went through Bull Run and Warrenton and on to 'Sky Line Drive'. Lunched, under a boiling sun at 'Big Meadows' on top of the ridge. Lovely views. Lunch well done—iced cocktails, and then each of us had a cardboard box containing an excellent picnic meal. We then drove on to Charlottesville, Ed., in his showman manner, getting more and more excited, holding forth on the beauties of the scenery as if he not only owned it but had painted it. Effect spoilt by Edward's head dropping between his knees and he fast asleep. Reception at Charlottesville University, built by Jefferson. Very beautiful. We were accompanied everywhere by 8 photographers, and Ed's voice was constantly to be heard, 'Now boys, line up here: they want to take a picture.' Then on to Monticello which is

* At the beginning of the Conference, the Russians and Americans had proposed to settle questions of peace and security by simple majority. Cadogan said Britain preferred a ⅔ majority, so as to avoid the appearance of trampling on the rights of smaller states. Cf. F.R.U.S., 1944, I, p. 729.

† Chinese Minister of Finance, 1938–44; brother-in-law of Chiang Kai-shek.

charming but I couldn't see it, as we were made to march and counter march by cinema operators. Then on to Ash Lawn, Monroe's House, where I gave the photographers the slip, but there wasn't very much to see. However, we all got mint juleps. Then on to Madison Cemetery, when Ed. said 'We'll drive past Montpelier' (Madison's house now owned by a Miss Dupont). So the cavalcade of 16 limousines and photographers and police swept up the drive. Ed said 'Hell: there's Miss Dupont in the porch'. And so she was, saying goodbye to a guest (who must have been surprised). So we all got out (a mixed party of about 50 British, Americans and Chinese, military, naval and civilian), and we were taken through the house and garden. A rather lovely (and large) old house, with some nice pictures, including Ben Marshalls. Finally we got away and arrived at Ed's house 'Horseshoe' about 6.30. Charming house, with a negro quartet singing spirituals on the lawn. He rushed us round a part of the place, including his Hereford cattle and his thousand and one turkeys. Then into a dinner 'à la fourchette'. Astonishing scene. Admirable food (Virginia hams, turkey, unlimited butter &c.) which one collected and took to an armchair or a sofa. Flashlight photographers followed one—also the negro 'spirituals'. And meanwhile the motor-bike police strolled about the house smoking cigarettes. All very pleasant but unintelligible. Mrs S. very nice, and 3 nice boys. Got Edward to make a move,* and we got back to Washington about 11.30, having covered v. nearly 300 miles.

['What a day!' exclaimed Cadogan in recounting all this to his wife. 'And what extraordinary people—quite charming, and kind to an unimaginable degree, in some ways rather like ourselves but (as you see) so utterly different.']

Monday, 11 September *Washington*

Ed. arrived about 2.45 and I had a talk with him. We must get on, if we can, during this pause, with the Chinese. I promised to talk to Gromyko. . . . Dominions at 4, till 5.30. They were nearly as tiresome as ever, but I again kept my temper. 6. private showing at Paramount of the Conference Film. Odd to see oneself, and to hear oneself talking. My voice sounded to me like Eddie's! Called on Gromyko, who is completely sticky about our beginning work with the Chinese. Back soon after 7. and rang up Ed., giving him account of my conversation with G. Told him that, at this stage, I thought we'd better not risk giving Soviet cause for complaint. He agreed. P.M. arrived Quebec. If he wants me, I may hear tomorrow.

* At which point the quartet broke into a ditty called 'Good News'.

Tuesday, 12 September *Washington*

Telegram from P.M. saying 'Do please come and stay a night 13th or 14th'.... Told Ed. of P.M.'s message. He didn't seem very enthusiastic.... Ed. went down to State Dept. and got back about 3, saying Hull thought it a 'tragic mistake' for me to go to Quebec. (Of course, he doesn't want to go himself.) His arguments were that Q. was 'ostensibly' a military meeting: it would be known I was there, and that would seem to inject into it diplomatic and political questions. Also, it would look as if President and P.M. were butting into D[umbarton] O[aks] against the Russians. I could do no more, or less, than put these considerations in a telegram to P.M., which Ed. agreed, adding that if P.M. didn't think these arguments decisive, he must talk to Pres.

Soon after 3, Steering-cum-Formulation Committee, till 5. We did something. But Gromyko is still awaiting word from Moscow on the main question.

By the way, this morning he sprung on us that his Govt. wouldn't have the Chinese associated with what we do here! Well, that's more Ed's headache than mine (as I told him).

Wednesday, 13 September *Washington*

Telegram from P.M., as I expected, v. indignant at Hull trying to stop me going to Q. Says A. starts today, which destroys at least one of Hull's arguments. Says I needn't do anything for 24 hrs. Says also that Pres. has invited Hull to Q. 10.30 Steering Committee. Ed asked me if I'd anything further from P.M. Told him. He said Hull had received no invitation so far. At meeting, Gromyko informed us his Government's final answer on voting question was definitely 'No'. So we all looked blue and discussed possible procedure, without finding any solution.... Had talk with Americans about the situation. Decided to call Formulation Committee and authorize our people to sound Sobolev on a *possible* compromise. Committee met about 5. I got back and saw Dominions at 5.30. Told them the truth, under seal of secrecy.... I go at noon tomorrow to Quebec unless there is anything definite to stop me. I *must* go to see A. in the present circumstances. Rang up Ed. and explained. He couldn't object. G.J. said Sobolev had shown some signs of being interested in our tentative compromise, but I doubt whether Kremlin will!

[Cadogan felt that to attempt the construction of a neat system, world-wide in its operation, was to chase a will o' the wisp. It was hardly likely, whatever the system might lay down, that two of the Great Powers would make war on the third. The Great Powers, and others, might well combine against a resurgence of German or Japanese aggression; they might equally devise a workable system to prevent smaller powers from making war upon each other. Beyond that point, he remained convinced that unless Russia, the U.S.A. and the Commonwealth could agree, no effective United Nations could be established.

The 'compromise' suggested that a Great Power should forgo the right to block investigation by the Security Council, or the formulation of a recommended settlement. A Permanent Member would, on the other hand, be able to veto a determination by the Council that a threat to security existed, or enforcement of the Council's decision.[11] Cadogan went to Quebec.]

Thursday, 14 September *Quebec*

Unpacked, and went round to Citadel. P.M. driving round the town in an open car (which he enjoys). . . . A. arrived about 6. Went and talked to him, and we both went to Citadel and had a chat with Pres. and P.M. Both seeming well, I thought. . . . dinner at Citadel at 8.30. Pres., P.M., A., Mackenzie King, Cherwell, Morgenthau* and self. Quite pleasant. But Pres. produced a film after, a v. bad one. A. (after 22 hrs. flying) slipped away before it. I felt bound to stay, and it went on till midnight!

Friday, 15 September *Quebec*

Citadel at 12. P.M., Pres., A., and at intervals Morgenthau and Cherwell, talked—or rambled—on a variety of things. It's quite impossible to do business this way. Stayed there for lunch—P.M., Clemmie, Pres., A. and Dick Law. Towards end of lunch, got on to Dumbarton Oaks. Both Pres. and P.M. rambled hopelessly. I tried to pin them down to the point, but they always wandered away. Lunch went on till 4. I came back to Hotel and had tea with Alan Brooke. Drafted a telegram to Washington about Dumbarton Oaks and gave it to A. to show to P.M. That may elicit some definite opinion. Also some notes of other subjects which they touched on this morning. A. went to dine at Citadel. Thank goodness I didn't, as there was to be a showing of the 'Wilson' film, which lasts 2 hours and 40 minutes; so they won't even *begin* talking much before 1 a.m.!

[Cadogan's visit to Quebec raised a serious question of American politics. A little while before, Stettinius had told the President, in Hull's presence, that the constant attendance of Harriman and Hopkins at international conferences had caused deep resentment in the State Department.

* H. J. Morgenthau, jr., U.S. Secretary of the Treasury, 1934–45.

Roosevelt, according to Stettinius's account, warmly agreed, admitted his error and promised that it should not recur. 'Quebec is to be entirely military; if any other subjects come up I shall call Cordell right away.' Within a few days Hull learned that not only Eden and Cadogan but also Morgenthau would be there. 'In Christ's name', exclaimed the furious Hull to Stettinius, 'what has happened to the man?'

The British Government had heard, before this meeting, of several plans designed to control German heavy industry. On 12 September, Hopkins suggested that it might be better to deprive Germany of her steel industry than to place the Ruhr under an international regime. Cadogan was not consulted on this subject during his brief stay in Quebec. He had the impression that the purpose was to regulate, rather than destroy, Germany's heavy industry, though he heard some talk of making the Germans live at what the President called a pastoral level. In deciding to support the 'Morgenthau plan', Churchill seems to have been swayed by economic arguments, in particular by the belief that British export trade would profit heavily, and by the prospect of disarming Germany efficiently.

Eden, whom the Prime Minister had not consulted before initialling, pointed out the objections. Hull, angry at Morgenthau's intervention, did likewise. It is still doubtful whether Roosevelt understood what he was initialling. Anyhow, the plan was stillborn.[12]]

Saturday, 16 September *Washington*

Found A. had got P.M. to pass my telegram and it had been sent off. . . . Back at [Washington] Embassy before 5 . . . Ed. turned up at 5.30. Told him of the little direction I'd got at Quebec: (1) Our Govt. don't support my compromise, and I must tell Gromyko that. (2) President's idea was to send out invitation to Conference, with the agreed document, leaving the disputed chapter blank. I always thought this was wrong, and he (and, I think, Hull) would prefer to say simply that we had agreed on a lot, but that some points were left over for further consideration. This is the best of a bad job. . . . 9.20 went to see Gromyko. Told him my Govt. didn't endorse my compromise. Had some discussion on procedure, and gathered he would come along on Ed's line.

Sunday, 17 September *Washington*

Ed. wanted meeting of Steering Committee at 4. I agreed. We met, and by 7 had agreed on (a) a communiqué for closing our talks (if possible on Tues.) and (b) a longer statement covering the document as so far agreed, to be issued some time after we have finished with Chinese. . . . Think we *may* finish with Russians Wed. and with Chinese Saturday, and then get away. All the American dreams of a United National Conference at the end of Oct. have melted.

Monday, 18 September *Washington*

Went to . . . cocktail party. A million people in a small, hot room, and a noise in which one couldn't hear oneself scream. A foretaste of Hell. . . . Heard Ed had been looking for me. Dashed up to Dumbarton Oaks, where he was lunching with Gromyko. He, of course, very fussed at possible result of our failure. He ought to have thought of that before! Suggested calling a Conference to settle the matter (I gathered this was old Hull's idea). I said that was quite out of the question.

Tuesday, 19 September *Washington*

Made a little progress with the text (which of course, doesn't matter now). But I discovered from Gromyko that his Government (a) would not close down our talks till they had agreed the ultimate communiqué and the text of the document, and (b) would not allow Chinese talks to begin, in any form, until we have closed down Soviet talks. This hopeless. I might be here for 10 weeks. Told Edward that, with his approval, I should telegraph to London tomorrow proposing I should come home, leaving Gladwyn in charge under him. He agreed.

Wednesday, 20 September *Washington*

Steering Committee at 4. Sat till nearly 7. Practically finished the document, leaving the big outstanding point unsettled. I had told Falla* to ring up London and ask when we should get a reply to our messages of the 17th. They said they thought a reply unnecessary in view of a telegram from Quebec (of which they gave the number). I hadn't got it, and had never seen it. Told Quebec to send it down. It arrived just as I was leaving the Oaks. It was a message from P.M. to A. reporting (probably incorrectly) what President had said to him (probably also incorrect) about future procedure. What a way of doing business! It had been sent off on the 18th, from Hyde Park [the President's house], and had not been repeated to me! So I came back and drafted a telegram trying to straighten things out, and asking for urgent instructions. I also sent another telegram saying I was wasting my time here and asking leave to come home next Tues. at latest.

Saturday, 23 September *Washington*

9.30–10.15 listened to F.D.R.'s speech. Very good electioneering stuff. It made Mrs. X. and Mrs. Y. *mad*—they itched all over. After

* P. S. Falla, then serving in F.O.; member of Cadogan's staff in New York, 1946–9.

that, talk went on much too long—till 5 mins. to 12. I wish people knew when they had, or should have had, enough of a bad thing.

Wednesday, 27 September *Washington*

10.30 meeting of Steering Committee. Gromyko made a few unimportant concessions and we agreed (surprisingly) on future procedure . . . 5.30 Dominions meetings (the last, I hope! And I must say they were very nice in their acknowledgement of what I had done for them.)

Thursday, 28 September *Washington*

10.30 saw British Press and spoke quite frankly to them. Hope they won't give me away! 11.30 Delegation meeting. 12 Left for White House to see President. Pa Watson* met me and explained I should see him 'in his room upstairs' and hoped I wouldn't say anything about it. The Pres. had slight throat trouble, due to speaking (he's only made one speech in the last 10 days), but it would be bad if anything got out about it. So I was eventually hoisted up in a lift to the 2nd Floor and found the Pres. in bed. The temperature in the room was about 90 and he was perspiring and not looking too well. But he seemed fairly cheerful. I said I'd listened with great pleasure to his speech and he said he'd enjoyed making it. Then we talked a bit about Dumbarton Oaks results. I said altho' we'd agreed 90%, there was a nasty snag in the remaining 10%. I *think* he understands this. He talked of the necessity of a top-level meeting to iron it out. Said Joe had agreed that a meeting was necessary. He (F.D.R.) proposes the Hague, or Stockholm or Scotland—in November. A propos of his speech, he said 'Fala' had received about 50 telegrams and letters!† As I left, I told him I'd been very well brought up and that I'd learnt not even to look at American elections, but that, as we were alone together, within 4 walls, I'd wish him all success. I don't think he's well and a lot turns on his health. . . .

Final meeting at the Oaks at 3.30. Mere formality, but I put on a little show for Ed., thanking him and praising him for his conduct in the Chair.

Friday, 29 September *Washington*

Inaugural meeting with the Chinese at 3. Drove there with

* The President's aide.

† Fala, the President's dog, was alleged to have been fetched from the Aleutians by a destroyer, at the President's order and the public expense. In one of his campaign speeches, Roosevelt said that although his family were accustomed to libellous attack, the dog resented it.

Edward. Read my usual little speech (written mostly by Prof. [C. K.] Webster). About an hour of photography after.

[In deference to the self-respect of the Chinese, it was thought necessary that the arrangements for the opening of talks with them should be as impressive as those of six weeks before. Halifax, who was about to take over the leadership of the British delegation, tried to impress on Cadogan afterwards how greatly the practice of sending a negotiator from home for each special occasion diminished the influence of the permanent representatives. Cadogan's answer is not recorded.[13]]

[*Sunday, 1 October*] *Friday, 29 September (cont.)* *London*

Arrived Victoria 3.50. T. there, looking well. Drove home, and had a tremendous gossip about everything, and unpacked my own things and the 'loot'. She seems well and cheerful. I have been a grandfather for about a week, or more!* Rather tired, but feel very well, and I've had a grand time. I hope T. has had some rest.

[Cadogan's performance at Dumbarton Oaks won him golden opinions in the United States, and laid the foundations for his work as the first permanent head of the British delegation at the U.N. He showed himself clear in argument, quick to grasp the points, precise in language; with all his detailed knowledge of the League's procedures, strengths and failures, a knowledge which no other delegate at the Conference began to rival, he spoke with exceptional authority. Stettinius, who formed a deep respect for his abilities, used to call Cadogan 'one of the strong men of Dumbarton Oaks'. 'His Majesty's Government', Churchill told Parliament, 'could have had no abler representative than Sir Alexander Cadogan and there is no doubt that a most valuable task has been discharged.'

The crucial question of the veto had to be adjourned to a meeting of the three heads of Government, and the draft Charter was understood not to be binding on governments. The memorandum which Cadogan circulated to the Armistice and Post-War Committee in November judged that the new organisation would not attract the full support of all states if a single power could frustrate its purposes by use of the veto. He still thought that his rejected compromise of September—essentially that permanent members should not possess a veto in the earlier stages of a dispute—would be the best solution. Meanwhile Churchill had inclined to the Russian view. It is characteristic of Cadogan that the diary does not indicate the nature of his compromise, which, when adopted by Roosevelt, became the agreed solution.[14]]

* Of Lavinia, daughter of Patricia and Gerald Coke.

Monday, 2 October

No great arrears. P.M. and A. off to Moscow on Sat. . . . A. arrived soon after 4 and I had discussion with him about various things. He asked whether I would come to Moscow. I said it would be as much a waste of my time as was Tehran. If you have an Ambassador there, you must use him, and it's no good my going. He agreed. Cabinet 5.30. Everything seems to be in pretty good shape. Only thing is that the Germans are ahead of us in jet-propelled fighters, But I hope they're too late.

[That night the resistance in Warsaw ceased. One of the last broadcasts, heard in London, said:

> 'We were treated worse than Hitler's satellites, worse than Italy, Roumania, Finland. May God, Who is just, pass judgment on the terrible injustice suffered by the Polish nation, and may He punish accordingly all those who are guilty. . . . Those who have died have conquered, and those who live on will fight on, will conquer and again bear witness that Poland lives when the Poles live.']

Tuesday, 3 October

Had hurried interview with A. about Dumbarton Oaks. He knows nothing about it, and it is most unsatisfactory that one can only occasionally sandwich in 5 mins' conversation with one's S. of S. about foreign affairs in between his other multifarious duties. We *must* get the A.P.W. Committee (and the Cabinet) to reach a decision this week about procedure. A. objected to the draft paper for the Committee, so I had to re-write it. . . . Got A. to agree draft for A.P.W. Committee. . . . tried to write suggestions as to what we *are* going to do about the future of the World. I *don't* like a nice, complete, logical 'Charter' which won't mean what it says. But I shall have some trouble with the Committee. Much better frankly say that for e.g. 5 years the 3 powers must run the world. They are the only people who *can*. Masses of correspondence and private business awaiting me.

Thursday, 5 October

3 p.m. A.P.W. Committee. Got them to recommend publication of Dumbarton Oaks scheme on Monday. They none of them knew what it was all about. This recommendation should be approved by Cabinet, or at least P.M., and as there probably won't be a Cabinet tomorrow, drafted minute from A. to P.M. urging publication. Americans are hot on it, and Winant rang me up. Discussion with X about the American 'directive' to Eisenhower about control of Germany. X probably right, but he's a hard-baked bureaucrat, quite

unimaginative and very obstinate. We have several like that. Only cure is to send them abroad to negotiate with other people who happen to hold diametrically opposite views, equally strongly. . . . Glad to see exchange of telegrams between Pres. and P.M. agreeing that they shouldn't discuss Dumbarton Oaks at Moscow. Thank heaven! None of them know anything about it, and they'd make a most *frightful* mess. Chinese have apparently submitted at Dumbarton Oaks, and are going to make no trouble.*

Friday, 6 October

12 Cabinet at H. of C. I had to sit through 1½ hrs.' discussion of Town and Country Planning! (and that takes up the whole of A's time so that we don't, for practical purposes, have a Foreign Sec. at all!) At 1.30 got Cabinet to agree to publication of Dumbarton Oaks document on Mon., subject to agreement with Soviet Government on para. 4 of the covering communiqué. We're trying to agree this with Moscow, who maintain discreet silence. . . . Caught A. at about 7., to finish off various things. He is leaving at 9.15 tomorrow for Bristol, to make a speech, and thereafter for Moscow. Complete confusion. He *can't* go on doubling these parts; F.O. can't work like this, and he agrees. But I don't know what's to be done about it.

[Churchill had told Roosevelt of his anxiety for another meeting between themselves and Stalin. At Dumbarton Oaks, an impasse had been reached on voting procedure, and the Russian claim to sixteen seats in the Assembly (one for each constituent Republic) had been referred to the heads of Government. No doubt it was Poland's needs, however, that the Prime Minister had chiefly in mind. When Roosevelt said he could do nothing about a meeting until after the Presidential Election, Churchill commented privately, with a sniff, that the Red Army would not await the result of the election. He and Eden therefore set off for Moscow, perhaps hoping to derive some extra purchase in their talks from the presence of a great Allied army on the mainland of Europe. The diversion of troops from Italy to the landings in the South of France, the tenacity of the German defence and the particularly unfavourable weather had caused the Italian campaign to bog down. There was now no serious prospect of an early Allied penetration from Italy into Austria and south-eastern Europe. 'Stalin', said Churchill gloomily, a few days before setting off for Moscow, 'will get what he wants. The Americans have seen to that. They haven't given Alex a dog's chance. He will do his best, but the cream of his army has been skimmed off.'

* The Chinese agreed to the publication, without modification, of the agreed proposals, and withdrew several supplementary proposals intended to define aggression and extend the jurisdiction of the International Court.

Eden began the Moscow talks by reproaching Molotov severely for the Russians' behaviour in Greece. Molotov had then to confess that Tito, who had been living under British protection on Vis, had been to Moscow. All the blame for this secrecy and deception, it appeared, lay with Tito; 'he was a peasant and did not understand anything about politics'. For the moment, and for war purposes only, it was agreed that Russia should have the dominant interest in Roumania and Bulgaria, Britain in Greece, and Russia and the Allies a half-share apiece in the affairs of Yugoslavia and Hungary.

On the issue of Poland little advance could be made. Eden represented to Churchill that this was a first-class issue, which might spoil Anglo-Russian relations. 'If people feel that Russia is putting in puppets and that everybody who doesn't agree with her is an enemy of Poland, they will be uneasy. Poland must be allowed to settle her own affairs.' Perhaps because he could hardly bear to contemplate the dissolution of the Grand Alliance, Churchill showed himself none too tender towards Polish claims. Mikolajczyk, Romer and Grabski were summoned from London on pain of being abandoned by the British. Thereupon Churchill pressed on Mikolajczyk a 'friendly discussion' with the Lublin Committee, who were palpably mere tools of Russia, and Russian annexation of all the lands east of the Curzon Line, including Lwow. He threatened that unless this frontier were accepted, Britain would wash her hands of the London Poles. 'Unless you accept the frontier you're out of business for ever!' he cried. 'The Russians will sweep through your country and your people will be liquidated. You're on the verge of annihilation. We'll become sick and tired of you if you continue arguing.' For some time Churchill berated Mikolajczyk and excoriated Polish blindness, stubbornness and folly. Mikolajczyk did not cringe. He said that he could not, without forfeiting much of his support, accept the Curzon Line publicly as a frontier, though he would take it as a line of demarcation for the time being. He saw Stalin, who seemed willing to agree to equal representation for the London and Lublin Poles in a new Government, and then returned to London.[15]]

Friday, 13 October

Nothing much from Moscow. We have scored something in regard to Bulgarian armistice and seem to be reaching some understanding in regard to Balkans generally. But nothing about Poland.

Sunday, 15 October

Saw some 'Planners' reports from which it seems unlikely that we can make our real thrust before end of Dec. Think the war will go on till April or May. I don't see how it ends.

Monday, 16 October

Not v. much news from Moscow, except that P.M. and A. have

nearly produced a Polish-Russian agreement, which sticks only over Lwow. Cabinet 5.30. Not v. much news. Certainly nothing bad, but we are in the middle of a pause, which barring unforeseen events, will last some months.

Thursday, 19 October

Raczynski at 11, mainly about the threatened mass murders at Oswiecim.* He asked about Moscow conversations, and I gave him vague outline, telling him Mikolajczyk would be back here 21st. Afterwards telegram from Moscow saying M. didn't want this known by Poles or anyone else. They ought to have thought of this before! However, I discovered Edward [Raczynski] had *not* told anyone, and wasn't going to! . . . Masses of telegrams from Moscow. Polish question *not* settled, but M. still seems to have hopes. Wild telegrams from A. telling me to damp down British, *and* Polish, Press! Went to see Brendan at 6.15 at H. of C. I think I impressed him with need for doing his damnedest.

Friday, 20 October

Message from Pres. to P.M. refusing to recognise de Gaulle as Provisional Govt.† I let myself go in a personal telegram to A., suggesting P.M. should tell Pres. that, as this is a vital British interest, we must take our own decision and tell Pres. that *we are* going to recognise, within a week. Poor A. won't dare put this to P.M.‡ I believe that, if he did so, Pres. would meekly follow. With the election imminent, he *can't* afford to be left out on a limb on this question. But of course P.M. would say that would disturb his relations with Pres. But it's nothing compared with various things the Pres. has done to *us*. However, there it is: I'm afraid it's useless, but I couldn't contain myself.

Saturday, 21 October

Massigli 11.30.§ Told him—perhaps indiscreetly—the true story of 'recognition'. By the way, woken up by Resident Clerk this morning to say that Caffery,|| in Paris, has been instructed by *State Dept.*

* More than 12,000 Poles were deported from Warsaw by the Germans to the death camp at Oswiecim. Mass executions began on 7 October. A rising of the prisoners had been brutally suppressed.

† The President preferred to wait, or so he said, until the French had set up a 'zone of the interior' and enlarged the Consultative Assembly. He would not be satisfied with a statement of intent by de Gaulle.

‡ In fact Eden had several times urged recognition. See, for example, *The Reckoning*, p. 471.

§ Recently appointed French Ambassador.

|| Jefferson Caffery, U.S. Ambassador in Paris, 1944–9.

to say U.S. Govt. are 'prepared' to recognise. God help us! Is this simple inefficiency and crossing of wires or are the U.S. trying to do us down? Anyhow, I thought Massigli had better know the truth. Aghnides 12.15, on Dumbarton Oaks. Injected into him the stuff I gave to van Kleffens and Bruce—do we want a polished, streamlined 'Charter' that doesn't mean what it says? 12.45 Cartier about starving Belgium. He gets quite worked up, but *I* can't feed Belgium. But I have stirred up Dept. to stick pins into SHAEF. It's going to be their headache if they have disorders and confusion in Belgium. . . . Telegram showing that [General] George Marshall has raised question of throwing in everything this year (including V.T. fuze—whatever that may be*) in hope of finishing. But doesn't it depend on Antwerp? P.M. due back tomorrow afternoon. Nothing more about recognition of French. Dined at home. News good all round, but I don't see signs of a decision *yet*.

Sunday, 22 October

Message this morning from U.S. Embassy that their Embassy in Paris has been instructed to 'recognise' tomorrow afternoon. So at once telegraphed to Duff to do the same! The ways of these Americans are too odd! I don't know whether this is only the State Dept.—not what the Pres. thinks. But I don't care: we're not going to be left out on a limb in this show. Telegram from A. saying I ought to explain to Massigli what had happened. I have replied that I had already done that yesterday morning! Lunch at home. Back at F.O. at 3.30 and sent minute down to meet P.M. at aerodrome telling him what had happened about recognition and what I had done. Home about 6. 6.30 P.M. rang up from Chequers. He seemed quite happy about it, but said that Russians would be annoyed. I said very likely but *we* had kept them informed of the whole comedy, and they would have seen it was not *our* fault! He seemed quite cheerful and said he was very well.

Monday, 23 October

P.M. on phone again at 9.30. He has just received a message from Pres. saying 'I will communicate with you again (about recognition of French Provisional Govt.) when Eisenhower announces establishment of interior zone, probably in two or three days' time.' But it's been *done*!! The man is out of touch. P.M. said it would be a good thing to put off for a day or two. I said might be, but present situation was that U.S. Embassy in Paris had their instructions, which they

* Proximity fuzes, which exploded the shell as it passed by the target or approached the ground.

would carry out. Obviously we could only clear it up at the other end, so I rang Winant, who promised to telephone. Unfortunately, it was then 5 a.m. in Washington. We plainly can't stop Duff and let the Americans get in ahead of us. No further word from Winant by lunch time, so I sent minute over to P.M., to catch him on his arrival, explaining situation. I'd arranged to flash a message to Paris after lunch if that was necessary. 3.30 Winant rang up to say, in American, 'Cleared everything: Schedule holding.' Passed this on to No. 10 and things took their course and we have *all*, thank God, Americans, British and Russians, recognised de Gaulle. At *last!* What a fuss about nothing! Due to that spiteful old great-aunt Leahy.* Hope he's feeling pretty sick! . . . 5.30 Cabinet. P.M. looks well and seems in good form. He didn't tell them much about his Moscow trip!

Wednesday, 25 October

4 Carcano.† These interviews are v. embarrassing. I can't say it's all the fault of that old lunatic Hull. I said anyhow it was no use discussing anything till after the American election. I suppose he'll telegraph that home and the Americans will read it and I shall be put on the spot!

Thursday, 26 October

P.M. rang up protesting against notes given him about France for his statement tomorrow. They certainly were silly. I hadn't seen them. Produced fresh version. Telegram from Duff saying French are going to invite P.M. and A. to Paris. Massigli hinted this yesterday and made personal suggestion of November 11. . . . 3 meeting with P.M. and the Poles. He pressing them to hurry on and go back to Moscow. Plain enough that Mik. has got nowhere—yet. News came of death of Archbishop of Canterbury. P.M. delighted—he said 'There's a total abstainer died of gout. How right we all are!'

Friday, 27 October

10.15 summoned to P.M.'s bedside, and went through his speech with him. He due to make it at 11, and didn't upheave himself out of bed till 10.40.

Saturday, 28 October

P.M. enquiring whether Poles have gone back to Moscow. I

* Admiral William D. Leahy, U.S. Ambassador to Vichy, 1940–2; Chief of Staff to President and member of Joint Chiefs of Staff, 1942–9.

† Argentine Ambassador.

reminded him they promised to report to him first—this weekend or at latest early next week. Of course that dear Mikolajczyk is havering and wobbling. I'm afraid he's weak as water. Meanwhile Raczynski was sent to talk to Bobbety yesterday (why?!) and Retinger to talk to A. Sinclair today. These manœuvres are as useless as they are silly. When will Poles learn *any* sense? Luckily both approaches were suitably repulsed. They're incurable idiots, and Poland will founder.

Monday, 30 October

11 Parade of Home Guards on Horse Guards Parade. Rather cold and draughty. Fine (43°) but cold Easterly breeze. John Anderson addressed the Parade. Not v. inspiring. In the middle I heard him suddenly saying to the rather motley and dilapidated ranks: 'We may be thankful that you were never called upon to go into action'! Sense of humour not John's strong suit! . . . Cabinet at 5.30. Had to tell P.M. of ridiculous Soviet note demanding that 'emigré' Polish Govt. should be replaced by Polish [Lublin] Committee on European Inland Transport Conference. He gave lines (rather violent) on which reply should be drafted. Got away about 7 and made draft for him. . . .*

Planners now give earliest date for defeat of Germany as Jan. 31—latest May 15. All depends on Antwerp—where we're doing fairly well. Last week 30 rockets—13 in London area—but only about 30 people killed. A good bang during Cabinet. Morrison told me the bang on Sat. evening was a rocket exploding *in the air* over Camberwell. Did practically no damage.

Tuesday, 31 October

11.30 Romer and Raczynski. Poles have done *nothing*—simply havering. Now put three questions to us. I said I'd try to get answers, which of course I couldn't give. But I must say delay was dangerous. Told them of Soviet demand for representation of Polish Committee on European Inland Transport Conference.

Wednesday, 1 November

No word from P.M. about my interview with Romer, so rang up Rowan and found they hadn't made him read it! Message at 12.45 to say he'd have a Cabinet on it this evening and meanwhile I was to stop Poles taking any irrevocable decision. This was easy, as I was

* Gousev was told that the British Government regarded this request, made while Churchill and Stalin were trying to compose differences between the Committee and the Government, as extraordinary.

lunching at Polish Embassy, and told Edward to hold them in check. Their Cabinet, as a matter of fact, put off till tomorrow. . . . Cabinet at 5.30. Decided to tell Poles (1) we would advocate full compensation in West even if Americans ran out (2) we would advocate Oder line (3) we would give a joint Anglo-Soviet guarantee of Polish independence and integrity.* Left Cabinet at 7 and did a draft which I sent over to P.M.

Thursday, 2 November

Went to P.M.'s bedside at 10.30. He had approved my draft reply to Romer's questions. I got it off to him before noon. P.M. said he wanted to see Mik. at 10 p.m. with all his Cabinet. I suggested he'd *offer* to Mik. to bring his colleagues *if* he wanted. P.M. agreed. Then spoke about telegram from Maclean reporting Tito-Subasic agreement. P.M. annoyed because it provided for Regents, which he didn't like. I pointed out that it acknowledged the Monarchy pending the plebiscite, and he agreed this was a good feature. Told me to bring the news to King Peter.† 2.30 Saw King Peter at Claridges. He said Subasic had no authority from him to sign an agreement. It is *not* signed—*yet*. 5 meeting with O.S. and others about set-up in Italy. I never understand these esoteric questions. Dined at home, washed up and at Annexe at 10. Mik., Romer and Edward. No others! Poles have done *nothing*. They didn't even have a Cabinet today. They really might have. We asked quick enough. P.M. knocked them about badly—and rightly. Finally gave them 48 hrs in which to say 'Yes' or 'No'. Think that's right. Told P.M. I was going away tomorrow.

[This meeting with the Poles lasted two hours. Churchill again demanded that Mikolajczyk fly back promptly to Moscow. 'Like a big sheep-dog, watch dog rather,' wrote Raczynski, 'he barked imperiously at his Polish flock, who were spared neither warning bites nor shafts of sarcasm.' After angry exchanges between Churchill and Mikolajczyk, there followed a confused discussion about the letter which Cadogan had just sent to the Poles. 'As to the joint guarantee, I admit that in the event of aggression by Russia on Poland, the British guarantee does not come into play', Cadogan said. 'But in that case, a Soviet aggression would be . . . a clear

* If possible with the U.S.A., and lasting until the establishment of the World Organisation.

† Churchill had been unfavourably impressed by Tito at a meeting in August, minuting to Eden that a great responsibility would rest on Britain at the end of the war, when all the arms in Yugoslavia would be in Tito's hands and might be used to subjugate the country. Pierson Dixon, who was present, records: 'It became apparent that Tito had swallowed the Ban, who, whenever he was asked for his opinion, merely reiterated or embroidered Tito's views.' Dixon, p. 103.

violation of international obligations by Russia. That alone is already some security.' 'How can you wait helplessly' demanded Churchill, 'as though you were paralysed? You are playing delaying tactics by posing still other new questions to us. . . . I have had enough of that and I withdraw my promises.' Cadogan's diary shows that he thought this rough treatment right; the Polish record indicates plainly that he did his best to smooth down acerbities and to give the Polish Cabinet time to reconsider. Mikolajczyk, however, had already found much difficulty with his colleagues. The Polish Cabinet decided on 3 November that it could not 'at present' accept the conditions demanded in Moscow.[16]]

Friday, 3 November

At F.O. by 10. P.M. had rung me up at 12.30 a.m. to say that before I went on my 'holiday' he wanted a record of last night. He also read me a further telegram, just in, from Maclean, showing that Tito and Subasic seem to have signed something. He told me to see King P. again. Began morning by dictating record of last night. . . . 12 King P. He sensible: said Subasic seemed to have done 'fairly well'. I encouraged him in this belief. . . . This morning, Edward rang up to say their Cabinet were meeting today and he thought they would reach a decision (!). He wanted to come round this afternoon to discuss with me the draft of what they decided. I sent back message to say I shouldn't be here. He must see O. Harvey who, after all, was in Moscow, and knows all about it. Briefed O.H. and left it in his hands. Pray Heaven I shan't be disturbed. I want 48 hrs. rest and others can do as well as I can on this job.

Monday, 6 November

3.15 talk with A. and Poles. Latter have got nowhere. . . . 5.30 Cabinet. News of attack on Moyne* had, I think, upset P.M. Anyhow, he in awful mood. Early in proceedings I went out to telephone for 5 min. When I came back, P.M. was saying to Amery 'Have you recovered your temper, or would you like to withdraw? I'm not going to sit here and be insulted by you'! Amery kept his temper and replied moderately. But he *can't* stay in Cabinet without an apology from P.M. Whole session stormy. We finally discussed Greece. Cherwell was tiresome and A. lost his temper with him. Max had a row with Anderson. However, finally agreement was reached on what to do about that. Cabinet adjourned at 8.10. The remaining 5 or 6 items weren't *touched.*

[The American Presidential election took place on 7 November. Roosevelt was re-elected as President of the United States for a fourth term of office.]

* Lord Moyne, Minister-Resident in the Middle East, was assassinated by Jewish terrorists in Cairo on 5 November.

Saturday, 11 November *Paris*

Cold and grey at first, but calm. Left Embassy with Diana* and drove to Tribune in Champs Elysées. 10.50 P.M. was driven past us with de G.—P.M. waving wildly. Tremendous reception. He laid wreath at Arc de Triomphe and then walked back in procession to our Tribune. He, de G., A. and Bidault† in front row: I just behind. Procession, which lasted a full hour, v. good. Pipers and Guards made a good effect, and the mounted Garde Républicaine in full uniform on very good horses. Enormous, enthusiastic and good-humoured crowd who, most of the time, chanted Chur-chill! In the middle, de G. turned round to me and said, sardonically, 'Vous voyez ce pays en révolution'. I had never said so—that was Roosevelt at Quebec! However de G. seemed—why, I don't know—to go out of his way to be v. gracious to me! Then moved off in procession to Clemenceau monument where P.M. deposited a wreath. (I drove with Chauvel,‡ who is more inaudible than Massigli—otherwise quite nice.) On to the Invalides, to Foch's tomb. The Veuve Foch there. We gazed dutifully at Napoleon's tomb. Lunch at Ministère de la Guerre. . . . De G. and P.M. spoke.

Talk after. De. G., Bidault, P.M., A. and myself. Went quite well, but decisions were avoided! Main topic rearmament of French army. . . . Left with Duff at 8.15 for dinner with de G. at his villa in Neuilly. Sat between Beatrice [Eden] and Mdlle. de G. After dinner de G. caught me and we sat and talked for about ¾hr. while the rest of the party went into a huddle at the other end of the room. De G. very reasonable. We talked about Syria, without getting down to the more contentious details, and about the 'Western European Bloc' on which he is *not* forthcoming owing (1) as he alleges, to Soviet suspicion (I told him why I thought this nonsense) and (2) to the fact that France would negotiate at a disadvantage while she was militarily weak. I said that any plan we might have was based on the assumption of a *strong* France.

[The Prime Minister discovered with unalloyed pleasure that his suite contained a golden bath, intended for the use of Goering; still better, the Foreign Secretary had only a bath of silver. In the discussions, almost every subject at issue was touched upon, but in a pleasant way. The most difficult question, taken up by Eden and Bidault on 12 November,

* Lady Diana Cooper, wife of the British Ambassador.

† Georges Bidault, Minister for Foreign Affairs in the Provisional Governments of 1944 and 1945.

‡ Jean Chauvel, Sec.-Gen. of the Ministry of Foreign Affairs 1945; French representative on the Security Council, 1949.

remained that of the Levant states. France had rejected the request of Syria and the Lebanon that she should relinquish control of the security police. Both states were refusing to make treaties which would give France special privileges.[17]]

Sunday, 12 November *Paris*

Lovely day. Wanted to walk to Quai, where had appointment at 10.30. But typists so slow in producing record of yesterday's conversation that I had to drive there. . . . Then talk between A., self, Duff, Bidault, Massigli, Chauvel. Nothing v. difficult, except Syria. Went on till 12.30. Sat in one of the rooms of the suite, reading telegrams while screams, in a crescendo of rage, of 'Sawyers'* from the P.M. echoed through the building. Bidault gave lunch at Quai . . . . Corbin there, and Jean Monnet, and had talk after with both. Went on with A. to have talk with de G. and Chauvel. Mostly about zones —and Tangier. 5.30 Hotel de Ville. Quite an impressive ceremony. Staircase lined with Garde Républicaine. P.M. given the 'Freedom' and replied in an ex tempore speech of about ¼ hr.—in *French!* Don't know what it conveyed to the natives, but it was very forceful, and tearful, with a lot of table-thumping! 6–7.30 a business talk with Chauvel at the Quai in a *freezing* room. The offices have got *no* heating! . . . Back at Embassy 7.30. Large cocktail party dominated by Noel Coward and Royal Artillery Band. 8.15 Dinner at Embassy. Sat between Bidault and Bogomolov.† While the table was being cleared and the rest had withdrawn, had long and violent and most friendly talk with B[idault] about Levant. Didn't move him an inch.

Monday, 13 November *Paris*

An Air officer, who said he was glad to meet me again—he had seen me at Wei-hai-wei—and observed it was curious that the Ambassador who 'ordered' the 'Eagle' to bomb the Chinese pirates should meet again the man who dropped the bombs! After lunch drove out to the Buc aerodrome, idea being that I should do a flight in a reconnaissance plane to see the bomb-damage. There found a charming and distinguished young R.A.F. pilot. . . . He tried to start up a 'Vigilant', but after winding at it for twenty min. (damned cold waiting), he gave it up and we took a 'Proctor', which was parked on the field—a tiny single-engined machine. Got it off and we flew to Trappes marshalling yard. An extraordinary sight. All the tracks blown up and locomotives flung about like children's toys.

* Mr Churchill's valet.

† Now Russian Ambassador to France.

Then along the Seine for a bit, and the Oise, to Pontoise and Creil. Occasionally my pilot would say 'Look isn't that beautiful?' and we would come down and circle round the twisted girders that were all that remained of a bridge. I don't think I saw a whole one, and I must have seen 20 destroyed. At Creil we saw the Flying Bomb site—a scene of devastation.

Tuesday, 14 November *Paris*

Went off about 11 to Villacoublay to find de Guingand,* who was going to fly me up to Brussels. Villacoublay an enormous aerodrome, and we couldn't find the plane. C. Peake was with me and we eventually found a 'Control Tower', which consisted of a wet and soggy tent. After putting through 15 telephone calls, C.P. eventually discovered that the plane was only about 400 yards away! Drove there through the mud and found de G[uingand] waiting. Got off about 11.55—v. comfortable plane—and arrived at 1. Drove to de G's villa and lunched there. After, his A.D.C. (American) Culver took me off to see Major Towle who is preparing the case against German atrocities in Belgium. He lectured me on what they had done at Breendonk. We then drove there (about ½ an hour). Cold and drizzly. We arrived at this awful place, and after waiting a bit for a Belgian guide with keys, went over the whole thing. *Everyone* ought to see it and know how the Germans behaved (which I couldn't possibly write down).

Thursday, 16 November *London*

V. good night and quite refreshed. Resumed usual routine. A. laid up with a temperature. Cold this morning—just about freezing point—and dull. Romer and Raczynski at 12.30. They are still awaiting reply from Washington, which they expect tomorrow. Fat lot of good it will do them! . . . Pres. is trying to put off meeting till January or even February. P.M. is suggesting that he come here and, if Joe won't come (as he won't), we ask him to send Molotov. Pretty wide attack today on Anglo-American front, which seems to be going all right. But the weather and the state of the ground over there (I saw some of that) pretty awful.

Saturday, 18 November

12.45 Konkin† (Frogface ill and Sobolev unfindable). Lectured him on Russian performance in N. Persia and asked him to try to get

* Maj.-Gen. Sir F. de Guingand, Chief of Staff, 21 Army Group, 1944–5.

† Counsellor at the Russian Embassy.

some explanation from his Government. He professed wide-eyed ignorance.

[In October Russia had asked for exclusive oil concessions in part of northern Persia. The request was refused on the grounds that Persia intended to grant no concessions until the war was over. The Russians had for some time been encouraging a separatist movement in the north. Now the unrest and discontent, doubtless aided by skilful distribution of funds, reached such a pitch that the Persian Prime Minister had to resign.

Britain and the U.S. supported the refusal of concessions. The Majlis, under the leadership of Dr Mossadeq, passed a resolution in the same sense.]

Sunday, 19 November

Pres. is protesting against early meeting—wants to put it off to end of Jan. I thought that, after the Election, we might find a burst of American activity. But they seem to be simply sitting back.

Monday, 20 November

Saw A. this evening and got him to agree that paper on Dumbarton Oaks should go forward to A.P.W. Committee—in my name as he is not sure he agrees with it. No more am I! But we *must* initiate a discussion on the subject.

Tuesday, 21 November

11.30 talk with A. about Russians in N. Persia. A. always gets the needle that he ought to 'do something', which is very natural in a young and rising politician, but there isn't really much more to be done. . . . 6. Cabinet. Battle [west of the Rhine] going all right—so far—but it doesn't look like being decisive, and may flicker out. It's going to be a *Hell* of a job finishing off the Germans. Rockets doing a good deal of damage, but not much worse than hitherto. . . . P.M. said he proposed to invite King and Cabinet to dine on eve of new session. Some people had advised him it was dangerous, so he had set the 'Prof' to work out the chances. He declared it to be 648,000 to 1 against. So the P.M.'s dinner is 'on'. As the P.M. said, 'the guests must come prepared to meet their Maker, bearing in mind the heavy odds against such meeting'.

Thursday, 23 November

Anglo-American Thanksgiving Celebration at Albert Hall at 7. Wish people wouldn't think of these things. Poor P.M. there, looking the picture of boredom. Crept away 8.30. . . . From a message he sent to Stalin, Winston still seems to think battle may produce decisive results. But it looks to me a bit boggy.

Friday, 24 November

Spent almost the whole morning . . . on this insane Educational Conference. A F.O. dept. . . . have been 'working' in a corner and, in true bureaucratic fashion, have been writing, at their leisure, endless minutes leading to *nothing*. I must get someone on to this job. . . . It's a disgrace: if one leaves bureaucrats alone for a moment, they do *nothing* except destroy any shred of reputation that the F.O. may have retained. I understood nothing of all that was told me, but hope I got a small move on. I am concerned at the general drift that the F.O. should take over all these fantastic things. We aren't a Department Store. . . . We are taking over remnants of M. of I., M.E.W., S.O.E. Are we competent to do so? We can't do it, and if we create new Depts. to grapple with it, isn't that frightful duplication? . . . Ike wants us to do something about propaganda to Germany. Realises—rather late—that 'unconditional surrender' was silly and baleful. Pres. rushed in with suggestion of a proclamation to the Germans. But is this the moment? Don't know what our 'gros bonnets' think of it. On a superficial view I should think it silly and untimely. We've made the mistake, and we've got to live with it!

[The Cabinet's agreement to a Polish western frontier on the Oder had been intended to strengthen Mikolajczyk's hands. Whether, in all the circumstances of Russia's advance, any British offer could have been sufficient is doubtful. On 21 November the Polish Cabinet learned that Roosevelt, although sympathetic, could not offer Poland a guarantee. Two days later Mikolajczyk resigned, finding among all parties save his own Peasant Party so hearty and unfeigned a mistrust of Russian intentions that they would agree to no concessions until the peace conference. Tomasz Arciszewski succeeded him, and was frigidly treated by the British Government.

Churchill said in Parliament that if

> the Polish Government had agreed to give up the disputed territory there would never have been any Lublin Committee. If Mr Mikolajczyk could have returned to Moscow early in November . . . with power to conclude an agreement on the frontier line, Poland might now have taken full place in the ranks of the nations contending against Germany and would have had the full support and friendship of Marshal Stalin and the Soviet Government.

These assumptions were soon to be disproved. They were never shared by the Ambassador to the Polish Government, Sir Owen O'Malley.

Saturday, 25 November

My birthday—I'm 60 and qualify for a pension. A. says he wants me to stay on, but I can't do so indefinitely.

Sunday, 26 November

Cold (32°) but fine. Easy morning. Not much news. Mikolajczyk's resignation seems to have been accepted, which wd. be the end of these silly Poles. Will he form another Govt.? . . . Walked to Cambridge Theatre. London Symphony Orchestra and Moiseiwitch. Strauss 'Don Juan' boring. Fauré's Pavane pretty. A Grieg which I liked v. much and Beethoven's 5th Symphony. Back at F.O. by 4.30.

Monday, 27 November

Cabinet 5.30 till after 8. Began on Spain. P.M. wandered off on to 'Western Bloc'. Think he can be cured of his worst misapprehensions —he really has got the wrong end of the stick. C's of S. and others admitted at 6.45 and we havered on till 8.10. Rockets are becoming rather tiresome. Battle seems likely to peter out. If so, good thing, to clear up S.W. Holland and put an end to rockets.

Thursday, 30 November

Sent for by A. at 10.30. Really hardly know what it was about. A typical interview for these days. He was talking on the telephone to Chief Whip. When he'd finished, he began to tell me he must make a statement in House next week about Poland, then had P.M. put thro' to him, then sprang up and dashed off to see latter. That is all I see, in three or four days, of my S. of S.!

Friday, 1 December

10.30 went to see P.M. (in bed) with Alexander, Lyttelton and Bevin, about Italian prisoners. P.M., who looked a bit ruffled, said 'Excuse me receiving you like this, but this is the morning after the night before'! He must have had a hell of a birthday party!

[Papandreou's Government entered Greece in October, on the Germans' retreat, with the small British force which Churchill had ordered to be made ready more than twelve months before. The administration had little authority outside Athens, and still less after the E.A.M. members withdrew from the Government in early December. Under an agreement made at Caserta in September, all the guerrilla forces in Greece had placed themselves under the Government, which had in turn entrusted their control to the British General Scobie. E.L.A.S., the military arm of E.A.M., soon showed that it had little intention of observing the Caserta agreement. Churchill, having paid a goodly price at Moscow for virtual control over Greece, reinforced Scobie in November. On 3 December a civil war began. Scobie ordered E.L.A.S. to evacuate Athens and the Piraeus. They retorted by mounting a determined effort to seize the capital. In the early hours of 5 December Churchill and Eden authorised Scobie to use all his forces against the rebels. Papandreou was urged to stand with the British and Leeper instructed: 'This is no time to dabble in Greek politics or to imagine that Greek politicians of varying shades can affect the situation.']

Wednesday, 6 December

A mess in Greece and a tangle in Italy. P.L[oxley] rang up at lunch time to say A.P.W. Committee may not take Dumbarton Oaks tomorrow! P.M. wants it to go straight to Cabinet. What a mess that would be! But I see Pres. now plumps for my 'compromise', and wants to get on with it, proposing another meeting. I should think we could do it by an exchange of telegrams. Gloomy telegram from P.M. to Pres. about progress of the war. Rather *too* gloomy, I think. Seems to me Germans are feeling the draught.

Thursday, 7 December

Found P.M. had banned A.P.W. Committee—so I needn't have come up! Met A. in Park, who told me this—and added 'I am not very much interested!' Doesn't catch enough votes at the moment, I suppose. Refused to take on ordinary work, which I left to O.S. . . . 3.30 went to see Bobbety about World Organisation. He about the only member of the Cabinet who knows *anything* about it, and takes fairly sensible line. He will send minute to P.M. pointing out we *must* consult Dominions, so as to reach a fairly early decision as to what *we* think and want. Of course none of them know, poor darlings! 'C' at 4.30 for a gossip. He off to Belgium. And he not so pessimistic as P.M. regarding present situation on western front.

Friday, 8 December

B.B.C. gave account of Greek Debate, which seems to have gone all right. What poisonous mischief makers there are. While waiting for dinner, I read . . . article in the 'New Statesman'—a thing I haven't done for 2 years or more. How anyone can write such distorted, biased and dishonest muck passes my comprehension. The 'N.S.' is addressed, I suppose, to more or less educated people. Are their readers really taken in by such dishonest and libellous trash? I suppose so, if the 'Times' readers can swallow the swill dished up to them . . . Barrington Ward is not capable of running a mussel stall. It's a tragedy that he should be, of all things, editor of the 'Times'.*

[The Prime Minister said that evening in the debate, in which the Government won a vote of confidence by 279 votes to 30:

> Poor old England! We have to assume the burden of the most thankless tasks, and in undertaking them to be scoffed at, criticised, and opposed from every quarter, but at least we know . . . what is our objective. It is that these countries shall be freed from the German armed power, and under conditions of normal tranquillity shall have a free universal vote to decide the Government of their country. . . .
>
> . . . We are told that because we do not allow gangs of heavily armed guerrillas to descend from the mountains and install themselves with all the bloody terror and vigour of which they are capable, in power in great capitals, we are traitors to democracy.
>
> . . . if I am not . . . dismissed . . . we shall persist in this policy of clearing Athens and the Athens region of all who are rebels against the authority of the constitutional government of Greece.

On 9 December further reinforcements were ordered to Athens. At that stage Greece was suffering an acute shortage of food and a runaway inflation. Communist guerrillas held the environs of Athens. A heavy attack was mounted on the British Embassy, and another attack, using missiles of a different kind, upon the British Government. The State Department had issued a sharp communique; and within a few days an American paper published a substantially correct version of Churchill's 'top secret' telegram to General Scobie of 5 December:

> Do not . . . hesitate to act as if you were in conquered city where a local rebellion is in progress. . . . We have to hold and dominate Athens. It would be a great thing for you to succeed in this without bloodshed if possible, but also with bloodshed if necessary.]

Monday, 11 December

Quiet morning. Cabinet at 12. P.M. not there, so we got thro' with reasonable expedition. No great news. Bevin complaining of deadlock on western front. But what's the good of complaining? P.M. would have slogged him over the ropes if he'd been there.

[Alexander, just arrived in Athens from Italy, telegraphed: 'The British forces are in fact beleaguered in the heart of the city.' He proposed to take the harbour at Piraeus and clear the road thence to Athens. On

* R. M. Barrington-Ward, Editor, 1941–8.

12 December, the War Cabinet gave him a free hand for all military measures. Alexander and Macmillan, who had accompanied him from Italy, supported the suggestion that Archbishop Damaskinos should assume the Regency. King George of the Hellenes refused—for the moment.]

Friday, 15 December

11.30 Aghnides, who is, genuinely I think distressed at his King's folly in refusing to appoint the Archbishop as Regent. He attributes everything to Pipinellis* who, he says, is a bad influence. 12—for nearly an hour—Philip [Noel] Baker,† N. Ronald, Hurcomb‡ and Archie [Clark] Kerr about this wretched Inland Transport business. P.B. airily says he wants to sign the agreement without the Russians (and *with* the London Poles). Says Russians 'won't mind'. But of course they will. We disagreed, and could only agree that the matter must be referred higher.... Saw A. for a minute about 6. He said Polish debate didn't go too well. Had some trouble with a draft for Cabinet about Dumbarton Oaks. Discussed it with G.J. and put it into final shape.

Saturday, 16 December

Telegrams from Athens urging we should press King to appoint Archbishop as Regent. Found P.M. had summoned Cabinet for 3 and A. motoring up from Country. (I had meant to go to Film!) ... Back at F.O. at 2.30. A. arrived 2.55. Saw him for 5 mins. What a way to do business! Cabinet agreed we couldn't yet force King to do anything unconstitutional. His own beastly Ministers, irrespective of what they say to *us*, advise *him not* to appoint Regent! Must wait and see whether our reinforcements change situation. Quite useful telegram from Pres. about Poland; he ready to urge Joe to hold his hand till 3-Power meeting. Cabinet over at 5. P.M. and A. saw King of Greece after. A. got back to F.O. at 6.55 to catch 7.18 train to Binderton. I had a word with him while he was flapping about the room collecting hat and coat. What a madhouse! However, I think we got the thing straight, and the decision is possibly not wrong.

Sunday, 17 December

A. rang up to say he had thought he ought to go to Athens. I asked why, and he said he would go to investigate situation and then

* Panayotis Pipinellis, chief of household of the King of Greece, 1942–6; Prime Minister, 1963.

† Philip J. Noel-Baker, Parliamentary Secretary to the Ministry of War Transport, 1942–5.

‡ C. W. (later Lord) Hurcomb; of the Ministry of War Transport.

make recommendation to King of Greece. I pointed out that he couldn't start without obtaining prior undertaking from King that latter would follow his advice, and that was just what he (King) would not give. Moreover, it's taking *too* much responsibility for him to dictate internal remedy in another country. Later he told me P.M. had said the same! It's his old trouble—the urge to *do* something, irrespective of the sense of it. V. dangerous.

Monday, 18 December

German offensive not too pleasant.* A. arrived at 11.50 for Cabinet at 12 on U.S. statement about Poland. Had to wait with him till 12.30. Sent off telegram,† and asked for telephone connexion. To Cabinet 12.30. They talking about other things. Just before 1, A. was able to put the matter to them. They agreed we should urge Americans to take our draft, or at least Edward's amendment. Telephone came through at 1.15. A. instructed Edward. . . . 4.20 talk with A. about Greece. He as usual, wants to 'do' something. I reminded him that Cabinet on Sat. wanted to await a development. There's been none. What does he *propose?* Nothing? He obviously annoyed. At Cabinet (5.30) P.M. took my line. If you decide to wait for a 'development' in 2 or 3 days, and if there isn't any on the 2nd day, that's no reason for 'doing' something rash and silly. Cabinet rambled on till 7.30.

[Cadogan told Colville that Churchill was making a deplorable impression in Cabinet because he would not read his papers and dwelt endlessly on Greek affairs. Asked in 1967 for permission to publish this fact, Cadogan said that he had no objection, provided it was also stated that no one had greater admiration than he for Churchill.[18]]

Wednesday, 20 December

Cabinet at 6. We meant to deal—amongst other things—with Dumbarton Oaks and Territorial Trusteeship.

Talked till 6.45 about military situation. This grave: it may shorten the war or may prolong it. But at present *very nasty.* Then a wrangle about Local Govt. till 7.50. Then World Organisation! A complete madhouse—P.M. knows *nothing* about it. A. merely said we wanted to consult Dominions. That's true, but not the whole story: we want

* The German thrust through the Ardennes, which split 12 Army Group, looked likely at one moment to reach the Meuse, cost some 70,000 American casualties and caused a severe setback to the Allied advance.

† Urging Roosevelt to send off his message immediately, since the Russians were likely at any moment to recognise the Lublin Committee as the Government of Poland.

to have a mind of our *own* and no one will give any attention to it. Just as utterly futile on Territorial Trusteeships. The old P.M. is failing.

Thursday, 21 December

Cabinet about Greece at 5.30. Too awful. P.M. rambled on till 7, stating with vehemence opinions based on no ascertained facts. He says 'I won't instal a Dictator'—'a Dictator of the Left'.* Even Attlee rose against this. He said 'We often heard you say that, but you haven't produced a scintilla of evidence in support of your thesis.' But there was nothing to be done. P.M. absolutely refused to put any pressure on the King to appoint a Regent. Refused even to see him again. Would agree only that we should ask (thro' Douglas Howard) if there was any news. Saw D.H. with A. after, and instructed him to ask for audience. Battle better, I hope. Germans—again I *hope*—rather at a standstill. P.M. said 'Today I think this battle is more likely to shorten the war than to prolong it.'

[Eden's diary too records that this was a very difficult Cabinet:

> W. has his knife into the Archbishop and is convinced that he is both a Quisling and a Communist. In fact, as Alec puts it neatly, he has taken the place of de Gaulle. Brendan was maddening and supported W. knowing absolutely nothing of the matter, and also attacked Leeper. This brought me out and I said that if Cabinet had no confidence in Leeper they had better say so and say the same of Foreign Secretary at same time. W. rejoined, rather mournfully for him, that there was no doubt of Cabinet's support of Foreign Secretary. What was in doubt was Cabinet's confidence in him. Embarrassing pause. But W. clung to his opposition to Regency of Archbishop, a 'dictatorship', as he insists on calling it.[19]

On the same day, Alexander telegraphed from Athens:

> I earnestly hope that you will be able to find a political solution to the Greek problem, as I am convinced that further military action after we have cleared the Athens–Piraeus area is beyond our strength.]

Friday, 22 December

Meeting with A. on Greece at 12. D. H[oward] had seen King last night. Latter had admitted having received further message from Papandreou (which he didn't show, tho' he showed others) advising *against* Regency. Aghnides says that it advised *in favour!* I said only

* That is, Archbishop Damaskinos, whom King George of Greece deeply mistrusted and who was alleged to be in close touch with E.A.M.

thing to do was (1) to tell Leeper to try and get from Papandreou text of his message, (2) to get Damaskinos to say what he would do about formation of a Govt. &c. if he *were* made Regent. This might be a weapon for us in the Cabinet against those who say (like Brendan) that this 'ambitious ecclesiastic' only wants to make himself Dictator.

[On that afternoon, Churchill and Eden again saw King George, who had clearly suppressed at least one telegram from Papandreou. Eden pressed upon the unconvinced Prime Minister the need for a Regency in Athens. A trusted Regent would be invaluable in setting up the broad-based Government, to include representatives of E.A.M., which the British desired for the post-armistice period; and would deprive E.A.M. of its principal weapon, the charge that the British intended to impose the King upon Greece.]

Sunday, 24 December *Thatched Cottage*

While I was shaving, the sun rose—as it does at Christmas, behind the church. A flame seemed to lick along the roof of the nave, and then an arc suddenly appeared. Not a cloud in the sky. It had froze a degree or two. From then till sunset, there wasn't anything like a cloud in the sky. I've never seen such a gorgeous day in winter. Looking up at the golden fleece of the winter jasmine, against a Neapolitan blue sky, one might have thought one was on the Riviera. Only a rather cold, light, northerly breeze.

Christmas Day *Thatched Cottage*

Just before we left for Church, Lawford rang up and from his cryptic remarks on the telephone I gathered that *both* P.M. and A. had gone away *somewhere*. Anyhow he said that I was 'in charge', but added that he thought there was no hurry. On returning from Church, I rang him up and suggested he should send down a Messenger. But he said there was really nothing much to report, and I managed to gather from him that they had gone to Athens! On the information that I have, this is silly, but there may have been developments that I know not of.

Tuesday, 26 December

10 o'c. news gave out P.M.'s and A.'s arrival in Athens. Not much news from the battle—what there is is not too good. Germans have been slowed up, but go slogging on, and no sign of a real counter-stroke from us. Air action on these last two lovely days has been on a large scale, but it doesn't *stop* the Germans. . . . One telegram from

P.M. but only reporting all-party meeting in Athens this afternoon. This already announced on wireless. Rang up O.S., but he had no more news and said nothing doing.

Wednesday, 27 December

One or two telegrams from Athens. A meeting was convened, but the prospects of its producing anything definite seem dim. P.M. staying in 'Ajax'.* 5.30 Cabinet. Battle seems stabilized more or less. But the Germans have attained their objectives in upsetting our plans, and so many of our troops have been drawn into the battle that I don't know that we've got sufficient for an effective counter-stroke. This may indeed prolong the war.

Thursday, 28 December

P.M. and A. leaving today and due back tomorrow. They haven't actually effected much, beyond getting all these ridiculous Parties to sit down together, but I think the fact of their going there will blunt criticism. Battle seems to have taken a good turn.

[These entries hardly do justice to the importance of the visit which Churchill and Eden had just made to Athens. Without meeting Archbishop Damaskinos, for whom he formed an immediate respect, Churchill was unlikely to press the King hard enough, in the sense long desired by Eden. By 28 December the Greek parties had all agreed that Churchill should ask King George to nominate the Archbishop as Regent. He would then form a Government without Communist members, continuing the fight against E.L.A.S. until a truce were requested or the Athens area cleared.]

Friday, 29 December

P.M. and A. got back soon after 5. Had talk with A. at 5.40 and Cabinet at 6, at which P.M. got authority to send for King of Greece tonight and put pressure on him to nominate Damaskinos as Regent. (King has just telegraphed to Papandreou saying he won't do this, but P.M. authorised by Cabinet to tell him that in that case we transfer our recognition to the Regency, so I don't believe he'll hold out, but it may be a stormy meeting.)

[It was. Not until 4.30 a.m. did the hapless King George, under threat of immediate disavowal by the British, appoint the Archbishop and promise 'not to return to Greece unless summoned by a free and fair expression of the national will'.

* The cruiser was anchored off the Piraeus.

Shortly afterwards E.L.A.S. made a truce. General Plastiras, a strong republican, replaced M. Papandreou as Prime Minister.]

Sunday, 31 December

Well, that's the end of *that* year. It's been a good one, but there's lots more to come yet. News is good. *This* offensive is stopped, and I believe we can stop any other. Can we turn it into a victory? By the way, broadcast last night showed King of Greece had capitulated. Lublin Committee also proclaimed themselves Provisional Government!

1945

Tuesday, 2 January

5 talk with A. about Greece. King has broken his word and told lies. Cabinet 5.30. Battle seems all right at present. Sinkings rather worse, but not bad. . . . Sent off telegrams to Athens, which Cabinet had approved, authorising R.L[eeper] to tell Damaskinos that the King had lied.

Wednesday, 3 January

A talk with him [Eden] and R. Stevenson about Yugoslavia. King P. raising niggling points about Tito-Subasic agreement. He must be told he's got to hold his nose and swallow the medicine. . . . A. saw King of Greece this afternoon, but haven't heard what happened. These Kings!

Thursday, 4 January

. . . 12 had longish talk with A. about forthcoming meetings. He agreed we *must* try to have a meeting of Foreign Ministers before the 'Big 3' meet. Otherwise nothing tangible will be done. They dine and wine, which is all very well, but nobody (least of all themselves) knows what, if anything, has been settled. We drafted minute to P.M. . . . 3 meeting of A.P.W. Committee on Dumbarton Oaks. I explained to them in about 10 mins. what it was all about, and they agreed sensibly on all we wanted. Cripps, O. Lyttelton and A. Sinclair helpful, and we got thro' in ¾ hr. Hope we can now push it thro' Cabinet.

[Eden's diary for that day observes:

> I am much worried that the whole business will be chaotic and nothing worth while settled, Stalin being the only one of the three who has a

clear view of what he wants and is a tough negotiator. P.M. is all emotion in these matters, F.D.R. vague and jealous of others.[20]]

Friday, 5 January

Just as I was going I was brought tiresome telegrams about Zervas* in Corfu, which necessitated consultation with A. in country. Tried to ring him up, but he was engaged—for 20 mins. I suppose P.M. (returned from France) rambling to him. Got through at 7.50. Settled it: but this is a *hopeless* way of doing business. . . .

By the way, my cigarettes arrived last night—6 days from Oxford St. to Arlington St. It's really too bad. And there's a letter in the 'Times' this morning congratulating the G.P.O. on their promptness and efficiency!

Sunday 7 January

P.M. agrees to propose a Foreign Secretaries' meeting preliminary to Big 3. But doubt whether he will get it. . . . Battle news is, I think, good, and Monty has broken out into a Press talk, which he must have enjoyed, and which, I think, shows confidence.

Monday, 8 January

A. arrives at 12.30. Summons a meeting on Greece at 12.45 (I am giving a lunch . . . at Savoy at 1.15!) *What* a way of doing business! This is all one sees of him. He strides about the room, gabbling, and I, at least, can't hear what he says. . . . Cabinet at 6. Battle seems to be going all right. But rockets are *bad.* We were under fairly constant bombardment all day, and no one can suggest any way of stopping it—short of German surrender! During the waffly talk at Cabinet, A. tries to get thro' some of his work and shoves papers under my nose, with hurried whispered comment, which I can't hear. (I'm not going v. deaf, yet!) This is *not* the way to do business. Home just before 8, dined and washed up. P.M. foresees at *least* 6 or 7 months more of war. I think he's optimistic!

[The Soviets had just recognised the Lublin Poles as the Provisional Government. Making no attempt to conceal his depression and pessimism, Cadogan told Raczynski on 7 January how he and others had hoped that the Russians would not make any such move before the forthcoming meeting at Yalta. Now they had done it and left the British to find out after the event.

* Head of the E.D.E.S. forces in Greece.

Cadogan [noted the Polish Ambassador] seemed to have no doubt that the Polish situation had got worse, both externally and internally. He had recent and detailed information about the Lublin regime, which apparently intended *inter alia* to impose the collective farm system. Each successive development would make it harder to turn the clock back; but he did not see how one could do anything about such events except deplore them, since Britain was in no position to deflect Russia from her course.[21]]

Tuesday, 9 January

Soviet Embassy, where I received Monty's and Ramsay's* insignia of the Order of Suvorov. Glass of vodka after. . . . Back at 4.45 to *masses* of work—avalanches of boxes. I have sent some back with reproaches.

Wednesday, 10 January

Talk with A, about 11, about Greece. Got a draft telegram to Athens which I took over to P.M. at 11.30. He in bed with a very untidy cold. Approved telegram. I tried to get out of the room, but he wandered on about a number of subjects till nearly 12. . . . Lots of work, and Depts. making it difficult by slinging *acres* of minutes. Have fulminated again.

Thursday, 11 January

Cabinet at 5.30. World Organisation on Agenda, so P.M. had got Carton de Wiart† in for a talk—so as to put off consideration of W[orld] O[rganisation]. Unluckily for him, that cock wouldn't fight—C. de W. spoke for 6½ mins. only. So P.M. plied him with questions. But even these gave out at 6.10, by when C. de W. had told us *nothing!* Unfortunately, A. had seen King Peter at 5.30, and had to report. This gave another splendid chance for procrastination. That silly youth maintains his pernickety objections to Subasić-Tito agreement, and thereby loses his throne. Moreover, he has already given his silly, and ill-drafted, statement to the Press,‡ which is as discourteous as ill-advised. Then the P.M. havered about Greece (which is going well) and raised many irrelevancies. Then he talked about the battle (which goes well) and Monty's disastrous press interview.§

* Adm. Sir B. M. H. Ramsay, naval commander in 'Overlord'.

† Now Prime Minister's military representative with Chiang Kai-shek.

‡ Saying that he would accept the Tito-Subasić agreement in principle, but must be able himself to appoint the Regents.

§ Of 7 January, when Montgomery, who had intended his remarks to be a contribution to Allied solidarity, conveyed the impression that the British had been largely responsible for stemming the German advance in the Ardennes.

Finally, at 7.10, all other subjects being exhausted, we took World Organisation. I had to explain what it was about. P.M. was lumped over the hurdle. Cripps played up. And we got through in under 10 mins.!

Friday, 12 January

Cabinet took 2 hrs. to do what I could have done in 20 mins. Our people in Greece have made rather a bloomer in signing truce without covering case of hostages. Upshot of Cabinet was that we put out a declaration saying no truce 'can be enduring or ripen into peace' unless hostages are liberated. I left at 5. Cabinet sat on ... till 7.30. A. lost patience at Cabinet. After ½ hour's waffle he offered to draft. Waffle went on for ½ hour and then P.M. said he would go out and draft. After he'd gone, A. made a scene saying 'What's the good of a F[oreign] S[ecretary] who isn't even trusted to draft a telegram?' He was fed up, and wouldn't go on, &c. But he calmed down. He got back at 7.30 and I got him to approve telegram to Athens and R. Stevenson and others came to talk about Yugoslavia. Silly little King shows *some* signs of coming to his senses and Subasić is exercising patience. But I don't see any way out of that tangle now.

Saturday, 13 January

News tonight good. The Ardennes go well and the Russians do seem to have launched a large, and so far successful, attack in S. Poland.

Monday, 15 January

Talked to N. Butler* about Levant. Think our Depts. are pretty bad, and have got into a groove. Shall have to do something about it. ... 5.30 Cabinet. P.M. not there at first, so Morrison and others made a stink about V2's. Agreed matter should be taken up by Defence Committee. P.M. came in about 6 and when we reverted to the subject the protagonists had lost their fire! Russian offensive seems good, tho' we don't know too much about it. Ardennes battle is all right now, but it hasn't turned into a triumph for us. Rundstedt,† after all, I suppose knows something about the art of war. A. had seen that silly little King Peter again, who's digging his toes in. A twig defying an avalanche, and a rather rotten twig too.

* Assistant Under-Sec. of State, F.O.

† Field Marshal C. R. G. von Rundstedt, German C.-in-C. in the West.

[King Peter accepted in principle the Tito-Subasić agreements of 1 November and 7 December 1944, but objected to the method of choosing the Council of Regency and to the surrender of interim powers of government to Tito's Council of National Liberation, a single political group.]

Tuesday, 16 January

12 Iranian, for a semi-audible wail about his country's tribulations. He wanted us to champion their cause at next Big 3 meeting. I gave him a diplomatic answer which amounted to 'perhaps'.

Wednesday, 17 January

I got my minute on Levant States into shape and gave it in to be typed. Will submit it tomorrow. I'm sure it's sensible. We *must* whack the Levant States on the head—gradually and gently if you like, but that's the way to begin. That's what Spears would *never* do. And I'm afraid Shone* is timid of doing it. . . . Russian news marvellous—they're tearing the guts out of the Germans. Warsaw has fallen. What must be the feelings of poor Edward [Racynski] and his friends at hearing the Polish anthems broadcast! It's no triumph for *them*, and *they* won't get back. What a tragedy!

Thursday, 18 January

Hear Winston had a success this morning with his speech and his (veiled) attack on the 'Times'. . . had an ovation.

[Churchill said he had never known a Government so maligned by the press, even by some of the most time-honoured and responsible journals, whose reckless partisanship on the Greek question made a hard task more difficult.]

Friday, 19 January

[11 Carandini,† on his return from Italy. He took 8 days—by air! There you are: that's air travel! He satisfied about political situation, but of course says Italians want 'moral' encouragement. 12 Massigli about French participation in 3-Power talks. I went so far as to say our attitude was 'bienveillant' but that we couldn't give an answer before consulting our Allies. Obviously things would be discussed final decision on which must have French concurrence—whether that was on E.A.C. or elsewhere. . . . Read Winston's speech, which was admirable. I am told his attack on the '*Times*' had terrific

* Sir Terence Shone, Minister to the Levant States from December 1944; Deputy to Cadogan at U.N.O. from 1948.

† Count Nicolo Carandini, Italian representative in London, 1944–7.

success. I hope someone will tie Barrington Ward and Ted Carr* together and throw them into the Thames. Good dinner. Russian news marvellous. They are tearing guts out of Germans and—once again—I think this beastly war may be over sooner than we think. After that! Our little advance seeps on. The Germans have had some success in Alsace, but I don't think that matters now. Wind, thank heaven, has dropped and it is deliciously quiet and peaceful—and reasonably warm—here.

Saturday, 20 January

T. and I fed chickens. 8 eggs. They are laying well. The pullets began the week before Christmas. More crumpets at tea, and a quiet read after. I must say, once one has torn oneself free from the toils of London, and packed and driven down here, this is a most refreshing rest. It makes me lazy and tho' I bring down work and correspondence, I don't do much of either! Russians news still wonderful. They've got Tilsit.

[On 19 January the deputy Prime Minister, Mr Attlee, complained to Churchill of the lack of method in the Cabinet's proceedings. 'I consider', he wrote, 'the present position inimical to the successful performance of the tasks imposed upon us as a Government and injurious to the war effort.' The Prime Minister was charged with showing scant respect for his colleagues' views on civil affairs. Frequently a long delay supervened before reports of Cabinet committees could be taken and even then it was 'very exceptional' for Churchill to have read them. Half an hour or more would be wasted in explaining what could have been grasped in two or three minutes' reading. 'Not infrequently a phrase catches your eye which gives rise to a disquisition on an interesting point only slightly connected with the subject matter.'

It appears that Beaverbrook and Bracken, upon whose undue influence Attlee also commented, said he was right. Mrs Churchill confirmed it. The Prime Minister received all this gloomily. Not until 4 p.m. did he beam at Jock Colville, throw aside the bedclothes and say, 'Let us think no more of Hitlee or Attler; let us go and see a film.' On 22 January he replied:

My dear Lord President,

I have to thank you for your Private and Personal letter of January 19. You may be sure I shall always endeavour to profit by your counsels.[22]]

Monday, 22 January

Masses of paper and faggots of files from A. marked 'A.C. please speak'. Couldn't catch him till 12.45, but then got thro' a number of

* Asst. Editor of *The Times*, 1941–5.

things. . . . 3 meeting with A. and others about Germany. V. unhelpful—he in a pet and annoyed by G. J[ebb]'s interventions—quite unjustifiably. Then, at 4, another quite useless meeting (because premature) on agenda for the Conference. Went on till 4.30. Tried to grapple with papers till 5.30 Cabinet. Cabinet as discursive and useless as usual. Got away at 7.45. . . . I had a *portmanteau* full of work. What a beastly life.

Tuesday, 23 January

Talk with A. and others on position created by that ridiculous King Peter having dismissed his Govt. last night. He's obviously down the drain. 11.45 Raczynski with a silly memo. from his Government suggesting postponement of frontier questions and establishment of an inter-Allied Military control in Poland! I observed that this was not very realistic and he, with a wry smile, agreed. . . . 12.55 (what an hour) a madhouse with A. and numerous others about Poland. However *some* sense resulted: clean the slate, remove Lublin *and* London 'Govts.' and set up something more generally acceptable to all. Don't know whether Joe [Stalin] will play on this. He *might*.

Wednesday, 24 January

4. Long talk with Mikolajczyk. He (perhaps too late?) sees sense. But we *might* form a *new* Govt. in Poland. The time has gone by for talk of 'fusion' of London with Lublin, but we *might* get a clean slate.* Depends on the mood in which we find Joe. . . . Russians 10 miles from Breslau!

Friday, 26 January

A. was playing about with telegrams about the Levant. Work is hopeless. One never has a quiet talk with A.: it is just a 10-min. flap between other engagements. How we carry on, I don't know. Must try to get opportunity to speak to him during forthcoming trip. Tarnowski† quite hopeless and I practically told him so. His memorandum (see Jan. 23) useless. Had he any other suggestions! No. When he tried to imply that it was up to us to save Poland, I reacted rather vigorously.

Saturday, 27 January

There's a mass to clear up—of 'Briefs'. These I refuse to look at.

* Cf. E. J. Rozek, *Allied Wartime Diplomacy*, pp. 336–7.

† Adam Tarnowski, Foreign Minister in the Arciszewski Cabinet, 1944–7.

They're of no use, and no one, at a Conference, bothers about them. The moles in Depts. look on them as the Bible. Winant at 5.15. Tried to spur him to urge his Govt. to be a little less woolly about Yugoslavia.* He may do something, but he's a spineless creature.

[The entries for 30 January to 17 February are taken from Cadogan's letters to Lady Theo.]

Tuesday, 30 January *A.C. to T.C.* *Malta*

We had a lovely flight yesterday. We got off the ground soon after 9.30, up into the sun, and by 12.30 I was eating lunch looking out at the dazzling snow-covered Pyrenees. We came on here (Malta) non-stop, landing at 4 o'clock—an average speed of round about 250 miles an hour. Our pilot hoped to do a record for a big 4-engined plane, as the wind was behind us most of the way. But as he had estimated the flight at 6 hours 5 minutes, and as we took about 6 hours 20 minutes, I'm afraid we probably didn't carry off the palm.

We came straight on board this cruiser ('Sirius') where we live in quite good comfort.

After tea, Anthony and I went for a bit of a walk. He is easily recognised by the crowd, which delights him, and we walk through crowds of hand-clapping Maltese dock workers.

No signs of Ed. yet, and I don't think he'll turn up till tomorrow. Anthony told me the P.M. said he (P.M.) would probably come today, as the weather forecast was good, with worse weather later.

This morning we heard he had arrived at 5 a.m. and was sleeping in his plane on the aerodrome! So I suppose he couldn't bear it any longer, and must have settled to start yesterday evening! *What* a man! But it bores Anthony frightfully, of course, taking the wind out of *his* sails. P.M. is living in another cruiser just across the harbour. He arrived on board about 10 this morning, but I think went to bed again.

So Anthony and Nicholas Lawford and Nevile Butler and the Captain and I went off for a drive about 11.

Malta certainly has been pretty well knocked about, and there's hardly anything unscarred. It's nice and warm in the sun, but a pretty cold wind. A few flowers coming out and crops beginning to show green. . . .

A lazy life, and I, personally, have done no work. But if Ed. arrives tomorrow I suppose we shall begin then. Poor Anthony has

* Eden and Cadogan feared that the possibility of a rift between the Allies was influencing King Peter to stand out against the Tito-Subasić agreement. F.R.U.S., 1945, vol. 5, p. 1190.

just been sent for by the P.M., and has pushed off in a boat (6 p.m.). I told him he'd probably be kept there till 3 in the morning and I, for one, shall *not* sit up for him.

I suppose we leave here for the next place on Friday. I don't think it should be more than 4 or 5 hours' flying. Harriman, who met us here, has seen it, and from his account it is probably pretty primitive. I gather the 'Tops' will be fairly comfortable—not so the lesser fry. I trust that I may be included in the former, but there are so many Generals, Admirals, Air Marshals and other Panjandrums, that I don't know!

It's nice to feel the sun a bit and to see fresh green and bright red earth, and even a few tentative little wallflowers. About one third of France seemed to be under snow, as far as we could see—we were above cloud a great part of the way.

The plane was comfortable, and they gave us an ambitious, though not frightfully good, lunch.

Wednesday, 31 January *A.C. to T.C.* *Malta*

The Bag seems to be going at midnight tonight, so I can continue.

Anthony got back from the P.M. about 7 yesterday evening with orders for me and him to dine with P.M. But we were promised we might go to bed at a reasonable hour, as he was going to play Bézique with Harriman.

P.M. felt ill on the way out, and proved to have a temperature of 102·4°. But was quite all right yesterday evening, cheerful and eating and drinking everything within reach. Personally, I think it's simply excitement! Our dinner consisted of Harriman, Moran, Anthony, Martin (P.M.'s private secretary), Sarah Oliver [Churchill], Thompson (P.M.'s A.D.C.) and the Captain of the 'Orion'. And we *did* get away soon after 10.30.

This morning was warmer, but dull. Anthony and Bob Dixon and I drove out into the country and had a walk there. Gen. Alexander came to lunch with us. He seems optimistic about the news, and can't see how the Germans can go on much longer. Then about 3.30 we had to leave for the airport to meet Ed. and H. Hopkins. Of course found on arrival there that the plane wouldn't be in for an hour or more. They eventually arrived and we brought Ed. and Harry to this ship, where they are staying, and gave them tea and a chat.

Thursday, 1 February *A.C. to T.C.* *Malta*

We had a large dinner with the Governor last night, about 30 or 40 people. We filed into a brightly lit dining room and took our places, and the lights were then switched off and we were left with a few heavily shaded candles. I don't like a glare, but this was overdoing it—so much so that I found that in helping myself to a vol au vent I only got bits of pastry and no chicken. . . .

Practically all this morning Anthony and I and Nevile Butler had discussion with Ed. and two of his henchmen. We got on very well and I don't think we're going to have any serious differences with *them*.

After an early tea, we drove out to the Governor's garden where we walked and picked and ate oranges!

Reports of our next destination are not encouraging. It sounds beastly, and *most* uncomfortable.

Most of us have to go and dine with the P.M. tonight, and I fear we shan't see our beds for *hours*.

Friday, 2 February *A.C. to T.C.* *Malta*

A lovely day again—even better than yesterday, and almost like summer.

But it was clouded at the beginning by the news we received at breakfast of the crash last night of the aircraft that was bringing Peter, two other members of the F.O., one of my young ladies and Anthony's detective. I'm afraid it's certain that all four men were killed: I'm not quite sure about the young lady. 14 out of 19 killed, apparently. It's the devil. I don't know when it will be published, and I can't yet find out how it happened.*

We've not had to work much today. The Pres. arrived in his cruiser this morning and steamed slowly past us to a berth next the P.M.'s cruiser. I haven't met him yet.

We had an Anglo-American lunch in this ship—a small one—we can't seat more than about 10.

We had a small dinner with the P.M. aboard his ship last night—P.M., Ed., Anthony, Harry Hopkins and self. P.M. seemed to be in good form and there was a spate of rambling talk on most subjects. Luckily it didn't last too late, and I was in bed before 12.30.

This afternoon Anthony, Nicholas and I drove out of the town and went for a walk along a coast road, and back for tea. Very pleasant. . .

Ed. in tremendous form: we make him make speeches to the ship's company and photograph him on all occasions, so he is quite happy!

* The aircraft missed Malta in mist, and crashed into the sea. Cadogan felt this event deeply, and especially the loss of his Private Secretary and 'very valued friend and helper', Peter Loxley.

We leave the ship tonight about 11, and are supposed to get off the ground at 12.30 a.m. tomorrow morning. Flight will take about 7 hours.

[At Malta, Eden pressed strongly for a firm Anglo-American stand on Poland. He found Stettinius and Hopkins 'fully alive' to the seriousness of the issue, and generally urged upon them, as he had done upon Churchill, the imprudence of making unrequited concessions to Russia. 'We found ourselves in complete agreement on all major points' says his diary for 1 February. Although the Foreign Secretary had asked for a longer conference, Roosevelt had refused to allow it. The President himself was available at Malta only for the inside of a day. Neither at lunch nor at dinner was any business done. Eden told Hopkins that 'we were going into a decisive conference and had so far neither agreed what we would discuss nor how to handle matters with a Bear who would certainly know his mind'. Though Cadogan's first impression was more favourable, Eden noted privately on that day that the President looked considerably older since their last meeting in September, and gave 'the impression of failing powers'.[23]]

Sunday, 4 February *A.C. to T.C.* *Alupka*

I certainly do seem to get to funny places during this war. This is quite the oddest.

We left the ship at Malta at about 11.30 p.m. on Friday night, and drove out to the airfield. Off the ground at 12.30 a.m. Very comfortable flight. I had quite a wide bed, and managed to sleep well. We were over the Black Sea when I woke, and crossed the coast and landed at a place called Saki about 8 a.m. I don't know how many planes we were in—all our military and other staffs, and all the Americans. It was well organised: the planes took off at regular intervals, and seemed to arrive at the other end, at the same spot, with exactly the same intervals.

There was thin and rather slushy snow on the ground, but no wind, and it wasn't very cold. We were met by Molotov and other swells and taken to a marquee, with a stove in it, where we ate caviare and drank vodka.

About 9 a.m.—or 11 a.m. by local time—Anthony and Harry Hopkins and I got off in a car to drive the 80 miles or so to this place. At first a bad road over dismal, flat, snow-covered country. But about half way we began to run into mountains, the road improved, the snow began to disappear and the country became interesting. Eventually the road tumbled down to the sea, and we were in a different country. Much warmer, cypress trees and villages with nice tiled roofs—rather like Italy. We then turned west (to our right) and drove for another hour or so, through the port of Yalta, dropping Harry H. at the American H.Q. at Livadia, the former Czar's Summer Palace, and then another 20 min. or so to this place (Alupka) which is almost the southern tip of the Crimea.

You never saw such a place. It was built by the Vorontsoff family in 1837, in what Baedeker so aptly describes as a combination of the Moorish and Gothic styles. You couldn't possibly imagine what it looks like. But its situation is superb, perched on a height looking over the sea, due south, with terraced gardens running right down to the beach. Behind, a pine forest clinging to the foot of a great rampart of rock 4,000 ft. high, which shelters us from the north. A cloudless day today with a hot sun. Schools of porpoises rolling about in the calm water. All entirely different from what I had expected. Hardly any flowers yet, but I should think the place would be lovely in about a month's time. There are the biggest magnolia trees I have ever seen.

To return to yesterday, when we arrived here (about 3 p.m.) we had an enormous lunch—more caviare and smoked salmon, more vodka and much food of all sorts, ending with tangerines. After that, Anthony and I retired to bed till dinner time! Dinner was another huge meal, in which all our staffs joined in. The P.M. didn't arrive till about dinner time—he had landed later than we did and had stopped for lunch somewhere on the way with Molotov. He must have dined in his own room, I think. We retired to bed fairly early.

I have got a small, but reasonably comfortable bedroom next to Anthony's, and I use his private bathroom, which is a convenience, as these are rather scarce. It's a big house, of indescribable ugliness—a sort of Gothic Balmoral—with all the furnishings of an almost terrifying hideosity. But it's well warmed. The food is good and the place is manned by Royal Marines and innumerable Russian waiters. So we do ourselves quite well. No work has, of course, yet begun. But I have got meetings after lunch today with Harry Hopkins and other Americans. Harry of course is ill, and wants me to go over to Livadia about 20 min. away. Uncle Joe, so far as I can make out, is somewhere in between. I should think this Conference will be a complete muddle, scattered as we are.

By the way, Anthony knows I want Washington! I don't know how, but I rather suspect Nicholas [Lawford]: I remember last time at Quebec the latter asked me about it and I told him I should like it. He may have been put up by Anthony to sound me! However, I haven't got it yet. Anthony announced in the car yesterday that he knew I wanted it: Harry gave a loud cry—whether of pain or pleasure, I don't know. So there it is. We dropped the subject, but as

Anthony knows my wish we can only leave it to see what he and the P.M. may decide about it. Edward apparently has definitely decided to leave this year.

Molotov suggests we shall stay here 5 or 6 days. Where we shall go then, I don't know. We *should* come straight home, but I expect Winston or Anthony will invent some other resort!

Must go now to an early lunch, in order to be in time for Harry's meeting.

Tuesday, 6 February *A.C. to T.C.* *Alupka*

I snatch a moment to scrawl a line.

I was so delighted with your first two letters, which arrived yesterday. I last wrote, I think, on Sunday.

That afternoon I went to Livadia for a chat with Harry Hopkins, who was in bed, and thereafter, at 5, we had a plenary session of the Conference, which lasted till about 7.30. We sat at a round table, with the Pres. presiding. He looks rather better than when I last saw him. But I think he is woollier than ever. Stalin looks well—rather greyer—and seemed to be in very good form. He and his Deputy Chief of Staff, General Antonov, gave us a survey of the military situation. I don't think that they told us an awful lot that we didn't know, but they did say that the Russian offensive would go on until the weather stopped it (middle or end of March) and that they would be prepared to discuss with us a summer campaign in case that might be necessary.

Yesterday wasn't such a good day from the point of view of weather. Our bright sun had gone, but it was calm and mild. I had a lot of work to do in the morning, but got out for a short stroll with Alexander, whom I like.

Then Anthony and I went off for lunch with Molotov to meet the Americans. The usual sort of lunch, with toasts all the time! I sat between Maisky* (in a sort of General's uniform) and Harriman. . . . Lunch went on till about 3.30 and we then had to go on to another plenary meeting at Livadia. Same party as yesterday, and we sat till 8 o'clock, dealing this time with political questions—or beginning to. It's always the same with these Conferences: they take *days* to get on the rails. The Great Men don't know what they're talking about and have to be educated, and made a bit more tidy in their methods. I think we're making some progress, but this place is still rather a madhouse. That's why my letter is rather incoherent—Anthony

* Assistant People's Commissar for Foreign Affairs since 1943.

flapping in and out and dropping papers all over the place, and Bob Dixon and Nicholas running in and out.

It's an awful bore our various Delegations being so scattered. It takes at least half an hour, especially at night, to drive from here to the Americans.

I wish I could describe this house. If I have a little more time some day, and less distraction, I will make the attempt. It was the H.Q. of Gen. von Manstein, the German C.-in-C., and Hitler gave it to him as a present! That is why it was hardly looted or damaged. But some of the decoration and furniture could do with a little of both!

Wednesday, 7 February *A.C. to T.C.* *Alupka*

Your letters are a great joy, and come regularly. Our daily 'Mosquito' service is pretty good, and I got your Sunday letter yesterday (Tues.).

Yesterday, after I closed my letter to you, we went off to a meeting of Foreign Secretaries at Livadia. On the whole, not bad, and we made a little progress.

I lunched with the President, P.M., Harry Hopkins, Harriman and Jimmy Byrnes (another American).* Quite agreeable and amusing, but not awfully useful. Harry is better, but he's never in very good condition and does nothing to take care of himself. He said he was all right when he left America, and kept all right until he saw the Pope!

After lunch Anthony and I walked a bit in the gardens at Livadia, till 4 o'clock, when we had another plenary meeting. Photographers opened the proceedings, and we then started a discussion about Dumbarton Oaks. I was terrified of what the P.M. might say, as he doesn't know a *thing* about it—he has always refused to look at it—and here he was plunging into debate! However, after a few flounderings, he really did fairly well. The Russians reserved their position, so nothing yet settled. We then had a wrangle about Poland, and I need hardly say nothing was settled *there.* Uncle Joe is in great form, though, and in quite genial mood. The President has certainly aged.

Thursday, 8 February *A.C. to T.C.* *Alupka*

I've started this letter early after breakfast, before the flap begins, or before it rises to its full fury.

Not that I've got an awful lot of news. We have reduced the Conference to such an orderly procedure that one day is very like another. We work in the morning till 11.30, when we have a meeting of Foreign Secretaries, followed by lunch. Yesterday this took place

* J. F. Byrnes, Director of Office of War Mobilisation 1943–5, Secretary of State 1945–7.

at the Russian HQ. Today we are acting as hosts. Then follows a meeting of the Big Three, which goes on usually till about dinner time.

We made some progress yesterday, and Uncle Joe showed signs of being accommodating both in regard to Dumbarton Oaks and Poland. The P.M. got rather off the rails. Silly old man—without a word of warning to Anthony or me, he plunged into a long harangue about World Organisation, knowing nothing whatever of what he was talking about and making complete nonsense of the whole thing. The worst of it was that what he said was completely contrary to the line already agreed with the Americans! However, I was able to explain privately to them that they needn't take it too tragically, that it didn't really mean anything and that we could clean up the mess afterwards.

I must say I think Uncle Joe much the most impressive of the three men. He is very quiet and restrained. On the first day he sat for the first hour and a half or so without saying a word—there was no call for him to do so. The President flapped about and the P.M. boomed, but Joe just sat taking it all in and being rather amused. When he did chip in, he never used a superfluous word, and spoke very much to the point. He's obviously got a very good sense of humour—and a rather quick temper!*

We are really very comfortable here. The Russians had 1,500 men working on this house for a fortnight before we came. Every pane of glass had to be put in and, I suspect, all the electric light. The latter works well, but there is a system of 'remote control' of lighting which is somewhat embarrassing. The lights in Anthony's room, his bathroom, and in the offices all turn on and off from a switchboard at the end of the passage! So that a Russian housemaid or a heavy-fingered Marine either plunge one in darkness or switch on the light at 6 a.m.! However, I think I'm curing them of that. Otherwise, everything is done for our comfort—bowls of fruit and bottles of mineral water in every bedroom. Also a decanter of vodka! The food is quite good though, as usual in Russia, rather monotonous. And of course they have to be trained in the matter of breakfast. Caviare and mince pies for breakfast are all very well once in a way, but they pall after a bit. However we have now drilled them into giving us omelettes and suchlike. No lack of eggs or butter.

As for our plans, I think the Conference will finish Sunday (11th), or Monday at latest. The P.M. talks of driving then to Sebastopol (about 2½ hours) where our ship lies, and spending the night on

* Cadogan noticed that he gave Maisky some 'savage nudges'.

board, and leaving by air the next day. I don't know where we shall go to. We *may* stop 24 hrs. in Athens, and we *may* go to Cairo for a few days and we *might* spend another day or two in Malta (though I think this last rather unlikely).

I should guess that we might be back in England at the earliest about Feb. 14th and at latest the 18th.

Our weather has been very good on the whole. A lot of bright warm sun, but yesterday and, so far, today a bit of wind from the East.

Friday, 9 February *A.C. to T.C.* *Alupka*

Stalin gave a dinner last night, but I'm glad to say that we have so many Chiefs of Staff and Supreme Commanders and an Ambassador, *and* Sarah, that I just missed fitting into a restricted number we were allowed to take to it! A great mercy, as I am tired of these silly toasts and speeches, and I could get a reasonably early bed! . . .

We leave here the 11th or 12th. I *think* Anthony and I go to Athens for 24 hours. He's delighted at the prospect of a little trip on his own, without the P.M. who will proceed to Alexandria, where we may join him for a day or two. P.M. has told Attlee that he expects to be back on the 18th.

I unfortunately left my slippers in the 'Sirius' and told the First Sea Lord he must do something about it. He has ordered the 'Sirius' to Athens, so I may find them there! Unless they've been pinched by the Steward.

P.M. seems well, though drinking buckets of Caucasian champagne which would undermine the health of any ordinary man. Otherwise, with the exception of Lord Leathers, who was knocked out for a day or two by the regime, we are all well so far, and flourishing.

Confusion in this office is now rising to a high pitch, and I have many things to do before going to a meeting at 11.30, so must stop.

Saturday, 10 February *A.C. to T.C.* *Alupka*

We really have made some progress. We have begun night sessions, and had a meeting of Foreign Secretaries at the Russian H.Q. last night, which went on till after midnight. But it was worth while, as we nearly succeeded in getting quite a decent arrangement about Poland, which I hope we can get over the last hurdle today. That will be the most important thing, if we can get that. Because after all, if we couldn't get a decent-looking Polish settlement, none of our other high-falutin' plans for World Organisation and suchlike would make much sense. . . .

Thank Goodness, we've given up the official lunches with toasts, after our midday meetings of Foreign Secretaries. It's a most tiresome and distracting habit. Molotov proposes a toast immediately the meal has begun. Someone has to reply and propose another. And so it goes on. One is always rising to one's feet and having to devise some silly remarks.*

We have practically fixed up with the Russians over Dumbarton Oaks, and I think that will go through. If so, there will be a United Nations Conference to finish it off, on April 25th. Ed. has arranged it all for San Francisco! Probably very pleasant at that time of year, but rather a long way to go. Anthony will have to go: I don't know whether I shall. Rather depends on what is going on elsewhere at the time.

The news seems good, and one can't help wondering how much longer the Germans can stand it.

Sunday, 11 February *A.C. to T.C.* *Alupka*

It has been a delight to get a number of letters from you. I do so look forward to the arrival of the Bag—about midnight.

Well, at last we are practically through. We had a pretty good rush all yesterday and I was up till 1.30 this morning drafting the Communiqué with Bridges and Americans. It has still to be approved by the Russians and formally blessed by a plenary meeting some time today.

Yesterday, at the afternoon meeting, at about 7.30, the President announced incidentally that he was leaving today at 3.0 p.m. It was pointed out by everyone else that it would be quite outside the limits of possibility to get everything tidied up in time. But the President remained quite unmoved although he could produce no sort of reason why he should leave today, or why at 3.0 p.m. Ed. of course said that it would be all right and that we could finish off the work in an hour. But then Ed. is completely inexperienced in these matters and very superficial. However, the President has since seen sense, and will stay till 6 p.m. today or, if necessary, tomorrow. But I think we shall be able to close the whole thing before 6.

I have never known the Russians so easy and accommodating. In particular Joe has been extremely good. He *is* a great man, and

* Cadogan noted gloomily that he generally had to propose the health of Vyshinsky, 'a great villain but quite a pleasant companion'. 'I don't care twopence about his health, and it goes against the grain to say anything pleasant about him. But it does me no harm.'

shows up very impressively against the background of the other two ageing statesmen. The President in particular is very woolly and wobbly.* Lord Moran says there's no doubt which of the three will go first.

Our enormous Chiefs of Staff party left yesterday, so we are somewhat reduced in numbers.

Our plan is to drive over to Sebastopol tomorrow and spend the night in the ship, leave next day (Tues.) by air for Athens, arriving there probably about 5.0 p.m. I think we spend a night there and go on to Alexandria. We still aim at getting back to London on the 18th.

I think the Conference has been quite successful. We have got an agreement on Poland which may heal differences, for some time at least, and assure some degree of independence to the Poles. We have agreed the Dumbarton Oaks plan, and we have got a number of other things settled, including an important agreement with the Russians about the treatment of our prisoners whom they liberate. I hope the world will be impressed!

The flap is now beginning, and I must stop.

I suppose we shall be sending back a Bag tomorrow which could carry another letter from me. After that, I don't know how you'll get another letter. I doubt whether one would go from Athens, but there may be daily communication from Alexandria.

(11 p.m.) We tidied up our Conference just before dinner tonight. P.M. left for Sebastopol this afternoon about 5. He said that, as weather reports were not good, he thought he would go on to Athens tomorrow. We were still at Livadia, half an hour away, trying to finish off our work, when he telephoned this from our HQ, adding that he had given orders for our luggage to be packed, so that we could follow him tonight to Sebastopol. So when I got back at 8 p.m., I found that my Marine batman had packed all the things I wanted. However, I've had them unpacked again, and have extracted a promise from Anthony that we don't start before 10.30 a.m. tomorrow. Must go to bed for a bit. My letters—like time—get shorter and shorter!

Monday, 12 February *A.C. to T.C.* S.S. *Franconia*

We had a pretty busy day yesterday, but got finished by about 7 p.m. In the middle of the proceedings I went to a lunch with the President, Winston, Joe, Anthony, Ed. and four or five others. Not too many toasts, luckily, but after lunch, as I was standing talking to

* 'The President', said Churchill at breakfast that morning, 'is behaving very badly. He won't take any interest in what we are trying to do.' (Moran, p. 231.)

someone, I felt a nudge, turned round and found Joe holding two glasses of brandy, and I had to drink 'no heeltaps' with him.

I got an early bed last night, and rather wanted it. We left Alupka at 10.30 a.m. and drove here—to Sebastopol. A lovely road the whole way, and it was fine and sunny. We passed Balaklava, and could see where the charge took place—rather a delicate subject with Russians, but we've reached the point of chaffing about it now.

Sebastopol, having been twice besieged in two years, is in a fine mess. It took us a long time to find our way through it to the port, but we finally got on board soon after 1.30. I joined Winston at a terrific lunch—dressed crab, roast beef, apple pie, washed down with excellent Liebfraumilch, and gorgonzola and port! He had come to the ship yesterday evening, arriving here after dark, so he wanted to go and charge about at Balaklava this afternoon. Molotov turned up at 3 to say good-bye, and we had to give him lunch and show him round the ship: didn't get rid of him till 4.

I then had a nap, and am now preparing for dinner. At present, the plan is to leave the ship at 9 a.m. tomorrow, and fly to Athens. Target date for return to England still 18th or 19th.

An extremely luxurious ship—all possible comforts. Wish I was sailing in her.

Tuesday, 13 February *A.C. to T.C.* S.S. *Franconia*

I need hardly say that, after dinner last night, plans were changed again. It had been arranged that the P.M. should stay here in the ship until tomorrow, while Anthony and I flew to Athens this morning. Anthony of course delighted at the idea of a trip on his own and not as a member of the P.M.'s suite. But the P.M. evidently had second thoughts about allowing Anthony to go gathering laurels on his own, and announced that he would come with us tomorrow—to Anthony's rage and horror. It's rather like travelling about with Melba and Tetrazzini in one company!

Anyhow, it's been really rather refreshing to have had a bit of a rest in great comfort here. You would have approved of me if you could have seen me this morning having breakfast in bed, eating a large fried fish and some excellent bacon, masses of butter, marmalade, coffee, oranges &c.! Rather a beastly day, but I did a good walk on deck. Then lunch with P.M., Sarah, Anthony and Alexander. We rose from the luncheon table at 4.10 p.m. There were only two alternatives (1) to go to bed and (2) to take a brisk walk. I did the latter, with Anthony.

P.M. in very good form, making a frightful noise at lunch. He had a great argument with Alexander, who was trying to plead that we must do the best we can to help the Italians. P.M. resisted this, so that Alexander was stung into saying that, after all, that was more or less what we were fighting this war for—to secure liberty and a decent existence for the peoples of Europe. P.M. said 'Not a bit of it: we are fighting to secure the proper respect for the British people!' And he's not entirely wrong either. . . .

I'm writing this between tea and film, at which I'm due in about half an hour. We should spend one, or more probably two nights in Athens, then on to Cairo, and back Sunday or at latest Monday. But one never knows!

The report of our Crimea Conference seems to have had quite a good reception in the Press, and I really think we did some quite useful things. On the whole it was great fun, and an unusual experience.

I must say this is a very nice ship. She has been carrying troops throughout the war, but for 6 days and nights 5,000 men worked on our quarters, which have been restored practically to the degree of pre-war luxury. We are waited on by hundreds of Marines and stewards. Altogether a great change from present-day standards in London. . . .

[Churchill argued at dinner that night for firmness with E.L.A.S. The Christmas truce, he now thought, had been a mistake; the Communists had committed atrocities; and Leeper had behaved weakly. (Moran, pp. 234–5.)]

Thursday, 15 February *A.C. to T.C.* *Athens*

We had a lovely day yesterday, marred somewhat by the fact that we had to get up at 7.30, dress, pack, breakfast and be off the ship by 9.00 a.m.

Rather beastly weather, cloudy, windy and rather cold. A 3-hour drive to the aerodrome, away from our mountains and over dreary snow-covered plains. Actually the snow disappeared by the time we reached the airfield, which is the most dreary spot you ever saw, swept by a cold wind. There, in the same old marquee, with its warm stove, vodka, caviare, &c. Winston arrived about a quarter of an hour after us. Then the usual national anthems, inspection of guard of honour and mutual compliments and, of course, a speech by Winston.

We finally got off the ground about 1.45 and almost at once flew into brilliant sunlight. We struck straight across the Black Sea, but unfortunately didn't pass over the Straits (I think one is now allowed to) but west of them. Soon we passed quite close to Mount Athos, flying about level with the top of it (about 6,000 ft.). It looked quite lovely, with the top half of it covered with snow, and the sea round about like sapphire and emerald. And the great snow-covered hump of Mount Olympus in the distance.

Our plane is faster than Winston's so, although he started ahead of us, we soon overhauled him and had to dawdle a bit so as not to land in front of him. Finally we had to circle 3 or 4 times over Athens and the Piraeus to let him get down. We got a very good bird's-eye view of the place, though nothing looks much from the air (except mountains). The Parthenon looked like a broken child's toy.

Directly after landing, we were put into cars and driven straight into Athens, to see the old Palace, which is well situated, perched on a terrace, with a great square below it. This was absolutely *packed* with people—I've never seen such a crowd. And I suppose I've never seen a crowd from above (as the King and Queen do from the balcony of Buckingham Palace) with everyone looking up. The effect is a sea of faces: it looks like one great stippled pink surface. Winston arrived with the Archbishop (Regent), and they had a terrific reception. Speeches of course, which Winston enjoyed enormously. Poor Anthony! All this would have been his if the P.M. hadn't butted in. But he was called for and made a little speech of his own, so let us hope that was some comfort.

It was the most lovely, cloudless evening, and quite warm. From the ground, the Acropolis and Parthenon certainly are superb.

We got here to the Embassy about 6.30 and had a cup of tea. Your letter of the day before (Tues.) was handed to me the moment I arrived.

After a bath and change, a dinner party of about 40. I sat between Alexander and Admiral Mansfield.* The Archbishop called at 10 and was closeted with the P.M. The latter went away, fortunately, about midnight, to sleep in his plane and get off to Cairo this afternoon.

After dinner, about 10.30, Sarah and Lord Moran and I and others drove up to the Acropolis (only about 5 minutes) to see the Parthenon floodlit. I've never seen anything more beautiful, and I must go back there today.

Must stop now (10 a.m.) as I've got meetings coming on.

I'll keep this letter open: I don't know when the Bag goes (if there is one: as the P.M. has left, it may have been laid off).

* Rear-Admiral J. M. Mansfield, commanded 15th Cruiser Squadron 1944–5.

Later (*7 p.m.*)

There is no 'Mosquito' from here today, so I'll keep this letter up to date and take it tomorrow to Cairo: I may be able to get it off from there tomorrow evening.

Most of this morning was taken up with discussions with Anthony, Macmillan, Alexander and Rex Leeper. After lunching here some of us went out to the Acropolis, with a Mr. and Mrs. Burn, who are both Greek archaeological experts, and proved very effective guides. It was a glorious day, without a cloud, and we spent a sun-drenched afternoon on that wonderful spot, which is even more beautiful than interesting, which is saying a great deal.

I have always heard that the light in Greece has some quality of its own, and it seems true. I was woken fairly early this morning by the brightest, clearest light that I have ever known, and at sunset this evening the colours of Mount Hymettus, which guards us from the north east, were perfectly lovely.

After the Acropolis, we drove out about 4 miles to Daphne, where there is an enchanting little Byzantine church, with remains of beautiful mosaics, and then on for 2 or 3 miles to the sea, on the bay of Eleusis. Back for tea, and read a bit after, and I am now preparing myself to go and dine with the Archbishop.

I'm very comfortable here, with a nice sunny bedroom and private bathroom attached.

Anthony spent what I hope was a happy afternoon, going round collecting cheers from troops! With the P.M. gone, he is having a little fun on his own. . . .

Friday, 16 February *A.C. to T.C.* *Cairo*

No 'Mosquito' from here, so must take this letter on with me, keeping it up to date.

The Archbishop gave us quite a good dinner. I sat between two members of the Government, one on my right quite pleasant and intelligent and speaking good English, but I had to devote most of my time to the old bore on my left, who only spoke French, which was beyond Gen. Scobie, who sat on the other side of him.

After dinner . . . Sideris* talked nonsense volubly, and A. lost his temper.† It was a perfectly hopeless discussion, but I think that the

* Georgis Sideris, Greek Finance Minister and Minister of Supplies.

† . . .'quite rightly', as Cadogan later noted. Eden's diary says 'I'm afraid that I was blunt to the verge of rudeness on the need for Greeks to bestir themselves. But they are now in the mood to rely entirely upon us, and that way lies disaster for them and for us. I had concerted general line with Rex [Leeper] beforehand, and he didn't seem unduly perturbed.' Eden, *The Reckoning*, p. 521.

Greeks gained from it the impression that we were getting tired of doing everything for them and that it was high time that they did something for themselves.

Into bed by 1 a.m.

A., Nicholas and Bridges went off at 7 a.m. to Corinth. I refused and instead went shopping with Bob Dixon. Bought some sponges, and then we did some sight-seeing—Theseum and Areopagus. Left for airfield at 12.20. Joined there by A. and party, and off the ground at 1.15. Arrived Cairo 4.45. (So can do Parthenon and Pyramids on the same day!)

Stopped at Mena villa about 5.15. Received by Grigg. Haile Selassie arrived at 6, and there was a not very stimulating conversation between him and P.M. (who has a cold). I talked after with Grigg* about Palestine and Levant, and A. and I then came on to the Embassy. Hot bath and change, and dinner at 9. 10.30 Paget and Holmes came in for a discussion on Levant. Shone was dining, so we had a regular confab., which led to no very heroic solutions, but was useful. Finished 12.30. Rather sleepy.

Saturday, 17 February *A.C. to T.C.* *Cairo*

This letter becomes a diary, as there are no means of sending it home that will get it there before we do. We had meant to start home tonight, but apparently even a 'Mosquito' can't land in England owing to thick weather. Lovely morning here. Started work at 9.30 and, before I'd finished, Bob Howe came in for a talk. Had to drive him out at 10.20, as I was due to start with A. for the Villa at 10.30, and I hadn't finished my work. Went out to Villa and picked up P.M. and we started for the Fayoum about 11.30. I drove with Ned Grigg, who talked shop, which I find v. tiring. However, our car broke down about half way, and we changed into another, in which Robin Hankey† was sitting in solitary state. That rather stopped the shop, and we discussed the birds and local conditions. Arrived 12.30 at the new Fayoum Hotel, where [King] Ibn Saoud [of Saudi-Arabia] and his followers (48 in number) were staying. Was presented to H[is] M[ajesty], who is an imposing figure, and we were given bitter coffee, which is beastly. After compliments, Ibn Saoud, P.M. and A. retired for a talk, and we waited for them till 2 p.m. Their party had been brought up on an American destroyer. They had demanded to embark 60 sheep. The Commander compromised on 6, but even so the Arabians had lit fires on the deck, at which to roast

* Sir Edward Grigg, now Minister of State Resident in Middle East.

† R. M. A. Hankey, British Embassy.

them, and had burnt large holes in the deck planking. At lunch, I sat between Medhurst* and Sheikh Yussuf Yasin. To make conversation, I asked the latter whether he had been comfortable on the trip. He said 'Yes, because I brought my tent with me'! And I discovered that he *had* pitched his tent on the quarter deck!

Left about 3.15, stopping at Miles' [Lampson's] country house on the way back. Arrived back at the villa at 5.30, and King Farouk appeared. I didn't take part, but had to attend a meeting at 6.30 with Shukri Quwatli, the Syrian President. We gave him a little plain, but polite speaking, which I hope will do him good. Dashed back with A. to the Embassy, changed and bathed and back to dinner at the Villa at 8.45. Sat next to Sarah, whom I found quite pleasant and interesting. A. insisted on coming away reasonably early, and it is now not more than 12.30 a.m. Weather over England hopeless, so neither we nor P.M. could start tonight. We *hope* to start tomorrow night.

[The King's suite included an astrologer, the Royal purse-bearer, the official food-taster, the chief and second servers of Ceremonial Coffee, 10 guards with sabres and 9 miscellaneous slaves, cooks, porters and scullions.

On the last day at Yalta the British learned that Roosevelt and Stalin had secretly negotiated a settlement of the terms on which Russia would come into the war against Japan. Eden had remarked to the Prime Minister in London, and to Stettinius at Malta, that since Russia would fight against Japan in her own interests, it would be needless to pay a high price for her belligerency. Territorial concessions to Russia in the Far East should be matched by Russian concessions elsewhere. The guiding principle of the American negotiations, of which Roosevelt kept Stettinius in virtual ignorance, ran on very different lines. It must be remembered that the development of the atomic bomb was not then completed. The U.S. Chiefs of Staff urgently desired Russia to fight against Japan, and Roosevelt agreed, in effect, to pay Stalin's price. China was not consulted.

Churchill was less hostile to this agreement than Eden, who urged upon him, in the presence of Stalin and Roosevelt, that Britain should not sign. They sent for Cadogan, who said that he entirely agreed with Eden. Nevertheless, Churchill signed, feeling that he would otherwise forfeit all influence in Far Eastern affairs. By no stretch of language could the agreement be called consonant with the declaration made about Chinese integrity at Cairo in November 1943. Roosevelt undertook to secure Chiang's consent, though it was clear that Stalin intended to insist on his terms whether or no Chiang objected.

The Polish question, however, was the most significant issue tackled at Yalta, for it had become the touchstone of Russian goodwill and honesty;

* Air Chief Marshal C. E. H. Medhurst, A.O.C.-in-C. Mediterranean, Middle East.

hence the importance of tying Stalin to clear declarations. On the Polish eastern frontier, he secured the easy acceptance of the Curzon Line, including Lwow. Poland, he said, could expand as far west as the Neisse, into regions where there were now no Germans 'as they had all run away'. Churchill and Roosevelt both thought that this proposal would give Poland an indigestible amount of German territory. The western frontier was therefore left for determination at the peace conference. Poland, said Churchill, must be free and sovereign, captain of her own soul. Stalin avowed that he wanted the same thing. It would be possible to hold free elections 'within a month unless there is some catastrophe on the front, which is improbable'. In order to overcome the impasses between the Lublin and the London Poles, the powers agreed on the reorganisation of the Provisional Government 'on a broader democratic basis, with the inclusion of democratic leaders from Poland itself and from Poles abroad. . . .'

Russia accepted the American proposal, which was in substance Cadogan's rejected compromise of the previous September, on voting in the Security Council; no longer pressed the demand for all sixteen Soviet Republics to have seats in the Assembly, but asked only for two; and made no attempt to interfere in Greek affairs. Churchill was able to postpone a decision on the dismemberment of Germany, and on the inordinate Russian demands for reparation; and to secure for France a zone in Germany and a seat on the Control Commission. The three powers pledged themselves to maintain unity for peace as for war, 'a sacred obligation which our governments owe to our peoples and to all the peoples of the world.' A Declaration on Liberated Europe set forth the 'right of all peoples to choose the form of government under which they will live' and looked to 'the earliest possible establishment through free elections of governments responsive to the will of the people.'

On his return to London, Churchill gave Ministers a vivid and ample account of Yalta, speaking warmly of Stalin and feeling sure that so long as Stalin lasted, Anglo-Russian friendship could be maintained. Several times, when pressed hard, he said 'Yes. I see the strength of argument. I will withdraw my proposal.' Dalton's diary records Churchill to have added: 'Poor Neville Chamberlain believed he could trust Hitler. He was wrong. But I don't think I'm wrong about Stalin.' Although no one could tell whether the Russians would honour their promise about a truly free and independent Poland, Churchill thought very significant a remark of Stalin: 'We are conscious of our great sins against Poland in the past, through occupation and oppression of that country.'

In Parliament, the Prime Minister, influenced by Stalin's behaviour over Greece, said confidently:

> The impression I brought back from the Crimea, and from all my other contacts, is that Marshal Stalin and the Soviet leaders wish to live in honourable friendship and equality with the Western democracies. . . .

I know of no Government which stands to its obligations, even in its own despite, more solidly than the Russian Soviet Government.

Cadogan's view, expressed to Halifax in a letter of 20 February, was also an optimistic one:

You will have been able to form your own opinion on the degree of success achieved. The P.M. and Anthony are well satisfied—if not more—and I think they are right. Of course Poles in London, and extreme right-wing M.P.s, criticise and grumble. All I can say is that, in the circumstances, I think we did much better by Poland than I, at least, could have thought possible before we left.

One wondered, before the Conference, what would be the effect on Stalin of his great military success. It might well have gone either way, but he was certainly more genial and more reasonable than I have ever seen him. There was no bluster: success, instead of going to his head, seemed to have given him the added assurance enabling him to take broad views and to be unafraid of making concessions. Long may it continue!

On the other hand, I am sorry to say that I was rather shocked at the President. He did not look well and was rather shaky. I know he is never a master of detail, but I got the impression that most of the time he really hardly knew what it was all about. And whenever he was called upon to preside over any meeting, he failed to make any attempt to grip it or guide it, and sat generally speechless or, if he made any intervention, it was generally completely irrelevant. It was really rather disturbing.

Ed. was of course as buoyant as ever. He occasionally let us down with a bump but that, I am persuaded, was simply because he didn't understand, and no one looked more surprised or distressed than he did when he noticed our crestfallen looks.

Harry Hopkins was, I think, helpful but rather under the weather. What exactly, he had been doing—or saying—in Paris and Rome, I was never able to determine with any certainty. He stoutly maintained that he had been misrepresented—a thing that happens to everyone on occasions.

On the whole, it was successful and a not unpleasant experience.[24]]

XI

February–August 1945

THE PERILS OF VICTORY

'The Crimea Conference', said Roosevelt on his return, '... spells—and it ought to spell—the end of the system of unilateral action, exclusive alliances, and spheres of influence, and balances of power and all the other expedients which have been tried for centuries and have always failed.'

It would have been nearer the mark to say that Yalta spelt a renewed lease of life for those expedients. Explaining his own pronouncements, Churchill wrote 'I felt bound to proclaim my confidence in Soviet good faith in the hope of procuring it'; and again, 'Our hopeful assumptions were soon to be falsified. Still they were the only ones possible at the time.' That is a large claim. It may well be true that by this stage Britain lacked the authority and influence to stand out for a different policy, or that it would have been imprudent to do so even had she possessed the power; but to announce that the three powers had set their hands 'to far-reaching engagements at once practical and solemn', and to believe that these assumptions were 'the only ones possible', when evidence to the contrary accumulated daily, made the inevitable change of course the more painful. On the very day after his speech, learning that the Russians had just demanded the dismissal of the Roumanian Prime Minister, Churchill said, 'I have not the slightest intention of being cheated over Poland, not even if we go to the verge of war with Russia.'

The Polish Government in London had already announced that it considered the Yalta terms 'as a fifth partition of Poland, now accomplished by her Allies'.

This prolonged debate about the frontiers and government of Poland was not simply a question of constitutional niceties or international decency; it was, as the Polish Ambassador himself put it to Eden,

> a contest for a territory rich in population and national resources, and occupying a key position on the map. If the U.S.S.R. could establish itself on a line from Stettin to Trieste, with the Czechoslovak fortress in the centre projecting into Germany, Europe would be exposed to heavy pressure which would prevent the restoration of the balance of power and the maintenance of peace.

Eden told Raczynski that if the Russians chose to ostracise Mikolajczyk there would be no agreement and Britain would not recognise the Polish Government. Russia must be assured of a friendly Polish Government which would oppose German attempts at revenge. He was hopeful that Soviet claims would not go beyond this point; yet later in the same talk the Foreign Secretary reflected ruefully on the other possibilities and described himself as less optimistic than Churchill and Cadogan. Before the end of March he minuted:

> I take the gloomiest view of Russian behaviour everywhere. We don't yet know how Russians will react to our last Anglo-American message, but if it is still negative a breakdown seems inevitable. Then there is Molotov's refusal to go to San Francisco [Conference] and Russian behaviour to Turkey. Altogether our foreign policy seems a sad wreck and we may have to cast about afresh.[1]

1945

Tuesday, 20 February

5–6 talk with A., Mikolajczyk and Romer about our Polish agreement. They of course exhibited no gratitude, and were merely critical and unconstructive—like all Poles. But at least they are ready to go to Moscow if invited. Telegraphed this to Moscow.

Wednesday, 21 February

3 interview between P.M. and [General] Anders.* Both rather lost their tempers at first, but calmed down later. It *may* have done some good, and they will meet again in a week. But it lasted 2½ hours, whereas all the business could have been done in 20 mins. 5.30 Gater† about 'Territorial Trusteeship'. After a Conference, one always has to spend a lot of time explaining to those who have no experience of Conferences why one has not been able to obtain 101% of what they set out to demand. However, Gater was not unreasonable and I enveloped him in clouds of warm and woolly words.

Thursday, 22 February

Cabinet, due at 6 put off till 6.30. Item 1 was 'man-power', which went on till 7.50. The P.M. cannot say 'Yes' or 'No'. Instead, he makes a long speech, of which, 5 mins. later, he produces a slightly differently worded version. Why all the Cabinet aren't mad, I can't think. Perhaps they are. I *long* for poor old Neville Chamberlain again. He *did* know how to conduct business! Got away at 8.5,

* Commander of Polish forces, Feb.–June 1945. Churchill told him that Britain had not guaranteed Poland's eastern frontier; according to Anders, he also said that as Polish troops were no longer necessary to the war effort, they could be withdrawn.

† Sir G. H. Gater, P.U.S., Colonial Office, 1939–47.

leaving Cabinet still sitting—and *rambling*. *How* have we conducted this war, with the P.M. spending *hours* of his own and other people's time simply drivelling, welcoming every red herring so as only to have the pleasure of more irrelevant, redundant talk?

Friday, 23 February

No news of our attack—except for the fact that it has been launched. It ought to succeed—there's nothing much against us, except the weather.

[Montgomery's troops reached the Rhine, north of Cologne, on 23 February, and the U.S. 9th Army crossed the Roer.]

Saturday, 24 February

3.15 walked into Green Park. Spent about 5 mins watching a baseball match. It's the silliest—and the dullest—game I've ever seen. I'd sooner play dominoes with mangold wurzels. Back at F.O. about 4. Yellow crocuses well out, some purple in flower and a few white. Forsythia just showing yellow. Not too much work. Home at 7.

Monday, 26 February

Talk with A., Bidault, Chauvel, Massigli and Duff [Cooper].* Don't think Bidault's much good. Quite a pleasant little man, but on the end of a string, the other end of which is held by de Gaulle. . . . O.S. and I went to Savoy for dinner to French. I luckily sat between Duff and Hoyer Millar,† so didn't have to talk French. . . . P.M., who was present, made innumerable and interminable speeches in French! Got away soon after 12 and in to bed at 1.

[From 27 February to 4 March Cadogan was on leave at the cottage. He had been suffering from minor ailments—several colds, followed by laryngitis and a bad cough—for nearly six months. Almost immediately after his return to London, his doctor insisted that he take two weeks' complete rest.]

Tuesday, 27 February *Thatched Cottage*

Punctured about 4 miles short of Sevenoaks. Found all my tools had been pinched. But found a charming and helpful lorry-driver, with whose help we changed tyre in about 20 mins. When I thanked him, he said 'That's all right, Pal'—so I couldn't offer him a tip.

* Respectively Eden, French Foreign Minister, Sec.-Gen. at the Quai d'Orsai, Ambassador in London and British Ambassador in Paris.

† F. R. H. Millar, then Counsellor at the F.O., later P.U.S.

Arrived at Cottage at 5.30. Had tea—excellent brioches—and T. and I walked round after. Yellow crocus in full bloom, many purple out. Winter jasmine still flowering, and one or two daffodils. Quite a lot of primroses, aconites flourishing and buds swelling up and bursting everywhere. Fine sunset, but one never knows and quite a nip in the air. Good dinner, and listened to news. Seems that the Govt. have had very little trouble so far, over Poland. Very nice to be here in the quiet and looking forward, I hope, to a few peaceful days. I've still got no voice but feeling well, if tired.

Thursday, 1 March *Thatched Cottage*

Reading Winston's Early Years*—v. good. Good dinner, and I feel better, but v. becolded. That may be right. News good: American 9th Army has taken München Gladbach. Govt. got a majority of 400 odd to 0.† 30 abstentions—mostly Conservatives—like Jock McEwen,‡ I suppose, who presume to criticise while confessing they know not what else to suggest. I have a suggestion for them—they should apply for the Chiltern Hundreds. . . . How I *hate* Members of Parliament! They embody everything that my training has taught me to eschew—ambition, prejudice, dishonesty, self-seeking, light-hearted irresponsibility, black-hearted mendacity. Feeling better tonight after dinner, and after above outburst!

[Despite the Yalta declaration on Liberated Europe, the Soviets put into office a puppet administration in Roumania after forcing King Michael to dismiss the all-party Government appointed in August 1944. British protests were vitiated to some degree by the 'percentage agreement' of the previous October (see page 672), but to a much greater degree by the presence of the Red Army in Bucharest.]

Tuesday, 6 March

Got away at 7.30 to draft message from P.M. to Stalin about Roumania (which is *bad*). Left it with Private Secretaries at 7.45, as Cabinet won't be over before 9. . . . Told O.S. about my sick-leave. Also A. He was dejected, as he said P.M. and he had thought of sending me out to Moscow to handle Polish situation (also bad). But I told him I didn't think that a good plan—for obvious reasons. I'll go if they really want it, but I don't think it would be right.

* *My Early Life.*

† On the Prime Minister's motion. On 28 February, 25 M.P.s had voted for an amendment regretting the decision to transfer Polish territory to Russia.

‡ Chairman of the Conservative Members' Committee, Dec. 1944–June 1945.

Wednesday, 7 March

3 talk with A. and others about (a) Roumania (b) Poland, as a result of which we put up this evening draft telegram from P.M. to Pres. . . . My huge parcel from Joe arrived and I brought it home. 6 botts. champagne, 8 botts. Vodka and 2 large tins caviare.

Thursday, 8 March

Brought home another parcel of Russian gift: 9 more Botts. of champagne, 1 of Vodka and a lot of cigarettes.

Americans are across the Rhine tonight!

Friday, 9 March

Bob Dixon came in about various things, including S[an] F[rancisco] Conference. I explained to him that I was not at all sure that I should go to it. A. has sent minute to P.M. proposing to take a row of politicians of various colours to take charge of the various Commissions. He adds at the end 'I shall take Sir A. Cadogan and Sir W. Malkin from the F.O.' But what am I going to *do* if I'm not a Delegate? I'm no stickler, but, after Dumbarton Oaks, I'm not going out as camp-follower, or boot-black to the bloody Delegation. I'm not going to be 'Sec. Gen'. I'm not going to sit on a hard chair behind Mr Dingle Foot. I started doing that at Geneva 22 years ago, and did it for ten years. I'm not going back to it. I'm not going to waste my time as I did at Tehran in 1943. I don't particularly want to go as a Delegate, but I'll go as nothing less, and they can dispense with my services if they like.

Monday, 12 March

News good, but not sensational. In the absence of *any* opposition in Germany, there won't be an Armistice Day or a surrender. It will peter out—slowly. In the process we shall slaughter and capture large numbers of Germans, but it's going to be tedious, and not dramatic.

Monday, 19 March

Bob Dixon rang up about S. Francisco. Didn't say much, but made it plain A. wants me to come out but *not* as a Delegate. Then what? Bob says he's sending me something in writing by the Messenger tomorrow. I'm not going unless I see a worth-while job. I'm no stickler about my personal position, but I am *not* going as a sort of Secretary of Delegation. I did that for long enough in my youth, and I'm not going to revert to it. If necessary—like Van—I shall claim a G.C.B., a Privy Councillorship, a Peerage and retirement!

Tuesday, 20 March

Messenger arrived about 3.45. Letter from Bob D[ixon] saying A. 'distressed' at idea of my not going to S. Francisco. Quite saw I couldn't be a S[ecretary] G[eneral]. Thought N. Butler might do this. I could go for the first part only, with A., and leave with him. I wrote back to say that if A. really wants me, I obey orders. I only wanted to make sure he had reflected (if he had time to spare from reflecting on much more important matters) on how the thing would work. N. B[utler] would make an excellent S[ecretary] G[eneral], if he were prepared to take on a job that I was given 22 years ago. If there's a string of puppet politician Delegates, who know nothing about the subject, to crowd all the Commissions, I don't see where I come in. I can hang about in the background, but that's just what I don't like, and what I don't think I ought to do. Bob says A. fears the world will think it very odd if I don't come. I think Americans, and others, will think it much odder if I turn up as a sort of 2nd Secretary. And the suggestion that I should leave with A., after the opening meetings—that's just the time I should have thought I should be wanted—shows that no one has thought out how the thing's going to work at all. It simply doesn't make sense. Upshot is that I'll go if ordered, but I think it's a mistake.

Wednesday, 21 March *Thatched Cottage*

A glorious summer day. T. and I walked down to bottom of fields, and sat there! After lunch, finished reading telegrams which came in box yesterday. We're getting *nowhere* on Poland, and Roumania doesn't look too nice! Then wrote letters and went out, about 3, to continue my clearing operations by the gooseberry bed. These went well and I produced an appearance of tidiness. . . . Quite an active and productive day. One of these days I must arrange for payment of my Surtax. But that will have to be a rainy day! Battle news, from all quarters, excellent. Organised fighting is going to be over in Europe before midsummer night.

Friday, 23 March *Thatched Cottage*

Messenger arrived about 2.45. Nothing more about my attendance at S. Francisco! . . . Note from Bill [Cavendish-Bentinck] showing that Monty's attack [across the Rhine] is timed for tomorrow. (We saw about 300 bombers going over about midday today.) Hope this weather holds—today was about the most perfect day I have ever known, and a lovely evening. I think the war is hastening to its end (I've said that before!) though I don't know how long sporadic, sniping resistance may last, nor how long it may take to mop up—and catch Hitler! But German supplies and communications are smashed and they've got no reserves.

Saturday, 24 March *Thatched Cottage*

Another midsummer day, with cool S.E. breeze. Monty attacked last night, and it seems to go well. P.M. there, of course. Not v. much air activity over here today, but this morning and after lunch considerable number of heavies went over in open formation—scattered all over the sky. I've never seen that before.

Monday, 26 March

Rather a rush mugging up Polish question for Cabinet at 5.30. (A. away with laryngitis) and a number of 'World Organisation' questions for A.P.W. Committee after. Got through Cabinet by 6.45—luckily, as P.M. was due back any minute, and we should have sat all night! Then A.P.W. Committee which settled a little—but not much. . . . Have to go now (10.30) to see P.M. and explain the Cabinet views on his draft telegram to Roosevelt about Poland. If he had been there, no-one would have raised a voice, but in his absence there was various criticism, which I shall have to expound to him!

[It had become obvious during March that the Soviet Government intended to allow the British and Americans very little say in Poland. Molotov's interpretation of the Yalta decisions differed alarmingly from theirs. He refused to allow their observers to visit Poland, paid no attention to the Polish leaders outside the Lublin Committee and in other ways played for time while the Russians took a grip of Poland. Since 8 March Churchill had been urging upon the unconvinced Roosevelt a joint intervention. Later in March, the Soviets demanded that only the Lublin Government should represent Poland at the San Francisco Conference. The British and Americans objected. Thereupon Molotov said he would not go. This was the situation on 27 March, when Churchill's telegrams went off. The first reminded Roosevelt that

> I advised critics of the Yalta settlement to trust Stalin. If I have to make a statement of facts to the House the whole world will draw the deduction that such advice was wrong; all the more so that our failure in Poland will result in a set-up there on the new Roumanian model. In other words, Eastern Europe will be shown to be excluded from the terms of the Declaration on Liberated Europe, and you and we will be excluded from any job of influence in that area.
>
> Surely we must not be manoeuvred into becoming parties to imposing

on Poland—and on how much more of Eastern Europe—the Russian version of democracy?

The second message suggested the lines upon which they should address Moscow. Roosevelt telegraphed to Stalin on 29 March:

> I must make it quite plain to you that any . . . solution which would result in a thinly disguised continuance of the present Warsaw régime would be unacceptable and would cause the people of the United States to regard the Yalta agreement as having failed.

On 1 April Churchill sent a parallel message.[2]]

Tuesday, 27 March

Saw A. . . . We went over to see P.M. about 12.45. Latter in bed. A. urged telegram be sent off. (P.M. had *not* made a redraft as promised last night. I must add to yesterday's record that I went to see P.M. at 10.30 last night. I told him of Cabinet suggestions, some of which he ignored. But he agreed message might be split in 2. But when he came to read it again, he said he thought he would re-draft it this morning. This he hasn't done.) About 1.15 P.M. agreed to send off at once the original message, but in 2 parts. . . . 5.15 Bob Dixon. Explained to him quite frankly why I don't want to go to 'Frisco. He said he had put all my reasons to A. Saw A. about 6.30 and raised point with him. He affected to be surprised that I should see any difficulty about my going. I said I was in his hands and at his orders, and if he required me to go, that was the end of it, but I thought it wrong. I fear I shall have to go. But 'Frisco may be blown out of the water altogether if Joe continues to behave like this. I said the tactic was to tell Pres. that if the Russians maintain their attitude, we could not support the 'President's compromise'.* I think P.M. may accept this. In that event, I believe Americans might postpone 'Frisco—they can't risk a break. . . . P.M. had a telegram this morning from Monty saying German army was beat. Looks as if this were true. But it may take some time to mop up and occupy the country. C. arrived for dinner. I had a bit of work to do, and Dr McCall called, and took a swab—under P.M.'s orders.

Monday, 2 April

Feel all right, but had *no* appetite during week-end. Better since I (yesterday) stopped eating McCall's horrible tablets. I put them on the fire instead.

* On voting in the Security Council.

Tuesday, 3 April

A. and P.M. between them have agreed that if Russia refuses to come to 'Frisco, owing to absence of Poland, that is a reason for holding the Conference in spite of all reasons to the contrary. I disagree, and must put my case to A. I think the opposite. But the 24 hrs. in the day are not enough to enable me to get thro' all I have to do.

Wednesday, 4 April

Wrote minute for A., who's still in country, pointing out that if Russians abstain from 'Frisco (*I* don't think they will) we really *can't* hold the Conference. Why P.M. and he think we must passes my comprehension. . . . 3.30 meeting with Dominions about Territorial Trusteeship. I can't make up my mind whether Evatt and Fraser are more stupid than offensive. . . .

A. is flapping on the telephone saying we can't go to 'Frisco and support 'President's Compromise' if Stalin won't play on Poland. I think he's right, but it's an awfully nasty decision. Bobbety sent a snorter in the same sense to P.M., but latter isn't at all converted. If 'Frisco is to be put off, that must be done in the next 48 hrs.

Thursday, 5 April

An emergency Cabinet on Joe's outrageous message to Pres. accusing us of having reached secret agreement with Germans behind his back. Pres. has sent v. good answer. P.M. submitted draft of supporting message. Quite good.

[Stalin's message referred to negotiations supposed to have taken place in Berne and to an agreement whereby Kesselring had undertaken to open the western front and permit the Anglo-American armies to move farther east, in return for easier peace terms. No such negotiations had been held or agreement made. 'Frankly', Roosevelt telegraphed to Stalin at the close of his rebuttal, 'I cannot avoid a feeling of bitter resentment toward your informers, whoever they are, for such vile misrepresentations of my actions or those of my trusted subordinates.'

In the previous month, sixteen Polish leaders had gone to Moscow, under written guarantee of their safety, for talks about the formation of an all-party Government. They disappeared without trace. On 5 April, Cadogan, gloomy and dispirited, told Count Raczynski that the Foreign Office had received no news of them and that he did not understand what the Russians were driving at. 'I replied that we would know soon enough, and he did not contradict me.'[3]]

Sunday, 8 April

A. rang up about Poland. I said we should have to give Stalin warning that we must make a statement to House. He will send minute to P.M. Also about French approach to us about Pact. P.M. says 'this is not the time to make a démarche to the French'. But of course that is not the point. *They* are making a démarche to *us*. And we ought not to snub them. A. said he would put this to P.M.

Monday, 9 April

Cabinet 5.30. I got away 7.30, with instructions to carry out Cabinet decisions. They *never* take a decision before 7.30, and by that time F.O. have gone home, so it's not too easy. I put it all on G. Millard,* and washed my hands of it. . . . Dominions meeting at 10. Being in the Chair, I rushed it through before midnight, and left it to others to draft report. This is really impossible. These bloody Dominions take up 6 hrs. of my working day, and then I get a gay little note from Moley [Sargent] asking when I expect him back. Have answered that he must be back on *Friday* and *I'm* going away. In bed by 1 a.m.

[President Roosevelt died on the afternoon of 12 April.]

Friday, 13 April

Message now from Truman that he would be delighted to see P.M. in Washington. So, when P.M. woke up about 6, there were hectic telephone conversations between A. and him. P.M. of course wanted to go. A. thought they oughtn't both to be away together (Monty announces that the war is over!) P.M. says he'll go and A. can stay. I told A. that, if P.M. goes, *he must*. (Otherwise I see I shall be put on a 'plane at 5 minutes' notice! Anyhow, it's right.) A. due to leave at 7.45. At that hour, no decision reached—P.M. said he would decide at aerodrome. Party due to get off ground at 8.30! Home at 8 and dined. Rang up Tommy at 9.30 and discovered P.M. had *not* gone! *Masses* of work, and P.M. has now (11.15 p.m.) just rung up to consult me about message to Stalin.

[Churchill deeply regretted in after years that he allowed himself to be persuaded not to go at once to Washington. Truman knew very little of international affairs, though he rapidly grasped the main problems and showed a most welcome power of decision. On his first day in the White House the new President was provided by the State Department with this accurate assessment:

The British long for security but are deeply conscious of their decline from a leading position to that of the junior partner of the Big Three and

* Asst. Private Sec. to Eden.

are anxious to buttress their position vis-à-vis the United States and Russia both by exerting leadership over the countries of Western Europe and through knitting the Commonwealth more closely together.[4]]

Saturday, 14 April

Looked at Truman's telegram about Poland with O.S. and [C.F.A.] Warner.* It wants a bit of amendment and we formulated this. We also formulated an alternative line. Truman's proposals merely continue the old wrangle. I think we may want to have something ready to forestall what I foresee—viz. an announcement by the Soviet that they have reached agreement with local Poles. Got this into some shape for telephoning to Chequers when (about 6.30) got 2 drafts of telegrams which P.M. has cooked up without waiting for our comments! These of course at variance with us. P.M wants to fall in at once with Truman's suggestion. How can one conduct affairs between Washington London ?! However, sent
Chequers
my criticisms of Truman to Chequers.... Call from Rowan seemed to show that P.M. was at least considering what I have sent him. Afraid I shall get no sleep.

War news marvellous. War is over, and it only a question of how long mopping-up lasts and whether (though I think this unlikely) there will be a surrender. A. and party arrived all right [in Washington] this afternoon.

Sunday, 15 April

Heard last night Molotov going to Washington. So was not surprised to get a telegram about midday from A. asking me to go tomorrow. Submitted to P.M., who approved. Michiels rang up to say P.M. would not receive Gerbrandy† at Chequers today, which distressed the latter, so rang up Chequers and got it fixed for 4 p.m.... To F.O. about 3.45. Cleared up all arrears and home 6.30... paid bills and settled up things. War news the same, tho' we are running up against some resistance.

[On Eden's instructions, Cadogan pointed out to the U.S. Ambassador the great political advantages which would accrue if the American forces could press forward and liberate Prague. Did the State Department agree? By the end of the month no answer had been received.

The entries for 18 April to 6 June are taken from Cadogan's daily letters to Lady Theo. He makes no mention of an incident on the outward

* Head of Northern Dept., F.O.

† Dr P. S. Gerbrandy, Netherlands Prime Minister, 1940–5.

journey, when the side door of the aircraft flew open. Sitting just forward of the door, he did no more than glance over his shoulder at the frantic efforts to shut it. A few minutes later, while the aircraft was still at no great height, the door suddenly unlatched itself again. Without troubling to look up from his book, Cadogan said to his neighbour, 'I don't think flying will really catch on until they make these machines less draughty.']

Wednesday, 18 April *A.C. to T.C.* *Washington*

We got off the ground punctually at 1 p.m. and found ourselves 9 hours later at the Azores! Apparently there were strong head winds on the northern course. The Azores are rather out of the way, but there was still a chance of getting on to Washington the same day. . . .

We spent no more than 2 hours there, and then left for Gander, in Newfoundland. Our plane was a good one—a 'Liberator'—but not too comfortable. There was one little truckle-bed at one end of the saloon in which we all sat, but it didn't look very inviting . . .; as a matter of fact I almost prefer sitting in a reasonably comfortable chair. But the chief inconvenience was that there was no heating, so that when, over a sea covered with ice floes and bergs, we had to go up to 12,000 ft. to avoid bumps, the temperature fell to zero Fahrenheit! However, we had flying suits and boots and any number of blankets, and I don't think any of us are any the worse. Personally, I feel very well.

We took 9 hours to get to Gander, landing there about 2.30 p.m. by local time. The Station Commander gave me tea—or rather, a drink! Gander a God-forsaken spot, pretty cold, with remains of snow lying about. We got off again at 4.30 p.m. and landed here about 12.30 a.m.—another 9-hr. flight. So we did 27 hours' flying out of 31! The Pilot was a bit sleepy at the end.

The Embassy . . . hadn't a spare room, but they had arranged with the New Zealand Minister to put me up in his Legation, next door to the Embassy—one can walk across the garden to it—and I am extremely comfortable there: good bed, and bathroom, breakfast in bed and all the things you like! . . . Slept like a log till I rang for my breakfast about 8.45. My host, Berendsen, I knew already and like. . . . Went on to the Embassy and saw Dorothy [Lady Halifax], who seems to be in good form, and later Edward, who is ditto. Anthony blew in just for a few minutes before going off to lunch with the Senate Foreign Relations Committee, after which he was going to stay at Ronnie Tree's house in Virginia till Saturday morning, before when Molotov will probably not be available for conversations.

A heavenly day here, and the place looks lovely, though the best blossom is almost over. Brilliant sun and sky and deliciously fresh air.

... Edward of course talked to me about his plans. He might, if pressed, come back here after his holiday, and stay till the end of the year! I'll find an opportunity to talk to Anthony some time.

Friday, 20 April *A.C. to T.C.* *Mirador, Greenwood, Va.*

[On 19 April] at 2.30 I took Tom [Bromley] shopping. But the shops are really almost as empty as in London. I managed to make up 1 doz. collars by taking 7 of one kind, 4 of another and 1 of another. I got a doz. handkerchiefs, but don't know how they will turn out. The only things in fairly good supply are socks. *No* shirts and *no* underclothing. Perhaps San Francisco may be better.*

We thought we shd. have to go back to Washington this morning. Molotov was reported from Alaska yesterday morning and was expected to arrive about noon today. But there was no further news of him this morning and we decided to go back for dinner only.

... P.M. getting rather annoyed, and sends messages to Anthony such as 'When you have finished your holiday in Virginia, there are matters of grave import that should be attended to in Washington, such as &c. &c.' As if *he* never went off on a jaunt.

I don't suppose we shall leave Washington much before Monday now, and shall probably stay one night on the way somewhere. Not sure where. Anthony wants to go to Tucson in Alabama, but Ed. is trying to drag us off to Ogden, Utah. I'm afraid that wherever Ed. is, we shall have brass bands, and shall have to inspect the Fire Brigade and open the flower show.

Sunday, 22 April *A.C. to T.C.* *Washington*

After despatching my letter to you yesterday morning, Anthony and I had a talk with Jumbo Wilson† and then went down to the State Department for a conversation with Ed., Joe Grew and Jimmy Dunn,‡ about (a) how to handle Molotov on Poland and (b) arrangements for the Conference. Molotov still miles away up in N.W. Canada. I think he must have been dawdling on purpose. It was plain he couldn't get here till this afternoon at earliest. Ed. in very good form and very pleased with himself.

... At 5.30 I had an appointment with Judge Rosenman at the

* Clothes were rationed in Britain.

† Field-Marshal Wilson was appointed head of British Military Mission in Washington after the death of Field-Marshal Sir John Dill.

‡ Of the U.S. State Dept.

White House. He was one of Roosevelt's intimate friends and is in charge of the 'War Criminals' question for the U.S. Government.

At the gate of the White House I was asked my business, said I had an appointment with Judge Rosenman and gave my name. The gatekeeper phoned to the House, and came back saying that that was all right and that Judge X was expecting me in the East Wing. I thought this was rather odd, but supposed Rosenman was busy, and drove round to the other end of the building.

I had been charged by John Simon to deliver a paper on War Crimes to Rosenman and to discuss it with him.

I was ushered in to Judge X, a heavy, owl-like creature, apologised for troubling him and handed him the paper, explaining that I was no great expert in these legal matters but was at his disposal for discussion. He said he knew nothing about them at all, took the paper and read it very slowly. He then put it down and after a long pause said to me in a booming voice 'What I say, Mr. Cadogan, is 'Let Justice Be Done',' and spat into the waste-paper basket. I agreed cordially, and said that was all right, but we had got to carry the matter a bit further.

He fixed his owlish gaze on me and began a very long and very slow sermon of which the text was the vital necessity of our 2 countries acting together. At least so I found out eventually. It took some time, as he began by telling me that he was from Kentucky and giving me a history of that State and a sketch of the main characteristics of its people. In the middle, a telephone message came to the effect that Judge Rosenman was awaiting me. But that had no effect on Judge X, who continued with his discourse until the end, expectorating intermittently into the waste-paper basket, which was of wood and fortunately watertight. We finally parted with mutual expressions of profound esteem, and I was ushered along through the basement of the White House to Judge Rosenman. He asked incredulously whether I had really been with Judge X and when I admitted I had, went into a fit of uncontrollable laughter, so I realised I had seen a character. What a people! Rosenman was very nice and quite business-like....

Nothing much this morning. Molotov expected about 6 this evening. Joe's performance in signing a treaty with the Warsaw Poles is pretty bad. I suppose that is why M. has been dawdling in Alaska and Canada. Anthony is *not* going to the airport to meet him and I *think* Truman is going to talk pretty straight to him.

[In 1943 the Allies had announced that the major German war criminals would be punished by their joint decision. The American and Russian Governments, it appears, favoured the judicial method, whereas the British Government (according to the paper which Cadogan gave to Judge Rosenman) preferred 'execution without trial in the case of Hitler and a number of arch-criminals associated with him'. However, the three Governments soon afterwards decided to set up the international military tribunal.]

Monday, 23 April *A.C. to T.C.* *Washington*

Molotov duly arrived about 6 yesterday evening.

I dined here with Anthony and 2 or 3 others, and at about 9.30 we went to the State Department for our first talk with Molotov. This lasted till about midnight, and got us *nowhere* at all. M. appears to have no instructions from Stalin—or pretends to have none—and is simply mulish on every point.

The question arises whether we can really go to San Francisco to urge the adoption of a plan admittedly based on Great Power co-operation when the Great Powers are so obviously at sixes and sevens. Ed. professes to agree that we might have to postpone the Conference, but the Americans are so dead set on the Conference that I doubt whether they'll really play along those lines. Ed. undertook that, if we made no progress this morning, he wd. mobilize the President to talk like a Dutch Uncle to Molotov.

After discussion with Anthony and the drafting of telegrams to London, I got into bed at 2 a.m. this morning.

We were at the State Dept. at 10 a.m. for a talk with the Americans before being joined by the Russian party at 10.30. Molotov as hopeless as ever, and we got *nothing* out of him. So we broke up soon after 12, and Ed. went over to the White House to see the President. We have now just had lunch here, and are waiting for a telephone call from him and, possibly, some guidance from London.

I personally think that it is pretty certain we shall leave here tomorrow morning and fly to Tucson (pronounced Tewson), stop the night there, and arrive in S. Francisco for lunch on Wednesday. . . .

Ed. summoned us about 3.30. We agreed to go on to S. Francisco (or Tucson) tomorrow morning, and to announce that we haven't completed our conversations here but that they will be continued in S. Francisco.

Meanwhile (it's now 6.30) we are dining early at 7.30 and having a further talk at 9 with Americans and Russians, mainly about arrangements for the Conference, in regard to which I am sure Molotov will be as bloody-minded as he has been on Poland!

[President Truman told Molotov in plain language what he thought of Russian behaviour. 'I have never been talked to like that in my life', said Molotov. 'Carry out your agreements and you won't get talked to like that,' retorted Truman.[5]]

Wednesday, 25 April *A.C. to T.C.* *San Francisco*

Since I closed my last letter to you, in Washington, we had a meeting at the State Dept. at 9 p.m. with Americans and Russians, on Poland. Molotov as sticky as usual. Then, about 9.30 we admitted China (T.V. Soong*) to discuss Conference arrangements. If I were to be honest, I should have to say that Molotov was only a *little* more forthcoming on this occasion. We broke up just before 12. Ed and Molotov went off to their planes to take off for San Francisco, but we went home to get some part of a night, at least, in bed.

... We ... arrived here 2.30 a.m. (1.20 a.m. local time *here*. These times are a bit puzzling, but they mean that we took about 16½ hours from Washington airport to S. Francisco airport.) Despite the hour, Ed. had arranged a brass band and a guard of honour! We had to motor about half an hour to this Hotel—a skyscraper affair. I have got a comfortable bedroom and bathroom and an office to myself, also well-appointed. I was in bed by 2.30 a.m. and woke up fresh and well this morning.

I should think S. Francisco is a wonderful town. It, like Rome, is built on 7 hills, only they are much steeper than the Roman! A marvellous situation and beautiful views from this Hotel. A dazzling sun, but a pretty strong wind (not cold), and I suspect that is the snag. It probably blows the whole time here.

We had a private meeting this morning with Americans, Russians and Chinese, about Conference arrangements, and found the Russians still pretty sticky. Molotov says he has a message from Joe about Poland, but that 'it hasn't been decoded yet'. So I reserve judgment until I have seen it.

Lunched with Attlee and Bob Dixon. In the afternoon the opening meeting of the Conference in the Opera House. Quite fantastic, with orchestral accompaniment. But you'll have read of that in the Press. This morning Ed. told us of the plans. He said that, before the proceeding began, there would be a military band to play martial airs. He continued 'I will conduct' and I thought he was going to say 'the Band', but he went on 'the Governor of California and the Mayor of San Francisco on to the stage'! However, he did his part,

* Chinese Minister of Foreign Affairs.

and his speech, very well. After that, at 6, we had a meeting with Dominions, and at 7, with our Delegation.

Friday, 27 April *A.C. to T.C.* *San Francisco*

Yesterday, . . . we started with a meeting of the 'Steering Committee'—all 45 Delegations—at which Molotov was most tiresome, wrangling about the Presidency of the Conference. The wrangle went on till 2.30. I got back to the Hotel and managed to get some lunch at 2.45 and then went back to the plenary meeting of the Conference at 3.30, for the beginning of the opening discussion. I had to go, as Anthony, amongst others, was speaking. And he did very well indeed, and had a most enthusiastic audience.*

We got home about 6. Anthony and Edward and I had a somewhat inconclusive discussion on Poland. Joe's reply has arrived, and is completely unsatisfactory. Don't know what we can do: I suppose we shall get comment from London.

Then Harriman† came round with a long rigmarole insinuating that the compromise on the question of the Presidency of the Conference which Anthony had proposed at the Steering Committee this morning had 'let Ed. down'. Fact is that the American Delegation don't know what they want, and Ed. doesn't understand what they *do* want: it had all been fixed with him beforehand. . . . [At 11] we had to go across and see Ed. (Anthony, Edward and I) at his hotel across the street. There we stayed till 12.30 a.m. patching up things and planning our future action. . . .

This morning at 10 a meeting of the Big Four about this wretched Presidency business. We, the Americans and Chinese lined up against Molotov. He wouldn't budge. However we adjourned to the 'Steering Committee' at 10.30. Another session lasting till 2.30. But it was satisfactory, as we got Molotov unanimously defeated over the Presidency and also over an attempt to get the Warsaw Poles invited to the Conference! I must say he took it quite well, and it will do him good.

Saturday, 28 April *A.C. to T.C.* *San Francisco*

Today began, as usual, with a meeting of our Delegation at 9.30, and then a Plenary Meeting of the Conference at 10.30. Poor Jan Masaryk made a speech. He is completely a prisoner of the Russians, Benes and most of his Govt. being held by Joe in Moscow, and he has

* For the text of this speech, see Eden, *Freedom and Order*, pp. 336–40.

† U.S. Ambassador in Moscow.

to say what he's told. He is very apologetic about it, but I tell him we all understand his position and sympathise. However, he took courage to put some quite good stuff into his speech this morning, and I thanked him for that.

I have met another little Czech, whom I used to know at Geneva, called Krno. He managed to escape into France from Czechoslovakia in 1940. Then France fell: he got to Bordeaux, where his wife died: he had to stop there 2 days to bury her, and so lost the last boat out. He drifted somehow to Dieppe, where he found a friend who provided him with false papers and employed him as a gardener. His house was destroyed by one of our bombs just before D. day, and the Resistance movement passed him on somehow to Paris, where he remained hidden till the Liberation. What experiences: but he looked just the same, and is now once more a Delegate of Czechoslovakia!

. . . All kinds of sensational things seem to be happening in the war, and it's really rather annoying to be out here. But there is a great move amongst influential Delegates, headed by Anthony, Smuts and others, to set a short-time limit to the Conference.

I've just come back from a talk with Anthony and Ed., about how to handle the admission to the Conference of the 2 Russian Republics. The Latin Americans will probably vote against, unless Molotov agrees to the admission of Argentina! The regular old Geneva 'marchandage'. We've arranged a meeting at 6.45 this evening between the Big Four and 3 representative Latin Americans, to try to solve it.

. . . I haven't had a chance of discussing my future with Anthony, and he's so upset by the Chelmsford [by-]election* that he thinks he'll be out of office in a couple of months: in which case he wouldn't be able to do me much good!

[The U.S. Government had still made no response to the British request that Eisenhower's forces should move quickly into Czechoslovakia. After consulting with Cadogan, Eden handed Stettinius a further note:

> In our view the liberation of Prague and as much as possible of the territory of western Czechoslovakia by United States troops might make the whole difference to the post-war situation in Czechoslovakia and might well influence that in nearby countries. On the other hand, if the western Allies play no significant part in Czechoslovakia's liberation that country may go the way of Yugoslavia.

* In which a candidate of Sir Richard Acland's Common Wealth party had defeated a Conservative.

Stettinius approved of this suggestion. Truman, however, decided that political considerations must not interfere with military. Although Prague could have been taken, the Allied forces therefore halted and left it to the Russians.[6]]

Sunday, 29 April *A.C. to T.C.* *San Francisco*

After closing my letter yesterday, I had to go to a meeting, with Anthony, with the Big Four and 3 representative Latin Americans.... The latter were refusing to vote for the admission now, to the Conference, of Molotov's 2 sham Republics, unless Molotov agreed equally to admit Argentina. Anthony had to go away in the middle and left me to fight the battle, which I did. Molotov said he wouldn't admit the Argentines unless we admitted his beastly sham Polish Government. Ed. and I flatly refused this, so we parted in a nice deadlock, which a committee will try to resolve tomorrow morning.

... Off to our concert, which was timed for 8.30. I enjoyed it very much—a Beethoven Concerto with Menuhin playing the violin, and a Tchaikowsky Symphony. Menuhin is certainly marvellous and the San Francisco Symphony Orchestra very good indeed.

This morning I went to Church in the Cathedral, which is almost next door to our Hotel. A very long service, 11–12.20. Edward read the lesson. After the Service the Bishop of California walked up to our pew, as we were leaving, followed by a camera man with flashlight. I shook the Bishop by the hand and then fled. Afterwards, I discovered that he had posed Edward at the lectern, in two poses, one looking down at the Book and the other looking up to Heaven. And then another pose on the Chancel steps!

When all that was over—but I forgot: the highlight of the Service was the collection. Large gold plates were handed round, in which dollar bills were heaped. These were then carried ceremoniously in procession to the altar, the stars and stripes and the flag of California were carried to the steps, and the 'star-spangled banner' was reverently played. Then we were allowed to get on with the rest of the Service. But this collection of the dollar bills was almost like the raising of the Host in a Roman Catholic Mass!

Monday, 30 April *A.C. to T.C.* *San Francisco*

Meetings of the different Committees of the Conference this morning from 9 a.m. till 2 p.m. Molotov being tiresome. We admitted his 2 beastly Republics, and he then opposed the admission of Argentina, arguing that if Argentina were admitted, his beastly

Warsaw Poles shd. also be admitted. This we flatly refuse: it's impertinent of him to demand it. However, we voted him down heavily at all stages. . . .

Then the spate of oratory in the 'General Discussion' was resumed, about 5 o'clock. But I can't stand the sound of it, even, it bores me so, and I returned home and polished off such little work as had accumulated.

Tuesday, 1 May *A.C. to T.C.* *San Francisco*

We are making some progress. The opening discussion may finish tonight. There is an after-dinner session (which I shall *not* attend), which may enable all the rest of the steam to be let off; in which case Commissions will begin tomorrow. Old Smuts, who fortunately is Chairman of one of the Commissions, has urged that their work must be completed within a fortnight, and he *may* be able to keep them to it. After that, the final Plenary ought not to last more than a few days.

Molotov is rather chastened, for the moment. His defeats on Division seem to have done him good. But he seems likely to return to Moscow shortly, and in his absence his underlings are likely to stone-wall.

I went to the beginning of the Plenary sitting this afternoon to hear old Smuts. He was quite good, but didn't say anything very original or striking. So far, I think Anthony is the success of the Conference, and is enjoying himself hugely, so surrounded wherever he goes, by photographers and autograph hunters that he really needn't wave to the crowd to encourage attention. I haven't got into the press much, and haven't seen any photograph or cuttings worth keeping!

I didn't stay at the meeting after Smuts had finished, but came back and had a meeting of my own here at 5, from which I've just come out. . . .

Edward has written to Winston that he is prepared to stay on in Washington till March or April, so that settles that—I shall be too old next year for them to appoint me there! And I don't see what else I can do but stay at the F.O., if they will keep me, as a pension is only half of full pay, which makes a difference. However, I may have a word about it with Anthony, if I can find a calm moment.

[On 28 April Mussolini and his mistress Clara Petacci were shot by partisans in Northern Italy, the bodies being strung up in a public square at Milan. Hitler, who had shortly before, and with justice, lamented his failure to hearken to reason, which would have imposed 'a brutal friendship as to Italy', survived his exemplar by a few hours only. Grand

Admiral Doenitz, to his astonishment, found himself appointed Hitler's successor.]

Wednesday, 2 May *A.C. to T.C.* *San Francisco*

This morning I went with Anthony to have a talk with Ed. and Molotov about Poland, but we got practically nowhere.

. . . We have a meeting of the Big Four tonight at 9 to discuss Dumbarton Oaks, so Anthony's dinner for Bidault, to which I am bidden, has to be at 7.15—an hour which is approaching.

What great doings in Europe! The 2 Dictators eliminated within 2 or 3 days of each other. It's a bore being away as, although we get *some* of the inside news transmitted to us here, we get nothing like what I should be seeing in London. I don't suppose you'll have great rejoicings, as the whole situation is coming about rather gradually. But if there is a Thanksgiving Service you must go as Lady Sargent!

Anthony talks of leaving about Monday week, and Attlee will probably have to go too. But I'm afraid I shall have to stay to look after Bobbety. However, there is a growing feeling that the thing can't be allowed to drag on beyond a certain point.

Thursday, 3 May *A.C. to T.C.* *San Francisco*

It is disconcerting to find that the 4 cannot at once agree on the amendments they want to make to their own Dumbarton Oaks draft. What we shall do with the shoals of amendments flowing in from all the other Delegations, I don't know. Squash them all, I hope. . . .

At 3 we had a meeting with Americans and Russians about War Criminals, for which my friend Judge Rosenman had come from Washington. The question of the major war criminals seems to be settling itself, as they seem to be getting bumped off satisfactorily in one way or another.

After that, I had to represent us in a sub-committee of this morning's Committee, to try to settle points of difference which we and the Americans had with Molotov. I found the latter completely sticky, and we adjourned about 5 o'clock with nothing really settled.

Friday, 4 May *A.C. to T.C.* *San Francisco*

The Russians seem more hopeless than ever on Poland, and this evening Molotov had to confess that the Soviet had arrested all the 15 Polish leaders with whom they were supposed to consult on the formation of a new Polish Government!

We shall have some angry words with them today.

Saturday, 5 May *A.C. to T.C.* *San Francisco*

After dinner [on 4 May] Ed. and Anthony sat Molotov down and cross-examined him about the arrest by the Soviet Government of the Polish leaders—a perfectly disgraceful performance. We have known since the end of March that the Soviet Government had collected these men for consultation about the formation of a new Polish government. Under the Yalta agreement, such consultations were to take place with the participation of ourselves and the Americans. But the Soviet did this behind our backs. For a month now we have been asking the Soviet Govt. what has been going on and where these men now are. They have always professed total ignorance. Now, having failed, I suppose, to intimidate them into doing what they want, the Soviet Govt. calmly tell us that they have arrested the lot! There was some quite plain speaking and Molotov looked more uncomfortable than I've seen him look before. We have put out a statement that, in the circumstances, we can't go on discussing Poland with them any longer. I'm afraid that won't do the poor Poles any good, but it will give the Russians a bad Press, I hope. How can one work with these animals? And if one can't, what can one hope for in Europe?

The P.M. seems to be highly incensed with them. (Incidentally, he seems to be aiming at an election in June.)

[On that day the Russians announced that the Poles would be tried on charges of organising 'diversionary tactics in the rear of the Red Army'; and Stalin telegraphed brusquely to Churchill:

> It appears from your message that you are not prepared to regard the Polish Provisional Government as the foundation of the future Government of National Unity, and that you are not prepared to accord it its rightful position in that Government. I must say frankly that such an attitude excludes the possibility of an agreed solution of the Polish question.

Upon this the Prime Minister commented to President Truman:

> . . . we should hold firmly to the existing position obtained or being obtained by our armies in Yugoslavia, in Austria, in Czechoslovakia, on the main central United States front, and on the British front, reaching up to Lübeck, including Denmark.[7]]

Sunday, 6 May *A.C. to T.C.* *San Francisco*

There certainly are beautiful flowers and flowering shrubs everywhere here, but today, when I suddenly saw a pink may-tree flowering, to remind me of England, it struck me that at this time of year England is pretty difficult to beat. One hears a lot of Californian scenes and flowers, but I don't know that they are better than fields of buttercups and horse-chestnut trees and may and lilac. But perhaps it's a better climate....

This week we ought to get down to work, and the Committees will, I hope, get to business. After a few days of that, it may be possible to guess how long the thing will last. Smuts and Anthony have demanded that the Committees finish their work in a fortnight. If that can be done, the whole thing should be over within 3 weeks. But I have my doubts. It's a not unpleasant Conference, but I don't like Conferences, and it's a great bore being away from England just now. However, if I can be home by the end of this month, I may still have most of the first summer of peace to enjoy, and we must try to spend as much time as we can at the cottage.

Ed. has just sent me some enormous photos of his dinner party, which will give you some more 'sticking in'. Otherwise I've got hardly any scraps, and no photographs. The population here are just crazy about autograph-hunting, and anyone even remotely connected with the Conference is assailed, on coming out of the Restaurant, or out of the Lift, by a crowd of children and grown-ups with autograph books, and one simply has to sign one's way through the crowd to gain one's liberty. It's a complete nuisance, and what can be the value or the interest to them, I can't imagine.

Tuesday, 8 May *A.C. to T.C.* *San Francisco*

I broke away just before 12 to get back here and hear the King's broadcast, which was at noon by our local time. We British had taken the Bar at the top of this building, on the 19th floor, a rather marvellous place with glass walls all round and wonderful views over the whole place. The radio was installed there and the King's speech came over very well. We couldn't drink his health, as the only form of celebration here in San Francisco is the closing of all Bars for 24 hours, and the drink was all locked away! Then we heard Anthony broadcasting for a few minutes from the Opera House here—quite good....

I'm afraid my letters are pretty dull. The Conference still moves very slowly, but I think it *will* move, but its daily doings are not thrilling, and there's been little of human interest. Perhaps I can arrange something more lively for the week-end.

Friday, 11 May *A.C. to T.C.* *San Francisco*

I was up early this morning. The whole Delegation were photographed and filmed at 9 a.m., under scorching arc-lamps, for about half an hour. I then had to talk to Anthony about various things. Amongst others he's had a number of jumpy telegrams from the P.M., who is evidently fussed about plans for the election and about an aggressive Russia sprawling over most of Europe. However, Anthony can't start back now before Sunday, anyhow. . . .

I shall shortly have a cocktail with Mr. Attlee, and then dine here quietly, I hope, after which I have a string of engagements running on till 11 p.m., of which the last will, I suppose, not finish before midnight.

A rather full, and dull, life as you see.

Saturday, 12 May *A.C. to T.C.* *San Francisco*

This morning I had a Committee meeting at 10.30. The Committee was discussing a fairly important point, the number of members of the Council. This discussion started yesterday and it looked as if the vote might go against us so we talked it out yesterday and prevented a vote being taken then. During the night, the Americans did what they could with their Latin American protégés and we got to work on ours. (I put in some work at Attlee's cocktail party, intimidating Saudi Arabians, Turks and others.) The result was that at this morning's meeting they all toed the line: all those who had proposed amendments withdrew them one after another, with the result that what we wanted went through unanimously! What a farce: but it's rather exhausting. . . .

On the whole our Delegation have got on pretty well I think. The Delegates, though they are of different parties (with an election pending) seem to get on quite well together: even the ladies don't fight each other. . . .

Anthony leaves tomorrow. The P.M. has been consulting him as to the election, whether to have it now (i.e. end of June) or October. I have advised Anthony it's better to have it now (though it is not my business) and that is his view too.

[Churchill had just telegraphed that Conservative opinion generally preferred a June election, 'although the Russian peril, which I regard as enormous, could be better faced if we remain united.' Eden replied on 12 May that all the signs pointed to greater international difficulties in October, by which time no further postponement would be possible:

> What therefore we have to balance is the limited advantage of prolonging Coalition on an uneasy basis until October against risk of an election at an even more dangerous period in international affairs than now and increased chances of a Socialist victory in October. . . . I hold

to the opinion . . . that from the national point of view the balance of the argument is in favour of an election in June.

Shortly afterwards, Attlee rejected the Prime Minister's proposal that the Coalition should continue until Japan's defeat. Thereupon Churchill resigned, the Labour Ministers left the Government, and a caretaker administration was formed. In tears, Churchill thanked members of the dissolving coalition for all they had done as a united band of friends. 'If ever such another mortal danger threatened', he added, maybe thinking of Russia, 'I am sure we should all do the same again. The light of history will forever shine on all your helmets.'[8]]

Sunday, 13 May *A.C. to T.C.* *San Francisco*

At about 12.30, we suddenly remembered that Winston was broadcasting, and we turned on the radio. He came through quite marvellously, just as if he were talking in the car. But we only got about 5 minutes of him, and then we were switched over to the New York Philharmonic Orchestra playing a Beethoven Sonata 'Sponsored by the Something Rubber Company'! Driving through the country to music rather gave me the impression that one was acting in a bad film.

Tuesday, 15 May *A.C. to T.C.* *San Francisco*

Since my last letter, I've spent a good deal of the time on Committees, and we *have* begun, on one of them at least, to make a little progress.

I generally sit next to the American, old Senator Tom Connally,* and we conspire together to try to whack obstructionists on the head. He has, of course, the usual Senator's gift of the gab and the usual senatorial habit of declaiming in stentorian tones. Quite ridiculous, but quite amusing and occasionally helpful. I tell him he's our heavy artillery and I am the sniper. It works quite well and we wiped the floor with a Mexican last night: I think we must have shut him up for a week or so. . . .

Winston is trying to arrange a meeting of the Big Three, though (owing to Truman's other preoccupations) it can't take place till early July, 'in some unshattered town in Germany'. I very much doubt whether Uncle Joe will come to a meeting in the British or American zones of occupation in Germany, and Winston says he won't go to the Russian zone. So it's all rather problematical at the moment. . . .

I am *hoping* that I might come home when the Committee work is over, which *might* be the end of next week. But I think I shall cross

* Chairman of the Senate Foreign Relations Committee, 1941–6.

America by train, which is more interesting and less tiring than by air. But of course it takes 4 days instead of 1. However, we shall see. Edward screams at the idea of my going, but there would be no point in my staying longer, and I'll get Anthony to telegraph for me!

Thursday, 17 May *A.C. to T.C.* *San Francisco*

This morning after our usual 9.30 huddle, I was fairly free, and at 11.30 went out for an hour's walk with Edward. He strides up and down the hills as though he wore 7-league boots, and I paddle alongside him as best I can. Very good exercise, and I'm all the better for that, and the air—of which there's plenty. It *always* blows all the time in San Francisco. . . . I had to go and prepare for a Committee due to meet at 3.30.

It was lucky I did so, as the Committee was due to discuss the critical point in the Draft Charter—the voting powers of the Council. And when we got there, that tiresome old New Zealand P.M., Fraser, without a word of warning to me, got up and said that he thought one of the Delegates of the Great Powers ought to explain the 'Yalta proposals'. Not too easy! Old Tom Connally of course doesn't know anything about it: Gromyko* told me he wasn't ready, and we couldn't expect much from the Chinese. So I had to step into the breach. I hope it was all right as, after I had finished, old Fraser moved that my speech should be printed and circulated to the Committee, to help them in their further discussion! I at once said that I would agree to that, provided I could revise the text before it was disseminated. (So I can get Will Malkin to put right anything I may have said wrong!). . .

I still think there *may* be a chance of finishing Committee work at the end of next week, and I have made Edward accept the fact that I leave here when that is over. I can get Anthony to telegraph for me. Ed. may set up a howl, but I can ignore that.

Friday, 18 May *A.C. to T.C.* *San Francisco*

Today, so far, has been pretty busy. Our usual Delegation meeting at 9.30, then a small committee at 9.45, consisting of the Belgian, the Greek and myself, on a point of drafting. While we were sitting in a quiet corner of a large room down at the Conference building, which we had found suitable for our confabulation, an American orderly came up and said 'Excuse me: are you the Uruguayan Delegation?' I said 'I am afraid not'. The Belgian accused the Greek of looking like a Uruguayan (as he might) as certainly neither he nor I did!

* Russian Ambassador in Washington.

Then a committee at 10.30, which lasted till lunch time, discussing the time-honoured question whether one can find a 'definition of aggression'. Of course one can't—not an automatic one: and one doesn't *want* automatic definitions. But it is the sort of idea which is very dear to the hearts of the sort of people who like these Conferences and like splitting hairs and wasting time on academic and perfectly useless questions. I put up old Connally to shoot at them, and he fired a few quite effective rounds. But the discussion dragged on, and eventually Berendsen, the New Zealander, chose to get up and make the regular sort of demagogic speech which he delights in. I lost my temper and went for him, which I enjoyed. He doesn't mind: I like him and we are very good friends!

Saturday, 19 May *A.C. to T.C.* *San Francisco*

A meeting of the Big Five, where we registered a little progress, as Gromyko, the Russian, had at last got his instructions from Moscow—not too bad, and I think we can settle up the worry with the Latin Americans over 'Regionalism', with the details of which I will not bore you!*

After that I had a sub-committee, at 3.30, of the Committee that deals with voting on the Council. They wanted to obtain from the Big Four an explanation of what was meant by the 'Yalta formula' on voting. I said we should be delighted to answer any questions, but as they didn't seem to agree on what they wanted to ask, I suggested that we Four should withdraw (and go for a walk) and the rest could stay behind and try to formulate their questions. They didn't like that a bit, but it brought the meeting, so far as I was concerned, to an end.

Sunday, 20 May *A.C. to T.C.* *San Francisco*

I had a meeting at 6. . . . Gromyko had got his instructions from Moscow, and they were more or less all right, so we fixed up 'Regionalism'.

Monday, 21 May *A.C. to T.C.* *San Francisco*

After lunching here I went with Edward to a meeting, at 2.30 of a thing called the 'Steering Committee', which is supposed to direct the work of the Conference. Its business today was to consider rules designed to speed up the work. The first half hour was taken up by Carcano, reading a speech on Argentine foreign policy, past and

* The Latin Americans, and other powers, were anxious to establish that regional organisations for defence should not be stultified by the exercise of a Great Power's veto.

present. Though what the Hell that's got to do with the Steering Committee, I'm blessed if I know. I could have killed him.

The Steering Committee *still* say they aim at getting committee work finished by the end of this week, but I'll bet *against*. I'm sure *my* committees won't have finished, unless they make some drastic change in the manner of their conduct of business.

Wednesday, 23 May

Old Smuts sent for me yesterday morning for a chat about things—mainly about voting powers of the Council, about which he's rather worried. I think he's all right himself on the subject but has been got at by Evatt, the Australian,* who's the most frightful man in the world; he makes long and tiresome speeches on every conceivable subject, always advocating the wrong thing and generally with a view to being inconvenient and offensive to us, and boosting himself. However, everyone by now hates Evatt so much that his stock has gone down a bit and he matters less.

Old Fraser, the New Zealander, is almost equally tiresome, but mainly from silliness: he's rather a dear old thing really, and at heart quite friendly. . . .

So I see we are going to plunge into an election. What with that and reduced bacon and fat rations, peace hasn't yet brought many blessings to our poor little island!

Thursday, 24 May *A.C. to T.C.* *San Francisco*

I had the usual crowded day yesterday, and the Committees are creaking along slowly. They waste a fearful amount of time. For instance, yesterday afternoon we had, by a lot of work behind the scenes, devised a formula satisfying the Latin-Americans on the subject of 'Regionalism', and all we needed to do was to bring it before the appropriate committee for approval. You would have thought that all that was necessary was to vote it through. But not a bit of it. One Latin-American Delegate gets up to express his approval, adding any mental reservations that he may have. So *all* 20 of them get up in turn. They all speak in Spanish (though all of them can talk English and French) so that every speech has to be interpreted *twice*—into French and English. It's enough to drive anyone mad. . . .

Things have been quite peaceful since Anthony left, and Edward remains quite calm. I don't see much of Bobbety, as practically all his time is devoted to 'Trusteeship', which means Mandates and Colonial policy, and is pretty tricky, and I leave that to him.

* Dr H. V. Evatt, Australian Minister of Foreign Affairs.

Friday, 25 May *A.C. to T.C.* *San Francisco*

Our remaining M.P. Delegates will have to go back the middle of next week. That makes Edward all the more insistent that I should stay to the end, but I argue with him that that doesn't make sense: once the Committees are over, he can get along perfectly with Bobbety: he won't want more Delegates, and there certainly won't be anything for *me* to do. I'll be wiring over the week-end about the probabilities in connexion with my plans.

You must have got my complaint if your voice is still wrong. I am very fit, and play 18 holes without turning a hair, and never feel tired, but even now, on some days, a slight croak intrudes into my voice. Perhaps that comes from arguing with foolish and obstinate Dagoes! . . .

We're reserving our final big fight on the voting powers of the Council for a sub-committee tomorrow and the Main Committee Monday and perhaps Tuesday. I shall mobilise Tom Connally to do the heavy business, but I may have to fire a shot or two myself. . . .

You say people in London don't think much of Truman. As a matter of fact, from what I've seen of what he's been doing, he seems to me awfully good—very practical and quick and helpful, with a mind of his own. (In these ways rather unlike his dear predecessor.) But it's early days to form a judgment.

Saturday, 26 May *A.C. to T.C.* *San Francisco*

This morning, usual meetings all the time. We have made some progress, and I think Committees will finish by middle of next week. I shall then make the most strenuous efforts to come home. The P.M. has just wired that all Ministers (including Cranborne) must be home by the 29th. Of course this can't be done—would leave Edward alone—and in that event I should have an awful tussle with him to get him to release me. But he's sending the right sort of reply—that the Ministers *must* stay till committees are over, which won't be many days, and that in any case Bobbety must stay to the end. If this last is approved, I *may* get away next week. . . .

Later, at 9, we've got a Big Four meeting on voting powers of the Council. I think we shall agree about that, so that it can come before a Committee on Monday and we can get a final decision on it in the course of a day or two. But we shall have all the little fellows yapping at our heels, and it won't be too easy. Of course one could crack the whip at them and say that if they don't like our proposals there just damned well won't be any World Organisation. But I don't know that that would pay, and it would have to be put tactfully.

Sunday, 27 May *A.C. to T.C.* *San Francisco*

Edward had a crowded cocktail party yesterday evening to celebrate the anniversary of the Anglo-Soviet Treaty. I spent most of the time arguing with Gromyko, whom I like personally, but who is quite wooden and mulish—mainly, I suppose because he's too frightened of Moscow to depart by a single hair's breadth from his instructions. . . .

After that, at 9.15, we had a meeting of the Big Four, about the eternal question of voting on the Council. I had to hold forth to them and try to prove—not unsuccessfully, I think—that they were being very silly. But I suppose Gromyko will have to refer to Moscow and wait for his instructions, which all delays matters.

Tuesday, 29 May *A.C. to T.C.* *San Francisco*

This morning we had a meeting of the Big Five, mainly to discuss how to shorten the Conference. We talked for 2 hours without achieving any result, so I'm afraid we made a negative contribution to the very desirable end we had in view.

We're stuck waiting for Gromyko to get his instructions from Moscow on the voting powers of the Council. I have telegraphed to London asking whether we may vote against him if he gets the wrong ones. But of course that wouldn't do much good, as I suppose the Soviet wouldn't join a World Organisation if we voted them down on a point that they affect to consider vital. But I don't see why we should vote for anything that we consider wrong, simply because the Russians are pig-headed. It's all very tiresome. If Gromyko gets the *right* instructions, things might go with a run. Anyhow, I can hardly see the Committees running over this week, and I hope to fly back.

Wednesday, 30 May *A.C. to T.C.* *San Francisco*

We are still stuck, waiting on these tiresome Russians. I'm glad to say I've just got authority from Anthony to vote against them if necessary—provided the Americans vote with us. That will give me some personal satisfaction even if it does no practical good.

I've got a Committee meeting at 8.30 this evening, though I don't quite know what it can do. I suppose we can always argue on points of procedure. I shall have to get up a row with someone, to keep myself awake.

I think everyone is getting rather bored. If only that would make them buck up and get the thing over!

Thursday, 31 May *A.C. to T.C.* *San Francisco*

I'm bored to tears: for several days nothing has been happening, and we are simply waiting on the Russians.

It's no good going on guessing as to when I can get away. If the Russians come out with the right answer, I could get away quickly: if they come out with the wrong one, that may mean another long delay, and I shall tell Edward I've had enough of kicking my heels in a Hotel. So in either event, I think it won't be long now, but it's no use prophesying. You'll know directly I finally start, and you'll expect me when you see me!

I had a committee last night 8.30–11 which made a little progress, and I put up old Tom Connally to have a row with the Australians, which made a lot of noise and was quite good fun for 10 minutes or so. Otherwise very boring.

Friday, 1 June *A.C. to T.C.* *San Francisco*

I fully mean to leave on Sunday night if nothing has developed, but I suppose that on Sunday morning Gromyko will produce some answer from his Government that, good or bad, will throw the Conference into a turmoil, and I shall have to put off my departure! It's really maddening. The only comfort is that I expect life would be Hell in the F.O.

Saturday, 2 June *A.C. to T.C.* *San Francisco*

Well, of course, as anticipated in my letter of yesterday, the storm burst on us last night, when Gromyko flat-footedly announced the 'wrong' answer by his Government. So there we are, right in the middle of the crisis, and I obviously can't leave *tomorrow*. I have just sent you a message by telegram explaining.

What we shall do, I don't know. We have telegraphed to London putting various alternatives. One is that the Conference should confess failure and adjourn. I doubt whether they will agree to that. They are more likely to tell us to go ahead with the rest of the Charter, leaving this crucial point open (as we did at Dumbarton Oaks). This might not take so very long but, taught by experience, I'm not making any prophesies. It's maddening.

However, from one point of view, I feel better: it's better to be in the middle of a crisis, and doing something, than simply sitting on one's haunches and waiting for the Russians to reply, doing nothing and kicking one's heels in the Hotel.

We had a meeting of the Big 5 all the morning, but got nowhere....

All this must be completely puzzling to you. It's simply arguing about words, on the surface, but it is of course a symptom of something much deeper—Russian suspicions and unwillingness to co-operate. How to cure those I really don't know. And I don't know whether it's better to have a good rough show-down with the Russians, or to attempt to go on coaxing them. I am inclined to think the former.

Of course it's hopeless trying to negotiate with Gromyko: he doesn't dare to change a comma without reference back to Moscow. The only man in his Delegation (Sobolev: Counsellor in London) who was at all reasonable was suddenly recalled to Moscow 2 days ago. I thought that was a bad sign. I expect he will have his head cut off.

[Gromyko insisted that a Permanent Member should be able, when not a party to a dispute, to veto its discussion by the Security Council. The United States, Stettinius retorted, would not sign a Charter on that basis. Harry Hopkins, in Moscow, persuaded Stalin to drop the demand.]

Sunday, 3 June *A.C. to T.C.* *San Francisco*

I received a telegram from Anthony first thing this morning, saying he had a duodenal ulcer, and that his Doctor had told him he must have a complete rest for a fortnight at least. So he wants me to come back as quickly as possible. I have told him that I can't leave immediately, in the midst of our crisis, but will come at the earliest possible moment—this week, it must be, I think.

The Conference flounders about and no one takes a grip of it and drives it along. Ed. is bad in that way. No one will face up to the problem presented to us by the Russians. We have meetings of the 5—we had another one this afternoon—but we discuss all sorts of silly little subjects, like the method of election of Deputy Secretaries General of the Organisation, and the one real topic is barred, as if it was something improper. Meanwhile the Press, of course, publish all the details and discuss it. Only *we* look foolish, doing and saying nothing about it. I've made Edward promise to press Ed. to do something about it tomorrow, to drag the matter into the open and try and deal with it.

Monday, 4 June *A.C. to T.C.* *San Francisco*

We had a meeting of the Big 5 this morning (preceded by a private talk with Ed. and some of his American henchmen) and it became so plain to me that they were just refusing to face facts and wobbling about, hoping vaguely that it would be 'all right on the night', that

I told Edward it was no use my staying on. One might play this game indefinitely without anything happening—except the Conference falling more and more into disrepute. I'm bound to say he agreed. Even Ed. admitted that, although he had twice stopped me going (I wasn't aware he had!) he couldn't ask me to stay any longer! So, barring unforeseen difficulties, I hope to be with you within the week. . . .

London won't be much fun, with Anthony laid up and Moley exhausted, but still it will be better than waiting vainly here.

Tuesday, 5 June *A.C. to T.C.* *San Francisco*

10.30 meeting of Executive Cttee. *whole* morning spent on discussing procedure and relative 'jurisdictions' of various organs of the Conference. Told Edward that had finally settled me to go. Edward and I had a good 5-min. talk with Jimmy Dunn and Ed., who agree we must get busy on planning our procedure, which provides for formal statement to the Conference of disagreement in the first place.

Wednesday, 6 June *A.C. to T.C.* *San Francisco*

A frightful meeting of Executive Cttee. at 10.30, which did little beyond re-opening all the questions of procedure and 'jurisdiction' which had been raised yesterday. Then they did dispose of 2 items, but only by referring to some other body!

[Cadogan thereupon left for home. 'It is quite right that he should go,' Halifax conceded, 'for the Foreign Office must be in sore trouble, but we shall miss him a lot here. The only compensation is that he will understand our problems when we throw them back at him.'

Stettinius, soon to be replaced as Secretary of State by J. F. Byrnes, wrote to Cadogan that morning:

> Your contribution to our work here has been invaluable. No one appreciates more than I do the extent to which you have been able to find the right answer to reconcile conflicting points of view.

The arrangements thrashed out at San Francisco showed many changes of detail, but few of substance, from those proposed in the Dumbarton Oaks draft. Much of the debate focused on the 'President's compromise' whereby, although a Great Power party to a dispute would not vote, the other four Permanent Members must agree before the Council could try to find a peaceful settlement. In other words, the Council's action in such an instance might be stopped by the abstention of one Great Power. The five resisted prolonged efforts of the smaller powers to abolish this 'hidden veto'.

The Charter, signed on 26 June, expressly recognised the right of self-defence, collective or individual; permitted regional groupings but made them clearly subordinate to the Council; and gave the General Assembly strictly limited functions. Desire for security against war, and reluctant agreement that the power to wage it on a large scale was now concentrated in a few powers, dominated the discussions. The United Nations, then, was not a World Government. On the contrary, its constitution turned on the frank recognition that unless the Great Powers agreed, it could do little.]

Thursday, 7 June *A.C. to T.C.* *Montreal*

Ran into storm near Cheyenne. Terrific flashes of green lightning. Pilot said he must land at Denver. Landed there about 2.30 a.m. Jacob* and an Admiral got rooms in a Hotel. I didn't—fortunately—as, after sitting for nearly 3 hours in a noisy waiting-room, found there was a 'plane leaving for New York at 5.30.... Our 'plane... raced to Chicago (at 200 m.p.h.) so we caught up a bit of time. Then on to N[ew] Y[ork] where we arrived at 6.30 instead of about 3. Rang up Cons[ul]-Gen[eral] and arranged to go to his flat. Shaved there and he took us to dine at the River Club. Off the ground at 10.30 and arrived Montreal 12.30 a.m. During the last half hour I noticed sparks streaming from our starboard engine exhaust, and after we landed I noticed them draining boiling liquid from it—so I was very glad we didn't have to fly further in *that* machine!

Saturday, 9 June

Commandant met us and gave us admirable breakfast, beginning with the freshest of fresh grilled herrings. Shaved and got off ground with Tom Bromley at 10.10 in a 'Dominie'. Arrived Hendon 12.45. T. there to meet me, which was a great joy. Lunched here. Unpacked and slept after. Dined here. Tired. It's a bit of a rush getting from S. Francisco to London (6,500 miles) from Wed. evening to Sat. morning!† T., thank goodness, seems well. Didn't go near F.O. Bob D[ixon] rang me up when I was asleep. Seems they're fairly calm.

Sunday, 10 June

Got to F.O. about 10.30. Nothing doing. Saw O.S., who looked all right. I said he must carry on for 2 or 3 days. He wants to go off on (long) leave. A. apparently not bad, but must rest. I must go down and see him, I think.... I've recovered from my trip, but still a bit sleepy!

* Lt.-Gen. Sir I. Jacob, Asst. Sec. (Military) to the War Cabinet.

† The completion of this journey of nearly 14,000 miles brought the distance covered by Cadogan on official business during the war to nearly 87,500 miles. With characteristic precision he kept a record accurate to the nearest mile.

Monday, 11 June

Resumed the usual treadmill (but have not officially notified my return to F.O., so don't get snowed under with papers!). . . Massigli at 3.30, very incensed at General Paget's goings-on which are, I should think, fully justified.* Promised to look into it.

Cabinet at 5.30. Some new faces—Harry Dalmeny, Arthur Salter, Donald Somervell, Llewellyn, Rob Hudson†—a funny crowd. P.M. looks rather pale, and indulged in a long monologue in a depressed undertone—all about the menace of Russia sprawling over Europe. Quite obvious, but nothing to be done about it. Long discussion about Reparations for which Walter Monckton‡ was present.

Tuesday, 12 June

Lunch at Mansion House for Ike. He made a v. good little speech from the balcony. Winston butted in after him. At lunch, sat between [Sir F.C.] Bovenschen and an unknown American, who seemed to have met me at Dumbarton Oaks. P.M. butted in again with an unscheduled speech. Ike replied v. well. . . . Discussion with T. about how to live in future. Want to get out of this flat, but where to go? Also I gather she doesn't care for the cottage, so we'd better sell that. But it's all very difficult and obscure and depressing.

Wednesday, 13 June

Michiels at 3.30. He rather jumpy. Had been over to Holland. Had found Klingendaal completely re-furbished and done up by Seyss-Inquart!§ House and garden re-done in perfect taste. Nothing removed from house—indeed some things added, including one or two Fragonards! Dutch Government claimed £4,000 from him. I don't know why—except that I suppose S. Inquart had dipped in to the Dutch Treasury for the re-furbishing! Massigli at 5.30 for a wail about the Levant. He wants a Franco-British agreement *before* a 3-Power or 5-Power meeting, but can't suggest on what lines.

Thursday, 14 June

4.45 discussion with Dick Law and others about captured German documents. I protested against a situation with which I am so often

* French reinforcements, sent by Gen. de Gaulle, had arrived at Beirut in May. At the end of the month fighting broke out in several parts of Syria. On 31 May Gen. Paget, then British C.-in-C. Middle East, was told to restore order. The French had to proclaim a ceasefire and withdraw from Damascus.

† Respectively Secretary of State for Scotland, Chancellor of the Duchy of Lancaster, Home Secretary, Minister of Food, Minister of Agriculture.

‡ Solicitor-General.

§ Nazi High Commissioner.

confronted—of being asked to give a decision without *any* elements of judgment. I don't know what these documents *are* or what they contain. How *can* I express a useful opinion? Woodward* undertook to have a representative number of them translated. We may then form a judgment. People really are too silly. Polish crisis, owing to Mik refusing to start for Moscow tomorrow because Witos† won't be there. Very tiresome. Sent off telegram to Moscow and explanatory minute to P.M. But this will probably spoil my week-end.

Friday, 15 June *Thatched Cottage*

Received minute from P.M. about zones: he wanted draft telegrams to Truman and Stalin, so I got them drafted and asked to see him before the Cabinet at 3. Lunched at home. Took drafts over to the annexe. Of course Winston sitting over lunch. About 2.55 was shown into drawing-room where I found Clemmie [Churchill] and unknown lady and Diana Cooper. P.M. came in about 3, kissed Diana good-bye and took me off in his car to No. 10. Told him I wanted to be away tomorrow, and he agreed. Tried then to get him to look at drafts, but he *would* talk—about the King wanting to come to Berlin. Took me into Cabinet room, where Cabinet assembled. Sat me next to him, and started—rather bemused—going through drafts. Meanwhile told Willink‡ to start talking about National Health Insurance Scheme. Didn't listen to that, but toyed with my drafts. Mercifully, he finished with them about 3.15. I went back to F.O. and finished off some papers—there's a merciful lull.... Shrubs doing well. Some apples. Still some strawberries left. Good currants and peas ripening. Broadcast by B. Bracken—very bad. Imitating Winston's style, and no stuff. Nice to be here. Hope I can have quiet 48 hrs.

Saturday, 16 June *Thatched Cottage*

Drove through Bodiam and Ewhurst and round by our oast-house. We are getting some peas and broad beans. Asparagus over. A few new potatoes. Some lovely delphiniums and some good lupin second blooms. Roses don't do much. Mik seems to have left for Moscow. King of the Belgians going back, and the Belgian Govt. resigning! Philip Baker talking the most *awful* rot on the wireless.

Sunday, 17 June *Thatched Cottage*

Gorgeous sunny day, with cool air. It is nice to go back to peace-time, with weather forecasts, which said, for today 'Drizzle: rain in

* Professor E. L. (later Sir Llewellyn) Woodward.

† A Polish delegate to Moscow who 'disappeared'. Cf. Churchill, vol. IV, p. 433.

‡ Minister of Health.

the south.' Where *do* they get their information from? Walked down the fields, then picked strawberries with T. We have had a very good crop. Read after lunch till nearly 3. Then picked beans and peas and lifted some new potatoes. Packed and changed and had tea at 5. Left 5.45. Home 7.40.... Usual business of unpacking, putting flowers in water, cooking, &c., and a box with a *mass* of work. I had had nothing to do last week, but the week-end seems to have boiled up. Mik is in Moscow.

Monday, 18 June

3.30 O. Harvey and Hall-Patch* about P.M.'s fretful minute on supplies to France. He silly on this subject. I'm all against giving *military* supplies in present circumstances, but we don't want an economic collapse in France. 6.45 Raczynski about trial of Poles in Moscow. It certainly looks bad—all accused making 'confessions'.† Meanwhile Mik seems happy, but he'll be in an impossible position if his associates are judicially murdered while he is talking with the Soviet Govt. Saw O. Harvey and Hoyer Millar about giving King Leopold facilities for return to Belgium. We can put him down on or near the Belgian frontier if necessary, but we mustn't go further. Approved telegram, to be submitted by telephone to P.M., who is still at Chequers. Dined at home. Not too much work.

Tuesday, 19 June

P.M. still down at Chequers and quiet, so far as I was concerned. A. rang me up on telephone, about P.M.'s idea of postponing 3-Power Conference for a month—till Aug. 15. Don't think there's any objection from *our* point of view. Gather we shall discuss this at Cabinet tomorrow. 10.45 Massigli, with various complaints about Levant. I impressed on him that only thing to do is to have a conference—preferably in London. 11.30 Carandini. He confident that Parri‡ will form a good Govt. Complained of difficulties of 'state of war'. I told him we were contemplating a Peace, but warned him this might come as a shock!... 5.30 long meeting about Far Eastern Planning. Rather exhausting, trying to push them to make some *concrete* and *practical* suggestions about things of which I am not expert (I am very bad at 'planning': it is to me as incomprehensible as futile).

* Sir E. L. Hall-Patch, Assistant Under-Secretary, F.O., 1944.

† 13 of the 16 Poles were found guilty and sentenced to various terms of imprisonment.

‡ Ferruccio Parri, successor to Bonomi and a leading member of the Italian Resistance; replaced by de Gasperi later in 1945.

Wednesday, 20 June

Raczynski, about a number of questions that will have to be faced if we transfer recognition to a new Polish Govt. 11.30 thinly attended meeting of Cabinet (under J. A[nderson]) where we polished off a few items before P.M. turned up, about 12. Then a long rambling talk about desirability of postponing Big 3 meeting in view of the Attlee-Laski imbroglio. Matter complicated by P.M. saying Attlee when he meant Laski, and vice versa! Decision deferred, anyhow till tomorrow. I undertook to re-word the messages to Truman and Stalin. I think in these days everyone, at the back of their mind, is searching how to turn everything to party advantage. Lunched at home. Frogface at 3 about sending officers into W. Germany for repatriation of Russians, and about captured German archives.

[Since the Potsdam Conference would open between the election (5 July) and the date when its result would become known, Churchill invited Attlee to accompany him. Attlee accepted; whereupon Professor Harold Laski, Chairman for that year of the Labour Party Executive, took it upon himself to announce 'It is of course essential that if Mr Attlee attends this gathering he shall do so in the role of an observer only.' There followed a published exchange of letters between Attlee and the Prime Minister. Attlee agreed, in effect, that he would take part at Potsdam as a member of the British delegation, though the Government alone would bear official responsibility for decisions.]

Thursday, 21 June

No sign of Winston today—I suppose he was busy with his broadcast for tonight. Nothing is in his mind—or anyone else's—but the Election. Haven't heard of any decision about the Conference.

Friday, 22 June

Telegrams from Moscow show Polish question probably settled. Spoke to [C.] Warner and Allen* about it and at 12.30 took over to P.M. draft telegram to Moscow authorising acceptance. P.M. still in bed. He agreed.† And rambled a good deal about the Election. He off to Chequers this afternoon. Then on Monday on a 4-day election-stomp. He asked me down to Chequers. I said it was awkward, as we have to lunch at Hatfield on Sunday. I might go on from there. . . . Alba at 3.30 on a mass of things. Told him we didn't want, at present,

* W. D. Allen, Assistant Head of Northern Dept., F.O.

† Sir A. Clark Kerr was told to accept the Polish settlement, emphasizing that Britain was not committed to recognise the new Government until assured that it had been formed in accordance with the Yalta agreement and was pledged to free elections.

to give a full-dress warning to Franco.* 5.30. Ferguson (on behalf of Kemsley) with reports (only just come thro') from their man in Bucharest. What were they to do about publishing? Said I'd let him know in a few days.

Sunday, 24 June

I went to F.O., clearing up some things, and left there 5.30 for Chequers. Arrived just before 7 (had to stop for petrol on the way). A beautiful evening and the country looked *lovely*—far lovelier than California. P.M. lying on lawn sunning himself, in Siren suit and 10-gallon hat. Cherwell there. Difficult to get P.M. down to business. He excited by his tour and his reception everywhere. Nervous about his voice, and started talking in stage whisper, but he soon forgot about it. Eventually got him to settle some things—most important being that we might press Bidault to come here to meet A. on Levant. 8.30 Sawyers appeared and said 'It's 8.30'. P.M. said 'My God, Sawyers! What *have* you been doing?' But we sat on. Went in at 8.45. Bathed and changed. Dinner about 9.15. Only P.M., Cherwell, Jack Churchill (who looks awful), Peck† and Tommy. Cold roast beef, mince pie and flaming brandy and lots of champagne, port and cognac. A damned bad film, after, ended at 1 and I to bed at 1.15.

Monday, 25 June

Same lovely weather. I breakfasted and down before 9.30. P.M. off on his campaign about 9.45. Met him on doorstep. He had read in press of de Gaulle's banning of Lady Spears' hospital,‡ and that had undone all I had done last night! Told him I would send him a note pressing the need for conference. . . . 5 Massigli, who plainly realises the asininity of de G's behaviour. Promised to try to have a statement for him at lunch tomorrow that may help to remove *some* 'misunderstandings'.

Tuesday, 26 June

Drafted minute to A. covering one to P.M. about Levant. Discussed it with R.I.C[ampbell] and Bob Dixon. I *must* bother A. with this.

* Hoare had proposed at the end of 1944 a warning to Franco that if he did not improve his Government, post-war relations between Spain and the Allies must suffer.

† J. H. Peck, Asst. Private Sec. to the P.M., 1940–6.

‡ It was widely believed that this mobile ambulance unit had been disbanded because de Gaulle was offended by its carrying a Union Jack in a parade. De Gaulle denied it and wrote to Lady Spears thanking her for her services.

Cadogan minuted that he suspected some of the difficulties with de Gaulle to be 'partly, at least, of our own making'. British policy towards Syria and the Lebanon remained substantially the same as before; to seek no special advantages in the Levant states, to promote, if possible, a treaty between them and France and then to withdraw British troops.[9]]

Wednesday, 27 June

No answer from A. about Levant—of course he can think of nothing but the Election, and his broadcast tonight. This bloody election cuts across everything, and all politicians come out—as I suppose they must—in their true colours. Poor devils!

Friday, 29 June

12 O.S. and Bob Dixon. Told them of the various problems, Poland (and our representation in Warsaw) and the Levant. Personally, don't think we shall get any useful decision out of the Govt. at the moment. But some things *must* be settled. Winston back, having finished his tour. But he, luckily, remained quiet.

Saturday, 30 June *Thatched Cottage*

Drove nearly 30 miles—slowly—a pleasant relaxation, and a *change!* Winston gave his last broadcast tonight. *Very* good, I thought. Dignified and forceful. Very little controversy, and no mud!

Monday, 2 July

11.15 Frogface, with demand from his Government to take part in Tangier discussions. I reminded him that Russia never had any part in the international régime we planned to restore. His Govt. demanded we should 'postpone' discussions due to begin in Paris tomorrow. I said we probably couldn't do this, but they would proceed 'without prejudice'. . . . 12.50 O. Harvey and Hoyer Millar about Soviet demand concerning Tangier discussions. Gave instructions for minute to P.M. Latter of course engrossed in election, but he *has* approved (a) our line on liquidation of London Polish Govt. and (b) my proposal to ask Bidault here (? when) for Levant discussions. . . . 4 Raczynski, with 2 Poles, Warner and Eady* on long and detailed discussion of liquidation of London Polish Govt. Rather difficult and v. depressing. Went on till 5.30.

Tuesday, 3 July

About 11.30 last night Warner rang me to say Truman wants to recognise new Polish Government midnight tonight. This is really

* Sir W. Eady of the Treasury.

rushing things. Told him to send reply urging at least 24 hours' delay.

10.30 Duff Cooper. He couldn't give much hope of de G[aulle] being reasonable.... 12.15 Massigli—as inaudible as usual. Just back from Paris. Himself in quite good mood but says he found 'air of pessimism'. Seems clear to me French won't agree to Tripartite discussion of Levant. Want a discussion 'à deux'—doubtless to give Levant States impression that we are getting together against them. Doubt if it's much good inviting Bidault here—to which P.M. has at last assented! 12.45 P.M. sent for me. He still in bed with rumpled hair. Got him to telegraph to Truman urging 24 hrs.' postponement of recognition of Warsaw....

Warner rang up to say Truman has deferred recognition for 48 hrs.—which is good!

[Russia had just demanded, in return for a new Turco-Soviet Treaty, the cession of territory, bases at the Straits and a revision of the Montreux Convention. Eden pressed Churchill hard by telephone on 4 July to enter a caveat forthwith. Although the Americans refused to move, the Prime Minister agreed to tell Turkey that the question must be taken up at Potsdam. In the same conversation, Eden pointed out that he was pledged to a free election in Poland and the representation of all parties in the Government: 'If we just had list voting [from a catalogue of candidates prepared by the Polish Government] it would be a farce. He kept repeating Truman wouldn't wait. I replied that our position was different. Americans knew little of Europe, we were of it and would be watched on this.'

Churchill nevertheless decided to recognise. Mikolajczyk was to be Minister of Agriculture in the new Government, with precious little support. Communists were to control the police. The Poles in London, including the Ambassador, refused to acquiesce. The question had been settled, said Raczynski to Cadogan, in a manner unworthy of great powers and inconsistent with the Yalta decisions.[10]]

Wednesday, 4 July

A crowded and tiresome day. People flapping in and out the whole time. Beastly grey weather. Michiels in the morning to complain about our 'Declaration' on Germany and to claim Holland should have a voice in settling Germany's western frontier. (Also complained about Tangier talks: here, I think, we've blundered.) O.S. for a long talk about his interview with A. yesterday. Latter getting restive and insists on putting a finger in the pie. If he's out of action, he ought to remain so. But he now wants to attach what I consider to be (and Soviet certainly will) a new condition to our recognition of Warsaw Govt. . . . P.M. objects to A.'s new condition. Rang up A. and told him he must settle it with P.M. It's hard enough when *no one* is in charge of F[oreign] A[ffairs], but it becomes impossible when *two* are.

R. Campbell called on return from Lisbon, and retirement. I almost envy him, but can't afford it! Masses of papers and all sorts of worries. Dined at home and worked long and hard. Heard, just before leaving F.O. that Will Malkin's 'plane was 6 hours overdue. I'm afraid this is bad. Carries also Capel Dunn, Miss Collard, Miss Cole-Hamilton and I believe 2 others of our ladies, Peel of I.O. and someone else. (Resident clerk has just rung up as I was writing this—10.45 p.m.—to say A[ir] M[inistry] have no news—this must be nearly 12 hrs. overdue.) This is Transport Command again. The Blitz was bad, but Transport Command are *much* worse. The tale of our dead is terrible and we *must* make a row about it. This loss, if so it proves, is really frightfully serious. Americans and Russians don't seem to have crashes. Why are we always slaughtered?

Thursday, 5 July

No news of 'plane. Fear the worst. Rang up Portal's Secretary, and got a letter from P. and an Air V[ice] M[arshal] has been keeping me informed, but they know practically nothing. 10.45 talk with O.S., Bob Dixon and Allen about recognition of Poland and A.'s misgivings. Apparently he had a sharp exchange with P.M. on telephone yesterday evening. He's wrong, I think. . . . Arranged with O.S. to go and see P.M. about 12.30. He in bed, and rumpled, but calm. At once rang up A. and I hoped he'd tell him we were going ahead with recognition. But he only enquired tenderly after A.'s health and told him not to come up before Mon. Then instructed O.S. and me to go ahead. Seems happy about election: says Central Office estimate a majority of 56 (but probably 80). Went back and rang up A. and told him we must go ahead, reserving right to discuss his point at Terminal.* He seemed quite happy.

Friday, 6 July

Very hot and fine again. Alba at 12—mainly about Tangier, on which I was quite firm. All the complications, including Soviet demand for participation, are due to Spanish unilateral action in 1940.† He quite saw the point. . . . 3 Cabinet, to which P.M. had bidden me (I had tried to cry off!) As there was no agenda, it went

* The codename for the Potsdam Conference.

† In occupying the International Zone at Tangier.

on for ever—P.M. havering about every subject on earth. Adjourned to the garden—and whiskies and sodas—at 5.30.... P.M. off tomorrow on holiday. A. due back Monday. G.Ll.G[eorge] and Oliver Lyttelton pretty optimistic about Election. Think P.M. is, too.

Tuesday, 10 July

Picked up A. at 12.20 for 12.30 Cabinet. He looks and seems quite well and cheerful. I condoled about his boy,* but he seems to bear that quite well, poor thing. Cabinet reviewed coal and food situation in Berlin. It's not so bad as indiscretions of some blockhead British officers make it seem.... Cabinet 3 till 4.45 on a variety of subjects. Sharp exchanges between P. J. Grigg† and Amery on India.

Wednesday, 11 July

Lunch with A., Joe Davies‡ and Winant. J.D. didn't give himself away and said nothing startlingly stupid. 5.15 talk with A. and others about 'Terminal' brief on Germany. Which is *not* very good, and he was rather jumpy about it. Depts. here overload themselves with words.... Their noses are pressed against tree-trunks so that they don't get a very good view of the forest. How do we find the perfect F.O. man, who is an excellent bureaucrat, something of a politician and human (I don't claim to be any of all three, but there are some excellent men who excel too much in *one* Department!) Lots of work and lots of interruptions. Have a lot (including 'Briefs' for Terminal) hanging over me.

Thursday, 12 July

Cabinet at 3. Italian Peace Treaty main point affecting us. Cabinet approved in principle. It *is* a relief to get work done efficiently—in the absence of the dear old Boy! Got through a good deal of work and 'Brief' reading.

[It had been agreed to negotiate a Peace Treaty with Italy as soon as the Germans surrendered. The terms now submitted to the Cabinet by Eden included Italian recognition of the independence of Ethiopia and Albania; the surrender of the Dodecanese to Greece and the Dalmation Islands to Yugoslavia; refusal of Yugoslav claims to Trieste and Gorizia; and the loss of Italy's former colonies.]

* Eden's son had been reported missing in Burma.

† The S. of S. for War had formerly been Finance Member of the Government of India.

‡ Formerly U.S. Ambassador in Moscow; special adviser to Truman at Potsdam Conference.

Friday, 13 July

12.15 Jimmy d'A[lba] to give him our answer about Mexican anti-Spanish resolution at S. Francisco. Told him that this formula might give Franco some comfort, but fact remains that Spain, with Franco, hadn't a dog's chance of admission to World Organisation. He delighted and said he would telegraph it to Franco!

[For the usual reason, Cadogan did not take his Diary to Potsdam. The entries for 15 to 31 July are extracted from his letters to Lady Theo.]

Sunday, 15 July *A.C. to T.C.* *Potsdam*

We flew over Antwerp and part of the Ruhr. Flying rather high, one couldn't see very much detail on the ground. There certainly were some good patches of devastation, but there were some towns and even large factories that didn't seem to show any signs of damage. I hardly saw a train moving anywhere in Germany, and nothing on the roads except military convoys.

I wrote to you from Yalta that that was the oddest spot I'd struck yet. In some ways I think this is odder. Here we are, in the midst of this devastated and denuded country, living in a little town of our own, consisting of villas set amidst trees (not unlike Le Touquet) with more or less every comfort of a somewhat rough and ready kind. My bedroom has a large balcony looking on to a garden which slopes down to a narrow lake—more like a wide river—with a bank opposite covered with pine-trees. My house, which I share with 5 or 6 others, is comfortable enough, though there's only one bathroom. However, I get my Marine to secure that for me when I want it. The house next door on one side is a mess where we have our meals, run by ATS* and none too good, but not too bad.

The house on the other side is a nice little modern house reserved for Anthony. The P.M. is the next one further on, really a charming house, though some of the decoration rather modern German. Then, several houses further on, is a drab and dreary little building destined to house Attlee! Very suitable—it's just like Attlee himself!

Altogether I suppose we have 25 or 30 houses, including another Mess—a larger one, where I dined last night. It has a large lawn sloping steeply down to the lake, and it was pleasant sitting there after dinner.

Masses of people have already arrived. Anthony and P.M. due today some time.

I believe this particular lot of villas belonged to the German UFA

* Auxiliary Territorial Service, later the Women's Royal Army Corps.

(Film) people. All Germans have of course been turned out. Where they've gone, no one knows. Can you imagine what we should feel if Germans and Japanese were doing this in England, and if we had all been bundled out to make way for Hitler and Co. to squat in our homes and decide our fate while we lived in holes in the rubble heaps of London? . . .

Driving from the airfield here, the road was lined with Russian soldiers (we're in an enclave in the Russian Zone)* and I saw very few natives, but it's quite noticeable that one sees only old people and children—the latter looking quite well nourished.

It's beautiful country—sandy with pines and birches and a chain of lakes.

Monday, 16 July *A.C. to T.C.* *Potsdam*

After writing yesterday, I spent the morning in Berlin. It's a staggering sight. The roads cleared, but no traffic on them. Hardly a house undamaged and 90% mere shells. I don't think it could ever be rebuilt. The whole thing would have to be pulled down and several million tons of rubbish carted away. I don't know what will happen, this winter, to the population living in the ruins. At present the sewers are mostly bust (with unpleasant results). There *is*, I believe a water-supply system, but the suffering and the disease will be awful.

Amongst other things we went to Hitler's Chancellery. At the main entrance there was a pile of rubble out of which were sticking medal ribbons, and occasionally decorations. I picked up a ribbon, and some people found Iron Crosses. I failed in that. But I gave 3 cigarettes to a Russian sentry who then pulled out from behind a door an old felt boot. I told him I didn't want boots, but he signed me to look inside and it was full of Iron Crosses! So I took one. We went into Hitler's study. It had been pretty badly damaged. There was the undercarriage of his enormous desk, with, alongside it, its marble top. (I've got a bit of that as a paper-weight!) In the banqueting hall a Russian sergeant climbed into the crystal chandelier (astonishingly still intact) and wrenched off a little crystal rosette for me! . . . Anthony arrived about 4 and I sat in his garden and reported to him on my talks with the Americans.

P.M. arrived about 7 and A. and I walked through the gate into his garden and found him and Mary [Churchill] and Monty there.

* Perhaps because he realised the significance of what had happened at Tehran, Churchill insisted that each delegation at Potsdam should have entirely separate quarters, with its own guards.

We were joined by Alex. I think he and Monty had hardly been together since N. Africa, so it was a historic reunion. . . .

P.M. delighted with Pres.

Lunched with P.M. Only A. and Archie Kerr there. Best fried fillets of real sole I've had for 6 years. I made the salad, which was successful!

We are now off—P.M., A. and I to Berlin. I don't necessarily want to see it again, but I want to hear the P.M.'s comments on Hitler's study!

Russians have only just arrived. I am seeing Molotov with A. at 6 this evening.

Very hot, blazing sun.

Tuesday, 17 July *A.C. to T.C.* *Potsdam*

After writing yesterday, I joined the P.M.'s convoy at 4 p.m., and we proceeded to Berlin. I drove with Mary and Bob Dixon. The P.M. only decided to go about an hour before, so there had not been much time to organise the trip very well. We were in charge, generally, of a Russian officer, who was not very efficient. We had to make a longish detour on the way into Berlin, as Pres. Truman was reviewing American Tank Divisions on the main Chaussée.

We stopped at the Reichstag building, which we inspected (outside only). We got out of the cars and wandered about, which I thought rather a questionable proceeding as there were no elaborate security measures and quite a number of Berliners. They seemed to take a vivid interest (Winston of course was recognised, as he kept a cigar in his mouth the whole time), but there were no obvious signs of hostility.

Then to the Chancellery, but we had a bad view of it: it was an awful scrimmage as our party had by then grown into a mob, swelled by Russian officers and officials and innumerable uniformed war correspondents. It was frightfully hot, milling about in such a crowd, stumbling over the dusty débris with which all the rooms and passages are littered.

I saw it much better, at my ease, the day before. I accompanied Winston into Hitler's study, but he didn't make much comment—perhaps he was too much overcome!

One thing was better, however, this time, as we went into the garden and down into Hitler's dug-out. Unfortunately the lighting system was out of order, and by the light of a single torch it was not easy to get a good view. We were shown the room in which, according to one story, Hitler died. Next door was another room said to have been Eva Braun's. On one table there was still a vase with a branch in it which had evidently been a spray of blossom.

At the exit from the dug-out there is a shallow crater where Hitler and Eva Braun were said to have been originally buried, and afterwards dug up and burnt. This is according to another story, of which there are many, but nobody knows the truth.

However, that is the scene of one of the world's greatest dramas, and it is certainly impressive.

About 6.30 A. and I went round to see Molotov and Vyshinsky and chatted for about three quarters of an hour. I don't think our conversation revealed anything of great interest. We were mainly discussing the agenda for the Conference, which as usual, refuses to begin. However, we shall have a meeting of the Big 3 this afternoon, and perhaps this delay gives us time to prepare and to coach our Chiefs, who have both been rather out of the picture for some time lately!

By the way, I forgot to say that we came back from Berlin yesterday afternoon direct along the main Chaussée. Truman's review was over, but his Tanks were still there. It was an impressive sight—a serried row of Tanks and armoured cars, side by side, only a yard or two separating each from its neighbour, and stretching for about a mile and a half.

[So far the Russians had ignored without serious attempt at explanation the Yalta agreements about free elections. The western frontiers of Soviet power had advanced about 750 miles, and the south-eastern frontiers some 600 miles. The Baltic States and the capitals of central and south-eastern Europe—Warsaw, Budapest, Bucharest, Sofia—lay within Russia's grasp. The Red Army was in partial occupation of Austria and Berlin. In Yugoslavia Tito lost no time in suppressing his opponents. As Goering remarked shortly before the end, the English had entered the war to prevent Germany from going into the East, not to have the East come to the Atlantic. Well might Churchill confess that he had never in his life been more worried by the European situation.

The British bargaining counters at Potsdam, as enumerated by the Foreign Secretary on 10 July, were the German fleet and merchant navy; credits; a substantial part of Germany's industry, including 70% of the steel industry; the Russians' desire for Italian ships and for access to the Eastern Mediterranean. These few cards Eden begged Churchill not to surrender without return. 'But he is again under Stalin's spell. He kept repeating "I like that man." I am full of admiration of Stalin's handling of him. I told him I was, hoping it would move him. It did a little.'

He minuted to the Prime Minister that day, 17 July:

> The truth is that on any and every point, Russia tries to seize all that she can and she uses these meetings to grab as much as she can get. . . . If we were to talk generously to the Russians this time about access to the wider oceans, I fear that they would only regard it as an indication that we had not been shocked by their demands on Turkey, and would proceed to make more and more demands on Persia and on other countries in the Middle East. . . . I am deeply concerned at the pattern of Russian policy, which becomes clearer as they become more brazen every day.[11]

In short, the consciousness of overwhelming common danger had gone, and with it the incentive to sacrifice and unity. The Allied armies had already withdrawn to their agreed zones.]

Wednesday, 18 July *A.C. to T.C.* *Potsdam*

The P.M., since he left London, has refused to do any work or read anything. That is probably quite right, but then he can't have it both ways: if he knows nothing about the subject under discussion, he should keep quiet, or ask that his Foreign Secretary be heard. Instead of that, he butts in on every occasion and talks the most irrelevant rubbish, and risks giving away our case at every point.

Truman is most quick and businesslike. He was only trying, at this first meeting, to establish a list of the questions we must deal with. Every mention of a topic started Winston off on a wild rampage from which the combined efforts of Truman and Anthony with difficulty restrained him.

So it was a pretty useless meeting, but these conferences always have their infantile complaints.

We didn't get back from the meeting till after 8.

The meetings take place in the Cecilien Hof, a palace that was built, I think, for Little Willie [Crown Prince Wilhelm of Germany] after his marriage. It stands in a lovely park (strewn with Russian sentries), but the house is pretty ugly. However it's very conveniently arranged for a conference.

I dined at the Mess (with the band of the Scots Guards playing on the lawn outside). A. dined alone with the P.M. and says he read him a lecture and in particular urged him to try to resist giving in to Stalin (who knows *exactly* how to manage him).

After dinner I had to go round for a discussion with the Americans—Jimmy Dunn and Doc. Matthews with a view to clearing up some of the mess made by the Big 3. But I got to bed before 12. . . .

Had a pretty good rush this morning preparing for the meeting of

Foreign Secretaries at 11 which lasted till 11.30. Quite useful, and we mapped out the course to some extent.

Lunched with A., Jimmy Byrnes* and Dunn there, and we talked shop all the time.

Big 3 at 4, and it went better. The P.M. had submitted to being coached a little bit. Some quite useful plain, but unheated, talk on Poland.

It went so efficiently that we got through our agenda by about 6—much to the P.M.'s annoyance, as he wanted to go on talking at random and was most disappointed—just like a child with its toy taken away from it. But Truman closed the proceedings!

Luckily they didn't repeat what they did yesterday evening—which was to lead us into a large dining-room the whole length of which was filled by an enormous table loaded with caviare, cold meat, turkeys, partridges, salads of all kinds &c. &c. with vodka and wines of all hues. Rather disgusting in the midst of a starving country!

[Dr Goebbels' machine had proclaimed unwearingly that Britain would end the war as the dependent of the U.S.A. Lend-lease had relieved the economy of the need to sustain a favourable balance of payments. Exports had dwindled to about a third of their pre-war level. The financial cost to Britain of the war is estimated at £25,000m. In 1944 and 1945, no more than 11s. in every £ spent was being found from revenue. Debts in sterling amounted to well over £3,000m., mainly owed to the countries in whose defence had been spent.

On 18 July Churchill spoke of this melancholy position to Truman, who listened with sympathy and spoke generously and justly of the immense debt owed to Britain for the time she fought alone. 'If you had gone like France, we might well be fighting the Germans on the American coast at the present time.'

On the same evening the Prime Minister, disregarding Eden's minute for the moment, told Stalin that he welcomed the prospect of Russia as a great sea power. Stalin promised free elections in all countries 'liberated' by the Red Army. This pledge Churchill was at first inclined to believe.[12]]

Thursday, 19 July *A.C. to T.C.* *Potsdam*

The usual rush this morning before a meeting of Foreign Secretaries at 11. We had quite a useful discussion—mainly on Government of Germany and the Polish Question. Things are setting straighter now—we have had time to prepare the work a bit, and I hope we shall get through a certain amount.

* Now Secretary of State.

Lunch with A., Molotov, Vyshinsky and Frogface came, and Archie Kerr. They were quite pleasant and festive.

Friday, 20 July *A.C. to T.C.* *Potsdam*

You tell me to hold my head up when I'm being photographed! But do you realise that there are 15 sizzling hot searchlights turned on us for about 10 minutes with 40 photographers taking shots the whole time? One can't pose continuously under those conditions, and one never knows which photograph will be selected for publication.

We had quite a fairly good 3-Power meeting yesterday afternoon. I can't say we accomplished much, but we had some quite frank talk, which does the Russians a power of good.

The President gave a 'Banquet' last night. Quite a good dinner and I sat between Joe Davies, who is not disagreeable, and another American, Bohlen.* The President had Winston on his right and Joe on his left—and Attlee opposite! Amongst the toasts, Winston proposed 'The Leader of the British Opposition—whoever he may be!'

After dinner the Americans produced a sergeant who was pianist in one of the New York Symphony Orchestras. He led off with Chopin's 'Polonaise', so I suggested to Molotov that we'd better hire him to play when we were discussing the Polish Question! Then Jimmy Byrnes played a little Chopin—not badly at all. All this on the terrace overlooking the lake, where it was quite pleasantly cool.

Truman is not quite the genial host that F.D.R. was, and the entertainment didn't go with a bang, but it was quite pleasant and ended about 10.45, so again I got to bed early.

It's warm again this morning, but filmy cloud keeps off the hottest rays of the sun.

We had a Foreign Secretaries' meeting this morning. Again we didn't achieve much, but A. spoke very well and firmly to the Russians about their behaviour in the Balkans. As I say, it does them good, and we had a quite genial lunch afterwards with Molotov in his house. Maisky was there.

Saturday, 21 July *A.C. to T.C.* *Potsdam*

I'm afraid we haven't been making as much progress as I had hoped, these last 2 days. It looks as if we may not finish on Wednesday. If we don't, Winston and Anthony will fly back on that day and

* C. E. Bohlen of the State Dept.

be back here on Friday. Whether I shall come back for 2 nights, or whether I should do more good staying here and trying to get the work in shape, I don't know. But it's not certain that we shall *not* finish, and even if we don't we should only have to carry on for 3 or 4 days after. I think Truman, and certainly Joe, will refuse to stay here indefinitely.

Last night I dined in the Mess and afterwards there was a concert on the terrace by the R.A.F. Symphony Orchestra. They are *extremely* good, all of them impressed from various Orchestras in England. It was very pleasant sitting on a lawn sloping down to the lake, on a perfect evening, listening to very good music. I did a little work after, and went early to bed.

This morning I started off at 9 to attend our parade in Berlin. It was a very good show. A stand had been put up on the main avenue in the Tiergarten leading up to the Siegessaüle. We all met there, and we (the Principal guests!) were put into little motor lorries that stretched right away nearly to the Brandenburger Tor. A very impressive sight, but we felt rather like French aristocrats being driven in tumbrils through the streets! We eventually got back to the saluting base, and then the whole show marched past, including some of the Grenadiers, to their regimental march.

When it was over we nipped into our cars and rushed back to the Conference, where we had a meeting of Foreign Secretaries at 12. It lasted till 2.30! I then lunched at Anthony's house (I'm sorry to say they have received news showing that their son is definitely lost). Then I had work to prepare for the Big 3 at 5. That went on till 7.30. All day we haven't achieved very much: we've been having a row with Joe about the Polish Western frontier, and trying to stop him bagging from the area he wants to allot to the Poles all the produce that it used to contribute to the supply of Germany. We, in the west of Germany, have got millions of Germans to feed and support, and if a great part of their normal source of supply is snaffled by Joe, our difficulties will be considerably increased.

[Churchill said that if the demand for the western Neisse frontier were accepted, Germany would lose one quarter of the arable land she had possessed in 1937. Between 8 and 9 million Germans would have to be removed. Stalin replied they had all left the area between the Vistula and the Oder.

At a later meeting the Chairman of the Polish National Council, M. Bierut, had the hardihood to suggest to Churchill that the Polish elections would probably be still more democratic than the British. Mikolajczyk told Eden that much of this talk was nonsense.[13]]

Sunday, 22 July *A.C. to T.C.* *Potsdam*

Again very little definite progress to report, but a lot of quite plain speaking may have cleared the ground a bit. Joe being very tiresome about the Polish Western frontiers. But it makes an awful rush, having to prepare for the morning meeting which goes on till after 1.30, swallow lunch and prepare for the afternoon meeting—which means giving Anthony sufficient material for him to be able to explain to Winston what it's all about. And this afternoon was more hectic than usual, as A. had arranged a little trip for himself to go round and collect salutes from British units (a little show of his own, in contrast to yesterday, when he rode in the *third* tumbril!) and only got back as the afternoon performance was due to start.

It got hotter and more and more oppressive this afternoon till a thunderstorm burst at about 5. All the streets of our village are littered with trees—there was a most frightful squall—and this evening there is a stream of water flowing down the gutter outside my house: I understand a fallen tree broke the water-main, so I suppose we shall have no bath water tomorrow.

As I was driving back from the meeting this evening, when I was half way out of the park of the Cecilien Hof, I was held up by Russian sentries at a cross-road. From the road on the left emerged a platoon of Russian tommy-gunners in skirmishing order, then a number of guards and units of the N.K.V.D. army. Finally appeared Uncle Joe on foot, with his usual thugs surrounding him, followed by another screen of skirmishers. The enormous officer who always sits behind Uncle at meetings was apparently in charge of operations, and was running about, directing tommy-gunners to cover all the alleys in the Park giving access to the main road. All this because Uncle wanted 5 minutes exercise and fresh air, and walked out to pick up his car 500 yards from the Palace! A curious comment on 'Democracy', and all the more curious considering the whole park is ringed and littered with sentries anyhow!

Monday, 23 July *A.C. to T.C.* *Potsdam*

It is now settled that we shall *not* be able to finish on Wednesday. P.M. and Anthony will leave us that afternoon. Meanwhile the Council of Foreign Secretaries will carry on, I taking Anthony's place, Byrnes and Molotov having graciously signified that that arrangement will be agreeable to them! It's a curse, but can't be helped. Winston says he will be back on Friday. That, of course depends on the election. If he has a comfortable majority over all parties, I have no doubt he will be back. If the Conservatives are the largest party, but with no clear majority over the others, I don't know what he'll do. I suppose he would come back here with Attlee. If Labour get a clear majority, I don't know what will happen. Winston need not, of course, resign until he has been beaten in the House, which couldn't be much before Aug. 10. But I doubt if he could come back here. Equally, Attlee would hardly come alone. So we must simply await result. Whenever the Conference resumes, it oughtn't to take a week to finish off. I don't know how long Joe and Truman can stay. The latter is *not* coming to London. Well, all this uncertainty is a great bore, but it always happens and there it is! . . .

We had the same sort of day today—Foreign Secretaries meeting in the morning and Big 3 in the afternoon. Both quite useful. Joe in a quite reasonable mood this afternoon. But one never knows, and things change from day to day.

I told you about our storm yesterday evening. My worst apprehensions proved true, and all water supply in our district ceased just before lunch. . . . There was a lime tree just outside the P.M.'s house which was bent over by the gale. It appears it must have been planted —I should think 80 years ago—just over the water main, on which its roots had got a complete grip. So when it bent it cracked the pipe. . . . P.M. very annoyed at not being able to have a bath. He says it is 'a most unwarranted act of Providence'.

Tuesday, 24 July *A.C. to T.C.* *Potsdam*

Usual routine—Foreign Secretaries at 11, who got through a certain amount. Then a Delegation of the Polish Government, including Mikolajczyk, were received at about 12.30, and we listened to them making their case for incorporating chunks of Germany into Poland until 2.30—all their statements being interpreted twice, into Russian and English. So I didn't get lunch, in Anthony's house, till about 3.

That didn't give much time before the Big 3 meeting at 5, which was quite useful—again with quite a lot of plain speaking. The principal topics were Russian behaviour in the Balkan states and Russian claims in regard to the Straits. . . .

P.M. and A. are off about lunch-time tomorrow. It was agreed this afternoon that the Conference wouldn't take more than 4 or 5 days to wind up once it resumes.

Later (10 p.m.)

Just back from Attlee's dinner. It was almost as bad as I expected. Vyshinsky was quite agreeable, but we were talking through interpreters, which doesn't help small talk. Frogface sat silent like a mountain (or a dunghill). Attlee addressed some remarks to him, in an effort to spur him into life. Frogface said 'Maybe so', once, and that was all.

[On this afternoon Truman told Stalin briefly that the atomic bomb had been successfully tested. Stalin merely said 'Thank you'. The British had already consented to the use of the bomb, partly because it would remove the need to pay a high price for Russian assistance in the Far East.]

Wednesday, 25 July *A.C. to T.C.* *Potsdam*

I had to be back at A's house at 10.30. Found no one there, so sat down to read a newspaper, but in about 5 minutes the Poles streamed in—dreadful people all of them, except Mikolajczyk. So I had to entertain them as best I could, and went on entertaining them—no signs of A. He didn't turn up till 11.30: had been dining with some military somewhere, lost his way, punctured &c. So then we got down to it, and talked shop till 1.30. Then filled the Poles (and ourselves) with sandwiches and whiskies and sodas and I went to bed at 2 a.m.

Today has been more peaceful. The Big 3 got out of bed in the morning (which doesn't suit either Winston or Joe) and met at 11. Considering all things, they were quite amiable. They left us at 12 and then followed a meeting of Foreign Secretaries, at which I impersonated A. We made Molotov agree one point anyhow. I got back soon after 1 and joined A. towards the end of his early lunch: he was due to leave for the airport at 2, and duly left.

I then got quietly down to the work of sorting out the mass of paper that always accumulates during a conference, and trying to find out where we stand and what, if anything, we have done so far. One ought always to have a pause like this in the middle of a conference, for taking stock: it's most useful.

Then for the first time for days, I walked out about 5.45 for an hour. One has to walk rather like a tiger, round and round one's cage, as, if one goes outside the British Sector, one is challenged at every yard by Russian sentries with tommy-guns. However, there's plenty of room and it was a lovely evening, and most refreshing. Then a little more work before dinner in the Mess. The R.A.F. pianist played for a bit after and I have now (10 p.m.) come back to my office to write this and to continue the process of clearing up, but shall go early to bed. I may have one meeting shortly, but it won't last long. I had one this afternoon with Walter Monckton and experts on Reparations, about which I understand *nothing*. . . .

It will be interesting tomorrow listening to the election results. Personally, I have an instinctive feeling that there may be some shocks for the Conservatives, but that's based on nothing.

[At the end of the morning Churchill explained to Stalin that he must now go to London. Whether or not he returned to Potsdam would depend on the election result. Stalin merely said, with a glance at the rather silent and mouselike leader of the Opposition, 'Mr Attlee does not look to me like a man who is hungry for power.'

In the event, Labour won 395 seats, a majority of more than 180.]

Thursday, 26 July *A.C. to T.C.* *Potsdam*

The election will have come as a terrible blow to poor old Winston, and I am awfully sorry for the old boy. It certainly is a display of base ingratitude, and rather humiliating for our country.

Where we stand now, I haven't an idea. I suppose Winston must resign at once: there's no point in his waiting to meet the House when his defeat is certain. If that is so, I suppose the King sends for Attlee tomorrow, and he forms a Government. In those circumstances I don't see how Attlee can return here tomorrow: surely he'd be too busy in London. Perhaps he could send a Foreign Secretary in a day or 2 (? Bevin). But it'll all be rather untidy. Or they may close the conference. Almost the only thing it has so far settled is to set up a Council of the 5 Foreign Ministers, to meet in London on Sept. 1st. The Conference might remit the rest of its work to that Council, but that wouldn't be very satisfactory.

I shall have to ring up London tonight, as I am due to meet my Foreign Secretary colleagues tomorrow morning, and I expect they will want a statement from me!

We've been peaceful here for the last 24 hours. This morning I and some others went to see the Neues Palais at Potsdam. Do you remember a hideous sort of ball-room with sea-shells encrusted on the walls? But the rest of it was better than my recollection of it. Then again to Sans Souci, which stands in the same park. It's very attractive and almost entirely undamaged. The Neues Palais has been rather knocked about, particularly the rather flamboyant outbuildings at the back of it. One of the 2 cupola'ed pavilions gutted by a bomb and the other knocked about by shell-fire. Then to the Garnison Kirche, which is in about the same state as the Guards' Chapel.* Frederick the Great and several other Emperors were buried there. A German lady whom we found picking about in the

* Destroyed by a V.1 'flying-bomb' on Sunday 18 June 1944.

ruins said she had heard their bodies had been removed, but she wasn't sure. I don't know how they could have been extracted from the wreckage I saw there.

[Despite the remark about his 'instinctive feeling', Cadogan had not expected a Conservative defeat. For all the irritable and exasperated observations in the Diary, felt admiration and affection for both Churchill and Eden; a sudden sense that a glorious epoch, in which he took quiet pride at having played his part, had come to its end; and dismay at the prospect of adjusting to a new regime. 'I've hardly got the resilience of youth to make a fresh start with a lot of new bodies', he told Eden, 'and I feel rather miserable.'

> But I do want just to write one line of thanks to you for all your help and kindness. You have been a great example and a good friend, and you leave behind you a host of friends in the Office to which I hope you will return soon, after I am gone from it, (though I suppose you'll be at No. 10!).

Eden replied:

> You and I have worked together in long spells at three different periods. For me this last has been the most stimulating of the three, though in all you were ever the wise and patient guide.
>
> I think that we have reason to feel proud of the work we did together in these war years and that history will write well of it. Certainly I could not have asked for a wiser or more loyal companion in arms, whether in battle against enemy forces or in argument with Allied ones! I shall always be deeply grateful, and I hope that for many years yet you will continue to guard and guide our international policy. . . . I am very glad that Bevin is to be my successor. He is the best man they have, and will hearken to you and the experience you bring.

Sir Alexander sent Churchill a letter of thanks for his inspired leadership in the dark days, of sympathy in defeat and of appreciation for unfailing kindness: 'It has been an unmitigated pleasure to serve you, and if I could feel that I had helped in any way, that would be an abiding satisfaction.'

Mr Churchill's reply is reproduced overleaf.]

Friday, 27 July *A.C. to T.C.* *Potsdam*

I had a telegram this morning early from Attlee saying he couldn't get here today, but would come tomorrow (he doesn't say whom he will bring with him) and conveying messages to Stalin and Truman. Also a personal message to me saying that he wants to get the

WESTERHAM 93.

CHARTWELL,
WESTERHAM,
KENT.

August 5, 1945.

My dear Alec,

Thank you so much for all you say in your letter. A very formidable event has occurred in Britain, and I fear it will diminish our national stature at a time when we most need unity and strength.

All the work you have done in this War has been excellent. I rejoice to feel you will still be at your post during years when an even heavier burden will descend upon your strong shoulders. You have indeed played a man's part in this glorious struggle, which we got into in one muddle and have come out of in another. Nevertheless the lustrum will glitter in future times.

Yours v[ery] sincerely,

Winston S. Churchill

The Hon.
Sir Alexander Cadogan, G.C.M.G., K.C.B.

Conference finished 'in 2 or 3 days', so the Foreign Secretaries, with whom he authorises me to act, are to get on as quickly as they can.

We are meeting at 4 this afternoon. In the circumstances there's not very much we can do, but there are perhaps a few loose ends that we could tie up. . . .

I am getting together a lot of documents to leave here by 'Mosquito' plane at 9.30, so that Attlee can read them on the way over in his plane tomorrow.

[At the meeting on the afternoon of 27 July, Molotov accused the Americans, not for the first time, of going back on the figure of $20,000m. for reparations. Byrnes said that this figure, accepted at Yalta only as a basis for discussion, was now meaningless; not least because the Russians had already taken much of the plant from that part of Germany which they now controlled.

On that evening, Byrnes spoke to Cadogan of a possible compromise: Russia should take reparations from her zone, and be allowed equipment to the value of $1500m. from the Western zones in return for the supply of coal and foodstuffs of equivalent value from German territory under her control; and Polish administration of all the territory up to the line of the eastern Neisse river should be accepted at once. Cadogan recommended this proposal to Attlee and Bevin. The latter tried to trade acceptance against satisfaction on other issues, and had some sharp exchanges with the Lublin Poles about the freedom and timing of elections. M. Bierut, their leader, eventually made some attempt to meet the British position. However, Mikolajczyk let the British delegation know on 30 July that Bierut's assurances had been deliberately designed to deceive. The British realised that although Byrnes's compromise suggested the eastern Neisse, the Poles and Russians were unlikely to accept anything less than the western Neisse.[14]]

Saturday, 28 July *A.C. to T.C.* *Potsdam*

Jimmy B. told me the President wanted to get away tomorrow (Sunday) night, so was in rather a hurry to finish the business! I think that will be quite impossible; however, I'm all for hurrying things up as much as possible. So I arranged provisionally there should be a meeting of the Big 3 after dinner tonight: our Ministers won't arrive here much before 7. I think they'll have to have individual talks with Truman and Stalin beforehand, so the meeting won't begin before 10, and will go on most of the night. And Truman likes going to bed at 10.30! Molotov of course agreed: Russians like sitting up all night.

Jimmy Byrnes gave me an outline (quite sensible) of how the

major outstanding problems of the Conference might be solved, and I must try to sell it to Attlee between the time of his arrival and this evening's meeting.

We had a quite futile meeting of the Foreign Secretaries yesterday afternoon, consisting mostly of a sharp duel between Molotov and Byrnes about reparations. I was quite content to let them fight it out! . . .

I think we may do better with Bevin than with any other of the Labourites. I think he's broadminded and sensible, honest and courageous. But whether he's an inspired Foreign Minister or not, I don't know. He's the heavyweight of the Cabinet and will get his own way with them, so if he can be put on the right line, that may be all right.

Sunday, 29 July *A.C. to T.C.* *Potsdam*

On the evening of 28 July I had a short talk with Attlee and Bevin, explaining the situation to them more or less. We then dined and went off to see the President and Byrnes at 9.45, and then on to Joe and Molotov. Joe was interested to know how to account for the election result. He asked whether it meant that the British were tired of the Japanese war! Then on to a meeting, at about 10.30, of the Big 3. Nothing very much happened. As usual there is some reluctance to grasp the larger nettles.

It was fortunate that Attlee had been here with Winston, following the Conference proceedings, so that one doesn't have to begin with him from scratch. Bevin has always taken an interest in foreign affairs and knows something about them. I think he is pretty sound on the whole. He has a tendency, of course, to take the lead over Attlee, who recedes into the background by his very insignificance. . . .

The Poles all came at 3 [on 29 July], to state their case. I went to sleep in the middle, as I had heard it all already—twice.

Then at 4.30 we went round to have a further chat with the President. There was to have been a Big 3 meeting at 4, but Joe is reported to be unwell and his doctor says he is not to go out of the house. I don't know for how long that will go on: we're consequently rather stuck at the moment.

I must say it's a bore beginning again with a new Administration. I don't mind old Bevin, but one had got used to the old ways and it's hard to adapt oneself to the new.

Monday, 30 July *A.C. to T.C.* *Potsdam*

This morning we had a Delegation meeting at 10, and then another dose of the Poles from 11.30 till 1. Lunched with Bevin.

Got through some accumulated work after—till nearly 4, when Jimmy Byrnes called on Bevin and we took him over afterwards to see Attlee. Mostly about Reparations—a very complicated subject which I find almost unintelligible—and the Polish Western frontier. Jimmy B. is a bit too active and has already gone and submitted various proposals to Molotov which go a bit beyond what we want at the moment.

Joe is still 'indisposed' but says he will be all right tomorrow. So at 5 we had a meeting of the Foreign Secretaries. Which sat till 9! But it *did* make a bit of progress, and I see some possibility of getting a real advance tomorrow. When, exactly, we shall finish, I really don't know. This week, I think.

Dined late in the Mess and have been clearing off work since.

The house I have taken over was occupied by the Chiefs of Staff. It has a marble statue of the Three Graces in the front garden, and I suggested to the 3 Chiefs of Staff that they should use it as a hat-rack—a charming idea, but I never went to see whether they adopted it.

Must go and see if the coast is clear, and, if so, toddle off to bed.

[Bevin sought further assurances from the Poles on the next afternoon, 31 July, when Bierut promised that free elections would be held no later than 'the early part of 1946'. Normal facilities would be allowed for foreign journalists. At 4 p.m., Attlee and Bevin announced that they accepted the extension of Polish administration to the western Neisse. Final settlement would await the peace conference. Russian troops, said Stalin, would largely be withdrawn from territory administered by Poland. The powers also contrived to patch up an agreement about reparations.]

Tuesday, 31 July *A.C. to T.C.* *Potsdam*

A Delegation meeting at 10, which didn't last too long, and I got through some work before going, with Bevin and Archie Kerr, to lunch with Molotov. The same food, the same drink and the same old toasts! But Molotov was quite cheerful and agreeable and it passed off pleasantly enough.

2.45 a final meeting with the Poles, at which we extracted from them (for what they may be worth) pledges about free elections and freedom of the Press &c. in return for large accessions of German territory.

Then the Big 3 at 4, where we jumped all the big hurdles—Reparations, Polish frontier &c.

There remain only a few minor questions which will not, I think, give undue trouble. We confidently expect to finish tomorrow and come home Thursday afternoon. . . .

That's the way most conferences go: all the difficulties pile up over a number of days, and then something suddenly loosens, and the whole thing breaks free.

We have not done too badly, I think. Joe has got most of what he wants, but then the cards were mostly in his hands, and we *have* got something, mainly in the matter of the treatment of Germany. . . .

Bevin will, I think, do well. He knows a good deal, is prepared to read any amount, seems to take in what he does read, and is capable of making up his own mind and sticking up for his (or our) point of view against anyone. I think he's the best we could have had.

He effaces Attlee, and at Big 3 meetings he does all the talking while Attlee nods his head convulsively and smokes his pipe.

I shall be glad to get away from here: it was novel and interesting for a bit, but one is rather a prisoner here in our Sector and one begins to get a sort of claustrophobia. . . .

Bevin says he does *not* want the F.O. Flat. I may be able to get it, but I don't know whether there are spare rooms for the daughters. (Also I must find out whether Bevin wants to keep me on!)

Thursday, 2 August

Delegation meeting at 10. Then Foreign Secretaries at 11. Byrnes talks too much and wastes time. But we polished off quite a lot. . . . Big 3 (or 2½!) at 4. Sat till about 7. Got thro' with a rush. Dined with Bevin and was back at Cecilien Hof at 9.30. Sat till 12.30 and really polished everything off, including Protocol and Communiqué.

['In politics', said Stalin during the conference, 'one should be guided by the calculation of forces.' The forces in central and south-eastern Europe, except in Greece and Turkey, were distributed so overwhelmingly in Russia's favour that there was little room for manœuvre. Despite repeated appeals, Molotov refused to consider the observation by the three Governments of elections in Italy, Greece, Bulgaria, Roumania and Hungary.

The conference agreed on a Council of the five Foreign Ministers to draft peace treaties, to deliberate upon other problems and to meet in London on 1 September. The three Governments would each consider 'in the near future, in the light of the conditions then prevailing, the establishment of diplomatic relations with Bulgaria, Finland, Hungary and Roumania, to the extent possible prior to the conclusion of peace treaties with those countries.' A peace settlement with Italy would be urgently sought, after which the three would support an Italian request to join the U.N. No promises were made about Russia's desire for access to the

Mediterranean or for a toehold in North Africa. Russian demands for a change in the Greek Government were successfully resisted. On the other hand, British complaints about Marshal Tito's proceedings received little support from the President and were not discussed after 30 July.

After the conference, Attlee telegraphed to the Dominions: 'I feel we have made considerable progress towards a better understanding between the three Governments, and that the decisions reached will provide a firm basis for a further advance.' On 20 August, however, Bevin told Parliament that in respect of Hungary, Roumania and Bulgaria, 'the impression we get from recent developments is that one kind of totalitarianism is being replaced by another.'[15]]

Friday, 3 August

There is much comment I should like to add on Potsdam, but I forget what, and I haven't time!

. . . 5.50 S. of S.—about appointments. Told him that, as far as I was concerned, he needn't be delicate about discussing my retirement or transfer. He said he didn't want to 'swop 'orses' at once. That's all right, but I should like to know something definite soon. Must give him time.

Saturday, 4 August

Sunny and v. hot. Massigli at 10.30 to cross-examine me about Terminal. But he wasn't critical—rather the reverse. Bevin off till Tues. so I did the same. As I was leaving at 11.30 N. Brook* rang up to say he was coming round to check the Protocol with me. I said he could damned well do it with someone else—*I* was not going to wait for such nonsense.

Monday, 6 August

Several showers. B.B.C. announced tonight the dropping of the first atomic bomb. Not many details yet as to its effect. (Joe had been told about it at Potsdam, but didn't seem to register much interest—perhaps he didn't believe in it! Wonder how he'll take the news!)

Tuesday, 7 August

At F.O. at 2.30, and started grappling with arrears. . . . Cabinet at 6. Funny-looking lot. Don't know half of them by sight. All sorts and

* Norman Brook of the Cabinet Office: from 1947 Secretary of the Cabinet.

shapes. Round, thin, white and black, wire-haired and smooth-coated. The old gentleman on my left (Lord Arnold, I think)* said, 'I am very ignorant: I don't know who you are'! I said 'My name is Cadogan', but I couldn't ask him who *he* was! Got away 6.30.

Wednesday, 8 August

Lunched Andersons. Sat between Ava [Lady Anderson] and Mrs. Barrington Ward. Winston and Clemmie there. W[inston] dominating the conversation, as usual, so we sat on till 3.15! He looks quite well. . . . Sent for to No. 10 at 9.30 about Russian declaration of war on Japan, which I heard of just before leaving F.O. Drafted public announcement and message to Joe.

Friday, 10 August

12 Talk with E[rnest] B[evin], O.S. and 1 or 2 others about his speech on foreign policy. He's got sound ideas—which we must encourage. Lunched at home. Inspected houses with T. This is a frightful gamble—will the house (uninhabited since 1940) fall down next week? Can one run a house? If it proved impossible, can one get in anywhere else? Am I going to be employed for some years yet (if I live)? Will that be at home or abroad?. . . Got back to F.O. at 3.30. Found special Cabinet had been sitting since 3 and my presence was required. Saw E.B. at 3.40—he had come back to summon Winant. Japs have surrendered, subject to keeping the Emperor in some kind of control. Sent off telegrams to Moscow, Washington and Chungking to get their reaction. Then went to Cabinet, till 4.30, wasting most of my time. Discussion of announcements, broadcasts, Parliament, public holiday, Day of Thanksgiving &c. I only warned them that we had got to fix up things first with our Allies. . . . S. of S. has agreed to R. I. Campbell as 'Deputy' for the Council of Foreign Ministers. But there is now to be a Cttee. of the Cabinet on Atomic Bomb. He is our obvious representative on *that*, and I doubt whether he can do both. Agreed to sleep on it. . . . What epochal events! And the bomb is a real one. It will be a complete revolution in human life, and the plans for 'nationalisation' of mines &c. may be the babblings of children.

* This was probably Lord Addison. Lord Arnold's obituary notice had appeared in *The Times* on the previous day.

Saturday, 11 August

11 Wellington Koo, with the expected demand that his [Chinese] Govt. should be consulted on Japanese surrender. Reassured him. . . . E.B. had half an hour's gossip with me. Said, incidentally, that he wanted me to stay on 'for a year'. Well, if I can stay the course. . . . Talk at 5 with R. I. Campbell and others about preparations for Council of Foreign Ministers. R.I.C. has accepted to act as 'Deputy' which means, I hope, that he will have to do all the foreign trips.

As regards Far East, we sent a telegram last night to U.S. saying we thought Emperor himself need not sign surrender. Telegrams from Chungking and Australia showing this would displease them. But hear tonight at 7.15 from Bob Dixon that Winant says Americans accept this modification and are going ahead, saying that the 4 Powers agree! So it's now up to the Japs. Nothing definite on 9 o'c. news.

Sunday, 12 August

Wish I was shooting grouse! V. stuffy, but not v. sunny. Still no answer from Japs, but they'll give in all right—they've no alternative.

Monday, 13 August

11 meeting with E.B., Duff [Cooper] and others about our policy regarding Levant, and France generally. E.B. very good. Went on till 12.30.

Tuesday, 14 August

Cabinet at 11. E.B. got approval for his Greek policy. Considered telegrams from Washington showing that Americans are going ahead on surrender terms &c., without showing much disposition to consult us. We must accept this, and if Dominions complain we can say that we, too, were not consulted. . . . 2.30 talk with E.B. and others about Italian policy. I think he's very wise and sound. . . . 4 Alba. Gave him—in reply to questions by his Govt.—some more straight talk. . . . Bob Howe about Angora leakages.* Snatch ought, of course, to be court-martialled, but I must think over this. 5.30 Bridges about arrangements for Foreign Secretaries' meeting. 5.45 Massigli, about further French association with Jap surrender; we must consult Washington. Got through some work, but brought home some stinkers. . . . Have just (10.45) heard from F.O. that Japs *have* surrendered. Cabinet sitting, but hope I shan't have to go!

* The reference is to the sale of photographed documents by Sir H. Knatchbull-Hugessen's valet, 'Cicero'.

Wednesday, 15 August

Wasn't disturbed last night! The news is out. Attlee gave it at midnight—Jap surrender. So that's that. Drizzly morning. Large crowds in Mall when I walked to F.O.—waiting for the King's procession to open Parliament. . . . The first of the 2 VJ days shows crowds of people wandering in millions aimlessly about. I wish they wouldn't demonstrate their joy by fire-crackers and petards. Surely we've had enough bangs in these last 6 years! . . . Home to hear the King. He did it v. well. It's something to have lived to hear this. I've heard a number of his broadcasts before, in different circumstances. Sometimes they seemed almost a mockery. I have heard them in Sloane Gardens, Lansdowne House and here. One day, one freezing day, I stood on an icy road outside a cottage and listened to the words coming thro' the window. Did I really believe the expressions of faith? I don't know: I hope so. It was hard sometimes. But here is the culmination. The problems in front of us are manifold and awful. But I've lived through England's greatest hour, and if I can see no falling away from that, I shall die happy.

[Keynes, who had negotiated most of the principal financial arrangements with the U.S.A. during the war, pointed out to the Cabinet that on account of foreign aid, mainly American, Britain was being enabled to overspend her income by £2,100m. p.a. Without such aid there was no hope of maintaining an equilibrium in the balance of payments. The Government should therefore assume a state of bankruptcy, initiate a policy of austerity and postpone its social and economic programme. Even if spending did not increase, American aid would still be necessary; but because Britain could not pay interest and begin early repayment of the principal, it must be sought as a gift, even at the price of accepting American policies disadvantageous to British trade.

A few days later, without consultation, the U.S. Government cut off Lend-lease abruptly.]

Thursday, 16 August

London not at its best, with scores of thousands of morons wandering about and doing not much more than obstruct traffic. But the threatening weather this evening may damp their ardour a bit. Read Keynes' paper today on our financial outlook. It is certainly grim reading! There are terrible times ahead of any Govt. in this country.

EPILOGUE
1945–1968

1945–1968
EPILOGUE

The collapse of Germany and Japan relieved the pressure at either extremity of the Russian empire, a fact which Stalin had not been slow to exploit in Central Europe, the Balkans, Northern Persia and the Far East. The only basis upon which Russia had co-operated effectively with the West since 1917 had disappeared, and with it the need for her to pay a price for collaboration. Great Britain had emerged from the war with heavy commitments in Germany, Austria, Italy, Greece, Turkey, Palestine and Egypt, not to mention her colonial territories in Asia and Africa. Some of these obligations could be shuffled off by the simple act of withdrawal, as in Palestine; others could be shed by the same method but at a much heavier price, as in India. Indian independence meant the loss of the mobile strategic reserve upon which Commonwealth defence east of Suez then turned.

Cadogan rapidly came to admire the resourcefulness, patience and broad views of his new master, Ernest Bevin; and by all accounts it did not take long for the Secretary of State, who had arrived at the Foreign Office somewhat suspicious of the P.U.S., to realise that he had an adviser of exceptional quality. Bevin's hopes of a new style of diplomacy, 'cards on the table, face upwards', waned during the autumn of 1945. At the meeting of Foreign Ministers held in London, Molotov behaved in his most mulish and obstructive manner. By 23 September Bevin had had enough. He told Cadogan that he proposed to "ave it out' with Molotov. This tactic, as readers of the Diaries will know, entirely accorded with Cadogan's ideas. Bevin duly told the Russian that he did not want the business to develop as it had done with Hitler, suspicion mounting on either side and neither ever speaking frankly. The result, at least in the short run, proved good; Molotov withdrew some Russian claims and promised to support some British ones. Soon, however, he upbraided Bevin for being less helpful than Churchill and Eden. When the Chancellor of the Exchequer asked how the conference was progressing, Bevin replied 'Like the strike leader said, "Thank God there is no danger of a settlement."' Having foreseen the impasse, Cadogan congratulated himself on so arranging matters that others bore the main burden, for the volume of work falling upon him this autumn felt greater than ever and he less inclined to face it. The Diary records in September: 'My life in London is that of a slave, and I'm too old', and in October, after a short holiday, 'Since 8.10 a.m. I've been driving along with never a spare minute (it is now 11.40 p.m.) and everything piling up.'[1]

Nor did the early performances of the United Nations Organisation lighten his gloom. It appeared, he wrote after a time-wasting preparatory Commission, 'a moderate parody of the League, with *all* the failings and no advantages, that I can see. It's dreadful, to me, that even the atomic bomb hasn't shaken people out of their old ways of thinking.'[2]

All these events occurred against a background of chronic economic weakness. The abrupt termination of Lend-lease left Britain unable to sustain her economy at home or overseas. On 21 August Cadogan recorded that Maynard Keynes gave Ministers a lecture as illuminating as gloomy. The gist was simple; without aid from the U.S.A., immediate economies abroad and an intense effort to increase exports, there was no hope of escaping a financial Dunkirk. At that stage Keynes felt confident that he could get an interest-free loan from the Americans. Bevin had demurred somewhat; and although Keynes presented the case in a masterpiece of lucid, persuasive and forceful reasoning, without bluster, threats, grovelling or exaggeration, his American counterparts did not then feel that fear of Russia and of Communist movements which soon saved the British from an impossible position in Europe. 'We are negotiating in Washington, repeat Washington', Keynes telegraphed: 'fig leaves that pass muster with old ladies in Threadneedle Street wither in a harsher climate.' Eventually he secured a credit of £1,100m., and a further large sum from Canada. By the time the American loan became available, it had been effectively devalued by a sharp rise in prices. At that stage Britain's dollar exports scarcely sufficed to pay for the tobacco which she imported from the U.S.A.

Meanwhile Mr Byrnes, who had replaced Stettinius as Secretary of State, had proposed without consulting London that the Foreign Ministers meet in Moscow during December. For the British, the proceedings were depressing on all counts. Nothing could have been less forthcoming than Molotov's attitude. Cadogan found the effort to determine American policy 'like trying to tickle a trout with highly oiled gloves'. Late on the evening of 20 December, he accompanied the Secretary of State to the Kremlin. Stalin looked well but rather slimmer than at Potsdam. Bevin, Sir Alec judged,

> did very well indeed, very frank and quite firm, while being polite, and cracking a few jokes. True, we got nothing definite out of Joe, but he promised to consider various suggestions, and my impression is that he might agree to one or two. Possibly he may have suddenly returned to Moscow in order to gain prestige by breaking the deadlock.[3]

Agreement of a sort was reached. While Cadogan did not undervalue it, he realised how wide was the rift already opened between the Great Powers. He had now been P.U.S. for a full eight years, the longest tenure of modern times. Clearly a move had to be made. No sooner had he learned, with disappointment, that he would not be sent to Washington than Attlee appointed him as the first British permanent representative to the United Nations. He left the Foreign Office to many warm tributes in February 1946, and was succeeded by Sir Orme Sargent.

* * *

It was already manifest that Russia would break the undertaking given at San Francisco not to obstruct wilfully the Security Council's business. Cadogan said as much to Gromyko in June: 'the trouble is that whereas my government give me some latitude, you haven't an inch of elbow-room.' 'Do you not agree', asked the Russian representative, 'that other things beside the veto are bringing the Council into disrepute?' 'Certainly, and principally the use of the Council for propaganda purposes.'

A previous attempt at a private talk had proved futile, Gromyko's responses being 'I do not know', or 'We shall see'. Cadogan used to remark wryly that he was a good guide to the Russians' inscrutability, since they always did the opposite of what he expected. They seemed so wooden and blundering that the observer found himself searching for some supremely cunning motive. Their timidity prevented all normal contact. They were forbidden to mix with the people, or with other delegations. They would not exchange views, presumably for fear of being reported back. Gradually Cadogan came to the conclusion that Russian policy was not clever or subtle. Had the cards been properly played, he believed, Communism might have controlled Italy and France. Instead, Russia squandered the ample goodwill which she had gathered in the war. She virtually gave the West the Treaty of Dunkirk and N.A.T.O.

At the U.N., any concession was interpreted by the Russian delegates as weakness unless explicitly traded against a counter-concession. The waste of time at the Security Council and at committees, the sub-committees they spawned and at numerous other meetings, had to be experienced to be believed. The Russians' mental processes seemed to be different, or at least their technique beyond Western understanding. 'How can ten men discuss with a ventriloquist's doll?' Cadogan enquired wearily after one wrangle. In the meetings of Commonwealth delegates, by contrast, a welcome and different atmosphere was found. Respect and goodwill prevailed; serious arguments were heeded even when agreement could not be reached. He came also to admire the behaviour of the Americans, on top of the world but never crowing about it.

As for countering Russia and her satellites, Cadogan thought it a mistake to indulge in biting language too often. The moment and the ground must be carefully chosen. When Gromyko and Manuilsky, the Foreign Minister of the Ukraine, charged that Britain and Greece were threatening the peace in the Balkans, Cadogan retorted that this was no way to use the Security Council. If accusations were flung down and inflammatory speeches made, the Charter would soon be nullified. After all, Russia had refused to join a commission to investigate conditions in Greece; British troops had sacrificed numerous lives to defend Greece against the Fascists some time before Russia, or the Ukraine, was forced into the war; and that campaign almost certainly postponed Germany's invasion of the Soviet Union. Conditions in Greece were not in nearly so sorry a plight as those in

> certain other European countries whose situations have not yet been investigated by the Council; and . . . would be better than they are if it were not for Communist pressure and propaganda inside her territory and along her borders.
>
> What Greece now needs is to be left alone. Her record during the war is second to none, and if all the records of all countries formerly under enemy occupation are to be searched, there are several statesmen now in power in countries near Greece whose past would contrast unfavourably with that of any member of the Greek Government.

As for Gromyko's charges, Cadogan told him curtly that to overstate a case is an elementary error:

> Mr Gromyko implied that Mr Bevin was using the British army to extirpate Greek trade unions. How can anyone expect such allegations to be taken seriously I cannot imagine.
>
> Mr Gromyko's trump card seemed to be that a plebiscite was held in Greece while the country was under occupation by foreign troops, and that this constituted foreign intervention.
>
> Is Greece the only country where elections or plebiscites have been held while foreign troops were on its soil? I seem to have heard of other cases.

A few days later the motion directing the Council to order Greece to cease 'threatening peace' was lost by 9 votes to 2. Bevin had meanwhile telegraphed:

> I read your speech on Manuilsky's motion with great satisfaction. Well done. By exposing their manœuvres in this way we may bring the Russians to realise that this game is not worth the candle.[4]

Since the Diaries which Cadogan kept daily at the U.N. will no doubt be published one day, when more of the official documents are available, it would be wrong to draw largely upon them here. The deadlock about disarmament; the unresolved quarrel over Kashmir, in which he thought India's conduct bad; the rows about the presence of Chiang's representative after the triumph of Communism in China; the bloody last stages of the British mandate in Palestine and the Arab states' onslaught upon Israel; the Russians' behaviour in Eastern Europe and the Berlin blockade; the endless droning debates and the repeated use of the veto, though not by Britain or the U.S.A.: all this formed a dismal experience for one who had been so intimately involved at Geneva and so prominent in drafting the Charter. Moreover, British diplomacy had to be conducted from a precarious position of over-commitment and economic instability. The American loan, finally available in the summer of 1946, was exhausted in a twelvemonth. Strict austerity was enforced at home, while successive Chancellors, Dr Dalton and Sir Stafford Cripps, warned their colleagues that overseas spending must be cut and risks reduced. And yet Cadogan contrived to exercise an influence at the U.N. out of all proportion to British material strength. Part of the explanation, of course, lies in America's willingness to shoulder the political, economic and military burdens in Europe, but as much in his own qualities and demeanour. He knew exactly how to present British interests in the manner which would identify them with the wishes of other governments, and how to sustain the general admiration for Britain's performance during the war. This was the peak of his career. Though busy, he was no longer harassed from morning till night. The Secretary of State and officials of the Foreign Office generally trusted his advice and allowed him much latitude.

In sum, Cadogan held a unique position at the U.N., derived from a blend of receptivity, debating skill, unmatched experience, knowledge of procedure and obvious desire to make the organisation work. A delegate of one of the Iron Curtain countries said:

> The person I respect mostly deeply at Lake Success is Cadogan. Obviously I do not share his views. But on the technical level of diplomacy and in point of ability and character, he is head and shoulders above the rest of them.

The Cadogans enjoyed great social prestige. Invitations to Hillandale, their home on Long Island, were highly prized. There they cultivated a pleasant and relaxed atmosphere for themselves and their many guests of every nationality: politicians, artists, musicians, members of other delegations and of the U.N. Secretariat. Those who asked Cadogan's help received courteous attention and excellent advice, delivered modestly, almost diffidently, in his matter-of-fact fashion. As dependable and unruffled at Lake Success as in Downing Street, he always sensed when colleagues had to carry out instructions which they disliked. If obliged to object, he would show by some phrase or gesture that he understood. There were even signs that Gromyko came to respect Sir Alec's powers as a debater, and Cadogan had no personal dislike of him, though he found Gromyko's behaviour maddening. He did not delude himself for a moment that his relations with Russian colleagues would affect Soviet policy; on the contrary, he recognised often that they were mere prisoners of instructions. So little margin for compromise or even for debate did this rigidity allow that it seemed hard to find any point of contact. 'It is like playing a card from your hand; your opponent then responds with a chessman.' When Gromyko accused him of inconsistency, Cadogan merely replied that the only inconsistency of which he was aware, a not unusual one, was between what he had said and what Gromyko said he had said.

At the Council, Cadogan's restraint and brevity contrasted with others' more flamboyant manners. In those days the proceedings were only broadcast, not televised.* Although Sir Alec never became as celebrated a public figure in the U.S.A. as his successor Gladwyn Jebb, his speeches were regarded by many as models; delivered in his dry, deliberate manner, with scarcely a glance at the script, or sometimes without a text, but with everything well-shaped and rounded. Of course, he remarked during the Security Council's debate on Czechoslovakia after the coup of 1948,

> it might be said that all these events were the outcome of spontaneous movements in the countries in question whose inhabitants became progressively convinced of the blessings of living under a totalitarian regime administered by a ruthless minority. Unfortunately, these upheavals generally seem to coincide with the visit to the country concerned of a high Soviet functionary from Moscow.

As Cadogan reflected upon the successive Russian moves in Eastern Europe, and warned of preparations for a stroke in Italy, he could hardly fail to be reminded of the events of ten years before, when another power had overwhelmed Czechoslovakia. Admittedly the basic conditions of international life in 1948 differed much from those of 1938. The risks and dangers, however, approximated. He remarked to Churchill that

> What forces itself on one's attention is the degree to which everything favours the evildoer, if he is blatant enough. Any honest Government fights (in peacetime) with two hands tied behind its back. The brilliant blatancy of the Russians is something that we can admire but cannot emulate. It gives them a great advantage.[5]

Towards the end of 1949 Bevin intimated that Cadogan should retire in the following summer, by which time he would have been in the Service forty-two years. Early in the New Year, Russia walked out of the Security Council. The sterility of the proceedings thereafter almost reconciled Cadogan to the pains of retirement and departure from America. He had not lost all faith in the U.N., for the machinery still seemed to him, after so many dispiriting experiences, well-conceived. As he used to remark, a fine violin is no more than an assemblage of wood and catgut. It takes a musician to conjure harmony from it, and if the player fails, there is no sense in blaming the instrument, still less in smashing it to matchwood. The U.N., unlike the League, would enjoy no golden age of goodwill and sincere allegiance. There would be no short cut, no royal road, probably no heroic solution; but rather, partial and perhaps experimental agreements with Russia, unless her appetite proved insatiable. For the moment, the West must build up its military power and hold on, showing that freedom, open debate and the right to criticise make for moral and material

* Cadogan's heartfelt 'Oh, my God', uttered when the chairman called upon a prolix delegate, was heard all over America.

advancement. 'Expect no easy or early solution' he said to undergraduates at McGill just before leaving the U.N.:

> . . . it may take generations to reach the goal and maybe even your generation will not look upon it, but if you remain firm in your faith and true to the dictates of your conscience and your heart, you will gain in strength and know that the battle is to be won at the last. . . . Seek truth above all. Have no illusions, face the truth. Truth brings courage.

Just after the Cadogans sailed for home, the Korean war began. By a happy chance, a U.N. commission was already in Korea and could report the facts quickly and Russia, being still absent from the Security Council, could not stultify the proceedings. The U.N. was therefore able to rise to its first great test. For a time, Cadogan believed that it might take on new life. Later, by about 1955, he concluded that the heady nationalism of the new members, compounding the conflicting interests of the Great Powers, largely deprived the Organisation of value.

* * *

Shortly after their return to England the Cadogans took a flat in Westminster and bought a cottage near Yateley, to which they generally repaired for weekends in the spring and summer. For a while, Sir Alexander found himself in the almost unbelievable position of having nothing to do. However, he was soon invited to join the boards of the National Provincial Bank and the Phoenix Assurance Company, and was nominated a Government Director of the Suez Canal Company.

Towards the end of 1950 King George VI intimated that he would like to give the Order of Merit in special recognition of Cadogan's work. No civil servant had previously received this honour. Cadogan, who made no attempt to conceal his pride and delight, received innumerable congratulations. Two he valued especially. The first came from Bevin, now mortally ill: 'You have earned it; you have served the State well. . . . Your help and guidance I always appreciated very much.' The second was written by Eden:

> This is indeed splendid news. The most gratifying of all honours, and in every way appropriate. I am so pleased, for nobody could have deserved it more; not only for these last years, but for a brilliant record of service. At least I have as much reason to know this as anybody, and more than anyone to be grateful for your help in such difficult years.

Cadogan replied:

> I shall always have the best recollections of the times when we worked together. If I was able to serve you, you gave me inspiration, and if I have ever done any good, I owe a large part of it to the lessons that I should have learned from you.[6]

In the summer of 1952, a new Chairman was needed for the B.B.C.'s Board of Governors. Churchill, recently returned to office, indicated dissatisfaction with the names submitted to him. 'Then what about Alec Cadogan?' said his Private Secretary, J. R. Colville. 'That would be *excellent*,' said the Prime Minister.

Cadogan, summoned to No. 10, found Churchill at his usual seat in the Cabinet Room. As he sat down, he saw on the blotter a sheet of names with his own at the top, and against it the legend 'Chairman'. The Prime Minister began a long and fascinating disquisition about the affairs of the world. Eventually he checked himself and came down to the immediate business, which he seemed to find less stimulating. The moment was a difficult one, for the B.B.C. was losing both its Chairman and its Director-General, Sir William Haley. Cadogan expressed doubts about his own suitability. Just in time he realised that an appeal to advancing age and increasing deafness might not be well received. Instead he represented the problems of coming in from the outside, with no experience on the Board and no knowledge of the Corporation. 'There *are* no qualifications,' said Churchill. 'All you have to do is to be fair.' 'And sensible, I suppose,' Cadogan added. Churchill nodded.

On his appointment Cadogan confessed to journalists that he had never seen a B.B.C. television programme, and that what he had seen of American television he disliked. The new Board's first important decision, 'perhaps the best they ever took' as he later described it, was to appoint Sir Ian Jacob to the post of Director-General. Cadogan had high respect and liking for him, dating from their contacts during the war, when Sir Ian had been General Ismay's senior assistant in the military section of the War Cabinet. He had worked at the B.B.C., with one short interval, since 1946. It was never Cadogan's habit in any of his posts to jog the elbows of those who bore the chief responsibility. He felt no inclination or need to break that rule during more than five years at the B.B.C. He normally went to the office at Broadcasting House three times a week. Much of the business was done by informal and unrecorded conversations with Jacob; 'It is very pleasant working with him, and he seems to suffer me gladly, though it must waste a lot of his time putting me wise.' It hardly needs to be said that all the ceremonial side of the Chairman's work was beautifully done. He presided over the Governors' Meetings well and prepared for them carefully, by mastering the papers and by preliminary discussion with colleagues known to feel strongly on this or that issue. He had only rare contacts with those who produced the programmes, partly because he did not wish to undermine the position of the Director-General, partly on account of his horror of wasting others' time and his own. He felt that he did not know enough to offer useful advice. His predecessor, Lord Simon of Wythenshawe, had said, 'You will find the B.B.C. an admirable machine.' That fact soon became obvious; and yet, as Cadogan recognised, there was more to the matter. Though the staff of the B.B.C. functioned with the precision of a machine, it was more importantly an assembly of talented individuals producing creative work of a high order.

All this is not meant to indicate that Cadogan saw no rôle for himself and his fellow-Governors beyond that of benevolent brooding. For instance, he thought in January 1953 that while the governments were discussing the creation of the Central African Federation it would be wrong for the B.B.C. to put out a critical talk by a former Minister. Sir Ian Jacob had already taken the same decision and the Chairman had only to back him. He wrote:

> It's not that I have any Party feelings, or that I want to 'muzzle' the B.B.C., but that I feel very strongly that it is indecent to have such a broadcast while a Conference is actually sitting on the matter. It is really sub judice. The Board today were a little bit tiresome on this question—or seemed to be inclined to be so—but I was very firm about it.

There were several other occasions when the Chairman insisted that the B.B.C.'s, and therefore the Governors', responsibility for the contents of programmes must be discharged in more than name. In some instances, especially the news bulletins, little could be done beyond general guidance and investigation of occasional complaints. In respect of talks and documentary programmes, he called for more careful scrutiny of texts and did not think it wrong to suggest occasional modifications. How, he asked, was the editorial responsibility of the Governors to be exercised if they never saw scripts in advance? 'They can only pick up bricks already dropped, which I find undignified and not very effective.' And on another occasion, 'It is wrong that the officials of the B.B.C. should think they are above all criticism. It is this attitude that is going to bring us trouble.'[7]

The first part of Cadogan's chairmanship coincided with the pressure to break the Corporation's monopoly in respect of television. He declined to involve himself or the B.B.C. in the political struggle, attracting from one Minister an accusation that the Corporation was being deliberately unhelpful and from protagonists on the other side the charge that it was betraying its responsibilities. Once the Television Bill had passed through Parliament in the summer of 1954, he accepted with regret that the B.B.C. had to lose many experienced and valued staff to the Independent Television Authority, but refused to see disaster in its establishment. The B.B.C., he believed, should support its essential principles; 'but if it did not fall in with changing habits, it might come to be regarded as merely cobwebby. . . . I would always resist competing in vulgarity or degeneration of the programmes.'

When, early in 1955, Sir Alec was told that scripts for a projected TV programme on nuclear warfare must be submitted in advance to the Government, he said at once that it would be both impossible and undesirable. Rather similar troubles arose about another programme which the B.B.C. was supposed to be maturing, a discussion between three former prisoners of war about their experiences in enemy hands. As it happened, there was no definite project of this kind. 'But it is plain that there is a move on to undermine our independence and relegate us to the position of an organ of the government, which would be fatal.'[8] The issue is worthy of mention because it illustrates Cadogan's conception of the B.B.C.'s position and his methods of handling such matters. The universal respect and the easy access to Ministers which he enjoyed were effectively used. Sir Alec let his attitude be known without placing anything on written record at this stage. Before a formal meeting took place in mid-February, the Secretary to the Cabinet had told Sir Ian Jacob that it was desired to let the correspondence die. Cadogan and Jacob found the Postmaster General, Lord de la Warr, and the Minister of Defence, Harold Macmillan, entirely reasonable. Each side explained its position, whereupon Sir Alec told Macmillan that while the B.B.C. would preserve its independence it would co-operate to the best of its ability. There the matter ended.

A few weeks later, Cadogan was asked to go to 10 Downing Street. He found Sir Winston in bed, with a small whisky and soda by his side and a budgerigar in a cage hanging from the ceiling. Cutting an enormous cigar, Churchill asked whether Cadogan would like one, or some whisky? He declined politely.

> On the floor by the side of the bed was a little metal pail with some water in it, destined presumably for the cigar ash and eventually for the stub. But as regards the ash at least, the P.M. did not seem to make much discrimination between the pail and the bed-clothes.

Sir Winston had been told that the B.B.C's news bulletins had been giving facts favourable to strikers of the Electrical Trades Union, but not presenting the other side fairly. Cadogan said that he did not believe it. The B.B.C. worked under an instruction from the Government to be impartial, and had to respect it. If the Corporation followed a line of its own, it might attract the ill-will of the E.T.U., with which there had already been other disagreements. Should the situation reach a point of crisis, the Government had only to ask for time on the air. After this the Prime Minister seemed to lose interest in the subject. He talked about his desire for four-power talks, to begin at the summit. 'I don't think he is wrong. I don't know what he hopes from any conversations. I have no hopes myself.'

Sir Winston also spoke of his intention to resign on the next day, and to leave public life for good. Cadogan expressed his genuine regrets, 'though I had realised that it had got to come some day. He was very friendly. Rather to my surprise, the budgerigar made no contribution to the discussion.'[9]

* * *

Cadogan's first three years as a Director of the Suez Canal Company passed more or less uneventfully. At least to outward appearances, the

Company stood at the pinnacle of its usefulness and success. With ample reserves, it had initiated a steady programme of improvements to the Canal and was acknowledged to run it well. Traffic and receipts grew yearly. Yet the real situation was less satisfactory. The concession ran only until 1968; as the size of ships using the waterway increased, the Directors had to ask themselves whether they should embark upon further and immensely expensive widening when the future looked so uncertain; the main physical security for the Company, the British garrison in the Canal zone, came under guerrilla attack, encouraged by the Egyptian Government. After hearing, just after the Egyptian denunciation in 1951 of the treaty with Britain, a distinguished authority describe these troubles as 'a red herring' and a 'temporary crisis', Cadogan remarked emphatically 'It's *not;* it's a manifestation of a very great and menacing and continuing nationalist movement throughout Asia and Africa. . . .'[10] He recognised that Eden, newly returned to the Foreign Office, must do his best to come to terms with this force.

Negotiations for an agreement to replace the treaty came to fruition only in the autumn of 1954, after King Farouk had been deposed by officers under General Neguib, who was in turn supplanted by Colonel Nasser. For the Suez Canal Company these were ominous developments, since the new treaty provided for the departure of British troops by 1956 and Colonel Nasser's attitude had become only too evident before he ejected Neguib. He had, indeed, roundly accused the President of the Company of inspiring a renewed complaint by Israel to the Security Council against Egypt's illegal prevention of the passage of her goods through the Canal; of influencing France's attitude towards the complaint; and of instigating the British Government's insistence during the treaty negotiations upon the principle of free use of the Canal.

Throughout 1955 the withdrawal of British forces from the Canal zone went steadily forward. In September Nasser arranged a large supply of fighters, bombers and tanks, nominally from Czechoslovakia but principally from Russia. The Company came under strong pressure from Cairo to make arrangements more satisfactory to Egypt's sensibilities and balance of payments. Meanwhile, negotiations for the construction of the Aswan Dam were proceeding between Egypt, the U.S.A., Britain, France, Germany and the World Bank. In the spring of 1956 the management of the Company learned that dark things, of which there might be a foretaste in June, were being prepared. Its fate was openly connected with the departure of British troops, the last of whom were due to go in mid-June. Early in that month, however, a settlement was reached in Cairo between the Company and the Egyptian Government. The latter expressed satisfaction at the services rendered by the Company, and reaffirmed their agreements.

However, the U.S. Government soon afterwards withdrew from the negotiations for the financing of the Aswan Dam, a step which entailed also the cancellation of the World Bank's contribution. A week later, on

26 July, the Egyptian Government seized without warning the West's most obvious and vulnerable asset in Egypt. To a delirious mob at Alexandria Nasser announced that by taking the revenues of the Company Egypt would have funds for the Dam. Proclaiming a battle against 'imperialism' and against its vanguard, Israel, he cried that Arab nationalism, afire from the Atlantic Ocean to the Persian Gulf 'feels its existence, its structure and strength'. The Company's *chefs de service* were instantly put under house arrest, the staff made to work under martial law, the workshops and other key points seized according to an obviously prearranged plan, and the Egyptian banks forced at gunpoint to yield up the Company's deposits. At once the British Cabinet decided that a man of Nasser's record could not be permitted, in the phrase of Sir Anthony Eden, now Prime Minister, 'to have his thumb on our windpipe', and that British interests in the Middle East must be safeguarded, if necessary by force and if necessary alone. It is perhaps best to say at this point that Cadogan shared Eden's view of Nasser as an unscrupulous demagogue of paranoic tendencies. He was not, and did not wish to be, privy to the Government's secrets in the next few months.

On 30 July Eden said in the House:

> No arrangements for the future of this great international waterway could be acceptable to Her Majesty's Government which would leave it in the unfettered control of a single power which could, as recent events have shown, exploit it purely for purposes of national policy.

'That', comments Cadogan's Diary, 'is a good formula and I only hope we are decided to take all measures necessary to assure it!'

Very soon it became clear that the assembly of a force in Malta and Cyprus would need several weeks. The Company was asked by the British and French Governments to keep the Canal working and the employees at their posts, although many wished to leave. The full Board, at its monthly meeting in Paris on 3 August, learned that the Commercial Directors had already given undertakings in this sense. It was generally agreed to be the right course. Meanwhile, Mr John Foster Dulles, the American Secretary of State, had arrived in London and said firmly that Nasser must be made to disgorge. For a spell it seemed that this might indeed be so. The French Government made encouraging statements to the Suez Canal Company. Mr Selwyn Lloyd, the Foreign Secretary, spoke confidently to some of the Directors on 10 August. On the same day Cadogan, who had the extraordinary experience of looking upon the crisis not only as an old friend of the Prime Minister and former head of the Foreign Office but also as a Government Director of the expropriated Company and as Chairman of the B.B.C., received a telephone call from Eden. It appeared that the Prime Minister of Australia, Mr Robert Menzies, wished to broadcast about the crisis and had been refused permission by a high official of the B.B.C., except on conditions. Eden took strong exception to this attitude. Cadogan equally thought it absurd. 'This really nonsense', records the Diary. He telephoned the Director-General and said that Menzies must be allowed to speak, 'no matter what our traditions and inhibitions might be'. By the evening it had been so arranged. Sir Anthony Eden thanked Cadogan for this promptitude.[11]

A few days later, the B.B.C. carried an interview with Major Salah Salem, about which complaints reached the Prime Minister. It was the eve of the conference, held in London, of the principal users of the Canal and signatories of the convention of 1888. Eden spoke to Sir Alexander about this broadcast; Cadogan said that he would enquire about it. He learned that the senior officials of the B.B.C. had already decided that no more transmissions of this kind would be made while the conference was sitting. During that day, 17 August, Cadogan received from Eden a letter, sent not as the official representation of a Prime Minister but as a personal comment. He had heard that the programme in which Major Salem spoke had given 'a deplorably misleading picture of British opinion as uncertain and hesitant'. Sir Anthony then gave an assurance which, in view of what has been said in the contrary sense since 1956, merits quotation:

> Of course the Government have no intention of interfering with the freedom of the B.B.C. to try and reflect, as well as educate, public opinion in this country. But I hope that the Governors will bear in mind the very heavy responsibility which rests on the B.B.C. at this crucial time when an international conference is meeting in London. Many people will judge the strength and determination of Britain by what they hear on the B.B.C.
>
> I do not need to tell you how grave the present crisis is for this country and the whole future of the western world.[12]

Cadogan viewed the business of Major Salem less seriously than did the Prime Minister. In the more substantial question of the B.B.C.'s responsibilities, there never was the slightest danger that Cadogan, of all people, would misapprehend his constitutional position or fail to uphold the B.B.C.'s freedom from interference so long as it behaved responsibly. The Board had to face, from mid-August, a position of especial difficulty. This was the first occasion since the war when the parties had split upon a prime issue of foreign policy. After the Governors had deliberated Cadogan saw Mr R. A. Butler, deputising for Eden, and Mr Hugh Gaitskell, the Leader of the Opposition, on 14 September, to explain the difficulty in which the B.B.C. might find itself. If requests for ministerial broadcasts could not be refused, nor could requests to reply. This was generally accepted.

Meanwhile, the international crisis simmered. The mission led by Menzies to Cairo after the London conference failed to make any progress; economic sanctions, as usual, proved ineffective; and the Russians took Egypt's side while Nasser played upon the obvious reluctance of the U.S. Government to support the British and French. In late August the Directors of the Canal Company were told that the Egyptians had anchored three old ships, two at Port Said and the other at Ismailia, filled with cement and ready to be sunk if the Western Powers attempted the re-occupation of the Canal Zone; and that the Egyptian authorities would probably scuttle the Company's two salvage ships, in order that they should not be used to clear the canal. It would be otiose to follow here the developments of September and October. When the issue was taken to the United Nations, the Security Council endorsed unanimously six principles, including free transit for all nations' goods through the Canal and the insulation of its operation from the politics of any country. The second part of the resolution, which dealt with the action needed to secure these principles, was vetoed by Russia.

It has been asserted that in late October Eden, furious at the B.B.C.'s behaviour, instructed the Lord Chancellor, Lord Kilmuir, to prepare an instrument which would enable the Government to take control (whatever that might mean) of the Corporation; that such a paper was drafted; and that Eden, finding it unsatisfactory, asked him to produce something stronger. There is no trace of anything of the kind in Cadogan's Diary for 1956, nor had he any recollection of it in 1968. True, it is suggested that on account of his supposedly close contacts with Eden and of a fear that he would be inclined to give way before the alleged intention of the Government, the 'facts' were kept from him. But it seems inconceivable that Sir Alec would not have learned of the intention, had it existed, and still more curious that the reported exchange between Eden and Kilmuir cannot be remembered by the latter's widow, now Lady de la Warr, or be found in his papers. Mr Edward Heath, then Chief Whip, knows nothing of it; nor, apparently, does any member of the Cabinet of 1956.

In any event, no instrument would have been needed, for the Government already had all the necessary powers. It is always possible that an official drafted the instructions which the Government was empowered to give, but no evidence of it has yet been brought forward. It is quite likely, though not corroborated by his papers, that Cadogan did not want evidence of disunity and recrimination at home broadcast to troops about to enter battle. The balance of the evidence is clear: that although the B.B.C. was inevitably subject to official pressures in the autumn of 1956, they were not of a kind which could convert it into a mouthpiece of the Government; and that the Government did not intend to depart from the private assurance given by Eden to Cadogan on 16 August.

Sir Alexander followed with some gloom the events of October, which appeared to show the Suez Canal Users' Association impotent and Nasser triumphant. It seemed that Egypt, after all the fuss, would be left in sole command of the Canal, and the others to retreat ignominiously. After Israel's mobilisation and attack on Egypt, Britain and France announced that they would intervene. Admitting all the risks and drawbacks, Cadogan approved that course, assuming that the military stroke would be accomplished within a day or two. He had particularly in mind the hopeless position in which Britain, guarantor of Jordan, would be placed if a general war developed and Israel moved against Jordan.

The Prime Minister was, of course, entitled in such circumstances to request time for a radio and television broadcast. Cadogan took a simple and consistent line; when and if this request was received, it must be granted at once, as must the expected counter-request from the Leader of the Opposition. In point of fact, the Prime Minister did not ask for time until 2 November; Sir Alec thereupon authorised a reply, which Gaitskell made on 4 November. Cadogan privately judged his performance 'disgraceful', but that is beside the point. On 8 November the Governors emphatically endorsed their Chairman's action.

In those days of tension it was hardly to be expected that the B.B.C. would escape charges of political bias. Undue prominence, many Conservatives believed, had been given to the views of newspapers and individuals hostile to the Government. Sir Peter Rawlinson raised a debate on this issue, an action widely but wrongly believed to have been instigated by the Whips' Office. Most of the time, however, was taken up by Colonel Wigg, who alleged that the B.B.C. was then 'a corruption of what it could become if there were honesty of purpose behind it'. Not only had the B.B.C. been 'indulging in Tory propaganda', but it had gone out of its way from the beginning of the crisis to 'withold the truth from the British people'. Sir Ian Jacob, in Colonel Wigg's view, was 'a Tory "stooge"', and Sir Alexander Cadogan 'a Foreign Office "deadbeat"'.[13] Colonel Wigg spoke for the better part of two hours. Mr Alport, Assistant Postmaster-General, defended the B.B.C. A senior official of the Corporation showed the transcript to Cadogan, who read it all through, uttered a pithy judgment on the habits of politicians and said that the Assistant P.M.G. seemed to have answered very well. The official confessed his distress and distaste at having to bring such material. Cadogan smiled at him and said 'Do you remember that advertisement "If you want to get ahead, get a hat?" We shall have to sponsor a variant: "If you want to fall behind, get a Wigg".'

After all the allegations of bias had been examined in detail, a full report came before the Governors on 22 November. 'The Board was unanimously of the opinion that the charges of bias in the members of the Staff were completely groundless, and that the output was "on the whole" unexceptionable'.

It need hardly be added that Cadogan, in his private capacity, bitterly regretted the failure or inability of the Anglo-French forces to secure their military objectives swiftly. The Permanent Under-Secretary at the Foreign Office, Sir Ivone Kirkpatrick, told him some time later that the ceasefire became inevitable when the U.S.A. and U.N. turned against Britain and France, and both Egypt and Israel accepted, with Britain divided and the Commonwealth cracking. Cadogan retorted that all this should have been foreseen.

He remained in office at the B.B.C., extending his tenure for some months at the Government's request, until the autumn of 1957. At the dinner which the Governors gave in his honour, he paid a warm and sincere tribute to them and the whole staff of the B.B.C. The Governors had put their views with moderation and had listened with respect to their colleagues. If differences of opinion had sometimes remained, rancour had not. Their meetings had reminded him of the gatherings which the Commonwealth delegates used to hold at the United Nations. 'If the B.B.C.', he declared, 'remains true to itself, maintains (and if possible improves) its standards and keeps its faith, I believe it has little to fear. If it were to abandon those and step down to fight in another arena, all its defences might be down.'

* * *

Although a full account of Sir Alec Cadogan's recreations—gardening, reading, ballet, music and painting—must await his biography, it would be a pity not to mention here the hobby to which he came latest but to which he devoted himself most keenly. Though he had always been fond of sketching, it was not until 1956, in his seventy-second year, that he began to paint. He took lessons with Mr Stanley Grimm, feeling apprehensive but excited. No activity, he discovered, calls for more intense concentration, or produces such ups and downs of hopefulness and despondency. 'I suppose', he remarked after no more than three days of tuition, 'one has to go through periods of frustration and disappointment. Anyhow, I am already better than the modern German painters at the Tate!' Or again, after a struggle to render some flowers to his satisfaction; 'Painting is rather like golf—some days one can hit the ball and the following day one is paralytic.'

It became his main recreation. He generally took his kit on holiday, when he would make sketches for conversion into finished works at home. In winter he had to make do, rather impatiently, with still life. Soon the flat was adorned with numerous of his paintings, much admired by visitors. On several occasions he exhibited. The best part of painting, he would say, was to catch a colour or a movement in a way which would recall the scene vividly years after and yet be distinctively different from a photograph; the most frustrating part to have a clear conception but be unable to realise it, a sensation which he had experienced in trying to capture the fleeting Cotswold honey-tones of Chipping Campden and Bourton-on-the-Hill.

All his life a devoted visitor to galleries, Cadogan found that he could never look at pictures for more than an hour. After that, so wholly had he absorbed himself in the colours and forms, his senses were sated. Among the painters of the last hundred years, he liked Corot, Whistler, Toulouse-Lautrec, Sisley and van Gogh, and Bonnard and Gaugin in patches; loved Monet; but did not care for Renoir or Cézanne. Since he did appreciate some of their contemporaries, however, he refused to label himself behind-the-times; 'I call myself eclectic, and condemn bad painting.' Early Picassos he could tolerate, but the rest he thought dreadful. 'They are ugly and silly enough in photographic reproductions, but when you see them in their crude colours the effect is—to me—indescribably depressing.' That was written after a visit to the Tate's exhibition in 1960. Other visits produced even more shattering effects. The Diary describes the 1964 exhibition of the art of the previous decade as

> the cruellest joke that has yet been played on the gullible and half-witted British public. The low point has been reached in an exhibit of 3 panels about 8 ft high and 3 ft wide, numbered and dated. They were all three identical—an absolutely plain wash of matt black. They were labelled 'abstract paintings'. . . . I like three piece suits, but I do *not* like three piece reclining female figures, especially when none of the separate chunks includes anything in the least resembling any part of the female human figure. What pathetic rubbish it all is! I look forward to the time (which I shall not see, but is not so far distant) when all this is exploded, and the very ample bins in the Gallery gardens labelled 'litter' will be bulging.[14]

* * *

In the last decade of his life Sir Alec Cadogan gradually shed his commitments. He left the Board of the Phoenix in 1960, regretting the end of interesting work and noting that he had never drawn a placed horse in the Derby sweep, and of the Bank a few years later. In 1961 he gave up the chairmanship of the Commonwealth-American Current Affairs Unit at the English-Speaking Union. 'Never', wrote its Director, 'could the hired man hope to have a kindlier or more considerate boss! I shall miss your calls, and our talks.'[15]

He continued to enjoy the ballet and occasional concerts, to paint well and to follow the affairs of the world with an expert's eye. The daily Diary he kept up almost to the end. After a serious illness in 1964, Cadogan realised that death could not be far off, a prospect which he faced with a silent prayer that he should not cumber the earth. He died in the summer of 1968, at the age of eighty-three. A week or two earlier, on the last occasion when he discussed the arrangement of this book, Sir Alexander Cadogan asked that the following tribute should conclude it:

> I have often wished that I could adequately put on record something that would convey what I feel I owe to my wife for all that she has been and done for me during near fifty-two years for which we have been married.
>
> I fear that I have not the gift of words that would enable me to do justice to the theme. But it has occurred to me that I might recall a little incident that happened two or three years ago, when I was accidentally

spurred to say some few words that put shortly something at least of what I feel, and I think those few words may express more than I could convey in a very long chapter.

We had a few friends lunching with us—amongst them a distinguished and very charming American lady whom we had known in New York and who was over here on a visit. She was sitting next to me and had been intently watching Theo who, at the other side of the table, was talking and laughing with a next-door neighbour. The American lady turned to me and said 'I suppose one would say that your wife's outstanding quality was her friendliness.' I said that that was certainly one of her outstanding qualities. 'And the others?' she enquired. 'Well,' I began, 'loyalty, courage'. . . 'Ah!' she interrupted, 'you have said the lot, haven't you?' I said that the tale didn't end there, but if I were to carry it further I should risk boring her, and would certainly embarrass Theo if ever she came to hear of it.

I hope I didn't sound too crushing: I think not: I certainly did not mean to be so. The American lady was of course only voicing a momentary and very pleasant impression, and was not attempting to give an appraisement of Theo's whole character and qualities, and I quite understood that, and I hope and believe that she knew I understood. I should regret it very much if she bore any resentment because I value very highly her friendship and sympathy.

Sometimes a momentary impression or stimulus can elicit a truer expression of one's feelings than any attempt at laborious composition. That is my reason for recalling this little incident. My tribute is of course incomplete and unworthy, but I very much doubt whether I could improve upon it, however much I tried.

A.C. June 1964.

NOTES AND BIBLIOGRAPHY

NOTES

Full details of published works are given in the Bibliography

INTRODUCTION *1884–1938* pages 1–20

1. Hon. Sir E. Cadogan, *Before the Deluge*, p. 5.
2. Macmillan, *Winds of Change*, p. 30.
3. Sir L. E. Jones, *An Edwardian Youth*, pp. 49, 64.
4. Hon. H. Nicolson, *Some People*, pp. 136–9, 148.
5. This account is based on reminiscences set down by Sir A. Cadogan in about 1964.
6. Sir A. Chamberlain to Cadogan, 17 June, 1926, C.P. H.E. Thanassis Aghnides and Mr V. Cavendish-Bentinck have kindly provided accounts of Cadogan's work as head of the League of Nations section.
7. Cabinet Paper 256 (27).
8. Cadogan's draft chapter 'First Disarmament Conference'.
9. Temperley, *The Whispering Gallery of Europe*, p. 108.
10. Cadogan to Lady Theo. 18 Feb. 1933.
11. Avon, *Facing the Dictators*, p. 27.
12. Cadogan to Eden, 1 Oct. 1933, C.P.
13. Cadogan to Simon, 30 Aug. 1934, F.O. 371/18101, F 5909/117/10.
14. Cadogan to Eden, 24 Jan. 1935, C.P.
15. Cadogan to Eden, 30 Apr. 1935, C.P.
16. Diary, 6 Aug. 1935.
17. Cadogan to Hoare, 19 Oct. 1935, F.O. 405/274, F 6654/427/10.
18. Cadogan to Hoare, 5 Dec. 1935, and minute of 4 Feb. 1936, F.O. 371/20241.
19. Cadogan's Diary, 1 Apr. 1936.
20. Cadogan to Eden, 13 May 1936.
21. Diary, 25 Sept. 1936.
22. Diary, 11 Sept., 3 Nov. and 24 Oct. 1936.
23. Diary, 27 Apr. 1937.
24. Minute by Cadogan, 28 May 1937, on C 3621/270/18, and Vansittart's comments, Vansittart Papers.
25. Woodward, *British Foreign Policy in The Second World War*, (1962), p. xxvi.
26. Cadogan to Eden, 24 Apr. 1943, C.P.

I *January–August 1938*, The Approach to Munich pages 30–39

1. Memorandum by the Chiefs of Staff for the Imperial Conference, May, 1937; F.O. 371/21160.
2. Feiling, *The Life of Neville Chamberlain*, pp. 323, 336.
3. Cadogan to Martin Gilbert, 14 Mar. 1962, C.P.
4. F 407/84/10 in F.O. 371/22106.
5. Cadogan to Eden, 12 Jan. 1938, F.O. 371/22395.
6. Cadogan to Eden, 13 Jan. 1938, C.P. Cf. the accounts in Avon, *Facing The Dictators*, and S. Welles, *The Time for Decision.*
7. Cadogan to Eden, 13 Jan. 1938, C.P.
8. Avon, *Facing the Dictators*, p. 555; record of a conversation with Lindsay, 17 Jan. 1938, Hull Papers.

I The Approach to Munich (*cont.*)

9. F.P. (36) 43, Cab. 27/626; F.P. (36), 21st meeting, Cab. 27/623.
10. Avon, *Facing the Dictators*, p. 574.
11. Cadogan to Avon, 3 Feb. 1967, C.P.
12. Minute by Cadogan, 16 Feb. 1938, F.O. 371/21526; Eden to Lindsay, 18 Feb. ibid.
13. Harvey, *The Diplomatic Diaries of Oliver Harvey*, pp. 422–3.
14. Chamberlain to Lady Chamberlain, 3 Mar. 1938, N.C.P.; Feiling, *The Life of Neville Chamberlain*, pp. 337–8.
15. Avon, *Facing the Dictators*, p. 600.
16. Cadogan to Templewood (Hoare), 26 Oct. 1951, C.P.; Halifax, *Fulness of Days* pp. 231–2.
17. Cadogan to Birkenhead, 12 Oct. 1964, C.P.
18. Halifax to Lindsay, 24 Feb. 1938, F.O. 371/21547.
19. Cadogan's draft to Lindsay, dated 'Feb., 1938', F.O. 371/21526.
20. Henderson to Halifax, C 1650/42/18, in F.O. 371/21656, 3 Mar. 1938.
21. Minute by Vansittart, 4 Mar. 1938, Vansittart Papers.
22. B.D., ser. III, vol. I, pp. 4–6.
23. ibid., pp. 21–2.
24. Feiling, *The Life of Neville Chamberlain*, pp. 341–2.
25. *Documents on German Foreign Policy* (= G.D.), ser. D., vol. 1, pp. 597–8.
26. C.O.S. 698 (revise), Cab. 53/37, 28 March 1938.
27. Feiling, *The Life of Neville Chamberlain*, pp. 347–8.
28. Parl. Deb., H. of C., vol. 333, cols. 1399–1413.
29. Minutes of 31 Mar. 1938, by Cadogan and Harvey on W 3835/13/98, F.O. 371/22509.
30. Cadogan to Halifax, 20 Apr. 1938, F.O. 800/313.
31. Cadogan to Henderson, 22 Apr. 1938, F.O. 800/269.
32. B.D., ser. III, vol. I, pp. 212–33.
33. ibid., pp. 260–1, 264, 273, 287, 627–8.
34. ibid., pp. 631–3.
35. ibid., pp. 585, 329–2, 334–5, 341, 356.
36. Henderson to Halifax, 24 May 1938, F.O. 800/313; B.D., ser. III, vol. I, pp. 412–4; Feiling, p. 354.
37. B.D., ser. III, vol. I, pp. 403–16.
38. ibid., pp. 496–8.
39. G.D., ser. D, vol. I, pp., 1145–6.
40. ibid., pp. 1150–1.
41. B.D., ser. III, vol. I, pp. 653–5.
42. Master of Elibank to Halifax, 19 June 1938, F.O. 800/313; B.D., ser. III, vol. I, pp. 584–9.
43. ibid., pp. 618–20.
44. Minutes by Vansittart, 6, 18 and 30 Aug. 1938, Vansittart Papers.

II *September 1938–March 1938*, Munich and Prague

1. Colvin, *The Chamberlain Cabinet*, pp. 141–5; Feiling, *The Life of Neville Chamberlain*, p. 357.
2. Minute by Vansittart, 13 Sept. 1938, Vansittart Papers; cf. his minute of 20 Sept. 1938, ibid.
3. Cited by Ian Colvin in *The Daily Telegraph*, 1 Jan. 1969.
4. Cadogan to Templewood, 26 Oct. 1951, C.P.
5. Minute by Cadogan on N 4601/533/63, F.O. 371/22276.
6. Templewood to Halifax, 21 Nov. 1951, T.P. XIX:12.
7. B.D., ser. III, vol. II, p. 277.
8. Duff Cooper, *Old Men Forget*, p. 228.

II Munich and Prague (*cont.*)

9. Phipps to Halifax, 14 and 16 Sept. 1938, F.O. 800/311; B.D., ser. III, vol. II, pp. 310, 311.
10. Minute by Cadogan to Halifax, 28 Nov. 1938, F.O. 800/396.
11. Minutes of the Cabinet, 17 Sept. 1938; Feiling, *The Life of Neville Chamberlain*, p. 368; B.D., ser. III, vol. II, pp. 338–40.
12. ibid., pp. 392–7, 405.
13. Minutes of 'Czechoslovakia Committee' and of the Cabinet, 24 Sept. 1938; B.D., ser. III, vol. II, p. 570.
14. The notes are in Halifax Papers, A4.410. 4.1; Cadogan to Birkenhead, 20 Jan. 1965, C.P.
15. B.D., ser. III, vol. II, pp. 550, 557.
16. N. Chamberlain, *In Search of Peace*, pp. 274–6;
17. C.O.S. 765 (Revise), 4 Oct. 1938.
18. Cadogan to Lord Francis-Williams, 9 Oct. 1965, C.P.
19. B.D., ser. III, vol. II, pp. 565–7.
20. Record of a conversation with Lindsay, 28 Sept. 1938, Hull Papers.
21. B.D., ser. III, vol. II, pp. 557, 562; Dalton, vol. II, P. 197.
22. B.D., ser. III, vol. III, pp. 320–2, 325–6.
23. Minute by Cadogan, 14 Oct. 1938, F.O. 371/21659.
24. F.R.U.S., 1938, vol. I, pp. 85–6; B.D., ser. III, vol. III, pp. 251–3.
25. Minute by Cadogan, 10 Oct. 1938, on F 10299/152/23, F.O. 371/22185.
26. Minute by Cadogan, 8 Nov. 1938, F.O. 371/21659.
27. F.P. (36), 32nd meeting; memorandum by Jebb, 19 Jan. 1939, Cab. 27/627.
28. B.D., ser. III, vol. III, pp. 285–311.
29. Memorandum by Jebb, 19 Jan. 1939, Cab. 27/627.
30. C 14809/62/18 in F.O. 371/21665; minutes by Vansittart and Cadogan, 7 and 10 Dec. 1938 on C 15084/42/18, F.O. 371/21657.
31. B.D., ser. III, vol. III, pp. 473–4, 478.
32. Kirkpatrick, *The Inner Circle*, pp. 137–9.
33. G.D. ser. D, vol. IV, pp. 530–2.
34. Memorandum by Jebb, 19 Jan. 1939, Cab. 27/627.
35. C.I.D. meeting of 22 Dec. 1938, Cab. 2/8.
36. B.D., ser. III, vol. III, pp. 496–502; minute by Cadogan, 9 Jan. 1939, F.O. 371/22289.
37. B.D., ser. III, vol. III, pp. 517–29.
38. *Ciano's Diary, 1939–1943*, pp. 9–10.
39. B.D., ser. III, vol. III, pp. 529, 524.
40. Memoranda by Halifax, Jebb and Cadogan, 17 and 19 Jan. 1939, C.P. (36) 74, Cab. 27/627.
41. F.R.U.S., 1939, vol. I, pp. 2–6.
42. B.D., ser. III, vol. IV, pp. 34, 70–1.
43. ibid, pp. 83–5.
44. Henderson to Cadogan, 16 Feb. 1939, F.O. 800/294; F.R.U.S., 1939, vol. I, pp. 14–17.
45. Chamberlain to Henderson, 19 Feb. 1939, Halifax to Henderson, 20 Feb. 1939, Henderson to Halifax, 22 Feb. 1939, F.O. 800/315.
46. Minute by Cadogan, 26 Feb. 1939, C 2/39/3, F.O. 800/294.
47. B.D., ser. III, vol. IV, pp. 123–4, 611–14, 188–99.
48. Minute by Cadogan, 1 Mar. 1939, on N 1459/1459/38, F.O. 371/23697.
49. B.D., ser. III, vol. IV, pp. 160–1.
50. Feiling, *The Life of Neville Chamberlain*, pp. 396–7; Halifax, *Fulness of Days*, p. 232.
51. B.D., ser. III, vol. VII, pp. 632–3.
52. ibid., pp. 270–2.

III *March–August 1939*, Floundering Into War

1. Colvin, *Vansittart in Office*, pp. 295–6.
2. Cadogan to Templewood, 10 Jan. 1953, T.P. 19: XII.
3. McLachlan, *Room 39*, p. 244; Strong, *Men of Intelligence*, p. 113.
4. Cf., for example, B.D., ser. III, vol. V, nos. 201 and 520, vol. VI, no. 35, with G.D., ser. D., vol. VI, nos. 239, 381, 511. Deakin and Storry, *The Case of Richard Sorge*, p. 221.
5. B.D., ser. III, vol. IV, pp. 366–7.
6. ibid., pp. 389–90; Irving, *Breach of Security*, pp. 28, 62; Cadogan's note on his talk with Tilea, 18 Mar. 1939, F.O. 371/23060.
7. B.D., loc. cit., pp. 402–3; minute by Cadogan, 24 Mar. 1939, on C 4311/421/62, F.O. 371/22944.
8. B.D., loc. cit., pp. 422–7, 457–63, 487–90.
9. Colvin, *Vansittart in Office*, pp. 304–10; Cadogan to Colvin, 7 June 1964, C.P.
10. Colvin, *The Chamberlain Cabinet*, pp. 196–7.
11. B.D., ser. III, vol. V, p. 642.
12. Cadogan to Colvin, 20 Jan. 1964.
13. McLachlan, *Room 39*, pp. 245 ff.
14. Colvin, *The Chamberlain Cabinet*, p. 200.
15. ibid., pp. 200–1.
16. B.D., ser. III, vol. V, pp. 239–40.
17. ibid., pp. 401–2.
18. Henderson to Cadogan, 10 May 1939, F.O. 800/294.
19. Minute of 15 May 1939, on N 2435/64/63, F.O. 371/23654.
20. B.D. ser. III, vol. V, pp. 639–47.
21. Cadogan to Halifax, 23 May 1939, F.O. 371/23066.
22. B.D., ser. III, vol. IX, pp. 98–9.
23. Loraine to Halifax, 16 May 1939, F.O. 800/319.
24. B.D., ser. III, vol. V, pp. 703–6; *Ciano's Diary, 1939–1943*, pp. 93–5.
25. C.O.S. reports 928, 18 June, and 931, 24 June, 1939; F.R.U.S., 1939, vol. iv, pp. 205–6.
26. Strang, pp. 174–5; minute by Cadogan, 30 June 1939, F.O. 371/23069.
27. Loraine to Halifax, 8 July 1939, F.O. 800/319.
28. Henderson to Cadogan, 4 July 1939, F.O. 800/294.
29. B.D., ser. III, vol. VI, pp. 456–60, 422.
30. Minutes by Cadogan and Chamberlain, 11 and 12 Aug. 1939, F.O. 371/23072.
31. B.D., ser. III, Vol. VII, pp. 32–3.
32. Halifax to Chamberlain, 19 Aug. 1939, F.O. 800/316.
33. Halifax, 'A record of Events before the War, 1939', F.O. 800/317.
34. B.D., ser. III, vol. VII, pp. 127–8.
35. Minutes by L. Collier, and R. A. Butler, 26 and 28 Aug. 1939, file N 4146, F.O. 371/23686.
36. B.D., loc. cit., pp. 227–9.
37. ibid., p. 282; Dahlerus, *The Last Attempt*, p. 74.
38. B.D., loc. cit., pp. 331–2.
39. ibid., pp. 351–4, 363–4.
40. ibid., pp. 376–7, 388–90.
41. ibid., pp. 432–3, 467, 450–1.

IV *September 1939–June 1939*, The Twilight War and the Collapse of France

1. Colvin, *The Chamberlain Cabinet*, pp. 256–8.
2. *Ciano's Diary, 1939–1943*, p. 141.
3. Minute of 26 Sept. 1939, F.O. 371/23846.
4. Loraine to Halifax, 13 Sept. 1939, F.O. 800/319.

IV The Twilight War and the Collapse of France (*cont.*)

5. Minute of 7 Sept. 1939, R 7151/2613/67, F.O. 371/23/53.
6. Cadogan to Birkenhead, 20 Jan. 1965.
7. B.D., ser. III, vol. VII, pp. 479–80.
8. G.D. ser. D, vol. VIII, pp. 140–5.
9. Undated minute by Cadogan, F.O. 800/325.
10. Woodward, *British Foreign Policy in the Second World War* (1970), vol. I, pp. 12–13.
11. G.D., loc. cit., pp. 275–6, 289.
12. Minute of 14 Oct. 1939, on C 16448, F.O. 371/23098.
13. Draft telegram to Bland, 19 Oct. 1939, C 16840, F.O. 371/23099.
14. For details see file C 17285, F.O. 371/23099.
15. On Hohenlohe see file C 17061, F.O. 371/23099.
16. G.D., loc. cit., pp. 399–400; cf. *Documenti Diplomatici Italiani*, ser. IX, vol. I, No. 878.
17. G.D., ser. D., vol. VIII, pp. 397–8.
18. Trevor-Roper, *The Philby Affair*, p. 124. Cf. Payne Best, *The Venlo Incident*, and *The Schellenberg Memoirs*, pp. 82–98.
19. Minutes by Halifax and Cadogan, 22 and 25 Mar. 1939, file C. 18883, F.O. 371/22986.
20. Minute by Cadogan, 6 Dec. 1939, N. 7198/57/38, F.O. 371/23678.
21. N 7171/7171/38, F.O. 34/6.
22. F.R.U.S., 1940, vol. I, pp. 1–4.
23. Lothian to Halifax, 3 Feb. 1940, F.O. 800/324.
24. *Ciano's Diary, 1939–43*, pp. 205–6.
25. Memorandum of 21 Feb. 1940, F.O. 800/322.
26. Halifax to Knatchbull-Hugesson, 21 Feb. 1940, F.O. 800/323.
27. For an account of these initiatives, see Bryans, *Blind Victory*, pp. 68–74, and H. Deutsch, *The Conspiracy Against Hitler in the Twilight War*, pp. 166–71. Bryans was in touch with von Hassell, formerly German Ambassador in Rome, who wanted a statement signed by Halifax.
28. For the record of this talk, see F.R.U.S., 1940, vol. I, pp. 78–80.
29. Quotation from Colvin's article, *The Daily Telegraph*, 1 Jan. 1971.
30. McLachlan, *Room 39*, pp. 82–3; Irving, *Breach of Security*, pp. 168–9.
31. Butler, *Grand Strategy*, vol. II, pp. 121–3.
32. Gamelin, *Servir*, vol. III, pp. 365–70; Butler, *Grand Strategy*, Vol. II, p. 139; Derry, *The Campaign in Norway*, chap. IX.
33. Cadogan to Chamberlain, 11 May 1940, and reply, 12 May 1940, Chamberlain Papers and C.P.
34. Churchill, *The Second World War*, vol. II, p. 24; F.R.U.S., 1940, vol. III, pp. 49–50.
35. Woodward, *British Foreign Policy in the Second World War* (1962), p. 52.
36. ibid., pp. 52–3.
37. Dalton's diary, 21 Aug. 1940.
38. Campbell to Halifax, 30 May and P.S. of 1 June 1940, F.O. 800/312.
39. Medlicott, *The Economic Blockade*, vol. I, chap. XII; Butler, *Grand Strategy*, vol. II, pp. 234–5.
40. C. de Gaulle, *The Call to Honour*, pp. 62–5.
41. *Ciano's Diary, 1939–1943*, p. 263.
42. Spears, *Assignment to Catastrophe*, pp. 501–22; for the meeting at Tours, see also Churchill, *The Second World War*, vol. II, chap. IX; Young, *Churchill and Beaverbrook*, pp. 145–7; *The Private Diaries of Paul Baudouin*, pp. 101–110; Woodward, *British Foreign Policy in the Second World War* (1970), vol. I, pp. 256–9.
43. Lord Halifax's diary, 8 Feb. 1941, A 7.8.19.

V *June 1940–May 1941,* A Year Alone

1. Churchill, *Marlborough*, vol. I, p. 535.
2. Spears, *Assignment to Catastrophe*, pp. 506–7.
3. Colville in Wheeler-Bennett, *Action This Day*, pp. 77–8.
4. Dalton's diary, 14 Nov. 1940.
5. Raczynski, *In Allied London*, p. 176.
6. de Gaulle, *The Call to Honour*, p. 167.
7. Messages of 15 and 16 June, F.O. 808/310.
8. Hoare to Halifax, 11 June 1940. T.P. XIII: 20.
9. Woodward, *British Foreign Policy in the Second World War* (1962), p. 165.
10. ibid., pp. 165–6; cf. record of a conversation with Lothian, and British memo., 27 June 1940, record of a further conversation and State Dept. memo., 28 June 1940, Hull Papers.
11. Amery's diary, 1 and 5 July 1940; Halifax to Hoare, 17 July 1940, T.P. XIII: 20.
12. Dalton to Halifax, 2 July 1940, Dalton Papers, envelope marked '17'.
13. Cf. Philby, *My Silent War*, pp. 18–19.
14. Dalton to Halifax, 10 Dec. 1940, Dalton Papers.
15. Conversation between Hull and Lothian, 12 July, 1940, Hull Papers; Woodward, *British Foreign Policy in the Second World War* (1962), p. 167.
16. Minute by Cadogan, 25 July, 1940, F.O. 800/322.
17. Woodward, *British Foreign Policy in the Second World War* (1970), vol. I, pp. 479–80.
18. ibid., pp. 481–7.
19. Amery's diary, 9 Aug. 1940.
20. Hoare to Chamberlain, 9 Sept 1940; Halifax to Hoare, 23 Aug. 1940, T.P. XIII: 20, Note by Dalton, 1 Oct. 1940, Dalton Papers, file marked '1940 miscellaneous'.
21. Cadogan to Hoare, 13 Sept. 1940, T.P. XIII: 17.
22. Halifax to Hoare, 26 Sept. 1940, T.P. XIII: 20.
23. Letters of 12 and 23 Oct. 1940, Chamberlain Papers and C.P.
24. Woodward, *British Foreign Policy in the Second World War* (1970), vol. I, pp. 487–500.
25. Sir M. Palairet to Halifax, 20 Dec. 1940, Vansittart Papers.
26. Lord Halifax's diary, 25 Nov. 1940, H.P. A7.8.3.
27. Minutes by Cadogan and Churchill, 12 and 15 Dec 1940, F.O. 800/312.
28. Halifax's diary, 17 Dec 1940, A7.8.3.
29. ibid., 19 Dec. 1940.
30. ibid., 20 and 23 Dec. 1940, A7.8.3, 6 Mar. 1946, A7.8.18.
31. Avon, *The Reckoning*, p. 285.
32. de Gaulle, *The Call to Honour*, pp. 150–2.
33. Enclosures to record of a conversation of 22 Jan 1941, with N. Butler, Hull Papers.
34. Woodward, *British Foreign Policy in the Second World War* (1970), vol. I, pp. 519–20.
35. This statement goes beyond that of Weygand, who states (*Recalled to Service*, pp. 309–12) that he decided to put the African Army into a state of war readiness.
36. Avon, *The Reckoning*, pp. 307–8.
37. Churchill, *The Second World War*, vol. III, chap. X, *passim;* enclosures to record of a talk with Halifax, 10 Feb. 1941, and record of a talk 3 Mar. 1941, Hull Papers.
38. Churchill, *The Second World War*, vol. III, appendix C.
39. Dalton's diary, 19 Feb. 1941.
40. Dixon, *Double Diploma*, pp. 67–70; Avon, *The Reckoning*, pp. 207–8; Churchill, *The Second World War*, vol. III, pp. 85–6.

V A Year Alone (*cont.*)

41. Churchill, *The Second World War*, vol. III, p. 86. The full texts of these exchanges are not yet available. It is not clear whether the telegrams printed by Churchill are identical with, or supplementary to, those summarised in Cadogan's entries for 28 Feb. and 1 Mar.
42. Woodward, *British Foreign Policy in the Second World War* (1970), vol. I, p. 537.
43. Cadogan to Halifax, 18 Mar. 1941, H.P.
44. Churchill, *The Second World War*, vol. III, p. 145; Woodward, *British Foreign Policy in the Second World War* (1970), vol. I, p. 541; Avon, *The Reckoning*, p. 227.
45. Amery's diary, 30 June 1941.
46. McLachlan, *Room 39*, pp. 242–3.
47. Churchill, *The Second World War*, vol. III, pp. 167ff; Irving, *Breach of Security*, p. 130; Deakin and Storry, *The Case of Richard Sorge*, pp. 225–6.
48. Craigie to Eden, 15 Apr. 1941, with record of a conversation with Halifax, 22 Apr. 1941, Hull Papers.
49. Cadogan to Halifax, 29 June 1941, H.P.
50. Dalton's diary, 19 Apr. 1941.
51. *Ciano's Diary, 1939–1943*, p. 342.
52. Kirkpatrick, *The Inner Circle*, pp. 169–85; Woodward, *British Foreign Policy in the Second World War* (1970), vol. I, p. 615.

VI *June–December 1941*, The Worldwide War

1. Dalton to Churchill, 24 Sept. 1941, Dalton papers, folder marked '1941'.
2. Dalton's diary, 7–11 July 1941.
3. Dalton to Attlee, 25 Sept. 1941, in folder marked 'Personal Papers A–Z, 1941 and 1942'.
4. Simon, *Retrospect*, pp. 261–3.
5. J. Colville in Wheeler-Bennett, *Action This Day*, p. 89.
6. Lord Halifax's secret diary, 11 Dec. 1941, H.P. A7.8.19.
7. Rozek, *Allied Wartime Diplomacy*, pp. 54–8.
8. Cadogan to R. A. Butler, 23 July 1941; I am grateful to Lord Butler for letting me see this letter.
9. Cadogan's record of 1962: 'Atlantic Meeting'.
10. F.R.U.S., 1941, vol. I. pp. 345–54.
11. Cadogan: 'Atlantic Meeting'.
12. Cadogan to Eden, 11 Aug. 1941, C.P.
13. Cadogan: 'Atlantic Meeting'.
14. Dalton's diary, 28 Aug. 1941.
15. ibid., 26 Aug. 1941.
16. I am indebted to Mr Valentine Lawford, who interpreted at the meeting, for this story.
17. Memorandum of 16 Oct. 1941, in Hull's record of a conversation with Halifax, 17 Oct. Hull Papers.
18. Churchill, *The Second World War*, vol. III, pp. 526–7.
19. *Stalin's Correspondence* (i.e. *Correspondence between the Chairman of the Council of Ministers, etc.*) vol. I, pp. 34–5.
20. Records of conversations between Hull and Halifax, 23–30 Nov. 1941, and attached papers, Hull Papers; Halifax's secret diary for the same period, esp. entry of 29 Nov. 1941, H.P. A7.8.19: cf. Hyde, *The Quiet Canadian*, pp. 213–4.
21. Connell, *Wavell*, vol. II, p. 41.
22. Woodward, *British Foreign Policy in the Second World War* (1962) pp. 190–1; Avon, *The Reckoning*, pp. 289–95.

VI The Worldwide War (*cont.*)

23. Avon, *The Reckoning*, p. 297.
24. F.R.U.S., 1941, vol. I, pp. 204–5.
25. Dalton's diary, 28 Jan. 1942.
26. Lord Halifax's diary, 4 Jan. 1942.

VII *January–September 1942*, Reverses

1. These passages about secret intelligence are based on Trevor-Roper, *The Philby Affair*, pp. 115–16; Philby, *My Silent War*, p. 38; Hyde, *The Quiet Canadian*, pp. 127–9, 215–16; *Ciano's Diary, 1939–1943*, for example the entries of 24 and 30 Dec. 1942; McLachlan, *Room 39*, p. 84; Irving, *Breach of Security*, p. 176; Kahn, *The Codebreakers*, p. 498.
2. Beaverbrook to Hoare, 17 Feb. 1942, and R. A. Butler to Hoare, 6 Mar. 1942, T.P. XIX: 13; Halifax's secret diary, 25 Mar. 1942, H.P.
3. Dalton's diary, 4, 5, 12, 22, 23 and 28 Feb. 1942; Dalton to Churchill, 23 Feb., Dalton to Cripps and to Attlee, 26 Feb. 1942; cf. Dalton, *The Fateful Years*, p. 386.
4. Avon, *The Reckoning*, p. 318; Churchill, *The Second World War*, vol. IV, p. 293; F.R.U.S., 1942, vol. III, pp. 527–8.
5. Woodward, *British Foreign Policy in the Second World War* (1962), p. 193.
6. Halifax's diary, 28 Mar. and 1 Apr. 1942, H.P.
7. Cadogan's memo. of 1963, 'Molotov's visit to London, May, 1942'; his diary entries, 12–15 May 1942; Young, *Churchill and Beaverbrook*, pp. 203, 244.
8. Avon, *The Reckoning*, p. 327; Irving, *Breach of Security*, p. 177.
9. For the text, see Cmd. 6368 of 1942; Cadogan's memorandum 'Molotov's visit'.
10. Eden (Avon), *Freedom and Order*, p. 159; Jasper, *George Bell, Bishop of Chichester*, pp. 270–1.
11. Kahn, *The Codebreakers*, pp. 473–6.
12. On Tobruk see Connell, *Auchinleck*, pp. 587–607; on the debate, Thomson, *Vote of Censure*.
13. Sir L. Rowan in Wheeler-Bennett, *Action This Day*, p. 256; Avon, *The Reckoning*, p. 339.
14. On the visit to Cairo, see Bryant, *The Turn of the Tide*, pp. 438–53; Tedder, *With Prejudice*, pp. 318–27; J. Connell, *Auchinleck*, pp. 685–74; and Churchill's account in *The Hinge of Fate*.
15. This interpolation is based on Cadogan's letters of the time to Lady Theo; on his memorandum of 1963 'Trip to Moscow with W.S.C., Aug., 1942'; his letter to Halifax, 29 Aug. 1942; Lord Moran, *Winston Churchill*, pp. 54ff; Bryant, *The Turn of the Tide*, pp. 460–2; Tedder, *With Prejudice*, pp. 330ff; Dalton's diary, 27 Aug. and 7 Sept. 1942.
16. Eden, *The Reckoning*, pp. 342–4.
17. Woodward, *British Foreign Policy in the Second World War* (1962), pp. 122–3.

VIII *October 1942–September 1943*, The Defeat of Italy

1. Avon, *The Reckoning*, pp. 350, 352; Bryant, *The Turn of the Tide*, p. 308. Cf. Dalton's diary, 10 Sept. and 10 Oct. 1942.
2. Woodward, *British Foreign Policy in the Second World War* (1962), pp. 199–200; Parl. Deb., H. of C., vol. 383, cols. 1943–4.
3. Woodward, *British Foreign Policy in the Second World War* (1962), pp. 433–5.
4. Hoare to Hankey, 20 Feb. 1942, T.P. XIX: 13; Trevor-Roper, *The Philby Affair*, p. 119; Philby, *My Silent War*, pp. 42–3: Hoare to Churchill, 10 Nov. 1942, T.P. XIII: 16.

VIII The Defeat of Italy (*cont.*)

5. de Gaulle, vol. II (i), pp. 79–80.
6. Moran, *Winston Churchill: The Struggle for Survival*, pp. 80–1.
7. Halifax's secret diary, 28 Aug. 1942, H.P. A.7.8.19.
8. On the Adana Conference, see Churchill, *The Second World War*, vol. IV, pp. 631–7; Moran, *Winston Churchill: The Struggle for Survival*, pp. 84–5; Avon, *The Reckoning*, pp. 363–4; Cadogan's memorandum of 1963, 'Ramshackle Conference'; Irving, *Breach of Security*, p. 182.
9. Woodward, *British Foreign Policy in the Second World War* (1962), pp. 218–9; Macmillan, *The Blast of War*, pp. 256–8.
10. Deakin, *The Brutal Friendship*, pp. 142–9; Kahn, *The Codebreakers*, p. 498; Dulles, *Germany's Underground*, pp. 130–1.
11. F.R.U.S., 1943, vol. III, pp. 332–3; Dalton's diary, 8 Feb. 1942.
12. Churchill, *The Second World War*, vol. IV, pp. 675–6.
13. Strang, *Home and Abroad*, pp. 72–3; Woodward, *British Foreign Policy in the Second World War* (1962), pp. 437–41, 443; Avon, *The Reckoning*, pp. 371–80; F.R.U.S., 1943, vol. II, pp. 54–5, vol. III, pp. 39–40.
14. Raczynski, *In Allied London*, pp. 140–3; Documents on Polish-Soviet Relations, pp. 530–2, 539–40; F.R.U.S., 1943, vol. III, p. 419.
15. Raczynski, *In Allied London*, p. 143.
16. Woodward, *British Foreign Policy in the Second World War* (1962), p. 205.
17. Avon, *The Reckoning*, pp. 386–7, 390–2; Halifax's secret diary, 22 May 1943; F.R.U.S., 1943, vol. II, pp. 116–17.
18. Amery's diary, 19 July 1940, 7 Aug. 1940; Amery to Churchill, 8 June 1943, Amery papers.
19. Woodward, *British Foreign Policy in the Second World War* (1962), pp. 239–43.
20. Avon's article in *The Daily Express*, 3 Jan. 1969; conversation betweeen Cadogan and the editor, 10 May 1968.
21. Avon, *The Reckoning*, pp. 393, 402.
22. Deakin, *The Brutal Friendship*, pp. 501–2; Woodward, *British Foreign Policy in the Second World War* (1962), p. 227.
23. Woodward, op. cit., pp. 228–9.

IX *September 1943–May 1944*, The Beginning of the End

1. Halifax's secret diary, 20 Nov. 1943, H.P. A7.9.19.
2. Hyde, *The Quiet Canadian*, p. 177; Philby, *My Silent War*, pp. 61–4; Trevor-Roper, *The Philby Affair*, pp. 78–9, 121; F. W. Winterbotham, *Secret and Personal*, p. 162; Woodward, *British Foreign Policy in the Second World War* (1962), p. 479.
3. Hoare to Churchill, 14 Oct. 1943, T.P. XIII: 16.
4. Woodward, *British Foreign Policy in the Second World War* (1962), pp. 381–2.
5. Churchill, *The Second World War*, vol. V, pp. 237–9.
6. See *The Times*' reports of 9 and 19 Oct. 1943 for the Senators' charges; Woodward, *British Foreign Policy in the Second World War* (1962), p. 395*n*.
7. Raczynski, *In Allied London*, pp. 171–2.
8. Avon, *The Reckoning*, pp. 418–20; Woodward, *British Foreign Policy in the Second World War* (1962), pp. 326–7.
9. Macmillan, *The Blast of War*, pp. 420–9.
10. Cadogan to Halifax, 10 Jan. 1944, H.P.; Stettinius, *Roosevelt and the Russians*, p. 212.
11. *The Times*, 20 Dec. 1968; *The Sunday Times*, 22 Dec. 1968 (see especially the remarks of Sir K. Strong); *The Memoirs of Lord Ismay*, p. 337.
12. Moran, *Winston Churchill: The Struggle for Survival*, pp. 132, 134; Wheeler-Bennett, *Action This Day*, p. 96; Avon, *The Reckoning*, pp. 426–9; Halifax's secret diary, 19 Dec. 1943, H.P. A7.8.19.

IX The Beginning of the End (*cont.*)

13. Moyzisch, *Operation Cicero, passim* but especially pp. 50, 52, 104 and the postscript by F. von Papen; Woodward, *British Foreign Policy in the Second World War* (1962), pp. 327–9.
14. Avon, *The Reckoning*, pp. 430–1; Woodward, *British Foreign Policy in the Second World War* (1962), p. 355.
15. Woodward, *British Foreign Policy in the Second World War* (1962), pp. 332–342; Churchill, *The Second World War*, vol. V, pp. 416–17.
16. Raczynski, *In Allied London*, pp. 178–9; Avon, *The Reckoning*, p. 434.
17. Avon, *The Reckoning*, p. 435; Woodward, *British Foreign Policy in the Second World War* (1962), pp. 278–9; for the texts of the statements see Raczynski, *In Allied London*, pp. 181–9.
18. *Stalin's Correspondence*, pp. 195–7; Woodward, *British Foreign Policy in the Second World War* (1962), pp. 280–4.
19. Woodward, *British Foreign Policy in the Second World War* (1962), pp. 284–6; Avon, *The Reckoning*, pp. 438–9.
20. Avon, *The Reckoning*, pp. 449–50.
21. *Stalin's Correspondence*, pp. 212–3; Woodward, *British Foreign Policy in the Second World War* (1962), p. 287; Avon, *The Reckoning*, p. 439.
22. Avon, *The Reckoning*, pp. 440–1.
23. Churchill, *The Second World War*, vol. V, Chap. XXX, *passim*.
24. Churchill, *The Second World War*, vol. V, p. 621; Halifax's secret diary, 31 Mar. 1944, H.P. A7.8.19.
25. Medlicott, *The Economic Blockade*, vol. II, pp. 570–5; Eden to Hoare, 23 Feb. 1944, T.P. XIII: 24; Woodward, *British Foreign Policy in the Second World War* (1962), pp. 367–70.
26. Raczynski, *In Allied London*, pp. 206–8.
27. Woodward, *British Foreign Policy in the Second World War* (1962), pp. 454–5; Avon, *The Reckoning*, pp. 442–3; Churchill, *The Second World War*, vol. V, p. 626.

X *June 1944–February 1945*, From Overlord to Yalta

1. de Gaulle, vol. II, pp. 219–22.
2. Cooper, *Old Men Forget*, p. 332.
3. Woodward, *British Foreign Policy in the Second World War* (1962), pp. 344–5.
4. Kolko, *The Politics of War*, p. 83.
5. Woodward, *British Foreign Policy in the Second World War* (1962), pp. 413–5.
6. Woodward, *British Foreign Policy in the Second World War* (1962), pp. 315–7; Halifax's secret diary, 22 Aug. 1944, H.P. A7.8.19.
7. Raczynski, *In Allied London*, pp. 303ff; Churchill, *The Second World War*, vol. V, Chap. 9, *passim*.
8. Woodward, *British Foreign Policy in the Second World War* (1962), p. 456.
9. For the U.S., British and Russian proposals see F.R.U.S., 1944, I, pp. 653–70, 670–93, 706–11; cf. Cmd. 6560, 1944.
10. Woodward, *British Foreign Policy in the Second World War* (1962), pp. 457–8: F.R.U.S., 1944, I, p. 782.
11. Woodward, *British Foreign Policy in the Second World War* (1962), p. 458.
12. Halifax's secret diary, 5 Oct., 17 Sept. 1944; Woodward, *British Foreign Policy in the Second World War* (1962), pp. 471–2.
13. Halifax's secret diary, 29 Sept. 1944.
14. Woodward, *British Foreign Policy in the Second World War* (1962), pp. 460–2; Webster, *The Art and Practice of Diplomacy*, pp. 70–83.
15. Moran, *Winston Churchill: The Struggle for Survival*, pp. 190–3, 200–3; Mikolajczyk, *The Pattern of Soviet Domesticity*, p. 109; Woodward, *British Foreign Policy in the Second World War* pp. 309–11.

X From Overlord to Yalta (*cont.*)

16. Raczynski, *In Allied London*, p. 240; Rozek, *Allied Wartime Diplomacy*, pp. 305–13.
17. Cooper, *Old Men Forget*, pp. 340–2.
18. J. R. Colville in Wheeler-Bennett, *Action This Day*, pp. 51–2.
19. Avon, *The Reckoning*, p. 500.
20. Avon, *The Reckoning*, p. 504.
21. Raczynski, *In Allied London*, pp. 261–2.
22. J. R. Colville in Wheeler-Bennett, *Action This Day*, p. 117; the two letters are in Attlee Papers, A.P. 2/2.
23. Avon, *The Reckoning*, pp. 509–12.
24. Dalton's diary, 23 Feb. 1945; Churchill, *The Second World War*, vol. VI, pp. 351–2; Cadogan to Halifax, 20 Feb. 1945, H.P.

XI *February–August 1945*, The Perils of Victory

1. J. R. Colville in Wheeler-Bennett, *Action This Day*, pp. 93–4; Raczynski, *In Allied London*, pp. 272–3; Avon, *The Reckoning*, p. 525.
2. Churchill, *The Second World War*, vol. VI, pp. 379–82.
3. Raczynski, *In Allied London*, pp. 185–6.
4. Truman, *Memoirs*, vol. I, p. 15.
5. Truman, *Memoirs*, vol. I, p. 82.
6. F.R.U.S., 1945, vol. IV, pp. 444–5.
7. For these and other telegrams, see Churchill, *The Second World War*, vol. VI, Chap. XXIX.
8. Avon, *The Reckoning*, p. 535; Dalton's diary, 27 May 1945.
9. Woodward, *British Foreign Policy in the Second World War* (1962), pp. 272–7.
10. Avon, *The Reckoning*, p. 544; Raczynski, *In Allied London*, p. 296.
11. Avon, *The Reckoning*, pp. 545–7.
12. Moran, *Winston Churchill: The Struggle for Survival*, pp. 273–5.
13. Churchill, *The Second World War*, vol. VI, pp. 573–7.
14. Woodward, *British Foreign Policy in the Second World War* (1962), pp. 548, 561–2.
15. Woodward, *British Foreign Policy in the Second World War* (1962), pp. 568–9.

Epilogue *1945–1968*

1. Cadogan's Diary, 29 Sept. and 23 Oct. 1945.
2. ibid., 24 Nov. 1945.
3. ibid., 20 Dec. 1945.
4. Bevin to Cadogan, 6 Sept. 1946, C.P.
5. Cadogan to Churchill, 6 Feb. 1948, C.P.
6. Eden to Cadogan and reply, 1 and 2 Jan. 1951, C.P.
7. Cadogan's Diary, 19 Jan. and 11 Dec. 1956.
8. ibid., 6 Jan. 1955.
9. ibid., 4 April 1955.
10. ibid., 15 Nov. 1951.
11. ibid., 10 and 11 Aug. 1956.
12. Eden to Cadogan, 16 Aug. 1956, C.P.
13. Parl. Deb., H. of C., ser. V, vol. 560, cols. 1023 ff. For an examination of the B.B.C's relations with the Government in 1956, see 'Eden, Suez and the B.B.C.—a reassessment' in *The Listener*, vol. 82, No. 2125 (1969).
14. Cadogan's Diary, 8 June 1964.
15. Ronald Fredenburgh to Cadogan, 16 Dec. 1961, C.P.

BIBLIOGRAPHY

(*a*) MS COLLECTIONS

Amery. Papers of Rt Hon. L. S. Amery (by courtesy of Rt Hon. Julian Amery, M.P.).

Attlee. Papers of Rt Hon. Lord Attlee (Churchill College, Cambridge).

Cadogan (C.P.). Papers of Sir Alexander Cadogan (by courtesy of Lady Theodosia Cadogan). There is a volume of Diary for each year from 1933 to 1967, but very little else for the period of Cadogan's official life.

Dalton. Papers of Rt Hon. Lord Dalton (British Library of Economics and Political Science).

Chamberlain (N.C.P.). Papers of Rt Hon. N. Chamberlain (by courtesy of Mr and Mrs Stephen Lloyd).

Halifax (H.P.). Papers of Rt Hon. Earl of Halifax. 2 collections; one in Public Record Office, London (F.O. 800 series), the other in Yorkshire (by courtesy of the 2nd Earl of Halifax).

Hull. Papers of Cordell Hull (Library of Congress).

Templewood (T.P.). Papers of Rt Hon. Sir S. Hoare, later Lord Templewood (Cambridge University Library).

Vansittart. Papers of Rt Hon. Lord Vansittart (Churchill College, Cambridge).

Webster. Papers of Prof. Sir Charles Webster (London School of Economics Library).

Public Record Office. Papers from the archives of the Foreign Office, Cabinet Office, Committee of Imperial Defence.

(*b*) PRINCIPAL COLLECTIONS OF PUBLISHED DOCUMENTS

Documents on Polish-Soviet Relations, 2 vols. (1961, 1970).

Foreign Relations of the United States (F.R.U.S.), normally 5 vols. p.a. (1938–45).

The Conferences at Cairo and Teheran (Washington, 1961).

The Conferences at Malta and Yalta (Washington, 1955).

The Conference at Potsdam (Washington, 1960).

Correspondence between the Chairman of the Council of Ministers and the Presidents of the U.S.A. and the Prime Ministers of Great Britain, 1941–5 (Moscow, 1957). (Abbreviated in source notes to '*Stalin's Correspondence*'.)

Documents on German Foreign Policy, ser. C, vols. I and II, ser. D, vols. I–XI. (Washington 1957, 1959, 1949–60.)

E. L. Woodward and R. Butler (eds.), *Documents on British Foreign Policy, 1919–39*, 3rd. ser., vols. I–IX (1949–55).

(*c*) SECONDARY SOURCES

This list does not purport to provide a comprehensive bibliography for international affairs in the period 1938–45. It does, however, include details of sources cited in notes or containing substantial references to Cadogan's work as P.U.S. The place of publication is London unless otherwise stated.

The page references for books which appear in the source notes refer only to the editions listed below and may not necessarily hold good for other editions.

Alperowitz, G. *Atomic Diplomacy* (New York, 1965).
Anders, Gen. W. *An Army in Exile* (1969).
Anon. 'Appeasement Reconsidered' in *The Round Table*, vol. LIII, 1963.
Armstrong, A. *Unconditional Surrender* (New Brunswick, 1961).
Ashton-Gwatkin, F. T. A. *The British Foreign Office* (Syracuse University Press, 1949).
Attlee, Rt Hon. C. R. *As it Happened* (1954).
Avon, Rt Hon. the Earl of. *See under* Eden.
Barman, T. *Diplomatic Correspondent* (1968).
Barnes, J. and Middlemas, K. *Stanley Baldwin* (1969).
Barros, J. *Betrayal from Within* (New Haven, 1969).
Bellush, B. *He Walked Alone* (The Hague, Monton, 1968).
Birkenhead, Earl of. *Halifax* (1965).
Blum, J. M. *From the Morgenthau Diaries*, 2 vols. (Boston, 1959, 1965).
Bonnet, G. *Quai d'Orsai, 1890–1961* (Paris, 1961); *Défense de la Paix* (Geneva, 1948).
Bor-Komorowski, T. *The Secret Army* (New York, 1951).
Bryans, J. Lonsdale, *Blind Victory* (1951).
Bryant, Sir A. *The Turn of the Tide* (1957); *Triumph in the West* (1959).
Bulloch, J. *M.I.5* (1963).
Burns, J. M. *Roosevelt, the Soldier of Freedom* (1970).
Butler, Sir J. R. M. *Grand Strategy*, vol. II (1957); *Lord Lothian* (1960).
Byrnes, J. F. *All in One Lifetime* (New York, 1958); *Speaking Frankly* (1947).
Bullock, A. *The Life and Times of Ernest Bevin*, vol. II (1967).
Cadogan, Hon. Sir E. *Before the Deluge* (1961).
Chamberlain, Rt Hon. N. *In Search of Peace* (1939).
Chapman, G. *Why France Collapsed.* (1968).
Chase, J. L. 'The Development of the Morgenthau Plan through the Quebec Conference' in *The Journal of Politics*, vol. XVI, 1954.
Churchill, Rt Hon. W. S. *Marlborough, His Life and Times* (1933–8). *The Second World War: I. The Gathering Storm* (1948); II. *Their Finest Hour* (1949); III. *The Grand Alliance* (1950); IV. *The Hinge of Fate* (1951); V. *Closing the Ring* (1952); VI. *Triumph and Tragedy* (1954).

Ciano, Count G. *Ciano's Diary, 1937–1938* (1952); *Ciano's Diary, 1939–1943* (1947); *Ciano's Diplomatic Papers* (1948).
Ciencala, A. M. *Poland and the Western Powers* (1968).
Colvin, I. *Chief of Intelligence* (1951); *Vansittart in Office* (1965); *The Chamberlain Cabinet* (1971).
Connell, J. *Auchinleck* (1959); *Wavell*, 2 vols. (1964, 1969).
Cooper, A. Duff, *Old Men Forget* (1953).
Craig, G. A. and Gilbert, F. (eds.) *The Diplomats* (Princeton, 1953).
Current, R. N. *Secretary Stimson. A Study in Statecraft* (New Brunswick, 1954).
Dahlerus, B. *The Last Attempt* (1948).
Dalton, H. *The Fateful Years* (1957).
Deacon, R. *A History of the British Secret Service* (1969).
Deakin, F. W. *The Brutal Friendship* (1962).
Deakin, F. W. and Storry, G. R. *The Case of Richard Sorge* (1966).
De Gaulle, C. *Memoirs*, 5 vols., inc. documents (1955–60).
Dennett, R. and Johnson, J. (eds). *Negotiating with the Russians* (Boston, Mass., 1951).
Deutsch, H. *The Conspiracy against Hitler in the Twilight War* (1968).
Dirksen, H. von. *Moscow, Tokyo, London* (1951).
Dixon, P. (ed.) *Double Diploma* (1968).
Dulles, A. W. *Germany's Underground* (New York, 1947).
Eden, Rt Hon. A. (Earl of Avon) *Freedom and Order* (1948); *Facing the Dictators* (1962); *The Reckoning* (1965).
Elibank, the Master of. 'Franklin Roosevelt: Friend of Britain' in *The Contemporary Review*, vol. 187, 1955.
Eubank, K. *Munich* (Naman, Oklahoma, 1963).
Fehrenbach, T. R. *F.D.R.'s Undeclared War* (New York, 1967).
Feiling, Sir K. *The Life of Neville Chamberlain* (1964).
Feis, H. *The Road to Pearl Harbor* (Princeton, 1950); *The China Tangle* (Princeton, 1953); *Churchill, Roosevelt, Stalin* (1957); *Between War and Peace: The Potsdam Conference* (Princeton, 1960); *Contest over Japan* (New York, 1967).
Fletcher, C. R. L. *Edmond Warre* (1922).
Francis-Williams, Lord. *A Pattern of Rulers* (1965).
Friedman, I. S. *British Relations with China, 1931–9* (New York, 1940).
Furnia, A. H. *The Diplomacy of Appeasement* (1960).
Gafencu, G. *Last Days of Europe* (1947); *Prelude to the Russian Campaign* (1945).
Gamelin, Gen. M. *Servir*, vols. II & III (Paris, 1946 & 1947).
Gardner, L. G. *Economic Aspects of New Deal Diplomacy* (Madison, 1964).
Gardner, R. *Sterling–Dollar Diplomacy* (Oxford, 1956).
Gehl, J. *Austria, Germany and the Anschluss* (1963).
Gilbert, M. *The Roots of Appeasement* (1966).
Gilbert, M. and Gott, R. *The Appeasers* (1963).
Goebbels, J. P. (trs. L. P. Lochner). *Diaries* (1948).

Gore-Booth, Rt Hon. Lord. Obituary notice of Sir A. Cadogan in *The Balliol College Record*, 1969.

Gowing, M. M. *Britain and Atomic Energy* (1964).

Gripenberg, *Finland and the Great Powers* (Lincoln, Nebraska, 1965).

Grisewood, H. *One Thing at a Time* (1968).

Gubbins, Maj.-Gen. Sir C. 'Resistance Movements in the War' in *Journal of the Royal United Service Institution*, vol. 93, 1948.

Hadley, W. W. *Munich: Before and After* (1944).

Hancock, Sir K. *Smuts: The Fields of Force* (Cambridge, 1968).

Halifax, Rt Hon. Lord. *Speeches on Foreign Policy* (1940); *Fulness of Days* (1957).

Harrod, R. F. *The Life of John Maynard Keynes* (1951); *The Prof.* (1959).

Hassell, U. von. *The Hassell Diaries* (New York, 1947).

Harvey, J. (ed.). *The Diplomatic Diaries of Oliver Harvey* (1970).

Henderson, Rt Hon. Sir N. *Failure of a Mission* (1940).

Hesse, F. *Hitler and the English* (1954).

Higgins, T. *Churchill and the Second Front* (New York, 1957).

Holborn, L. W. (ed.). *War and Peace Aims of the United Nations* (Boston, 1948).

Hooker, N. H. (ed.). *The Moffat Papers* (1956).

Hull, C. *The Memoirs of Cordell Hull*, vol. II (1948).

Hutton, J. B. *Hess* (1970).

Hyde, H. Montgomery. *The Quiet Canadian* (1962); *Cynthia* (1966).

Irving, D. J. C. (ed.). *Breach of Security* (1968); *Accident* (1967).

Ismay, Rt Hon. Lord. *The Memoirs of Lord Ismay* (1960).

James, R. Rhodes. *Chips: The Diaries of Sir Henry Channon* (1967).

Jasper, Canon R. C. D. *George Bell, Bishop of Chichester* (1967).

Jones, F. C. *Japan's New Order in East Asia* (1954).

Jones, Sir L. E. *A Victorian Boyhood* (1955); *An Edwardian Youth* (1956);

Jones, T. *A Diary with Letters* (1954).

Kahn, D. *The Codebreakers* (1966).

Kelly, Sir D. *The Ruling Few* (1952); *The Hungry Sheep* (1955).

Kirkpatrick, Sir I. *The Inner Circle* (1959).

Knatchbull-Hugessen, Sir H. *Diplomat in Peace and War* (1949).

Kolko, G. *The Politics of War* (1968).

Korbel, J. *Poland between East and West* (Princeton, 1963).

Kordt, E. *Wahn und Wirklichkeit* (Stuttgart, 1947); *Nicht aus den Akten* (Stuttgart, 1950).

Kot, S. *Conversations with the Kremlin and Dispatches from Russia* (1963).

Lawford, V. 'Three Ministers' in *The Cornhill Magazine*, No. 1010, 1956–7.

Leahy, Admiral W. D. *I Was There* (1950).

Leasor, J. *Rudolf Hess* (1962).

Leeper, Sir R. *When Greek meets Greek* (1950).

Leith-Ross, Sir F. W. *Money Talks* (1968).

L'Etang, Dr H. *The Pathology of Leadership* (1969).

Leverkuehn, P. (trs. R. H. Stevens and C. Fitzgibbon). *German Military Intelligence* (1954).

Liddell Hart, Captain Sir B. H. 'Churchill in War' in *Encounter*, vol. XXVI, 1966.
Lie, T. *In the Cause of Peace* (New York, 1954).
Lubbock, P. (ed.) *The Diary of Arthur Christopher Benson* (1926); *Shades of Eton* (1928).
MacLean, F. *Disputed Barricade* (1957).
MacLeod, Rt Hon. I. *Neville Chamberlain* (1961).
MacLeod, Col. R. and Kelly, E. (ed.). *The Ironside Diaries* (1962).
MacKenzie, F. R. 'Eden, Suez and the B.B.C.—a reassessment' in *The Listener*, vol. 82, No. 2125, 1969.
Macmillan, Rt Hon. H. *Winds of Change* (1966); *The Blast of War* (1967).
Maisky, I. M. (trs. A. Rothstein) *Who Helped Hitler?* (1964); *Memoirs of a Soviet Ambassador: The War, 1939–43* (1967).
McLachlan, D. *Room 39* (1968).
McNeill, W. H. *America, Britain and Russia: Their Co-operation and conflict, 1941–6* (1953).
Medlicott, W. N. *The Economic Blockade*, 2 vols. (1952); *The Coming of War in 1939* (1963); *British Foreign Policy since Versailles* (1968); *The Search for Agreement with Germany* (1969).
Mikolajczyk, S. *The Pattern of Soviet Domination* (1948).
Minney, R. J. *The Private Papers of Hore-Belisha* (1960).
Moran, Lord. *Winston Churchill: The Struggle for Survival* (1966).
Morton, H. V. *Atlantic Meeting* (1943).
Mosely, P. E. 'Techniques of Negotiation' in *Negotiating with the Russians* (Boston, 1951); *The Kremlin and World Politics* (New York, 1960).
Moyzisch, L. C. *Operation Cicero* (1969).
Murphy, R. *Diplomat Among Warriors* (1964).
Namier, Sir L. B. *Europe in Decay*, (1950); *In the Nazi Era* (1952); *Diplomatic Prelude* (1948).
Nicolson, Hon Sir H. *Some People* (1934); 'The Foreign Service' in *The British Civil Servant* (ed. W. A. Robson) (1937); *Diplomacy* (1942).
Northedge, F. S. *The Troubled Giant* (1966).
O'Malley, Sir O. *The Phantom Caravan* (1955).
Payne Best, S. *The Venlo Incident* (1950).
Philby, K. *My Silent War* (1968).
Pratt, J. W. *Cordell Hull*, 2 vols. (New York, 1964).
Raczynski, Count E. *In Allied London* (1962).
Reynaud, P. *In the Thick of the Fight* (1955).
Ritter, G. (trs. C. T. Clark) *The German Resistance* (1958).
Robbins, K. *Munich 1938* (1968).
Rock, W. R. 'Grand Alliance or Daisy Chain: Opinion and Policy towards Russia, April–August, 1939' in L. P. Wallace and W. C. Askew (eds), *Power, Public Opinion and Diplomacy* (Durham, N. C., 1959).
Rothfels, H. (trs. L. Wilson). 'Resistance Begins' in *The Road to Dictatorship* (1964).

Rozek, E. J. *Allied Wartime Diplomacy* (New York, 1958).

Russell, R. D. *A History of the U.N. Charter: The Role of the United States, 1940–5* (Washington, 1958).

Schellenberg, W. *The Schellenberg Memoirs* (1956).

Sherwood, R. E. *The White House Papers of Harry L. Hopkins*, 2 vols. (1948–1949).

Simon, Rt Hon. Lord. *Retrospect* (1952).

Smith, G. *American Diplomacy during the Second World War* (1965).

Snell, J. L. (ed.). *The Meaning of Yalta* (Baton Rouge, 1956).

Spears, Maj.-Gen. Sir E. L. *Assignment to Catastrophe* (1956).

Stettinius, E. R. *Roosevelt and the Russians* (1950).

Strang, the Rt Hon. Lord. *The Foreign Office* (1955); *Home and Abroad* (1956); *The Moscow Negotiations, 1939* (Leeds, 1968); *War and Foreign Policy, 1939–45* (2 lectures delivered at the London School of Economics, March, 1965).

Strong, Maj.-Gen. Sir K. *Men of Intelligence* (1970).

Taylor, A. J. P. *The Origins of the Second World War* (1963).

Tedder, Marshal of the R.A.F. Lord. *With Prejudice* (1966).

Teichova, A. 'Great Britain in European Affairs, March 15 to Aug. 21, 1939' in *Historica*, vol. III, 1961.

Temperley, Maj.-Gen. A. C. *The Whispering Gallery of Europe* (1938).

Templewood, Rt Hon. Lord. *Ambassador on Special Mission* (1946); *Nine Troubled Years* (1954).

Thomson, G. M. *Vote of Censure* (1967).

Thompson, L. *The Greatest Treason* (New York, 1968).

Thorne, C. *The Approach of War, 1938–9* (1961).

Tilley, Sir J. and Gaselee, S. *The Foreign Office* (1933).

Trevor-Roper, H. R. *The Philby Affair* (1968).

Truman, H. *Memoirs*, 2 vols. (1955–6).

Umiastowski, R. *Poland, Russia and Great Britain, 1941–5* (1946).

Vandenberg, A. H. *The Private Papers of Senator Vandenberg* (Boston, 1952).

Vere-Hodge, E. R. *Turkish Foreign Policy, 1918–48* (Ambilly-Annemasse, 1950).

Watt, D. C. *Personalities and Policies* (1965).

Webster, Sir C. 'Munich Reconsidered' in *International Affairs*, vol. 37, 1961; *The Art and Practice of Diplomacy* (1961).

Weizsacker, E. von. *Memoirs* (1951).

Welles, S. *A Time for Decision* (1944).

Weygand, Gen. M. (trs. E. W. Dickes) *Recalled to Service* (1952).

Whalen, R. J. *The Founding Father* (New York, 1964).

Wheeler-Bennett, Sir J. *Munich, Prologue to Tragedy* (1948); *The Nemesis of Power* (1953); *John Anderson, Viscount Waverley* (1962); (ed.) *Action This Day* (1968).

Williams, T. D. 'Negotiations leading to the Anglo-Polish agreement of 31 March, 1939' in *Irish Historical Studies*, vol. X, 1957.

Wilmot, C. *The Struggle for Europe* (1952).

Wilson, T. A. *The First Summit* (Boston, 1969).
Winant, J. G. *A Letter from Grosvenor Square* (1947).
Winterbotham, F. W. *Secret and Personal* (1969).
Woodward, Sir E. L. 'The origins of the Second World War' in *The Listener*, vol. LXXII, 1964; 'Some reflections on British Policy, 1939–1945' in *International Affairs*, July, 1955; *British Foreign Policy in the Second World War* (1962), *British Foreign Policy in the Second World War*, vol. I (1970).
Wrinch, P. N. *The Military Strategy of Winston Churchill* (Boston, 1961).
Young, K. *Churchill and Beaverbrook* (1966).

APPENDIXES

A. Lists of Abbreviations and Codenames

B. List of Principal Characters

APPENDIX A

Lists of Abbreviations and Codenames used in the Diaries

(a) *Persons*	(see also List of Principal Characters, Appendix B)
A.	Anthony Eden (Also: A. E.)
Bobbety	Lord Cranborne
Brendan	Brendan Bracken
E.B.	Ernest Bevin
H.B.	L. Hore-Belisha
R.A.B.	R. A. Butler
S.B.	Lord Baldwin
R.H.C.	Sir Ronald H. Campbell
R.I.C.	R. I. Campbell
W.S.C.	Winston Spencer Churchill
Duff	Duff Cooper
Ed.	Edward R. Stettinius
A.E.	Anthony Eden (Also: A.)
Frogface	F. T. Gousev
Gladwyn	Gladwyn Jebb (Also: G.J.)
G.	Gromyko
G.	Gillian, Cadogan's daughter
Ll. G.	David Lloyd George
H.	Lord Halifax
H.H.	Harry Hopkins
N.H. Nevile H.	Sir Nevile Henderson
O.H.	Oliver Harvey (Also: Oliver. But see also Oliver: Oliver Stanley)
Ike	General Dwight D. Eisenhower
Maurice I.	Maurice Ingram
Joe Uncle Joe	Stalin
G.J.	Gladwyn Jebb (Also: Gladwyn)
A.C.K.	Sir Archibald Clark Kerr
I.K. Kirk.	Ivone Kirkpatrick

Leithers	Sir F. Leith-Ross
Rex L.	Sir Reginald Leeper
M.M. M.MacD.	Malcolm MacDonald
Mik.	S. Mikolajczyk
Musso	Benito Mussolini
W.M.	Sir Will Malkin
Oliver	Oliver Harvey (Also: O.H. But see also Oliver: Oliver Stanley)
Oliver	Oliver Stanley (Also: O.S. But see also O.S.: Sir Orme Sargent), and Oliver: Oliver Harvey)
L.O.	Sir Lancelot Oliphant
O'M.	Sir Owen O'Malley
Rib.	Joachim von Ribbentrop
R.	President Franklin D. Roosevelt
L.R.	Sir F. Leith-Ross
Snatch	Sir H. Knatchbull-Hugesson
Stett.	Edward R. Stettinius
C.K.S.	Chiang Kai-Shek
David S.	Sir David Scott
J.S.	Sir John Simon, later Lord Simon
O.S.	Sir Orme Sargent (But see also O.S.: Oliver Stanley)
O.S.	Oliver Stanley (Also: Oliver. But see also O.S.: Sir Orme Sargent)
W.S.	Sir William Strang
T. Theo	Lady Theodosia Cadogan
Tommy	Commander C. R. Thompson
Van.	Sir Robert Vansittart
Horace W. H.W. H.J.W.	Horace Wilson
W.	Winston Spencer Churchill

(b) *Other abbreviations*

A.A.	Anti-aircraft ('ack-ack') guns
Amgot	Allied Military Government of Occupied Territories
A.O.C.-in-C.	Air Officer Commanding in Chief
A.P.W.	Armistice and Post-War Committee
A.R.W.	Air raid warning
B.E.F.	British Expeditionary Force
C.A.S.	Chief of the Air Staff
C.D.A.	Chief Diplomatic Adviser

Ch.d'A.	Chargé d'Affaires
C.I.D.	Committee of Imperial Defence
C.I.G.S.	Chief of the Imperial General Staff
C.-in-C.	Commander-in-Chief
C.O.S. / C's of S.	Chiefs of Staff
D.C.N.S.	Deputy Chief of Naval Staff
D.M.I.	Directory of Military Intelligence
D.N.I.	Director of Naval Intelligence
D.O.	Dominions Office
E.A.C.	European Advisory Commission
E.A.M.	The Greek 'National Liberation Front'
E.D.E.S.	The Greek 'National Democratic Army'
E.L.A.S.	The Greek 'People's National Army of Liberation'
F.C.N.L.	French Committee of National Liberation
F.P.C.	Foreign Policy Committee
G.O.C.	General Officer Commanding
H.M.G.	His Majesty's Government
J.I.C.	Joint Intelligence Committee
L. of N.	League of Nations
M.A.	Military Attaché
M.E.W.	Ministry of Economic Warfare
M.F.A.	Ministry of Foreign Affairs
M. of I.	Ministry of Information
N.I.C.	Non-Intervention Committee
P.H.P.	Post Hostilities Planning Sub-Committee
P.Q.	Parliamentary Question
P.U.S.	Permanent Under-Secretary
P.W.E.	Political Warfare Executive
R.M.O.	'Royal Marine' Operation
S.H.A.E.F.	Supreme Headquarters Allied Expeditionary Force
S.O.E.	Special Operations Executive
S. of S.	Secretary of State
T.U.C.	Trades Union Congress
U.N.R.R.A.	The United Nations Relief and Rehabilitation Administration
V1	German flying bomb
V2	German rocket bomb
V.C.A.S.	Vice-Chief of the Air Staff
V.C.I.G.S.	Vice-Chief of the Imperial General Staff
V.C.N.S.	Vice-Chief of the Naval Staff

(c) *Codenames of Operations*

Agreement	The abortive raid on Tobruk, September 1942.
Anvil	Allied landings in the South of France, 1944, later named 'Dragoon'.
Avalanche	Amphibious assault on Naples (Salerno).
Brisk	An early plan (1941) for the occupation of the Azores.
Catapult	The seizure or destruction of all accessible French ships in July 1940.
Crossbow	The Committee set up to deal with measures against pilotless 'V' weapons.
Culverin	Operations against North Sumatra.
Dragoon	Allied landings in the South of France, 1944.
Gymnast	Occupation of French North Africa (later named 'Torch').
Hardihood	???
Husky	The Capture of Sicily.
Lifebelt	Operations against the Azores.
Menace	Occupation of Dakar.
Mandibles	Operations against the Dodecanese Islands.
Overlord	The liberation of France in 1944 and the landing in Normandy.
Puma	A plan to occupy the Canary Islands.
Round-up	Liberation of France in 1943 (later developed as 'Overlord').
Shrapnel	A plan for the occupation of the Cape Verde Islands.
Sledgehammer	Plan for attack on Brest or Cherbourg in 1942.
Torch	Allied invasion of French North Africa in 1942.
Trident	The Washington Conference, 1943.
Quadrant	The Quebec Conference, 1943.
Whipcord	Plan for the invasion of Sicily (abandoned October 1941).

APPENDIX B

List of Principal Characters appearing in the Diaries

Aghnides Thanassis: worked for the League of Nations, 1919–1942; Secretary for Foreign Affairs in Greek Cabinet, 1942–3; Greek Ambassador in London, 1942–7.

Amery Leopold S.: First Lord of the Admiralty, 1922–4; Secretary for the Colonies, 1924–9, for Dominion Affairs, 1925–9, for India and Burma, 1940–5.

Anderson Sir John, 1st Viscount Waverley: Governor of Bengal, 1932–7; Lord Privy Seal, 1938–9; Home Secretary and Minister of Home Security, 1939–40; Lord President of the Council, 1940–3; Chancellor of Exchequer, 1943–5.

Attlee Clement R., 1st Earl: Leader of the Opposition, 1935–40, 1951–5; Lord Privy Seal, 1940–2; Secretary for Dominion Affairs, 1942–3; Lord President of the Council, 1943–5; Deputy Prime Minister, 1942–1945; Prime Minister, 1945–51.

Beaverbrook Lord: Newspaper proprietor; Minister for Aircraft Production, 1940–1; Minister of State, 1941; Minister of Supply, 1941–2; Lord Privy Seal, 1943–5.

Beneš Eduard: Czechoslovak representative at Paris Peace Conference, 1919; Foreign Minister, 1918–35; President, 1935–8; in 1941 became President of exiled Czech Government in London, returning to Prague in 1945.

Bonnet Georges: held Cabinet rank from 1926; French Minister of Foreign Affairs, 1938–9; Minister of Justice, 1939–40.

Bracken Brendan, 1st Viscount: M.P., 1929–51; newspaper proprietor; Parliamentary Private Secretary to Churchill, 1940–1; Minister of Information, 1941–5.

Brooke Field-Marshal Sir Alan F., 1st Viscount Alanbrooke: G.O.C.-in-C. Southern Command, 1939, 1940; Commander of Second Army Corps, B.E.F., 1939–40; C.-in-C. Home Forces, 1940–1; C.I.G.S., 1941–6.

Butler	R.A., 1st Baron: Parliamentary Under-Secretary of State at India Office, 1932–8, at F.O., 1938–41; Minister of Education, 1941–5; Chancellor of the Exchequer, 1951–5; Lord Privy Seal, 1955–7; Home Secretary, 1957–62; Deputy Prime Minister, 1962; Foreign Secretary, 1963–4.
Byrnes	James, F.: Director of Office of War Mobilisation, U.S.A., 1943–5; Secretary of State, 1945–7; Governor of South Carolina, 1951–5.
Cadogan	Sir Alexander George Montagu: born 25 Nov. 1884, younger son of 5th Earl Cadogan; educated at Eton and Balliol; entered Diplomatic Service 1908; several short spells of service abroad before 1914; married, 1912, Lady Theodosia Acheson, daughter of 4th Earl of Gosford (1 son, 3 daughters); head of League of Nations section at F.O. before appointment as Minister at Peking, 1934–5, and Ambassador, 1935–6; Deputy Under-Secretary of State, F.O., 1936–7; Permanent Under-Secretary, Jan. 1938–Feb. 1946; Permanent Representative of H.M.G. to the United Nations Organisation, 1946–1950; retired, 1950. Government Director of the Suez Canal Co., 1951–7; Chairman of the Governors of the B.B.C., 1952–7; director of the Phoenix Assurance Co. and of the National Provincial Bank, 1951–1964. Died 9 July 1968.
Chamberlain	Neville: Director of National Service, 1917; various Ministerial offices, 1922–9; Chancellor of the Exchequer, 1931–7; Prime Minister, 1937–40; Lord President of the Council, 1940.
Chiang Kai-Shek	Chairman of the National Government, 1928; Chairman of the National Military Affairs Council, 1932–46; President of the Executive Yuan, 1935–8, 1939–45; Chairman of Supreme National Defence Council, 1919–47; President of Republic of China, 1948–9; resumed Presidency in Formosa, 1950.
Churchill	Sir Winston S.: numerous Ministerial offices, 1905–1922; Chancellor of Exchequer, 1924–9; First Lord of the Admiralty, 1939–40; Prime Minister and Minister of Defence, 1940–5; Prime Minister, 1951–5.
Ciano	Count Galeazzo: son-in-law of Mussolini; Italian Minister for Foreign Affairs, 1936–43; Ambassador to Vatican, 1943; executed, 1944.
Cooper	A. Duff, 1st Viscount Norwich: junior posts at War Office and Treasury, 1928–35; Secretary for War,

1935–7; First Lord of the Admiralty, 1937–8; Minister of Information, 1940–1; Minister of State in Far East, 1941–2; British representative with the F.C.N.L., 1943–4; Ambassador to France, 1944–7.

Corbin A. Charles: French Ambassador in Madrid, 1929–1931; Ambassador in Brussels, 1931–3; Ambassador in London, 1933–40.

Cranborne Viscount (later Marquess of Salisbury): Parliamentary Under-Secretary, F.O., 1935–8; Secretary for Dominions, 1940–2, 1943–5; Lord Privy Seal, 1942–1943; Leader of the House of Lords, 1942–5, 1951–7; Lord President of the Council, 1951–7.

Cripps Sir R. Stafford: Ambassador in Moscow, 1940–2; Lord Privy Seal and Leader of the House of Commons, 1942; Minister of Aircraft Production, 1942–1945; President of Board of Trade, 1945–7; Minister of Economic Affairs, 1947; Chancellor of Exchequer, 1947–50.

Daladier Edouard: French Prime Minister and Minister of War, 1933; Prime Minister and Minister for Foreign Affairs, 1934; Prime Minister and Minister of National Defence, 1938–40; Minister for Foreign Affairs, 1939–40.

Dalton Dr Hugh, 1st Baron: Parliamentary Under-Secretary, F.O., 1929–31; Minister of Economic Warfare, 1940–2; President of Board of Trade, 1942–5; Chancellor of Exchequer, 1945–7.

De Gaulle General Charles: Under-Secretary for National Defence, June 1940; Chief of Free French, then President of French National Committee, London and Brazzaville, 1940–2; President of French Committee of National Liberation, Algiers, 1943; President of Provisional Government of the French Republic, 1944–6; recalled to power 1958; President, 1959–69.

Dill Field-Marshal Sir John: G.O.C.-in-C. Aldershot, 1937–9; Commander I Corps in France, 1939–40; Vice-C.I.G.S., April 1940; C.I.G.S. May 1940–1; principal British representative on Combined Chiefs of Staff's Committee, Washington, 1941–4.

Drummond Sir Eric: see Perth.

Eden R. Anthony, 1st Earl of Avon: Parliamentary Under-Secretary, F.O., 1931–3; Lord Privy Seal, 1934–5; Minister without Portfolio, 1935; Foreign Secretary, 1935–8; Dominions Secretary, 1939–40; Secretary for War, 1940; Foreign Secretary, 1940–5, 1951–5;

Leader of the House of Commons, 1942–5; Prime Minister, 1955–7.

Franco General Francisco: C.-in-C. Spanish Moroccan Army, 1935; C.-in-C. Canary Islands, 1936; led revolt against Spanish Government, 1936; Head of Spanish State since 1939.

Gamelin General Maurice: Vice-President, Conseil Supérieur de la Guerre and chef d'état-major général, 1935–8; chef d'état-major général de la défense nationale, 1938; C.-in-C. Land Forces until superseded by Weygand, May 1940.

Goering Field-Marshal Hermann: participant in the putsch of 1923; President of the Reichstag, 1932; Air Minister and C.-in-C. German Air Force, 1933–45; Prime Minister of Prussia and Minister of the Interior, 1933; Commissioner for the 4-Year Plan, 1936; Member Ministerial Council for Reich Defence, 1939; President General Council for War Economy, 1940.

Gousev Feodor Tarasovich: Chief of the Second European Department of the People's Commissariat for Foreign Affairs, 1939–42; Russian Ambassador in London, 1943–6.

Grandi Count Dino: Italian Minister for Foreign Affairs, 1929–32; Ambassador in London, 1932–39; Minister of Justice, 1939–43.

Halifax Viscount, later 1st Earl: Viceroy of India, 1926–31; Lord Privy Seal, 1935–7; Lord President, 1937–8; Foreign Secretary, 1938–40; Ambassador in Washington, 1941–6.

Hankey Sir Maurice, later Lord: Secretary to the Cabinet and to the Committee of Imperial Defence, 1916–1938; Minister without Portfolio in the War Cabinet, 1939–40; Chancellor of the Duchy of Lancaster 1940–1; Paymaster-General, 1941–2.

Harriman W. Averell: President Roosevelt's special representative in London, March 1941; chairman of special mission to Russia, 1941; U.S. representative in London of Combined Shipping Adjustment Board, 1942; U.S. Ambassador to U.S.S.R., 1943–6, to Britain, 1946; Secretary of Commerce, 1946–8; numerous high offices since.

Harvey Oliver C., later 1st Baron: Private Secretary to Eden and Halifax, 1936–9; Minister at British

Embassy, Paris, 1939–40; seconded to Ministry of Information; Private Secretary to Eden, 1941–3; Acting Assistant Under-Secretary of State, 1943–6; Deputy Under-Secretary (Political), 1946–8; Ambassador in Paris, 1948–54.

Henderson Sir Nevile: entered Foreign Service, 1905; Minister at Belgrade, 1929–35, and at Buenos Aires, 1935–7; Ambassador in Berlin, 1937–9.

Hitler Adolf: enlisted in Bavarian infantry 1914; saw active service on the Western Front; founder of Nazi Party; Chancellor of the Reich from 1933; Head of State from 1934; C.-in-C. German Fighting Forces, from 1938; Personal Commander of the Army from 1941; Supreme War Lord from 1942; committed suicide 1945.

Hoare Sir Samuel, 1st Viscount Templewood: Secretary for India, 1931–5, for Foreign Affairs, 1935; First Lord of the Admiralty, 1936–7; Home Secretary, 1937–9; Lord Privy Seal, 1939–40; Secretary for Air, 1940; Ambassador to Spain, 1940–4.

Hopkins Harry; U.S. Secretary of Commerce, 1938–40; Special Adviser and Assistant to President Roosevelt to 1945.

Hull Cordell: member of U.S. House of Representatives, 1907–21, 1923–31; Senator, 1931–3; Secretary of State, 1933–44; Nobel Peace Prize, 1945.

Jebb Gladwyn, later 1st Baron Gladwyn: Private Secretary to Permanent Under-Secretaries of State, 1937–40; Ministry of Economic Warfare with temporary rank of Assistant Under-Secretary, August 1940; Acting Counsellor in F.O., 1941; head of the Reconstruction Department, 1942; Counsellor, 1943; Acting Secretary-General, United Nations, February 1946; Deputy Under-Secretary, F.O., 1949–50; succeeded Cadogan at the U.N., 1950–4; Ambassador in Paris, 1954–60.

Kennedy Joseph P.: Chairman, Securities Exchange Commission, 1934–5; U.S. Maritime Commission, 1937; U.S. Ambassador in London, 1937–41.

Kirkpatrick Sir Ivone: entered Diplomatic Service 1919; First Secretary at British Embassy in Berlin, 1933–8; Director of Foreign Division, Ministry of Information, 1940; Controller, European Services of B.B.C. 1941; Assistant Under-Secretary of State, F.O., 1945; Permanent Under-Secretary of State, F.O., 1953–7; Chairman of I.T.A., 1957–62.

Laval Pierre: French Prime Minister, 1931–2; Foreign Minister, 1934–5; Prime Minister and Foreign Minister, 1935–6; Deputy Prime Minister and Minister of Information, 1940; Prime Minister and Foreign Minister, 1942–4; executed 1945.

Law Richard, 1st Baron Coleraine: Financial Secretary, War Office, 1940–1; Parliamentary Under-Secretary of State, F.O., 1941–3; Minister of State, 1943–1945; Minister of Education, 1945.

Leeper Sir Reginald W. A.: Counsellor, F.O., 1933; Head of the News Department, F.O.; Acting Assistant Under-Secretary of State, August 1940; Ambassador to Greek Government in Cairo, 1943, and in Athens, 1944–6.

MacDonald Malcolm J.: Secretary for the Dominions, 1935–8, 1938–9; Secretary for the Colonies, 1938–40; Minister of Health, 1940–41; High Commissioner in Canada, 1941–6; thereafter numerous other posts in the oversea Commonwealth.

Maisky Ivan M.: Russian Ambassador in London, 1932–43; Assistant People's Commissar for Foreign Affairs, 1943–6.

Mikolajczyk Stanislav: Vice-President, Polish Peasant Party; Vice-Chairman, Polish National Council, 1939–41; Deputy Prime Minister and Minister of the Interior, 1941–3; Prime Minister, 1943–4; Deputy Prime Minister, 1945–7.

Molotov Vaycheslav M.: Chairman of Council of People's Commissars, 1930–41; Deputy Chairman of Council of Ministers of U.S.S.R., 1941–57; Commissar, later Minister, for Foreign Affairs, 1939–49.

Mounsey Sir George, A.: Assistant Under-Secretary of State, F.O., 1929–40.

Mussolini Benito: Socialist agitator and journalist, 1904–15; President, Council of Ministers, 1922–6; Head of the Government and Prime Minister, 1926–43; Minister for Foreign Affairs, 1924–9, 1932–6, and numerous other offices, including Ministries of the Interior and War; deposed 1943; rescued and reinstated at Hitler's instance; executed 1945.

Oliphant Sir Lancelot: Deputy Under-Secretary of State, F.O., 1936–9; Ambassador at Brussels, 1939–40; captured and interned in Germany, 1940–1; resumed duties in London, October, 1941; retired 1944.

Perth Earl of (earlier Sir Eric Drummond): entered F.O. in 1900; first Secretary-General of the League of Nations, 1919–33; Ambassador at Rome, 1933–9; resigned in July 1940 from appointment as Chief Adviser on Foreign Publicity to the Ministry of Information.

Phipps Sir Eric C.: entered Diplomatic Service 1889; Ambassador in Berlin, 1933–7; Ambassador at Paris, 1937–9.

Pound Admiral Sir Dudley: C.-in-C. Mediterranean, 1936–1939; First Sea Lord, 1939–43.

Raczynski Count Edward: Polish Ambassador in London, 1934–45; Acting Polish Foreign Minister, 1941–2; Minister of State in charge of Foreign Affairs in Cabinet of General Sikorski, 1942–3.

Reynaud Paul: French Minister of Finance, 1938–40; Prime Minister 1940; Minister of Foreign Affairs and Defence, 1940; interned by Vichy Government, 1940–2; interned by Germans, 1942–5.

Ribbentrop Joachim von: Ambassador of the Reich, 1935; led German delegation to London naval talks, 1935; Ambassador in London, 1936–8; Foreign Minister, 1938–45; executed 1946.

Roosevelt Franklin D.: Democratic Senator, 1911; Assistant Secretary of the Navy, 1913–20; Governor of the State of New York, 1929–33, President of the United States of America, 1932–45.

Salazar Dr Antonio de Oliveira: Portuguese Prime Minister, 1932–68; Minister of War and Interior, 1936–44; Minister for Foreign Affairs, 1936–47.

Sargent Sir Orme: entered F.O. in 1906; Assistant Under-Secretary of State, 1938–9; Deputy Under-Secretary, 1939–46; succeeded Cadogan as Permanent Under-Secretary, F.O., 1946–9.

Sikorski General Wladyslaw: Polish Prime Minister, 1922–3; Minister of Military Affairs, 1923–5; C.-in-C. Polish Army 1939–43, and Prime Minister, 1941–43.

Simon Sir John, later 1st Viscount: Home Secretary, 1915–16; Foreign Secretary, 1931–5; Home Secretary, 1935–7; Chancellor of Exchequer, 1939–40; Lord Chancellor, 1940–5.

Smuts Field-Marshal Jan C.: member of Imperial War Cabinet in First World War; South African Prime Minister 1919–24, 1939–48.

Stalin	Generalissimo Joseph V.: Joined Tiflis Marxist Social Democratic Organization, 1898; founded *Pravda*, 1911; in October Revolution, 1917; elected General Secretary of Central Committee of Communist Party of Soviet Union, 1922; Marshal of the Soviet Union, 1943; Generalissimo, 1945.
Stanley	Oliver: related by marriage to Cadogan, he was President of Board of Trade, 1937–40; Secretary for War, 1940; for the Colonies, 1942–5.
Stettinius	Edward R.: Lend-lease Administrator, U.S.A., and Special Assistant to President Roosevelt, 1941–3; Under-Secretary of State, 1943–4; Secretary of State, 1944–5; U.S. representative in Security Council and Chairman U.S. delegation in General Assembly of U.N., 1945–6.
Strang	William, later 1st Baron: entered F.O. 1919; head of Central Department, F.O., 1937–9; Assistant Under-Secretary of State, 1939–43; British representative on European Advisory Commission, 1943–5; political adviser to C.-in-C. British Forces in Germany, 1945–7; Permanent Under-Secretary, F.O. German Section, 1947–9; succeeded Sargent as Permanent Under-Secretary, 1949–53.
Tito	Marshal Josip Broz; Leader of Yugoslav Partisan forces after German invasion; Marshal of Yugoslavia and President of National Liberation Committee, 1943; Prime Minister and Minister of National Defence, 1945–53; President from 1953.
Truman	Harry S.: Vice-President of U.S.A. 1944; President, 1945–53.
Vansittart	Sir Robert, later 1st Baron: entered Diplomatic Service 1902; Principal Private Secretary to Prime Minister, 1928–30; Permanent Under-Secretary, F.O., 1930–7; Chief Diplomatic Adviser to H.M.G., 1938–41.
Wilson	Sir Horace: entered Civil Service 1900; Chief Industrial Adviser to H.M.G., 1930–9; seconded to the Treasury for duties with Baldwin and Chamberlain, 1935–40; Permanent head of Civil Service, 1939–42.
Winant	John Gilbert: Director of International Labour Office, 1938–41; U.S. Ambassador in London, 1941–6; U.S. representative on European Advisory Commission, 1943–7.

INDEX

Lightning Source UK Ltd.
Milton Keynes UK
UKOW01f1604170817
307483UK00004B/356/P

9 780571 269853